ENCYCLOPEDIA OF DOMESTIC VIOLENCE

ENCYCLOPEDIA OF DOMESTIC VIOLENCE

NICKY ALI JACKSON
EDITOR

Routledge
Taylor & Francis Group
New York   London

Routledge
Taylor & Francis Group
270 Madison Avenue
New York, NY 10016

Routledge
Taylor & Francis Group
2 Park Square
Milton Park, Abingdon
Oxon OX14 4RN

© 2007 by Taylor & Francis Group, LLC
Routledge is an imprint of Taylor & Francis Group, an Informa business

Printed in the United States of America on acid-free paper
10 9 8 7 6 5 4 3 2 1

International Standard Book Number-10: 0-415-96968-9 (Hardcover)
International Standard Book Number-13: 978-0-415-96968-0 (Hardcover)

Visit the Taylor & Francis Web site at
http://www.taylorandfrancis.com

and the Routledge Web site at
http://www.routledge.com

CONTENTS

EDITORIAL BOARD MEMBERS

LIST OF CONTRIBUTORS

Elaine J. Alpert Boston University

Georgia J. Anetzberger Cleveland State University

Christina Antonopoulou University of Athens

Martha E. Banks ABackans DCP, Inc.

Raquel Kennedy Bergen Saint Joseph's University

L. René Bergeron University of New Hampshire

LaVerne A. Berkel University of Missouri–Kansas City

Teri Bernades California State University, Fresno

E. Sue Blume Independent Scholar

Bette L. Bottoms University of Illinois at Chicago

Tod W. Burke Radford University

Sondra Burman University of Oklahoma–Tulsa

María Bustelo Complutense University

Jacquelyn C. Campbell Johns Hopkins University

Bonnie E. Carlson University at Albany, State University of New York

Janice E. Clifford Auburn University

Wendy P. Crook Florida State University

Theodore P. Cross RTI International

Lanette P. Dalley Minot State University

Clarissa Freitas Dias Georgia State University

Tracy L. Dietz University of Central Florida

David DiLillo University of Nebraska–Lincoln

Patricia Duffy-Feins University of Oklahoma–Tulsa

Donald G. Dutton University of British Columbia

Miriam K. Ehrensaft Columbia University

Jessica L. Ekhomu Georgia State University

Elizabeth B. Erbaugh University of New Mexico

Edna Erez Kent State University

Patricia E. Erickson Canisius College

Ruth L. Fischbach Columbia University

Bonnie S. Fisher University of Cincinnati

Gail Flint West Virginia State University

David Fontes Independent Scholar

Venessa Garcia Kean University

Shirley Garick Texas A&M University–Texarkana

Richard J. Gelles University of Pennsylvania

Nancy Glass Oregon Health & Science University

Ann Goetting Western Kentucky University

Pamela Goldberg Independent Scholar

Denise Kindschi Gosselin Western New England College

Dee L. R. Graham University of Cincinnati

Carolyn E. Gross Lynchburg College

John Hamel John Hamel & Associates

Samantha K. Hamilton Independent Scholar

Robert D. Hanser University of Louisiana at Monroe

Kathleen M. Heide University of South Florida

Amy Holtzworth-Munroe Indiana University

Wendelin Hume University of North Dakota

Sherina Hume University of North Dakota

Peter R. Ibarra Syracuse University

Silvina Ituarte California State University, East Bay

Nicky Ali Jackson Purdue University

John P. Jarvis Federal Bureau of Investigation

Jana L. Jasinski University of Central Florida

Janet R. Johnston San Jose State University

Josephine A. Kahler Texas A&M University–Texarkana

Kristen Kuehnle Salem State College

Karel Kurst-Swanger State University of New York at Oswego

Hamid R. Kusha East Carolina University

Mindie Lazarus-Black University of Illinois at Chicago

Arlene Istar Lev Choices Counseling and Consulting and University at Albany,
    State University New York

Mark I. Levy University of California, San Francisco

Polly Loeber University of South Florida

Frances Ma California State University, Fresno

Linda MacDonald Independent Scholar

Greg Martin Lynchburg College

Kimberly A. McCabe Lynchburg College

N. Jane McCandless University of West Georgia

Michelle R. McCauley Middlebury College

Sarah J. McLean University at Albany, State University of New York

Elizabeth Corzine McMullan University of Southern Mississippi

Nancy Meyer-Emerick Cleveland State University

Janet Mickish Mickish Consulting

Sharon Mihalic University of Colorado at Boulder

Alison Miller Independent Scholar

J. Mitchell Miller University of South Carolina

Stephanie Mines The TARA Approach for the Resolution of Shock and Trauma

Ronald S. Morgan, Jr. Blackwell–Thurman Criminal Justice Center and Texas State University–San Marcos

Kelley Moult University of Cape Town

Cynthia J. Najdowski University of Illinois at Chicago

Nancy Nason-Clark University of New Brunswick

Lisa S. Nored University of Southern Mississippi

Michelle Oberman Santa Clara University

Robbin S. Ogle University of Nebraska at Omaha

Godpower O. Okereke Texas A&M University–Texarkana

Shelley N. Osborn University of California, Riverside

Stephen S. Owen Radford University

Teresa F. Parnell Independent Scholar

Joseph E. Pascarella University of Maryland

Pamela K. S. Patrick Capella University

Corinne Peek-Asa University of Iowa

Alison R. Perona Independent Scholar

Andrea R. Perry University of Nebraska–Lincoln

Maureen Pirog Indiana University, Bloomington

Daniel Price Providence College

Peter Racheotes Texas A&M University–Texarkana

Lisa A. Rapp-Paglicci University of South Florida, Lakeland

Edna I. Rawlings University of Cincinnati

Saundra L. Regan University of Cincinnati

Albert R. Roberts Rutgers, The State University of New Jersey

Lorie Rubenser Sul Ross State University

Sophia Sakoutis Saint Xavier University

Jeanne Sarson Independent Scholar

Beth M. Schwartz Randolph–Macon Woman's College

Phyllis W. Sharps Johns Hopkins University

Sara H. Sinal Wake Forest University

Dick Sobsey University of Alberta, Canada

Daniel Jay Sonkin Independent Practice

Erin Sorenson Chicago Children's Advocacy Center

Loretta J. Stalans Loyola University

Evan Stark Rutgers, The State University of New Jersey

Suzanne K. Steinmetz Indiana University–Purdue University

Jan E. Stets University of California, Riverside

Murray A. Straus University of New Hampshire

Anne Sullivan Salem State College

Rita Swan Children's Healthcare Is a Legal Duty, Inc.

Jason S. Ulsperger Arkansas Tech University

Melissa Valentine Columbia University

Carmen Valiente Hospital Clinico San Carlos de Madrid

Edward D. Vargas Indiana University, Bloomington

Michael S. Vaughn Sam Houston State University

Holly E. Ventura University of South Carolina

Patricia Villavicencio Hospital Clinico San Carlos de Madrid

Lenore E. A. Walker Nova Southeastern University

Harvey Wallace California State University, Fresno

Charles Walton Lynchburg College

Neil Websdale Northern Arizona University

Carolyn M. West University of Washington

Deborah Wilson Southern Arkansas University

Alissa Pollitz Worden University at Albany, State University of New York

Shiho Yamamoto California State University, Fresno

Joanne M. Yednock Lynchburg College

Alice G. Yick Capella University

Rachel Zimmer Schneider University of Akron

FOREWORD

In 1971 the *Journal of Marriage and the Family* published a special topic issue on family violence. The editor commented in the introduction that the articles were the first on that topic to have been published since the journal began in 1938. Subsequently, there has been an exponential growth in research on all aspects of domestic violence (Straus 1992). One indicator of the large research effort to understand the causes and consequences of domestic violence and to develop evidence-based methods of prevention and treatment is that there are now entire journals that focus on one or more aspects of family violence. These include:

Abuse, Violence, Maltreatment and Neglect
Child Abuse and Neglect
Journal of Child Sexual Abuse
Journal of Child Sexual Abuse and the Law
Journal of Elder Abuse and Neglect
Journal of Emotional Abuse
Journal of Family Violence
Journal of Interpersonal Violence
Violence Against Women
Violence and Victims

In addition to these specialized journals, a great deal of research on domestic violence is published in more broadly focused journals. Like the *Journal of Marriage and the Family*, they had not previously published research on domestic violence, or, like the *Journal of Family Psychology,* did not exist in 1971.

The explosive growth of family violence research cannot be explained on the basis of an increase in wife beating or physical abuse of children because the evidence indicates they have been decreasing (Finkelhor & Jones in press; Gelles & Straus 2006; Straus & Gelles 1986). Rather, the growth exemplifies the social construction of a social problem, or what Gusfield (1963) calls a "moral passage." This was brought about by changes in American society and resulting changes in the disciplines of criminology, pediatrics, psychology, social work, and sociology.

The work of a pediatrician, Henry Kempe, is generally credited with alerting the medical and social work professions to what Kempe called the "battered baby syndrome" (Kempe *et al.* 1962). The efforts of pediatricians and social workers were important in creating public recognition of child abuse as a widespread social problem (Nelson 1984; Pfohl 1977). A decade later, the women's movement brought about a similar transformation of the public perception of wife beating (Roy 1977; Steinmetz & Straus 1974). The rapid emergence of public concern and research on these and other aspects of domestic violence reflect several major social changes that were occurring at the time. I will list some of them in approximate chronological order:

- The social activism of the 1960s, which championed oppressed groups, was extended to the oppression of children and women.
- The rising homicide, rape, and assault rates from 1960 to 1980, violent political and social protests and assassinations, and the Vietnam War sensitized people to violence.
- Disenchantment with the traditional family in the 1960s and 1970s facilitated the recognition of negative features of family life, including violence.
- Studies by Levinger (1966) and O'Brien (1971, No. 2925, 1966) demonstrated that violence was a factor in 40% of divorces.
- The growth in paid employment by married women provided the economic means for women to escape the abuse that had long been tolerated. The increased legal, economic, and social acceptability of divorce also helped make it possible to no longer tolerate abusive behavior.
- Professions with a stake in family intervention grew rapidly. For example, the American

Association of Marriage and Family Therapists went from 3,375 members in 1975 to 12,302 in 1985.

- Social-activist baby boomers were entering graduate school, and they were interested in using sociology as a means of social activism. A growing number of them were women. Among the results were more attention to gender roles and research on oppression of women by men, including violence used in maintaining male dominance (Straus 1973, 1976; Yllo & Bograd 1988; Yllo & Straus 1984).

- The women's movement made rape and then battering central issues in the mid 1970s and created a new public consciousness of these ancient cruelties. The movement also created two new social institutions: rape crisis centers and shelters for battered women. Both did more than provide medical and psychological assistance and safety. They were also ideologically important because they concretized and publicized phenomena that had previously been ignored (Straus 1974).

- There was a convergence of certain aspects of the conservative agenda of the period with the agendas of the feminist movement and of sociologists engaged in research on family violence. The conservative demand for "law and order" and use of punishment to correct social problems coincided with the demands of women to end the virtual immunity of wife beaters from legal sanctions. The sexual repression that is a traditional aspect of conservatism also coincided with feminist campaigns against pornography.

- Changes in theoretical perspectives in sociology put the consensus model of society under attack by conflict theory. The inevitability of conflict in all human groups, including the family, was recognized, along with the possibility of violent conflict.

- Certain enduring characteristics of sociology as a discipline meshed with these historical circumstances. One of these characteristics is the tradition of seeing sociology as a vehicle for social improvement. This tradition is especially strong in the United States, where many early sociologists were ordained ministers. A concern for the underdog and liberal political leanings are also part of the sociological tradition. Finally, sociology has a strong debunking tradition (Berger 1973). Research on family violence was consistent with these three elements of the culture of sociology. It

held out the hope of improving families and society, it came to the rescue of oppressed women and children, and it debunked the view of the family as a "haven."

Not even the most dedicated scholar, much less students, practitioners, and the general public, can know what is in the treasure trove of information created by the torrent of research in response to these social changes. The *Encyclopedia of Domestic Violence* helps solve this problem. It summarizes a vast body of knowledge that provides a better understanding of a key human institution—the family. The family is both the place where a typical person is most likely to find love and support and also the place where a typical person is most likely to be a perpetrator or victim of violence. As previously indicated, we are well on the way to reducing the violent aspect of family life. There are short-term ups and downs, but the long-term trend is a major decrease in partner violence and child abuse. The *Encyclopedia of Domestic Violence* provides information, which, when applied, can help accelerate that trend.

MURRAY A. STRAUS

References

Berger, P. L. (1973). *Invitation to sociology: A humanistic perspective*. Woodstock, NY: Overlook Press.

Finkelhor, D., & Jones, L. (In Press). Explaining the decline in crimes against children, child abuse & child victimization. *Special Issue of Journal of Social Issues*.

Gelles, R. J., & Straus, M. A. (2006). Introduction to the transaction edition." In Murray A. Straus, Richard J. Gelles, and Suzanne K. Steinmtez (1980 [2006]) Behind closed doors: Violence in the American family, pp. 1–20. Piscataway, NJ: Transaction.

Gusfield, J. R. (1963). *Symbolic crusade: Status politics and the American temperance movement*. Urbana: University of Illinois Press.

Kempe, C. H., Silverman, F. N., Steele, B. F., Droegmueller, W., & Silver, H. K. (1962). The battered-child syndrome. *Journal of American Medical Association, 181*, 17–24.

Levinger, G. (1966). Sources of marital dissatisfaction among applicants for divorce. *American Journal of Orthopsychiatry, 26* (October), 803–807.

Nelson, B. J. (1984). *Making an issue of child abuse: Political agenda setting for social problems*. Chicago: University of Chicago Press.

Pfohl, S. J. (1977). The discovery of child abuse. *Social Problems, 24* (February), 310–323.

Roy, M. (Ed.). (1977). *Battered women: A psychosociological study of domestic violence*. New York: Van Nostrand, Reinhold.

Steinmetz, S. K., & Straus, M. A. (1974). *Violence in the family*. New York: Harper & Row.

Straus, M. A. (1973). A general systems theory approach to a theory of violence between family members. *Social Science Information, 12* (3), 105–125.

Straus, M. A. (1974). "Foreword." In R. J. Gelles (Ed.), *The violent home*. Newbury Park, CA: Sage.

Straus, M. A. (1976). Sexual inequality, cultural norms, and wife-beating. In E. C. Viano (Ed.), *Victims and society* (pp. 543–559). Washington, DC: Visage Press.

Straus, M. A. (1992). Sociological research and social policy: The case of family violence. *Sociological Forum, 7* (2), 211–237.

Straus, M. A., & Gelles, R. J. (1986). Societal change and change in family violence from 1975 to 1985 as revealed by two national surveys. *Journal of Marriage and the Family, 48*, 465–479.

Yllo, K., & Bograd, M. (Eds.). (1988). *Feminist perspectives on wife abuse*. Newbury Park, CA: Sage.

Yllo, K., & Straus, M. A. (1984). Patriarchy and violence against wives: The impact of structural and normative factors, *Journal of International and Comparative Social Welfare 1*, 16–29.

INTRODUCTION

Domestic violence remains a relatively new field of study among social scientists. Only within the past 4 decades have scholars recognized domestic violence as a social problem. Initially, domestic violence research focused on child abuse. Thereafter, researchers focused on wife abuse and used this concept interchangeably with domestic violence. Within the past 20 years, researchers have acknowledged that other forms of violent relationships exist, including dating violence, battered males, and same-sex domestic violence. Moreover, academicians have recognized a subcategory within the field of criminal justice: victimology (the scientific study of victims). Throughout the United States, colleges and universities have been creating victimology courses, and even more specifically, family violence and interpersonal violence courses.

The media have informed us that domestic violence is so commonplace that the public has unfortunately grown accustomed to reading and hearing about husbands killing their wives, mothers killing their children, or parents neglecting their children. While it is understood that these offenses take place, the explanations as to what factors contributed to them remain unclear. In order to prevent future violence, it is imperative to understand its roots. There is no one causal explanation for domestic violence; however, there are numerous factors which may help explain these unjustified acts of violence. Highly publicized cases such as the O.J. Simpson and Scott Peterson trials have shown the world that alleged murderers may not resemble the deranged sociopath depicted in horror films. Rather, they can be handsome, charming, and well-liked by society. In addition, court-centered programming on television continuously publicizes cases of violence within the home informing the public that we are potentially at risk by our caregivers and other loved ones. There is the case of the au pair Elizabeth Woodward convicted of shaking and

killing Matthew Eappen, the child entrusted to her care. Some of the most highly publicized cases have also focused on mothers who kill. America was stunned as it heard the cases of Susan Smith and Andrea Yates. Both women were convicted of brutally killing their own children. Many asked how loving mothers could turn into cold-blooded killers. This encyclopedia will address this issue along with many others.

The encyclopedia will educate the reader that domestic violence takes on many forms. Through recent scientific study, it is now known that domestic violence occurs within different types of households. The purpose of creating an *Encyclopedia of Domestic Violence* is to have available a comprehensive, one volume, state-of-the-research, easy-to-read compilation of a wide variety of domestic violence topics. This groundbreaking project will be the first ever publication of an encyclopedia of domestic violence. Editing this type of project was an enormously exhaustive task. The first step in putting together a volume of this sort was to create a list of topics. Topics included entries that have been given a great deal of consideration by scholars (i.e., wife abuse, child abuse, date rape), as well as those which have largely been ignored by scholars (i.e., battered males, domestic violence by law enforcement officers, pseudo-family violence). The second step was to locate potential contributors who are experts on these selected topics. Authors were chosen based on their scholarly reputations within their respective fields of study.

The *Encyclopedia of Domestic Violence* can be divided into seven categories: (1) victims of domestic violence, (2) theoretical perspectives and correlates to domestic violence, (3) cross-cultural and religious perspectives, (4) understudied areas within domestic violence research, (5) domestic violence and the law, (6) child abuse and elder abuse, and (7) special topics in domestic violence.

Victims of Domestic Violence

Initial research recognized wives as victims of domestic violence. Thereafter, it was acknowledged that unmarried women were also falling victim to violence at the hands of their boyfriends. Subsequently, the term "battered women" became synonymous with "battered wives." Legitimizing female victimization served as the catalyst in introducing other types of intimate partner violence.

Theoretical Perspectives and Correlates to Domestic Violence

There is no single causal factor related to domestic violence. Rather, scholars have concluded that there are numerous factors that contribute to domestic violence. Feminists found that women were beaten at the hands of their partners. Drawing on feminist theory, they helped explain the relationship between patriarchy and domestic violence. Researchers have examined other theoretical perspectives such as attachment theory, exchange theory, identity theory, the cycle of violence, social learning theory, and victim-blaming theory in explaining domestic violence. However, factors exist that may not fall into a single theoretical perspective. Correlates have shown that certain factors such as pregnancy, social class, level of education, animal abuse, and substance abuse may influence the likelihood for victimization.

Cross-Cultural and Religious Perspectives

It was essential to acknowledge that domestic violence crosses cultural boundaries and religious affiliations. There is no one particular society or religious group exempt from victimization. A variety of developed and developing countries were examined in understanding the prevalence of domestic violence within their societies as well as their coping strategies in handling these volatile issues. It is often misunderstood that one religious group is more tolerant of family violence than another. As Christianity, Islam, and Judaism represent the three major religions of the world, their ideologies were explored in relation to the acceptance and prevalence of domestic violence.

Understudied Areas within Domestic Violence Research

Domestic violence has typically examined traditional relationships, such as husband–wife, boyfriend–girlfriend, and parent–child. Consequently, scholars have historically ignored non-traditional relationships. In fact, certain entries have limited cross-references based on the fact that there were limited, if any, scholarly publications on that topic. Only since the 1990s have scholars admitted that violence exists among lesbians and gay males. There are other ignored populations that are addressed within this encyclopedia including violence within military and police families, violence within pseudo-family environments, and violence against women and children with disabilities.

Domestic Violence and the Law

The Violence against Women Act (VAWA) of 1994 helped pave domestic violence concerns into legislative matters. Historically, family violence was handled through informal measures often resulting in mishandling of cases. Through VAWA, victims were given the opportunity to have their cases legally remedied. This legitimized the separation of specialized domestic and family violence courts from criminal courts. The law has recognized that victims of domestic violence deserve recognition and resolution. Law enforcement agencies may be held civilly accountable for their actions in domestic violence incidents. Mandatory arrest policies have been initiated helping reduce discretionary power of police officers. Courts have also begun to focus on the offenders of domestic violence. Currently, there are batterer intervention programs and mediation programs available for offenders within certain jurisdictions. Its goals are to reduce the rate of recidivism among batterers.

Child Abuse and Elder Abuse

Scholars began to address child abuse over the last third of the twentieth century. It is now recognized that child abuse falls within a wide spectrum. In the past, it was based on visible bruises and scars. Today, researchers have acknowledged that psychological abuse, where there are no visible injuries, is just as damaging as its counterpart. One of the greatest controversies in child abuse literature is that of Munchausen by Proxy. Some scholars have recognized that it is a syndrome while others would deny a syndrome exists. Regardless of the term "syndrome," Munchausen by Proxy does exist and needs to be further examined. Another form of violence that needs to be further examined is elder abuse. Elder abuse literature typically focused on abuse perpetrated by children and caregivers. With increased life expectancies, it is now understood that there is greater probability for violence among elderly intimate couples. Shelters and hospitals need to better understand this unique population in order to better serve its victims.

Special Topics in Domestic Violence

Within this encyclopedia, there are entries that may not fit clearly into one of the aforementioned categories. Therefore, they will be listed in a separate special topics designation.

How to Use this Book

The *Encyclopedia of Domestic Violence* provides a **simple, alphabetically-arranged reference guide** to a variety of topics written by leading international scholars. Both the **List of Entries A–Z** and the **Thematic List of Entries** will prove useful in directing readers to topics of interest covered at length. The end of each entry includes cross-references (**See also**) so that the reader may search other entries of similar interest within the book. Each entry also contains a list of **References and Further Reading,** including sources used by the authors of the entries as well as additional work of scholarship and other resources that may be of great use to the reader. As the overarching topic of domestic violence is complex, covering a range of issues that are distinct and yet often deeply interrelated, a **thorough, analytical Index** assists the reader in finding information on specific topics appearing across different entries throughout this volume. This is a breakthrough project as there has never been a similar encyclopedia of this scope published to date. This publication will allow scholars the information to share their research and study new topics in the field.

Acknowledgments

This encyclopedia has been an arduous project. It has taken a great deal of time and energy to create this powerful resource. For this reason, I give many thanks to Mark Georgiev and Susan Cronin with Routledge. Without Mark's suggestion to put together this encyclopedia, this project would never have been developed. I am most grateful to Susan Cronin for ensuring a secure schedule to help me get through this extensive project. Her assistance was invaluable.

I would also like to thank all of the contributors to this project, particularly Dr. Tod Burke for his continued support during this time. Their time and commitment to this project was generously given. I am also grateful for Dr. Murray Straus' generosity in agreeing to write the foreword. His dedication to the field is apparent and greatly appreciated. Before working on this encyclopedia I had not been in contact with Dr. Jan Mickish since my college days at Ball State University; my interest in domestic violence can be traced to her victimology course. She has been an inspiration.

Personally, I have many people to thank. My parents, Dr. Mir Masoom and Firoza Ali have helped shape the meaning of family. Also, my siblings, Nancy, Mimi, and Ishti, have played a major role in my life. I would like to thank my mother-in-law, Dorothy Jackson and father-in-law, Ralph Jackson and his wife, Connie Jackson for accepting me unconditionally into their families. I would also like to thank Amy, Laura, Lily, Nicole, Eilis, Gail, Elizabeth, Marie, Julie, Cathy, and Margaret who helped get through this project with laughter. I can't forget Sharon who is the greatest friend any person can have. And yes, Amy I do believe we are soul sisters from two different worlds.

Most importantly, I must thank my husband and children for their support. Rhys and Bryn, you are amazing children. To my husband, Ralph, you have been very patient and helpful in getting this encyclopedia off the ground. Thank you for all those hours of proofing and editing my work. Your support has never gone unnoticed. I hope that this encyclopedia will be shared with other emergency room physicians, such as yourself, in order to better understand and treat your patients. We are blessed to have our amazing family even when life isn't so perfect! My love for you is immeasurable. Thank you.

NICKY ALI JACKSON

LIST OF ENTRIES A–Z

THEMATIC LIST OF ENTRIES

Victims of Domestic Violence

Battered Husbands
Battered Wives
Battered Women: Held in Captivity
Battered Women Who Kill: An Examination
Cohabiting Violence
Date Rape
Dating Violence
Intimate Partner Homicide
Intimate Partner Violence, Forms of
Marital Rape
Mutual Battering
Parricide
Spousal Prostitution
Stalking
Workplace, Domestic Violence in

Theoretical Perspectives and Correlates of Domestic Violence

Animal Abuse: The Link to Family Violence
Assessing Risk in Domestic Violence Cases
Attachment Theory and Domestic Violence
Battered Woman Syndrome
Batterer Typology
Bullying and the Family
Coercive Control
Control Balance Theory and Domestic Violence
Cycle of Violence
Depression and Domestic Violence
Education as a Risk Factor for Domestic Violence
Exchange Theory
Feminist Theory
Homelessness, The Impact of Family Violence on
Identity Theory and Domestic Violence
Intergenerational Transfer of Intimate Partner
    Violence
Popular Culture and Domestic Violence
Post-Incest Syndrome

Pregnancy-Related Violence
Social Class and Domestic Violence
Social Learning Theory and Family Violence
Stockholm Syndrome in Battered Women
Substance Use/Abuse and Intimate Partner
    Violence
Victim-Blaming Theory

Cross-Cultural and Religious Perspectives

Africa: Domestic Violence and the Law
Africa: The Criminal Justice System and the
    Problem of Domestic Violence in West Africa
African American Community, Domestic
    Violence in
Asian Americans and Domestic Violence: Cultural
    Dimensions
Child Abuse: A Global Perspective
Christianity and Domestic Violence
Corporal Punishment, Religious Attitudes toward
Cross-Cultural Examination of Domestic Violence
    in China and Pakistan
Cross-Cultural Examination of Domestic Violence
    in Latin America
Cross-Cultural Perspectives on Domestic Violence
Cross-Cultural Perspectives on How to Deal with
    Batterers
Dating Violence among African American Couples
Greece, Domestic Violence in
Human Rights, Refugee Laws, and Asylum
    Protection for People Fleeing Domestic Violence
Jewish Community, Domestic Violence within the
Medical Neglect Related to Religion and Culture
Minorities and Families in America,
    Introduction to
Multicultural Programs for Domestic Batterers
Native Americans, Domestic Violence among
Qur'anic Perspectives on Wife Abuse
Rule of Thumb
Rural Communities, Domestic Violence in

Understudied Areas within Domestic Violence Research

Domestic Violence and the Law

Child Abuse and Elder Abuse

Special Topics in Domestic Violence

AFRICA: DOMESTIC VIOLENCE AND THE LAW

Domestic violence is a form of aggression perpetrated by one family member against another. It includes a pattern of behaviors involving physical, sexual, economic, and emotional abuse, used alone or in combination, by an intimate partner often for the purpose of establishing and maintaining power and control over the other partner (Human Rights Watch 1995). Studies have shown that women are the primary victims of domestic violence (Greenfeld 1998; Neubauer 1999; Rennison and Welchans 2000). This is particularly true of women in Africa, where studies show that 35 to 75 percent of women are victims of violence at the hands of fathers, husbands, intimate partners, or male members of their families at some point in their lives (AFROL News 2002; Hajjar 2004; Human Rights Watch 2003; Mulama 2005; Okereke 2002). Given this situation, this article examines the role the law plays in the problem of domestic violence in Africa.

First and foremost, most African countries do not have specific laws prohibiting domestic violence and the associated gender-specific abuses women and girls suffer in Africa. The South African 1998 Domestic Violence Act is a notable exception in that it prohibits not only domestic violence but rape within marriage and other forms of violence in both marital and nonmarital relationships, including abuses by parents, guardians, other family members, and anyone who resides with the victim (Human Rights Watch 2003a). In Mauritania, a Protection from Domestic Violence Act was passed in 1997 (Bowman 2003). Additionally, as a result of pressure from the United Nations, African Union, World Health Organization, international and domestic human rights organizations, international and domestic nongovernmental organizations (NGOs), and human rights activists from around the world, a number of countries (including Ghana, Kenya, Nigeria, Tanzania, and Uganda) have drafted domestic violence bills which are at various stages of parliamentary discussions (Human Rights Watch 2005; Sarpong 2002). Other countries, such as Senegal, Tanzania, and Zimbabwe have laws prohibiting violence against women and girls, but such laws are rarely enforced. Even the constitutions of several countries in Africa guarantee equal rights to all citizens, including clauses that bar discrimination on the basis of sex; however, as Human Rights Watch (2000)

1

points out, the governments of African countries have failed to enforce existing laws and implement policies that reflect the principles of gender equality found in both regional and international human rights documents.

Although passing gender-sensitive laws that reflect the principles of human rights found in international documents such as the Convention on the Elimination of All Forms of Discrimination against Women (UN CEDAW 2000) and regional documents such as the Protocol to the African Charter on Human and People's Rights on the Rights of Women in Africa of the African Union are moves in the right direction, such laws become mere formalities if they are not enforced. For example, in 1998, the Ghanaian Parliament passed the Criminal Code Amendment Bill banning all forms of ritualized enslavement, but according to Aird (2003), ritualized forced labor is still practiced in Ghana. Similarly, female genital mutilation—a practice that is widespread in Africa—has been outlawed in twelve countries, but according to the Ark Foundation Ghana (2005) and Human Rights Watch (2002), the practice still goes on, and perpetrators have been prosecuted only in Burkina Faso, Ghana, Senegal, and Sierra Leone. Further, in Uganda, the 1972 Succession (Amendment) Decree, intended to recognize women's right to inherit from their husbands and fathers, and the 2003 Land Act (Amendment) Bill, intended to provide widows greater protection from eviction from their matrimonial homes following the death of their husbands, are usually not enforced. Tanzania's Marriage Act of 1971 prohibits corporal punishment of wives by husbands and grants spouses equal rights to property acquired through joint efforts. In practice, however, Tanzanian women are still denied these rights (González-Brenes 2004). Furthermore, the Penal Code in Zambia prohibits virtually all abuses associated with sexual violence, coercion, and discrimination based on sex, but these provisions are not enforced by the state (Human Rights Watch 2003a). From the foregoing, it is evident that enforcing existing statutes while drafting new legislations would stem down the tide of domestic abuse in Africa.

Also relevant to the problem of domestic violence in Africa is the fact that most African countries have multiple legal systems: statutory law, civil law, customary law, and religious law. When these legal systems conflict, as they often do, the dictates of customary law and/or religious law are generally adhered to. For example, in Cameroon, marital rape is recognized as an offense under statutory law but tolerated under customary law because it is culturally accepted that consent to marriage constitutes unlimited consent to sexual intercourse (Human Rights Watch 2002 and 2003a; Tetchiada 2005). Further, rape, according to Hajjar (2004), is a punishable offense in every Muslim society, but under dominant interpretations of *Sharia,* forced sex within marriage is not an offense. Also, in Sierra Leone and Cameroon, the statutory age of marriage is twenty-one and fifteen, respectively, while under Islamic and customary laws in both countries, a girl is marriageable at twelve (Human Rights Watch 2003d). In Nigeria, the Criminal Code stipulates that the age of marriage is sixteen, but under customary law, girls can be married off at twelve; in Ethiopia, the age of marriage according to statutory law is eighteen, but under customary law, girls can be married off at the tender age of eight (United Nations 2002). Further, civil law in Liberia prohibits polygyny but customary law permits men to have two or more wives simultaneously (U.S. Department of State 2004). In light of the above, the problem of domestic violence in Africa is partially due to the conflicts that exist among the multiple legal systems that operate in Africa.

Another area where the law in Africa tends to contribute to the problem of domestic violence is in its stance to rape. There is generally a narrow definition of the crime of rape in most African countries (Gyau 2004; Okungu 2003). The laws in many countries (East Timor, Liberia, Nigeria, Sierra Leone, Tanzania, Zambia, Zimbabwe), when referring to "sexual violence," specifically talk about rape as the penetration of a female victim's vagina by a male perpetrator's penis; at times, the definition goes further to require ejaculation for the elements of the crime of rape to be complete (Advocates for Youth 2005; Amnesty International 2004 and 2005a; Klein 2004; Nduna 2004). Acts of forced oral or anal sex or penetration by foreign objects are not considered rape. The confusion in rape laws in Africa is worse in Sierra Leone, where the rape of a person over the age of sixteen is considered a felony and carries a maximum sentence of life imprisonment, but the rape of a thirteen-year-old girl is misconstrued as a misdemeanor and carries a maximum sentence of two years. Even more confusing is the fact that to be classified as rape in both cases, the victim must have been a virgin, because forced sexual intercourse with a nonvirgin is not considered rape in Sierra Leone (Standley 1999). Also, statutory law in Sierra Leone requires that all serious criminal cases be tried under general law, but rape cases are frequently prosecuted under customary law, under which the alleged perpetrator is generally required to pay "virgin money" to the family of his victim and to the chiefs who oversee such cases. In Muslim communities, the "virgin victim" is sometimes forced to marry the offender, as a girl or woman who is not a virgin is considered less eligible for marriage (Human Rights Watch 2003d). In other countries, the rules of evidence require the corroborating testimony of a witness to the sexual assault before a rape survivor's statement can be admissible in court (Amnesty International 2005b; Hajjar 2004). Consequently, families of rape survivors in those countries seek monetary compensation rather than criminal prosecution.

In some ways, statutory laws in Africa discriminate against women and in so doing contribute to the problem of domestic violence. For example, Article 7 of the Trade Code in Cameroon allows a husband to oppose his wife's right to work if the protest is made in the interest of the household and family, and according to Articles 1421 and 1428 of the Civil Code, women are not fully entitled to use, enjoy, or sell their own property. Article 1421 grants husbands the right to administer communal property, which means that the husband has the legal right to sell or mortgage the couple's property without the wife's consent (UN CEDAW 2000). Also, Section 361 of the Penal Code in Cameroon criminalizes adultery, but the provisions differ depending upon whether the adulterer is the wife or the husband. The law provides that "any married woman having sexual intercourse with a man other than her husband shall be punished" and that "any married man having sexual intercourse in the matrimonial home, or habitually having sexual intercourse elsewhere, with a woman other than his wife or wives, shall be punished" (International Women's Rights Action Watch 1999). While in the case of women *all* adultery is a criminal offense, for men, it is or is not a crime depending on the venue or frequency.

Under the Personal Status Code of Morocco and Egypt, women are treated as legal minors and denied the legal autonomy to conclude their own marriage contracts. The code establishes male authority over female members of the family (Alami 1992). Furthermore, women in Africa seeking to formally terminate violent marriages through divorce face enormous legal obstacles. In most countries, a woman cannot simply accuse her husband of adultery to terminate their marriage; she must couple her claim with a claim of cruelty and/or desertion or claim that the adultery was incestuous or bigamous. There is no such legal requirement for men. Marriage and divorce laws in Uganda discriminate against women and contravene constitutional guarantees for nondiscrimination, equal protection of the

law, and equal rights in marriage, during marriage, and at its dissolution. For example, Section 27 of Uganda's Divorce Act stipulates that if a wife's adultery is the cause of a divorce, a court may order that all or part of her property be settled for the benefit of the husband and/or the children (Human Rights Watch 2003a). There is no such provision for men. Nationality laws in Egypt, Liberia, Morocco, Nigeria, and Zambia also discriminate against women. While men from these countries can transmit their nationality to their children wherever they are born and whoever their mothers are, women, on the other hand, do not have the same right (International Women's Rights Action Watch 1999). Furthermore, immigration rules in Nigeria require that a wife obtain her husband's endorsement before she can be issued an international passport and that for the children to be endorsed on her passport, their father must give written consent (Embassy of Nigeria 2005).

Religious laws in Africa are also discriminatory against women and as a result can contribute to the prevalence of domestic violence. *Sharia* tends to be interpreted in ways that give men power over women family members; dominant interpretations of *Sharia* treat women as legal minors and accord men the status of heads of their families with guardianship authority over and responsibility for women. As a result, women have a duty to obey their guardians—husbands, fathers, or other male heads of the family (Hajjar 2004). Consequently, a male legal guardian of an adult woman can oppose her choice of husband (Human Rights Watch 2001). Also, under the *Sharia* penal code in Nigeria—as in other African countries with large Muslim populations—a husband has the right to beat his wife as long as the beating does not result in grievous harm, which is defined as loss of sight, hearing, power of speech, facial disfigurement, or other life-endangering injuries (Women's International Network 1998). In effect, while divorce is a permissible option to end a marriage under Islam, in many largely Islamic countries, it tends to be treated as a male prerogative; women can easily be divorced but not seek divorce (Amnesty International 2005a and 2005b). Additionally, dominant/fundamentalist interpretations of *Sharia*, according to Hajjar (2004), allow men to have up to four wives, to whom they have unabridged sexual access and who cannot refuse, because such refusal can be conceived as a defiance of their duties and can give rise to accusations of disobedience, thereby triggering legal justification for beating. Such interpretations are evident in decisions handed down by *Sharia* courts in predominantly fundamentalist countries. For example, an appellate *Sharia* court in Nigeria upheld a sentence of death by stoning against a woman for having sex outside marriage, while setting free the man she allegedly had sex with on the ground that the court lacked sufficient evidence to prosecute him for the alleged adultery (Human Rights Watch 2001). This growing Islamic fundamentalism led the Egyptian government to amend its constitution in 1981 to provide that the principles of *Sharia* would constitute the main source of legislation in Egypt (Hajjar 2004). There is no doubt that such legislations would adversely affect women.

Another way the law could affect the incidence of domestic violence in Africa is in its recognition of customary laws and practices. Due to the multiplicity of ethnic origins and cultural differences reflected in the various beliefs and practices found in most African countries, national governments allow local governments and authorities to interpret and apply local norms and values to issues that arise from within their communities without interference as long as such norms and values pass the "repugnancy test." This test, according to Okereafoezeke (2001), is the government's legal requirement that for a customary law to be enforced, it must neither be repugnant to natural justice, equity, and good conscience nor be contrary to any written law. Since African traditional society is highly patriarchal, the resulting body of customary laws is highly discriminatory against women (U.S. Department of State 2005a). For example, under African customary law, a man can marry two or more wives simultaneously and can divorce any one of them without any verifiable justification (Human Rights Watch 2001). Women have no such right. Also, once married, an African woman is considered her husband's inheritance property, comparable to her spouse's personal property and real estate, and upon his death, she herself can be inherited by her husband's brother (AFROL News 2004; Human Rights Watch 2003c; U.S. Department of State 2004). As an old custom, wife inheritance was a way for men to take responsibility for their dead brothers' children and household, but the fact that it can be and is frequently forced on the woman contributes to the problem of domestic violence against women in Africa.

Most marriages under customary law require the family of the prospective husband to pay a "bride price," or dowry, in the form of money or a gift to the family of the prospective wife (U.S. Department of State 2005a and 2005b). Historically, this payment indicated appreciation for the characteristics and skills of the bride and a bonding of the two families and the extended family on both sides. Now, a bride price is frequently regarded simply as payment for a commodity and, as in any commercial transaction, entitles the husband—essentially, the buyer—to full ownership rights over his acquisition (Amnesty International 2005b). As property, many women married under customary law have no authority within what is seen as the man's home (Amnesty International 2005a). According to human rights organizations and the United Nations, this practice subjugates women to the unbridled authority of their husbands because it reinforces the inferior status of women within customary marriages (League of Democratic Women 2005; United Nations 2002) and forces women to remain in abusive relationships (Okereke 2002). Furthermore, under customary law, husbands have numerous grounds for divorce available to them, including infidelity, infertility, adultery, witchcraft, or insubordination. The grounds available to wives are limited to impotence, excessive cruelty, and desertion.

Also under customary marriage laws, spouse abuse is not a legitimate ground for divorce. In fact, interviews by Human Rights Watch and other human rights organizations across Africa show that neither men nor women see anything wrong with a husband beating his wife every now and then (Human Rights Watch 2001, 2002, 2003c). The League of Democratic Women (2005) holds that in addition to approving of physical abuse of wives, women also perpetrate psychological violence on other women, especially in the observance of widowhood rites, which include shaving the woman's head bald; making her sit/sleep on the floor for a certain length of time; making her drink water used to bathe the corpse; making her jump over the corpse/grave; making her sit/sleep with the corpse; making her eat from a broken plate and not allowing her to wash the hand used to eat; expecting her to cry/wail early in the mornings; keeping her in seclusion or restricting her movement for a certain period of time; making her take an oath of innocence; and disinheriting her of property acquired with her deceased spouse. In contrast, a widower is showered with sympathy and compassion on the death of a wife. To console him, a woman could be procured for the widower even on the night of the wife's death to keep him "company."

Although most African countries do not have laws specifically prohibiting domestic violence and related gender-specific violence perpetrated against women and girls, it can be argued that the greatest problem with regard to domestic violence in Africa is nonenforcement of existing laws and constitutional provisions that bar discrimination on the basis of sex. By the same token, amending laws that directly or indirectly discriminate against women would be a move in the right direction.

GODPOWER O. OKEREKE

See also **Africa: The Criminal Justice System and the Problem of Domestic Violence in West Africa; Cross-Cultural Examination of Domestic Violence in China and Pakistan; Cross-Cultural Examination of Domestic Violence in Latin America; Cross-Cultural Perspectives on Domestic Violence; Cross-Cultural Perspectives on How to Deal with Batterers; South Africa, Domestic Violence in**

References and Further Reading

Advocates for Youth. "Sexual Abuse and Violence in Sub-Saharan Africa," 2005. http://www.advocatesforyouth. org/publications/factsheet (accessed August 11, 2005).

AFROL News. "Half of Nigeria's Women Experience Domestic Violence," 2002. http://www.afrol.com/articles/ 16471 (accessed August 6, 2006).

———. "Gender Profiles: Liberia," 2003. http://www.afrol. com/categories.women/profiles/Liberia_women.htm (accessed June 10, 2005).

———. "Gender Profiles: Cameroon," 2004. http://www. afrol.com/Categories/Women/profiles/cameroon_women. htm (accessed June 10, 2005).

Aird, S. C. "Ghana's Slaves to the Gods." *Human Rights Brief: A Legal Resource for the International Human Rights Community* 7, no. 1 (2003). http://www.wcl.amer ican.edu/hrbrief/v7i1/ghana.htm (accessed August 6, 2006).

Alami, Dawoud S. *The Marriage Contract in Islamic Law in the Sharia and Personal Status Laws of Egypt and Morocco.* Herndon, VA: Brill Academic Publishers, 1992.

Amnesty International. "Liberia: No Impunity for Rape—A Crime against Humanity and a War Crime," 2004. http:// web.amnesty.org/library/index/engafr340172004 (accessed August 6, 2006).

———. "Nigeria: Level of Violence against Women in the Home Shockingly High," 2005a. http://www.amnesty.ie/ user/content/view/full/3900 (accessed August 6, 2006).

———. "Nigeria: Unheard Voices," 2005b. http://web.am nesty.org/library/index/ENGAFR440042005 (accessed June 25, 2005).

Ark Foundation Ghana. "Domestic Violence Facts and Figures," 2005. Gender Centre on Violence against Women and Children in Ghana. http://www.h-net.org/~attaboah/ ark/information/facts_figures.htm (accessed August 28, 2005).

Bowman, Cynthia Grant. "Theories of Domestic Violence in the African Context." *Journal of Gender, Social Policy, and the Law* 11, no. 2 (2003): 847–863. http://www. wcl.american.edu/journal/genderlaw/11/bowman.pdf? rd=1 (accessed August 6, 2006).

Embassy of Nigeria (The Hague, Netherlands). "Passport," 2005. http://www.nigerianembassy.nl/passport.htm (accessed August 6, 2005).

González-Brenes, Melissa. "Domestic Violence and Household Decision-Making: Evidence from East Africa." Ph.D. diss., Department of Economics, University of California, Berkeley, 2004. http://www.polisci.ucla.edu/ wgape/papers/7_Gonzalez.pdf (accessed August 6, 2006).

Greenfeld, L. A. *Violence by Intimates: Analysis of Data on Crimes by Current or Former Spouses, Boyfriends, and Girlfriends.* Washington, DC: U.S. Department of Justice, 1998.

Gyau, Isabella. "Ghana: Marital Rape Under the Spotlight." Accra, Ghana: Inter Press Service News Agency, 2004.

Hajjar, Lisa. "Domestic Volence and *Shari'a*: A Comparative Study of Muslim Societies in the Middle East, Africa and Asia," 2004. http://www.law.emory.edu/IFL/thematic/ violence.htm (accessed May 10, 2005).

Human Rights Watch [HRW]. "The State Response to Domestic Violence and Rape in South Africa," 1995. http://www.hrw.org/reports/1997/safrica/Safrica-03.htm (accessed July 2, 2005).

———. "International Human Rights and Tanzanian Law," 2000. *HRW country reports.* http://www.hrw.org/reports/ 2000/tanzania/Duhweb-08.htm (accessed July 2, 2005).

———. "Human Rights Watch World Report 2001," 2001. Women's Rights Division. http://www.hrw.org/wr2k1/ africa/index.htm (accessed July 2, 2005).

———. "Defending Human Rights Worldwide: World Report," 2002. http://www.hrw.org/wr2k2/africa.html (accessed July 2, 2005).

———. "Just Die Quietly: Domestic Violence and Women's Vulnerability to HIV in Uganda." *HRW* 15, no. 15(A) (2003a). http://www.hrw.org/reports/2003/ uganda0803 (accessed August 6, 2006).

———. "Suffering in Silence: The Links between Human Rights Abuses and HIV Transmission to Girls in Zambia," 2003b. http://www.hrw.org/reports/2003/zambia (accessed August 6, 2006).

———. "Policy Paralysis: A Call for Action on HIV/AIDS-Related Human Rights Abuses against Women and Girls in Africa," 2003c. http://www.hrw.org/reports/ 2003/africa1203 (accessed July 2, 2005).

———. "We'll Kill You If You Cry: Sexual Violence in the Sierra Leone Conflict." *HRW* 15, no. 1(A) (2003d). http://hrw.org/reports/2003/sierraleone (accessed August 6, 2006).

———. "Uganda: Domestic Relations Bill Would Save Lives," 2005. http://hrw.org/english/docs/2005/05/31/ uganda11051.htm (accessed August 15, 2005).

International Women's Rights Action Watch. "Country Reports: Cameroon," 1999. http://iwraw.igc.org/publi cations/countries/cameroon.htm (accessed June 8, 2005).

Klein, Jacques Paul. "Conference on Gender Justice in Post-Conflict Situations." United Nations Mission in Liberia, 2004. http://www.womenwarpeace.org/issues/justice/gen der_justice_conference.htm (accessed June 10, 2005).

League of Democratic Women. "For the Health of Women, for the Health of the World: No More Violence," 2005. http://www.cwgl.rutgers.edu/16days/about.html (accessed June 10, 2005).

Mulama, Joyce. "Domestic Violence in East Africa: Violence against Women Defies Laws, Education Campaigns," 2005. http://www.ipsnews.net/africa/interna.asp?idnews= 27798 (accessed July 5, 2005).

Nduna, Sydia. "Inter Agency Lessons Learned Conference: Prevention and Response to Sexual and Gender-Based Violence in Zambia." United Nations High Commission for Refugees, 2004.

Neubauer, D. W. *America's Courts and the Criminal Justice System,* 6th ed. Belmont, CA: West/Wadsworth, 1999.

Okereafoezeke, Nonso. "Judging the Enforceability of Nigeria's Native Laws, Customs, and Traditions in the Face of Official Controls." *Southern Regional Seminar in African Studies,* Spring 2001.

Okereke, Godpower. "Incidence of Physical Spouse Abuse in Nigeria: A Pilot Study." *Institute of African Studies Research Review* 18, no. 2 (2002) (University of Ghana, Legon). http://www.peacewomen.org/news/news%20 archive/2003/August/culture.html

Okungu, Vincent R. "Culture of Sexual Violence Pervades Continent," 2003. Women's International League for Peace and Freedom. http://www.peacewomen.org/news/ news%20archive/2003/August/culture.html (accessed July 10, 2005).

Rennison, C. M., and S. Welchans. *Intimate Partner Violence.* Washington, DC: U.S. Department of Justice, 2000.

Sarpong, Sam. "Views and News on Peace, Justice and Reconciliation in Africa. Ghana: Striving to Flush out Domestic Violence," 2002. http://www.newsfromafrica. org/newsfromafrica/articles/art_809.html (accessed June 20, 2005).

Standley, Jane. "South Africa Targets Domestic Violence," 1999. British Broadcasting Corporation. http://news. bbc.co.uk/1/hi/world/africa/566160.stm (accessed April 16, 2005).

Tetchiada, Sylvestre. "Rights—Cameroon: Report Paints Bleak Picture of Women's Lives," 2005. Inter Press Service News Agency. http://www.ipsnews.net/africa/interna. asp?idnews=22820 (accessed June 10, 2005).

UN CEDAW [United Nations Committee on the Elimination of Discrimination against Women]. "Initial Reports of States Parties: Cameroon," 2000. http://www.un.org/ womenwatch/daw/cedaw/cedaw23/cameroon.pdf (accessed August 6, 2006).

United Nations. "East Africa: Special Report on Violence against Women," 2002. *IRIN News.org.* http://www.irin-news.org/report.asp?ReportID=24161&SelectRegion =East_Africa&SelectCountry=EAST_AFRICA (accessed June 10, 2005).

U.S. Department of State. *Country Reports on Human Rights Practices: Liberia.* Bureau of Democracy, Human Rights, and Labor. Washington DC: Author, 2004.

———. *Human Rights Report on Nigeria for the Year 2004.* Washington, DC: U.S. Bureau of Democracy, Human Rights, and Labor, 2005a.

———. "Country Report: Ghana, 2004," 2005b. http:// www.state.gov/r/pa/ei/bgn/2860.htm (accessed June 10, 2005).

Women's International Network. "Family Violence in Lagos, Nigeria." Lagos: Author, 1998.

AFRICA: THE CRIMINAL JUSTICE SYSTEM AND THE PROBLEM OF DOMESTIC VIOLENCE IN WEST AFRICA

Domestic violence is a form of aggression perpetrated by a family member or an intimate partner, usually male, on another family member or partner, usually female. According to Amnesty International (2004), domestic violence is a problem the world over and affects one in every three women; this translates into approximately one billion women who have been beaten, coerced into sex, or otherwise abused in their lifetime. This problem is particularly pernicious in Africa, where both international and regional human rights and gender-sensitive documents have not been implemented by the governments of the various countries (Human Rights Watch 2002). This article examines how the criminal justice systems in West

African countries respond to the problem of domestic violence in the subregion.

Laws are made by legislatures and enforced by the police, and when violators are arrested, the courts interpret the law and assign punishment accordingly. It follows, then, that before the police and subsequently the courts can get involved in the problem of domestic violence, the law must prohibit this behavior. However, among West African countries, only Mauritania has specific domestic violence legislation in place (Amnesty International 2004). Article 297 of the Senegalese Penal Code, amended in 1999, punishes violence against women by imprisonment of one to five years (Center for Reproductive Law and Policy 2001). Ghana and

Nigeria both have draft legislations designed to make domestic violence illegal in their countries (Human Rights Watch 2005). As of this writing, the rest of the countries in West Africa have yet to draft domestic violence legislations (Amnesty International 2004). Without specific domestic violence legislation which prescribes the responsibilities of the officials of the criminal justice system, the victims will continue to suffer (Archer 2002). By the same token, the constitutions and sometimes civil laws of the various West African countries guarantee equality before the law and forbid discrimination based on sex, race, religion, class, ethnicity, or language; despite this, women continue to experience extensive societal discrimination, especially in rural areas, where women generally are confined to traditional roles. For example, though the Ghanaian Parliament banned the practice of customary servitude (known as *Trokosi*) in 1998, the practice still goes on (Aird 2003). Also, female genital mutilation has been outlawed in many West African countries (including Burkina Faso, Gambia, Ghana, Guinea, Ivory Coast, Mauritania, Niger, Senegal, and Togo), but the practice continues and prosecutions are few (Human Rights Watch 2003c). Further, despite the 1985 Agrarian and Land Reform Legislation in Burkina Faso—which established equality between men and women and granted women the right to own land—in practice, women in this country are still denied this right (Center for Reproductive Law and Policy 2001). Commitment on the part of the governments of the various countries to enforcing the provisions of the constitutions and, in some cases, civil laws of their respective countries would stem the tide of domestic violence within the West African subregion. Such commitment would include providing funds for gender-sensitive training of criminal justice officials and outlining the responsibilities of each part of the criminal justice system.

Further, it has been charged that some laws in West African countries are narrow and in some instances ambiguous, and as a result are confusing to even criminal justice officials (Human Rights Watch 1995). For example, rape laws in Liberia, Nigeria, and Sierra Leone provide a narrow definition of the crime of rape that requires penetration of the vagina by a man's penis for the elements of the crime to be complete (Advocates for Youth 2005; Amnesty International 2005a; Human Rights Watch 2003c). Acts of forced oral or anal sex or penetration by foreign objects are not considered rape. According to Human Rights Watch (2003d), this discrepancy in rape laws is worse in Sierra Leone, where the law holds that unlawful carnal knowledge of a girl over the age of 16 is a felony but unlawful carnal knowledge of a 13-year-old girl, whether with or without her consent, is a misdemeanor. To be classified as a crime in either case, the victim must be a virgin, because forced sexual intercourse with a nonvirgin in Sierra Leone is not considered rape (Standley 1999). Similar confusion exists in Senegal, where the rape of a person over the age of 16 is a felony but the rape of younger girls is misconstrued by the police and the judiciary as unlawful carnal knowledge, which makes the act a misdemeanor. To improve the handling of domestic violence by the criminal justice system, any inherent confusion in the law as well as narrow definitions of the crime of rape must be given attention.

In evaluating how the criminal justice system handles the problem of domestic violence in West Africa, it is necessary to note that several statutes in many West African countries discriminate against women. For example, in Cameroon, civil law allows a husband to oppose his wife's right to work in a separate profession if the protest is made in the interest of the family. Also, while Cameroonian law gives a woman the freedom to organize her own business, it allows her husband to end such commercial activity by notifying the clerk of the commerce tribunal of his opposition (Human Rights Watch 2002). These laws, in effect, subjugate women to the authority of men. In addition, the law in many West African countries either tolerates marital rape or does not recognize it as a crime. In Cameroon, for example, marital rape is recognized as an offense under statutory law but tolerated under customary law because it is culturally accepted that consent to marriage constitutes unlimited consent to sexual intercourse (Human Rights Watch 2002 and 2003a; Tetchiada 2005). The law permits men in West Africa to have two or more wives simultaneously but does not allow polyandry. Spousal abuse is not a legal and sufficient ground for divorce (Gambia is an exception). Further, the law in some countries even permits husbands to beat their wives (New York University School of Law 2004). In Nigeria, for example, the Penal Code permits husbands to "correct" their wives as long as such "correction" does not result in grievous harm, which is defined as loss of sight, hearing, power of speech, facial disfigurement, or other life-endangering injuries (Women's International Network 1998). Under this type of legal discrimination, it should not be surprising that the police in Nigeria as well as within the subregion do not intervene in "family affairs" except in the case of serious bodily harm or murder (Amnesty International 2004).

The law also discriminates against women in the manner in which it punishes people who assault others. For example, the Criminal Code for Southern Nigeria prescribes different sentences for the crime of assault depending on whether the victim of the attack is a man or a woman. Whereas assault on a man is a felony and carries a prison term of three years, assault on a woman is a misdemeanor and carries a prison term of two years (Amnesty International 2004). Also, Section 361 of the Penal Code in Cameroon criminalizes adultery, but the provisions differ depending upon whether the adulterer is the wife or the husband. The law holds that "any married woman having sexual intercourse with a man other than her husband shall be punished" and that "any married man having sexual intercourse in the matrimonial home or habitually having sexual intercourse elsewhere, with a woman other than his wife or wives, shall be punished" (International Women's Rights Action Watch 1999). In effect, for a man to be punished for adultery, the act must either take place in the matrimonial home or be habitual. But, in the case of a woman, all acts of adultery are criminal. Also, nationality laws in Liberia and Nigeria allow men from these countries to transmit their nationality to their children wherever they are born and whoever their mothers are. Women, on the other hand, are not given the same privilege (International Women's Rights Action Watch 1999). Furthermore, immigration rules in Nigeria require that a married adult woman wishing to obtain an international passport must secure her husband's endorsement before such a passport can be issued to her and if she wants the children to be endorsed on her passport that she presents their father's written consent (Embassy of Nigeria 2005). Rules of this nature make the intervention of the criminal justice system in cases of domestic violence problematic. Additionally, whereas divorce is a permissible option under the marriage and divorce laws of West African countries, it tends to be treated as a male prerogative. A woman cannot be granted divorce on the ground of adultery or abuse alone; she must accompany either claim with cruelty and/or desertion. Men, on the other hand, can divorce their wives without any verifiable justification (Amnesty International 2005b). In effect, women can easily be divorced but not seek divorce. So, when the spirit and/or the letter of the law clearly discriminates against women, there is very little that criminal justice officials can do to fight domestic violence.

Criminal justice officials in various countries in West Africa have been accused of maintaining a dismissive, unsympathetic, or nonchalant attitude toward the problem of domestic violence within the subregion (Amnesty International 2005a and 2005b). Human Rights Watch (1997) has charged that the police do not see domestic abuse as a "real" crime but as a family matter in which the state has no right to intervene (AFROL News 2002). Court officials are said to be complacent in dealing with victims of domestic abuse who seek their assistance (U.S. Department of State 2004) and judges are said to blame the victims of domestic abuse for their own victimization (Amnesty International 2005b). The criminal justice system as a whole has even been accused of discriminating against women in the subregion (U.S. Department of State 2004). Relative to the above, the following need to be taken into account. Each country within the subregion is made up of multiple ethnic groups whose customs, traditions, norms, values, beliefs, practices, dialects, and languages are different to say the least. To be sensitive to this ethnic pluralism, the governments allow customary laws to operate alongside civil or general laws as long as such customary laws pass the "repugnancy test," which is the government's legal requirement that for a customary law to be enforced, it must neither be repugnant to natural justice, equity, and good conscience nor be contrary to any written law (Okereafoezeke 2001).

It is common experience in these countries that the law in theory and the law in practice remain estranged; customary law is actually given precedence over civil or general law in case of conflict. Since the state allows the police and the courts (especially those in the rural areas) to operate in accordance with local norms and values, interviews conducted by both Amnesty International (2005b) and Human Rights Watch (2003c, 2003d) reveal that victims of domestic violence (including sexual violence) and their families do not report such abuses to the police but rather seek informal (mostly financial) settlements. It is postulated that this reluctance to report abuses to the police is due to negative experiences with the criminal justice system, especially with the police. Also, customary norms and practices in the various countries (especially in the rural areas) either do not see anything wrong with wife beating or tolerate the behavior. Consequently, both men and women see spouse abuse as normal (Human Rights Watch 2003c); women especially see domestic violence as another burden they must bear (League of Democratic Women 2005). Since the officials of the criminal justice system are products of the same culture, it should be expected that they too would not see anything wrong with a man beating his wife. While this does not justify the abuse or excuse either police or judicial inactivity with reference to this problem, it does indicate that the government of each country needs to embark on a public awareness campaign to educate the public about the ills of certain norms, traditions, customs, and values, as well as the costs of domestic violence to the society at large. It also indicates that the governments need to pass domestic violence legislation detailing the responsibilities of all citizens, the police, court officials, prosecutors, judges, social workers, and counselors, as well as providing and funding shelters for abused women and children.

The public's reluctance to report abuses to the police also indicates that the governments of West African countries need to pay attention to those customary norms, values, beliefs, and practices that are prejudicial toward women and girls and that make them vulnerable to abuse. For example, whereas statutory laws among West African countries set the age of marriage at between 15 and 21, under the customary laws of the various countries girls are marriageable at 12 and, in some instances of arranged and forced marriages, younger (Human Rights Watch 2003b). Along the same line is the custom that requires the family of a prospective husband to pay a "bride price," or dowry, in the form of money or a gift to the family of the prospective wife (U.S. Department of State 2005a and 2005b). Historically, this payment indicated appreciation for the qualities and skills possessed by the bride and served to cement the relationship between the two families and their respective extended families. Currently, this symbolic gesture is assumed to be equivalent to payment for a commodity and, as in any commercial transaction, entitles the husband—the buyer—to full ownership rights over his "purchase" (Amnesty International 2005b). Having been "bought," many women married under customary law have no authority within what is seen as the man's home (Amnesty International 2005a). According to human rights organizations and the United Nations, this practice subjugates women to the unbridled authority of their husbands because it reinforces the inferior status of women within customary marriages (League of Democratic Women 2005; United Nations 2002) and forces women who cannot repay the dowry to remain in abusive relationships (Okereke 2002). Another customary practice that contributes to the abuse of women and as a result needs to be given legislative attention by the governments of West African countries is wife inheritance. Once a bride price has been paid, the woman is considered the property of the husband. When he dies, the widow is often unable to collect any inheritance; indeed, since she herself is considered part of the man's inheritance property, she could be inherited by another male family member, often against her will (AFROL News 2004). If a

woman is customarily considered to be her husband's property and can be inherited by another male family member on the death of her husband, there is not much the police can do for her if she is a victim of abuse; they might even be apt to escort her back to her abusive husband or family, to whom she belongs.

Also hampering a positive relationship between abused women and the police and criminal justice system in West Africa is the growing incidence of religious fundamentalism. Fundamentalist and dominant interpretations of Islamic law, *Sharia,* in countries with large Muslim populations (such as Nigeria and Sierra Leone) treat women as legal minors and accord men the status of heads of their families with guardianship authority over and responsibility for women (Human Rights Watch 2001). These interpretations allow men to have up to four wives, to whom they have unabridged sexual access and who cannot refuse, because such refusal can be conceived as a defiance of their duties and can give rise to accusations of disobedience, thereby triggering legal justification for beating (Hajjar 2004). In these countries, *Sharia* tends to be interpreted in ways that give men power over women family members. As a result, women have a duty to obey their guardians-husbands, fathers, or other male heads of the family; failure to do so could result in violence (Hajjar 2004, p. 9). Such fundamentalist interpretations are evident in decisions handed down by *Sharia* courts in Nigeria. For example, an appellate *Sharia* court in northern Nigeria upheld a death by stoning sentence against a woman for having sex outside marriage, while setting free the man she allegedly had sex with on the ground that the court lacked sufficient evidence to prosecute him for the alleged adultery (Human Rights Watch 2001). Under the Maliki School of Thought, dominating interpretation of *Sharia* penal codes in the twelve northern states in Nigeria which have introduced them since 1999, pregnancy is considered sufficient evidence to condemn a woman to death, but a mere oath by the man denying having had sexual intercourse with the woman is often considered sufficient proof of innocence unless four independent and reputable eyewitnesses declare his involvement in the act of voluntary intercourse (Amnesty International 2004). The fault here is not with the police or the criminal justice system failing to protect women or discriminating against women, but with the federal government for allowing such fundamentalist/dominant interpretations of religious tenets to prosper.

This article asserts that the criminal justice system in West Africa does not take the problem of domestic violence within the subregion seriously. The authors believe that this is mainly due to the lack of domestic violence legislation and gender-sensitive laws; preference given to statutory and customary laws that discriminate against women and girls; prevalence of customs, traditions, beliefs, and practices that are prejudicial toward women and girls; and the inability of the governments of West African countries to check the growing incidence of religious fundamentalism and ethnic intolerance.

GODPOWER O. OKEREKE and
PETER RACHEOTES

See also **Africa: Domestic Violence and the Law; African American Community, Domestic Violence in; Asian Americans and Domestic Violence: Cultural Dimensions; Cross-Cultural Examination of Domestic Violence in China and Pakistan; Cross-Cultural Examination of Domestic Violence in Latin America; Cross-Cultural Perspectives on Domestic Violence; Cross-Cultural Perspectives on How to Deal with Batterers; Dating Violence among African American Couples; Greece, Domestic Violence in; Minorities and Families in America, Introduction to; South Africa, Domestic Violence in**

References and Further Reading

Advocates for Youth. "Sexual Abuse and Violence in Sub-Saharan Africa," 2005. http://www.advocatesforyouth.org/publications/factsheet (accessed August 11, 2005).

AFROL News. "Gender Profiles: Cameroon," 2004. http://www.afrol.com/Categories/Women/profiles/cameroon_women.htm (accessed June 10, 2005).

Aird, S. C. "Ghana's Slaves to the Gods." *Human Rights Brief: A Legal Resource for the International Human Rights Community* 7, no. 1 (2003). http://www.wcl.american.edu/hrbrief/v7i1/ghana.htm (accessed August 6, 2006).

Amnesty International. "Making Violence against Women Count: Facts and Figures," 2004. http://web.amnesty.org/library/Index/ENGACT770362004 (accessed August 6, 2006).

———. "Nigeria: Level of Violence against Women in the Home Shockingly High," 2005a. http://www.amnesty.ie/user/content/view/full/3900 (accessed August 6, 2006).

———. "Nigeria: Unheard Voices," 2005b. http://web.amnesty.org/library/index/ENGAFR440042005 (accessed June 25, 2005).

Archer, Raymond. "Ghanaian Women Demanding Protection from Violence." *Women's eNews*. Accra, Ghana, 2002. http://www.womensenews.org/article.cfm?aid=886 (accessed August 6, 2005).

Center for Reproductive Law and Policy. "Women of the World: Laws and Policies Affecting Their Reproductive Lives," 2001. http://www.crlp.org/pub_bo_wowafrica.html#online (accessed August 3, 2005).

Embassy of Nigeria (The Hague, Netherlands). "Passport," 2005. http://www.nigerianembassy.nl/passport.htm (accessed August 6, 2005).

Hajjar, Lisa. "Domestic Violence and *Shari'a*: A Comparative Study of Muslim Societies in the Middle East, Africa and Asia," 2004. http://www.law.emory.edu/IFL/thematic/violence.htm (accessed May 10, 2005).

Human Rights Watch. "The State Response to Domestic Violence and Rape in South Africa," 1995. http://www.hrw.org/reports/1997/safrica/Safrica-03.htm (accessed July 2, 2005).

———. "The State Response to Violence against Women," 1997. http://www.hrw.org/reports/1997/safrica/Safrica-03.htm (accessed August 7, 2005).

———. "Human Rights Watch World Report 2001: Africa," 2001. http://www.hrw.org/wr2k1/africa/index.html (accessed July 2, 2005).

———. "Africa Overview," 2002. *World Report 2002*. http://www.hrw.org/wr2k2/africa.html (accessed July 2, 2005).

———. "Just Die Quietly: Domestic Violence and Women's Vulnerability to HIV in Uganda." *HRW* 15, no. 15(A) (2003a). http://www.hrw.org/reports/2003/uganda0803 (accessed August 6, 2006).

———. "Suffering in Silence: The Links between Human Rights Abuses and HIV Transmission to Girls in Zambia," 2003b. http://www.hrw.org/reports/2003/zambia (accessed August 6, 2006).

———. "Policy Paralysis: A Call for Action on HIV/AIDS-Related Human Rights Abuses against Women and Girls in Africa," 2003c. http://www.hrw.org/reports/2003/africa1203 (accessed July 2, 2005).

———. "Women and Girls under Sierra Leonean Law," 2003d. http://www.hrw.org/wr/africa/index/html

———. "Uganda: Domestic Relations Bill Would Save Lives," 2005. Women's Rights Division. http://hrw.org/english/docs/2005/05/31/uganda11051.htm (accessed August 15, 2005).

International Women's Rights Action Watch. "Country Reports: Cameroon," 1999. http://iwraw.igc.org/publications/countries/cameroon.htm (accessed June 8, 2005).

League of Democratic Women. "For the Health of Women, for the Health of the World: No More Violence," 2005. http://www.cwgl.rutgers.edu/16days/about.html (accessed June 10, 2005).

New York University School of Law. "Strategies for Combating Domestic Violence: Ghana and Sierra Leone," 2004. http://www.law.nyu.edu/newscalendars/2004_2005/RTKseries/afadzinu.html (accessed August 6, 2006).

Okereafoezeke, Nonso. "Judging the Enforceability of Nigeria's Native Laws, Customs, and Traditions in the Face of Official Controls." *Southern Regional Seminar in African Studies,* Spring 2001.

Okereke, Godpower. "Incidence of Physical Spouse Abuse in Nigeria: A Pilot Study." *Institute of African Studies Research Review* 18, no. 2 (2002) (University of Ghana, Legon).

Standley, Jane. "South Africa Targets Domestic Violence," 1999. British Broadcasting Corporation. http://news.bbc.co.uk/1/hi/world/africa/566160.stm (accessed April 16, 2005).

Tetchiada, Sylvestre. "Rights—Cameroon: Report Paints Bleak Picture of Women's Lives," 2005. Inter Press Service News Agency. http://www.ipsnews.net/africa/interna.asp?idnews=22820 (accessed June 10, 2005).

United Nations. "East Africa: Special Report on Violence against Women," 2002. *IRIN News.org*. http://www.irinnews.org/report.asp?ReportID=24161&SelectRegion=

East_Africa&SelectCountry=EAST_AFRICA (accessed June 10, 2005).

U.S. Department of State. "Country Reports on Human Rights Practices: Liberia," 2004. Washington, DC: Bureau of Democracy, Human Rights, and Labor.

———. "Human Rights Report on Nigeria for the Year 2004," 2005a. Washington, DC: U.S. Bureau of Democracy, Human Rights, and Labor.

———. "Country Report: Ghana, 2004," 2005b. http://www.state.gov/r/pa/ei/bgn/2860.htm (accessed June 10, 2005).

AFRICAN AMERICAN COMMUNITY, DOMESTIC VIOLENCE IN

According to the 2000 Census, there were over 34 million Americans who identified as African American. This group constitutes over 12 percent of the U.S. population (U.S. Bureau of the Census 2001). As a group, they are very diverse and differ greatly from each other in socioeconomic status, education level, racial identity, acculturation, family structure, and political affiliation (Sue and Sue 2003). For example, while roughly 20 percent of African Americans live in poverty, about one-third are considered middle or upper class. While one-third of African American men are involved in the criminal justice system, one out of seven African American families earned more than $50,000 per year (Hildebrand, Phenice, Gray, and Hines 1996). Since the 1970s and 1980s, when violence against women first became viewed as a critical social issue, scholars have begun to examine racial and ethnic differences in the incidence and severity of violence. A growing focus of this inquiry has been domestic violence in the African American community.

Intimate Partner Violence in the African American Community

Although violence against men does occur, women are much more likely than men to be the victims of violence (Tjaden and Thoennes 2000). According to the National Violence against Women Survey (NVWS) (Tjaden and Thoennes 2000), 22 percent of women surveyed reported being physically assaulted by a current or former spouse or partner in their lifetime, compared with 7 percent of men reporting such assaults. Similarly, violence against women tends to be intimate partner violence (IPV); 64 percent of the women compared with 16 percent of the men in the NVWS who reported being raped, physically assaulted, or stalked were victimized by a current or former spouse/intimate partner. In fact, femicide, the homicide of women, is among the leading causes of death for African American women between the ages of 15 and 44 (Centers for Disease Control and Prevention 2005), and many of these femicides are committed by the victims' intimate partners (Campbell et al. 2003). Another potential consequence of IPV is increased rate of HIV infection among African American women who are abused (Lichtenstein 2004). For example, in one study of a predominantly African American sample of HIV-infected women, the author concluded that risk for HIV infection was increased because these women were trapped in abusive relationships with HIV+ men and were not able to negotiate sexual activity with their partners. Due to these types of disparities in IPV, most of the research in this area has focused on violence toward women, including the literature addressing domestic violence in the African American community.

Among the most cited studies that examined domestic violence, or IPV, among African Americans were the First and Second National Family Violence Surveys. In the first study conducted in 1975, Straus, Gelles, and Steinmetz (1980) reported that black husbands reported higher rates of severe violence and overall violence toward their wives than did white husbands; in black families the rate of overall wife abuse was 169 per 1,000, compared with 112 per 1,000 for white families. For severe acts of violence toward wives, the rate for blacks was 113 per 1,000 versus 30 per 1,000 for whites. Straus and his colleagues also examined wife-to-husband abuse and found that black wives reported severe violent acts toward their husbands at nearly twice the rate of white wives (76 per 1,000 compared with 41 per 1,000). This pattern of findings was replicated in the second survey conducted ten years later, in 1985 (Straus and Gelles 1986), which found that black families reported higher rates of overall husband-to-wife abuse (169 per 1,000) and wife-to-husband abuse (204 per 1,000) compared with white families (107 per 1,000 and 116 per 1,000, respectively). Based on these data, questions were raised about whether African Americans were actually more violent in general than whites. Subsequent research has resulted in oftentimes confusing and seemingly contradictory findings, with some studies reporting similarities between IPV rates between blacks and whites, and others reporting increased risk of IPV toward black women compared with white women (West 2002a).

Some of the differences found in this literature are attributable to the confounding effects of socio-economic variables, such as neighborhood disadvantage (Benson, Wooldredge, Thistlethwaite, and Fox 2004), and low education and employment status, particularly for the perpetrators of interpersonal violence against African American women. For example, in an examination of risk factors for femicide in abusive relationships, Campbell et al. (2003) reported that the strongest sociodemographic risk factor for femicide was the abuser's lack of employment. The abuser having a college (versus high school) education or a college degree while searching for work were found to be protective factors against femicide. When these sociodemographic factors were included in regression models, the race/ethnicity of abusers and victims failed to have independent effects on femicide. As stated by the authors, "unemployment [of the abuser] appears to underlie increased risk often attributed to race/ethnicity" (p. 1092). Benson and his colleagues also found that differences between white and African American women's risk of violence decreased substantially (although still remained significant) when taking into account neighborhood disadvantage (e.g., percentage of residents unemployed, on public assistance, and living below the poverty line).

Risk Factors for Intimate Partner Violence against African American Women

Factors associated with African American women's ability to leave abusive relationships include having their own home and their own source of income (Lichtenstein 2004), further highlighting the importance of sociodemographic factors in understanding IPV among African American women. Sociodemographic circumstances are also among the most commonly reported risk factors for IPV among African American women. "African-Americans are economically and socially disadvantaged, which places them at greater risk for IPV" (West 2004, p. 1489). Closely related to economic disadvantage is the fact that many African American women are marginalized, making them vulnerable to multiple traumatic experiences (West 2004). Other risk factors may include stereotypes and myths about African American women that may affect their help-seeking. Stereotypes of the black superwoman may discourage an African American woman from seeking help because she might subscribe to the belief that she should be strong enough to endure or stop the violence directed toward her. Similarly, African American women, cognizant of the stereotypes that portray them as aggressive, masculine, dangerous, and promiscuous (Bell and Mattis 2000), may avoid seeking help out of fear that they will be blamed for the abuse. They may also be seen as less legitimately needful of help because of their darker skin and potentially larger size and the perception that they are more likely to fight back (Bell and Mattis 2000). These stereotypes may also present African American women as needing to be controlled by their men, which may foster IPV as well (Bell and Mattis 2000; Hampton, Oliver, and Magarian 2003). Alcohol-related problems are also risk factors for IPV among African Americans (Benson et al. 2004; Campbell, Sharps, Gary, Campbell, and Lopez 2002).

Cultural and Community Factors

Other risk factors for IPV seem culturally specific to African American women. In her interviews with black battered women jailed for illegal activity, Richie (1994) used life history interviews to distinguish this group of women from (a) white battered women in jail and (b) black women in jail who had not been battered. Comparison of their responses allowed Richie to identify experiences unique to this group of black battered women. Compared with the nonbattered black women, the black women who were battered reported a notable sensitivity to the social and economic position of African American men. This concern for African American men prompted a desire to protect them from a racially unjust criminal justice system, resulting in fewer attempts to call the police or get other forms of help. Participants also reported feeling the need to provide opportunities to their men to help them feel more powerful, oftentimes doing so by relinquishing much of their own power. Because of poor treatment of black men by white men, and because black women were often able to find employment when their male counterparts could not, these women felt a sense of privilege compared with their male partners, and felt compelled to accept the violence.

While it is important to hold men responsible for the violence they inflict on women, it is also important to understand some of the contexts in which this violence might develop. As stated by King (1997), discussions of African American male violence should not take place outside of the context of understanding the treatment of African Americans in this country. In particular, he points to significant features of the African American experience in America, like chattel slavery, institutionalized racism, lynching, higher rates of execution in the criminal justice system, police brutality, and poverty. These injustices may cause feelings of frustration and hopelessness in African American men, and may lead to alcohol and drug use and low socioeconomic attainment. Perceived and real differences in earning potential between black men and women can also be a source of frustration and tension in a relationship, where the man does not feel able to fulfill society's prescribed role for him as wage-winner; this frustration and tension may also lead to violence (West 2002a). Similarly, racial discrimination toward black men may lead to decreased access to resources and opportunities, causing stress and violence among black men. Oliver (2000) summarizes an argument by Staples (1982), which states that this anger and frustration toward society becomes displaced and their wives and girlfriends bear the burden of it. Similarly, Hampton et al. (2003), in describing the cultural and community context of domestic violence in the African American community, note that African American men, particularly those of lower social status, have adopted alternative ways of exerting their "manhood" because the traditional ways (e.g., being the financial provider) have been unattainable for them; these alternatives to establishing manhood may include violence.

Other scholars have written about beliefs held by many in the African American culture that may increase women's risk of IPV. One is the so-called shortage of eligible black men that might cause some women to consider "man sharing," which increases a man's power over a woman (Lichtenstein 2004), or may discourage a woman from leaving an abusive relationship out of fear of not finding another partner. Another is the negative portrayal of African American women in some popular music, particularly gangsta rap, which often advocates violence as an acceptable method of relating to and controlling women (Bell and Mattis 2000).

Residing in violent communities can also increase risk for intimate partner violence for African American women because residence in such communities increases the likelihood of a woman being exposed to other types of violence (West 2002a) and may isolate her from potential sources of support (Benson et al. 2004; Hampton et al. 2003). Deteriorating environmental conditions in communities also weakens that community's ability to influence and control the behavior of its residents. In these communities, violence becomes an acceptable way to respond to interpersonal conflict, and typical social controls such as churches and neighbors are no longer able to influence IPV (Benson et al. 2004). Similarly, African American women experiencing IPV who are also involved in illicit drug use quickly become isolated from the potentially supportive communities that may provide assistance in escaping the abuse (Hampton et al. 2003).

Theories of Intimate Partner Violence

Several theories of violence against women have emerged. Among them is feminist theory, which posits that women are abused by men because of the patriarchal and sexist values advocated by society and its institutions (e.g., media, legal system). These values are rooted in a history of ordained violence against women, which included viewing women and girls as the property of their husbands and fathers and gave men the right to chastise or reprimand their wives by hitting them.

Several critiques of feminist theory emerged from African American and other scholars (e.g., Collins 1991; West 1999) who stated that the theory did not address the unique history and experiences of African American women and was therefore inadequate in describing the experiences of African American women, including their experiences of abuse. Because its primary focus was addressing male oppression of women, feminist theory has been criticized for catering only to the experiences of white middle-class women and ignoring the experiences of women of color and the poor. So, although feminist theory has challenged white male supremacy, it has also been accused of stifling the experiences and ideas of black and other marginalized women (Collins 1991) who live at the intersection of sexism and racism. This dual minority status, or position as both woman and black in society, sets the stage for a unique set of experiences and presents unique challenges for black women that the traditional feminist literature does not address. The theory's focus on male privilege also does not adequately address IPV among lesbians, and in particular, lesbians of color, who exist at the intersection of racism, sexism, and heterosexism. According to T. C. West, another problem with feminist theory in addressing IPV against African American women is that it equates black and white men's male privilege relative to women, ignoring the pervasive culture of racism that impacts black, and not white, men's status in society. As argued by Collins (1991), T. C. West (1999), and others (e.g., hooks 1989; Richie 1994), in order to fully understand the experiences of black women, including those affected by IPV, critique must occur not only on issues of gender, but also on issues of race, class, and sexual orientation.

Black feminist thought emphasizes the importance of race, gender, and class oppression; in doing so, it "fosters a fundamental paradigmatic shift in how we think about oppression" and "[embraces] a paradigm of race, class, and gender as interlocking systems of oppression" (Collins 1990). It further acknowledges African American women as both self-defined and self-reliant and places a strong emphasis on the acquisition of knowledge as a way of combating oppression (Collins 1990). Emphasis is placed not only on changing the consciousness of individuals, but also on altering society's political and social institutions in order to support needed change.

The inclusive examination of multiple forms of oppression also allows one to examine the relative salience of each of a number of identities. According to hooks (1989), race, class, and sex determine a woman's position in life and whether she will be dominated or will have the power to dominate. C. M. West (2004) explains that "when compared to poor women and lesbians, social class and heterosexual privilege can protect middle class or heterosexual Black women from some types of aggression. At the same time, racism can make it difficult for Black women, regardless of their economic status and sexual orientation, to escape racially based . . . violence" (p. 226). Black feminist theory also recognizes that black women may be more susceptible to violence in many settings (e.g., intimate relationships, communities) because of their position at the intersection of oppressions (West 2002a).

Richie's (1994, 1996) theory of gender entrapment provides a framework for explaining illegal activity among battered women of color and incorporates four levels of analysis: social (examines societal structures and practices), individual (considers how human behavior is influenced by intimate relationships), community (examines the influence of community norms and values on behavior), and intrapsychic (considers how internal psychological processes affect meaning-making). This theory, which attempts to incorporate the combined effects and intersection of gender identity, cultural determinants of behavior, violence, and crime, is one more example of the comprehensive approaches and models needed to understand phenomena such as IPV against African American women.

Prevention, Intervention, and Treatment

Ways to reduce violence against African American women have been proposed. Some address the social inequities experienced by African American men (see Hampton et al. 2003) and call for a reduction in joblessness and underemployment among African American men through high school retention programs and through job information and placement centers. Community-based interventions designed to educate men and boys about manhood and womanhood and that challenge the prevailing and damaging stereotypes about African American men and women have also been proposed. These community-based programs, which can be offered through local churches or fraternities, will be most effective if they successfully combat societal and cultural norms that subjugate and oppress women.

Throughout the African American IPV literature, there exist several calls for culturally competent treatment of African Americans who are affected by IPV. Successful treatment will require both the therapist and the client to reject stereotypes of the dangerous African American woman and accept her vulnerability; it may also be necessary for practitioners and service providers treating African American women to help them grieve the loss of their "superwomen" identities. The healers in IPV interventions may also be required to serve as advocates for their clients (Bell and Mattis 2000), potentially assisting them as they navigate the criminal justice system and helping them to secure the resources necessary for them and their children to live safe and violence-free lives. Bell and Mattis further assert that culturally competent interventions with African American victims of interpersonal violence should be consistent with a client's culture, including themes and topics most directly relevant to African American women, particularly religion and spirituality. This culturally sensitive treatment and incorporation of religion and spirituality should not include challenges to women's religious beliefs, but rather should provide a safe place where women can explore and critically examine their own beliefs (Bell and Mattis 2000). Treatment of religious women may also include referrals to or collaborative work with religious leaders who have been trained in dealing with domestic violence issues, allowing women to explore their religious and spiritual issues (Jordan 2002).

C. M. West (1997) provides several recommendations for culturally appropriate assessment and treatment for women of color who experience IPV. She notes that a comprehensive assessment of race and ethnicity should be conducted, during which time clients can identify their primary ethnic identity (e.g., West Indian vs. black), which may allow for a better understanding of their worldview. Additionally, both objective (income, education) and subjective (perceived social status) measures of socioeconomic status should be assessed, as should family structure, which might include an assessment of family members' roles and the family's social support network. West also notes that it is critical to assess family members' previous experiences with violence, including community violence, war, and lynchings. Suicidality and cultural coping strategies, including family rituals and other sources of strength, should also be assessed. Treatment should include legal assistance, provision of safety, helping women to regain a sense of control, and the validation of her experiences and feelings (West 1997). Additionally, practitioners should assist women in developing and strengthening their social support networks, and may use literature, art, and music as opportunities to reflect on their experiences (West 2002b).

Other recommendations for practice and education are provided by Campbell et al. (2003). These include using a strengths-based approach to interventions, increasing the number of African American workers to help African American victims of IPV, and focusing on injury prevention. Oliver (2000) discusses how aspects of African American popular culture, which include the common experiences, beliefs, and values among black people, could be used to increase awareness of the problem of IPV among African Americans and to potentially improve the effectiveness of IPV interventions. Facets of this popular culture include its heroes, music, common history of racism, and the black church. Oliver identified several mediums in the black popular culture that may be effectively used to combat issues of IPV in the community. For example, attendance at gospel musicals or black gospel plays is

becoming increasingly popular among African Americans. These plays often address issues of relevance to black Americans and can be used to facilitate domestic violence prevention and intervention. According to Oliver, shows like *How to Treat a Black Woman* and *Why Good Girls Like Bad Boys* have already addressed IPV. Another potential medium is black radio, which serves as a source of communication and dissemination of black popular culture (Oliver 2000). Oliver describes the potential for radio programming and black disk jockeys to impart information and generate discussion about IPV in the black community. Finally, black music can be used in treatment with African American women through discussion of the lyrics relevant to IPV or other personal and relational issues relevant to African American women.

The Black Church

The role of the black church in addressing and combating IPV among African American women has been discussed by many scholars. Some scholars have noted that the church has been and can be a detriment to ending violence because of the patriarchal structure of most churches, the use of some scriptures to support the subjugation of wives by their husbands, or by ignoring the problem of IPV altogether (Fortune 2000). However, the church can also be a tremendous source of strength and support for African American women experiencing partner abuse (Bell and Mattis 2000). Similarly, prayer and faith can both be impediments to traditional help-seeking as well as provide support to IPV victims (West 1997). Because African American women may turn to their faith or religion in time of trouble, including IPV (Berkel, Furlong, Hickman, and Blue 2005), the church can be central to addressing issues of violence among its members.

Because of its position of esteem in the African American community, the church has a unique opportunity to effectively provide education about IPV and support for its victims, many of whom regularly attend church (Jordan 2002). This education and support may be in the form of helping both victims and offenders to understand the true meaning and context of scriptures often used to justify male domination over women. For example, Jordan asserts that the church must address the theological justifications often used for violence toward women and provide accurate interpretations of biblical texts that address male–female relationships. Another critical issue is the gender imbalance in church leadership. When women have more leadership positions in the church, issues affecting them, like IPV, are more likely to get addressed. According to Jordan, the black church is in a position not only to address domestic violence directly through providing shelter and resources for victims of IPV, but to address many of the contextual factors that might increase risk for IPV, such as unemployment, underemployment, and alcohol abuse. T. C. West (1999) further contends that black churches should denounce violence against women and challenge the culture of many churches that supports male domination.

Coping Strategies and the Process of Survival

Much of the data on African American women victimized by IPV focus on their incidence of battering. Also needed is an understanding of their coping strategies and processes of survival (West 2004). Using a womanist framework, Taylor (2004) interviewed twenty-one self-identified African American women survivors of IPV to determine how they understood and labeled their experiences and how they moved beyond simply surviving to thriving. The first of the six themes related to survivorship-thriving that were identified was sharing secrets/shattering silences. The cultural value of not "putting one's business in the street" was recognized as an impediment to their safety. The process of healing began for many women through speaking out about their abuse, either with family members and friends, or with therapists in individual or group therapy. hooks (1989) states that black people are often taught not to speak out and to remain silent, perhaps out of a fear of rejection or isolation. But, according to hooks, and echoed by the survivors in this study, speaking out can be an act of resistance and can challenge a system of domination.

Reclaiming the self, or resisting society's definition of who they were and who they were supposed to be, was another theme identified. Being able to define one's self and identify one's own course served to empower these women. Renewing the spirit was the third theme identified, and referred to women's need to resurrect their spirits, which had died or were dying as a result of the abuse. This spiritual healing was essential to their overall health and recovery. This finding underlies the importance of spirituality in the lives of African American women in general, as well as those who have experienced IPV. As stated by others (e.g., Bell and Mattis 2000), in order to provide culturally competent service to African American women who are victims of IPV, practitioners must address

spiritual and/or religious issues. The fourth theme identified was self-healing through forgiveness, which was achieved gradually and only after obtaining some distance from the relationship. The forgiveness of their partners was seen as a personal victory and was central to the participants' self-healing.

The final two themes, finding inspiration for the future and self-generativity by engaging in social action, address the development of a sense of hope and empowerment, which are critical advances for women who previously had felt both hopeless and powerless. Based on these findings, the author recommends that interventions with African American women with a history of IPV include a focus on spirituality, forgiveness, safe places to share their stories, and opportunities for activism (Taylor 2004).

Areas for Future Research

One area in the African American IPV literature requiring critical attention is the topic of battering among lesbians (West 1998). According to Robinson (2002) and others, in many ways the dynamics of lesbian battering are very similar to nonlesbian battering. According to Robinson, the cycle of violence is often similar, the victims of abuse are often isolated from their friends, families, and other potential sources of support, and for some lesbian couples, one or both partners may have problems with alcohol. Lesbian battering also differs, however, in very important ways. First, the threat of being outed is a significant concern for lesbians who have not come out to members of their family, coworkers, or landlords. Internalized homophobia or fear of homophobic reactions by others may also discourage lesbians from seeking help.

C. M. West (2002, 2004) provides several other recommendations for future research in the area of domestic violence in the African American community. First, researchers should limit the number of simple black–white comparisons in partner abuse and focus more on the inclusion of more diverse samples of black women. Currently, much of the IPV literature focuses on the experiences of low-income women, which results in a paucity of information about middle- and upper-class women. Research on protective factors and resiliency are also needed (West 2004). Other recommendations include broadening the definitions of violence to include both emotional and verbal abuse (West 2002a), and stereotypes held by both victims and helpers (West 2002b). Campbell et al. (2003) also call for future research that generates and tests multidimensional causal models of violence and research that examines the impact of batterer intervention programs on batterers and couples. More community-based studies that address sociodemographic factors like employment status, single parenthood, education, substance abuse, support systems, and history of abuse are also needed (Campbell et al. 2003).

Although research in the area of IPV in the African American community has grown considerably in the last decade and has expanded our knowledge of the experiences of African Americans—particularly women—and violence, more research is needed to provide an in-depth understanding of the multiple factors that may foster or eliminate violence between intimates. To address this critical issue, scholarship and intervention strategies must continually incorporate and expand their understanding of the influence of multiple forms of oppression and culture on violence between intimates.

LaVerne A. Berkel

See also **Dating Violence among African American Couples; Minorities and Families in America, Introduction to; Multicultural Programs for Domestic Batterers; Native Americans, Domestic Violence among; Rural Communities, Domestic Violence in**

References and Further Reading

Bell, Carl C., and Jacqueline Mattis. "The Importance of Cultural Competence in Ministering to African-American Victims of Domestic Violence." *Violence against Women* 6, no. 5 (2000): 515–532.

Benson, Michael L., John Wooldredge, Amy B. Thistlethwaite, and Greer Litton Fox. "The Correlation between Race and Domestic Violence Is Confounded with Community Context." *Social Problems* 51, no. 3 (2004): 326–342.

Berkel, LaVerne A., Adielle N. Furlong, Anika A. Hickman, and Erika L. Blue. "A Qualitative Examination of Black College Women's Beliefs about Abuse in Relationships." *Professional Psychology: Research and Practice* 36, no. 3 (2005): 283–290.

Campbell, Doris W., Phyllis W. Sharps, Faye Gary, Jacqueline C. Campbell, and Loretta M. Lopez. "Intimate Partner Violence in African-American Women." *Online Journal of Issues in Nursing* 7, Manuscript #4 (2002). http://www.nursingworld.org/ojin/topic17/tpc17_4.htm (accessed August 7, 2006).

Campbell, Jacquelyn C., Daniel Webster, Jane Koziol-McLain, Carolyn Block, Doris Campbell, Mary Ann Curry, et al. "Risk Factors for Femicide in Abusive Relationships: Results from a Multisite Case Control Study." *American Journal of Public Health* 93, no. 7 (2003): 1089–1097.

Centers for Disease Control and Prevention. *National Violence Statistics Reports*, 2005. http://www.cdc.gov/nchs/data/nvsr/nvsr53/nvsr53_17.pdf (accessed August 30, 2005).

Collins, Patricia H. "Black Feminist Thought in the Matrix of Domination." In *Black Feminist Thought: Knowledge, Consciousness, and the Politics of Empowerment*, edited by Patricia H. Collins. Boston: Unwin Hyman, 1990, pp. 221–238.

———. *Black Feminist Thought: Knowledge, Consciousness, and the Politics of Empowerment*. New York: Routledge, 1991.

Fortune, Marie M. "Religious Issues and Violence against Women." In *Sourcebook on Violence against Women*, edited by Claire M. Renzetti, Jeffrey L. Edleson, and Raquel K. Bergin. Thousand Oaks, CA: Sage Publications, 2000, pp. 371–385.

Hampton, Robert, William Oliver, and Lucia Magarian. "Domestic Violence in the African-American Community: An Analysis of Social and Structural Factors." *Violence against Women* 9, no. 5 (2003): 533–557.

Hildebrand, Verna, Lillian A. Phenice, Mary M. Gray, and Rebecca P. Hines. *Knowing and Serving Diverse Families*. Englewood Cliffs, NJ: Prentice-Hall, 1996.

hooks, bell. *Talking Back: Thinking Feminist, Thinking Black*. Boston: South End Press, 1989.

Jordan, Lynda M. "Domestic Violence in the African-American Community: The Role of the Black Church." In *Religious Healing in Boston: Reports from the Field*, 2002. http://www.hds.harvard.edu/cswr/research/RHHI/healing_reports/05.Jordan.pdf (accessed August 7, 2006).

King, Anthony O. "Understanding Violence among Young African-American Males: An Afrocentric Perspective." *Journal of Black Studies* 28, no. 1 (1997): 79–96.

Lichtenstein, Bronwen. "Domestic Violence, Sexual Ownership, and HIV Risk in Women in the American Deep South." *Social Science and Medicine* 60, no. 4 (2004): 701–714.

Oliver, William. "Preventing Domestic Violence in the African-American Community: The Rationale for Popular Culture Interventions." *Violence against Women* 6, no. 5 (2000): 533–549.

Richie, Beth E. "Gender Entrapment: An Exploratory Study." In *Reframing Women's Health*, edited by Alice Dan. Thousand Oaks, CA: Sage Publications, 1994, pp. 219–232.

———. *Compelled to Crime: The Gender Entrapment of Battered Black Women*. New York: Routledge, 1996.

Robinson, Amorie. "'There's a Stranger in This House': African-American Lesbians and Domestic Violence." *Women in Therapy* 25, no. 3/4 (2002): 125–132.

Staples, Robert. *Black Masculinity: The Black Male's Role in American Society*. San Francisco: Black Scholar Press, 1982.

Straus, Murray, and Richard J. Gelles. "Societal Changes in Family Violence from 1975 to 1985 as Revealed by Two National Studies." *Journal of Marriage and the Family* 48 (1986): 465–479.

Straus, Murray, Richard J. Gelles, and Suzanne K. Steinmetz. *Behind Closed Doors: Violence in the American Family*. Garden City, NY: Doubleday, 1980.

Sue, Derald W., and David Sue. *Counseling the Culturally Diverse: Theory and Practice*, 4th ed. New York: John Wiley & Sons, 2003.

Taylor, Janette Y. "Moving from Surviving to Thriving: African-American Women Recovering from Intimate Male Partner Abuse." *Research and Theory for Nursing Practice: An International Journal* 18, no. 1 (2004): 35–50.

Tjaden, Patricia, and Nancy Thoennes. *Full Report of the Prevalence, Incidence and Consequences of Violence against Women*, 2000. http://www.ncjrs.gov/pdffiles1/nij/183781.pdf (accessed August 7, 2006).

U.S. Bureau of the Census. *Population Profile of the United States*. Washington, DC: U.S. Government Printing Office, 2000.

West, Carolyn M. "Partner Violence in Ethnic Minority Families," 1997. http://www.agnr.umd.edu/nnfr/research/pv/pv_ch7.html (accessed August 7, 2006).

———. "Leaving a Second Closet: Outing Partner Violence in Same-Sex Couples." In *Partner Violence: A Comprehensive Review of 20 Years of Research*, edited by Jana L. Lasinski and Linda M. Willians. Thousand Oaks, CA: Sage Publications, 1998, pp. 163–183.

———. "Black Battered Women: New Directions for Research and Black Feminist Theory." In *Charting a New Course for Feminist Psychology*, edited by Lynn H. Collins and Michelle R. Dunlap. Westport, CT: Praeger/Greenwood, 2002a, pp. 216–237.

———. "'I Find Myself at Therapy's Doorstep': Summary and Suggested Readings on Violence in the Lives of Black Women." *Women and Therapy* 25, no. 3/4 (2002b): 193–201.

———. "Black Women and Intimate Partner Violence: New Directions for Research." *Journal of Interpersonal Violence* 19, no. 12 (2004): 1487–1493.

West, Traci C. *Wounds of the Spirit: Black Women, Violence, and Resistance Ethics*. New York: New York University Press, 1999.

ANALYZING INCIDENTS OF DOMESTIC VIOLENCE: THE NATIONAL INCIDENT-BASED REPORTING SYSTEM

Domestic violence continues to exist in American society in spite of legislative and community-level strategies aimed at eradicating this social problem. Likewise, prevention and intervention efforts by professionals in the fields of law enforcement, public health, and social work have been met with some success. One particular challenge to addressing issues related to domestic violence is the lack of knowledge about the nature and extent of the problem in American communities. Correspondingly, this arises, in part, from the inconsistencies in definitions of circumstances and behaviors used to categorize incidents as domestic violence.

Addressing Definitional Issues of Domestic Violence

In attempting to address these challenges, two important definitional issues are pertinent. First is the question of what constitutes domestic violence. In addressing this question, it is important to consider the changing nature of interactions within various interpersonal relationships. The relationships that individuals maintain in contemporary society are varied and often elude clear definitional categories.

Relationship classifications most often used in both crime data and other survey data typically fall into the categories of "family," "acquaintance," "stranger," and "unknown" (Federal Bureau of Investigation [FBI] 1992, 2004). Some argue that these categories pose problems as to the mutual exclusivity and collective exhaustion of many relationships that exist among individuals. In certain situations, individuals initially seeming to be strangers are not truly complete strangers; they may, in fact, be acquaintances. That is, they may be relative strangers, but not absolute strangers (e.g., the grocery bagger, the video store clerk, public transportation passengers).

The second question concerns the definition of what constitutes violent behavior. Recognizing the extent of violent behavior is a challenge, as the classification of various types of acts may differ across law enforcement reporting mechanisms. While behavior that shows evidence of criminal injuries is certainly reflective of violence, in some instances similar behavior may not result in criminal injuries. Similarly, other actions, such as intimidation or verbal threats, while not producing physical injuries, may constitute violent behavior depending on the categorization of these actions. Regardless of the degree of injury, some of these conflicts may go unreported. Even when these incidents are brought to the attention of law enforcement, they may not be classified as involving domestic disputants. In certain situations, determination of what constitutes violence may also be based upon the consequence of the behavior rather than an absolute standard. These classification and reporting problems are not restricted to domestic violence. Often measuring other socially defined behaviors and interactions involves similar ambiguities.

Historical Reporting

In the past, definitional aspects of domestic violence were less of a concern than obtaining reliable information on these victimizations. What was known about these conflicts was derived mainly from anecdotal information, victim accounts, or cases that made headlines in the local or national media. Aspects of this problem continue to persist into the twenty-first century. However, beginning in the early 1990s, pursuant to inception of the Violence against Women Act, efforts to collect more systematic information about domestic violence included the use of the Uniform Crime Reporting (UCR) of the Federal Bureau of Investigation (FBI) and the National Criminal Victimization Survey (NCVS), in addition to various large- and small-scale surveys.

These efforts were designed to gauge the frequency of occurrences and to more fully describe the nature of the conflicts and injuries that occur between disputants in domestic settings. While these sources are informative, questions have been raised at times about the accuracy of the results, as they sometimes have appeared inconsistent or contradictory. For example, according to the Centers for Disease Control and Prevention (2003, p. 1) nearly 5.3 million intimate partner violence victimizations occur each year. However, UCR statistics report as few as approximately 258,000 of such criminal victimizations on average (FBI 2004, p. 342). Many of these reporting disparities, however, are likely of more of a technical than a substantive nature. For example, differences in what is considered a domestic conflict and what is considered criminally violent behavior are often at issue. Varying definitional debates at least partially explain variances in the data that often inform policy and practice discussions regarding the incidence and prevalence of domestic violence (for a similar debate pertaining to general crime reporting, see FBI 2004, pp. 502–504).

To study domestic homicide, the Supplementary Homicide Report (SHR) of the UCR is often examined to provide information about the dynamics of lethally violent events. These data not only contain the critical relationship categories noted above, but also describe some of the circumstances (e.g., weapon use, location of incident) and demographics (age, sex, race) of the disputants in these incidents. Data for 2003 show 1,804 (12.5 percent) victims of homicide at the hands of a family-related offender and an additional 4,401 (30.5 percent) victims of homicide by an offender who was identified as an acquaintance (FBI 2004, p. 21). Additionally, these data reveal that in incidents in which the victim knew her assailant, about 29 percent involved related offenders (FBI 2004, pp. 18–23). While the SHR allows for more detailed examination of criminal behavior resulting in death than the UCR, unfortunately it does not provide information about other forms of nonlethal assaultive behavior, ranging from intimidation to aggravated assault incidents.

Through examination of various official measures (i.e., UCR and SHR), one gains some information to more fully comprehend the nature and extent of some forms of domestic violence. However, it must be noted that such information is representative only of those incidents known to the police. One important exception to this is the self-report household survey, the NCVS, which for the year 2003 conveyed that the estimated proportion of completed criminal stranger violence not reported to police was about 36 percent, and unreported violence involving nonstrangers was 47 percent (U.S. Department of Justice 2005, Table 93). This clearly reflects the fact that some victims are either reluctant or unwilling to disclose to law enforcement their victimization. Additionally, while some incidents of domestic violence may and do come to the attention of other authorities or community assistance centers, the UCR (and most police data relating to criminal behavior) does not give any specific indication of the noncriminal behaviors that occur (i.e., forms of verbal or psychological abuse).

The Promise of the National Incident-Based Reporting System

The existence of more comprehensive law enforcement reporting mechanisms that allow for in-depth analysis of various aspects of domestic violence incidents could prove useful in the development of more effective laws and programs aimed at curbing these events. To this end, one development that may assist in the understanding of the dynamics of these violent encounters is the FBI's National Incident-Based Reporting System (NIBRS).

The NIBRS is a complete redesign of the original UCR summary reporting data system. This relatively new reporting system to be used by all law enforcement agencies across the United States includes up to fifty-three data elements (including weapon use, location type, injuries suffered, etc.) and allows for recording of forty-six different criminal offenses that may occur in a criminal incident (FBI 1992 and 1999). The importance of these data is that they are incident, rather than offense, oriented. That is, in any given criminal incident, all the criminal offenses that occurred in the incident as well as all associated information pertaining to victims, offenders, property loss, offense type and dynamics, and any arrestee associated with that incident is reported in the NIBRS. Additionally, all person crimes (homicide, rape, aggravated assault, robbery, simple assault, and intimidation) reported require documentation of circumstances of the incident (e.g., weapons used, presence of substances used by the offender including both alcohol and drugs), relationship categories for all victims and offenders, injuries sustained, and victim and offender demographics (age, race, sex, and residency), as well as the location of the incident. Lastly, many of these attributes are available for all offenders, all victims, all offenses, and all arrestees reported in the incident.

This wealth of information compared with previous criminal offense data is a remarkable advance but also poses a number of computational challenges (Akiyama and Nolan 1999). The computational issues aside, this detailed information has afforded a number of recent efforts to explore the dynamics of domestic violence that show the promise of data of this nature. For example, Thompson, Saltzman, and Bibel (1999) showed that in Massachusetts 10 percent of women victims had experienced more than one offense in the incident. Moreover, they found that when it came to female victims, intimate partners were more likely than nonpartners to commit simple assault, intimidation, and aggravated assault (Thompson et al. 1999, p. 163).

Additionally, a report from the FBI utilizing 1998 NIBRS data showed 1.6 million criminal incidents reported. Of these, 421,493 victims of violent offenses were identified and 112,042 victims of violence were found to have related offenders involved. Considering these numbers, about 27 percent of all violence was determined to be family related (FBI 1999, p. 280). More recent analyses of NIBRS data reported even larger percentages, with 43 percent of

incidents of violence having occurred among family members (FBI 2004, p. 342).

Studies of this nature may provide better insights as to the structure of domestic violence and assist in the formulation of policies and practices associated with combating these situations. For example, analyses of the time, location, and day of domestic violence incidents as well as the nature and scope of behaviors that are common to these incidents may assist social service agencies, community prevention efforts, and law enforcement to coordinate more effective response plans to calls of domestic conflicts.

Limitations of the National Incident-Based Reporting System

While the promise of NIBRS is considerable compared with previous efforts to examine crime and specifically domestic violence, it is important to note that NIBRS is not a panacea to the information and reporting needs associated with the many challenges of domestic violence. As of 2005, there was no direct mechanism in NIBRS for identifying repeated incidents of domestic violence that commonly occur in abusive intimate partner relationships. Moreover, as noted earlier, the codes used in NIBRS, like those used in other reporting systems, have limitations such as designations for workplace victimizations, location codes lacking specificity, and injury classifications that are somewhat restrictive. As such, analyses of certain types of domestic violence may be obscured.

Lastly, as with other official record systems, the lack of reporting of incidents to law enforcement results in a proportion of these criminal events remaining unaccounted for. This is likely the explanation for much of the differences among police data, health statistics, and ad hoc surveys. Complicating this situation, NIBRS remains to be fully implemented across the country, with these data as of 2004 reflecting reports from twenty-five states covering 20 percent of the U.S. population (FBI 2004). In fact, much of the data reported are from small to medium-sized rural jurisdictions. Therefore, the patterns revealed to this point in the data are more likely reflections of these types of jurisdictions rather than of urban jurisdictions that are not as of this point reporting in NIBRS.

Tempering this limitation are the increases in NIBRS participation by law enforcement agencies nationwide and the increased emphasis on enhancement of crime reporting content and frequency in support of initiatives to combat terrorism.

NIBRS reporting may well benefit from these efforts. As such, information systems pertaining to the dynamics of domestic violence as well as other domestic crime problems may similarly advance.

These developments may provide for more analysis and better opportunities to formulate effective strategies for confronting not only domestic violence but also a number of other crime problems. The difficulties of obtaining uniform data on the incidence of domestic violence are not limited to the issues noted above either. In fact, it is unrealistic to expect that a single large-scale national reporting system would be able to provide all the information that authorities, citizens, advocates, and others would desire and make such information available on a regular basis. This said, the NIBRS perhaps shows the most promise for moving toward a more comprehensive and detailed source for data pertaining to domestic violence and also a large number of criminal behaviors that may be precursors to later violence, theft, and destruction of property.

JOHN P. JARVIS and JANICE E. CLIFFORD

See also **Conflict Tactics Scales; Measuring Domestic Violence**

References and Further Reading

Akiyama, Yoshio, and James Nolan. "Methods for Understanding and Analyzing NIBRS Data." *Journal of Quantitative Criminology* 15, no. 2 (1999): 225–238.

Bachman, Ronet. "A Comparison of Annual Incidence Rates and Contextual Characteristics of Intimate-Perpetrated Violence against Women from the National Crime Victimization Survey (NCVS) and the National Violence against Women Survey (NVAWS)." *Violence against Women* 6, no. 8 (2000): 839–867.

Centers for Disease Control and Prevention. "Intimate Partner Violence: Fact Sheet," 2005. www.cdc.gov \ncipc\factsheets\ipvfacts.htm (accessed August 7, 2006).

Chilton, Roland, and John Jarvis. "Victims and Offenders in Two Crime Statistics Programs: A Comparison of the National Incident-Based Reporting System (NIBRS) and the National Crime Victimization Survey (NCVS)." *Journal of Quantitative Criminology* 15, no. 2 (1999): 193–205.

Chu, Lawrence D., and Jess F. Kraus. "Predicting Fatal Assault Among the Elderly Using the National Incident-Based Reporting System Crime Data." *Homicide Studies* 8, no. 2 (2004): 71–95.

Federal Bureau of Investigation. *Uniform Crime Reporting Handbook: NIBRS Edition.* Washington, DC: Author, 1992.

———. *Crime in the United States 1998.* Washington, DC: Author, 1999.

———. *Crime in the United States 2003.* Washington, DC: Author, 2004.

Finkelhor, David, and Richard Ormrod. "Child Abuse Reported to the Police." *Juvenile Justice Bulletin.* Washington, DC: U.S. Department of Justice, Office of Justice Programs, Office of Juvenile Justice and Delinquency Prevention, 2001.

Maxfield, Michael. "The National Incident-Based Reporting System: Research and Policy Applications." *Journal of Quantitative Criminology* 15, no. 2 (1999): 119–149.

Orchowsky, Stan, and Joan Weiss. "Domestic Violence and Sexual Assault Data Collection Systems in the United States." *Violence against Women* 6, no. 8 (2000): 904–911.

Schwartz, Martin D. "Methodological Issues in the Use of Survey Data for Measuring and Characterizing Violence against Women." *Violence against Women* 6, no. 8 (2000): 815–835.

Snyder, Howard N. *Sexual Assault of Young Children as Reported to Law Enforcement: Victim, Incident, and Offender Characteristics.* Bureau of Justice Statistics. Washington, DC: U.S. Department of Justice, Office of Justice Programs, 2000. NCJ 182990.

Thompson, Martie P., Linda E. Saltzman, and Daniel Bibel. "Applying NIBRS Data to the Study of Intimate Partner Violence: Massachusetts as a Case Study." *Journal of Quantitative Criminology* 15, no. 2 (1999): 163–180.

Tjaden, Patricia, and Nancy Thoennes. *Full Report of the Prevalence, Incidence, and Consequences of Violence against Women: Findings from The National Violence against Women Survey.* Washington DC: U.S. Department of Justice, 2000. NCJ 1883781.

U.S. Department of Justice. *Criminal Victimization in the United States: 2003 Statistical Tables* from the National Criminal Victimization Survey. Washington, DC: Office of Justice Programs, Bureau of Justice Statistics, 2005. NCJ 207811. http://www.ojp.usdoj.gov/bjs/pub/pdf/cvus 03.pdf (accessed August 7, 2006).

ANIMAL ABUSE: THE LINK TO FAMILY VIOLENCE

Animal abuse or animal cruelty is a complex, multidimensional phenomenon, which only recently has come to the attention of researchers and the general public. Popular television shows such as *Animal Cops* and *Animal Precinct* have brought the problem of animal mistreatment to the general public. These shows document the work of animal welfare professionals and bring to life the horrific treatment some animals endure at the hands of their owners. Animals are victimized in many ways, sometimes by deliberate acts of violence and other times by more passive neglect. Regardless, animals suffer real physical and emotional pain and sometimes die as a result of abuse.

Animal mistreatment is an important issue for a number of reasons. Ironically, a society that embraces socially accepted practices such as hunting and fishing also reveres its animals. Marked by the large number of homes and farms that have at least one pet, animals are an integral part of American life. There is no universal agreement as to whether or not animals should be used for experimental purposes, or as an indispensable part of the human diet, or for sport or entertainment, etc. However, many would agree that animals, especially those deemed as pets, are deserving of our respect and worthy of proper treatment. Animals are capable of feeling both physical and emotional pain and are victimized, much like humans are, by mistreatment, sometimes with tragic consequences. Therefore, protecting animals from mistreatment has desirable social value.

Second, research has found consistent evidence that animal abuse, in its various forms, is linked to interpersonal violence. In particular, there appears to be a clear link between animal mistreatment, child abuse and neglect, and intimate partner violence. Promoting a better understanding of animal abuse will only shed greater light on the critical factors associated with violence among humans, and in particular, violence within families. Therefore, animal welfare officials, veterinarians, mental health practitioners, law enforcement personnel, and criminologists have much to gain by working together to protect both animals and people. A social commitment to protecting animals is also a commitment to protecting people.

Historically, public policy addressing the plight of animals has evolved from an initial focus on animals as property with economic value to a more humane approach concerned with the overall physical and emotional welfare of animals. The first statute to address the actual welfare of animals was passed in New York State in 1866 as a result of the advocacy efforts of Henry Bergh, a wealthy New York City philanthropist. Although animal cruelty laws had existed prior to this time, statutes tended to reflect concern over only those animals that had established financial worth, and "cruelty" applied only when someone other than the owner mistreated the animal. The purpose of such laws was to assist property owners in protecting their property. Henry Bergh, appalled by the cruelty he observed toward some animals in New York City, organized the American Society for the Prevention of Cruelty to Animals (ASPCA) and was ultimately successful in spearheading policy change across the nation. In fact, the assistance of the ASPCA was sought in the landmark case of Mary Ellen Wilson in 1874. Mary Ellen was a 9-year-old child who was abused by her legal custodians. Since no laws existed to protect Mary Ellen from her abusers, the ASPCA intervened, arguing that Mary Ellen was part of the animal kingdom and therefore was deserving of protection like other animals. Later that year, the New York Society for the Prevention of Cruelty to Children (SPCC), one of the nation's first child welfare organizations, was founded.

Although great strides have been made over time to protect animals from abuse and neglect, much work is left to be done. Animal welfare laws vary widely from state to state. Definitions of abuse vary; diverse social standards exist regarding what is considered appropriate minimum levels of care, proper shelter, humane training methods, disciplinary practices, etc. In addition, there are differing views on how stray, wild, livestock, and companion animals ought to be treated. Differing views regarding animal treatment are embedded in both cultural and religious traditions; therefore, there is no clear consensus on what constitutes animal abuse.

Although animals are still considered property, both state and federal lawmakers have recognized the need to protect animals from acts of cruelty and have enacted legislation to address both acts that cause deliberate harm as well as neglect. Most states have provisions making animal cruelty a felony; however, other states consider such acts misdemeanors. Many laws exclude accepted practices such as hunting and trapping of wildlife and animal husbandry. Also, many laws exclude animals used in legitimate research. As the research on the connection between animal and human violence continues to mount, some states have responded with additional legislation. For example, requiring persons convicted of animal abuse to undergo psychological evaluation or counseling, granting veterinarians who report cases to authorities immunity from civil or criminal litigation, and promoting cross-system training and reporting of potential abuses by caseworkers responsible for the protection of children and adults.

Enforcement of animal cruelty laws varies across the states. In some jurisdictions, enforcement is left to local law enforcement officials. In other jurisdictions, state and local governments grant authority to animal welfare officials such as humane officers or animal control officers to enforce abuse laws. Since there is no uniformity in how animal cruelty laws are enforced, there is also no uniform methodology for measuring the prevalence of animal cruelty or neglect. Even though authorities document cases that have been reported to them, animal cruelty is not systematically monitored like other crime types. Studies have examined animal mistreatment among specific populations of people; however, no national studies have been conducted which attempt to estimate the prevalence of different forms of animal mistreatment in the general population. Therefore, we are aware only of cases that have involved the authorities.

Forms of Animal Abuse

The mistreatment of animals takes many different forms. Like humans, animals can be physically or sexually abused, neglected, or intentionally tortured and killed. Emotional or mental abuse or neglect is also an inherent problem among animal cruelty cases; however, documenting that an animal has suffered emotionally or mentally is often a difficult

task, especially if no other signs of abuse are present. Animal abuse also encompasses both acts of commission and acts of omission. Acts of commission are considered those in which the animal owner or caretaker does something to cause injury or harm to the animal, while acts of omission are those in which the owner or caretaker fails to do something for the animal, which ultimately results in harm.

There is currently no universal typology to describe the various ways animals are abused. As described earlier, this is complicated by the fact that state laws vary in their definition of what an animal is and what constitutes cruelty, abuse, and neglect. For the sake of simplicity, several different categories of animal abuse are described here, including physical abuse, sexual abuse, and neglect. These categories of animal abuse have the closest link to interpersonal violence and family violence in particular. It should be noted, however, that animal mistreatment can be manifested in a variety of ways with varied motivations.

Physical Abuse

The physical abuse of animals can involve a wide range of injurious acts. Physical abuse requires an active engagement of maltreatment. Animals suffer from being hit, kicked, burned, poisoned, whipped, disfigured, dismembered, stabbed, stoned, shot, trapped, strangled, thrown, etc. Animals may also be physically abused if their movement is restricted for long periods of time, have been restrained in an inhumane manner, or are living in overcrowded conditions. Also, animals are at risk for injury when disciplinary practices or training methods involve physical punishment. In some instances, animals die as a result of such physical abuse. The term "peticide" refers to situations in which family pets have been purposefully killed, often as a result of or in conjunction with other forms of family violence.

A wide range of animals can fall prey to physical abuse, including wild, stray, and livestock animals as well as pets such as birds, cats, dogs, fish, turtles, etc. Animal cruelty statutes generally do not protect all species of animals, and definitions of what types of creatures are worthy of protection are generally defined in statute.

Individual motivations for physically abusing an animal vary widely. In some cases, incidents of physical abuse are intentional, overt acts to cause specific harm to the animal. In these types of cases, the abuser gains some form of satisfaction from torturing or teasing the animal. In other cases, especially those involving other forms of family violence, deliberate acts of cruelty toward animals is intended to instill fear and emotionally harm one or more family members. Animals are abused as a tool to threaten and terrorize intimate partners, children, or siblings. In many cases, the animal being victimized is a family pet. Most would consider such acts to constitute animal cruelty.

In other cases, animals may be physically abused as a result of commercial exploitation in which animals are forced to engage in fighting, breeding, experimentation, sporting, or excessive labor, etc. The intention is not to harm the animal specifically but to use the animal for economic benefit, often with little regard to the animal's well-being. In these cases, animals are physically abused as a result of some type of commercial enterprise. Animals are often mistreated in settings such as circus and other entertainment venues in which animals are expected to perform, companies that use animals for the testing of products such as pharmaceuticals and cosmetics, dog and horse racing, and companies that prepare animals for slaughter for human consumption. Although these types of activities are socially acceptable, there is concern that animals are treated in a fair and humane manner, minimizing their pain and suffering. Animal welfare legislation exists to protect such animals. Outside of these legal commercial activities, animals, especially dogs and roosters, endure physical abuse by being forced into fighting. Animal fighting is an illegal practice and is often specifically addressed in animal cruelty legislation. However, the link between commercial exploitation and interpersonal violence has not yet been addressed by the research literature.

Regardless of motivation, most state statutes utilize the word "cruelty" to describe situations in which animals are deliberately injured and those that are harmed from reckless or neglectful behavior. Therefore, the term "animal cruelty" often refers to a broad range of acts and/or practices that are deemed cruel and inhumane.

Sexual Abuse

The sexual abuse of animals is a phenomenon that is not well understood by clinical practitioners or researchers. Very little is known about the prevalence of sexual activity between humans and animals; however, research suggests that the engagement of animals in various levels of sexual activity may be more common than previously recognized. In fact, sexual contact between humans and animals has been documented throughout history in art and literature. Even the earliest of civilizations have depicted humans and nonhumans

engaging in sexual activity in cave drawings and tomb paintings.

Although evidence of sexual contact between humans and animals has been established in various societies and continues into contemporary times, this form of sexual behavior is still considered deviant by mainstream society. As a consequence, many states have explicit language making such contact illegal. Penal codes address sexual contact with animals under specific laws making bestiality illegal, under broader animal cruelty statutes, or under the more generic category of sodomy. Although some laws do not specifically outlaw sexual contact with animals, most laws do provide avenues for prosecution when it can be determined that an animal has been physically injured as a result of such sexual activity.

The animals most likely to be used for sexual gratification by humans include pets such as dogs and cats, and animals found on farms, such as horses, goats, sheep, pigs, hens, etc. These animals are the most accessible, since they are not living in the wild. In cases of family violence, the animals most likely to be sexually victimized are those to which family members have a special attachment. All kinds of sexual contact are possible, including use of the animal for human masturbation, masturbation of the animal, oral sex, and intercourse. Although not all sexual contact involves physical injury, injuries such as vaginal or rectal tears, discharge or bleeding, and internal trauma are indicative of abuse in animals. These are consistent with the types of injuries found in human victims of sexual assault. In addition, changes in an animal's behavior and demeanor may suggest sexual abuse.

The use of animals for the sexual pleasure of humans is a controversial matter. Regardless of visible injury to animals and the various motivations individuals may have for engaging animals in sexual activity, some consider any sexual act with an animal to be harmful to animals and therefore an animal welfare concern. Others, such as researchers and clinicians, are concerned about bestiality as a companion behavior to other problematic behaviors in both children and adults. Since research has found evidence linking sexual contact with animals as a consistent feature among other aggressive, violent behaviors toward humans, its role in interpersonal violence cannot be underscored. Yet, others argue that bestiality is a more complex phenomenon and is not necessarily a direct link to psychological or pathological social behavior. They argue that not everyone who engages in sexual activity does so to harm animals or humans, nor do they necessarily view all such acts as harmful to animals. There appears to be a wide range of reasons and motivations for engaging in various forms of sexual fantasy or sexual behavior with animals. Further research is warranted.

As a controversial matter, the terms "bestiality" and "zoophilia" are often used interchangeably to describe the engagement in sexual activity with animals by humans. However, some argue that the terms really refer to different levels of attachment to animals. "Bestiality" refers specifically to sexual acts with animals, while "zoophilia" or "zoosexual" refers to a broader interest or attachment to animals. Those who are actively involved in relationships with animals, including sexual contact, refer to themselves as zoophiles. Many zoophiles see their involvement with animals as a lifestyle or orientation. The term "zoophilia" is considered one of many paraphilias noted by mental health professionals. The term "paraphilia" is assigned to signify individuals who have atypical sexual interests and are sexually aroused by nontraditional objects or situations. These sexual interests are generally considered taboo by society at large. Although some paraphilias, especially those involving a lack of consent or those considered criminal, are considered potentially dangerous, many paraphilias are not inherently dangerous or necessarily harmful. The American Psychiatric Association (1994) in its *Diagnostic and Statistical Manual of Mental Disorders,* fourth edition (DSM-IV), considers paraphilias problematic when the sexual behavior causes significant distress or impairment in social, occupational, or other areas of functioning. Researchers have further defined sexual desires and practices into more distinct forms of sexual involvement. Examples include: *formicophilia* (sexual activity involving very small animals such as ants, insects, frogs, etc.), *mixoscopic zoophilia* (sexual interest in watching animals copulate), and *zoosadism* (sexual pleasure derived from torturing or killing animals or forcing intimate partners or others to engage in sexual activity with animals).

Neglect

The vast majority of cases brought to the court system for animal cruelty involve active neglect. Animal neglect refers to situations in which animals have not been provided adequate food, shelter, or medical care. It may also involve the failure to euthanize an animal when medically necessary. In cases of neglect, animals endure physical injury as a result of neglectful or careless behavior on the part of the animal owner or caretaker.

Animals that are neglected are often in very poor physical condition and suffer from a variety of ailments. Animals that are not provided with adequate food or water usually have poor body weight and, in severe cases, look visibly malnourished or starved. Providing proper food for the species is also important because animals that have been given improper food can also suffer from starvation.

Animals whose grooming care is neglected experience a number of problems, including the matting of hair coat, loss of hair or feathers, long nails or hooves, and decaying teeth and other dental problems. Open flesh wounds are common when animals are subjected to collars, chains, or harnesses that are not fitted properly or left on continuously. In some cases, the collar actually becomes embedded in the skin of the animal, causing the animal great pain. Animals may also be infested with parasites, which are organisms that live off the animal as a host. Animals may be exposed to external parasites due to poor living conditions, or internal parasites, which are transmitted through excrement or food. Animals may suffer from severe skin irritation exhibited in itching or sores, referred to as mange. Mange is a general term used to describe a variety of skin conditions caused by the infestation of different kinds of mites.

Animals also suffer when their medical care is neglected. Untreated injuries, illnesses, or diseases can have disastrous consequences for animals, leading to problems such as blindness, loss of limbs, or death. Overall poor living conditions, evidenced by inadequate space, light, and ventilation, poor sanitation, or excessive numbers of animals in confined spaces can complicate the consequences of such neglect.

Of particular concern are individuals who accumulate large numbers of animals, often referred to as animal collectors or animal hoarders. Animals living in these conditions are at great risk of neglectful care and often pose a public health problem for all those living on the property or perhaps even the surrounding community. Animal owners who fail to provide the minimum standards of care, fail to act on the deteriorating conditions as the animal population grows, and are unable to cope with the negative consequences such an environment would have on humans living with the animals are considered animal hoarders. In many cases, animal hoarders are not only not able to care for the animals, but are not able to care for themselves or others as well. Children, the elderly, and the disabled are more likely at risk for being neglected in these circumstances. Self-neglect, especially among the elderly, is also a common feature of hoarding. Animal hoarders tend to be older, female, and socially isolated.

The public health concern regarding animal hoarding cannot be underestimated. Animal hoarders often have dozens to hundreds of animals living with them in single family homes, apartments, or trailers. Commonly, cats, dogs, birds, and farm animals are involved. Often dead animals have not been properly disposed of and may be found dispersed around the home, or found in freezers, sheds, or garages. Homes are usually found in complete disarray and disorganization, with excessive clutter, failed utilities, lack of running water, piles of garbage strewn about, and human and animal urine and feces covering the surfaces of the living space. As a result, homes might also be infested with insects and rodents.

It is difficult to comprehend the extreme level of squalor some hoarders and their families live in. In most cases, the health and safety of both humans and animals is in jeopardy. Humans exposed to such conditions are at great risk of developing multiple health conditions, compounded by the inability to maintain proper nutrition or personal hygiene in such unsanitary environments. Of particular concern is the risk of contracting zoonotic diseases. Zoonotic diseases are those caused by infectious agents that are transmitted between animals and humans, generally through urine, feces, blood, milk, or saliva. Individuals who have pre-existing health problems associated with their immune systems are at greatest risk of contracting additional illnesses as a result of the unsanitary conditions. An additional danger consists of high levels of ammonia exposure for those living in the home. In severe cases, the air quality is so toxic that animal welfare officials must wear protective gear and use special breathing equipment to be able to safely enter the homes. Municipalities may have to condemn the home, and in some cases destroy the building. Also, neighboring homes, businesses, schools, etc., may experience health risks associated with animal hoarding.

Animal hoarding is not well understood by the psychiatric community. It is believed that animal hoarding is associated with mental illness; however, no specific diagnosis exists in the literature to date. Hoarding behavior in general is symptomatic of obsessive-compulsive disorder (OCD) and obsessive-compulsive personality disorder (OCPD). Animal hoarding is also manifested in a variety of psychiatric conditions. Described as a multifaceted mental health problem, it may be linked to limitations in information processing, decision making, and distorted thinking regarding possessions and hoarders' ability to properly care for their animals. It is associated with dementia, delusional disorders, impulse control disorders, and attachment disorders. There is some evidence that histories of child abuse, neglect, or dysfunction within the family is associated with animal hoarding later in life. This link should be researched more fully.

Animal Abuse: The Link to Family Violence

The past several decades have been marked by increased interest in the link between animal mistreatment and interpersonal violence. Reasons behind animal mistreatment and violence against humans are complex and varied; therefore, it is difficult to determine the exact pathways of how these two social problems are related. The research evidence does not confirm a causal relationship, nor can it confirm that one form of violence is always a precursor to another. For example, not all children who exhibit cruel acts toward animals grow up to be violent offenders; however, many serial killers and other violent offenders acknowledge having committed such acts as children.

However, the evidence is clear that there is a strong connection that should not be minimized. When humans are vulnerable to abuse and neglect, animals are likely to be as well. When animals are identified as being abused or neglected, it is feasible that humans may also be at risk of victimization. The risk within abusive families appears to be of greatest concern. Yet, little has been done to document the extent, on a large-scale basis, of the conditions in which animal mistreatment exists within abusive family environments. Animal welfare officials have long known that many victimized animals live with problematic families. At the same time, child and adult protective caseworkers and domestic violence advocates have observed or heard reports from their clients that animals have been mistreated. Most states have no protocols or formal policy to address the cross-system issues inherent when both animals and humans are at risk of abuse.

Yet, the evidence is mounting that reforms are warranted. Policy and programmatic approaches to intervention in animal abuse and family violence require collaboration and integration across systems. A commitment to continued research is necessary and likely to increase our understanding of what factors influence violent behavior and provide guidance on how best to protect both people and animals from abuse and neglect.

Though research on the connection between animal abuse and family violence is still evolving, several themes have surfaced.

First, animal abuse appears to be a consistent feature among violent families, particularly those families in which children and intimate partners are also abused. Animals become additional victims within the household. Studies have attempted to measure the frequency with which the coexisting problems of family violence and animal abuse occur. Studies have found that in families that have exhibited child maltreatment or intimate partner violence, a majority had also exhibited cruel acts toward animals (Ascione 1998; DeViney, Dickert, and Lockwood 1983). In a study of same-sex partners, Renzetti (1992) found that 38 percent of the women with pets reported maltreatment of a pet by their abusive partner. In the case of sibling abuse, the torturing or killing of a pet was considered a form of emotional abuse targeted toward a sibling (Wiehe 1997). In the case of elder abuse, little is known about the prevalence of animal maltreatment, with the exception of the self-neglect that is consistently found with animal hoarding.

It is theorized that abusers use violence against animals as a tool to control, threaten, taunt, or coerce family members. Victims have reported that abusers, in particular partners or fathers, had threatened, hurt, or killed one or more of their pets. Animals become vulnerable targets for a number of reasons. It is not uncommon for survivors of family violence to find their belongings, e.g., toys, clothing, games, music, destroyed by a family member, and in that sense, animals are victimized because they are a prized possession. It is a way that abusers can further emotionally harm victims. Threats or actual acts of abuse may be enacted to terrorize or frighten the victim, or to coerce the victim into doing something, such as staying in the relationship, etc. Animals can easily be victimized, because they generally cannot fight back, nor can they report such actions to the authorities. For human survivors of abuse, witnessing the abuse of one's own pet compounds the trauma of living in a violent home. Signs of pet abuse or peticide may also serve as a marker for lethality in abusive relationships and should, therefore, be taken very seriously by authorities.

Second, juvenile offenders, particularly those displaying violent behaviors, often have exhibited cruelty toward animals throughout childhood. Many young offenders are diagnosed with *conduct disorder,* which is defined by the DSM-IV as "a repetitive and persistent pattern of behavior in which the basic rights of others or major age-appropriate societal norms or rules are violated" (American Psychiatric Association 1994: 90). As a common symptom of conduct disorder, research suggests that abuse of animals may occur early in childhood, before other symptoms of conduct disorder emerge. Therefore, when young children exhibit cruel behavior toward animals, it should not be ignored, for it may serve as a marker for more destructive behavior to come in the future (Ascione 2001). Other common symptoms exhibited by young people with conduct disorder include fire setting, destruction of property, bullying, and cruel acts toward people.

Studies reveal that the motivations for youth engaging in cruel behavior toward animals are varied (Ascione, Thompson, and Black 1997). In some cases, youth participate in cruelty as a result of peer pressure, to lessen boredom or depression, to escape an animal phobia, or to incite an animal to self-injury. In other cases, youth engage in animal abuse as a more direct result of being exposed to interpersonal violence. Children may kill an animal to protect it from being tortured by someone else or may do so as a result of modeling the behavior of others. Animals may also be harmed during play, as the child reenacts violence he or she has previously observed. Some children are forced into hurting an animal by another person or may abuse or threaten to abuse an animal to terrorize a sibling, etc. Children who abuse animals are often abused and neglected themselves. Such children are exposed to corporal punishment and physical and sexual abuse and have witnessed domestic violence. The cycle of violence is then displaced onto helpless animals.

In addition to being an indicator of child maltreatment, cruelty toward animals by children may serve as a rehearsal for violence against humans later in life and should not be minimized. Psychological evaluations of children should consistently include an assessment of propensity toward animal abuse, thereby providing the best opportunity for early intervention and delinquency prevention.

Third, concern over animals may prevent some family members from seeking help or leaving an abusive relationship. In a study of women residing at a domestic violence shelter in Utah, Ascione (1998) found that 18 percent of the women with pets had reported that concern over the welfare of their animals had prevented them from seeking shelter sooner. Women were concerned about the safety of the animals and having to find another home for their pets in order to find safe, suitable housing for themselves. In addition, some women were concerned about having to place a pet with a neighbor or having to abandon a pet to keep it secure from the abusive partner. Since most domestic violence shelters do not have provisions for animals or collaborative arrangements with animal welfare organizations, these findings suggest the critical need for the development of such partnerships.

Fourth, animals may be helpful in the therapeutic process to help heal the trauma of family violence. Animal-assisted therapy is used successfully with both children and adults in a variety of settings. Also referred to as "pet therapy," animal-assisted therapy has been helpful to patients suffering from terminal illnesses, disabilities, depression, and other mental illnesses and/or behavior problems. Animals have also been utilized in a variety of ways to help the elderly. Pet therapy has many therapeutic benefits. It can help child and adult offenders rebuild empathy and compassion. It can help reduce the effects of social isolation. For young children who have been abused and neglected or have witnessed repetitive acts of violence, pet therapy can offer an opportunity to reestablish trust and help victims identify and disclose their feelings.

In summary, animal mistreatment is a significant social problem that needs to be addressed with as much fervor as other criminal justice concerns. Like family members, animals are physically assaulted, sexually abused, and neglected. Some are tortured and killed. Understanding that animal abuse may serve as a marker for other forms of family violence should elevate the level of concern. Until recently, these two issues have been dealt with as discrete problems by law enforcement, mental health professionals, animal welfare officials, veterinarians, and others concerned. Researchers call for more formal collaboration between animal welfare professionals, law enforcement, and protective agencies, as well as cross-training about the co-occurring problems. Few family violence programs address the issue of animal mistreatment concurrently with the problems associated with family violence. Few animal welfare programs engage protective agencies or family violence specialists in their response to investigate abuse and neglect or to rescue animals. It is imperative that a continued investment be made to explore the connection in greater depth.

KAREL KURST-SWANGER

See also **Ritual Abuse–Torture in Families; Substance Use/Abuse and Intimate Partner Violence**

References and Further Reading

American Psychiatric Association. *Diagnostic and Statistical Manual of Mental Disorders,* 4th ed. Washington, DC: Author, 1994.

Arluke, Arnold, Randy Frost, Luke Carter, Jane Nathanson, Gary Patronek, Michelle Papazian, and Gail Steketee. "Health Implications of Animal Hoarding." *Health and Social Work* 27, no. 2 (May 2002): 125–137.

Arluke, Arnold, Jack Levin, Luke Carter, and Frank Ascione. "The Relationship of Animal Abuse to Violence and Other Forms of Antisocial Behavior." *Journal of Interpersonal Violence* 14, no. 9 (September 1999): 963–975.

Ascione, Frank R. "Battered Women's Reports of Their Partners' and Their Children's Cruelty to Animals." *Journal of Emotional Abuse* 1, no. 1 (1998): 119–133.

———. "Animal Abuse and Youth Violence." *Juvenile Justice Bulletin.* Washington, DC: Office of Juvenile Justice Delinquency Prevention, 2001. NCJ 188677.

Ascione, Frank R., and Phil Arkow, eds. *Child Abuse, Domestic Violence and Animal Abuse: Linking the Circle of Compassion for Prevention and Intervention.* West Lafayette, IN: Purdue University Press, 1999.

Ascione, Frank R., Teresa Thompson, and Tracy Black. "Childhood Cruelty to Animals: Assessing Cruelty Dimensions and Motivations." *Anthrozoos* 10 (1997): 170–177.

Ascione, Frank R., Claudia V. Weber, and David S. Wood. "The Abuse of Animals and Domestic Violence: A National Survey of Shelters for Women Who Are Battered." *Society and Animals* 5, no. 3 (1997): 205–218.

Becker, Fiona, and Lesley French. "Making the Links: Child Abuse, Animal Cruelty and Domestic Violence." *Child Abuse Review* 13 (2004): 399–414.

Beetz, Andrea M. "Bestiality/Zoophilia: A Scarcely Investigated Phenomenon between Crime, Paraphilia, and Love." *Journal of Forensic Psychology Practice* 4, no. 2 (2004): 1–36.

Boat, Barbara W. "The Relationship between Violence to Children and Violence to Animals: An Ignored Link?" *Journal of Interpersonal Violence* 10 (June 1995): 229–235.

DeViney, Elizabeth, Jeffrey Dickert, and Randall Lockwood. "The Care of Pets Within Child Abusing Families." *International Journal for the Study of Animal Problems* 4 (1983): 321–329.

Flynn, Clifton P. "Exploring the Link between Corporal Punishment and Children's Cruelty to Animals." *Journal of Marriage and the Family* 61 (November 1999): 971–981.

Kellert, Stephen R., and Alan R. Felthous. "Childhood Cruelty toward Animals Among Criminals and Noncriminals." *Human Relations* 38 (1985): 1113–1129.

McClellen, Jon M., Julie Adams, and Donna Douglas. "Clinical Characteristics Related to Severity of Sexual Abuse: A Study of Seriously Mentally Ill Youth." *Child Abuse and Neglect* 19 (October 1995): 1245–1255.

Merz-Perez, Linda, and Kathleen M. Heide. *Animal Cruelty: Pathway to Violence against People.* New York: Altamira Press, 2004.

Miletski, Hani. "Bestiality/Zoophilia—An Exploratory Study." *Scandinavian Journal of Sexology* 3, no. 4 (December 2000): 149–150.

Patronek, Gary. "Hoarding of Animals: An Under-Recognized Public Health Problem in a Difficult-to-Study

Population." *Public Health Report* 114, no. 1 (January-February 1999): 81–87.

Peretti, Peter O., and Maurice Rowan. "Variables Associated with Male and Female Chronic Zoophilia." *Social Behavior and Personality* 10, no. 1 (1982): 83–87.

Renzetti, Claire M. *Violent Betrayal: Partner Abuse in Lesbian Relationships*. Newbury Park, CA: Sage Publications, 1992.

Wiehe, Vernon R. *Sibling Abuse: Hidden Physical, Emotional, and Sexual Trauma*. Thousand Oaks, CA: Sage Publications, 1997.

Williams, Colin J. "Zoophilia in Men: A Study of Sexual Interest in Animals." *Archives of Sexual Behavior* 32, no. 6 (December 2003): 523–536.

ASIAN AMERICANS AND DOMESTIC VIOLENCE: CULTURAL DIMENSIONS

Who Are Asian Americans?

The term "Asian" is widely used for those individuals who have ethnic ties to Asia, which includes the Far East, Southeast Asia, and the Indian subcontinent. This would consist of countries such as China, Japan, Korea, Vietnam, Cambodia, Thailand, India, Pakistan, and the Philippines. "Pacific Islands" refers to Hawaii, Guam, and Samoa, and other islands in the region. The concept of "Asian American" (and sometimes "Asian/Pacific Islander American") has been employed for statistical purposes, and although Asian Americans share some physical and cultural similarities, in no way does this term capture the tremendous diversity within this group. There are over twenty-five Asian/Pacific Islander groups; each group has a different migration history to the United States, and the socio-political contexts of their respective homelands vary widely from each other. Asian Americans are also different in terms of their acculturation levels, length of residency in the United States, their languages, their English-speaking proficiency, education attainment, socioeconomic status, and religion. There are approximately thirty-two different languages that exist within the Asian American category group; and sometimes within a single Asian subgroup (i.e., Chinese), multiple dialects exist.

According to the U.S. Census (2004), there are 11.9 million Asian and Pacific Islanders living in the United States. This constitutes 4.2 percent of the U.S. population. It is estimated that by the year 2020, there will be a 145 percent to 177 percent increase from 1990. The Chinese are the largest Asian American group, comprising 24 percent of the U.S. Asian population, followed by Filipinos (representing 18 percent) and Asian Indians (representing 16 percent). A third of Asian Americans were born in the United States, and similar proportions are foreign born but U.S. citizens and foreign born but not U.S. citizens.

Invisibility of Domestic Violence in Asian American Communities

"Intimate violence," "domestic violence," "wife beating," "partner abuse," and "spousal abuse" are terms that are used interchangeably, but they do have different political connotations. These terms are used within the context of women's issues, which were brought to the public's attention by the feminist movement of the 1960s in the United States. The term "domestic violence" will be used in this entry and will refer primarily to female victims of male perpetrators. While it is also recognized that abuse can occur in both heterosexual and homosexual relationships, the emphasis here will be on heterosexual relationships.

In the 1970s, crisis hotlines for rape and sexual assault victims as well as the first battered women's shelter were established. Although domestic violence was clearly portrayed as a women's issue, this early domestic violence movement was criticized for not capturing the voices and needs of ethnic minority women. In part, this was because the women's movement consisted primarily of white women. They argued that gender inequities and power imbalances were the main causes of domestic violence for *all* women, regardless of color. Other structural and cultural factors such as racism, ethnocentrism, class, and poverty were not taken into account in how they worked alongside gender in influencing domestic violence. Ethnic minority women, including Asian American women, remained invisible, and scholars, researchers, and practitioners often concluded that domestic violence did not affect Asian American and immigrant communities.

Several factors have contributed and continue to contribute to the invisibility of domestic violence in Asian American communities. First, Asian Americans and immigrants generally underutilize Western social and mental health services or tend not to use them at all. Furthermore, there are few organizations that provide culturally appropriate and sensitive services staffed with professionals who are linguistically competent, especially when it comes to communicating in a wide range of dialects, to service this population. Therefore, cases of domestic violence may not necessarily come to the attention of mainstream service providers and authorities. Second, the "model minority myth" has been applied to Asian Americans, which has distorted the public's perceptions of them. The "model minority myth" disseminates the view that Asian Americans have "made it" and have become successful, particularly in the areas of educational and occupational achievements. This myth clouds the fact that there are many social problems in Asian American communities, and as a result, such problems tend to be ignored. Third, racism, prejudice, and discrimination have also contributed to the invisibility of domestic violence among Asian Americans. Many Asian Americans opt to keep silent about incidences of domestic violence because they fear further racial attacks and discrimination. Abused Asian women who seek help often end up feeling discriminated against and marginalized in settings that are not sensitive to their culture and ethnicity. In addition, they also realize that their batterers are more likely to be unjustly treated by the police and judicial systems. Finally, cultural factors also play a role in impeding Asian American women from disclosing experiences with domestic violence. This will be discussed later in this article.

Taking Culture into Account When Examining Domestic Violence

Demographic shifts in the United States highlight the need to take culture into account when investigating social problems. Culture, race, and ethnicity have become forefront issues in America. It has been estimated that by 2050, ethnic minority groups will comprise almost half (47.5 percent) of the total U.S. population. Whites will most likely be a minority group by the year 2056. This multicultural shift calls for policymakers and service providers to adequately meet the needs of ethnic minorities.

The life experiences and social realities of Asian American and immigrant women are very different from those of white women. Some have argued that gender brings women of all colors together, and to some extent that may be true; however, it cannot be denied that other factors, such as racism, prejudice, discrimination, oppression, language barriers, and different cultural values and belief systems, will influence how victimization is experienced. Some Asian American or immigrant women may face unique obstacles, which are not necessarily part of the social realities of white domestic violence victims. For example, language barriers or lack of English language proficiency can exacerbate the difficulties Asian American or immigrant women experience in navigating the U.S. legal system and accessing services. In other cases, the legal status of Asian immigrant women can complicate the already complex dynamics of domestic violence. In some domestic violence cases, husbands who are U.S. citizens who sponsor their Asian non-U.S. resident wife may threaten to withdraw their sponsorship. The victim is then reluctant to report the abuse for fear she will be deported back to her homeland and lose custody of her children.

Culture and ethnicity are important social categories that impact attitudes toward domestic violence. For example, to what extent do individuals approve the use of violence against women? Are there certain situations in which individuals are more likely to approve the use of domestic violence? How is domestic violence defined? Attitudes, definitions, and beliefs justifying violence are often examined because they are considered to be risk factors to violence and can guide prevention efforts. Gender role beliefs (views about women's and men's roles) are intertwined with cultural belief systems, and it has been documented that patriarchy and male privilege are linked to violence against women.

Focus groups were conducted with Laotian, Khmer, Vietnamese, and Southeast Asian Chinese men and women to explore their perceptions of physical violence toward spouses. Attitudes varied somewhat among the four ethnic groups. Physical violence against wives was deemed unacceptable in the Chinese group, but the Chinese men reported using indirect and nonviolent means to control their wives. On the other hand, the Vietnamese appeared more tolerant of physical violence—the women believed it was to be tolerated periodically, and the men admitted to hitting their wives when they were angry. Both the Khmer and Laotian participants stated that physical violence in marriages was common and tolerated.

In a large study of 507 Chinese, Korean, Vietnamese, and Cambodian adults in the northeastern region of the United States, differences in attitudes toward domestic violence among these four Asian subgroups were examined. Among all four groups, in general, wife abuse was not sanctioned; however, the use of violence was justified in certain situations, such as a wife's unfaithfulness, her nagging, her refusal to cook or keep the house clean, or her making fun of her partner. The Vietnamese and Cambodians were more likely to endorse male privilege and also more likely to justify the use of wife abuse. Interestingly, among Koreans, age of immigration was related with endorsing the use of marital violence. This study showed that cultural beliefs about women's roles and male privilege influence attitudes toward wife abuse; however, there were variances in attitudes among Asians, which are influenced by an array of contextual factors such as immigration, sociopolitical conditions of their homelands, and level of education.

Feminist theory has argued that patriarchal ideologies influence violence against women. In a telephone survey of forty-seven South Asian women, the researchers were interested in whether patriarchal beliefs predicted perceptions of abuse. A vignette was read to participants describing a wife (from India) making dinner for her husband. They got into an argument whereby he accused her of making too many long-distance telephone calls. She denied it, stating that it was he who was making the calls. The husband lost his temper, pushed her, and slapped her on the face. She was holding a bowl with hot curry, which spilled and burned her foot. Is this scenario perceived as abuse? More than half of the women in this study stated that this Indian woman was a domestic violence victim, though those who endorsed patriarchal beliefs were less likely to state that the woman in the vignette was a domestic violence victim.

In another study, 289 Chinese American and 138 white undergraduate college students were surveyed to examine how students defined various acts of aggression and the extent to which they agreed that certain situations justified dating violence. The findings showed that Chinese American students were less likely to define dating violence in terms of psychological aggression compared with their white counterparts. Second, Chinese American students were more likely than the white students to agree that dating violence was justified in cases where the woman was caught having an affair, was drunk, screaming hysterically, unwilling to have sex, nagging, or flirting with someone else, and if the man was in a bad mood.

These findings were similar to results from another study that looked at gender differences in attitudes toward dating violence among 171 Filipino college students on a university campus. Although in general both Filipino males and females agreed that psychological aggression constituted dating violence, males did so to a significantly lesser degree. Again, while overall, Filipino students did not believe that dating violence was warranted under various circumstances, Filipino male students were more likely to justify violence if the female intimate partner/date was found flirting with another guy or having an affair. In both studies involving Chinese and Filipino college students cited here, it was speculated that in general, we live in a culture that sanctions retributive justice. Furthermore, culture affects how the world is interpreted. In certain Asian cultures, like the Chinese culture, aggression is condemned and looked down upon because of Chinese cultural norms that promote harmony and self-restraint in social relationships. Paradoxically, violence against women is condoned because of traditional views that place Asian women in subservient positions in the family and in society.

Finally, it is also crucial to examine culture in domestic violence because culture and ethnicity can influence help-seeking behaviors. In general, ethnic minorities are more reluctant to seek outside professional help, which may be attributed to their suspiciousness toward mental health and social services that are based on Western theoretical paradigms. Logistical factors such as financial limitations and inconvenient operational hours of many mental health and social service organizations also play a role affecting help-seeking behaviors. Finally, help-seeking behavior is in part influenced by the individual's definition and understanding of the phenomenon, which is ultimately influenced by culture. If, according to the study described above, Chinese American college students are less likely than their white counterparts to define psychological abuse as dating violence, they may also be less likely to label the phenomenon as a problem and ultimately less likely to seek help. Ultimately, race, culture, and ethnicity influence how one perceives the world.

Prevalence of Domestic Violence in Asian American Communities

Since the 1990s, more empirical research has been done in the area of domestic violence and Asian American and immigrant women. The majority of these research studies have relied on using non-probability sampling designs, which means it is not possible to get true prevalence rates. However, these studies offer us a glimpse of the scope of domestic violence in Asian American communities. Table 1 provides a summary of some of the studies that have been done looking at different Asian American subgroups and the scope of different components of domestic violence. These studies indicate that domestic violence does exist in Asian American communities.

Domestic Violence in an Asian Cultural Context

Culture plays a role in influencing attitudes sanctioning, minimizing, or masking domestic violence. Culture can be defined as patterns of behaviors and customs such as food, dress, music, and the arts—the observable components of culture. They are passed down from generation to generation through verbal communication, instruction, and general observation. Yet, culture does not consist merely of practices or rituals, but it also exists in intangible forms such as language; artistic expression; religion; political, economic, and social structures; norms of behavior; and values. Culture also encompasses a worldview, which in turn encompasses assumptions and perceptions about the world and how it guides individuals' behaviors and responses to their environment. It is not clear to what extent traditional Asian cultural values infuse the behaviors of Asian Americans living in the United States or how long it takes for Asian immigrants to begin adopting Western values, but it is known that acculturation is not a linear process whereby immigrant ethnic minorities move in stages in adopting the behaviors of their new environment. Culture is enduring, and cultural adaptation is not merely a process in which one selectively chooses to maintain and adhere to certain values and to discard others. Therefore, it is important to keep in mind that Asian American and immigrant women may adhere to more Eastern values and belief systems, while others are more acculturated and may endorse more Western values.

Women's Status and Roles

In Asia, patriarchal norms influence much of the social order and structure. Patriarchy involves the transmission of power and authority from father to eldest son, with key decision making and authority revolving around the male members. Consequently, relationships are based on a hierarchy involving traditional gender roles. The husband is the head of the household, the primary breadwinner, and the decision maker. The wife is the caretaker of the husband, his family, and the children. Girls are socialized to be dutiful, virtuous, and submissive wives who ultimately become mothers in order to bear sons so that the family name can be perpetuated. These views about women and their roles are also influenced by Confucian principles. For example, one major Confucian tenet, "Three Submissions," asserts that females are first to be subservient to their fathers before they are married, then to their husbands, and finally to their eldest son when widowed. Socialized early on with the notion that Asian women have no other options but to be wives and mothers, many battered Asian women find it difficult to terminate abusive relationships. These rigid gender role expectations are colored with moral nuances (i.e., being a good mother), and it leaves women bearing all the responsibility. Terminating the marriage may mean leaving the children behind, and if women opt for this route, they might subject themselves to criticisms of being a "bad mother." An Asian domestic violence victim not only bears the pressure of having to live up to the ideal image of a woman and fulfilling her duties but is also pressured to maintain the family. Ostracism and criticism can ensue if she does not fulfill her responsibilities.

In many Asian countries, there is a preference for having sons so that the family lineage is preserved, which can be done only by having a son perform the ancestral worship rituals. Sons also serve as a social security system for elderly parents, since daughters are married off and reside with their husbands' families. Therefore, wives experience great pressure to have sons, and those who cannot produce sons are humiliated, publicly shamed, and sometimes beaten. The devalued status of women in Asia still exists, as demonstrated by China's one child policy, which was designed to curb the increasing population growth. Because of Chinese families' desire to have sons, demographers are discovering that many baby girls are unaccounted for. Couples who give birth to baby girls often abandon or kill them so that they can adhere to the one child policy and still have a son. Such a climate fosters and condones violence against women.

Hierarchical Relationship Patterns

In Asian cultures, patterns of relationships are characterized by hierarchy. In Western societies, however, relationships are more likely to be egalitarian. In other words, the structure of Asian society is vertical, reflecting the influence of Confucianism. Confucianism has been described as a philosophy that emphasized peace, hierarchy, and order. Confucius arrived in China during a period of economic, political, and moral confusion, and he advocated a highly structured and hierarchical society, where everyone was ascribed specific roles. Proper conduct would naturally flow from this structure. His most well known philosophy describes five basic social relationships between (1) sovereign and subject, (2) father and son, (3) elder and younger brother, (4) husband and wife, and (5) friend and friend. A husband, for example, is deemed the authority figure. His primary responsibility is to provide for and protect the family. In turn, the wife must submit, be loyal, and fulfill her obligations to her husband. A focus group with Asian women and men found that these values may influence attitudes toward violence. Some Asian men, for example, believe that they have the responsibility of disciplining their wives, with physical violence being one mechanism of discipline.

Collectivistic Orientation and Loss of Face

In the United States and many Western societies, autonomy and individualism are the guiding philosophies. Individuals are socialized and reinforced to be self-sufficient and independent, and personal success and achievement are highly valued. Conversely, Asian cultures are characterized as collectivistic. In other words, one's identity, behaviors, and successes are rooted in collective units such as the family and community. Roles are interdependent and inextricably woven into social structures. Therefore, a decision made by an individual must take into account the whole (i.e., family) rather than merely the individual's needs. Shameful behaviors do not merely reflect on the individual but ultimately on his/her entire family, lineage, and even community. One of the major barriers confronted by Asian domestic violence victims in seeking assistance is that they are ashamed about the abuse. In part, this stems from societal myths that disseminate the misconception that domestic

violence victims must have in some way provoked the violence, and consequently, victims deserve the abuse.

However, the concept of guilt and shame can take on different connotations in different cultures. In Western culture, the guilt rests on the individual, and the individual bears the ramifications. However, in traditional Asian cultures, such as those of China, Japan, and Korea, "loss of face" means disgrace and loss of respect not only for the individual but also the immediate family and the entire ancestral lineage. Again, this is rooted in the collectivistic orientation described above. It is believed that the successes and failures are due to the blessings or anger of their ancestors, and similarly, positive and negative behaviors are believed to impact future generations. Therefore, Asian domestic violence victims may be reluctant to disclose the abuse for fear of shaming their families and communities.

Religious Orientations: Intersection with Cultural Values

A victim's religious beliefs may also be a cultural barrier to seeking assistance in domestic violence situations. Buddhism, the dominant religion in many parts of Asia, emphasizes the importance of perseverance and endurance and that life is a cycle, with each state linked to another. Its doctrine is tied to the Four Noble Truths: (1) Life is painful; (2) Pain originates from desire; (3) For pain to end, desire must end as well; and (4) The path to the end of pain is righteous living. The ultimate state is Nirvana, which is a peaceful state, absent of desire. There is an emphasis on fatalism; that is, all human beings must bear whatever trials and challenges that have been placed in the journey of life. This is the essence of *karma*, a Buddhist doctrine which advocates that all life is subject to suffering. This fatalistic orientation has colored attitudes toward help-seeking in domestic violence cases, where many Asian domestic violence victims remain silent about the abuse and do not seek help because they believe that they have to persevere and that violence is part of their fate.

Taoism is considered both a religion and philosophy. The individual is regarded as an autonomous being but interconnected with the natural forces of life. One does not necessarily attempt to alter one's environment; rather, the objective is to seek harmony with the natural order of things through rituals. The ultimate goal is to find peace and union between the individual and the cosmic forces of nature, aiming for harmony for the good of the whole. This religious and philosophical orientation

Table 1 Scope of Domestic Violence in Asian American Communities

Asian American Subgroup	Summary of Research Study	Scope of Domestic Violence	Source
Korean Americans	N = 256 Korean American couples, telephone interviews.	19 percent of Korean Americans experienced at least one incident of minor physical assaults by a spouse during the year.	Kim, Jae Yop, and K. T. Sung, "Conjugal Violence in Korean American Families: A Residue of the Cultural Tradition." *Journal of Family Violence* 15, no. 4 (2000): 331–345.
	N = 150 Korean adult married women. Face-to-face surveys, convenience sampling in Chicago.	60 percent of Korean women reported some form of spousal abuse.	Song-Kim, Young I. "Battered Korean Women in Urban United States." In *Social Work Practice with Asian-Americans,* edited by Sharlene M. Furuto, Renuka Biswas, Douglas K. Chung, Kenji Murase, and Fariya Ross-Sheriff. Newbury Park, CA: Sage Publications, 1992, pp. 213–226.
Filipino Americans	N = 171 Filipino male and female university students; self-administered surveys.	58.9 percent of Filipino females and 41.1 percent of Filipino males reported they experienced physical violence by a dating partner since they started dating.	Agbayani-Siewert, Pauline, and Alice Yick Flanagan. "Filipino American Dating Violence: Definitions, Contextual Justifications and Experiences of Dating Violence." *Journal of Human Behavior in the Social Environment* 3, no. 3/4 (2001): 115–133.
Chinese Americans	N = 262 Chinese American male and female adults; Asian surname sampling in Los Angeles County. Administered telephone surveys.	81 percent reported verbal abuse in last 12 months and 85 percent for lifetime; 6.8 percent reported physical spousal abuse in last 12 months and 18 percent for lifetime.	Yick, Alice G. "Domestic Violence in the Chinese American Community: Cultural Taboos and Barriers." *Family Violence and Sexual Assault Bulletin* 15 (1999): 16–23.

	$N = 181$ Chinese women in Boston, random sample using sampling frame from the Boston census; telephone surveys.	14 percent reported partner violence during lifetime.	Hicks, Madeline H., and Z. Li. "Partner Violence and Major Depression in Women: A Community Study of Chinese Americans." *Journal of Nervous and Mental Disease* 191, no. 11 (2003): 722–729.
Japanese Americans	$N = 211$ women of Japanese descent in Los Angeles completed face-to-face interviews. Two methods of estimating prevalence were assessed. One was a conventional method and the other asked if respondents perceived that the acts were abusive.	51 percent of the sample reported physical violence and 75 percent reported emotional abuse. However, with the additional criteria of asking respondents if they perceived the acts as abusive, the prevalence rates decrease (i.e., 39 percent for physical violence and 50 percent for emotional abuse).	Yoshihama, Meiko. "Domestic Violence against Women of Japanese Descent in Los Angeles: Two Methods of Estimating Prevalence." *Violence against Women* 5, no. 8 (1999): 869–897.
South Asians	$N = 62$ (20 South Asians, 22 Hispanics, and 20 African Americans). Recruited from domestic violence programs. Administered face-to-face interviews.	63 percent of South Asians reported having objects thrown at them, being choked, or slammed against wall; 73 percent reported being punched, pushed, or shoved.	Yoshioka, Marianne R., Louisa Gilbert, Nabila El-Bassel, and Malahat Baig-Amin. "Social Support and Disclosure of Abuse: Comparing South Asian, African American, and Hispanic Battered Women." *Journal of Family Violence* 18, no. 3 (2003): 171–180.
Vietnamese	$N = 10$ Vietnamese women; purposive sampling; in-depth face-to-face interviews.	80 percent experienced some form of emotional abuse within last 12 months.	Bui, Hoan N., and Merry Morash. "Domestic Violence in the Vietnamese Immigrant Community: An Exploratory Study." *Violence against Women* 5, no. 7 (1999): 769–794.

often results in Asian domestic violence victims implicitly accepting the abuse, and at times, criticizing and ostracizing those who shake the status quo. Consequently, Asian American domestic violence victims may relegate their own needs in order to preserve harmony, as conflict or confrontations are culturally (and/or philosophically) dissonant.

Practical Implications for Counselors

With all clients, building rapport or engagement is an integral part of the clinical process. However, when working with Asian American and immigrant domestic violence victims, particularly those who may be less acculturated, counselors need to convey authority, credibility, and legitimacy. Many Asian American or immigrant clients come into counseling believing that the counselor will quickly identify the problem and provide a solution. When the counselor does not do so, he or she loses legitimacy in the eyes of the client. Therefore, the counselor needs to overtly establish authority. Employing professional titles, displaying diplomas and professional licenses are some examples of overtly establishing legitimacy. Furthermore, obtaining sufficient information about the client and family and offering some explanation of the cause of the client's problems can facilitate credibility. Consequently, counselors need to be very knowledgeable about domestic violence (from both a victim's and a perpetrator's perspective) and have strong links to community resources such as medical, family, and financial services, social services, legal assistance, and child care and immigration aid services. Clients will expect to take away something concrete (i.e., a solution), which is reinforced by cultural values of pragmatism. On the other hand, if the counselor focuses too much on facilitating emotional disclosure, Asian clients are more likely to terminate counseling prematurely.

When working with Asian American and immigrant domestic violence victims, it is also important to acknowledge their feelings of guilt and shame. The shame, and in this case, loss of face, stems from two sources—the emotional turmoil caused by the abuse, and the fact that the victim has had to seek outside assistance, particularly for issues considered to be private, sensitive family matters. Consequently, it is crucial for counselors to help victims work through their ambivalence about seeking help as well as their guilt for feeling that they are at fault for the abuse.

Empowering Asian American and immigrant domestic violence victims is another component

of work with this population. However, it is important for counselors to keep in mind that the term "empowerment" is a social construction used in the fields of feminist studies, domestic violence, and the helping professions. Empowerment is based on principles of autonomy, individualism, and self-determination, which are primarily Western ideologies and are at times dissonant with traditional Asian values that revolve around collectivism, such as importance of the family, community, marriage, and relegating one's own needs for the greater good. Therefore, counselors should not immediately coach Asian or Asian American domestic violence victims to leave the marriage, because it may not be congruent with their value systems. As with all domestic violence victims, their voices have been silenced, and it is vital to have their voices heard and to respect and support their decisions. Part of this entails educating them about what abuse entails, the dynamics of abuse, and facilitating and linking them to both informal and formal services.

ALICE G. YICK

See also **Cross-Cultural Examination of Domestic Violence in China and Pakistan; Cross-Cultural Perspectives on Domestic Violence; Cross-Cultural Perspectives on How to Deal with Batterers; Minorities and Families in America, Introduction to; Multicultural Programs for Domestic Batterers; Qur'anic Perspectives on Wife Abuse; Social Learning Theory and Family Violence**

References and Further Reading

Ahmad, Farah, Sarah Riaz, Paula Barata, and Donna E. Stewart. "Patriarchal Beliefs and Perceptions of Abuse among South Asian Immigrant Women." *Violence against Women* 10, no. 3 (2004): 262–282.

Anderson, Michelle J. "License to Abuse: The Impact of Conditional Status on Female Immigrants." *Yale Law Journal* 102 (1993): 1401–1430.

Bradshaw, Carla K. "Asian and Asian American Women: Historical and Political Considerations in Psychotherapy." In *Women of Color: Integrating Ethnic and Gender Identities in Psychotherapy,* edited by Lillian Comas-Diaz and Beverly Greene. New York: Guilford Press, 1994, pp. 72–113.

Chung, Douglas K. "Asian Cultural Commonalities: A Comparison with Mainstream Culture." In *Social Work Practice with Asian Americans,* edited by Sharlene Furuto, Renauka Biswas, Douglas K. Chung, Kenji Murase, and Fariyal Ross-Sheriff. Newbury Park, CA: Sage Publications, 1992, pp. 27–44.

D'Andrade, Roy G. "Cultural Meaning Systems." In *Culture Theory: Essays on Mind, Self, and Emotions,* edited by Richard A. Shweder and Robert A. LeVine. Cambridge: Cambridge University Press, 1984, pp. 88–119.

Dobash, R. Emerson, and Russel P. Dobash. *Violence against Wives: A Case against the Patriarchy.* New York: Free Press, 1979.

Green, James W. *Cultural Awareness in the Human Services: A Multi-Ethnic Approach,* 3rd ed. Boston: Allyn and Bacon, 1999.

Greenblat, Cathy S. "'Don't Hit Your Wife. . . Unless. . .': Preliminary Findings on Normative Support for the Use of Physical Force by Husbands." *Victimology* 10 (1985): 221–241.

Ho, Christine. "An Analysis of Domestic Violence in Asian American Communities: A Multicultural Approach to Counseling." *Women and Therapy* 9, no. 1 (1990): 129–150.

Jackson, Anita P., and Ferguson B. Meadows. "Getting to the Bottom to Understand the Top." *Journal of Counseling and Development* 70 (1991): 72–76.

Jung, Marshall. *Chinese American Family Therapy: A New Model for Clinicians.* San Francisco: Jossey-Bass, 1998.

Kanuha, Valli. "Women of Color in Battering Relationships." In Comas-Diaz and Greene, eds., *Women of Color,* 428–454.

Kurz, Demie. "Social Science Perspective in Wife Abuse: Current Debates and Future Directions." *Gender and Society* 3, no. 4 (1989): 489–505.

Lavizzo-Mourey, Risa, and Elizabeth R. Mackenzie. "Cultural Competence: Essential Measurements of Quality for Managed Care Organizations." *Annals of Internal Medicine* 1124 (1996): 919–921.

Lee, Evelyn. "Asian American Families: An Overview." In *Ethnicity and Family Therapy,* edited by Monica McGoldrick, Joe Giordano, and John K. Pearce, 2nd ed. New York: Guilford Press, 1996, pp. 227–248.

Lee, Mo-Yee. "Understanding Chinese Battered Women in North America: A Review of the Literature and Practice Implications." *Journal of Multicultural Social Work* 8, no. 3/4 (2000): 215–241.

Lee, Mo-Yee, and Phylllis F. M. Law. "Perceptions of Sexual Violence against Women in Asian American Communities." *Journal of Ethnic and Cultural Diversity in Social Work* 10, no. 2 (2001): 3–25.

Masaki, Beckie, and Lorena Wong. "Domestic Violence in the Asian Community." In *Working with Asian Americans: A Guide for Clinicians,* edited by Evelyn Lee. New York: Guilford Press, 1997, pp. 439–451.

Ong, Paul, and Suzanne J. Hee. "The Growth of the Asian Pacific American Population: Twenty Million in 2020." In *The State of Asian Pacific America: Policy Issues to the Year 2000,* edited by Paul Ong. Los Angeles: LEAP Asian Pacific American Public Policy Institute and UCLA, Asian American Studies Center, 1993, pp. 11–24.

Pedersen, Paul. "Balance as a Criterion for Social Services for Asian and Pacific Islander Americans." In *Handbook of Social Services for Asian and Pacific Islanders,* edited by Noreen Mokuau. Westport, CT: Greenwood Press, 1991, pp. 37–57.

Richie, Beth E., and Valli Kanuha. "Battered Women of Color in Public Health Care Systems: Racism, Sexism, and Violence." In *Wings of Gauze: Women of Color and the Experience of Health and Illness,* edited by Barbara Blair and Susan E. Cayleff. Detroit: Wayne State University Press, 1993, pp. 288–299.

Riley, Nancy E. "Chinese Women's Lives: Rhetoric and Reality." *Asia Pacific Issues* 25 (1995). Honolulu: East-West Center.

Rimonte, Nilda. "A Question of Culture: Cultural Approval of Violence against Women in the Pacific-Asian Community and the Cultural Defense." *Stanford Law Review* 43 (1991): 1311–1326.

Roy, Susan G. "Restoring Hope or Tolerating Abuse? Responses to Domestic Violence against Immigrant Women." *Georgetown Immigration Law Journal* 9, no. 2 (1995): 263–290.

Shibusawa, Tazuko. "Japanese American Parenting." In *Culturally Diverse Parent–Child and Family Relationships: A Guide for Social Workers and Other Practitioners,* edited by Noreen B. Webb. New York: Columbia University Press, 2001, pp. 283–303.

Sokoloff, Natalie J., and Ida Dupont. "Domestic Violence at the Intersection of Race, Class, and Gender: Challenges and Contributions to Understanding Violence against Marginalized Women in Diverse Communities." *Violence against Women* 11, no. 1 (2005): 38–64.

Sue, Donald W., and David Sue. *Counseling the Culturally Different: Theory and Practice.* New York: John Wiley & Sons, 1990.

Tang, Catherine S., Day Wong, and Fanny M. Cheung. "Social Construction of Women as Legitimate Victims of Violence in Chinese Societies." *Violence against Women* 8, no. 8 (2002): 968–996.

Tran, Carolee GiaoUyen, and Kunya Des Jardins. "Domestic Violence in Vietnamese Refugee and Korean Immigrant Communities." In *Relationships Among Asian American Women,* edited by Jean Lau. Washington, DC: American Psychological Association, 2000, pp. 71–96.

Uba, Laura. *Asian Americans: Personality Patterns, Identity, and Mental Health.* New York: Guilford Press, 1994.

U.S. Census. "We the People: Asians in the United States: Census 2000 Special Reports," 2004. http://www.census.gov/prod/2004pubs/censr-17.pdf (accessed April 13, 2005).

Wong, Roger R. "Divorce Mediation among Asian Americans: Bargaining in the Shadow of Diversity." *Family and Conciliation Courts Review* 33, no. 1 (1995): 110–128.

Yick, Alice. "Domestic Violence Beliefs and Attitudes in the Chinese American Community." *Journal of Social Service Research* 27, no. 1 (2000): 29–51.

———. "Feminist and Status Inconsistency Theory: Application to Domestic Violence in Chinese Immigrant Families." *Violence against Women* 7, no. 5 (2001): 545–562.

Yick, Alice, and Pauline Agbayani-Siewert. "Dating Violence Among Chinese American and White Students: A Sociocultural Context." *Journal of Multicultural Social Work* 8, no. 1/2 (2000): 101–129.

Yoshioka, Marianne R., Jennifer DiNoia, and Komal Ullah. "Attitudes toward Marital Violence: An Examination of Four Asian Communities." *Violence against Women* 7, no. 8 (2001): 900–926.

ASSESSING RISK IN DOMESTIC VIOLENCE CASES

Victims of domestic violence face different kinds of risks. Perpetrators are the most obvious source of risk. Risk assessment procedures seek to identify the most dangerous perpetrators. However, victims also face risks associated with the delivery of various system services including law enforcement, the judicial system, emergency medical services, and so on. For example, a battered woman's risk of dying from her injuries may be far greater in a rural community where emergency services take longer to arrive. It is also the case that lethal domestic violence occurs much more frequently in poorer neighborhoods with fewer resources. Social problems such as poverty, unemployment, and alcohol and drug addiction may also be seen as elevating the risk of dying from domestic violence.

The odds of predicting which victims of domestic violence will eventually die as a result of their victimization are rather low. Domestic violence usually precedes intimate partner homicide. However, there are over a million domestic violence assaults reported to police each year, compared with a thousand to two thousand deaths by domestic homicide. Therefore, identifying cases that will escalate to the occurrence of the abuse victim's death is an inexact science at best. Nevertheless, risk assessment and management are integral and important aspects of the delivery of all kinds of services to victims.

Definitional Issues

In any analysis of risk it is important to ask the question, "Risk of what?" In other words, are risk assessors exploring the possibility of death or serious injury or a felonious assault as opposed to a misdemeanor assault? It is also important to bear in mind the duration of risk and how that risk may change over time. For example, one might talk about an elevated risk of homicide during a divorce or the process of physical separation between intimate partners. Alternatively, it is possible the risk will last until the abusive partner moves out of town, or it might last for the rest of the victim's life.

It is also important to realize that victims of domestic violence may see great danger in certain forms of abusive behavior directed at themselves or others that might not register on risk assessment instruments, might not qualify as violence under the criminal code, or might not result in the kinds of injuries that would warrant a visit to a hospital emergency room. Put simply, risk assessment must examine the victims' own perception of the meaning of abusive behaviors they experience. These risks may often take discreet, subtle, and highly idiosyncratic forms. One example here might be some form of emotional abuse that a victim might perceive as indicative of potentially homicidal behavior, which to the untrained eye may appear innocuous. These subjective dimensions of risk remind us that it is not just the physical acts of violence that contribute to one's appreciation of potential danger but rather what violence and emotional abuse mean to victims and others and the context within which these various transgressions occur.

Most often risk assessments rely upon information derived from victim reports. However, given the complex and multidimensional nature of risk, it is advisable that risk assessments tap into a wide variety of informants and sources of information. For example, comprehensive risk assessments might involve asking questions of perpetrators, victims, family members, neighbors, friends, workplace peers, and various service providers. This is time-consuming and in practice rarely done.

The risk posed by a particular perpetrator changes. Some risk assessments attempt to transcend a flat, one-off evaluation of danger by examining risk on an ongoing basis or at least assessing it at multiple points in time. The rolling/longitudinal risk assessment and management strategies are much more difficult to conduct and raise some very difficult issues. For example, if there are multiple sources of information on a perpetrator of domestic violence, one might expect the multiple agencies that contribute such data to all have access to the ongoing risk score. However, if the perpetrator is currently being prosecuted, then the broad availability of data regarding the case might compromise the prosecution. The access of agencies to sensitive case information might also compromise the safety of victims of domestic violence.

Police officers attending domestic violence scenes may have neither the time nor the skill to elicit detailed and highly idiosyncratic information pertaining to risk. Thoughtful risk assessments must fit into the busy schedules of those working specifically with victims of domestic violence. In a very practical way, such assessments ought not be prohibitively long.

The asking of open-ended questions usually elicits much more information from victims and provides an opportunity for the development of some rapport between interviewer and victim. In these scenarios risk assessors may pay more attention to demeanor, listening skills, body language, and choice of words. Interviews such as these may be more likely to unfold between an advocate and a victim. The data emerging may be much more idiosyncratic and therefore less amenable to statistical analysis. However, it may tell the advocate/risk assessor much more about the compromises and difficulties the victim faces.

Most risk assessors realize that no instrument should form the exclusive basis for safety planning and that listening to victims is essential. Nevertheless, thoughtfully constructed risk assessment instruments have the potential to enlighten both victims and service providers alike. Although little research has been conducted as of this writing on how risk assessment affects intervention, recidivism, and death rates, anecdotal evidence suggests that risk scores exert pressure on multiple service providers and may encourage them to be more careful. It is also the case that conversations about risk involve a shared language and thus may enhance coordinated community responses to domestic violence.

Notwithstanding all these possible benefits, two questions arise (Websdale 2005a, 2005b). First, because risk assessment involves triaging, is it likely even if "high-risk" cases are identified that resources will be available to increase protection? Second, in situations where victims reject safety-planning advice based on risk assessments or choose to follow another path, does society set them up for blame?

Red Flags or Risk Markers

Researchers appear to have identified characteristics of cases in which domestic violence victims die. Digging deeply into that small population of domestic violence homicides uncovers a number of factors that do not seem to surface as frequently or with the same level of intensity in everyday (nonlethal) cases. Risk assessors search for these red flags in everyday cases and use their presence as a possible sign of increased danger. Researchers are agreed that this is not foolproof science. Indeed, lethal outcomes might depend upon other extraneous variables, such as the quality of emergency medical services or the distance from a major hospital.

Notwithstanding these caveats, certain red flags loom large in both the research literature and in risk assessment instruments (Campbell et al. 2003a, 2003b; Websdale 2000). These red flags are outlined below.

A Prior History of Intimate Partner Violence

The first and most important red flag is a prior history of intimate partner violence (Campbell et al. 2003a; Websdale 1999; Wolfgang 1958). Under this broad umbrella of "prior history" some researchers note the predictive significance of particular forms of violence such as "choking" and "forced sex" (Campbell 2003b). Using data from the Danger Assessment Instrument, Campbell et al. (2003b: 17) found that compared with the control group of abused women, murdered women were forced to have sex 7.6 more times and were 9.9 times more likely to be choked.

"Stalking" appears as a prominent correlate in a number of works. According to the research of McFarlane et al. (1999: 300), "Stalking is revealed to be a correlate of lethal and near lethal violence against women and, coupled with physical assault, is significantly associated with murder and attempted murder."

A prior history of intimate partner violence may include the use of a weapon. According to Campbell et al.'s Danger Assessment study, abused women who were "threatened or assaulted with a gun or other weapon were 20 times more likely than other women to be murdered." The mere presence of a gun in the home meant that an abused woman "was six times more likely than other abused women to be killed" (Campbell et al. 2003b: 16).

Although prior intimate partner violence in many of its guises powerfully informs the debate on risk, it is also the case that significant numbers of women who die report no prior history of violence that researchers are able to later identify. For example, the Chicago Women's Health Risk Study reports that in one in five cases of men killing female intimates, researchers uncovered no evidence of prior intimate partner violence (Block 2003: 5).

Pending or Actual Separation or Estrangement

The extant research literature contends that women experience an increased risk of lethal violence when they leave intimate relationships with men (Browne 1987; Wilson and Daly 1993). More recent research from Campbell et al.'s eleven-city case control study found, "Women who separated from their abusive partners after cohabitation experienced increased risk of femicide, particularly when the abuser was highly controlling" (2003a: 1092).

Obsessive Possessiveness or Morbid Jealousy

The research literature consistently identifies obsessive or morbid jealousy as central to intimate partner homicides. For example, Daly and Wilson (1988: 202–205) point to the role of male sexual proprietariness in homicides in India, Uganda, Zaire, and Samoa. Easteal (1993: 109) discusses obsessive or pathological jealousy in terms of the perpetrator seeing his partner as part of his own identity. Consequently, any threat of the female leaving threatens the man's identity. The emphasis with this red flag is firmly on "extreme" or "morbid" forms of jealousy.

Making Threats to Kill

Threats to kill constitute one of the most consistent correlates of intimate partner homicide when compared with abused women in general (Browne 1987; Campbell et al. 2003b: 17; Hart 1988). "Women whose partners threatened them with murder were 15 times more likely than other women to be killed" (Campbell et al. 2003b: 16).

Batterers' threats to take their own lives, perhaps as a means of gaining some control in the relationship, also appear as risk indicators for homicide. Barbara Hart, J.D., a leading advocate for battered women, sees batterers' suicidal threats, ideations, and plans as very significant risk markers (Hart 1988: 242). These and other risk markers become all the more onerous if the battered woman plays a "central role . . . in the batterer's universe . . . . Especially if the loss of the battered woman represents or precipitates a total loss of hope for a positive future." Hart bases her insights on what she calls "experiential data" rather than statistical research.

Paradoxically, in Campbell et al.'s eleven-city case controlled study of femicide, the researchers found that "[t]hreatened or attempted suicide by either males or females . . . were not found to be predictors of intimate partner homicide. However, there was an increased risk of homicide when the man is suicidal and there has not been any physical abuse" (Campbell et al. 2003b: 16).

Alcohol and Drug Use

It is a widely held belief that excessive alcohol and, to a lesser extent, drug use accompany intimate partner violence. In predicting dangerous and lethal outcomes, these variables figure prominently on nearly all risk assessment forms. Campbell et al. (2003b: 17) found that women whose partners became "drunk every day or almost every day" were 4.1 times more likely to die than battered women whose partners did not engage in this behavior.

Unemployment

Recent research reveals a clear association between unemployment and intimate partner homicide. One group of researchers comments that the "abuser's lack of employment was the only demographic risk factor that significantly predicted femicide risks after we controlled for a comprehensive list of more proximate risk factors, increasing risks 4-fold relative to the case of employed abusers" (Campbell et al. 2003a: 1092). This statistical research is a fine start, but more research is needed that indicates what being unemployed means to victims, perpetrators, and others.

Stepchildren

According to Wilson and Daly (1998: 226), the presence of children of other unions constitutes "a major risk marker for violence against wives." Campbell et al. (2003a: 1092) note that "instances in which a child of the victim by a previous partner was living in the home increased the risk of intimate partner homicide."

Neil Websdale

See also **Child Maltreatment, Interviewing Suspected Victims of; Elder Abuse, Assessing the Risks of; Fatality Reviews in Adult Domestic Homicide and Suicide; Healthcare Professionals' Roles in Identifying and Responding to Domestic Violence; Intimate Partner Homicide; Police Response to Domestic Violence Incidents**

References and Further Reading

Block, C. R. "How Can Practitioners Help an Abused Woman Lower Her Risk of Death?" *NIJ Journal*, no. 250 (2003): 4–7.

Browne, A. *When Battered Women Kill*. New York: Free Press, 1987.

Campbell, Jacquelyn C., et al. "Risk Factors for Femicide in Abusive Relationships: Results from a Multisite Case Control Study." *American Journal of Public Health* 93, no. 7 (2003a): 1089–1097.

———. "Assessing Risk Factors for Intimate Partner Homicide." *NIJ Journal*, no. 250 (2003b): 14–19.

Daly, Martin, and Margo Wilson. *Homicide*. Hawthorne, NY: Aldine de Gruyter, 1988.

Easteal, Patricia W. *Killing the Beloved: Homicide between Adult Sexual Intimates*. Canberra: Australian Institute of Criminology, 1993.

Hart, Barbara. "Beyond the Duty to Warn: A Therapist's Duty to Protect Battered Women and Children." In *Feminist Perspectives on Wife Abuse,* edited by K. Yllo and M. Bograd. Newbury Park, CA: Sage, 1988, pp. 234–248.

McFarlane, Judith M., J. C. Campbell, S. Wilt, C. J. Sachs, Y. Ulrich, and Xiao Xu. "Stalking and Intimate Partner Femicide." *Homicide Studies* 3, no. 4 (1991): 300–316.

Websdale, N. *Understanding Domestic Homicide*. Boston: Northeastern University Press, 1999.

———. "Lethality Assessment Tools: A Critical Analysis." VAWnet. Violence against Women Grants Office Applied Research Series, 2000.

———. "R and B: A Conversation between a Researcher and a Battered Woman about Domestic Violence Fatality Review." *Violence against Women* 11, no. 9 (2005a): 1186–1200.

———. "Battered Women at Risk: A Rejoinder to Jacquelyn Hauser's and Jacquelyn Campbell's Commentaries on R and B." *Violence against Women* 11, no. 9 (2005b): 1214–1221.

Wilson, Margo I., and Martin Daly. "Spousal Homicide Risk and Estrangement." *Violence and Victims* 8 (1993): 271–294.

Wolfgang, Marvin E. *Patterns of Criminal Homicide*. Philadelphia: University of Pennsylvania Press, 1958.

ATTACHMENT THEORY AND DOMESTIC VIOLENCE

Over the past thirty years since the 1970s, the treatment of choice for perpetrators of domestic violence has not evolved much. Most programs consist of either cognitive-behavioral therapy (e.g., Dutton 1998; Sonkin 2003), feminist-based reeducation (Pense and Paymar 1993), or a combination of the two. Other models, such as those of family systems and psychodynamics (Dutton and Sonkin 2003), have been described but are less common in practice. The reason for this is that state laws that have been advocated by activists generally mandate the type of interventions providers must include in their programs, and these requirements usually are based on the feminist reeducation model, such as that offered by the Domestic Abuse Intervention Project, which has come to be known as the Duluth Model. Although some scholars and practitioners are attempting to challenge these traditional ways of approaching perpetrator treatment (see, e.g., Dutton and Nichols 2005), domestic violence intervention has experienced little change in recent decades.

Many states have mandated the Duluth Model into the law, even though numerous evaluations of this model have found that program participation had no impact on recidivism (Davis, Taylor, and Maxwell 1998; Feder and Forde 1999; Levesque 1998; Shepard 1987, 1992). One outcome of having legislated a particular form of intervention is that there has been a stagnancy in the field, resulting in minimal innovation and change over the last decades of the twentieth century. What is most disturbing is that this stagnancy continues despite research suggesting that the current intervention models are having only a moderate effect on treatment outcome (Babcock, Green, and Robie 2004).

The purpose of this article is to propose an expansion of the common conceptualization of domestic violence from a primarily behavioral-social/political perspective to a model that considers recent findings in developmental and social psychology as well as neuropsychology. While this article will focus primarily on male perpetrators, many of the principles of attachment theory and neurobiology presented here can be applied to women perpetrators (Babcock, Miller, and Siard 2003; Leisring, Dowd, and Rosenbaum 2003) and victims (Henderson, Bartholomew, and Dutton 1997; Morgan and Shaver 1999).

ATTACHMENT THEORY AND DOMESTIC VIOLENCE

Attachment Theory Overview

In his landmark trilogy *Attachment and Loss,* the British psychiatrist John Bowlby (1969, 1973, 1980) posited a theory of development that contradicted the prevailing psychoanalytic theories of the time and proved to be a revolutionary way of understanding the nature of the attachment bonds between infants and their caregivers (Bretherton 1992). In his observations of infants separated from their mothers and fathers during hospitalizations, he saw the dire effects of separation distress on the emotional state of the child. According to the theory, attachment is governed by a number of important principles. First, alarm of any kind, stemming from an internal (such as physical pain) or external source (such as a loss of contact with a caregiver), will activate what Bowlby called the "attachment behavioral system." Bowlby believed that this system was one of four behavioral systems that are innate and evolutionarily function to ensure survival of the species. The distress produced by the stimulus directs and motivates infants to seek out soothing physical contact with the attachment figure. Once activated, only physical attachment with the attachment figure will terminate the attachment behavioral system. As Cassidy (1999) describes, the infant is like a heat-seeking missile, looking for an attachment figure that is sufficiently near, available, and responsive. When this attempt for protection is met with success, the attachment system deactivates, the anxiety is reduced, the infant is soothed, and play and exploration can resume. When these needs are not met, the infant experiences extreme arousal and terror. When the system has been activated for a long time without soothing and termination, the system can then become suppressed. If the system is activated and inconsistently soothed, it can become exquisitely sensitive and reactive. Bowlby reported observations he made of 15- to 30-month-old children separated for the first time from their mothers. He witnessed a three-phase behavioral display: protest, despair, and detachment. He concluded from these observations that the primary function of protest was to generate displays that would lead to the return of the absent parent. This expression of negative emotion may be viewed as an attempt to recapture the attachment figure that can soothe tension and anxiety at a developmental stage where the child cannot yet self-soothe. Through this signaling, the attachment figure is told that she is wanted and/or needed. When the attachment figure is sufficiently *unresponsive* to the infant's call for help, insecure patterns of attachment develop that may set the stage for interpersonal problems later in life.

Mary Ainsworth was the American psychologist who brought Bowlby's theory to the United States and developed a method, the Strange Situation, of assessing infant attachment (Ainsworth, Blehar, Waters, and Wall 1978). Originally three patterns were observed—secure, anxious-avoidant, and anxious-ambivalent—but later on a fourth category, disorganized, was described. Since Ainsworth's original studies, it has been found that attachment pattern rates are fairly consistent across cultures—approximately 65 percent secure and 35 percent insecure (van IJzendoorn and Sagi 1999). The Strange Situation is a laboratory procedure used to assess infant attachment status. The procedure consists of eight episodes of separation and reunion. The infant's behavior upon the parent's return is the basis for classifying the infant into one of three attachment categories. The secure infants experienced distress at the separation and were unable to resume exploration and play. When the parent returned, the infant showed distress but was able to quickly settle down and return to exploration. Another group of infants showed distress at neither separation nor reunion. These infants were termed anxious-avoidant. Although they seemed unaffected by the separation and reunion process, their results on physiological measures showed that they were clearly in distress. A third category of infants were extremely distressed at separation and at reunion. However, these infants were not able to return to play and exploration, like the secure infants, when their parents tried to soothe them. They clung to their parents and often demonstrated anger and aggression. These infants were termed anxious-resistant.

Originally researchers described three categories (secure, anxious-avoidant, and anxious-resistant), though some infants studied were termed "cannot classify." Main and Solomon (1986) looked more closely at these unclassifiable infants and found that some children were particularly ambivalent upon reunion with their attachment figure, both approaching and avoiding contact. These infants appeared to demonstrate a collapse in behavioral and attentional strategies for managing attachment distress (Hesse and Main 2000). They didn't display an organized strategy for coping with attachment distress, so these infants were termed *disorganized.* When researchers asked why these children were both seeking protection from their caregivers while at the same time pulling away, they discovered that a large percentage of these infants were experiencing abuse by their caregiver. Main and Hesse (1990) wrote that these infants were experiencing "fear without solution." Another sub-group of disorganized infants, however, were not experiencing abuse by their caregivers, which the researchers found to be a curious anomaly. It was discovered that these caregivers had experienced abuse by their parents, but that abuse was still unresolved (Hesse, Main, Yost-Abrams, and Rifkin 2003). Upon close examination, it was discovered that when the infant was in need of protection, the caregiver became frightened (as evidenced by his or her turning away or making subtle frightening faces at the infant). It is believed that attachment disorganization occurs when a parent acts either frightening or frightened in response to the infant's need for protection.

Adult Attachment

In the 1980s, the field of adult attachment began to evolve. This occurred for several reasons. First, many attachment labs were conducting research on the continuity of attachment status over time. Researchers were also becoming interested in the long-term effects of secure and insecure attachment on interpersonal functioning. As the research in child, adolescent, and adult attachment evolved, new methods of assessing attachment status were needed. Main and Goldwyn (1993), at the University of California, Berkeley, developed the Adult Attachment Interview (AAI). The interview has been utilized in hundreds of studies worldwide to assess adult attachment states of mind.

In longitudinal studies, 80 percent of children assessed in the Strange Situation as infants were given the same AAI classification as young adults (Fraley 2002; Waters, Hamilton, and Weinfield 2000). In approximately 20 percent of the cases, the attachment status changes over time (usually from insecure to secure, but sometimes the other way). The term "earned security" is used for those individuals who were assessed as insecure as infants but assessed as secure as adults (Roisman, Padron, Sroufe, and Egeland 2002). When a child changes from insecure to secure, it is most likely as a result of a relationship. This makes sense because insecurity grows out of relationships, so one would expect "earned security" to grow out of relationships. The AAI data have also been utilized to examine the relationship between the parent's attachment status and the attachment relationship between that parent and her/his infant (Main and Goldwyn 1993). The most robust predictor of the attachment

pattern between the infant and her/his parent is the attachment status of the parent—as high as 80 percent predictability.

Social psychologists have studied attachment in adult relationships and its relationship to interpersonal (Fraley and Shaver 2000) and group processes (Rom and Mikulincer 2003). Out of this track came a large body of social-psychological research on attachment *style* (rather than attachment *status*, the term used by developmental psychologists) and interpersonal functioning. Self-report measures have been developed that could be quickly administered to a larger group of subjects and scored relatively easily. Attachment is deconstructed differently, depending on the measure. For example, the Experiences in Close Relationships Scale measures attachment patterns based on two continuums, anxiety and avoidance (Brennan, Clark, and Shaver 1998). The Relationship Status Questionnaire, developed by Bartholomew and Horowitz (1991), measures attachment in a way that is more in line with Bowlby's initial conceptualization: internal working models of self and others. Although there was some initial conflict between the consistency between self-report measures and interview methods, recent studies have suggested that these different assessment tools may have more consistency than originally thought (Shaver, Belsky, and Brennan 2000).

A number of important findings have emerged from the research on attachment. Attachment is a form of dyadic emotion regulation (Mikulincer, Shaver, and Pereg 2003; Sroufe 1995). Infants are not capable of regulating their own emotions and arousal and therefore require the assistance of their caregiver in this process. How the infant ultimately learns how to regulate his/her emotions will depend heavily on how the caregiver regulates his/her own emotions and displays sensitivity or attunement to the infant's emotional state (Fonagy, Target, Gergely, and Jurist 2002; Stern 1985). Another important finding was that attachment is not a one-way street. As the caregiver affects the infant, the infant also affects the caregiver. This process is referred to as "mutual regulation" (Tronick 1989). The caregiver is not only aware through observation of the infant's emotional state, but also feels the infant's emotions, which allows for even greater sensitivity.

The Neurobiology of Attachment

Bowlby believed that attachment was a biologically based behavioral system (Bowlby 1988). However, it wasn't until the 1990s, the decade of the brain, with the development of sophisticated scanning techniques, that we were able to literally look into the brain and better understand how this behavioral system actually functioned. Magnetic resonance imaging (MRI) studies of infants have indicated that a rapid and significant brain growth spurt occurs from the last trimester of pregnancy through the second year. The volume of the brain, particularly the right brain, increases rapidly during the first two years (Schore 1994). The right brain has been linked with self-regulation, the enhancement of self/other emotion regulation, and the implicit self, all of which are shaped by these attachment experiences (Fonagy 2001; Schore 1994). During this time, the infant is developing important neural capacities that critically affect interpersonal functioning. Certainly these first two years are both a time of opportunity and a time of vulnerability (Siegel 1999).

What are the mental capacities that are developing in the infant's right brain during this critical period? Siegel (1999) states that early childhood experiences with caretakers allow the brain (the right prefrontal cortex in particular) to organize in specific ways, which forms the basis for later interpersonal functioning. The immature infant brain uses the mature functions of the caregiver's brain to develop these important neural capacities, which include: body mapping, reflective function, empathy, response flexibility, social cognition, autobiographical memory, and emotion regulation. Given this list, a well-developed right prefrontal cortex is critical to experiencing healthy interpersonal relationships. It may also be the biological basis of the attachment behavioral system. The lack of development of this part of the brain and the need for parental interaction explains why there would be such a high correlation between a parent's attachment status and the infant's attachment status.

Because the vast majority of perpetrators of domestic violence have insecure attachment (Dutton 1998), it is important for clinicians to understand what specific neural capacities may be lacking in their clients and to develop interventions that specifically address those deficits. In addition, if secure attachment in parents is most likely going to imbue secure attachment in children (good affect regulation capacities), then the same may be true about psychotherapy. The better therapists are at regulating their and their client's affect, the more likely their clients will become "earned secure."

The neurobiology findings suggest that the techniques typically utilized to effect change in treatment, such as interpretation, education, and skill building, may not be sufficient to bring about lasting (one may even say neurobiological) change in psychotherapy clients. Schore (2003a, 2003b) suggests that the right-brain to right-brain attunement that occurs between a parent and an infant is primarily a nonverbal, nonintellectual process. He suggests that psychotherapists appreciate this fact if they want to make an impact on the neural capacities of the right brain. The right hemisphere processes information quite differently from the left hemisphere (Trevarthen 1996). The right-hemisphere specialization in affective awareness, expression, and perception is critical to clinicians who are helping people learn to regulate affect more adaptively. However, the language of the right hemisphere is different from the left. As opposed to the left hemisphere, whose linguistic processing and use of syllogistic reasoning looks for logical, linear cause-effect relationships, the language of the right hemisphere is nonverbal and body oriented (Siegel 2001). It would follow that changing these capacities of right-prefrontal functioning will necessarily involve a nonverbal and body-awareness component.

Attachment Theory and Domestic Violence

Don Dutton's (1988, 1994) groundbreaking studies on batterer typology and intervention found that there were different types of batterers needing different types of interventions. Other domestic violence researchers (Babcock, Jacobson, Gottman, and Yerington 2000; Hastings and Hamberger 1988; Holtzworth-Munroe, Smart, and Hutchinson 1997; Saunders 1987) have found the same differences. As Dutton (1994) began to incorporate attachment measures into his interview protocol, it became clear that different patterns of attachment also began to emerge. Approximately 40 percent had dismissing attachment (as compared with 25 percent in the nonclinical population), 30 percent preoccupied attachment (as compared with 10 percent in the nonclinical population), and 30 percent disorganized attachment (as compared with 5 percent in the nonclinical population). Dutton utilized a self-report measure developed by Kim Bartholomew, the Relationship Scales Questionnaire (RSQ) (Bartholomew and Shaver 1998). These findings were corroborated by the research conducted by Holtzworth-Munroe et al. (1997), who utilized both the RSQ and AAI in their research with perpetrators and found similar results with both measures. What these data suggest is that domestic violence perpetrators have higher rates of attachment insecurity than the general population and that incorporating attachment theory into treatment may ultimately help increase outcome data and facilitate the process of clients developing "earned security."

These data also prove that batterers represent a heterogeneous population and that different interventions may be necessary for different clients depending on how they regulate attachment distress. For example, batterers with a dismissing attachment status downregulate affect, so interventions need to focus on helping these individuals identify disavowed affect and learn constructive ways of expressing feelings and needs in a relationship context. Conversely, preoccupied clients, who have learned to upregulate attachment distress, need to learn how to self-soothe when activated and not depend solely on their attachment figures to soothe them via proximity maintenance.

Disorganized batterers have learned that interpersonal relationships are dangerous. They have learned to regulate attachment distress through approach and avoidance. When these forces are strongest, it can result in a breakdown in cognition and affect, resulting in uncontrollable rage and dissociation. These individuals need to address previous traumas and losses in order to break the disorganized processes that contribute to aggression and violence. One study found increased success (Saunders 1996) when batterers who have experienced childhood abuse were given psychodynamic treatment models that emphasize resolution of childhood abuse dynamics. Although the goal of domestic violence treatment for each of these attachment categories is similar—cessation of violence—how that goal is achieved will differ depending on how each client typically regulates attachment distress.

Developing the Therapeutic Alliance with Batterers

The most robust predictor of change in psychotherapy is not the techniques or even the brilliant interpretations that therapists devise, but the relationship between the client and the therapist (Horvath and Greenberg 1989; Luborsky 1994; Stern 2004). Bowlby (1969) believed that intimate attachments to other human beings are the hub around which a person's life revolves. From these intimate attachments, a person draws strength and enjoyment of life. Bowlby also believed that one such attachment might be a person's therapist. Bowlby (1988) described the five tasks of attachment-informed psychotherapy. One of those tasks is to explore the relationship with a psychotherapist as an attachment figure. Bowlby believed that the therapist would be viewed as an attachment figure regardless of whether or not the client was aware of this fact. And like the patterns of attachment that emerged in the stressful Strange Situation procedure, the natural ruptures and reunions that occur in psychotherapy that are likely to activate the attachment behavioral system of the client will become grist for the therapeutic mill.

Because more perpetrators of domestic violence have had particularly negative experiences in their family-of-origin attachment relationships, simply walking into the therapist's office is likely to cause some degree of anxiety. In this unusual type of relationship, clients have the opportunity to have these reactions and patterns of attachment brought to their attention, to reappraise their functionality and learn new methods of regulating attachment distress.

How does one facilitate the process of attachment in psychotherapy? Therapists are trained to focus primarily on verbal communication in the therapeutic encounter, but just as the expression of infant distress is largely nonverbal, so, too, much of the communication between client and therapist occurs on the nonverbal level. The more therapists are able to adaptively regulate their own emotional reactions to clients, the better they will be able to attend and respond to their clients' signals. Therefore, it is critical that therapists working with perpetrators are able to read nonverbal signals, interpret them correctly, respond quickly and appropriately, and help slowly and gently bring these emotions to awareness so that perpetrators can learn adaptive ways of regulating them. Contingent communication begins when the client sends a signal to the therapist. These signals are both verbal and nonverbal (facial expressions, body movements/gestures, tone of voice, timing and intensity of response, etc.). The therapist needs to recognize the signal, interpret it correctly, and send back a message to the client that these signals have been seen. This response is not simply a mirror of what was received (e.g., I see that you are angry); the therapist must send a message that not only was the original signal received and interpreted and is being responded to, but that a part of the therapist has been communicated to—that part, of course, which is the therapist's caring, concern, or empathy. When this contingent communication occurs, the client not only feels understood but feels connected to another person, and the process continues. Trevarthen (1993) contends that contingent communication is the basis of healthy, collaborative communication and facilitates positive attachments.

This seems so elementary, yet what these scholars and practitioners suggest is that the ability to read and interpret these nonverbal signals is more than a therapeutic trick the therapist occasionally pulls out of his or her bag. It is the basis of developing the therapeutic alliance, which in turn is the key to positive therapy outcome. Many perpetrators of domestic violence enter into therapy under duress and emotionally difficult situations (such as a separation or divorce). It is critical that therapists listen closely as well as look for nonverbal signals and respond starting with the first contact in a sensitive and caring fashion. So much of domestic violence literature emphasizes confrontation of minimization and denial, and though it is important to address these issues, it is probably more important to attend to the client's emotional state and respond in an empathic and helpful way. Just walking into the therapist's office is going to trigger attachment distress for most clients. Add to this the fact that the client is being forced to attend therapy and that he may be anxious about losing his family. Attending to the therapeutic alliance is going to give the therapist more leverage later on to deal with the other issues in therapy, such as denial, minimization, and inspiring commitment to behavior change.

Observation of the client is key to noticing these changes in states of mind. But because much of interpersonal communication goes on below the radar or outside of one's consciousness, there will be many instances when recognition of signals is not sufficient. As mentioned earlier, Tronick (1989) states that affect in the attachment relationship is a two-way street: The infant is affected by the parent and the parent is affected by the infant. In other words, the parent feels what the infant is feeling. There is research suggesting that a particular part of the prefrontal cortex, called the *mirror neuron system,* is responsible for this phenomenon (Iacoboni, Woods, Brass, Bekkering, Mazziotta, and Rizzolatti 1999). The mirror neuron system is hypothesized to be the biological basis of our ability to experience empathy (Preston and de Waal 2002). This system allows the brain to simulate an emotional response observed in others, and this process does not have to be conscious. In other words, one can feel what others feel simply by observing their signals, and this process occurs whether we are conscious of it or not. Therefore, another way therapists can learn to be sensitive to a client's emotional state is by being attuned to their own emotional state when in a client's presence. To complicate matters, changes in the therapist's state of mind will be picked up by the client's mirror neuron system and will either exacerbate or reduce their anxiety. This close attention to the process of contingency is critical not only to the development of the therapeutic relationship, but to helping the client learn more adaptive affective regulation skills as well. When a patient feels empathized with by the other, he experiences a deep sense of being understood, which contributes to positive feelings associated with close relationships. When the therapist is regulating his or her affect in a constructive manner, the client will learn how to do the same, whether it's made explicit or not.

Affect Regulation in the Treatment of Perpetrators

Over the past fifteen years, the affective neurosciences have evolved primarily because of improved imaging techniques that have also allowed us to better understand how emotion and cognition work together to create the experience of feeling (Damasio 1999; Panksepp 1998). Additionally, these imaging techniques have elucidated how the two hemispheres of the brain may operate very differently in important domains of psychological functioning such as memory (Kandel 1999; Tulving 1993) and emotion (Davidson 2003). Although most batterer intervention programs consider improved affect regulation abilities to be paramount in their treatment goals, many clinicians utilize interventions that reflect obsolete notions of emotion and its regulation.

What are emotions? Emotions are packages of solutions handed down by evolution to assist organisms to solve problems or endorse opportunities (Damasio 1999). All emotions are involved either directly or indirectly in the organism's management of life. The purpose of emotions is to promote survival, with the net result being to achieve a state of well-being (Ryff, Singer, and Love 2004), versus some state of neutrality. Emotions can be broken down into three categories: primary, background, and social (Damasio 1999, 2003; Siegel 1999). The primary emotions were those originally described by Darwin (1872/1965): anger, sadness, happiness, surprise, disgust, fear. These emotions are characterized by a quick onset, burst, and rapid decay. This is not to say that these primary emotions can't last for a long period of time; for example, they could be constantly stimulated by an ongoing emotionally "competent stimulus" (a term Damasio uses to refer to the external or internal stimulus that evokes the emotional response). "Background emotions" are those one experiences when one arises in the morning and feels a strong sense of possibility for the day (or the opposite), or when someone is asked how she is feeling and the response is simply "good" or "bad." They are often thought of in simple ways— you feel good or not good. These emotions are present in the background and may exert their influence on us throughout the day, though we may not necessarily be aware of them. Background emotions may set a certain emotional temperature, which may in turn affect how one experiences a primary emotion. Social emotions are extremely complex— they may be an amalgam of primary emotions but are triggered during a social interaction. Emotions such as compassion, shame, contempt, resentment, awe, jealousy, or altruism may be thought of as combinations of primary emotions or ones that have their own unique configuration and purpose. Like the primary and background emotions, these emotions may also become activated without conscious awareness, and will exert their influence on the person's behaviors and cognitions.

Another important characteristic of emotions is that they generally occur in the body first, not just the muscles or specific organs, but the viscera and the internal chemistry of the body. Damasio (1999) has demonstrated that there is a dedicated system within the spinal cord for transmitting information about emotion from the body to the brain. There are particular trigger points in the brain for specific types of emotions (such as the amygdala for fear, or the ventral medial prefrontal cortex for certain social emotions), and these structures can activate behavioral solutions without the mind knowing it's experiencing an emotion at all. This means that there are times when we are in the process of emoting in a rather "thoughtless" manner. This fact helps us to understand how emotions get communicated nonverbally without our awareness.

Feeling occurs when a person becomes consciously aware of the fact that he is in the process of experiencing emotion (Damasio 1999, 2003). Feeling occurs in the prefrontal cortex, which has a region specifically dedicated to recognizing changes in the body. The orbital prefrontal cortex is thought to be involved in this body mapping process, which would allow for the sensing of emotion. Damasio considers the feeling of emotion similar to a sense—not unlike smell, hearing, sight, touch, and taste. *Feelings* reveal to us the state of the organism at any particular point in time. Feelings allow us to make decisions about how to respond to emotions; they allow us the opportunity to make a choice. The process of emoting does not end in a neutral state, but the goal of the process of emoting is to end in a state of well-being (Damasio 2003; Urry et al. 2004).

The affect regulation strategies that batterers learned in childhood don't ultimately result in feelings of well-being, but in more frustration and distress, particularly when those strategies are placed in the relationship context. For example, a preoccupied client's dependency on his partner to soothe his fears of loss and neediness through clinging or preoccupied anger ultimately drives the partner away, producing even greater feelings of loss and anxiety. Likewise, a dismissing client's over-reliance on independence and apparent devaluation of attachment to deal with his fears of closeness only leads to greater feelings of loneliness when others perceive him as not needing intimacy.

In treating perpetrators of violence, therapists need to help them become more aware of their different types of emotions (the process of feeling) and how those emotions interact with each other, by strengthening their body-mapping capacities of the prefrontal cortex. In addition, by identifying the competent stimuli that trigger the different emotions in the first place, they can better predict when an emotion is likely to be triggered. Of course, these stimuli can be external to the person (such as criticism from a spouse or defiance by a child), but it can also be internal (such as a memory from childhood that is triggered by a criticism by a spouse). By appreciating the range of their emotions, clients can benefit from therapy by learning a new emotional vocabulary, so as to better know themselves and communicate more effectively with others. More adaptive regulation strategies will lead to feelings of well-being, which will ultimately reinforce these strategies. By making clients more aware of their emotional processes, therapists give them the opportunity to make better decisions about how to cope with their emotional responses (Bechara, Damasio, and Damasio 2000).

Because emotions often occur without the person knowing (having a *feeling*), the therapist is at a disadvantage without the assistance of a brain scanner that would indicate that a client is in the process of emoting. However, because the body is so directly involved with the emotional process, and usually responds before the emotion is felt, the bodily changes that occur could be recognized by the therapist, who can in turn bring this awareness to the client. The typical signs that an emotion is occurring include changes in facial expression (Ekman and Friesen 1978), eye gaze, tone of voice, bodily motion, and timing of response

(Siegel 1999). Therefore, therapists would need to pay careful attention to these nonverbal cues in their clients and carefully bring this to their client's attention. Likewise, as described earlier, therapists can make use of their own emotional reactions (those activated by the mirror neuron system) to better understand their clients' states of mind. Confrontation, though it can at times be useful, is generally not helpful when a person is unaware of his emotional state. A gentle and supportive approach can help to raise the client's awareness of his emotional state, whether in the context of group, individual, or couples psychotherapy. Because of their history of deactivating or hyperactivating attachment distress (or a combination of both in cases of disorganized attachment), these clients will need consistent and sensitive attunement by the therapist to learn to recognize and tolerate all of their emotional states and develop new strategies for regulating them.

Left Brain/Right Brain

Another exciting concept in the affective neurosciences is the notion that different parts of the brain specialize in different capacities. Neuroimaging technology has made it increasingly clear that the different hemispheres of the brain (right and left), even of the same neurostructures, may have different functions. Richard Davidson (2004) has found differences in the patterns of activation of the prefrontal cortex with regard to approach and avoidance emotions. His studies have included brain scans of monks who have studied with the Dalai Lama (Davidson 2000). He found that these individuals had particularly positive outlooks on life, and this was reflected by difference in the activation of their right and left prefrontal cortexes. Individuals who have an overall positive outlook on life are more likely to have higher left-to-right prefrontal activation in response to problem solving, as compared with individuals who have a more negativistic outlook on life (who have a lower left-to-right ratio of activation). In other words, some people do really see the glass as half full and others really see it as half empty. What is most interesting about Davidson's work is that the pattern of activation can be changed through mindfulness techniques. Individuals with secure attachment are likely to have this more positive outlook, whereas individuals with insecure attachment are more likely to possess a negative outlook. These data suggest that an important part of psychotherapy with perpetrators may include teaching certain clients mindfulness techniques in the service of developing more effective affect regulation strategies. If emotion begins in the body, then training the mind (the prefrontal cortex in particular) to be more mindful of the body and its changes will help a person become more aware of their emotions. Perpetrators with moderate to severe affective disorders who participate in meditation and other, similar practices report that these activities dramatically increase feelings of well-being and, when practiced consistently, can have a long-lasting effect.

Summary

Attachment theory is a useful lens through which to understand perpetrator behavior. It explains how early childhood experiences have led to a particular way of experiencing close relationships. It also helps therapists to see how, depending on the attachment status of the client, interventions will need to be developed to address their specific needs and that cookie cutter approaches will not advance the profession. The attachment findings make it clear that domestic violence is not just a result of social conditioning; if anything, it is at least the interaction between psychological conditioning and the social context. Therefore, while social changes are necessary, violence will never stop as long as the psychological and biological factors are minimized or altogether ignored.

What neurobiology findings suggest is that the regulation of affect, particularly with individuals with insecure attachment, is much more complex than early theories of intervention have suggested. Developing skills in adaptive regulation of both negative and positive emotional states involves learning to recognize an emotionally competent stimulus—identifying the different types of emotions that are activated in the body—and how consciousness is necessary to allow the individual to *feel* the emotion and finally make adaptive choices with regard to responding to the emotional stimulus. Most importantly, the notion that the final goal of this complex process is to achieve a state of well-being, rather than simply neutrality or some resting state of quiescence, is one of the rewards of the change in the strategies.

DANIEL JAY SONKIN

See also **Control Balance Theory and Domestic Violence; Exchange Theory; Feminist Theory; Identity Theory and Domestic Violence; Popular Culture and Domestic Violence; Social Learning Theory and Family Violence**

References and Further Reading

Ainsworth, M. D. S., M. C. Blehar, E. Waters, and S. Wall. *Patterns of Attachment: A Psychological Study of the Strange Situation.* Hillsdale, NJ: Erlbaum, 1978.

American Psychological Association [APA] Presidential Task Force on Violence and the Family. *Violence and the Family: Report of the American Psychological Association Presidential Task Force on Violence and the Family.* Washington, DC: APA, 1996.

Babcock, J. C., C. E. Green, and C. Robie. "Does Batterers' Treatment Work?: A Meta-Analytic Review of Domestic Violence Treatment Outcome Research." *Clinical Psychology Review* 23 (2204): 1023–1053.

Babcock, Julia C., Neil S. Jacobson, John M. Gottman, and Timothy P. Yerington. "Attachment, Emotional Regulation, and the Function of Marital Violence: Differences between Secure, Preoccupied, and Dismissing Violent and Nonviolent Husbands." *Journal of Family Violence* 15, no. 4 (2000).

Babcock, J. C., S. A. Miller, and C. Siard. "Towards a Typology of Abusive Women: Differences between Partner-Only and Generally Violent Women in the Use of Violence." *Psychology of Women Quarterly* 27 (2003): 153–161.

Bartholomew, K., and L. M. Horowitz. "Attachment Styles Among Young Adults: A Test of a Four-Category Model." *Journal of Personality and Social Psychology* 6 (1991): 226–244.

Bartholomew, K., and P. R. Shaver. "Methods of Assessing Adult Attachment: Do They Converge?" In *Attachment Theory and Close Relationships,* edited by J. A. Simpson and W. S. Rholes. New York: Guilford Press, 1998, pp. 25–45.

Bechara, Antoine, Hanna Damasio, and Antonio Damasio. "Emotion, Decision Making and the Orbitofrontal Cortex." *Cerebral Cortex* 10 (2000): 295–307.

Bowlby, J. *Attachment and Loss: Vol. 1. Attachment,* 2nd ed. London: Hogarth Press, 1969.

———. *Attachment and Loss: Vol. 2. Separation.* New York: Basic, 1973.

———. *Attachment and Loss: Vol. 3. Loss, Sadness, and Depression.* New York: Basic Books, 1980.

———. *A Secure Base: Clinical Applications of Attachment Theory.* London: Routledge, 1988.

Brennan, K. A., C. L. Clark, and P. R. Shaver. "Self-Report Measures of Adult Romantic Attachment: An Integrative Overview." In *Attachment Theory and Close Relationships,* edited by J. A. Simpson and W. S. Rholes. New York: Guilford, 1998.

Bretherton, Inge. "The Origins of Attachment Theory: John Bowlby and Mary Ainsworth." *Developmental Psychology* 28, no. 5 (1992): 759–775.

Cassidy, J. "The Nature of the Child's Ties." In *Handbook of Attachment: Theory, Research, and Clinical Applications,* edited by J. Cassidy and P. R. Shaver. New York: Guilford Press, 1999, pp. 355–377.

Damasio, A. *The Feeling of What Happens: Body and Emotion in the Making of Consciousness.* New York: Harcourt Brace, 1999.

———. *Looking for Spinoza: Joy, Sorrow, and the Feeling Brain.* Orlando, FL: Harcourt, 2003.

Darwin, C. *The Expression of Emotion in Man and Animals.* Chicago: University of Chicago Press, 1872/1965.

Davidson, Richard. "Affect Style, Psychopathology and Resilience: Brain Mechanisms and Plasticity." *American Psychologist* 55, no. 11 (2000): 1196–1214.

———. "Darwin and the Neural Bases of Emotion and Affective Style." *Annals of the New York Academy of Sciences* 1000 (2003): 316–336.

———. "What Does the Prefrontal Cortex 'Do' in Affect: Perspectives on Frontal EEG Asymmetry Research." *Biological Psychology* 67 (2004): 219–233.

Davis, R. C., B. G. Taylor, and C. D. Maxwell. "Does Batterer Treatment Reduce Violence? A Randomized Experiment in Brooklyn." *Justice Quarterly* 18 (1998): 171–201.

Dutton, D. G. "Profiling Wife Assaulters: Some Evidence for a Trimodal Analysis." *Violence and Victims* 3, no. 1 (1988): 5–30.

———. "Patriarchy and Wife Assault: The Ecological Fallacy." *Violence and Victims* 9, no. 2 (1994): 125–140.

———. *The Batterer.* New York: Harper Collins, 1995.

———. *The Abusive Personality: Violence and Control in Intimate Relationships.* New York: Guilford Press, 1998.

Dutton, Don, and Tonia Nicholls. "The Gender Paradigm in Domestic Violence Research and Theory: Part 1—The Conflict of Theory and Data." *Aggression and Violent Behavior* 10, no. 6 (2005): 680–714.

Dutton, Don, and Daniel Sonkin, eds. *Intimate Violence: Contemporary Treatment Innovations.* New York: Haworth Publishing, 2003.

Ekman, P., and W. V. Friesen. *The Facial Action Coding System.* Palo Alto, CA: Consulting Psychologists Press, 1978.

Feder, L., and D. R. Forde. "A Test of Efficacy of Court Mandated Counseling for Convicted Misdemeanor Domestic Violence Offenders: Results from the Brouward Experiment." Paper presented at the Sixth International Family Violence Research Conference, Durham, NH, 1999.

Fonagy, P. *Attachment Theory and Psychoanalysis.* New York: Other Press, 2001.

Fonagy, P., M. Target, G. Gergely, and E. J. Jurist. *Affect Regulation, Mentalization and the Development of the Self.* New York: Other Press, 2002.

Fraley, R. Chris. "Attachment Stability from Infancy to Adulthood: Meta-Analysis and Dynamic Modeling of Developmental Mechanisms." *Personality and Social Psychology Review* 6, no. 2 (2002): 123–151.

Fraley, R. Chris, and Phillip Shaver. "Adult Romantic Attachment: Theoretical Developments, Emerging Controversies, and Unanswered Questions." *Review of General Psychology* 4, no. 2 (2000): 132–154.

Ganley, A. *Participants Manual: Court-Mandated Therapy for Men Who Batter: A Three Day Workshop for Professionals.* Washington, DC: Center for Women Policy Studies, 1981.

Hastings, J., and K. Hamberger. "Personality Characteristics of Spouse Abusers: A Controlled Comparison." *Violence and Victims* 3 (1988): 31–48.

Hazan, C., and P. R. Shaver. "Romantic Love Conceptualized as an Attachment Process." *Journal of Personality and Social Psychology* 52 (1987): 511–524.

Hazan, C., and D. Zeifman. "Pair Bonds as Attachments: Evaluating the Evidence." In *Handbook of Attachment: Theory, Research, and Clinical Applications,* edited by J. Cassidy and P. R. Shaver. New York: Guilford Press, 1999, pp. 336–354.

Henderson, A. J. Z., K. Bartholomew, and D. G. Dutton. "He Loves Me, He Loves Me Not: Attachment and Separation Resolution of Abused Women." *Journal of Family Violence* 12, no. 2 (1997): 169–192.

Hesse, Erik, and Mary Main. "Disorganized Infant, Child, and Adult Attachment: Collapse in Behavioral and Attentional Strategies." *Journal of the American Psychoanalytic Association* 48, no. 4 (2000): 1097–1127.

Hesse, E., M. Main, K. Yost-Abrams, and A. Rifkin. "Unresolved States Regarding Loss or Abuse Have 'Second Generation' Effects: Disorganization, Role-Inversion, and Frightening Ideation in the Off-spring of Traumatized, Non-Maltreated Parents." In *Healing Trauma,* edited by M. Solomon and D. J. Siegel. New York: Norton, 2003.

Holtzworth-Munroe, Amy, Gregory L. Smart, and Glenn Hutchinson. "Violent Versus Nonviolent Husbands: Differences in Attachment Patterns, Dependency, and Jealousy." *Journal of Family Psychology* 11, no. 3 (1997): 314–331.

Horvath, A. O., and L. S. Greenberg. "Development and Validation of the Working Alliance Inventory." *Journal of Counseling Psychology* 36 (1989): 223–233.

Iacoboni, M., R. P. Woods, M. Brass, H. Bekkering, J. C. Mazziotta, and G. Rizzolatti. "Cortical Mechanisms of Human Imitation." *Science* 286 (1999): 2526–2528.

Jones, Alison Snow, Ralph B. D'Agostino, and Edward W. Gondolf. "Assessing the Effect of Batterer Program Completion on Reassault Using Propensity Scores." *Journal of Interpersonal Violence* 19, no. 9 (2004): 1002–1020.

Kandel, Eric R. "Biology and the Future of Psychoanalysis: A New Intellectual Framework for Psychiatry Revisited." *American Journal of Psychiatry* 156 (1999): 505–524.

Leisring, Penny A., Lynn Dowd, and Alan Rosenbaum. "Treatment of Partner Aggressive Women." In Dutton and Sonkin, eds., *Intimate Violence,* 2003.

Levesque D. "Violence Desistance Among Battering Men: Existing Intervention and the Application of the Transtheoretical Model for Change." Unpublished doctoral dissertation. Department of Psychology, University of Rhode Island, 1998.

Luborsky, L. "Therapeutic Alliances as Predictors of Psychotherapy Outcomes: Factors Explaining the Predictive Success." In *The Working Alliance: Theory, Research, and Practice,* edited by A. O. Horvath and L. S. Greenberg. New York: John Wiley and Sons, 1994, pp. 38–50.

Main, M., and R. Goldwyn. *Adult Attachment Classification System.* Unpublished manuscript, University of California, Berkeley, 1993.

Main, Mary, and Erik Hesse. "Parents' Unresolved Traumatic Experiences Are Related to Infant Disorganized Attachment Status: Is Frightened and/or Frightening Parental Behavior the Linking Mechanism?" In *Attachment in the Preschool Years: Theory, Research, and Intervention,* edited by Mark T. Greenberg and Dante Cicchetti. Chicago: University of Chicago Press, 1990, pp. 161–182.

Main, Mary, and Judith Solomon. "Discovery of an Insecure-Disorganized/Disoriented Attachment Pattern." In *Affective Development in Infancy,* edited by T. Berry Brazelton and Michael W. Yogman. Westport, CT: Ablex Publishing, 1986, pp. 95–124.

Mikulincer, M., P. R. Shaver, and D. Pereg. "Attachment Theory and Affect Regulation: The Dynamics, Development, and Cognitive Consequences of Attachment-Related Strategies." *Motivation and Emotion* 27, no. 2 (2003): 77–102.

Morgan, Hillary, and Phillip Shaver. "Attachment Processes and Commitment to Romantic Relationships." In *Handbook of Interpersonal Commitment and Relationship Stability,* edited by J. Adams and W. Jones. New York: Kluwer Academic/Plenum Publishers, 1999.

Panksepp, J. *Affective Neuroscience: The Foundations of Human and Animal Emotions.* New York: Oxford University Press, 1998.

Pense, Ellen, and Michael Paymar. *Education Groups for Men Who Batter: The Duluth Model.* New York: Springer Publications, 1993.

Roisman, Glen, Elena Padron, L. Alan Sroufe, and Byron Egeland. "Earned-Secure Attachment Status in Retrospect and Prospect." *Child Development* (July/August, 2002).

Rom, E., and M. Mikulincer. "Attachment Theory and Group Processes: The Association between Attachment Style and Group-Related Representations, Goals, Memories, and Functioning." *Journal of Personality and Social Psychology* 84 (2003): 1220–1235.

Rosenbaum, A., and P. A. Leisring. "Beyond Power and Control: Towards an Understanding of Partner Abusive Men." *Journal of Comparative Family Studies* 34, no. 1 (2003): 7–22.

Ryff, Carol D., Burton H. Singer, and Gayle Dienberg Love. "Positive Health: Connecting Well-Being with Biology." *Philosophical Transactions of the Royal Society of London, Bulletin* 359 (2004): 1383–1394.

Saunders, D. "Are There Three Different Types of Men Who Batter? An Empirical Study with Possible Implications for Treatment." Paper presented at the Third National Family Violence Research Conference, July 6–9, Durham, NH, 1987.

———. "Feminist-Cognitive-Behavioral and Process-Psychodynamic Treatments for Men Who Batter: Interaction of Abuser Traits and Treatment Models." *Violence and Victims* 11, no. 4 (1996): 393–414.

Schore, A. N. *Affect Regulation and the Origin of the Self: The Neurobiology of Emotional Development.* Mahwah, NJ: Erlbaum, 1994.

———. *Affect Dysregulation and Disorders of the Self.* New York: Norton, 2003a.

———. *Affect Regulation and the Repair of the Self.* New York: Norton, 2003b.

Shaver, Phillip R., Jay Belsky, and Kelly Brennan. "The Adult Attachment Interview and Self-Reports of Romantic Attachment: Associations Across Domains and Methods." *Personal Relationships* 7 (2000): 25–43.

Shaver, Phillip, and Mario Mikulincer. "Attachment-Related Psychodynamics." *Attachment and Human Development* 4 (2002): 133–161.

Shepard, M. "Interventions with Men Who Batter: An Evaluation of a Domestic Abuse Program." Paper presented at the Third National Conference on Domestic Violence, University of New Hampshire, 1987.

———. "Predicting Batterer Recidivism Five Years After Community Intervention." *Journal of Family Violence* 7, no. 3 (1992): 167–178.

Siegel, D. J. "The Developing Mind: How Relationships and the Brain Interact to Shape Who We Are." New York: Guilford Press, 1999.

———. "Toward an Interpersonal Neurobiology of the Developing Mind: Attachment Relationships, 'Mindsight,' and Neural Integration." *Infant Mental Health*

Journal 22 (2001): 67–94 (special edition on contributions of the decade of the brain to infant psychiatry).

Sonkin, D. J. *Domestic Violence: The Court-Mandated Perpetrator Assessment and Treatment Handbook*. Sausalito, CA: Author, 2003.

Sonkin, D. J., and M. Durphy. *Learning to Live Without Violence: A Handbook for Men* (rev. ed.). Volcano, CA: Volcano Press, 1997.

Sroufe, L. A. *Emotional Development: The Organization of Emotional Life in the Early Years*. New York: Cambridge University Press, 1995.

Stern, Daniel. *The Present Moment in Psychotherapy and Everyday Life*. New York: W. W. Norton, 2004.

Trevarthen, C. "The Function of Emotions in Early Infant Communication and Development." In *New Perspectives in Early Communicative Development,* edited by J. Nadel and L. Camaioni. London: Routledge, 1993, pp. 48–81.

———. "Lateral Asymmetries in Infancy: Implications for the Development of the Hemispheres." *Neuroscience and Biobehavioral Reviews* 20 (1996): 571–586.

Tronick, E. "Emotions and Emotional Communication in Infants." *American Psychologist* 44 (1989): 112–119.

Tulving, E. "Varieties of Consciousness and Levels of Awareness in Memory." In *Attention, Selection, Awareness, and Control: A Tribute to Donald Broadbent,* edited by A. Baddeley and L. Weiskrantz. London: Oxford University Press, 1993, pp. 283–299.

Urry, H. L., J. B. Nitschke, I. Dolski, D. C. Jackson, K. M. Dalton, C. J. Mueller, M. A. Rosenkranz, C. D. Ryff, B. H. Singer, and R. J. Davidson. "Making a Life Worth Living: Neural Correlates of Well-Being." *Psychological Science* 15 (2004): 367–372.

van IJzendoorn, M. H., and A. Sagi. "Cross-Cultural Patterns of Attachment: Universal and Contextual Dimensions." In *Handbook of Attachment,* edited by J. Cassidy and P. R. Shaver. New York: Guilford, 1999, pp. 713–734.

Waters, Everett, Claire Hamilton, and Nancy Weinfield. "The Stability of Attachment Security from Infancy to Adolescence and Early Adulthood: General Introduction." *Child Development* 71, no. 3 (2000): 678–683.

B

BATTERED HUSBANDS

The lens through which a society views itself plays a critical role in how it identifies, measures, and interprets a social problem, the mechanisms used to disseminate the findings, and the types of programs developed to address the problem. Acceptance of the status quo is jarred when isolated facts that are incongruent with a common view are identified as social problems and gain public attention. The public awareness of battered husbands went through such a transformation. Although most social services and law enforcement agencies were aware of instances of battered husbands, they tended to define the cases that they knew of as unique. It was only after the article on the battered husband syndrome (Steinmetz 1977–78) appeared and drew attention to this phenomenon that it began to be defined as a problem. However, considerable controversy continues to surround this topic, and as a result, services and programs for battered husbands are still very limited.

Denying the Findings

Probably underlying much of the controversy is the fact that the phenomenon of the battered wife has been intricately linked to feminist theory regarding patriarchy. Unwilling to recognize the problem of battered husbands and concerned that attention would be drawn away from the problem of battered wives, some radical feminists attempted to punish those who brought attention to this problem. For example, researchers who had written on battered husbands were verbally harassed and had their characters defamed. Attempts were made to prevent scholars from getting tenure or to rescind their funding. One scholar received verbal threats and anonymous phone calls threatening to harm her children, and when invited to speak at a domestic violence conference sponsored by the American Civil Liberties Union, bomb threats were received. This is ironic, since the women making such threats were vigorously denying that women could be violent.

After the publication of studies on battered males, numerous articles or letters to journal editors often appeared in which the goal was to discredit the findings—a phenomenon that continues into the start of the twenty-first century. The Conflict Tactic Scales (CTS) were considered to be flawed and especially problematic when all physically violent acts were combined into a single score, possibly camouflaging the more violent acts by men. However, not only are statistics on husband abuse obtained via CTS similar to data collected by other means, there is considerable similarity between husbands and wives when comparing the specific acts of violence. For example, a study of 516 emergency room admissions, using the Index of Spouse Abuse, found that 28 percent of men compared with 33 percent of women had experienced physical violence.

In an attempt to discredit this information, an assumption was made that husbands started the fights and women who used violence did so in self-defense. However, numerous studies found that in about one-half of the couples, both used violence, and in about one-fourth of the couples, only the wife was violent. Studies that specifically asked who started the fight indicated that wives often initiated violence at a rate equal to or, in some studies, exceeding that of their husbands. For example, in their 1985 study, Murray Straus, Richard Gelles, and Suzanne Steinmetz asked couples which partner initiated the violence. Although both males and females reported that wives were more likely to initiate violence than were husbands, reports from women indicated a larger gap (43 percent of male-initiated compared with 53 percent of female-initiated violence).

Even when it was acknowledged that husbands and wives might be victims of similar acts, it was assumed that husbands would experience very little injury because of their greater size, weight, and strength, factors which would also enable them to inflict greater injury. Studies asking about injury (i.e., questions about pain level and injuries requiring medical care) have reported that husbands are injured at equal or greater levels than wives and report similar levels of pain.

Even as the existence of battered husbands became acknowledged, the violence that husbands experienced was seen as inconsequential. For example, one researcher described the abuse of husbands by their wives as relatively modest, because 86 percent of the respondents (wives) in his study never hit their husbands. Another researcher reported that 29 percent of the wives battered their husbands, 15 percent used violence against their spouses when in a battering relationship, and 5 percent continued this violent behavior after they had left that relationship and entered into a non-battering one. This researcher concluded that battered men are not a problem. What makes this last study interesting is that it was based on a sample of battered women, not a large national sample of men and women.

Historical Background

Although battered husbands as an academic topic is barely three decades old at the start of the twenty-first century, accounts in court records, newspaper articles, and preambles to laws suggest that domestic violence in America dates back at least as far as the arrival of the Pilgrims. For example, during the colonial period, Massachusetts law required that cohabitation be peaceful, and yet there were numerous examples that this requirement was not always met. As noted by Steinmetz (1977–1978), these records documented incidents in which both wives and husbands were victims of abuse by their spouses. Examples from the colonial period include the excommunication of Mary Whorten by the First Church of Boston because she defamed and beat her husband and committed other abusive acts. One man in Plymouth colony kicked his wife off of a stool, causing her to fall into the fire. Another woman, Joan Miller, not only cursed and beat her husband, but was also charged with encouraging their children to beat him.

Throughout history, laws were written to give men the power to control their wives by use of violence. However, there were also examples in which society considered the wife justified in using physical force against her husband. One such example was a post-Renaissance custom called *charivari*. This noisy demonstration was intended to shame and humiliate males who engaged in behavior that was considered to be a threat to the patriarchal community's social order. In France, the husband who "allowed" his wife to beat him was made to wear an outlandish outfit and ride a donkey around the village. The Britons strapped the beaten husband into a cart and paraded him through booing crowds; they also punished the abusive wife by public humiliation (Steinmetz and Lucca 1988).

There have also been numerous instances of women abusing men in the comics. These comics often depict the husband as deviating from the masculine cultural ideal of strength, self-assertion, and intelligence and assuming the character traits which have been culturally ascribed to women. Therefore, the wife was justified in chastising her husband, even if this took the form of humiliation and violence, because he had not fulfilled his culturally prescribed role. As early as the late 1890s and early 1900s, comic strips such as the *Katzenjammer Kids* and *Bringing Up Father* depicted the husband who endured physical and verbal abuse from his wife. The popularity of these domestic-relations comics was most likely sustained because they approximated, in a less serious manner, common family situations. It is also likely that these comics allowed men and women to carry out in the fantasy world those actions which they were unable to carry out in their own lives (Steinmetz 1977–1978; Steinmetz and Lucca 1988).

An examination of twenty consecutive editions of all comic strips appearing in the nine leading newspapers in New York City during October 1950 found that wives initiated more violence (10 percent versus 7 percent) and rarely were the recipients of violence (1 percent versus 14 percent). Saenger (1963) found that 39 percent of wives were victims of hostile attacks and violence compared with 63 percent of husbands who were the victims of these attacks. This was the same era in which the families on television shows such as *Father Knows Best* and *Leave It to Beaver* were portrayed as the ideal.

Current Statistics

Before providing some statistics on battered husbands, it is important to identify exactly what will be covered in this article. It will be limited to acts perpetrated by women that were intended to inflict physical harm or did inflict physical harm on their husbands or male partners. It will not address violence between lesbian and gay partners, lesbian battering, date violence, date rape, sexual violence, female-perpetrated rape, and domestic homicide. For simplicity, both married couples and common-law/cohabiting couples will be referred to as husband and wife.

Across studies of spouse abuse, differences between husbands and wives as victims of the abuse depend on who participated in the study and the questions asked. For example, data collected from individuals residing in a shelter for abused women would reveal a higher percentage of severely abused women compared with the general population. Even among large-scale studies, there are differences that reflect different goals of the studies. Information collected by the U.S. Department of Justice's National Crime Victimization Survey (Rennison 2003) asked individuals about being a victim of a series of violent crimes (rape, sexual assault, robbery, aggravated assault, and simple assault). This study found that 3.6 per 1,000 women, compared with 0.5 per 1,000 men, experienced simple assault in which the spouse was the perpetrator. For aggravated assault the differences between male and female victims was considerably smaller (0.7 per 1,000 women were victims compared with 0.3 per 1,000 men). Even though wives were victimized to a greater extent by spouses than

were husbands, the phenomenon of battered husbands is clearly indicated as a significant problem even in a general crime survey that does not focus on acts that occurred in a family setting.

How Much Violence

The earliest information on spousal abuse was obtained from smaller studies that did not represent the general population. At a time when wife abuse was just starting to be recognized as a social problem, these studies provided evidence that husbands were also victims. The studies found that husbands were as likely to be abused as wives and that wives frequently used violence more often (Steinmetz 1987). Although these are small samples, the results are similar to larger studies discussed below.

Several large studies using samples that were scientifically selected (Straus and Gelles 1990; Straus, Gelles, and Steinmetz 1980) or used sophisticated methodology to enhance the study (O'Leary, Barling, Arias, Rosenbaum, Malone, and Tyree 1989) discovered that not only did the rates of husband abuse often equal or exceed that of wife abuse, but wives used violence more frequently.

The first large-scale national study conducted by Straus and colleagues collected data from 2,143 persons (about half of whom were men) in 1975 (Straus et al. 1980). The researchers found that in just under half of the families, both spouses had committed a violent act (mutual violence). However, in 23 percent of the couples, the wife was the only one who had been violent. Not only did a greater percentage of women engage in violence, they also used more severe violence (wife abuse occurred in 3.8 out of 100 families versus 4.6 per 100 families for husband abuse).

A decade later, in 1985, Straus and colleagues obtained data on over 6,000 individuals and found that while husband abuse showed a slight increase, there was a 21 percent decline in wife abuse. A third national study, of 1,970 families, was conducted by Straus and colleagues in 1992. A comparison of the 1985 and 1992 statistics for wife and husband abuse found that husband abuse remained virtually the same but wife abuse declined by 37 percent.

A longitudinal study of physical violence of 393 couples, conducted by O'Leary and colleagues (1989), obtained self-reports of aggression at three times: a month prior to the marriage and at eighteen and thirty months after the marriage. Data from both husbands and wives were obtained for each time period. Thus, the researchers were able to compare the husbands' reports of victimization with the wife's report of perpetrating the violence and vice versa. A summary measure of overall violence computed for one month prior to marriage indicated that 31.2 percent of men and 44.4 percent of women reported that they committed acts of violence against the future spouse. A similar trend was noted at eighteen months after marriage (26.8 percent of men versus 35.9 percent of women), and thirty months after marriage (24.6 percent of men versus 32.2 percent of women). At each time period, wives used more violence than did husbands.

Individual acts revealed a similar pattern. A greater percentage of women reported using less serious acts of violence ("throwing something," "slapping," and "pushing") at each time they were interviewed. However, they also reported using more severe violence than their husbands at all three time periods. For example, more women "kicked, bit or hit with their fist" than men prior to marriage (12.6 percent of women versus 3.4 percent of men), eighteen months after marriage (10.8 percent versus 3.9 percent), and thirty months after marriage (7.6 percent versus 2.7 percent). No men and 1.1 percent of the women reported that they "beat up" their spouse prior to marriage and 0.4 percent of the men and 1.1 percent of the women "beat up" their spouse at thirty months of marriage. Considering all of the severe acts of violence measured at three time periods, women were *more* violent in all but one act—0.8 percent of both men and women reported that they "beat up" their spouses at eighteen months after marriage. Furthermore, women were found to engage in violence against their partners even though the partner had never been violent.

International Trends

Abuse of husbands is not limited to the United States. In a cross-cultural study of domestic violence, battered husbands were identified in Israel, Puerto Rico, Finland, Belize, and Canada (see Steinmetz 1987, Table 6, for a complete listing of the data). The data in this study were based on small samples collected in the mid-1970s. Most were collected from junior/senior high school or college students reporting their mothers' and fathers' behavior.

Several trends were noted. First, for most countries the percentages of husbands and wives using violence were fairly similar. Only in Puerto Rico was husbands' violence nearly double that of wives' violence. Couples in Finland averaged a fairly low rate of spousal violence—just over 2 percent—being committed by husbands and wives alike. Israeli couples living in cities committed an average

of 7.6 and 7.4 acts of violence for males and females, respectively. (However, Israeli couples living on the kibbutzes not only had considerably higher rates of violence, but wives were considerably more violent than were their husbands [9.9 percent for husbands versus 12.6 percent for wives].) Similar results have been found in numerous countries, such as Great Britain, Korea, Mexico, India, Hong Kong, Brazil, and Singapore.

An Australian study of 804 men and 839 women (Headey, Scott, and de Vaus 1999) asked about violence between spouses that occurred in the previous year. They found that a higher percentage of men were victims of all types of violence (5.7 percent of males compared with 3.7 percent of females), although the differences were not statistically significant (i.e., they could have occurred by chance). Interestingly, they also found that 54 percent of respondents who experienced violence reported having assaulted their spouse.

A trend appeared in which it was clear that men and women had different perceptions regarding violence. Just under 2 percent of both men and women reported that the violence resulted in "pain as bad as hitting one's thumb with a hammer or worse," but a higher percentage of men reported needing first aid (1.8 percent of men versus 1.2 percent of women) or treatment by a doctor or nurse (1.5 percent of men versus 1.1 percent of women). Although women reported less injury, a higher percentage of battered women called the police or other government authority (1.7 percent of women versus 1.3 percent of men). The authors summarized their study by noting that men and women were as likely to report being physically assaulted by their spouses, and both were as likely to admit being violent themselves.

Data from the 2005 report "Family Violence in Canada," which is a series produced annually by *Statistics Canada,* estimated that 7 percent of Canadians in a current or previous marriage or common-law union experienced spousal violence during the preceding five-year period. Women were more likely to experience more serious types of violence from their intimate partner (being beaten, choked, threatened with a gun or knife, or having a gun or knife used against them) than men (23 percent of women versus 15 percent of men) and were more likely to report being injured (44 percent versus 18 percent). Female victims were more likely to express fear for their lives (34 percent versus 10 percent) and to change their daily activities because of the violence (29 percent versus 10 percent). However, 15 percent of the men reported being beaten, threatened, or attacked with a gun or knife by their wives, 18 percent reported being injured, 10 percent feared for their lives, and 10 percent changed their daily activities. The researchers also discovered that although the rates of abused husbands were unchanged since the previous report, wife abuse had declined.

Sommer, Barnes, and Murray (1992) collected data on spousal violence in Canada in 1989–1990 and conducted follow-up interviews in 1991–1992. The researchers discovered that women were more physically abusive than their husbands and were considerably more likely to have initiated various acts of violence. For example, when asked who initiated violence by throwing an object at his or her spouse, a greater number of women had engaged in this behavior (16.2 percent versus 4.6 percent). Likewise, a greater number of wives initiated violence by slapping, kicking, or punching (15.8 percent versus 7.3 percent) or by striking their spouse with a weapon (3.1 percent versus 0.9 percent).

The overall violence measures of this study indicated that roughly 39 percent of husbands were abused compared with about 26 percent of wives. Wives' use of violence against their husbands has been viewed as acts of self-defense. Abused wives appeared to require medical care more frequently than did abused husbands (14.3 percent of husbands versus 21.4 percent of wives). However, these researchers found that while nearly 10 percent of the women reported that their actions were committed in self-defense, nearly 15 percent of the men reported self-defense as the reason for using violence against their wives.

Why Men Don't Report

Given the considerable similarity between the use of violence by wives and husbands, why has there been so little attention paid to the problem of husband abuse? One reason, discussed earlier, is that awareness and prevention of wife abuse has become part of a political agenda supported by feminist activist groups, while awareness and prevention of husband abuse has not yet been similarly embraced as an important political or social issue. A study or article on husband abuse often produces an immediate reaction, such as an attempt to discredit the study. Therefore, the media attention that was instrumental in gaining the funding for hotlines, shelters, and programs to help abused women has not been forthcoming to provide assistance to men who have been battered.

Men are less likely to call the police and report the abuse unless medical attention is needed. Since men are expected to be able to defend

themselves—especially against women—they are embarrassed to report and fear that they will not be believed. Noting the lack of attention to battered men in the legal field, Kelly (2003) reported that feminist lawyers initially used the battered woman's syndrome to justify self-defense by women who killed or attempted to kill violent males, but it is now reflected in gender-based laws defining arrests, prosecution, and punishment of batterers. Kelly reported that one study found that when wives called the police because they were being abused, their husbands were frequently threatened with arrest and actually arrested in about 15 percent of the cases. However, no woman in this study was ever threatened or actually arrested when the man called the police. Furthermore, in over 41 percent of the cases studied, the violent husband was ordered out of the home, but no woman who was violent was given such an order by the police. Most surprising, the battered husband was quite likely to be arrested when he called the police, since it was assumed that the male was the perpetrator in the domestic violence incident.

However, another reason why battered husbands do not report violence is that they tend to redefine the actual violence that has occurred. The husband may rationalize that it was his fault—he did something to set off his wife. He may claim that his wife is a very good person and that it was some outside source such as stress at work, mental health problems, or alcohol abuse that caused her to take such actions. The outcome of the violence as defined by the husband may also be rationalized in one of the following ways: "It was just a few bruises," "It really didn't hurt," "I would leave if the violence got too bad."

In the late 1970s, Steinmetz attended a conference shortly after the publication of her article "The Battered Husband Syndrome," which was receiving a lot of media attention. A family scholar commented that he did not believe there were really battered husbands and then described the violence he had endured from his own ex-wife, including being hit with a board and stabbed with a knife. Not only had he experienced extreme violence, but this family scholar had not considered himself to be a battered husband. When asked about this, he replied that he knew that he could leave when things got really bad—which he did.

Why Men Don't Leave

Like the family scholar mentioned above, many men "know" (or at least believe) that they can leave their violent wives; to them, this means that they are not "battered," which they define as being trapped. A review of numerous studies as well as anecdotal reports suggests that many men are clearly under the delusion that they can leave, when in reality they lack a job, a source of income, transportation, alternative housing, and other resources that are needed in the event of a breakup.

The reasons why battered husbands remain in a violent relationship are similar in many respects to the reasons given by battered wives. First are economic concerns. Leaving may mean establishing a separate household as well as providing child support. Concern for the safety of his children, toward whom the wife is also violent, is another reason some men stay. They remain in the home in order to protect the children because they are concerned that if they left, the wife might get custody, putting the children in even greater danger. Finally, in a manner similar to that expressed by battered women, battered husbands may hold out the hope that the violence will end.

The frequent definition or characterization of victimization as a female experience can have a serious impact on the battered male's masculine identity, making him feel that it is his fault and that he has character flaws. These men also fear further isolation, a fear the abusive wife may exploit in order to maintain control of her husband. This isolation operates on two levels. First, it keeps the matter private from the prying eyes of family, friends, and neighbors. Second, which is probably more destructive, it limits the victim's contact with others who could confirm that he is actually being abused. This isolation can also be used as a form of punishment. When the victimization that the male is experiencing is revealed to a family member or friend, further contact, even phone calls, are no longer permitted. Thus, he becomes emotionally trapped in a violent relationship.

Conclusion

Studies based on samples of women who responded to an advertisement or are in battered women's shelters clearly document the existence of wife abuse. However, even in these nonscientific samples of women, battered husbands have been identified. Studies based on large national samples or general statistics collected by various government entities not only support the existence of battered husbands, but find that they are victimized in equal or even greater numbers than wives.

Ignoring the existence of battered husbands results in a lack of resources for men. Moreover, this position also denies women who are violent legitimate access to resources that might reduce the stress and conflict that results from the multiple roles faced by women today. Most important, ignoring husband abuse constitutes a failure to recognize that many of these families have children who witness this violence.

Research in the late 1970s and early 1980s noted a difference in level of injury that women and men experienced. It was estimated that 7 percent of wives but only 0.6 percent of husbands experienced severe physical abuse. Three reasons were suggested for this difference. First, women were socialized to have better impulse control and therefore tend to stop their violent behaviors before causing serious injury. Second is the myth that women instigate the violence by using verbally abusive behavior—they are "asking for it." Third, men are usually larger and stronger; therefore, even when the same behaviors are reported, e.g., a slap, the level of injury could differ considerably.

A quarter century later, these findings need to be reexamined. First, numerous studies find that women are considerably more likely to use violence on their children and elderly relatives for whom they are providing care. Second, considerable research on violence between lesbian partners further challenges the idea that women have better impulse control and documents women's ability to use violence. Third, rather than women being physically abused by their husbands as a result of their verbally annoying behavior, recent data suggest that wives are as likely as husbands to initiate the conflict by using physical violence. Furthermore, although wife abuse has declined considerably between 1975 and 1992, husband abuse has remained constant or shown a small increase.

Fortunately, there is a small but growing trend in which feminist scholars and service providers are recognizing that males are experiencing considerable violence, and they are discussing options for addressing this issue. Males are fathers, husbands, brothers, and sons. It is as hurtful for them to experience violence perpetrated by their wives as it is for mothers, wives, sisters, and daughters to experience violence perpetrated by their husbands. Only when violence by all members of the family can be openly addressed will society gain a better understanding of the dynamics of domestic violence and be able to develop prevention, intervention, and treatment programs that ensure a healthy, violence-free environment for all families.

SUZANNE K. STEINMETZ

See also **Batterer Typology; Children Witnessing Parental Violence; Date Rape; Dating Violence;**

Dating Violence among African American Couples; Domestic Homicide in Urban Centers: New York City; Factors Influencing Reporting Behavior by Male Domestic Violence Victims; Gay and Bisexual Male Domestic Violence; Intimate Partner Homicide; Intimate Partner Violence in Queer, Transgender, and Bisexual Communities; Lesbian Battering; Male Victims of Domestic Violence and Reasons They Stay with Their Abusers; Mutual Battering; Sexual Aggression Perpetrated by Females

References and Further Reading

Cook, Philip W. *Abused Men: The Hidden Side of Domestic Violence.* Westport, CT: Praeger, 1997. Written for the general public, this book provides a wealth of information.

F.A.C.T. Information: Domestic Violence. http://www.fact.on.ca/Info/info_dom.htm. A valuable online source listing research articles. For a comprehensive review of a large number of articles, essays, and editorials, see the following entry: Martin S. Feibert, "References Examining Assaults by Women on Their Spouses or Male Partners: An Annotated Bibliography." http://www.fact.on.ca/Info/dom/martinfi.htm.

Headey, Bruce, Dorothy Scott, and David de Vaus. "Domestic Violence in Australia: Are Men and Women Equally Violent?" *Australian Social Monitor* 2, no. 3 (1999). http://www.fact.on.ca/Info/dom/heady99.htm (accessed August 9, 2006).

Kelly, Linda. "Disabusing the Definition of Domestic Abuse: How Women Batter Men and the Role of the Feminist State." *Florida State University Law Review* 30, no. 4 (2003): 791–855. http://www.law.fsu.edu/journals/lawreview/downloads/304/kelly.pdf (accessed August 9, 2006).

MenWeb. http://www.batteredmen.com. This is an excellent online source for summaries of research, services, and general information.

O'Leary, K. Daniel, Julian Barling, Ileana Arias, Alan Rosenbaum, Jean Malone, and Andrea Tyree. "Prevalence and Stability of Physical Aggression between Spouses: A Longitudinal Analysis." *Journal of Consulting and Clinical Psychology* 57, no. 2 (1989): 263–268.

Rennison, Callie M. "Intimate Partner Violence, 1993–2001." U.S. Department of Justice, 2003. http://www.ojp.usdoj.gov/bjs/pub/pdf/ipv01.pdf (accessed August 9, 2006). NCJ 197838.

Saenger, Gerhart. "Male and Female Relations in the American Comic Strip." In *The Funnies: An American Idiom,* edited by D. M. White and R. H. Abel. Glencoe, IL: The Free Press, 1963, pp. 219–231.

Sommer, Reena, Gordon E. Barnes, and Robert P. Murray. "Alcohol Consumption, Alcohol Abuse, Personality and Female Perpetrated Spouse Abuse." *Personality and Individual Differences* 13, no. 12 (1992): 1315–1323.

Steinmetz, Suzanne K. "The Battered Husband Syndrome." *Victimology: An International Journal* 2 (1977–1978): 499–509.

———. "Family Violence: Past, Present, and Future." In *Handbook of Marriage and the Family,* edited by Marvin B. Sussman and Suzanne K. Steinmetz. New York: Plenum, 1987, pp. 725–765.

Steinmetz, Suzanne K., and Joseph S. Lucca. "Husband Battering." In *Handbook of Family Violence,* edited by Vincent B. Van Hasselt, Randall L. Morrison, Alan S. Bellack, and Michel Hersen. New York: Plenum Press, 1988, pp. 61–87.

Straus, Murray A., and Richard J. Gelles. "Societal Change and Change in Family Violence from 1975 to 1985 as Revealed by Two National Surveys." In *Physical Violence in American Families,* edited by Murray A. Straus and Richard J. Gelles. New Brunswick, NJ: Transaction Publishers, 1990, pp. 113–131.

Straus, Murray A., Richard J. Gelles, and Suzanne K. Steinmetz. *Behind Closed Doors: Violence in the American Family.* Garden City, NY: Anchor/Doubleday, 1980.

Szabo, Paul. *Tragic Tolerance of Domestic Violence.* This book, published in 1998, was written by a Member of Parliament in Canada. The complete book is available free from http://www.fact.on.ca/tragic_t/tragic_t.htm.

BATTERED WIVES

Since the 1970s significant progress has been made in documenting the nature and extent of different types of woman battering, as well as in the implementation of emergency shelters, 24-hour crisis hotlines, transitional housing, legal aid, criminal justice responses, and social services aimed at reducing the prevalence of this widespread problem. According to recent statistics, these interventions have led to some decreases in the number of reported incidents. However, much work remains to be done if the goal is to eliminate woman battering and intimate partner violence from large segments of American society in future decades.

This article traces the historical background and summarizes the key contemporary issues impacting battered wives and other abused partners, such as legislative reforms, emergency shelters and other social services, innovative policies and programs, and criminal justice responses aimed at lessening and eventually eliminating intimate partner abuse.

Historical Perspective

Battered wives, also known as abused women, beaten women, victims of intimate partner violence, and victims of spousal or partner abuse, have existed for centuries. Historically, in Roman times as well as in the fourteenth through seventeenth centuries in European countries and North America, a wife was viewed as her husband's property. Husbands were allowed to punish and discipline their wives through corporal punishment and other methods. By 1885 in the United States, one of the first official protective responses for women who were abused came about when the Chicago Protective Agency for Women was established to provide legal assistance for rape victims, and to advocate for and shelter women who were victims of physical abuse at the hands of their husbands. Between 1915 and 1920, twenty-five cities followed Chicago's pioneering lead in developing agencies for the protection of abused women (Pleck 1987; Roberts 1996).

The point of departure for the battered women's movement is the mid-1970s, when it became more widely recognized as a social problem in England and the United States. In 1971 the first emergency shelter for battered wives was opened in West London, England, by Erin Pizzey. It was called Chiswick Women's Aid. In 1972 two shelters were opened in the United States: Women's Advocates in St. Paul, Minnesota, and Haven House in Pasadena, California. By the mid-1970s, battered wives and feminist advocates began to speak publicly about the physical batterings women endured in their abusive marriages, often from a painful personal perspective, and grassroots and social service organizations such as the Salvation Army began to set up emergency shelters and safe home networks for battered wives.

The services provided included peer counseling, crisis intervention programs, group counseling and social support, legal aid and advocacy of reforms in courtroom procedures, and emergency shelters for battered women and their children (Roberts 1981). By the late 1970s, the first national survey of and services guide to eighty-nine shelters for battered women and their children, *Sheltering Battered Women,* was completed (Roberts 1981).

In 1974, Judge Marjory D. Fields, a former legal-aid attorney at the Brooklyn Legal Services

Corporation, discovered that a large number of her clients had called the police after being battered by their husbands or ex-husbands. However, the police frequently refused to respond to these emergency calls, viewing each situation as a private family conflict rather than an illegal act. Judge Fields was so outraged by the lack of action from police officers that she gave a *New York Times* reporter her story, which appeared in newspapers across the United States. Shortly after the media attention, the New York City police department (NYPD) created special police crisis intervention teams—which included women police officers and police social workers—to respond to domestic violence complaints.

Four important events occurred in 1976. The first book on the topic was published under the title *Battered Wives*. In this early publication, the author, Del Martin, one of the founders of the National Organization of Women (NOW), argued that violence against wives is deeply ingrained in societal sexism, and almost all men view woman as their property. At around the same time, *MS.* magazine published an issue with the cover story "Battered Wives: Help for the Secret Victim Next Door," with a large cover photo of a battered woman with a black eye. In this same year, Pennsylvania became the first state to establish a statewide coalition against domestic violence and to pass important legislation providing for orders of protection for domestic violence victims. Also in 1976, the first national conference on battered women was held in Milwaukee, sponsored by the Milwaukee Task Force on Battered Women.

Several years later, two significant events led to widespread social, legal, and law enforcement reforms. The first was the 1983 Minneapolis experimental study indicating that arresting batterers deters further family violence; the second was the landmark U.S. Supreme Court decision in the *Thurman v. Torrington Police Department* case, which held the police liable for their negligence in failing to protect Tracy Thurman from severe and repeated injuries inflicted by her husband.

The most far-reaching legislation—the Violence against Women Act (VAWA)—was passed in 1994 as part of the Violent Crime Control and Law Enforcement Act. This significant legislation authorized $1.2 billion over a five-year period for state and local criminal justice programs and social services to assist battered women and sexual assault victims. The funding was increased substantially in October 2000, when the United States Congress reauthorized VAWA II with $3.3 billion in funding through 2005 for a continuum of services, including concrete social services, crisis intervention and counseling, legal assistance, and training of police, prosecutors, judges, domestic violence advocates, public defenders, and social workers specifically oriented toward victims of domestic violence, sexual assault, and stalking (Roberts 2002). VAWA III was reauthorized by the U.S. Congress and signed into law by President George W. Bush on January 5, 2006 (National Task Force to End Sexual and Domestic Violence against Women 2006).

Scope of the Problem

Every nine seconds somewhere in the United States, a woman is assaulted or abused by an intimate partner. The number-one cause of women's injuries is abuse at home (Roberts and Roberts 2005, p. 4). Woman battering/intimate partner violence has a lifetime prevalence estimate of 25 percent of American couples. As a result, it is viewed as a pervasive and serious criminal justice and public health problem in American society today (Roberts 2002). The scope of the problem is illustrated by recent national estimates which indicate that approximately eight million women are abused by intimate partners in their homes each year (Roberts 2002). Intimate partner violence causes more injuries to women victims than accidents, muggings, and cancer deaths combined. Pregnancy is a risk factor for battering; as many as 37 percent of obstetrics patients are physically abused during pregnancy. Sixty percent of all female homicides are related to domestic violence.

The human cost of domestic violence is almost impossible to accurately estimate. Woman battering costs society billions of dollars annually in terms of medical bills and lost wages due to absenteeism and disabilities. It is impossible to measure the long-term physical and mental health costs to the children who witness marital violence. Carlson and Lehman (1998) reported that 60 to 75 percent of youths growing up in violent homes suffered from depressive and anxiety disorders and manifested aggression and antisocial behavior, delinquency, and violent acts.

Definition of Domestic Violence Terms

Woman battering, or *intimate partner abuse,* refers to the intentional abuse of adult women at least eighteen years of age who are involved in a relationship in which they are the victim of abuse by their intimate partners. The most frequent types of physical battering include slapping, grabbing, pushing, shoving, hair pulling, kicking, choking, biting, head banging, throwing objects at, whipping with a belt, and striking with a bat. The most severe abuse usually involves weapons such as knives, cars, bats, guns, and rifles. Recent studies indicate that 90 percent of spouse/partner abuse victims are women (Roberts 1996).

Date abuse refers to unwanted physical abuse and/or a pattern of emotional abuse in dating relationships. Abusive acts include pushing, shoving, slapping, throwing objects at, punching, hair pulling, kicking, biting, scratching, choking, head banging, whipping with a belt, striking with a knife, cutting with a nail file or scissor, and hitting with a heavy object (e.g., a lamp, a baseball bat, a golf club).

A restraining order or order of protection is a court order signed by a judge which usually forbids the alleged batterer from making contact with the victim; in some cases, the court order specifies the distance that the abuser must maintain from the victim who requested the order. Depending on the state law, the restraining order may mandate that the abusive spouse/partner immediately vacate the residence, refrain from terroristic threats or further abusive acts, pay support for the victim and minor children, and/or be court-mandated to participate in a group counseling program aimed at ending the violence (both the abusive partner and the victim may be court-mandated to attend and complete treatment).

The Emergence and Growth of Shelters for Battered Women and Their Children

Since the emergence of the battered women's movement in the 1970s and the opening of the first emergency shelters for battered women, the movement has come a long way, with several billion dollars in federal funding through the VAWAs I, II, and III; mandatory and warrantless arrest laws in many states of the union; and a network of over 2,000 emergency shelters and victim assistance, crisis intervention, legal aid, and social service programs for battered women. During the past three decades, as a result of increased awareness of the chronic and severe nature of battering relationships, short-term shelters have grown in both numbers and the scope of services provided. In the mid-1970s, there were only a half dozen shelters for battered women; by January 2001 there were over 2,000 such shelters throughout the United States. In the late 1970s, the most frequent types of services available in shelters were twenty-four hour crisis hotlines and emergency housing.

Once a woman was ready to leave the shelter, she was usually given referrals to welfare and/or legal advocacy depending on her individual needs, but little else (Roberts 1998, p. 60). By the 1990s, services had been expanded to include additional components, particularly support groups and legal advocacy for the women, and education, crisis counseling, and trauma treatment for the children. In addition, executive directors of family crisis programs and shelters began hiring clinical social workers and licensed master's-level counselors to provide mental health treatment to battered women. Outreach has been expanded to include specialized training for police officers and prevention efforts at local middle schools, high schools, and colleges on date abuse and acquaintance rape. Major changes in the staffing of shelters have taken place from the original grassroots movement of former battered women and paraprofessionals to the utilization of trained clinicians and managers, many of whom have bachelor's and/or master's degrees (Roche and Sadoski 1996). By 2005, approximately 500 comprehensive family crisis programs had secured funding for transitional second-stage communal housing, usually lasting from six months to one year, as well as vocational training and job placement service.

Advocacy groups and statewide domestic violence coalitions also came a long way in the last decades of the twentieth century. Women's advocacy groups and statewide domestic violence coalitions emerged in the late 1970s and early 1980s. These highly organized and dedicated advocacy groups/coalitions helped community members, community leaders, and legislators to recognize that domestic violence was a serious public health and social problem. As of 2001, the National Coalition against Domestic Violence and the National Network to End Domestic Violence and its fifty state coalition members had received an annual federal funding appropriation of $90 million (Roberts 2002).

Shelters for battered wives and their children can provide an exit point for ending a battering relationship and a promising entry point to a new beginning for abused women who are determined to break the cycle of violence and change their lives. Moreover, they provide a safe place to stay as well as crisis intervention, advocacy, and a supportive environment (Roberts 2002). Battered women who are successful in ending the abusive relationship usually gain necessary ego strength and self-confidence from domestic violence advocates and clinicians. Crisis intervention is frequently used to help battered women (see Roberts 2006, for further information on the popular seven-stage crisis intervention model).

Although important progress was made during the decades of the 1980s and 1990s, much remains to be done in the twenty-first century. The most underserved groups seem to be children of battered women, abused women living in rural areas, elderly battered women, lesbian battered women, Asian American battered women, Latino battered women, Orthodox Jewish battered women, and poor battered women in dire need of transitional second-stage housing (Roberts 1998).

Police

Most police calls for domestic violence come from women who have been abused by their partners several times before. In most cases, several months or years of abuse pass as the women suffer in silence. Then, as a result of a crisis precipitant (e.g., a life-threatening injury to themselves, an injury to their child, or a specific terroristic threat), they seek help from relatives, neighbors, or friends. At that point, some are helped to leave the batterer permanently. However, in the beginning (following the earliest incidents of abuse), the majority of battered women believe the batterer's apologies and false promises and remain dependent on the batterer by staying in the relationship, particularly when they have children. However, an acute crisis event usually takes place during the first few months or years of the relationship, resulting in the police being called.

Police responding to incidents of domestic violence are faced with several important decisions with possible hazardous consequences. If an assault occurs in a particular state or jurisdiction, and the police officer called to the scene does not make an arrest, is the officer violating an individual's right to equal protection under the law? If the officer makes an arrest, will it have a deterrent or escalation effect? With certain types of batterers, will arresting and detaining the batterer in jail lead to an escalation of the number of life-threatening battering incidents?

Throughout the United States, England, and Canada, there has been a major shift in police attitudes and responses to domestic violence calls. Often the batterer is arrested when the abused woman shows visible signs of injuries, the police or neighbors of the victim overhear terroristic threats, or there is probable cause to believe a crime has been committed. Several research studies have indicated that arrest and prosecution alone are not effective in reducing woman battering by abusive partners. Mandatory arrest seems to reduce future battering by minor offenders, but it has the opposite effect on more serious offenders—resulting in an escalation of violence, particularly when the couple is unmarried and the batterer is unemployed (Roberts 2002). More specifically, the Milwaukee police experimental study of 1,200 domestic violence cases indicated that among individuals with a high stake in conformity (married and employed), arrest reduces the annual rate of subsequent violence by 25.2 percent. Among those with a low stake in conformity (unmarried and unemployed), arrest is associated with a 53.5 percent increase in the annual rate of subsequent violence (Sherman 1992). Arrest alone does not deter domestic violence in the long term. Arrest and protective orders are an important part of a comprehensive approach to lessening and eventually eliminating domestic violence. However, a full continuum of services are necessary, including court-mandated batterers' counseling, transitional housing, vocational training and placement, mental health treatment, crisis intervention, prosecution, and support groups.

ALBERT R. ROBERTS

See also **Battered Woman Syndrome; Battered Woman Syndrome as a Legal Defense in Cases of Spousal Homicide; Battered Women, Clemency for; Battered Women: Held in Captivity; Marital Rape; Rule of Thumb; Social, Economic, and Psychological Costs of Violence; Violence against Women Act**

References and Further Reading

National Task Force to End Sexual and Domestic Violence against Women. "Violence against Women Act Reauthorization," 2006. http://www.vawa2005.org (accessed August 9, 2006).

Pleck, E. *Domestic Tyranny: The Making of Social Policy against Family Violence from Colonial Times to the Present.* New York: Oxford University Press. 1987.

Roberts, A. R. *Sheltering Battered Women: A National Study and Service Guide.* New York: Springer Publishing Co., 1981.

———. *Battered Women and Their Families.* New York: Springer Publishing Co., 1984.

———. "Introduction: Myths and Realities Regarding Battered Women." In *Helping Battered Women: New Perspectives and Remedies,* edited by A. R. Roberts. New York: Oxford University Press, 1996, pp. 3–12.

———. "The Organizational Structure and Function of Shelters for Battered Women and Their Children: A National Survey." In *Battered Women and Their Families,* edited by A. R. Roberts, 2nd ed. New York: Springer Publishing Co., 1998, pp. 58–75.

———. ed. *Handbook of Domestic Violence Intervention Strategies: Policies, Programs and Legal Remedies.* New York: Oxford University. Press, 2002.

———. Crisis Intervention Network website, 2006. http://www.crisisinterventionnetwork.com/index.html (accessed August 9, 2006).

Roberts, A. R., and S. Burman. "Crisis Intervention and Cognitive Problem Solving Therapy with Battered Women: A National Survey and Practice Model." In *Battered Women and Their Families,* edited by A. R. Roberts, 2nd ed. New York: Springer Publishing Co., 1998, pp. 3–28.

Roberts, A. R., and B. S. Roberts. "A Comprehensive Model for Crisis Intervention with Battered Women and Their Children." In *Crisis Intervention Handbook: Assessment, Treatment, and Research,* edited by A. R. Roberts, 2nd ed. New York: Oxford University Press, 2000, pp. 177–208.

———. *Ending Intimate Abuse: Practical Guidance and Survival Strategies.* New York: Oxford University Press, 2005.

Roche, S. E., and P. J. Sadoski. "Social Action for Battered Women." In *Helping Battered Women: New Perspectives and Remedies,* edited by A. R. Roberts. New York: Oxford University Press, 1996, pp. 13–30.

Sherman, L. W. *Policing Domestic Violence.* New York: The Free Press, 1992.

BATTERED WOMAN SYNDROME

Introduction

Battered woman syndrome (BWS) is a term that was first used in the mid-1970s to describe the psychological effects that happened to women who were physically and sexually abused and psychologically maltreated by an intimate partner (Walker 1979). The definition of BWS, like those of most terms used in the field of domestic violence, often depends on what discipline or theory a person subscribes to. For example, a psychologist or other mental health professional might use the definition of a syndrome that appears in the current classification system, which is the *Diagnostic and Statistical Manual of Mental Disorders,* fourth edition, text revision (DSM-IV-TR) (American Psychiatric Association [APA], 2000). A law enforcement officer or an attorney might use the legal definition of domestic violence that appears in the criminal statutes, which differ from country to country or even state to state. A shelter worker or domestic violence advocate might use the definition that appears in the domestic violence injunction statutes. A divorce lawyer might use the definition that appears in the family law statutes or in case law in that particular jurisdiction. A medical doctor might use the definition in her or his hospital protocols.

The beliefs of helpers and their philosophy about sex roles may also impact on the definition of what actions are serious enough to cause a psychological reaction. For example, a law enforcement officer might not pay attention to someone said to call a woman bad names, as this is not against the law, while a psychologist, who understands the harm that such behavior can cause, might give it more credence. Some battered women's advocates do not want to label the psychological effects that are noted in these women with a formal diagnosis, usually for reasons that have some truth; labeling often causes stereotyped negative images (Dobash and Dobash 1998). This is especially true in the mental health field, where many people fear being labeled as "crazy." Labeling can also cause misdiagnosis, so that the battered woman who demonstrates a psychological reaction after being abused cannot get appropriate assistance from professionals (Dutton et al. 2005). For example, a religious leader or emergency room nurse might not recognize a psychological reaction as coming from domestic violence, but for different reasons. The emergency room nurse who works with bleeding trauma victims who have broken bones and serious head injuries might have a different threshold for what constitutes serious harm, while the religious leader might blame the victim for not being a better wife. The psychologist or psychiatrist who is not trained in understanding the battered woman (or the child exposed to domestic violence) might misdiagnose a psychological reaction to domestic violence based only on the observable signs and symptoms and not the context in which the reaction occurred.

The inconsistency of definitions in the field of domestic violence has made it difficult to understand and treat women's psychological effects that come from being battered in their own homes. In addition, battered women come from all walks of life, and some of them have other mental disorders in addition to the psychological effects from being battered. In some cases, these mental disorders worsen when living with intimate violence. For example, Dutton et al. (2005) suggest that BWS is not broad enough to diagnose and treat all the symptoms that battered women might demonstrate. This causes even further confusion in both the mental health and domestic violence fields. To complicate matters even more, many feminist researchers now call domestic violence "intimate partner violence." Having one definition that everyone who works in the field recognizes and accepts would go a long way to getting battered women and other victims of intimate partner violence (i.e., men are victims too, albeit in less than 10 percent of known cases) better access to the interventions that they need.

What Is a Psychological Syndrome?

The DSM-IV-TR (APA 2000) defines a *syndrome* as a collection of signs and symptoms that commonly appear in people who have a particular disorder. A *sign* is defined as something that is observable by the diagnostician whether or not reported by the individual. A *symptom* is defined as something that is reported by the person, whether or not it is observable by the diagnostician. In this case, BWS is a collection of signs and symptoms, some of which are observable by others and some of which are experienced and reported by the battered woman herself. Most of these signs and symptoms are similar to others in the category that lists the psychological effects from experiencing a trauma, especially a trauma that is believed to be able to cause someone to die or be seriously harmed. The DSM category used in this classification system is called acute stress disorder (ASD) if the psychological effects last less than one month, and post-traumatic stress disorder (PTSD) if they last more than one month. Some clinicians suggest that PTSD is not an appropriate diagnostic category to use for BWS, especially when women are still in the relationship and the violence has not stopped (Dutton et al. 2005). However, it is important to understand that past PTSD symptoms continue to have an impact on present and future abuse in that victims reexperience the trauma as if it were reoccurring, even when it is not. Therefore, cognitively and emotionally, anyone with PTSD can be expected to react in a similar manner whether or not the actual violence is in the past or is current or anticipated.

BWS, like battered child syndrome, rape trauma syndrome, and Vietnam War syndrome, has some differences from typical, onetime environmental trauma, such as may be experienced in an earthquake, a tidal wave, or even a terrorist attack (Walker 1994). Perhaps the major difference in the dynamics or context of the relationship comes from the repeated nature of violence in the family or during state-sponsored conflicts. Family violence has even further differences from the violence of state-sponsored conflicts such as civil wars because the "enemy" is also someone who is or was a loved one. In domestic violence, research has discovered a cycle of violence that is further described below.

Diagnostic and Statistical Manual of Mental Disorders

The criteria for a DSM diagnosis of PTSD include three thresholds that must be met and three categories of signs and symptoms. The first group of criteria comprise those symptoms that demonstrate high levels of arousal of the autonomic nervous system, which are often measured by parameters of anxiety, fearfulness, nervousness, jumpiness and hypervigilance to further trauma, frequent crying, sleep and eating disorders, and difficulty with concentration and attention. The second group of criteria are those symptoms that demonstrate a distancing from the trauma and emotional numbing, such as avoidance of people, places, and things that remind the person of the abuse whenever possible (including keeping the batterer calm); depression; denial; minimization; dissociation; and other ways of psychologically "running away," as would be expected in a dangerous situation. Sometimes victims become counterphobic and face the danger head on, rather than succumb to the paralysis or depression seen in others. The third set of criteria includes those that keep victims reexperiencing the abuse in their minds, such as with flashbacks, intrusive memories, and dreams. This includes those who intentionally use alcohol and other substances to try to keep from experiencing the pain, as if the events were reoccurring.

Those who have experienced PTSD from domestic violence and have developed BWS also have difficulties in three other areas. These are in interpersonal relationships, due to isolation and problems with power and control issues, body image, and sexuality. It is believed that the isolation of the battered woman in the relationship and the numbing of emotions create difficulties in her interpersonal relationships even after the abuse has stopped.

Loss of trust in and bitter feelings of betrayal by the person who once loved her enter into the difficulties she has in building new intimate relationships. Batterers abuse the power and control that couples normally share in intimate relationships, causing the woman to have difficulties knowing where the boundaries are between her own choices and those actions the man coerces her into doing. The battered woman shelter and other psychoeducational groups prove to be very useful in helping women reestablish trusting friendships and family connections.

Definitions of Battered Woman Syndrome

The psychological definition of BWS calls it a syndrome that includes the three criteria of the DSM diagnosis of PTSD (reexperiencing the event, avoidance and numbing of responsiveness, and hyperarousal) and the three additional effects that have been measured through the empirical study of hundreds of battered women (Walker 1984/2000). As described above, these additional effects disrupt interpersonal relationships caused by the batterer's imposed isolation and abuse of power and control toward the woman, difficulties with body image and somatic concerns, and sexual and intimacy problems. New studies demonstrate that these symptoms constitute BWS in women in many different countries.

Cycle of Violence

Legal cases define BWS as PTSD and the addition of what has been described as the dynamics of battering relationships. The dynamics of the relationship usually include evidence of a cycle of violence and some description of the relationship between the parties. A three-phase cycle of violence that follows after the courtship, or "honeymoon period," is identifiable in many but not all domestic violence relationships.

Courtship Period

It is well known that the courtship period in domestic violence relationships is characterized by extremely flattering and loving behavior by the batterer. Often, women say that the initial impression made by the batterer was not one that they liked, due to his sense of self-importance, entitlement, or even aggressive behavior toward others. However, he seeks them out, and his attention and loving behavior becomes attractive to them. Their descriptions include a lot of what is now being called "aggressive courtship" tactics, including frequent telephone calls, refusal to accept no for an answer, and increased inducements toward enjoyment and doing fun things. Frequently, the batterer has a sense for what buttons to push in a woman, being solicitously helpful in solving a difficult problem she has or being an ever so sympathetic listener to her stories. He may share intimate details about himself, particularly about earlier abuse or injustices he suffered, which may give the woman reason to believe that she can help him feel better about himself. These behaviors also begin to create a dependency for the woman on the batterer, and perhaps for some batterers, a dependency on the woman.

The women describe waiting for the man's telephone calls, which may start out on a daily basis and escalate to five to ten a day. Initially this is part of the excitement of a new relationship, but eventually its purpose is to create intimacy and check on where she is and what she is doing. As he spends more time with the woman, she becomes more isolated from others. Eventually, he begins to regulate her contacts with her friends and family. In many relationships, battered women have more contact with the man's friends or family than their own. Sometimes this is easier, as her family and friends may not like the man or how he treats her. Other times, the man may shower gifts on the woman's family in an attempt to cause them to ignore his negative behavior. Once the man is sure he has "seduced" the woman, and the intimacy is set in place, the cycle of violence begins.

Phase One: Tension-Building Period

The first phase is a period of tension that builds. There are lots of small abuse incidents that often produce psychological harm. Each time an incident occurs, the woman may do something to stop it from going any further, and the tension starts to resolve, but the feeling of danger does not go away completely. There is an uneasy feeling in anticipation of the next incident, which pushes the tension level up further, until finally there is a period of inevitability, and the explosion occurs. In some relationships, the period of tension becomes associated with feelings of danger, so that any behavior that is reminiscent of earlier incidents can set off the anticipatory feelings in the woman. Sometimes the incidents are connected together—for example, if she violates rules he has established—while other times they occur with long intervals of time between them, so there may not be any perception of their connection. The most successful time to separate the couple and avoid the explosion is early during the tension-building period; once it approaches or reaches the period of inevitability, the explosion is difficult to stop.

Phase Two: Acute Battering Incident

The second phase—when the explosion occurs— is the shortest period and has the highest risk of physical or sexual harm. Some argue that the batterer is out of control during this period, while others believe that the batterer's behavior is intentional. During this phase, the man uses physical abuse and threats of further harm or even death directed toward the woman or her family to force her to "listen to him." Batterers often justify their abuse by insisting that they are teaching the woman important lessons that she needs to get along in life.

In some relationships, the second phase starts slowly, with pushing, shoving, shaking, hair pulling, and perhaps a slap or two, escalating to more serious assaults. In other cases, choking, threats of further harm, and being held captive at gunpoint may begin quickly, making it clear that this person has probably engaged in dangerously violent behavior previously.

The second phase may come rapidly after the first phase or it may punctuate long periods of tension-building types of incidents after some situational crisis. The introduction of a new baby, a crisis at work, having to move, or even children reaching a new developmental stage, such as entering their teens, can trigger a change in the cycle in these relationships.

Phase Three: Loving Contrition

The risk of danger is usually temporarily over during the third phase, which is the reinforcing period where loving behavior and contrition are demonstrated. For many women the reduction in tension and feelings of danger serves as reinforcing in itself. Some batterers apologize in nonverbal ways, such as with gifts, being less argumentative, exercising more self-control, or doing something they know will please the woman. Others may never say or do anything to convey their apologies. This third phase becomes reinforcing for the woman just because there is an absence or lowering of the tension and danger in the relationship, often bringing with it the positive memories of the courtship period.

Some women describe incidents that at first appear loving but turn out to be very aggressive and controlling despite their initial appearance. For example, one woman told of how her husband surprised her with a new Cadillac when she got out of the hospital. However, she later found out that he had not paid for it but rather left it for her to scrape together the money to make the monthly payments. In another example, a woman had been asking her partner to help her do some landscaping around the house. Instead of making it a joint project, her partner went out and bought a roomful of plants that she then had to spend several days planting or they would have withered and died. Some behavior starts out to be nice, but the batterer gets so grandiose that it inevitably becomes annoying and even dangerous for the woman. A typical example might be taking the woman on a surprise trip where the partner does not know where he is going, refusing to get directions, and ending up driving around lost for hours. Most battered women are so grateful to have some time without feeling as if they are "walking on eggshells" that they accept the good intentions of their partner and do not dwell on the negative aspects of these types of incidents.

As the relationship progresses, the third phase changes and becomes less reinforcing. Here women describe more perfunctory apologies or none at all. The tension may go down, but never to zero. Once the woman becomes aware that the man could have killed her or caused her to die during the acute battering incidents, she may never be sufficiently relaxed around him again, and the reinforcers of the relationship change significantly for her. This is the point at which she may begin to prepare to terminate the relationship.

Types of Abuse

Physical Abuse

Physical abuse described by battered women ranges from pushing and shoving, slapping, hitting, throwing her against walls, throwing objects in the room at her or on the floor, all the way to life-threatening incidents including stabbing and shooting her. Most studies use a checklist of possible violent acts and some estimate how frequently each occurs in the relationship. Some studies suggest that the violent behavior tends to increase over time (Walker 2000/1984) while others find that it may stay quite stable or even decrease on its own initiative (O'Leary 1993). Sonkin (2006) has developed a useful assessment tool for measurement.

It is often difficult to get an accurate picture of all the physically abusive incidents that have occurred in a domestic violence relationship because of the difference in how men and women report violent incidents. The perpetrator often will report only incidents in which he intentionally used physical violence. So, if he shoved his partner out of his way in an aggressive manner and she fell down and hurt herself, it may not count as a battering incident to the man. However, if a woman unintentionally kicks the man while she is sleeping, she usually will report that incident as domestic violence. This disparity in gender report causes some studies to overestimate the amount of aggressive behavior used by women and underestimate the amount used by men in domestic violence relationships.

In addition to differences in reporting because of intentionality, women minimize their reports of physical abuse toward themselves if they are not injured. Many incidents of what is sometimes called "low level" domestic violence go uncounted. Some have estimated that by the time an arrest is made, as many as thirty-five physically abusive incidents may have occurred. Some studies have simply counted aggressive acts without putting them into context, resulting in reports that women use as much violence toward men as men use toward women. However, when examining this issue more carefully, it is clear that one slap from a woman does not cause the same injury to a man as does one slap from him to her. Women are more likely to be the recipients of more injuries even when there is mutual violence in the relationship. It is the woman who is more often seen in the emergency room or doctors' offices after a domestic violence incident, when they seek medical help. When the man does seek medical attention, it is more likely for very serious injury such as gunshot or knife wounds, often received as a result of their initiating the aggressive behavior, followed by the woman attempting to defend herself.

Interestingly, teenage girls appear to be using more aggressive behavior against other people than had previously been reported. The media has been portraying these girls as bad, mean, and violent without looking at the context during which these incidents have occurred. An examination of several hundred girls who had been arrested and placed in a detention center over a five-year period found that almost 85 percent had experienced or been exposed to domestic violence in their homes, causing them to develop PTSD as measured by several standardized tests. The higher their PTSD scores, the angrier they were, and the more they expressed their anger outwardly, resulting in aggressive behavior (Walker, Robinson, Dorsainville, Ipke, and Coker 2005). However, over half of them denied having been abused during the interviews. Studies like this support the early studies that violence begets more violence, at least when it occurs in families. While this trend of more aggressive behavior in adolescent girls has been noted internationally, statistics suggest that only a small percentage of them continue using aggressive behavior once they get out of their teenage years. It is thought that the biological changes and brain development that occur in the late teens and early twenties has some mediating effect on the girls' aggressive behavior. Research is needed to determine whether these girls, like their predecessors, also have a higher risk of becoming battered women in their intimate relationships.

Sexual Abuse

Sexual abuse, which occurs in almost one-half of the domestic violence relationships studied, may come at any point in the cycle. Sometimes the woman initiates sex as a means to calm down the batterer during the tension-building period and is able to postpone the second phase for as long as possible. In some countries sexual abuse in a marital relationship, or marital rape, is neither legally prosecutable nor religiously defined because the act of marriage is considered an open consent for the couple to have sexual relations whenever it is desired, usually by the man. Nonetheless, there are new laws that forbid marital rape and give the woman the right to say no if she does not want to have sex at a particular time. These are usually used when the couple is separated and the man forcibly rapes the woman.

The man's sexually aggressive behavior is commonly reported by the battered woman, usually beginning during the courtship period and often sporadically occurring during the relationship, frequently after an argument or battering incident. This behavior can range from embarrassing the woman in front of others with crude jokes or disclosures about their sex life to grabbing her breasts or buttocks in public and criticizing her dress at an important function. As the man's jealousy over the woman's possible attraction to other men is such a common theme in domestic violence relationships, anything that causes him to become jealous can be used to begin another acute battering incident. After a while, the women report, they do not want to attend events such as company parties or family receptions for fear that the man will become sexually jealous and an explosion will occur.

There are reports of some batterers demanding that their partners participate in unusual sex acts such as sex with objects, animals, and even third parties. It is not uncommon for the man to record these behaviors on video and then threaten to expose the woman by showing the pictures to others. Some men force their wives into prostitution and then control the money they earn. Other men have forced women to obtain other sex partners for the man's own use. Women describe themselves as giving in to coercion to engage in these sexual practices in order to stop the men from escalating their violence. The women's feelings of guilt and emotional distress afterward, especially if the act was recorded, are similar to those of rape victims.

Psychological Abuse

The most prevalent form of abuse that occurs in battering relationships is psychological in nature. It is often called the glue that holds together the pattern of violence in the relationship. There are many different ways to assess for psychological abuse, perhaps because most people feel that they have been taken advantage of, ignored, humiliated, embarrassed, or in some other way psychologically maltreated. Therefore, it is important to differentiate psychological abuse in intimate partner relationships from the psychological dynamics and effects of a dysfunctional but not abusive relationship. One of the most often confused areas is where one partner emotionally wounds the other by betrayal with another person. In most cases, this involves betrayal with another sexual partner. While this type of betrayal is not necessarily part of a battering relationship, the issue of jealousy is one that co-occurs frequently with domestic violence, with the batterer inappropriately jealous of the woman if she even looks at another man. The man may control what clothes the woman will wear, often wanting her to look sexy for him but not for anyone else. Acute battering incidents commonly follow attendance at a party when the man becomes angry with the woman for even talking to another man. The woman may also be jealous of the man's behavior toward other women. Sometimes her jealousy is more justified than his is toward her. The most likely way for the batterer to let the woman go is when he has found another partner.

Amnesty International's Definition of Torture

In assessing behaviors that constitute psychological abuse, it is possible to use the Amnesty International definition of torture regarding prisoners of war. Under this definition, aspects of psychological abuse include attempts to control someone's mind, isolation, creating a dependency on the captor, hypnosis or brainwashing, debilitation by withholding food or interrupting sleep, humiliation and name-calling, forced drug administration, and threats of further harm to the captive or others, all offset by occasional indulgences. The pattern outlined in the Amnesty International list of behaviors is similar to the pattern seen in the cycle of abuse described above, with "occasional indulgences" serving the same role as the third phase, or period of loving contrition. Using a checklist of these behaviors, jealousy and overpossessiveness, financial control, and other power and control methods are seen on a daily basis in most domestic violence homes.

Impact on the Children

Perhaps one of the most difficult areas in which to intervene is in stopping the toll that the exposure to domestic violence takes on the children of a couple. Findings in psychological studies attest to the effects that interfere with children's normal development by causing cognitive, emotional, and behavioral changes. Children as young as two years have been seen repeating their father's attempts to control their mother's behavior, and their increasing levels of anxiety have been measured while they were observing adults in angry verbal fights. Most battered women try to protect their children from exposure to their abusive fathers, but when questioned, the children acknowledge hearing the fights, even if they were in their bedrooms trying to sleep. Psychological tests indicate that these children may even develop PTSD themselves from this exposure.

Most battered women state that one of the reasons for staying in the relationship is to make sure the children have a father in the home. Others who have tried to terminate the relationship state that they returned because they were less able to protect their children from the mood swings of the typical abuser. Divorce courts are not able to protect the children and, in fact, may create or increase their PTSD by forcing shared parenting requirements on the abusive parent. Batterers must always be in control, or they will use whatever tactics are necessary to gain control, even if they are hurtful to the child.

Intervention

It has been difficult for mental health professionals to intervene in domestic violence relationships without the fear of making it more dangerous for those in the family or the community. A perusal of the local news will demonstrate the higher risk for

homicide and suicide, especially when a separation has occurred.

Public Health Model

Given the high frequency of homes in the community where domestic violence occurs, some have suggested applying a public health model of prevention to try to stop the continued abuse. The three parts to the prevention model include primary, secondary, and tertiary levels of activities. In primary prevention, no one is singled out for services, but the entire community is eligible. For example, a movie or television program that talks about the dangers of domestic violence would serve a good educational function for the entire community. If there are, for example, teenage girls who may have been exposed to violence in their homes, then targeting them with a special presentation to teach them to avoid getting involved with an abuser might be another prevention strategy.

Secondary prevention targets those people who have already been exposed to an abuser. Psychotherapy or survivor therapy groups run by domestic violence shelters or rape crisis centers constitute secondary prevention strategies. The goal is to lessen the impact that exposure to domestic abuse has had on people, especially women, though men can also benefit. Secondary prevention strategies for the male abuser include anger management programs and offender-specific treatment groups. Usually secondary prevention strategies are offered on an outpatient basis and people use them as needed. However, it is typical for batterers to be court-ordered into treatment, while battered women who do not commit any offenses are not required to attend, although many do on a voluntary basis. Sometimes psychotropic medication, outpatient psychotherapy groups, or individual psychotherapy also may be used by a battered woman to help her to heal.

Tertiary-level treatment removes the individual from the community temporarily. Battered women are removed from the community when living in a battered women's shelter or in a hospital. Batterers are removed from the community when they are placed in jail or prison. In many communities that have a pro-arrest policy, the batterer is arrested upon probable cause, denied bond at the time of arrest, and held until the next regularly scheduled hearing in front of a judge. This may be just overnight or it might last for several days, depending on the severity of the physical abuse, any prior arrests that the batterer might have, and the assessment of the current risk of dangerousness. If there has been a conviction, the tertiary intervention might be a prison sentence of one year or longer. Unfortunately, it is rare for there to be offender-specific treatment programs in jail or prison.

LENORE E. A. WALKER

See also **Battered Woman Syndrome as a Legal Defense in Cases of Spousal Homicide; Battered Women, Clemency for; Battered Women: Held in Captivity; Battered Women Who Kill: An Examination; Batterer Typology; Cohabiting Violence; Cycle of Violence; Stockholm Syndrome in Battered Women**

References and Further Reading

American Psychiatric Association. *Diagnostic and Statistical Manual of Mental Disorders,* 4th ed., text revision. Washington, DC: Author, 2000.

Dobash, R. E., and R. P. Dobash. *Rethinking Violence against Women.* Sage Series on Violence against Women. Thousand Oaks, CA: Sage Publishers, 1998.

O'Leary, K. D. "Through a Psychological Lens: Personality Traits, Personality Disorders, and Levels of Violence." In *Current Controversies on Family Violence,* edited by R. J. Gelles and D. R. Loeske. Newbury Park, CA: Sage, 1993, pp. 7–30.

Sonkin, Daniel. *Domestic Violence Resources,* 2006. www.daniel-sonkin.com (accessed August 10, 2006).

Walker, L. E. *The Battered Woman.* New York: Harper & Row, 1979.

———. *The Battered Woman Syndrome.* New York: Springer, 1984/2000.

———. *Abused Women and Survivor Therapy: A Practical Guide for the Psychotherapist.* Washington, DC: American Psychological Association, 1994.

Walker, L. E. (chair), M. Robinson, A. Dorsainville, U. Ipke, and K. Coker. *Born to Be Wild: Media Portrayal of Bad Girls.* Symposium presented at the Annual Meeting of the American Psychological Association, Aug. 2005, Washington, DC.

BATTERED WOMAN SYNDROME AS A LEGAL DEFENSE IN CASES OF SPOUSAL HOMICIDE

"Battered woman syndrome" (BWS) is a descriptive term that refers to a pattern of psychological and behavioral symptoms found in women living in abusive relationships. Battered women sometimes use physical force to kill their batterers. These women may be charged with a criminal offense. When women are charged with murder or manslaughter for killing their batterer, they often do not deny having committed the act, but rather claim the act was committed in self-defense. In some cases, battered women may claim that they were insane at the time of the killing. Evidence of BWS may be offered to substantiate the claims of self-defense and insanity. Therefore, there is no specific legal defense called "the BWS defense"; rather, evidence about battering and its effects is offered to assist the jury in its determination of the guilt or innocence of the defendant based on the claims of self-defense or insanity.

BWS has been used as a defense in criminal cases since the late 1970s. However, its introduction to support claims of self-defense and insanity in cases of spousal homicide raises many empirical, normative, and legal questions. Battered women's advocates express concerns about the use of the term "syndrome" to describe the response of women who kill their batterers. These advocates argue that the use of the term "syndrome" serves to stigmatize battered women defendants because it appears to indicate that battered women have some sort of medical condition or psychological disorder. In addition, some behavioral science research questions the underlying empirical research used to support the claim that a specific, identifiable syndrome affects women who have been subjected to continuous physical abuse by their intimate partners. Finally, many psychologists, legal scholars, and attorneys challenge the use of

BWS as evidence at trial, especially when the defense counsel uses expert witness testimony to support battered women's defense claims.

This article will examine the use of BWS in cases of spousal homicide by considering: (1) the definition of BWS, (2) the claim that BWS is a form of post-traumatic stress disorder (PTSD), (3) the legal standard for claims of self-defense, including the problems with using BWS to support such claims, (4) the legal standard of insanity and the problems with using BWS to support such claims, (5) the use of expert witnesses to support claims of BWS, and (6) the legal standards and issues surrounding the admissibility of expert witness testimony concerning BWS. In examining these issues, the word "spouse" will include married couples as well as partners who live together and are not legally married. It will also include recently separated partners as well as divorced partners.

Definition of BWS

BWS is associated with the pioneering research of feminist psychologist and researcher Dr. Lenore Walker. She introduced the term in her 1979 book *The Battered Woman,* based on her initial findings from a nonrandom sample of 110 predominantly white and middle-class battered women who had contacted social service agencies. On the basis of her research, Walker advanced a psychological theory of the process of victimization of battered women. She posited that not all battered women develop BWS. Rather, the syndrome refers to women who have been, on at least two occasions, the victim of physical, sexual, or serious psychological symptoms by a man with whom they have had an intimate relationship. Walker identified BWS as comprising two distinct components: (1) a cycle of violence and (2) learned helplessness.

The cycle of violence refers to a three-stage, repetitive cycle that occurs in battering relationships. The first stage is the *tension-building stage,* which consists of a gradual buildup of minor abusive incidents (largely verbal and psychological abuse) in which women attempt to placate the batterer. This stage is eventually followed by an *acute battering stage,* in which the severity of the abuse increases and women are subjected to a violent battering incident. Following the acute battering stage is a calm, *loving, contrite stage* in which the batterer apologizes for his behavior. The batterer's behavior in this third stage encourages the woman to believe that he will reform and influences her to remain in the relationship. Walker identified this third phase as the one that most victimizes women psychologically, because inevitably the cycle of violence recurs. Battered women become demoralized as they realize that the batterer has once again fooled them into believing that he will change. Although Walker did not hypothesize a specific time frame to define the cycles or the phases within it, she argued that the cycle is eventually repeated, and over time the violence escalates in both severity and frequency.

The second component of Walker's theory of BWS is learned helplessness. Learned helplessness explains the psychological paralysis that Walker argued prevents some women from leaving their batterers. Walker maintained that learned helplessness occurs in a domestic violence situation when battered women cannot rest assured of their own safety because, regardless of their own efforts, they face the batterer's unpredictable, abusive behavior. Over time, as the violence escalates, women begin to live in a constant state of fear, believing that there is no escape from their situation. This fear is typically reinforced by the batterers' threats that if they attempt to leave or seek help, he will subject them to even greater abuse or kill them and their children. In addition, the batterers' controlling behavior often causes the women to isolate themselves from family and friends. Walker also argued that social and economic factors, such as the women's emotional and financial dependency on their batterers, societal norms stressing the importance of marriage, and the lack of effective social and legal remedies to end the battering, prevent women from leaving these relationships. Battered women believe that there is no way for them to prevent the violence; therefore, they simply give up and accept the abuse, or in some cases, resort to violence and kill their batterers to free themselves from the abuse.

Battered Woman Syndrome as a Form of Post-Traumatic Stress Disorder

After Walker published her research, some empirical data emerged that cast doubt on her explanation of why women kill their batterers. More specifically, some research indicated that victims of abuse often contact other family members and seek the assistance of the legal system for help as the violence from their batterers escalates. This research also indicated that when battered women sought outside help, they were confronted with insufficient help sources, a legal system that did not address their issues, and societal indifference.

The lack of practical options, combined with victims' lack of financial resources, made it likely that battered women would stay in abusive relationships. In contrast to this research demonstrating battered women's active help-seeking behavior, Walker's theory of BWS emphasized women as becoming passive and helpless in the face of repeated abuse.

An alternative conceptualization of BWS emerged in the 1980s when the American Psychiatric Association added post-traumatic stress disorder (PTSD) as a classification in the *Diagnostic and Statistical Manual of Mental Disorders,* third edition (DSM-III), the foremost manual used by mental health professionals to diagnose mental illness. Although the DSM-III did not recognize BWS as a distinct mental illness or disorder, many experts regarded BWS as a subcategory of PTSD. The DSM's fourth edition (DSM-IV), published in 1994, retains PTSD as a mental disorder and often uses it as a reference in cases of spousal homicide to attempt to demonstrate that BWS is a form of PTSD.

The PTSD theory as applied to battered women does not exclusively focus on battered women's perceptions of helplessness or ineffective help sources to explain why battered women stay with their abusive partners. Instead, the theory focuses on the psychological disturbance that an individual suffers after exposure to a traumatic event. The diagnostic criteria for PTSD include a history of exposure to a traumatic event, as well as the following symptoms: intrusive recollection, avoidant/numbing, and hyperarousal. In individuals suffering from PTSD, the traumatic event is a dominant psychological experience that evokes panic, terror, dread, grief, or despair. Flashbacks of battering incidents are examples of intrusive recollection symptoms that battered women may display. The avoidant/numbing symptom consists of the emotional strategies that individuals with PTSD use to reduce the likelihood that they will expose themselves to traumatic stimuli or, if exposed, minimize their psychological response. These strategies can be behavioral (e.g., avoiding situations in which the battering is likely to be encountered), cognitive (e.g., using disassociation to cut off the conscious experience of the trauma-based memories of battering incidents), or emotional (e.g., using psychic numbing to separate the cognitive and emotional aspects of the experience). The hyperarousal symptoms closely resemble those seen in panic and generalized anxiety disorders; however, hypervigilance and startle responses are unique to PTSD. The hyperarousal vigilance symptom refers to the

response of victims' autonomic nervous systems, which signal battered women that they and/or their children are in danger. In addition, persons repeatedly victimized and repeatedly placed in harm's way become irritable, lose the ability to concentrate, and may experience panic attacks. These feelings can become so intense that victims appear paranoid, and it is claimed that battered women, suffering from PTSD, may become convinced that the batterer will kill them at any time.

In the case of spousal homicide, defense counsel may introduce evidence attempting to prove that the battered woman defendant displays the symptoms of PTSD and that these symptoms are a result of the repeated battering that she experienced from her partner. However, considering BWS as a form of PTSD remains a controversial issue. Researchers indicate that while some women who experience continuous battering may experience the symptoms that are diagnosed as PTSD, others do not. Moreover, feminists argue that linking BWS to PTSD presents an image of battered women as mentally ill, and does not emphasize the social conditions of the power and control issues among batterers that served to create the situations of domestic violence experienced by battered women. Feminists have been especially vocal in their criticism of this medicalization effect in situations in which battered women have killed their partners and PTSD is used to support a claim of self-defense. These critics charge that viewing battered women as mentally disordered when they assert self-defense diminishes battered women's claims that their actions were reasonable given their situation.

The Claim of Self-Defense

Women who kill their batterers may claim that the killing was committed in self-defense. The law considers self-defense an act of justification. This means that the legal system does not consider someone who kills in self-defense morally culpable; it concludes that the action was correct under the circumstances. The claim of self-defense requires battered women defendants to demonstrate that their actions meet the legal standards for a claim of self-defense. However, legally using self-defense to justify the killing of partners by battered women is controversial and often problematic because of the kind of evidence that the defense offers at trial to prove its case and because of the jury's perception of the battered woman's situation at the time of the killing.

The law of the state where the killing took place defines the legal standard for a claim of self-defense.

Most states define self-defense in terms of four traditional requirements. First, at the time of the act, the defendant must have believed that he or she was in imminent danger of unlawful bodily harm. Second, the defendant must have used a reasonable amount of force to respond to the threatened danger. Third, he or she cannot have been the aggressor. Fourth, under some circumstances the defendant must have had no opportunity to retreat safely. Essentially this means that where individuals cannot resort to the law in response to violence from others, they may use reasonable force to protect themselves from physical harm.

In many cases in which women kill their batterers, these traditional criteria of self-defense are not met. For example, in the majority of cases, battered women who kill their abusers do not attack during a direct confrontation but rather when no "imminent" threat may seem apparent to an outside observer. Battered women may kill their mates during a lull in the violence or when the batterers are sleeping. Battered women may use a knife or gun while the abuser was unarmed. In addition, though most states do not require the victim to retreat when attacked, when battered women kill their abusers there is usually a long history and pattern of violence in their relationship with the batterers. This raises the question of why battered women do not leave violent relationships earlier. Proponents of BWS maintain that these departures from the traditional expectations of self-defense law can be explained by the psychological dynamics involved in intimate violent relationships. These psychological dynamics may be introduced at trial, often with the testimony of an expert witness.

Another controversial application of BWS concerns its use to support the battered woman defendant's contention that her employment of deadly force was reasonable. In some states, courts may accept the history of abuse and, in particular, the nature of that abuse, as important factors for understanding the reasonableness of the defendant's belief in the need to use deadly force. In other states, the relevant comparison for judging the defendant's actions is "a reasonable battered woman" rather than the ordinary reasonable person. These courts have responded to the concern of researchers who note that in deciding what is "reasonable," traditional criminal law utilizes the "ordinary man" as its reference point, in which the assault typically occurs during a single violent episode and the assailant is often a stranger to the victim. This point of reference fails to fully capture the battered woman's circumstance. The violence that the battered woman faces is continual and at the hands of an intimate partner rather than a stranger. Furthermore, the woman is generally not on equal physical grounds with the batterer, thus explaining why the force that the woman uses against her spouse usually involves the use of a deadly weapon.

The other major obstacle to achieving a claim of self-defense is that the lay public, from which jurors are chosen, may harbor misconceptions regarding the causes and effects of intimate partner violence. Jurors may believe that violence in the relationship fulfills the needs of each of the partners or that the woman defendant could have left her abuser if she truly objected to the abuse. Beliefs such as these may make it difficult for jurors to understand how a woman might have a perception of imminent fear. Although the law in most states does not require the defendant to attempt to escape from the situation or to leave the relationship earlier, the woman's failure to do so may still influence the juror's evaluations of the reasonableness of her actions. Jurors' beliefs about intimate partner violence and the lack of fit between the woman's actions and the existing laws of self-defense can make it difficult for the defense to establish that the woman's behavior in killing her abuser was reasonable.

The Defense of Insanity

In some cases, battered women who kill their abusers will claim the defense of insanity. Battered women who claim an insanity defense allege that their mental capacity was impaired at the time of the criminal act, in contrast to a defense of self-defense, in which battered women claim that they acted in response to a reasonable perception of danger. This insanity defense is referred to legally as "defense of excuse" rather than a defense of justification. An excuse defense refers to situations in which the defendant doesn't deny that she committed the crime, but rather states that she is not responsible for it, typically on grounds of lacking volition over her free will, as in the case of a claim of insanity. The defense of insanity requires that a defendant have a serious mental illness at the time of the criminal act. Furthermore, in most states, the legal standard for insanity is a narrow one, requiring that the defendant's mental condition impaired her mental capacity to such an extent that she did not understand the nature and consequences of what she was doing or did not understand that what she was doing was wrong. This defense is used much less frequently in cases of spousal homicide than is the claim of self-defense, but when the condition of legal insanity is offered as a defense, testimony by experts can be offered to explain how BWS and its associated symptoms may have precluded the victim from knowing right from wrong or appreciating the consequences of her actions at the time of the criminal act.

Although BWS has been used to support a defense of insanity, critics argue that its use is misplaced because the extent to which the syndrome causes mental illness cannot be determined by clinicians and because BWS, as it was articulated by Walker, does not entail a loss of ability to understand the nature or consequences of what one is doing or the failure to appreciate right from wrong at the time the crime was committed. In addition some legal scholars claim that the use of BWS to support a defense of insanity creates judicial confusion because doing so suggests a biological/medical basis for the condition, rather than a social or behavioral basis. These critics also charge that this pathological view of BWS is further suggested when it is linked to PTSD. The pathological view stands in marked contrast to the view that battered women act in self-defense when they kill their abusers. Therefore, these critics assert that using BWS to support a claim of insanity argues against the idea that battered women's actions are reasonable given their circumstances, and instead encourages courts to see them as helpless.

The Use of Expert Witness Testimony in Cases Involving Battered Women

In cases of spousal homicide, both the prosecution and the defense can present evidence of BWS in a variety of ways. The defendant can testify about her experiences as a battered woman, and both the prosecution and the defense can call witnesses to testify on their behalf. One of the most important kinds of testimony in cases of spousal homicide is the use of expert witness testimony. Expert testimony is legally defined as the opinion evidence of someone who possesses special skill or knowledge in some science, profession, or business which is not common to the average person and is possessed by the expert by reason of special study or experience. In cases of spousal homicide where the defense asserts a claim of self-defense or insanity, the expert typically used is a psychologist or psychiatrist. Both the prosecution and the defense can introduce expert witness testimony on battering and its effects in cases of spousal homicide. The defense utilizes expert witness testimony to support its claims of insanity or self-defense. It may also

utilize expert witness testimony in conjunction with the sentencing phases of a trial as a mitigating factor to lessen the sentence the defendant will receive. The prosecution may use expert witness testimony in cases of spousal homicide to explain such matters as battered women's lack of cooperation or recantation. The expert witness does not determine the ultimate issues, such as whether it was reasonable for the battered woman to believe that she was in imminent danger. Rather, the purpose of expert witness testimony is to provide the judge or jury with an alternative perspective for interpreting a woman's actions. Specifically, the role of the expert witness is to provide information relevant to inferences they will have to make about the woman's state of mind at the time of the killing, such as why she may have perceived herself to be in a situation of imminent danger, even if she was not under direct attack at the time of the killing.

The earliest case to consider the use of expert witness testimony regarding BWS was *Ibn-Tamas v. United States,* in 1979. Ibn-Tamas was married to a husband who beat her often and who had a history of violence toward women. While she was pregnant, her husband beat her; in response, she shot and killed him. She was charged with murder in the second degree and claimed self-defense. At trial a psychologist testified on her behalf on BWS. The trial judge refused to let the testimony be heard, stating that the victim/husband was not on trial. The Washington, DC, appeals court reversed the ruling and stated that an expert can testify where subject matter is beyond the understanding of the average layman. Since the *Ibn-Tamas* case, research indicates that the nature of the information that the expert conveys may vary in the extent to which it specifically addresses the defendant's behavior. Much of this variation is explained by the laws in different states and the court's interpretation of those laws concerning the introduction of expert witness testimony. In some instances, the court may allow the expert to explain the general research findings regarding battered women and to provide a clinical opinion on whether the woman on trial exhibits the syndrome. Typically, the expert is not permitted to offer an opinion on the woman's perceptions at the time of the killing. In other instances, however, the expert has been allowed to offer evidence only about the general research findings regarding battered women, without offering an opinion as to whether the defendant fits the profile of a battered woman. In some cases, courts may refuse to permit such opinion evidence. In these latter instances, jurors are left to infer, on the basis of other trial testimony, whether the defendant exhibits BWS and whether the implications that derive from it apply to her behavior.

Legal Standards and Issues Concerning Expert Witness Testimony

Expert testimony on BWS must meet a number of legal requirements before the court decides to admit it as evidence. Clearly the testimony must be relevant to the issues or facts of the case, but in addition, expert testimony must satisfy three other criteria. First, the expert must be sufficiently skilled and qualified to testify about BWS. Typically the court determines whether the expert is qualified on the basis of the education and experience of the expert. Second, the proposed evidence must be deemed scientifically reliable. Third, the testimony must provide the jury with unique information that is beyond their common understanding of BWS and its effects. While the first criterion is a rather straightforward one, the second and third require additional explanation in terms of both the general legal standard and its applicability to situations involving the use of BWS in cases of spousal homicide.

There are no universal standards employed by courts to determine whether the basis upon which the expert testimony given in sufficiently reliable. For many years, the standard used by most courts was the *Frye* standard (*Frye v. United States,* 1923) which requires that the scientific validity of the evidence must be generally accepted by experts in the particular field of inquiry. However, more recently, federal courts and many state courts have employed the *Daubert* standard (*Daubert v. Merrell Dow Pharmaceuticals, Inc.,* 1993). In *Daubert,* the Supreme Court ruled that in federal courts the *Frye* test had been superseded by the adoption, in 1973, of Rule 702 of the *Federal Rules of Evidence,* which provides that a witness qualified as an expert by knowledge, skill, experience, training, or education may testify in the form of an opinion if the scientific, technical, or other specialized knowledge would assist the jury to understand the evidence or to determine a fact in issue. The Court emphasized that the testimony must be grounded in the methods and procedures of science. The Court concluded that evidence grounded in science could establish reliable evidence. Today, while all federal courts follow the *Daubert* standard, states are divided, with some following *Daubert* while others follow *Frye.*

Whether courts use the *Daubert* or *Frye* standard, the reliability of BWS evidence remains a controversial issue. Supporters point to the fact that BWS evidence has achieved considerable recognition within the legal and behavioral science community. The American Psychological Association (APA) has endorsed the validity of the syndrome in amicus briefs it filed in homicide cases of battered women. In the noted case of *State v. Kelly,* the APA concluded that the underlying theories used by the experts were well developed and well recognized, had previously been applied in other contexts, and had simply been adapted to the study of battered women (*State v. Kelly,* Amicus Brief, p. 255). In *Kelly,* the New Jersey Supreme Court held that the existence of battered spouse syndrome was relevant to the honesty and reasonableness of a woman's claim that she believed she was in imminent danger of death or serious injury. Additional support is found in numerous cases in which courts have permitted testimony on BWS. A research report published in 1995 by the National Clearinghouse for the Defense of Battered Women (NCDBW) indicated that expert testimony on battering and its effects is admissible, at least to some degree, in each of the fifty states and the District of Columbia, though eighteen states had excluded expert testimony in some cases. Of the nineteen federal courts that had considered the issue, all but three had admitted testimony on battering and its effects in at least some cases. Expert testimony on battering and its effects was most readily accepted by state courts in cases involving traditional self-defense situations—that is, where a battered woman kills her spouse during a direct confrontation. The NCDBW report also found that a vast majority of states found expert testimony to be admissible to prove that the defendant had been a battered woman or that she suffered from BWS. Other findings include that nearly 70 percent of the states have found expert testimony relevant to supporting a self-defense claim and that nearly 70 percent of the states agree that expert testimony is relevant to the issue of the defendant's state of mind at the time of the killing.

The findings and support for the reliability of BWS have been criticized on several grounds. The first critique concerns the two core components of the theory: the cycle of violence and the application of learned helplessness to battered women. These criticisms point to the fact that not all cases involving battered women contain a tension-building stage and a loving, contrite stage. Therefore, it appears from the data gathered on battered women that not all couples go through the cycle of violence articulated by Walker. Some research has also found little support for the applicability of learned helplessness to explain battered women's behavior. This research points to the fact that the majority of women engage in a variety of responses in an attempt to end the abuse. More generally, critics point to the fact that the majority of research on battered women has been limited to clients of shelters for battered women who are not necessarily representative of all battered women.

A second criticism concerning the reliability of BWS concerns whether BWS is a diagnostic category. This issue surfaces when an expert wishes to go beyond describing the general characteristics of BWS and instead offers an opinion about whether the defendant actually suffers from the syndrome. As indicated earlier, BWS is not a diagnosable mental disorder, though some researchers have classified the BWS as a form of PTSD; therefore, the expert may have difficulty articulating a diagnosis and may be challenged by the prosecution if a diagnosis is offered. This criticism can be avoided if the expert describes only the dynamics and consequences of spousal abuse and the similarity between the woman's actions and these phenomena without offering a diagnosis.

In addition to issues concerning the reliability of BWS, the major reason for permitting expert testimony is that it provides jurors with information beyond what is commonly understood. Researchers have questioned whether lay and expert opinions on this issue are significantly different from each other. Some research that compares the knowledge of experts and laypersons has found significant differences in their beliefs about BWS. For example, compared with the experts, laypersons are less likely to believe that a battered woman would be persuaded to remain in the relationship by the abuser's promises in the loving, contrite stage. They were less likely to believe that using deadly force was the only way that women could protect themselves. Laypersons were also more likely to believe that battered women are abused because they are emotionally disturbed. Other research suggests that the general public has become more educated about domestic violence and BWS; therefore, the jury could be fairly well informed on these issues and not need the assistance of expert witness testimony.

Conclusion

BWS as a defense in cases of spousal homicide has gained wide acceptance but remains a controversial issue. Battered women who claim self-defense are more likely to be successful in using BWS to substantiate their claims in situations of direct confrontation with the batterer. In other situations, jurors are more likely to question the claim of self-defense. Battered women who kill their partners are less likely to use the defense of insanity because they must prove that they did not know what they were doing at the time or that what they were doing was wrong. Finally, the use of expert witness testimony concerning BWS can assist the jury in understanding the dynamics of domestic violence and its effects on battered women. However, some researchers and legal scholars remain skeptical about the admissibility of BWS as evidence at trial. These critics question whether BWS is a "syndrome" that can be accurately diagnosed in women who assert their battering experiences as explanations for spousal homicide.

PATRICIA E. ERICKSON

See also **Battered Husbands; Battered Woman Syndrome; Battered Women, Clemency for; Battered Women Who Kill: An Examination; Cohabiting Violence; Compassionate Homicide and Spousal Violence; Cycle of Violence; Domestic Homicide; Domestic Homicide in Urban Centers: New York City; Expert Testimony in Domestic Violence Cases; Fatality Reviews in Adult Domestic Homicide and Suicide; Judicial Perspectives on Domestic Violence; Legal Issues for Battered Women**

References and Further Reading

Browne, Angela. *When Battered Women Kill*. New York: Free Press, 1987.

Downs, Donald A. *More Than Victims: Battered Women, the Syndrome Society, and the Law*. Chicago: University of Chicago Press, 1996.

Ewing, Charles P. *Battered Women Who Kill: Psychological Self-Defense as Legal Justification*. Lexington, MA: Lexington Books, 1987.

Gerdes, Louise, ed. *Battered Woman*. San Diego, CA: Greenhaven Press, 1999.

Leonard, Elizabeth D. *Convicted Survivors: The Imprisonment of Battered Women Who Kill*. Albany: State University of New York Press, 2002.

Morrissey, Belinda. *When Women Kill: Questions of Agency and Subjectivity*. New York: Routledge, 2002.

Parrish, Janet. *Trend Analysis: Expert Testimony on Battering and Its Effects in Criminal Cases*. National Clearinghouse for the Defense of Battered Women, for the National Association of Women Judges for the project "Family Violence and the Courts: Exploring Expert Testimony on Battered Women" (no. A-93-018.DEF), 1994.

Ogle, Robbin S., and Susan Jacobs. *Self Defense and Battered Women Who Kill: A New Framework*. Westport, CT: Praeger Publishers, 2002.

Stewart, Mary W. *Ordinary Violence: Everyday Assaults against Women*. Westport, CT: Bergin and Garvey, 2002.

Walker, Lenore E. *The Battered Woman*. New York: Harper & Row, 1979.

———. *Terrifying Love: Why Battered Women Kill and How Society Responds*. New York: HarperCollins, 1990.

———. *The Battered Woman Syndrome*. New York: Springer Publishing, 2000.

Cases

Ibn-Tamas v. United States, 407 A.2d 626 (1979).

State v. Kelly, 478 A.2d 364 (1984).

BATTERED WOMEN, CLEMENCY FOR

Introduction

Leaving an abusive relationship is difficult for many women. On average, battered women attempt to leave abusive partners approximately five to seven times before they are successfully out of the relationship (Ferraro 1998). There are some women, however, who even after numerous attempts to leave have been unable to get away from their violent partners. Leonard (2002), in interviews with incarcerated battered women who had killed their partners, found that they had tried almost every avenue to seek help. This included turning to friends, family, mental health personnel, law enforcement agencies, medical professionals, members of religious organizations, and battered women's shelters and hotlines. Many of these same women also tried to file for legal separation or divorce. Their attempts to leave or seek help often resulted in the abusive partner becoming more violent. Walker (1989) reported that the batterer often has the mindset that he would rather kill than be left by his partner. Furthermore, many of the agencies (i.e., police, courts, hospitals, and churches) that these women turned to were not able to help due to a lack of understanding about the nature of domestic violence.

When such agencies fail to help, many women feel that they are left deciding between their own lives and the lives of their violent partners (Walker 1989). Death of one of the partners in battering relationships is not uncommon. Statistically, women are more likely than men to be victims of lethal violence by their intimate partners (Browne 1987; Walker 1984). For example, the U.S. Department of Justice (2000) reported that in 1998, 72 percent of homicide victims in intimate relationships were women. When looking at this rate between 1976 and 1997, the female intimate homicide rate remained stable. However, between 1997 and 1998, females killed by their male intimate partners rose by 8 percent. On the other hand, the male intimate homicide rate (males killed by their female intimate partners) decreased by 60 percent between 1976 and 1998. Some professionals attribute this decrease to the increased availability of battered women shelters and crisis centers (Ammons 2003; Browne 1987). These statistics reveal that women are much more likely to be victims of domestic homicide, and their chances of being a victim of lethal violence have not declined over the last few years.

Studies have found that men are more likely to kill when their partners try to leave the relationship (Block and Christakos 1995; Walker 1989), while battered women are more likely to kill in self-defense (Block and Christakos 1995; Gagnè 1998; Leonard 2002; Walker 1989). Walker (1989) reported that very few of the battered women she interviewed who committed homicide killed out of jealousy or revenge. Most battered women who killed reported that they had done so out of fear for their lives. According to their accounts, they had endured emotional, verbal, physical, and sexual abuse before they had killed their partners. They explained that if they had not killed their partners, their partners would have killed them (Beattie and Shaughnessy 2000; Gagnè 1998; Walker 1989).

Gender Bias in the Legal System

Even though it appears that most battered women who kill do so in self-defense, the legal system is often extremely hard on them. Usually women who kill their intimate partners have no prior criminal record (Browne 1987; Walker 1989), yet, these women often receive long and severe sentences (Browne 1987). The claim that battered women are getting away with murder is unfounded (Osthoff 2001). Even with the legal recognition of battered woman syndrome (BWS) in the courts, a large majority (70–80 percent) of abused women charged with killing their partners accepted plea bargains or were convicted and given long sentences in prison rather than having their cases go to trial or being acquitted (U.S. Bureau of Justice Statistics 1995).

Introduced into the criminal justice system in the 1980s, BWS has been used in some states to help explain (through expert testimony) the battered woman's state of mind at the time of a violent incident. BWS is used as a way to explain the reasonableness that the battered woman feared for her life. While BWS is not a defense in itself, it is used to support a legal claim of self-defense (Dutton 1996). In order to do this, an expert on domestic violence is called to testify in court about the effects of battering (Osthoff 2001).

As of 1994, every state in the United States allowed some degree of expert testimony on BWS into the courts (Parrish 1994). However, prior to the acceptance of expert testimony in court, many battered women were not allowed at their trials to reveal the horrific abuse they had endured in their relationships. They were told they could talk about only the events at the time of the killing and therefore were unable to provide a description of the context in which the killing occurred.

Gender Bias in Self-Defense Law

Many feminist legal scholars and battered women advocates have stated that there is an apparent gender bias within the legal system (Gillespie 1989; Schneider 2000). One example of this gender bias is in self-defense law. Historically, women have been viewed as men's property and therefore had no independent legal standing (Pleck 1987). Women are socialized to seek help and protection from men. In this context, women should have no reason to learn how to defend themselves. The primary purpose of self-defense law was the right of individuals to protect themselves or their property from an intruder. Self-defense law was not designed with women's experiences or violence in intimate relationships in mind (Gillespie 1989).

There are two main assumptions in self-defense law. The first is that the person who acted in self-defense did so as a reasonable person. In other words, anyone else in that situation would have acted in the same way. This standard of reasonableness used in some states is based on male status and does not take into account women's experiences. This is considered an objective reasonable person standard (Ogle and Jacobs 2002). If the defendant's behavior is inconsistent with that of a reasonable person (white, middle-class, heterosexual male), she did not act in self-defense.

Scheppele (2004) disagrees with the use of one standard and instead argues that there need to be multiple standards of reasonableness. For instance, a white, lower-income woman with two children in a battering relationship is going to see her options or choices differently from those of a white, middle-class man. The choice to leave or stay in a violent relationship is affected by her lack of income, her lack of social status as a woman (i.e., wage gap, lack of affordable child care), her gender socialization (i.e., caretaker, passive, responsible for success of relationships), and her smaller physical stature as a woman. If she is a woman of color, this brings in other issues, such as dealing with racial prejudice and discrimination. Therefore, some states (Ohio, North Dakota, and Washington) use a subjective reasonable person standard (Ogle and Jacobs 2002). The subjective standard assesses whether the person truly felt she was in imminent danger. The jury must ask themselves if the defendant is really telling the truth when she says she feared for her life (Ogle and Jacobs 2002). Just as with the objective reasonable person standard, there has also been dissent about the subjective reasonable person standard. The legal system worries that with the subjective standard, anybody could argue self-defense and state that he or she was in imminent danger. Therefore, there has been a move toward trying to combine the two standards. When states do so, they will assess imminent danger based on a reasonable person similar to the defendant, with comparable resources and knowledge. Thus, a battered woman could be compared with other battered women (Ogle and Jacobs 2002). No states have actually adopted the blending of the two standards, though cases in Ohio, Oklahoma, and South Dakota have applied the idea of combining the objective and subjective standards (Ogle and Jacobs 2002).

The second assumption of self-defense law is that the person acted as he or she did because of a belief of being in imminent danger. "Imminent danger" means that in that moment in time, the person feared for his/her life. This assumes that the defense should occur *during* an attack, not before or after, and that once the attack is over, the victim is no longer in imminent danger. Imminent danger in abusive relationships is experienced as a constant for many battered women who are in fear for their lives over time, not just during a violent episode (Gillespie 1989).

One other area of self-defense law that is biased against women is the assumption that the two people fighting are of equal size, height, weight, and physical build. Furthermore, self-defense law states that excessive force should not be used to defend oneself. Only if the attacker is armed can an individual use a weapon to defend him/herself (Gillespie 1989). When applying this to a violent intimate relationship, it does not take into account that a person's body can be used as a weapon. Walker (1989) found that weapons had not injured most of the abused women she interviewed, but instead the injuries had resulted from their partner's own fists. Many of these women reported being thrown across the room, hit, punched, kicked, stomped on, and choked. For these women, using a gun or a knife was the only way they could successfully defend themselves (Ogle and Jacobs 2002).

However, in most contemporary societies, women are not taught to use firearms (Gillespie 1989). Many battered women who use a weapon to defend themselves do not fully comprehend the lethality of it. There have also been instances in which battered women shot or stabbed their partners not once, but numerous times, claiming that they truly believed that their partner was invincible and that he could never be killed (Walker 1989). According to self-defense law, these women used "excessive force," which is defined as more force than is necessary to defend oneself (Gillespie 1989).

If juries are told to assess whether or not a battered woman killed in self-defense based only on the legal criteria, the abused woman could easily be convicted of homicide rather than justifiable homicide (Gillespie 1989). A defendant must prove she acted in perfect self-defense to get a not-guilty verdict. Perfect self-defense requires that the defendant truly believes she was acting in part to save her life and that her belief of imminent danger was realistic based on an objective standard (Ogle and Jacobs 2002). As stated earlier, this objective standard may vary from state to state. If, however, she shows that she truly believed she was in danger but her state of mind was not reasonable, she could be found guilty of imperfect self-defense and charged with varying degrees of homicide (Ogle and Jacobs 2002). One response to this bias in self-defense law has been the use of BWS to aid in the defense of

battered women who use violence against their partners.

Clemency for Battered Women

One of the early questions the battered women's movement dealt with was how to help battered women who had killed or attempted to kill their partners. Activists lobbied for the inclusion of BWS testimony in court hearings in cases in which battered women had killed their abusive partners. Because it took so long for the battered women's movement to effect changes in the legal system, activists had to change their focus on how to help battered women who were incarcerated. Activists argued that abused women who had killed their partners were imprisoned unlawfully and that it was important for the state to reconsider these cases and grant these women clemency. Clemency has been defined as a "generic legal term that includes any executive act that reduces or alleviates a penalty for a crime" (Gagnè 1998, p. 29). Many battered women's advocates view clemency as a way to provide justice for abused women who had been unable to defend themselves using the BWS in court.

The decision to grant a battered woman clemency is not always easy. The United States has afforded governors and presidents both political and legal power in this regard. The purpose of clemency is to ensure that our legal system is working effectively and justly. It may be considered one of the checks and balances of our judicial system. However, because governors and presidents are also political actors, they are influenced greatly by public opinion (Ammons 2003). The public's voice is usually the loudest when it comes to granting clemency to cases involving a homicide. It could be political suicide for governors or presidents to appear soft on crime. Therefore, the governor or president must justify his/her decision to the public and reassure society that a dangerous criminal is not being released (Ammons 2003).

Ohio was the first state to allow a mass clemency review of imprisoned women for crimes related to their history as victims of battering. Dagmar Celeste (wife to then Ohio governor Richard Celeste) was instrumental in this first attempt at a mass clemency for battered women (Gagnè 1998). In 1990, Governor Celeste granted clemency to 25 battered women in Ohio. By the end of his term, he had granted clemency to a total of 28 incarcerated battered women (27 were commuted; 1 on parole was pardoned) (Ammons, 2003). There were two other states that followed suit with mass clemencies for battered women convicted of crimes. Governor William Donald Schaefer granted clemency to 8 battered women in Maryland in 1991, and Kentucky governor Brereton Jones granted clemency to 9 battered women in 1996 (National Clearinghouse for the Defense of Battered Women 2003). Overall there have been a total of 125 battered women granted clemency from twenty-three states (42 of these from Ohio, Maryland, and Kentucky).

Ammons (2003) followed up with the governors of the states that granted clemency to these battered women, finding that they had a variety of reasons for why they granted these women clemency (e.g., illness, punishment too severe, BWS, sufficient time served, ineffective counsel). The most cited reason was that the governors felt that these women were "trapped in relationships because of a mental deficiency, a 'syndrome'" (p. 557). The second most cited reason was that these women had been unable to tell about the battering in their relationships at the time of the trial. Rather than the governors justifying these women's actions, they excused them based on the abuse they had endured and society's failure to help them.

It is important to keep in mind that all of these women (with the exception of the one woman in Ohio) had their sentences commuted. A commutation replaces the original punishment/sentence with a less severe one (Sheehy, Reinberg, and Kirchwey 1991). Thus, many of these women still had to serve some type of sentence and/or go before the parole board. Appearing before the parole board was not always a guarantee that parole would be granted. A commutation also does not exonerate the person of the crimes he/she has committed. These battered women still had to deal with having a felony conviction that stripped away many of their civil liberties and made it difficult for them to find employment and housing.

Clemency and Recidivism

Even though these women have difficulties finding employment with a felony conviction, the majority have been able to live violence-free lives. There was great public upheaval over granting convicted battered women clemency because many in society worried that these women would kill again. Ammons (2003) researched the recidivism rate for the twenty-eight women in Ohio who were granted clemency in 1990. The overall recidivism rate for female violent offenders was 23 percent. The clemency recipients' recidivism rate for a felony murder was 0 percent. Ammons found that one woman

had a drug-related charge against her and another woman a property offense. Two women have since passed away (Schneider 2006). The rest of these women are leading crime-free lives.

Issues Confronting Women Who Do Get Clemency

Gagnè (1998) conducted a qualitative study with women who had been incarcerated in the Ohio prison system for killing their abusive partners and received clemency. Gagnè interviewed eleven of the twenty-five women who were granted clemency in Ohio in 1990 soon after they were released from prison. The interviews revealed that women who received clemency felt that killing their abusive partner had been their only option. They said they had felt trapped and that they had had no other viable options to stop the abuse. They also felt that if they had not killed their abusive partners, they would have been killed instead. Furthermore, these women discussed at length how they felt they had been victimized repeatedly by unsympathetic social service agencies as well as the judicial system.

Another study on battered women's lives after clemency was conducted by Beattie and Shaughnessy (2000). They conducted oral history interviews in 1995 with nine battered women who became eligible for parole at the Kentucky Correctional Institution and were granted clemency. All of the women talked about lives filled with childhood abuse (most often sexual) and how this abuse continued into adulthood when they entered into intimate relationships. These women described relationships filled with horrific abuse and communities where no one seemed to care. They spoke of contacting authorities and being victimized repeatedly by people who refused to do anything. For example, one woman told the story of her community being so afraid of her partner that when she would call the police, the police would stand at the bottom of her driveway and yell at her husband. The police in this instance were so terrified of this man that they would not come face to face with him. As a result they let him abuse his wife for years and did nothing to stop him.

The interviews in both studies revealed that these battered women felt they had killed in self-defense to end the abuse. They tried to seek help before they acted and were unsuccessful. They feared for their lives and felt they had no options. These women also spoke of great inequities within the criminal justice/legal system during their questioning, arrest, sentencing, and trial. Many were unfamiliar with the court system and were terrified of losing their children (which was often used as a threat). They spoke of inadequate representation and attorneys who were not sensitive to battered women. Some of the women talked about being scared to talk about the battering because their attorney was a male. Others talked about their attorney dismissing the battering and not wanting to bring it up because he/she was not familiar with laws pertaining to battered women (Beattie and Shaughnessy 2000; Gagnè 1998).

Once these women were given the opportunity to apply for clemency and were granted it, they spoke of their lives after prison. Because in both Ohio and Kentucky these women were not pardoned (removal of felony conviction and exoneration), but instead had their sentences commuted (replacement of less severe punishment), they still had a felony conviction on their record (Sheehy, Reinberg, and Kirchwey 1991). This had a huge impact on their life after clemency, as it was difficult for them to find employment, housing, and assistance. These women struggled with reestablishing their relationships with their children, and many suffered from depression and anxiety. The majority commented that without the help of their family, they could not have made it on their own (Beattie and Shaughnessy 2000; Gagnè 1998).

One of the most difficult things women granted clemency had to deal with was having a prison record. Due to the fact that in both states the women had their sentences commuted and were not pardoned, their felony convictions stayed with them. This influenced everything in their lives outside of prison, from gaining employment to obtaining adequate housing to how individuals (family, friends, and community workers) related to them. In Gagnè's (1998) sample, none of the women were able to go back to the places where they had been employed prior to their incarceration due to their felony convictions. In both studies the women talked about how finding employment was one of the most difficult challenges and that they relied heavily on family for financial support after release from prison.

Related to finding employment is finding adequate housing. One of the conditions of leaving prison is often to report the address where you will live outside of prison. For many women, this is the only prerelease planning they are given (O'Brien 2001). Most of the women in both studies reported living with family after release. However, there were a couple of women who had no family and had to rely on halfway homes. These women had been in prison most of their lives for killing their abusive stepfathers and had a really hard time adjusting to life outside of prison, since that was the life they knew best (Gagnè 1998).

Another major hurdle the clemency recipients had to deal with was reuniting with their children. In some cases, due to parole conditions, the women were not allowed to see their children. In other situations the children were still very angry and blamed their mothers for their own victimization by their fathers, stepfathers, or mothers' boyfriends. Some women dealt with older children who had become caught up in their own abusive relationships, and these women had to figure out how to help in a way that was not too aggressive. The women tried very hard to reconnect with their children, but it was not something that came easy. This experience is common for mothers who have served time in prison (Hunter 2005).

Some women also had to contend with the family of the abusive partners they had used violence against. One woman in Beattie and Shaughnessy's (2000) study reported that due to parole conditions, she could not contact her abuser's family; however, they continued to contact her through harassing phone calls. Another clemency recipient from Ohio talked about the fear of seeing her abusive partner, who had survived the attack. Because of victim's rights, he was contacted when she was let out of prison, yet she had no protection from him (Gagnè 1998).

These women also had to deal with the decision of whether to get involved in another intimate relationship. The majority talked at great length about their fear of commitment and mistrust of everyone. One woman spoke of still wearing her wedding ring because she still felt controlled by her husband even though he was dead (Beattie and Shaughnessy 2001). Some women from both studies ended up in abusive relationships again. Some of these women were able to get out of these relationships, while others were still trying to figure out how to disentangle themselves from the vicious cycle of abuse. Gagnè (1998) reported that the women who had had abusive childhoods (especially sexual abuse) had an extremely hard time moving into a life free of abuse. Many of the women chose not to have any intimate relationships because of a lack of trust.

Granting clemency to incarcerated battered women is only a small step in providing justice for battered women who defend themselves. Because of their felony convictions, it is not easy for these women to enter back into society. They are continually victimized over and over again as they are denied employment, housing, and custody of their children, repeatedly reinforcing the fact that they are on their own. Prior to incarceration, many of these women dealt with poverty, racism, and sexism. Post-prison they face the same barriers, and now they have a felony conviction to contend with as well (Richie 2001). Gagnè (1998) found that support groups in prison aided in the reintegration of women back into society post-prison. However, Richie (2001) reported that the counseling, support groups, mental and physical health care, and educational/employment services that prisons offer are minimal. Many of the women in Richie's study (incarcerated for a variety of offenses, not just killing/attempting to kill battering partners) stated that they were not prepared at all for life after prison. They suffered from PTSD and multiple mental and physical health issues, and those with addiction problems had difficulty maintaining sobriety.

Issues Confronting Women Denied Clemency

Women who are denied clemency are confronted with the reality that the governor and/or parole board do not justify or excuse their actions to use violence against their battering partner. Schneider (2006) interviewed eleven incarcerated battered women in Ohio who were denied clemency. These women, just as the women who received clemency, reported lives filled with abuse. They were also confronted with societal indifference and felt that the abuse they endured was condoned. They reported that they felt their lives or their children's lives were in danger and that they had had no other choice but to kill in self-defense. Unfortunately, many of these women spoke of inadequate attorneys and witnesses who testified against them in their trials. Furthermore, these battered women were not like the "stereotypical battered woman." They had character flaws (i.e., they drank alcohol or used drugs, they'd had extramarital affairs, and they denied the abuse their children endured from their partner), which hurt them in their trials as well as in the clemency proceedings.

These women continue to live their lives incarcerated within a system which they reported is not rehabilitative. They stated that rehabilitation came from inside each person. They reported that some prison support groups were available, but because most of the women have life sentences, they have completed the majority of the programming and there is very little left for them to take while in prison. Many of them have tried to further their education by completing their general equivalency degree (GED) and taking college courses. Unfortunately, due to budget cuts and overcrowding at the prison, much of the college programming has been cut. For example, prisoners are no longer able to earn a college degree in the Ohio prisons, only certificates. They have taken it upon themselves to start battered women support groups and have started to look at themselves as survivors rather than victims. However, this change in identity is a double-edged sword. When these women go before the parole board, the board does not want to hear that they have survived years of abuse and were justified in defending themselves. Therefore, most of the women have life sentences and remain in prison, where the parole board continually denies them an exit to the outside world.

Furthermore, these women struggled with not being able to see their children. Most of the children ended up living with family. Unfortunately, some living situations for these children have been as abusive as their home life prior to their mother going to prison. Some of the children were bounced around from one foster home to the next. Some of the women have been able to keep in touch with their children, while others have struggled with the reality that they may never see their children again. These women have missed out on their children's entire childhoods, as many were sent to prison when their children were just in elementary school. Reestablishing a relationship with their children will most likely be very difficult, if and when they are released from prison.

If these women do get out of prison, they will face many of the same challenges that the women who received clemency faced. However, these women will be unable to say to their communities that they were legally justified or excused for killing (or attempting to kill) their violent partners or family members. These women will most likely have difficulty finding employment, will have little social support, and will be faced with communities that view them as killers.

Conclusion

Clemency is a way to ensure our legal system is really just and fair. It is a way to provide "justice . . . when you get what you deserve, mercy . . . when you don't get what you deserve, or grace . . . when you get what you don't deserve" (Ammons 2003, p. 551). Clemency gave a voice to battered women and allowed society to hear about the abuse these women endured. Unfortunately, society has heard very little about the hardships these women encountered after clemency or the structural factors that affected battered women who were denied clemency. Many feminist scholars feel that clemency is just one small step toward equality for women and that there is much more that needs to be done

(Beattie and Shaughnessy 2000; Gagnè 1998; Schneider 2006).

One clemency recipient in Gagnè's (1998) study stated that she wanted her life back along with her freedom and that she feels she has neither since she has been out of prison. She has struggled with alcohol addiction, lack of employment, physical and mental health problems from the abuse in her past, and frustration with her inability to obtain adequate housing because of her felony record. Society obviously needs to do much more to support battered women. It is not enough to just give them a "get out of jail free card"; society must also provide the services they so greatly need and are unable to obtain.

There needs to be more research on life after clemency, and these women's stories must be told to the public. This information could help alleviate sources of strain and aid in helping incarcerated women adjust to life outside once they are released from prison. Furthermore, these women's stories also need to be shared so that the public understands what clemency means and that there is empirical support that shows that these women are not career criminals. Ammons (2003) found that the assumption that battered women are dangerous criminals is unfounded and that these women's violent actions were isolated incidents. Policymakers must hear these women's stories so as to understand the changes needed in our criminal justice system, hospitals, churches, and neighborhoods.

RACHEL ZIMMER SCHNEIDER

See also **Battered Woman Syndrome; Battered Women Who Kill: An Examination; Batterer Intervention Programs; Batterer Typology; Cohabiting Violence; Dating Violence; Divorce, Child Custody, and Domestic Violence; Domestic Violence Courts; Expert Witnesses in Domestic Violence Cases; Fatality Reviews in Adult Domestic Homicide and Suicide; Intimate Partner Homicide; Shelter Movement; Stalking; Victim Blaming Theory**

References and Further Reading

Ammons, Linda L. "Why Do You Do the Things You Do? Clemency for Battered Incarcerated Women, a Decade's Review." *American University Journal of Gender and Social Policy and Law* 11 (2003): 533–566.

Beattie, L. Elisabeth, and Mary Angela Shaughnessy. *Sisters in Pain: Battered Women Fight Back.* Lexington: University Press of Kentucky, 2000.

Block, Carolyn Rebecca, and Antigone Christakos. "Intimate Partner Homicide in Chicago Over 29 Years." *Crime and Delinquency* 41 (2003): 496–526.

Browne, A. *When Battered Women Kill.* New York: Free Press, 1987.

Dutton, Mary Ann. "Impact of Evidence Concerning Battering and Its Effects in Criminal Trials Involving Battered Women." In *The Validity and Use of Evidence Concerning Battering and Its Effects in Criminal Trials.* Washington, DC: U.S. Departments of Justice and Health and Human Services, 1996.

Ferraro, Kathleen. "Battered Women: Strategies for Survival." *In Public and Private Families: A Reader,* edited by Andrew J. Cherlin. Newbury Park, CA: Sage, 1998.

Gagnè, Patricia. *Battered Women's Justice: The Movement for Clemency and the Politics of Self-Defense.* New York: Twayne Publishers, 1998.

Gillespie, Cynthia K. *Justifiable Homicide: Battered Women, Self-Defense, and the Law.* Columbus: Ohio State University Press, 1989.

Hunter, Vicki. *Transitions in Mothering: The Social Construction of Motherhood and Its Implications for the Experiences of Recently Released Mothers.* Doctoral dissertation, Kent State University, 2005.

Leonard, Elizabeth Dermody. *Convicted Survivors: The Imprisonment of Battered Women Who Kill.* Albany: State University of New York Press, 2002.

National Clearinghouse for the Defense of Battered Women. "Clemency Organizing Projects." Philadelphia: Author, 2003.

O'Brien, Patricia. *Making It in the "Free World": Women in Transition from Prison.* Albany: State University of New York Press, 2001.

Ogle, Robbin S., and Susan Jacobs. *Self-Defense and Battered Women Who Kill: A New Framework.* Westport, CT: Praeger, 2002.

Osthoff, Sue. "When Victims Become Defendants: Battered Women Charged with Crimes." In *Women, Crime, and Criminal Justice,* edited by Claire Renzetti and Lynne Goodstein. Los Angeles: Roxbury, 2001.

Parrish, Janet. *Trend Analysis: Expert Testimony on Battering and Its Effects in Criminal Cases.* National Clearinghouse for the Defense of Battered Women/National Association of Women Judges for the project "Family Violence and the Courts: Exploring Expert Testimony on Battered Women" (no. A-93-018.DEF), 1994.

Pleck, Elizabeth. *Domestic Tyranny: The Making of Social Policy against Family Violence from Colonial Times to the Present.* New York: Oxford University Press, 1987.

Richie, Beth E. "Challenges Incarcerated Women Face as They Return to Their Communities from Life History Interviews." *Crime and Delinquency* 47 (2001): 368–389.

Scheppele, Kim Lane. "Inequality and Gender: The Reasonable Woman," 2004. In *Philosophy of Law,* edited by Joel Feinberg and Jules Coleman. Belmont, CA: Wadsworth.

Schneider, Elizabeth M. *Battered Women and Feminist Lawmaking.* New Haven, CT: Yale University Press, 2000.

Schneider, Rachel Zimmer. *Battered Women and Violent Crime: An Exploration of Imprisoned Women before and after the Clemency Movement.* Doctoral dissertation, University of Akron, 2006.

Sheehy, Lisa, Melissa Reinberg, and Deborah Kirchwey. *Commutation for Women Who Defended Themselves against Abusive Partners: An Advocacy Manual and Guide to Legal Issues.* Philadelphia: National Clearinghouse for the Defense of Battered Women, 1991.

U.S. Bureau of Justice Statistics. *Spouse Murder Defendants in Large Urban Counties*. Washington, DC: Author, 1995.

U.S. Department of Justice. *Homicide Trends in the U.S.: Intimate Homicide*. Washington, DC: Author, 2000.

Walker, Lenore. *The Battered Woman Syndrome*. New York: Springer, 1984.

———. *Terrifying Love: Why Battered Women Kill and How Society Responds*. New York: Harper & Row, 1989.

BATTERED WOMEN: HELD IN CAPTIVITY

From a sociological feminist perspective, a battering relationship is one of captivity, and battered women are survivors of terror. Battering is an obsessive campaign of coercion and intimidation designed by a man to dominate and control a woman, which occurs in the personal context of intimacy and thrives in the sociopolitical climate of patriarchy. For the woman it is a terrifying process of progressive entrapment into an intimate relationship of subjection that is promoted and preserved by a social order steeped in gender hierarchy—a social order in which mainstream ideology and social institutions and organizations, including the criminal justice system, the church, social service and medical institutions, the family, and the community, recognize male privilege and accordingly relegate a secondary status to women.

Sometimes physical violence is incorporated into the battering agenda. When less risky intimidation strategies such as yelling, threatening, stalking, and harming the family pet fail, a man may have to resort to assaulting his mate—with all implied potential for serious injury or even death—in order to maintain control over her. In the face of defiance or even simple resistance on the part of the woman, or perhaps because he for some reason independent of the woman's behavior perceives a threat to his control, he may feel forced to appeal to her most basic need for physical safety. That is what battering is all about: a man using male privilege derived from a patriarchal social structure to coerce a woman, sometimes through fear for her very life, into an exploitive intimate relationship that holds her hostage and in servitude to his personal needs and desires. With the weight of society behind him, a man is able to gain deference, and all that goes with it, from a woman.

Men are able to intimidate and coerce women to their benefit because society favors men and thwarts women at every turn (Acker 1989; Lorber 1994: 298). It orchestrates women's emotional and economic dependence on men. Girls are taught to believe that in order to be whole they must please and be desired by men. The socialization of women emphasizes the primary value of being a good wife and mother at the expense of personal achievement and satisfaction in other realms of life. It is no surprise, then, that United States women who are employed full-time earn, on average, about 75 percent of the amount earned by their male counterparts. Indeed, women are programmed to willfully play into a social order that minimizes their value and sense of self-worth and oppresses them.

Battering takes two: a man and a patriarchy. Battering is comprehensive in that it includes both interpersonal and societal forms of gendered abuse. It represents the convergence of one man (the batterer), obsessed with controlling a particular woman and willing to abuse her to gain and maintain that control, with a social order that delivers that woman to him and helps hold her there as hostage. Patriarchal culture creates a generalized climate of risk in which all men are allowed to, and particular men will, batter women. Battered women, then, constitute one of the numerous categories of women (including victims of stalking, sexual harassment, incest, and rape) who fall prey to men's individual as well as collective oppression.

Using this sociological definition of battering, there can be no battered men: Men can be treated unfairly and even severely abused by women, but they cannot be battered, because to be battered requires a social order antagonistic to one's gender. To be battered means to be blocked by the gendered nature of society from escaping an abuser. Simplistically stated, men cannot be battered because they can leave their abusers. In a patriarchal society, a woman cannot hold a man captive through conventional dynamics of romantic intimacy. Hypothetically, men could be battered, but only in a matriarchal society—if one were to exist. In the meantime, one can only imagine such a state of affairs the likes of which is depicted by Gerd Brantenberg (1985) in her fictional account of a fishing village named Egalia. The ideal, of course, would be an equalitarian society, where no one could be battered.

From the perspective offered here, battered women can be viewed as political prisoners because their captivity is a political act or process in that it operates as both a manifestation and a reinforcement of social-structured power imbalance. With the more conventional forms of politically based hostage-taking, where operatives of terrorist governments or special interest groups overpower military or civilian personnel, the power imbalance is one between governments and/or special interest groups, whereas with battering, the power imbalance is sourced in gender inequality.

This interpretation of battered women as hostages and survivors of terror has occupied a niche in feminist scholarship since the emergence of the neo-feminist movement in the 1970s. One path has been to explore battered women's psychological processes as explanations for their captivity. Some neo-feminist writings rejected traditional psychological theories that suggested that battered women love and remain with their abusers because of female masochism, in favor of an alternate interpretation attributing such behavior to the woman's psychological response to power imbalance. These feminist scholars explained the battered woman experience as an example of the Stockholm Syndrome, which is a framework developed to account for the paradoxical psychological responses of hostages to their captors (Dutton and Painter 1981; Finkelhor and Yllo 1985; Hilberman 1980). With the discovery of the Stockholm Syndrome and its eventual application to the understanding of woman abuse in the context of intimacy, one psychological theory was replaced with another. And in that sense, the woman continued to be blamed for her victimization.

The Stockholm Syndrome is a survival strategy observed among a variety of captives in hostage-taking situations, including concentration camp prisoners, cult members, prisoners of war, and physically and/or emotionally abused children. It is characterized by a relationship of solidarity initiated by the captive with his or her captor perhaps in a subconscious attempt to gain the captor's sympathy and leniency. The syndrome is named after the 1973 robbery of the Kreditbanken at Norrmalmstorg, Stockholm, Sweden, in which four bank employees were held hostage for six days by two men. During that time, the hostages and their captors bonded bidirectionally. After six days of being bound with dynamite and being generally mistreated, several hostages actually resisted rescue attempts, believing that their captors were protecting them from the police. Afterward, they refused to testify against their captors. Following the release of the hostages, one of the women became engaged to one of the captors, and another hostage initiated a "defense fund" for the legal expenses of the captors.

Four conditions give rise to the Stockholm Syndrome: (1) perceived threat to one's physical or psychological survival and the belief that the captor(s) will carry out the threat, (2) perceived small kindnesses from the captor(s) to the captive(s) (allowing the captive to live is enough), (3) isolation from perspectives other than those of captor(s), and (4) perceived inability to escape. The Stockholm Syndrome model predicts that when hostages are faced with these four conditions, they may forge a strong emotional bond with their captor(s) as well as an antipathy toward authorities working for their release. They will claim to love their captor(s) for their show of kindness during captivity. For example, the kidnapped hitchhiker Colleen Stan, who was held captive and tortured by Cameron Hooker for seven years, some of those years closed up in a wooden box, justified her love for Cameron with stories of his kindnesses, including his once bringing her an extra plate of pancakes. How wonderful he was for that kindness, she thought. After all, he could have killed her, but instead he gave her an extra plate of food (McGuire and Norton 1988).

It is the contention of this author that all battered women are hostages, but that not all battered women have fallen prey to the Stockholm Syndrome. Every battered woman, according to the definition offered here, is held captive by a man who chooses to use his male privilege derived from a patriarchal society to hold her in servitude. A woman's psychological processes, including those designated as Stockholm Syndrome, can fortify her social-structural captivity. Essentially it is the gendered nature of society that holds her captive, but that captivity can be reinforced by psychological processes.

ANN GOETTING

See also **Battered Woman Syndrome; Battered Woman Syndrome as a Legal Defense in Cases of Spousal Homicide; Battered Women, Clemency for; Battered Women Who Kill: An Examination; Cycle of Violence; Lesbian Battering; Social Class and Domestic Violence; Stockholm Syndrome in Battered Women**

References and Further Reading

Acker, Joan. "Making Gender Visible." In *Feminism and Sociological Theory,* ed. Ruth A. Wallace. Thousand Oaks, CA: Sage, 1989.

Brantenberg, Gerd. *Egalia's Daughters: A Satire of the Sexes.* Seattle: Seal Press, 1985.

Brownmiller, Susan. *Against Our Will: Men, Women, and Rape.* New York: Simon and Schuster, 1975.

Dutton, Don, and Susan Lee Painter. "Traumatic Bonding: The Development of Emotional Attachments in Battered Women and Other Relationships of Intermittent Abuse." *Victimology* 6, nos. 1–4 (1981).

Finkelhor, David, and Kersti Yllo. *License to Rape: Sexual Abuse of Wives.* New York: Holt, Rinehart and Winston, 1985.

Goetting, Ann. *Getting Out: Life Stories of Women Who Left Abusive Men.* New York: Columbia University Press, 1999.

Graham, Dee L. R., and Edna Rawlings. "Bonding with Abusive Dating Partners: Dynamics of Stockholm Syndrome." In *Dating Violence, Women and Danger,* ed. Barrie Levy. Seattle: Seal Press, 1991.

Hilberman, Elaine. "Overview: The 'Wife-Beaters' Wife' Reconsidered." *American Journal of Psychiatry* 137, no. 11 (1980).

Lorber, Judith. *Paradoxes of Gender.* New Haven, CT: Yale University Press, 1994.

MacKinnon, Catherine A. "Feminism, Marxism, Method and the State: Toward a Feminist Jurisprudence." *Signs* 8, no. 4 (1983).

McGuire, Christine, and Carla Norton. *Perfect Victim: The True Story of "The Girl in the Box."* New York: Dell Publishing, 1988.

Walker, Lenore E. *The Battered Woman.* New York: Harper and Row, 1979.

BATTERED WOMEN WHO KILL: AN EXAMINATION

Since the 1990s, there has been a growing interest in the battered woman and the violence that permeates her life. Battering is a difficult topic, because it exists in the privacy of the family home, grows in silence and shame, and has historically been acceptable and even expected from male heads of households. In reality, the very large majority of battered women do not resort to killing their abusers in order to survive. In fact, far more women are killed each year by their abusers. Most of these women suffer devastating injuries in silence and simply attempt to placate their abusers, hoping to reduce the amount and severity of the beatings. However, each year a small number of abused women do kill their abusers as a last resort. Most of these women have attempted to seek help from family, community, and criminal justice resources, with negative results. Oftentimes, the failure of these resources has the unintended effect of increasing the amount and severity of the violence. This leaves some women believing that they are alone in their situation and must decide between their survival and death.

In discussing this phenomenon, this article will explore the research available on the following topics:

- History of battering legality
- Women and homicide
- Battering and homicide
- Battered women who kill
- Two theories on why battered women kill

History of Battering Legality

In order to understand why a battered woman would resort to killing her abuser, it is first necessary to examine the failure of resources attempting to address battering. Battering flourishes even though it is now illegal, because these resources fail to stop it entirely. One of the reasons that resources fail is the history of battering and society's difficulty with criminalizing formerly acceptable behavior.

Throughout most of world history, women have not only been treated as second-class citizens, but also considered property of their fathers, husbands, and other male family members rather than as citizens in their own right. This has been the case under the secular law as well as the tenets of most of the religions of the world. Historically, religious institutions were responsible for defining and performing social control. Most of these traditions demand or at least support the submission of all family members to the control of the male head of household. Consequently, they require this male to take responsibility for maintaining control and discipline of family members by whatever means necessary, including corporal punishment (Belknap 1992; Davidson 1977; Dobash and Dobash 1979; Gordon 1989; Gosselin 2000; Ogle and Jacobs 2002; Pleck 1983, 1987).

For example, some scholars point to the specificity of the Bible concerning the subordination of women to men and the need for men to use corporal punishment in order to maintain control over and protect the chastity of their women (Davidson 1977; Davis 1971; Gosselin 2000; Masters 1964). Other scholars note that in medieval times, the church required men to maintain complete and absolute control of wives and children and advised that failure to do so would result in their own punishment by the church (Dutton 1998; Masters 1964; Pushkareva 1997). Some of these scholars indicate that the church went as far as to warn men to be careful not to beat women and children about the head, because this could cause irreparable damage to their property (Masters 1964).

As secular governments began to take responsibility for social control, little changed with regard to the status or treatment of women. For example, under Roman civil law, women were property just like slaves, without legal or human rights. Male ownership included the right to buy, sell, punish, or impose death on his property (Gosselin 2000; Masters 1964). Gosselin (2000) notes that in the French civil code of the late 1700s women were declared to be legal minors for the entirety of their lives and the property of their fathers or husbands. Such laws also required corporal punishment of wives, including punching, kicking the body, and permanent disfigurement—especially injuries that were easily observable by others in order to increase her shame (Dobash and Dobash 1978; Gosselin 2000; Pagelow 1984).

When Blackstone codified the British common law in 1768, he included rules on the status of women and the use of corporal punishment to control them. This code says that man and woman become one entity by marriage and the woman's legal existence ceases (Dobash and Dobash 1979;

Gosselin 2000; Pagelow 1984). Even more specifically, it establishes the "rule of thumb" indicating that a husband had the legal right and responsibility to control and punish his wife but that he should do so with a rod no bigger around than his thumb (Dutton 1998; Gosselin 2000; Ogle and Jacobs 2002; Pagelow 1984; Ulrich 1991). Of course, this code formed the foundation for law established by Britain in the United States and remained in place there in similar form until the late twentieth century.

In essence, battering has long been a well-established tradition in both religion and secular government throughout the world. Even though some governments have made battering illegal, it continues to flourish everywhere, alongside rape, as a successful method of controlling women. Unfortunately, most efforts to address battering have consisted mainly of women's support groups, shelters, and hotlines, rather than a coordinated social and legal systemic attack on battering and batterers, which would have a broader reach and likely be more effective.

Women and Homicide

There has been quite a bit of research done on women who kill, likely because murder is an aggressive, violent act that falls considerably outside the passive, submissive role expectations for women. This extreme variation has enticed researchers since the nineteenth century. Consequently, social science research provides a significant amount of information on women who kill, and this article will attempt to give a useful overview of these findings.

Women do not often kill; in fact, only about 10 percent of homicides in any given year are committed by women. When women kill, they most often kill intimates: husbands, lovers, or children. The large majority of these killings are actually battered women killing their abusers in order to survive (Browne 1987; Dobash, Dobash, Wilson, and Daly 1992; Federal Bureau of Investigation 1993, 1998; Hart 1991, 1996; Ogle and Jacobs 2002). As a result, homicides committed by women, as opposed to those by men, present fairly consistent characteristics and circumstances (Browne 1987; Browne and Williams 1989; Ewing 1987; Goetting 1988; Jones 1980; Jurik and Winn 1990; Ogle and Jacobs 2002; Ogle, Maier-Katkin, and Bernard 1995; Wolfgang 1958). Women most often kill in the home, likely because they spend much more time in the home than men (Goetting 1988; Ogle et al. 1995; Totman 1978). Women generally kill alone without co-conspirators, and their victims have usually provoked the homicidal attack (Browne 1987; Ewing 1987; Goetting 1988; Jones 1980; Ogle et al. 1995; Roberts 1996; Wolfgang 1958). These killings generally involve explosive, sudden aggression rather than a planned attack (Browne 1987; Ewing 1987; Goetting 1988; Jones 1980; Ogle et al. 1995; Roberts 1996; Wolfgang 1958). In addition, women killers tend to be more socially conforming and traditional in their sex roles and relationships than other women (Blackman 1988; Browne 1987; Ewing 1987; Goetting 1988; Jones 1980; Ogle et al. 1995; Ogle and Jacobs 2002; Widom 1979). These women often indicate that they were suffering from severe depression and despair when they committed the homicide (Browne 1987; Ewing 1987; Goetting 1988; Jones 1980; Ogle et al. 1995; Ogle and Jacobs 2002; Piven and Cloward 1979; Totman 1978; Widom 1979).

Homicides committed by women of a lower socioeconomic class are higher in number, as are homicides committed by women of color (i.e., about eight murders by a woman of color for every one murder by a white woman) (Block and Christakos 1995; Mercy and Saltzman 1989; Websdale 1999). However, these killings do not vary much from the above pattern (Dawson and Langan 1994; Ewing 1987; Goetting 1988; Jones 1980; Ogle et al. 1995; Ogle and Jacobs 2002). It should be noted that some scholars believe that this difference in homicide rates is a result of socioeconomic status rather than race or ethnicity (Centerwall 1984; Stark and Flitcraft 1996). These patterns represent a rich picture of the characteristics of homicides committed by women and have provided scholars with sufficient information to formulate theories on why battered women kill.

Battering and Homicide

Although there is yet to be agreement among researchers, there is evidence in the research to support the existence of two types of domestic violence. Johnson (1995) attempts to delineate these two specific types of battering relationships: (1) common couple violence and (2) patriarchal terrorism. *Common couple violence* involves minor violence and reciprocity of assaults between partners. In other words, both parties participate in the violence toward each other. This type of violence occurs less often and generally only when the couple is experiencing an extremely stressful situation. *Patriarchal terrorism* involves the victim being systematically terrorized by the other partner. In this

type of battering, the violence is both more serious and more frequent. The qualitative data on battered women indicate that these may be the cases most likely to escalate to homicides. The most common victim of homicide in a battering relationship is the battering victim. In the United States, about two or three thousand women are killed each year by their batterers. In contrast, only about five hundred battered women kill their abusers each year. There is evidence that these numbers may be decreasing where social and legal resources are more successful (Browne and Williams 1989; Bureau of Justice Statistics 1998; Websdale 1999). However, there is also evidence that a significant number of battering homicides may never be recorded as such because the batterer has been successful at hiding the situation, the police fail to record the battering, or the relationship is early in the battering process and these issues remain hidden. It should also be noted that the largest percentage of murdered battered women (about 60 to 70 percent) are killed by their batterers while trying to leave the situation. These are referred to as "separation attacks" (Bachman and Saltzman 1994; Browne 1987; Copelon 1994; Felder and Victor 1996; Klein 1996; Mahoney 1991; Ogle and Jacobs 2002). Of course, there are a significant number of women killed at the climax of a battering incident as well. When battered women kill, it is generally after they have been provoked by their batterers/victims and see no alternative for survival.

Battered Women Who Kill

Battered women live in a world quite different from their nonvictimized counterparts. It is a world filled with tension, distrust, violence, and fear. Aldarondo and Straus (1994) identified ten risk factors for marital violence. They note the willingness to use violence at all, dependency, violent behavior outside the home, and physical violence in the family of origin as major factors. They also note the importance of marital rape, possession or use of weapons, abuse or killing of pets, psychological abuse, and threats used to solve problems or control the partner. These characteristics have also been identified by other researchers studying battering in general (Straus and Gelles 1986, 1990; Straus, Gelles, and Steinmetz 1980). While this set of general characteristics of battering relationships indicates an environment of fear and violence, other studies have shown even more difficult circumstances for battered women who kill their abusers.

Research indicates that battered women who kill their abusers live in a world that is even more intimidating. Browne (1987) did a study comparing her sample of battered women who had killed their abusers with Walker's 1979 sample of battered women who had not killed their abusers. She found several significant differences in the cases of battered women who killed their abusers. She identifies a higher frequency of violence in these cases and more serious injuries as a result. These cases more often involved serious sexual abuse, high levels of isolation of the victim, frequent substance abuse, and frequent threats to kill the victim. She also notes higher levels of hopelessness among these victims, particularly those who had attempted to leave or get assistance and had failed, leaving them feeling entrapped in the violence. This adds support to Johnson's (1995) claim that there are two types of battering relationships and each has somewhat different characteristics. All of this research has led some scholars to develop theories on battering and battering homicides.

Two Theories on Why Battered Women Kill

Lenore Walker was one of the first scholars to devote her efforts to understanding the battering relationship. In 1979, she published a book detailing the pattern of battering that she discovered from working with battered women. This pattern is referred to as the *cycle of battering,* or the cycle of violence. This cycle consists of three phases. First, Walker identified a period of tension building in these relationships, where the batterer emotionally abuses the victim with intimidation and threats. Victims generally react to this abusive behavior by attempting to placate the batterer in order to avoid the threatened violence. The second phase consists of the actual battering incident. The third phase consists of contrition, whereby the batterer apologizes for the violence and attempts to convince the victim that it will not happen again, in order to prevent the victim from leaving the relationship. Walker followed up this work in 1984 with a book explaining her theory of why women stay in battering relationships and how this can result in a homicide. This theory is called *battered woman syndrome.* In this theory, Walker argues that over time, battered women develop learned helplessness. This means that as the cycle reoccurs over time, the battered woman learns that nothing she does has an influence on the battering. It becomes inevitable regardless of her response to the threats. The victim feels helpless and entrapped in the violence. Some victims simply give up

and expect to die; others continue in this mode until they believe that they are going to be killed and then resort to killing their abusers in order to survive.

Battered woman syndrome has become well accepted in the legal community as a supplement to self-defense strategies for battered women who have killed their abusers. It is similar to arguing that the battered woman was slowly driven to a form of temporary insanity, resulting in her homicidal behavior. In essence, battered woman syndrome is a partial excuse for committing homicide; however, it is not a legal justification. In other words, it may reduce her responsibility for the homicide and mitigate the punishment, but it does not legally justify the homicide.

Battered woman syndrome has also received significant criticism over the past twenty years. For example, it is hard to argue in court that the defendant made a reasonable decision while claiming that she was temporarily insane. Ogle and Jacobs (2002) argue that this theory focuses only on psychology and only on the victim, as if the victim were the problem to be explained. They claim that this theory ignores all of the cultural, social, structural, and situational variables that are inherent parts of any interaction between people. Consequently, they utilize an interaction perspective to explain battering and escalation to homicide.

Ogle and Jacobs (2002) borrow the cycle of battering from Walker and use it as the framework for understanding how interactions occur over time in a battering relationship and how these interactions might escalate to a homicide. They argue that the tension-building phase creates negative affect (i.e., bad feelings like anger, fear, or despair) for both the batterer and the victim. The batterer temporarily relieves his tension by battering the victim, but the victim lives in a constantly increasing, high state of arousal. When people experience such feelings, they normally utilize their personal coping mechanisms to end the tension or at least manage it. Since women are generally socialized against the use of aggression, they are likely to begin coping by appeasing the batterer to keep him calm and reduce the likelihood of violence. For example, the victim may try to do everything just as the batterer wants it, hoping that this will prevent another beating. When another battering incident occurs, she has learned that her actions will not stop the violence. At this stage, some women will try physical self-defense, which usually results in more serious injuries. But again the batterer will apologize and promise not to do it again. Most women will believe this contrition for a while because they so desperately want it to be true. When the tension building and battering continue to occur, the victim often responds by utilizing her personal coping resources to attempt to end the violence. For example, she may call her parents for advice or talk to a trusted friend about the situation. These coping efforts by the victim will signal a loss of control to the batterer and he will respond by increasing the tension and violence in order to regain complete control of both the victim and the relationship.

As the violence continues, the victim will no longer believe the apologies offered by the batterer. At this point, the contrition phase is going to dissipate or disappear entirely because the victim doesn't believe it, and therefore it is no longer useful to the batterer. He will focus his control efforts on intimidation, threats, and violence. At this stage, fear significantly increases for the victim. In addition, when contrition disappears from the battering cycle, all that is left is tension building and battering incidents. So, while the batterer relieves his tension by battering, the victim lives in a constant high state of fear waiting for the next threat and beating. In essence, at this stage, there are no nonconfrontational periods for the victim—it could happen at any time. Most victims respond reasonably to this escalation by going outside their personal resources to social or public resources for help. This may involve calling the police, a battering hotline, a shelter, a divorce lawyer, or a counselor for assistance. Since public knowledge of the batterer's behavior can have serious social and criminal justice consequences, he will feel at greater risk than before. The batterer reacts to these victim coping efforts in two ways.

First, he will act to block any further use of these resources. For example, he may threaten to kill the dog or beat the kids if she calls her parents, the police, or a counselor again; sell the car, so she has no transportation; gather up important papers that she would need to have in order to leave; or reduce her access to money. Second, the batterer will react by increasing the frequency and intensity of the violence in order to regain complete control of the victim and the relationship. With each progression of the battering cycle, the chance of desistance by the batterer diminishes because success in regaining and maintaining control is self-reinforcing. In other words, each time the batterer is successful at blocking resource use and regaining control, he is more convinced of his superiority and omnipotence. Ogle and Jacobs (2002) are not arguing that the victim does not experience trauma in this battering

process, but rather that it is perfectly reasonable for a victim in this situation to view it as progressively more lethal.

At this point, the victim knows that any effort to utilize outside assistance will put her and her children in an extremely high-risk situation. Most of these victims are very courageous; they will make multiple attempts to obtain outside assistance from social resources and will bear the intensified violence when those resources do not successfully end the battering.

Unfortunately social resources to assist battering victims are not particularly abundant or successful. Battered woman shelters are few and far between and severely underfunded. In the United States, there are three times as many animal shelters as there are battered woman shelters (Senate Judiciary Committee 1992). There are about 1,200 battered woman shelters in the United States serving thousands of women each year, but their services are requested by about two million women each year (ibid.). Having the batterer arrested may create temporary safety, but most victims find themselves later facing an even angrier batterer who is not intimidated by a protection order (Klein 1996). Neighbors don't call the police when they hear the commotion for fear of violating someone's privacy or giving the batterer reason to aggress toward them. Clergy and counselors sometimes fail to recognize the level of danger in these situations and convince victims to try to work out differences. Doctors do not always question the victim in a safe environment where she can give honest answers. Worse yet, insurance agencies reserve the right to cancel life and health insurance on women and children living in battering situations; of course, the only way they obtain such information is by the victim reporting the battering to some social service agency. So in order to get help, battered women have to be willing to be mistreated by the system. Unfortunately, all too often, when battered women do what they are told to do to end the violence, such as use social resources or leave the situation, they are punished by the system, and some are killed by their batterers in separation attacks.

After the victim has made multiple attempts to utilize these social resources and watched them fail, it is not unreasonable to expect the victim to view herself as alone in the situation. It is not unreasonable that she will resign herself to kill or be killed to end the violence. Since women generally are physically smaller and have less strength than their male partners, their self-defense will almost always have to involve a weapon. It is also likely that to be successful in protecting themselves and ending the violence, they will have to act before their batterers initiate one of their attacks, during what the courts call a nonconfrontational period. Ogle and Jacobs (2002) argue that if juries were exposed to this interactional information about the battering relationship over time, they would be more willing to accept a self-defense justification for battered women who kill their abusers even if they do so prior to the next attack.

ROBBIN S. OGLE

See also **Battered Woman Syndrome; Battered Woman Syndrome as a Legal Defense in Cases of Spousal Homicide; Battered Women: Held in Captivity; Intimate Partner Homicide; Mutual Battering; Stages of Leaving Abusive Relationships**

References and Further Reading

Aldarondo, E., and Murray A. Straus. "Screening for Physical Violence in Couple Therapy: Methodological, Practical, and Ethical Considerations." *Family Process* 33 (1994): 425–439.

Bachman, Ronet, and Linda E. Saltzman. *Violence against Women: A National Crime Victimization Survey Report.* Washington, DC: U.S. Department of Justice, 1994. NCJ 154348.

Belknap, Joanne. "Perceptions of Women Battering." In *The Changing Roles of Women in the Criminal Justice System,* edited by Imogene L. Moyer, 2nd ed. Prospect Heights, IL: Waveland Press, 1992, pp. 181–201.

Blackman, Julie. "Exploring the Impacts of Poverty on Battered Women Who Kill Their Abusers." Paper presented at the American Psychological Association meeting in Atlanta, GA, 1988.

Block, Carolyn R., and Antigone Christakos. "Intimate Partner Homicide in Chicago over 29 years." *Crime and Delinquency* 41 (1995): 496–526.

Browne, Angela. *When Battered Women Kill.* New York: The Free Press, 1987.

Browne, Angela, and Kirk R. Williams. "Exploring the Effect of Resource Availability and the Likelihood of Female Perpetrated Homicides." *Law and Society Review* 23, no. 1 (1989): 75–94.

Bureau of Justice Statistics. *Violence by Intimates: Analysis of Data on Crimes by Current or Former Spouses, Boyfriends, and Girlfriends.* Washington, DC: U.S. Department of Justice, 1998. NCJ 167237.

Centerwall, Brandon S. "Race, Socioeconomic Status, and Domestic Homicide, Atlanta, 1971–1972." *American Journal of Public Health* 74 (1984): 813–815.

Copelon, Rhonda. "Recognizing the Egregious in the Everyday: Domestic Violence as Torture." *Columbia Human Rights Law Review* 25, no. 2 (1994): 291–367.

Davidson, Terry. "Wife Beating: A Recurring Phenomenon Throughout History." In *Battered Women: A Psychological Study of Domestic Violence,* edited by Maria Roy. New York: Penguin Books, 1977, pp. 19–57.

Davis, Elizabeth G. *The First Sex.* New York: Penguin Books, 1971.

Dawson, John M., and Patrick A. Langan. *Murder in Families.* Washington, DC: U.S. Department of Justice, 1994. NCJ 143498.

Dobash, R. Emerson, and Russell P. Dobash. "Wives: The 'Appropriate' Victims of Marital Violence." *Victimology: An International Journal* 2, no. 3–4 (1978): 426–442.

———. *Violence against Wives: A Case against the Patriarchy.* New York: The Free Press, 1979.

Dobash, R. Emerson, Russell P. Dobash, Margo Wilson, and Martin Daly. "The Myth of Sexual Symmetry in Marital Violence." *Social Problems* 39, no. 1 (1992): 71–91.

Dutton, Donald G. *The Domestic Assault of Women: Psychological and Criminal Justice Perspectives,* 3rd ed. Vancouver, BC: UBC Press, 1998.

Ewing, Patrick. *Battered Women Who Kill: Psychological Self-Defense as Legal Justification.* Lexington, MA: D. C. Heath, 1987.

Federal Bureau of Investigation. *Uniform Crime Reports: Crime in the United States 1992.* Washington, DC: Author, 1993.

———. *Uniform Crime Reports: Crime in the United States 1997.* Washington, DC: Author, 1998.

Felder, Raoul, and Barbara Victor. *Getting Away with Murder: Weapons for the War against Domestic Violence.* New York: Simon and Schuster, 1996.

Goetting, Ann. "Patterns of Homicide Among Women." *Journal of Interpersonal Violence* 3 (1988): 3–20.

Gordon, Linda. *Heroes of Their Own Lives: The Politics and History of Family Violence.* New York: Penguin Books, 1989.

Gosselin, Denise K. *Heavy Hands: An Introduction to the Crimes of Domestic Violence.* Upper Saddle River, NJ: Prentice Hall, 2000.

Hart, Barbara. *Testimony on the Family Violence Prevention and Services Act.* Congressional Reauthorizing Hearing, 1991.

———. "Battered Women and the Criminal Justice System." In *Do Arrests and Restraining Orders Work?* edited by Eva S. Buzawa and Carl G. Buzawa. Thousand Oaks, CA: Sage, 1996, pp. 98–114.

Johnson, Michael P. "Patriarchal Terrorism and Common Couple Violence: Two Forms of Violence against Women." *Journal of Marriage and the Family* 57 (May 1995): 283–294.

Jones, Ann. *Women Who Kill.* New York: Holt, Rinehart, and Winston, 1980.

Jurik, Nancy C., and Russ Winn. "Gender and Homicide: A Comparison of Men and Women Who Kill." *Violence and Victims* 5, no. 4 (1990): 227–242.

Klein, Andrew R. "Re-abuse in a Population of Court-Restrained Male Batterers: Why Restraining Orders Don't Work." In *Do Arrests and Restraining Orders Work?* edited by Eva S. Buzawa and Carl G. Buzawa. Thousand Oaks, CA: Sage, 1996, pp. 192–213.

Mahoney, Margaret. "Legal Images of Battered Women: Redefining the Issue of Separation." *Michigan Law Review* 90, no. 1 (1991): 1–94.

Masters, Robert E. L. "Misogyny and Sexual Conflict." In *The Anti-sex: The Belief in the Natural Inferiority of Women: Studies in Male Frustration and Sexual Conflict,* edited by Robert E. L. Masters and Eduard Lea. New York: Julian Press, 1964, pp. 3–52.

Mercy, James A., and Linda E. Saltzman. "Fatal Violence among Spouses in the United States, 1976–1985."

American Journal of Public Health 79, no. 5 (1989): 595–599.

Ogle, Robbin S., and Susan Jacobs. *Self Defense and Battered Women Who Kill: A New Framework*. Westport, CT: Praeger, 2002.

Ogle, Robbin S., Daniel Maier-Katkin, and Thomas J. Bernard. "A Theory of Homicidal Behavior among Women." *Criminology* 33, no. 2 (1995): 173–193.

Pagelow, Mildred D. *Family Violence*. New York: Praeger, 1984.

Piven, Frances Fox, and Richard A. Cloward. "Hidden Protests: The Channeling of Female Innovation and Resistance." *Signs: Journal of Women in Culture and Society* 4 (1979): 461–487.

Pleck, Elizabeth H. "Feminist Responses to 'Crimes against Women,' 1868–1896." *Signs: Journal of Women in Culture and Society* 8, no. 3 (1983): 451–470.

———. *Domestic Tyranny: The Making of Social Policy against Family Violence from Colonial Times to Present*. New York: Oxford University Press, 1987.

Pushkareva, Natalia. *Women in Russian History: From the Tenth to the Twentieth Century,* edited and translated by Eve Levin. Armonk, NY: M. E. Sharpe, 1997.

Roberts, Albert R., ed. *Helping Battered Women: New Perspectives and Remedies*. New York: Oxford University Press, 1996.

Senate Judiciary Committee. *Violence against Women: A Week in the Life of America,* 1992. 102nd Congress, 2d sess. S. Rept. 118, 26 (1992).

Stark, Evan, and Anne Flitcraft. *Women at Risk: Domestic Violence and Women's Health*. London: Sage, 1996.

Straus, Murray A., and Richard J. Gelles. "Societal Change and Change in Family Violence from 1975 to 1985 as Revealed by Two National Surveys." *Journal of Marriage and the Family* 48, no. 3 (1986): 465–479.

———. *Physical Violence in American Families: Risk Factors and Adaptations to Violence in 8,145 Families*. New Brunswick, NJ: Transaction Books, 1990.

Straus, Murray A., Richard J. Gelles, and Suzanne K. Steinmetz. *Behind Closed Doors: Violence in the American Family*. Garden City, NY: Anchor Press/Doubleday, 1980.

Totman, Jane. *The Murderess: A Psychological Study of Criminal Homicide*. San Francisco: R. and E. Research Associates, 1978.

Ulrich, Laurel T. *Good Wives: Image and Reality in the Lives of Women in Northern New England, 1650–1750*. New York: Vintage Books, 1991.

Websdale, Neil. *Understanding Domestic Homicide*. Boston: Northeastern University Press, 1999.

Widom, Cathy S. "Female Offenders: Three Assumptions about Self Esteem, Sex Role Identity, and Feminism." *Criminal Justice and Behavior* 6 (1979): 365–382.

Wolfgang, Marvin E. *Patterns of Criminal Homicide*. Philadelphia: University of Pennsylvania Press, 1958.

BATTERER INTERVENTION PROGRAMS

There are basically four therapeutic approaches to treating interpersonal partner violence: same-sex group therapy (for example, a group of males sent to therapy by the criminal justice system), couples therapy (which focuses on the interaction between the two members of the couple), "psychoeducational" groups (again, mandated by the criminal justice system but having a different focus than treatment groups), and intimate abuse circles (an innovative form of restorative justice that involves public apology to a small group and/or apology to the victim) (Mills 2003; Strang and Braithwaite 2002). Psychoeducational groups do not view intimate partner violence as having psychological causes but as being a case of male power and control (Pense and Paymar 1993) that requires attitude adjustment. For this reason, this approach does not refer to "treatment" but rather to intervention and is designed with male perpetrators in heterosexual relationships in mind. It is legally required in many states (Tolman 2001), although many researchers have complained that the approach is not informed by research on perpetrators, that is, it does not have a complex picture of the subtypes of perpetrators, even within a heterosexual male group (see Maiuro et al. 2001; Dutton and Sonkin 2003; Hamel 2005). For example, the notion that "attitudes" drive violence is naive. Large survey studies (e.g., Simon et al. 2003) find that only 2.1 percent of males in the United States agree with the statement "A man is justified in using violence to keep his mate in line." Even studies on male perpetrators obtain mixed results on whether attitudes predict use of intimate partner violence (see Dutton, in press). It may well be that attitudes are changed by violent men to be more consistent with their behavior (Bem 1972).

Psychoeducational Interventions

The Duluth Domestic Abuse Intervention Project (DAIP) designed an intervention program to be applied to men who had assaulted their female partners but who were not going to receive jail time. The objective of the program was to ensure the safety of the women victims (i.e., protection from recidivist violence) by "holding the offenders accountable" and by placing the onus of intervention on the community to ensure the woman's safety. The curriculum of the Duluth model was developed by a "small group of activists in the battered woman's movement" (p. xiii) and was designed to be used by paraprofessionals in court-mandated groups. It is now one of the most commonly used court-sanctioned interventions for men convicted and having mandatory treatment conditions placed on their probations. This is true in many U.S. states and Canadian provinces. The curriculum of the model stresses that violence is used as a form of "power and control," and a "Power and Control Wheel" has become a famous insignia of the program. This wheel depicts various forms of abuse (physical, financial, sexual, emotional) as emanating from a need in the abuser to have power over the abuse victim. Also, the need for power and control is seen as being an exclusively male problem. As the authors put it, "[Men] are socialized to be dominant and women to be subordinate" (p. 5). Hence, the "educational" aspect of the program deals with male privilege that exists in patriarchal structures such as those in place in North American countries. The DAIP view of female violence is that it is always self defensive. "Women often kick, scratch and bite the men who beat them, but that does not constitute mutual battering" (p. 5). Male battering stems from beliefs which are themselves the product of socialization. These include the beliefs that the man should be the boss in the family; that anger causes violence; that women are manipulative; that women think of men as paychecks; that if a man is hurt, it is natural for him to hurt back; that smashing things isn't abusive; that "women's libbers" hate men; that women want to be dominated by men; that men batter because they are insecure; that a man has the right to choose his partner's friends and associates; and that a man can't change if the woman won't (pp. 7–13). According to the manual, the basis for these beliefs came from a sample of five battered women and four men who had completed the Duluth program.

Outcome studies, which measure recidivism (the success or failure of a treatment after completion, usually assessed either by new police reports or by interviews with the previous victim), have been carried out on the Duluth model. Four separate studies (Davis, Taylor, and Maxwell 1998; Feder and Forde 1999; Levesque 1998; and Shepard 1992) essentially found that men completing Duluth treatment were just as likely as untreated control subjects to reoffend. When treatment ends, violence returns. It seems that clients privately reject the Duluth model's proposals while publicly realizing that they have to comply with the system. Furthermore, dropout rates are very high for such programs, ranging from 40 to 80 percent (McCloskey, Sitaker, Grigsby, and Malloy 2003). One reason may be that such programs do not form a "therapeutic bond" with the client and can be highly judgmental, promoting a philosophy that the client does not see as fitting his situation.

The single most predictive factor for successful therapeutic outcome (realizing that the Duluth model is not therapy but required of many mental health practitioners) is the therapeutic relationship (see, for example, Luborsky 1984; Schore 2003). However, it becomes extremely difficult to form a positive relationship when the therapist is required to disbelieve clients' reports of acts of violence by the partner; indeed, therapists can lose their certification with probation if they don't confront their clients enough and tell them that they have a "power entitlement" when the clients feel powerless in the world, and are considered enabling or manipulated when they advocate for their clients' continued treatment.

One must balance confrontation with support, belief, and caring in order to develop a solid therapeutic alliance. Building a therapeutic alliance without colluding with dangerous acting-out behaviors is one of the greatest challenges facing treatment providers working with domestic violence perpetrators. Because so many of these individuals experienced abuse by authority figures, the process of building a trusting relationship is particularly difficult.

According to Lester Luborsky of the Penn Psychotherapy Project, the therapeutic alliance may be defined as "that point in the therapeutic relationship when the client on one hand elevates the therapist to a position of authority, but on the other hand believes that this power and authority is shared between them, that there is a deep sense of collaboration and participation in the process.

In this way a positive attachment develops between the client and the therapist" (Luborsky 1984).

Cognitive-Behavioral Treatment

Cognitive-behavioral treatment (CBT) of intimate partner violence is based on the assumption that beliefs or cognitions about violence and its causes sustain a habit of intimate violence and that by challenging and changing these beliefs, abusive behavior can also be stopped. CBT is implemented in a same-sex group with one or two therapists. Treatment typically lasts for sixteen to fifty-two weeks on a once-a-week basis. The treatment is far broader in its targeting of abusive beliefs than is psychoeducational intervention. Topics covered in CBT groups include the following:

- Focus on the unacceptability of abuse:
  Confrontation of beliefs and behavioral choices
  Emphasis on attitudes and choices

- Generation of client agreement with the unacceptability of abuse:
  Generation of a "Violence Contract" (getting the clients to write out their personal violence policy—the conditions under which they believe the use of violence is acceptable)
  Generation of commitment to therapy

- Skills training:
  Emotional labeling
  Anger management (including keeping anger diaries)
  Self-soothing (stress reduction skills)
  Redirecting power needs
  Assertiveness awareness

- Focus on specific "problem" emotions:
  Dealing with anger, jealousy, anxiety, depression

- Attitudinal challenge:
  Attitudes toward the use of violence
  Attitudes toward women
  Violence potential awareness

- Managing contact with partner:
  Crisis strategies
  Connection of learned patterns in family of origin to present dysfunctional action patterns

Therapists typically attempt to confront abusive behaviors while forming and maintaining a therapeutic bond (sportive milieu) with the client.

Dutton (in press) has developed a "blended CBT" model that expands the targets of CBT to include identity disturbances (called borderline personality organization), trauma, substance abuse, and insecure attachment. Research had shown that all four are risk factors for abusiveness, what Dutton (2003) called the associated features of abuse. As of this writing, no evaluation has been done of programs utilizing this expanded focus.

Evaluations of earlier CBT models showed the following. Babcock, Green, and Robie (2004) conducted a meta-analytic study of twenty-two studies of treatment outcome. (Meta-analysis combines several or all known studies to arrive at an overall evaluation.) For Duluth treatment, the effect size (differences in success of treatment groups and control groups in remaining violence-free after treatment) was .19. (An effect size of .20 is considered small, of .40 moderate, and of .75 large.) Comparisons between CBT and Duluth were not significant. However, "pure" Duluth models were hard to find; as the authors of this study state, "modern batterer groups tend to mix different theoretical approaches to treatment, combining feminist theory of power and control as well as specific interventions that deal with anger control, stress management and improved communication skill" (p. 1045).

The effect size of .34 for most therapeutic outcomes, also reported by Babcock, Green, and Robie (2004), is less than optimal. The average effect size in psychotherapy studies is .85, but it is substantially lower for court-mandated treatment. By standards of court-mandated client populations, however, this is an average result. By expanding the focus of treatment in a blended model, this outcome may improve.

Couples Therapy

Several studies have found couples therapy effective with violent couples (Brannen 1994; Heyman and Schlee 2003; Klein 1991; O'Leary, Heyman, and Neidig 1999). Obviously the form of treatment is dictated by an assessment of violence levels and danger but to rule it out *a priori,* as the Duluth model does, operates against treatment efficacy.

The decision regarding whether an individual or a couples approach to therapy is best may depend on the client. A partner who has a history of violence in several relationships may be a conflict generator capable of creating the system pattern in the current relationship, as observed by the systems therapist. Certainly an "abusive personality" requires extensive therapeutic work at an individual level before couples treatment seems viable.

Also, as some therapists have shown (Richter 1974), an individual is capable of generating entire interaction patterns within a family on the basis of his or her own pathology. Richter describes how a paranoid personality who holds power in a family can generate a shared paranoia in the entire family system. Men with abusive personalities, one may suspect, are conflict generators in all their intimate relationships, regardless of the personality or style of their female partner. Of course, such men may also pick women with their own backgrounds of abuse victimization and personality disorders. Therefore, obtaining detailed social histories of clients and their partners is recommended prior to embarking on a systems approach. If a male batterer has a history of violence with women that predates his current relationship, or strong indicators of an abusive personality, couples treatment may not be advisable. Where the female feels threatened by the man's violence potential or where violence is still recent, couples therapy might be delayed until the man has successfully completed an anger management program and has been violence free for a lengthy period. In general, where the violence and conflict seem specific to the present relationship, couples treatment may be more useful after the man's anger treatment.

Neidig and Friedman (1984) begin their description of their couples treatment program by stating that "abusive behavior is a relationship issue but it is ultimately the responsibility of the male to control physical violence." Their view is that approaches which attribute total responsibility to either party lead to blaming, which compounds the problem. According to these authors, it does so by beginning a chain of retributional strategies by the victim and the aggressor whereby each tries to "get even" for the other's most recent transgression. A systems approach avoids blaming by getting couples to think of the causes of violence from a circular feedback perspective rather than a linear one. This leads to "constructive interventions in the escalating process" which permit each partner to accept a portion of the responsibility. Having said that, however, Neidig and Friedman assign "*ultimate* responsibility to the male for controlling violence" [emphasis added], as a recognition that both parties are not equal in physical strength. If a man is responsible for his violence, then why is he not to blame if he acts violently? One answer may be that his violence occurred in a state of high arousal when he perceived no alternatives to the actions he took. Therapeutically, a couples approach and an individual approach have a fundamental disagreement: The couples approach tries to reduce blame, and the individual approach tries to increase responsibility.

Cascardi and Vivian (1995) found that in the majority of couples clients seeking marital therapy, both partners engaged in aggressive acts, though the woman got the worst of it. Vivian and Langhinrichsen-Rohling (1994) classified couples seeking therapy as (1) mild bidirectional, in which about 50 percent report low-level aggression (pushes, slaps, grabs) committed by both husband and wife, (2) moderate, and (3) severe wife victimization, in which 30–40 percent report high levels of wife victimization and much lower levels of husband victimization. This leads to the same question posed by Stets and Straus (1992): What happens to violent couples in which the female is the predominant aggressor? These couples do not appear to seek marital therapy. Interestingly, only a small percentage (6–14 percent) of women seeking marital therapy report physical violence as a problem, despite reports from the Conflict Tactics Scale (CTS) revealing higher levels of physical aggression in the marriages.

Heyman and Schlee (2003) assessed for levels of aggression prior to their treatment program and found that very few couples reported severe levels of aggression (p. 145). When someone was injured or fearful or when the husband was in denial, the couple was screened out. They did not comment on wives in denial. Post-treatment assessment revealed significant drops in aggression and increases in reported marital adjustment by both parties. The reduction in aggression was still significantly lower than its pre-treatment level one year after cessation of treatment. Complete cessation was found among 26 percent of the couples one year later. Additionally, reductions occurred in a substantial subgroup.

Klein (1991) did a follow-up on a ten-week conjoint (couples) therapy group. The results were mixed: 80 percent of the couples were violence free at a two-month follow-up, but 80 percent were continuing to be verbally abusive. However, the sample was small and the follow-up period too short.

Stith, Rosen, McCollum, and Thomsen (2004) also found significant reductions in male violence recidivism six months after couples treatment cessation in a study of forty-two couples (only 25 percent recidivated). This was in a couples group-therapy format. In an individual-couples format, 43 percent recidivated. In a nontreated control, 66 percent recidivated. By comparison, in a treatment outcome study done on the Duluth model, Shepard (1987, 1992) found a 40 percent recidivism rate in a six-month follow-up of Duluth clients, higher than most control recidivism levels, and Dutton (1987) found a recidivism rate of 16 percent (or 84 percent complete cessation) based on wives' reports for a CBT court-mandated group for men. Rosenfeld (1992) found that wives' reports of husbands' violence revealed four times as much violence as police reports. (This does not mean that four times as many men were being violent, but that the violent men were more violent than the police realized.) Stith, Rosen, and McCollum (2003) reviewed six outcome studies of couples treatment and concluded that they were at least as effective as so-called traditional treatment.

Treatment Groups for Female Perpetrators

Evidence is beginning to show that women are as violent as men and that the profiles of female abusers are the same as those of male abusers (Archer 2000; Moffitt, Caspi, Rutter, and Silva 2001; Ehrensaft, Moffitt, and Caspi 2004; Babcock and Dutton, in press). Henning, Jones, and Holdford (2003) found that both women and men in court-mandated treatment had adverse childhood experiences and high levels of personality and mood disorder. Borderline personality disorder, which Dutton (2003) noted as being central in male batterers, was even more frequent in female batterers. Hence it seems that blended CBT groups designed for male abusers may prove to be most effective with female abusers.

Intimate Abuse Circles

Linda Mills (2001), in a thoughtful and provocative article in the *Harvard Law Review,* argues that state intervention itself has become abusive to "victims" who don't want that intervention. Battered women, she argues, are safest and feel most respected when they willingly partner with state officials to prosecute domestic violence crimes. Mandatory state interventions do not allow clinical healing to occur. The unwanted state intervention replicates "rejection, degradation, terrorization, social isolation, missocialization, exploitation, emotional unresponsiveness and close confinement that are endemic to the abusive relationship" (p. 551). Mills advocates what she calls a "survivor-centered approach," which focuses on listening to the woman, discussing the options with her, and leaving control of the outcome in her hands.

This approach can involve what are called *intimate abuse circles,* involving conferences between victims and perpetrators in the midst of a caring community chosen by both the victim and the perpetrator. These "restorative justice circles" have been tried in South Africa, New Zealand, the United States, and Canada. As a group and by consensus, a contract is developed to restore to the victim what has been lost (e.g., dignity, property). The contract must be agreeable to both sides and is prepared only after two events have occurred: First, there has been a full examination of the impact of the violence on those most affected; and second, violent offenders express remorse for their actions. This is referred to as the "healing process." Conferences can be formed only with the consent of both parties and the participation of the care community. It is a radical alternative to the "adversarial" justice system now in place, in which both sides spin the truth to self-advantage. Braithwaite provides considerable empirical evidence indicating high levels of victim satisfaction; this process leaves victims feeling empowered by their participation in the conference. The offender's apology offers symbolic reparation and enhanced empathy for the offender (sometimes as a prerequisite for making the apology). Strang and Braithwaite (2002) report that the use of justice circles in Indianapolis had a 40 percent lower recidivism rate than a control group (after six months) and a 25 percent lower recidivism rate after twelve months. A quasi-experimental study in Winnipeg among "serious adult offenders" produced a recidivism rate one-third that of the matched control group. A similar improved reduction in recidivism is reported in a study from New Zealand (Strang and Braithwaite 2002). The only evaluation available as of this writing on the application of justice circles to family violence is a study in Newfoundland by Burford and Pennell (1998), reported in the Strang and Braithwaite book. It found "marked reduction in both child abuse/neglect and abuse of mothers after the intervention." Thirty-two families who underwent the restorative justice intervention reduced violence by 50 percent in the year after the intervention; by comparison, thirty-one control families saw violence increase.

Caution must be employed here, though; the use of intimate abuse circles in domestic violence treatment probably requires that participants be screened (by criminal justice officials) for psychopathology prior to using this system. Also, the couple has to have access to the "caring community" group that Mills describes. It should be added that victim veto and careful monitoring of community group composition by criminal justice professionals are necessary to ensure that no "stacking" of the community group occurs.

As a summary statement, it must be said that no one treatment modality is so superior that others can be eliminated. What is more important is the fit between participants (the abusive couple) and the treatment or intervention system. Psychoeducational models and/or intimate abuse circles may work better with immigrant groups among whom cultural values upholding patriarchy are at odds with the host culture. Couples therapy may be better suited to mutually violent couples. CBT is probably better for individuals who habitually use violence but should be augmented with attention to the features of abusiveness described above.

DONALD G. DUTTON

See also **Batterer Typology; Cross-Cultural Perspectives on How to Deal with Batterers; Domestic Violence Courts; Electronic Monitoring of Abusers; Mutual Battering; Protective and Restraining Orders**

References and Further Reading

Babcock, J., J. Waltz, N. Jacobson, and J. M. Gottman. "Power and Violence: The Relation between Communication Patterns, Power Discrepancies and Domestic Violence." *Journal of Consulting and Clinical Psychology* 61, no. 1 (1993): 40–50.

Bem, D. J. "Self-Perception Theory." In *Advances in Experimental Social Psychology,* edited by L. Berkowitz. New York: Academic Press, 1972.

Burford, G., and J. Pennell. *Family Group Decision Making Project: Outcome Report.* St. John's Newfoundland, Memorial University of Newfoundland, 1998.

Davis, R. C., B. G. Taylor, and C. D. Maxwell. "Does Batterer Treatment Reduce Violence? A Randomized Experiment in Brooklyn." *Justice Quarterly* 18 (1998): 171–201.

Dutton, D. G. *The Abusive Personality: Violence and Control in Intimate Relationships.* Revised paperback ed. New York: Guilford Press, 2003.

————. *The Domestic Assault of Women.* 3rd ed. Vancouver: University of British Columbia Press, in press.

Dutton, D., and D. Sonkin. *Intimate Violence: Contemporary Treatment Innovations.* New York: Haworth Press, 2003.

Ehrensaft, M., P. Cohen, and J. Johnson. "Development of Personality Disorder Symptoms and the Risk for Partner Violence." *Journal of Abnormal Psychology* 115, no. 3 (2006): 474–483.

Ehrensaft, M. K., T. E. Moffitt, and A. Caspi. "Clinically Abusive Relationships in an Unselected Birth Cohort: Men's and Women's Participation and Developmental Antecedents." *Journal of Abnormal Psychology* 113, no. 2 (2004): 258–271.

Feder, L., and D. Forde. "A Test of Efficacy of Court Mandated Counseling for Convicted Misdemeanor Domestic Violence Offenders: Results from the Broward Experiment." Paper presented at the International Family Violence Research Conference, Durham, NH, 1999.

Hamel, J. *Gender Inclusive Treatment of Intimate Partner Abuse: A Comprehensive Approach.* New York: Springer, 2005.

Henning, K., A. Jones, and R. Holdford. "Treatment Needs of Women Arrested for Domestic Violence: A Comparison with Male Offenders." *Journal of Interpersonal Violence* 18, no. 8 (2003): 839–856.

Heyman, R., and K. Schlee. "Stopping Wife Abuse via Physical Aggression Couples Treatment." In *Intimate Violence: Contemporary Treatment Innovations,* edited by D. Dutton and D. Sonkin. New York: Haworth Press, 2003.

Klein, P. "Efficacy of Conjoint Group Treatment in Therapy for Spouse Abuse." Unpublished doctoral dissertation, Pacific School of Psychology, Palo Alto, CA, 1991.

Levesque, D. "Violence Desistance among Battering Men: Existing Intervention and the Application of the Transtheoretical Model for Change." Unpublished doctoral dissertation, University of Rhode Island, 1988.

Luborsky, L. *Principles of Psychoanalytic Therapy: A Manual for Supportive-Expressive Treatment.* New York: Basic Books, 1984.

McCloskey, K. A., M. Sitaker, N. Grigsby, and K. A. Malloy. "Characteristics of Male Batterers in Treatment: An Example of a Localized Program Evaluation Concerning Attrition." *Journal of Aggression, Maltreatment and Trauma* 8, no. 4 (2003): 67–95.

Mills, L. *Insult to Injury: Rethinking Our Responses to Intimate Abuse.* Princeton, NJ: Princeton University Press, 2001.

Moffitt, T., A. Caspi, M. Rutter, and P. Silva. *Sex Differences in Antisocial Behaviour: Conduct Disorder, Delinquency, and Violence in the Dunedin Longitudinal Study.* Cambridge and New York: Cambridge University Press, 2001.

Pennell, J., and G. Burford. "Feminist Praxis: Making Family Group Conferencing Work." In *Restorative Justice and Family Violence,* edited by H. Strang and J. Braithwaite. Cambridge and New York: Cambridge University Press, 2002.

Pense, Ellen, and Michael Paymar. *Education Groups for Men Who Batter: The Duluth Model.* New York: Springer Publications, 1993.

Richter, H. *The Family as Patient.* New York: Farrar, Straus and Giroux, 1974.

Schore, A. *Affect Regulation and Repair of the Self.* New York: Norton, 2003.

Shepard, M. "Predicting Batterer Recidivism Five Years after Community Intervention." *Journal of Family Violence* 7, no. 3 (1992): 167–178.

Stith, S. M., K. H. Rosen, and E. E. McCollum. "Effectiveness of Couples Treatment for Domestic Violence." *Journal of Marital and Family Therapy* 29 (2003): 407–426.

Stith, S. M., K. H. Rosen, E. E. McCollum, and C. J. Thomsen. "Treating Intimate Partner Violence Within Intact Couple Relationships: Outcomes of Multi-Couple Versus Individual Couple Therapy." *Journal of Marital and Family Therapy* 30 (2004): 305–318.

Strang, H., and J. Braithwaite. *Restorative Justice and Family Violence.* New York: Cambridge University Press, 2002.

BATTERER TYPOLOGY

Male Violence against an Intimate Female Partner

Physical aggression against an intimate partner is a serious problem. While both men and women engage in physical aggression in their intimate relationships, male aggression is generally found to have more negative consequences than female aggression, in terms of physical injury, partner fear, and other psychological sequelae (e.g., post-traumatic stress disorder [PTSD], depression). Thus, the focus in this article is on male violence toward an intimate partner, or husband violence. The potential causes of husband violence can be considered from a variety of levels, including those of societal and cultural variables, family and dyadic interactions and relationships, and individual characteristics of the violence perpetrator. To date, many studies, examining a wide variety of individual characteristics (e.g., psychopathology, behaviors and social skills, attitudes), have demonstrated differences between maritally violent and nonviolent men, suggesting that it is important to consider individual characteristics of violent men. Such individual characteristics are emphasized in existing batterer typologies.

Initial research in this area generally consisted of studies comparing men who had engaged in violence against an intimate partner with men who had not (i.e., violent vs. nonviolent sample study designs). However, as researchers gained experience with maritally violent men, they began to agree that differing levels and types of husband aggression exist and that maritally violent men differ from one another in a variety of ways. For example, it is clear that some men, often labeled batterers, engage in severe physical violence and usually also engage in other forms of male control and aggression (e.g., psychological and/or sexual abuse); their violence is likely to result in wife fear and injury. In contrast, some men engage in lower levels of violence, to which a variety of terms have been applied (e.g., minor violence, common couple violence, situational violence).

As research has made it clear that samples of maritally violent men are heterogeneous, varying along theoretically important dimensions, it has been assumed that our understanding of husband violence can be advanced by drawing attention to these differences. Comparing subtypes of violent men with each other, and understanding how each type differs from nonviolent men, should help us to identify different underlying processes resulting in violence. By thus better understanding the correlates and causes of varying types of male aggression, batterer typologies might also lead to improved outcome in batterer intervention and treatment, helping us to identify the men most likely to benefit from various interventions and to develop interventions matched to the needs of differing subtypes of violent husbands.

Batterer Typologies

Given such goals, Holtzworth-Munroe and Stuart (1994) conducted a comprehensive review of then available batterer typologies. Across these studies, we observed that batterer subtypes could be classified along three descriptive dimensions: (1) the severity/frequency of the husband's marital violence, (2) the generality of the man's violence (i.e., marital only or extrafamilial), and (3) the batterer's psychopathology or personality disorder characteristics. Using these dimensions, we proposed that three subtypes of batterers would be identified. First, family-only (FO) batterers were predicted to engage in the least marital violence, the lowest levels of psychological and sexual abuse, and the least violence outside the home. Men in this group were predicted to evidence little or no psychopathology. Second, dysphoric/borderline (DB) batterers were predicted to engage in moderate to severe wife abuse. Their violence would be primarily confined to the wife, although some extrafamilial violence might be evident. This group would be the most psychologically distressed and the most likely to evidence characteristics of borderline personality disorder (e.g., extreme emotional lability; intense, unstable interpersonal relationships; fear of rejection). Finally, generally violent/antisocial (GVA) batterers were predicted to be the most violent subtype, engaging in high levels of marital violence and the highest levels of extrafamilial violence. They would be the most likely to evidence characteristics of antisocial personality disorder (e.g., criminal behavior, arrests, substance abuse).

Holtzworth-Munroe and Stuart (1994) then integrated several intrapersonal theories of aggression into a developmental model of these differing types of husband violence. This model proposed that correlates of male violence that were both distal/historical (e.g., violence in the family of origin, association with delinquent peers) and proximal (e.g., attachment/dependency, impulsivity, social skills in marital and nonmarital relationships, and attitudes [both hostile attitudes toward women and attitudes supportive of violence]) might serve as varying risk factors for differing batterer subtypes.

Based on this model, we predicted that among maritally violent men, FO batterers would evidence the lowest levels of risk factors. The violence of FO batterers was proposed to result from a combination of stress (personal and/or relationship) and low-level risk factors (e.g., modeling of marital violence in the family of origin, lack of relationship skills), so that on some occasions during escalating marital conflicts, these men would perpetrate physical aggression. Following such incidents, however, their low levels of psychopathology and related problems (e.g., low impulsivity, low attachment dysfunction), combined with their lack of hostility toward women and lack of positive attitudes toward violence, would result in remorse and prevent their aggression from escalating. Our newer conceptualization of this subtype suggests that it might also be appropriate to consider the role of dyadic factors in understanding the violence of FO batterers.

In contrast, DB batterers were hypothesized to come from a background involving parental abuse and rejection. From such childhood experiences, these men were expected to have difficulty forming a stable, trusting attachment with an intimate partner. Instead, they would be very jealous and highly dependent upon, yet fearful of losing, their wives. They would tend to be impulsive and lack marital skills and have hostile attitudes toward women but positive attitudes toward violence. Their early traumatic experiences might lead to borderline personality organization, anger, and insecure attachment which, when frustrated, result in violence against the adult attachment figure (i.e., their romantic partner or wife).

Finally, GVA batterers were predicted to resemble other antisocial, aggressive groups. Compared with the other subtypes, they were expected to have experienced high levels of family-of-origin violence and association with deviant peers. They would be impulsive and lack both marital and nonmarital relationship skills, have hostile attitudes toward women, and view violence as acceptable. Their marital violence was conceptualized as a part of their general use of aggression and engagement in antisocial behavior.

To test the proposed typology, we conducted a study of men, recruited from the community, who had been physically aggressive toward their wives in the past year. We included men who had engaged in a wide range of violence. Using measures of the three descriptive dimensions (marital violence, general violence, personality disorder), the three predicted subgroups of violent men (FO, DB, and GVA) emerged, along with one additional subgroup, which we labeled low-level antisocial (LLA). The three predicted subgroups generally differed as hypothesized on both the descriptive dimensions and the model correlates of violence (i.e., childhood home environment, association with deviant peers, impulsivity, attachment, skills, and attitudes). The LLA group had moderate scores on measures of antisociality, marital violence, and general violence. On many measures, this group had higher scores than FO men but lower scores than GVA men.

In addition to our own study, other recent batterer typologies have usually been consistent with the proposed typology. Thus, across studies from multiple laboratories, the existing research suggests that using some or all of the proposed descriptive dimensions (i.e., severity/frequency of marital violence, generality of violence, psychopathology/personality disorder), the proposed batterer subtypes will be identified and generally will differ in a theoretically consistent manner.

Given that the proposed subtypes can be identified at one point in time, then an important follow-up question becomes: How stable, over time, are the violence and related characteristics and behaviors of the differing batterer subgroups? Some researchers initially suggested that the subtypes of maritally violent men, identified cross-sectionally, represent different phases of marital violence, with violent husbands progressing from a less violent subtype to a more severely violent subtype. Such predictions were derived from the assumption that husband violence, once begun, inevitably escalates in frequency and severity. Contradicting this notion, however, are several longitudinal studies suggesting that the initial severity level of husband violence is the best predictor of violence continuation and that men engaging in low levels of violence do not necessarily escalate their violence level over time. Thus, rather than hypothesizing that the subtypes represent phases in the escalation of relationship violence, we suggested that the violence levels of subtypes of maritally violent men should continue to differ over time. More severely violent men would continue to engage in more marital violence and related relationship abuse (e.g., sexual and psychological aggression), while less severely violent men would maintain lower levels of abuse or even desist from relationship violence over time.

To examine such issues in our typology study, we reassessed men approximately three years after their initial assessments. As predicted, the aggression of men who initially engaged in lower levels of violence was less stable over time than that of more severely violent men. In fact, among men still having at least monthly contact with their partners (i.e., the opportunity for continued violence), 40 percent of FO batterers and 23 percent of LLA batterers desisted from violence over a three-year period, but only 7 percent of GVA batterers and 14 percent of DB batterers desisted from violence.

Though these data suggest that the FO group may be a stable one, they should not be interpreted to mean that all men who engage in low levels of physical aggression will not escalate to more severe violence. Instead, the data suggest that among men engaging in low levels of violence, those who resemble FO batterers, in terms of evidencing low levels of other risk factors (e.g., little concurrent psychopathology or generally violent behavior, low risk from other risk factors such as impulsivity and negative attitudes), may continue to have a low risk of marital violence over time. In contrast, we would predict that a man who has, to date, engaged in only low levels of marital violence but who resembles a more violent subtype, such as the GVA subgroup, on risk factors (e.g., criminal behavior, delinquent friends, substance abuse, impulsivity, problematic attitudes) is at high risk to perpetrate escalating levels of marital aggression over time.

A related question regards the stability of batterer characteristics that are theoretically linked to a man's use of violence. We predicted that the initial subtype differences, observed on measures of theoretically relevant individual characteristics, would continue to differentiate the subtypes over time. This prediction was based on our implicit hypothesis that the relationship violence of severely violent men is related to stable individual characteristics of these men. Indirectly, our model suggests that the individual characteristics of some men put them at high risk for perpetrating severe relationship violence; in these relationships, the man is viewed as the cause of the relationship violence and is likely to carry his violence forward, across time and across relationships. Thus, the individual characteristics of these men that are theoretically linked to their use of violence (e.g., antisociality, insecure attachment, impulsivity) should remain relatively constant across time. In contrast, the low levels of violence perpetrated by our least violent subgroup, while reflecting some individual characteristics of the man, may also be related to dyadic factors (e.g., marital conflict), life stressors (e.g., job loss), and the cultural acceptability of low levels of relationship aggression. If correct, then men in the least violent subgroup are not necessarily men in the early phases of developing a lifelong pattern of escalating relationship aggression, but rather, over time, should use violence inconsistently and should continue to evidence low levels of risk factors for relationship violence (e.g., reporting less psychopathology, less positive attitudes toward violence, less impulsivity than other subtypes).

Many of our longitudinal study findings supported our hypotheses that the subtypes would continue to differ in men's individual characteristics assumed to be related to their use of violence. While not all group differences reached statistical significance, across time and as predicted, men in one or both of the more severely violent subtypes (GVA and DB) reported more continuing problems than the less violent men (FO and/or LLA) on a variety of measures, including:

- highest level of wife injury (for wives of both GVA and DB batterers),
- highest levels of impulsivity (both GVA and DB batterers),
- most positive attitudes toward violence and most hostile attitudes toward women (both GVA and DB batterers),
- the highest scores on measures of borderline personality disorder characteristics, fearful/preoccupied attachment, jealousy and dependency on the spouse, and being most likely to seek psychological help (DB batterers), and
- highest levels of problems resulting from substance use and the highest number of new arrests (GVA batterers).

One related issue emerging from recent typology research is the question of whether the GVA and DB subgroups are distinct. Outside of our lab, one group of researchers identified a pathological subtype that scored high on measures of both antisocial and borderline personality disorders. Similarly, in our study, the GVA and DB groups did not always differ significantly. Part of the problem in differentiating these two subgroups is that both are predicted to be similar in their levels of marital aggression and on several model correlates of violence, including impulsivity, positive attitudes toward violence, and negative attitudes toward women. Yet, over time, the GVA and DB groups in our study did differ on some variables. For example, GVA batterers were the most likely to be arrested, and DB batterers scored highest on a measure of jealousy and spouse-specific dependency and were the most likely to have been treated for depressive symptoms.

While our study findings do not conclusively resolve this debate, they do suggest the potential importance of two types of personality-related characteristics (i.e., antisociality and borderline) when studying husband violence. Indeed, considering antisocial behavior, it is possible to conceptualize three of our violent subtypes (FO, LLA, and GVA) as falling along a continuum of antisociality (e.g., FO batterers have the lowest levels of violence, antisocial behavior, and risk factors; GVA batterers have the highest; and the LLA group has intermediate levels). The DB group, however, could not be easily placed along this continuum, as it had the highest scores on variables that clustered in a theoretically coherent manner (i.e., fear of abandonment, preoccupied/fearful attachment, dependency). This has led us to argue that both dimensions (antisociality and borderline personality characteristics) are needed to describe all of the subgroups.

In summary, current batterer typology research suggests that identifying subtypes of maritally violent men is a useful method to account for the heterogeneity among maritally violent men on theoretically important variables that may remain relatively consistent across time. Yet one can ask whether these subgroups are true diagnostic categories that identify underlying taxonomical differences across subtypes of batterers, or whether, while some men are prototypes of the different subtypes, the majority of batterers fall along dimensions of theoretical importance rather than forming distinctly identifiable groups. The answers to such questions await further research, but we currently believe that both dimensional and categorical approaches to conceptualizing the data should be considered.

Assuming that one wishes to use a categorical approach, and thus to identify subgroups of men in clinical or research work, we have been asked to provide subgroup cut-off scores on the measures we used to identify subgroups of maritally violent men. Based on pilot work with various samples, however, we are concerned that cut-off points may not be generalizable from one setting to another.

Thus, at this time, we believe that absolute cut-off scores cannot be provided to identify subtypes until further research is conducted. Instead, cut-off scores for each sample need to be established.

Clinical Implications of the Typology

Given concerns about the potentially low overall effectiveness of batterers' treatment, one hope is that a batterer typology might allow us to distinguish subtypes likely to benefit from treatment from those unlikely to improve following clinical intervention. Indeed, recent findings suggest that standard batterer treatment programs may be ineffective for certain subtypes of maritally violent men. Specifically, researchers have found that GVA batterers are the most likely to drop out of treatment and the most likely to recidivate following treatment. In contrast, FO batterers are the most likely to complete treatment and to remain violence free afterward.

Another idea is that treatment outcome might be improved by matching interventions to batterer subtypes. For example, in a study comparing cognitive-behavioral-feminist treatment to a process-psychodynamic reatment, researchers found that batterers scoring high on an antisocial measure did better in the structured cognitive-behavioral intervention, while batterers scoring high on a measure of dependency did better in the other intervention. While it is premature to recommend particular interventions for various subtypes of batterers, we can generate hypotheses for future testing.

When considering the DB subtype, the one study discussed suggests that process-psychodynamic interventions might be useful, as might interventions developed for borderline personality disorder or that focus on past traumas and affect regulation. In addition, given their high levels of psychological distress, it may prove beneficial to provide DB batterers entering batterer programs with adjunct medication, such as antidepressants, or individual therapy for their immediate psychological distress. When considering GVA batterers, the available research on treatments for violent offenders and individuals with antisocial personality disorder suggest that many currently available interventions (e.g., insight oriented) are not effective, while other interventions (i.e., cognitive-behavioral approaches) deserve more study. In addition, it may be important to consider new interventions developed in other fields, such as criminal justice efforts (e.g., close monitoring of offenders in the community), and to directly address the other potentially relevant problems prevalent among this subgroup (e.g., substance abuse).

Given their lower levels of behavioral, personality, and criminal problems, we have hypothesized that FO, and perhaps LLA, batterers would be the most likely to benefit from existing batterer treatment programs (e.g., cognitive-behavioral approaches including anger management and feminist approaches encouraging these men to examine gender roles). Finally, couples with an FO-batterer husband may be the only physically aggressive couples for whom conjoint couples therapy would be appropriate, as this group of men often resembles maritally distressed men who do not perpetrate violence, and the risk factors that characterize FO batterers (e.g., skills deficits) are often directly addressed in available conjoint therapy programs.

Issues for Further Consideration

Many important issues in this area remain unresolved and require further examination. One is the question of the meaning and impact of low-level husband violence. Low levels of physical aggression (e.g., FO batterers) are so prevalent as to be almost statistically normative in our culture, and we do not understand how less violent men differ from men who are experiencing marital conflict but who do not engage in physical aggression. It is thus tempting to assume that low levels of aggression do not lead to any more negative outcomes than does marital distress alone. However, recent longitudinal studies of newlyweds suggest that even relatively low levels of physical aggression may be highly detrimental to relationship functioning, even perhaps predicting marital dissolution better than does marital distress or negative marital communication. Thus, we believe that lower levels of male physical aggression continue to deserve attention.

Also, it is now time to examine the potentially differing impacts on women (and children) of being in a relationship with differing subtypes of batterers. For example, in our study, we found increasing group differences in wives' marital satisfaction over time, with the wives of more severely violent men reporting more relationship distress. Study of other negative consequences for women (e.g., depression) should be conducted, as should studies of possible negative consequences for the children (e.g., child abuse) in these homes.

An important criticism of existing batterer typologies is that they focus so heavily on individual characteristics of violent men (e.g., psychopathology) that are relatively distal predictors of violence. While typologies tend to emphasize characteristics of the individual, one must remember that husband violence occurs in the context of interpersonal relationships, communities and subcultures, and society. For example, it is important to note that batterer typologies have been developed only in Western countries, primarily the United States. Whether such typologies will be replicated in other cultures is a question requiring empirical investigation. It is possible, given the role of societal factors (e.g., patriarchy, availability of guns) in shaping the expression of husband violence, that existing typologies will require modification in other cultures. For example, in societies in which husband violence is widely viewed as acceptable, there may be a weaker link between husband violence and psychopathology. Similarly, minimal attention has been paid to the possible impact of ethnic and socioeconomic group variability on typologies. As another example, the generalizability of existing batterer typologies to same-sex relationships has not been examined.

At the opposite end of the spectrum, one could examine more immediate variables related to how stable characteristics (e.g., personality variables, motivations) are expressed in a given situation. Consider the DB subgroup: How is an insecure attachment style activated in a particular situation? And once activated, how do fears of abandonment translate into violence? Does the man act in rage, experiencing emotional dysregulation, or in a calculated manner, to prevent his partner from leaving him? It will be important to understand why, for each subtype of batterer, violence emerges within an ongoing dyadic relationship and within particular situations.

The field needs prospective studies to identify the developmental pathways resulting in different subtypes of violent husbands. In such studies, researchers could examine constructs assumed to predict the use of violence among samples of adolescents or children (e.g., characteristics of antisocial and borderline personality disorders) and then observe the relationship between these variables and the emergence of relationship violence as study participants enter intimate relationships. Similarly, future researchers could study the process of desisting from violence. Several longitudinal studies suggest that some men, particularly those who engage in "minor" violence, desist. This issue might have clinical implications if it can suggest techniques that men have found useful in refraining from violence. Indeed, longitudinal studies of the predictors of violence and violence desistance could help guide future violence prevention efforts. Ultimately, rather than waiting to intervene with cases of serious levels of partner violence, it would be better to work to prevent the onset and escalation of physical aggression within intimate relationships. To do so, we must continue to better understand the predictors of varying types of husband violence.

AMY HOLTZWORTH-MUNROE

See also **Animal Abuse: The Link to Family Violence; Assessing Risk in Domestic Violence Cases; Battered Husbands; Battered Woman Syndrome; Children Witnessing Parental Violence; Education as a Risk Factor in Domestic Violence; Social Class and Domestic Violence; Stockholm Syndrome in Battered Women; Substance Use/Abuse and Intimate Partner Violence; Victim-Blaming Theory**

References and Further Reading

Holtzworth-Munroe, A., and J. C. Meehan. "Typologies of Men Who Are Maritally Violent: Scientific and Clinical Implications." *Journal of Interpersonal Violence* 19 (2004): 1369–1389.

Holtzworth-Munroe, A., J. C. Meehan, K. Herron, U. Rehman, and G. L. Stuart. "Testing the Holtzworth-Munroe and Stuart (1994) Batterer Typology." *Journal of Consulting and Clinical Psychology* 68 (2000): 1000–1019.

———. "Do Subtypes of Maritally Violent Men Continue to Differ Over Time?" *Journal of Consulting and Clinical Psychology* 71 (2003): 728–740.

Holtzworth-Munroe, A., and G. L. Stuart. "Typologies of Male Batterers: Three Subtypes and the Differences among Them." *Psychological Bulletin* 116 (1994): 476–497.

Lynam, D. R. "Looking Earlier in the Lifecourse for the GVA: Comment on Holtzworth-Munroe and Meehan." *Journal of Interpersonal Violence* 19 (2004): 1410–1440.

Prentky, R. A. "Can Sex Offender Classification Inform Typologies of Male Batterers?: A Response to Holtzworth-Munroe and Meehan." *Journal of Interpersonal Violence* 19 (2004): 1405–1411.

Saunders, D. G. "The Place of a Typology of Men Who Are Maritally Violent Within a Nested Ecological Model." *Journal of Interpersonal Violence* 19 (2004): 1390–1395.

Widiger, T. C., and S. N. Mullins-Sweatt. "Typology of Men Who Are Maritally Violent: A Discussion of Holtzworth-Munroe and Meehan." *Journal of Interpersonal Violence* 19 (2004): 1396–1400.

BULLYING AND THE FAMILY

Family violence and its many forms is certainly not a new phenomenon. It has existed since the beginning of time and very likely will continue until the end of time. Throughout history women and children have been subjected to horrific acts of cruelty and violence at the hands of male-dominated social systems. Siblings were not immune from committing such acts against family members. There is growing recognition that such events may not be gender specific, but rather may encompass to varying degrees participation as victimizer and/or victim by any family member. The purpose of this article is to explore aspects of what is widely being recognized as bullying in the family.

Definition

Bullying in the family is a form of domestic violence that can occur between marital partners (heterosexual or homosexual), parents and children (in either direction), and siblings. Bullying occurs when one person, the more powerful, attempts to degrade, abuse, or control the other, less powerful person. The ultimate goal of the family bully is domination, power, and control of one or more family members.

Forms of Family Bullying

Most often the abuse takes the form of psychological tormenting of the victim. This may include constant criticism for real or imagined infractions, usually of minor importance, consistently blaming the victim at any opportunity, and refusing to value and appreciate the individual. This may also include emotional and verbal abuse (to undermine self-esteem and confidence), intimidation, and humiliation. Emotional abuse tends to be the most common form of bullying behavior in the family. Emotional abuse by siblings toward other siblings usually includes an older, more powerful sibling victimizing younger, weaker brothers and sisters.

There have been cases, however, where older physically or mentally challenged siblings have been victimized by younger brothers and/or sisters. This type of abuse is perhaps the most damaging in the long term; it may lead to withdrawal, depression, antisocial behaviors, and the emotional abuse of others later in life.

Social abuse is another tactic employed by the family bully. This tactic is utilized to isolate the victim from socially interacting with friends and family. It may take the form of preventing the victim from leaving the home, forbidding phone use, verbally degrading the victim in front of others, not allowing contact with others, or making the victim accountable for his/her whereabouts at all times. This can lead to fear of others and to psychological dependence upon the family bully.

Financial abuse is used as another form of bullying. This method involves the bully taking complete control of the finances—his own and the victim's—in order to completely control the situation. This may include depriving the victim of money necessary for survival on a daily and long-term basis.

Sexual abuse is a coercive method which leads to unwanted sexual activity. This form of bullying is all about power and control over another. This includes sexual assault, rape, and accusations of infidelity by the bully toward the victim. Long-term consequences may include sexual dysfunction in later life, domestic violence, crime, substance abuse, and suicide.

There is the potential for physical abuse as well. This may include, but is not limited to, threats, assault resulting in injury, beatings with the hands or other objects, or any attempt to control, hurt, or intimidate the victim. Damage or destruction of property should also be included in this category. Child victims of physical abuse bear not only physical indicators of that abuse but emotional scarring as well. In many cases performance at school is affected adversely, language development may be impaired, and the child may have difficulty nurturing healthy relationships with peers.

Manipulation of family members is a tactic employed effectively by the family bully. Pitting family members against one another, the bully is able to keep everyone off balance, which gives the bully the control they continually seek. The bully derives satisfaction and even pleasure starting arguments which lead to hostility and other forms of destructive behavior while at the same time doing his best to remove himself from the conflict. Emotional manipulation—making people feel guilty about their actions, opinions, or beliefs—is employed as well. Elderly family members as well as the very young are quite vulnerable to this form of exploitation. Gossip spreading and innuendo about other members of the family by the bully is used as a form of harassment and control. This serves to undermine and isolate the bully's intended victim(s). This also leads to an environment of hostility and distrust in which the bully may rise to the top in order to appear to be above reproach and the hero of the day.

Characteristics of the Family Bully

Interestingly enough, family bullies also tend to project their shortcomings onto others. This allows them to avoid the reflection necessary to own up to their own inadequacies and the effort necessary to correct them. The projection takes the form of blaming, criticizing, and maligning others to keep the focus of attention off of the bully. The bully tells much about himself through his negative commentary of others. Other behavioral descriptors apt to characterize the bully include:

- Deceptive
- Charming
- Articulate
- Superficial
- Highly verbal
- Emotionally immature
- Untrustworthy
- Sexually immature
- Incapable of intimacy
- Prejudiced
- Compulsive
- Attention seeking
- Controlling
- Evasive
- Vindictive
- Manipulative
- Aggressive
- Arrogant
- Subtle
- Petty
- Selfish
- Self-absorbed
- Quick to misinterpret the actions or language of others
- Highly defensive
- Given to extreme mood swings
- Unpredictable
- Adroit at lying and believable

Family History

A number of child-rearing styles and family dynamics are evident in the creation of the family bully. Children learn first from their family the expectations, behaviors, and either effective or ineffective ways of interacting with others. Children who come from backgrounds which are authoritarian, harsh, and physically punitive tend to manifest bullying behaviors in later life. These children tend to be ineffective in establishing healthy relationships with others due to the inappropriate manner (i.e., physical aggression) in which they first learned to interact. Families that tend to overly control, dominate, and shame their children also tend to produce bullies in later life. The type of parental role model also plays a factor in building bullying behavior. Parents who are overly aggressive and abusive to each other set the tone for future interactions of their children with their peers and later with their own families. Again, these children model their own behavior to exactly what they see in the home as a tool to get what they want. This negative cycle of behavior affects siblings and parents, and may spill over into the school environment as well. It can lead to anxiety, depression, and various forms of antisocial behavior. Siblings from these types of environments also tend to victimize each other.

Children who lack attachment to parents, are neglected or abused, and/or come from highly volatile and dysfunctional environments are under a great deal of stress as a result of the lack of predictability around them. Likewise, children from extremely permissive environments are at risk as well. These children will tend to resort to the same tactics they see successfully used in this environment to gain some semblance of control and stability. Unfortunately, this tends to ripple out into other areas of their lives, such as school, work, and eventually their own families. This is very much a cyclic phenomenon.

As a long-term result, family bullies tend to have no conception of the feelings or needs of others. The physical, emotional, and psychological well-being of their victims are totally irrelevant to them and in many cases are used as strategies of attack and eventual conquest. The spouse who terrorizes or intimidates and the child who oppresses and dominates siblings or other family members are both driven by the compulsive and destructive need for control. Although they appear compassionate and caring, in reality they are toxic and destructive to themselves and their families.

Family Types

Research has identified three kinds of families and their relationship to bullying. The three types of family structures are the brick-wall, the jellyfish, and the backbone. The brick-wall family is concerned with order, control, obedience, and a hierarchy of power. The jellyfish family lacks a core family structure and exists within a laissez-faire atmosphere. The backbone family provides consistent control with an opportunity for discovery.

The brick-wall family instills in the children that power is obtained through intimidation. To win in this world, one must obtain and maintain power over subordinates. Power results from the actions of physical violence and threats. The bully is most likely a product of a brick-wall family.

Two different types of jellyfish families exist. The first type is one in which the parents, in an attempt to please their children, fail to provide strict rules of conduct. In this type of family, the child becomes his own master. A child who has never been led to feel he must work for what he or she desires expects those desires to be fulfilled simply upon request and may bully a smaller or weaker child into submission. In the other type of jellyfish family, the parents, again in an attempt to please their children, assume all of the responsibilities for their children. A child raised in this environment may be perceived as an easy target to bullies, as he is labeled the "mama's boy" of the classroom, thus becoming vulnerable to the intimidations of other students. In one type of jellyfish family, the child becomes the bully. In the other, the child becomes the victim.

In the backbone family, the child learns through caring but consistent rules and punishment, which parents utilize in order to empower and teach their children. These children will most often feel respect for themselves, their parents, and others. Through these families, communications lines are open and there exist caring for the other family members and respect for each other. The child from the backbone family is least likely to be involved in bullying as the bully or as the victim.

Effects of Family Bullying

Once the initial confrontation between bully and victim has taken place or has been suggested, the element of threat of further aggression exists. Both the bully and the victim know that the bullying will continue and that it is unrealistic to expect that a bullying encounter is merely a single event. Both

BULLYING AND THE FAMILY

the victim and the bully know that the much popularized media story of a victim standing up to and defeating his bully is essentially a myth. The victim now realizes his vulnerabilities and unfortunately so does the bully. With the threat of further aggression, the bullying continues.

The element that exists after an incident of bullying is terror. Bullying is a systematic action intended to intimidate and maintain dominance over a victim or victims. Once terror has been established, the bully can act without fear of retaliation and, in many cases, the action will escalate to more severe forms of abuse both in terms of emotional abuse and physical abuse. In some cases, this escalation of bullying may also be in the form of sexual abuse. The victim is always awaiting another attack and remains in a state of emotional terror. This state of terror facilitates the continuation of bullying.

The effects of family bullying on children are manifested in different ways depending on the child and the circumstances. Emotional symptoms include:

- Feeling guilty for the abuse and for not stopping it
- Grieving for family and personal losses
- Having conflicting feelings toward parents or other family members
- Experiencing fear of abandonment, the unknown, or personal injury
- Feeling angry about the violence and chaos in their lives
- Becoming depressed, feeling helpless and powerless
- Being embarrassed about events and dynamics at home

Perceptual symptoms of children affected by family bullying include:

- Believing that they are responsible
- Blaming others for their own behavior
- Believing that it is acceptable to bully others to get what they want
- Not asking for what they need or want
- Not trusting others
- Having very rigid beliefs about what it means to be a man, a woman, a husband, or a wife

Behavioral symptoms include:

- Becoming an overachiever or underachiever
- Refusing to go to school
- Showing more concern for others than for self
- Becoming exceptionally aggressive or passive
- Wetting the bed or having nightmares

- Seeking excessive attention
- Demonstrating "out of control" behavior

Social symptoms include:

- Being isolated from friends and relatives
- Having relationships that are frequently stormy
- Having poor conflict resolution and anger management skills
- Becoming excessively involved in social activities
- Being passive with peers or bullying peers
- Engaging in exploitative relationships either as perpetrator or victim
- Playing with peers in an exceedingly rough manner

Physical symptoms include:

- Complaining about headaches, stomachaches, etc.
- Seeming anxious and having a short attention span
- Being tired or lethargic
- Regressing in developmental tasks
- Seeming desensitized to pain
- Engaging in high-risk play and activities, abusing or mutilating themselves

For many individuals who bully, bullying is only the beginning of their perpetration of violence. Studies on bullying suggest that bullies are six times more likely to commit violent crimes than nonbullies. In addition, child bullies who are not stopped may mature to be adult bullies who provoke fear in their families and often in their coworkers. It is not unusual for an individual who bullied others as a child to continue that behavior and even further the aggression in terms of domestic violence and child abuse.

Studies have also suggested that individuals who engage in antisocial behaviors as children may also continue these actions as adults. In fact, according to many criminologists and criminal justice practitioners, an "early onset" of violent behavior is one of the best predictors of the frequency, seriousness, and duration of offending. In general, individuals who begin aggressive bullying toward others at the age of seven are more likely to continue with actions of violence than individuals who began aggressive bullying at the age of fifteen.

Adult victims of family bullies also may manifest such symptoms as:

- Clinical depression
- Anxiety
- Gastric problems
- Unspecified aches and pains

- Injury
- Loss of self-esteem
- Relationship problems
- Drug and alcohol abuse
- Suicide

Post-Traumatic Stress Disorder

Over the years the victim(s) of prolonged family bullying may manifest symptoms of post-traumatic stress disorder (PTSD). This psychiatric disorder can occur following the experience of or witnessing life-threatening events or violent personal assaults. It can also result from a series of non-life-threatening negative events over a prolonged period in which the victim cannot escape or chooses not to leave. These may include incidents of humiliation, rejection, betrayal, emotional abuse, physical abuse, loss of control, and disempowerment.

The symptoms are marked by clear physiological and psychological changes in the individual. This disorder is complex in that it usually manifests itself in concert with various other psychic disorders such as depression, drug and alcohol abuse, short-term memory loss, emotional numbness, and loss of concentration in the sufferer. Unfortunately, this disorder is frequently linked to job loss, crime, family disharmony, divorce, ineffective parenting, and a general inability to nurture and sustain effective interpersonal relationships. In addition, victims can experience general discomfort throughout their bodies, such as dizziness, headaches, digestive problems, angina, insomnia, and problems with their immune systems. At present, there is no cure for this disorder. The recovery process for victims of family bullies often takes years, and in cases involving PTSD, the victim may never fully recover.

Theories to Explain Bullying

In explaining the action of bullying, three perspectives are utilized—biological, psychological, and social. Specifically, to explain bullying, the physical trait perspective is offered as a biological explanation; sociopathy is offered from the social-psychological perspective; and the theory of social learning is offered from the social perspective.

Physical Traits

Since before the publication of Lombroso's *The Criminal Man* (1876) and up through today, individuals have attempted to categorize persons by their physical appearance and their asserted propensity to act strangely or violently. William Sheldon (1949) in his *Varieties of Delinquent Youth* applies that philosophy to young people. Sheldon maintained that there existed three categories of body types and that each type had its own unique associated temperament. Specifically, the types of body builds were: (1) endomorph, (2) mesomorph, and (3) ectomorph.

The endomorph body type was soft and round with a tendency to put on body fat. Its associated temperament was one of a relaxed nature that was slow to react and tolerant of others. The mesomorph body type was one of massive strength and defined muscular development. Its associated temperament was assertive with a desire for power and dominance. These individuals were often considered ruthless and indifferent to pain (theirs or others). The ectomorph body type was thin and frail. Its associated temperament was one of inhibition and social isolation.

In applying Sheldon's body types to the behavior of bullying, one asserts that the bully is the mesomorph. The mesomorph is an individual with not only the physical build and strength to intimidate and provoke fear in others, but also the personality or temperament to desire dominance over others. The target or victim of a bully, based on Sheldon's theories, is most likely the ectomorph. The victim is perceived to be physically vulnerable and lacks the social integration or ability to form and sustain the social bond to peers that may reduce his/her likelihood of becoming a target.

Sociopathy

One social-psychological explanation that is applied to criminal and delinquent behavior is that of sociopathy. The terms *psychopathy* and *antisocial personality* are considered synonymous with sociopathy. Sociopaths are characterized as selfish, impulsive, and emotionally unattached. As these individuals do not feel sympathy or empathy toward others, they often are the perpetrators of many crimes of violence over their life course. The cause of sociopathy is uncertain. Some researchers look toward the concept of a neurological defect as the cause, some seek explanation from the experience of an emotional trauma during childhood, and some look to the family. However, it is suggested that, in some cases, youths who begin bullying will continue the action throughout their life course. Such a youth may be classified as a sociopath.

Social Learning

Developed in the 1970s as a revision of Sutherland's concept of differential association, social learning theory is an attempt to explain behaviors as a result of reinforcement and punishment. Like Sutherland's concept, Aker's social learning theory maintains that deviant behavior is learned and that it is a direct outcome of instrumental conditioning and imitation. Instrumental conditioning, which relies upon reinforcement and punishment, allows a behavior to continue once it has been reorganized and imitated from observing the original source.

In discussing the action of bullying, a potential bully observes another bully and then initiates his or her own action of bullying, with instrumental conditioning supporting the behavior. Specifically, in Aker's (1985) social learning perspective, behavior increases if either a reward is received or a punishment is removed. A bully who obtains power and control over his target and does not receive any sort of punishment will continue bullying. If neither the target nor the bystanders intervene, bullying continues. The original action of bullying, as discussed above, is usually viewed within the family.

Characteristics of Victims and Bystanders

Although bullies may have a positive perspective on themselves, victims do not. Victims of bullies tend to suffer from low self-esteem, are insecure, and are often unwilling to defend themselves. Whereas the parents of bullies often allow the child to become independent at an early age, often in order that these parents may have more time to focus upon themselves, the victims of bullies may come from homes with very overprotective parents and are allowed few friends outside of the family.

From a victimological perspective, bullying is explained under the foundation of *victim precipitation,* which asserts that victims (either passively or actively) provoke their attacks. In cases of bullying, victims passively precipitate the action merely through their physical appearance or behaviors. In support of their actions, many bullies blame their victims for their attacks. Bullies perceive their victims as physically weaker, "nerds," and "afraid to fight back." These victims do not report the bullying; hence, the bully is given permission (through omission) to continue.

It has been suggested with regard to bullying that there are no "innocent" bystanders. Those who observe the bullying either support it or are neutral to it. Researchers have suggested that there are six different types of bystanders, all with a different dynamic:

1. *The bully.* As discussed previously, he/she rules through threats of violence and intimidation.
2. *Followers or henchmen.* These take part in the bullying but are not the initiators of the action.
3. *Supporters.* They enjoy observing the bullying but do not take part in it.
4. *Disengaged onlookers.* They assert that the bullying of someone else is not their concern.
5. *Possible defenders.* These believe that the target of the bullying activity should be defended.
6. *Defenders.* Those unique individuals who actually attempt to help the victim of the bully (and his followers/henchmen). Although popular media may contradict the reality, in cases of bullying there exist few defenders.

Conclusion

The consistent theme evident in all forms of bullying in families is the intention of the bullies to humiliate the victims and achieve complete control over their lives. Bullying is a complex and multifaceted dynamic that tends to manifest in multiple forms in American society. Bullying in the family may indeed be related to other types of bullying in our culture. The consequences of being victimized by a bully vary with the individual and the severity and duration of the bullying. However, it is suggested that bullying not only affects the victim, but also, for instance, an entire school environment. Bullying disrupts classes and redirects the attention of the teachers away from teaching. A teacher who must constantly monitor the activities of one student is not focused upon teaching. It must also be acknowledged that although the overwhelming majority of victims of bullying in schools are students, there are some victims of bullies who are teachers, nurses, and/or school administrators.

Bullying may have both short- and long-term consequences for the victim. Short-term consequences can include psychological distress, physical illness, a lack of concentration on schoolwork, and a fear of attending school. Long-term consequences can include low self-esteem, depression, and a reduced capacity for learning.

Often, in many cases of bullying, the victims display behaviors of anxiousness, nervousness, and worry. In other cases, victims themselves become aggressive toward other nonbullying students. Students who are victims of bullying spend much of the time during their school day planning how not to be a victim. For example, a student who is concerned about being victimized in the bathroom may choose not to eat or drink during the day for fear of having to go to the bathroom, or may request permission to go to the bathroom during class time while the other students remain in the classroom. A student worried about victimization on the playground may act out in class to avoid being allowed to go outside and therefore stay inside under the supervision and protection of the teacher. For these students, educational learning is limited, and for the victims who cannot plan for their protection on school grounds, absenteeism becomes an issue.

Statistics indicate that 15 percent of U.S. students with persistent absences report bullying as their initial reason for missing school. Students who are not attending school are not learning. Schools which receive funding based upon the number of students in attendance suffer financially when students are afraid to come to school. Therefore, bullying, directly and indirectly, can pose one set of problems for the victim and another set for the educational system.

It has been suggested that many of the youths who were bullies in their schools were later members of street gangs. This is especially true for females. Reportedly, female gang members were even more likely than males to have been bullied at home and then to bully someone else at school. It is also suggested that involvement in bullying—as bully or victim—was related to juvenile involvement in violence and weapons. As publicized in the media since the 1990s, bullying can lead to severe consequences, such as school shootings like those at Columbine High School in Colorado.

In some rare cases of bullying, victims are initially the target of verbalized bullying; however, the verbal abuse escalates into physical abuse. Therefore, the victims are forced to fight to defend themselves and are often injured during these confrontations. Bullying is often the root of other forms of violence. In other rare cases of bullying, the victim decides that the only way to end the victimization is to kill the perpetrator. As is seen in cases of domestic violence, the victim, after a history of abuse at the hands of the perpetrator, kills the abuser either during a conflict or prior to his/her perception of a future conflict.

In addition, adolescents who have been bullied are isolated and, oftentimes, very angry. Their natural inclination is to gravitate toward others with similar experiences. This may result in friendships with other victims of bullies and sometimes develops into antisocial attitudes that may manifest in destructive behavior, including self-destructive

behavior and even suicide. Although most people perceive the Columbine incident as a mass shooting by two students, it was in fact a planned suicide. Prior to shooting their classmates, teachers, and ultimately themselves, Eric Harris and Dylan Klebold had recorded suicide messages to their families on videotapes. In each of these boys' accounts, they acknowledged that they would commit suicide. Hence, before entering Columbine, before attempting to ignite the first explosive, and before shooting the first students, the end result was intended to be a suicide, which many individuals, including the shooters and the media, attributed to bullying by classmates.

Unfortunately, this type of behavior is usually ignored by society unless it spills over into physical or sexual abuse or the victim is killed. Fundamental social and cultural mores must change if the insidious and destructive behavior of bullying within the family and within the school system is to be eradicated.

GREG MARTIN

See also **Child Abuse: A Global Perspective; Child Abuse and Neglect in the United States: An Overview; Child Neglect; Children Witnessing Parental Violence; Christianity and Domestic Violence; Control Balance Theory and Domestic Violence; Pseudo–Family Abuse; Sibling Abuse**

References and Further Reading

ABCNews.com. "Serious Bullying," November 29, 2001. http://abcnews.go.com.
Addington, L. A., S. A. Ruddy, A. K. Miller, J. F. DeVoe, and A. K. Chandler. *Are America's Schools Safe? Students Speak Out. 1999 School Crime Supplement.* Washington, DC: US Department of Education, 2002 (NCES-2002-331).
Agnew, R. *Juvenile Delinquency: Causes and Control.* Los Angeles: Roxbury, 2001.
Akers, R. L. *Deviant Behavior: A Social Learning Approach.* Belmont, CA: Wadsworth, 1973.
———. *Deviant Behavior: A Social Learning Approach,* 3rd ed. Belmont, CA: Wadsworth, 1985.
Arnette, J. L., and M. C. Walsleben. *Combating Fear and Restoring Safety in Schools.* Washington, DC: U.S. Department of Justice, 1998.
Bandura, A. *Social Learning Theory.* Englewood Cliffs, NJ: Prentice Hall, 1977.
Barkan, S E. *Criminology. A Sociological Understanding,* 2nd ed. Upper Saddle River, NJ: Prentice Hall, 2001.
Barone, F. J. "Bullying Can Be Prevented." In *School Violence,* edited by J. L. Bender, B. Leone, B. Szumski, D. M. Haugen, and B. Stalcups. San Diego, CA: Greenhaven, 2000, pp. 119–123.
Batsche, G. M., and H. M. Knoff. "Bullies and Their Victims: Understanding a Pervasive Problem in the Schools." *School Psychology Review* 23, no. 2 (1994): 165–174.

Bethel v. Fraser, 478 U.S. 675 (1986).

Casella, R. "What Is Violent about 'School Violence'? The Nature of Violence in a City High School." In *Preventing Violence in Schools: A Challenge to American Democracy,* edited by J. N. Burstyn et al. Mahwah, NJ: Lawrence Erlbaum Associates, 2001.

Charach, A., D. Pepler, and S. Ziegler. "Bullying at School: A Canadian Perspective. A Survey of Problems and Suggestions for Intervention." *Education Canada* 35, no. 1 (1995): 12–18.

CNN.com. "School Offers Deal to Accused Students," May 21, 2003. http://www.cnn.com/2003/education/05/20/highschool.hazing.ap/index.html.

Coloroso, B. *The Bully, the Bullied, and the Bystander.* New York: HarperCollins, 2003.

Cooper, D., and J. L. Snell. "Bullying: Not Just a Kid Thing." *Educational Leadership* 60, no. 6 (2003): 22–25.

Cornell, D. G., and A. B. Looper. "Assessment of Violence and Other High-Risk Behaviors with a School Survey." *School Psychological Review* 27 (1998): 317–330.

Crick, N. R., J. F. Casas, and H. C. Ku. "Relational and Physical Forms of Peer Victimization in Preschool." *Developmental Psychology* 35 (1999): 376–385.

Cunningham, P. B., and S. W. Henggler. "Implementation of an Empirically Based Drug and Violence Prevention and Intervention Program in Public School Settings." *Journal of Clinical Child Psychology* 30, no. 2 (2001): 221–232.

Curran, D. J., and C. M. Renzetti. *Theories of Crime,* 2nd ed. Needham Heights, MA: Pearson Education Company, 2001.

Davis v. Monroe County Board of Education, 525 U.S. 1065 (1999).

Derksen, D. J., and V. C. Strasburger. "Media and Television Violence: Effects on Violence, Aggression, and Antisocial Behaviors in Children." In *School Violence and Society,* edited by A. M. Hoffman. Westport, CT: Praeger, 1996, pp. 61–78.

Dertzon, J. H. "Antisocial Behavior and the Prediction of Violence: A Meta-Analysis." *Psychology in the Schools* 38, no. 1 (2001): 93–106.

Dreikurs, Rudolf, with Vicki Soltz. *Children: The Challenge: The Classic Work on Improving Parent-Child Relations—Intelligent, Humane and Eminently Practical.* New York: Plume, 1920/1991.

Ericson, N. *Addressing the Problems of Juvenile Bullying.* Washington, DC: U.S. Department of Justice. Office of Juvenile Justice and Delinquency Prevention, 2001 (FS-200127).

Espelage, Dorothy L., and Susan M. Swearer, eds. *Bullying in American Schools: A Social-Ecological Perspective on Prevention and Intervention.* Mahwah, NJ: Lawrence Erlbaum Associates, 2003.

Farrington, D. P. "Understanding and Preventing Bullying." In *Crime and Justice: A Review of Research,* vol. 17, edited by M. Tonry. Chicago: University of Chicago Press, 1993, pp. 381–458.

Garbarino, J., and E. DeLara. "Words Can Hurt Forever." *Educational Leadership* 60, no. 6 (2003): 18–21.

Gottfredson, G. D., and D. C. Gottfredson. *Victimization in Schools.* New York: Plenum, 1985.

Hare, R. D. "Psychopathy: A Clinical Construct Whose Time Has Come." *Criminal Justice and Behavior* 23, no. 1 (1996): 25–54.

Hart, S. D., and R. J. Dempster. "Impulsivity and Psychopathy." In *Theory, Assessment, and Treatment,* edited by C. D. Webster and M. A. Jackson. New York: Guilford, 1997, pp. 212–232.

Haugaard, J. J., and M. M. Feerick. "The Influence of Child Abuse and Family Violence on Violence in the Schools." In *School Violence and Society,* edited by A. M. Hoffman. Westport, CT: Praeger, 1996, pp. 79–99.

Henry, D. B., P. H. Tolan, and D. Gorman-Smith, "Longitudinal Family and Peer Group Effects on Violence and Nonviolent Delinquency." *Journal of Child Clinical Psychology* 30, no. 1 (2001): 172–186.

Holmes, S. R., and S. J. Brandenburg-Ayers, "Bullying Behavior in Schools: A Predictor of Later Gang Involvement." *Journal of Gang Research* 5, no. 2 (1998): 1–6.

Killias, M., and J. Rabasa. "Weapons and Athletic Constitutions as Factors Linked to Violence among Male Juveniles: Findings from the Swiss Self-Reported Delinquency Project." *British Journal of Criminology* 37, no. 3 (1997): 446–457.

Lantendre, G. K. "Disruptions and Reconnections: Counseling Young Adolescence in Japanese Schools." In *The Challenge of Eastern Asian Education,* edited by W. K. Cummings and P. G. Altbach. Albany: State University of New York Press, 1992.

Lawrence, R. *School Crime and Juvenile Justice.* New York: Oxford University Press, 1998.

Lombroso, C. *The Criminal Man.* Milan: Hoepli, 1876.

MacDonald, I. M. "Violence in Schools: Multiple Realities." *Alberta Journal of Educational Research* 43 (1997): 142–156.

McCabe, K. A. *Child Abuse and the Criminal Justice System.* New York: Peter Lang, 2003.

McDermott, J. "High Anxiety: Fear of Crime in Secondary Schools." *Contemporary Education* 52 (1980): 18–23.

McKenzie, V. Michael. *Domestic Violence in America.* Lawrenceville, VA: Brunswick Publishing, 1995.

Murakami, Y. "Bullies in the Classroom." In *Transcending Stereotypes: Discovering Japanese Culture and Education,* edited by B. Finkelstein, A. Imamura, and J. Tobin. Yarmouth, ME: Intercultural Press, 1991.

Nolin, M., E. Davies, and K. Chandler. "Student Victimization at School." *Journal of School Health* 66 (1996): 216–226.

Oliver, R., J. H. Hoover, and R. Hazler. "The Perceived Roles of Bullying in Small-Town Midwestern Schools." *Journal of Counseling and Development* 72, no. 4 (1994): 416–419.

Olweus, D. *Bullying at School: What We Know and What We Can Do.* Cambridge, MA: Blackwell, 1993, 2003.

Olweus, D., and S. Limber. *Bullying Prevention Program.* Boulder, CO: Institute of Behavioral Sciences, University of Colorado, 1999.

Pagelow, Mildred Daley, with Lloyd W. Pagelow. *Family Violence.* New York: Praeger, 1984.

Pellegrini, A. D., M. Bartini, and F. Brooks. "School Bullies, Victims, and Aggressive Victims: Factors Relating to Group Affiliation and Victimization in Early Adolescence." *Journal of Educational Psychology* 91 (1999): 216–224.

Phillips, D. "Airplane Accident, Murder, and the Mass Media: Toward a Theory of Imitation and Suggestion." *Social Forces* 58, no. 3 (1980): 1001–1024.

Phillips, D., and L. Carstensen. "Clustering of Teenage Suicides after Television News Stories about Suicide." *New England Journal of Medicine* 315 (1986): 685–689.

Rutger, C., M. E. Engels, M. Dekovic, and W. Meeus. "Parenting Practices, Social Skills and Peer Relationships in Adolescence." *Journal of Social Behavior and Personality* 30 (2002): 3–18.

Sheldon, W. *Varieties of Delinquent Youth.* New York: Harper and Brothers, 1949.

Smith, P., and P. Brain. "Bullying in School: Lessons from Two Decades of Research." *Aggressive Behavior* 26 (2000): 1–9.

Smith, P., and S. Sharpe. "The Problem of School Bullying." In *School Bullying: Insights and Perspectives,* edited by P. Smith and S. Sharpe. New York: Routledge, 1994.

Stephens, R. D. "National Trends in School Violence: Statistics and Prevention Strategies." In *School Violence Intervention: A Practical Handbook,* edited by A. P. Goldstein and J. C. Conoley. New York: Guilford Press, 1997, pp. 72–90.

Tinker v. Des Moines, 393 U.S. 503 (1969).

Toch, H., and K. Adams. *The Disturbed Violent Offender.* New Haven, CT: Yale University Press, 1989.

White, M. *The Material Child: Coming of Age in Japan and America.* New York: Free Press, 1993.

Williams, J., C. Lawton, S. Ellis, S. Walsh, and J. Reed. "Copycat Suicide Attempts." *Lancet* 2, no. 8550 (1987): 102–103.

C

CAREGIVER VIOLENCE AGAINST PEOPLE WITH DISABILITIES

No one knows the precise number of people with disabilities who experience violence or abuse each year, but the number of cases per year in the United States is probably well in excess of 2,000,000. This includes most of the estimated 500,000 to 2,000,000 cases of elder abuse, about one-third of the estimated 3,000,000 cases of child abuse, and a large but unknown number of offenses among adults with disabilities in their middle years of life.

The majority of perpetrators of these offenses are paid or family caregivers. Some of these cases fall within a traditional definition of domestic violence, but many others do not. Large numbers of people with disabilities require assistance from a variety of caregivers, and violence or abuse often takes place within these caregiving relationships. It is important to note that the large number of offenses committed by caregivers cannot be interpreted as a blanket condemnation of caregivers as a group. The vast majority of both paid and family caregivers render a valuable service to both society as a whole and to the individuals they serve without perpetrating violence or abuse.

Caregivers may be traditional family members, paid assistants, or volunteers. While violence by natural, adoptive, or foster care family members is included within most definitions of family and domestic violence, violence by other caregivers may or may not be included, depending on the nature of the definition of "family" being used. Older and narrower definitions that require a relationship by blood or legally binding marriage appear to exclude many of these caregiving relationships, but more modern definitions based on potentially enduring, intimate, and interdependent relationships clearly include a broader range of caregiving relationships.

Many people with disabilities are highly dependent on personal care assistants or other care providers. Caregivers and the individuals who receive care from them often develop strong emotional bonds that go beyond physical and financial interdependence. Caregiving relationships often involve a high degree of intimacy. For example, assistance is frequently required for dressing, bathing, or using the toilet and frequently requires close physical contact between the assistant and the individual requiring care. The duration of these relationships is highly variable, but many last for decades and continue after fromal employment ends. In many cases, caregivers have their own keys to the homes of their clients, and in a considerable number of cases, members of extended families also enter into a second relationship as paid or volunteer caregivers. Considering all of these factors, no clear line can be drawn between caregiving and family relationships, and it is more meaningful to view caregiving relationships along a continuum from less to more family-like, depending on characteristics of the individual situation.

All infants and young children require care from adults, and many adults require care again later in life when age or the accumulated effects of illness or injury reduce independence. In addition, individuals with significant mental or physical disabilities may require various levels of care from others throughout their lives. Much of the violence commonly categorized as child abuse and elder abuse occurs within the context of these caregiving relationships.

In relatively recent years, there has been a growing recognition of violence against people as another category of maltreatment commonly linked to caregiving relationships. Because disability is increasingly prevalent among people with advancing age and because most elder abuse is perpetrated against people who are vulnerable because of some degree of mental or physical disability, almost all cases of elder abuse also can be categorized as violence against people with disabilities. About 30 percent of all children who experience substantiated child abuse and neglect also have diagnosed disabilities. Some studies have reported that as many as two-thirds of children in the child welfare system or foster care have diagnosed disabilities, and children in foster care experience higher rates of abuse than the general population. While much of the violence against people with disabilities could also be classified as child abuse or elder abuse, many adults with disabilities who are too young to be considered elders also become victims of violence or abuse. While there has been much more scholarly study of child abuse and elder abuse than of violence against people with disabilities, the scholarly consideration of violence against people with disabilities has emerged as an overlapping field of study that provides its own unique framework extending across all age groupings.

While foster care is primarily a system of care for children, many adults with developmental disabilities who require care or supervision are also placed in foster homes. The adult foster care system places adults in existing homes and families rather than large institutions or group homes. The creation of foster families for adults with disabilities has generally been an important step toward improving their quality of life, but like other kinds of families, foster families of adults with disabilities may also be dysfunctional, abusive, and violent.

Adding to the large number of people with disabilities in foster homes or who have home-care aides spending time in their homes, there is an entire spectrum of living alternatives that have been generated for people who require care ranging from family-like to institutional. As a result, it is difficult and perhaps inherently arbitrary to draw a clear line between family and institutional living. Assisted living facilities, subsidized adoption, intentional communities, small and stable group home placements, and a variety of other living arrangements have some characteristics of family living and some characteristics of institutional care. For example, some large corporations create a network of small homes that care for one, two, or three individuals with disabilities in what is intended to be a family-like environment.

A wide variety of other individuals may interact with people with disabilities in roles characterized by care, supervision, and significant intimacy. For example, paratransit bus drivers often interact with riders in ways that involve considerable caregiving. They often serve the same riders day after day. They frequently assist their riders in and out of their homes and in some cases go into their homes with them. They commonly come in close contact with their riders as they secure their wheelchairs and fasten their seatbelts. They are sometimes expected to supervise and protect their riders. As a result, these individuals are placed in the role of caregiver as well as driver.

According to the Department of Labor Statistics, 625,770 people employed as home care aides provided services for individuals of all ages who required personal-care assistance in 2002. Furthermore, home health care is the most rapidly expanding segment of the health care industry. This number does not include skilled professionals such as nurses and therapists who provide additional home-care services for individuals who require procedures such as respiratory therapy. As a result, millions of American families have health providers in their homes anywhere from one to forty hours per week, and a few have home-care aides who live with them on a full-time basis. In some cases, families recruit and hire their own assistants, but most home-care aides work for large corporations that provide services under contract.

While large companies have a number of advantages, such as the ability to arrange for substitute caregivers if the primary home-care aide is unable to work, they often have the major disadvantage from the families' perspective of giving families little control over who enters their home.

One high-profile and tragic case illustrating this problem occurred when John W. Ward, a thirty-two-year-old man with cerebral palsy, and his grandmother were both stabbed to death by a home-care worker sent to his home by Trusted Health, Inc. in 1991. The hiring agency had failed to conduct a background check on the health care aide they hired to care for vulnerable people, and after the aide was apprehended for this murder, his six previous felony convictions were revealed to the family. In their defense against a negligence suit that followed the deaths, Trusted Health argued that there was no industry standard on conducting background checks. A Massachusetts jury, however, awarded $26.5 million to the estate of John Ward (*Ward v. Trusted Health*, 1991, Suffolk Superior Court, No. 94-4297). While this decision sent a clear message to service providers regarding their responsibility to screen home-care workers, relevant court decisions have been mixed, and some courts have ruled that prohibiting people fromerly convicted of violent crimes from caregiving occupations is an unconstitutional denial of the right to work.

While many caregiving relationships are healthy and beneficial to all parties, violence, exploitation, and abuse are also common. In many cases, abuse by caregivers is similar to other froms of domestic violence. Physical, emotional, and sexual violence are common. In addition to these types of violence, some caregivers subject people with disabilities to what has been termed "disability-related abuse." For example, rearranging the furniture to make it difficult for a person who is visually impaired to navigate in his own home or moving a wheelchair so that a person with impaired mobility has to drag herself across the floor can be disruptive, dangerous, and humiliating. Even a brief hesitation or delay in restoring function to the respirator of an individual whose breathing depends on assistance can communicate a powerful death threat. Abusive caregivers may also withhold medication from people with disabilities or overmedicate them as froms of abuse.

Abusive Caregivers

Caregiving often involves and sometimes requires exercising some degree of control over the person in care. For example, many people with cognitive or emotional disabilities may need supervision in order to protect them in certain situations. Many caregivers, however, have difficulty limiting their controlling behavior to situations in which it is actually required. Even when the person receiving care is cognitively intact and emotionally healthy, physical disabilities may make the individual so dependent on the caregiver that extreme power imbalances exist. For some abusive caregivers, this control becomes a means to an end, such as financial gain or reduced work demands. For example, a caregiver may be employed to help a person with a physical disability bathe, and the caregiver may use physical or sexual violence, psychological abuse, or rough handling to ensure that the individual will not want to be bathed. Then the caregiver can sleep or watch television rather than working. Similarly, the caregiver may coerce the person in care to hand over his or her bank card and personal identification number in order to get cash or make purchases on a bank account.

In other cases, excessive control becomes an end in itself, and the caregiver gains psychological gratification through the total domination of the person receiving care. Caregivers addicted to controlling others may do a very good job or very poor job of meeting their clients' physical needs. They may resort to physical violence, but implicit or explicit threats often replace physical violence once domination is established. These abusive caregivers may even see their own use of physical violence as a sign of their failure to establish total control. Many abusive caregivers have difficulty coping with authority figures and suffer from pathologically low self-esteem. They seek out vulnerable people as a way of regaining a sense of control and raising their self-esteem through their demonstration of authority over them.

In some cases, the caregivers who exercise this kind of extreme and unhealthy control have been or currently are victims of domestic violence themselves. They have been dominated and controlled by a violent spouse or parent and feel that they have little control over their own lives. By employing their own violence to establish domination over a vulnerable person in their care, they redirect their displaced anger toward vulnerable victims and gain a feeling of being in greater control of their own lives through their demonstration of control over a more vulnerable person. The redirection of displaced anger may also play a role when caregivers, angry with the agency that employs them but afraid to confront their more powerful supervisors, channel their anger toward the people in their care.

Substance abuse problems also play a role in disinhibiting violence or sexual aggression among some caregivers. Some individuals who are successful in managing their own antisocial impulses under normal conditions lose impulse control under the influence of alcohol or other drugs.

In addition, some people with disabilities exhibit aggression or other behavior that is difficult for caregivers to manage, and there may be times when caregivers must use physical force or restraint to protect themselves, the individual with a disability, or a third party. A legitimate need to use physical force or restraint does not justify the use of excessive force or violence. In some caregivers, the need to exercise occasional control in the interest of the individual with a disability becomes a stimulus or excuse for violence.

Abusive caregivers are sometimes categorized as corrupt or predatory. Corrupt caregivers do not enter a caregiving relationship with the intention of being abusive. They often assume the role of caregiver with a genuine desire to help others or simply as an opportunity for employment. Once in the position of caregiver, however, they succumb to temptation and other pressures. Many caregivers are surprised to find themselves experiencing sexual attraction to their clients or impulses to hurt their clients. These feelings, however, are so common among caregivers that they must be considered as normal, and the distinction between healthy caregiving and abusive caregiving is probably more a function of the individual's ability to manage these feelings than it is related to the presence or absence of these feelings. Clear codes of conduct, training, availability of counseling for caregivers, good supervision, and a number of other factors can reduce the risk of violence against people with disabilities by this group of offenders.

In sharp contrast to these corrupt offenders, predatory caregivers seek out caregiving relationships and employment in order to access vulnerable people as victims. Their violence is more planned and organized. When their abusive behavior is identified by one employer, they often simply move to another agency that provides caregiving services. This pattern of behavior is sometimes facilitated by agencies that are willing to write letters of recommendation for staff they suspect of abuse in order to rid their own agency of a problem. Training, counseling, and clear codes of conduct appear to have little effect on the potential for abuse among these offenders. It is often difficult to prove the abuse committed by these individuals because they choose their victims carefully, are often adept at covering their tracks, and frequently make an excellent impression on employers and other authority figures.

Some people with disabilities lack the communication skills to complain about their treatment, and some who have intellectual or psychiatric disabilities are unaware that they have a right to better treatment. Many who know they are being abused and who are capable of complaining are fearful to do so for a variety of reasons. Some fear personal retribution from the abusive caregiver. Some fear service disruption or service denial by the agencies that serve them if they complain about services. Others are afraid that a new caregiver may be worse than the one they have, or simply feel too humiliated to tell about their victimization.

The delivery of home health care and support services has become a major industry in many parts of the world. For example, in the United States in 2004, about 7,800 companies were approved by Medicare to provide home health care services. During that year, Medicaid payments for home nursing reached $11.6 billion. This represents only a fraction of the entire industry, because it does not include care provided through other programs or private hiring. Industry standards for the protection of clients from abuse by caregivers remain poorly defined, but generally agencies are expected to take reasonable measures to manage foreseeable risks.

While there has been relatively little systematic study of abuse of people with disabilities by caregivers outside institutional settings, a few studies have attempted to address this issue. Ulicny and colleagues surveyed individuals with disabilities who required attendant care. They found that approximately 40 percent had experienced some from of abuse or exploitation, including 10 percent who had experienced physical violence by paid caregivers. Another study, by Mathias and Benjamin, included interviews of 271 Californians with disabilities who were receiving caregiving service from paid workers who were not family members. They also interviewed 240 clients who received care from paid family members and who reported significantly less maltreatment. Within the previous twelve months, 12.7 percent of those receiving care from non–family members reported being neglected compared to 5.5 percent of those receiving care from family members. In the same period 9.6 percent of those receiving care from non–family members reported their caregivers yelling at them, compared with 5.6 percent of those receiving care from family members.

In addition, among those receiving care from non–family members, 7.2 percent believed that their caregivers had taken money or other items belonging to the client, 5.7 percent had been injured by a caregiver, 3.6 percent had been threatened, and 3.4 percent had experienced unwanted sexual advances from their caregivers. Among those receiving care from paid family members, the rates were 0.8 percent, 4.3 percent, 2.1 percent, and 1.3 percent, respectively. While this and other research suggests that paid family caregivers provide a safer alternative than caregivers who are not members of the traditional family, some government programs disqualify family members from being paid as caregivers. Violence by paid caregivers affects people with disabilities at every stage of life, but because disabilities affect a larger percentage of the population as age increases and because elderly people are less likely to have unpaid family caregivers, it is a particularly common problem among older adults.

Industry standards, selective hiring, and police checks appear to be useful strategies for reducing violence by paid caregivers. Staff training, supervision, and counseling for paid caregivers also appear to be useful in reducing risk. However, chronic staff shortages and high staff turnover make it difficult to maintain employment standards.

Patterns of Caregiver Abuse

Violence by caregivers can be physical, sexual, or psychological. Some extreme froms of neglect should probably be viewed as violence when they are used as threat or intimidation or when they are intended to harm. As a result of the very high levels of dependency experienced by some people with disabilities, some behavior can produce substantially different results. The following discussion provides a few examples of patterns of abusive behavior that are uniquely related to disability and caregiving.

Many people with disabilities depend on caregivers to administer or assist with their medications. Caregivers may deny or delay medication or may provide less than the appropriate doses. Sometimes, this occurs because an addicted caregiver is taking the medication for personal use or a caregiver is stealing the medication to sell or give to an associate. In other cases, this occurs to create distress or anxiety in the person with the disability or even to create a crisis and stir up some excitement. *Munchausen syndrome by proxy,* a psychological disorder in which caregivers simulate or create illnesses or injuries, may explain some of these cases. Denying medication to an epileptic or diabetic person may result in the individual sleeping excessively and therefore being easier to manage; it may also result in serious harm or even death. Similarly, caregivers may overdose their clients on medications in order to make them more manageable.

Caregiver violence against people with disabilities appears to have a unique relationship to spousal violence. All family relationships involve some degree of caregiving, but the presence or emergence of a disability may radically alter caregiving needs and the balance of power within families. These changes are sometimes accompanied by the initiation of violence or substantial changes in a previously abusive relationship. For example, in many families, one person, most frequently a woman, carries out the primary caregiving role, but the ability to provide care for others or for herself may be compromised by acquired disability. As a result, the fromer caregiving roles may reverse, requiring significant adjustment by all family members. In some cases, the spouse who is forced to assume more responsibility as a caregiver may resent or have difficulty filling this new role and respond with abuse or violence.

In other families, an abusive and violent relationship results in the domination of one spouse by another, usually the domination of the wife by the husband. However, husbands are often older than wives and frequently acquire disability as a result of injuries or disease at earlier ages. As a result, a violent and domineering spouse may become vulnerable and dependent on his or her fromer victim. In some relationships, this can lead to a role reversal, and the fromer victim becomes the abuser.

Another related from of violence may occur when caregivers allow or encourage one individual with a disability to act violently against another. This may occur as a result of simple neglect or a variety of other motives, such as reducing one's own demands as a caregiver by reassigning one's duties to a more able resident. For example, in a classic case, a small care home took in just two clients, a vulnerable sixteen-year-old girl with developmental disabilities and a violent twenty-year-old sex offender with a behavioral disorder. Because she lacked the necessary skills to leave the group home without supervision and the staff was unwilling or unable to take her swimming, they entrusted the vulnerable sixteen-year-old to the sex offender, with the tragic and predictable result of murder.

Conclusion

People with disabilities rely heavily on a variety of family and nonfamily caregivers. While most caregiving relationships are healthy and beneficial, they frequently provide a context for abuse. Patterns of abuse within caregiving relationships are variable. Careful screening and training of people who work as caregivers of vulnerable people help to reduce the risk of violence by caregivers.

DICK SOBSEY

See also **Elder Abuse and Neglect: Training Issues for Professionals; Elder Abuse by Intimate Partners; Elder Abuse Perpetrated by Adult Children; Filicide and Children with Disabilities; Women with Disabilities, Domestic Violence against**

References and Further Reading

Anetzberger, G. J., B. R. Palmisano, M. Sanders, D. Bass, C. Dayton, S. Eckert, et al. "A Model Intervention for Elder Abuse and Dementia." *Gerontologist* 40, no. 4 (2000): 492–497.

Awadallah, N., A. Vaughan, K. Franco, F. Munir, N. Sharaby, and J. Goldfarb. "Munchausen by Proxy: A Case, Chart Series, and Literature Review of Older Victims." *Child Abuse and Neglect* 29, no. 8 (2005): 931–941.

Benedict, M. I., S. Zuravin, M. Somerfield, and D. Brandt. "The Reported Health and Functioning of Children Maltreated While in Family Foster Care." *Child Abuse and Neglect* 20, no. 7 (1996): 561–571.

Finkel, P., M. Fishwick, K. L. Nessel, and D. Solz. "Sexuality and Attendant Care: A Panel Discussion." In *Sexuality and Physical Disability: Personal Perspectives,* edited by D. G. Bullard and S. E. Knight. St. Louis: C. V. Mosby, 1981, pp. 111–123.

Fisher, J. W., and C. B. Dyer. "The Hidden Health Menace of Elder Abuse: Physicians Can Help Patients Surmount Intimate Partner Violence." *Postgraduate Medicine* 113, no. 4 (2003): 21–24, 30.

Hansberry, M. R., E. Chen, and M. J. Gorbien. "Dementia and Elder Abuse." *Clinics in Geriatric Medicine* 21, no. 2 (2005): 315–332.

Harden, B. J. "Safety and Stability for Foster Children: A Developmental Perspective." *Future of Children* 14, no. 1 (2004): 30–47.

Hazen, A. L., C. D. Connelly, K. J. Kelleher, R. P. Barth, and J. A. Landsverk. "Female Caregivers' Experiences with Intimate Partner Violence and Behavior Problems in Children Investigated as Victims of Maltreatment." *Pediatrics* 117, no. 1 (2006): 99–109.

Matthias, R. E., and A. E. Benjamin. "Abuse and Neglect of Clients in Agency-Based and Consumer-Directed Home Care." *Health and Social Work* 28, no. 3 (2003): 174–184.

McFarlane, J., R. B. Hughes, M. A. Nosek, J. Y. Groff, N. Swedlend, and P. Dolan Mullen. "Abuse Assessment Screen-Disability (AAS-D): Measuring Frequency, Type, and Perpetrator of Abuse toward Women with Physical Disabilities." *Journal of Women's Health and Gender Based Medicine,* 10, no. 9 (2001): 861–866.

Milberger, S., N. Israel, B. LeRoy, A. Martin, L. Potter, and P. Patchak-Schuster. "Violence against Women with Physical Disabilities." *Violence and Victims* 18, no. 5 (2003): 581–591.

Nosek, Margaret A. "Sexual Abuse of Women with Physical Disabilities." In *Women with Physical Disabilities: Achieving and Maintaining Health and Well-being,* edited by D. M. Krotoski, M.A. Nosek, and M.A. Turk. Baltimore: Paul H. Brookes, 1996, pp. 153–173.

Smith, J. M. "Foster Care Children with Disabilities." *Journal of Health and Social Policy* 16, no. 1–2 (2002): 81–92.

Sobsey, D. *Violence and Abuse in the Lives of People with Disabilities: The End of Silent Acceptance.* Baltimore: Paul H. Brookes, 1994.

Sullivan, P. M., and J. F. Knutson. "Maltreatment and Disabilities: A Population-Based Epidemiological Study." *Child Abuse and Neglect* 24, no. 10 (2000): 1257–1273.

Ulicny, G. R., G. W. White, B. Brandford, and R. M. Mathews. "Consumer Exploitation by Attendants: How Often Does It Happen and Can Anything Be Done About It?" *Rehabilitation Counseling Bulletin* 33, no. 3 (1990): 240–246.

Yativ, N. "Nanny, Lies, and Videotape: Child Abuse and Privacy Rights Dilemmas." *Pediatrics* 115, no. 6 (2005): 1791–1792.

Young, M. E., M. A. Nosek, C. Howland, G. Chanpong, and D. H. Rintala. "Prevalence of Abuse of Women with Physical Disabilities." *Archives of Physical Medicine and Rehabilitation* 78, no. 12 (1997): S34–S38.

CHILD ABUSE: A GLOBAL PERSPECTIVE

Child abuse and neglect affects millions worldwide, and the issues surrounding this social problem are remarkably similar regardless of economic resources or political structure. However, although this tragic social issue exists in most countries, the kinds of abuse and neglect and the ways they are defined, prevented, and treated vary significantly from country to country. Many countries appear to be in a state of flux regarding this issue, striving to create definitions of abuse and neglect within their cultural contexts, while seeking adequate distinctions between acceptable discipline and child rearing practices and inappropriate practices that should be defined as maltreatment. In addition to these crucial definitional issues, experts in many countries note their frustration with the lack of resources available to tackle the problem of child abuse and neglect (Schwartz-Kenney, McCauley, and Epstein 2001).

The United Nations Convention on the Rights of the Child

The Convention on the Rights of the Child (CRC), one of the many United Nations Agreements on Human Rights, seeks to provide a common definitional understanding of child abuse and neglect and an organized and consistent framework for protecting children around the world regardless of sex, religion, social origin, or country of residence. The CRC was developed over a ten-year period and was opened for signature and ratification in 1989 (United Nations Children's Fund [UNICEF] 1989). It bans discrimination against children and provides for special protection and rights appropriate to minors. Governments that have ratified the CRC state that they have a clear commitment to protecting and ensuring the human rights of children, as defined in the convention. By signing, each country also becomes accountable to the international community to follow the set of standards and obligations described in detail within the document. Specifically, the convention states that children have the right to survival; to develop to their fullest; to be protected from harm, including abuse and exploitation; and to participate fully in family, cultural, and social life. In addition, the convention includes guidelines governing health care, education, and legal, civil, and social services. Finally, countries may choose to ratify two optional protocols governing the involvement of children in armed conflict and child sexual exploitation through the sale of children, child prostitution, and child pornography.

The CRC is one of the most successful of the United Nations' human rights initiatives. One hundred and ninety-two countries have ratified the convention. Only two members of the United Nations—the United States and Somalia—have yet to ratify the CRC, although both countries have indicated their intent to do so by fromally signing the convention. Somalia has been unable to ratify this document because it lacks a recognized government, and an extensive examination is currently under way in the United States to determine whether the CRC is consistent with existing state and federal laws and practices. The CRC has proven effective worldwide, prompting changes in legislation and policy in numerous countries. However, despite near-global acceptance of the CRC, it has not yet created unifrom global legal refroms.

Global Unifromity Not Yet Achieved

Consider, for example, the issue of child testimony. In cases of child abuse and neglect, children must provide testimony in court because the child is often the sole witness to the crime. The need for testimony creates a countervailing difficulty, in that forcing the child to recount his or her experiences may prove traumatic to the child, and having the child testify in the presence of the alleged abuser may prove frightening to the child, resulting in further trauma or inaccurate testimony. Countries vary greatly in their approaches to these problems (see Bottoms and Goodman 1996, which provides an international perspective on child abuse and the use of children's testimony within legal systems). In Canada, children are allowed to testify via closed-circuit television, or behind a screen in the courtroom, if the judge believes that the child witness cannot testify as accurately under the standard courtroom conditions. A similar accommodation is available in thirty-six of the seventy-two courts in England and Wales, in which the child can testify in an adjacent room accompanied by a supportive adult (see Bull and Davies, in Bottoms and Goodman 1996). Live-link television is also available to child witnesses in New Zealand, Scotland, and Australia. These accommodations are freely available when a country's legal system does not guarantee a defendant the right to cross-examine witnesses or confront his or her accusers.

In the United States, where the rights to cross-examine and confront one's accusers is guaranteed by the U.S. Constitution, judges are required to protect these rights and cannot freely allow a child witness to testify outside of court from a less public location. However, in the United States, the rights to confront and cross-examine witnesses are not absolute, and U.S. judges do have the authority to accommodate child witnesses under certain circumstances. In those instances in which in-court testimony is required, it may be possible for the child witness to turn away from the defendant while testifying, while still allowing the defendant to see the witness. States vary as to the accommodations allowed to child witnesses, and the decision to allow such accommodations is frequently left to the discretion of the judge. As a result, the accommodations that can be obtained are often dependent on the presiding judge (Myers 1996).

ISPCAN Surveys

The International Society for the Prevention of Child Abuse and Neglect (ISPCAN) has conducted numerous worldwide surveys to obtain a global perspective of the characteristics of and responses to child abuse. ISPCAN's goal in conducting this research is to provide infromation from a global perspective, from which programmatic changes can be identified and implemented based on successes and problems in this area around the world. Its latest survey was released in 2004 (ISPCAN 2004). For most of its research, the Society's response rate has been approximately 50–70 percent. In the 2004 survey, of the ninety-four countries invited, sixty-four countries provided infromation. The respondent countries represent a diverse group, including countries from Africa, the Americas, Asia, Europe, and Oceania. Because of this great diversity, the ISPCAN survey provides a truly global perspective of the problem of child abuse and neglect.

Accordingly, the summary below is based primarily on the Society's comprehensive survey research, as well as two other resources that provide infromation on the global view of child abuse (Bottoms and Goodman 1996; Schwartz-Kenney, McCauley, and Epstein 2001).

Prevalence of Definitional Diversity

To assess similarities and differences in definitions of child abuse and neglect, the ISPCAN researchers listed behaviors and conditions and asked responders to indicate whether the behaviors or conditions would be labeled abuse or neglect in his or her country. The survey reveals many similarities in definitions of abuse and neglect (ISPCAN 2004). For example, all of the responding countries agree on the illegality of sexual abuse, although how sexual abuse is defined differs from country to country. Most countries also included in their definition of abuse such behaviors and conditions as child prostitution, children living on the street, physical beating of a child by an adult, foster care abuse and neglect, and abandonment by caretakers. However, despite these similarities, the ISPCAN survey reveals wide variations in defining the problem of child abuse and neglect.

Regional differences in definitions of child abuse or neglect are particularly dependent upon differences in cultural and religious values. For instance, behaviors such as failure to secure medical care, female circumcision, and physical discipline are not labeled as child abuse or neglect in regions where these behaviors are included in cultural or religious practices. Asian and African countries were less likely to define female infanticide as abuse than countries in the Americas, Europe, or Oceania.

Among the diverse views of child abuse and neglect, physical discipline of children produced the most widely varied response. Only 46 percent of countries surveyed considered physical discipline of children to be an abusive act. In those countries where physical discipline is not considered abuse, parents and teachers impose corporal punishment that would readily be labeled as abuse elsewhere. For instance, in Sri Lanka, an education ordinance is still in effect from 1939 that permits caning of students in Government Schools.

Other variations in definitions of abuse and neglect seem to stem from economic status—whether a country is developed or developing. Many developed countries define a number of resource-based behaviors and conditions as abuse or neglect (e.g., lack of basic necessities such as food, clothing, or shelter; forcing a child to beg; abuse or neglect committed within a school, daycare center, or psychiatric center; parental substance abuse that affects the child; psychological neglect; parental mental illness), where many developing countries do not. Essentially, when countries are faced with extreme economic hardship, as many developing countries are, such resource-based behaviors are often unavoidable and, therefore, are not considered abusive. Bottoms and Goodman (1996) suggest that cross-cultural differences in definitions of abuse and neglect may be related to the different resources available to each country to deal with the problem and corresponding differences in the relative emphasis that each country places on the issue. For example, in India, many children are considered lucky simply to have a roof over their head and someone to take care of them, a situation which leads to a relative de-emphasis on the degree of kindness received from the caretaker. Accordingly, India has a significantly high population of street children, many of whom are exploited by adults through working, begging, and prostitution (see Segal in Schwartz-Kenney et al. 2001). By contrast, in the more affluent Sweden, it is illegal to spank a child.

Accordingly, in more developed countries, definitions of abuse frequently have a broader scope than definitions in less developed countries. However, even in some developed countries, commonly accepted definitions may be of only recent vintage. In Spain, commonly used and agreed upon definitions of abuse were not developed until 1987. The legislative act outlined different situations that could be indicative of child abuse and lead to child protection intervention by government child protection agencies. The covered situations included inappropriate protection or maltreatment of children by guardians. Definitions of physical abuse included any nonaccidental behavior by parents that leads to physical harm or placing a child at risk of physical abuse. After the legislative act, professional handbooks were developed to assist child protection agencies in classifying cases. Spain's definitions are consistent with those used in many other European countries and America (see de Paul and Gonzalez in Schwartz-Kenney et al. 2001).

In England, physical abuse includes instances in which children are subject to actual injury, failure to prevent injury, or placing a child in a situation in which he or she is likely to experience injury. Neglect may be persistent or severe, as well as the failure to protect from exposure to danger. Sexual abuse is more loosely defined and includes instances of actual or likely sexual exploitation of children (see Stainton-Rogers and Roche in Schwartz-Kenney et al. 2001).

Global Variations in Available Services

The ISPCAN respondents reported great differences in services available to intervene when abuse was present. These differences were in the type of interventions available (e.g., services for children or services for parents). More developed countries (e.g., United States, Canada) provide a wider array of services compared with developing countries (e.g., India, Rwanda, South Africa). Looking at all responding countries as a whole, services were most often made available to children, rather than parents. When services were available for parents, European countries provided therapy and home visits, which were often not available in African countries. These differences therefore parallel those between economic statuses in terms of definitions: More developed countries are likely to cast a wider net around the issues, with respect to both scope and services, than less developed countries. Differences between developed and developing countries also emerged in connection with prevention strategies, with most differences arising in the areas of availability of services overall and greater access to health care and home-based strategies. ISPCAN respondents most often cited limited resources, decline in family support, and family privacy as factors that limited greater prevention of abuse and neglect. Many African nations cited the influence of poverty, availability of health services, and dependency on finances from other countries as reasons why prevention efforts were not more extensive.

In addition to the presence of services, ISPCAN researchers also assessed the adequacy of the services available. Regional differences again emerged, with those from Africa and the Americas reporting lower adequacy of service compared with Asian and European respondents. This difference is likely due in part to how "adequate" is defined in each responding country.

Differences based on developmental status also appear with respect to funding sources of services. When services were available, they were most often provided through non-governmental organizations (NGOs), private foundations, hospitals, and service agencies, rather than universities, religious organizations, or businesses. Only rarely were services provided by relief organizations such as the

Red Cross. However, in developing countries, NGOs and international relief organizations provided more funding than in developed countries. Funding for developed countries more often came from national and local governments.

When preventative measures were available, the ISPCAN respondents most often reported strategies such as advocacy, professional training, media campaigns, and prosecution. However, even where these strategies were in place, many responding countries indicated that the strategies were not effectively reducing the occurrence of child abuse and neglect. When the available strategies are compared based on developmental status, developed countries were more likely to provide individual-level preventative strategies, such as risk assessment, home-based services, and home visitation, as well as community-based strategies such as universal health care and preventative medical care. The lack of these strategies in less developed countries is most likely due to lack of resources or funds available to provide these services to all those in need.

With regard to investigations of suspected cases of abuse or neglect, wide variations exist even within individual countries. For instance, in the United States, investigation procedures differ from state to state. Australia was the first country to attempt to create a national strategy for approaching the problem of child abuse and neglect. There, child abuse and neglect is categorized under one of four categories: neglect or abandonment, physical abuse, emotional abuse, or sexual abuse. Once reported, independent committees are responsible for investigating all reports of suspected abuse (Schwartz-Kenney et al. 2001).

The ISPCAN researchers attempted to examine the prevalence of child abuse and neglect within countries indirectly, by attempting to measure the well-being of children from country to country. The well-being of individual children is related to child abuse and maltreatment because the well-being of a child is usually directly related to the willingness and ability of a caretaker to adequately meet a child's basic needs. When those basic needs are not met, children suffer, and, in severe situations, the mortality rate of children will significantly increase. To this end, the ISPCAN survey measured adopted the same measure of well-being used by UNICEF in its State of the World's Children Report (UNICEF 2004). The measure is called the Under-Five Mortality Rate (U5MR) and is used as a measure of child well-being because the death of a child often results due to a parent or

guardian's unwillingness or inability to meet a child's basic needs, or due to a government's failure to provide sufficient health care, or finally due to overall societal neglect. Results from the ISPCAN report indicate that poverty, children living on their own, inadequate health care systems, acceptance of corporal punishment, and the need for family privacy all significantly related to children's overall well-being. The most important factor governing child well-being was whether a country had a reporting system of abuse in place and whether parental services were available when abuse was reported. Accordingly, most experts see general public awareness of abuse as one route to increased intervention and prevention. Fortunately, all countries but one indicated an increase in awareness of child abuse neglect during the ten years preceding ISPCAN's 2004 survey.

Awareness at the Public and Governmental Levels

To increase awareness, some countries have implemented public awareness campaigns, which seemed effective in Africa, the Americas, and Asia. In Europe, awareness was increased more through professional education. The ISPCAN report also noted that awareness was also affected, though less often, by media profiles of child deaths and through the efforts of NGOs. These last types of awareness factors did not differ between developed and developing countries.

The ISPCAN survey asked respondents to indicate if and how their country maintained records of cases of child abuse and neglect as well as public awareness of the problem. They found that a significant number of countries (68 percent) conducted population surveys, many conducted public opinion polls (67 percent), with fewer monitoring an official count of cases (57 percent). Of the countries that did maintain specific infromation concerning the number of child abuse and neglect cases, most included physical, sexual, neglect, and psychological maltreatment within the database. Developmental status differences did emerge, with developing countries using public opinion polls more often than developed countries. These public opinion polls allow the developing countries to maintain infromation about awareness and how residents define abuse, but with much lower expense involved. All countries but one indicated an increase in public awareness of abuse and neglect over the last decade. Developed countries reported greater public awareness of ways to protect children from abuse and neglect than developing countries.

The history of legislative recognition of the problem within countries illustrates the global diversity in recognizing and addressing the problem. In Australia, the problem of child abuse and neglect was recognized over 100 years ago when the Offences against the Person Act was passed, creating harsh consequences for those who commit crimes against children (see Shrimpton, Oates, and Hayes, in Bottoms and Goodman 1996). In Canada, there was also little social or legal recognition of the needs of children until the end of the nineteenth century (Mia, Bala, and MacMillan 2001). The same time frame can be found in England and Ireland, where the National Society for the Prevention of Cruelty to Children began its work at the end of the nineteenth century (see Stainton-Rogers and Roche, in Schwartz-Kenney 2001). In contrast, in Hong Kong, statutory protection of children from abuse focused primarily on sexual exploitation against girls, until 1951, when the protection of Women and Juveniles Ordinance was enacted (see Ho in Bottoms and Goodman 1996).

ISPCAN's 2004 survey reports that 81 percent of responding countries have an official governmental policy on child abuse and neglect. One-third of those policies were in place before 1980, and 41 percent were enacted between 1990 and 2000. The policies usually include criminal penalties for abusing a child and provisions for state response to abuse, such as removing a child from the abusive environment. Most policies also included infromation on mandatory and voluntary reporting laws. Countries reporting no national policy included Hong Kong, Saudi Arabia, Syria, Australia, and Romania. Only one-third of the official policies required intervention services for abusers, and two-thirds included resources for prevention services. The report indicates that the lack of focus on intervention is likely due to the increase in defining child abuse as a crime rather than a mental health problem and to the lower cost of prevention (e.g., parenting education and family support services) compared with intervention (e.g., ongoing therapy). Although most countries reported official policies for responding to reports of abuse and neglect, only one-third of all countries noted that these policies were implemented consistently. More than half of the countries also maintained a database for the number of cases of abuse, specifically physical, sexual, neglect, and psychological maltreatment. Regional differences emerged regarding reporting laws, with African and Asian countries less likely to have mandatory reporting laws. The lack of mandatory reporting is likely due, again, to the limited resources available in these regions.

BETH M. SCHWARTZ and
MICHELLE R. MCCAULEY

See also **Child Abuse and Juvenile Delinquency; Child Neglect; Child Sexual Abuse; Christianity and Domestic Violence; Corporal Punishment, Religious Attitudes toward; Ritual Abuse–Torture in Families; Rule of Thumb; Worldwide Sociolegal Precedents Supporting Domestic Violence from Ancient to Modern Times**

References and Further Reading

Bottoms, B. L., and G. S. Goodman. *International Perspectives on Child Abuse and Children's Testimony: Psychological Research and Law.* Thousand Oaks, CA: Sage Publications, 1996.

ISPCAN. *World Perspectives on Child Abuse,* 6th ed., 2004. http://www.ispcan.org/wp/index.htm (accessed August 13, 2006).

Schwartz-Kenney, B. M., M. McCauley, and M. Epstein. *Child Abuse: A Global View.* Westport, CT: Greenwood Publishing, 2001.

United Nations Children's Fund (UNICEF). "Convention on the Rights of the Child," 1989. http://www.unicef.org/crc/crc.htm (accessed August 13, 2006).

———. "State of the World's Children Report: Children Under Threat," 2004. http://www.unicef.org/publications/index_24432.html (accessed September 15, 2005).

CHILD ABUSE AND JUVENILE DELINQUENCY

Introduction

So much attention has been given by researchers and professionals to the critical link between child abuse and juvenile delinquency that most would assume that child abuse causes later juvenile delinquency and wonder why there is still a discussion of the issue. Early research suggested that this was a simple relationship. Widom (1989) and Smith and Thornberry (1995) found evidence of this relationship initially. However, more recent studies have found that the relationship between child abuse and juvenile delinquency is more multifaceted and intriguing than originally thought. Additionally, newer studies have begun to recognize the association between children's abuse within the family and exposure to domestic violence and the development of juvenile delinquency. This article will delineate and explain the intricate relationship between child abuse and juvenile delinquency, as well as describe the latest infromation regarding the relationship between youth exposure to domestic violence and the later development of juvenile delinquency.

Definitions

One common discrepancy found throughout the literature in this area is the lack of consistent definitions among terms. Child abuse, juvenile delinquency, and domestic violence are described and labeled differently within research studies, resources on the Internet, and searches throughout university libraries. Oftentimes domestic violence is termed *family violence, spousal abuse,* or *intimate partner violence,* whereas child maltreatment may be defined and categorized into specific froms of abuse. As broad as the term *child abuse* is, there are still wavering discrepancies among the definitions of sexual abuse, neglect, physical abuse, and emotional and/or psychological maltreatment.

The Child Abuse Prevention and Treatment Act (CAPTA) is the law (P.L. 93–247) that provides a foundation for a national definition of child abuse and neglect. CAPTA defines child abuse and neglect as "at a minimum, any recent act or failure to act on the part of a parent or caretaker, which results in death, serious physical or emotional harm, sexual abuse or exploitation, or an act or failure to act which presents an imminent risk of serious harm."

Sexual abuse is "inappropriate adolescent or adult sexual behavior with a child. It includes fondling a child's genitals, making the child fondle the adult's genitals, intercourse, incest, rape, sodomy, exhibitionism, sexual exploitation, or exposure to pornography." Physical abuse is "the inflicting of a non-accidental physical injury upon a child. This may include burning, hitting, punching, shaking, kicking, beating, or otherwise harming a child. It may, however, have been the result of over-discipline or physical punishment that is inappropriate to the child's age." Psychological maltreatment is "a pattern of caregiver behavior or extreme incidents that convey to children that they are worthless, flawed, unloved, unwanted, endangered, or only of value to meeting another's needs. This can include parents or caretakers using extreme or bizarre froms of punishment or threatening or terrorizing a child. The term 'psychological maltreatment' is also known as emotional abuse, verbal abuse, or mental abuse." Neglect is "the failure to provide for the child's basic needs. Neglect can be physical, educational, or emotional. Physical neglect can include not providing adequate food or clothing, appropriate medical care, supervision, or proper weather protection (i.e., providing a heated living environment or coats when it is cold). Educational neglect includes failure to provide appropriate schooling or special educational needs, or allowing excessive truancies. Psychological neglect includes the lack of any emotional support and love, chronic inattention to the child, or exposure to spouse abuse or drug and alcohol abuse" (Administration for Children and Families 2005). Finally, a juvenile delinquent is a minor who commits one or more froms of antisocial behavior. Most state codes define juvenile delinquency as behavior that is in violation of the criminal code and is committed by a youth who has not reached adult age (Roberts 2004).

Child Abuse

In 2000, there were over 880,000 reports of child maltreatment to Child Protective Services (Administration for Children and Families 2005). Fifty-two percent of the victims were female, 55 percent were white, 28 percent were black, 12 percent were Hispanic, and 5 percent were other races. Nineteen percent of victims were age two or younger, 52 percent were age seven or younger, and 7 percent were age sixteen or older. The vast majority (80 percent) of perpetrators were parents of the victims. An estimated 1,077 children died as the result of maltreatment and approximately 16 percent of victims in substantiated or indicated cases were removed from their homes. The most common from of child abuse is neglect, followed by physical, and then sexual abuse (Snyder and Sickmund 1999).

A growing body of knowledge suggests that child abuse is a causal contributor to many emotional and behavioral problems, including juvenile delinquency (Lemmon 1999). The long-standing effect of child abuse in juveniles has been well documented, and previous studies suggest a pattern of abuse and neglect as a precursor to later offending behavior in both adolescents and adults (Crittenden and Ainsworth 1989; Smith and Thornberry 1995; Widom 1989). Studies have found that abused youth are referred to the juvenile justice system more often than their nonabused and nonneglected counterparts and are also significantly younger at the time of initial referral (Lemmon 1999). In addition, abused youth are more often persistent and violent offenders as compared with nonabused youth, who are more likely infrequent, low-risk offenders (Lemmon 1999). Boswell (1995) found that 72 percent of violent youth residing within the juvenile justice system had experienced emotional, physical, sexual, or ritual-type abuse, with 27 percent having been subjected to two or more types.

Child abuse does help shed light on why some juveniles engage in delinquency. However, not all children who are abused go on to engage in juvenile delinquency, and not all juvenile delinquents have histories of child abuse. This infromation suggests that child abuse by itself is not a cause of juvenile delinquency. Rather, a more complex explanation is required.

Data support the conclusion that there are many common pathways, not just one specific variable, which may lead a youth toward delinquent behavior. Influential factors include: child abuse victimization; exposure to domestic violence; association with delinquent peers; parents with poor parenting skills; lack of parental bonding; availability of drugs and firearms; and community disorganization (Hawkins, Herrenkohl, Farrington, Brewer, Catalano, and Harachi 1998). These factors are termed *risk factors*; the more risk factors the youth or family has, the higher the likelihood of the youth engaging in delinquency. These risk factors are interrelated. For instance, the availability of drugs and firearms is related to high levels of community disorganization; poor parenting skills open up the opportunity for the youth to associate with delinquent peers. Consequently, child abuse is one risk factor for juvenile delinquency, but certainly not the only one. Risk factors should also not be confused with predetermination, in that having a risk factor does not mean that one will automatically become a juvenile delinquent. Many children who are abused do not engage in delinquency when they reach adolescence, and some have no long-term effects from the abuse.

Types of Abuse Relating to Types of Delinquency

All abuse is not the same. Various froms of abuse result in different reactions and behaviors by youth. The tendency for persons to commit crime will differ based on the specific maltreatment experienced. Studies illustrate that experiencing specific child maltreatment can justifiably result in the exhibition of the similar type of offending behavior later on (Hamilton, Falshaw, and Browne 2002). For example, Dutton and Hart (1992) reported that a childhood of physical abuse could possibly progress in comparable types of criminal activity. Whereas those who experience sexual abuse may later become sexually violent, a person may not become a sexual abuser unless he or she has experienced some from of sexual trauma (Bagley, Wood, and Young 1994; Dutton and Hart 1992; Ford and Linney 1995; Prendergast 1991).

Children who are victims of neglect are at the highest risk of becoming delinquent, with the highest probability, 1 in 10, in becoming involved in criminal activity, whereas physical abuse victims were reported to have a 9.3 percent chance (1 in 11) of becoming delinquent. Physical abuse victims, though, do engage in more aggressive and violent types of delinquency (Zingraff, Leiter, Johnson, and Myers 1994), and physical abuse lends a unique risk to girls for violent offending, in that physically abused girls are over seven times more likely to commit a violent offense than nonabused girls (Herrera and McCloskey 2001).

Herrenkohl, Huang, Tajima, and Whitney (2003) found abusive discipline to be as detrimental as physical abuse. This type of abuse included paddling or severe spanking which left marks or bruises. Children disciplined in this manner developed violent attitudes, later became involved with violent peers, and subsequently exhibited violent behavior of their own.

Sexual abuse victims often engage later in nonaggressive sexual offenses compared with physical abuse victims, who evince higher aggression (Mouzakitis 1981). However, there appears to be a direct association between sexual abuse and delinquency in girls. Fifty-six percent of the girls studied in California's juvenile justice system reported past sexual abuse (Acoca 1998), and Finkelhor and Baron (1986) found sexual abuse rates for girls in juvenile justice and mental health settings to be substantially higher than those in the general population (Okamoto and Chesney-Lind 2004). Studies have found that girls contend with sexually abusive homes by running away, thereby exposing themselves to further abuse, associations with delinquent peers, or survival delinquency (stealing, etc.) (Chesney-Lind and Sheldon 2003).

It is important to note, however, that few if any of these abuses occur separately and apart from one another; rather, most abused children suffer from a combination of multiple maltreatments. For example, physical abuse usually is accompanied by verbal taunts and name-calling. Ney, Fung, and Wickett (1994) studied froms of child maltreatment including neglect and physical, sexual, emotional, and verbal abuse and found that less than 5 percent of occurrences of these types of abuse transpired alone. Researchers Smith, Berkman, and Fraser (1980) suggest that experiencing both physical abuse and neglect leads to a greater propensity to commit violent offenses.

A more comprehensive understanding of child abuse suggests that various types of abuse occur simultaneously. Those who experience multiple froms of abuse simultaneously are at greater risk for later delinquent behavior and other negative outcomes (Hamilton, Falshaw, and Browne 2002). However, it is unlikely that a specific type of child abuse would transfrom a juvenile into a specific type of offender.

Severity of Abuse

The type of abuse is an important risk factor, but the severity of the abuse is also critical in understanding the nexus between child abuse and juvenile delinquency. Unfortunately, not much is known about the relationship between the severity of abuse and the later development of delinquent behaviors. Initial findings suggest that more extensively or harshly mistreated youth consistently exhibit higher rates of delinquency; however, there is not a linear relationship between the phenomena (Smith and Thornberry 1995). It is also important to note that youth react differently to abuse. Some are deeply affected by more minor froms, while others seem able to withstand and adapt to more severe froms. Another difficulty in understanding this relationship is attempting to measure the severity of abuse and obtaining the precise amount of severity as seen by the youth. In other words, who is to determine how severe abuse is? Clearly, further research is needed.

Persistent or Repeat Abuse

While being abused on one occasion is cause for concern, many youth are repeatedly or persistently abused by the same or multiple perpetrators. Child Protective Units have distinguished approximately one quarter of their case loads as being children who will be revictimized. Once a child has been victimized twice, the risk of another victimization is then doubled (Hamilton, Falshaw, and Browne 2002). Studies have found that youth who had experienced persistent abuse were more likely to engage in more severe delinquency than those who had one abuse incident. Additionally, youth victimized by different perpetrators both inside and outside the family were more likely to engage in violent and/or sexually offending behavior (Hamilton, Falshaw, and Browne 2002). Some scholars postulate that each subsequent abuse exacerbates the effects from the previous incidents, placing the youth at further risk for serious long-term effects, including serious delinquency.

Adolescent Abuse

Though most studies have focused on the relationship between child abuse and juvenile delinquency, adolescent abuse is receiving increased attention, and further attention to this topic is warranted. Official estimates indicate that the amount of adolescent abuse equals or exceeds the amount of child abuse, with approximately 47 percent of the known cases of abuse being perpetrated against adolescents even though they account for only 38 percent of the total population of people under age eighteen (Garbarino 1989). Abused adolescents are more likely than nonabused adolescents to be arrested (Ireland, Smith, and Thornberry 2002),

CHILD ABUSE AND JUVENILE DELINQUENCY

and researchers hypothesize that abused adolescents may translate experiences of maltreatment into delinquent behavior.

Abuse of children is relevant to delinquency by young adolescents, but does not have a strong correlation to offending by older youths. However, abuse of adolescents is a key explanatory factor of violence for both young and older adolescents (Benda and Corwyn 2002). On one hand, this suggests that abuse of young children does not necessarily have long-term devastating impacts—one cannot assume that all abused children will become adult offenders. However, it does suggest that adolescent abuse may have longer, more critical consequences and that persistent abuse occurring throughout childhood and adolescence may have a dire projection for adulthood.

Theoretical Foundation for the Relationship between Child Abuse and Juvenile Delinquency

The *social development model* (SDM) is a comprehensive and integrative theory which incorporates suppositions from social control theory, social learning theory, and differential association theory. The theory attempts to more specifically explain the pathways from child abuse to juvenile delinquent behavior (Catalano and Hawkins 1996; Herrenkohl, Huang, Tajima, and Whitney 2003). SDM suggests that children learn behaviors and attitudes at an early age and then find like-minded individuals, groups, and units to interact and bond with. These friends or groups further reward or punish particular behaviors and attitudes. The bond to the group becomes very important and affects behavior by influencing how the youth thinks about the costs or benefits of any behavior.

In a positive light, children learning positive behaviors and healthy attitudes from their families will more likely find positive friends to interact and bond with. These friends will support further healthy behaviors and punish negative behaviors and attitudes, and this bonding within the group will act as an outside parental control. Strong bonds fromed with prosocial peers or supports (such as school or church) will lessen the likelihood of risk for negative behaviors.

Herrenkohl et al. (2003) hypothesized that physical child abuse may generate negative behaviors and attitudes in children and negatively impact the child–parent attachment. This may weaken the youth's commitment to prosocial activities and attitudes and increase the association with antisocial peers. Attachments to antisocial groups and peers directly elevate the risk for negative behaviors via modeling,

reinforcement, and bonding. Bonding with these peers reduces the likelihood of positive influences as well as the likelihood of behaving positively. Clearly, all youth will have positive and negative influences in their lives, but the balance of prosocial and antisocial influences within a youth's life will determine his or her preponderance for engaging in either positive or negative behaviors. Studies have supported this theory, finding that abused youth are more supportive of the use of violence and have more violent attitudes, which in turn is predictive of involvement with antisocial peers and violent behavior (Hawkins et al. 1998).

Exposure to Domestic Violence

It is estimated that 10–20 percent of American children are at risk for exposure to domestic violence each year (Carlson 2000). Exposure to domestic violence can entail witnessing firsthand violence in the home, hearing violence, being in a parent's arms while they are being hurt, being held hostage during the incident, being forced to participate in the abuse of a parent, and/or being used to spy on a parent (Edleson 1999). Children who are exposed to violence in the home have been found to exhibit more aggressive and delinquent behaviors and more anxiety, post-traumatic stress symptoms, depression, and temperament problems than their counterparts who did not experience violence in the home (Edleson 1999; Hughes 1998; Maker, Kemmelmeier, and Peterson 1998; Sternberg et al. 1993). In addition, children exposed to violence are more likely to have increased risks for drug and alcohol problems (Berenson, Wiemann, and McCombs 2001).

Any exposure or combination of exposures can be damaging and may result in long-term negative effects and trauma. However, exposure to domestic violence has differing impacts on children, based on the circumstances of the violence and/or the characteristics of the child. For instance, children who are exposed to frequent and severe froms of violence, who fail to observe parents engage in appropriate conflict resolution, who are younger, who have fewer coping skills and/or a support network tend to have more distress and long-term problems than children who do not meet these criteria (Carlson 2000; Edleson 1999; Hughes, Graham-Bermann, and Gruber 2001).

There also appears to be varying degrees of specific responses to each parent. A child's relationship with his/her battering father can be confusing. The child expresses affection toward the father while simultaneously feeling hatred, pain, resentment, and disappointment regarding the offending behavior (Peled 1998). A child's relationship with his/her mother is a potential and significant factor in determining the effects of exposure to domestic violence. Some researchers report that a mother's poor mental health functioning may have a negative impact on how the child experiences violence in the home. A negative bond between mother and child may further exacerbate the effects of the exposure and again leave the child open to relationships with negative peers or adults.

Exposure to Domestic Violence and Child Abuse

Many times exposure to domestic violence in itself can be labeled as child neglect or abuse. But domestic violence and physical child abuse are also known to overlap (Appel and Holden 1998) and can occur as separate incidents over time. Evidence suggests that youth exposed to both domestic violence and child abuse, either independently or at the same time, exhibit more serious problem behaviors and have been found to be more violent than those who experience only one from of trauma (Carlson 1991; Edleson 1999; Hughes 1998; O'keefe 1994b; Silvern et al. 1995; Sternberg et al. 1993). Childhood abuse and exposure to domestic violence also plays a role in predicting violent behavior in adults. For example, studies suggest that male batterers tend to have been raised in homes where domestic violence occurred and were found to have been seriously physically abused and/or to have witnessed weapons violations between adults (Rivera and Widom 1990; Rosenbaum and O'Leary 1981; Spaccarelli et al. 1995; Widom 1989).

Exposure to domestic violence results in traumatic effects on children that are distinct from the effects of child abuse, but multiple exposures to violence and victimization interact and intensify the negative impact on children. In another words, the more exposure to violence children have over the course of their development, the more likely they are to engage in violent offending as adolescents and later as adults (Nofziger and Kurtz 2005). To predict juvenile offending, one must look at the volume of exposure, severity, and types of victimization experienced throughout childhood. This exposure may lead to violent behavior in a number of ways. First, exposure to violence may lead to an increased susceptibility to a violent belief system. This in turn perpetuates and justifies violent behavior as acceptable and/or provides an appropriate resolve during conflict. Also, a youth's social support network that involves peers who use or are involved in violence may promote the youth's perception of acceptable violent behavior as well as provide opportunities for violence to occur (Nofziger and Kurtz 2005).

In addition, repeated exposure also teaches children to handle anger and disagreements by using violence as opposed to prosocial tactics. Frequent reinforcement of this concept by family and/or friends makes changing behaviors more difficult later on.

Risk and Protective Factors for Juvenile Delinquency: The Context of Child Abuse and Exposure to Domestic Violence

Risk factors are behaviors, characteristics, and/or conditions present in the child, parent, family, or community that will likely contribute to the development of juvenile delinquency, while protective factors are strengths and resources that appear to mediate or serve as a "buffer" against risk factors. As mentioned earlier, child abuse and exposure to domestic violence are both strong risk factors for the later development of juvenile delinquency. The relationship, however, is complex and not easily explained. One of the reasons for this complexity is that child abuse and exposure to domestic violence happen in conjunction with other risk and protective factors which may exacerbate or diminish the effects of violence on the child. To fully understand the intricate relationship between child abuse and exposure to violence and juvenile delinquency, it is important to delineate these risk and protective factors.

On an individual level, risk factors for juvenile delinquency include: hyperactivity, concentration problems, restlessness, risk taking, aggressiveness, delinquent peers, gang membership, and beliefs and attitudes favorable to antisocial behavior. The more risk factors a child has, the more likely he or she will be to develop delinquency. When these risk factors are added to exposure to domestic violence or child abuse, the cumulative effects can be serious.

On a family level, risk factors include: parental criminality, poor parenting practices, low levels of parental involvement, poor family bonding, high family conflict, and, as mentioned previously, child abuse and domestic violence. Clearly, the development of delinquent behavior becomes more likely if several of these factors are present concurrently.

On the community level, risk factors include: poverty, community disorganization, availability of drugs and firearms, adults involved in crime, and community violence. The likelihood of developing delinquent behaviors increases as risk factors are compounded and interact to exacerbate the situation. Consider a child who experiences child abuse who also has difficulties with hyperactivity and lives in poverty in a violent neighborhood. In addition, the type, timing, and severity of the abuse also influence the likelihood of this child developing delinquent behaviors.

Risk factors, however, do not explain the entire context of the correlation between child abuse, exposure to domestic violence, and the later development of juvenile delinquency. Protective factors are also present in this context and work to mitigate or buffer the child from the effects of negative risk factors. Some of these protective factors include: bonding to one positive adult, a support system, small family size, good parenting skills, and lack of criminal behavior and/or substance abuse by parents. Studies have indicated that a secure, warm relationship with a positive adult can significantly buffer the effects of multiple risk factors and can help children adjust to negative life events (Kruttschnitt, Ward, and Sheble 1987). It is preferable that bonding occur with the parent or guardian, but it can also occur with another positive adult, such as a teacher. Likewise, a positive support system such as friends, relatives, or community who are able to encourage and sustain the child can also mediate the effects of various risk factors. In addition, small family size (fewer than four children) can help the child by allowing ample time for individual bonding and interacting with parents. A smaller family size also reduces parental stress and encourages positive parenting practices, which can help mediate difficulties and assist children in adapting to changes and solving problems. Positive parenting practices include being aware of appropriate child development and using positive tactics to illicit positive behaviors. Finally, parents who have attitudes and beliefs contrary to violence, criminal behavior, and substance use and who express these attitudes to their children help shield them from negative influences.

Risk and protective factors help shed light on the relationship between child abuse, exposure to domestic violence, and the later development of delinquency by highlighting the complexity of the context in which children develop. There will always be children who develop delinquent behaviors after exposure to minimal risk factors and others who do not develop these behaviors despite compounding risks. It is not a clear, linear relationship, and this makes prediction of later juvenile delinquency difficult at best.

Conclusion

This article provides a general overview of the association between childhood abuse, exposure to domestic violence, and the later development of juvenile delinquency. The infromation is not conclusive or definite; there are many questions remaining. However, it provides an initial understanding of the complexity of this relationship. Child abuse and exposure to domestic violence are each risk factors for the later development of juvenile delinquency. However, neither is necessarily a direct causal explanation for delinquency, in that not all children abused or exposed to violence will engage in delinquency, while some children who were never abused or exposed to violence will develop delinquent behaviors. Studies have indicated that neglect and physical abuse are particularly potent risk factors for later violent offenses, while the relationship between sexual abuse and later offenses is still unclear.

Child abuse and exposure to domestic violence should also be considered on a continuum rather than as a dichotomy of abused/exposed or not abused/not exposed. The number of times a child was abused, whether there were multiple types of abuse (verbal and physical, etc.), how severe the abuse was, and how long the abuse persisted are all crucial variables in predicting the likelihood of developing delinquent behaviors. Finally, it should be recognized that multiple risk and protective factors are constantly interacting and provide a context for understanding the development of juvenile delinquency. It is not the expected path for a child subjected to abuse or exposed to domestic violence to develop delinquent behaviors, yet this does occur in many instances when the context is especially dire or additional risk factors are present.

LISA A. RAPP-PAGLICCI and POLLY LOEBER

See also **Children Witnessing Parental Violence; Cycle of Violence; Intergenerational Transfer of Intimate Partner Violence; Social, Economic, and Psychological Costs of Violence; Social Learning Theory and Family Violence**

References and Further Reading

Acoca, L. "Outside/Inside: The Violation of American Girls at Home, on the Streets, and in the Juvenile Justice System." *Crime and Delinquency* 44, no. 4 (1998): 561–589.

Administration for Children and Families. "National Clearinghouse on Child Abuse and Neglect Infromation," 2005. http://nccanch.acf.hhs.gov/index.cfm.

Appel, A., and G. Holden. "The Co-Occurrence of Spouse and Physical Child Abuse: A Review and Appraisal." *Journal of Family Psychology* 12, no. 4 (1998): 578–599.

Bagley, Christopher, Michael Wood, and Loretta Young. "Victim to Abuser: Mental Health and Behavioral Sequels of Child Sexual Abuse in a Community Survey of Young Adult Males." *Child Abuse and Neglect* 18 (August 1994): 683–697.

Benda, Brent, and Robert Corwyn. "The Effect of Abuse in Childhood and in Adolescence on Violence among Adolescents." *Youth and Society* 33, no. 3 (2002): 339–365.

Berenson, Abbey, Constance Wiemann, and Sharon McCombs. "Exposure to Violence and Associated Health-Risk Behaviors among Adolescent Girls." *Archives of Pediatrics Adolescent Medicine* 155, no. 11 (2001): 1238–1242.

Boswell, G. *The Prevalence of Abuse and Loss in the Lives of Section 53 Offenders.* London: Princes Trust, 1995.

Carlson, Bonnie. "Children Exposed to Intimate Partner Violence: Research Findings and Implications for Intervention." *Trauma, Violence, and Abuse* 1, no. 4 (2000): 321–340.

Catalano, Richard F., and David J. Hawkins. "The Social Development Model: A Theory of Antisocial Behavior." In *Delinquency and Crime: Current Theories,* edited by J. D. Hawkins. New York: Cambridge University Press, 1996, pp. 149–197.

Chesney-Lind, Meda, and Randall Sheldon. *Girls, Delinquency and Juvenile Justice,* 3rd ed. Belmont, CA: Wadsworth, 2003.

Crittenden, P., and M. Ainsworth. "Child Maltreatment and Attachment Theory." In *Child Maltreatment: Theory and Research on the Causes and Consequences of Child Abuse and Neglect,* edited by Dante Cicchetti and Vicki Carlson. New York: Cambridge University Press, 1989, pp. 432–463.

Dutton, Donald G., and S. D. Hart. "Evidence for Long Term, Specific Effects of Childhood Abuse and Neglect on Criminal Behavior in Men." *International Journal of Offender Therapy and Comparative Criminology* 36 (1992): 129–137.

Edleson, Jeffrey L. "Children's Witnessing of Adult Domestic Violence." *Journal of Interpersonal Violence* 14, no. 8 (August 1999): 839–870.

Finkelhor, David, and L. Baron. "Risk Factors for Child Sexual Abuse." *Journal of Interpersonal Violence* 1 (1986): 43–71.

Ford, Michelle E., and Jean Ann Linney. "Comparative Analysis of Juvenile Sexual Offenders, Violent Nonsexual Offenders, and Status Offenders." *Journal of Interpersonal Violence* 10 (March 1995): 56–70.

Garbarino, James. "Troubled Youth, Troubled Families: The Dynamics of Adolescent Maltreatment." In *Child Maltreatment: Theory and Research on the Causes and Consequences of Child Abuse and Neglect,* edited by Dante Cicchetti and Vicki Carlson. New York: Cambridge University Press, 1989.

Hamilton, Catherine, Louise Falshaw, and Kevin Browne. "The Link between Recurrent Maltreatment and Offending Behavior." *International Journal of Offender Therapy and Comparative Criminology* 46, no. 1 (2002): 75–94.

Hawkins, James, Todd Herrenkohl, David Farrington, D. Brewer, R. Catalano, and T. Harachi. "A Review of Predictors of Youth Violence." In *Serious and Violent Juvenile Offenders: Risk Factors and Successful Interventions,* edited by Rolf Loeber and David Farrington. Thousand Oaks, CA: Sage, 1998, pp. 106–146.

Herrenkohl, Todd I., Bu Huang, Emiko A. Tajima, and Stephen D. Whitney. "Examining the Link between Child Abuse and Youth Violence." *Journal of Interpersonal Violence* 18, no. 10 (October 2003): 1189–1208.

Herrera, Veronica M., and Laura Ann McCloskey. "Gender Differences in the Risk for Delinquency among Youth Exposed to Family Violence." *Child Abuse and Neglect* 25 (2001): 1037–1051.

Hughes, Honore. "Psychological and Behavioral Correlates of Family Violence in Child Witnesses and Victims." *American Journal of Orthopsychiatry* 58 (January 1998): 77–90.

Hughes, Honore, Sandra Graham-Bermann, and G. Gruber. "Resilience in Children Exposed to Domestic Violence." In *Domestic Violence in the Lives of Children: The Future of Research, Intervention, and Social Policy,* edited by Sandra Graham-Bermann and Jeffrey Edleson. Washington, DC: American Psychological Association, 2001, pp. 67–90.

Ireland, Timothy O., Carolyn A. Smith, and Terence P. Thornberry. "Developmental Issues in the Impact of Child Maltreatment on Later Delinquency and Drug Use." *Criminology* 40, no. 2 (May 2002): 359–396.

Kemshall, Hazel, and Jacki Pritchard, eds. *Good Practice in Working with Victims of Violence.* Philadelphia: Jessica Kingsley Publishers, 2000.

Kruttschnitt, Candace, David Ward, and Mary Ann Sheble. "Abuse-Resistant Youth: Some Factors That May Inhibit Violent Criminal Behavior." *Social Forces* 66, no. 2 (1987): 501–519.

Lemmon, John. "How Child Maltreatment Affects Dimensions of Juvenile Delinquency in a Cohort of Low-Income Urban Youths." *Justice Quarterly* 16, no. 2 (1999): 357–376.

Loeber, Rolf, and David Farrington, eds. *Child Delinquents: Development, Intervention, and Service Needs.* Thousand Oaks, CA: Sage, 2001.

Loseke, Donileen, Richard Gelles, and Mary Cavanaugh, eds. *Current Controversies on Family Violence.* Thousand Oaks, CA: Sage, 2005.

Maker, Azmaira H., Markus Kemmelmeier, and Christopher Peterson. "Long-Term Psychological Consequences in Women of Witnessing Parental Physical Conflict and Experiencing Abuse in Childhood." *Journal of Interpersonal Violence* 13, no. 5 (October 1998): 574–589.

Mouzakitis, Chris Michael. "An Inquiry into the Problem of Child Abuse and Juvenile Delinquency." In *Exploring the Relationship between Child Abuse and Delinquency,* edited by R. J. Hunner and Y. E. Walker. Montclair, NJ: Allanheld, Osmun and Co., 1981.

Ney, Phillip G., Tak Fung, and Adele Rose Wickett. "The Worst Combinations of Child Abuse and Neglect." *Child Abuse and Neglect* 18, no. 9 (September 1994): 705–714.

Nofziger, Stacy, and Don Kurtz. "Violent Lives: A Lifestyle Model Linking Exposure to Violence to Juvenile Violent Offending." *Journal of Research in Crime and Delinquency* 42, no. 1 (February 2005): 3–26.

Okamoto, Scott, and Meda Chesney-Lind. "Understanding the Impact of Trauma on Female Juvenile Delinquency and Gender-Specific Practice." In *Juvenile Justice Sourcebook,* edited by Albert Roberts. New York: Oxford University Press, 2004, pp. 381–394.

O'keefe, Maura. "Linking Marital Violence, Mother-Child/Father-Child Aggression, and Child Behavior Problems." *Journal of Family Violence* 9 (March 1994): 63–78.

Peled, Einat. "The Experience of Living with Violence for Preadolescent Witnesses of Woman Abuse," 1998. http://infotrac.galegroup.com.proxy.usf.edu.

Prendergast, W. E. *Treating Sex Offenders in Correctional Institutions and Outpatient Clinics: A Guide to Clinical Practice.* New York: Hayworth Press, 1991.

Rapp-Paglicci, Lisa, Albert Roberts, and John Wodarski, eds. *Handbook of Violence.* New York: Wiley and Sons, 2002.

Rivera, B., and C. Widom. "Childhood Victimization and Violent Offending." *Violence and Victims* 5 (1990): 19–35.

Roberts, Albert, ed. *Juvenile Justice Sourcebook.* Oxford, MA: Oxford, 2004.

Rosenbaum, A., and D. K. O'Leary. "Children: The Unintended Victims of Marital Violence." *American Journal of Orthopsychiatry* 51 (1981): 692–699.

Silvern, Louise, Jane Karyl, Lynn Waelde, William F. Hodges, Joanna Starek, E. Heidt, and K. Min. "Retrospective Reports of Parental Partner Abuse: Relationships to Depression, Trauma Symptoms and Self-Esteem among College Students." *Journal of Family Violence* 10 (June 1995): 177–202.

Smith, C. P., D. J. Berkman, and W. M. Fraser. *Reports of the National Juvenile Justice Assessment Centers.* Washington, DC: American Justice Institute, 1980.

Smith, Carolyn, and Terrence Thornberry. "The Relationship between Child Maltreatment and Adolescent Involvement in Delinquency." *Criminology* 3, no. 3 (1995): 451–481.

Snyder, Nancy, and M. Sickmund. *Juvenile Offenders and Victims: 1999 National Report.* Washington, DC: Office of Juvenile Justice and Delinquency Prevention, 1999.

Spaccarelli, Steve, J. Douglas Coatsworth, and Blake S. Bowden. "Exposure to Serious Family Violence among Incarcerated Boys: Its Association with Violent Offending and Potential Mediating Variables." *Violence and Victims* 10 (1995): 163–182.

Sternberg, Kathleen J., Michael E. Lamb, Charles Greenbaum, Dante Cicchetti, Samia Dawud, Rosa Manela Cortes, Orit Krispin, and Fanny Lorey. "Effects of Domestic Violence on Children's Behavior Problems and Depression." *Developmental Psychology* 29, no. 1 (1993): 44–52.

Widom, Cathy Spatz. *The Intergenerational Transmission of Violence.* New York: Harry Frank Guggenheim Foundation, 1989.

Wiebush, Robert. *Preventing Delinquency Through Improved Child Protection Services.* Washington, DC: U.S. Department of Justice, 2001.

Zingraff, Matthew T., Jeffrey Leiter, Matthew C. Johnson, and Kristen A. Myers. "The Mediating Effect of Good School Perfromance on the Maltreatment-Delinquency Relationship." *Journal of Research in Crime and Delinquency* 31, no. 1 (February 1994): 62–91.

CHILD ABUSE AND NEGLECT IN THE UNITED STATES: AN OVERVIEW

Child abuse continues to be a major concern in the United States. Reports of child maltreatment have increased dramatically over the last decades of the twentieth century, in part because of better reporting. During 2003, 2.9 million referrals regarding over 5 million children were made to child protective services. Approximately 30 percent of these reports were subsequently substantiated (United States Department of Health and Human Services [USDHHS] 2005). Given the staggering number of child maltreatment reports, it is not surprising that the U.S. Advisory Board on Child Abuse and Neglect (1990) characterized child maltreatment in America as a "national emergency." Fortunately, it appears that the incidence of actual child victimization has dropped slightly, from 14.7 per 1,000 children in 1996 to 12.4 per 1,000 children in 2003 (USDHHS 2005). This article provides a brief overview of the history and prevalence of child abuse in America as well as federal laws regarding abuse.

Background on Child Abuse and Neglect in the United States

During the late eighteenth and early nineteenth centuries, there was little focus on physical or sexual abuse of children in the United States, and no focus on emotional abuse. The typical societal response to child abuse and neglect at this time involved either ignoring the abuse or, in some instances, removing the child from the family, with indigent children being placed in institutions, foster homes, or situations working as apprentices in factories or on farms (Giovannoni 1989; Schene 1996). Legislation specifically designed to protect children from physical maltreatment was limited. One of the earliest cases of physical abuse in the United States to receive widespread attention was the 1874 case of Mary Ellen, a young girl who was seriously abused by her adoptive parents. Although the little girl had been repeatedly beaten and malnourished, existing laws made it difficult for the state to remove the child from her home. The case generated significant media attention and led to the establishment of the Society for the Prevention of Cruelty to Children in 1875 (Zigler and Hall 1989).

Sexual abuse was rarely identified during this period, even though it clearly occurred, as numerous articles published in American medical journals during the nineteenth century discussed children with venereal diseases—usually syphilis and gonorrhea. As late as 1889, some professionals suggested that children had contracted these diseases through nonsexual contact, such as breast-feeding, hugging, or the sharing of eating utensils and bedding (Taylor 1985). This assumption allowed doctors to diagnose and treat children with venereal diseases without acknowledging a violation of society's incest taboo.

The first federal legislation to protect children was passed in 1935 as part of the Social Security Act, marking the first time the federal government provided funding for child welfare services (USDHHS 1988). Under the Social Security Act, suspected child abuse could be reported to child protection agencies. Mandatory reporting requirements and widespread social awareness of the problem, however, still did not emerge until the 1960s, when Kempe, Silverman, Steele, Droegemueller, and Silver (1962) identified the "battered child syndrome." This research provided working medical definitions for physical abuse and encouraged the medical community to report physical examinations that suggested abuse (see also Bain 1963; Fontana, Donovan, and Wong 1963). This work, along with other studies during this period, resulted in swift changes. By 1966, all states had enacted laws requiring physicians to report suspected abuse (Kalichman 1993). Soon thereafter, the types of abuse that required mandatory reporting expanded to include emotional and nutritional maltreatment, as well as suspected sexual abuse. Concurrently, the number of professionals identified as mandatory reporters broadened beyond just doctors to include human service professionals such as teachers, therapists, and social workers (Giovannoni 1989).

With the Child Abuse Prevention and Treatment Act of 1974 (CAPTA) the United States created a federal definition of child abuse and neglect with guidelines and standards for mandatory reporting. CAPTA defined child abuse and neglect as:

> The physical or mental injury, sexual abuse, negligent treatment, or maltreatment of a child under the age of 18 by a person who is responsible for the child's welfare under the circumstances which indicate the child's health or welfare is harmed or threatened thereby as determined in accordance with regulations prescribed [Child Abuse Prevention and Treatment Act of 1974, 42 U.S.C. § 5106g (4) (1974)].

This broad definition provided a comprehensive view of child abuse that increased governmental and public awareness and response. In 1996, Congress changed the federal definition of "child abuse and neglect" to read as follows:

> [T]he term "child abuse and neglect" means, at a minimum, any recent act or failure to act on the part of a parent or caretaker, which results in death, serious physical or emotional harm, sexual abuse or exploitation, or an act or failure to act which presents an imminent risk of serious harm [42 U.S.C. §5106g(2) (1999)].

Prevalence of Abuse in the United States

Compared with many other countries, the United States has good data on the incidence of child maltreatment, particularly after 1990. This is in part due to the 1988 amendments to CAPTA, which mandated that the Department of Health and Human Services (DHHS) acquire and maintain data on the prevalence and types of abuse. To this end, the United States seeks to collect information about every case of child maltreatment reported to child protective services, which in 2003 amounted to approximately 2.9 million referrals. Of these, approximately one-third of the cases were substantiated, resulting in the victimization of approximately 960,000 children, of whom approximately 1,500 died from the maltreatment. The majority (60.9 percent) of cases of child maltreatment in the United States in 2003 were of neglect. However, physical abuse accounted for 18.9 percent of child victims, sexual abuse 9.9 percent, and emotional abuse 4.9 percent. Because each state has slightly different laws, 17 percent of the cases are identified as "other" in the federal records (USDHHS 2005).

Although the data in the United States are much better than in many other countries, the exact number of children affected each year is difficult to determine. The prevalence numbers provided by DHHS are not exact, in part because a particular child may have experienced multiple types of abuse, all accounted for in a single incident report. Additionally, a particular child may be the subject of multiple investigations in a year. Scholars have repeatedly suggested that these rates underestimate the actual incidence of maltreatment, with some arguing that perhaps half of all cases are not reported. Additional support for this view comes from national research surveys which have asked adults to retrospectively report whether they were abused as children. These surveys reveal much higher levels of abuse than those reported by DHHS. In particular, childhood sexual victimization is reported by approximately one in four women and by approximately one in ten men (e.g., Elliot and Briere 1995; Epstein and Bottoms 1998).

Risk Factors of Abuse and Neglect in the United States

Although abuse in the United States occurs across all levels of parental class, income, and education, there are several factors related to increased risk of victimization. Experiences of abuse tend to be related to parental class and family income, or socioeconomic status (SES), with violence occurring more often in homes with lower SES (e.g., Pelton 1981; Sedlack and Broadhurst 1996; Straus 1994; Straus, Gelles, and Steinmetz 1980) and in single-parent homes. Although the overall rate of child victimization in the general population is low (1.2 percent of children), the rate is almost twice that for African American, Pacific Islander, and American Indian children (2.04 percent, 2.14 percent, and 2.13 percent, respectively) compared with white children (1.1 percent). It is difficult to know how this latter finding should be interpreted. Minority status is correlated with SES, thus it is possible that these findings are being driven by the fact that a large percentage of minority children live in lower-SES homes. Additionally, it is possible that there is bias such that maltreatment occurring in minority families is more likely to be brought to the attention of child protective services than the same treatment occurring in white families.

Also related to prevalence of victimization is a child's age and gender. Specifically, children in their first three years of life have the highest rates of victimization. Further, three-quarters of the children killed by abuse were under age four (USDHHS 2005). In addition, girls are more likely to experience abuse than boys, but boys are more likely to receive particularly serious injuries (Sedlack and Broadhurst 1996).

Investigating Abuse in the United States

Throughout the United States, child protective services receive approximately 50,000 calls a week alleging abuse. Approximately one-third of these referrals are dismissed immediately without investigation, and the remaining two-thirds are investigated. It is estimated that, on average, each investigation worker will handle sixty-one investigations per year. However, this number is based on reports from only twenty-eight states and does not take into account the wide variability between urban and rural populations as well as different resources available at different locations (USDHHS 2005).

Mandated federal reporters, such as child care providers, medical personnel, teachers, and mental health/social service professionals, submit the majority of referrals (USDHHS 2005). In 2003, the largest number, over 17 percent, came from educational personnel and child care providers. In the United States, individual states may define aspects of abuse and neglect slightly differently. Thus, once a referral is made, the exact investigation progresses as a function of the particular state guidelines. Typically, after a referral is made and determined to be worthy of an investigation, an investigator will visit the alleged victim at home or in school to interview the child. In addition, siblings, parents, and others who have considerable contact with the child or family (e.g., teachers) might be interviewed to provide information about the child's situation and level of risk. Additional in-depth assessments including medical examinations may be conducted if the investigator believes the situation warrants this (Pecora 1991).

An abuse investigation may produce a variety of outcomes, but the three main outcomes are *substantiated, unsubstantiated,* and *indicated.* Substantiation means that the abuse has occurred, the family is in need of assistance, and the child requires protection. Typically, in substantiated cases, either the identified perpetrator or the child victim is removed from the home, and additional social services are provided to the family. In 2003, of the investigated cases, 26.4 percent were substantiated (USDHHS 2005). If investigators did not find enough evidence to support child maltreatment charges, the case is considered unsubstantiated. The majority (57 percent) of cases investigated in 2003 fell into this category. However, even in unsubstantiated cases, the agency may refer the family for education and prevention counseling. Finally, in some states, the child protective services may return an *indicated* finding. This states that although there was not enough evidence for substantiation, there is reason to believe that the child may have been, or is, at risk for maltreatment. Approximately 4 percent of investigated cases resulted in an indication finding in 2003. Notably, under this system, the closest an alleged perpetrator can come to being "cleared" is to have the case classified as unsubstantiated; investigators rarely, if ever, conclude or report that abuse has not, in fact, occurred.

Children Who Testify

When a case goes to court, a child's testimony may be critical, because the child is often the sole witness to the events in question. In the United States, it is necessary for a witness to be deemed competent to take the stand. Although the majority of states have adopted the Federal Rules of Evidence Rule 601, which presumes that all persons are competent to testify regardless of age, it is always possible that a child's competence will be challenged. In states that have not adopted Rule 601's presumption, the competence of a child witness will be determined during a pretrial hearing. State laws differ with regard to the age at which a child no longer requires such a hearing. However, generally beginning at ten to fourteen years of age, a hearing is no longer required for a child. During a competency hearing, the child witness's understanding of the truth and what a lie is will be assessed. Historically, the court has found children competent when they demonstrate an understanding of the difference between a truth and a lie.

In the last two decades, a number of reforms have been proposed and implemented to accommodate child witnesses. These reforms are designed to obtain accurate information from potentially abused children. For example, many states have created community-based "Children's Advocacy Centers" in which experts in many fields (e.g., law, mental health, child protection) work together in making decisions about the investigation, treatment, and prosecution of child abuse cases (National Children's Advocacy Center 1999). These programs are focused on helping children through the process of a trial. In addition to ensuring that the best investigative procedures are followed, these professionals facilitate medical and mental health referrals for child victims. The interviewers at these centers are specially trained to use the most recent research in child psychology to increase a child's recall without being coercive or misleading. Often, the use of such a center results in fewer total number of interviews for the child. This is important because research has found that repeated interviews increase the chances of a child reporting inaccurate information.

Other suggested innovations for use with child abuse victims include allowing a child to testify using closed-circuit television and one-way mirrors so she or he does not have to be in the presence of the alleged perpetrator. This suggestion is controversial given that in the United States, a defendant has a constitutional right to face her or his accuser. However, in *Maryland v. Craig* (1990) the U.S. Supreme Court suggested that the use of this type of intervention may be considered appropriate on a case-by-case basis when a child would not be able to provide credible testimony without it. Additionally, given the anxiety that can be produced by the experience of being in court, some communities have established "court schools," or programs that educate a child victim about the trial process ahead of time (e.g., Doueck, Weston, Filbert, Beekhuis, and Redlich 1997). Other communities have excluded spectators from the courtroom and/or allowed a parent or loved one to be next to the child for social/moral support while he or she testifies (see Goodman et al. 1992).

Services

Child protective services offer many different types of responses for families and children after abuse has occurred. Remedial services include family and individual counseling and foster care. In 2003, approximately 57 percent of child victims—over 500,000 children and their families—received some type of post-event remedial services. A number of factors predict whether a child will receive post-event services. Children who have been prior victims of maltreatment, are victims of multiple types of maltreatment, or are disabled are more likely to receive services than those without such experiences. Race was also an important predictor of the provision of services in 2003. White children were less likely than African American and Hispanic children to be referred for post-event services. In addition, children abused or maltreated by their mothers are more likely to receive service than those maltreated by their fathers (USDHHS 2005).

In addition, over 200,000 children were placed in foster care in 2003. There are a number of factors related to the decision to remove a child from his or her home. Similar to other services, children who had been prior victims of maltreatment were more likely to be placed in foster care compared with children for whom this was a first finding of maltreatment. Child victims who were disabled were more likely to be placed in foster care than nondisabled children. Again, race played an important role in this situation, with African American children

36 percent more likely to be placed in foster care than white children. Finally, children abused or maltreated by their mothers, compared with those maltreated by their fathers, were more likely to be placed in foster care (USDHHS 2005). In addition to those children who were removed from their homes because of maltreatment, approximately 70,000 children, later determined to not be victims, were placed in foster care during the process of investigating their cases.

Child protective services also provided educational services to *prevent* child abuse and neglect. In 2003 it is estimated that almost two million children and families received preventative services. These services are typically provided to families deemed at risk for abuse or neglect. They include education about child development and child rearing practices, substance abuse treatment, respite care, housing assistance, and counseling (USDHHS 2005).

Perpetrators of Abuse

When all types of maltreatment (neglect and abuse) are considered, perpetrators are more likely to be female (58.2 percent) than male (41.8 percent). Additionally, the female perpetrators are on average slightly younger (average age of thirty-one years) compared with male perpetrators (average age of thirty-four years). In general, the majority of the perpetrators were parents (80 percent). The fact that parents are the most common perpetrators is in part related to the fact that neglect is the most common form of child maltreatment in the United States. In 2003, neglect accounted for 69 percent of all maltreatment, and parents are responsible for the majority of neglect (62 percent) that occurs. Relatives and unmarried partners were the next most frequent perpetrators of overall maltreatment (6 percent and 4 percent, respectively). However, when physical and sexual abuse are evaluated apart from neglect, parents are not the primary perpetrators. Only 11 percent of physical abuse and less than 3 percent of sexual abuse involved parents. The perpetrators in these cases were likely to be familiar others in the child's life (USDHHS 2005).

Legal Ramifications for Convicted Perpetrators of Child Abuse

Often cases of child abuse are not taken to criminal court but are decided instead in family or civil court. If a case goes to criminal court and the perpetrator is convicted, sentencing will differ from state to state. The sanction will be based on the act or type of violation and the age of the child

victim. For example, in Vermont the criminal code states that a person convicted of sexual assault of a minor younger than sixteen years of age "shall be imprisoned for not more than 20 years, or fined not more than $10,000, or both" [13 V.S.A. § 3253(a)(3)]. The Arizona criminal code draws finer age distinctions by providing that sexual assault of a minor who is fifteen years of age or older is punishable by a presumptive sentence of seven years imprisonment, while the sexual assault of a minor between the ages of twelve and fifteen is punishable by a presumptive sentence of twenty years imprisonment, and sexual assault of a minor younger than twelve years of age is punishable by life imprisonment without hope of parole until at least thirty-five years of the sentence have been served [Ariz. Rev. Stat. §§ 13-1406(B), 13-604.01(C), and 13-604.01(A)]. Each state differs with regard to the mandatory minimum sentencing for sexual abuse, but most require that a convicted perpetrator serve a minimum number of years prior to gaining eligibility for parole (Bulkley et al. 1996).

Prevention

Edward Zigler at Yale University's Child Study Center has suggested that to prevent child abuse and neglect, it is necessary to focus resources on family education and support to alleviate family stressors such as poverty (McCauley, Schwartz-Kenney, and Epstein 2001). For example, unemployment and job loss have been repeatedly linked to increases in child abuse (Scannapieco and Connell-Carrick 2005). Perhaps because of the additional financial stressors, children in single-parent households are more likely to experience abuse. It is not clear how society can help families reduce these stressors, but it is clear that doing so would be helpful in preventing child maltreatment.

National agencies and corporations often sponsor outreach programs aimed at preventing child abuse. For example, the Freddie Mac Foundation, Doris Duke Charitable Foundation, and Ronald McDonald House Charities each donated over $250,000 last year to the Healthy Families America Program. This program, and others like it, focus efforts on home visits for families with young children and educational outreach. Healthy Families America (2006) is involved in over 450 communities in the United States and Canada. They report that over 90 percent of families contacted accept their services. Programs like this seek to foster a supportive environment for families with newborns by enlisting the help of professionals and neighbors (Rabasca 1999). Getting the community involved may be key to the success of a prevention program. Parents view community-based programs as less threatening and less stigmatizing than government-sponsored programs. Healthy neighborhoods are also related to a reduction in child maltreatment. Children in families who interact with their neighbors and experience strong informal social support from the neighborhood are less at risk for abuse and neglect (Scannapieco and Connell-Carrick 2005).

In addition to family-focused prevention, school-based child sexual abuse prevention programs educate children about personal safety. These programs teach children about personal safety, appropriate and inappropriate touching, and saying no, as well as how to resist if abuse against them is attempted. Finally, these programs inform children of where they can get support if needed. It is hoped that children who receive this type of training will be empowered to resist abuse. Training has also been used to decrease the chances that a child will abuse others. To this end, some prevention programs have included empathy training, problem solving, and anger management. The type of programs and topics included in the training will depend on the age of the children involved. Training programs for younger children use puppets and dolls, while those targeting older children may use lectures and role-playing (Kohl 1993). It is unclear the extent to which these interventions and programs are effective in reducing the incidence of child maltreatment. It does appear that children learn about prevention from the different training approaches (Finkelhor and Strapko 1987).

Conclusions

Child abuse remains a large problem in the United States. The positive news is that although the number of reports made each year has increased, the number of substantiations has decreased. In addition, many communities are becoming involved in proactive programs for parents and children to help reduce the chances of abuse. One can hope that the recent decline in maltreatment and increase in prevention mark the beginning of a permanent trend.

MICHELLE R. MCCAULEY and
BETH M. SCHWARTZ

See also **Child Abuse: A Global Perspective; Child Neglect; Child Sexual Abuse; Children Witnessing Parental Violence; Corporal Punishment, Religious Attitudes toward; Filicide and Children with Disabilities; Incest; Medical Neglect Related to Religion and Culture; Mothers Who Kill; Munchausen by Proxy Syndrome; Parental Abduction; Sibling Abuse**

References and Further Reading

Ariz. Rev. Stat. §§ 13-1406(B), 13-604.01(C), and 13-604.01(A) (1999).

Bain, K. "The Physically Abused Child." *Pediatrics* 31 (1963): 895–898.

Child Abuse Prevention and Treatment Act, 42 U.S.C. §5106g(4) (1974).

Child Abuse Prevention and Treatment Act, 42 U.S.C. § 5101 et seq (1974).

Child Abuse Prevention and Treatment Act, 42 U.S.C. §5106g(2) (1999).

Child Abuse Prevention and Treatment Act Amendments of 1995, 104 S.Rpt 117 (July 20, 1995).

Doueck, H. J., E. A. Weston, L. Filbert, R. Beekhuis, and H. F. Redlich. "A Child Witness Advocacy Program: Caretakers' and Professionals' Views." *Journal of Sexual Abuse* 6 (1997): 113–132.

Epstein, M. A., and B. L. Bottoms. "Memories of Childhood Sexual Abuse: A Survey of Young Adults." *Child Abuse and Neglect* 22 (1998): 1217–1238.

Fontana, V. J., D. Donovan, and R. J. Wong. "The 'Maltreatment Syndrome' in Children." *New England Journal of Medicine* 269 (1963): 1389–1394.

Giovannoni, J. "Definitional Issues in Child Maltreatment." In *Child Maltreatment,* edited by D. Cicchetti and V. Carlson. Cambridge, England: Cambridge University Press, 1989, pp. 3–37.

Goodman, G. S., E. P. Pyle-Taub, D. P. H. Hones, P. England, L. K. Port, L. Rudy, and L. Prado. "The Effects of Criminal Court Testimony on Child Sexual Assault Victims." *Monographs of the Society for Research in Child Development* 57 (1992) (Serial No. 229): 1–163.

Healthy Families America website, 2006. http://www.healthyfamiliesamerica.org/about_us/index.shtml (accessed August 13, 2006).

Kalichman, S. C. *Mandated Reporting of Suspected Child Abuse: Ethics, Law, and Policy.* Washington, DC: American Psychological Association, 1993.

Kempe, C., F. Silverman, B. Steele, W. Droegemueller, and H. Silver. "The Battered-Child Syndrome." *Journal of American Medical Association* 181 (1962): 17–24.

Kohl, J. "School-Based Child Sexual Abuse Prevention Program." *Journal of Family Violence* 8 (1993): 137–150.

Maryland v. Craig, 110 S. Ct. 3157 (1990).

Pecora, P. J. "Investigating Allegations of Child Maltreatment: The Strengths and Limitation of Current Risk Assessment Systems." *Child and Youth Services* 15 (1991): 73–92.

Pelton, L. H., ed. *The Social Context of Child Abuse and Neglect.* New York: Human Sciences Press, 1981.

Rabasca, L. "Child-Abuse Prevention Efforts Still Too Few." *APA Monitor.* Washington, DC: American Psychological Association, 1999, p. 30.

Scannapieco, M., and K. Connell-Carrick. *Understanding Child Maltreatment: An Ecological and Developmental Perspective.* New York: Oxford University Press, 2005.

Schene, P. "Child Abuse and Neglect Policy: History, Models, and Future Directions." In *The APSAC Handbook on Child Maltreatment,* edited by J. Briere, L. Berliner, J. A. Bulkley, C. Jenny, and T. Reid. Thousand Oaks, CA: Sage, 1996, pp. 385–397.

Sedlack, A. J., and D. D. Broadhurst. *The Third National Incidence Study of Child Abuse and Neglect.* U.S. Department of Health and Human Services. Washington, DC: U.S. Government Printing Office, 1996.

Straus, M. A. *Beating the Devil Out of Them: Corporal Punishment in American Families.* New York: Lexington Books, 1994.

Straus, M. A., R. Gelles, and S. Steinmetz. *Behind Closed Doors: Violence in the American Family.* Garden City, NY: Doubleday, 1980.

Taylor, K. J. "Venereal Disease in Nineteenth-Century Children." *Journal of Psychohistory* 12 (1985): 431–463.

U.S. Advisory Board on Child Abuse and Neglect. *Child Abuse and Neglect: Critical First Steps in Response to a National Emergency.* Washington, DC: Government Printing Office, 1990.

U.S. Department of Health and Human Services. *Child Maltreatment 2003.* Washington, DC: U.S. Government Printing Office, 2005.

13 V.S.A. § 3253(a)(3) (1999).

Zigler, E., and N. W. Hall. "Child Abuse in America." In *Child Maltreatment,* edited by D. Cicchetti and V. Carlson. Cambridge, England: Cambridge University Press, 1989, pp. 38–75.

CHILD MALTREATMENT, INTERVIEWING SUSPECTED VICTIMS OF

Many children are victims of violence in the home. Over three million cases of sexual abuse, physical abuse, and neglect are officially reported each year, but most experts believe that far more cases of child maltreatment go undisclosed and undiscovered. Many children also suffer the trauma of witnessing acts of violence to family members, including their parents and siblings.

Cases involving child maltreatment, domestic violence, and related crimes are often complicated from an investigative perspective, because they involve testimony from child witnesses and complex emotional motivations that could promote denials or recantations. Therefore, the police, social service, and prosecutorial agencies involved in such cases use special strategies for investigation. For example, many prosecutors' offices employ highly trained attorneys who specialize in these cases. The cases might also be prosecuted vertically, meaning that one attorney is assigned to the case from investigation through trial, fulfilling traditional investigative and prosecutorial roles and also acting as a facilitator. The vertical prosecutor coordinates efforts and strategies and ensures communication among case participants—efforts that can result in more successful prosecutions.

A child's report can be a key piece of evidence in such investigations. This is especially true in cases of child sexual abuse because there is often little corroborating evidence. Thus, it is critically important that children's reports in legal (i.e., forensic) contexts be accurate. In an investigation, children's eyewitness reports are obtained during a forensic interview. This is sometimes referred to as a *victim-sensitive interview,* a label acknowledging that the interview needs to be sensitive to and accommodating of children's special needs.

Child forensic interviews are usually performed by professionals such as social workers, police, and prosecutors but can also be performed by medical professionals or special child advocates. In many communities, forensic interviews are performed at a children's advocacy center. The goals of these centers include limiting trauma for suspected abuse victims and their families, reducing the number of times children are interviewed, and ensuring that children receive nonsuggestive, yet thorough, forensic interviews in a sensitive and child-friendly manner. These centers often coordinate multidisciplinary team investigations of child abuse cases by housing representatives of all agencies involved (police, prosecutors, child and family services, and sometimes medical professionals). Within this context, one interview that serves all partner agencies' purposes is conducted, avoiding the need for multiple interviews which could further traumatize child witnesses. It also increases the probability that the forensic interviewers will be specifically trained in child-sensitive techniques. Thus, the advocacy-center model has the potential to increase the integrity of investigations involving child witnesses—an assumption researchers are currently testing.

During a forensic interview with a suspected child victim or child witness, an investigator will attempt to obtain a comprehensive report, including details about the alleged incident and offender, other possible victims or witnesses, and the location and context of the event. The best forensic interviewers use well-established, empirically validated techniques that facilitate children's reports of actual events and minimize false reports. Good interview techniques facilitate two crucial goals: detecting actual abuse, so that children can be protected from further injury; and ruling out abuse that did not occur, so that innocent individuals are not falsely accused.

Optimal Interview Techniques

Child-sensitive interview techniques have been empirically validated by researchers, often psychologists by training, who are concerned with understanding children's capacity to give accurate reports and using that information to develop techniques to improve children's accuracy. Specifically, in controlled experiments, researchers vary interview techniques and determine their effects on children's accuracy, which includes both children's ability to recall information from memory and their ability to resist false suggestions about events that never happened. Researchers also study individual child factors and situational factors that modify the effectiveness of interview techniques.

Generally, research shows that good techniques for conducting a child forensic interview include building rapport with a child before questioning, maintaining a socially supportive rather than intimidating atmosphere during the interview, remaining impartial and open-minded about what might have occurred throughout the interview rather than having fixed hypotheses about what happened, using developmentally appropriate language rather than complex sentences and advanced vocabulary, asking the most open-ended questions possible instead of narrow questions suggesting information that might be untrue, and using nonsuggestive interview aids such as drawings and anatomically detailed dolls only when necessary. A discussion of some of these and other elements that compose a good forensic interview follows.

Rapport Building

Establishing a positive, trusting relationship between the forensic interviewer and the child serves to set the stage for the interview, provides the interviewer with the opportunity to assess the child's abilities and response style, and allows the child to relax. Asking a child to freely recall neutral, nonstressful events familiarizes the child with the interview format, which consists of the investigator posing open-ended questions to elicit descriptive accounts and using more directive questions only when further inquiry is required. This initial interview phase also allows the interviewer to evaluate the child's social, cognitive, and language skills and emotional state. Research shows that during this early phase of the forensic interview and throughout the interview to come, an interviewer's use of warm vocal tones, supportive eye contact, frequent smiling, rapport building, and relaxed body posture helps to create a supportive environment and increases children's resistance to suggestion.

Question Suggestiveness

A significant concern when interviewing children is the issue of suggestiveness. Both adults and children provide more accurate reports when interviewed with open-ended questions rather than misleading questions, and when interviewed in a noncoercive rather than an intimidating context. Misleading questions introduce inaccurate information or suppositions that the child did not previously disclose. These questions are problematic because children may subsequently include the misinformation in accounts of their experiences, contaminating their reports.

Misleading questions become especially problematic when they occur in conjunction with a variety of contextual or situational factors. Children are most vulnerable to suggestion when, for example, they have been told inaccurate information prior to being interviewed; they are interviewed with questions that are not age-appropriate; they are asked misleading questions by an interviewer who is biased, who has a position of authority, or who is emotionally intimidating and nonsupportive; or they are asked misleading questions repeatedly either within the same interview or across multiple interviews.

To avoid potential suggestibility, investigators use the least leading, most open-ended types of questions. Such questions contain little information and allow children to provide extensive, detailed accounts of their experiences. Freely recalled information is often quite accurate. Even so, using only open-ended questions without providing any cues for children risks that some details of the child's story might be omitted. This hazard is especially relevant when children are very young or reluctant to disclose their abuse, a situation that is not uncommon. In such cases, interviewers employ more focused (but not misleading) questions to help children maintain their concentration and search their memory for details. The best interviewers balance the risks associated with using more directive or cued questions against the risks of missing a disclosure of actual abuse.

It is important to note that although even adults are sometimes suggestible, there are predictable age trends in suggestibility, with preschoolers usually being more suggestible than older children. Even so, increasing age does not always lead to increased accuracy. In fact, some studies show that older children can be more inaccurate than younger children when reporting events that might be considered embarrassing or that they have been told to keep secret. This is because older children are more likely than very young children to understand that some things, such as talking about genitalia, are embarrassing. They are also more cognitively capable of understanding and heeding an adult's threat to secrecy.

Interview Aids

Interview aids are sometimes valuable tools for communicating with children during a forensic interview because they help children describe the event being investigated. Some of the most common aids include freehand drawings, anatomically detailed drawings or diagrams, and anatomically detailed dolls. These tools are most useful for clarifying already-established disclosures from older children. Research reveals that these aids can be problematic, however, for preschool-aged children because, compared with older children, they are more suggestible and their language abilities and symbolic skills are not yet developed enough to understand that drawings and dolls represent specific people. Interview aids are particularly problematic when used in conjunction with misleading questions and when presented to children who have not yet been interviewed with open-ended questioning techniques.

Inconsistencies and Questioning about Repeated Incidents

During a forensic interview, or across multiple interviews (which are not recommended but sometimes unavoidable), children might make inconsistent statements. Research illustrates that some inconsistencies are normal for children and do not necessarily indicate inaccurate reporting.

Discrepancies may result from limited language or cognitive skills. Also, what seems like an inconsistency in reporting details of an event might reflect a child recounting multiple episodes of abuse. Like adults, children who experience multiple occurrences of a similar event develop memories for common, central elements of repeated events, rather than detailed memory for each individual event. That is, they develop and become dependent upon a generalized "script" for the event. Consequently, multiple experiences of stressful events can reinforce children's memories for central aspects of the events but harm their memory for peripheral, tangential details. As a result, children might have difficulty isolating memories of a specific event from memories of other similar events. To counter the effects of this potential challenge, interviewers sometimes ask about the most recent event or use children's own memory markers (e.g., an event happened near a holiday) to help them remember more details about particular incidents.

Truth and Lies

It is important that children's statements be validated to the extent possible with age-appropriate techniques. Asking children directly whether they understand the difference between truth and lies, however, is not a good technique. Research reveals that, even though children might not be able to define or express the difference between such abstract concepts, they can still be reliable witnesses. A better approach is for the interviewer to ask children about independently verifiable facts (e.g., the child's teacher's name) and facts that are critical to the investigation (e.g., description of the location where the alleged events took place). Other investigators can then either corroborate or refute such statements.

Delayed Disclosure and Recantation

Children sometimes delay in reporting their or loved ones' maltreatment, or they sometimes even recant their initial reports of maltreatment. This can happen either before, during, or after a forensic interview. Delays in reports of actual abuse may be linked to shame and embarrassment, fear of not being believed, fear of police involvement, fear of reprisal from threatening perpetrators, feelings of being responsible or blameworthy for the incident, or fear of separation from caregivers. False recantations may be linked to the same factors. Of course, some recantations are true. Trained forensic investigators are aware of this possibility and conduct an impartial examination of recantations and denials. Interviewers will question a recanting child about his or her initial statements and recantations, and gather information about circumstances of the recantation and original statements. If the interviewer discovers that a recantation was improperly encouraged by another person or was part of a deliberate effort to discourage the investigation, the interviewer will question the child about those circumstances. If, however, the child sustains the recantation and there is no evidence of improper motivation, the interviewer will accept the possibility that the recantation is true and question the child about his or her motivations for the false disclosure.

Special Accommodations for Individual Differences among Children

Research reveals that children's accuracy, suggestibility, and ability to communicate differ as functions of many factors, such as age, cultural background, and intellectual and emotional abilities/disabilities. Skilled interviewers will recognize and accommodate such factors during a forensic interview.

For example, as previously mentioned, age is a powerful predictor of children's abilities in investigative interviews. Age is not always a perfect indicator of developmental level because children achieve developmental landmarks at somewhat varying ages, and consequently even children a year or two apart in age can differ dramatically in terms of ability. In any case, good forensic interviewers treat young children and children at an early developmental stage with great care, interviewing them as soon as possible after a report at a time of day when they are normally awake and alert, and taking extra care to build rapport and to monitor their attention span to see if breaks are needed. Interviewers will also reassure young children that a caretaker is nearby or even allow a support person to be with children during an interview (although this person should be unable to signal the child about the accuracy of responses).

Further, compared with older children, younger children have less developed language and memory skills, as well as less capacity to understand what information might be significant in a forensic interview or to understand that the suspected abuse incident was wrong. Compared with older children, young children also give less information in response to open-ended questions, thus requiring more specific questions. Even so, suggestive and misleading questions should be avoided. Also,

questions should contain simple vocabulary and be constructed cleanly (without unnecessary phrases or clauses, ambiguous pronouns, etc.). Young children are particularly vulnerable to complex questions because, even though they may not understand them, they may try to answer anyway, providing inaccurate information.

There are also unique concerns when interviewing older children and adolescents. As noted previously, although older children have better memory skills and are less suggestible than younger children, they are also more aware of complex social and emotional issues. Older children, especially adolescents and teenagers, might be more reluctant than younger children to disclose embarrassing information, which they have perhaps been told to keep secret or which might lead to family disruption.

There are many other individual differences among children that can affect a forensic interview. Children with disabilities are far more vulnerable to maltreatment than nondisabled children, and depending on the type of disability, they may need special accommodations. For example, a disabled child's mental age might be less than his or her chronological age, necessitating interview techniques used with younger children to guard against suggestibility (e.g., using very direct questions and reminding the child frequently that he or she can disagree if anything said is either incorrect or misunderstood). To determine what type of accommodation is necessary, prior to an interview, the interviewer will gather information about the nature of the disability; the type and extent of impairment; how the child adapts to new environments and people; how the child manages anxiety; and whether the child is taking any medication that could influence his or her behavior, ability to communicate, or memory.

Good forensic interviewers will also be aware of a child's cultural background, which can have implications for understanding events in the child's life, how the child and family react to the child's victimization, and the child's and family's attitudes toward the investigation. Also, children who have been severely traumatized by abuse or maltreatment may need special accommodations during an interview. Much research in the field of children's eyewitness testimony is currently focused on the effect of these and other individual differences (e.g., attention skills, temperament) on children's memory and suggestibility. Future research will surely bring many developments relevant to understanding children's vulnerabilities and accommodating individual difference factors in the investigative interview.

Forensic Interview Protocols and Training

Although there are variations on interview style and content, all good forensic interviews contain the basic elements outlined herein. Several specific interview protocols have been developed that prescribe a certain style of questioning. These protocols provide empirically sound and thorough instruction for performing forensic investigations. Among these are the "stepwise interview," developed by Yuille and colleagues, the "cognitive interview," designed by Fisher and Geiselman, and the "NICHD investigative interview protocol," developed by Lamb, Sternberg, and other researchers at the National Institute of Child Health and Human Development. These protocols generally instruct interviewers to begin with rapport building, then use very open-ended questions (sometimes a specific set of scripted questions), gradually building toward more specific questioning. Highly directive questions are recommended only if open-ended questions are unsuccessful at eliciting responses, and all protocols caution against badgering children with potentially misleading, suggestive questions that could elicit false reports. Studies reveal that compared with nonstandard interviews, these types of protocols increase the amount of accurate information obtained from children. Numerous agencies and organizations across the country offer training for child welfare professionals that embody these techniques (e.g., the American Professional Society on the Abuse of Children, the National Child Protection Training Center).

Conclusion

Reports obtained from children are critical evidence in many investigations. Therefore, it is extremely important that the most successful and reliable methods are implemented when interviewing children. By using techniques that encourage and facilitate children's reports, interviewers protect children who may be experiencing abuse or maltreatment and simultaneously help prevent false allegations from threatening the rights of innocent individuals. By continuing to do research on these topics, social scientists ensure that there is an adequate research base to guide interviewers and ensure justice.

BETTE L. BOTTOMS, ALISON R. PERONA, ERIN SORENSON and CYNTHIA J. NAJDOWSKI

See also **Child Neglect; Child Sexual Abuse; Healthcare Professionals' Roles in Identifying and Responding to Domestic Violence; Incest; Munchausen by Proxy Syndrome; Post-Incest Syndrome; Training Practices for Law Enforcement in Domestic Violence Cases**

References and Further Reading

American Professional Society on the Abuse of Children. *Guidelines for Psychosocial Evaluation of Suspected Sexual Abuse in Young Children* (Revised). Chicago: Author, 2002.
Bottoms, Bette L., and Gail S. Goodman, eds. *International Perspectives on Child Abuse and Children's Testimony: Psychological Research and the Law.* Newbury Park, CA: Sage, 1996.
Bottoms, Bette L., Margaret B. Kovera, and Bradley M. McAuliff, eds. *Children, Social Science, and the Law.* New York: Cambridge University Press, 2002.
Eisen, Mitchell, Jodi A. Quas, and Gail S. Goodman, eds. *Memory and Suggestibility in the Forensic Interview.* Mahwah, NJ: Erlbaum, 2002.
Faller, Kathleen C. *Evaluating Children Suspected of Having Been Sexually Abused.* Thousand Oaks, CA: Sage, 1996.
Goodman, Gail S., and Bette L. Bottoms, eds. *Child Victims, Child Witnesses: Understanding and Improving Testimony.* New York: Guilford, 1993.
Goodman, Gail S., Robert E. Emery, and Jeffrey J. Haugaard. "Developmental Psychology and Law: Divorce, Child Maltreatment, Foster Care, and Adoption." In *Handbook of Child Psychology: Vol. 2, Cognition, Perception, and Language,* edited by W. Damon (series ed.), D. Kuhn, and R. S. Siegler (vol. eds.), 5th ed. New York: Wiley, 1998, pp. 775–874.
Goodman, Gail S., Elizabeth P. Taub, David P. Jones, Patricia England, Linda K. Port, Leslie Rudy, and Lydia Prado. "Testifying in Criminal Court." *Monographs of the Society for Research in Child Development* 57, no. 229 (1992).
Myers, John E. B. *Evidence in Child Abuse and Neglect Cases,* 3rd ed. New York: Wiley, 1997.
Myers, John E. B., Lucy Berliner, John Briere, C. Terry Hendrix, Carole Jenny, and Theresa A. Reid, eds. *APSAC Handbook on Child Maltreatment,* 2nd ed. Thousand Oaks, CA: Sage, 2002.
Pence, Donna, and Charles Wilson. *Team Investigation of Child Sexual Abuse: The Uneasy Alliance.* Newbury Park, CA: Sage, 1994.
Poole, Debra A., and Michael E. Lamb. *Investigative Interviews of Children: A Guide for Helping Professions.* Washington, DC: American Psychological Association, 1998.

CHILD NEGLECT

Many researchers believe that child neglect, or a failure to provide for some basic need of a child, is one of the most common forms of child abuse. Although society has advanced in many ways in addressing child abuse, neglect, which is related to the care of children, has not been an area that has kept pace with those advances. Parents still fail to seek medical assistance, provide proper nutritional meals, and ensure that their children attend school. Whether it is explained as ignorance on the part of parents or callousness, many individuals in America today feel that there is some degree of responsibility on the part of society to protect all children (McCabe 2003).

Of all the categories of child abuse (physical, sexual, emotional abuse, and neglect), neglect has probably received the least amount of attention from researchers. The reasons for this lack of attention include the fact that neglect is not seen as being as important or as detrimental to the child's well-being as other forms of abuse. Another reason is that neglect is less dramatic and fails in the shock factor that is often required to "STOP ABUSE" (Garbarino and Collins 1999). In addition, neglect does not lend itself to a quick solution or short-term evaluations of success. Addressing neglect involves a long process of teaching parents to identify, first, the basic needs of a child and then avenues for satisfying those basic needs (Crosson-Tower 2002); thus, researchers interested in empirical assessments opt for focusing on another category of abuse. Finally, neglect, although defined in some of the literature, is still quite subjective in its identification in that what one individual may recognize as neglect, another individual may not. However, this does not infer that neglect is less important than the other categories of child abuse.

It has been estimated that the majority of all child victims of physical, sexual, and emotional abuse are also victims of neglect and that more child deaths from maltreatment or abuse are associated with neglect than with any other type of abuse (McCabe 2003). In addition, it is estimated that over one-half of the child abuse cases reported to law enforcement agencies within the United States are cases of neglect. Unfortunately, neglect does not lend itself to an easy confirmation.

All children are potential victims of neglect; however, certain children have been identified as being at a higher risk. In considering gender, boys are at a higher risk for physical neglect than girls (McCabe 2003). In considering the family characteristics of neglected children, those of single parents are at a greater risk of physical neglect than children of two-parent families; children in large families are more likely to be victims of physical neglect; and children from the lowest-income families are more likely victims of educational neglect (Barkan 2001). One must be aware of the fact that there are many types of neglect, with each type addressing a specific area in the child's life, and that often some of these types of neglect continue to be unrecognized or ignored.

Types of Neglect

The types of neglect can be divided into four general categories: physical, educational, emotional, and supervisional. These categories, although appearing mutually exclusive, may overlap, as most children who are victims of neglect are actually victims of one or more different categories of neglect. For example, a child who is not being supervised on a regular basis is also probably not being sent to school on a regular basis.

By definition, *physical neglect* refers to the caretaker's inability to reduce or prevent the child's likelihood of physical harm (Crosson-Tower 1999). This form of neglect includes a refusal to allow or a delay in the seeking of health care for the child; failing to provide adequate nutrition for the child; a disregard for the child's personal hygiene and/or an inability to provide a sanitary home for the child; a disregard for the child's safety; and the risk to an unborn child due to the use of drugs and/or alcohol by the mother during pregnancy. In other words, physical neglect addresses the neglect of any part of a child's life that may result in physical injury or illness to that child.

Historically, and from a legal perspective, the most common example of physical neglect is a caretaker's choice to refuse medical treatment of an ill or injured child (Wallace 1999). Established in the late 1800s in the case of *In Heinemann's Appeal,* the

Supreme Court of Pennsylvania (1880) supported the principle that states may intervene in the best interest of the child when parents fail to provide medical care. Through this ruling, a child does not have to suffer without relief from illness or injury if the parents refuse medical treatment; in these cases, the state may order the treatment of the child.

A failure to provide adequate nutrition and personal hygiene is another example of neglect and is of common concern for law enforcement and social services. One memoir on the topic of child physical neglect is David Pelzer's (1995) best-selling *A Child Called It*. Pelzer's account of starvation at the hands of his mother brought to the public consciousness the existence of child neglect and the importance of agency intervention.

In addition, the medical community has identified a condition called *nonorganic failure to thrive syndrome*, in which a caretaker's not knowing how to properly feed a baby or failing to provide an adequate amount of milk/formula for the baby results in the delayed development of the child or in some cases the death of the child (English 1978). Failure to Thrive recognizes that all neglect is not intentional; however, with or without intent, the outcome for a neglected child may be death, and Failure to Thrive constitutes physical neglect.

The failure to maintain a safe home, to "baby-proof" a home, or to ensure that a child utilizes a car safety seat may also constitute neglect. Children may ingest common poisons in the home, fall from the top of staircases, or drown in a couple of inches of bath water. The caretakers who choose not to take the proper precautions to protect their children may face prosecution in family court, and lawsuits can be filed in civil court even though the neglect may not be intentional. In Washington, D.C., in November of 2001, the family of a disabled child who died in a Delaware nursing home filed a $120 million lawsuit against the nursing home based upon neglect, on the claim that caretakers at the facility failed to provide for the special needs of the child.

Finally, one of the latest concerns is in the area of prenatal care. In particular the failure of a mother to seek prenatal care for her unborn baby and the use of drugs and alcohol by the mother while pregnant may also be reasons for the criminal charge of physical neglect. This is a topic of liability in the criminal courts, and in many states the definition of a child has been rewritten to include an unborn child (or fetus), which introduces another dimension to child neglect—the drug addicted mother.

Educational neglect refers to the caretaker's failure to provide an education or a means of education to the child (Crosson-Tower 1999). Included in this category of neglect are allowing chronic school truancy, failing to enroll the child in school, and disregarding a child's special education needs. Each of these examples of educational neglect is reason for prosecution in U.S. court systems.

All children in the United States are required to attend school. In turn, parents are required to register their children for school. In some cases of educational neglect, parents fail to register their children or fail to send them to school. Thus, as seen from a legal perspective, the parent, who fails to ensure that his or her child attends school, is guilty of educational neglect.

Finally, another aspect of educational neglect involves the situation of a mentally challenged child or a child with a learning disability and a parent or caretaker who makes little or no effort in an attempt to ensure that child an education or educational progress (Crosson-Tower 1999). Their rights as U.S. citizens afford all children the opportunity of education. Parents are responsible for ensuring that their children seize that opportunity.

The emotional neglect of children may be, in the case of threats or intimidation, classified as emotional abuse. However, for the purpose of this discussion, *emotional neglect* includes inadequate nurturance and affection, the abuse of another person in the presence of the child, and a refusal to provide psychological care by the parent or caretaker (National Center on Child Abuse and Neglect [NCCAN] 1993). Child development consists of a series of stages, and each stage provides a new or additional set of circumstances for the emotionally neglected child. The child who is not nurtured and shown affection but simply ignored has an unstable foundation for a "normal" relationship. The child who never experiences positive contact between parent and child is unaware of this type of relationship and, in many cases, is unable to initiate the process of bonding with other individuals.

In some cases of emotional neglect, an older child who did not receive the love and attention from his/her parents makes a conscious effort to fulfill that role for the younger siblings. In these cases, the child becomes the nurturer and essentially the caretaker to the younger siblings. In other families where emotional neglect exists, the roles of parent and child are undefined and blurred; thus, the child becomes the nurturer to the parents. However, despite this initiative to maintain family closeness, such children usually have little self-value and will oftentimes view themselves as not capable of attracting or maintaining a loving relationship. It is not unusual for these children to drift in and out of relationships as adults, as they were not exposed to the stability of a family life.

Some researchers view emotional neglect as one of the most damaging phenomena in a child's life (Wallace 1999). In addition to the physical condition of Failure to Thrive, which may result from emotional neglect, many researchers have asserted that children who are unloved demonstrate neediness and general feelings of fear of abandonment or rejection later in life (Miller-Perrin and Perrin 1999). These children, who have little value in themselves, often become either the victims or perpetrators of domestic violence (Barkan 2001).

Neglect in terms of supervision is the failure to adequately supervise a child (NCCAN 1993). *Supervisional neglect* includes abandonment (both long-term and short-term) as well as the expulsion of the child from his/her residence without providing adequate alternative housing. Also included under the category of supervisional neglect are cases in which a child is allowed to stay away from the home overnight or for extended periods of time without the caretaker's knowledge of the child's location (NCCAN 1993). In many cases of supervisional neglect, children will simply leave home and, as the parents/caretakers are not in the habit of attending to his/her whereabouts and do not even miss them at first, are not reported to law enforcement officials as missing or as runaways (Crosson-Tower 2002).

Probably one of the most debated hypotheses in the discussion of supervisional neglect is the notion that decreased supervision increases the likelihood of delinquency. The notion that unsupervised youths are more likely to be involved in illegal activities (Bynum and Thompson 2002) or, more generally stated, that inadequate supervision in the home helps to explain delinquent behavior outside of the home is a common philosophy. In the absence of caretaker supervision, the child becomes accustomed to acting as he/she desires without giving thought to the consequences. It is an unfortunate case of a lack of adequate supervision when a child is injured or killed or inflicts injury upon or kills another person.

Indicators of Neglect

Just as there are many indicators of child physical, sexual, and emotional abuse, there are also many indicators of neglect. School officials are most likely to be involved in identifying a neglected child.

In fact, in most states, educators, because of their positions, are mandated reporters of child abuse and neglect and must accept their responsibility in reporting possible cases of abuse.

Neglect manifests itself in two forms—either in physical injury or through behavioral indicators. However, it must be acknowledged that although the following characteristics are indicators of neglect, they are not always the result of neglect. Just as with any type of child abuse, those investigating such charges should weigh all the facts prior to pronouncing neglect.

One of the more common physical indicators of neglect is poor physical development. Research has revealed that neglected children often produce poor growth patterns (Crosson-Tower 1999; Wallace 1999). These children will be smaller than other children of the same age, and neglected children will often be below the fifteenth percentile of their growth range for their age and sex. In many cases, related to lack of physical development, a neglected child may appear to be constantly hungry or even to suffer from malnutrition. These children may steal food or hoard food and eat (when they are allowed) as though they were starved. In many cases of neglect, the children are in various stages of starvation. In addition, and as is commonly the case, the child's hygiene is also a good indicator of neglect. In particular, a child with poor hygiene, a smell of urine, rotten teeth, head lice, and/or other unattended physical or medical problems may also be a victim of neglect (Crosson-Tower 2002).

Finally, in many cases, child neglect produces a child who suffers from constant fatigue or sleepiness. This child, because of lack of food or of shelter, may seem always tired and in need of sleep. Again, in most cases, the individuals who are in the positions to recognize the physical signs of neglect are the child's teachers.

Often, long before the physical indicators of neglect are revealed, the behavioral indicators will be present. A child who lacks self-confidence or self-worth and has poor relationships with peers may be a victim of neglect (Wolfe, McMahon, and Peters 1997). Behavioral indicators of neglect include begging for food, being socially withdrawn or destructive, and eliciting negative responses to gain attention (Crosson-Tower 2002). Other behavioral indicators related to the education of the child include being developmentally behind other children in the same age group in the understanding of concepts or the advancement of motor skills, difficulties with language comprehension (as generally their interactions have been through one- or two-word statements such as

"No," "Get out," or "Shut up"), and overall lower intelligence (Crosson-Tower 2002). Finally, neglected children are often self-destructive, destructive to other people, or destructive to other's property (Wallace 1999).

In many cases, neglected children are expected to assume the role of caretaker for their younger siblings. A child who appears to be mature for his/her age in actions or who acknowledges responsibilities in the home such as cooking dinner for the family or the bathing of siblings may be neglected. Children who are neglected rarely see school as a necessary part of their lives; therefore, a child who is often tardy or absent from school may also be a victim of neglect. Later, of course, most of these neglected children simply drop out of school completely. Finally, a child who appears to be generally depressed or withdrawn may be a victim of neglect.

Just as the parents are responsible for the care of their children, they are also the most likely source of neglect. However, one cannot discuss neglect by parents or caretakers as simply a result of a failure to fulfill their role. Neglect must be addressed in regard to the dynamics behind the caretaker inability to care for their child. From that perspective, most research would assert that child neglect is a result of three different types of parental and family characteristics: the parent/caretaker's developmental history and personality, the characteristics of the family and child, and environmental influences (Crosson-Tower 1999).

Explaining Neglect

The first attempt to explain the causes of neglect is from the perspective of the caretaker's own developmental history and personality (Gaudin 1993). Caretakers themselves who have grown up in an environment of neglect are likely to neglect their own children. Just as with other forms of abuse and the cycle of violence (Walker 1979), neglect is often a generational outcome. These acts of neglect are often a result of the parent not knowing or understanding, for example, that a three-year-old child is not an appropriate caretaker for an eight-month-old baby (Wolfe et al. 1997) or that by leaving a five-year-old alone in a home overnight or for several days constitutes abandonment (Wallace 1999). Many of these caretakers were raised in an environment of child "responsibility" and therefore see nothing wrong with repeating the pattern.

One must also consider the personality or physical condition of the caretaker in the explanation of neglect. Caretakers—in particular, mothers, who are the most likely perpetrators of neglect—may suffer from depression or have an impulsive personality in which such actions as sleeping for days or not providing meals for the child may result in child neglect. Some caretakers are apathetic and some are psychotic (Crosson-Tower 2002). A caretaker's substance abuse or mental disadvantage may also promote neglect of the child in the household (Gaudin 1993). Finally, caretakers who themselves are physically ill may not be able to provide for the child's basic needs; in turn, the child is neglected (McCabe 2003).

The second attempt to explain neglect focuses on the characteristics of the family and the child (Gaudin 1993). Just as the personality traits of the caretaker may be used to explain child neglect, so may the personality of the child and the characteristics of the family structure. Just as two adults may have a personality conflict, the child and his/her caretaker may also clash. In addition, children who are introverts (e.g., those who demand little attention) or who do not have the ability to request help from a caretaker (because of some physical or mental handicap) may become neglected. Children who are one of many in a family (especially if they are not the oldest or the youngest) may also be neglected, and children from single-parent homes, simply because of the limitations of time on one parent, may also be victims of neglect (Gaudin 1993). As applies to this text, children who are members of a family in which domestic violence is present may also be victims of child neglect.

The third explanation of neglect is related to environmental influences or sources of stress outside of the family. Families that are isolated from other family members or the community itself lack all outside resources when it comes to child care. In these families, the children are at high risk for neglect.

Finally, economics is another source of stress on the family (Gaudin 1993). With both parents working or, in the case of a single-parent household, with the one parent working perhaps multiple jobs, there is little time for the children. These so-called "latchkey children" are often victims of neglect.

It is unfortunate that neglect may result in children feeling hungry, in pain, or afraid to be alone; however, there are other consequences of neglect (both short- and long-term), of which society may not be fully aware. Often neglect manifests itself in actions other than disruptive school behavior or withdrawn personalities. Children who are neglected may suffer from sleep problems, weight loss or weight gain, and poor social relations. They may suffer from frequent illnesses or be labeled hypochondriacs (McCabe and Martin 2005). The neglected children may turn to drugs or alcohol as an escape from their situation or to promiscuous sexual behavior to gain attention. In addition, neglected children may become runaways or throwaways if their parents decide that their presence in the home is no longer convenient (Bynum and Thompson 2002).

Later in life, it is not uncommon for neglected children to become adults who are unable to relate to their own children or adult partners; thus, they continue the cycle of neglect. They may also be involved in drug or alcohol abuse, which again reduces the likelihood of their positive interactions with their families. Also, adults who were neglected as children may partake in violent activities such as crime or domestic violence.

Conclusion

Child neglect is not a new topic for those whose jobs place them in positions of daily contact with children; however, the problem has no simple solution. In cases of physical, sexual, or emotional abuse, interventions often focus on ending the abuse; however, neglect, because of its underlying dynamics of family structure, personalities, and environmental influences, does not equate with a simple fix.

In the United States, more child fatalities are associated with neglect than any other form of child abuse (McCabe 2003), and most efforts by law enforcement and departments of social services are focused simply upon physical neglect. Only through education and intervention may the problem of child neglect be addressed. Only through the involvement of interested parties will the problem of child neglect be solved.

KIMBERLY A. MCCABE

See also **Child Abuse: A Global Perspective; Child Abuse and Juvenile Delinquency; Child Abuse and Neglect in the United States: An Overview; Child Maltreatment, Interviewing Suspected Victims of; Munchausen by Proxy Syndrome; Shaken Baby Syndrome**

References and Further Reading

Barkan, Steven. *Criminology. A Sociological Understanding,* 2nd ed. Upper Saddle River, NJ: Prentice Hall, 2001.

Bynum, J. E., and W. E. Thompson. *Juvenile Delinquency: A Sociological Approach,* 5th ed. Boston, MA: Allyn and Bacon, 2002.

Crosson-Tower, C. *Understanding Child Abuse and Neglect,* 4th ed. Boston, MA: Allyn and Bacon, 1999.

———. *When Children Are Abused: An Educator's Guide to Intervention.* Boston, MA: Allyn and Bacon, 2002.

Garbarino, J., and C. C. Collins. "Child Neglect: The Family with the Hole in the Middle." In *Neglected Children: Research, Practice, and Policy,* edited by H. Dubowitz. Thousand Oaks, CA: Sage, 1999, pp. 1–23.

Gaudin, J. M. *Child Neglect: A Guide for Intervention.* Washington, DC: U.S. Department of Health and Human Services. Administration for Children and Families, 1993. HHS-105891730.

McCabe, K. *Child Abuse and the Criminal Justice System.* New York: Peter Lang, 2003.

McCabe, K., and G. Martin. *School Violence, the Media, and Criminal Justice Responses.* New York: Peter Lang, 2005.

Miller-Perrin, C., and R. Perrin. *Child Maltreatment: An Introduction.* Thousand Oaks, CA: Sage, 1999.

National Center on Child Abuse and Neglect [NCCAN]. *Child Neglect: A Guide for Intervention.* Washington, DC: U.S. Department of Health and Human Services. Administration for Children and Families, 1993. HHS-105891730.

Pelzer, David. *A Child Called It.* Deerfield Beach, FL: Health Communications, Inc., 1995.

Walker, L. E. *The Battered Woman.* New York: Harper & Row, 1979.

Wallace, H. *Family Violence: Legal, Medical, and Social Perspectives,* 2nd ed. Boston, MA: Allyn and Bacon, 1999.

Wolfe, D. A., R. J. McMahon, and R. D. Peters. *Child Abuse: New Directions in Prevention and Treatment Across the Lifespan.* Thousand Oaks, CA: Sage, 1997.

CHILD SEXUAL ABUSE

Historical Perspective

Child sexual abuse (CSA), a social problem of endemic proportions, has existed in all historical eras and societies (Conte 1994; Fergusson and Mullen 1999; Wekerle and Wolfe 1996; Wolfe 1999). Since antiquity, anecdotal records (e.g., legal, artistic, philosophical, and literary accounts) have documented activities that would today be classified as CSA (deMause 1974; Kahr 1991; Olafson, Corwin, and Summit 1993). For instance, a sizable portion of adults in ancient Greek and Roman cultures openly engaged in what is now considered pederasty or rape (deMause 1974; Kahr 1991). Although adult–child sexual encounters have occurred throughout history, perceptions of such practices have fluctuated, ranging from societal acceptance (adult–child sex viewed as healthy or justifiable) to rejection (adult–child sex believed to be inappropriate or abusive) (Barnett, Miller-Perrin, and Perrin 1997; Kahr 1991; Olafson et al. 1993). With this oscillation of cultural ideologies, establishing behaviors as sexually abusive has not been an additive or linear process. Rather, scholars have called attention to cycles of "recognition (or 'discovery') and suppression" that, until the 1970s, largely obscured public awareness of the magnitude of the problem (Conte 1994; Olafson et al. 1993). In the late nineteenth and early to mid-twentieth centuries, for example, physicians (e.g., Tardieu), psychoanalysts (e.g., Freud), and researchers (e.g., Kinsey) had, to some extent, discovered and documented sexual victimization in their patients. Representative of the general sentiment at the time, however, these findings were subsequently minimized, discounted, or justified, resulting in victim blame and a cycle of "suppression" (Bolen 2001; Conte 1994; Olafson et al. 1993). Sigmund Freud's work perhaps best exemplifies the "recognition and suppression" cycle (Fergusson and Mullen 1999). Specifically, although Freud initially publicized the reality of CSA with his "seduction theory," he later rescinded this account, indicating that most of the alleged instances were false and that children, via the Oedipal complex, exhibit a natural and erotic sexual desire toward their opposite-sex parent (Bolen 2001; Olafson et al. 1993; Tharinger 1990). In one explanation of Freud's "suppression," Bolen (2001) highlighted the Victorian social and political atmosphere which encased Freud and concluded that he "effectively colluded with a society that wished to deny the existence of child sexual abuse" (p. 20).

This cycle of "recognition and suppression" regarding the sexual abuse of children was disrupted in part by two events more associated with the physical abuse of children. The first of these events was the inception of the child protection movement in New York State. Imbued within a culture where children were viewed as parental property and where family lives were kept discreetly out of public view, the establishment of formal child protection reflected the convergence of several salient factors, particularly related to the 1874 case of Mary Ellen, a girl who experienced physical and psychological cruelty by her stepmother (MacMillan 2000; Wolfe 1999). In contrast to the majority of cases at that time, which went undetected or were ignored, a culmination of necessary ingredients—including the persistent voices of advocates for Mary Ellen, public concern, and a political and social atmosphere more prepared for reform—enabled Mary Ellen's story to affect legal change. Contrary to the "suppression" cycle that typically followed, the tragedy of Mary Ellen's case contributed to the founding of the New York Society for the Prevention of Cruelty to Children (NYSPCC), which paralleled the already flourishing Society for the Prevention of Cruelty to Animals and was the first child protection organization (Barnett et al. 1997; NYSPCC 2000; Wolfe 1999). This late-nineteenth-century event signified that the protection of children against physical abuse and neglect was an idea that had begun to take root.

A second watershed event that ultimately helped to draw attention to the problem of sexual abuse was the publication of the seminal study by Kempe, Silverman, Steele, Droegemueller, and Silver (1962). This study, on the physical abuse of children, scientifically documented medical injuries resulting from child abuse and focused particular attention on the presumed pathology of maltreating parents. In the aftermath of Kempe et al.'s (1962) landmark publication, several factors (e.g., enhanced societal awareness of child maltreatment, the effects of the Vietnam war and the concomitant raising of "social consciousness" of the era, the growth of the women's movement) coalesced and again provided impetus for increased recognition of CSA as a pervasive problem for children and adult survivors (Bolen 2001, p. 21; Fergusson and Mullen 1999; Finkelhor 2002, p. xii; Olafson et al. 1993).

Even after the problem of CSA became widely recognized and reached the mainstream of public awareness in the 1970s, the topic has remained controversial. For instance, despite increased media and research attention on CSA throughout the 1980s and 1990s, these two decades (and onward into the twenty-first century) witnessed a backlash that engendered skepticism about the magnitude and long-term sequelae of CSA (Fergusson and Mullen 1999; see also the meta-analysis of Rind, Tromovitch, and Bauserman 1998), as well as the validity of CSA allegations (Bowen 2001; Olafson et al. 1993). The impact of this "child abuse backlash," which is evidenced via increasingly visible and organized "opposition" groups (e.g., attorneys, websites, and layperson or legal groups specifically geared to those who believe they have been falsely accused of perpetrating CSA), complicates scientific inquiry and professional advocacy/practice (Finkelhor 2002, p. xiv). Despite these controversies, however, the sexual abuse of children has been referred to as "one of the defining cultural themes of our age" (Fergusson and Mullen 1999, p. 1), a phenomenon that ultimately "emerged from the cloak of social secrecy and [has] become a leading concern of mental health professionals" (Cole and Putnam 1992, p. 174).

Definition of Child Sexual Abuse

Ever since the recognition in the 1970s of the sexual mistreatment of children as a widespread problem, professionals have wrestled with how to conceptualize and define CSA (Haugaard 2000). Although formulating a universally accepted definition is complicated by several theoretical and ideological considerations, some agreement has emerged among professionals regarding the defining features of sexual abuse. These characteristics are captured by the most recent Child Abuse Prevention and Treatment Act (CAPTA), which defines CSA as "the employment, use, persuasion, inducement, enticement, or coercion of any child to engage in, or assist any other person to engage in, any sexually explicit conduct or simulation of such

conduct for the purpose of producing a visual depiction of such conduct; or the rape, and in cases of caretaker or interfamilial relationships, statutory rape, molestation, prostitution, or other form of sexual exploitation of children, or incest with children" (National Center on Child Abuse and Neglect [NCCAN], 2005a, p. 1). In addition to this legal conceptualization, many researchers distinguish sexual offenses involving contact (e.g., penetration) or noncontact (e.g., child pornography, exhibitionism) (American Psychological Association 2001; Hansen, Hecht, and Futa 1998). Definitions also encompass the age differential between the perpetrator and the victim, with victims of CSA (in contrast to those of statutory rape or adolescent sexual assault) generally being under sixteen years of age and perpetrators being at least five years older (Hansen et al. 1998). Notably, the age differential becomes less important if force is involved in the sexual abuse incident (Berliner and Elliott 2002).

Prevalence

Just as establishing an operational definition of CSA is difficult, obtaining accurate incidence and prevalence rates of CSA is also challenging. Data collection methods (e.g., self-report versus interview methodology), measurement variations (e.g., single-item versus in-depth measures of CSA), study design issues (e.g., prospective versus retrospective design, sampling techniques), and extraneous factors (e.g., underreporting, response rates) all obscure estimates (Goldman and Padayachi 2000; Putnam 2003). Despite these hurdles, researchers have sought to uncover estimates of CSA in the general population through national incidence studies and self-report data.

National Incidence Study

The government-mandated National Incidence Study (NIS) represents perhaps the most expansive attempt to ascertain the incidence of CSA in the United States (Sedlak and Broadhurst 1996). Sedlak (2001) points out that children who come to the attention of the legal system as a result of abuse or neglect exemplify only the "tip of the iceberg" (p. 6). For this reason, the third National Incidence Study (NIS-3) measures maltreatment according to a five-tier system, which involves substantiated child protective services (CPS) reports and the reports of trained teachers, courts, police, and hospital personnel, as well as cases indicated by other agencies. Further, NIS-3 evaluates child maltreatment against two standards: the Harm

Standard (i.e., the child has already suffered known harm as a result of abuse/neglect) and the Endangerment Standard (i.e., the child [who has experienced maltreatment] is at high risk for developing abuse-related consequences or has yet to evidence known sequelae) (Sedlak and Broadhurst 1996). Results from NIS-3 reflecting 1993–1994 data indicated that 217,700 children experienced CSA according to the Harm Standard and 300,200 via the Endangerment Standard, both reflecting substantial increases from NIS-2 (Sedlak and Broadhurst 1996); the most current data collection as of this writing (NIS-4) is currently under way and will conclude sometime in 2008 (National Incidence Study 4, 2005). Finally, another national database utilizing reports to child protective agencies, the National Child Abuse and Neglect Data System (NCANDS) revealed per capita child maltreatment rates of 12.4 per 1,000 children, with 10 percent of those being sexual abuse victims (NCCAN 2005b).

Self-Report Data

Although NISs provide an indication of the magnitude of CSA, they probably underestimate rates of sexual victimization because of a heavy reliance on cases that come to the attention of the legal and child protective systems (e.g., Walch and Broadhead 1992). In contrast, retrospective surveys of adults (particularly with representative community samples) may gain access to individuals whose abuse never came to the attention of the legal system. In reviewing sixteen such studies, Gorey and Leslie (1997) found that the prevalence of CSA in nonclinical samples in the United States is 22.3 percent for women and 8.5 percent for men. When they included only studies with a 60 percent or higher response rate, the percentages for women and men dropped to 16.8 percent and 7.9 percent, respectively (even more conservative rates were shown with stricter inclusion criteria). The authors concluded that the "truth" likely falls between these estimations (p. 395). As can be seen, CSA prevalence rates vary, depending on factors such as the methodology employed, the type of sample, and the instrument used. For example, in their review of the literature, which included community-based and convenience samples, Fergusson and Mullen (1999) estimated that the most inclusive rates of CSA (which included noncontact experiences) ranged from 8.0 to 62.1 percent for women and 3 to 29 percent for men, though the majority of studies estimated between 15 and 30 percent for women and 3 and 15 percent for men. Results from another national study, utilizing a randomized

telephone sampling, found that 27 percent of women and 16 percent of men met the most liberal criteria for CSA (Finkelhor, Hotaling, Lewis, and Smith 1990). These results were similar to a national sample by Briere and Elliott (2003), who indicated that 32.3 percent of women and 14.2 percent of men were classified as sexually abused. In Finkelhor's (1993) estimate, sexual abuse is likely to be present in approximately one in four girls and one in ten boys. Finally, although the NIS-3 indicated that CSA rates had increased substantially in recent years, this finding has not been consistent. Jones, Finkelhor, and Kopiec (2001), for example, discussed contrary indicators that CSA had declined by 39 percent. Specifically, they (among others) noted that it is challenging to determine whether the rates of CSA have actually diminished or whether definitional criteria and research methodologies are responsible for these patterns (Jones et al. 2001; Leventhal 2001).

Demographic Factors Associated with Child Sexual Abuse

Victim Characteristics

In addition to examining overall prevalence rates, researchers have also explored whether CSA trends emerge based on various demographic characteristics. For example, regarding victim gender, the majority of studies indicate that girls experience sexual abuse at much higher rates than boys. Indeed, girls not only are three times more likely to experience CSA under both the Harm and Endangerment Standards used in NIS-3 (Sedlak and Broadhurst 1996), but also are more likely to experience forceful and injurious sexual abuse (Levesque 1994). In a study examining international prevalence rates, Finkelhor (1994) found that, overall, gender findings tended to parallel those in the United States, with girls experiencing a significantly greater likelihood of being sexually victimized (between one and a half and three times more likely). Despite these trends, it is important to note that boys still constitute a significant minority of CSA victims and may in fact be underrepresented in studies (Finkelhor 1993).

Similar to relatively consistent gender findings, results concerning age of the victim indicate that CSA risk and age increase simultaneously, with the highest risk being in mid to late childhood, between the ages of six and eleven years (Putnam 2003; Sedlak and Broadhurst 1996). In their review of the literature, Fergusson and Mullen (1999) indicated that, for girls, CSA peaks at between ten and twelve years of age; these authors, however, cautioned that underreporting or undiscovered incidents may be more prevalent before that time. Finkelhor (1993) indicated that although CSA occurs at every age level, risk appears to manifest around ages six to seven years and be most common at around age ten. Thus, it appears that middle and later childhood are the most common times for CSA to onset, or at least to be acknowledged or discovered. Socioeconomic status (SES) is an additional demographic variable of interest. Most studies to date have not substantiated a drastic impact of SES (Finkelhor 1993; Putnam 2003). Thus, although CSA may pose a greater risk for girls and children in their middle years, it has been documented in every social stratum.

Perpetrator Characteristics

As in the case of victim gender, certain trends also have emerged regarding perpetrator gender. Namely, men make up the large majority of perpetrators of sexual abuse both in the United States (Finkelhor et al. 1990; Sedlak and Broadhurst 1996) and internationally (Finkelhor 1994). However, women do constitute a portion of CSA perpetrators, and the role of female perpetrators should not be discounted. In addition to gender, the relationship of the perpetrator to the victim tends to extend across the gamut of possible relationships. In the NIS-3, perpetrators of CSA included birth parents (approximately 25 percent) and individuals other than biological parents or those serving in parental roles (approximately 75 percent) (Sedlak and Broadhurst 1996). Notably, according to Berliner and Elliott (2002), CSA by family members seems to be overrepresented in clinical settings.

Consequences of Child Sexual Abuse

Developmental Framework

Part of the complexity surrounding CSA stems from the heterogeneity of its short- and long-term correlates. According to Nash, Hulsey, Sexton, Harralson, and Lambert (1993), there is no emergent "delimited replicable pattern of sequelae" associated with early abuse (p. 276). Instead, CSA may impact victims according to a more "nonspecific" symptom pattern. Thus, the mental health consequences of CSA cannot be placed into a single diagnostic classification within the *Diagnostic and Statistical Manual of Mental Disorders* (American Psychiatric Association 2000; Finkelhor 1990). Furthermore, while some victims experience a wide range of adverse emotional, behavioral, and interpersonal sequelae, others appear asymptomatic (Cicchetti and

Toth 2000; Cole and Putnam 1992; Finkelhor 1990; Kendall-Tackett, Williams, and Finkelhor 1993). This variation in outcomes can be understood within a developmental framework (Cicchetti and Toth 2000; Cole and Putnam 1992; DiLillo, Perry, and Fortier, in press; Wolfe 1999). That is, as infants and children progress through various phases of development, they must confront and master a range of stage-salient tasks (Cicchetti 1989; Cicchetti and Toth 2000; Cole and Putnam 1992; Wolfe 1999). In the absence of significant environmental or biological adversity, most individuals will progress along expected developmental pathways. Early sexual abuse, however, represents a substantial form of interpersonal trauma and, as such, may impede normal developmental processes, setting the stage for possible short- and long-term adjustment difficulties (Cole and Putnam 1992; Wolfe 1999).

Short-Term Sequelae

Overall, the research has revealed that the immediate aftermath of CSA often engenders a wide array of consequences but that boys and girls, with few exceptions, appear to be impacted by CSA in many of the same ways (Finkelhor 1990). According to Wolfe and Birt's (1997) review, there are several "sets" of findings related to the short-term sequelae of CSA, including: (1) increased internalizing and externalizing difficulties in CSA victims, (2) the presence of a range of behavioral and emotional problems that relate directly to the CSA, the home environment, or both, and (3) the risk of post-traumatic stress disorder (PTSD) symptomatology and sexuality difficulties. A fourth area that may be useful to consider is the differentiated mental health and interpersonal sequelae, both of which appear to be impacted even in the immediate aftermath of CSA. Paralleling the aforementioned "sets" of short-term difficulties are findings that victims experience increased depression (e.g., Swanston, Plunkett, O'Toole, Shrimpton, Parkinson, and Oates 2003), anxiety (e.g., Chaffin, Silovsky, and Vaughn 2005; Spataro, Mullen, Burgess, Wells, and Moss 2004), personality disorders (Spataro et al. 2004), suicidal ideation (e.g., Martin, Bergen, Richardson, Roeger, and Allison 2004), nightmares (Mannarino and Cohen 1986; NCCAN 2003), guilt, anger, and fear (Barnett et al. 1997), somatization (Emiroğlu, Kurul, Akay, Miral, and Süha 2004), and attachment-related problems (e.g., Shapiro and Levendosky 1999). PTSD symptomatology appears to be particularly salient among victims (e.g., Kendall-Tackett et al. 1993; NCCAN 2003). In the area of externalizing difficulties, the experience of CSA is related to self-injury (Kendall-Tackett et al. 1993), academic/school trouble (Barnett et al. 1997), behavioral problems (Kendall-Tackett et al. 1993), bed-wetting (NCCAN 2003), problem eating behaviors (NCCAN 2003), delinquency and aggression (Swanston, Parkinson, O'Toole, Plunkett, Shrimpton, and Oates 2003), running away (NCCAN 2003), and a range of sexualized behaviors (Barnett et al. 1997) (see excellent reviews by Hecht and Hansen 2001; Kendall-Tackett et al. 1993; and Paolucci, Genuis, and Violato 2001).

In addition to these internalizing and externalizing difficulties, CSA sequelae also manifest in the interpersonal and physiological realms. Regarding interpersonal functioning, CSA has been linked to difficulties in interpersonal relationships, including poor social adjustment (Friedrich, Urquiza, and Beilke 1986) and developmentally inappropriate sexual behaviors and disturbed attitudes related to sexuality (Kendall-Tackett et al. 1993; NCCAN 2003; Tharinger 1990). Studies have also documented several physiological or neurobiological linkages, such as diminished salivary cortisol levels in recently abused children (King, Mandansky, King, Fletcher, and Brewer 2001), earlier onset of menarche (Vigil, Geary, and Byrd-Craven 2005), increased sympathetic nervous system activity, and a range of neurobiological sequelae (see Putnam 2003 for review).

There is also evidence that certain symptoms are more likely to emerge when the abuse is perpetrated during specific developmental stages. For example (although perhaps due to methodological/measurement issues), internalizing symptoms such as depression and anxiety are reported less frequently in early childhood but emerge with greater frequency in adolescence (Berliner and Elliott 1996). In a separate review of childhood versus adolescence findings, Arias (2004) indicated that children were more likely to experience problems related to school, attention, social skills, and aggression, whereas adolescents were at greater risk for delinquency/violence, sexual problems, substance use, and self-injurious behavior. Finally, in Kendall-Tackett and colleagues' (1993) review of CSA sequelae, the authors overviewed the most commonly occurring symptoms at various developmental levels, including preschool-aged children (anxiety, nightmares, PTSD, internalizing, externalizing, and inappropriate sexual behavior), school-aged children (fear, neurotic/general illness, aggression, nightmares, school difficulties, hyperactive behaviors, and regression), and adolescents (depression, withdrawal, suicidality/self-injurious behaviors, somatization, illegal activity, running away, and substance use).

Long-Term Sequelae

In addition to short-term sequelae, investigators have illuminated a myriad of adult mental health as well as behavioral, societal, and physical correlates of CSA (NCCAN 2005c). Among these long-term mental health sequelae are elevated levels of psychopathological symptomatology, such as depression (e.g., Denov 2004; Hill, Davis, Byatt, Burnside, Rollinson, and Fear 2000; Jackson, Calhoun, Amick, Maddever, and Habif 1990; Hunter 1991; Roberts, O'Connor, Dunn, Golding, and the ALSPAC Study Team 2004), anxiety (Greenwald, Leitenberg, Cado, and Tarran 1990; Steel, Sanna, Hammond, Whipple, and Cross 2004), PTSD (Putnam 2003), obsessive-compulsive disorder (Steel et al. 2004), and personality disorder concerns or diagnoses, including antisocial and borderline (Callahan, Price, and Hilsenroth 2003; Putnam 2003). Additional cognitive and behavioral effects include suicidal ideation and suicide attempts (Anderson, Tiro, Price, Bender, and Kaslow 2002; Read, Agar, Barker-Collo, Davies, and Moskowitz 2001), dissociation (Putnam 2003), substance use/abuse (Denov 2004; Molnar, Buka, and Kessler 2001), somatization (Polusny and Follette 1995; Putnam 2003), disordered eating behaviors (Putnam 2003; Smolak and Murnen 2002), risk of aggression toward others, including one's children (DiLillo, Tremblay, and Peterson 2000), diminished self-esteem (Hunter 1991; Jackson et al. 1990), and academic/vocational difficulties (Arias 2004). At a broader societal level, victims of CSA have been found to have higher health care costs and lower self-perceptions of good health (Arias 2004). A meta-analysis conducted by Paolucci et al. (2001), for example, found that PTSD, depression, suicide, sexual promiscuity, victim–perpetrator cycle, and poor academic performance all represented, to varying degrees, substantially elevated risks for CSA survivors.

More recently, interest has increased in exploring the associations between a history of childhood maltreatment and adult interpersonal functioning. Within this domain, adult survivors of child maltreatment are more likely not only to display social maladjustment in dating and extracurricular activities (Jackson et al. 1990), but also to experience greater overall relationship dysfunction in comparison with nonmaltreated individuals. This dysfunction may include decreased relationship satisfaction and trust, as well as a greater likelihood of infidelity and relationship instability or termination (Colman and Widom 2004; Denov 2004; DiLillo 2001; DiLillo and Long 1999; Hunter 1991). Child maltreatment also appears to be related to the occurrence of physical violence in adult dating and marital relationships (Barnett et al. 1997; DiLillo, Giuffre, Tremblay, and Peterson 2001). DiLillo et al. (2001), for example, found that women with a history of CSA were more likely to be involved in relationships characterized by minor and severe forms of interpartner aggression (e.g., breaking things, hitting/kicking, beating), as well as greater amounts of bidirectional, reciprocal (i.e., male-to-female and female-to-male) acts of violence. Research in this area also suggests that sexual abuse during childhood is associated with problems related to sexual functioning, including preoccupation with sexuality, negative attitudes toward sex, fear of intimacy, unrestricted sexual behavior, sexual dissatisfaction, and sexual maladjustment (Davis, Petretic-Jackson, and Ting 2001; Meston, Heiman, and Trapnell 1999; Noll, Trickett, and Putnam 2003; Rumstein-McKean and Hunsley 2001).

Recent literature has helped to elucidate factors that accompany CSA and its correlates. For example, researchers documented the frequent co-occurrence of maltreatment subtypes (e.g., high overlap between sexual abuse and physical abuse) (Davis et al. 2001; Dong, Anda, Felitti, Dube, Williamson, Thompson, Loo, and Giles 2004; Higgins and McCabe 2000). Similarly, it appears that the long-term effects of CSA are cumulative, with symptom presence and severity increasing as more forms of maltreatment are experienced (Anderson et al. 2002; Clemmons, DiLillo, Martinez, DeGue, and Jeffcott 2003; Higgins and McCabe 2000, 2003). Finally, when considering long-term sequelae, there are many concomitant or intervening factors that may mediate or moderate the impact of the consequences associated with CSA (e.g., Beitchman, Zucker, Hood, DaCosta, Akman, and Cassavia 1992; Nash et al. 1993; Rind et al. 1998). For example, childhood family environment has been shown to be more chaotic, dysfunctional, and conflictual in victims of CSA (Bennett, Hughes, and Luke 2000; Long and Jackson 1994). It has been documented that the long-term sequelae of CSA diminish in significance after accounting for family environment issues (Rind et al. 1998). However in most cases, even when these mediating and moderating variables are controlled, an array of CSA sequelae remain (Molnar et al. 2001; Sachs-Ericsson, Blazer, Plant, and Arnow 2005).

Current Controversies Related to CSA

Although there is a general consensus that CSA is a prevalent and deleterious societal phenomenon, several issues, such as ritualistic/satanic abuse, accuracy of children's testimony in court regarding CSA, children's suggestibility and adults' false memories surrounding CSA experiences, and multiple personality disorder, remain controversial or unresolved (Fergusson and Mullen 1999; Wolfe and Birt 1997). Professional groups commenting on each of these "hot topics" demonstrate distinctly polarized viewpoints. In the area of recovered memory, for instance, professionals often display inclinations toward one of two positions, promoting either the belief that so-called "recovered memories" are often accurate representations of the past, or the belief that it is essentially impossible to forget (or repress) and subsequently recover a memory of early abuse (Farrants 1998). Further complicating this division, research in the area of recovered memory has both supported and debunked aspects on both sides of this issue, thereby inflaming each viewpoint (Farrants 1998). In commenting on ritual abuse, Gallagher (2001) notes the paradox that the various parties involved in the debates regarding CSA "are passionately committed to upholding the welfare and interests of children and survivors. However, if this is to be done, then all of us working in this area must be equally committed to finding out the truth irrespective of our preconceptions and beliefs" (p. 84). This comment reflects the notion that even though the topic of CSA generates passionate debate, the underlying goals—to prevent abuse and assist victims—must be achieved by advancing science and identifying commonalities.

Summary

Since antiquity, children have experienced sexual abuse by adults. Following a period of alternately being recognized then suppressed, CSA ultimately garnered public attention in the aftermath of Kempe et al.'s (1962) study on the physical abuse of children. Since that time, attempts to define CSA have remained difficult and fraught with differing professional opinions. Nonetheless, research focusing on the prevalence and consequences of CSA has confirmed that it is a widespread societal problem with a range of negative intra- and interpersonal outcomes across the lifespan. At the same time, some victims of CSA seem to suffer few ill effects. To date, the intersection of research and policy work has placed CSA in the public consciousness by underscoring its magnitude and adverse correlates. Following closely behind the widespread recognition of CSA as a serious societal problem, various controversies, such as the existence of recovered memories, emerged among professionals and laypersons alike. Understanding of CSA and its consequences will best be furthered by a commitment to objective scientific inquiry and a focus on commonalities of the various parties interested in the protection and well-being of children.

ANDREA R. PERRY and DAVID DILILLO

See also **Bullying and the Family; Child Abuse and Juvenile Delinquency; Child Maltreatment, Interviewing Suspected Victims of; Child Neglect; Incest; Post-Incest Syndrome; Prosecuting Child Abuse; Ritual Abuse–Torture in Families; Sibling Abuse; Victim-Blaming Theory**

References and Further Reading

American Psychiatric Association. *Diagnostic and Statistical Manual of Mental Disorders,* 4th ed., text revision. Washington, DC: Author, 2000.

American Psychological Association. "Understanding Child Sexual Abuse: Education, Prevention, and Recovery," 2001. http://www.apa.org/releases/sexabuse.

Anderson, Page L., Jasmin A. Tiro, Ann W. Price, Marnette A. Bender, and Nadine J. Kaslow. "Additive Impact of Childhood Emotional, Physical, and Sexual Abuse on Suicide Attempts among Low-Income African American Women." *Suicide and Life-Threatening Behavior* 32, no. 2 (2002): 131–138.

Arias, Ileana. "The Legacy of Child Maltreatment: Long-Term Health Consequences for Women." *Journal of Women's Health* 13, no. 5 (2004): 468–473.

Barnett, Ola W., Cindy L. Miller-Perrin, and Robin D. Perrin. *Family Violence Across the Lifespan: An Introduction.* Thousand Oaks, CA: Sage Publications, 1997.

Beitchman, Joseph H., Kenneth J. Zucker, Jane E. Hood, Granville A. DaCosta, Donna Akman, and Erika Cassavia. "A Review of the Long-Term Effects of Child Sexual Abuse." *Child Abuse and Neglect* 16, no. 1 (1992): 101–118.

Bennett, Susan E., Honore M. Hughes, and Douglas A. Luke. "Heterogeneity in Patterns of Child Sexual Abuse, Family Functioning, and Long-Term Adjustment." *Journal of Interpersonal Violence* 15, no. 2 (2000): 134–157.

Berliner, Lucy, and Diana M. Elliott. "Sexual Abuse of Children." In *The APSAC Handbook on Child Maltreatment,* edited by John Briere, Lucy Berliner, Josephine A. Bulkley, Carole Jenny, and Theresa Reid. Thousand Oaks, CA: Sage Publications, 1996, pp. 51–71.

———. "Sexual Abuse of Children." In *The APSAC Handbook on Child Maltreatment,* 2nd ed., edited by John E. B. Myers, Lucy Berliner, John Briere, C. Terry Hendrix, Carole Jenny, and Theresa A. Reid. Thousand Oaks, CA: Sage Publications, 2002, pp. 55–78.

Bolen, Rebecca M. *Child Sexual Abuse: Its Scope and Our Failure.* New York: Kluwer Academic/Plenum Publishers, 2001.

Briere, John, and Diana M. Elliott. "Prevalence and Psychological Sequelae of Self-Reported Childhood Physical and Sexual Abuse in a General Population Sample of Men and Women." *Child Abuse and Neglect* 27, no. 10 (2003): 1205–1222.

Callahan, Kelley L., Jennifer L. Price, and Mark J. Hilsenroth. "Psychological Assessment of Adult Survivors of Childhood Sexual Abuse Within a Naturalistic Clinical Sample." *Journal of Personality Assessment* 80, no. 2 (2003): 173–184.

Chaffin, Mark, Jane F. Silovsky, and Christy Vaughn. "Temporal Concordance of Anxiety Disorders and Child Sexual Abuse: Implications for Direct Versus Artifactual Effects of Sexual Abuse." *Journal of Clinical Child and Adolescent Psychology* 34, no. 2 (2005): 210–222.

Cicchetti, Dante. "How Research on Child Maltreatment Has Informed the Study of Child Development: Perspectives from Developmental Psychopathology." In *Child Maltreatment: Theory and Research on the Causes and Consequences of Child Abuse and Neglect,* edited by Dante Cicchetti and Vicki Carlson. New York: Cambridge University Press, 1989, pp. 377–431.

Cicchetti, Dante, and Sheree L. Toth. "Developmental Processes in Maltreated Children." In *46th Annual Nebraska Symposium on Motivation: Motivation and Child Maltreatment,* edited by David J. Hansen. Lincoln: University of Nebraska Press, 2000, pp. 85–160.

Clemmons, John C., David DiLillo, Isaac G. Martinez, Sarah DeGue, and Michelle Jeffcott. "Co-occurring Forms of Child Maltreatment and Adult Adjustment Reported by Latina College Students." *Child Abuse and Neglect* 27 no. 7 (2003): 751–767.

Cole, Pamela M., and Frank W. Putnam. "Effect of Incest on Self and Social Functioning: A Developmental Psychopathology Perspective." *Journal of Consulting and Clinical Psychology* 60, no. 2 (1992): 174–184.

Colman, Rebecca A., and Cathy S. Widom. "Childhood Abuse and Neglect and Adult Intimate Relationships: A Prospective Study." *Child Abuse and Neglect* 28, no. 11 (2004): 1133–1151.

Conte, Jon R. "Child Sexual Abuse: Awareness and Backlash." *Future of Children* 4, no. 2 (1994): 224–232.

Davis, Joanne L., Patricia A. Petretic-Jackson, and Ling Ting. "Intimacy Dysfunction and Trauma Symptomatology: Long-Term Correlates of Different Types of Child Abuse." *Journal of Traumatic Stress* 14, no. 1 (2001): 63–79.

deMause, Lloyd, ed. *The History of Childhood: The Untold Story of Child Abuse.* New York: Peter Bedrick Books, 1974.

Denov, Myriam S. "The Long-Term Effects of Child Sexual Abuse by Female Perpetrators: A Qualitative Study of Male and Female Victims." *Journal of Interpersonal Violence* 19, no. 10 (2004): 1137–1156.

DiLillo, David. "Interpersonal Functioning among Women Reporting a History of Childhood Sexual Abuse: Empirical Findings and Methodological Issues." *Clinical Psychology Review* 21, no. 4 (2001): 553–576.

DiLillo, David, Dawn Giuffre, George C. Tremblay, and Lizette Peterson. "A Closer Look at the Nature of Intimate Partner Violence Reported by Women with a History of Child Sexual Abuse." *Journal of Interpersonal Violence* 16, no. 2 (2001): 116–132.

DiLillo, David, and Patricia J. Long. "Perceptions of Couple Functioning among Female Survivors of Child

Sexual Abuse." *Journal of Child Sexual Abuse* 7, no. 4 (1999): 59–76.

DiLillo, David, Andrea R. Perry, and Michelle Fortier. "Child Physical Abuse and Neglect." Chapter to appear in *Comprehensive Handbook of Personality and Psychopathology, Volume 3: Child Psychopathology,* edited by Robert T. Ammerman and Michel Hersen. New York: John Wiley and Sons, in press.

DiLillo, David, George C. Tremblay, and Lizette Peterson. "Linking Childhood Sexual Abuse and Abusive Parenting: The Mediating Role of Maternal Anger." *Child Abuse and Neglect* 24, no. 6 (2000): 767–779.

Dong, Maxia, Robert F. Anda, Vincent J. Felitti, Shanta R. Dube, David F. Williamson, Theodore J. Thompson, Clifton M. Loo, and Wayne H. Giles. "The Interrelatedness of Multiple Forms of Childhood Abuse, Neglect, and Household Dysfunction." *Child Abuse and Neglect* 28, no. 7 (2004): 771–784.

Emiroğlu, Fatma Neslihan Inal, Semra Kurul, Aynur Akay, Süha Miral, and Eray Dirik. "Assessment of Child Neurology Outpatients with Headache, Dizziness, and Fainting." *Journal of Child Neurology* 19, no. 5 (2004): 332–336.

Farrants, Jacqui. "The 'False Memory' Debate: A Critical Review of the Research on Recovered Memories of Child Sexual Abuse." *Counselling Psychology Quarterly* 11, no. 3 (1998): 229–238.

Fergusson, David M., and Paul E. Mullen. *Childhood Sexual Abuse: An Evidence Based Perspective.* Thousand Oaks, CA: Sage Publications, 1999.

Finkelhor, David. "Early and Long-Term Effects of Child Sexual Abuse: An Update." *Professional Psychology: Research and Practice* 21, no. 5 (1990): 325–330.

———. "Epidemiological Factors in the Clinical Identification of Child Sexual Abuse." *Child Abuse and Neglect* 17, no. 1 (1993): 67–70.

———. "The International Epidemiology of Child Sexual Abuse." *Child Abuse and Neglect* 18, no. 5 (1994): 409–417.

———. "Introduction." In *The APSAC Handbook on Child Maltreatment,* 2nd ed., edited by John E. B. Myers, Lucy Berliner, John Briere, C. Terry Hendrix, Carole Jenny, and Theresa A. Reid. Thousand Oaks, CA: Sage Publications, 2002, pp. xi–xvi.

Finkelhor, David, Gerald Hotaling, I. A. Lewis, and Christine Smith. "Sexual Abuse in a National Survey of Adult Men and Women: Prevalence, Characteristics, and Risk Factors." *Child Abuse and Neglect* 14, no. 1 (1990): 19–28.

Friedrich, William N., Anthony J. Urquiza, and Robert L. Beilke. "Behavior Problems in Sexually Abused Young Children." *Journal of Pediatric Psychology* 11, no. 1 (1986): 47–57.

Gallagher, Bernard. "Ritual Abuse: A Response to Colman." *Child Abuse Review* 10, no. 2 (2001): 83–84.

Goldman, Juliette D. G., and Usha K. Padayachi. "Some Methodological Problems in Estimating Incidence and Prevalence in Child Sexual Abuse Research." *Journal of Sex Research* 37, no. 4 (2000): 305–314.

Gorey, Kevin M., and Donald R. Leslie. "The Prevalence of Child Sexual Abuse: Integrative Review Adjustment for Potential Response and Measurement Biases." *Child Abuse and Neglect* 21, no. 4 (1997): 391–398.

Greenwald, Evan, Harold Leitenberg, Suzana Cado, and Matthew J. Tarran. "Childhood Sexual Abuse:

Long-Term Effects on Psychological and Sexual Functioning in a Nonclinical and Nonstudent Sample of Adult Women." *Child Abuse and Neglect* 14, no. 4 (1990): 503–513.

Hansen, David J., Debra B. Hecht, and Kristine T. Futa. "Child Sexual Abuse." In *Handbook of Psychological Treatment Protocols for Children and Adolescents,* edited by Vincent B. Van Hasselt and Michel Hersen. Mahwah, NJ: Erlbaum, 1998, 153–178.

Haugaard, Jeffrey J. "The Challenge of Defining Child Sexual Abuse." *American Psychologist* 55, no. 9 (2000): 1036–1039.

Hecht, Debra B., and David J. Hansen. "The Environment of Child Maltreatment: Contextual Factors and the Development of Psychopathology." *Aggression and Violent Behavior* 6, no. 5 (2001): 433–457.

Higgins, Daryl J., and Marita P. McCabe. "Multi-Type Maltreatment and the Long-Term Adjustment of Adults." *Child Abuse Review* 9, no. 1 (2000): 6–18.

———. "Maltreatment and Family Dysfunction in Childhood and the Subsequent Adjustment of Children and Adults." *Journal of Family Violence* 18, no. 2 (2003): 107–120.

Hill, Jonathan, R. Davis, M. Byatt, E. Burnside, L. Rollinson, and S. Fear. "Childhood Sexual Abuse and Affective Symptoms in Women: A General Population Study." *Psychological Medicine* 30, no. 6 (2000): 1283–1291.

Hunter, John A., Jr. "A Comparison of the Psychosocial Maladjustment of Adult Males and Females Sexually Molested as Children." *Journal of Interpersonal Violence* 6, no. 2 (1991): 205–217.

Jackson, Joan L., Karen S. Calhoun, Angelynne E. Amick, Heather M. Maddever, and Valerie L. Habif. "Young Adult Women Who Report Childhood Intrafamilial Sexual Abuse: Subsequent Adjustment." *Archives of Sexual Behavior* 19, no. 3 (1990): 211–221.

Jones, Lisa M., David Finkelhor, and Kathy Kopiec. "Why Is Sexual Abuse Declining? A Survey of State Child Protection Administrators." *Child Abuse and Neglect* 25, no. 9 (2001): 1139–1158.

Kahr, Brett. "The Sexual Molestation of Children: Historical Perspectives." *Journal of Psychohistory* 19, no. 2. (1991): 191–214.

Kempe, C. Henry, Frederic N. Silverman, Brandt F. Steele, William Droegemueller, and Henry K. Silver. "The Battered-Child Syndrome." *Journal of the American Medical Association* 181, no. 1 (1962): 17–24.

Kendall-Tackett, Kathleen A., Linda M. Williams, and David Finkelhor. "Impact of Sexual Abuse on Children: A Review and Synthesis of Recent Empirical Studies." *Psychological Bulletin* 113, no. 1 (1993): 164–180.

King, Jean A., Deborah Mandansky, Susie King, Kenneth E. Fletcher, and Judith Brewer. "Early Sexual Abuse and Low Cortisol." *Psychiatry and Clinical Neurosciences* 55, no. 1 (2001): 71–74.

Leventhal, John M. "A Decline in Substantiated Cases of Child Sexual Abuse in the United States: Good News or False Hope?" *Child Abuse and Neglect* 25, no. 9 (2001): 1137–1138.

Levesque, Roger J. R. "Sex Differences in the Experience of Child Sexual Victimization." *Journal of Family Violence* 9, no. 4 (1994): 357–369.

Long, Patricia J., and Joan L. Jackson. "Childhood Sexual Abuse: An Examination of Family Functioning." *Journal of Interpersonal Violence* 9, no. 2 (1994): 270–277.

MacMillan, Harriet L. "Child Maltreatment: What We Know in the Year 2000." *Canadian Journal of Psychiatry* 45, no. 8 (2000): 702–709.

Mannarino, Anthony P., and Judith A. Cohen. "A Clinical-Demographic Study of Sexually Abused Children." *Child Abuse and Neglect* 10, no. 1 (1986): 17–23.

Martin, Graham, Helen A. Bergen, Angela S. Richardson, Leigh Roeger, and Stephen Allison. "Sexual Abuse and Suicidality: Gender Differences in a Large Community Sample of Adolescents." *Child Abuse and Neglect* 28, no. 5 (2004): 491–503.

Meston, Cindy M., Julia R. Heiman, and Paul D. Trapnell. "The Relation between Early Abuse and Adult Sexuality." *The Journal of Sex Research* 36, no. 4 (1999): 385–395.

Molnar, Beth E., Stephen L. Buka, and Ronald C. Kessler. "Child Sexual Abuse and Subsequent Psychopathology: Results from the National Comorbidity Survey." *American Journal of Public Health* 91, no. 5 (2001): 753–760.

Nash, Michael R., Timothy L. Hulsey, Mark C. Sexton, Tina L. Harralson, and Warren Lambert. "Long-Term Sequelae of Childhood Sexual Abuse: Perceived Family Environment, Psychopathology, and Dissociation." *Journal of Consulting and Clinical Psychology* 61, no. 2 (1993): 276–283.

National Clearinghouse on Child Abuse and Neglect. *Recognizing Child Abuse and Neglect: Signs and Symptoms*. Washington, DC: US Department of Health and Human Services, 2003.

———. *Definitions of Child Abuse and Neglect: State Statutes Series 2005*. Washington, DC: US Department of Health and Human Services, 2005a.

———. *Child Maltreatment 2003*. Washington, DC: US Department of Health and Human Services, 2005b.

———. *Long-Term Consequences of Child Abuse and Neglect*. Washington, DC: US Department of Health and Human Services, 2005c.

National Incidence Study (NIS) 4. Website, 2005. https://www.nis4.org/nishome.asp (accessed August 14, 2006).

New York Society for the Prevention of Cruelty to Children (NYSPCC). "NYSPCC 125th Anniversary, 2000." http://www.nyspcc.org/beta_history/index_history.htm.

Noll, Jennie G., Penelope K. Trickett, and Frank W. Putnam. "A Prospective Investigation of the Impact of Childhood Sexual Abuse on the Development of Sexuality." *Journal of Consulting and Clinical Psychology* 71, no. 3 (2003): 575–586.

Olafson, Erna, David L. Corwin, and Roland C. Summit. "Modern History of Child Sexual Abuse Awareness: Cycles of Discovery and Suppression." *Child Abuse and Neglect* 17, no. 1 (1993): 7–24.

Paolucci, Elizabeth O., Mark L. Genuis, and Claudio Violato. "A Meta-Analysis of the Published Research on the Effects of Child Sexual Abuse." *Journal of Psychology* 135, no. 1 (2001): 17–36.

Polusny, Melissa A., and Victoria M. Follette. "Long-Term Correlates of Child Sexual Abuse: Theory and Review of the Empirical Literature." *Applied and Preventive Psychology* 4, no. 3 (1995): 143–166.

Putnam, Frank W. "Ten-Year Research Update Review: Child Sexual Abuse." *Journal of the American Academy of Child and Adolescent Psychiatry* 42, no. 3 (2003): 269–278.

Read, John, Kirsty Agar, Suzanne Barker-Collo, Emma Davies, and Andrew Moskowitz. "Assessing Suicidality in Adults: Integrating Childhood Trauma as a Major Risk Factor." *Professional Psychology: Research and Practice* 32, no. 4 (2001): 367–372.

Rind, Bruce, Philip Tromovitch, and Robert Bauserman. "A Meta-Analytic Examination of Assumed Properties of Child Sexual Abuse Using College Samples." *Psychological Bulletin* 124. no. 1 (1998): 22–53.

Roberts, Ron, Tom O'Connor, Judy Dunn, Jean Golding, and the ALSPAC Study Team. "The Effects of Child Sexual Abuse in Later Family Life; Mental Health, Parenting and Adjustment of Offspring." *Child Abuse and Neglect* 28, no. 5 (2004): 525–545.

Rumstein-McKean, Orly, and John Hunsley. "Interpersonal and Family Functioning of Female Survivors of Childhood Sexual Abuse." *Clinical Psychology Review* 21, no. 3 (2001): 471–490.

Sachs-Ericsson, Natalie, Dan Blazer, E. Ashby Plant, and Bruce Arnow. "Childhood Sexual and Physical Abuse and the 1-Year Prevalence of Medical Problems in the National Comorbidity Survey." *Health Psychology* 24, no. 1 (2005): 32–40.

Sedlak, Andrea J. *A History of the National Incidence Study of Child Abuse and Neglect*. Washington, DC: US Department of Health and Human Services, 2001.

Sedlak, Andrea J., and Diane D. Broadhurst. *Executive Summary of the Third National Incidence Study of Child Abuse and Neglect*. Washington, DC: Department of Health and Human Services, 1996.

Shapiro, Deborah L., and Alytia A. Levendosky. "Adolescent Survivors of Childhood Sexual Abuse: The Mediating Role of Attachment Style and Coping in Psychological and Interpersonal Functioning." *Child Abuse and Neglect* 23, no. 11 (1999): 1175–1191.

Smolak, Linda, and Sarah K. Murnen. "A Meta-Analytic Examination of the Relationship between Child Sexual Abuse and Eating Disorders." *International Journal of Eating Disorders* 31, no. 2 (2002): 136–150.

Spataro, Josie, Paul E. Mullen, Philip M. Burgess, David L. Wells, and Simon A. Moss. "Impact of Child Sexual Abuse on Mental Health: Prospective Study in Males and Females." *British Journal of Psychiatry* 184, no. 5 (2004): 416–421.

Steel, Jennifer, Lawrence Sanna, Barbara Hammond, James Whipple, and Herbert Cross. "Psychological Sequelae of Childhood Sexual Abuse: Abuse-Related Characteristics, Coping Strategies, and Attributional Style." *Child Abuse and Neglect* 28, no. 7 (2004): 785–801.

Swanston, Heather Y., Patrick N. Parkinson, Brian I. O'Toole, Angela M. Plunkett, Sandra Shrimpton, and R. Kim Oates. "Juvenile Crime, Aggression and Delinquency after Sexual Abuse." *British Journal of Criminology* 43, no. 4 (2003): 729–749.

Swanston, Heather Y., Angela M. Plunkett, Brian I. O'Toole, Sandra Shrimpton, Patrick N. Parkinson, and R. Kim Oates. "Nine Years after Child Sexual Abuse." *Child Abuse and Neglect* 27, no. 8 (2003): 967–984.

Tharinger, Deborah. "Impact of Child Sexual Abuse on Developing Sexuality." *Professional Psychology: Research and Practice* 21, no. 5 (1990): 331–337.

Vigil, Jacob M., David C. Geary, and Jennifer Byrd-Craven. "A Life History Assessment of Early Childhood Sexual Abuse in Women." *Developmental Psychology* 41, no. 3 (2005): 553–561.

Walch, Anne G., and W. Eugene Broadhead. "Prevalence of Lifetime Sexual Victimization among Female Patients." *Journal of Family Practice* 35, no. 5 (1992): 511–516.

Wekerle, Christine, and David A. Wolfe. "Child Maltreatment." In *Child Psychopathology,* edited by Eric J. Mash and Russell A. Barkley. New York: Guilford Press, 1996, 492–537.

Wolfe, David A., ed. *Child Abuse: Implications for Child Development and Psychopathology.* Thousand Oaks, CA: Sage Publications, 1999.

Wolfe, Vicky V., and Jo-Ann Birt. "Child Sexual Abuse." In *Assessment of Childhood Disorders,* 3rd ed., edited by Eric J. Mash and Leif G. Terdal. New York: Guilford, 1997, pp. 569–623.

CHILDREN WITNESSING PARENTAL VIOLENCE

The psychic pain and debilitating effects, both short- and long-term, experienced by children who witness parental violence frequently goes unnoticed by others. These children are also the victims of domestic violence, even though they may not be direct targets of the abuse. They are being maltreated, whether intentionally or unintentionally, by incapacitating inattention, indifference, and/or neglect of their developmental well-being.

Observations of such cruelty between loved ones can produce enduring emotional and psychological scars of such great magnitude that children who are exposed to domestic violence (in this case, parental violence against another parent) are traumatically harmed by these acts. Their feelings and emotional responses often go unnoticed, and the enormity of their distress is overlooked or disregarded as attention is focused on the battered and the batterer. Yet their suffering and damage can be extensive, when lingering memories of violence between their parents become long-lasting burdens. Their lives, from a young age, are vulnerable to continuous dread and expectations of spontaneous terror and danger. In reaction, trust and unquestioning devotion to the parental bond and other important relationships frequently become shaken and unstable. These children, as innocent victims, too frequently carry the punishing marks of parental conflict through many trying years to come, even into adulthood.

Estimates of the number of children who witness domestic violence annually in the United States vary greatly. A Harvard Medical School report (Harvard Mental Health Letter 2004) cites between two and three million; an earlier study (Horton, Cruise, Graybill, and Cornett 1999), from three to ten million. When considering how many domestic violence occurrences go unreported, the greater number may be considered more accurate. It is likely that for many years, a vast number of children were negatively affected by these events and most went unattended. But there also is evidence of resilient children—those whose external supports, internal resources, and adaptive coping mechanisms have counteracted the expected emotional wounds of witnessing parental violence. The strengths of these children provide hope that many more can be helped to learn to avoid the anticipated fate of those less strong and hence less fortunate.

Witnessing Abuse and Violence: Children's Maltreatment at Home

Jaffe, Wolfe, and Wilson (1990) provide a historical perspective of the public's attitudes toward family violence in the United States, including that which affects children who witness its impact. It has only been since the 1970s that the acknowledgment of and serious concern over wife battering has been openly publicized. For the most part, family secrets of beatings and conflicts have been kept under wraps, very often ignored or neglected by police and other investigative organizations. These were "family problems" and considered within the private domain; therefore, they were given undeserved immunity from examination, inquiry, and prosecution. Yet the abuse was occurring widely. Langley and Levy (1977) published a telling book of this incidence and its troubling effects entitled *Wife*

Beating: The Silent Crisis, and Walker's 1979 exposé of *The Battered Woman* created a stir with its identification and description of battered woman syndrome. Concern about children witnessing the brutality of one parent and the helplessness of the other began surfacing in print in the 1980s and even more so in the 1990s. Prior to this time, there was only sporadic mention of children witnessing parental violence. It had been taken for granted that children were harmed only when they themselves were physically or sexually abused.

Maltreatment of children can be the result of different factors, many of which have to do with the interaction among stressors of daily life. Consider the parent who loses his job, worries about failing his responsibilities to the family, cannot face life as it has become, and increases his drinking to temporarily forget the trouble he has caused everyone (including himself). He is depressed, guilt-ridden, angry, and frustrated. The lack of financial security due to unemployment undoubtedly exacerbates the situation. The negativity and disarming changes in mood will be felt by others around him, especially his wife and children. As a result of this discord, tempers rise, personalities clash, hurtful statements are made, and violent behaviors erupt.

Understandably, children in the crossfire of escalating parental disputes frequently become the victims of circumstances beyond their control. The fierceness and cruelty of the perpetrator of the abuse, as well as the dismaying response of the parent attacked, will compound the fears and repercussions for these children. During these periods of crisis, physical and emotional abuse and neglect replace the nurturing and expressions of affection that are displayed by caring parents. The severity of damaging effects can be profound. Studies have reported that in the aftermath, children who are observers of parental violence will suffer effects similar to those suffered by children who have themselves been physically maltreated (Fantuzzo, McDermott, and Noone 1999; Kilpatrick and Williams 1997). Research findings have also shown that it is not unusual for these child witnesses to be at greater risk of being targets of physical abuse (Chamberlain 2001). They live in an environment where danger might spontaneously erupt.

For a young child observing parental assaults, safety and security are jeopardized, and inescapable feelings of vulnerability surface periodically. Severe problems coping with everyday life can develop across the life span, regardless of a child's age at the time of the violent events. The results of witnessing or even hearing violent interactions between parents can be felt during a temporary lull in such attacks and even after the violence, or the children's exposure to it, has ended. The development of behavioral, physical, emotional, and social problems speaks to the enormity of the distress these children experience. Regressive and maladaptive reactions to traumatic acts of violence, particularly by and toward intimate family members, are notable. For example, children may respond by returning to the behaviors of an earlier period of development, such as bed-wetting, thumb-sucking, and temper tantrums. Sleep disturbances, nightmares, anxiety, irritability, depression, and recurrent flashbacks of traumatic events may be all-encompassing (Burman and Allen-Meares 1994). These symptoms have been described as evidence of post-traumatic stress disorder (PTSD), which can result from bearing witness to horrific sights (Graham-Bermann and Levendosky 1998).

Consequently, it is not surprising that adjustment problems may emerge in reaction to the traumas observed and/or experienced in the form of disrespectful, disturbing, and disruptive acting-out behaviors at home, school, or in the neighborhood. Often mistakenly attributed to other motives and reasons, these forms of conduct disorders should initiate an investigation into the child's possible exposure to domestic violence. If overlooked, impairments in functioning may occur in teen and even adult years. Environmental cues can serve as reminders of past traumas, thereby arousing images of the suppressed turmoil. Such intrusions of memories of abusive events into consciousness can be unrelenting. A movie, a television show, a book, a few lines from a story, or a photo can tap such memories. However, it should be emphasized that much depends on the seemingly innate capabilities, learned coping behaviors, and extent of buffering supports and aids available to lessen the damaging influence of the past on present and future functioning. In this manner, the stress-producing and debilitating symptoms of PTSD can thus be mitigated.

Theory-Driven Assessments

Numerous theories can be explored that would help to explain behaviors, events, and phenomena interrelated with themes of domestic violence involving child witnesses. Theoretical frameworks assist in making sense of the complexity of human behaviors and attitudes and their relationship to the world around them. Applying several well-known theories on learning and early life span development to a typical child witness's experience can serve as a guide to assessments and interventions. These theories highlight the importance of early care, stability, and security in developing sound mental health and satisfactory performance throughout the life span.

Social Learning Theory

How behaviors are learned in families is aptly demonstrated by viewing parental models and the offspring who emulate their actions. Bandura (1977) developed the concept of social learning that emphasizes modeling, imitation, and observational learning as noteworthy aspects of acquiring behaviors. Children are highly influenced by the people closest to them, especially parental figures and other caretakers. Exposure to intimate violence during the developmental years could thus create a pattern of paralyzing fear, numbing detachment, and the repetition of abuse in present and future years. This pattern is illustrated by the cycle of violence that permeates from one generation to the next (Burman and Allen-Meares 1994).

A child observing the beatings her mother endured might develop an intense fear that, like her home environment, the world outside is also dangerous. This in turn leads the child to believe that safety and love are not assured and that women are powerless and helpless against the dominance of men, who are generally stronger and larger than they are. It may explain the child witness's timidity and desire to isolate herself rather than play and socialize with others. She feels more secure in her own world of daydreams, devoid of the pain and suffering she observed her mother experiencing. When reality is too stressful, creating a fantasy world may be a coping mechanism for the child who witnesses parental violence. The extent and duration of the child's detachment and ability to withstand these fears can depend on the strengths the child sees in the parent confronting the abuse. The abused parent who protects the child and herself by seeking help and finding a way out of their hostile and dangerous environment serves as a good role model for the child to emulate.

Attachment Theory

John Bowlby's contribution to early life development comes from his research into bonding between infants and mothers, who are seen as the primary caregivers (McMillen 1992). The theory accentuates the importance of nurturing, responsive, and stable relationships that develop during a child's early exploration and interaction with others in his or her environment. Bowlby proposed that a secure attachment between mother and child is necessary for the child's psychological and emotional health and well-being.

During domestic violence episodes, parents are unavailable to allay their children's fears and attend to their needs. Witnessing and reacting to parental violence can elicit extreme anxiety, disbelief, and loathing in children. Depending on the child's age, helplessness and guilt at not being able to intervene and stop the abuse of a loved one can become too much to bear. It is not unusual for such experiences to provoke confused loyalty and devotion toward either or both parents, as the strength of the attachment and trust that had been developed invariably wavers. It creates a growing emotional and physical distance in the child that increases the probability of the impairment of present and future relationships outside the home. The child's sense of safety and trust can be restored if the battering ends.

Erikson's Stages of Psychosocial Development

Actively resolving psychosocial crises throughout the life span (from infancy through old age) is necessary for the development and continuation of a healthy personality and identity, according to Erik Erikson (1982). As would be expected, the foundation for the ability to resolve crises in later stages of life is developed in the early psychosocial stages, from infancy until school age (six years old). These are the years when children are home more often, becoming aware of their surroundings and learning a sense of right and wrong. Under healthy and affirming conditions, their sense of trust with reliable caregivers is strengthened. This sets the stage for building attachments and trusting relationships in the future, which is very important for optimal functioning. During these preschool years, emerging self-confidence, autonomy, and ego strength result in an independent ability to make choices and be self-directed (Seifert, Hoffnung, and Hoffnung 2000). However, if the child is being raised in a punitive, abusive, and/ or neglectful home, the development of the child's ability to overcome psychological and social barriers and conflicts can be thwarted.

The ability of the child witness to develop trusting relationships and rapport with others could be hampered even in adulthood. The child has been subjected to viewing and hearing the cruelty between his or her parental role models. The child witness may come to believe that this is the way adults settle conflicts; this makes it difficult for the child to internalize a sense of right and wrong, justice and compromise. A female child who witnesses the abuse of her mother may identify with her mother's experience and might correlate being a female to being a victim and accepting the passive role. For the child witness to gain the ego strength and self-confidence to solve problems would depend on a satisfactory resolution of the family crises, in which safety and security would be attained.

The Therapeutic Experience

Therapeutic services for witnesses of parental battering are critically needed. The consequences of neglecting this aspect of a child's family experience can weigh heavily on him or her. Children have various ways of expressing their feelings about family violence; some may not be directly linked to the violent episodes. There is the likelihood that images of the violence have been internalized, whether this has been openly discussed with the child or not. Therefore, erratic behaviors and symptoms of acute emotional change or impairment at home, school, a shelter (where children accompany a parent), or another public setting should be considered signs of possible traumatic experiences in the household. These phenomena must be assessed in a safe environment, where trust and rapport with the child can be established. Assuring the child that he or she will be protected and have the freedom to explore memories and emotions without negative repercussions is crucial to encouraging the child's self-disclosure. When a child's family bonds and trust have already been violated, this becomes quite a challenge to overcome.

Play therapy with dolls, expressive art, storytelling, games, and photographs may initiate discussion of painful feelings associated with the abuse witnessed. Carlson (2000) emphasizes the importance of assisting children to acknowledge the violence in their homes and to realize that they are not to blame for these harmful actions. Treatment should include instructions in problem solving and ways of taking safety precautions, in simple, easily understood terms and age-appropriate language. A young child can be taught to call 911 in times of need. Running to a neighbor's house for help, while making sure it is safe to do so, is also an important strategy to teach these children.

The child witness might experience confusion and guilt resulting from competing feelings of anger and loyalty toward the parent who instigated the violence. Working with the child witness requires a nonjudgmental conveyance of an understanding of the difficulty he or she is placed in and the assurance that it is okay to sustain regard for this parent, while decrying the abusive behaviors. Worrying about the safety of the abused parent will place a heavy burden on the child. Paradoxically, the child might harbor displaced feelings of anger and shame toward the victimized parent, who may be viewed as weak and ineffective. Assisting the abused parent to take charge of the situation and engage in constructive decision making and problem solving can help turn this parent into a strong role model for the child to emulate. Therefore, empowering the victimized parent to recognize and utilize his or her own strengths in making plans to stop the violence and secure safety for him/herself and the children is of utmost importance. In addition to individual and group counseling, both the parent and the child should be referred to physical, mental, and social resources in the community. These resources can offer much needed ongoing supportive structures.

The Fallacy of "No Place Like Home"

For too many vulnerable children and their caretakers, the home environment lacks safety and security. Communities are plagued with violence, not only in the streets but also in private, in homes where unresolved mental health issues and reactions to stressors are played out. Domestic violence arising from relationship conflicts, poverty, crime, unemployment, substance abuse, discrimination, and unequal opportunities are problems that can be explosive, in both urban and rural areas. When anger and hostility escalate, especially as a result of uncontrollable factors, those in dependent and subordinate positions become convenient targets.

Severe abuse knows no borders. Women and children in upscale neighborhoods will experience similar dangers and fears to those experienced by women and children in less affluent neighborhoods (Weitzman 2000). Nevertheless, abusers' aggressive behaviors are more likely to stay hidden when protective mechanisms at their disposal serve to maintain reputations, allay the stigma, and keep the perpetrators safer from prosecution.

Increasingly, the media bring disturbing images into view. Over time, people can become desensitized to violence as a result of overexposure to such images. However, child witnesses to parental violence are exposed to violent acts not just on television but in their own lives, between the people they most love and depend on. Witnessing parental violence is traumatic, and images and memories of such violence can stay with and harm child witnesses throughout their lives.

The necessity of prevention and early recognition of domestic violence and maltreatment of children cannot be overemphasized. Helping parents resolve their problems and conflicts in a constructive manner, while learning effective parenting skills, is critical to improving their children's ability to function, as well as their own. Whether it is used for a complete or a temporary separation, visiting a shelter is an important first step for immediate safety and supportive resources. It provides a caring, supportive environment and "time out" to contemplate beneficial choices that can alter the victim's present and future situation. Recognizing and acknowledging personal strengths can carry them through, despite the calamities experienced. To all who suffer, the journey out of harm's way takes a measure of hope and optimism and the reaching out for assistance to acquire a better life.

SONDRA BURMAN and PATRICIA DUFFY-FEINS

See also **Battered Woman Syndrome; Bullying and the Family; Child Abuse and Juvenile Delinquency; Child Neglect; Coercive Control; Divorce, Child Custody, and Domestic Violence; Inmate Mothers: Treatment and Policy Implications; Intergenerational Transfer of Intimate Partner Violence; Intimate Partner Violence, Forms of; Stages of Leaving Abusive Relationships**

References and Further Reading

Bandura, Albert A. *Social Learning Theory*. Englewood Cliffs, NJ: Prentice-Hall, Inc. 1977.
Burman, Sondra, and Paula Allen-Meares. "Neglected Victims of Murder: Children's Witness to Parental Homicide." *Social Work* 39 (1994): 28–34.
Carlson, Bonnie. "Children Exposed to Intimate Partner Violence: Research Findings and Implications for Intervention." *Trauma, Violence, and Abuse* 1 (2000): 321–342.
Chamberlain, Linda. "Domestic Violence and Child Abuse: Ten Lessons Learned in Rural Alaska." *Policy and Practice of Public Human Services* 59, no. 1 (2001): 33–38.
Dulmus, Catherine N., and Carolyn Hilarski. "Children and Adolescents Exposed to Community Violence." In *Handbook of Violence*, edited by Lisa A. Rapp-Paglicci, Albert R. Roberts, and John S. Wodarski. New York: John Wiley and Sons, 2002, pp. 129–147.
Erikson, Erik. *The Life Cycle Completed: A Review*. New York: Norton, 1982.
Fantuzzo, John W., Paul McDermott, and Megan Noone. "Clinical Issues in the Assessment of Family Violence Involving Children." In *Assessment of Family Violence*, 2nd ed., edited by Robert T. Ammerman and Michel Hersen. New York: Wiley, 1999.
Graham-Bermann, Sandra A., and Alytia Akiko Levendosky. "Traumatic Stress Symptoms in Children of Battered Women." *Journal of Interpersonal Violence* 13 (1998): 111–128.
Harvard Mental Health Letter. "Children as Witnesses and Victims." *Harvard Mental Health Letter,* Boston: Harvard Health Publications, 2004.
Horton, Connie B., Tracy K. Cruise, Daniel Graybill, and J. Yvette Cornett. "For Children's Sake: Training Students in the Treatment of Child Witnesses of Domestic Violence." *Professional Psychology: Research and Practice* 30 (1999): 88–91.
Jaffee, Peter, David A. Wolfe, and Susan K. Wilson. *Children of Battered Women*. Newbury Park, CA: Sage, 1990.
Kilpatrick, Kym L., and Leanne M. Williams. "Post-Traumatic Stress Disorder and Anxiety in Child Witnesses to Domestic Violence." *American Journal of Orthopsychiatry* 67 (1997): 639–644.
Langley, Roger, and Richard C. Levy. *Wife Beating: The Silent Crisis*. New York: E. P. Dutton, 1977.
McMillen, J. Curtis. "Attachment Theory and Clinical Social Work." *Clinical Social Work Journal* 20 (1992): 205–218.
Seifert, Kevin L., Robert J. Hoffnung, Michele Hoffnung. *Lifespan Development,* 2nd ed. Boston, MA: Houghton Mifflin, 2000.
Walker, Lenore. *The Battered Woman*. New York: Harper and Row, 1979.
Weitzman, Susan. *Not to People Like Us: Hidden Abuse in Upscale Marriages*. New York: Basic Books, 2000.

CHRISTIANITY AND DOMESTIC VIOLENCE

Christians consider the family to be a sacred institution. In fact, celebrating the virtues of family life and family values has become a cardinal feature of the contemporary Christian message in North America and beyond. So powerful is the nostalgia for family togetherness that keeping families intact and ensuring that the family unit is strong serves to undergird many of the activities that take place during the weekly routine of congregational life in churches that are otherwise markedly diverse from a theological point of view. The strength and vitality of the local parish, affectionately labeled the *church family,* is sometimes gauged by how fully members look out for each other in the face of a culture that is perceived to be ambivalent, or even hostile, to their life choices. Amidst all the enthusiasm for the family, there is a stark reality that must be faced. While the Christian family may be sacred, sometimes it is not safe.

Violence affects scores of church families. Millions of women around the world—many of them Christian believers—have been battered. Most abused women, whether or not they are religious, feel alone. Since abuse often occurs in the privacy of the home, others in the community or the church can be lulled into believing it is not happening. As a result, victims feel faceless and nameless; silence and secrecy abound. Yet, for religious women, there is often an added sense of betrayal: They may feel that not even God has heard their cry for help.

A holy hush pervades many religious settings when it comes to the topic of domestic violence. Even finding the right words to describe what has happened in a violent outburst between a husband and a wife can be contentious. Given the sociopolitical landscape regarding the issue of abuse in the family context, perhaps it is not too surprising that naming the issue becomes a political act. By and large, clergy and other religious leaders prefer the term "family violence," downplaying the gender power imbalance. Moreover, many religious leaders are reluctant to condemn wife abuse from the pulpit and confuse reconciliation between a victimized woman and her abusive partner as evidence of recovery, believing that since the violence has stopped (often only temporarily), the home is now a safe place for each family member.

The Religion and Violence Research Team at the Muriel McQueen Fergusson Centre for Family Violence Research at the University of New Brunswick in eastern Canada has been studying abuse in families of faith for over fifteen years (Stirling, Cameron, Nason-Clark, and Miedema 2004). The team's research has sought to explore the relationship between woman abuse and faith communities, from the perspective of religious leaders, abused women, community resources (including transition houses) and congregations (Nason-Clark 1997, 2004). The research is coupled with a social action strategy including print resources for abused religious women (Nason-Clark and Kroeger 2004), congregations (Kroeger and Nason-Clark 2001), and developing a website (RAVE, Religion and Violence E-learning [Ruff n.d.]) that provides immediate information and other e-learning opportunities specifically for pastors and other religious leaders.

Through a variety of methodologies—including mailed questionnaires, in-depth interviews, community consultations, focus groups, and telephone surveys—the Religion and Violence Research Team have become acquainted with how violence impacts upon parishioner and pastor alike. While survey data explored how often, and under what circumstances, clergy were called upon to assist in situations involving abuse, personal interviews with religious leaders revealed both the advice and referral practices offered to those seeking clerical help. The research team learned both of the struggle of the pastoral counselor, poorly equipped for the task at hand, and yet pushed to provide more pastoral care (Nason-Clark 2000a), and the struggle of a religious woman who feels abandoned by her family, her faith, and even her God (Nason-Clark 1999). As a result, many religious leaders who do respond compassionately to victims and their families find themselves caught between an ideology of the family they are meant to uphold and the reality of families in extreme crisis (Nason-Clark 1996). In light of this, what happens in the average Christian church when there is a disclosure of abuse close to home? Is there still a holy hush, or has the silence been shattered?

The phrase "holy hush" is not meant to suggest that clergy directly dismiss an abused woman's call for help or diminish the severity of her distress. Rather, the most direct evidence of silencing occurs through the paucity of information available to women in faith communities about abuse, and the relatively obscure referencing to abusive acts in the burgeoning Christian family literature (Nason-Clark 1997). With limited training in counseling and virtually no background in understanding the severity or impact of abuse, many clergy find themselves caught in the cross-fire between enthusiastic support of family unity and the reality of families in pain. Since naming the issue clearly poses problems for the average pastor, and direct preaching against such violence rarely occurs, by default the reality of woman abuse is silenced. Clerical leaders are often reluctant to place responsibility for abuse solely on the shoulders of the violent partner, preferring instead to locate the problems and their eventual solutions within the broader family unit. Only among the most experienced clergy are there appropriate and adequate referral networks offering cooperation and collaboration between sacred and secular sources of support for abused women and their children (Hong and Wiehe 1974; Weaver 1993). Yet, in many church communities, there is a rumbling that cannot be silenced (Nason-Clark 1999).

When clerical leaders proclaim that God abhors violence, offer advice that is supportive and accurate, and use their religious authority to bring the "healing balm of Gilead" to a woman's physical, emotional, and spiritual pain, a religious woman's healing journey is augmented. When those with spiritual credentials fail to ask a victimized woman if she is afraid, fail to see her emotional or financial vulnerability, or misunderstand her sense of hopelessness, obstacles are placed on the road toward her healing and wholeness. The Religion and Violence Research Team has found that abused religious women generally require assistance that uses both the language of contemporary culture and the language of the spirit as they seek solace and support in the aftermath of battery.

The remainder of this article will address three particular questions related to the theme of Christianity and domestic violence. While none of the answers will be exhaustive, each will point to some factors impacting the interface between abuse and the contemporary Christian church. Since research and scholarship in this important area is just beginning to surface, there is ample room for development from activists, social scientists, and theologians working alone or in partnership with one another (Nason-Clark 2005).

Inhibitions on Christian Community-Wide Awareness of Abuse

The first question to address is, What are some of the central features of the Christian tradition that inhibit community-wide efforts to raise awareness about violence against women and to encourage abused women to seek safety and assistance? When the tragedy of wife abuse is combined with the passion of a religious ideology, there are concerns both on the part of those who approach the issue from a spiritual perspective and those adopting a secular perspective. Religious leaders fear that abused women in their congregations will be told to leave behind their community of faith as they journey toward a life free from the violence of the past. Community advocates fear that religious leaders will minimize the violence in an attempt to "keep the family together." There is fear and skepticism on both sides (Bearman-Hall and Nason-Clark 1997). Yet, in order to most effectively assist women of faith who are victimized by their partners, bridges need to be built between the "steeple and the shelter" (Nason-Clark 2000b). The language of contemporary culture and the language of spirituality, when used in tandem with each other, will augment, rather than thwart, a religious woman's search for help and wholeness in the aftermath of violence at home (Nason-Clark 2005).

While researchers are still in the early stages of learning about the relationship between religion and wife abuse (Brinkerhoff, Grandin, and Lupri 1992; Knickmeyer, Levitt, Horne, and Bayer 2003), victim safety must be paramount for religious as well as secular caregivers. Statistics Canada (2005) reports that in 2004, 12 percent of female victims turned to a clergy member for some form of support. For groups that harbor a particular mistrust of secular society, the impact of nonsupport from their community of faith is especially pronounced, e.g., abused Amish and Mennonite women whose abuse was ignored or tolerated by their church leaders and who were silenced and abandoned by their faith communities (Espenshade 2004a, 2004b; Espenshade and Alexander 2004a, 2004b). Other researchers, such as Buxton (2000), claim that victims who find their way to the sanctuary seeking help will find a double-edged sword: The people of the church will be loving and caring, but the church will not be a safe place to discuss violence or to disclose its reality.

A major criticism of the impact of religious belief in connection with family violence is based upon the strong patriarchal ideology of conservative Christian and other fundamental faith traditions which serve to "keep women submissive." Indeed, religious belief or practice can act as a root cause of violence (Dobash and Dobash 1979). Several scholars point to the mutually reinforcing relationship between patriarchy and religious traditions (Battaglia 2001; Brown and Bohn 1989).

Moreover, religious victims of abuse sometimes receive conflicting advice from secular and religious professionals (Shannon-Lewy and Dull 2005), in large measure because secular sources often have little understanding of the importance of the victim's beliefs, particularly at a time of crisis in her life. Additionally, those in the secular therapeutic community may attribute her abuse to her religion, believing that it is her faith that reinforces passivity and acts as a detriment to any effective confrontation of the abuse (Bearman-Hall and Nason-Clark 1997; Horton and Williamson 1988; Nason-Clark 1997, 2000a, 2000b). While unintentional, inappropriate responses of faith leaders may cause far more harm than good to victims of abuse (Horne and Levitt 2003).

Just as the victim's needs may not adequately be met, so too the church may fail to meet the needs of men who act abusively by reinforcing their grip on power in their intimate relationships and failing to recognize those specific needs that must be met for significant change to commence (Fleming 1986; Livingston 2002). Since the clerical focus is often on the sanctity of marriage, any threats to the marriage, such as separation and divorce, are met with resistance (Alsdurf and Alsdurf 1989; Miles 2002).

Ammons (1999) claims that in a similar vein to the courts—which have been slow to recognize the illegality and inhumanity of spousal abuse—many religions have been slow to reevaluate their traditions and reluctant to acknowledge their culpability in turning a blind eye to domestic violence. Moreover, they are averse to actively challenging any of the ideological underpinnings that might be regarded as support for violence against women within the belief structures (Ammons 1999; Brown and Bohn 1989; Fortune 1991).

Yet there is reason for cautious optimism as one reads of theologians working to clarify notions of headship and submission (see, for example, Kroeger and Beck 1996, 1998; Kroeger and Nason-Clark 2001; and the groundbreaking work of Rev. Dr. Marie Fortune and the Faith Trust Institute [2006], established in 1977). Moreover, faith-based organizations in the United States are increasingly offering batterer intervention programs to violent religious men, and in Canada secular agencies are beginning to consider the importance of spirituality in the lives of men who have acted abusively (Fisher-Townsend 2006).

The Vulnerability of Abused Religious Women

In what ways are religious women more vulnerable when abused? Where strong religious faith interweaves with the family unit, it is common to observe that many of the patterns impacting abusive relationships within mainstream society are exacerbated, such as the fear, the isolation, and the covenant proclaimed before God at the marriage ceremony. Although there is no compelling evidence that abuse happens more frequently or that its forms are more severe in families of faith, religious women are more vulnerable after abuse takes place. In short, they are less likely to leave, are more likely to believe that the abuser can and will change his violent ways, frequently voice reservations about seeking respite in a community-based transition house or shelter, and commonly express guilt—believing they have failed their families and even God in not being successful in making their marriages work (Nason-Clark 2004). To be sure, most women victims are reluctant to see their marriages end, but, for women of strong spiritual conviction, these beliefs are commonly and strongly reinforced by a religious ideology that sees women's role in the home as pivotal to her sense of self-worth, believes that happy families build strong nations, and accepts divorce with great reservation. Central Christian notions such as forgiveness or women's identity with Jesus the sacrificial lamb stymie her ability to grasp the full extent of her current suffering or to even sound a cry for help. Could battering be her "cross to bear"?

Any discussion of the healing journey of religious victims of abuse eventually ends up on the doorstep of Christian beliefs surrounding forgiveness. The famous cry of Jesus from the cross, "Father, forgive them; for they do not know what they are doing" (Luke 23:34), is often portrayed as the exemplary pattern that abuse victims ought to imitate as they approach their aggressors. Yet, forgiveness does not eradicate the pain of the past, nor does it erase the implications to follow. Rather, when forgiveness is placed within a broader context of the journey from victim to survivor, it is achieved when the events of an abusive past no longer control the future and the victim is freed from the complicated web of anger and despair (Nason-Clark and Kroeger 2004).

But achieving this fine balance is extremely difficult. Marie Fortune (1991) believes that forgiveness is the very last step on the healing journey, the top rung on the ladder of a woman's valiant effort to overcome the brokenness of her past. As such, it cannot precede justice or the offender's accountability for his violent ways. Interestingly, premature forgiveness actually thwarts the very goals it may be trying to achieve: the possibility of healing and growth for both perpetrator and victim. Any pressure, religious or otherwise, on the victim to quickly "forgive and forget" must be avoided. Yet, forgiveness, it might be argued, is the most charitable and compassionate gift that religious groups can offer victims in their midst (Fortune 1988). However, forgiveness should be approached carefully: It cannot be put on a timetable by someone other than the victim herself, and never should forgiveness be touted as a guarantee for safety or protection. Religious professionals need to ensure that they do not employ language which suggests that once forgiveness is sought and granted, the life for the family returns to normal, as if the abuse never happened.

The Role of Faith-Based Agencies in Dealing with Abusers

The third question to be asked is whether there is a specific role for faith-based agencies in bringing religious men to accountability for their abusive behavior. As connections between religion and wife abuse are uncovered, several issues have become clear. North American courts are increasingly referring perpetrators of wife abuse to batterer treatment or intervention programs. Researchers Healey, Smith, and O'Sullivan (1998) demonstrate that 80 percent of clients in batterer programs are referred by court mandate. While women of faith who have been victimized want the violence to end, they often hope that there can be reconciliation of their marital relationships within the context and support of their faith communities. They live in family situations that may not be peaceful and safe, yet their faith traditions highlight family unity and celebrate the divinely ordained nature of family life (see Ruff 2006). In interviews with women of faith experiencing abuse, Boehm, Golec, Krahn, and Smyth (1999) found that many religious

women spoke of their spiritual anguish in the midst of abuse at home. To offer hope to abused religiously committed women, it is important that therapeutic staff condemn the abuse they have suffered using the language of their faith traditions (Nason-Clark and Kroeger 2004). Yet, secular therapists report that they find it frustrating to work with religious clients, in part because they find themselves often unsuccessful in challenging their seemingly erroneous religion ideation (Whipple 1987). Consequently, this leaves a significant gap in the ability of community-based services to meet the needs of the religious. Fitting into this niche are faith-based services for victims and perpetrators.

An essential feature of a faith-based intervention program is the ability of therapeutic staff who are knowledgeable of sacred texts and various religious traditions to counter any use of religion to support abuse in intimate relationships. Men in a faith-based intervention program cannot justify their violent behavior by using the language of their faith tradition. Here, the rationale of any abusive man that his belief system encourages or even justifies the abuse he has meted out on his victim will not be tolerated.

It may be that faith-based services differ not only in content but also in the constituency that they serve. In a recent study, Nason-Clark, Murphy, Fisher-Townsend, and Ruff (2003) found that men who sought help from a faith-based agency were more likely than those enrolled in a secular program to report demographic characteristics suggestive of life stability (e.g., currently married, older, higher educational and employment levels), yet they were as likely as other abusive men to abuse alcohol or drugs. Interestingly, men in the faith-based program under study were more likely than others to have witnessed or experienced violence in their childhood homes.

Yet, in areas of the United States that are highly religious, researchers have found that even in secular programs religious justification for violence occurs. In two secular Texas batterer intervention programs, it was revealed that men of faith appealed to the Bible as support for their violent ways. "The most common word they used was submit: She will not submit, she did not submit, she should submit" (Shupe, Stacey, and Hazlewood 1987).

If men of faith who act abusively are to be challenged to alter their violent ways, it is essential that their religious convictions and misunderstandings be addressed in an environment where their faith is not attacked, they cannot justify their actions based upon their faith traditions, and they can share experiences with men who have a common worldview. It cannot be overstated: If perpetrators hold their faith in high esteem, in order for their violence to stop, it must be condemned using the language of religious conviction, rooted in the Scriptures they believe to be sacred.

Conclusion

Violence against women knows no boundaries—not of color, ethnicity, class, religion, or region. Rich women, poor women, educated women, beautiful women, frail women, spiritual women, indeed all categories of women can and have been victims of aggression at the hands of someone who promised before God to love, cherish, and care for them under and through all circumstances. The words "until death do us part" are meant to convey the sense that the covenant of marriage is forever, witnessed by friends, family, and the Creator of life itself.

When men act abusively toward their partner, the promise unravels. The journey toward healing and wholeness for religious victims is replete with both secular and sacred overtones—as are its causes and the factors that reinforce it. Breaking the cycle of violence in the family requires both the language of secular culture and the language of the spirit. Researchers and activists alike must unravel the many layers involved in the interface of faith, family, and fear for victimized women and their children. The time has come to shatter the silence.

NANCY NASON-CLARK

See also **Corporal Punishment, Religious Attitudes toward; Cross-Cultural Perspectives on Domestic Violence; Jewish Community, Domestic Violence within the; Medical Neglect Related to Religion and Culture; Qur'anic Perspectives on Wife Abuse; Rule of Thumb; Worldwide Precedents Supporting Domestic Violence from Ancient to Modern Times**

References and Further Reading

Alsdurf, James, and Phyllis Alsdurf. *Battered into Submission: The Tragedy of Wife Abuse in the Christian Home.* Eugene, OR: Wipf and Stock Publishers, 1989

Ammons, Linda L. "What's God Got to Do with It? Church and State Collaboration in the Subordination of Women and Domestic Violence." *Rutgers Law Review* 51 (1999): 1207–1288.

Battaglia, Lisa Jeanne. "Conservative Protestant Ideology and Wife Abuse: Reflections on the Discrepancy between Theory and Data." *Journal of Religion and Abuse* 2, no. 4 (2001): 31–45.

Beaman-Hall, L., and Nancy Nason-Clark. "Partners or Protagonists? The Transition House Movement and Conservative Churches." *Affilia: Journal of Women and Social Work* 12, no. 2 (1997): 176–196.

Boehm, Reinhild, Judith Golec, Ruth Krahn, and Dianne Smyth. *Lifelines: Culture, Spirituality and Family Violence. Understanding the Cultural and Spiritual Needs of Women Who Have Experienced Abuse.* Edmonton: University of Alberta Press, 1999.

Brinkerhoff, M. B., E. Grandin, and E. Lupri. "Religious Involvement and Spousal Violence—The Canadian Case." *Journal for the Scientific Study of Religion* 31, no. 1 (1992): 15–31.

Brown, J., and C. Bohn, eds. *Christianity, Patriarchy and Abuse: A Feminist Critique.* Cleveland, OH: The Pilgrim Press, 1989.

Buxton, Rod. "Domestic Violence in the Church: 'There Is an Elephant in the Sanctuary and No-One Is Talking about It.'" *Didaskalia* 12, no. 1 (2000): 51–75. (The results of a Manitoba survey.)

Dobash, R. P., and R. E. Dobash. *Violence against Wives: A Case against the Patriarchy.* New York: Free Press, 1979.

Espenshade, Linda. "Beliefs, Culture Can Perpetuate Abuse in Families, Churches," 2004a. *Intelligencer Journal,* July 12, 2004.

———. "The Ties That Bind Can Form the Noose," 2004b. *Intelligencer Journal,* July 13.

Espenshade, Linda, and Larry Alexander. "Abused Wives Feel Abandoned by Church," 2004a. *Intelligencer Journal,* July 13.

———. "Hidden in Plain Sight: Domestic Abuse among Amish and Mennonites Often Ignored, Even Tolerated among Church Leaders," 2004b. *Intelligencer Journal,* July 12.

Faith Trust Institute. Website, 2006. www.faithtrustinstitute.org (accessed August 14, 2006).

Fisher-Townsend, B. "Changing Violent Religious Men: The Intersection of the Criminal Justice System, Batterers' Intervention Programs, and Faith-Based Services and Supports." Department of Sociology, University of New Brunswick, Fredericton, 2006.

Fleming, Steven R. "Competent Christian Intervention with Men Who Batter." In *Women, Abuse and the Bible: How Scripture Can Be Used to Hurt or Heal,* edited by C. C. Kroeger and J. Beck. Grand Rapids, MI: Baker Books, 1986.

Fortune, M. *Violence in the Family: A Workshop Curriculum for Clergy and Other Helpers.* Cleveland, OH: Pilgrim Press, 1991.

Healey, K., C. Smith, and C. O'Sullivan. 1998. *Batterer Intervention: Program Approaches and Criminal Justice Strategies.* Issues and Practices in Criminal Justice. National Institute of Justice/Office of Justice Programs. Washington, DC: U.S. Department of Justice.

Hong, B. A., and V. R. Wiehe. "Referral Patterns of Clergy." *Journal of Psychology and Theology* 2 (1974): 291–297.

Horne, Sharon G., and Heidi M. Levitt. "Shelter from the Raging Wind: Religious Needs of Victims of Intimate Partner Violence and Faith Leaders' Responses." *Journal of Religion and Abuse* 5, no. 2 (2003): 83–98.

Horton, A., and J. Williamson, eds. *Abuse and Religion: When Praying Isn't Enough.* New York: D. C. Heath and Company, 1988.

Knickmeyer, Nicole, Heidi M. Levitt, Sharon G. Horne, and Gary Bayer. "Responding to Mixed Messages and Double Binds: Religious Oriented Coping Strategies of Christian Battered Women." *Journal of Religion and Abuse* 5, no. 2 (2003): 29–54.

Kroeger, C., and N. Nason-Clark. *No Place for Abuse: Biblical and Practical Resources to Counteract Domestic Violence.* Downers Grove, IL: InterVarsity Press, 2001.

Kroeger, C., and J. R. Beck, eds. *Women, Abuse, and the Bible: How Scripture Can Be Used to Hurt or to Heal.* Grand Rapids, MI: Baker Books, 1996.

Kroeger, C. Clark, and J. Beck. *Healing the Hurting: Giving Hope and Help to Abused Women.* Grand Rapids, MI: Baker, 1998.

Livingston, David. *Healing Violent Men: A Model for Christian Communities.* Minneapolis: Fortress Press, 2002.

Miles, A. *Domestic Violence: What Every Pastor Should Know.* Minneapolis: Fortress Press, 2002.

Nason-Clark, N. "Religion and Violence against Women: Exploring the Rhetoric and the Response of Evangelical Churches in Canada." *Social Compass* 43, no. 4 (1996): 515–536.

———. *The Battered Wife: How Christians Confront Family Violence.* Louisville, KY: Westminster John Knox Press, 1997.

———. "Shattered Silence or Holy Hush: Emerging Definitions of Violence against Women." *Journal of Family Ministry* 13, no. 1 (1999): 39–56.

———. "Making the Sacred Safe: Woman Abuse and Communities of Faith." *Sociology of Religion* 61, no. 4 (2000a): 349–368.

———. "The Steeple or the Shelter? Family Violence and Secularization in Contemporary Canada." In *Rethinking Church, State and Modernity: Canada between Europe and the USA,* edited by D. Lyon and M. Van Die. Toronto: University of Toronto Press, 2000b.

———. "When Terror Strikes at Home: The Interface between Religion and Domestic Violence." *Journal for the Scientific Study of Religion* 42, no. 3 (2004): 303–310.

———. "Linking Research and Social Action: Violence, Religion and the Family. A Case for Public Sociology." *Review of Religious Research* 46, no. 3 (2005): 221–234.

Nason-Clark, N., and C. Clark Kroeger. *Refuge from Abuse: Hope and Healing for Abused Christian Women.* Downers Grove, IL: InterVarsity Press, 2004.

Nason-Clark, Nancy, Nancy Murphy, Barbara Fisher-Townsend, and Lanette Ruff. "An Overview of the Characteristics of the Clients at a Faith-Based Batterers' Intervention Program." *Journal of Religion and Abuse* 5, no. 4 (2003): 51–72.

Ruff, L. "Religiosity, Resources and Regrets: Variations amongst Conservative Protestant Mothers." Department of Sociology, University of New Brunswick, Fredericton, 2006.

———. "Religion and Violence E-Learning (RAVE)," n.d. http://www.peaceandsafety.com/RAVE%20Newsletter%20Feb%2006.pdf (accessed August 14, 2006).

Shannon-Lewy, Colleen, and Valerie T. Dull. "The Response of Christian Clergy to Domestic Violence: Help or Hindrance?" *Aggression and Violent Behavior* 10 (2005): 647–659.

Shupe, Anson, William A. Stacey, and Lonnie R. Hazlewood. *Violent Men, Violent Couples: The Dynamics of Domestic Violence.* Lexington, MA: D. C. Heath and Company, 1987.

Statistics Canada. *Family Violence in Canada: A Statistical Profile 2005,* edited by J.-A. Brzozowski. Ottawa: Canadian Centre for Justice Statistics, 2005.

Stirling, Mary Lou, C. Ann Cameron, Nancy Nason-Clark, and Baukje Miedema, eds. *Understanding Abuse: Partnering for Change.* Toronto: University of Toronto Press, 2004.

Weaver, Andrew J. "Psychological Trauma: What Clergy Need to Know." *Pastoral Psychology* 41 (1993): 385–408.

Whipple, V. "Counseling Battered Women from Fundamentalist Churches." *Journal for Marital and Family Therapy* 13, no. 3 (1987): 251–258.

COERCIVE CONTROL

Variously referred to as coerced persuasion; conjugal, patriarchal, or intimate terrorism; nonphysical abuse; emotional abuse; indirect abuse; psychological abuse; and mental or psychological torture, coercive control describes the pattern of sexual mastery by which abusive partners, typically males, employ different combinations of violence, intimidation, isolation, humiliation, and control to subordinate adult victims. In marked contrast to the incident-specific definition of physical assault that dominates domestic violence research and intervention, coercive control is ongoing, extends through social space as well as over time, exploits persistent sexual inequalities, and focuses its regulatory tactics on enforcing stereotypic sex role behaviors. Although coercive control can cause physical injury and psychological trauma, its harms tend to be cumulative rather than incident specific and include the suppression of autonomy and basic personal liberties as well as violations of physical integrity. Despite the fact that coercive control is not currently classified as a crime, it is the context for abuse in which a majority of victims seek outside assistance. The discrepancy between the pattern of abuse for which most women seek help and the prevailing equation of battering with incidents of physical violence helps explain why such current policies as arrest, court protection orders, batterer intervention programs, and emergency shelter have largely failed to reduce the prevalence or incidence of woman battering.

The Theory of Coercive Control

The coercive control model developed from applications of learning theory to the experiences of persons undergoing severe restraint in nonfamilial settings, particularly hostages, prisoners of war (POWs), inmates, mental patients, and members of religious cults. The parallels between these experiences and abuse extend from the tactics deployed to similarities between the proximate consequences for battered women and the harms experienced by other groups who suffer extreme forms of personal or institutional subjugation.

In their efforts at "thought reform" with American prisoners during the Korean War, the Chinese Communists used "coerced persuasion," a technique by which a person's self-concept and resistance was broken down ("unfreezing"), the controller's altered picture of reality was substituted ("changing"), and then the new view of reality was installed ("refreezing"), typically through "random, noncontingent reinforcement by unpredictable rewards and punishments." In the late 1970s, two feminist psychologists, Camella Serum and Margaret Singer, noticed that batterers employed these same or similar techniques, placing their partners in a "coercive control situation" of childlike dependency on the controllers. Psychologist Steven Morgan labeled wife abuse "conjugal terrorism" and noted the "remarkable" resemblance between the attitudes and behavior of the violent husband and those of the political terrorist. Building on this work, another psychologist, Lewis Okun (1986) wrote what remains the definitive chapter on the coercive control theory of woman battering. Drawing an extended analogy between coerced persuasion, the experience of women being conditioned to prostitution by their pimps, and the experiences recounted to him in his counseling work with abusive men and battered women, Okun emphasized the "breakdown" of the victim's personality in the face of severe external threats and isolation and highlighted the extreme emotional

and behavioral adaptations to this process, ranging from guilt, loss of self-esteem, identification with the controller's aggressiveness, and fear of escape to difficulty planning for the future, detachment from violent incidents, and overreaction to trivial incidents. Importantly, Okun shifted the explanation for the victim's reactions from her predisposing personality or background characteristics to the power dynamics mediated by the violent interaction. Although he stressed that any "normal" person would respond to coercive control tactics in a similar way, he emphasized the systemic nature of the oppression, not the extraordinary nature of the violence itself. Okun also identified social isolation as a key component of coercive control and linked it to "torture" ("conjugal terrorism"), threats, and the larger pattern of control by which batterers constricted their victims' decision-making powers and, in some cases, prohibited all independent decisions. He described how batterers controlled women's access to information (including censorship of mail and phone calls), exhausted them physically (e.g., by keeping them awake at night), and limited their movement, often to the point of forcibly confining them.

The next important contribution to the theory was by Ann Jones, a feminist author and journalist. In *Next Time, She'll Be Dead* (1994), Jones extended the analogy between the control skills men deployed in battering and similar techniques used with hostages, inmates, and American POWs, drawing on the human rights literature rather than on learning psychology. In a dramatic table, she juxtaposed the Amnesty International "chart of coercion" and comments by shelter residents to illustrate such methods as "isolation," "monopolization of perception," "induced debility and exhaustion," "threats," "occasional indulgences," "demonstrating 'omnipotence,'" "degradation," and "enforcing trivial demands." In addition to highlighting the extreme psychological effects of violence, Jones noted that thoroughgoing coercion could be accomplished without physical violence.

The movement to counsel batterers was another important source of coercive control theory. Feminist pioneers Del Martin, Susan Schechter, and Ann Jones embraced a definition of wife-beating as controlling behavior that created and maintained an imbalance of power between the batterer and the battered woman. Following this lead in 1977 when he founded Emerge in Boston, one of the nation's first counseling programs for violent men, David Adams construed battering as "controlling behavior" and defined any act as violent that causes the victim to do something she does not want to do, prevents her from doing something she wants to do, or causes her to be afraid. Counselors at Emerge confronted men's "control skills" as well as their excuses for violence, asked their clients to keep "control logs" (built around a checklist of violent and controlling behaviors), and assessed their intent by the intimidating and controlling effects of their behavior on women's autonomy. Moreover, in recognizing that control consisted of an array of "skills," Emerge helped demystify the belief that dominance was intrinsic to masculinity rather than a carefully selected, instrumental way to "do masculinity." In a related development, the Domestic Abuse Intervention Program (DAIP) in Duluth, Minnesota, used video portrayals to sensitize men to their control patterns. The reasoning by Emerge and DAIP was refreshingly straightforward: Since men "learned" the tactics they deployed to subordinate their partners, they could be helped to "unlearn" them when appropriate sanctions were combined with reeducation.

The rationality of coercive control was spelled out most completely by Lundy Bancroft (2002). In *Why Does He Do That?* Bancroft identified the collection of comforts and privileges that made control over women desirable to abusive men, including the "heady rush of power" that provided intrinsic satisfaction; "getting his way," especially when it matters the most; the availability of someone to take his problems out on; free labor from her and leisure and freedom for him; being the center of attention, with priority given to his needs; financial control; ensuring that his career, education, or other goals are prioritized; the public status of partner and/or father without the sacrifices; and the enjoyment of a double standard whereby he is exempt from rules that apply to her.

Another piece of the puzzle was provided by Ann Jones, this time working with a collaborator, longtime advocate Susan Schechter. In *When Love Goes Wrong* (1992) Jones and Schechter adapted the categories of coercive control theory, referred to batterers as "controlling partners" rather than as violent men, and defined abuse as "a pattern of coercive control that one person exercises over another in order to dominate and get his way." While it was widely understood that "power and control" are the aims of woman abuse, Jones and Schechter made clear that "control" tactics were also its primary means. They provided a lengthy checklist of these tactics, roughly modeled after the widely disseminated "power and control wheel" developed by DAIP in Duluth, juxtaposing various aspects of psychological abuse (such as

"moodiness, anger, and threats," "denying your perception," and "shifting responsibility") to such structural constraints as "control through money," "limiting contact with other people," and control "through decision making." "Physical and sexual violence" appeared last on their list. Sandwiched among the better-known control tactics on the Jones and Schechter checklist was "picking out your clothes," "telling you what to wear," "forbidding you to shop," and other constraints specific to women's devalued gender roles. If regulating a woman's dress or shopping seem trivial compared with burning her with cigarettes, including these tactics revealed that coercive control is "gendered."

Components of Coercive Control

Coercion includes acts of physical or sexual assault, threats, or other acts of intimidation used to directly compel or dispel a particular response by inducing pain, injury, and/or fear. Although the violence in coercive control can be fatal or cause serious injury, it is generally minor and distinguished from other types of assault by its frequency—often including hundreds of assaultive incidents—its duration, its routine or even ritual nature, and the fact that its effects are cumulative rather than incident specific.

Control encompasses forms of regulation, isolation, and exploitation that limit a victim's options, transfer her resources to the controller, ensure her dependence on him, and maximize the benefits of personal service. Control tactics affect this outcome through three means primarily: by monopolizing the tangible and intangible resources needed to develop and enjoy personhood; by orchestrating a partner's behavior through "rules"; and by eliminating opportunities for the victim to garner outside support. Though control may include transparent forms of exploitation or confinement (such as taking a partner's money or locking her in the house), it can be harder to identify when it is mediated by rules (such as forbidding her to work) or structural deprivations or when it targets behaviors such as cooking or cleaning that are already normatively constrained by identification with women's default status as housewives and caretakers. Decisional autonomy is so taken for granted in many of these activities that their restriction passes without notice.

Intimidation in coercive control achieves the desired levels of fear, compliance, "loyalty," and dependence primarily through threats, surveillance, and degradation. Intimidation may properly be termed "psychological abuse" because it reduces the victim's sense of worth and psychological efficacy, often inducing an image of the perpetrator as bigger than life. Threats run the gamut from holding a gun to a woman's head and detailing how she will be killed to signals of impending harm that are recognized only by the victim, such as a raised eyebrow or a tapping of the foot. Among the most frightening are threats that have such an ambiguous referent ("you made me jealous"), anonymous threats (including so-called "gaslight" games designed to make a victim think she's crazy), and the use of force against property or other persons that communicate what a partner is capable of doing if a woman disobeys. Indirect threats can also be directed at the woman through the children, a dynamic of "child abuse as tangential spouse abuse" (contributor's own term).

Surveillance, a second form of intimidation, makes coercive control portable, allowing it to extend through social space, making physical separation relatively ineffective as a way to end abuse. Stalking is the most prominent of a range of surveillance tactics designed to deprive the person of the right to privacy or to freely negotiate public and private spaces. Criminal law prohibits certain forms of surveillance (such as "stalking" and electronic eavesdropping). But the range of tactics batterers employ to watch their partners and intrude on their social and private lives goes far beyond anything currently considered criminal. For instance, an important intimidation technique involves micro-surveillance, where the controlling partner may subdivide ordinary behaviors such as sleeping, eating, cleaning, or making love into component parts, set performance rules for each component, and monitor their enactment. Controllers may steal or read diaries; search drawers for "sexy" clothes; measure the toilet paper, the breakfast cereal, or the height of the bed cover off the floor; and inspect underwear to detect disloyalty. Another facet of intimidation involves chronic insults and shaming. Typically introduced as a test of loyalty, a sign of ownership, a form of discipline, or a means of isolation, shaming involves demonstrating a victim's subservience through public humiliation, denying her self-respect, marking (as with tattoos, burns, or bruises), and the enforcement of a behavior or ritual that is either intrinsically humiliating or is contrary to the woman's nature, morality, or best judgment.

Isolation, the third tactical component of coercive control, is designed to prevent disclosure, instill dependence, express exclusive possession, monopolize a victim's skills and resources, and keep the victim from mustering the help or resources needed for independence. Controllers isolate victims within and from those arenas that provide the moorings of social identity, including friends, family, coworkers, and professional helpers, eviscerating a woman's selfhood and constraining her subjectivity. By cutting women off from alternative sources of information and support and inserting themselves between victims and the "world," batterers become their primary source of interpretation and validation. In extreme cases, this can elicit a "Stockholm syndrome," where the victim so completely internalizes her partner's view that she sees, knows, and experiences herself only as he sees her and believes that only he can protect her. In order to placate their partners, prove their loyalty, or counteract their partners' jealousy, abused women may also isolate themselves by quitting work or school or cutting themselves off from friends and family. When victims seek out "safety zones" where they can contemplate their options, controllers pursue them, "entering" and trying to sever each new social connection in "search and destroy" missions.

Because coercion relies on the proximate application of force, it compromises scope for immediacy. By contrast, control makes up in scope of effect what it lacks in immediacy. In control, where the element of compulsion is often implied by the "or else" presumption rather than being made explicit, the victim's volition is constrained indirectly by the batterer's dictating preferred choices, monopolizing time or access to information (called "monopolization of perception" in the torture literature), limiting the options available, and depriving the victim of the support needed to exercise independent judgment.

Batterers employ control to instill dependence, as a means to exploit their partner's capacities and resources for personal gain and gratification, to prevent escape or disclosure, and to enforce stereotypic gender roles consistent with ideals of male dominance. Control is effective because it simultaneously constrains the sphere where independent action is possible and deprives the battered woman of the resources needed for such action. Control tactics are the direct cause of dependence in abusive relationships. In traditional societies where women are denied alternatives to dependence on men and their behavior is prescribed by religion, law, and/or culture, physical abuse is usually sufficient to actualize women's obedience in personal life. But in societies where women are formally equal to men and reject "bad bargains" in relationships in large numbers, men who insist on securing sex-linked privileges must do so directly, personally, and without the expectation of institutional support. This is why coercive control is increasingly replacing partner assault as the chosen mode of entrapping women in personal life.

Control tactics target the basic necessities needed to survive, including money, food, sex, drugs, sleep, housing, transportation, and communication with the outside world. But if control over necessities constitutes its material foundation, the most insidious dimension of coercive control involves extending exploitation, prohibition, and regulation to minute facets of everyday life, particularly those associated with women's devalued status as caretakers, homemakers, and sexual property. The regulation of women's everyday behavior is accomplished through explicit or implicit "rules" that govern not merely what they do but how they do it; what they can and cannot say and to whom; whether, when, and where they go out; and how and to whom they make love. In the controller's mind, rules give abuse the aura of rationality and disguise its authorship: It is because she has broken the rules, or an "agreement," or acted "crazy" that she must be punished. The batterer not only makes the rules, but judges violations and enforces sanctions. The functional appeal of rules is their economy and the illusion of order and rationality they provide the batterer. Control skills are perfected slowly through trial and error as behaviors and excuses that have been standardized within cultures are adapted to the unique circumstances in millions of relationships, often over months or years.

Empirical Dimensions of Coercive Control

The existence of coercive control could be deduced from the fact that violence alone fails to account for critical facets of battering, including why it is ongoing; why the battering presented at service sites or reported to crime surveys looks so different from the "abuse" picked up by general population surveys; why female victims (but not male victims) become "entrapped" and develop a complex of psychological, behavioral, medical, and psychosocial problems seen among no other population of assault victims; and why interventions predicated on a violence-based definition of abuse have universally failed to reduce the problem, let alone prevent it.

Sociologist Michael Johnson (1995) was the first to recognize that the different pictures of "violence" that emerged from population surveys and service sites reflected different types of abuse. In contrast to the "common couple" or "situational" violence picked up by the surveys, what was being seen by shelters, police, and the courts was "intimate terrorism," where control as well as violence was used. Evan Stark further subdivided violence into ordinary "fights" and "partner assaults," where violence (but not control) was used to hurt or control a partner rather than to resolve a conflict. Johnson (2001) showed that the vast majority of women who used shelters (79 percent) or sought court assistance (68 percent) suffered from "intimate terrorism" rather than domestic violence.

Studies drawn from other service settings suggest that coercive control is the context for somewhere between 50 and 80 percent of the abuse seen by police, courts, and batterer intervention programs. Among the men arrested for domestic violence crimes in Quincy, Massachusetts, 38.1 percent admitted that they had prevented their partners from freely coming and going in their daily routine, 58.5 percent said that they denied their partners access to money and other resources, and almost half reported restricting their partners in three or more additional ways (Buzawa, Hotaling, Klein, and Byrne 1999). Abused women in a representative sample of 734 Aid to Families with Dependent Children recipients in Massachusetts were eight times more likely than nonabused women (16 percent vs. 2 percent, respectively) to report that a current or former boyfriend would not let them go to school or work (Allard, Albelda, Colten, and Cosenza 1997). The extent of control in these relationships is suggested by the remarkable finding that fully 36 percent of the residents at one shelter reported not having a single supportive or recreational experience during the month prior to the interview (Forte, Franks, Forte, and Rigsby 1996). Realizing the possible importance of "domination behaviors" in measuring the success of counseling for batterers, psychologist Richard Tolman (1992) devised a scale of psychological "maltreatment" and then used a factor analysis to distinguish a dimension of "Dominance Isolation" from "Verbal Emotional Abuse," a distinction that was supported in subsequent research. Items reflecting gender role expectations loaded with the domination/isolation factor. In a preliminary test of his measurement scale, Tolman documented the use of control tactics among a convenience sample of 207 battered women and 407 largely unrelated offending men, reporting that 75–95 percent of the battered women had experienced ten of the items and 50–75 percent of the women "endorsed" at least six of the behaviors. Only three control items—not being allowed to work (35 percent), being kept from medical care (29 percent), and being threatened with having the children taken away (44 percent)—were reported by fewer than half of the victims.

The only population data available on coercive control as of this writing come from the Finnish national sample. One in three of the battered women identified were restricted from seeing friends and family, as many as one in four (16–26 percent) were prevented from making financial decisions or shopping, and almost half (41–49 percent) were continually humiliated (Piispa 2002, p. 888).

There is mounting evidence that coercive control is the most dangerous context for woman battering, not merely the most common. A sophisticated multicity study identified two factors that predicted fatality in abusive relationships better than all factors other than the presence of a firearm: whether the couple had separated after having lived together, and whether an abuser was "highly controlling" in addition to being violent (Glass, Manganello, and Campbell 2004). When these factors were combined, the chance that an abused woman would be killed by her partner was nine times higher than when these factors were not present.

Even in the absence of violence, control tactics can elicit the profile associated with battering. In the Finnish national population study cited above, the highest incidence of mental health and behavioral problems was reported by a group of generally older women who had been physically abused in the past but had not been reassaulted for at least seven years. Compared with those who were in short-term, currently violent relationships, these women were three times as likely to report "fear" (91 percent vs. 39 percent), four times as likely to feel "numbness" (78 percent vs. 18 percent), and more likely to experience other similar feelings, strongly suggesting that their partners had merely replaced physical abuse with coercive control. Finally, in an ingenious study, psychologist Cynthia Lischick found that a measure of coercive control was far better at predicting the level of fear and entrapment in a population of young, unmarried, and multicultural women than the Conflict Tactics Scale, the most commonly used measure of domestic violence. Remarkably, where 29 percent of the partners of the "battered" women used both minor and severe violence and 15 percent used only minor violence, the majority of the partners (56 percent) had never physically abused their partners.

The Gendered Nature of Coercive Control

Violent women are no less likely to seek control over their partners than violent men. Moreover, violent women in counseling are as likely as their male counterparts to use violence because they are jealous, to get their partners to do what they want, to "punish" partners, and "to feel more powerful" (Kernsmith 2005). Male victims of female violence also report that their partners used a variety of control strategies such as "monitoring my time" or "interfering with my relationships with other family members," although these tactics are reported far more often by female victims (Phelan, Hamberger, Guse, and Edwards 2005). Despite these data, there is no evidence that any substantial population of men are victims of the same pattern of coercive control by female partners or suffer comparable harms to their liberty. This is because women's vulnerability to entrapment in personal life is due to the larger status inequalities they bring to relationships and their default consignment to a round of domestic responsibilities even in lieu of direct control. Since men cannot be unequal to women the same as women are disadvantaged relative to them, they can exploit inequality in relationships in ways that women cannot. Thus, even though many women hit, intimidate, control, or demean men, the substance, meaning, and consequence of these tactics are completely different when they are used in combination to oppress women. It is this fusion of social and personal constraint that gives coercive control its gendered theme and organizes its delivery around stereotypic sex roles. It is unclear whether similar structural constraints are imposed in abuse by same-sex or transgender partners.

How Victims Respond

In response to coercive control, victims attempt to establish outside supports and seek "moments of autonomy" in "safety zones" where they feel free to consider their options. Many victims try to exercise "control in the context of no control" by hurting themselves rather than waiting to be hurt, an explanation for the high rates of substance abuse and suicidality among battered women (Stark and Flitcraft 1996). Controllers react by pursuing victims into these spaces ("search and destroy" missions) and trying to close them off, both literally by locking a victim in the house or a room and by monitoring her movements and relationships when she is on her own. The outcome of coercive control is a condition of unreciprocated authority that victims experience as entrapment.

Entrapment due to coercive control may explain a number of problems left unresolved by the domestic violence paradigm, such as why abusive relationships endure, why battered women suffer a range of medical, behavioral, and psychosocial problems seen among no other population of assault victims, and why arrest, batterer intervention programs, and a range of other interventions that are incident specific fail to stem either the level or the extent of woman abuse to any degree.

Coercive control deprives victims of the right to autonomously express their unique endowments in the world, thereby disabling a vast store of life-energy and creativity that is critical to the exercise of citizenship, women's personal development, and the well-being of families, communities, and society. For this reason, coercive control is more appropriately thought of as a "liberty crime" than as a crime of assault. Implicit in this understanding—and in the broadening of domestic violence laws required to encompass coercive control—is the right of its victims to a liberatory response.

EVAN STARK

See also **Battered Woman Syndrome; Batterer Typology; Feminist Theory; Social Learning Theory and Family Violence; Stockholm Syndrome in Battered Women**

References and Further Reading

Allard, Mary Ann, Randy Albelda, Mary Ellen Colten, and Carol Cosenza. *In Harm's Way? Domestic Violence, AFDC Receipts, and Welfare Reform in Massachusetts.* Executive Summary of the Report from the University of Massachusetts, Boston. McCormack Institute and Center for Survey Research at the University of Massachusetts, 1997.

Bancroft, L. *Why Does He Do That? Inside The Minds of Angry and Controlling Men.* New York: Putnam, 2002.

Buzawa, E., G. Hotaling, A. Klein, and J. Byrne. *Response to Domestic Violence in a Proactive Court Setting. Final Report.* Washington DC: National Institute of Justice, 1999.

Forte, J. D. M. Franks, J. Forte, and D. Rigsby. "Asymmetrical Role Taking: Comparing Battered and Nonbattered Women." *Social Work* 41, no. 1 (1996): 59–74.

Glass, N., J. Manganello, and J. C. Campbell. "Risk for Intimate Partner Femicide in Violent Relationships." *DV Report* 9, no. 2 (2004): 30–33.

Kernsmith, P. "Exerting Power or Striking Back: A Gendered Comparison of Motivations for Domestic Violence Perpetration." *Violence against Victims* 20, no. 2 (2005): 173–186.

Johnson, M. P. "Patriarchal Terrorism and Common Couple Violence: Two Forms of Violence against Women." *Journal of Marriage and the Family* 57 (1995): 283–294.

———. "Conflict and Control: Symmetry and Asymmetry in Domestic Violence." In *Couples in Conflict,* edited by A. Booth, A. Crouter, and M. Clements. Mahwah, NJ: Erlbaum, 2001.

Jones, A., and S. Schechter. *When Love Goes Wrong.* New York: HarperCollins, 1992.

Lischick, C. W. "Coping and Related Characteristics Delineating Battered Women's Experiences in Self-Defined, Difficult/Hurtful Dating Relationships: A Multicultural Study." Unpublished PhD diss., Rutgers University, Newark, NJ, 1999.

Okun, L. *Woman Abuse: Facts Replacing Myths.* Albany: State University of New York Press, 1986.

Phelan, M. B., R. L. K. Hamberger, C. E. Guse, and S. Edwards. "Domestic Violence among Male and Female Patients Seeking Emergency Medical Services." *Violence and Victims* 20, no. 2 (2005).

Piispa, M. "Complexity of Patterns of Violence against Women in Heterosexual Partnerships." *Violence against Women* 8, no. 7 (2002): 873–901.

Stark, E., and A. H. Flitcraft. *Women at Risk: Domestic Violence and Women's Healthcare.* Thousand Oaks, CA: Sage, 1996.

Tolman, R. M. "The Development of a Measure of Psychological Maltreatment of Women by Their Male Partners." *Violence and Victims* 4, no. 3 (1989): 159–177.

COHABITING VIOLENCE

Cohabitation is when two partners integrate their residence, property, and daily lives without legally marrying. During the twentieth century, the courtship culture of European immigrants in the United States steadily diminished and cohabitation has become increasingly more acceptable in social circles. Regardless of one's ethical perspectives, the recent growth in cohabitation has serious implications for the institution of marriage as well as child rearing and domestic violence. This article will discuss the current trends in cohabitation, compare the differences between cohabitation and marriage, remark on nonmarriageable men and domestic violence, and lastly discuss current policies pertaining to cohabitation.

Current Demographic Trends

The U.S. Census Bureau estimated that in the year 2000 there were 105.5 million households in the United States. Of those households, about 5 percent, or 5.5 million couples, lived together but were unmarried. This figure is up from the previous 3.2 million estimated unmarried couples in the prior 1990 census. Among the 5.5 million cohabiting couples, about one in nine were same-sex, predominantly male couples.

While the percentage of cohabiting couples at any point in time is not remarkably high, particularly when compared with other social phenomena like nonmarital births, Bumpass and Lu (2000) report that currently over half of all marriages are preceded by cohabitation. This reflects the tendency for Americans to live together and "test the waters" before tying the knot. This conclusion is reinforced by Bumpass, Sweet, and Cherlin (1991), who have shown that cohabiters are more likely to be young, childless couples. In their historical overview of cohabitation, they show that cohabiting couples were dominated by individuals with less than a high school education in the 1930s and 1940s but that the 1970s and beyond saw a growth in cohabitation among all educational groups. From this perspective, cohabitation is commonplace and far more socially accepted than it was just fifty years ago.

The majority of unmarried, cohabiting couples, nearly 80 percent, live in metropolitan areas. Among same-sex couples, this percentage is even higher (85.3 percent). These figures are slightly lower for married couples, with 78.5 percent living in metropolitan areas. Within metropolitan areas, however, unmarried couples are more likely than married couples to reside in the central city (35.7 versus 24.3 percent for married and unmarried couples, respectively). Among same-sex couples, 41.6 percent live in central cities.

A higher percentage of all households consist of unmarried couples in the western United States than in any other region of the country. In descending order, these percentages are 10.2 in the West, 9.6 in the Northeast, 8.9 in the Midwest, and 8.4 in the South. The same pattern exists when looking strictly at same-sex cohabiting couples.

In absolute terms, California has more cohabiting households than any other state, followed by New York, Florida, Texas, and Pennsylvania. As a percentage of all households, however, the districts/states with the highest percentages of cohabiting couples are the District of Columbia (20.8 percent), Nevada (12.6 percent), Alaska (12.5 percent), and Vermont (12.5 percent). There is considerable cross-state variation in these figures. In contrast, the states with the lowest percentages of cohabiting couples include Utah (5.2 percent), Alabama (6.1 percent), Arkansas (6.7 percent), Kansas (6.9 percent), and Oklahoma (6.9 percent). This state variability in household composition is even more pronounced when looking at same-sex couples, ranging from a low of 0.5 percent of all households in Iowa, North Dakota, and South Dakota to a high of 5.1 percent in the District of Columbia.

Using data from 1979 through 1987, Roberts (1987) shows that most cohabiters report higher rates of domestic violence than married couples. This is disturbing given the sheer volume of victimizations reported in the National Crime Victimization Survey (2003). During 2001 alone, it is estimated that there were 691,710 nonfatal violent victimizations committed by current or former spouses, boyfriends, or girlfriends. The majority of victims were females. In 2000, a total of 1,247 women and 440 men were killed by an intimate partner. In decreasing order, other crimes committed by intimate partners include assault, aggravated assault, robbery, and rape/sexual assault.

Cohabitation Versus Marriage

For young adults, cohabitation seems attractive because it allows couples to receive many of the benefits of marriage, such as the sharing of expenses and household responsibilities. This is especially attractive for young couples in large metropolitan areas where the costs of living are constantly rising. Additional benefits of cohabitation include emotional support, a safe-sex partner, and the ability to spend time with a partner to confirm lifelong commitment. Cohabiting couples can learn about their partners without any legal or religious commitments.

There are some distinctive differences between younger and older cohabiting couples. King and Scott (2006) find that older cohabiters are less likely to make plans to eventually marry. Older cohabiters also report significantly higher levels of stability and quality in their relationships compared with younger cohabiters. These authors suggest that older unmarried couples view cohabitation as a substitute for marriage, while younger cohabiters view cohabitation as a preface to marriage.

Like marriage, however, cohabitation is not without risks and costs. Risks are assumed when debts and assets are combined (e.g., leases signed, property and household goods purchased). Psychological uncertainties are more pronounced: Studies show that cohabiting couples are more likely to feel that their relationship is not as steady as that of married couples. Furthermore, when children are involved, the potential risks and costs of cohabitation increase. Raley, Frisco, and Wildsmith (2005) show that children who lived with cohabiters did significantly worse in educational achievement and attainment than children raised with divorced or remarried mothers. Thompson, Hanson, and McLanahan (1994) found that children who lived with an unmarried mother and her partner were more likely to suffer behavioral problems and achieve lower academic success than children reared by married parents.

When queried about how life would change if they were to marry, cohabiters report that there would be few changes (Bumpass et al. 1991). There were two exceptions: When males were asked about their independence, one-third of the respondents felt that they would no longer be free to do what they wanted; additionally, a large proportion of all respondents felt that their economic and emotional security would be better if they were married.

To understand how cohabiters' behavior might differ from that of married or divorced couples, Deleire and Kalil (2005) used Consumer Expenditure data to examine the expenditure patterns of cohabiting partners. The authors suggest that cohabiting parents allocate a greater amount of their budget to adult goods such as alcohol and tobacco and a smaller amount to education. This evidence might suggest a relationship between cohabiting and substance abuse. Testa, Livingston, and Leonard (2003) investigated this phenomenon and found that in fact women who cohabited were more likely to be exposed to drug use and domestic violence.

Newcomb and Bentler (1980) examined sixty-eight marriages and looked specifically at whether or not the couples had lived together prior to marrying. They found no differences in marital satisfaction or divorce rates between the two groups. However, among those couples who eventually divorced, those who had lived together prior to marriage reported experiencing less marital distress.

In their study of the urban underclass in Chicago, Wilson, Aponte, and Neckerman (1985) argued that the increase of urban poverty was due to low marriage rates because of a shortage of "good"

eligible men. Using a Marriageable Pool Index (MPI), which is a ratio of employed black males per 100 black females, the authors showed that in fact there was a shortage of good, hardworking, eligible, employed, black men. Black urban men in the areas studied by these authors were disproportionately involved in drugs and violent crime, and experienced high incarceration rates. A complementary explanation of the low marriage rates in these areas is found in the work of Edin and Kefalas (2005), who examined why poor mothers in Philadelphia chose single motherhood or cohabitation over marriage. They found that many poor women revered marriage as a very special institution but feared that they would not live up to the expectations associated with it.

Finally, using the National Longitudinal Survey of Youth to examine the economic effects of cohabiting couples after dissolution, Avellar and Smock (2005) found that women's economic standing sharply declined after separation. Such an economic decline is also common among married couples who divorce and is responsible for pushing a large proportion of women and children into poverty.

Literature on Violence in Cohabiting Relationships

Numerous articles have been written on cohabiting and violence. Levinger (1965) proposed a model of marital cohesiveness and dissolution which predicted higher levels of violence in ongoing marriages than in cohabiting relationships. Yllo and Straus (1981) challenged Levinger and showed that with the exceptions of high-income and older (over age thirty) unmarried couples, cohabiters were more likely to commit acts of violence in comparison with their married counterparts. Higher rates of violence among cohabiting couples have been found by other researchers. For example, using Canadian homicide data, Wilson (1993, 1995) found that women in cohabiting relationships were at a greater risk of being killed by their partners than were women who were married. In fact, Shackelford (2001) found that women in cohabiting relationships were nine times more likely to be killed by their partners than were women who were in marital relationships.

Stets (1991) studied the role of isolation and aggression in cohabiting relationships and found that a lack of social control and some demographic characteristics help explain aggression among cohabiters. Literature on social control and intimate violence is not new (Brownmiller 1975; Carmody and Williams 1987; Pagelow 1981; Riger and Gordon 1981; Stanko

1985; Williams and Hawkins 1989). Social control can be derived through either formal or informal processes. Traditional formal control has relied on the use of legal sanctions as a deterrence to crime. Individuals internally evaluate the expected value (benefits and costs) associated with committing acts of domestic violence. Some researchers argue that formal controls, particularly the expected costs associated with legal sanctions, have little effect on the reduction of intimate violence (Paternoster 1987). These researchers argue that informal social controls play a more pivotal role in the reduction of violence. Such informal social control agents, or "eyes on the street," include family, peers, and subordinates.

Studies show that intimate partners use violence to influence or control their cohabiting partners. The social psychology literature (Goode 1971; Pruitt and Rubin 1986; Stets and Burke 1996; Tedeschi 1970; Tedeschi and Felson 1994) shows that coercion and conflict through verbal communication usually precede the actual act of violence.

Demographic characteristics that seem to be important correlates of violence in cohabiting relationships include not only age and income, but also education and race. For example, Sorenson (1996) found that people with less than a high school education were 40 percent more likely to report intimate partner violence than those with a high school education. Surprisingly, college graduates were only 30 percent less likely to report partner violence than those with a high school diploma. Cunradi, Caetano, and Schafer (2002) estimated that annual household income has the biggest influence on the probability of inflicting violence toward a cohabiting partner. Additionally, Caetano and Schafer (2002) found income to have the greatest influence on the probability of committing acts of violence among cohabiting relationships.

Race is a strong correlate of intimate partner violence in numerous studies (Gelles 1982; Gil 1970; Hampton, Gelles, and Harrop 1991; Newberger, Reed, Daniel, Hyde, and Kotelchuck 1977; Turbett and O'Toole 1980). Moreover, these studies not only suggest that race and socioeconomic class are strong predictors for domestic violence between married and cohabiting couples, but the reporting of such acts vary across racial groups. For example, minorities from patriarchal, male-dominated societies (Latinos) tend to underreport domestic violence incidences compared with Anglo-Americans.

Policy Response

Some states have laws prohibiting unmarried couples from cohabiting. In May 2005, newspapers around the United States released the news that the American Civil Liberties Union (ACLU) was to challenge a 200-year-old North Carolina law which prohibited unmarried couples from living together, although rarely enforced. North Carolina is one of seven states that still prohibit the practice. The other six states are Virginia, West Virginia, Florida, Michigan, Mississippi, and North Dakota.

Most states have instituted common law clauses or cohabitation contracts which try to establish the rights and obligations that cohabiting couples would gain if married. Only two states have visibly failed to recognize these cohabitation contracts: Illinois (*Hewitt v. Hewitt,* 394 N.E.2d 1204 [1979]) and Georgia (*Rehak v. Mathis,* 238 S.E.2d 81 [1977]).

In applying the laws related to domestic violence, the U.S. court system does not differentiate between cohabiters and married couples. The only real distinction comes when property, children, and debt are involved. In most state circuit courts, there are few protections for unmarried couples.

Since the 1990s there has been widespread advocacy for protecting all women in domestic relationships. The U.S. Department of Justice in 1995 established the Office of Violence against Women to help implement the 1994 Violence against Women Act, which was later updated in 2000. This office leads a nationwide effort to stop domestic violence in local communities and tribal territories through grant monies. The purpose of these grants is to encourage states to reorganize their criminal justice systems so that local communities can create partnerships and increase the reporting of domestic violence cases. Additionally, Congress has passed the Victims of Trafficking and Violence Prevention Act of 2000 to combat illegal trafficking of women and children. This legislation secures that women and children will not be coerced into underground sex markets.

Conclusion

Cohabitation is steadily increasing in the United States, and will continue to increase as society redefines the concept of marriage. Unfortunately, women in cohabiting relationships are at a higher risk of violent victimization by their partners. This is particularly true for younger couples, low-income couples, and couples with low educational attainment. For unmarried cohabiting couples with children, the impacts of violence spill over into the next generation and can result in maladaptive child behaviors, as well as fuel the intergenerational transmission of violence. While public awareness and public policy have made great strides with legislative and community-level responses, the high rates of abuse in cohabiting and marital relationships continue to pose serious challenges for policymakers.

MAUREEN PIROG and EDWARD D. VARGAS

See also **Battered Woman Syndrome; Date Rape; Dating Violence; Intimate Partner Violence, Forms of; Mutual Battering; Stalking**

References and Further Reading

Avellar, Sarah, and Pamela J. Smock. "The Economic Consequences of the Dissolution of *Cohabiting* Unions." *Journal of Family and Marriage* 67 (2005): 315–327.

Axinn, William G., and Arland Thornton. "The Relationship between Cohabitation and Divorce: Selectivity or Causal Influence?" *Demography* 29 (1992): 357–374.

Bennett, Neil, Ann Blanc, and David Bloom. "Commitment and Modern Union: Assessing the Link between Premarital Cohabitation and Subsequent Marital Stability." *American Sociological Review* 53 (1988): 127–138.

Booth, Alan, and David Johnson. "Premarital Cohabitation and Marital Success." *Journal of Family Issues* 9 (1988): 255–272.

Brown, Susan L. "Union Transitions among Cohabitors: The Significance of Relationship Assessments and Expectations." *Journal of Marriage and the Family* 62 (2000): 833–846.

Brownmiller, Susan. *Against Our Will: Men, Women and Rape.* New York: Simon and Schuster, 1975.

Bumpass, Larry L., and Hsien-Hen Lu. "Trends in Cohabitation and Implications for Children's Family Contexts in the U.S." *Population Studies* 54 (2000): 29–41.

Bumpass, Larry L., James A. Sweet, and Andrew Cherlin. "The Role of Cohabitation in Declining Rates of Marriage." *Journal of Marriage and the Family* 53 (1991): 913–927.

Capser, Lynne N., and Suzanne M. Bianchi. *Continuity and Change in the American Family.* Thousand Oaks, CA: Sage Publications, 2002.

Carmody, Dianne C., and Kirk R. Williams. "Wife Assault and the Perceptions of Sanctions." *Violence and Victims* 2 (1987): 25.

Cohan, Catherine, and Stacey Kleinbaum. "Toward a Greater Understanding of the Cohabitation Effect: Premarital Cohabitation and Marital Communication." *Journal of Marriage and Family* 64 (2002): 180–192.

Cunningham, John D., and John K. Antill. "Cohabitation and Marriage: Retrospective and Predictive Comparisons." *Journal of Social and Personal Relationships* 11 (1994): 77–94.

Cunradi, Carol B., Raul Caetano, and John Schafer. "Socioeconomic Predictors of Intimate Partner Violence among White, Black, and Hispanic Couples in the United States." *Journal of Family Violence* 17 (2002): 377–389.

Deleire, Thomas, and Ariel Kalil. "How Do Cohabiting Couples with Children Spend Their Money?" *Journal of Family and Marriage* 67 (2005): 286–329.

DeMaris, Alfred, and K. Vaninadha Rao. "Premarital Cohabitation and Subsequent Marital Stability in the United States: A Reassessment." *Journal of Marriage and the Family* 54 (1992): 178–190.

Edin, Kathryn, and Maria Kefalas. *Promises I Can Keep: Why Poor Women Put Motherhood Before Marriage.* Berkeley and Los Angeles: University of California Press, 2005.

Forste, Renata, and Koray Tanfer. "Sexual Exclusivity among Dating, Cohabiting, and Married Women." *Journal of Marriage and the Family* 58 (1996): 33–47.

Gelles, Richard J. "Child Abuse and Family Violence: Implications for Medical Professionals." In *Child Abuse,* edited by E. H. Newberger. Boston: Little, Brown, 1982, pp. 55–67.

Gil, David G. *Violence against Children: Physical Child Abuse in the United States.* Cambridge: Harvard University Press, 1970.

Goldscheider, Frances, Arland Thornton, and Linda Young-DeMarco. "A Portrait of the Nest Leaving Process in Early Adulthood." *Demography* 30 (1993): 683–699.

Goode, William J. "Force and Violence in the Family." *Journal of Marriage and the Family* (November 1971): 624–635.

Gordon, Michael, and Susan J. Creighton. "Natal and Nonnatal Fathers as Sexual Abusers in the United Kingdom: A Comparative Analysis." *Journal of Marriage and the Family* 50 (1988): 99.

Graefe, Deborah, and Daniel Lichter. "Life Course Transition of American Children: Parental Cohabitation, Marriage, and Single Motherhood." *Demography* 36 (1999): 205–217.

Hampton R. L., Richard J. Gelles, and J. Harrop. "Is Violence in Black Families Increasing? A Comparison of 1975 and 1985 National Survey Rates." In *Black Family Violence,* edited by R. L. Hampton. Lexington, MA: Lexington Books, 1991, pp. 3–18.

Jackson, Nicky Ali. "Observational Experiences of Intrapersonal Conflict and Teenage Victimization: A Comparative Study among Spouses and Cohabitors." *Journal of Family Violence* 11 (1996): 191–203.

Jackson, Nicky Ali, and Gisele Casanova Oates. *Violence in Intimate Relationships: Examining Sociological and Psychological Issues.* Boston: Butterworth-Heinemann, 1998.

King, Valarie, and Mindy E. Scott. "A Comparison of Cohabiting Relationships among Older and Younger Adults." *Journal of Marriage and Family* 67 (2006): 271–554.

Laumann, Edward O., John H. Gagnon, Robert T. Michael, and Stuart Michaels. *The Social Organization of Sexuality: Sexual Practices in the United States.* Chicago: University of Chicago Press, 1994.

Levinger, George. "Marital Cohesiveness and Dissolution: An Integrative Review." *Journal of Marriage and the Family* 27 (1965): 19–28.

Malkin, Catherine, and Michael Lamb. "Child Maltreatment: A Test of Sociobiological Theory." *Journal of Comparative Family Studies* 25 (1994): 121–133.

Manning, Wendy, and Daniel Lichter, "Parental Cohabitation and Children's Economic Well-Being." *Journal of Marriage and the Family* 58 (1996): 998–1010.

Manning, Wendy D., and Pamela J. Smock. "First Comes Cohabitation, Then Comes Marriage." *Journal of Family Issues* 23 (2002): 1065–1087.

Margolin, Leslie. "Child Abuse and Mother's Boyfriends: Why the Overrepresentation?" *Child Abuse and Neglect* 16 (1992): 541–551.

Morrison, Donna Ruane, and Amy Ritualo. "Routes to Children's Economic Recovery After Divorce: Are Cohabitation and Remarriage Equivalent?" *American Sociological Review* 65 (2000): 560–580.

National Domestic Violence Hotline. http://www.ndvh.org.

National Online Resource Center on Violence against Women. http://www.vawnet.org.

Newberger, Eli H., Robert B. Reed, Jessica H. Daniel, James N. Hyde, and Milton Kotelchuck. "Pediatric Social Illness: Toward an Etiologic Classification." *Pediatrics* 60 (1977): 178–185.

Newcomb, Michael D., and P. M. Bentler. "Assessment of Personality and Demographic Aspects of Cohabitation and Marital Success." *Journal of Personality Assessment* 44 (1980): 11–24.

Office of Justice Programs, Bureau of Justice Statistics. *Criminal Victimization in the United States, 1992.* U.S. Department of Justice, 1994, p. 31. NCJ-145125.

———. *Intimate Partner Violence, 1993–2001.* U.S. Department of Justice, 2003. NCJ 197838.

O'Keefe, Maura. "Racial/Ethnic Differences among Battered Women and their Children." *Journal of Child and Family Studies* 3 (1994): 283–305.

Pagelow, Mildred Daley. *Woman-Battering: Victims and Their Experiences.* Beverly Hills, CA: Sage Publications, 1981.

Paternoster, Raymond. "The Deterrent Effect of the Perceived Certainty and Severity of Punishment: A Review of the Evidence and Issues." *Justice Quarterly* 4 (1987): 173.

Popenoe, David, and Barbara Dafoe Whitehead. "Should We Live Together? What Young Adults Need to Know about Cohabitation before Marriage." *The National Marriage Project,* Rutgers University, 2002.

Pruitt, Dean G., and Jeffrey Z. Rubin. *Social Conflict: Escalation, Stalemate, and Settlement.* New York: Random House, 1986.

Raley, Kelly R., Michelle L. Frisco, and Elizabeth Wildsmith. "Maternal Cohabitation and Educational Success." *Sociology of Education* 78 (2005): 144–164.

Rhoads, Steven E. *Taking Sex Differences Seriously.* San Francisco: Encounter Books, 2004.

Riger, Stephanie, and Margaret T. Gordon. "The Fear of Rape: A Study in Social Control." *Journal of Social Issues* 37 (1981): 71.

Roberts, Albert R. "Psychosocial Characteristics of Batterers: A Study of 234 Men Charged with Domestic Violence Offences." *Journal of Family Violence* 2 (1987): 81–93.

Robins, Lee, and Darrel Regier. *Psychiatric Disorders in America: The Epidemiologic Catchment Area Study.* New York: The Free Press, 1991.

Shackelford, Todd K. "Cohabitation, Marriage and Murder." *Aggressive Behavior* 27 (2001): 284–291.

Smock, Pamela. "Cohabitation in the United States: An Appraisal of Research Themes, Findings, and Implications." *Annual Review of Sociology* 26 (2000): 1–20.

Sorenson, Susan B., Dawn M. Upchurch, and Haikang Shen. "Violence and Injury in Marital Arguments: Risk Patterns and Gender Differences." *American Journal of Public Health* 86 (1996): 35–40.

Stanko, Elizabeth A. *Intimate Intrusions: Women's Experience of Male Violence.* London: Routledge and Kegan Paul, 1985.

Stets, Jan E. "Cohabiting and Marital Aggression: The Role of Social Isolation." *Journal of Marriage and the Family* 53 (1991): 669–680.

———. "The Link between Past and Present Intimate Relationships." *Journal of Family Issues* 14 (1993): 236–260.

Stets, Jan E., and Peter J. Burke. "Gender, Control and Interaction." *Social Psychology Quarterly* 59 (1996): 193–220.

Stets, Jan E., and Maureen A. Pirog-Good. "Violence in Dating Relationships." *Social Psychology Quarterly* 50 (1987): 237–246.

———. "Patterns of Physical and Sexual Abuse for Men and Women in Dating Relationships: A Descriptive Analysis." *Journal of Family Violence* 4 (1989): 63–76.

Stets, Jan E., and Murray A. Straus. "The Marriage License as a Hitting License: A Comparison of Assaults in Dating, Cohabiting, and Married Couples." *Journal of Family Violence* 4 (1989): 161–180.

Stiffman, Michael. "Household Composition and Risk of Fatal Child Maltreatment." *Pediatrics* 109 (2002): 615–621.

Tedeschi, James T. "Threats and Promises." In *The Structure of Conflict,* edited by P. Swingle. New York: Academic Press, 1970, pp. 155–192.

Tedeschi, James T., and Richard B. Felson. *Violence, Aggression, and Coercive Actions.* Washington: APA Books, 1994.

Testa, Maria, Jennifer A. Livingston, and Kenneth E. Leonard. "Women's Substance Use and Experiences of Intimate Partner Violence: A Longitudinal Investigation among a Community Sample." *Addictive Behaviors* 28 (2003): 1649–1664.

Thompson, Elizabeth, T. L. Hanson, and S. S. McLanahan. "Family Structure and Child Well-Being: Economic Resources Versus Parental Behaviors." *Social Forces* 73 (1994): 221–242.

Thomson, Elizabeth, and Ugo Colella. "Cohabitation and Marital Stability: Quality or Commitment?" *Journal of Marriage and the Family* 54 (1992): 259–267.

Treas, Judith, and Deirdre Giesen. "Sexual Fidelity among Married and Cohabiting Americans." *Journal of Marriage and the Family* 62 (2000): 48–60.

U.S. Census Bureau. "Married-Couple and Unmarried-Partner Households, 2000." *Census 2000 Special Reports,* 2003.

Waite, Linda J., and Maggie Gallagher. *The Case for Marriage: Why Married People Are Happier, Healthier, and Better Off Financially.* New York: Doubleday, 2000.

Waite, Linda J., Frances Goldschieder, and C. Witsberger. "Nonfamily Living and the Erosion of Traditional Family Orientations among Adults." *American Sociological Review* 51 (1986): 541–554.

Whitehead, Barbara, and David Popenoe. "The State of Our Unions 2002." *The National Marriage Project,* Rutgers University, June 2002.

Williams, Kirk R., and Richard Hawkins. "The Meaning of Arrest for Wife Assault." *Criminology* 27 (1989): 163.

Wilmoth, Janet, and Gregor Koso. "Does Marital History Matter? Marital Status and Wealth Outcomes among Preretirement Adults." *Journal of Marriage and the Family* 64 (2002): 254–268.

Wilson, James Q. *The Marriage Problem: How Our Culture Has Weakened Families.* New York: HarperCollins, 2002.

Wilson, Margo, Martin Daly, and Christine Wright. "Uxoricide in Canada: Demographic Risk Pattern." *Canadian Journal of Criminology* 35 (1993): 263–291.

Wilson, Margo, Holly Johnson, and Martin Daly. "Lethal and Nonlethal Violence against Wives." *Canadian Journal of Criminology* 37 (1998): 331–361.

Wilson, William J., R. Aponte, and K. Neckerman. "Joblessness Versus Welfare Effects: A Further Reexamination." In *The Truly Disadvantaged: The Inner City, the Underclass, and Public Policy*. Chicago: University of Chicago Press, 1985.

Wu, Zheng. "Premarital Cohabitation and Postmarital Cohabiting Union Formation." *Journal of Family Issues* 16 (1995): 212–232.

Yllo, Kersti, and Murray A. Straus. "Interpersonal Violence among Married and Cohabiting Couples." *Family Relations* 30 (1981): 339–347.

COMMUNITY RESPONSE TO DOMESTIC VIOLENCE

The Importance of a Community Response

When one considers domestic violence, one too often assumes that violence within a family is a private problem, an issue to be resolved by the persons involved. Certainly, domestic violence has costs for the victim. Included in such costs are the serious physical injuries and the psychological damage that a victim suffers, as well as a victim's feelings of powerlessness, hopelessness, and fear. However, the negative impact of domestic violence extends far beyond the family and affects the entire community in which it occurs. For example, a community absorbs financial costs when police must intervene in domestic disputes or serve warrants to abusers. Also, communities absorb costs for the judicial prosecution of the abuser. Because domestic violence remains the number one reason women seek emergency medical care, a community also assumes some of the costs for a victim's medical treatment. Further, when children are socialized in a violent home environment, the social costs for a community increase exponentially.

Children who are exposed to domestic violence can experience both immediate and lifelong effects. First is the fact that children who grow up in violent homes are more likely to become abusive adults. Additionally, these same children are at greater risk for physical abuse, sexual abuse, and neglect. These children are often lonely and isolated from other children; they often struggle with behavioral problems, mental health problems, and school problems. Coupling the judicial and medical costs with the costs that children pay,

there is no doubt that domestic violence is a public issue and requires a response from the larger community.

Many communities across America have taken steps to respond to domestic violence. Within these communities law enforcement officers have been specially trained to respond to domestic violence situations and enforce laws that protect victims and children. In the same fashion, prosecutors and judges have committed themselves to taking a strong stand against perpetrators of domestic violence and have increased efforts to prosecute and punish abusers. Even medical personnel and community leaders have been trained to take action in situations where it is suspected that the victim's injuries are a result of domestic violence. Perhaps one of the most important steps in a community's response is the formation of an emergency shelter.

History of the Shelter Movement

Historians of the shelter movement recognize that work with battered women probably began in Bologna, Italy, ca. 1563. During that time women knew which convent in town would hide them from their batterers or which convent would send them to safe space in another town. However, more recent history recognizes the work of Erin Pizzey, who in 1971 organized a group of women to create a community center for homeless women and children in London, England. While not initially intended, this same center later offered refuge to battered women. Inspired by both Pizzey's work and the rise of feminism's second wave, emergency shelters began to be developed by grassroots organizations in the United States in the 1970s. The first shelter to be opened in the United States was founded in 1974 in St. Paul, Minnesota. Since that time, over 2,000 shelters have been opened around the nation.

Domestic Violence Shelters

Created for the purpose of helping female victims of domestic violence, emergency shelters provide a temporary safe space and physical safety for battered women and their children. Along with this safe space are the necessary food, clothing, and personal amenities needed by victims. This immediate and temporary shelter is, for many victims, an important step toward leaving an abusive relationship. Yet, supplying food, clothing, and shelter on a limited-time basis is not always enough to resolve the personal problems that a victim faces or the social problems that domestic violence creates for the larger community. Thus, over the past twenty-five years emergency shelters have added a comprehensive list of victim and community services to their agendas.

Today many shelters offer a 24-hour crisis hotline that anyone may dial to receive information and advocacy concerning domestic violence. Shelters also offer individual and group counseling, as well as support groups for both mothers and children. Shelters sometimes provide court advocacy, helping victims secure legal and protective services. In addition, shelters often serve as advocates for a victim's medical services, financial assistance, vocational training, and job placement. For many shelters, transitional housing has been added: housing that allows victims to extend their stay in agency-owned secure housing while gaining the resources for independence.

Along with a change in services there has been a shift in the composition of shelter staffs. What once were staffs of local volunteers are now staffs of volunteers and trained professionals who offer educational programs and advocacy work within the community. Undoubtedly, the shelters' staffs have raised the awareness of many community members by educating the public about issues surrounding domestic violence. Beyond teaching the public that domestic violence is a punishable crime, shelter staffs have lobbied for legislative actions that would protect and provide for victims. Perhaps one of the most important pieces of legislation is the Violence against Women Act of 1994, which provided $1.62 billion in funding over a six-year period, broadening the range of services and counseling available to women who were victims of abuse.

Future Challenges

After more than a quarter-century of laborious work by many activists and other concerned citizens, one might conclude that emergency shelters are an integral part of communities around the nation and available to anyone who is victimized by domestic violence. Yet, the reality is that emergency shelters are not available in every community. While there are more than 2,000 shelters in the nation at the start of the twenty-first century, current estimates suggest that the number of domestic violence victims continues to exceed the capacity of existing shelters.

There are many reasons to explain the shortage of emergency shelters. One of the most obvious and important challenges to face is increasing each community's understanding of domestic violence. Though the consciousness of many community members has been raised, persons who work with and on behalf of victims of domestic violence can attest to the fact that far too many community members do not understand the objective facts about domestic violence. For example, many people still believe that "If she didn't like it, she would leave," or ask: "Why does she stay?" Many people blame the victim. Unfortunately the attitude of "blaming the victim" places the responsibility for combating the problem of domestic violence squarely on the shoulders of the victim and slows a collective community response.

Even for those communities that have public support for the creation of an emergency shelter there is the immediate problem of securing government funding and local philanthropic support. Undoubtedly, funding on the federal and state levels has improved over the course of a decade. In fact, the total budget for some shelters is now secured through federal and state funding. However, there remain too many shelters that do not receive adequate funding from state or federal government, too many shelters that have had their budgets trimmed by state legislatures, and too many shelters that must depend upon the generosity of local community members to keep their doors open and provide necessary services. Without adequate funding, shelters are limited in the resources that can be provided to victims and are challenged when trying to find professionals to fulfill these services.

As shelters continue to face funding problems, some also face the problems of being understaffed and being unable to gain cooperation from other community agencies and unsupportive community members. Furthermore, shelters are not dispersed evenly throughout the nation. At greatest risk for not having access to a shelter are rural women. Factually speaking, rural women are often in the position of traveling miles to reach safe space. Elderly women, lesbians, and Hispanic women, as well as women from other minority populations, also face difficulty when they seek help from shelters that are less inclusive. Further, many shelters are not prepared to accommodate the needs of women with disabilities.

In spite of the challenges that shelters face, they have been rated as the most effective and helpful resource for victims of domestic violence and remain the only hope for many women and children living in violent situations. It is thus imperative that communities around the nation seriously consider the development of safe spaces for victims of domestic violence. It is important that these same communities come to recognize the challenges that shelters face and attempt to learn from past mistakes. It is only with a sincere community response that society can combat the violence that exists and prevent this violence from spilling over into the next generation.

N. JANE MCCANDLESS

See also **Batterer Intervention Programs; Cross-Cultural Perspectives on Domestic Violence; Mandatory Arrest Policies; Worldwide Sociological Precedents Supporting Domestic Violence from Ancient to Modern Times**

Further Reading

Bowen, Linda, Victoria Gwiasda, and M. Mitchell Brown. "Engaging Community Residents to Prevent Violence." *Journal of Interpersonal Violence* 3 (2004): 356–367.

Chanley, Sharon, Jesse J. Chanley, Jr., and Heather E. Campbell. "Providing Refuge: The Value of Domestic Violence Shelter Services." *American Review of Public Administration* 4 (2001): 393–413.

Domestic Violence Awareness: Stop the Cycle of Violence: What You Can Do. Washington: U.S. Department of Justice, 1996.

Murphy-Milano, Susan. *Defending Our Lives: Getting Away from Domestic Violence and Staying Safe.* New York: Anchor, 1996.

Roberts, Albert R., ed. *Battered Women and Their Families: Intervention Strategies and Treatment Programs.* New York: Springer, 1998.

Roberts, Albert R., and Sarah J. Lewis. "Giving Them Shelter: National Organizational Survey of Shelters for Battered Women and Their Children." *Journal of Community Psychology* 6 (2000): 669–681.

COMMUNITY RESPONSE TO GAY AND LESBIAN DOMESTIC VIOLENCE

Perceptions of Domestic Violence

Most people generally define domestic violence as a social problem between men and women. Specifically, it is believed that domestic violence involves men physically, sexually, or emotionally assaulting women with the specific intent of causing them harm. Therefore, domestic violence is frequently considered a problem that occurs only between men and women—with men engaged as batterers and women engaged as victims. This understanding of domestic violence is linked to society's gendered socialization process wherein one learns that it is appropriate, and sometimes even expected and

required, for a man to engage in violent activity. Defining women as the polar opposite of men, societal norms perpetuate the belief that being a woman is not defined by acts of violence, but by acts of compassion. One is taught that women are caretakers, kind and emotional people who rarely, if ever, respond aggressively and violently. These same gender messages are further reinforced by cultural images depicting men as the ones who fend off the enemy through violent actions, and women as the ones prepared to comfort the men when the violent confrontation has ended. The corollary to this is that such messages reinforce a heterosexual norm. If such gender stereotypes do not, in reality, apply to all men and women who identify as heterosexual, still less do they apply to men and women who identify as gay or lesbian. Furthermore, if one has not been taught about gay or lesbian domestic violence, if one has not read about gay or lesbian domestic violence, if one has not viewed depictions of gay and lesbian domestic violence in popular entertainment, or if the community is not engaged in gay and lesbian domestic violence prevention efforts, then surely it must not exist.

Domestic Violence in Gay and Lesbian Relationships

When one utilizes a newer terminology, substituting the term "intimate partner violence" for "domestic violence," one can begin to understand that this type of violence is not an issue of being male or female, but is an issue of power. One can come to recognize that violence can occur in gay and lesbian relationships. In fact, studies have reported that the levels of violence found in both gay and lesbian relationships mirror the amounts of domestic violence found in heterosexual relationships. While the numbers are not exact, researchers consistently argue that between 25 and 40 percent of both heterosexual and gay/lesbian couples have engaged in acts of violence with an intimate partner. Also, as with heterosexual couples, acts of domestic violence within gay and lesbian relationships include a myriad of harmful actions, from physical and sexual assaults to financial and emotional abuse. These acts of domestic violence have high costs for gay and lesbian victims, just as they do for victims in heterosexual relationships. Costs to all victims of domestic violence include physical injuries, psychological and emotional damages, and feelings of powerlessness, hopelessness, and fear.

Acknowledging the rates, types, and costs of violence in all situations of domestic violence, there still exist differences between acts of domestic violence within heterosexual couples versus gay and lesbian couples. One difference is found in specific ways in which gays and lesbians may be vulnerable to abuse. For example, while the gay or lesbian abuser, just like the heterosexual abuser, may push, shove, hit, and kick, the gay or lesbian abuser might also use threats of "outing" his or her partner. For those persons who are accepting of alternative lifestyles, it is difficult to image how "outing" someone can be abusive. However, for the victim who does not live an open lifestyle,

who fears for loss of family ties, the loss of professional networks, or backlash from the larger community, this single threat produces anxiety and fear. Scholars have also argued that HIV/AIDS plays a role in some domestic violence situations within the gay community. While HIV/AIDS is certainly not a problem exclusive to the gay population, studies have reported that HIV-positive men have higher rates of being abused than all others in the gay community.

Responding to Gay and Lesbian Domestic Violence

Because domestic violence is not only a serious social problem within the heterosexual community, but also a serious social problem within the gay and lesbian community, it is imperative that every victim regardless of sexual orientation have someone to turn to for help. Intervention by a third party is vitally important in helping any victim escape a violent situation. Unfortunately, however, those who often serve as third parties for members of the heterosexual community are not always inclusive of gay and lesbian victims of domestic violence.

Law enforcement officers are among the most important resources for victims of domestic violence, as it is an officer who is frequently the first responder in such situations. For that reason, law enforcement personnel are specially trained to respond to domestic violence situations, though such training centers on domestic violence involving heterosexual couples. The officer's role in these cases is simple: to enforce the laws that protect the victim and her or his children. However, for gays and lesbians, it is often intimidating and/or discouraging to report acts of domestic violence to law enforcement. More often than not, law enforcement officers are not specially trained to deal with domestic violence situations among gay and lesbian couples, making it difficult for an officer to define—and therefore to properly, sensitively, and effectively respond to—same-sex domestic violence. Without an understanding of such situations it becomes too easy for law enforcement to define an act of lesbian domestic violence as a "catfight" between two women, or an act of gay domestic violence as just another fight between two men. Studies have also indicated that gays and lesbians who report acts of domestic violence are often confronted with the arresting officer's homophobia or disdain for the gay/lesbian lifestyle. As harsh as it sounds, sometimes it is too easy for the arresting officer to walk away, believing that persons who live "that way" deserve what they get. The end result is that when a law enforcement officer does not intervene and leaves the victim in the abusive situation, the victim is further traumatized.

In the same fashion, prosecutors and judges have committed themselves to taking a strong stand against perpetrators of domestic violence in heterosexual relationships and have increased efforts to prosecute and punish abusers. However, in cases of gay and lesbian domestic violence, the law is not always helpful. Scholars have pointed out the negative impact of states defining marriage as "a union between two persons of the opposite sex" and attempts at the federal level to create a constitutional amendment banning gay marriage. Prohibiting states from recognizing a relationship between two adults living together outside of the legalized union of marriage often means that they cannot be granted the same legal rights as two adults who are married. Therefore, if domestic violence laws are written to indicate that domestic violence reflects violence between "married people," gays, lesbians, and, in some cases, heterosexual couples who are cohabiting do not have legal grounds to use such laws. While gays and lesbians can invoke the use of less weighty laws, such as misdemeanor assault charges, the use of domestic violence charges often carry more severe penalties. Further, few states offer domestic violence laws that allow gays and lesbians the right to secure a restraining order against an abusive partner, apply for a protective order, or prosecute their batterer.

Like law enforcement officers, medical personnel and community leaders have also been trained to take action in situations where it is suspected that the victim's injuries are the result of domestic violence. However, like law enforcement personnel, few professionals in these fields have been trained in issues relevant to gay and lesbian domestic violence. If the same homophobia found in the general population is played out in the responses of professionals who assist domestic violence victims, gay and lesbian victims have little hope of receiving an effective response to their immediate situation.

Perhaps one of the most important steps in a community's response to domestic violence is the funding and establishment of shelters where victims are offered safe space and physical safety from their abusers. The reality is, however, that emergency shelters are not generally prepared to deal with gays and lesbians seeking refuge from situations of domestic violence. Too often shelter staffs are trained to think of acts of domestic violence in terms of men abusing women, leaving lesbians and, even more so, gay males feeling unwelcome. It is

the rare domestic violence shelter that has the facilities, or the willingness, to offer safe space to a gay male who has been abused. Without access to a shelter, the victim of domestic violence does not have access to information, advocacy, counseling, support groups, legal and protective aid, or any number of services that shelter staffs provide.

In cases of gay and lesbian domestic violence, if the criminal justice system, the medical institution, and the staffs at emergency shelters cannot or will not respond to or meet the needs of the victim, many gays and lesbians are left with only the option of turning to family and friends for help. Again, however, this is not always possible for many. If friends or relatives do not know that the individual is gay or lesbian, or do not approve of the gay or lesbian lifestyle, there is little, if any, support to be offered. Without some understanding of the dynamics of domestic violence, even one's closest friends can harbor a victim-blaming attitude and wonder what the victim did to deserve the abuse; this difficulty is also faced by many heterosexual domestic violence victims. This fosters the belief that the violence is the fault of the victim and that it is the victim, not the abuser, who must change her or his behaviors.

Change for the Future

With few resources available to victims of gay and lesbian domestic violence, it is not surprising to find advocates calling for change. Some of the most comprehensive recommendations for change have come from the National Coalition of Anti-Violence Programs. These recommendations call for, among other things, an expansion of existing community-based services for domestic violence victims and their inclusion of services for gay and lesbian victims of domestic violence. It is imperative that the services provided for heterosexual victims of domestic violence be extended to gay and lesbian victims. Preventative education aimed at gays and lesbians is also necessary. Educational programming that addresses the existence and dynamics of gay and lesbian domestic violence must be established for all professionals who assist domestic violence victims. Most importantly, the law must protect all victims of domestic violence and hold all abusers accountable for their actions. Helping the victim is vital, but holding the abuser accountable for her or his actions is one of the most important steps toward ending the violence.

Without challenging societal perceptions of victims and perpetrators of domestic violence and without taking seriously the recommendations for future changes toward assisting all victims and ending domestic violence in all relationships, a significant portion of the population is left to face a very serious, and sometimes deadly, situation on their own. This is unacceptable and unnecessary, as everyone has the right to live their lives free from violence.

N. JANE MCCANDLESS

See also **Community Response to Domestic Violence; Gay and Bisexual Male Domestic Violence; Gay Domestic Violence, Police Attitudes and Behaviors toward; Gender Socialization and Gay Male Domestic Violence; Lesbian Battering; Same-Sex Domestic Violence: Comparing Venezuela and the United States; Victim-Blaming Theory**

Further Reading

Burke, T., and S. Owen. "Same-Sex Domestic Violence: Is Anyone Listening?" *Gay and Lesbian Review Worldwide* 13, no. 1 (2006): 6.

Kaschak, E. "Intimate Betrayal: Domestic Violence in Lesbian Relationships." *Women and Therapy* 23, no. 3 (2001): 1.

Landolt, M., and D. Dutton. "Power and Personality: An Analysis of Gay Male Intimate Abuse." *Sex Roles* 37, no. 5/6 (1997): 335.

McClennen, J. "Domestic Violence between Same-Gender Partners." *Journal of Interpersonal Violence* 20, no. 2 (2005): 149.

Renzetti, C. M. *Violent Betrayal: Partner Abuse in Lesbian Relationships*. Newbury Park, CA: Sage, 1992.

Seelau, E., S. Seelau, and P. Poorman. "Gender and Role-Based Perceptions of Domestic Abuse: Does Sexual Orientation Matter?" *Behavioral Sciences and the Law* 21 (2003): 199.

COMPASSIONATE HOMICIDE AND SPOUSAL VIOLENCE

On average, intimate partners kill approximately 2,000 Americans every year. According to the Bureau of Justice Statistics (Rennison 2002), spouses, ex-spouses, and other intimate partners were responsible for 42 percent of the homicides of female victims and 9 percent of homicides of male victims for which an offender was determined between 1976 and 2002. Although only 24 percent of all homicide victims during those years were female, 63 percent of the victims killed by intimate partners were female. Although the annual numbers of intimate-partner homicides decreased between 1976 and 1998, the percentage of victims who were women increased steadily from 54 percent to 72 percent over this period. Among the many diverse and complex motives for intimate-partner homicide, compassion is the alleged motive in a relatively small but rapidly increasing number of cases each year.

Compassionate homicide is defined as the killing of one individual by another with the stated intention of reducing the physical or mental suffering of the individual who dies. Compassionate homicide is sometimes subdivided into two categories: euthanasia and mercy killing. The term *euthanasia* is used more frequently in terms of homicides in medical settings and for those that are legally sanctioned. The term *mercy killing* is used more frequently to describe those homicides that occur outside of medical settings, are carried out in secrecy, and are not legally sanctioned. The distinctions between euthanasia and mercy killing, however, are inconsistent, and the terms are often used interchangeably. Compassionate homicide is considered to be voluntary when the individual who is killed requests or consents to die and involuntary when the individual who is killed does not request or consent to die. Death may result from an act of commission or an act of omission. In most cases, the physical or mental suffering considered to justify compassionate homicide is the result of a terminal disease or chronic disability, but any form of suffering might be considered grounds for compassionate homicide.

Assisted suicide is a distinct but closely related phenomenon. Assisted suicide refers to the taking of one's own life with the help of another individual. It differs from voluntary compassionate homicide because the individual dies as a result of his or her own actions. For example, assistance may consist of supplying the individual with a lethal dose of medication or a weapon with the knowledge that he or she intends to commit suicide; but actions by an individual that actually result in another person's death, with or without that individual's consent, cannot be properly construed as assisted suicide, since they meet the technical definition of homicide. In practice, the line between assisted suicide and compassionate homicide often blurs. Interactions with others influence individual intentions, and the line between assistance and coercion is often unclear. For example, an individual may anticipate that he will instinctively fight for his life even as he states that he wishes to die, and thus asks another person to restrain him if he attempts to remove a suffocating object from his face. Most states have specific laws against assisting in another person's suicide or counseling another person to commit suicide. Some other states do not have specific laws but prosecute assisted suicide under common law. Oregon permits physician-assisted suicide under specified conditions, and a few other states have no criminal prohibition of assisted suicide as of 2005.

The term *acquiescent suicide* sometimes has been used to refer to acts of suicide, with or without assistance, in which the individual chooses to die as a result of succumbing to the social influence. This might include the expectations of significant others that the individual should die or the message implicit in some institutional environments that life is essentially over. Although some specific cases may involve violations of other laws, the concept of acquiescent suicide has no standing in criminal law; however, it is an important phenomenon from psychological, sociological, and ethical perspectives. In some cultures, widows may kill themselves to acquiesce to societal expectations of the sacrifice of the widow's life when the husband dies, as in the Indian custom of Sati. Fear of being forcibly killed by other members of the community or of living in shame in a community that views a widow as immoral for continuing to live may be powerful suicidal influences, even when they have not been overtly expressed. Similarly, the expectation that a person with a disability should die rather than become a burden on family or the state may result in acquiescent suicide. Intimate partners sometimes exert incredible dominance and control, particularly in abusive relationships. The ultimate expression of submission to this kind of dominance may be an acquiescent suicide on command of the dominant partner.

In most places, both assisted suicide and compassionate homicide are illegal acts. Some forms of assisted suicide and euthanasia, however, are permitted in Oregon, the Netherlands, Belgium,

and a few other jurisdictions. In addition, the U.S. Supreme Court has determined that while there is no constitutional right to assisted suicide, states may pass laws permitting and regulating assisted suicide. Finally, courts have endorsed some forms of compassionate homicide, such as withholding life-prolonging treatment from an individual who is close to death or who makes a competent choice to refuse treatment, even where compassionate homicide and assisted suicide have otherwise been prohibited. In addition, various actions that meet the technical definitions of compassionate homicide or assisted suicide are tolerated in many countries, in spite of the fact that they are officially criminal offenses.

Advocates for assisted suicide and compassionate homicide argue that people should be able to exercise choice about when to die, that the criminalization of these acts results in unnecessary suffering, and that the potential for abuse and error can be controlled by procedural safeguards. Critics of these acts suggest that the potential for error and abuse is too high and impossible to adequately control, that in many cases the individuals who are killed do not request or consent to die, and that suicide is typically an irrational act. Critics argue that legalizing the killing of other human beings based on intentions invites abuse, while advocates argue that society already justifies some killings based on intention in the case of self-defense.

The intent of people who engage in compassionate homicide or assisted suicide is often unclear and subject to conflicting interpretations. For example, in one case, staff members who killed nursing home patients were defended as acting from compassion to end the patients' suffering. Evidence presented at trial, however, indicated that they chose their victims based on the first letter of their last names, not based on suffering or compassion. Criminal profilers suggest that the real intentions of mercy killers are often very different from the stated intentions of relieving suffering. The *Crime Classification Manual*, a handbook for criminal profiling and forensic psychology, classifies these acts as "Mercy Homicide (s)." According to these experts:

> Death at the hand of a mercy killer results from the offender's claim/perception of victim suffering and what the offender believes is his or her duty to relieve it. Most often, the real motivation for mercy killing has little to do with the offender's feelings of compassion and pity for the victim. The sense of power and control the offender derives from killing is usually the real motive. (Douglas, Burgess, Burgess, and Ressler, 1992)

The *Manual* also points out that mercy killers often go on to commit multiple or serial killings. Since motivations can never be directly observed and behavior is typically the product of multiple and complex factors, it is impossible to determine with certainty what motivational factors are present, the relative importance of various motivational factors, or how these various factors interact in a particular case. In addition, when the person who kills and the person who is killed are members of the same family, many other potential motivations may be present. For example, economic considerations may influence the decision-making process when an inheritance is at stake or when the costs of continued medical care would be substantial.

Humphry and Wickett (1990) present a history of mercy killing from their perspective as advocates for compassionate homicide and assisted suicide. They analyzed 151 cases of euthanasia and defined mercy killing as the taking of a loved one's life to relieve suffering. These cases typically involved husbands killing wives and occasionally wives killing husbands. Many of these spousal cases involved double suicides or murder-suicides, and those cases involved almost exclusively husbands and wives. Humphry and Wickett reported that in more than 80 percent of euthanasia cases, a dominant male partner killed a spouse and that the most frequent method of killing was firearms. They suggest that the demands of caring for a spouse with a severe illness or disability may be too great and that the killing of a spouse may function as much to release the caregiving spouse from the burden of care as to release the individual who is ill or disabled from further suffering. This suggests an obvious potential conflict of interest when mercy killing or assisted suicide occurs within a spousal relationship and raises questions about when spousal euthanasia serves as a convenient rationale for common murder or a vulnerable partner being driven to suicide.

Other analyses have confirmed the finding that more women than men die by assisted suicide, and women usually are assisted to die by men. This finding is particularly striking considering that women are likely to be younger than their spouses and are typically in better health for their age. Some analysts suggest that when women are no longer viewed as valuable sexual partners because of their age or as efficient homemakers because of their illness or disability, they are disposed of as having outlived their usefulness. Osgood and Eisenhandler (1994) present an analysis of assisted and acquiescent suicide from the perspective of suicidology. They suggest that gender issues and the lack of reasonable alternatives play important roles. In their view many women are more vulnerable to assisted suicide because they are often economically dependent on men, dominated by their male partners, and encouraged by society to view their own value as a function of their ability to take care of others. This gender analysis suggests that wives typically assist their husbands who are ill or disabled by taking care of them, but husbands typically assist their wives who are ill or disabled by encouraging them or assisting them to die.

Nevertheless, it should be pointed out that many feminists are strong supporters of an individual's right to die at a time of one's own choosing and of legalization of assisted suicide and euthanasia. For many women, the right to choose how and when to die and the right to choose death to avoid mental or physical suffering are extensions of the principle of choice and control over their own bodies and lives.

High-Profile Cases

Many cases of assisted suicide and compassionate homicide have been at the center of considerable controversy. The following cases received a great deal of public and media attention for a variety of reasons, and subsequently had influence on the public debate. The cases presented here were chosen, in part, to represent the diversity of circumstances and attributes of cases of spousal euthanasia and assisted suicide. It should be noted that the cases that attained the highest profiles are not likely to be typical of the cases that occur most frequently. Cases typically gain high profiles because the individuals involved are already famous, because the alleged offenders are charged, or because they become the subject of a book or play. Only a tiny minority of cases involve people who are already famous or have books written about them, and in many cases, no one is ever charged or the case is dismissed before trial. Many others are settled by plea agreements. Of cases that do reach trial, a few lead to murder or manslaughter convictions with prison sentences, and a few result in acquittals. Most appear to end in convictions for crimes other than murder, with suspended sentences or probation.

In 1920, Frank C. Roberts was charged in Michigan for poisoning his wife Katie Roberts, who had multiple sclerosis. He pleaded guilty and was sentenced to life in prison. He appealed, however, arguing that he had only assisted his wife by preparing the poison, which she drank willingly. Since she had died as a result of suicide, he argued that he

185

could not be an accessory to suicide because suicide was not a crime in Michigan. The court heard arguments that the law that treated assisted suicide like murder was antiquated and cruel. The Michigan Supreme Court, however, upheld the sentence, since Roberts had been charged with and pled guilty to murder, not accomplice to suicide, for his part in his wife's death.

The Roberts case may have been the first American trial over assisted suicide, and it received widespread national and international attention. Wolfgang Liebeneiner's film *I Accuse (Ich klage an)* (1941) presented a trial with obvious parallels to the Roberts' trial. In the film, a loving husband is tried for murder because he reluctantly poisoned his wife, who had multiple sclerosis. It ends with the husband accusing society of being the real criminals for enforcing an outmoded law that results in unnecessary suffering. *I Accuse* received international acclaim, including a gold medal at the Venice Film Festival. Long after the end of World War II, Liebeneiner (1965) remained adamant that "*I Accuse* . . . was no Nazi propaganda film, but on the contrary a document of humanity in an inhuman time" (p. 149). Nevertheless, most experts consider this film to have been among the most sophisticated tools of Nazi propaganda, intended to promote public acceptance for the massive Nazi euthanasia program that exterminated approximately 275,000 people with disabilities and eventually evolved into the Holocaust.

In 1958, author Lael Wertenbaker published *Death of a Man,* describing how she helped her husband, who had cancer, kill himself in France. The book received considerable attention and was made into a Broadway play called *A Gift of Time* in 1962. The play, starring Henry Fonda and Olivia de Havilland, brought more attention to the topic. *Death of a Man* was the first of a series of autobiographical accounts of assisted suicides, and also provides an example of a wife participating in the death of a husband, which occurs less frequently than husbands participating in the deaths of their wives.

In 1983, novelist, social critic, and euthanasia advocate Arthur Koestler, who was seventy-seven years old and had Parkinson's disease and leukemia, committed suicide. He indicated that he did not want to continue to live in a debilitated state. His third wife, Cynthia, who indicated that she could not live without him, committed suicide along with him, though Cynthia was twenty-one years younger and healthy. At the time, even some advocates for compassionate homicide raised concerns over her willingness to follow her husband to the grave.

Critics of compassionate homicide and assisted suicide viewed Cynthia Koestler's death as an acquiescent suicide, imposed on her by the expectations of others. Some feminists saw this act as a variation of the Indian custom of Sati, in which widows immolate themselves on their husband's funeral pyre, the ultimate expression of a belief system in which women are valued only as caregivers for their husbands. In their view, Koestler had treated his wife and the family dog—which he also killed when he committed suicide—in much the same way. This concern over whether Cynthia Koestler's death was truly voluntary was exacerbated some time after Koestler's death when there were a number of accusations that Koestler had been a repeated rapist who enjoyed battering and bullying women. Koestler was quoted as saying that he carefully selected women he could dominate and control: "I always picked one type; beautiful Cinderellas, infantile and inhibited, prone to being subdued by bullying" (in Cockburn 1998, p. 9). Nevertheless, others argued that Cynthia Koestler was an intelligent adult who made an autonomous choice to die and that her choice should be respected rather than questioned or demeaned. From this perspective, suicide should be respected as an autonomous and rational act for avoiding mental as well as physical suffering, and grief or loneliness are presented as equally valid reasons for suicide as are illness or disability.

In 1985, Roswell Gilbert killed his wife, Emily, who had Alzheimer's disease. He shot her once in the head at close range, but when she didn't die he went to get another bullet, reloaded, and shot her a second time. The couple had been married for fifty-one years when he killed her. Many people and most published stories suggested that this was an act of love by a devoted husband, but others raised questions about his motivation, suggesting that he simply wanted to rid himself of the responsibility of caring for an ailing wife. While there was no question about the fact that Emily Gilbert had needed care due to her Alzheimer's disease, she was not yet in a state of severe debilitation, and she was certainly not in a terminal state. In the end, Gilbert was convicted of murder by a Florida jury and sentenced to seventy-five years in prison with a requirement to serve twenty-five years before being considered for parole. He was granted clemency and released in 1990, and died in 1994.

Derek Humphry and Ann Wickett, who cofounded the Hemlock Society and collaborated as authors on a number of works advocating for the acceptance of assisted suicide and euthanasia, were also at the center of their own controversy.

Humphry participated in the death of his first wife, who had breast cancer, helping her commit suicide in 1975. Ann Wickett helped Humphry write *Jean's Way,* an emotionally wrenching account of his wife's illness and suicide that portrayed assisted suicide in a very positive light. Subsequently, Ann Wickett and Derek Humphry married, but after Wickett developed breast cancer and underwent surgery in 1989, she claimed that Humphry was trying to coerce her to commit suicide. Humphry and Wickett parted ways. In the midst of the bitter dispute, Wickett claimed that Humphry had actually murdered his first wife, and Humphry claimed that Wickett had been responsible for her parents' deaths. Formerly an advocate for assisted suicide and euthanasia, Wickett recanted much of her previous support for the "right to die" and joined forces with anti-euthanasia advocates before killing herself at age forty-nine with a drug overdose and leaving a note blaming Humphry for driving her to suicide. Humphry claimed that she was simply mentally unbalanced.

In 1997, in a case that clearly tested the limits of the mercy-killing defense, Gaye Elisabeth Lock was beaten to death with a hammer by her husband, Peter Lock, who then ransacked the house in an attempt to blame the crime on an intruder. Although Gaye Lock was not ill or disabled and the brutal nature of the murder did not convey an act of compassion, her husband's lawyer and a psychiatrist defended his actions as a mercy killing. They argued that Lock knew that his wife would be severely distressed when she found out that he had failed to file her tax returns for her. Rather than allow her to suffer, he acted out of compassion. While admitting that his thinking was distorted, they argued that his intentions were compassionate even if his reasoning was faulty. This rationale attempted to present two choices: (1) to accept Lock's actions as reasonable acts of compassion, or (2) to assume that his belief that he was acting compassionately was so unreasonable that he could not be fully responsible for his actions. Some members of the jury may have agreed with the former or latter view, since the trial ended with a hung jury. A second jury convicted Lock and sentenced him to a mandatory life sentence. The court of appeal ordered a third trial. In the end, the prosecution withdrew the murder charge and accepted a plea of manslaughter with a maximum of eight years in prison.

No case has received more attention than that of Michael and Terri Schiavo. Unlike most previous cases, this case did not involve the determination of whether actions already carried out should be viewed as criminal; it involved determining whether the husband should be empowered to act on his wife's behalf to end her life by having her life-sustaining feeding tube removed. The bitter battle between Terri Schiavo's parents, who wanted to preserve her life, and her husband, who wanted to end it, was reflected in parallel debate in the media and by the public. There were only a few facts that both sides agreed upon. In 1990, Terri Schiavo, who was twenty-six years old, experienced a cardiac arrest. The cardiac arrest seemed to be caused by a potassium imbalance, but there was some uncertainty about exactly what caused the imbalance. Paramedics, who considered the situation unusual, called police, who found no evidence of a crime. Terri Schiavo sustained severe brain damage and never fully regained consciousness. While there was some disagreement about the degree of her impairment, there was no doubt that she was severely impaired and totally dependent on others for care, which included tube feeding. In June 1990, her husband, Michael, was appointed guardian without any objection from other family members. In November 1992, the court awarded more than $1,000,000 for medical malpractice to Michael and Terri Schiavo. During the trial, Michael Schiavo indicated his willingness to care for and seek rehabilitation for his wife. By February 1993, however, Michael Schiavo and Terri Schiavo's parents were engaged in conflict. In May 1998, Michael Schiavo petitioned to have his wife's feeding tube removed to bring about her death. Between that time and Terri Schiavo's death on March 31, 2005, there were repeated court decisions, administrative interventions, and even the creation and nullification of special laws. In the end Michael Schiavo had the phrase "I kept my promise" inscribed on his wife's grave marker. For those who see him as a hero determined to fulfill a promise to his wife, these words are inspiring; for those who view him as a villain determined to control his wife's destiny, the words are chilling.

This case, like most others, is hinged on intentions. One side considered Michael Schiavo to be a loving husband, who acted with the best of intentions to carry out his wife's directions not to prolong her life in a state of extreme dependency. From this perspective, who would be better able to make this difficult decision than a loving husband? The other side considered Michael Schiavo as acting from selfish motives to dispose of a wife he now considered to be burdensome. From this perspective, who would be a worse choice to hold the power of life or death over a woman than a "husband" who has moved on to live with and have children by another woman? Each side could summon indirect evidence that seemed to support its view. Intentions, however, are never directly observable, and wherever the truth lies in this particular case, a general assumption of best or worst intentions applied to all cases will always produce errors.

All of these cases are characterized by ambiguity about intentions and assumptions about whose lives are worth preserving and whose lives would be better ended. There is simply no way for society to allow spouses to exercise control of life or death over each other for the best of purposes without providing an easy mechanism for concealing the worst intentions.

A Disability Rights Perspective

While some individuals with chronic illnesses, terminal illnesses, or disabilities have chosen death by assisted suicide or advocated in favor of assisted suicide, most disability rights organizations and leaders have taken strong positions against assisted suicide and various forms of compassionate homicide. There are a number of reasons for this opposition. First, they believe that there is and can be presented considerable objective evidence of widespread social bias against people with disabilities. They believe that decisions to end the lives of people with disabilities will inevitably be influenced by this bias. The simple assumption that most members of society believe that severe disability or illness may be a legitimate reason for killing someone out of compassion, while other real and imagined sources of suffering (e.g., poverty, racial discrimination, loneliness) are not, probably reflects this bias. Second, they believe that permission to choose death will inevitably lead to undue influence to choose it. This undue influence may come from spouses, the health care system, health insurance companies, or society in general. Third, they believe that spouses and others who might make the decisions to end the lives of people with disabilities are often in a conflict of interest. For example, a husband who has been taken care of by his wife for most of his adult life and is confronted with caring for *her* may have difficulty discerning whether she would not want to go on living like this or whether he does not want to go on being a caregiver.

Finally, many people with acquired disabilities, such as spinal cord injuries, point out that the initial adjustment period is difficult, and that they had times when they would have chosen suicide; but having survived that initial adjustment, however, they are thankful that they were not assisted or encouraged to end their lives. They feel that legitimizing this option would not only have left them vulnerable to the misdeeds of others, it may have led to a catastrophic mistake at their most vulnerable moment.

Beyond the advocacy leadership for people with disabilities, however, support for physician-assisted suicide among people with disabilities is more variable. Gill and Voss (2005), for example, found that among a sample of people with a wide variety of disabilities, attitudes toward legalization of physician-assisted suicide were only slightly less positive than those in the general population, with the majority favoring legalization. Among a subsample with multiple sclerosis, however, a group considered to be particularly likely to personally face issues regarding life or death, support for legalization was much lower, although even in this group 41 percent approved of legalization. Support was much lower among women than among men with disabilities and much lower among African Americans and Hispanics than among whites. These findings are consistent with some general trends.

These trends suggest that many people see potential benefits and also potential risks. They can imagine that there might be some circumstance in which life is so painful or unpleasant that they would prefer a seemingly "easy" death. They can also imagine circumstances in which they might be driven or manipulated toward death, or even simply murdered. If they focus on the possible benefit and ignore the risks, compassionate homicide appears an attractive option. If they focus on the risks and ignore the benefit, so-called compassionate homicide appears to be a deadly pretense for murder. Not surprisingly, the people who have been socially and economically advantaged feel confident about managing the risks. People who have been disadvantaged socially and economically worry more about the risks. People who are healthy and able-bodied assume that they would prefer death to disability and dependency. Research clearly demonstrates, however, that people with disabilities value their lives and rate their quality of life just as high as people without disabilities. To men and women who have always had strong, loving relationships with their spouses, the knowledge that their spouses can end their lives if they become debilitated may be a source of comfort. For millions of other women or men who have been bullied or abused by a spouse, giving that spouse the power of life or death over them is a potential nightmare.

From a disability rights perspective, society's willingness to see the killing of a spouse with a disability as an act of love while seeing other spousal killings as ultimate acts of domestic violence is a clear reflection of social devaluation. All people suffer, and many things can have a negative impact on one's quality of life. Many people suffer as a result of poverty, discrimination, addictions, abuse, social isolation, homelessness, stress, depression, and a variety of other causes. If compassionate homicide is a legitimate alternative for addressing quality of life issues related to disability, it is a legitimate response to issues related to these other threats to quality of life. From the disability rights perspective, assisting suicide of people with disabilities while engaging in suicide prevention for others is a subtle form of extermination.

Intimate Partner Violence and Disability

In addition to intimate partner homicide, which was discussed previously, nonlethal intimate partner violence is extremely common. It produces a vast number of injuries, many of which lead to significant disabilities. In the United States, there are approximately 1,000,000 victims of nonlethal domestic violence reported each year, and researchers estimate that there are an additional 3,000,000 unreported victims each year. About 85 percent of these victims are women. Approximately 25 percent of all women report that they have been victims of intimate partner violence at some time during their lives, although the percentage varies from 18 to 50 percent in various studies. The percentage of men reporting domestic violence in various studies varies from about 10 to 25 percent.

Approximately 63 percent of women who report intimate partner violence have physical injuries, but the number of these injuries resulting in long-term disabilities is unknown. Violence is identified as the cause of approximately 20 to 30 percent of all spinal cord injuries and 10 to 20 percent of brain injuries. In addition, people who sustain brain injuries as a result of violence typically are left with more severe disabilities and encounter more difficulties in rehabilitation. Women who experience intimate partner violence are also more likely to suffer from depression and to have suicidal ideation. Women who have been victims of intimate partner violence report significantly lower quality of life and significantly higher rates of impaired physical health than women who have no history of victimization by an intimate partner. Regardless of the cause of their disabilities, women and men with disabilities are more likely to be abused than women and men without disabilities.

This tangle of relationships between violence and disability has important implications for so-called spousal mercy killings and assisted suicides. Even if one could assume that these killings always took place within the context of a healthy and loving marriage, issues of intentions would be difficult to assess. If one is to believe these statistics that emerge reliably from a large body of research, however, one is forced to conclude that many mercy killings, assisted suicides, and acquiescent suicides occur within the context of preexisting family violence and that some will be committed by spouses whose previous violent attacks caused the disability of the spouse that he or she so compassionately eliminates.

Summary

Compassionate homicide and assisted suicide often occur in the context of spousal relationships. In the majority of cases, husbands kill wives, but in a significant minority of cases, wives kill husbands. These cases can be presented as the loving acts of spouses who cannot allow their beloved partners to continue suffering or who reluctantly assist their spouses to die when they have come to a rational decision to do so. The same cases can be presented as the cold-blooded crimes of spouses who use the convenient fact of their partner's illness or disability to conceal their crimes as acts of mercy or who drive a vulnerable spouse to suicide. It is likely that the truth behind some cases lies close to one extreme, the truth behind some others lies at the other extreme, and the truth behind many lies somewhere between these extremes.

DICK SOBSEY

See also **Domestic Homicide; Elder Abuse by Intimate Partners; Elder Abuse, Consequences of; Fatality Reviews in Adult Domestic Homicide; Filicide and Children with Disabilities; Parricide; Women with Disabilities, Domestic Violence against**

References and Further Reading

Annas, G. J. "Physician-Assisted Suicide—Michigan's Temporary Solution." *New England Journal of Medicine* 328, no. 21 (1993): 1573–1576.
Cockburn, A. "Beat the Devil: The Rapist and the Snitch." *The Nation* 267, no. 17 (1998): 9.
Gill, C. J., and L. A. Voss. "Views of Disabled People Regarding Legalized Assisted Suicide Before and After a Balanced Informational Presentation." *Journal of Disability Policy Studies* 16 (2005): 6–15.

Humphry, D., and A. Wickett. *The Right to Die: An Historical and Legal Perspective of Euthanasia.* Eugene, OR: The Hemlock Society.

Liebeneiner, W. Letter. *Nazi Cinema.* New York: Macmillan Publishing, 1965, pp. 149–151.

"Lifetime and Annual Incidence of Intimate Partner Violence and Resulting Injuries—Georgia, 1995." *Morbidity and Mortality Weekly Report* 47, no. 40 (1998): 849–853.

Marker, A. *Deadly Compassion.* New York: Avon Books, 1993.

Oberhardt, M. "Husband Obsessed by Death and Taxes." *Courier Mail,* September 11, 2001, p. 5.

Osgood, N. J., and S. A. Eisenhandler. "Gender and Assisted and Acquiescent Suicide: A Suicidologist's Perspective." *Issues in Law and Medicine* 9, no. 4 (1994): 361–374.

Smith, W. J. *Forced Exit.* New York: Times Books, 1997.

CONFLICT TACTICS SCALES

The Conflict Tactics Scales (CTS) are the most widely used instrument for identifying domestic violence. There are two main versions of the CTS: the CTS2 (Straus, Hamby, Boney-McCoy, and Sugarman 1996) is the version measuring violence against a partner in a dating or marital relationship. The CTS2 has scales to measure victimization and perpetration of three tactics that are often used in conflicts between partners: physical assault, psychological aggression, and negotiation; and scales to measure injury and sexual coercion of and by a partner.

The CTSPC is the version of the CTS (Straus, Hamby, Finkelhor, Moore, and Runyan 1998; Straus and Hamby 1997) for measuring maltreatment of a child by parents. The CTSPC has scales to measure physical assault (with subscales for corporal punishment and physical abuse), psychological aggression, and use of nonviolent discipline techniques. There are also supplementary questions on neglect, sexual abuse, and discipline in the past week. In this article, "CTS" will be used when the sentence applies to all versions of the instrument, and CTS2 and CTSPC will be used to refer to those specific versions.

Both the CTS2 and the CTSPC have versions for child respondents and for adult recall of tactics used between their parents (Straus website, 2006). The CTS2 has been translated into many languages. Both versions of the CTS can be obtained from Western Psychological Services.

Theoretical Basis of Conflict Tactics Scales

Conflict theorists such as Louis Coser and Ralph Dahrendord argue that conflict is an inevitable and valuable aspect of all human association because conflict is part of the process by which inequities and problems are corrected. What is harmful is not the conflict itself, but use of coercion, including force and violence, as a tactic for resolving conflicts. In order to understand this perspective, it is necessary to distinguish between two closely related yet clearly different phenomena, both of which are often called conflict: "conflict of interest" and "conflict management." When conflict theorists talk about the ubiquity of conflict, they are referring to conflict of interest, that is, to the fact that members of a social group, no matter how small and intimate, are each seeking to live out their lives in accordance with personal agendas that inevitably differ. These differences range from the trivial, such as which TV show to watch at eight, to major life events such as whether to move to a new house. On the other hand, conflict management, or what for purposes of the CTS is called "conflict tactics," refers to the method used to resolve the conflict. Two families can have the same conflict but differ vastly, and with profound consequences, in how they deal with these conflicts. One family might resolve the issue of which TV program to watch by rotation, another by "first one there," and another by threat of force by the physically strongest.

Measurement Strategy of the Conflict Tactics Scales

A Behavioral Measure

The CTS consists of a list of behaviors directed toward a partner or a child. It deliberately excludes attitudes, emotions, and cognitive appraisal of the behaviors. These are crucial for some research and clinical purposes but must be measured separately.

The value of a behavioral instrument is illustrated by a study which first asked about violent behaviors experienced, and then asked about cognitive appraisal. It found that more than a third of women who reported being victims of one or more violent acts did not regard themselves as having experienced "physical abuse," as a "victim of violence," or as a "battered woman" (Hamby and Gray-Little 2000). This discrepancy between the behavior and the cognitive appraisal of the behavior is important for understanding family violence and for designing programs of prevention and treatment. However, it is possible to identify the discrepancy only if there is an instrument such as the CTS which obtains the behavioral data.

The CTS2 questions are presented in pairs. The first question in the pair asks respondents to indicate how often they carried out each item in the referent period. The second asks how often the partner carried out each behavior. The response categories ask for the number of times each action occurred during the past year, ranging from "Never" to "More than 20 times." The default referent period is the past twelve months, but other referent periods, such as "since starting in this program," can be used. The five CTS2 scales and examples of a minor and a severe question in each scale are:

> *Physical Assault:* "I slapped my partner." "I punched or hit my partner with something that could hurt."
>
> *Injury:* "I had a sprain, bruise, or small cut because of a fight with my partner." "I needed to see a doctor because of a fight with my partner, but I didn't."
>
> *Psychological Aggression:* "I shouted or yelled at my partner." "I stomped out of the room or house or yard during a disagreement."
>
> *Sexual Coercion:* "I insisted on sex when my partner did not want to (but did not use physical force)." "I used force (like hitting, holding down, or using a weapon) to make my partner have sex."
>
> *Negotiation:* "I said I cared about my partner even though we disagreed." "I suggested a compromise to a disagreement."

Symmetry of Measurement

The CTS measures the behavior of both the respondent and the respondent's partner. This does not assume symmetry in the behavior; it only makes it possible to investigate the degree of symmetry or asymmetry. Most research and clinical uses of the CTS benefit from having data on the behavior of both partners in a relationship. This applies even when it might seem that only information on the behavior of one of the partners is needed, such as when the CTS is used to measure progress in a treatment program for male batterers. Research has shown that cessation of violence by one partner is influenced by whether the other partner also stops hitting (Feld and Straus 1989; Gelles and Straus 1988). Thus, when monitoring a treatment program, it is crucial to know the extent to which the partner has also ceased acts of physical and psychological aggression. In addition, for reasons that are not yet understood, the sensitivity of the CTS (as measured by disclosure rate) is lower in studies, such as the National Violence against Women Survey, that used only the victimization questions.

Severity Level

All CTS scales measuring maltreatment have subscales for less severe and more severe behaviors, based on the presumed greater harm resulting from acts in the severe subscale. The distinction between minor and severe assaults is roughly parallel to the legal distinction in the United States between "simple assault" and "aggravated assault." That conceptually based classification has been supported by factor analyses and by a growing recognition that the etiology and treatment of occasional minor violence may be quite different than the etiology of repeated severe assaults (Gelles 1991; Holtzworth-Munroe and Stuart 1994; Johnson and Ferraro 2000; Straus and Gelles 1990). Severity of violence is also measured by the frequency of the acts and by whether an injury results. A national survey of Canadians (Laroche 2005) demonstrated that the CTS can be used to identify what Johnson calls the terroristic level of violence (Johnson and Ferraro 2000).

Clinical Interpretation and Norms

The CTS is also used for clinical assessment (Aldarondo and Straus 1994). Because even one instance of physical assault is a behavior that calls for remedial steps, a basic clinical assessment indicates whether there is a score of 1 or higher on the physical assault scale. In addition, there is information for many clinical and general population samples in the CTS Manual (Straus, Hamby, and Warren 2003), in the core papers on the CTS, and in many publications by others. These rates, mean scores, and standard deviations can be used to evaluate specific cases or categories of cases. In addition to the scale scores, each CTS item should be examined because of the different implications of, for example, slapping as compared with punching, or insisting on sex compared with physically forcing sex.

Reliability and Factor Structure

Internal Consistency Reliability

Alpha coefficients of reliability for the CTS2, reported in forty-one articles, are tabulated in Straus (2005). The coefficients ranged from .34 to .94, with a mean of .77. A study of the CTS2 in seventeen nations found similar results (Straus 2004). The occasional low alpha coefficient occurred when the behavior measured by some of the items, such as attacking a partner with a knife or gun, was absent or nearly absent in some samples.

There are less data on the internal consistency reliability of the CTSPC because this instrument is less widely used. In the seven articles which provided reliability data, the alpha coefficients ranged from .25 to .92, with a mean of .64. The coefficients below the convention of .70 are for the severe violence subscale and reflect the near zero rate of extremely abusive acts in some samples.

Temporal Consistency

Temporal consistency, as measured by a test-retest correlation or intraclass correlation, is arguably the most important aspect of reliability because low temporal consistency imposes an upper limit for validity. However, it is rarely reported, probably because it requires testing the same subjects on two closely spaced occasions. As a result, for the CTS2, test-retest correlations have been located for only two samples. The coefficients for the various scales ranged from .49 to .90 with a mean of .72. For the CTSPC, no studies were located that provide data on test-retest reliability. However, three studies provide data on the parent–child version of the original CTS. The coefficients range from .49 (McGuire and Earls 1993) to .70 and .79 (Johnston 1988) to .80 (Amato 1991). Because the CTSPC is so similar to the original CTS, those results probably apply to the CTSPC as well.

Validity

Content Validity

The steps to achieving content validity included developing the questions on the basis of qualitative interviews and suggestions and reviews by experienced researchers and clinicians. Each question is based around an example of the behavior being measured, such as punching a partner or a child.

For punching to be invalid, it would be necessary to conclude that it is not an act of violence.

Like most tests, the CTS includes only a sample of the universe of possible violent acts. This is analogous to a spelling test that includes only a sample of the total number of words that a child in the seventh grade should know how to spell. Although the behaviors in the CTS may be valid, the method used to select behaviors to include in the CTS did not guarantee that they are an adequate sample of violent behaviors. One indication that they are an adequate sample comes from a study by Dobash and Dobash (1984), who are among the most strident critics of the CTS. They used qualitative methods to identify typical violent acts. Their list of violent acts is almost identical to the items in the CTS.

Sensitivity and Confounding with Social Desirability

Sensitivity. An instrument's sensitivity is its ability to detect the occurrence of a phenomenon. Sensitivity is a critical aspect of validity. It is especially important for self-report measures of socially undesirable behaviors such as those measured by four of the five CTS2 scales. When the CTS is administered according to the standard instructions, it obtains many times more disclosure of violence than the most widely used measures, such as the National Crime Victimization Survey and rates of cases reported to Child Protective Services.

Confounding with Social Desirability. Many studies have found low correlations between the CTS and "social desirability" scales (Sugarman and Hotaling 1996). These scales measure the degree to which respondents are reluctant to disclose socially undesirable behavior. The fact that there is little correlation between scores on a social desirability scale and the CTS2 was confirmed by data from the International Dating Violence Study data for students at thirty-one universities. This study found that the mean correlation with a social desirability scale was −.17 for the physical assault scale (range = −.03 to −.23) and −.09 for injury (range = .00 to −.23) (Straus and International Dating Violence Research Consortium 2004). These relatively low correlations suggest that scores on the CTS reflect real differences in violence, rather than differences in willingness to disclose socially undesirable behavior. Nevertheless, analysis of the CTS, like analysis of all self-report data on socially undesirable behavior, should include a control for score on a social desirability scale.

Agreement between Respondents

Because the main threat to the validity of the CTS is failure to report violent behaviors that actually occurred, the degree of agreement between the reports of different participants is an important type of validity data. A number of studies have investigated the degree of agreement between partners in a relationship, and between data provided by parents about violence to a child and data provided by the child. A meta-analysis of agreement between partners summarizing results from nineteen samples which obtained CTS data from both partners and forty-three samples which obtained the data on both partners from just one of the partners found correlations that averaged about .50 (Archer 1999).

Construct Validity

Construct validity refers to the association between the measure in question and other variables for which prior research or theory predicts a relationship. It follows that the construct validity of the CTS can be assessed by the degree to which the CTS produces findings that are consistent with theoretical or empirical propositions about the variables the CTS purports to measure. There are literally hundreds of studies providing such evidence. For parent-to-child violence, see Straus and Hamby (1997). For measures of partner violence, a few examples from the National Family Violence Surveys and the International Dating Violence Study will be mentioned.

Many hypothesized "risk factors" have been found to be related to partner violence as measured by the CTS (Gelles and Straus 1988; Straus and Gelles 1990), including:

- Inequality between partners, and especially male dominance
- Poverty and unemployment
- Stress and lack of community ties
- Youthfulness
- Heavy drinking

Experience of corporal punishment as children and neglectful behavior by parents were both found in a study of university students in seventeen countries to be independently associated with an increased probability of violence to a dating partner as measured by the CTS (Douglas and Straus 2006; Straus and Savage 2005).

Limitations of the Conflict Tactics Scales

The CTS is both the most widely used measure of family violence and also the most widely criticized. Extensive critical examination is appropriate for any widely used instrument because, if the instrument is wrong, then a great deal of research will also be wrong. In the case of the CTS, however, the most frequent criticisms reflect ideological differences rather than empirical evidence. Specifically, many feminist scholars reject the CTS because studies using this instrument find that about the same percentage of women as men assault their partners. This contradicts the feminist theory that partner violence is almost exclusively committed by men as a means to dominate women, and is therefore taken as prima facie evidence that the CTS is not valid. Ironically, the fact that the CTS has provided some of the best evidence confirming the link between male dominance and partner violence and other key aspects of feminist theory of partner violence (Coleman and Straus 1990; Straus 1994) has not shaken the belief that the CTS is invalid.

Another irony is that despite these denunciations, many feminist researchers use the CTS. However, having used the CTS, they reaffirm their feminist credentials by routinely inserting a paragraph repeating some of the erroneous criticisms. These criticisms are then cited in other articles as though there were empirical evidence. Anyone reviewing these studies would have the impression that there is a large body of empirical evidence showing the invalidity of the CTS, whereas there is only endless repetition of the same unvalidated opinions. Because of space limitations, only a few examples will be mentioned and rebutted. Others are documented elsewhere (Straus and Gelles 1990).

Erroneous Criticisms

The CTS Measures Only Conflict-Related Violence. Although the theoretical basis of the CTS is conflict theory, the introductory explanation to participants specifically includes expressive and malicious violence. It asks respondents to answer questions about the times when they and their partners "disagree, get annoyed with the other person, want different things from each other, or just have spats or fights because they are in a bad mood, are tired or for some other reason." In the past twenty-five years this criticism has been repeated in over one hundred publications, giving the appearance of a well-established limitation. However, no empirical evidence has been provided showing that only conflict-related violence is reported. In fact, where there are both CTS data and qualitative data, as in Giles-Sims (1983), it shows that the CTS elicits malicious violence as well as conflict-related violence.

Equates Acts That Differ Greatly in Seriousness. As shown previously in this entry, exactly the opposite is a key characteristic of the CTS. The physical assault scale, like all the CTS maltreatment scales, differentiates between less severe acts of violence, such as slapping and throwing things at a partner, and more severe acts such as punching, kicking, and choking, and the CTS provides the opportunity to weight the scores by the frequency of these behaviors.

Context and Consequences Are Ignored. The idea that the CTS physical assault scale is defective because it does not take into account the context, meaning, causes, and consequences of the violent acts is analogous to declaring a reading ability test invalid because it does not provide data on why a child reads poorly (such as limited exposure to books at home or test anxiety), or for not measuring the harmful effects of reading difficulty (such as low self-esteem or dropping out of school).

Context and consequences are extremely important, but they must be measured separately from the behavior they presumably cause to be able to test theories about context effects. This includes information on whether the assault was in self-defense or retaliation or was provoked by domineering behavior, verbal taunting, or other psychological aggression. For example, because the CTS has a separate measure of psychological aggression, Murphy and O'Leary (1989) were able to test the theory that psychological aggression against a partner is associated with an increased probability of physical violence.

Some Actual Limitations

Covers Only a Limited Set of Violent Acts. The brevity of the CTS makes its use possible in situations which preclude a longer instrument. However, its brevity is also a limitation because it means that the subscales are limited to distinguishing minor and severe levels of each of the tactics. For example, with only eight items, the psychological aggression scale cannot provide subscales for separate dimensions such as rejecting, isolation, terrorizing, ignoring, and corrupting.

Response Categories Are Unrealistic. The CTS asks respondents how many times they and their partners did each of the acts in the past year (or some other referent period). This is satisfactory to provide estimates of how many times severe and rarely occurring events such as punching a partner or a child have happened. However, for events that

can occur daily or several times a week, such as spanking or slapping a child (Giles-Sims, Straus, and Sugarman 1995), parents cannot be expected to accurately estimate how many times this behavior occurred in the past year. Nevertheless, thousands of respondents around the world have provided these estimates, and these data have been successfully used to identify cases which are low or high compared with other respondents. These response categories enabled Giles-Sims (1983) to estimate that women in the shelter she studied had been assaulted an average of sixty-nine times in the preceding year. This is more than ten times greater than the six times in the previous twelve months experienced by women in the National Family Violence Survey who had been assaulted that year (Straus and Gelles 1990).

Underreporting. Although the CTS has repeatedly been found to uncover higher rates of partner violence than other instruments, these rates are nonetheless lower-bound estimates because of underreporting. In addition, a meta-analysis (Archer 1999) found that although both men and women underreport, the extent of underreporting is greater for men. Perhaps the most serious type of underreporting is by partners or victims of partners who engage in repeated severe assaults that often produce injuries. Although such extreme violence is only a tiny percentage of partner violence, the perpetrators and the victims of such acts are the ones in most urgent need of intervention. This problem is a limitation of survey research on partner violence rather than a unique problem of the CTS.

Obtains Maltreatment Data for Only the Current Partner or Caregiver. The CTS2 asks for information about relationships with the current or most recent partner, and the CTSPC about the current caregiver of the child. Thus, the CTS does not provide information about the history of victimization or perpetration.

Injuries Not Directly Linked to Assaults. The injury scale does not provide information on which assault caused each of the injuries in the scale. Research to understand the processes resulting in injury could obtain this information by expanding the CTS to ask each of the injury items for each assaultive behavior reported.

Administration, Testing Time, and Scoring

Administration

Experience with the CTS indicates low refusal rates, even in mass surveys such as the 1985

National Family Violence Survey, which had an 84 percent completion rate (Gelles and Straus 1988). The CTS can be administered in many ways, including in-person interview, telephone interview, self-administered questionnaire, and computer-administered questionnaire. Studies that compared in-person with telephone interviews of the CTS have found equivalent results. A study comparing paper-and-pencil self-administered questionnaires with computer-administered questionnaires also found general equivalence (Hamby, Sugarman, and Boney-McCoy, 2005). There is a picture-card version of the CTSPC for use with young children (Straus website, 2006).

Testing Time

The testing time for the full CTS2 is twelve to fifteen minutes. A shorter alternative is to administer only the three core scales (physical assault, psychological aggression, and negotiation). This produces an instrument that has the same coverage and takes about the same time as the original CTS (seven to ten minutes). It is not advisable to shorten the scale by including only the victimization or only the perpetration questions. This obtains only half of the information needed to understand partner violence, and even for that half, it reduces the disclosure rate. A second alternative is to use the CTS2 short form (Straus and Douglas 2004), for which testing time is approximately three minutes. Both of these alternatives have important limitations. The first alternative means no data on injury and sexual coercion. The second alternative obtains information on all five scales, but at the cost of detecting only about half as many cases as when the full-length scales are used.

Scoring

There are many ways to score the CTS. Each is suited to different circumstances. They are described in a paper on scoring (Straus website, 2006) and in the core publications on the CTS (Straus et al. 1996; Straus et al. 1998; Straus and Douglas 2004). Because of space limitation, only four will be mentioned.

Prevalence. For the scales with highly skewed distributions, and for which it is important to identify even a single occurrence of the behavior, such as the physical assault, injury, and sexual coercion scales, the "prevalence" score or rate is the most usual choice. This is simply an indication of whether any one or more of the acts in the scale have been committed. In the aggregate, this results in the

percentage who were violent, injured a partner, or coerced sex.

Frequency. This is the number of times the behavior occurred in the past year. A limitation of this score is that, for general population samples, the distribution is so skewed that the mean is not an appropriate measure of central tendency. In addition, unless a normalizing transformation is used, the frequency score does not meet the assumptions of parametric statistical tests. On the other hand, a sample of known offenders or victims will not have 85 or 95 percent with a score of zero, and the frequency score can be very useful for measuring the chronicity of maltreatment.

Severity Level and Mutuality Types. The severity level classifies each case into three categories: *none, minor only,* or *severe.* The mutuality types classify each case as *respondent only, partner only,* or *both.* The mutuality types may be particularly useful in couples therapy because over a hundred studies have found that when there is violence, 50 percent or more of the time it is by both partners (Archer 2000; Straus and Ramirez in press).

Contributions of the Conflict Tactics Scales to Understanding Family Violence

The twentieth anniversary commemorative issue of the *Journal of Interpersonal Violence* included an article entitled "Top 10 Greatest 'Hits'" (Langhinrichsen-Rohling 2005). The list of hits begins, "Greatest Hit Number 1: He Gave Us a Tool to Look Behind Closed Doors." It goes on to say, "In 1979, Straus created a measure, the Conflict Tactics Scale (CTS), which lit a fire to the domestic violence field. The CTS was revolutionary because it allowed researchers to quantitatively study events that had often been ignored culturally and typically took place in private." The CTS made possible national surveys on the prevalence of family violence in the United States and other countries, such as the two National Family Violence Surveys (Straus and Gelles 1990), the National Violence against Women Survey, and the National Survey of Child and Adolescent Well-Being. Between the first study using the CTS (Straus 1973) and 2005, about 600 research papers and at least ten books reporting results based on the CTS were published. Between 1995 and 2005, four to six articles reporting results obtained using the CTS were published every month.

Every measuring instrument has limitations and problems, and the CTS is no exception. These limitations need to be considered when interpreting results from the CTS, or when choosing an instrument to measure family violence. Fortunately, there are comprehensive compendia which describe over 100 measures of different aspects of violence (Dahlberg, Toal, and Behrens 1998; Hamby and Finkelhor 2001; Rathus and Feindler 2004). They facilitate examining alternatives to the CTS or choosing additional instruments to measure aspects of violence that are not covered by it.

MURRAY A. STRAUS

See also **Analyzing Incidents of Domestic Violence: The National Incident-Based Reporting System; Measuring Domestic Violence**

References and Further Reading

Aldarondo, Etiony, and Murray A. Straus. "Screening for Physical Violence in Couple Therapy: Methodological, Practical, and Ethical Considerations." *Family Process* 33 (1994): 425–439.

Amato, Paul R. "Psychological Distress and the Recall of Childhood Family Characteristics." *Journal of Marriage and the Family* 53 (1991): 1011–1019.

Archer, John. "Assessment of the Reliability of the Conflict Tactics Scales: A Meta-Analytic Review." *Journal of Interpersonal Violence* 14, no. 12 (1999): 1263–1289.

———. "Sex Differences in Aggression between Heterosexual Partners: A Meta-Analytic Review." *Psychological Bulletin* 126, no. 5 (2000): 651–680.

Coleman, Diane H., and Murray A. Straus. "Marital Power, Conflict, and Violence in a Nationally Representative Sample of American Couples." In *Physical Violence in American Families,* Edited by M. A. Straus and R. J. Gelles. New Brunswick, NJ: Transaction Publications, 1990.

Dahlberg, Linda L., Susan B. Toal, and Christopher B. Behrens. *Measuring Violence-Related Attitudes, Beliefs, and Behaviors among Youths: A Compendium of Assessment Tools.* Atlanta: Division of Violence Prevention, National Center for Injury Prevention and Control, Centers for Disease Control and Prevention, 1998.

Dobash, Emerson R., and Russell P. Dobash. "The Nature and Antecedents of Violent Events." *British Journal of Criminology* 24, no. 3 (1984): 269–288.

Douglas, Emily M., and Murray A. Straus. "Assault and Injury of Dating Partners by University Students in 19 Nations and Its Relation to Corporal Punishment Experienced as a Child." *European Journal of Criminology* 3, no. 3 (2006): 293–318.

Feld, Scott L., and Murray A. Straus. "Escalation and Desistance of Wife Assault in Marriage." *Criminology* 27, no. 1 (1989): 141–161.

Gelles, Richard J. "Physical Violence, Child Abuse, and Child Homicide: A Continuum of Violence, or Distinct Behaviors?" *Human Nature* 2, no. 1 (1991): 59–72.

Gelles, Richard J., and Murray A. Straus. *Intimate Violence.* New York: Simon & Schuster, 1988.

Giles-Sims, Jean. *Wife Battering: A Systems Theory Approach.* New York: Guilford Press, 1983.

Giles-Sims, Jean, Murray A. Straus, and David B. Sugarman. "Child, Maternal and Family Characteristics Associated

with Spanking." *Family Relations* 44, no. 2 (1995): 170–176.

Hamby, Sherry L., and David Finkelhor. *Choosing and Using Child Victimization Questionnaires.* Washington, DC: Office of Juvenile Justice and Delinquency Prevention, 2001.

Hamby, Sherry L., and Bernadette Gray-Little. "Labeling Partner Violence: When Do Victims Differentiate among Acts?" *Violence & Victims* 15, no. 2 (2000): 173–186.

Holtzworth-Munroe, Amy, and Gregory L. Stuart. "Typologies of Male Batterers: Three Subtypes and the Differences among Them." *Psychological Bulletin* 116, no. 3 (1994): 476–497.

Johnson, Michael P., and Kathleen J. Ferraro. "Research on Domestic Violence in the 1990s: Making Distinctions." *Journal of Marriage and the Family* 62, no. 4 (2000): 948–963.

Johnston, Mildred E. "Correlates of Early Violence Experience among Men Who Are Abusive toward Female Mates." In *Family Abuse and Its Consequences: New Directions in Research,* edited by G. T. Hotaling, D. Finkelhor, J. T. Kirkpatrick and M. A. Straus. Newbury Park, CA: Sage, 1988.

Langhinrichsen-Rohling, Jennifer. "Top 10 Greatest 'Hits': Important Findings and Future Directions for Intimate Partner Violence Research." *Journal of Interpersonal Violence* 20, no. 1 (2005): 108–118.

Laroche, Denis. "Aspects of the Context and Consequences of Domestic Violence—Situational Couple Violence and Intimate Terrorism in Canada in 1999." Government of Quebec, 2005.

McGuire, Jacqueline, and Felton Earls. "Exploring the Reliability of Measures of Family Relatons, Parental Attitudes, and Parent–Child Relations in a Disadvantaged Minority Population." *Journal of Marriage and the Family* 55 (1993): 1042–1046.

Murphy, Christopher M., and K. Daniel O'Leary. "Psychological Aggression Predicts Physical Aggression in Early Marriage." *Journal of Consulting and Clinical Psychology* 57, no. 5 (1989): 579–582.

Rathus, Jill H., and Eva L. Feindler. *Assessment of Partner Violence.* Washington, DC: American Psychological Association, 2004.

Straus, Murray A. "A General Systems Theory Approach to a Theory of Violence between Family Members." *Social Science Information* 12, no. 3 (1973): 105–125.

———. *Bibliography and Tabular Summary of Publications on the Revised Conflict Tactics Scales (CTS2 and CTSPC).* Durham, NH: Family Research Laboratory, University of New Hampshire, 2005.

———. website. http://pubpages.unh.edu/~mas2 (accessed August 15, 2006).

Straus, Murray A., and Emily M. Douglas. "A Short Form of the Revised Conflict Tactics Scales, and Typologies for Severity and Mutuality." *Violence and Victims* 19, no. 5 (2004): 507–520.

Straus, Murray A., and Richard J. Gelles. *Physical Violence in American Families: Risk Factors and Adaptations to Violence in 8,145 Families.* New Brunswick, NJ: Transaction Publications, 1990.

Straus, Murray A., and Sherry L. Hamby. "Measuring Physical and Psychological Maltreatment of Children with the Conflict Tactics Scales." In *Out of the Darkness: Contemporary Research Perspectives on Family Violence,* edited by G. Kaufman Kantor and J. Jasinski. Thousand Oaks, CA: Sage, 1997.

Straus, Murray A., Sherry L. Hamby, Susan Boney-McCoy, and David B. Sugarman. "The Revised Conflict Tactics Scales (CTS2): Development and Preliminary Psychometric Data." *Journal of Family Issues* 17, no. 3 (1996): 283–316.

Straus, Murray A., Sherry L. Hamby, David Finkelhor, David W. Moore, and Desmond Runyan. "Identification of Child Maltreatment with the Parent–Child Conflict Tactics Scales: Development and Psychometric Data for a National Sample of American Parents." *Child Abuse and Neglect* 22 (1998): 249–270.

Straus, Murray A., Sherry L. Hamby, and W. Louise Warren. "State-to-State Differences in Social Inequality and Social Bonds in Relation to Assaults on Wives in the United States." *Journal of Comparative Family Studies* 25, no. 1 (1994): 7–24.

———. *The Conflict Tactics Scales Handbook.* Los Angeles: Western Psychological Services, 2003.

———. "Cross-Cultural Reliability and Validity of the Revised Conflict Tactics Scales: A Study of University Student Dating Couples in 17 Nations." *Cross-Cultural Research* 38, no. 4 (2004): 407–432.

Straus, Murray A., and International Dating Violence Research Consortium. "Prevalence of Violence against Dating Partners by Male and Female University Students Worldwide." *Violence against Women* 10, no. 7 (2004): 790–811.

Straus, Murray A., and Ignacio Luis Ramirez. "Gender Symmetry in Prevalence, Severity, and Chronicity of Physical Aggression against Dating Partners by University Students in Mexico and USA." *Aggressive Behavior,* in press.

Straus, Murray A., and Sarah A. Savage. "Neglectful Behavior by Parents in the Life History of University Students in 17 Countries and Its Relation to Violence against Dating Partners." *Child Maltreatment* 10, no. 2 (2005): 124–135.

Sugarman, David B., and Gerald T. Hotaling. "Intimate Violence and Social Desirability: A Meta-Analytic Review." *Journal of Interpersonal Violence* 12, no. 2 (1996): 275–290.

CONTROL BALANCE THEORY AND DOMESTIC VIOLENCE

Introduction

Domestic violence, or intimate partner violence (IPV), is a contemporary social problem that has evolved from a husband's legal right to discipline his wife through physical means (Lutze and Symons 2003: 321). Historically, the judicial system protected the right of the husband; however, as the women's movement gained influence, the courts began to treat IPV as the serious and pervasive problem that it is (Lutze and Symons 2003: 321, 324). While studies show that there are specific groups who are victimized with greater frequency than others—for example, women who are members of minority groups, or those who live in urban areas (U.S. Department of Justice 1998: 13–15), IPV is not exclusive, that is, it can affect anyone, regardless of age, sex, culture, socioeconomic status, or race. Therefore, society must continue to develop effective means to address violence between partners.

Before solutions can be found, the etiology of the problem must be understood. In the case of this critical issue, criminological theories should be applied to better understand IPV and how best to control it. This article applies Charles Tittle's control balance theory to occurrences of domestic violence; in doing so, it seeks to explain not only instances of IPV, but also victims' responses to the violence that they are experiencing and suggests possible means of addressing IPV.

Statement of Problem

On March 28, 2003, in a case that garnered widespread media attention in Austin, Texas, Ortralla Mosley was stabbed to death on her high school campus, and her ex-boyfriend Marcus McTear was accused of the crime (Gilbert 2003). He was later sentenced to a forty-year determinate sentence (Smith 2003). In a 2003 *Austin American Statesman* article discussing IPV (Gilbert 2003), Veranda Escobar was profiled. She survived her violent relationship, but not before it left her confined to a wheelchair. In 2002, Michael Edward Hill was stabbed to death by his girlfriend in what appeared to be an attempt by the woman to defend herself from Hill, who had four prior convictions for domestic violence assaults (Osborn 2002).

The cases of Mosley and Escobar illustrate what could happen when a person is either unable or unwilling to attempt to end the circumstances that place her at risk of being a victim of IPV. The case of Michael Edward Hill, on the other hand, appears to represent the end result of a violent relationship and the attempt by a victim of IPV to end the relationship by desperate means. Each of these cases, however, raises questions as to what causes IPV, what may prevent women from escaping violent relationships, and what may cause them to feel compelled to escape the violence by killing or assaulting the person who victimizes them.

In his assessment of the policy issues that surround IPV and, more particularly, the specific policy of mandatory arrest in domestic violence cases, Drew Humphries (2002: 91) presented a summary of the connection between control and IPV for policymakers: "Policymakers should recognize that victim control is a core policy issue, which originates from the unique character of intimate violence." His suggestion is that criminological theory can aid in the creation of public policy that would benefit victims and help in reducing instances of IPV. Considering Humphries' statement regarding the importance of control in cases of IPV, it is possible that the application of Tittle's control balance theory, which generally holds that a person's proclivity toward criminal acts is based on his or her need to obtain control of a given situation (Tittle 1995: 135), could present a means to reduce IPV. Specifically, the theory could be applied to encourage the creation of legitimate means for victims to escape violent relationships so as to avoid a case like that of Michael Edward Hill.

Charles Tittle's Theory of Control Balance

Tittle's theory of control balance states that a person lives his or her life in one of three states: control surplus, control equilibrium, or control deficit (Lilly et al. 2002: 98). He predicts deviance by positing that "[t]he amount of control to which an individual is subject, relative to the amount of control he or she can exercise, determines the probability of deviance occurring as well as the type of deviance likely to occur" (Tittle 1995: 135). This is called the *control ratio* (Lilly et al. 2002: 98; Piquero and Hickman 2003: 284). Tittle's thesis is that a person is moved toward deviance, as a result of an imbalance in the control ratio, when

three situations exist simultaneously: predisposition, motivation, and opportunity.

An individual is predisposed toward deviance when the balance of control is somehow not equal. The inequality may favor the individual (a control surplus) or may not favor the individual (a control deficit) (Piquero and Hickman 2003: 284). In the former case, the individual is predisposed toward delinquent behavior that expresses exploitation, plunder, and defiance, while in the latter case, the person acts in a manner that expresses defiance, submissiveness, or predation (Lilly et al. 2002: 99; Piquero and Hickman 2003: 284). Examples of such delinquent acts for those in control surpluses can be found in financial, or white-collar, crime, where an individual with a considerable amount of resources and control exercises his control illegally in order to achieve more control or financial reward. In cases of delinquent acts by those in a control deficit, a group of people who, for instance, feel that they are being treated badly by the government may turn to vandalism, graffiti, or other property crimes in order to gain some modicum of control.

According to control balance theory, the second prong required for delinquency is motivation. Tittle (2000: 320) states that the motivation for delinquency could come from the imbalance that exists in control. The result of the motivation would be deviance in order to overcome the deficit or enlarge the surplus (Lilly et al. 2002: 99). Other possible sources for motivation could be a situation or issue that causes the need to act in a delinquent manner in order to remedy the situation or issue (Piquero and Hickman 2003: 282).

Much like other criminological theories, such as opportunity theory (see Lilly et al. 2002: 57) and routine activity theory (see Lilly et al. 2002: 234), the existence of motivation or predisposition alone is not sufficient to cause delinquent behavior. As in the opportunity and routine activity theories, according to control balance theory, there is a third element required. In order for delinquency to take place, one must have the opportunity to commit an offense (Lilly et al. 2002: 99).

After all three prongs of the theory are satisfied, one may engage in delinquency that is said to be a result of an issue of control imbalance. Conversely, if there is no imbalance in control—that is to say, if equilibrium of control exists—deviant behavior is less likely to take place (Lilly et al. 2002: 98) because of the absence of predisposition, and possibly of the motivation that may come from the unequal balance of power.

Exploring Intimate Partner Violence

The Law

In order to understand the meaning of IPV, it is helpful to know the applicable law that makes such violence an offense. Texas law defines IPV under two separate sections of code. The first section addresses dating violence, which is, in general terms, an assaultive act between individuals currently engaged in or previously engaged in a dating relationship (Texas Family Code § 71.0021). The second statute addresses family violence, which encompasses assaultive acts between individuals who are members of the same family or household (Texas Family Code § 71.004). These definitions, when combined with that of assault, which generally states that an assault takes place when a person "intentionally, knowingly, or recklessly causes bodily injury to another" (Texas Penal Code § 22.01 (A)(1)), create the foundation for charging an individual with an offense based on an act of IPV. The IPV laws adopted by the state of Texas are similar to statutes enacted in other states that have enlarged the scope of assaults covered by domestic violence laws beyond that of the traditional marital relationship (Lutze and Symons 2003: 319).

Relevant Statistics

Clearly, IPV is a serious issue in criminal justice, and the above-cited cases of Mosley, Escobar, and Hill illustrate this reality quite well. Furthermore, it is an issue that affects people nationwide (McFarlane, Wilson, Malecha, and Lemmey 2000: 167). Statistics collected by the U.S. Department of Justice lend support to the perspective that IPV is widespread. From 1992 to 1996, an average of 8 in 1,000 women and 1 in 1,000 men were victims of IPV (U.S. Department of Justice 1998: 3). In 2001, over 690,000 instances of IPV were reported through the National Crime Victimization Survey (U.S. Department of Justice 2003: 1). In the same year, 20 percent of the violent acts experienced by women and 3 percent of the violent acts experienced by men were a result of IPV (U.S. Department of Justice 2003: 1). A 1998 study by the Department of Justice (1998: 4) shows that "[a]lthough less likely than males to experience violent crime overall, females are five to eight times more likely than males to be victimized by an intimate." Due to the prevalence of violence against women, this article will address the issue of IPV from the perspective of a female victim and male batterer, a position supported by some theorists, who believe that IPV is a more significant problem for women than for men (McFarlane et al. 2000: 166–167; Melton and Belknap 2003: 332).

The Root of Intimate Partner Violence

Research has tied IPV to a relationship that contains "a *pattern* of intimidation and control that includes the use of physical violence by one person against another" (Wright 2000: 5, emphasis in original). This pattern may result in manifestations of violence of a physical and/or sexual nature, attempts by the abuser to control his intimate partner's lifestyle or finances, or attempts by the batterer to isolate his intimate partner from other social contacts (Wright 2000: 6–7). In terms of examining IPV from the perspective of Tittle's theory, the key issue is the *control* serving as an impetus for violence.

Control Balance Theory and Intimate Partner Violence

An issue at the core of IPV is control. The surplus of control is generally in the hands of the batterer, while the victim experiences a deficit of control (Wright 2000: 5–8). Parallel this with Tittle's theory and the potential connection between theory and the crime of IPV begins to appear.

Control Balance and the Batterer

The batterer in an IPV situation exercises great control over his victim, and this control is expressed through a number of different outlets, including psychological abuse (Henning and Klesges 2003: 866–868; Wright 2000: 6–7). This psychological abuse takes the form of verbal threats and abuse and psychological manipulation of the victim by the batterer (Henning and Klesges 2003: 862) and allows the abuser to believe that he is increasing his control over the victim (Henning and Klesges 2003: 868). Another area of control for a batterer is that of the couple's finances, which requires the victim to accede to the will of the abuser in order to have financial means, which allows control in that if the victim has no means to support outside activities, she finds it difficult to engage in any (Wright 2000: 6–7). These two control methods are illustrative of the many ways that an abuser controls his victim.

Tittle's control balance theory states that deviant behavior by the individual who has a control surplus is undertaken as a means of expanding the surplus of control (Lilly et al. 2002: 99). IPV by

CONTROL BALANCE THEORY AND DOMESTIC VIOLENCE

the batterer appears to be consistent with the part of Tittle's theory that outlines the potentially delinquent acts employed by the party with the surplus in control in order to extend that control. Supported by a patriarchal view of intimate relationships (which still exists, but has been losing popular acceptance since the 1970s) wherein men have certain powers and privileges, including total control of the intimate relationship (Lutze and Symons 2003: 321), it becomes easy for the batterer to engage in the deviant behavior (i.e., physical violence) because he perceives that his level of control allows it, as there are no factors that exist to restrain him (Piquero and Hickman 2003: 286–287).

The Victim and Control Balance

The position of the individual who experiences a deficit in control is a difficult one, because of the constant reminder of lack of control. Two examples given of control methods employed by batterers in IPV situations were psychological control and financial control. Regarding psychological abuse, a study by Henning and Klesges (2003: 869) indicated that such a mechanism of control causes the victim to feel at greater risk for additional violence. In the case of the latter example, with financial control in the hands of the abuser, the victim could feel as though she is powerless to escape the abusive relationship (Wolf, Ly, Hobart, and Kernic 2003: 124; Wright 2000: 7, 12). In both situations, the flow of control seems to be constant in favor of the abuser, and there appears to be little that the victim can do to gain control for herself in the relationship.

At the heart of control balance theory are the possible criminogenic implications of the control imbalance. This applies to the victim in IPV as much as it does to the batterer. Control balance theory holds that the individual with a deficit in control also has the potential to act in a delinquent manner to attempt to achieve a balance in control (Lilly et al. 2002: 99).

When a victim is subject to the control of her batterer, is experiencing physical abuse, and perceives an inability to gain control, one response is an increase in depression and hopelessness (Campbell and Soeken 1999: 23; Clements, Sabourin, and Spiby 2004: 34). This response, however natural, diminishes the victim's ability to care for herself (Campbell and Soeken 1999: 35) and possibly exacerbates the control imbalance and the potential for future violence against the victim (Piquero and Hickman 2003: 299).

The most dramatic means that can be employed by a victim of IPV in order to gain control in a violent relationship is to respond to violence with physical violence. According to control balance, such a response would fall into the category of delinquent behavior. This is supported by Melton and Belknap's study of violent relationships between intimate partners. One finding of their study that replicated other scholarly literature is that women tend to use violence in intimate partner relationships in order to oppose the violence that they are experiencing from their batterers (Melton and Belknap 2003: 345). The case of Michael Edward Hill, presented in the introduction to this article, illustrates the lengths to which a victim may be pushed in order to correct the balance of control and escape a violent situation. As stated previously, Hill, who had a record of convictions for offenses of IPV, was stabbed by his partner and died from his wounds. This event mirrors Jeffery Adler's study of homicides perpetrated by wives against their husbands at the turn of the twentieth century in Chicago. His study found that many of the killings took place after a considerable amount of abuse by the batterer-turned-victim (Adler 2002: 877). This is a powerful illustration of Tittle's theory at work that calls for attention by policymakers and people of all walks of life in society.

Implications for Criminal Justice and Social Policy

With a link between control balance theory, the offense of IPV, and the potential violent responses of the victim established, the mission of policymakers and society in general is to take this link and translate it into meaningful policy initiatives to address IPV. Policymakers should take note of the fact that individuals who experience a deficit of control are at a high risk of victimization (Piquero and Hickman 2003: 295–296) and could respond to that deficit by violent means (Adler 2002: 877; Melton and Belknap 2003: 345). This criminal response by the victim is strongly suggested by Henning and Feder (2004: 78–79) as a reason for the increasing number of arrests of women in IPV cases. Individuals who understand the connection between control balance and IPV and the foregoing statement about control deficit, victimization, and violent responses by victims should recognize that the implication for criminal justice and social policy is to aid the victim in achieving a balance in control by nonviolent means.

Social Support as a Control Mechanism for Victims

One step in giving women control over the relationship is to help them gain an understanding of their ability to take control, and to help them overcome the feeling of a lack of control. According to one study, there is an irony present in the psychological mechanisms of control employed by batterers, in that they may actually have the unintended impact of pushing the victim away from the potentially physically abusive situation (Henning and Klesges 2003: 868). In this circumstance, it is hoped that a victim, if provided with appropriate social supports, will be able to find an opportunity to gain control in a nondelinquent manner.

One study points out a problem with obtaining social supports, which is that many women in violent relationships were unaware of the resources that were at their disposal (Fry and Barker 2001: 338). Many of the social supports that are offered to victims of IPV are provided through shelters and other professional services. In Austin, Texas, there are a number of these professional resources available, including the SafePlace program, which provides shelter and counseling for victims of domestic violence, the Women's Advocacy Project, which provides legal information for IPV victims, and the Family Violence Protection Team, which is a consolidated "one-stop shop" where legal assistance is available and law enforcement and the prosecutors' offices are accessible (Sylvester, Shirley, Mueller, and Clark 2004). The implications are clear: The development of programs that provide aid to victims and potential victims of IPV should be encouraged, and the general public's awareness that professional services exist should be ensured. Finally, victims and potential victims of IPV must be directly targeted by these services. This can be done in a number of ways, one of which is effective publicity. Formal resources aimed at reducing domestic violence should be advertised at places where individuals who are at risk of being victims of IPV are found, such as schools, workplaces, and college campuses. As stated above, individuals in lower socioeconomic brackets are at high risk of being victims of IPV; as a result, places like unemployment-assistance centers, shelters, and food banks should also be targeted as places where information about IPV resources can be distributed. Both creating resources and shedding light on the problem of IPV should be explored as a means of encouraging victims and potential victims to obtain support in acquiring control in their relationships in a nonviolent manner.

Another area of social support of which a victim of IPV could avail herself comes in the form of aid from friends and family members, described in literature as "front-line helpers" (West and Wandrei 2002: 972). The value of professional violence intervention programs is in no way questioned here; however, it is hoped that by highlighting a complementary form of social support, professional support providers can consider extending their mission to educating the public at large. One question often aimed at victims of IPV seeks reasons as to why they did not leave the deteriorating relationship (Wright 2000: 10). Many of the reasons relate to their lack of control, which is caused by the controlling behaviors of their partner (Wright 2000: 12; Zoellner et al. 2000: 1095). The possibility exists that some of the first individuals outside of the abusive relationship who could notice the abuse or at least the change in the relationship between the victim and her abuser are the victim's friends and family. These people are in a unique position to note changes in the victim and her behaviors, which may indicate a deteriorating or abusive relationship. They could provide some of the support needed to allow the victim of IPV to gain the control necessary in order to escape the relationship. The implication here is to sufficiently educate the public as to not only the signs and symptoms of an unhealthy relationship, but also as to the appropriate responses when these signals are noted (West and Wandrei 2002: 977, 984). These responses could include providing financial or emotional support to the victim in order to empower her to gain the control needed to leave the relationship, and absolutely *should* include advising the victim to seek professional support, in the form of either assistance from a professionally run program or intervention by law enforcement, when necessary.

Involving Law Enforcement in a Violent Situation to Gain Control

When the control imbalance in a relationship is such that physical violence takes place, law enforcement must be involved in the situation in order to protect both the health and the safety of the victim and her rights in the judicial process. Among the major barriers that keep a victim from contacting law enforcement are physical acts of the batterer that restrain her from seeking aid (Wolf et al. 2003: 124). There are also a number of other factors that exist that make a victim either unwilling or hesitant to contact law enforcement when she is assaulted by her partner.

One subset of these factors that create unwillingness or hesitation is found in the victim herself, or in the particular situation of IPV. These factors include the victim's inaccurate belief that the violence must result in physical marks; a hesitation, on the part of the victim, to report an incident that involved sexual assault or injuries to the intimate parts of her body; cultural differences to which the victim ascribes that appear to condone IPV; the very fragile emotional condition of the victim who has been subjected to both psychological and physical control and abuse; and the financial dependence of the victim on the batterer (Wolf et al. 2003: 124). The worst-case scenario regarding access is that because of one or many of these factors, a woman who is otherwise unrestrained from contacting law enforcement does not *feel* able to call the police and replies to the violence inflicted on her with additional violence.

A second subset of factors that creates hesitation to involve law enforcement relates to the reaction of police to an IPV case. Female victims of IPV are sometimes arrested when they attempt to defend themselves (Henning and Feder 2004: 78; Humphries 2002: 91–96; Melton and Belknap 2003: 345) in an effort to gain control and safety. If a victim feels that she stands a substantial risk of being arrested in the course of an IPV incident where she has defended herself, or has been arrested in the past due to a similar situation, she may be far less likely to contact law enforcement (Henning and Feder 2004: 78; Wolf et al. 2003: 124). These arrests could stem from police use of mandatory arrest policies, which have drawn the attention of scholars (Henning and Feder 2004: 69). In their study of female victims of IPV in Memphis, Tennessee, Henning and Feder (2004: 77–78) concluded that many of the women victims who were actually arrested for the IPV offense did not fit the mold of such a perpetrator (that is, they had a low level of criminality and associated risk factors), and they suggest that some of these women were arrested for defending themselves.

Other factors that relate to victims' hesitation to involve law enforcement include poor experiences with police officers in their response to previous violent incidents, including not arresting the batterer; the victim's feeling that her situation is not important to the police; the perception that the responding officers could bond with the abuser; and the victim's perceived inability to communicate with the officers due to a language barrier (Wolf et al. 2003: 125). The statistics collected by the Department of Justice (2000: 7) regarding nonreporting of IPV cases are interesting. Of women victimized between 1993 and 1998, 35 percent did not report because they felt that the incident was a private matter, 19 percent because they were afraid of reprisal, and 2 percent because they were unsure as to whether or not a crime had actually occurred. However, the most startling statistic presented was that 13 percent did not report because they felt that the police either were biased, would not bother to take action, or would be ineffective in their response (U.S. Department of Justice 2000: 7). This appears to infer a crisis of confidence in the police on the part of victims of IPV and suggests that action must be taken to truly make police a viable resource for victims in their attempt to escape a violent relationship.

There are two different sets of potential policy responses that address the involvement of law enforcement in IPV cases. The first, again, is to strengthen education—of the public and of law enforcement personnel. Educating potential victims of IPV will allow them to fully understand their right to seek help from law enforcement (Wolf et al. 2003: 128). This should also extend to educating the potential first responders (i.e., family and friends) to be aware of signs of abuse so that they can assist the victim in overcoming the fears and hesitations that seem to inhibit involving law enforcement.

Many of the suggestions made thus far relate directly to the victim. In the case of involvement of law enforcement, the changes in policy also come from the police. These changes include: effectively training officers in how to respond to IPV incidents, especially as it pertains to gathering sensitive information from the victim; ensuring that translators are readily available in order to serve all segments of the community; appropriately identifying the batterer in the relationship, as opposed to mis-identifying as batterer the victim who is defending herself; and enforcing any mandatory arrest laws or policies that exist in a jurisdiction (Humphries 2002: 92, 94; Stephens and Sinden 2000: 534, 545–546; Wolf et al. 2003: 127–128). Another change involves the mandatory arrest policy itself. The suggestion in this situation is to give law enforcement the discretion to perform a thorough investigation of the situation in order to accurately determine who the abuser is, including reviewing the arrest histories of the parties and any prior domestic violence calls for service involving the parties to a given IPV case (Henning and Feder 2004: 78). This would hopefully lead to law enforcement looking beyond arresting the individual who appeared to cause the most damage in a mutual combat situation. Each of these areas of focus is designed to create an image of and response from law enforcement that engenders confidence on the part of the victim and permits her to feel free to utilize police service as a means of gaining control in an IPV situation.

Seeking Control through the Judicial Process

After a case of IPV is reported to the police, both the accused and the victim begin to wend their way through the judicial system, which only relatively recently began to respond to IPV as a serious problem (Lutze and Symons 2003: 322). The victim's perceived legal power can serve as a very effective tool in gaining control in a situation of IPV (Miller 2003: 712) and present another nonviolent alternative to gaining such control. A victim does not tend to feel comfortable being involved in the criminal justice system in an IPV case if she does not perceive that the potential outcome of the legal proceedings will be appropriate to the situation (Wolf et al. 2003: 125; Wright 2000: 14) or that it will leave her vulnerable to reprisals from the batterer (Wolf et al. 2003: 126). As a result, the judicial system's response to IPV must be examined to ensure that it provides a victim with maximum protection, of both her person and her rights.

One means that a woman has at attempting to gain control over her batterer through the judicial process is by obtaining an order of protection. According to a study published in the *Journal of the American Medical Association,* 20 percent of victims of IPV obtain orders of protection (Holt et al. 2002: 589). This number seems to be rather low, and other scholarly literature identifies the process of obtaining the order, which has the potential to be time-consuming and unduly burdensome on the victim, as a barrier to seeking this important protection (Zoellner et al. 2000: 1092). While no process of law should be undertaken hastily, the challenge for policymakers is to create a means by which a victim can avail herself of the protection of the legal system in a reasonable manner without having to expend unnecessary energy to do so.

A second issue relating to the criminal justice system is found in the laws and sanctions that deal with IPV. There has been a notable increase in legislation designed to aid the victim in IPV situations (Lilly 2002: 179), and in states that target IPV through legislation, a study has found that there is an impact on domestic violence (Dugan 2003: 303). As a result, the implication is that legislative bodies should enact laws that aggressively address IPV *and that are well enforced* in order to provide for the safety of the victim (Dugan 2003: 305; Lutze and Symons 2003: 324).

As with accessing law enforcement, becoming an active advocate for oneself in the criminal justice system requires that the victim become involved in a system with which, more likely than not, she is unfamiliar. The victim's experience with that system will greatly impact the amount of control that she perceives she can gain by participating in the judicial process and can impact her choice to continue to involve the courts as a nondelinquent means of gaining control in a violent relationship, as opposed to responding with further violence. The inference here is that an effective advocacy program should be implemented so that victims have some form of guidance in navigating the legal processes that surround being victimized by one's partner, which would provide positive support to the victim, and this inference is supported by scholars (Marano 2003).

Conclusion

In the case of IPV, the opportunity exists to explain both the origin of the crime (control) and the criminal act (violence), as well as to suggest possible ways to address the crime, through control balance theory. Applying the theory allows one to identify violence in a relationship on the part of a batterer as his attempt to extend his control over his victim, while the victim's physical responses are explained as attempts to gain control in a violent relationship due to the victim's belief that there are no other legitimate ways to acquire control. This presents the challenge of creating legitimate means of obtaining control that are accessible to the victim and are perceived favorably by her as effective in helping her gain the control necessary to escape the cycle of violence without resorting to violence herself. Some of the methods that should be considered involve increasing, and making accessible, social services and educational programs, improving police responses to IPV, and focusing the judicial system on the safety of the victims as well as the rights of the accused.

Michelle Hughes Miller (2004: 68), a sociologist at Southern Illinois University–Carbondale, states that "to be a survivor, women victims have to survive both their own victimization and the system of justice." The application of control balance theory to IPV clearly illustrates the centrality of the issue of control in such cases. More importantly, it highlights the importance of the role of the entire community, policymakers, criminologists, and the public at large, in addressing the crime by providing to victims legitimate, nonviolent means of gaining control to survive IPV.

RONALD S. MORGAN, JR.

See also **Attachment Theory and Domestic Violence; Battered Woman Syndrome; Coercive Control; Exchange Theory; Social Learning Theory and Family Violence; Victim-Blaming Theory**

References and Further Reading

Adler, J. "I Loved Joe, But I Had to Shoot Him: Homicide by Women in Turn-of-the-Century Chicago." *Journal of Criminal Law and Criminology* 92 (2002): 867–897.

Campbell, J., and K. Soeken. "Women's Responses to Battering over Time: An Analysis of Change." *Journal of Interpersonal Violence* 14 (1999): 21–40.

Clements, C., C. Sabourin, and L. Spiby. "Dysphoria and Hopelessness Following Battering: The Role of Perceived Control, Coping, and Self-Esteem." *Journal of Family Violence* 19 (2004): 25–36.

Dugan, L. "Domestic Violence Legislation: Exploring its Impact on the Likelihood of Domestic Violence, Police Involvement, and Arrest." *Criminology and Public Policy* 2 (2003): 283–312.

Fry, P., and L. Barker. "Female Survivors of Violence and Abuse: Their Regrets of Action and Inaction in Coping." *Journal of Interpersonal Violence* 16 (2001): 320–342.

Gilbert, J. "School Killing Puts Focus on Abuse of Teens," 2003. *Austin American Statesman*, April 7. http://www.statesman.com/metrostate/content/metro/reagan/0407parents.html (accessed May 1, 2004).

Henning, K., and L. Feder. "A Comparison of Men and Women Arrested for Domestic Violence: Who Presents the Greater Threat?" *Journal of Family Violence* 19 (2004): 69–79.

Henning, K., and L. Klesges. "Prevalence and Characteristics of Psychological Abuse Reported by Court-Involved Battered Women." *Journal of Interpersonal Violence* 18 (2003): 857–871.

Holt, V., M. Kernie, T. Lumley, M. Wolf, and F. Rivara. "Civil Protection Orders and Risk of Subsequent Police-Reported Violence." *Journal of the American Medical Association* 288 (2002): 589–594.

Humphries, D. "No Easy Answers: Public Policy, Criminal Justice, and Domestic Violence." *Criminology and Public Policy* 2 (2002): 91–96.

Lilly, J., F. Cullen, and R. Ball. *Criminological Theory: Context and Consequences,* 3rd ed. Thousand Oaks, CA: Sage Publications, 2002.

Lutze, F., and M. Symons. "The Evolution of Domestic Violence Policy through Masculine Institutions: From Discipline to Protection to Collaborative Empowerment." *Criminology and Public Policy* 2 (2003): 319–328.

Marano, L. "Access to Legal Aid Lowers Domestic Abuse," 2003. http://www.lanwt.org/yb/accright.asp (accessed September 15, 2004).

McFarlane, J., P. Wilson, A. Malecha, and D. Lemmey. "Intimate Partner Violence: A Gender Comparison." *Journal of Interpersonal Violence* 15 (2000): 158–169.

Melton, H., and J. Belknap. "He Hits, She Hits: Assessing Gender Differences and Similarities in Officially Reported Intimate Partner Violence." *Criminal Justice and Behavior* 30 (2003): 328–348.

Miller, J. "An Arresting Experiment: Domestic Violence Victim Experiences and Perceptions." *Journal of Interpersonal Violence* 18 (2003): 695–716.

Miller, M. Review of "Convicted Survivors: The Imprisonment of Battered Women Who Kill." *Homicide Studies* 8 (2004): 66–68.

Osborn, C. "Victim Had a Volatile History," 2002. *Austin American Statesman,* April 28. http://www.statesman.com/specialreports/content/specialreports/homicides/0428hill.html (accessed May 1, 2004).

Piquero, A., and M. Hickman. "Extending Tittle's Control Balance Theory to Account for Victimization." *Criminal Justice and Behavior* 30 (2003): 282–301.

Smith, J. "McTear Admits Murder, Gets Maximum Sentence," 2003. *Austin Chronicle,* June 13. http://www.austinchronicle.com/issues/dispatch/2003-06-13/pols_feature5.html (accessed September 15, 2004).

Stephens, B., and P. Sinden. "Victims' Voices: Domestic Assault Victims' Perceptions of Police Demeanor." *Journal of Interpersonal Violence* 15 (2000): 534–547.

Sylvester, J., R. Shirley, B. Mueller, and K. Clark. Presentation at "Raising Voices Raising Issues: An Educational Forum for Candidates and the Public on Family Violence," September 12, 2004.

Texas Family Code. http://www.capitol.state.tx.us/statutes/fa.toc.htm (accessed May 1, 2004).

Texas Penal Code. http://www.capitol.state.tx.us/statutes/pe.toc.htm (accessed May 1, 2004).

Tittle, C. *Control Balance: Toward a General Theory of Deviance.* Boulder, CO: Westview, 1995.

———. "Control Balance." In *Explaining Criminals and Crime: Essays in Contemporary Theory,* edited by R. Paternoster and R. Bachman. Los Angeles: Roxbury, 2000, pp. 157–179.

U.S. Department of Justice. *Violence by Intimates: Analysis of Data on Crimes by Current or Former Spouses, Boyfriends, and Girlfriends.* Washington, DC: Bureau of Justice Statistics, 1998.

———. *Intimate Partner Violence.* Washington, DC: Bureau of Justice Statistics, 2000.

———. *Intimate Partner Violence, 1993–2001.* Washington, DC: Bureau of Justice Statistics, 2003.

West, A., and M. Wandrei. "Intimate Partner Violence: A Model for Predicting Interventions by Informal Helpers." *Journal of Interpersonal Violence* 17 (2002): 972–986.

Wolf, M., U. Ly, M. Hobart, and M. Kernic. "Barriers to Seeking Police Help for Intimate Partner Violence." *Journal of Family Violence* 18 (2003): 121–129.

Wright, A. *Defending Battered Women: A Manual for Criminal Defense Lawyers.* Austin, TX: Women's Advocacy Project, 2000.

Zoellner, L., N. Feeny, J. Alvarez, C. Watlington, M. O'Neill, R. Zager, and E. Foa. "Factors Associated with Completion of the Restraining Order Process in Female Victims of Partner Violence." *Journal of Interpersonal Violence* 15 (2000): 1081–1099.

CORPORAL PUNISHMENT, RELIGIOUS ATTITUDES TOWARD

Corporal punishment, defined as discipline that intentionally causes physical pain, has been meted out to children throughout recorded history in most cultures, but its frequency is declining, and seventeen countries, beginning with Sweden in 1979, have banned it completely.

In the nineteenth century the founder of the Baha'i faith prohibited corporal punishment of children in his scriptures. Some scholars say Baha'i was the first religion to oppose corporal punishment. The United Methodist Church is the first Christian denomination to take an official position against corporal punishment. The church passed resolutions in 2004 discouraging parents from hitting children and calling upon states to prohibit corporal punishment in schools, day-care centers, and residential facilities for children. However, while a few religions have spoken out against corporal punishment, others not only permit it, but declare it to be divinely mandated.

While few denominations have taken a position against corporal punishment, individual clerics and devout believers have written that Jesus' teachings advocate respect for children and training without striking them. End Physical Punishment of Children has posted several such statements on the Internet (Center for Effective Discipline website 2006). Jesus is presented as leading by example in Teresa Whitehurst's book *How Would Jesus Raise a Child?*, by Christians for Nonviolent Parenting (Project NoSpank website 2006), and by Christian parents Sue and Steve Lawrence (website 2006), using the qualities of the beatitudes to nurture the internal moral compass of individuals, including children. Jesus valued affirming, nurturing relationships above legalistic rules, they say.

The Catholic Church in the United States does not have a national policy on corporal punishment, but six calls to Catholic dioceses in different regions of the country found that all now prohibit corporal punishment in Catholic schools. Nearly all said the policy related to theological teaching on the dignity of the human person. Judaism does not interpret the verses in Proverbs as authority to hit children with implements, nor does it believe that children are born into original sin. Israel prohibits all corporal punishment of children.

Several studies have shown both the practice of and belief in corporal punishment to be much higher among fundamentalist Protestants. Researchers for ReligiousTolerance.org (website 2006) found that they are the only religious group that publishes doctrinal justifications for corporal punishment. Many fundamentalists believe that hitting children is sanctioned or mandated by the Bible. They cite these verses in the Old Testament's Proverbs as authority for their belief, specifically Proverbs 3:11–12, 13:24, 19:18, 20:30, 22:15, and 23:13–14. Proverbs 23:13–14 claims that if you beat a child with a rod, he will not die, but instead will have his soul saved. Verses from Proverbs have been used to justify, advocate, or encourage various forms of corporal punishment by parents against children. One sermon advises parents to "wound" the child with corporal punishment because Proverbs 20:30 says a wound cleanses away evil. Punishment by prying the child's mouth open and putting Tabasco sauce on the tongue or clipping a clothespin on the tongue is recommended for verbal defiance, biting, and lying in Lisa Whelchel's book *Creative Correction*. She cites Proverbs 10:31 about a "perverse tongue" being "cut out" and other Bible verses as authority for such methods. The publisher of Whelchel's book is Focus on the Family, founded by James Dobson, the most prominent Christian advocate of corporal punishment.

No recorded words of Jesus recommend corporal punishment or the subjugation of children. No New Testament verses say that children should be struck with the hand or with implements. In Hebrews 12, Saint Paul speaks of fathers "chastening" and "correcting" their sons as an analogy for the trials Christians encounter in their spiritual growth, but the verses do not indicate that chastening should be physical. Paul says that children should honor and obey their parents (Ephesians 6:2–4) but also says that fathers should not anger or discourage their children (Colossians 3:20). Paul does, however, set forth an authoritarian model for the family with wives and children subjugated to the adult males. A few verses after declaring that women should keep silent in churches and be in subjection, he says that fathers must rule their households and keep their children in subjection in order to be able to take care of the church (1 Timothy 3:4–5).

Several scholars indicate that conservative Protestants' approval of corporal punishment is based on their beliefs that the Bible is inerrant and has the answers to all human concerns, children are born with original sin, and an apocalypse, or "rapture," is coming soon. Many fundamentalists advocating corporal punishment read Proverbs as a literal injunction to hit children with implements. They reject advice from secular parenting books because they believe the Bible has the correct advice on all matters. Their determination that the Bible is the literal, absolute word of God leads to an insistence on authoritarian relationships. They fear that sensuality and libertarianism in popular culture threaten their ability to impart religious values to their children. They do not see the government as supporting their parenting ideals, but rather as interfering with them. They believe that babies are born sinful and naturally inclined to rebel against God and their parents. Reflecting the divine order, they expect that men should be in control of their wives and children. A child's reluctance or refusal to obey a parent's order is as offensive as Satan's original rebellion against God. Corporal punishment is sacralized as a divine mandate. Parents must break a child's will in order for the child and parents to be saved from hell on judgment day, which they expect to arrive in the near future. Fundamentalists are more likely than others to hold images of God stressing punishment and judgment.

Fear of rebellion is prominent among fundamentalists. Dobson recommends that parents be flexible and use various nonviolent discipline methods for most problem behaviors of children, but for "willful disobedience" he believes that corporal punishment should be a parent's first resort and that a parent must "win decisively."

Many, but not all, fundamentalist advocates of corporal punishment recommend striking children with implements rather than the hands so that the parents' hands will be perceived as instruments of love. Some emphasize that corporal punishment must be continued until the child's will is broken, as shown when the child "accepts" the punishment. Some advocates warn that children may cry during corporal punishment as a strategy of rebellion and should then be hit harder.

Several advocates present corporal punishment as a ritual with firm directions about how to do it, what to use, when to stop, and what to do afterward. Dobson recommends holding the child close after he or she accepts the punishment, assuring the child of the parent's love, and then praying with the child in confession that everyone has sinned and asking for God's forgiveness.

Articles on the Christian Parent's Network (website 2006) say that parents have a religious duty to do battle against a child and win. Corporal punishment gives children "a foretaste of the potential terror and pain of eternal separation from God," one says. Another warns parents not to have sympathy for the child when they hit him or her and accuses nonspanking parents of laziness.

Several fundamentalist advocates for corporal punishment place important caveats on its use. The majority say that parents should never strike a child in anger or frustration, for then they will be displaying loss of control. They say that children will develop their image of God from the parents' behavior and therefore parents should show both love for their children and punishment of sin that is inevitable and consistent.

Dobson and others set age limits. Corporal punishment should not be used on babies younger than fifteen months and rarely if ever used on children more than ten years old, they say. Some fundamentalist leaders, however, recommend hitting infants with switches because they are born with the sin of rebellion, and the earlier that corporal punishment is started, the easier it will be to control them later.

While several scholars believe that a hierarchical, authoritarian model of sacred and secular relationships and strict gender roles contribute to endorsement of corporal punishment, the Mormons are an interesting counterexample. The Church of Jesus Christ of Latter-day Saints (the Mormon Church) has an all-male priesthood, to which every boy over the age of twelve may belong. Gender-prescribed roles are a map to salvation and the basis of hierarchy and distinction in church doctrine. The child training literature of this patriarchal religion, however, is radically different from that of fundamentalist Protestants. The Mormon Church's sacred scriptures do not express the doctrine of original sin, nor do they view children as inherently rebellious or recommend corporal punishment to break their will. Joseph F. Smith, the Church's tenth president, advised parents to "use no lash and no violence" with their children. Gordon Hinckley, the fifteenth president, said, "I have never accepted the principle of 'spare the rod and spoil the child. . . .' Children don't need beating. They need love and encouragement." The Church's magazine *Ensign* publishes articles calling corporal punishment ineffective and promoting other methods of discipline. Rates of child abuse and neglect in Utah, which has a large Mormon population, are below the national average, and Utah has outlawed corporal punishment in schools.

Several studies indicate that religious belief is a better predictor of corporal punishment than socioeconomic status. Features of the larger society, however, may shape religious beliefs or parenting practices. For example, rates of corporal punishment and of religious belief are both high in the African American community. While there may be a causal relationship between those two factors, several scholars have found that racism, urban violence, and high rates of incarceration are causes of corporal punishment among African Americans. Many of these parents spank their children severely because they want to protect them from street violence and from the punishments of a white power structure.

Critics of corporal punishment say that most injuries and even deaths due to physical abuse of children begin as discipline. Beatings have gone on for hours because children would not apologize or meet another parental demand. Some say that a religious rationale increases the emotional harm done by corporal punishment. Insisting that the physical pain comes because of love and that a supernatural being has ordered it compounds the assault on the child's sense of self. The parent's love is conditioned upon stripping the child of will.

Critics also point out that hitting children with implements makes the parent less aware of the force being used. They find the claim that parents may win salvation by hitting their children insidious. Some claim that even the conservative Protestants' emphasis on hitting without anger is harmful. They feel that this religious group has made corporal punishment a ritual in which the parent becomes emotionally detached and irresponsible on the assumption that he is acting as God's agent. Furthermore, the doctrines of supernatural evil and original sin may lead adults to believe the child is demon possessed and to attempt an exorcism. Children have been tortured and killed because of belief in demon possession.

Most research on the impact of corporal punishment is criticized as unscientific and misleading by proponents and opponents alike. The many variables involved make scientific conclusions difficult. Elizabeth Gershoff reviewed eighty-eight studies of corporal punishment with sixty-two years of data and found that corporal punishment was associated with ten negative outcomes for children and that the only positive effect was short-term compliance. Robert Larzelere, however, found that corporal punishment confined to loving parents' infrequently giving toddlers a few swats on the buttocks was beneficial. One study found that persons who believe that the entire Bible is literally true have more unrealistic expectations of children and less empathy toward children's needs than nonliteralist Christians. Another found that fundamentalist Protestants who are involved in their churches spend more time participating in their children's activities and talking to them than other parents. The quality of the total parent–child relationship influences the impact of corporal punishment.

Public Policy

Twenty-eight states prohibit corporal punishment in public schools. Most of them also outlaw it in state-licensed day-care and residential facilities for children. Only two of those states, Iowa and New Jersey, prohibit corporal punishment in parochial schools. New Jersey became the first state to abolish corporal punishment in the schools, in 1867, and Massachusetts became the second state, in 1972.

Many fundamentalists lobby for school personnel to have a legal right to hit children. The trend, however, is to prohibit it in more public schools, partly because of civil liability. In nine of the twenty-two states that allow corporal punishment by state law, more than half of the students are in school districts that have banned it. In the 1999–2000 school year, Texas had the highest percentage and number of children given corporal punishment by school staff, with 73,994 instances. By 2005, however, the school districts of Austin, Dallas, Ft. Worth, Houston, San Antonio, and many other Texas cities had prohibited corporal punishment.

Forty Christian schools filed suit to overturn the United Kingdom's ban on all school corporal punishment, charging that it prevented them from teaching morals to their students and interfered with religious freedom. The European Court of Human Rights and U.K. courts ruled against them. In South Africa 196 Christian schools brought a similar challenge; the South African Constitutional Court ruled against them.

In 2005 Brookline, Massachusetts, passed a non-binding resolution stating that it is local policy to discourage parents and other caretakers from using corporal punishment on children. Brookline is reportedly the first municipality in the United States to do so. Given the strength of U.S. religious conservatism and the lack of consensus in scholarship, the United States is highly unlikely to ban corporal punishment of children by parents in the foreseeable future.

RITA SWAN

See also **Christianity and Domestic Violence; Medical Neglect Related to Religion and Culture; Munchausen by Proxy Syndrome; Ritual Abuse–Torture in Families**

References and Further Reading

Bartkowski, John, and Christopher Ellison. "Divergent Models of Childrearing in Popular Manuals: Conservative Protestants vs. the Mainstream Experts." *Sociology of Religion* 56, no. 1 (1995): 21–34.

Capps, Donald. *The Child's Song: The Religious Abuse of Children.* Louisville: Westminster John Knox Press, 1995.

Center for Effective Discipline website. www.stophitting.org (accessed August 16, 2006).

Christian Parent's Network website. http://www.christian-parents.net (accessed August 16, 2006).

Corpun website. World Corporal Punishment Research. http://www.corpun.com (accessed August 16, 2006).

Dobson, James. *The New Dare to Discipline.* Wheaton, IL: Tyndale, 1992.

Ellison, Christopher. "Conservative Protestantism and the Corporal Punishment of Children: Clarifying the Issues." *Journal for the Scientific Study of Religion* 35, no. 1 (1996): 1–16.

Ellison, Christopher, and John Bartkowski. "Religion and the Legitimation of Violence: Conservative Protestantism and Corporal Punishment." In *The Web of Violence: From Interpersonal to Global,* edited by Jennifer Turpin and Lester Kurtz. Urbana and Chicago: University of Illinois Press, 1997, pp. 45–67.

Ellison, Christopher, John Bartkowski, and Michelle Segal. "Do Conservative Protestants Spank More Often? Further Evidence from the National Survey of Families and Households." *Social Science Quarterly* 77, no. 3 (1996): 663–673.

Gershoff, Elizabeth. "Corporal Punishment by Parents and Associated Child Behaviors and Experiences: A Meta-Analytic and Theoretical Review." *Psychological Bulletin* 128, no. 4 (2002): 539–579.

Gershoff, Elizabeth, Pamela Miller, and George Holden. "Parenting from the Pulpit: Religious Affiliation as a Determinant of Parental Corporal Punishment." *Journal of Family Psychology* 13, no. 3 (1999): 307–320.

Greven, Philip. *Spare the Child: The Religious Roots of Punishment and the Psychological Impact of Physical Abuse.* New York: Alfred A. Knopf, 1991.

Grille, Robin. *Parenting for a Peaceful World.* Alexandria, Australia: Longueville Media, 2005.

Hines, Denise, and Kathleen Malley-Morrison. *Family Violence in the United States: Defining, Understanding, and Combating Abuse.* Thousand Oaks, CA: Sage Publications, 2004.

Kimmel, Tim. *Grace-Based Parenting.* Nashville: W. Publishing Group, 2004.

Larzelere, Robert. "Child Outcomes of Nonabusive and Customary Physical Punishment by Parents: An Updated Literature Review." *Clinical Child and Family Psychology Review* 3, no. 4 (2000): 199–221.

Lawrence, S., and S. Lawrence website. http://www.parentinginjesusfootsteps.org (accessed August 16, 2006).

Project NoSpank website. http://www.nospank.net (accessed August 16, 2006).

ReligiousTolerance.org website. http://www.religioustolerance.org (accessed August 16, 2006).

Straus, Murray. *Beating the Devil Out of Them: Corporal Punishment in American Families and Its Effects on Children.* New Brunswick, NJ: Transaction Publishers, 2001.

Whelchel, Lisa. *Creative Correction: Extraordinary Ideas for Everyday Discipline.* A Focus on the Family book. Carol Stream, IL: Tyndale House, 2000.

Whitehurst, Teresa. *How Would Jesus Raise a Child?* Grand Rapids, MI: Baker Books, 2003.

CROSS-CULTURAL EXAMINATION OF DOMESTIC VIOLENCE IN CHINA AND PAKISTAN

Since the 1970s there has been an emerging concern for violence against women. It has been shown that much of the violence perpetrated against women occurs in the home and/or at the hands of someone known to the female. While many Western and developed nations have been committed to the study of domestic violence, it has only recently achieved global priority. Although researchers have been more diligent in collecting data on various areas of domestic violence in North America, data seem to suggest that family violence dynamics are fairly similar from one nation to the other (Walker 1999). The global significance of domestic violence, and specifically violence against women, has been recognized as a major international issue. Rather than consisting of isolated occurrences, it would seem that domestic violence is a problem that transcends both culture and national identity. Indeed, domestic assaults of women share many commonalities across a wide range of otherwise diverse cultures. These common aspects must be examined to gain a broader understanding of a problem that is encountered in cultures throughout the world. One such commonality is that violence against women has, in general, been touted as gender based in occurrence and etiology. Indeed, Walker (1999) points out that "where women and girls are the primary targets of male abuse, violence cannot be eradicated without looking carefully at the gender socialization issues that facilitate such violence in the home" (p. 22). Indeed, any strategy to end violence will have to deal with eliminating those social causes that support and condone violence against women. This means challenging the underlying attitudes that support male aggression, renegotiating the meaning of gender, and redefining the balance of power held between women and men at all levels of society (Walker 1999).

It is with this in mind that a comparison of Chinese and Pakistani cultures will demonstrate an emergence of common themes. Similarities and differences between these cultures exist which serve to modify the nature and occurrence of domestic violence against women. In both cases, a common connection develops where patriarchy and female subservience seem to correlate with the onset of domestic violence. In each of these Asian cultures, as in many other cultures worldwide, there seems to be little societal concern about female assault within the home. Indeed, such assaults are frequently held to be a private matter for the family. These views are not unlike those held in the United States and England before the women's movement of the late 1960s and early 1970s. In fact, many similarities can be observed between the current experiences of these Asian cultures and the past experiences of Western nations. Further, just as with previous developments in the United States and England, there is a slow cultural shift toward consideration for the victim of family violence. While outdated beliefs regarding roles of perpetrator and victim are still maintained in many parts of both countries, there are changes occurring. These changes in both

countries will be illustrated after comparing the more traditional beliefs and problems associated with domestic violence in China and Pakistan.

Traditional Chinese Values Regarding Domestic Violence

In Chinese culture, family lines are based on patriarchal family structures, and men are therefore endowed with a strong sense of importance and entitlement (Lee and Au 1998). Because Chinese cultural values support male supremacy and dominance over women, male violence against women in the form of physical abuse is often justified based on culturally acceptable reasons (Hanser 2001; Lee and Au 1998). Because family name and honor is paramount and because the individual well-being is held to be subordinate to family well-being, it is extremely difficult for many Chinese women or families to disclose the existence of abuse (Hanser 2001; Lee and Au 1998). Such cultural factors exacerbate the problems involved with intimate partner violence, creating a tenuous process in attempting to eradicate it.

Modern Developments in China Regarding Domestic Violence

Parish, Wang, Laumann, Pan, and Luo (2004) conducted a study that has supplied the first national analysis of intimate partner violence in China, including prevalence by perpetrator and severity; risk factors; and general, sexual, and reproductive health correlates of violence among men and women. Parish et al. (2004) used data from the 1999–2000 Chinese Health and Family Life Survey, which included a nationally representative sample of the adult population aged twenty to sixty-four. From their research, Parish et al. (2004) found that many risk factors for partner violence in China are similar to those in other countries. Like women in other countries, Chinese women are at increased risk of partner violence when their male partner is of low socioeconomic status and when either partner uses alcohol (Parish et al. 2004). Likewise, Parish and colleagues found evidence for a link between patriarchal beliefs and hitting. Acceptance of the belief that "men should lead in sex and women should follow" is at best an imperfect measure of only one set of possible patriarchal values. Nevertheless, this belief is associated with increased male-on-female and reduced female-on-male hitting.

Despite the strictures of traditional culture, it would appear that the social climate is changing quite rapidly. Indeed, one large-scale change is that the central government as well as nongovernmental organizations have started to place great importance on ending domestic violence. Though there is still no unified law against domestic violence in China, legislation has emerged in many provinces and cities throughout the nation (*People's Daily* 2001). For example, in Liaoning and Hunan provinces, local people's congresses have passed regulations to curb domestic violence, and Shaanxi Province is expected to follow suit shortly. At this point, at least thirteen provinces, regions, cities, and counties in China have passed local regulations to prevent domestic violence (*People's Daily* 2001). And official statistics indicate that about 90 percent of the counties, cities, and provinces in China have established legal counseling centers for abused women (*People's Daily* 2001).

Further, the China Law Society recently published a national survey urging the establishment of legislation against domestic violence (*China Daily* 2002). According to this survey, domestic violence has become publicly recognized as a social problem in China, where one-third of the country's 270 million households cope with domestic violence (*China Daily* 2002). Amazingly, an average of 100,000 households are torn apart by domestic violence each year.

Traditional Problems with Domestic Violence in Pakistan

Within the nation of Pakistan, violence against women and domestic violence are commonly reported to occur (Human Rights Watch 1999). Women in Pakistan face the threat of multiple forms of violence, including physical and sexual abuse, by both family members and state agents (Human Rights Watch 1999). The worst victims were found to be those falling within the poor and middle classes, as their lack of financial resources make them particularly vulnerable to both the state and criminals alike. Women in Pakistan are also subject to oppressive customs and mores inside the home, such that the most endemic form of violence faced by Pakistani women is domestic violence (Human Rights Watch 1999).

Research on domestic violence in Pakistan indicates that it is a structural rather than causal problem. It is the structure of the family that leads to or legitimizes the act. This structure is mirrored and confirmed in the structure of society within Pakistan, and condones the oppression of women while tolerating male violence as one of many means to maintain the dominant power balance (Human

Rights Watch 1999). Indeed, numerous customs exist which result in lethal consequences for women at the hands of their husbands or their husband's relatives.

One type of domestic violence that seems to be more peculiar to Pakistan and some other Islamic nations is the practice of what are termed "honor killings" (Mayell 2002). This practice, referred to as *karo kari,* calls for the woman to be summarily killed due to being guilty of an illicit liaison. It should be noted that *karo kari* has been found to occur throughout all parts of Pakistan (Human Rights Watch 1999). Each year, it is estimated that hundreds of women are murdered by their families in order that the family can save its honor. Honor killings are perpetrated for a wide range of offenses. Marital infidelity, premarital sex, flirting, or even failing to serve a meal on time can all be perceived as impugning the family honor. Though the media in Pakistan make frequent reports of this occurrence, it is still difficult to get exact data on honor killings because the murders frequently go unreported and the perpetrators unpunished, and the concept of family honor seems to justify the act (Mayell 2002).

In addition to perceived blemishes against the family honor, many of these killings may be motivated by the fact that the dowry from the marriage is not considered adequate. Complicity by other women in the family and the community strengthens the concept of women as property and the perception that violence against family members is a family issue and not a judicial one. Mayell (2002) notes that "in a society where most marriages are arranged by fathers and money is often exchanged, a woman's desire to choose her own husband—or to seek a divorce—can be viewed as a major act of defiance that damages the honor of the man who negotiated the deal" (p. 2). Further, when women are accused by family members of bringing dishonor to their families, they seldom have the ability to demonstrate their innocence.

In these cases, the public, police, and government officials seem lax in holding the husband accountable by conviction (Human Rights Watch 1999). State responses seem to be somewhat lacking, and domestic violence cases are seldom addressed by the police or the criminal justice system. As is the case with many countries across the world, domestic violence is seen as a private family matter, not subject to government intervention, with criminal responses being extremely unlikely (Human Rights Watch 1999). Rates of domestic violence in Pakistan are alarming, estimated at between 70 to 90 percent over the course of the woman's life span (Human Rights Watch 1999).

Modern Research and Developments in Pakistan Regarding Domestic Violence

First and foremost, it should be noted that domestic violence is not a crime in Pakistan (Manzoor 2004). Indeed, it is commonly accepted that every man has the right to beat his wife, daughter, or sister. Likewise, it is estimated that roughly 5,000 women die annually from various forms of domestic violence (Manzoor 2004). Further, thousands are badly injured, maimed, and/or disabled. According to a survey conducted by a leading English-language newspaper in Pakistan, roughly 90 percent of all women polled reported facing some form of domestic violence (Manzoor 2004).

The tenets of *Shari'a* (Islamic law) hold that men are allowed to beat their wives or daughters, particularly if it is designed to protect the family honor from the possible deficiencies or character flaws that the woman is purported to have (Hajjar 2000). These beliefs are further reinforced by the sermons of the mullahs, who routinely disseminate this belief system regarding marriage and women's rights.

The vast majority of victims of domestic violence in Pakistan (including those who are victims of attempted honor killings) have no way of getting legal protection (Manzoor 2004). One reason for this is that the police do not consider domestic violence as a crime (again, the male police are likely to enforce the tenets of *Shari'a*) and typically refuse to register cases dealing with family issues. In fact, it is often the case that the police encourage and/or force victims to come to a compromise with their own families. Likewise, there are very few shelters in Pakistan, leaving victims with little or no ability to flee the violence perpetrated against them (Mayell 2002).

Research on domestic violence issues in Pakistan is not widespread but is becoming a topic that is drawing more attention from the global arena. One study conducted by Shaikh (2003) found that nearly 97 percent of women interviewed reported being victims of some form of domestic violence at one point or another throughout their lifetimes. Further, many of these women also reported multiple types of violence, from verbal to sexual abuse. Verbal abuse was found to be the most frequent form, while the use of a weapon such as a gun or knife was found to be the least common type of violence indicated. Among those women who had ever been pregnant, roughly 25 percent reported that violence had increased during their pregnancy, while 51 percent reported a decrease in the amount of domestic violence that had occurred. Also, nonconsensual sex was reported by 47 percent of the women who were interviewed. Though it would appear that domestic violence does indeed occur with some degree of frequency (Shaikh 2003), it should be noted that there were no significant findings related to the educational or income level of the victims or the abusers.

An earlier study on domestic violence in Pakistan by Shaikh (2000) assessed the prevalence and type of domestic violence by conducting interviews with male subjects. This cross-sectional survey found that 32.8 percent admitted that they had slapped or hit their wives at times throughout the duration of their marriage. Further, another 77.1 percent admitted to forcing nonconsensual sex on their wives (Shaikh 2000). This of course amounts to marital rape, though this is not a recognized crime in Pakistan (Shaikh 2000).

From these data-driven studies, it becomes clear that domestic violence is a problem by the admittance of both the potential victims and the potential perpetrators. Each study found substantial support that domestic violence is a serious issue, even though both asked fairly intrusive questions of both male and female subjects. Taken together, this is strong indication that problems with domestic violence are considered commonplace among the population in Pakistan.

Conclusion

As is readily discerned, perceptions among Asian cultures regarding domestic violence can vary quite significantly. Where some cultures tend to retain acknowledged violence solely within the family, as in the case of China, others, such as Pakistan, are more openly callous and nonchalant when addressing domestic violence focused against women. It would appear that the role of patriarchy is central to the social customs of both China and Pakistan. However, the religious basis of *Shari'a* in Pakistan has created a much more dangerous and lethal set of social practices of domestic abuse. While the People's Republic of China appears to be modernizing its concept of women's rights and, correspondingly, the social need to eradicate domestic abuse, the nation of Pakistan seems to continue to have a social climate that condones the practice. The difficulty in making social change where an exploited group is given fair and humane treatment is counterbalanced by the claims of many developing nations that the United States is behaving in an ethnocentric manner when it crafts policy that is designed to encourage countries to provide equality and humane treatment among its citizens. Resolving this dilemma between traditional culture and modern Westernized beliefs about women and the "balance of power" with family systems will be the challenge of those who hope to remove the occurrence of family violence from the homes of not only Asian nations, but a wide array of developing nations around the world.

ROBERT D. HANSER

See also **Africa: Domestic Violence and the Law; Asian Americans and Domestic Violence: Cultural Dimensions; Cross-Cultural Examination of Domestic Violence in Latin America; Cross-Cultural Perspectives on Domestic Violence; Greece, Domestic Violence in; Jewish Community, Domestic Violence within the; Minorities and Families in America, Introduction to; Multicultural Programs for Domestic Batterers; Qur'anic Perspectives on Wife Abuse; Spain, Domestic Violence in; Worldwide Sociolegal Precedents Supporting Domestic Violence from Ancient to Modern Times**

References and Further Reading

Burney, S. *Crime or Custom: Violence against Women in Pakistan*. New York: Human Rights Watch, 1999.
China Daily. "Domestic Violence Tackled," 2002. http:// www.china.org.cn/english/government/49704.htm.
Hajjar, L. "Domestic Violence and *Shari'a*: A Comparative Study of Muslim Societies in the Middle East, Africa and Asia," 2000. www.law.emory.edu/IFL/thematic/ Violence.htm.
Hanser, R. D. "A Cross-Cultural Examination of Domestic Violence." *Criminal Justice International* 17, no. 48 (2001): 9–10, 30.
Lee, M., and P. Au. "Chinese Battered Women in North America: Their Experiences and Treatment." In *Battered Women and Their Families: Intervention Strategies and Treatment Programs,* edited by A. R. Roberts, 2nd ed. New York: Springer, 1998, pp. 448–482.
Manzoor, R. "Musharraf's Hypocrisy Won't End Violence to Women." Socialist Movement Pakistan, 2004. http:// www.geocities.com/socialistparty/Women/Pakistan.htm.
Mayell, H. "Thousands of Women Killed for Family 'Honor.'" *National Geographic News*. Washington, DC: National Geographic Society, 2002. http://news.national geographic.com/news/2002/02/0212_020212_honorkilling. html.
Parish, W. L., T. Wang, E. O. Laumann, S. Pan, Y. Luo. "Intimate Partner Violence in China: National Prevalence, Risk Factors, and Associated Health Problems." *International Family Planning Perspectives* 30, no. 4 (2004). http:// www.guttmacher.org/pubs/journals/3017404.html.
People's Daily. "China to Curb Domestic Violence," 2001. http://english.people.com.cn/english/200005/06/ eng20000506_40251.html.
Shaikh, M. A. "Domestic Violence against Women: Perspective from Pakistan." *Journal of the Pakistani Medical Association,* no. 9 (2000): 312–314.
———. "Is Domestic Violence Endemic in Pakistan?: Perspectives from Pakistani Wives." *Pakistan Journal of Medical Sciences* 19, no. 1 (2003).
Walker, L. "Psychology and Domestic Violence around the World." *American Psychologist* 54, no. 1 (1999): 21–29.

CROSS-CULTURAL EXAMINATION OF DOMESTIC VIOLENCE IN LATIN AMERICA

Violence against women has become a focal concern for international organizations such as the United Nations (2005) and the World Health Organization (2005). Due to this international focus, cultural issues have taken a central role in understanding factors that contribute to violence against women in various countries. Violence against women has been shown to frequently occur in the home and/or be committed by someone closely known to the victim (Walker 1999). This phenomenon is one of the strongest common factors recognized among a wide range of cultures (Walker 1999). Within many Latin American cultures the occurrence of domestic violence has been shown to be fairly frequent (World Health Organization 2005). It has been found in almost thirty nations in this region of the world (Creel 2005). Despite the fact that many Latin American countries have passed laws against domestic violence, it would appear that the victims are not well served in this region of the world (Creel 2005). Likewise, a substantial amount of survey research has been conducted in various Latin American countries and it has been found that roughly 10 to 50 percent of women in Latin America report being physically assaulted by their male partner (Creel 2005). It is with this in mind that this article will provide an examination of the various cultural aspects specific to Latino families faced with domestic violence while at the same time providing a brief comparison of selected Latin American countries to demonstrate several common beliefs produced by the cultural underpinnings shared among these nations (Hanser 2001). Although each of these nations has its own distinct history of cultural development, there are several commonalities that exist among many Latin American countries (Hanser 2001).

Spanish is, of course, the commonly shared language among Latinos (except for Brazilians, who typically speak Portuguese), and most subscribe to the Roman Catholic Church (Garcia-Preto 1996a). There is also an emphasis on spiritual values and an expressed willingness to sacrifice material satisfactions for spiritual goals. Moreover, the concepts of *machismo* and *marianismo* are common social constructs in many Latin American cultures; these two constructs serve to organize gender roles for both males and females within a primarily patriarchal value system (Garcia-Preto 1996a, 1996b). In the United States, machismo has a negative connotation and is used to describe sexist behavior of Latino men (Garcia-Preto 1996a). Culturally, however, machismo emphasizes self-respect and responsibility for protecting and providing for the family (Garcia-Preto 1996a). But this value can become negative when it leads to possessive demands and expectations that absolute authority be given to the man. This machismo also holds that a man must always be ready for sex and must possess a great deal of sexual prowess (Garcia-Preto 1996a, 1996b). In many Latin American countries, the male head of the household is expected to protect the females of the house, while the female members are expected to play a subservient role in relation to the male family head (Shusta, Levine, Harris, and Wong 2005).

It should also be noted that in nations such as El Salvador, Nicaragua, and Colombia, citizens are frequently traumatized by guerilla warfare and political strife (Shusta et al. 2005). This has a significant impact on the behavior of both men (affecting their levels of aggressive response to environmental stressors) and women (who often present with symptoms of trauma, some profound enough to be diagnosed as post-traumatic stress disorder) in these war-torn nations. Likewise, the violence associated with wartime rape and other atrocities have been reported in these countries, and this creates a landscape of violence that essentially minimizes the effects of internal family violence that may occur in these Latin American nations.

In addition, there is a social paradox in that female virginity is highly valued in many Latin cultures and it is up to the man to protect the honor of female family members (Garcia-Preto 1996b). Naturally, the effects of wartime rape have impacted this value system and the status of women in affected families. Traditionally, in many Latino cultures, if a woman has sex before marriage, she will lose the respect of others and bring dishonor to herself and to her family (Garcia-Preto 1996b). This cultural distinction between *doñas* (ladies) and *putas* (whores) has been very concrete (Garcia-Preto 1996b). Thus again, the effects of wartime rape on girls and women living within the family systems of these countries lay the groundwork for blame and justification of abuse among the male figures of the family, while also bringing a sense of shame to the men who could not protect the female members of their families more adequately.

Perhaps the most significant value these nations share is the importance of family unity, welfare, and honor (Garcia-Preto 1996a, 1996b). In this respect, there is a strong emphasis on the group rather than the individual. In many Latin cultures, social interactions are guided by the concept of *personalismo,* which means that relationships are more important than accomplishments (Garcia-Preto 1996a, 1996b). This results in a deep sense of family commitment, obligation, and responsibility. In fact, the family is responsible for protection and caretaking for life, provided the person remains a member of the family system. The family is an extended system that includes not only blood and marriage relations, but even *compadres* (godparents) and *hijos de crianza* (adopted children); this is regardless of legal custody considerations by the godparents or legal adoption arrangements for the children (Garcia-Preto 1996b). Similarly, caring for *hijos de crianza* is a practice whereby children are transferred from one family system to another within the social network during times of crisis (Garcia-Preto 1996b). This practice is not considered neglectful and has been observed in cases where problems with family violence are experienced. Strong religious values that hold marital unions to be absolute, and Latino cultural values that hold family cohesion as paramount, have created great difficulty for many victims of domestic violence who might wish to leave abusive relationships. This has likewise provided a façade behind which the true nature and extent of such violence has remained hidden within many of these nations.

Domestic Violence in Chile

In Chile, domestic violence advocates contend that the country's culture has fostered, even supported outright, domestic violence against women (McWhirter 1999). Machismo, alcoholism, and a prevailing social permissiveness toward family violence have perpetuated a virtual disintegration of relationships between spouses and other family members (McWhirter 1999). In the Chilean belief system, it is commonly held that a man may appropriately demonstrate expressions of love through violent acts (McWhirter 1999). Further, Chilean women typically define themselves in terms of their relationships to others, performing socially prescribed roles that often involve service to others (i.e., cooking and cleaning). Therefore, a woman's self-worth is based on how well she fulfills her relationship role with others (McWhirter 1999). Because of the acceptance of male-initiated violence, and because a woman's self-worth is so closely attached to her perceived success in maintaining domestic relationships, there remain few options by which women can evade domestic violence perpetrated against them.

These cultural factors were intensified during Augusto Pinochet's dictatorship (1973–1990), which began with the overthrow of the democratically elected government (McWhirter 1999). This regime was responsible for state-sponsored violence that often included the sexual abuse and exploitation of women (McWhirter 1999). Since women were seen as central to family cohesion, the torture of these women was intended to disjoint dissident families (McWhirter 1999). Brutal violence, including that against women, has been accommodated within the Chilean culture (McWhirter 1999). Due to this accommodation to violence, and since men are viewed as the authority figure within the home, women and children are at high risk for domestic violence within Chilean homes (McWhirter 1999).

Domestic Violence in Mexico

As is the case with many Latino cultures, norms in Mexican society tend to connect machismo with male identity. Affiliation and cooperation are stressed within Mexican families, and clear hierarchies are supported within the family system (Falicov 1996). This hierarchy is based on a patriarchal formation of gender roles, with gender double standards being replete throughout Mexican society (Falicov 1996; Carrillo and Goubaud-Reyna 1998). Social status for a woman rises when she becomes a mother, making a woman's identity all the more dependent upon her family relationships (Falicov 1996). Another similarity between Mexican culture and other Latino cultures is the fact that Roman Catholicism provides continuity for the vast majority of families (Falicov 1996). For many of these followers, Catholicism is a private affair centered on marriage and fertility, the sanctity of mothers, etc., with guilt and shame about sinful acts or thoughts being common inner experiences (Falicov 1996). This results in a bonding agent that essentially glues women into the family structure. Mexican batterers, on the other hand, have been reported to frequently engage in excessive drinking that is highly correlated with abusive behavior (Carrillo and Goubaud-Reyna 1998).

The image of the Latino male as authoritarian, drunk, and womanizing is espoused through many Mexican cultural proverbs, songs, and the media, especially telenovelas (Spanish-language soap operas) (Carrillo and Goubaud-Reyna 1998). These social messages tend to reinforce the double standard that Mexican batterers often expect (Carrillo and Goubaud-Reyna 1998). Though the values of machismo emphasize positive aspects such as loyalty, respectability, integrity, courage, and responsibility to family, the social role likewise provides Mexican men with a rationale to engage in behaviors that demonstrate their authority and dominance within the family (Carrillo and Goubaud-Reyna 1998). This translates into the use of violence as a legitimate means for Mexican batterers to maintain command, respect, and obedience from family members. For women who are in such abusive families, family expectations shaped by cultural and religious beliefs ensure that most will succumb to such abuse.

Evidence of these dynamics of family violence in Mexican culture was found in a 2004 study in Mexico conducted by Collado (2005). Collado sought to examine the dynamics of domestic violence in rural areas of Mexico. This type of research is fairly important for two reasons. First, the rural parts of Mexico tend to be the areas where old patriarchal values are most strongly adhered to, thus exacerbating power dynamics associated with domestic violence. Second, it is in the rural parts of Mexico that domestic violence is less frequently reported to (and thus detected by) Mexican police.

This study investigated three different rural communities and sought to determine the means by which social control was used with women (Collado 2005). It examined other corollary factors such as coping strategies, the availability and use of social support, and other forms of adaptation used by women who are involved in violent intimate relationships (Collado 2005). This study confirmed that these communities maintain very strict and traditional gender roles that hinge on the division of labor in and out of the home. According to Collado, the main factors associated with domestic violence were alcoholism, community gossip, the male partner's infidelity, lack of economic resources, and the failure of women to fulfill expectations associated with traditional general roles.

Legal Reforms in Costa Rica

It should be noted that there are legal and judicial reforms occurring throughout various countries in Latin America. Due to substantial civil unrest and corresponding sexual violence toward women by various guerilla factions, media attention is increasingly focused on violence against women in these regions. Further still, there is a slow movement toward acknowledging the rights of women in many Latin American countries. For example, in Costa Rica, the Law against Domestic Violence, passed in 1996, provides for protective measures that are enforced without the need for full criminal or civil proceedings (Creel 2001). This law targets anyone who inflicts psychological, physical, or sexual violence on any relative. The perpetrator may be ordered out of the home and restricted from having access to the victim (Creel 2001). The perpetrator is also banned from caring for or raising children and is not allowed to possess weapons. Additionally, he may be ordered to pay for family support despite his mandated separation from the family. In 1996 alone, over 7,000 legal cases involving domestic violence were reported (Creel 2001). Further, Costa Rica has created a forum known as the National Plan to Treat and Prevent Intra-Family Violence (Creel 2001). This initiative seeks to provide for an integrated set of services and interventions available to victims of domestic violence. This initiative has succeeded in raising public awareness and sensitivity to domestic violence issues and has provided for numerous shelters and crisis hotline services (Creel 2001). Training of professionals and conducting research on domestic violence are also included in this initiative (Creel 2001).

Conclusion

Latino nations have many common connections among their cultural dynamics. Among these connections, a history of Spanish colonization, Roman Catholicism, family codes of loyalty, and gender role expectations seem most pronounced. Each of these common aspects serves as a potential explanation for much of the domestic violence that occurs against women within these cultures. On one hand, these norms and mores hold many positive functions within these societies. On the other hand, and in a paradoxical sense, these cultural belief systems elevate one half of the society while potentially subjugating the other half through a system of patriarchy that can entrap women in abusive family relationships. The social changes that many developing Latino cultures experience have led to an increased awareness of women's rights in this region. Though many countries in Latin America have laws against domestic violence, and social reforms are still in the beginning stages, it is nevertheless encouraging to see that cultural change is directed toward the ultimate eradication of domestic violence. These changes reflect the growing global sentiments as the rights of women and children are brought into primary focus around the world.

ROBERT D. HANSER

See also **Africa: Domestic Violence and the Law; Asian Americans and Domestic Violence: Cultural Dimensions; Cross-Cultural Examination of Domestic Violence in China and Pakistan; Cross-Cultural Perspectives on Domestic Violence; Greece, Domestic Violence in; Jewish Community, Domestic Violence within the; Minorities and Families in America, Introduction to; Multicultural Programs for Domestic Batterers; Spain, Domestic Violence in; Trinidad and Tobago, Domestic Violence in; Worldwide Sociolegal Precedents Supporting Domestic Violence from Ancient to Modern Times**

References and Further Reading

Bonilla-Santiago, G. "Latina Battered Women: Barriers to Service Delivery and Cultural Considerations." In *Helping Battered Women: New Perspectives and Remedies,* edited by A. R. Roberts. New York: Oxford University Press, 1996, pp. 229–234.

Carrillo, R., and R. Goubaud-Reyna. "Clinical Treatment of Latino Domestic Violence Offenders." In *Family Violence and Men of Color: Healing the Wounded Male Spirit,* edited by R. Carrillo and J. Tello. New York: McGraw-Hill, 1998, pp. 53–73.

Carrillo, R., and J. Tello, eds. *Family Violence and Men of Color: Healing the Wounded Male Spirit.* New York: Springer Publishing Company, 1998.

Collado, M. E. "Cultural Meanings of Domestic Violence in Rural Areas of Mexico," 2005. http://apha.confex. com/apha/133am/techprogram/paper_117052.htm.

Creel, L. "Domestic Violence: An Ongoing Threat to Women in Latin America and the Caribbean," 2001. http://www.prb.org/Template.cfm?Section=PRB& template=/ContentManagement/ContentDisplay.cfm& ContentID=4744 (accessed August 16, 2006).

Ellsberg, M., T. Caldera, A. Herrera, A. Winkyist, and G. Kullgren. "Domestic Violence and Emotional Distress among Nicaraguan Women: Results from a Population Based Study." *American Psychologist* 54 (1999): 30–36.

Falicov, C. J. "Mexican Families." In *Ethnicity and Family Therapy,* edited by M. McGoldrick, J. Giordano, and J. Pearce, 2nd ed. New York: Guilford Press, 1996, pp. 169–182.

Ferrer, D. V. "Domestic Violence in Latino Cultures." In *Battered Women and Their Families: Intervention Strategies and Treatment Programs,* edited by A. R. Roberts, 2nd ed. New York: Springer, 1998, pp. 106–123.

Garcia-Preto, N. "Latino Families: An Overview." In *Ethnicity and Family Therapy,* edited by M. McGoldrick, J. Giordano, and J. Pearce, 2nd ed. New York: Guilford Press, 1996a, pp. 141–154.

———. "Puerto Rican Families." In *Ethnicity and Family Therapy,* edited by M. McGoldrick, J. Giordano, and J. Pearce, 2nd ed. New York: Guilford Press, 1996b, pp. 183–199.

Hanser, R. "Domestic Violence in Selected Latin American Countries." *Criminal Justice International* 17, no. 54 (2001): 5–6, 26–27.

McWhirter, P. T. "La violencia privada: Domestic Violence in Chile." *American Psychologist* 54, no. 1 (1999): 37–40.

Shusta, M., D. R. Levine, P. R. Harris, and H. Z. Wong. *Multicultural Law Enforcement: Strategies for Peacekeeping in a Diverse Society,* 3rd ed. Upper Saddle River, NJ: Prentice Hall, 2005.

United Nations. *United Nations Division for the Advancement of Women.* New York: United Nations, 2005. http://www.un.org/womenwatch/daw.

Walker, L. "Psychology and Domestic Violence around the World." *American Psychologist* 54, no. 1 (1999): 21–29.

Watts, C., and C. Zimmerman. *Violence against Women: Global Scope and Magnitude.* The Lancet Publishing Group, 2002. http://www.hawaii.edu/hivandaids/Violence_ Against_Women__Global_Scope_and_Magnitude.pdf (accessed August 16, 2006).

World Health Organization. *World Health Organization Violence Prevention Activities, 2002–2004.* Washington, DC: World Health Organization, 2005.

CROSS-CULTURAL PERSPECTIVES ON DOMESTIC VIOLENCE

Introduction

Despite diverse cultural traditions seen in family life around the globe, a common thread of domestic violence weaves through nearly every culture worldwide. Societies which maintain rigid gender roles that define masculinity or male honor in terms of dominance are strongly associated with violence against women. Concern for the physical and mental safety of victims makes domestic violence an international human rights issue, yet it is essential to understand the cultural context for the abuse.

Violence around the World

In one form or another, domestic violence has been documented in almost every country and in every socioeconomic class. A statement issued by the United Nations General Assembly in 1993 described domestic violence against women as "physical, sexual, and psychological violence occurring in the family including battering, sexual abuse of female children in the household, dowry-related violence, marital rape, female mutilation, and other traditional practices harmful to women" (United Nations General Assembly 1993). However, local definitions of abuse and violence vary widely, so determining the actual prevalence of domestic violence within specific cultures is difficult. Full recognition of violence is prevented by cultural attitudes about male dominance and honor, rigid gender roles, failure to report abuse due to shame, concern over not being believed, and fear of retribution.

In many patriarchal societies, it is accepted that a man has a right to discipline his wife using physical means. The majority of villagers interviewed in Ghana, for example, stated that it was appropriate for a man to physically chastise his wife (Fischbach and Herbert 1997). Attitudes reported among the Japanese have shown that men and women of all classes and educational levels accept that men are entitled to batter their wives (Magnier 2002). In Islamic countries, women suffer violence from their husbands or male relatives, a practice allowed by religious text and institutionalized social norms (Douki et al. 2003). Even previously in the United States, which now has a progressive domestic violence policy, the "Rule of Thumb" law did not prevent a man from striking his wife; it only dictated the thickness of the instrument with which he could strike her (Eckert 2001). Severe and ongoing domestic violence has been documented in every culture, with the exception of rare, isolated, preindustrial, and nonpatriarchal societies.

Domestic violence is a serious threat in cultures under extreme duress due to poverty and lack of education or opportunity. Aboriginal women in Australia credit the many examples of violence and sexual assault toward women in their community to the poverty brought on by loss of lands, resources, and self-determination that arose from the colonization of Aboriginal lands (Perry 2001). Native American cultures report similar abuse among communities with severe poverty and hardship (Wahab and Olson 2001).

Violence takes on culturally specific forms when linked with traditional issues of honor and sexuality. For example, acid throwing has become an urgent safety issue for women in Middle Eastern cultures. Rejected suitors avenge their honor by attacking their would-be wives with sulfuric acid, causing serious pain and permanent disfigurement. India has seen an alarming number of dowry-related deaths (a woman may be killed because her dowry is too small). Often the death is made to appear as a kitchen accident by the husband or husband's family in collusion with local authorities. Female genital mutilation (infibulation) is practiced extensively in Africa and is common in some cultures in the Middle East. The cultural beliefs surrounding the mutilation means that it is often seen as a significant initiation rite or status change, associated with festivities and gifts. Many countries worldwide consider a woman as the property of her husband, particularly with regard to her sexuality. Since a woman is not allowed to choose if or when to engage in sexual relations with her husband, particularly in some African and Hispanic cultures where it is common for the husband to have unprotected sex outside of the marriage, she is at high risk of HIV/AIDS exposure. In cultures where virginity determines the woman's worth, the stigma of rape can be particularly devastating. Case studies from Bangladesh note numerous women beaten, murdered, or driven to suicide because of the dishonor that rape brings upon the family (Fischbach and Herbert 1997).

Consequences

Though the appearance of and attitudes toward violence vary from culture to culture, the worldwide health consequences of domestic violence do not. Domestic violence is a significant cause of preventable death, injury, incapacity, and mental illness for women in every culture. Victims of domestic violence sustain genital infections, broken bones, third-degree burns, lacerations, disfiguring scars, and other bodily injuries.

Around the world, women are at risk for domestic violence during every phase of life. As infants, female children are killed (infanticide) or are subject to physical, sexual, and psychological abuse. In some cultures, girls are at risk for incest as well as female genital mutilation from family members. Violence in adolescence expands to include date rape, courtship violence, and dowry-related death. Marital rape and sexual assault increase the risk of HIV/AIDS and other sexually transmitted diseases, as well as unwanted pregnancy. In times of war, armies have used rape as a means of controlling the minds and bodies of the people they seek to conquer; rape enables the victors to demoralize their enemy, further asserting their power ("Viewpoint" 1999). Elderly women are at risk both for violence and for neglect from related caregivers on whom they are dependent; and in extreme cases, they are victims of forced suicide.

Harm inflicted by domestic violence is not limited to physical injury. Exposure to even one episode of violence experienced or witnessed or even the perceived threat of violence is enough to produce mental trauma with lasting effects. Women who are abused are significantly more likely to suffer from depression, alcohol abuse, and post-traumatic stress disorder, and are at increased risk for suicide (Fischbach and Donnelly 1996). Importantly, these symptoms are not limited to only Western cultures that typically understand and commonly treat mental illness. A study conducted among the Kalahari Bushmen found that victims of domestic battering suffered from symptoms classified as post-traumatic stress disorder (McCall and Resick 2003).

Besides the risk of death, physical injury, and mental health disorders, consequences of domestic violence reach beyond the abused woman, resulting in intergenerational consequences for families, communities, and cultures. For example, boys who witness violence perpetrated against their mothers are more likely to batter their partners as adults. Girls who grow up witnessing or experiencing violence in the home are likely to tolerate abuse from partners as adults. Secrecy within the family keeps these abuses hidden and private, reinforcing behaviors that undermine women's autonomy, their potential as individuals, and their worth as members of their culture and society.

Human Rights

While data on the nature and extent of intimate partner violence directed against women are slowly gathered, human rights organizations increasingly recognize the universality of the threats posed to a woman's fundamental right to life and liberty and freedom from fear and want. Although human rights abuses tend to increase in environments of extreme poverty, scarcity, and social and economic oppression, violence against women is found to occur in nearly every society regardless of socioeconomic class.

As domestic violence becomes defined as an international human rights issue, effective intervention and prevention is focusing on two approaches: education and contact with health care professionals. Health care professionals are often the primary and perhaps only point of contact with public services for battered women. These professionals, if properly trained, are in the best position to identify abusive situations and counsel the victim. Widespread education will be a key factor in changing societal attitudes and empowering women to gain control over their lives and to wield sufficient influence and power to make changes which will lead to improvements in their sense of dignity, their physical and mental health, and their overall well-being.

Research

Effective strategies for eliminating the threat and reality of violence in women's lives must be informed by research that is culturally specific and comprehensive. Researchers need to recognize and be sensitive to particular cross-cultural differences in interpretation of violence. This type of research is particularly challenging in that it must be comparable to the work of researchers in other parts of the world, and thus researchers must first agree on a common vocabulary and lexicon so that they are evaluating the same problems. Quantitative data are needed from every region to identify

the magnitude and impact of the problem, as are qualitative data to improve understanding of domestic violence as a social process in local contexts.

Several international organizations including the World Health Organization (1997) and the United Nations have sponsored cross-cultural research on domestic violence, identifying universal risk factors such as low socioeconomic status, young age of partners, excessive alcohol use, and cultural attitudes (Fischbach and Herbert 1997). Even though abuse and violence vary across cultures, recognizing universal contexts is essential for research and ultimately for designing strategies for intervention and prevention.

Conclusion

While the gravity of domestic violence across cultures is obvious, data currently are not available to assess accurately its prevalence, severity, and culturally significant differences (Cousineau and Rondeau 2004). Given this, it is difficult to fully understand and appreciate the magnitude of the problem and recommend potential solutions. The complexities of cross-cultural definitions and behaviors are full of ambiguity in understandings and interventions; the challenge is to be informed and culturally sensitive in order to decrease intimate domestic violence in a significant and meaningful way.

RUTH L. FISCHBACH and MELISSA VALENTINE

See also **Africa: Domestic Violence and the Law; African American Community, Domestic Violence in; Asian Americans and Domestic Violence: Cultural Dimensions; Cross-Cultural Examination of Domestic Violence in China and Pakistan; Cross-Cultural Examination of Domestic Violence in Latin America; Cross-Cultural Perspectives on How to Deal with Batterers; Greece, Domestic Violence in; Jewish Community, Domestic Violence within the; Minorities and Families in America, Introduction to; Multicultural Programs for Domestic Batterers; Native Americans, Domestic Violence among; Qur'anic Perspectives on Wife Abuse; Rural Communities, Domestic Violence in; Spain, Domestic Violence in; Trinidad and Tobago, Domestic Violence in; Worldwide Sociolegal Precedents Supporting Domestic Violence from Ancient to Modern Times**

References and Further Reading

Cousineau, Marie-Marthe, and Gilles Rondeau. "Toward a Transnational and Cross-Cultural Analysis of Family Violence." *Violence against Women* 10, no. 8 (2004): 935–949.
Douki, Saida, F. Nacef, A. Belhadj, A. Bouasker, and R. Ghachem. "Violence against Women in Arab and

Islamic Countries." *Archives of Women's Mental Health* 6, no. 1 (2003): 165–171.

Eckert, S. "Domestic Violence: Rule of Thumb." *Pennsylvania Medicine* 104, no. 5 (2001): 12–15.

Fischbach, Ruth, and Elizabeth Donnelly. "Domestic Violence against Women: A Contemporary Issue in International Health." *Society, Health, and Disease* 18 (1996): 316–341.

Fischbach, Ruth, and Barbara Herbert. "Domestic Violence and Mental Health: Correlates and Conundrums within and across Cultures." *Social Science Medicine* 45, no. 8 (1997): 1161–1176.

Magnier, Mark. "Battery, Behind the Shoji Screen." *Los Angeles Times,* Jan. 29, 2002, p. A1.

McCall, George, and Patricia Resick. "A Pilot Study of PTSD Symptoms among Kalahari Bushmen." *Journal of Traumatic Stress* 16, no. 5 (2003): 445–450.

Perry, Michael. "Australia's Aboriginal Women Call for End to Abuse." *Reuters.* June 21, 2001.

United Nations General Assembly. "The Declaration on the Elimination of Violence against Women." Resolution No. A/RES/48/104. February 23, 1994.

"Viewpoint: Armies at War Use Rape as a Weapon." *National NOW Times* (Fall 1999). http://www.now.org/nnt/fall-99/viewpoint.html (accessed August 16, 2006).

Wahab, Stephanie, and Leonora Olson. "Intimate Partner Violence and Sexual Assault in Native American Communities." *Trauma, Violence, and Abuse* 5, no. 4 (2004): 353–366.

World Health Organization. "Violence against Women: A Priority Health Issue." July, 1997.

CROSS-CULTURAL PERSPECTIVES ON HOW TO DEAL WITH BATTERERS

Domestic violence victims and offenders represent all ethnicities and races. The United States is a culturally diverse society, and the problem of domestic violence and how to deal with batterers should be examined across these different cultures. When discussing an issue in relation to the major ethnic groups found in America, it is important to remember that only generalities can be used, as there is great diversity within each ethnic group as well. The main ethnic communities found in the United States, and covered in this article, include Native Americans, African Americans, Hispanic Americans, and Asian Americans.

The breaking of a law or the commission of an act which is classified as breaking a norm or as being antisocial can cause society to react with a sanction against the offender. What is deemed an appropriate sanction for a particular act, such as domestic violence, varies from culture to culture. There has been little systematic research conducted and few clinical interventions developed specific to populations of color. While some aspects of domestic violence may supersede culture, cultural considerations need to be made when developing community response mechanisms and designing treatment or other interventions.

Acknowledging that domestic violence exists in minority cultures may be viewed as criticizing a culture itself. Cultural members may fear that the dominant society will use any information about domestic violence to reinforce negative stereotypes. Race is not always an indicator of who is at risk of domestic violence. as many of the statistics are generally consistent across racial and ethnic boundaries. One of the important differences is that domestic violence is thought to be more prevalent among immigrant women, who already face unique legal, social, and often economic problems compared with U.S. citizens.

Cultural dynamics may affect the woman's acceptance of domestic violence as a part of her "role." The same dynamics may discourage her from "leaving" her partner. The partner may in turn view his behavior as normal. Many minority women have a distrust of the court system and may believe that only men or those who are wealthy or have ties to the government will be believed or helped. Immigrant women may also fear deportation if they seek help or try to find a program for their batterers.

Many minority groups have a deep-seated distrust of the dominant culture and thus may believe

CROSS-CULTURAL PERSPECTIVES ON HOW TO DEAL WITH BATTERERS

that the police, social services, courts, and other institutions will not actually act in a protective fashion, and so they will not seek help. The stress of racism, discrimination in employment opportunities, and other economic inequalities may create additional barriers to the victim's being able to leave or the batterer's changing of his violent behavior. Even simply the lack of bilingual personnel may prevent minorities from utilizing available services. Additionally, many services ignore or negatively label cultural beliefs which may be helpful in addressing interpersonal violence.

Minority batterers may view therapy or treatment programs as another attempt by the dominant culture to be oppressive and controlling. This view may contribute to underutilization of treatment and premature dropout of those who do use the services. If one of the goals of the program is to raise self-esteem, providers should address cultural oppression as an important factor.

Many who provide treatment services to minority groups have the conviction that attempting to change behavior without recognizing their unique beliefs, traditions, and cultural differences results in inaccurate perceptions and limited success. By fostering admiration of one's culture and stressing the importance of cultural connectedness, perhaps the ability to modify the offender's behavior will improve. Until quite recently, much of the focus on cross-cultural issues relating to work with batterers has been found only at the grassroots level within a small number of varied male batterer programs. Only now are researchers finding that ethnicity and culture are critically important in designing treatment interventions for offenders. Recognizing differences in history, experiences of racism and oppression, as well as cultural and religious beliefs is important in designing responses.

The nature, extent, and meaning of "family" and its support differs among various racial and cultural groups. Even when dealing with minority batterers, the main goal of safety for all family members must remain. Oppression is not an excuse for violence; of course, a great many minority individuals are victims of racism yet do not resort to domestic violence. It should be stressed that it is important not to overgeneralize and assume that all members of a specific ethnic group think or act alike.

Native Americans

According to Census 2000 there are currently 2.5 million American Indians and Alaska Natives in the United States. There is little research on domestic violence batterer programs in Native

communities. In addition to difficulty accessing services, Native American victims and batterers may also face the complex issue of jurisdiction, which depends on where the crime was committed, who committed the crime, and what exact crime was committed.

To many Native Americans, family is part of a broad kinship and tribal network, and its strength is based on interdependence and group affiliation, so a high value is placed on cooperation and harmony. While most Native Americans do not condone domestic violence, they do view it differently than does the mainstream Anglo culture. Because of extended kinship networks and the general view that there is relative equality and interdependence between men and women, violence in the family is not seen as a gender or feminist issue, where the man alone is to blame. Since both men and women bear responsibility for domestic violence, shelters and court systems that seem to blame and punish the man, while not helping to resolve the underlying problem and ignoring the woman's behavior, are typically avoided.

Some alternative approaches to the intervention of the dominant society's criminal justice system include tribal justice systems, restorative justice which turns to community support rather than the formal legal process to provide group conferencing, and sentencing circles. In tribal communities there is typically a large supportive group of people able to help both the victim and the offender. If the batterer was told to leave the community temporarily, when reentering the community the offender has to ask forgiveness from the direct victim as well as any indirect victims, such as other family members and friends as well as their community. While the tribe has a say in what will happen to the offender, in many tribes the direct victim also has a say; in other tribes the direct victim has no say in the matter. Depending on the traditional practices of the tribe involved, forms of redress for the victim of domestic violence will often include some type of offering by the batterer to the victim for the benefit of the tribe and to appease the spiritual beings associated with the tribe.

When working with Native Americans, counselors may wish to allow longer periods of silence, as is normal within the culture, and they may have greater success by posing general guiding questions rather than direct ones. Due to the complexity of the issue of domestic violence among Native Americans, a number of community resources may need to be involved in batterer programs, including tribal health, social services, law enforcement, legal assistance, mental health services, and addiction treatment centers.

Hispanic Americans

The Hispanic population in the United States is mainly young, and two-thirds are concentrated in the states of California, New York, and Texas. The United States has 35.3 million Hispanics, which is the fifth largest such population in the world. Latinas and Latinos in the United States come from various countries throughout Central and South America as well as the islands of Cuba and Puerto Rico. Some Latino families have been in the United States for generations, while others have arrived only recently.

Many Hispanic American cultures value group affiliation and sharing in the community. Even children are often viewed as belonging to the collective group of elders, so that no one would be unloved or not respected. Despite their diverse backgrounds, Hispanics tend to view any type of child abuse very negatively, although they are rather tolerant of domestic violence. Many Latinos value a linear approach to problems and prefer to comprehend relationships in the more solid terms of traditional "roles" rather than the abstract concept of "equality." Thus Latinas may be less likely to view themselves as victims, and both Latinas and Latinos are less likely to seek help. While overall rates of domestic violence are similar between Hispanics and non-Hispanics, young Hispanic females experience higher rates of violence than non-Hispanics. Hispanic women also experience higher rates of sexual abuse by their significant others than non-Hispanic women.

Family is very important to Latino groups. Family is more important than the individual and is a source of pride, self-esteem, and self-worth. The emphasis on family can protect against violence and stress from the outside world but it can also make an individual unwilling to admit abuse and seek help with dysfunctional behaviors for fear that it might harm or bring shame to the family unit. Some Hispanics may have difficulty communicating to English speakers and may fear exposing members of their community to investigation regarding immigration status. There may also be a hesitance to involve an "outsider" and possibly threaten the family's integrity.

Latino families often adapt to incorporate the immigration of other family members. They typically are involved in their Latino neighborhoods, so much of their socialization takes place in the barrios. They take pride in their heritage, and there is usually a strong involvement in and allegiance to the Catholic Church. As Catholicism is the primary religion of Hispanics, many abusive Latinos will turn to their priest for advice and assistance with their violence rather than seeking batterer services offered through a shelter or other program in the community. While some churches are ready to help victims with their plight, few are ready to offer services to the batterers.

Hispanic culture is also influenced by the concepts of *machismo* and *marianismo*. Machismo includes concepts of honor, courage, and a man's obligation to be head of the family and provide for it. The negative side of machismo can be men's use of violence to fulfill their role and an unwillingness to seek or accept help or services from outsiders. Marianismo is the female ideal of being like the Virgin Mary in terms of morality, integrity, or spiritual strength and self-sacrifice for the family. This norm may encourage women to tolerate abuse and pain in order to keep their family together. Many Latinas assume that violence is a part of marriage and the husband has the right to use physical discipline on her. They may also assume that if they told extended-family members of their abuse, they would not receive support and understanding but instead would bring shame to the entire family.

When working with Hispanic Americans, sensitivity to patriarchal family patterns, the importance of developing rapport, and the incorporation of spiritual practices may be advised. Factors to address include language barriers, experiences of racism and discrimination, lack of awareness of available services, viewing the violence as a private family matter, and fear of deportation. Due to the complexity of the issue of domestic violence among Hispanic Americans, a number of community resources may need to be involved in batterer programs, including religious services, public health, social services, interpreter services, law enforcement, legal assistance, mental health services, and addiction treatment centers.

African Americans

According to Census 2000, there are 35.5 million African Americans in the United States, which is 13 percent of the total U.S. population. There seems to be a considerable range of tolerance of domestic violence in the African American community. This range of views probably stems from the differences in culture between African Americans who are descendents of slaves brought to this country, descendents of black freemen, and twentieth-century immigrants.

Traditionally, African American women had roles similar to Native American women, in which they were separate from but cooperatively interdependent with men. From pre-slavery days to the present time, African American women have endured hardship and discrimination to provide for their families. This stereotypical role may lead African American women to sacrifice their own needs and safety to take care of others.

Many African Americans value kin-structured networks where there is support both within and between families. While households are often quite adaptable and willing to care for children of friends, two-parent relationships in which both parties are treated equally are also valued. Many African American adults are steadfastly optimistic that things will be better for their children and succeeding generations. The children themselves are often resilient and able to take part in the dominant culture while respecting the values of their black heritage.

The propensity for domestic violence is not an African American biological or cultural trait. African Americans are disproportionately influenced by the societal factors of low income, unemployment, inadequate education, and urban crowding, which are correlated with higher rates of domestic violence. It should be recognized that African Americans are harmed by the police at much higher rates than whites, so their trust in batterer services offered by, affiliated with, or working in conjunction with the criminal justice system may understandably be lacking. There is evidence that African Americans may commit more physical domestic violence than members of other ethnicities, though the influences of poverty, education, health, and employment rates are important variables as well.

Whether the current rates of domestic violence in African American communities are traced back to white colonization and slavery or to current institutionalized racism, macro-level societal attitudes and policies (as with all minority violence) need to be examined and adjusted according to the needs of these communities. Additionally, assistance and guidance at the individual level for victims and for batterers need to be provided. African Americans view themselves in terms of their role within the bigger group rather than as individuals, so this role needs to be a focus in batterer intervention programs. There may also be an emphasis on the importance of extended family and cultural spirituality. When working with African American batterers, the value of extended family and the batterers' roles in it should be recognized, and

attention should be paid to nonverbal cues given by the client as well as by the counselor in return.

Asian Americans

Census 2000 showed 11.9 million Asians in the United States, making up 4.2 percent of the U.S. population. Within the broad category of *Asian American,* there are more than twenty-four specific group affiliations, though Chinese and Filipino are the most common. Each Asian American group has a distinct culture and a different migration history. Many Asians are influenced by Confucian values which emphasize patriarchy, emotional control, duties, and obligations. Other Asians are typically Catholic, though others are influenced by Hindu and Buddhist traditions. Thus Asian Americans represent a very broad and diverse set of religions, a diverse range of ethnicities, and a diverse range of countries and cultures of origin.

Many Asian communities have strong patriarchal values that devalue women and girls and emphasize the importance of obedience. Suffering is seen as important in building a strong character, and harmony is valued over conflict. Many female Asian Americans may not report abuse in an effort to maintain harmony in the family and to avoid bringing shame to their family and community by involving outsiders. Many of these women may feel intense shame and anger about their abusive situations and do not wish to tell anyone about them; instead, they accept them as fate. Many Asian American males may view their behavior as acceptable and even expected according to cultural norms.

A number of factors contribute to the typical underreporting of domestic violence in Asian American communities. These factors, like those faced by Hispanic Americans, include language barriers, experiences of racism and discrimination, lack of awareness of available services, a "private matter" viewpoint, and fear of shame and/or deportation. Asian Americans tend to be quite accepting of physical punishment of children and are less likely to offer praise or public signs of affection. These views carry over into domestic violence; in fact, in many Asian languages there is no term for "domestic violence."

Individuals from Asian cultures typically do not include in their way of thinking psychological abuse as a type of domestic violence. They also tend to be more accepting of greater amounts of physical violence, depending on the circumstances, before they consider it abuse. If a woman flirts with another man or argues with her husband, physical force may be considered an appropriate response. This tolerance of abuse and blaming the victim may make many Asians less likely to view the way they are treated or the way they treat others as abuse and make them less likely to report the abuse or seek services for battering or advice from programs in the larger community. When working with Asian Americans, counselors should appreciate their concern with privacy, hierarchical family roles, and a strong relatedness between emotional problems and physical ailments.

Immigrants

Being a battered immigrant woman in America heightens the emotional trauma of domestic violence; the lack of culturally competent services and resources compounds the difficulty of escape. Some of the barriers that immigrant women face include personal issues such as shame and fear, institutional barriers such as strict immigration and welfare policies, and cultural barriers such as accepting their fate and gender role or the unacceptability of divorce.

Domestic violence victimization is thought to be more prevalent among immigrant women, who may have higher rates because they come from cultures which tend to accept domestic violence. Additionally, immigrant women may have less access to social services. The penalties and protections of the American legal system may not apply to them, or they may fear deportation if they turn to the legal system. Even legal residents distrust official channels based on their experiences with the systems in their native countries, where only those who were wealthy, had ties to the government, or were male were believed. There may also be language barriers, and victimized immigrant women may not have access to bilingual services to obtain financial assistance or food, be able to report a complaint to the police, or understand proceedings in court. Many immigrant women may not know basic survival skills such as how to drive a car or use public transportation. They also may not know how to use the phone or read a newspaper to locate a job or housing.

Strict immigration policies may make it difficult for women to leave an abusive spouse or sponsor, especially if they wish to have custody of a child born in America. Additionally, immigrant women may have been sending money to their parents or siblings in their country of origin. Being forced to leave the abuser would end this source of support for their family.

Batterers are typically aware of the plight of the immigrant victim. Some batterers will use these concerns to their advantage to further their control over the victim and ensure compliance. Other batterers may not realize that their behaviors are considered abusive in the United States, and even if they do realize it, they may fear seeking help due to their own or their spouse's immigration status. Due to the complexity of the issue of domestic violence among immigrants, a number of community resources may need to be involved in batterer programs, including a wide variety of interpreter services, literacy education, religious services, public health, social services, employment assistance, law enforcement, immigration services, legal assistance, and mental health services.

To address the issue of domestic violence among minorities, both citizens and immigrants, several improvements could be made. Beyond offering bilingual services for victims and batterers, workers in the system should reach out to those who could use their services and explain what the services provide and how to obtain them. Culturally sensitive service providers need to build trust with the minority communities, understand how social and cultural discrimination against the minority group has impacted that group over time and how strengths within the minority culture can be used to facilitate change. Workers should take the first step toward bridging any barriers, racial or otherwise. Partnerships with immigrant and minority communities should be made so that close relations can be maintained, and needed adjustments to batterer and other programs will be recognized as early as possible.

Minority-group values and histories may explain the presence of violence, but they do not excuse it. Each minority group comprises a diverse set of communities. All minority groups have been subjected to racism and discrimination at a societal level. Efforts should be made to address poverty, racism, and other societal problems faced by minority communities on a large scale. Rather than simply incarcerating men of color who commit domestic violence and sending the abused wives to shelters, communities may benefit from integrating discussions of and services for victims and batterers into the ethnic community settings. Better options such as the development of batterer programs in lieu of incarceration may be viewed as a positive step as long as victims' safety is ensured.

WENDELIN HUME

See also **African American Community, Domestic Violence in; Asian Americans and Domestic**

Violence: Cultural Dimensions; Batterer Intervention Programs; Cross-Cultural Examination of Domestic Violence in Latin America; Minorities and Families in America, Introduction to; Multicultural Programs for Domestic Batterers; Native Americans, Domestic Violence among

References and Further Reading

Dasgupta, Shamita Das. "Women's Realities: Defining Violence against Women by Immigration, Race, and Class." In *The Criminal Justice System and Women: Offenders, Prisoners, Victims, and Workers,* edited by Barbara Raffel Price and Natalie J. Sokoloff, 3rd ed. New York: McGraw-Hill, 2004, pp. 361–373.

Malley-Morrison, Kathleen, and Denise A. Hines. *Family Violence in a Cultural Perspective: Defining, Understanding, and Combating Abuse.* Thousand Oaks, CA: Sage Publications, 2004.

Presser, Lois, and Emily Gaarder. "Can Restorative Justice Reduce Battering?" In Price and Sokoloff, eds., *The Criminal Justice System and Women,* 2004, pp. 403–418.

Walker, Samuel, Cassia Spohn, and Miriam DeLone. *The Color of Justice: Race, Ethnicity, and Crime in America,* 3rd ed. Belmont, CA: Wadsworth/Thompson Learning, 2004.

CYCLE OF VIOLENCE

Since the late 1970s, researchers and theorists have focused increased attention on the widespread problem of domestic violence in contemporary society. Research has shown that domestic violence cuts across racial, ethnic, religious, and socioeconomic lines. In particular, researchers have sought to identify the factors associated with intimate violence in an effort to develop theories explaining the causes of battering.

One of the most widely cited theories in the domestic violence literature is Lenore Walker's cycle of violence. According to Walker, the cycle of violence is characterized by three distinct phases which are repeated over and over again in the abusive relationship. As a result, domestic abuse rarely involves a single isolated incident of violence. Rather, the abuse becomes a repetitive pattern in the relationship.

The first stage in the cycle of violence is *tension building*. During the tension-building stage, the victim is often subjected to less serious nonviolent forms of abuse, such as threats and insults. Victims soon come to realize that the verbal threats usually precede physical violence and will therefore attempt to delay its onset. For example, the victim may act compliant in the hope of mollifying the batterer and avoiding a violent outburst, but eventually the inevitable occurs, namely, the physical assault.

The second stage in the cycle of violence is *acute battering*. The acute-battering stage is marked by uncontrolled physical aggression, which may be extremely violent in nature. It is during the acute-battering stage that victims are most likely to sustain injuries ranging from bruises, cuts, broken bones, disfigurement, and miscarriage to loss of life. The acute-battering stage, however, tends to be abrupt. The violent episode usually lasts only a few minutes.

Immediately following an acute-battering incident, the abuser usually acts remorseful. Walker describes this third stage in the cycle of violence as *loving and contrite,* or the "honeymoon" stage. The batterer is apologetic as well as attentive to the victim. The abuser may shower the victim with gifts, compliments, and sincere promises that it will never happen again. The victim becomes reassured that the perpetrator loves her and that the relationship can be salvaged. The victim may actually begin to feel responsible for the violent outburst. Predictably, the third stage ends, tension building resumes, and the cycle of violence persists.

Escalation Theory

As the cycle of violence continues, victims report that they are less successful in delaying the onset of the acute-battering stage and that the abusers become less remorseful with each new incident of violence. Many researchers have observed that the violence also tends to increase in severity over time. More specifically, escalation theory posits that the battering becomes increasingly more violent with each successive incident. Consequently, the risk of personal injury increases with the number of events of less serious violence.

Research has found that over time the violence increases in frequency and severity. For example, a study examining domestic homicide patterns in Kansas City discovered that in approximately 90 percent of the domestic homicide cases, police had responded to at least one call for service at the address of the victim or suspect in the two years prior to the murder. It was further reported that in about 50 percent of the domestic homicide cases, police had responded to five or more calls. Comparable results were reported for domestic aggravated assaults. Similar findings were found in studies examining domestic disturbance calls in other cities, including Boston and Minneapolis.

Beginning in the 1980s, researchers began to focus attention on same-sex battering. These studies lend further support to the cycle of violence theory as well as the escalating violence thesis. Studies found that intimate violence among lesbians tends to be characterized by what Elizabeth Leeder refers to as "chronic battering." As with heterosexual couples, lesbian victims experience domestic abuse that is repetitive in nature and escalates over time. Many battered lesbians have reported that the violence was preceded by a tension-building phase and followed by a period of contrition. In addition, a significant number of battered lesbians have communicated that the abuse grew more intense and serious over time. For gays and lesbians, serial incidents tend to involve more serious personal crimes than first-time incidents, including assault with and without a weapon, attempted assault with and without a weapon, and rape. Furthermore, being victimized more than once increases the likelihood of injuries that require outpatient care or hospitalization. These findings suggest that gays and lesbians, like their heterosexual counterparts, experience escalating violence that intensifies and becomes more serious over time.

Collectively, these studies provide evidence of escalating violence in all types of abusive relationships. Researchers have begun to explore the consequences of living under a constant threat of danger. It is believed that as the violence increases in frequency and severity, victims of intimate violence often exhibit diminished hope, less self-esteem, and more fear.

The Effects of Escalating Violence

Research indicates that there are both short-term and long-term psychological consequences for battered intimates. Lenore Walker found that the repeated cycle of violence led to severe psychological symptoms, such as sleep disturbances, eating problems, fatigue, and indicators of stress, i.e., headaches, back pain, high blood pressure, and heart problems. She identified a pattern of psychological consequences that developed in women exposed to chronic battering. Walker introduced the concept of the battered woman syndrome, which is characterized by a pattern of learned helplessness, reexperiencing of the trauma, intrusive recollections, generalized anxiety, low self-esteem, and social withdrawal.

Low self-esteem and feelings of powerlessness have been consistently reported in victims of battering. Survey research with clinical samples have identified numerous other psychological problems: anxiety, depression, anger and rage, nightmares, dissociation, somatic problems, sexual problems, and addictive behaviors. Overall, 75 to 80 percent of victims in these samples suffered depression.

Suicidal ideation is greater for women experiencing assault. Murray Straus and Richard Gelles compared a sample of victimized women with a sample of women experiencing no violence. The seriously assaulted women reported two times the number of headaches, four times the rate of depression, and five and a half times more suicide attempts. A number of researchers have found that nearly half of battered women contemplate suicide. It has been estimated that greater than 20 percent of domestic violence victims actually attempt suicide. Victims often report that with increasing isolation from support networks such as family and friends, they became more vulnerable. They also experience increasing negative attitudes toward their partners, decreasing hope for changing the violence, and feelings of there being no escape other than suicide.

The psychological consequences of powerlessness and depression also contribute to the difficulty some battered women have leaving a relationship. When victims leave, however, escalating violence can occur during the separation. "Separation assault" often results from retaliation attempts or jealousy. Most women who are murdered by their partners are killed when they separate from the batterer.

Social consequences of battering are pervasive. Businesses lose about $100 million annually in lost wages, sick leave, absenteeism, and nonproductivity as a result of domestic violence. The violent male partner often resents the woman's job because it is an area of her life that he cannot control. The abuse then has an effect that spills over into the workplace setting. Abused women miss many days of work due to psychological coercion and physical injury. They have far greater problems with lateness, interruption, and harassment by the batterer on the job than do other workers.

Health care costs for treating victims of domestic violence are estimated to be at least $3 billion to $5 billion annually. The emergency room is the first place that many abused women find themselves after an outburst of violence; and between one-fifth and one-third of women who are treated in hospital emergency rooms are victims of battering. Between 20 and 50 percent of women admitted for emergency surgery have been assaulted by a male partner.

Domestic violence is a special risk to pregnant women. Battering often escalates when there is a change of some kind in the home, and pregnancy may trigger such an increase. It has been estimated that as many as 37 percent of all obstetrical patients are abused. Injury can trigger premature labor. Also, battered women are four times more likely to have low-birth-weight babies and twice as likely to miscarry as other women. Abuse of pregnant women is a leading cause of infant mortality and birth defects.

The costs of domestic violence account for almost 15 percent of the annual total crime costs, while family homicide is projected to cost $1.7 billion annually. In addition to direct costs of police intervention, courts devote a large amount of time to issuing protection orders, protecting victims, and housing the most serious offenders.

The Legal System's Response

It is obvious that domestic violence produces many negative consequences. The most serious is domestic homicide. Women are far more likely than men to be killed by an intimate. As many as three out of four domestic homicides are committed against female victims. It is estimated that between 1,000 and 1,600 women are killed each year by male partners. A significant number of these victims were murdered after enduring years of abuse. Unfortunately, the legal system may have contributed to the escalating violence experienced by victims of partner abuse by refusing to treat such violence as a criminal offense.

For centuries, the physical punishment of women by their husbands was socially condoned. Under common law, the *rule of thumb* specified the extent of physical force that a husband was permitted to use against his wife. A husband was allowed to hit his wife with a rod no thicker than his thumb.

During the late nineteenth century, the suffragist movement focused attention on the plight of female victims of domestic violence. Simultaneously, many states began enacting laws prohibiting wife battering. These laws, however, often amounted to mere paper statutes, existing on the books but not enforced by the criminal justice system. For example, several states prevented police from arresting a batterer unless they witnessed the violence firsthand. Other states adhered to the stitch rule, whereby police would be allowed to arrest a husband accused of battering if the injuries sustained by the victim were serious enough to require stitches. Police typically responded to domestic violence by temporarily separating the parties for a cooling-down period. Police rarely arrested the batterer.

As a result, victims of domestic violence did not receive adequate protection from the criminal justice system. This in turn may have contributed to the pattern of escalating violence characterizing many abusive relationships. In the early 1970s, the women's movement lobbied for legislative reforms and stronger criminal sanctions. At the same time, researchers also began to advocate that the criminal justice system take domestic violence seriously by arresting the batterer.

In 1986, Lawrence Sherman and Richard Berk conducted the infamous Minneapolis Domestic Violence Experiment. They discovered that arresting batterers resulted in the least amount of repeat violence. As noted previously, a study of homicides in Kansas City showed that police had been warned by multiple or repeated domestic violence calls to the residence, now the crime scene of a murder.

These findings indicate that police should respond to domestic violence incidents by arresting the batterer to deter escalating violence. Many states have subsequently adopted mandatory and pro-arrest policies. The ability of mandatory arrest to reduce escalating violence is debatable. The Minneapolis experiment has been replicated numerous times with mixed results. Some research has found that arrest actually intensifies the violence. Other studies have revealed that only certain types of batterers are deterred by arrest. Nevertheless, many victim advocates continue to insist that arrest is the most successful response for deterring repeat violence. As a result, mandatory arrest has emerged as the standard response to domestic violence in American society.

Another criminal justice reform that is designed to protect victims of partner abuse from further violence is the warrantless arrest. It allows police to arrest batterers who violate restraining orders without securing a warrant. Warrantless arrests have the potential to decrease intimate partner violence and reduce opportunities for domestic homicide.

These reforms show that the criminal justice system is more committed than ever to protecting victims of domestic violence. It should, however, continue to explore additional interventions that may successfully reduce escalating violence as well as prevent domestic homicides.

ANNE SULLIVAN and KRISTEN KUEHNLE

See also **Battered Woman Syndrome; Education as a Risk Factor for Domestic Violence; Intergenerational Transfer of Intimate Partner Violence; Social Class and Domestic Violence; Stages of Leaving Abusive Relationships**

References and Further Reading

Bell, Holly. "Cycles with Cycles: Domestic Violence, Welfare, and Low-Wage Work." *Violence against Women* 9, no. 10 (2003): 1245–1262.

Berry, Dawn Bradley. *The Domestic Violence Sourcebook*. Los Angeles: Lowell House, 1998.

Breedlove, Ronald, G. Marie Wilt, James Bannon, John Kennish, Donald Sandker, and Robert Sawtell. "Domestic Violence and the Police: Kansas City." In *Domestic Violence and the Police Studies: Detroit and Kansas City*, Washington, DC: Police Foundation, 1977.

Donnellan, Craig. *Confronting Domestic Violence*. Cambridge: Independence Educational Publishers, 2002.

Leeder, Elizabeth. "Enmeshed in Pain: Counseling the Lesbian Battering Couple." *Women and Therapy* 7 (1988): 81–99.

Mills, Linda G. *The Heart of Intimate Abuse: New Interventions in Child Welfare, Criminal Justice, and Health Settings*. New York: Springer Publishing, 1998.

Sherman, Lawrence, and Richard Berk. "The Specific Deterrent Effects of Arrest for Domestic Assault." *American Sociological Review* 49 (1984): 261–272.

Straus, Murray, and Richard Gelles. "Societal Change and Change in Family Violence from 1975 to 1985 as Revealed by Two National Surveys." *Journal of Marriage and the Family* 48 (1986): 465–479.

U.S. Department of Justice. *Stop the Cycle of Violence: What You Can Do*. Washington, DC: Author, 1997.

Walker, Lenore. *The Battered Woman*. New York: Harper & Row, 1979.

———. *The Battered Woman Syndrome*. New York: Springer Publishing, 1984.

Wiehe, Vernon R. *Understanding Family Violence: Treating and Preventing Partner, Child, Sibling and Elder Abuse*. Thousand Oaks, CA: Sage Publications, 1998.

D

DATE RAPE

Date rape is the lay term that captures the phenomenon of rape perpetrated by an assailant who knows his victim. While legislators had never excluded such perpetrators, except for husbands, who were excluded in marital rape exemptions, from the legal definition of rape, appellate courts had demonstrated great difficulty in letting stand the rape convictions of men who had known their victims. Susan Estrich, a feminist jurisprudential scholar, assumed the task of analyzing case law to make transparent the legal reasoning appellate judges used to overturn the rape convictions of these men. In the 1970s, Estrich herself was raped when a stranger put an ice pick to her throat. She ultimately learned that she had been "really" raped because her assailant was a violent stranger. The experience of discussing the crime with police and prosecutors who would distinguish her "real rape" from the rapes of women who were "asking for it" led Estrich to begin researching the cases of "not real" rape.

Rape unmodified is a legal offense typically perpetrated by men against women. It is nonconsensual sexual intercourse with force or threat of force. As jurisdictions began modernizing their rape statutes, they began broadening the categories of sexual assault prosecutable under their newer "sexual deviant assault" legislation. Under the new statutes it became possible for sexual crimes perpetrated against men (most commonly by other men) to be prosecuted. Legislative reforms attempted to capture people's experience of sexual crimes. But the criminal justice processing of these cases lagged behind the intent of reformers in cases where the assailant knew the victim. Did a woman's speech or conduct indicating "no" mean the sex was nonconsensual if the woman was not physically injured? Did a man's taking of a woman's car keys when she was in an unfamiliar and dangerous neighborhood constitute sufficient force? Legal processing reflected a lingering social problem: Between a man and a woman who know each other, the cultural gaze remained on the woman and what she did to bring sexual attention to herself rather than on the man's conduct that culminated in a crime.

Over the course of time, "date rape" has come to be more commonly called "acquaintance rape." Whereas the concept of date rape seems to limit the phenomenon to people who have some sort of relationship, conceptualizing the event as acquaintance rape broadens the field to the cases of parties who know each other, lack a relationship appropriate to sexual intimacy, yet have unwanted sex forced upon the victim.

Women who know their assailants often assume some blame or complicity in the attack. In the 1980s, psychologist Mary Koss and her associates framed questions to college students to capture the actual behavior they had engaged in or had had forced upon them, without labeling the events as rape. In that way, one in every twelve men admitted to having forced intercourse or attempting to force intercourse, with virtually none of the men identifying themselves as rapists. Women identified attacks on them without conceptualizing the attacks as rape. The Koss analysis revealed that one in four college women had been the victim of rape or attempted rape and that 84 percent of these women knew their assailants. Ultimately the study was criticized as both exaggerating the date rape problem yet underreporting its extent. Research of date rape has continued to focus on college students and young people. The subject would benefit from research done on a representative sample of Americans to capture the depth and frequency of the phenomenon.

In light of the pace of legal reforms and of the dearth of large-scale empirical research on acquaintance rape, perhaps the most pressing and accessible project for students, scholars, and practitioners is the undermining of rape myths that continue to fester in Western culture. The first set of right-of-access myths rely on a male perspective that interprets nonsexual behavior as an opening to sexual behavior. For instance, the belief that if a woman agrees to go to her date's home or apartment, or, in a famous case, his hotel room on their first date, that she is willing to have sex. Or the belief that how a woman dresses or presents herself is meant to lure sexual handling rather than simply reflect her taste in fashion. Right-of-access myths also depend on pushing agreed upon activity to non-agreed upon extremes. Agreeing to a ride, drinks, or even some sexual activity needs to be accepted at face value rather than converted into traps that bar women from rejecting any other attention. Cultural rape myths also revolve around creating specious distinctions among women. The nonraped are women who can successfully resist rape because they want to, whereas the raped are women of less stellar reputations (and apparently physical abilities), women who subconsciously want to be attacked, or women who are vindictively lying about men. Finally, people are more comfortable thinking of the rapist as some brutish Other when the very phenomenon of date and acquaintance rape arises from the men who commonly surround a woman's life.

Men intent on extracting sex from their dates have traditionally used alcohol to facilitate the crime. In the Koss study, 73 percent of the assailants and 55 percent of the victims had used alcohol or other drugs prior to the attack. However, three drugs have become more common in facilitating date rape. Rohypnol (flunitrazepam), GHB (gamma hydroxybutyric acid), and Ketamine (ketamine hydrochloride) are colorless, odorless, and tasteless. Rohypnol ("roofies") comes in pill form and dissolves in liquid. GHB comes in forms as varied as pills, white powder, and liquid. Ketamine is a white powdery substance. Besides rendering victims vulnerable, each of these drugs distorts memory, further protecting the rapist from prosecution. In the current state of law and culture, women are still their own best first defense.

NICKY ALI JACKSON and SOPHIA SAKOUTIS

See also **Battered Wives; Battered Woman Syndrome; Child Sexual Abuse; Dating Violence; Incest; Lesbian Battering; Marital Rape; Pseudo-Family Abuse; Sexual Aggression Perpetrated by Females; Sibling Abuse**

References and Further Reading

Bergen, Raquel Kennedy. *Issues in Intimate Violence.* Thousand Oaks, CA: Sage Publications, 1998.
Estrich, Susan. "Rape." *Yale Law Journal* 95, no. 6 (1986): 1087–1184.
————. *Real Rape*. Cambridge, MA: Harvard University Press, 1987.
Francis, Leslie, ed. *Date Rape: Feminism, Philosophy, and the Law*. University Park, PA: University Press, 1996.
Koss, Mary. "Hidden Rape: Sexual Aggression and Victimization in the National Sample of Students in Higher Education." In *Violence and Dating Relationships: Emerging Social Issues,* edited by Maureen Pirog-Good and Jan Stets. New York: Praeger, 1988, pp. 145–168.
Malamuth, Neil M. "Rape Proclivity among Males." *Journal of Social Issues* 37, no. 4 (1981): 138–157.
Warshaw, Robin. *I Never Called it Rape*. New York: Harper Perennial, 1994.

DATING VIOLENCE

"Dating" is a conventional term describing the process of forming and maintaining intimate relationships. This romantic process typically begins during adolescence and extends throughout the adult life span. Society generally views dating as carefree, romantic, and trouble free, yet this is far from the truth. The U.S. Department of Justice noted that women aged sixteen to twenty-four were most vulnerable to intimate partner violence. In addition, females who were physically abused by a date during adolescence were more likely to experience dating violence during their freshman year in college.

When considered within the context of initial intimate relationship formation, the adolescent years become the focus of the rituals and practices associated with initial courtship and dating. Dating also sets the stage for formation of social and interpersonal skills such as exploring intimate social interactions, male/female roles, communication styles, and problem-solving skills. However, coupled with immaturity and inexperience, adolescents are also more apt to use less than prosocial strategies for dealing with relational conflict such as verbal put-downs or physical aggression. Furthermore, such early unhealthy dating relationships have far-reaching consequences. Adolescent girls who disclosed being physically or sexually abused by a boyfriend were twice as likely to smoke, drink, use illegal drugs, and engage in behavior indicative of an eating disorder (e.g., binging and purging). Consequently, how dating partners are viewed and treated forms the backdrop to developmental, social, and cultural forces associated with the incidence and patterns of dating violence. Clearly, violence during dating represents a significant contemporary issue with historical overtones and a social problem that warrants study separate from domestic violence.

Historical Perspective

During colonial times, courtship was infused with economic motivations for marriage, since marriage was viewed as essential to sustaining communities and social institutions, which were in turn clearly linked to expectations that older family members would be cared for. Over time, the roles of men and women during courtship came to reflect "traditional" definitions of male and female behavior, with men assuming authority over women. How violence within such relationships was addressed was often clouded with secrecy, shame, and embarrassment and reflected prevailing social and cultural conventions.

Prior to the twentieth century, courtship was a chaperoned activity among adolescents and young adults or took place as part of supervised social or religious events. Emotional or romantic interactions were explored carefully, often requiring various forms of deception to evade the watchful eyes of elders or parents. As Americans entered the 1900s, public dating became more acceptable, with males and females going on "dates" without chaperones yet with expectations that the male would protect the weaker female, who was in his care. Today, by the age of fourteen or fifteen, the majority of adolescents have had some experience with dating. Unlike in earlier times when courtship was facilitated by parents through matchmaking, today's adolescents meet and form romantic relationships with significantly greater degrees of freedom. While there is variation across ethnic and cultural populations within the United States, adolescents as well as adults now form intimate relationships with the help of friends who serve as matchmakers, through dating services advertised on television, radio, and the Internet, and through computer-mediated technologies. Alongside the changes in perspectives regarding the definition of dating and courtship that have evolved through the start of the twenty-first century, adolescents and young adults have become the most vulnerable population subject to dating violence.

The social problem of domestic violence became highly publicized in the early 1970s in the United States when the women's movement was at its height. The domestic violence agenda, however, did not focus on intimate violence among adolescents. As early as the late 1950s, a researcher examined male aggression dating relationships and found that 30 percent of the women had experienced attempted or completed forced sexual intercourse while on a high school date. However, it was not until the early 1980s when a study by James

Makepeace found that 20 percent of college students experienced dating violence. This study was considered a landmark, and "dating violence" was publicly acknowledged as a serious social problem and launched many empirical studies in this area. Around the same time, Susan Brownmiller's book *Against Our Will: Men, Women, and Rape,* launched the term "date rape." All of this was set against the backdrop of activism and feminism during the 1970s.

Scope of Dating Violence

It is estimated that one-third of the violence that occurs among youth takes place within a dating relationship. Within the span of a year's time, such violence will repeat at least once. In the National Longitudinal Study of Adolescent Health, 61 percent of fifteen-year-old males and 66 percent of fifteen-year-old females stated that they had been in a romantic relationship during the previous eighteen months. What is disturbing about these statistics is that by age fifteen, some of these adolescents will have had an experience of violence perpetrated by a dating partner.

In one study of eighth- and ninth-grade students, a quarter of the sample disclosed having experienced nonsexual dating violence, and 8 percent revealed that they had experienced sexual dating violence. In a national study on violence in adolescent romantic relationships, 32 percent of the adolescents disclosed some type of violence in the eighteen months preceding the interview. Twelve percent of the respondents reported being the victims of physical violence, usually accompanied by psychological violence.

Among university studies, the prevalence of dating violence is also high, and both males and females are victims. In one study, 20–40 percent reported one or more assaults in the last twelve months. In another study, examining Chinese American and white college students' victimization experiences, student subjects were recruited in psychology and ethnic studies courses. Surveys asked students if they had ever experienced any physical violence in a dating relationship since they'd started dating. The Chinese American students were a bit older when they'd started dating (around sixteen), while the white students had started dating at fifteen years of age. Slightly more than 20 percent of the Chinese American students disclosed experiences of physical dating violence compared with 31 percent of the white students. Given that the average ages of the Chinese American and white students were twenty and twenty-two,

respectively, and given that the dating violence occurred within a five- to seven-year dating span, these incidences of violence are high.

Psychological abuse in the context of dating relationships is equally as damaging to the victim as is physical or sexual abuse. While consensus about a single definition of psychological abuse within dating relationships is elusive, there is no controversy about its impact on the person who is the target of such behavior. Lasting emotional scarring, while invisible, can result in lifelong distress and suffering.

Psychological abuse perpetrated within dating relationships is common. One study found that over three-quarters of college women experienced psychological abuse during a six-month period, and 91 percent experienced this form of emotional violence over their dating lifetime. Sexual assault in the context of dating is also common. A national study of college females found that 54 percent had experienced some form of sexual aggression by a dating partner at least once since the age of fourteen. Oftentimes, these incidences go unreported, given the shame that surrounds dating violence. In addition, victims often blame themselves for somehow instigating the violence. Unfortunately, the prevalence of societal myths about rape (i.e., blaming victims' alleged provocative attire and promiscuity) continues. These myths prevent many dating violence victims from reporting sexual assault and battery to appropriate authorities.

Definitions of Dating Violence

Definitions of dating violence are influenced by a complex array of factors that reflect social, cultural/racial, political, familial, legal, geographic/regional, and personal perspectives. Currently, the term "dating" is used to describe a romantic dyadic relationship formed for the purpose of interacting and engaging in social activities. "Dating" is used with heterosexual and homosexual dyadic romantic relationships and applies to individuals of all ages. Dating continues until one or both partners end the relationship or until the relationship progresses to a more involved state such as cohabitation, engagement, or marriage. Depending on the prevailing social mores and expectations, the dating relationship may be exclusive and monogamous or only one of several dating relationships that a person maintains. Other terms used to describe the dyadic romantic relationship include "hooking up," "hanging out," or more formally, "courtship." Central to the dating relationship is mutuality or reciprocity; i.e., the capacity of both partners to invest emotionally in the relationship.

Violence that occurs in a dating relationship can consist of various forms of physical, verbal, and/or psychological victimization. When sexual assault is excluded, dating violence can be defined as any harmful action taken against a dating partner, including: physical violence such as pushing and shoving; slapping, hitting, or kicking; beatings ranging from a single episode with minimal injury to severe battery associated with life-threatening risk to the victim. Verbal and psychological abuse can entail verbal threats to harm and threats using weapons such as knives, guns, objects, or other forms of potential injury to intimidate and control the targeted person.

Dating violence may be associated with a single conflict occurring within a romantic relationship or may characterize a pattern of addressing conflict in the relationship. When violence occurs, it often is a reflection of the power and control dynamic between partners and can be directly influenced by a history of, or exposure to, violence between intimate partners; e.g., witnessing parental domestic violence. Research exploring dating violence may focus on heterosexual male-on-female dating violence as the definition of the problem or use other definitions that broaden the scope of violence in dating relationships, e.g., violence in gay or lesbian relationships.

What Are the Similarities and Differences between Dating and Domestic Violence?

Dating violence shares a number of common features with domestic violence. In both dating and marital relationships, couples invest a tremendous amount of time with each other. Personal information is shared, and each party becomes familiar with the other's strengths and limitations. It has been argued that these characteristics of intimate relationships make it fertile for violence.

The dynamics of power and control exist in both dating and domestic violence. Batterers employ threats, verbal manipulation and put-downs, and physical and sexual violence to control their partners. Just as the dynamics of the abuse are similar, victims in both dating and domestic violence situations face the same obstacles in terminating the abusive relationship. In both cases, the victim may still love the perpetrator, hoping that he/she will change. Victims are also fearful of retaliation, as victims of both dating and domestic violence are most at risk of physical injury and homicide when they make deliberate attempts to end the relationship. For example, 1,247 women during the year 2000 were killed by an intimate partner.

Despite the similarities, there are unique, distinct differences between dating and domestic violence. In dating violence, both males and females are equally at risk for physical and psychological violence, as prevalence estimates for both genders are similar. This speaks to the mutuality of violence among youths and at times among adults as well. In addition, in a dating relationship, the adolescent victim is not necessarily cohabitating under the same roof with their dating partner, and typically, there is no economic relationship that binds the couple. For adults in violent dating relationships, however, financial dependence often becomes a factor, particularly as this is often a similar barrier for domestic violence victims in terminating the relationship. In the majority of dating violence cases in adolescence, the requirement of providing for the well-being of offspring is not present. However, in adult dating relationships in which violence emerges as a central problem, children of one or both partners are placed at risk through exposure to adult acts of violence, and violence can be perpetrated against the children. Furthermore, legal options are a bit more limited for dating violence victims, as only thirty-nine states and the District of Columbia offer the option of protective orders for dating violence victims.

Conclusion

Experts in the field of dating violence argue that understanding its unique characteristics can be beneficial in developing prevention efforts and can form the foundation for adolescent education and early intervention efforts during these crucial developmental years. Due to the nature of adolescent development and the co-occurring increase in risk for violence during early dating experiences, it is imperative that public awareness be increased regarding the impact of this often hidden, yet devastating and potentially lethal problem. Furthermore, since there appears to be a trend toward lowering the initial dating age to the pre-teen years, education and prevention efforts need to target youths at younger ages. Partnering with parents, schools, and civic organizations as well as religious, health, and educational services and institutions will be vital in this endeavor.

ALICE G. YICK and PAMELA K. S. PATRICK

See also **Battered Wives; Battered Woman Syndrome; Battered Women, Clemency for; Date Rape; Dating Violence among African American Couples; Lesbian Battering; Marital Rape**

References and Further Reading

Agbayani-Siewert, Pauline, and Alice Yick Flanagan. "Filipino American Dating Violence: Definitions, Contextual Justifications and Experiences of Dating Violence." In *Aspects of the Asian American Experience: Diversity within Diversity,* edited by Namkee G Choi. Binghamton, NY: Haworth Press, 2001, pp. 115–133.

Carlson, Bonnie E. "Dating Violence: A Research Review and Comparison with Spouse Abuse." *Social Casework* 68 (1987): 16–23.

Close, Sharron M. "Dating Violence Prevention in Middle School and High School Youth." *Journal of Child and Adolescent Psychiatric Nursing* 18, no. 1 (2005): 2–9.

Connolly, Jennifer A., and A. M. Johnson. "Adolescents' Romantic Relationships and the Structure and Quality of Their Interpersonal Ties." *Personal Relationships* 3 (1996): 185–195.

Family Violence Prevention Fund. "The Facts on Teenagers and Intimate Partner Violence." http://endabuse.org/resources/facts/Teenagers2.pdf (accessed August 17, 2006).

Feiring, Candice, and Wyndol C. Furman. "When Love Is Just a Four-Letter Word: Victimization and Romantic Relationships in Adolescence." *Child Maltreatment* 5, no. 4 (2000): 293–298.

Ferguson, Carroy U. "Dating Violence as a Social Phenomenon." *Violence in Intimate Relationships: Examining Sociological and Psychological Issues*, edited by Nicky A. Jackson and Giselle C. Oates. Boston: Butterworth-Heinemann, 1998, pp. 83–118.

Foshee, Vangie A., George F. Linder, Karl E. Bauman, et al. "The Safe Dates Project: Theoretical Basis, Evaluation Design, and Selected Baseline Findings. Youth Violence Prevention: Description and Baseline Data from 13 Evaluation Projects." *American Journal of Preventive Medicine* 12, no. 5 (1996): 39–47.

Halpern, Carolyn T., Selene G. Oslak, Mary L. Young, Sandra L. Martin, and Lawrence L. Kupper. "Partner Violence among Adolescents in Opposite-Sex Romantic Relationships: Findings from the National Longitudinal Study of Adolescent Health." *American Journal of Public Health* 9 (2001): 1679–1685.

Henton, June, Rodney Cate, James Koval, Sally Lloyd, and Scott Christopher. "Romance and Violence in Dating Relationships." *Journal of Family Issues* 4 (1983): 467–482.

Hickman, Laura J., Lisa H. Jaycox, and Jessica Aranoff. "Dating Violence among Adolescents: Prevalence, Gender Distribution, and Prevention Program Effectiveness." *Trauma, Violence, and Abuse* 5 (2004): 123–142.

Howard, Donna E., and Min Qi Wang. "Risk Profiles of Adolescent Girls Who Were Victims of Dating Violence." *Adolescence* 38, no. 149 (2003): 1–13.

Kanin, Eugene J. "Male Aggression in Dating-Courtship Relations." *Journal of Sociology* 63 (1957): 197–204.

Koss, Mary P., Christine A. Gidycz, and Nadine Wisniewski. "The Scope of Rape: Incidence and Prevalence of Sexual Aggression and Victimization in a National Sample of Higher Education Students." *Journal of Consulting and Clinical Psychology* 55 (1987): 162–170.

Mahlstedt, Deborah L., and Lesley A. Welsh. "Perceived Causes of Physical Assault in Heterosexual Dating Relationships." *Violence Against Women* 11 (2005): 447–472.

Makepeace, James. "Courtship Violence among College Students." *Family Relations* 30 (1981): 97–102.

———. "Gender Differences in Courtship Violence Victimization." *Family Relations: Journal of Applied Family and Child Studies* 35 (1986): 383–388.

Marcus, Robert F. "Youth Violence in Everyday Life." *Journal of Interpersonal Violence* 20 (2005): 442–448.

Neufeld, Jonathan, John R. McNamara, and Melissa Ertl. "Incidence and Prevalence of Dating Partner Abuse and Its Relationship to Dating Practices." *Journal of Interpersonal Violence* 14 no. 2 (1999): 125–136.

Smith, Page H., Jacquelyn W. White, and Lindsay J. Holland. "A Longitudinal Perspective on Dating Violence among Adolescent and College-Age Women." *American Journal of Public Health* 93, no. 7 (2003): 1104–1109.

Strauss, Murray. "Prevalence of Violence against Dating Partners by Male and Female University Students Worldwide." *Violence Against Women* 10 (2004): 790–811.

Suarez, Kathryn E. "Teenage Dating Violence: The Need for Expanded Awareness and Legislation." *California Law Review* 82 (1994): 423–471.

Sugarman, David B., and Gerald T. Hotaling. "Dating Violence: Prevalence, Context, and Risk Markers." In *Violence in Dating Relationships: Emerging Social Issues*, edited by Maureen A. Pirog-Good and Jan E. Stets. New York: Praeger Publishers, 1989, 3–31.

West, Carolyn, M. and Suzanna Rose. "Dating Aggression among Low Income African American Youth." *Violence Against Women* 6, no 5 (2000): 470–494.

Wolfe, David A. and Candice Feiring. "Dating Violence through the Lens of Adolescent Romantic Relationships." *Child Maltreatment* 5, no. 4 (2000): 360–364.

Yick, Alice, and Pauline Agbayani-Siewert. "Dating Violence among Chinese American and White Students: A Sociocultural Context." *Journal of Multicultural Social Work* 8, no. 1/2 (2000): 101–129.

DATING VIOLENCE AMONG AFRICAN AMERICAN COUPLES

Dating violence, also referred to as *courtship violence* or *premarital abuse,* can occur across all racial/ethnic groups. However, African Americans are overrepresented in demographic categories that are at increased risk for dating violence. Although this racial group is socially and economically diverse, according to the 2000 U.S. Census, black Americans on average are younger, more likely to be impoverished, and less likely to be married than their non-Hispanic white counterparts. Consequently, much of the intimate partner violence experienced by black Americans will occur in nonmarital relationships. As reported by the National Crime Victimization Survey, between 1998 and 2002 more African Americans were victimized by boyfriends or girlfriends (17.2 percent) than by spouses (10.9 percent).

Despite the elevated risk of dating violence among African American couples, research on this topic has been limited and plagued with methodological problems, including definitional limitations and problems with how data have been collected, analyzed, and interpreted. Researchers, often using small samples of African Americans, have focused primarily on dating violence among high school and college students. As a result, less is known about violence among black couples who are older, cohabitating, or involved in same-sex partnerships. The definition of dating violence, which is often narrowly defined, has been inconsistent across studies. For example, several researchers focused only on victimization or used a single item to measure dating violence (e.g., "Has a boyfriend or date ever threatened to or actually hurt you physically?"). Consequently, it has been difficult to compare rates of violence across studies or to identify the types of physical, verbal, psychological, and sexual violence inflicted and sustained by black dating couples. Once the data have been collected, researchers have often neglected to consider gender differences in the injury level, nature, and circumstances of the violence. The failure to consider the association between socioeconomic status and dating violence has been particularly problematic.

What appear to be racial differences in rates of violence may, in fact, be social class differences.

Prevalence of Dating Violence

Similar to their white American counterparts, dating violence among African American couples can occur across the lifespan, often beginning in middle school or high school. During the 1993 academic year, the Centers for Disease Control and Prevention administered the Youth Risk Behavior Survey to 3,805 high school students, which included 677 black males and 829 black females. Physical and sexual victimization and perpetration were measured by such items as, "During the last thirty days were you physically beaten up by the person you date or go out with?" and "Has anyone ever forced you to have sexual intercourse even when you did not want to?" Approximately 9 percent of black girls had inflicted or sustained physical dating violence. A small number (3 percent) of the black girls were sexual aggressors, while significantly more (16 percent) were victims of sexual assault. In contrast, 8 percent of black boys had beaten up a date and 6 percent had been physically assaulted themselves in the month prior to the survey. Equal numbers (9 percent) of black boys had been victims or perpetrators of sexual assault.

Dating violence may continue into the college years. Clark and associates surveyed 311 African American undergraduates (76 males and 235 females). Students were asked to indicate how frequently during the previous year they or their partner had used dating violence to resolve a conflict. Verbal aggression was defined as insulting or swearing at the other person; refusing to talk to the other person; and saying something to spite the other person. More than 90 percent of males and females were victims or perpetrators of verbal aggression. Physical aggression was assessed using the following items: pushed, grabbed, or shoved; slapped, hit with something; choked; used a gun or knife. Comparable rates of physical victimization were reported by males (33 percent) and females

(41 percent). However, more females (47 percent) than males (35 percent) used at least one physically aggressive action against a dating partner. Pushing, slapping, or hitting were the most frequently used forms of physical aggression inflicted and sustained by both genders.

Dating violence also has been reported among couples who are engaged to be married. Boye-Beaman and colleagues surveyed 123 black couples immediately upon completion of their marriage license application. Mild aggression was defined as pushed, grabbed, or shoved, and moderate aggression as slapped or hit. Couples rated the frequency with which the husband engaged in each behavior over the course of their relationship. One-half of these black couples reported male aggression during their courtship. More specifically, 19 percent reported mild aggression and 30 percent experienced moderate aggression.

Despite what appears to be gender parity in reported rates of dating violence, it is premature to conclude that aggression in black male–female premarital relationships is mutual combat or a gender-neutral phenomenon. Using a sample of 171 low-income African American youths enrolled in a job training program, researchers Carolyn West and Suzanna Rose discovered significant gender differences in the types of violence inflicted and sustained. Significantly more men than women perpetrated severe forms of sexual aggression, such as attempted rape. In addition, men were more likely to make their partners feel inferior or to degrade them. In comparison, the women were more likely to have their feelings hurt by a partner and to be victims of severe physical and sexual aggression, including choking and attempted rape. Self defense may explain why these young women were significantly more likely to threaten, slap, hit, or throw objects at their partners. Taken together, the research suggests that dating violence is gendered. Alternatively stated, female-initiated violence should not be excused and male victimization should not be minimized. However, when one considers the severity of violence and extent of injuries, it appears that women are the primary victims.

Risk Factors and Consequences of Dating Violence

African American couples consistently reported higher rates of dating violence across studies. For example, McLaughlin and colleagues surveyed 150 African American and 458 white couples upon completion of their application for a marriage license. The rates of mild aggression were comparable across ethnic groups. Both black and white men (23 percent and 19 percent, respectively) had pushed, grabbed, or shoved their future wives. However, the rates of moderate aggression were quite different. One-quarter (25 percent) of black men had slapped their partner compared with 12 percent of white men.

Based on these findings, it should not be concluded that black Americans are biologically or culturally more prone to dating violence than other ethnic groups. Rather, these results suggest that African Americans are economically and socially disadvantaged, which places them at an increased risk for all forms of violence. Racial differences in rates of dating violence frequently disappear, or become less pronounced, when economic factors are taken into consideration.

In addition, exposure to violence in other contexts may partially account for elevated rates of dating violence among African Americans. Black men who were involved in community violence—as witnesses, participants, or victims—committed more dating violence. In some cases, exposure to violence in the family of origin predicted the initiation of dating violence by black youths but was not as strongly associated with dating violence initiation among white adolescents. However, the connection between family violence and dating violence appears to be influenced by race, gender, socioeconomic status, and family structure. Foshee and her associates found that the strongest association between mothers' use of corporal punishment and dating violence initiation was among those whose mothers had low levels of education. Being hit with the intention of harm predicted dating violence perpetration by black adolescents living in two-parent households, but not those living in one-parent households. Witnessing parental violence, on the other hand, predicted dating violence perpetration by black adolescents living in one-parent households, but not by those living in two-parent households.

Other researchers found an association between more approving attitudes toward dating violence and exposure to rap music and videos. Johnson and his colleagues divided their sample of low-income African American youths into two groups. One group viewed nonviolent rap videos, which contained images of women in sexually subordinate roles. The second group did not view any videos. Next, both groups read a story that involved teen dating violence perpetrated by a hypothetical male who shoved his girlfriend after she kissed another boy. Acceptance of violence was measured by such items as "Should John have pushed and shoved his girlfriend?" Acceptance of the use of violence did not vary as a function of video exposure for males. The boys who did not view rap videos were equally accepting of dating violence as boys who were exposed to the videos. In contrast, black girls who were exposed to the videos showed greater acceptance of dating violence in the scenario than girls who did not see the videos. However, it is not known if exposure to sexualized images of black women increases the risk of dating violence in the lives of black adolescents. Future research on the links between premarital abuse and popular culture, in the form of music and media, is required.

Premarital abuse can undermine the mental and physical health of some victims. Salazar and colleagues measured physical, emotional, and verbal dating violence among 522 low-income African American adolescent females who resided in a southern city. Most physically abused girls (69 percent) were extremely upset over the incident. Victims also reported less social support from friends and family, lowered self-esteem, depression, and a more negative body image. Using this same group of black adolescent girls, Wingood and associates discovered that 18 percent had been physically abused—defined as punched, hit, or pushed by a boyfriend—in the six months prior to the survey. When compared with their nonvictimized counterparts, abused girls were 2.8 times more likely to have a sexually transmitted disease and half as likely to use condoms consistently. These unhealthy sexual practices can elevate the risk of AIDS/HIV and contribute to unplanned pregnancy and reproductive health problems.

African American women may face additional challenges when they attempt to terminate their abusive dating relationships. Some black women fear that disclosing violence will reinforce negative stereotypes, such as the belief that African American relationships are inherently dysfunctional. The perceived scarcity of eligible black men can make other women reluctant to end violent partnerships. Despite these challenges, April Few and Patricia Bell-Scott discovered that black college women were able to successfully terminate their violent relationships. After they identified their victimization, they separated from the abusive partner and sought support from family members and friends. Utilizing self-help books, spirituality, and therapy also fostered their healing process.

Intervention and Prevention

According to researchers, improving the employment status, job conditions, and economic well-being of African Americans should drastically reduce the rates of dating violence. Limiting exposure to child abuse, violence in the family of origin, and community violence should also reduce dating violence among black couples. Finally, education is important. Sexual assault and dating violence programs should begin in middle school. Based on preliminary research, these programs effectively increase black students' knowledge about dating violence and improve their attitudes, making them less accepting of premarital abuse. A special effort should be made to reach black boys, who are sometimes reluctant to discuss intimate relationships. Single-sex groups may increase their comfort level. If dating violence does occur, middle-school children anticipate seeking parental and peer support. Effective intervention requires that parents, community members, and public and social service providers be prepared to assist these children. Culturally sensitive education should be provided to adolescents and young adults as well. Research suggests that black male undergraduates are receptive to rape prevention programs, particularly if these programs include culturally sensitive content, such as specific information about race-related rape myths. However, primary prevention is the ultimate goal. It is necessary to reach black youths and young adults before coercive dating patterns are established and to give them tools to prevent relationship conflict from escalating.

CAROLYN M. WEST

See also **African American Community, Domestic Violence in; Cohabiting Violence; Date Rape; Dating Violence; Education as a Risk Factor for Domestic Violence; Minorities and Families in America, Introduction to; Social Class and Domestic Violence**

References and Further Reading

Boye-Beaman, Joni, Kenneth E. Leonard, and Marilyn Senchak. "Male Premarital Aggression and Gender Identity among Black and White Newlywed Couples." *Journal of Marriage and the Family* 55 (1993): 303–313.

Clark, M. L., Joyce Beckett, Mabel Wells, and Delores Dungee-Anderson. "Courtship Violence among African American College Students." *Journal of Black Psychology* 20, no. 3 (1994): 264–281.

Foshee, Vangie A., Susan T. Ennett, Karl E. Bauman, Thad Benefield, and Chirayath Suchindran. "The Association between Family Violence and Adolescent Dating Violence Onset." *Journal of Early Adolescence* 25, no. 3 (2005): 317–344.

Johnson, James D., Mike S. Adams, and Leslie Ashburn. "Differential Gender Effects of Exposure to Rap Music on African American Adolescents' Acceptance of Teen Dating Violence." *Sex Roles* 33, nos. 7/8 (1995): 597–605.

Malik, Shaista, Susan B. Sorenson, and Carol S. Aneshensel. "Community and Dating Violence among Adolescents." *Journal of Adolescent Health* 21, no. 5 (1997): 291–302.

Malley-Morrison, Kathleen, and Denise A. Hines, eds. *Cultural Perspective: Defining, Understanding, and Combating Abuse.* Thousand Oaks, CA: Sage Publications, 2004.

McLaughlin, Iris G., Kenneth E. Leonard, and Marilyn Senchak. "Prevalence and Distribution of Premarital Aggression among Couples Applying for a Marriage License." *Journal of Family Violence* 7, no. 4 (1992): 309–319.

Pierce-Baker, Charlotte. *Surviving the Silence: Black Women's Stories of Rape.* New York: W.W. Norton & Company, 1998.

Salazar, Laura F., Gina M. Wingood, Ralph J. DiClemente, Delia L. Lang, and Kathy Harrington. "The Role of Social Support in the Psychological Well-Being of African American Girls Who Experience Dating Violence Victimization." *Violence and Victims* 19, no. 2 (2004): 171–186.

Valois, Robert F., John E. Oeltmann, Jennifer Waller, and James R. Hussey. "Relationship between Number of Sexual Intercourse Partners and Selected Health Risk Behaviors among Public High School Adolescents." *Journal of Adolescent Health* 25, no. 5 (1999): 328–335.

West, Carolyn M., ed. *Violence in the Lives of Black Women: Battered, Black, and Blue.* Binghamton, NY: Haworth Press, 2002.

West, Carolyn M., and Suzanna Rose. "Dating Aggression among Low Income African American Youth." *Violence Against Women* 6, no. 5 (2000): 470–494.

Wingood, Gina M., Ralph J. DiClemente, Donna McCree, Kathy Harrington, and Susan L. Davies. "Dating Violence and the Sexual Health of Black Adolescent Females." *Pediatrics* 107, no. 5 (2001): 1–4.

DEPRESSION AND DOMESTIC VIOLENCE

Introduction

Depression is highly correlated with domestic violence. Physical, emotional, and sexual abuse experienced or observed can traumatize mental well-being; for this reason, it is not surprising that high rates of depression or depressive symptoms are documented in the victim, perpetrator, and witness of abuse. When treating depression, therefore, it is necessary to provide an integrated, comprehensive approach that considers the potential for family violence.

Depression and the Victim

Victims of domestic violence experience harm beyond that of the actual battering. Abused and battered women are significantly more likely than nonvictims to suffer from major depression, alcohol and substance abuse, generalized anxiety, post-traumatic stress disorder, and obsessive-compulsive disorder. The trauma-related effects are intensified when the abuser is someone the victim depends on, loves, or trusts.

Depression is a significant mental health problem for women because of its prevalence, persistence, recurrence, and interference with well-being and performance of everyday activities. Women classified as depressed are six to seven times more likely to have experienced severe partner abuse than women who are not classified as depressed (Hegarty et al. 2005). High levels of abuse increase risk for depression and anxiety over the life span. Conversely, a decrease in actual or threatened abuse among victims of domestic violence is associated with a lowered prevalence of depression (Kernic et al. 2003).

It is essential that professionals providing care to at risk populations recognize the mounting evidence associating depression with domestic violence. Appropriate therapeutic and precautionary intervention should then be made available to prevent potentially life-threatening situations. Doctors should be alert to the serious possibility of partner abuse whenever they are treating a patient with depressive symptoms. Time and patience need to be dedicated to probing the patient's social context to identify the cause of the depression or depressive symptoms rather than just prescribing psychoactive medications that merely mitigate symptoms or obscure the root causes. Furthermore, treating only the symptoms of depression experienced by a victim of abuse reinforces the belief that the fault, and therefore the fix, is within the victim instead of within the abusive situation.

Failure to recognize the underlying social context for depressive symptoms can lead to increased risk of injury and deepening depression for the victim. Prescribing sedatives, tranquilizers, or antidepressants for a woman who is in a dangerously abusive or battering situation can dull the reflexes and senses she needs to protect herself (Fischbach and Herbert 1997). She must be fully alert to take safety precautions for herself and her children and, if necessary, to make and carry out an escape plan to get to a safe shelter.

High rates of depressive symptoms are found also in specific populations at risk for family and partner violence, such as the elderly, same-sex partners, adolescents in dating relationships, pregnant women, and children in abusive homes. The elderly may be at increased risk for depressive symptoms because of declining financial resources or deteriorating health, but when compounded with violence, abuse, or neglect from caregivers or family members, elderly persons consistently show severe signs of depression and anxiety (Dyer et al. 2000). Homosexual couples often are at increased risk for depression due to internalized homophobia and reactions to other social pressures; this stress may contribute to the depressive context in same-sex intimate partner violence (Goglucci 1999). Adolescents involved with an abusive partner report increased levels of depressed mood, substance use, antisocial behavior, and, in females, suicidal behavior (Roberts et al. 2003). Similarly, pregnant women are at risk for increased violence during pregnancy: It is estimated that one in five women will be abused during pregnancy (Weiss 2005). Being victimized while pregnant is associated with depression during pregnancy as well as severe postpartum depression (Jasinski 2004).

Recognizing that depression can be both a cause and a result of domestic violence should encourage the victims to make changes in their living arrangements that will lead to improvements in their sense of health and mental well-being. As a cause of violence, the despondency of a depressed victim may provoke the batterer, which can trigger further mistreatment. This in turn can result in deepening the victim's depression, leading to a paralyzing inability to make lifesaving choices that would preserve her physical and emotional well-being.

Depression and the Batterer

Perpetrators of domestic violence also often exhibit high rates of depression and depressive symptoms.

Interviews with the partners of patients who are seen in emergency rooms for signs and symptoms of abuse have shown that risk factors for perpetrating intimate partner violence include current depression, as well as race, living with a partner, and substance abuse (Lipsky et al. 2005). The majority of abusers surveyed by Stith et al. (2004) reported depression, alcoholism, or drug addiction at the time of committing an abusive act. Understanding that the abusers often show high levels of depression may be useful to health care professionals in identifying perpetrators of domestic violence, especially in primary care or emergency room settings.

Evidence indicates that depression brought on by stressful life events may also be connected to an increased risk of being a batterer, even in relationships that previously were free from physical confrontation. For example, in the period leading up to and during separation and divorce, new instances of violence, as well as increased violence, are reported (Toews 2003). In times of high stress where depressive symptoms could be expected, e.g., during natural disasters or prolonged unemployment, women are at increased risk for physical abuse from their partners (Norris 2005).

Though females are less likely than males to be perpetrators of intimate partner violence, abusing females are nonetheless also found to show high levels of depression. In Watson's study of ten female perpetrators, 50 percent of the women had histories of major depression, post-traumatic stress disorder, or substance abuse (Watson 2001).

While some argue that the high correlation and temporal relationship of depression with domestic violence suggest a causal relationship, others are concerned that blaming depression for the violent or abusive acts reduces the batterer's accountability. They posit that most men who batter their partners and children do not exhibit generalized violence outside of their domestic relationships, even when depressed or under stress. This suggests that partner violence is a pattern of control that includes verbal and physical abuse, threats, psychological manipulation, and sexual coercion, rather than random, isolated acts of violence caused by depression or mental illness (Adams 2003).

Depression and the Witness

Estimates of the number of children who observe domestic violence perpetrated against their mothers range from 3.3 million to 10 million children every year. This engenders grave consequences because witnessing domestic violence, like directly experiencing it, also predicts depression. There is increasing evidence that a child who is exposed to domestic violence against his or her mother is more likely to experience depression, behavior problems, and physical complaints (Wolf 2002). These children are affected in ways similar to children who are abused, revealing signs of helplessness, powerlessness, and conflicting feelings toward the perpetrator. Younger children exhibit higher emotional and psychological distress than older children, suggesting that they have not developed critical coping skills for their age. These early traumatic observations can handicap children when they need to deal with future problems, putting them at risk for depression throughout their lives.

Internalized depressive feelings of powerlessness and helplessness in child witnesses of family violence can appear in adolescence as extreme and dangerous behaviors such as drug and alcohol abuse, truancy, and sexual promiscuity (Herrera 2002). Female adolescents who witnessed battering against their mothers tend toward depression and internally destructive behaviors with an increased risk of suicide. Male adolescents are likely to exhibit depression and other psychological stresses through violent and aggressive outlets. Those who witnessed domestic violence as children continue to exhibit high levels of depressive symptoms as adults (Reinherz et al. 2003).

Observing even a threat of violence can have the same potent consequences as witnessing violent acts against another. Research examining the negative psychological impact of childhood exposure to family violence has found that observed threats of violence and current heavy drinking were the most potent predictors of depression in women. Among men, observing threats of violence predicted current heavy drinking, while directly experiencing violence predicted depression and also put the men at risk for perpetrating violent behavior in their own future relationships (Trocki and Caetano 2003).

Recognizing the intergenerational cycle of abuse and depression among victims, batterers, and witnesses means that domestic violence cannot be regarded as a private matter. Domestic violence perpetuates itself with devastating effects on individuals as well as on society.

Conclusion

Depression is regarded as one of the world's leading mental health problems. In addition to impairing patient well-being, depression imposes a significant societal burden in terms of both direct costs (e.g., for treatment) and indirect costs (e.g.,

absenteeism, lost productivity, and increased risk for other medical illnesses). The alarming prevalence of depression among victims, perpetrators, and witnesses of domestic violence demands continuing epidemiological study to substantiate the causal relationship and to direct health professionals to examine social factors when treating the symptoms of depression. Psychoactive medication should be prescribed with care so as not to jeopardize the ability of victims of violence to protect themselves. The consequences of domestic violence are urgent public health challenges that require a strong societal commitment to providing the expertise, resources, and services to treat, intervene, and free victims from the destructive intergenerational cycles of violence and depression.

RUTH L. FISCHBACH and MELISSA VALENTINE

See also **Female Suicide and Domestic Violence; Neurological and Physiological Impacts of Abuse; Postpartum Depression, Psychosis, and Infanticide; Social, Economic, and Psychological Costs of Violence**

References and Further Reading

Adams, David. "Treatment Programs for Batterers." *Clinics and Family Practice* 5, no. 1 (2003).

Dyer, Carmel Bitondo, Valory N. Pavlik, Kathleen Pace Murphy, and David J. Hyman. "The High Prevalence of Depression and Dementia in Elder Abuse or Neglect." *Journal of the American Geriatrics Society* 48, no. 2 (2000): 205–208.

Fischbach, Ruth, and Barbara Herbert. "Domestic Violence and Mental Health: Correlates and Conundrums within and across Cultures." *Social Science and Medicine* 45, no. 8 (1997): 1161–1176.

Goglucci, Nina Marie. "Domestic Violence in Lesbian Relationships." *Dissertation Abstracts International: Section B: The Sciences and Engineering* 60, no. 9-B (2000): 4963.

Hegarty, Kelsey, Jane Gunn, Patty Chondros, and Rhonda Small. "Association between Depression and Abuse by Partners of Women Attending General Practice: Descriptive, Cross Sectional Survey." *British Medical Journal* 328, no. 7440 (2004): 621–624.

Herrera, Veronica Marina. "Family Influences on Adolescent Depression and Delinquency: Gender Differences in Risk." *Dissertation Abstracts International: Section B: The Sciences and Engineering* 62, no. 9-B (2002): 4219.

Jasinski, Jana. "Pregnancy and Domestic Violence: A Review of the Literature." *Trauma, Violence, and Abuse* 5, no. 1 (2004): 47–64.

Kernic, Mary A., Victoria L. Holt, Julie A. Stoner, Marsha E. Wolf, and Frederick P. Rivara. "Resolution of Depression among Victims of Intimate Partner Violence: Is Cessation of Violence Enough?" *Violence and Victims* 18, no. 2 (2003): 115–129.

Lipsky, Sherry, Raul Caetano, Craig A. Field, and Shahrzad Bazargan. "The Role of Alcohol Use and Depression in Intimate Partner Violence among Black and Hispanic Patients in an Urban Emergency Department." *American Journal of Drug and Alcohol Abuse* 31, no. 2 (2005): 225–242.

Norris, Fran H. "Prevalence and Impact of Domestic Violence in the Wake of Disasters." *Disasters and Domestic Violence: A National Center for Post-Traumatic Stress Disorder Fact Sheet.* Department of Veterans Affairs, 2005. http://www.ncptsd.va.gov/facts/disasters/fs_domestic.html.

Reinherz, Helen Z., Angela D. Paradis, Rose M. Giaconia, Cecilia K. Stashwick, Garrett Fitzmaurice. "Childhood and Adolescent Predictors of Major Depression in the Transition to Adulthood." *American Journal of Psychiatry* 160, no. 12 (2003): 2141–2147.

Roberts, Timothy A., Jonathan D. Klein, and Susan Fisher. "Longitudinal Effect of Intimate Partner Abuse on High-Risk Behavior among Adolescents." *Archives of Pediatrics and Adolescent Medicine* 157, no. 9 (2003): 875–881.

Stith, Sandra M., Douglas B. Smith, Carrie E. Penn, David B. Ward, and Dari Tritt. "Intimate Partner Physical Abuse Perpetration and Victimization Risk Factors: A Meta-Analytic Review." *Aggression and Violent Behavior* 10, no. 1 (2004): 65–98.

Toews, Michelle L., Patrick C. McKenry, and Beth S. Catlett. "Male-Initiated Partner Abuse during Marital Separation Prior to Divorce." *Violence and Victims* 18, no. 4 (Aug 2003): 387–402.

Trocki, Karen F., and Raul Caetano. "Exposure to Family Violence and Temperament Factors as Predictors of Adult Psychopathology and Substance Use Outcomes." *Journal of Addictions Nursing* 14, no. 4 (2003): 183–192.

Watson, Carol Julianne. "Female Perpetrators of Domestic Violence: A Pilot Study." *Dissertation Abstracts International: Section B: The Sciences and Engineering* 61, no. 9-B (2001): 5011.

Weiss, Robin Elise. "Domestic Violence in Pregnancy," 2005. http://pregnancy.about.com/cs/domesticviolence/a/domesticviol.htm.

Wolf, Angela Marie. "The Effect of Exposure to Domestic Violence on Children: A Longitudinal Examination of Children's Outcomes." *Dissertation Abstracts International: Section B: The Sciences and Engineering* 63, no. 5-B (2002): 2627.

DISSOCIATION IN DOMESTIC VIOLENCE, THE ROLE OF

The Dissociative Batterer

The battering cycle begins with a dissociative condition in the batterer. The spouse abuse process is a "dance" in which the cyclical batterer switches into different ego states, and his partner follows him in the dance by developing corresponding ego states of her own. The two most prominent states of the batterer are anger and normalcy. Each state has its characteristic emotions and behavior. Heightened emotional states are the key to the batterer's dissociative switches (Sutker 1994, p. 101).

Walker (1979) traces the buildup, discharge, and contrition phases in the cycle of spousal abuse. During the buildup phase, the batterer's criticism of his partner gradually escalates. In the discharge phase, he acts out his uncontrolled rage by battering his partner. After the discharge phase comes the contrition phase, during which the batterer may express remorse for his actions and promise it will never happen again and/or he may justify his behavior as a result of stress or his partner's alleged provocations. Once the rage is fully discharged, the abuser may be relatively pleasant until the buildup begins once more. The three phases are explored more fully below. For the purposes of simplicity in writing, the batterer is referred to throughout this entry as "he" and the victim/spouse as "she," but it is important to be aware that both victims and batterers can be of either sex.

The batterer is often an upstanding member of the community. This is his conscious self-image, the only part of his behavior which he experiences as ego-syntonic. The feedback he receives from sources other than his spouse (i.e., colleagues, neighbors, others in the community) indicates that he is indeed a respectable and admirable person. He may appear helpful, somewhat unassertive, and deferential to authority. Dutton and Golant (1995), experts on domestic violence, note that even researchers and scholars in the field may have a difficult time understanding how men who seem to "have it all together" on the outside can be so abusive at home. Not until they interviewed the wives of abusers who presented as "normal" to the outside world did they realize how physically and emotionally abusive such men could be.

Dutton (1995, pp. 82–84) found that batterers' childhoods were characterized by humiliation, embarrassment, and shame. Factors related to battering, in order of importance, were paternal rejection, the father's inability to express warmth toward the child, physical and verbal abuse by the father, and rejection by the mother. Dutton argues that being shamed by one's father is prime among the parental actions that may generate abusiveness in men. Batterers' relationships with their mothers are high on both warmth and rejection, from which Dutton concludes that they were "angrily attached." Dutton (1995) notes that the original motive for anger is to reestablish soothing contact; thus anger follows unmet attachment needs. Fearfully attached children often develop a lifelong style of reacting to their fear of the loss of intimacy with anger. Spouses' accounts of their batterers suggest that the angry side of their partners' personality is distinctly different from their normal personality. The batterer appears to have an angry ego state which emerges in response to an attachment threat but is not his usual deportment.

With regard to partners of domestic batterers, research indicates that they do not all fit one psychological profile. Some studies suggest that those who stay for some time in abusive relationships have only one thing in common: They believe in the importance of maintaining the family unit.

The Psychological Contract between the Batterer and Victim

The batterer's assaults on his partner usually begin during the first year of their relationship, when the positive feelings are strongest. To both parties, the violence appears to be an anomaly, something that is completely out of character for the one who committed it. Since the batterer does not see himself as the kind of person who would act violently toward someone he loves, he considers his violent behavior to be the result of external influences. Initially, both partners believe that the violence will never happen again, since it contradicts the positive aspects of their relationship. When it recurs, both partners look to the present rather than the past for the cause of their problems. The batterer attributes his switch into this angry, violent mode to his wife's behavior, which he believes to be the trigger for his violence toward her.

At this point, the battered woman becomes aware that there is a discrepancy between the seemingly wonderful man she believed her partner to be and the angry, violent side of his personality that appears only behind closed doors. The relationship continues to appear normal outside the home, while an entirely new and terrifying reality presents itself within the home. Since no one else may be exposed to the abusive side of her partner, the battered woman may begin to doubt her perceptions of him. The victim of domestic violence often accepts a major portion of the blame because she has been taught to do so. She stops believing that the violence will simply stop happening and starts believing that the end of her abuse is contingent upon her altering her behavior. She still sees the violence as inconsistent with her partner's character and, therefore, avoidable. She has accepted her partner's core belief that future outbreaks of violence depend upon her behavior, not his.

The psychological contract between the batterer and his spouse maintains that his emotional well-being depends on her. If he is distressed, he considers it her fault. She may reason that since he becomes violent only when he is home with her, she causes the violence; her partner reinforces this belief. Typically, the victim tries to change her behavior to ameliorate her abuser and to stop his violent behavior.

Why Doesn't She Leave?

Those who have not experienced domestic violence firsthand often question why battered women do not leave abusive relationships and, when they do leave, why so many return to their spouses. There are data to suggest that battered women may stay with or return to their abusers because of the dissociation of memories into "chains" characterized by different extreme emotional states.

When the wife accepts that it is her responsibility to make her husband happy, the dissociative process is initiated. Most literature has focused on the battering phases within the home; however, a key to understanding the dissociative nature of the cycle may be in taking a closer look at the situation outside the home, where the battering spouse is consistently charming, pleasant, and thoughtful. The extreme contrast between the person the abused partner sees outside the home and the person who appears in the home is an important factor in encouraging the development of a dissociative process in the abused partner. Even if she may have initially been an emotionally integrated person, the repetitive nature of the phases causes her to split her memories into state-dependent chains. The abused spouse is intermittently in a terrifying environment in which she must comply with someone who exercises power over her in order to avoid further physical harm. She responds by developing different personae, each characterized by a different primary emotion and a different belief system. Like the batterer, she does not forget what happens during the violent episodes, but rather she tends to minimize his behavior and hope for the best between episodes.

The Phases of the Abuse Cycle from the Perspective of Dissociation Theory

The Buildup Phase

During the buildup phase, the batterer's ego state marked by his negative emotions begins to rise to the surface. The batterer will often experience chronic depression and resentment. These emotions affect his wife and sometimes their children, especially when a "trigger" provides a reminder of the emotions of past trauma. For example, a husband who had been sexually abused as a child may develop a regular pattern of picking a fight with his spouse within a few hours after sexual intimacy, even if the sex itself was satisfactory.

The abused spouse's primary emotions during the buildup phase are anxiety and pity. She tries to determine the likelihood that her partner will be triggered into the full emergence of his abusive personality. She patiently listens to her spouse as he blames her for things that are not her fault, and she takes responsibility for triggering his violent mood by her behaviors. She permits chronic personal boundary violations in the hope of avoiding a violent situation.

During the buildup phase, the battered spouse represses her own anger, but her hurt feelings caused by the verbal abuse build up, until she withdraws emotionally or physically. Jones (1994, pp. 95, 185) describes this dissociative process in the woman as follows: "From the first moment a man abuses her, a woman begins, in some sense, to leave—emotionally, spiritually, physically. Abused women describe this process of going underground within themselves, hiding out inside, lying low until they can emerge, like some moth shedding caterpillar skin, becoming themselves. Escapees say 'Now I'm myself again.' A general withdrawal goes on, and the batterer, who is exquisitely sensitive to abandonment, notices it."

The Discharge Phase

As the batterer's internal discomfort builds to a peak, he becomes extremely verbally abusive toward his spouse. She begins to detach herself, partly because her hurt feelings are also trying to surface, and partly in order to be able to concentrate on complying with his demands so as to avoid a more serious situation. The batterers Dutton (1995) studied appeared to have outbursts of rage triggered by a sense that their partners were moving away from them, emotionally or physically. They frequently had "delusions of impending abandonment." In experiments involving the videotapes of spousal discussion, batterers became angriest in response to videos in which the woman was in control and was moving away emotionally from her husband. These videos did not have this effect on nonbattering men. Dutton concludes that emotional distance appeared to trigger the batterers' violence.

The switch from the buildup phase into the discharge phase is quite visible, and most battered women can describe it. Something seems to snap, and the husband seems to become a different person. His demeanor and expression change. At this point, nothing will prevent him from attacking his wife. The only questions are how long the attack will last and how serious it will be.

In the early part of the discharge phase, when the victim's partner is tormenting, threatening, and interrogating her, the victim experiences extreme fear. When the abuser's anger reaches its peak, all of the victim's emotions are suppressed and she moves into "survival mode." Her energy becomes focused on calculating such things as where to fall and how to keep the children from overhearing the fight. She may dissociate and feel that she is leaving her body. Just after the violence stops, her extreme fear returns. This experience becomes chained together with all of her other memories of abuse at the hands of her husband; these memories are remembered vividly in the immediate aftermath of a violent episode. This is the time when she is most likely to leave, especially if there has been outside intervention (e.g., a witness to the incident tells her she is not crazy when she reports that her partner is violent). However, if threats have been made regarding what will happen if she leaves (e.g., he will kill her, he will kill himself, he will abduct the children), her awareness of danger is also very high. In addition, she is exhausted and unable to think clearly after enduring the violence. She may become paralyzed, "blanking out" in response to her internal conflict between fear of the consequences of staying and fear of the consequences of leaving.

The Postdischarge Phase

After his negative emotions have been discharged, the batterer's state changes. His violent side recedes and the batterer is faced with explaining his violent behavior. Because he feels shame, he rationalizes his ego-dystonic behavior—sometimes blaming it on "stress," sometimes blaming his spouse for provoking him. As the violent side of his personality recedes further inside, the details of the abuse are gradually forgotten by the abuser. He is once more able to see himself as a nice person who experienced a temporary aberration.

Walker describes the postdischarge phase as a "honeymoon phase" in which the batterer behaves in a kind and nurturing manner. He seduces his partner into believing that he is still loving and that he will change his behavior. The batterer is even more likely to appear remorseful if his spouse has actually left. Many scholars assume that the batterer's behavior at this point is a conscious manipulation. However, if the batterer is viewed as dissociative, a different interpretation is possible: The violent side of his dual personality has receded, allowing the charming side to come to the fore. The good side has no understanding of the bad side. When faced with interventions from the outside world, he is in the venue where he has always functioned as a pleasant (nonviolent) man.

During the postdischarge phase, the abused wife experiences relief and gratitude. Her husband becomes remorseful, solicitous, tender, and nurturing at the very moment when she most needs it. The needs he does not meet at other times are finally being met. Because all of his negative emotion has been discharged, she is able to feel secure—he is not currently vulnerable to another episode of violence. Her emotional experience of security becomes chained with all her previous memories of being secure with him. She remembers how he treated her in the early stages of their relationship, how he behaves toward her in public, and all the previous honeymoon phases of their relationship.

The remorseful period does not occur in all batterers, especially if the abused wife does not leave. Some batterers just go into a period of postviolence during which they blame their victims for their behavior in order to remove their own sense of shame, while others withdraw into themselves to "cool off." Yet even without a remorseful phase, the batterer's character in the outside world provides sufficient contrast with his violent self to produce dissociative memory chains in both himself and his partner.

Helping an Abused Spouse to Leave or to Stay Away

Most people who provide assistance to victims of spousal abuse try to give them logical reasons for

leaving the relationship or for not returning to an abusive partner; they are sometimes bemused by how easily the victims are seduced back into the relationship. However, if the dissociative nature of the victim's experiences is taken into account, her behavior becomes more comprehensible. When she is in the outside world and her partner is acting like a model husband, the victim of spousal abuse is unable to clearly recall what his abusive personality is like. Because of this dissociation, treatment should focus on blending the victim's memories from the buildup, discharge, and postdischarge phases of the cycle.

A major task in treatment is getting the battered woman to learn how to remember the abuse when her spouse is being supportive, and the supportiveness when he is being abusive. To accomplish this, the following interventions have proven helpful:

- Have the abuse victim keep a journal, instructing her to divide it into different sections that correspond with the different phases of the abuse cycle. She should keep her journal each day in the appropriate section throughout the phases of the relationship. Then have her read material daily from the sections which contain material from phases which are different from the one she is currently experiencing. The journal will also help the patient access material for use in therapy, as it is much easier for her to access images from the present phase of the cycle than from other phases.

- After the abused spouse is able to access images from phases other than the one she is currently in, hypnotically interweave images from each phase of the relationship. Use Eye Movement Desensitization and Reprocessing (EMDR) or a similar technique with images from the different phases, then overlay the images and have the spouse attempt to see both at once.

- Use Emotionally Focused Therapy or Gestalt therapy techniques with the abused spouse, placing the imagined abusive partner in two or more different chairs, one for his abusive self, one for his public self, and others as needed. The purpose is for her to recognize that all aspects of her partner always exist.

Children in the Abusive Home

The batterer as a parent often intentionally interferes with the bond between his wife and their children. If he in his abandonment panic cannot have comfort from his spouse, he will not allow her to be a source of comfort to their children, because that would make him see that his spouse can be a source of comfort.

When his spouse fails to meet the batterer's needs for comfort, the batterer may turn to his children, trying with them, as he did with his wife, to get the nurturing he missed as a child. If the batterer has chosen his children as objects of attachment and comfort, he is likely to abuse them as well, and to interfere with his partner's ability to comfort them, abusing her even more for attempting to protect them from his abuse or tending to them afterward. He may escalate his abuse of the children if she questions his behavior or his authority. Hurting the children is a way to hurt their mother, and if she does not intervene, knowing that the outcome could be worse if she does, the children may see her as being complicit in their abuse.

What does it do to a child to be placed in this kind of situation? The child is exposed to more than one father—the frightening one, the nurturing one, and the regular one shown outside the home. The child is also exposed to a terrified and helpless mother as well as a nurturing one, who appears only when the father is not around. Children need to be able to provide comfort for both parents as well as to keep themselves safe. They need to be ready to deal with whatever parental ego state they are confronted with. These children are also likely to develop different ego states to deal with the different states of the abusive parent. In that way, like their mothers, they can enjoy being with the nurturing father without memories of the frightening father causing a level of anxiety that might actually precipitate the frightening father's appearance.

Baker and O'Neil (1996) discuss attachment failure triads that occur when a child lives with a "frightened-frightening" parent. If the father is intermittently abusive and the mother is unavailable for comfort, the child may use dissociation to develop (1) a secure ego state for dealing with the protecting father, (2) a traumatized ego state for dealing with the threatening father, and (3) an avoidant or resistant ego state for dealing with the unavailable mother.

A child who develops alternating attachments to his or her parents may become "stuck to" one parent, either father or mother, for a period of days while refusing the other parent. If a situation requires the child to spend time with the parent he or she is not "stuck to," the parent who is the current object of attachment may physically have to force the child away and hand him or her over to the other parent. The child will then switch allegiance. The child is able to tolerate thinking that one parent is the "good guy" but is unable to grasp the complexity of the situation and therefore reduces it to simplicity by allowing an awareness of only one parent at a time.

In many cases, the batterer attempts to turn the children against the other parent. He may tell them that their mother deserved the abuse, giving them his side of the story. The children may be able to evade his abuse by listening supportively to him and even berating their abused parent themselves. They come to believe that if they take the abuser's side, they could be protected from harm. Indeed, the abuser may make them take sides, calling them in as witnesses in some dispute and pointing out to them how bad their mother is. The only safe place for a child in a spouse-abusing household is in the arms of the abuser.

The abusive parent needs desperately to see himself as the "good guy" and as being justified in his behavior. Therefore, he has to convince the only witnesses, the children, of his view of the situation. They know that their safety is contingent upon their acceptance of the abuser's viewpoint and their rejection of their other parent. If the love of the nonabusive parent is not conditional, but is frequently unavailable because of the abuse, the children need to dissociate their awareness of the actual situation in order to obtain whatever love he or she can. Keeping safe from the frightening parent (whether the father or the mother) involves accepting that parent's verbal explanation that the other parent is the "bad guy," even though the child's own observations indicate otherwise. The child also has to keep the secret of what life is like at home. This is a prime breeding ground for dissociation, or at least of the development of fairly separate ego states, which can emerge later when, as adults, they enter into intimate relationships.

As a result, the children may adopt the abusive parent's anger as their own, and genuinely believe the other parent to be the monster of the abusive parent's imagination. Even at a very young age, they may begin to verbally abuse one parent the way the other parent does, or exhibit uncontrollable rages against her. In order for this behavior to stop, such children must come to realize that all the rage that they have been carrying against the abused parent belongs to the *abusive* parent rather than to themselves.

Summary: The Dissociative Dance

As the battering spouse goes through the phases of the abuse cycle, his partner develops parallel states which link together in separate chains of memory. The abuse victim feels anxiety and pity during the buildup phase, enters into a survival and coping mode marked by a lack of emotion and dissociation from the body during the discharge phase, experiences extreme fear just before and just after the battering, and feels a sense of relief and security during the postdischarge or "honeymoon" phase. During the "honeymoon" phase, as well as when she is with her partner in the outside world, the victim has only hazy recollections of the battering and buildup phases. Thus she is able to enjoy the relief periods without contamination from memories of violence, continue to love her spouse, and maintain the marriage. However, such dissociation prevents her from leaving when this might be the best course of action. When he becomes a parent, the abuser often interferes with his wife's bond with their children, substituting himself as both abuser and comforter. He thus creates the dissociative splits which enable his children to repeat the dissociative dance of domestic violence when his children become adults.

ALISON MILLER

See also **Identity Theory and Domestic Violence; Victim-Blaming Theory**

References and Further Reading

Baker, Su, and John O'Neil. "Transference and Countertransference Revisited: The Interplay of Trauma and Attachment in the Process of Therapy with Dissociative Disorders." Workshop presented at the 13th International Fall Conference of the International Society for the Study of Dissociation, 1996.

Dutton, D. *The Domestic Assault of Women.* Vancouver, BC: UBC Press, 1995.

Dutton, D., and S. K. Golant. *The Batterer: A Psychological Profile.* New York: Basic Books, 1995.

Jones, Ann. *Next Time, She'll Be Dead: Battering and How to Stop It.* Boston: Beacon Press, 1994.

Miller, Alison. "The Dissociative Dance of Spouse Abuse." *Treating Abuse Today* 8, no. 3 (1998): 9–18.

Sutker, L. W. "When Dissociation Is Called Denial: Differences in Treatment Approaches to Dissociative Phenomenon in Victims and Offenders." *Proceedings of 3rd Annual Victoria Child Sexual Abuse Symposium,* 1994, 100–105.

Walker, L. *The Battered Woman.* New York: Harper & Row, 1979.

Weldon, Michelle. *I Closed My Eyes: Revelations of a Battered Woman.* Center City, MN: Hazelden, 1999.

DIVORCE, CHILD CUSTODY, AND DOMESTIC VIOLENCE

Approximately 50 percent of all first marriages in the United States end in divorce. The rate of divorce is even higher among second marriages. Approximately 1,000,000 children are affected each year by divorce. Determination of where a child will live after a parental divorce and whether the child will have ongoing contact with the noncustodial parent and on what schedule are important issues. Although only about 10 percent of first-marriage divorces where there are minor children involve a legally disputed child custody case, these are often the mostly highly contentious and hostile of situations, in which children are exposed to tremendous conflict. Accordingly, accusations of domestic violence (i.e., violence between adult intimate partners) are not uncommon in such contested custody disputes. Even when "custody" or primary residential responsibility for a child is not legally disputed, the presence of spousal violence significantly impacts postdivorce matters. Most notably, custody and visitation laws often promote the notion that parents should be given equal access to children as well as equal say in decision making. When parents get along well or at least are able to put aside their own differences for the sake of their children, these notions are appropriate. However, achieving equal access and decision making usually requires a high level of contact, communication, and negotiation between the parents. This can be quite difficult even in cases where there is no domestic violence. Expecting that level of cooperation to occur where there has been domestic violence may be unrealistic and potentially damaging or even life threatening for the children and the spouse-victim.

Impact of Divorce and Domestic Violence on Children

Divorce is a difficult situation for children. The effects of divorce on children can be devastating, although there are certainly broad individual differences in children's abilities to assimilate this and other traumas in their lives. Discussion of the research on the immediate impact of divorce as well as the impact on children's life-span adjustment is beyond the scope of this article. However, in general, children whose parents divorce may have additional problems, such as conduct disorders like defiance and aggression; signs of psychological maladjustment such as depression, anxiety, and fear; lower academic achievement; increased social difficulties; and poor self-concept. Evidence suggests that such problems may continue into adulthood, with adult children of divorce scoring lower on various indices of well-being. It should be noted that differences are not large between the adult children of divorced and nondivorced parents and that the two groups overlap a lot. However, in studies, some adult children of divorce report it as having been a severe stressor which resulted in substantial impairment and decline in their well-being. Adult children of divorce may display lower psychological well-being and more behavior problems. They may have achieved less education and have lower job status and a lower standard of living. Lower marital satisfaction and higher divorce rates have also been reported among adult children of divorce.

The long-term effects of divorce often result from the presence of multiple changes and problems surrounding the divorce which seem to compound children's postdivorce negative adjustment. For instance, factors such as parental absence, economic hardship, associated life changes, poor emotional adjustment in parents, and poor parenting skills all increase the likelihood that a child will have difficulty adjusting. A child will usually have a more difficult time adjusting to the divorce when he has to move from his residence, change schools, can no longer participate in extracurricular activities due to financial constraints, loses regular contact with a parent and/or extended family members, and has to give away a pet because the new apartment complex does not allow pets. Adjustment problems may first take the form of noncompliance, aggression toward peers, and difficulty concentrating on schoolwork, which then leads to additional problems making friends with new classmates, building relationships with new teachers, and obtaining passing grades in school. More research is needed to determine under what conditions divorce is most harmful and what factors might mitigate the damage to children immediately following the divorce and later in life. One area that is quite clear in the literature is the impact of interparental conflict on children. In those cases in which a child witnesses conflict between the parents, even if nonviolent, the child will have a more difficult adjustment. Experiencing the stress and trauma of a divorce along with exposure to ongoing emotional and verbal abuse between parents or directed from one parent to another may be especially damaging to the child's ability to function on a day-to-day basis and to continue thriving developmentally, psychologically, socially, and academically.

Exposure to domestic violence may include children witnessing actual incidents of violence between parents or parent figures or seeing the aftermath of an incident such as a parent's arrest, injuries, or emotional distress. Children may feel responsible for "causing" the fight, especially when a domestic violence incident appears to begin with a dispute over disciplining the child, money for children's needs, or other child-related issues. Children may be further involved in the domestic violence when they try to intervene between their parents or when they call the police. Just as with divorce, the impact of exposure to domestic violence on children is also variable because of many factors. However, once again, children experiencing the stress of exposure to interparental violence may exhibit more externalizing and internalizing behavior problems than children who have not been exposed to such violence. Children exposed to domestic violence may show more aggressive behavior in their school and community. They may display depression, anxiety, fears, phobias, insomnia, tics, bed-wetting, and low self-esteem. In school, problems with impaired ability to concentrate and difficulty with schoolwork can occur, as well as lower overall achievement. Just as with divorce, the coexistence of multiple risk factors is more important in predicting problems than the presence of any single factor alone. Children exposed to domestic violence are likely to do more poorly when uprooted from their homes and separated from their family members and have to experience the sight of their mothers responding poorly under conditions of great stress. In addition, negative outcomes are more likely for children exposed to both domestic violence and child maltreatment. Unfortunately, children exposed to violence between the intimate partners in their lives are also at greater risk of being directly abused both physically and sexually. There is increasingly negative psychological impact on children from nonviolent interparental conflict, exposure to physical aggression between parents, and abuse directed at the children.

Needless to say, when children are exposed to both divorce and domestic violence, the immediate as well as long-term impact on their adjustment can be dramatic. With traumatic experiences such as parental divorce or exposure to domestic violence, certain factors can lessen the negative impact. In the area of domestic violence exposure, the support of a parent or other adult who models good problem solving, intact parenting and coping skills by the victimized parent, and a safe haven at school, church, or community center can all be helpful. In addition, whenever possible, minimizing other changes in the child's life is important. The research literature regarding divorce, as well as clinical experience with families who have experienced divorce, suggests that children do best when there is a low level of conflict between parents, when they maintain contact with both parents, when each parent copes well emotionally with the divorce and remains available to the children, and when there are a minimal number of divorce-related changes in their lives (economic hardship, moving, changing schools, etc.). Unfortunately, these areas of stability that can so assist children with continuing to thrive even through adversity are especially problematic when divorce is combined with domestic violence between the parents. The characteristics of the individual child will also have a significant mitigating effect on the impact of divorce, the exposure to domestic violence, and, in some cases, the experience of child abuse.

Clearly, it is important in these situations for the court to be aware of the programs and services that may be beneficial to the victim, the batterer, and also the children. These may include intervention programs which directly address the batterer's violence, support programs and counseling services for the victim, counseling services for the children, and financial assistance to maintain as much stability in the children's lives as possible. Victims may have diminished capacity to parent due to their victimization. They may need support and assistance in improving their parenting competence. Continued education of volunteers and other laypeople as well as professionals about domestic violence is important as well, so that children are surrounded with understanding and supportive individuals at school and in the community.

When Battered Victims Leave

There are many reasons that battered victims do not always leave after the first sign of emotional abuse or the first battering incident. One reason is that when victims have children, it is not uncommon for the batterer to have repeatedly threatened to take them from the victim through legal means in a divorce or to abscond with the children. Victims have often been told over and over by their batterers that they are unfit and terrible parents. Threats to seek custody and constant demeaning of victims' parenting skills often leave them fearful of leaving the violent home for fear of losing their children. The victim may also fear that even if she does not lose custody of her children, the children might not be safe in the care of the father. This may be due to ongoing concerns about the batterer's parenting skills and his direct abuse of the children. Once she is no longer present during their time with the father, she cannot act as a buffer between the father and the children. In addition, she may fear that his emotional state will deteriorate if she leaves. In fact, the batterer may have threatened the physical safety of the victim and their children if the victim tries to leave. Battered women are at greater risk for being killed when they resist or fight back. The ultimate method of fighting back is leaving the relationship, which in many cases puts battered women at an even greater risk of being seriously physically harmed or even killed by their batterers.

When battered women do successfully leave, this unsettles the entire twisted family balance. Battering men may fall apart when their victims leave, because their own insecurities and low self-esteem may render them unable to tolerate the rejection of a departing spouse. "Possession" of the children, even for brief periods, may be used by the father to torment and threaten their mother, the battering victim. The batterer may reenter an intimate relationship with another woman rapidly, creating additional stress in the co-parenting situation. Threats to seek custody of the children often continue after the separation as a way to maintain power over the other parent. If the batterer cannot reestablish control in any other way, he may in fact seek legal custody as a means to regain control. Even without seeking actual custody, ongoing conflict in the form of a variety of tactics might be manifested through the co-parenting relationship that the court requires of both the batterer and the victim. This may include such actions as constantly threatening court filings, refusing to provide basic information about the children's care, refusing to disclose the children's location during visitation, removing the children from school or day care randomly and without notice, threatening not to return the children after visitation, regularly returning the children late from visitation, refusing to allow the mother to speak to the children during the visitation, and many other tactics. The pattern of control does not usually end after the separation or even after the legal divorce.

Child Custody Determinations and Shared Parenting Expectations

Children's well-being is a concern of society at large. Because the quality of parenting received throughout childhood significantly affects such well-being, the public has an interest in promoting positive parenting practices. In the divorce process, parents sometimes have difficulty maintaining the same quality of parenting, meeting the physical and financial needs of their children, and establishing a co-parenting relationship in the midst of the emotional tension that often characterizes the dissolving marital relationship. In addition, to continue effectively meeting children's needs from two households, the roles each parent is expected to take must shift somewhat. On a practical level, the legal responsibilities for raising a child as well as the parental rights that go along with those responsibilities must be divided or clarified in some manner so that parents who share in those rights and responsibilities know what they need to do. Furthermore, this ensures that the children's needs are met without interruption and that their right to access to their parents is similarly addressed.

Historically, children were considered the property of their fathers, who had absolute power over them as well as the legal obligation to care for them. Mothers essentially had no legal rights. Thus there was a presumption of paternal custody for a very long time, but that began to slowly shift in the nineteenth and twentieth centuries due to a variety of historical trends. These included changes in British law to suggest that children under the age of seven years should be in the primary custody of their mothers and that older children should have visitation rights with their mothers. The "tender years doctrine," as it is commonly known, presumed that mothers were better able to nurture and care for children, especially young ones. In America, some states began to adopt their own statutes based on this English common law. The increasing concern for children's rights and welfare evident in many changes in other areas of the law influenced such trends as well. Also, the Industrial Revolution led fathers and mothers into defined roles that would remain static for decades: the father as financial provider and the mother as child caretaker. Women's increasing legal status in the United States in the early twentieth century also contributed. Essentially the maternal preference for child custody became as firmly entrenched as the paternal preference had been previously. Needless to say, exceptions have and always will occur to such trends; nonetheless, a well-established expectation that children, especially young ones, would be in the primary care of their mothers after a divorce continued for decades.

In the mid- to late twentieth century, as divorce rates began to rise and more mothers entered the workforce, the concept of a primary maternal caretaker began to weaken. More gender-neutral laws began to replace those gender-specific laws that had once been based on paternal property and later on maternal nurturance. The Uniform Marriage and Divorce Act in the early 1970s suggested a "best interest of the child" standard instead of a "tender years doctrine" as the basis for child custody decisions. Essentially it was proposed that the court give direction for the custody, care, and education of children as deemed necessary in their best interest. The court was to consider all relevant factors in making such determinations. The "best interest of the child" standard was adopted by states in various individualized forms. Custody decisions became based, theoretically, on consideration of the needs of the child rather than the gender of the parent. This standard asks courts to establish the custody and visitation arrangement that will best provide for the health, education, and welfare of minor children whose parents are divorcing. States have continued to operate generally under this principle, although vast differences occur in how the best interest of the child is to be determined and implemented. Even the terminology used to describe the custodial arrangements for children differ from state to state. Essentially, nearly all states distinguish on some level between legal custody and physical custody. *Legal custody* refers to the decision-making right and power regarding children, while *physical custody* refers to the physical care and supervision of the children or their living arrangements on a day-to-day basis. Legal custody is often expected to be shared by parents, although the sole right to make all decisions or decisions in a specific area regarding a child may be granted to one parent. Physical custody may range from one parent having the children the majority of the time to equal contact with both parents.

Examples of variations of custody terminology from state to state include rotating custody, shared parent responsibility, primary residential responsibility, sole legal custody, sole physical custody, joint legal custody, joint physical custody, divided custody, and split custody. The term "joint custody" is commonly used in the state statutes and in the literature discussing topics related to child custody. *Joint physical custody* means that each parent is awarded significant periods of time in which the child resides with each or is under her or his care and supervision. The time might not be exactly equal, but the idea is to ensure the child frequent and continuing contact with both parents. Joint legal custody means that the parents are to share in the decision-making rights, responsibilities, and authority relating to the health, education, and general welfare of the child.

In summary, in recent decades the movement in child custody has been away from a mother-dominated custodial arrangement to greater involvement of both parents in the form of joint custody (or a similar concept). This important topic of how to "divide" the rights and responsibilities of parents who are not residing together, while maintaining the focus on the child, has spawned much research, scholarly writing, professional opinion statements, and parent testimonials throughout the scholarly and popular media. Most would agree that the ongoing involvement of both parents in all aspects of children's lives is important for their growth and development. Exactly how to accomplish that goal while also providing the child with a sense of stability is the subject of much debate. Regardless of how that is done, joint-custody type of arrangements tend to work best when parents get along quite well, share information easily, live in close proximity, and cooperate at a high level. This presents substantial problems when there is violence by one or both parents.

Parents who cannot agree on custody and access are then subject to the legal criteria for determining custody outcomes adopted by their state. Many states have adopted a list of criteria to be considered by the court in determining the child's best interests in a child custody dispute. Common criteria include the relationship of the child with each parent, the mental and physical health of the parent, the moral fitness of the parent, the desire to maintain the stability of the current arrangement, and the capacity of the parent to provide for the material needs of the child. The preference of the child is considered by some states. Additional criteria commonly used by state courts are based in the willingness of the custodial parent to allow contact with the other parent, to promote a relationship with the other parent, and to cooperate in decision making. For instance, the Florida statutes include the following criteria: (1) the parent who

is more likely to allow the child frequent and continuing contact with the nonresidential parent, (2) the willingness and ability of each parent to facilitate and encourage a close and continuing parent–child relationship between the child and the other parent. If a battered spouse is fearful of the batterer and does not feel she has the capacity to negotiate and safely compromise with him, then she is not likely to look favorable to the court in some of these areas.

Some states have recognized that policies promoting equal access and decision making may not in fact promote the children's best interest when it exposes them to ongoing parental conflict and violence. Many states require that courts consider the history of domestic violence when making decisions regarding child custody, visitation, and decision-making powers. Even when domestic violence is to be considered in determinations of child custody and visitation, the decisions are left very much to an individual judge's discretion. Therefore, some states have gone further and require the judge to issue written findings in the decisions about his or her consideration of the domestic violence issue. Some states have gone still further and create a presumption against the batterer having custody of the children that must be overcome if he seeks custody. In other words, once the court determines the existence of domestic violence, the batterer must show why it is still in the children's best interest to be with him.

A generally positive trend in divorce processes in all states is toward nonlitigious resolution of matters regarding child custody, financial support, and division of property and assets. In contrast to legal decisions imposed by judges, parents have more satisfaction with and more respect for decisions in which they have input. The opportunity to be heard and to influence the outcome of their parenting agreements often leads to greater satisfaction with the divorce process and greater likelihood of complying with those decisions. Hence, a variety of alternative dispute resolution methods have been attempted, including mediation. The mediation process is one in which a trained neutral third party helps promote decision making between the parents. This may be done with or without the presence of an attorney. The mediator assists parents in reaching agreements regarding the division of time with their children, decision making, and other responsibilities of caring for their children that become incorporated as the parenting agreement in the final divorce decree. Mediation is often less expensive, more expeditious, and more sensitive to the emotional aspects of a divorce than is litigation in a courtroom. Therefore, mediation is commonly suggested and in some jurisdictions required in family law cases before a judge will hear a case. Unfortunately, when used with people of unequal bargaining power, the result may be agreements which reflect that inequality.

Alternative dispute resolution methods are an important advancement, though in domestic violence cases they may not be better solutions, especially if the mediator or other professional involved is uneducated or unprepared to deal with such cases. It is helpful to note that specific training in domestic violence is required for mediators and mental health professionals in some states. However, even with educated professionals, the use of mediation when there is a history of domestic violence is controversial. Some would argue that the power dynamics present in the history of the couple's relationship can never be overcome and that the victim will not only remain at an unfair disadvantage in the negotiations but her and/or the children's safety might be compromised. There is concern that any agreement reached might be the result of intimidation, coercion, or fear of later retaliation. Some states exempt cases involving domestic violence from mandatory mediation. It should be noted, however, that this does not always provide the assistance that a victim might need. Due to lack of financial resources, the victim may be left without legal representation and thus trying to negotiate an agreement with the batterer on her own or in front of a judge who may not have knowledge of the couple's history of domestic violence or who may not fully understand the implications of that history.

At a minimum it is expected that mediators screen for the presence of domestic violence and make a determination of whether it is appropriate to proceed. The more chronic and severe the violence, the more caution is warranted. If mediation proceeds, all available safeguards for the victim should be provided. These might include separate waiting rooms, separate arrival and leaving times, and even separate sessions for the batterer and victim. The presence of supportive third parties or court deputies in a courthouse mediation program might be necessary.

Even when children are safeguarded by statutory reference to consideration of domestic violence in child custody decisions, there are still issues with visitation between the children and the batterer that must be considered. Some cases will result in no perpetrator/child contact, some in only supervised contact, and some in a regular visitation schedule. Exposure of the child to the violence as well as to the power and control dynamics in the

parental relationship must end. Whether a child's loss of contact with the batterer father as a result of divorce or an injunction is positive or negative for the child depends on a variety of factors. These include whether the father is abusive to the child in ways other than exposing the child to domestic violence, the parent's other parenting skills, the quality of the relationship between the father and the child, and the batterer's ability to take responsibility for his actions. First and foremost it must be determined whether the child is safe visiting with the father. If not, denial of visitation rights to perpetrators of violence or supervised visitation should be implemented.

Unfortunately supervised visitation can be logistically difficult and often expensive when conducted by supervision programs or facilities. However, when not provided by those programs, supervised visitation is usually provided by family or friends who have not been trained to handle visitation situations that could be harmful to the child. When unsupervised visitation is either determined to be safe for the children or is ordered in spite of allegations of domestic violence, additional safety concerns are raised regarding the victim, who will have contact with the batterer when the children are exchanged between the two homes. Special consideration needs to be given to how those exchanges occur in order to minimize the opportunity for conflict. This might include exchanges at day care or school, exchanges in a public or official place such as a store or police station, or use of a monitored exchange program, which again will involve a cost. When a regular visitation schedule is court ordered in such cases, the order should be very specific with regard to the contact schedule so as to minimize the opportunity for disputes.

Even after the divorce case has been resolved legally, ongoing disputes may still arise, especially when shared parenting is the outcome. An individual who was once able to use coercion, intimidation, or violence to resolve disputes or to get his way will have great difficulty reaching agreements and compromises. In these scenarios, services such as co-parenting counseling, cooperative parenting programs, and parenting coordination are sometimes considered. Once again, such services may place the victim and children at risk if the batterer's history of violence and other abuse are not addressed with the help of appropriate services. In those situations in which the court believes that a regular visitation schedule and shared parenting is appropriate in spite of the allegations of domestic violence, it may at least be necessary to assign specific areas of decision-making responsibility to the victim-parent to minimize the areas subject to issues of power and control. In addition, ongoing judicial monitoring might be the only alternative in those situations for addressing ongoing disputes rather than any mental health or alternative dispute resolution approaches.

Domestic violence may present in different patterns, a full discussion of which is beyond the scope of this article. However, from a judicial standpoint, when weighing issues of child custody and visitation in the context of some type of domestic violence allegation, it is important to ascertain as well as possible what type of abusive relationship occurred between the parents, as that may guide case management decisions. Each pattern of violence can affect children's development and the nature of their relationships with their mothers and their fathers in different ways. Of course, if a professional has all of the available information about both parents, it may not be difficult at all to distinguish the pattern or type of abuse; however, this occurs only rarely. The suggestions above may be useful for any intimate relationship in which there has been physical violence and/or conflict resolution that centered primarily or solely around power and control, though this article is concerned primarily with those cases in which there has been ongoing or episodic male-initiated battering against wives and mothers which began early in the relationship and continued intermittently or continuously throughout the duration of the marriage. These men's physical attacks can be quite severe and they may become extremely dangerous when their wives separate from the marriage. In the midst of separation or divorce, they tend to deny or minimize their abuse and place blame for their violence on their wives, which can have serious consequences regarding the custody and safety of their children.

TERESA F. PARNELL

See also **Attachment Theory and Domestic Violence; Batterer Intervention Programs; Batterer Typology; Child Neglect; Child Sexual Abuse; Children Witnessing Parental Violence; Domestic Violence Courts; Parental Abduction; Stages of Leaving Abusive Relationships**

References and Further Reading

Berhrman, Richard, ed. "The Future of Children." *Children and Divorce* 4, no. 1 (1994). The David and Lucile Packard Foundation.

———. "The Future of Children." *Domestic Violence and Children* 9, no. 3 (1999). The David and Lucile Packard Foundation.

Dutton, M. A. *Empowering and Healing the Battered Woman: A Model for Assessment and Intervention.* New York: Springer Publishing Company, 1992.

Family Violence Prevention Fund website. http://www.endabuse.org (accessed August 17, 2006).

Gelles, R., and D. Loseke. *Current Controversies on Family Violence.* Newbury Park, CA: Sage Publication, 1993.

Institute for Family Violence Studies website. http://familyvio.ssw.fsu.edu (accessed August 17, 2006).

Institute on Violence, Abuse, and Trauma website. http://www.fvsai.org (accessed August 17, 2006).

Jaffe, P., D. Wolfe, and S. K. Wilson. *Children of Battered Women.* Newbury Park, CA: Sage Publications, 1990.

Johnston, J., and L. Campbell. *Parent–Child Relationships in Domestic Violence Families Disputing Custody.* Newbury Park, CA: Sage Publications, 1993.

Kaser-Boyd, N., and F. Mosten. *The Violent Family: Psychological Dynamics and Their Effect on the Lawyer–Client Relationship.* Thousand Oaks, CA: Sage Publications, 1993.

Magana, H., and N. Taylor. *Child Custody Mediation and Spouse Abuse: A Destructive Study of a Protocol.* Newbury Park, CA: Sage Publications, 1993.

Maxwell, J. *Mandatory Mediations of Custody in the Face of Domestic Violence: Suggestions for Courts and Mediators.* Thousand Oaks, CA: Sage Publications, 1999.

Medline Plus website. http://www.nlm.nih.gov/medlineplus/divorce.html (accessed August 17, 2006).

O'Keefe, M. *Predictors of Child Abuse in Maritally Violent Families.* Thousand Oaks, CA: Sage Publications, 1995.

Thoennes, N., P. Salem, and J. Pearson. *Mediation and Domestic Violence: Current Policies and Practices.* Thousand Oaks, CA: Sage Publications, 1995.

DOMESTIC HOMICIDE IN URBAN CENTERS: NEW YORK CITY

Domestic homicide in New York City (NYC) often increases and decreases with the overall rate of homicide and murder of the general population of the city; however, there are differences in the rate and types of domestic homicide in large urban areas such as NYC. Homicide in general in NYC, as in the rest of the United States, began to rise steadily beginning in the early 1960s, reached a peak in the early 1980s, then rose again to another peak in the early 1990s. Then, beginning in the early 1990s, homicide and murder in NYC, as in most other urban centers in the United States, began to decline steadily. According to the Federal Bureau of Investigation's annual Uniform Crime Report (UCR), the rate of homicide decreased 64 percent from 1990 to 2002. Criminology experts are continually debating the reasons for this significant crime decrease.

Measuring the scope of domestic homicide and proportion and variations with the overall rate of murder is a complex task because of difficulties encountered in categorizing and defining "domestic homicide." Also, measuring domestic homicide is a relatively new phenomenon because of the relatively recent recognition and acknowledgment of domestic violence as a social problem. This recognition and acknowledgment has placed greater accountability on the police and law enforcement to properly investigate and record domestic violence incidents and prevent future occurrences. Additionally, more resources have become available to domestic violence victims from social services in recent decades, thereby heightening the awareness and subsequently the reporting of domestic violence. These factors make studying and determining long-term trends of domestic violence an onerous task.

Although police and law enforcement now have a greater degree of accountability, different police and law enforcement agencies have different definitions of what constitutes "domestic" homicide. Defining domestic homicide in a particular jurisdiction depends on legally defined relations as well as circumstantial, situational, and spatial factors surrounding the criminal incident. *Legally defined relations* refer to relationships between persons that constitute a "domestic" environment according to the legal code. For example, are domestic violence incidents limited to males and females who are legally married? This traditional relationship is the paradigm of domestic violence (i.e., the abusive male spouse repeatedly assaulting his lawfully wed wife inside their shared dwelling) and ultimately the type of domestic homicide that most persons envision. The inverse of this traditional stereotype is the female spouse ultimately defending herself and murdering her abusive husband out of self-defense or long-suffering post-traumatic stress disorder as a result of the abuse. However, legal and relational characteristics and domestic homicide are much more complex.

Domestic relationships also include persons who are living together, regardless of gender, in the same household. A domestic relational characteristic may also include persons who are legally married but estranged from each other, or couples never legally married but estranged. This type of living arrangement engenders a significant amount of domestic homicide because the relationship is in decline and often one party is emotionally overwhelmed and prompted by despair to commit homicide. Domestic violence also includes parents assaulting their children and vice versa and siblings assaulting each other or other family members. Victims of domestic homicide tend to be younger than average homicide victims. According to murder research conducted by Mike Maltz (1998), the most dangerous period in a female's life is during the first five years of her life, because the likelihood that she will be murdered by a family member or caregiver is the highest during those years. Also included is the extended family, such as cousins and in-laws. Close friends or persons who are not related yet live in the same household are another relational factor related to domestic homicide.

Circumstantial and situational characteristics also beget problems in defining and analyzing the scope of domestic violence and homicide. For example, the reason that precipitated a family or domestic homicide may also be a great unknown to the police and law enforcement investigators. In some cases of domestic violence, there is a pre-planned motive, and the victim-offender relationship is easily known. However, most domestic homicides involve some form of victim precipitation such as an argument or violence leading up to the homicide. For example, although the homicide should not be mitigated, domestic homicide is often the result of a vicious argument that has increased to the next level of violence on the continuum often aggravated by the victim, offender, or both under the influence of alcohol or drugs. Often in some jurisdictions, if a homicide has been determined to have been justified by self-defense, it is not counted as a murder, thereby muddling the scope of the problem.

Spatial circumstances regarding the location of the homicide are also an issue when attempting to measure and analyze the crime. Is the physical location of the homicide (home or dwelling) the lone factor? Often persons currently or formerly involved in a relationship may get into an encounter in a public area or at a third-party location. Therefore, the spatial location of the incident becomes an issue when measuring domestic violence homicide.

The UCR's Supplementary Homicide Report (SHR) is the standard in recording homicides for statistical and analytical purposes. The SHR list of victim-offender relationship categories highlights the difficulties of gauging the extent of domestic homicide. There are twenty-one categories of relationships that can be defined as domestic, not including a category entitled "Acquaintance." According to the SHR, the police knew the relationship between the victim and offender in two-thirds of the cases in all homicides occurring from 1976 through 2002. Nationally, domestic homicide comprised 43.8 percent of homicides in which the relationship was known. The national rate is significantly higher than the rate in NYC (9 percent) over the same time period.

This could be due to the high percentage of immigrants in NYC. The percentage of immigrants as part of the total population of NYC is 36 percent, compared with the national average of 11 percent. The problems of measuring domestic violence are particularly acute in urban centers such as NYC because of the increased percentage of immigrants. Immigrants may not trust the authorities, and there may also be cultural and language barriers preventing them from seeking help. Female victims in immigrant communities may be reluctant to report violence or seek intervention from the police or social services; ultimately their abuse may lead to a homicide.

The differences may also reflect the diversity of living arrangements and rate of violent crime in urban centers such as NYC. For example, the average of victims who were related to the offender as a "husband" or "wife" was over 8 percent nationally but less than 2 percent in NYC. Additionally, the likelihood of homicide during the commission of a robbery or burglary is increased in urban areas, lessening the percentage rate of domestic homicides.

Domestic homicide in urban centers such as NYC does present a different crime problem than domestic homicide in suburban and rural areas. The differences are based on the demographics of the population, the living arrangements, and the provincialism of police and law enforcement authorities who are mandated to investigate initial incidents and make proper referrals to other authorities charged with preventing future occurrences of domestic violence. Recognition of domestic violence in general has heightened the awareness of the problem, although cultural and definitional barriers persist, making domestic homicide in urban areas a perennial social problem.

JOSEPH E. PASCARELLA

See also **African American Community, Domestic Violence in; Asian Americans and Domestic Violence: Cultural Dimensions; Battered Women Who Kill: An Examination; Cohabiting Violence; Fatality Reviews in Adult Domestic Homicide and Suicide; Intimate Partner Homicide; Intimate Partner Violence in Queer, Transgender, and Bisexual Communities; Jewish Community, Domestic Violence within the; Minorities and Families in America, Introduction to; Mothers Who Kill; Police Response to Domestic Violence Incidents**

References and Further Reading

Fox, James A. "Uniform Crime Reports: Homicide Reports, 1976–2002, Study no. 4179." http://www.icpsr. umich.edu/cgi-bin/bob/newark?study=4179.

Maltz, Michael D. "Visualizing Homicide: A Research Note." *Journal of Quantitative Criminology* 15, no. 4 (1998): 397–410.

New York City Department of City Planning. "Immigrant New York in the New Millennium." *The Newest New Yorkers, 2000*. City of New York, 2002. http://www.nyc. gov/html/dcp/html/census/nny.shtml (accessed August 17, 2006).

DOMESTIC VIOLENCE BY LAW ENFORCEMENT OFFICERS

Introduction

Society has now come to the knowledge that domestic violence is a serious preventable crime. Researchers have concluded that domestic violence crosses all socioeconomic classifications. A rich man may beat his wife in the same way that a poor man does. Society also has come to understand that a person in any profession, whether a doctor, lawyer, judge, or even a police officer, may commit an act of domestic violence. By the same token, an individual of any background or profession may also be the victim of domestic violence. However, the issue of domestic violence by law enforcement officers has become a controversial topic among researchers, professionals, and the media, though several researchers have examined the dynamics of domestic violence committed by law enforcement officers.

Definition of Domestic Violence

No one single definition of domestic violence exists. Different authorities include different forms of violence within their definitions. For the purpose of this entry, "domestic violence" is a broad term that includes threats or violent acts against an existing or former intimate partner. The term "law enforcement officer," for the purpose of this article, refers to a police officer. This is because victims of domestic violence by police officers are in a very different situation than that of other victims of domestic violence. The term "intimate partner," for the purpose of this article, is defined as someone, of the same or opposite sex, with whom the officer has or had a relationship with, including dating, marriage, cohabitation, or parenting/raising a child. This definition is very similar to that used by the International Association of Chiefs of Police (IACP) in their policy on domestic violence by law enforcement (International Association of Chiefs of Police 2003). A serious flaw with the IACP's policy was its failure to include elder abuse and all forms of child abuse among the forms of domestic violence within its definition. Domestic violence by law enforcement officers includes, but is not limited to, physical, sexual, emotional, and financial abuse.

Feminine pronouns will be generally used to indicate the victim or abused party throughout this article. This does not mean that males are not victims of domestic violence. In fact, some studies indicate that male victims of domestic violence, particularly spousal abuse, are far more common than imagined. However, female victims of domestic violence generally suffer from more severe and long-lasting abuse than male victims.

Extent

The extent of domestic violence by law enforcement officers is still unknown, though researchers have conducted studies to explore its extent. Because police officers hold a special place in society, it is assumed that they will always obey all laws and regulations. Therefore, some people may expect the prevalence rate of domestic violence by law enforcement officers to be lower than that of the general population. However, according to the IACP, domestic violence among law enforcement officers occurs as frequently as among the general population.

Researchers conducted a study on the extent and nature of domestic violence by officers in a large western police department. This study involved 353 sworn police officers. Researchers found that 4.8 percent of the officers admitted that they engaged in domestic violence and that 7.4 percent reported having been a victim of domestic violence (Klein and Klein 2000).

Ryan (n.d.) examined the extent of domestic violence in the police family. This study used a survey of 210 police officers and self-reported data obtained from tests that were taken by applicants for law enforcement positions with several law enforcement agencies. The survey found that 54 percent of the officers knew an officer who engaged in domestic violence. The self-reported data showed that 10 percent of respondents (148 candidates) admitted that they had engaged in acts of violence toward a spouse or intimate partner, including slapping and punching. Male respondents were 67.6 percent of the sample, and 32.4 percent were female. Subsequent investigation of these candidates found that only one of the 148 candidates who engaged in violent acts became a police officer.

One study by Neidig and his colleagues (1992) examined the prevalence rate of domestic violence among sworn law enforcement officers (Neidig 1992). This study involved a series of surveys of 385 male officers, 40 female officers, and 115 female spouses of officers who were attending a national law enforcement conference. Researchers found that approximately 40 percent of all the officers reported at least one incident of domestic violence within the last year.

In the second study, Neidig (1992) surveyed 891 male officers, 32 female officers, and 119 spouses attending another conference. This group of officers was of a higher rank than those surveyed at the first conference. The result indicated a lower percentage of domestic violence by the higher-ranking of officers. However, 24 percent of the male officers and 22 percent of the female officers still reported at least one incident of domestic violence in their personal relationships within the preceding year.

No agreement on the prevalence rate of domestic violence by law enforcement officers exists among authorities. This may be because different authorities have different definitions of domestic violence or differences in their methodologies.

Effects on Victims

Danger. Victims of abuse by law enforcement officers face special dangers that civilian victims do not. These dangers include the officers' familiarity and experience in using weapons, their police training regarding subduing suspects, their ability to access information that is not normally available to citizens, their knowledge of the criminal justice system, and their fear of losing their job as a result of any conviction.

Unique Access to Information. Police officers have special training regarding accessing information. This includes the locations of shelters and other community support groups. By training and experience, they are able to conduct investigations that result in gaining information about such services. Thus they will be able to identify the location of the victim, family, and friends as well as any other persons who might be inclined to help the victim.

Training. Law enforcement officers receive special training regarding surveillance, investigation, and use of force. This training, especially in the area of use of force, may make them especially dangerous, since they will know how to use weapons such as their duty-issued handguns, batons, and handcuffs, as well as their own hands.

Police Culture and Department Response. In the event the victim files a complaint, the responding officers may not want to do anything, since they may know and have worked with the batterer. They may be less sympathetic to the victim and more supportive of their fellow officer. Police culture may foster a belief that things that happen in the family stay within the family and are not to be reported officially. Nine hundred and elven calls may be handled differently when the victim identifies the offender as a police officer. Emergency protection orders in many jurisdictions are issued by police officers, who may be reluctant to issue such an order against his/her own.

Loss of Job. In many departments, a conviction of a misdemeanor would be sufficient for the department to terminate the officer's employment. Even assuming the conviction of a misdemeanor by itself would not be sufficient to cause an officer to lose his or her job, there are other consequences that affect an officer's employment if convicted in a domestic violence case. The Lautenberg Amendment prohibits any individual who is convicted of committing domestic violence from owning a firearm (18 U.S.C. 992 (d)(9) 1997). Since owning and possessing a firearm is a requirement of almost all law enforcement positions, the officer will be unable to carry out the required duties. The victim may be reluctant to report the abuse because of fear that the officer may lose his job. The offender may also react more violently toward the victim out of that same fear.

Linkage between Police Officers and Other Professionals. Dispatchers, prosecutors, and even judges may be reluctant to pursue proceedings against an officer they know and have worked with for a number of years. The prosecutor's decision to proceed or file charges of battery against an officer may be influenced by the police reports, collection of any evidence, and other factors.

Knowledge of Criminal Justice System. Police officers know how the criminal justice system works. They can use this knowledge against the victim. For instance, police officers would know when courts are busy and can ask for continuances. They also know which judges are hard and which ones are lenient when it comes to domestic violence cases.

Assumption of Credibility of Police Officers. By the very nature of their training and job, police officers carry distinct credibility with citizens, fellow officers, and other professionals in the criminal justice system. Officers have been trained in how to testify in court hearings and therefore are very credible witnesses. When it comes to deciding whom to believe—a police officer accused of domestic violence or the alleged victim making the accusation—many will want to believe the police officer.

Police Officer as the Victim. When the victim is a police officer, the process becomes more complex. A female officer's victimization may be viewed by other officers as a sign that she is weak or not competent. Other officers may also be concerned that she is a whistleblower. Her safety on the job may also be jeopardized, because fellow officers who are friends of the abuser may not respond as quickly to her request for help or backup.

Long Arm of the Law. Hiding from law enforcement is difficult. Because the officer is aware of where shelters or other support groups are located and is trained in investigation, he may be able to follow the victim's trail as she moves from location to location. Therefore, fleeing or hiding from an abuser who is also a police officer is difficult if not impossible.

Suicide and Homicide as Threats. Average citizens are not trained in the use of firearms and may not lose their jobs even if they are convicted of domestic violence. Because the officer is trained in the use of weapons and may fear loss of his job, there is a heightened risk that he may take the life of the victim, kill himself, or kill both the victim and himself.

Standards and Remedies. The traditional response to battering by the criminal justice system may not be available to the officer. For instance, some jurisdictions or judges may be reluctant to place the officer in a batterers' program, where he may be in a group that includes persons he has previously arrested for domestic violence.

Causes of Domestic Violence by Law Enforcement Officers

The issue of why law enforcement officers engage in domestic violence is controversial among scholars and professionals. Little, if any, consensus exists among researchers regarding the cause of domestic violence by law enforcement officers. Several researchers have examined the factors that have an impact on police officers in an attempt to find specific influences that may contribute to domestic violence within police families. Three factors that may be part of the pressures faced by police officers and that may cause them to engage in acts of domestic violence are stress, personality and behavior, and police culture.

Stress

Many scholars believe that police stress has no limits or boundaries. The primary stressors for police officers consist of the continuous exposure to traumatic events and tragedies experienced by victims of crime, the attitude of perpetrators, and the risk of physical danger that exists all the time in police work. Any stress experienced by police officers during duty hours may result in increased stress within the family system as well (Wallace 2005).

The nature of police work is highly stressful. Police officers may confront traumatizing events at any time on duty. Mullins and McMains (2000) examined the correlation between post-traumatic stress disorder (PTSD) resulting from witnessing or experiencing traumatic events and domestic violence committed by law enforcement officers. Individuals with PTSD suffer from various types of psychological and behavioral symptoms, which may include nightmares, feelings of self-doubt, and extreme anxiety or fear. Mullins and McMains believe that there exists a positive correlation between PTSD and domestic violence by police officers. They acknowledge that further study must be conducted to understand this relationship.

Personality and Behavior

Some authorities have examined the possibility that certain personalities or behavioral characteristics of police officers contribute to domestic violence within police families (Wallace 2005). These researchers found that police officers place a high value on cognitive functioning, responsibility, and self-confidence. They also found that these officers have guarded, moralistic, rigid, and controlling personalities. Other researchers examined individual cases and results of psychological screening tests to explore profiles of abusive police officers compared with those of nonabusive officers (Inwald, Traynor, and Favuzza 2000). The researchers state that officers who engage in domestic violence within the family may have feelings of social failure or a sense of loss of control (often influenced by drug and/or alcohol abuse). They concluded that alcohol/substance abuse, low self-esteem, and antisocial behaviors contribute to domestic violence committed by law enforcement officers (Inwald, Traynor, and Favuzza 2000).

Police Culture

It is important to discuss the basics of police culture in order to understand the special situation faced by victims of abuse by officers. Understanding police culture would help professionals to be sensitive to the needs of victims of domestic violence by law enforcement officers and respond appropriately to these needs.

One of the most important basics of police culture is a sense of power (Wetendorf and Davis 2003). Law enforcement officers are tasked with the responsibility of enforcing laws in society. Therefore, they are considered to be the "good guys," and those who break the laws or challenge them are regarded as the "bad guys." In order to keep these "bad guys" under control, law enforcement officers are trained to consider themselves to be smarter and tougher than normal citizens. Officers are armed with weapons, wear uniforms, and use special equipment. They have the power to take control over an individual by using their authority.

Another basic concept of police culture is loyalty and the code of silence. Law enforcement officers face potential life-or-death situations on a daily basis. Facing such situations together fosters bonds of solidarity among police officers; they are united by bonds of loyalty and will defend each other. The complexity and dynamics of police activities sometimes require police officers to use their discretion when responding to certain situations. Additionally, the solidarity of the group creates the code of silence among officers. This code of silence, which still exists in some departments, is an unofficial acknowledgment that no officer blames or implicates another officer who is accused of wrongdoing.

Law enforcement officers rely on their individual authority and power as well as the solidarity of the group and the code of silence. Wetendorf and Davis (2003) state that this makes it difficult for the criminal justice system to hold some officers accountable. As a result, some officers come to consider themselves as having an ultimate power over others (Wetendorf and Davis 2003).

Sgambelluri (2000) examined the literature of several aspects of police culture, including isolation, need for control, entitlement, loyalty, rugged individualism, and authoritarian spillover. He concluded that the police culture itself encourages isolation, a sense of entitlement, authoritarianism, and a need for control, characteristics which are often present in a domestic abuser. However, Sgambelluri also noted that although police work and culture have a clear impact on officers' attitudes and behaviors, they do not cause domestic violence by police officers (Sgambelluri 2000).

The Lautenberg Amendment

One of the most influential laws that have affected the issue of domestic violence by law enforcement is the provision of the Omnibus Consolidated Appropriations Act of 1997, known as the Lautenberg Amendment to Title 18, United States Code 922 (d)(9). This law explicitly prohibits any individual who is convicted of domestic violence from owning a firearm. It specifically prohibits possession of a firearm by a police officer with a misdemeanor conviction of domestic violence. Though this law does not exempt the police officer, other federal gun control laws do exempt even those officers who are convicted of any kind of felony crime (Nathan 2000). The Lautenberg Amendment applies to all local, state, and federal law enforcement officers and to all misdemeanor convictions, including those that occurred before its enactment on September 30, 1996.

Law Enforcement Response to Domestic Violence by Law Enforcement

Response to domestic violence by law enforcement officers varies from department to department. Some police departments have established a clear "zero tolerance" policy on domestic violence by officers, while others have unclear policies or have not established any policy. One study found that in most law enforcement agencies, allegations of domestic violence by law enforcement officers were frequently handled informally (Lott 1995). This study also found that most agencies did not make an official complaint of these allegations or maintain records of the incidents.

Between 1990 and 1997, the Los Angeles Police Department handled 227 alleged cases of domestic violence by police officers. Only 91 of these allegations were classified as sustained or proven cases. Of these 91 cases, only 4 resulted in conviction of criminal charges. Of the four convictions, only one officer was suspended from duty, for a mere fifteen days, and another had his conviction expunged (*Domestic Violence in the Los Angeles Police Department* 1997).

The IACP has addressed the issue of domestic violence within the police community. This international group of law enforcement officers is concerned about professionalism within the law enforcement community. The organization holds an annual meeting and publishes research that focuses on various law enforcement issues. In 1998, the IACP released a draft policy on domestic violence by law enforcement in an attempt to assist police agencies in developing effective policies for dealing with it. The draft policy was revised and released in July 2003 and is based on the principles of (1) prevention and training, (2) early warning, (3) intervention, (4) responsibility, (5) incident response protocols, (6) victim safety and protection, and (7) post-incident administrative and criminal decisions.

Prevention and Training

Comprehensive prevention and education will assist departments to accomplish zero tolerance against the issue of police officer domestic violence. One of the most important means of prevention is establishing a corroborative relationship with other professionals, including victim advocates, shelter staff, hotline crisis workers, social workers, and others who work with victims of domestic violence. Departments should actively collaborate with these professionals in order to establish an implementation strategy and effective training for officers. It is important for comprehensive training to cover basic topics such as the dynamics of domestic violence and departmental response protocol. Additionally, the efforts of the prevention and training program should be reinforced regularly.

Early Warning

It is critical for departments to minimize the risk of police officer domestic violence when they screen candidates during the hiring process. In order to identify individuals who may engage in domestic violence, the department should ask all candidates about past arrests, investigations, or convictions for any crimes related to domestic violence during the screening process. During the background investigation of officer candidates, the department should look for any history of violence. Additionally, the department should conduct a psychological examination even if a candidate's background investigation does not find a history of violent acts. This examination will indicate whether a candidate has abusive tendencies.

Intervention

The department should ensure that all officers have a clear understanding of the department policy on domestic violence. It should ensure that officers' family members are aware of the policy by creating opportunities such as family orientations. Providing information to officers' families will encourage them to identify potentially problematic behaviors or report incidents of domestic violence. It should be noted that it may be difficult to reach family members when an officer is abusive and controlling. Therefore, information regarding the issues of domestic violence by officers should also be available to family members through other means such as an outreach campaign.

Responsibility

Departments, supervisors, and officers must understand their responsibilities to handle the issue of domestic violence by officers. When partners or family members of police officers notice anything that may indicate possible violent behavior, they may contact fellow officers or supervisors about their concern. The department should ensure that all employees of the department are able to properly respond to such informal contacts. They should be knowledgeable and able to recommend available resources such as referral or counseling services for officers or their family members. It is ideal for the department to have a policy or formal system to respond to partners' or family members' concerns. Confidentiality of information or of any report should be required to protect the officer's partner or family member from potential violence. Additionally, the department should be wary of officers who defend fellow officers who are accused of domestic violence.

Supervisors should be sensitive to subordinate officers' potentially problematic behaviors, which may include excessive power and control issues, aggressiveness, or deteriorating work performance. Such behaviors can be indicators of domestic violence. If a supervisor observes these indicators, it is important for him or her to take proper actions, such as documenting the officer's problem, informing the chief of the problem, or ordering the officer to seek counseling or a batterer program.

All officers should clearly understand their department's policy on domestic violence by law enforcement officers and be aware of their responsibilities. They should understand what the repercussions may be if they do not report information about another officer's engaging in domestic violence or if they attempt to interfere with domestic violence cases brought against fellow officers.

Incident Response Protocols

A department should establish a clear incident response protocol for responding to domestic violence by law enforcement officers. 911 dispatchers should have instructions on how to respond to domestic violence cases involving a police officer. This will ensure that information will be sent to the proper supervisors. It will also prevent the call from being handled informally.

The dynamics of a domestic violence situation involving a law enforcement officer may become complex when a relationship exists between responding officers and the officer who is accused of domestic violence. These dynamics may involve mutual respect or rank differences between officers. Therefore, the responding officers should be directed to report to a supervisor who is of higher rank than the accused officer. Additionally, a supervisor who is in charge of the scene must respond to the call and coordinate all decision making, including crime scene documentation, arrest decisions, and weapon removal.

When the victim and the abuser are both police officers, standard domestic violence response and investigation procedures must be pursued. The department should ensure the safety and privacy of the abused police officer. It is important that referrals to confidential domestic violence services are made available to the abused officer. In addition, special attention must be paid to the victimized officer so that the reported domestic violence case does not have any negative impact on the performance and evaluation of the abused officer.

Victim Safety and Protection

Victims of domestic violence by law enforcement officers face unique situations. Police officers may be well known in the community and well respected among fellow officers. In these situations, the victim may feel powerless and may not be willing to seek police assistance. Thus the department must provide partners and family members with a variety of information within the community, including advocacy resources, designated principle contacts, and victim safety advocates. The department also should ensure that the victim receives information regarding victim's rights, applicable laws on domestic violence, and the procedures for obtaining a restraining order if the victim wishes to do so.

It is important for the department to establish a designated principal contact for victims of domestic violence by police officers. The designated principal contact person must ensure that the victim is informed about all elements of departmental procedures and policies, including the department policies regarding victim confidentiality and its limitations.

Departments must always be aware of the possibility that domestic violence situations may become worse when an abusive officer finds out that the victim has reported the domestic violence incident. This could result in extremely violent behaviors by the abuser, such as committing homicide and/or suicide. The department must assist the victim in developing plans to handle the situation through a safety plan and danger assessment.

Post-Incident Administrative and Criminal Decisions

Once an abusive officer has been arrested, the department must pay careful attention to the case in order to properly handle it. Three steps should be followed for the consideration of post-incident administrative and criminal decisions: administrative investigation and decisions; criminal investigation and decisions; and termination procedures. The first two processes should be conducted in a separate but parallel manner.

First, the department should assign its internal affairs division or appoint an investigator to conduct a post-incident administrative investigation. Based on the administrative investigation, the department must make a decision regarding whether weapons should be seized. Although many departments have a wide range of policies, it is critical for the victim's safety that decisions on administrative sanctions are made as soon as possible. It is recommended that any officer who is found through an administrative investigation to have engaged in domestic violence be terminated from the department.

Second, a special unit for domestic violence should be assigned to conduct the criminal investigation of the accused officer. If a department does not have such a unit, the criminal investigations team or the detective division can be used to conduct the criminal investigation. All information found during the investigation must be forwarded to the prosecutor's office. This information may include all documentation regarding previous concerns about the officer's problematic or abusive behaviors, damage or injuries of the victim, and danger assessment findings.

Third, once the administrative or criminal investigations conclude that the officer should be terminated, the officer must be notified in person and in writing by the department. When the officer is notified of his termination from the department, such notification should include a list of available support services for the terminated officer. It is also important for the department to notify the victim that it intends to terminate the officer prior to the actual termination. This notification allows the victim to take appropriate steps to protect herself from abusive acts by the officer (International Association of Chiefs of Police 2003). Sometimes, after the criminal investigation, the victim may indicate her desire to drop the criminal charge against the abusive officer. However, some jurisdictions have policies that allow prosecutions to go forward without the consent of the victim.

Conclusion

Domestic violence by law enforcement officers continues to be a controversial subject among researchers, professionals, and the media. Society looks to law enforcement personnel for protection from harm; one is shocked and dismayed to learn that an officer has become violent toward a member of his or her family.

Researchers' best estimates indicate that domestic violence occurs as frequently among law enforcement officers as it does among the general population. Victims of domestic violence by law enforcement officers face special dangers that are unique to police culture. For instance, law enforcement officers have special training regarding accessing information, conducting surveillance, and using weapons and physical force.

Additionally, victims must overcome the secrecy and loyalty of police culture when filing charges of domestic violence against law enforcement officers. Police culture accepts and defends its own members and looks with distrust upon outsiders. Officers are loyal to each other because of the nature of their work and the dangers they face together on a daily basis.

The IACP has recommended a model code for departments dealing with domestic violence by law enforcement officers. It establishes processes and procedures for handling these types of cases. Many departments have begun to adopt this code in part or in full. This is a significant step forward for both law enforcement officers who commit acts of domestic violence and for their victims. However, more training, knowledge, and support is still needed.

SHIHO YAMAMOTO and HARVEY WALLACE

See also **Battered Woman Syndrome; Batterer Typology; Coercive Control; Marital Rape; Military Families, Domestic Violence within; Stockholm Syndrome in Battered Women; Victim-Blaming Theory**

References and Further Reading

Domestic Violence in the Los Angeles Police Department: How Well Does the Los Angeles Police Department Police Its Own? Domestic Task Force, Office of the Inspector General, 1997.
International Association of Chiefs of Police. *Domestic Violence by Police Officers*. 2003.
Inward, Robin, William Traynor, and Vicki Favuzza. "Psychological Profiles of Police and Public Safety Officers Accused of Domestic Violence." In *Domestic Violence by Law Enforcement Officers,* edited by Donald C. Sheehan. Washington, DC: U.S. Department of Justice, Federal Bureau of Investigation, 2000, pp. 209–224.
Klein, Robin, and Constance Klein. "The Extent of Domestic Violence within Law Enforcement: An Empirical Study." In Sheehan, ed., *Domestic Violence by Law Enforcement Officers*, 2000, pp. 225–232.
Lott, Lonald D. "Deadly Secrets: Violence in the Police Family." *FBI Law Bulletin* (1995): 12.
Mullins, Wayman C., and Michael J. McMains. "Impact of Traumatic Stress on Domestic Violence in Policing." In Sheehan, ed., *Domestic Violence by Law Enforcement Officers*, 2000, pp. 257–268.
Nathan, Alison J. "At the Intersection of Domestic Violence and Guns: The Public Interest Exception and the Lautenberg Amendment." *85 Cornell L. Rev.* 822, 2000.
Neidig, Peter H. "Interspousal Aggression in Law Enforcement Families: A Preliminary Investigation: 15 Police Studies." *International Review of Police Development* 30 (1992a).
———. "FOP Marital Aggression Survey: Interspousal Aggression in Law Enforcement Personnel Attending the FOP Biennial Conference." *National Fraternal Order of Police Journal* 5 (1992b).
Ryan, Jr., Andrew H. "The Prevalence of Domestic Violence in Police Families." In Sheehan, ed., *Domestic Violence by Law Enforcement Officers*, 2000, pp. 297–308.
Sgambelluri, Anthony V. "Police Culture, Police Training, and Police Administration: Their Impact on Violence in Police Families." In Sheehan, ed., *Domestic Violence by Law Enforcement Officers,* 2000, pp. 309–322.
Wallace, Harvey. *Family Violence, Legal, Medical, and Social Perspectives*, 3rd ed. Boston: Allyn & Bacon, 2005.
Wetendorf, Diane, and Dottie L. Davis. "The Misuse of Police Powers in Officer-Involved Domestic Violence." *Advocate and Officer Dialogues: Police-Perpetrated Domestic Violence*. Fort Wayne, IN: Davis Corporate Training, 2003.

Cases and Statues Cited

Omnibus Consolidated Appropriations Act of 1997 (the Lautenberg Amendment) 18 U.S.C. 922 (d)(9).

DOMESTIC VIOLENCE COURTS

Domestic violence courts are specialized to address the complex issues presented in domestic violence cases. These courts utilize approaches that reflect a significant departure from those of traditional courts. While no single model of a domestic violence court is used by all states, domestic violence courts across the United States share a similar philosophical orientation regarding their role and function. Rather than simply determining facts, applying the law, defending rights, and assigning punishment according to legal rules and procedures, these courts recognize that victim safety is as important as perpetrator accountability. As such, judges and court personnel need to be sensitive to such issues as the risk of future violence to the victim and her children, the victim's fear and sometimes reluctance to testify, and the need to link victims to services in the community that will help them rebuild their lives, free from violence.

This article will discuss the formation of domestic violence courts by examining the unique features of domestic violence cases that led to their formation. It will also examine how domestic violence courts differ from traditional courts, especially in terms of their core principles. In addition, this article will describe three different models of domestic violence courts, analyzing the advantages and limitations of each. Finally, we will examine the major criticisms of domestic violence courts, focusing on problems with some of the programs typically used by them.

Unique Characteristics of Domestic Violence Cases

Derived from English common law, the American legal system had a long tradition of regarding domestic violence as a private family matter, not subject to criminal prosecution. Early American courts held that husbands acted within their rights when they beat and abused their wives in response to what husbands described as their wives' "misbehavior." This view of domestic violence as a private family matter stemmed from a larger body of law and social custom that denied women a separate identity of their own. Indeed, the American legal system did not criminalize domestic violence until the late nineteenth century. It was not until 1871 that a state court, the Supreme Court of Alabama, in *Fulgham v. State,* determined for the first time that a husband did not have the right to beat his wife. In the years following this decision, several states began adopting laws against domestic violence that made wife beating a crime. Despite these laws, individual opinions held by judges and prosecutors regarding the appropriate role of law in private family matters frequently meant that courts did not enforce these laws.

In the 1970s, the feminist movement focused attention on battered women, leading to some changes in the criminal justice response to domestic violence. The attention drawn by the feminist movement to domestic violence resulted in legal reforms that emphasized the need for court intervention in these matters. The emphasis of these new reforms was on applying sanctions to the batterer through such measures as the enactment of civil order of protection statutes, criminal contempt orders to enforce protection orders, and laws mandating the arrest of batterers. State-funded shelters began to appear as well as batterer intervention programs. However, these reforms did not reduce the number of domestic violence cases.

Critics argued that the reason for the persistence of domestic violence could be explained in part by the limitations in the practices and procedures of traditional courts. One limitation was the inadequacy of orders of protection (restraining orders) to prevent further abuse. Orders of protection impose restrictions on a person's future behavior. The order may require that there be no contact between the parties, order an abuser to relinquish any firearms, grant possession of a shared residence to the victim, and address such issues as child custody, visitation, and support. Often victims obtained orders of protection through the civil side of the legal system. Victims often appeared *pro se* because they lacked the financial resources to retain an attorney. While orders of protection represented an important legal remedy, they were not always the most effective means for preventing future violence. Research indicated that batterers often violated orders of protection, sometimes with tragic results, such as the murder of the victim and her children.

A second criticism directed at traditional courts concerns the inherent complexity of domestic violence cases. Domestic violence cases involve complex issues of family dynamics and emotional relationships between the parties. Many domestic violence victims have suffered previous attacks by their batterers, and there may be strong emotional ties between the victim and the batterer because of issues such as the victim's economic dependence on the batterer and the likelihood that she will have continuing contact with him because of their children. However, criminal courts frequently processed domestic violence cases, especially low-injury or noninjury incidents, in the same manner that they handled other crimes, even though many low-injury domestic violence cases later escalated into high-injury or homicide cases that the legal system could have prevented with effective sanctions at the outset.

A third criticism of traditional courts concerns the barriers that victims encountered in attempting to have effective participation in the criminal justice system. Law enforcement and court personnel often viewed battered women as responsible for the crimes committed against them because they failed to leave the relationship after the batterer had previously harmed them. In addition, domestic violence victims were often reluctant witnesses against their batterers because they feared retaliation. Prosecutors were often reluctant or unwilling to prosecute batterers because of the unwillingness by the victims to cooperate or because of beliefs that women would only return to the abusive relationship.

A final criticism concerned the fragmented nature of the criminal justice system when confronted with domestic violence cases. The criminal justice system depends upon the effective coordination of law enforcement officers, court personnel, and judges. However, these personnel frequently display varied levels of motivation, training, and sensitivity to issues surrounding domestic violence. For example, while a court might demonstrate a willingness to prosecute domestic violence cases, police may be indifferent to responding to such calls or may be ineffective in responding to the needs of victims.

Core Principles of Domestic Violence Courts

Domestic violence courts reflect the growth of other specialty or problem-solving courts in contemporary society, such as drug treatment courts and mental health courts. Common to all problem-solving courts are the goals of solving underlying problems and avoiding a recurrence of criminal behavior. Problem-solving courts require a new view of the judicial process, one in which judges use their authority, in part, to motivate individuals to accept services and then to monitor compliance with them. Problem-solving courts typically focus on a defined population of offenders and rest on an assumption that it is pointless and an inefficient use of resources to send addicts, the mentally ill, and others with ongoing behavioral issues through a revolving door of incarceration and release. Problem-solving courts are also known as therapeutic courts because these courts view crimes and other dysfunctional behaviors as rooted in behavioral, emotional, and psychological disorders that will recur unless individuals address underlying problems.

Problem-solving or therapeutic courts originated in the late 1980s with the emergence of a legal perspective known as therapeutic jurisprudence. Arising originally from mental health law, therapeutic jurisprudence is a scholarly, interdisciplinary movement toward legal reform. The basic principle underlying therapeutic jurisprudence is that law is a social force that has inevitable and often unintended consequences for the mental health and psychological functioning of those it affects. These consequences may have either therapeutic effects that enhance an individual's social functioning, or negative, anti-therapeutic effects. Scholars define "therapeutic" very broadly to include any effects that improve the psychological, physical, or emotional health of the person. The goal of therapeutic jurisprudence is to increase the therapeutic effects of the law while decreasing its anti-therapeutic effects. In order to accomplish this goal, therapeutic jurisprudence examines the costs and benefits of the law's effect on the mental and physical health of an individual through a social science lens. It assesses the costs and benefits of enforcing laws by evaluating the overall consequences on individuals in society. This assessment should reveal whether laws are accomplishing their public policy goals.

Domestic violence courts are problem-solving courts that generally share many of the ideas embodied in therapeutic jurisprudence. However, one important difference is that domestic violence courts center on the principles of victim safety as well as defendant accountability and rehabilitation. This means that while domestic violence courts must uphold the basic principles of protecting defendants' rights, providing a fair and impartial hearing as well as opportunities for rehabilitation, domestic violence courts also focus on providing avenues for the safety of victims and their children.

Courts manifest this emphasis on safety by linking victims and their children to services while they are participating in the judicial process. This does not mean that the court acts as a direct service provider, but rather that the structure of the court enables it to link victims to advocates who can meet with victims to provide needed services, such as emergency shelter, counseling, economic assistance, legal assistance, and services for children. The services provided are noncompulsory; the emphasis is on victims determining their own needs. In addition to services, domestic violence courts keep victims informed about all aspects of the case, such as its status and the terms of an order of protection.

In order for courts to hold batterers accountable and attempt their rehabilitation, they must closely monitor defendants to ensure that they comply with all court conditions and that they face swift and certain consequences if they fail to do so. This requires that judges and other criminal justice personnel have accurate and up-to-date information concerning all issues that bear on the case, such as the defendant's criminal history, whether the defendant is attending court-mandated programs, and any violations of an order of protection. Typically, domestic violence courts bring defendants back for regular review or status hearings during the duration of court proceedings. During status hearings, judges review reports to the court from agencies that traditionally monitor defendants, such as probation programs. Domestic violence courts also develop sentencing models for handling cases that will promote offender accountability. This can include sentences that contain court-ordered conditions and monitoring by agencies to ensure compliance with court-mandated conditions. This type of sentencing is especially important when the court does not incarcerate the batterer. For example, domestic violence courts can include such conditions as mandated participation in a batterers' intervention program, parenting skills programs, and substance abuse treatment.

Domestic violence courts typically accomplish the goals of victim safety and offender accountability through *coordinated community responses*. The need for such responses grew out of the recognition that a significant lack of coordination and systemic response to intimate partner violence probably put many victims at greater risk because there were few standards, little consistency, and even less institutional accountability among agencies in a community. While coordinated efforts may take a variety of forms, they generally include a variety of system partners, including but not limited to judges and judicial officers, law enforcement, prosecutors, defense attorneys, advocates for children, victim advocates, shelter providers, corrections, probation, parole, and child protective services. Coordinated community responses typically embrace the following ideas. First, the emphasis is on community partnerships to develop effective work plans. Second, these efforts focus on providing community intervention projects that provide direct services to batterers from entry into to exit from the system. Third, task forces or coordinating councils provide assessments of community needs and recommendations for changes. Fourth, coordinated community responses provide mechanisms for training, technical assistance projects, and community initiatives. Ideally, successful, coordinated community responses send the message that the system will protect victims and hold batterers accountable.

Models of Domestic Violence Courts

There are diverse models of domestic violence courts. Some handle all criminal and civil cases involving domestic violence. Others handle only civil matters, only criminal domestic violence cases, or only misdemeanor criminal cases. Other court systems have dedicated teams of prosecutors that work only on domestic violence cases. Dedicated courts and prosecutions have many advantages. Since the same judges or prosecutors hear all domestic violence cases, these individuals are able to gain expertise in the issues and ensure more consistency in the treatment of cases. They are likely to be more sensitive to the needs of victims and can direct them to community resources. Dedicated courts or prosecution teams can process cases more quickly, thus reducing the opportunity for the batterer to intimidate his partner into abandoning the charges. In addition, judges who consistently deal with domestic violence cases will see repeat offenders, who will consequently expect increasing penalties and greater accountability.

While there is significant variation in how domestic violence courts are structured, there are a number of important similarities that enable them to identify themselves as separate and distinct from other courts. Whether civil or criminal, domestic violence courts pay particular attention to how cases are assigned, the need to screen for related cases, who performs intake-unit functions, the need to provide services to victims and batterers, and the monitoring of batterers. Some examples of different models of domestic violence courts can illustrate this point.

In one model, the court may specialize in handling civil protection orders. A full-time dedicated judge may handle these cases, or judges who rotate through the court calendar will preside over the cases, but the calendar is always specialized. This model includes a fully dedicated court that handles only civil protection orders all the time, as well as a court that devotes perhaps one day a week to focus on these cases. This model offers many of the advantages that a domestic violence court can provide, such as increased safety for victims, educated judges, and access to advocacy. On the other hand, this structure is limited because it generally allows for follow-up monitoring only when there is a violation of the order of protection. While it is possible for the court to conduct a more intensive follow-up, there are usually no conditions imposed beyond compliance with the order of protection that would trigger court monitoring. Some civil protection courts also handle related civil matters. This provides these courts with the ability to handle custody and visitation matters concerning children of the parties.

One of the more common models for domestic violence courts segregates criminal cases for specialized, concentrated handling by one or more judges. Most states have created specialized misdemeanor domestic violence courts. Some states have created courts that handle only felony abuse cases, while others have created courts that handle both misdemeanors and felonies. Since domestic violence defendants tend to have repeated and often escalating cases, when courts can hear both misdemeanor and felony cases a clearer picture of these defendants emerges. Compliance follow-up is more likely to occur in a criminal model because these courts have mechanisms to facilitate such follow-up, such as probation or incarceration. On the disadvantage side, just as a purely civil court cannot address criminal cases that may be occurring, a criminal-only court does not address related civil cases that may be ongoing.

A third model attempts to address the disadvantages raised in the previous models by combining domestic violence cases and related matters. These courts, often known as integrated domestic violence courts, or IDV courts, recognize that both victims and perpetrators often have related issues before the court, such as a criminal matter, an order of protection, child support, custody, or divorce. This type of model addresses more comprehensively the issues that families dealing with domestic violence face. The court has access to complete information on a family, lending itself to consistency of orders and outcomes. For example, if the judge issues an order of protection, that same judge will make a child visitation order that is compatible with the order. However, one problem with IDV courts is the difficulty of keeping civil and criminal matters separate. For example, the attorneys in both cases may work on a resolution for both cases at the same time. Another disadvantage of this model is that if participants do not like a particular judge, they are nevertheless dependent on that judge for decisions on every aspect of their various cases.

Criticisms of Domestic Violence Courts

Critics argue that the very act of creating a separate domestic violence court creates potential benefits as well as potential disadvantages. Four potential disadvantages or criticisms are especially noteworthy. First, creation of separate courts may be a result of an overreaction to the uniqueness of domestic violence cases, especially in terms of attempts to provide services for the batterer. The struggle between those who think that domestic violence cases should be set apart for special treatment and those who think that individual treatment can create the perception that the justice system is treating domestic violence perpetrators less seriously than other criminals is difficult to reconcile. Critics argue that if the community perceives that domestic violence courts are more likely to use diversion or counseling instead of holding batterers accountable for their behavior, then the community may lose faith in the ability of these courts to address domestic violence cases effectively.

A second criticism concerns the multidisciplinary approach embedded in many domestic violence courts. This approach involves numerous parties with a variety of perspectives, beliefs, and goals. Police officers, judges, prosecutors, victim advocates, and social service agencies may all be involved in a single domestic violence case. As a result, although there may be theoretical agreement that victim safety and defendant accountability are the primary goals of abuse intervention, the potential exists for creating conflict on a practical level in the actual implementation of interventions designed to further these goals. For example, through criminalization of domestic violence, the legal system validates women's experiences by treating domestic violence crimes as seriously as stranger crimes. However, despite improvement in recent years, many officials still apply the law half-heartedly. In some instances, systematic gender bias or a reluctance to change the traditional justice system exists, resulting in insensitivity to victims despite innovative programs created to enhance sensitivity and to prevent victim mistreatment. For example, some judges may hesitate to mandate batterer intervention programs for men who have job and travel constraints. Prosecutors may also play a large role in promoting domestic violence laws or, alternatively, in limiting the use of such laws. When time and resources run low, some prosecutors prioritize their cases and discourage battered women from going forward with prosecution. Conversely, situations exist in which a city's system has a sincere desire to implement domestic violence programs and policies, but case-specific circumstances dictate otherwise.

A third criticism concerns the uncertainty that exists over the effectiveness of batterer intervention programs. Most mainstream batterer programs, which are often court-mandated as an alternative to incarceration, utilize a group approach requiring batterers to attend weekly group sessions run by program staff and composed of other batterers. Each of these programs, however, may vary in overall length and number of sessions, as well as content of the curriculum. Although researchers have conducted several evaluation studies of batterer intervention programs, the outcome is inconclusive as to whether they actually result in reduced levels of violence. Moreover, a source of controversy involves the use of valuable domestic violence resources on services for perpetrators. Many battered women's advocates object to spending money on long-term interventions for batterers when doing so diverts limited funds away from services for battered women. Advocates argue that with the effect of batterer programs so indeterminate, battered women are losing resources to interventions that may not even benefit them.

A fourth criticism concerns the impact of alternative legal sanctions on the recidivism rate of domestic violence offenders. Traditionally, legal sanctions included arrest and incarceration in serious cases of domestic violence, with courts giving perpetrators in less serious cases less punishment. Domestic violence courts, however, have promoted not only a greater variety of legal sanctions, with the advent of alternative sentences such as court-mandated counseling, but also greater severity of sanctions in cases that previously went unpunished, such as mandatory arrest, more stringent monitoring of defendant behavior by the court, and greater enforcement of orders of protection through criminalization of violations. However, research concerning whether such approaches deter future domestic violence is inconclusive. For example, traditionally experts considered arrest to be the

primary tool for deterrence in domestic violence cases because of the 1980 Minneapolis Domestic Violence Study that found a dramatic decrease in repeat domestic violence incidents following arrest. Since that time, however, other studies have produced conflicting results. Furthermore, in the context of domestic violence courts, the newly created courts have taken straightforward legal sanctions and intertwined them with a host of other factors, making it difficult to assess the impact of any given legal sanction. Therefore, it is not known what legal sanctions, if any, actually deter future cases of domestic violence.

Conclusion

Domestic violence courts represent a potentially significant approach to dealing with the complexity characteristic of most domestic violence cases. The principles of offender accountability and victim safety provide domestic violence courts with important challenges to develop programs and monitoring that address both principles. Using dedicated resources and having coordinated community responses are important steps toward making domestic violence courts effective.

PATRICIA E. ERICKSON

See also **Battered Women, Clemency for; Batterer Intervention Programs; Community Response to Domestic Violence; Divorce, Child Custody, and Domestic Violence; Electronic Monitoring of Abusers; Legal Issues for Battered Women; Mandatory Arrest Policies; Police Response to Domestic Violence Incidents; Training Practices for Law Enforcement in Domestic Violence Cases; Violence against Women Act**

References and Further Reading

Buzwa, Eve, and Carl G. Buzwa. *Domestic Violence: The Criminal Justice Response*. Thousand Oaks, CA: Sage Publications, 2002.
Roberts, Albert. *Handbook of Domestic Violence Intervention Strategies*. New York: Oxford University Press, 2002.
Sack, Emily. *Creating a Domestic Violence Court: Guidelines and Best Practices*. San Francisco: Family Violence Prevention Fund, 2002.
Tsai, Betsy. "The Trend Toward Specialized Domestic Violence Courts: Improvements on an Effective Innovation." *Fordham Law Review* 68 (2000): 1285–1326.
Winick, Bruce, and David B. Wexler. *Judging in a Therapeutic Key: Jurisprudence and the Courts*. Durham, NC: Carolina Academic Press, 1996.

E

EDUCATION AS A RISK FACTOR FOR DOMESTIC VIOLENCE

Domestic violence is an epidemic that knows no boundaries and does not discriminate based upon religion, race, or even gender. Throughout the years scholars and practitioners have learned more about the epidemic and have become aware of some risk factors that may increase an individual's chance of being a domestic violence victim. Recognizing the risk factors has become helpful in the attempt to identify those individuals who are more at risk than others. These factors are not intended to serve as a definition of who or what domestic violence victims can and cannot be. It is extremely important to keep in mind that anyone can be a victim of domestic violence regardless of whether or not she or he meets the characteristics identified as risk factors within this article.

Throughout the years researchers have made significant strides concerning domestic violence. They have studied many risk factors that practitioners can now use to successfully identify victims of domestic violence. The ability to recognize these factors has proven valuable to the many professionals who come into contact with victims of domestic violence because it helps them properly identify victims and provide them with the assistance they need. Studying risk factors also allows domestic violence experts to learn more about the phenomenon and develop better ways to address this problem. In addition to identifying risk factors, this research has helped identify protective factors associated with the prevention of domestic violence. The discovery of both risk and protective factors will lead to further research that will help professionals better understand this epidemic and find new ways of managing it.

One of the risk factors associated with domestic violence is being female. Research has indicated that females are more likely to be victims of domestic violence than males. This does not mean that men cannot be victims; it simply means that women are more often victims than men. Furthermore, much of the research conducted concerning domestic violence has focused on heterosexual couples, though domestic violence is something that can and does affect anyone, regardless of sexual orientation or gender.

Another risk factor associated with domestic violence is being a minority female. This does not mean that whites or minority males cannot be victims of domestic violence. The risk factor of race simply indicates that minority women are victimized at higher rates than their white counterparts.

A third risk factor associated with domestic violence is the discrepancy between education, income, or occupational status between partners. In 2003 a study conducted by T. Lane appeared in the journal *Perspectives on Sexual and Reproductive Health* that determined that women have different risk factors for emotional and physical abuse. This study indicated that certain risk factors are linked to physical abuse, whereas others are linked to emotional or verbal abuse. Education was one of the risk factors linked with physical violence. This does not mean that the victim cannot experience both forms of abuse; it is just more likely that physical violence will occur when the education risk factor exists (Lane 2003).

This article will focus primarily on education as a risk factor associated with domestic violence. Education as a risk factor includes the lack of education of the victim, lack of education of the offender, or discrepancies between education levels, income, or occupational status between victims and their offenders. Sometimes the risk factors tend to be intertwined with one another, as in the case of education level, income, and status. Conversely, education has also been cited as being a protective factor.

Lack of Education

Most research concerning risk factors has indicated that lack of education is a risk factor for domestic violence. Lack of education is generally defined as having earned less than a high school diploma, although some studies include those with less than a college degree in their definition. It has been noted that women with less education experience domestic violence at higher rates than women who have achieved a higher level of education. In the simplest of terms, those individuals with less than a college education are at a higher risk of being victims of domestic violence than those with a college degree. This does not mean that people with higher levels of education cannot be victims of domestic violence; it simply means that the risk of being a victim of domestic violence is greater for those with less than a high school or college education. As previously stated, domestic violence does not discriminate when it comes to victims, and risk factors such as a victim's education level merely act as tools to help practitioners identify those people who are more likely to be affected than others.

Lack of education is also a risk factor associated with perpetrators of domestic violence. Most research that has focused on education as a risk factor has indicated that males with lower levels of education than their partners are more likely to be domestic violence offenders than those with an equivalent level of education. Most research indicated that these offenders were primarily male, although females are certainly not exempt. The common belief is that communication skills are sharpened with added levels of education; those with lower levels of education may resort to violence due to the inability to properly communicate anger or frustration (Jeyaseelan et al. 2004).

The Threat of Education

Although lack of education is one of the risk factors associated with domestic violence, a difference in a couple's education level is another. A difference in educational status can be defined as one partner having a higher level of education than the other. This disparity can exist on various levels. Most studies do not specify the amount of educational difference between partners, only that one exists. The educational discrepancy may be as minor as one partner having a high school education and the other not. This difference may also be wider, i.e., one partner has less than a high school education and the other has an advanced college degree.

A person's education level is often associated with earning ability and status in society. For this reason an offender may perceive his partner's educational achievement as a threat. This perception is often not valid, but the offender cannot be convinced otherwise. The abuser will often feel threatened by this discrepancy and will resort to perpetrating psychological and physical forms of domestic violence on his victim in order to regain control over her. If one partner tries to pursue a higher level of education, the other may feel threatened and try to prevent her success through various means. This difference in educational status may cause the abuser to feel threatened by the possibility that his partner will obtain a higher level of status within society than he could ever obtain.

The Importance of Education

Education is a very valuable tool in contemporary society. The amount of formal education a person receives will usually determine what type of lifestyle he or she will be able to lead and how much income he or she will be able to earn. Another common risk factor associated with domestic violence is income level, and it is easy to see how this goes hand in hand with the educational risk factor.

The less formal education a person has, the less likely he or she is to earn competitive wages. In an aggressive job market, those with more education and work-related experience will be employed first. Those with less formal education are subjected to lower-paying jobs or, even worse, unemployment. This may create a situation of dependency for those with less education if they are prone to earn less income and may not be able to support themselves or their children on their own. If abuse already exists in the relationship, the lack of education and strained income provides the abuser with an upper hand in feeding upon the victim's vulnerability. This vulnerability is compounded when there are dependents involved. Many victims of domestic violence stay in their situations due to feelings of necessity. The victim has often been isolated from friends and family by the abuser, and this unequal financial arrangement further fuels her sense of dependency and reluctance to leave. The victim may be unable to seek employment that makes leaving the relationship financially feasible, or unable to seek any employment at all; a 2003 study of barriers to employment in metropolitan Detroit stated that domestic violence was one of those barriers (Allard et al. 2003). Domestic violence has been listed as a barrier not only to employment but also to education which may lead to employment, as discussed further on in this article.

Education provides one with opportunities to learn new things. Most colleges provide students with an opportunity to expand their knowledge in particular subject areas in order to pursue a career. Knowledge is not the only advantage to an increased educational level. Along with more knowledge on particular subjects comes expertise required by various professions. Education is an absolute requirement for those persons wanting to enter the medical field. There is specific knowledge that must be gained in order for a person to become a successful professional, such as a medical doctor, architect, or research scientist. Typically those with higher levels of education have more opportunities for advancement. An individual's status in society is dependent on several factors, including professional status, income level, and educational level. The college experience also allows individuals the opportunity to meet new people and gain new perspectives on life. This includes gaining a new perspective on what is acceptable and unacceptable with regard to relationships. It is also believed that education provides an individual with an increased

ability to rationalize in everyday life, resulting in the ability to make better life decisions. Those with more education are also believed to be able to communicate better, and this ability may serve as a protective factor against domestic violence (Jeyaseelan et al. 2004).

Barriers to Education

Some individuals simply do not have the desire to further their level of education. There are others who have experienced barriers that prevent them from pursuing a higher level of education. These barriers can include but are not limited to: not being able to afford tuition; not being able to afford child care services; not being able to juggle work and school; not being able to find an employer willing to work around their school schedule; having to care for siblings or other relatives following the death of a family member; or caring for a terminally ill family member. Often people who have experienced barriers become easily discouraged and believe that this is just something they must accept. Domestic violence is also a barrier to education.

One of the common themes that exist among victims of domestic abuse is isolation. This means that their abusers will try to keep them from having any outside contacts or support from outside sources—including preventing them from continuing their education. Isolating the victim gives the abuser power over her. This can be accomplished in a variety of ways, not the least of which is through use of physical force. Often emotional abuse accompanies physical abuse, and the abuser may succeed in convincing the victim that she is not smart enough to succeed in school. The abuser may also prevent the victim from going to school through the control of available finances.

Conquering the Barriers to Education

Some of the barriers that prevent individuals from attaining higher levels of education can be overcome if a person genuinely desires to do so. The General Educational Development Diploma (GED) is available to those individuals who never completed high school. Most public libraries offer classes that will help people obtain their GED or can refer them to alternate resources that can also help them reach this goal. Those who wish to pursue a college education but feel that they cannot afford it should be referred to the U.S. Department of Education's website to explore the different types of financial aid available. Most states have an agency designed to help parents complete their educational goals by defraying some child care expenses. Some colleges offer child care services for their students at reduced rates. Family housing is also available at some colleges and universities for students and their immediate family.

ELIZABETH CORZINE MCMULLAN

See also **Battered Woman Syndrome; Batterer Typology; Coercive Control; Intergenerational Transfer of Intimate Partner Violence; Social Class and Domestic Violence; Social Learning Theory and Family Violence; Workplace, Domestic Violence in**

References and Further Reading

Allard, Scott W., Richard M. Tolman, and Daniel Rosen. "The Geography of Need: Spatial Distribution of Barriers to Employment in Metropolitan Detroit." *Policy Studies Journal* 31, no. 3 (2003): 293–307.

Jeyaseelan, L., Laura S. Sadowski, Shuba Kumar, Fatma Hassan, Laurie Ramiro, and Beatriz Vizcarra. "World Studies of Abuse in the Family Environment: Risk Factors for Physical Intimate Partner Violence." *Injury Control and Safety Promotion* 11, no. 2 (2004): 117–124.

Lane, T. "Women Have Different Risk Factors for Verbal, Physical Partner Abuse." *Perspectives on Sexual and Reproductive Health* 35, no. 2 (March/April 2003): 106–107.

U.S. Department of Education website. http://www.ed.gov.

ELDER ABUSE, ASSESSING THE RISKS OF

Assessing the risks of elder abuse involves applying what has been discovered about this type of abuse through research to detect problems before they become serious, or before they emerge at all. Researchers have uncovered certain risk factors, as they are called, which are really characteristics of victims, perpetrators, or environments that suggest the possibility of the occurrence of elder abuse. In a given situation in which one notices such risk factors, elder abuse may not have happened yet. Indeed, it may never happen. However, the circumstances are ripe for the problem to surface.

Identifying and assessing risk factors requires those in contact with older adults to maintain a high level of suspicion and remain watchful and alert to instances or signs of elder abuse. This will allow clinicians and caregivers who provide care to older adults to take measures to reduce the risk of abuse occurrence.

Importance of Risk Factors

Identifying risk factors is at the heart of problem prevention. More specifically, in order to stop a problem from happening, it is important to know what is causing or could potentially cause the problem. By removing the cause, it may be possible to prevent the occurrence, or at least reoccurrence, of the problem.

It is difficult to determine through research the causes, exactly, of elder abuse. Because empirical demonstration of cause and effect has not been achieved with regard to elder abuse, it is more appropriate to use the term "risk factors" rather than "causes" to describe conditions that appear to be closely linked with abuse according to theories of the presumed causation of elder abuse.

The risk factors of elder abuse provide a framework for developing individual and community strategies for problem prevention. For example, social isolation is a widely regarded risk factor for abuse occurrence. Problem prevention in this regard may involve increasing social contact and support for older adults. On an individual level, this might mean arranging for friendly visitors to spend time with a homebound and vulnerable elder on a regular basis. On a community level, it might mean establishing a publicly funded Senior Companion Program, whereby low-income people age fifty-five and above are linked with frail elders for in-home socialization and limited assistance.

Looking for risk factors also contributes to problem detection. Detecting elder abuse represents an attempt to answer three interrelated questions pertaining to particular situations with older adults. First, have there been known occurrences of elder abuse? This involves identifying specific *examples* of abuse occurrence—for example, abuse situations that are personally observed or reported by the victim or some other knowledgeable source. Examples of physical elder abuse include slapping, shoving, or beating an older adult.

The second question is, Is elder abuse suspected? Answering this question involves identifying signs, symptoms, or indicators of abuse occurrence. *Signs* represent the consequences or effects of elder abuse—e.g., for physical abuse, signs might include bruises, lacerations, and broken bones. However, signs can have origins other than abuse occurrence. Bruises, for instance, can result from accidental falls or even certain medications. Therefore, unlike examples, signs are not conclusive and require delving deeper into investigating the situation. Known (as evidenced by examples) or suspected (as suggested by signs) elder abuse is the usual precondition for referring a situation to authorities under state adult protective services or elder abuse reporting laws.

The third question one should ask is whether elder abuse is likely in a particular situation. This involves identifying the presence of risk factors for abuse occurrence. These "red flags" suggest that conditions are such that elder abuse may take place and that consequently one should be on the lookout for examples and signs of it. For example, alcoholism on the part of the adult child who serves as the elderly person's primary caretaker is a risk factor for physical abuse. When combined with the adult child's financial dependency on and co-residence with the elderly person, the probability of abuse occurrence is high.

Finally, risk factors are prompts for elder abuse assessment. The presence of risk factors or signs necessitates a thorough evaluation of the situation, the possible victim, and the suspected or potential perpetrator. Assessments serve multiple purposes. They allow one to appraise the need for assistance, the urgency of that need, the availability of assistance resources, and priorities for extending assistance. Assessments are used to consider the nature of the elder abuse as well as such risk-factor domains as mental and cognitive status, recent family or life crises, and financial issues. They can be layered. For example, identifying an elderly person's feelings of depression may suggest the need for application of depression symptom scales or even psychiatric evaluation.

Understanding Risk Factors

The presence of risk factors increases the chance that elder abuse will occur. Correlatively, this usually means that the higher the number of risk factors present in any situation, the greater the probability of abuse occurrence. Similarly, longer exposure to risk factors also enhances the likelihood of abuse occurrence. Returning to the earlier identified risk factors for physical abuse noted above, alcoholism alone on the part of the potential or suspected perpetrator is not nearly as powerful a risk factor for elder abuse as it is when combined with his or her financial dependence on the victim and the victim's social isolation. Likewise, the continuance of these risk factors over time makes it more and more likely that elder abuse will happen, and when it does, that it will be repeated.

To understand elder abuse risk factors, several points should be kept in mind. First, there have been few studies to date which explore elder abuse risk factors using acceptable research designs. Typically, investigations lack a comparison group of some kind and/or collect data from sources other than victims or perpetrators. These deficits mean that researchers do not have a clear theory on what constitutes the risk factors for elder abuse and do not know the relative importance among proposed risk factors for predicting the problem.

Second, existing research suggests that risk factors may differ by form of elder abuse. This implies variation in etiology and problem intervention by abuse form as well. For instance, physical abuse and neglect are two of several forms of elder abuse. Physical abuse is the infliction of injury or pain on an older adult by a trusted person, such as a spouse, adult child, or other caregiver. Neglect is the failure of a caregiver to provide a dependent older adult with necessary goods or services. These concepts of abuse involve different behaviors. In addition, they often suggest different relations between victim and perpetrator and result in different consequences. It is understandable that risk factors for physical abuse will not be the same as those for neglect. Rosalie Wolf, Michael Godkin, and Karl Pillemer (1986) discovered this in their pioneering study of the subject. In evaluating 328 cases of elder abuse, they found victims of physical abuse to be more independently functioning but suffering from poor emotional health; perpetrators had a history of mental illness or alcoholism, recent decline in health or mental status, increased dependency on the victim, and poor relations with the victim. In contrast, victims of neglect had problems performing daily living tasks and diminished capacity in both orientation and memory; perpetrators found victims to be a source of stress and exhibited no dependency issues.

Third, no one risk factor is sufficient to indicate the probability of elder abuse. Instead, risk factors in combination and complex interaction provide the condition for abuse occurrence. Additionally, risk factors lack a single source, thereby making the search for risk factors in specific situations even more challenging. Risk factors reside in characteristics of the victim, perpetrator, and/or environment. Those of the perpetrator tend to be more predictive of abuse occurrence than those of the victim. Environmental risk factors can be either situational or cultural in nature. For instance, using the previously identified risk factors for physical abuse, emotional problems represent a risk factor for the victim, while mental illness and alcoholism represent risk factors for the perpetrator. Co-residence represents a situational or environmental risk factor. Social isolation may be a cultural risk factor, if, for example, it originates from being a member of a stigmatized minority, such as gays or lesbians.

Fourth, risk factors relate to theoretical explanations for elder abuse. Many such explanations have been suggested, but none have been rigorously tested. An example of a theoretical explanation that may have relevance to neglect is role theory, which posits that neglect results from a lack of ability or willingness on the part of a caregiver to provide appropriate and sufficient assistance.

Lastly, conceptual models have been proposed for integrating elder abuse risk factors. An early one offered by Eloise Rathbone-McCuan and Joan Hashimi (1982) considers isolators in the lives of victims. Isolators can be biophysical, psychological, economic, or social. They render older adults vulnerable to elder abuse by diminishing their resources or providing barriers to accessing help. More recently, Georgia Anetzberger (2000) proposed a conceptual model in which elder abuse is primarily a function of perpetrator characteristics and secondarily of victim characteristics. These characteristics merge and provide the underlying etiology for abuse occurrence. Context is important in this model as well, initially the context that brings the victim and perpetrator in contact with one another and later the context that triggers abuse occurrence. To illustrate these two kinds of contexts: Co-residence may bring the victim into contact with the perpetrator; refusal of the victim to comply with the expectations of the perpetrator may trigger abuse occurrence. In this situation,

an elder abuse perpetrator may think, "When I was a kid, my parents said that as long as I was under their roof, I had to do what was asked of me. Now Mom is under my roof, and I am in control."

Risk Factors for Elder Abuse

Risk factors for elder abuse reflect characteristics of the victim, perpetrator, and environment. In addition, a set of risk factors relate to cultural norms. Research on the various characteristics may be minimal, deficient, and challenging to carry out or analyze. However, research is nearly nonexistent on risk factors for elder abuse related to cultural norms, and even more difficult to conduct. Nevertheless, characteristics of the larger society provide the milieu for elder abuse. All people are social beings, and it is through group interaction that one is socialized to become a member of society. During this process, one learns certain responses as normative activities. Select responses produce a context rich for abuse occurrence.

Risk Factors for Victims

Elder abuse can happen to any older adult. Still, some seem to be at greater risk than others. The characteristics that appear to make older adults most vulnerable are those which reduce their functional capacity or spawn problem behaviors. Sometimes these two types of characteristics are related.

Reduced functional capacity can result from frailty, poor health, physical or mental impairment, or disability. Its effects may leave older adults unable to fend off or escape from elder abuse, and in some instances may even render them unable to recognize the seriousness of the problem. In addition, reduced functional capacity can render older adults dependent for care on others who are ill-equipped to provide it or resentful about having to do so. Finally, reduced functional capacity can limit an elderly person's ability to seek help. For instance, mental illness may make them suspicious of outside assistance, sensory loss may inhibit use of telephones or other communication devices to signal need, and cognitive impairment may limit the ability of older adults to problem-solve and thereby identify sources of help and make contact with them.

Problem behaviors can originate in cognitive impairment, mental illness, or personality traits. Personality traits which seem to render older adults most vulnerable to elder abuse include hostility, aggression, and passivity. For example, in a study conducted in the Netherlands (Comijs, Pot, Smit, and Jonker 1998), victims of physical, verbal, and financial abuse showed higher levels of aggression along with more passive and avoidant coping styles than did nonvictims. Similarly, perpetrators often perceive the behavior of victims as demanding, disagreeable, complaining, and uncooperative. According to one physically abusive adult child, he becomes angry and violent toward his elderly father when he "argues with me, talks back, gets contrary."

Dementia is a disorder that often results in both reduced functional capacity and problem behavior. It is one of only a handful of elder abuse risk factors that has been validated by substantial evidence. *Dementia* is a term used to describe a decline in mental functioning severe enough to bring about significant incapacity in such areas as memory, decision making, and judgment. There are many diseases which can cause dementia. Some are progressive and irreversible. The most common of these is Alzheimer's disease, which represents half of all cases of dementia in older adults.

Various studies have shown a two to three times greater prevalence of physical abuse by family caregivers of persons with dementia. The care recipients also abuse the caregivers in 16 to 33 percent of these situations. Indeed, over half of persons with dementia are reported to be physically or verbally aggressive during the course of the disorder.

The National Elder Abuse Incidence Study conducted by the National Center on Elder Abuse (1998) found that three-fourths of identified victims had some degree of confusion, typically resulting from Alzheimer's disease or other dementia. Family caregivers of persons with dementia report aggression as the most serious problem they confront. It can precipitate institutionalization. Catherine Hawes (in Bonnie and Wallace 2003) found that in nursing home settings, staff view aggression by residents as purposefully hurtful and intentional attempts to be difficult. When residents abuse staff, staff are five times more likely to reciprocate.

Risk Factors for Perpetrators

Characteristics of the perpetrator represent the dominant risk factors for elder abuse. They are better predictors of the problem than victim or environmental characteristics. There is compelling evidence that perpetrator pathology and dependency particularly contribute to abuse occurrence. More controversial, and far less substantiated by empirical study, are such other risk factors as caregiver stress and the cycle of violence.

Perpetrator pathology can take several forms, with alcoholism and mental illness most commonly cited in the research literature. Various case control investigations suggest that alcoholism is frequently found among elder abuse perpetrators. More than nonabusers, elder abusers are likely to use alcohol, to consume it regularly, and to be self-identified or identified by others as having an alcohol problem. Although the precise relationship between alcoholism and elder abuse is unclear, several propositions have been offered. Alcoholism may provide an excuse for unacceptable behavior. It may remove inhibitions and increase impulse response. It may foster dependency between perpetrator and victim, leading to resentment and hostility. Actually, it may be that all three of these factors are linked. More specifically, mistreating an older adult breaches social taboos. Those who do so risk severe negative reaction, and perhaps criminal penalty. Alcoholism provides the vehicle for overcoming the taboo, committing the act, and rationalizing it away. It also provides the justification for the perpetrator being financially and otherwise dependent on the victim. This may be especially true when alcoholism is viewed as a disease, rather than self-selected behavior. Personal responsibility is less likely to be an expectation under these circumstances.

Mental illness and emotional distress on the part of the perpetrator are risk factors for elder abuse. Several studies have shown that perpetrators are more likely to have a diagnosed mental illness, especially depression, and more likely to have been psychiatrically hospitalized. They also are more likely to express emotional distress, often related to interaction with the victim. Besides depression, other forms of mental illness identified among perpetrators include schizophrenia, personality disorder, and anxiety. There also may be a complex interaction between mental illnesses like depression or anxiety and elder abuse, where one fosters the other, without a clear sense of which happened first.

Perpetrator dependency is most likely to involve financial or housing needs, although dependency can take other forms, including psychological and social. Perpetrators are frequently financially dependent on their victims for food and other life essentials. They may expect victims to support their habits, addictions, and dreams. Additionally, perpetrators often require the shelter provided by their victims. The reasons for this dependency are complex and may include personality traits such as selfishness and greed or may relate to the unemployment or underemployment of the perpetrator; indeed, because of alcoholism, mental illness, or other dysfunction, the perpetrator may be unemployable. The victim, as a family member, ordinarily feels obligated to offer assistance, only to find that it becomes the source of frustration and conflict. For example, an unemployed, alcoholic son may reside in the home of his eighty-year-old father and depend on the older man for food and spending money. Yet, the son becomes angry and abusive whenever his father tells him to stop drinking and get a job. The grandsons of the victim, who are the sons of the perpetrator, regularly visit, timing this with the arrival of their grandfather's Social Security and pension checks. They expect money to finance their drug habits and become abusive to both their father and grandfather when they are not given the amount demanded.

Other perpetrator characteristics have been suggested as risk factors for elder abuse. They include poor health and lack of empathy for older people. The most popular among the other suggested risk factors are caregiver stress and the cycle of violence, neither of which has been substantiated as a risk factor for elder abuse through research. Caregiver stress or burden was the favorite explanation for elder abuse during its early recognition as a health problem and an aspect of family violence, beginning in the mid- to late 1970s. The demands associated with providing care to frail or impaired older adults, the necessity of juggling multiple roles and responsibilities, and the lack of resources to accomplish caregiving tasks were seen as contributing to abuse occurrence. The appeal of naming stress as a risk factor was threefold:

1. Experiencing stress was nearly universal among caregivers and, perhaps as a result, blameless. This made elder abuse more understandable. It was something anyone was capable of inflicting, and since it was related to caregiving, it was amenable to resolution through supportive services.
2. Systems already were in place to provide supportive services for those experiencing stress. Nothing new had to be developed.
3. The origins of elder abuse were found in the frailty or impairment of older adults. This perception tended to reinforce long-standing American ageism and stereotyping of persons with disabilities. It also reinforced a "blame the victim" notion that was gaining momentum at the time. However, with rare exceptions, research has not found that elder abusers are more stressed or burdened by caregiving than nonabusers.

Called by various names, including transgenerational or intergenerational abuse, the cycle of violence remains an important explanation for child abuse. According to this theory, abused children grow up to be child abusers themselves. Applied to elder abuse, the explanation suggests that children abused by their parents or other relatives grow up to abuse these very people when they are vulnerable in later life. As of this writing, only a couple of studies have addressed this issue. Neither found evidence to support it. Still, the notion seems to have some popular appeal. Some scholars, as well as some elder abusers who had been victims of child abuse, would argue that being abused as a child can lead someone to commit elder abuse as an adult.

Environmental Risk Factors

The most important environmental risk factors are shared living arrangements and social isolation. Research and anecdotal evidence suggest that living alone is a protection against elder abuse. Conversely, sharing a residence with someone increases the likelihood of abuse occurrence. Co-residence promotes contact and, therefore, possible tension and conflict between people. The greater the proximity and intimacy of the contact and the longer it takes place, the greater the probability of discord and abuse when co-residence is combined with perpetrator and victim risk factors.

Social isolation is another validated elder abuse risk factor. Both victims and perpetrators tend to have fewer social contacts and lower levels of social support than those not affected by elder abuse. In some instances, isolation is perceived, as opposed to real. Still, for those convinced of this perception, the effect can be the same as if it were. They feel alone, without sources of necessary assistance or reassurance. Social isolation also means that others are not present to monitor interactions between perpetrator and victim, diffuse tensions, or identify and report abuse occurrence. Isolation can happen for any number of reasons, such as marginalized lifestyle, estrangement from family and friends, and poor health or disability. It also can be imposed upon the victim by the perpetrator as a form of psychological abuse, to create conditions for undue influence or to prevent abuse detection.

Cultural Risk Factors

Elder abuse is widely regarded as a global problem. However, there is some evidence to suggest that its forms, meanings, and prevalence may vary by country. In part, this may reflect differences in cultural norms, particularly as they relate to attitudes toward and treatment of vulnerable populations. Although unsubstantiated by research, some gerontologists believe that American values promoting violence, material acquisition, youth, and individualism contribute to elder abuse. Likewise, American attitudes of ageism and stereotyping of persons with disabilities create a climate in which older and disabled people are ignored or regarded as less than human. The American emphasis on personal and family responsibility also means that those incapable of taking care of themselves or their relatives have fewer sources of outside help available than in other developed countries. Moreover, using these outside sources of help can result in feelings of guilt or shame, because it contradicts cultural ideals.

Risk Factor Screening and Assessment

Detecting possible elder abuse is a precursor for preventing occurrence or reoccurrence and treating any manifestations of the problem. Screening or risk assessment instruments aid in the detection process. There are a number of instruments or tools that screen or assess elder abuse risk factors. Nearly all are developed for clinicians, such as physicians or social workers. Some are designed for use in specific clinical settings, like hospitals or home care agencies. Some also are focused on revealing only select forms of elder abuse, such as the Conflict Tactics Scales for physical or psychological abuse and the Elder Assessment Instrument for neglect or inadequate care.

Elder abuse screening or risk assessment instruments are important for three reasons. First, they provide assurance that important clues in elder abuse detection are not missed. Screening or risk assessment instruments are used to identify commonly recognized varieties of elder abuse and to describe their characteristics. Second, instruments provide a framework for gathering data on older adults and their circumstances. They foster a more complete and accurate collection of essential information about the elderly. Third, data gathered through instrumentation tends to be more useful for research and court proceedings.

Clinicians need to assume a greater role and responsibility in detection and reporting, because others who come in contact with elder abuse situations often cannot or do not do so. According to findings from the *2004 Survey of State Adult Protective Services* (National Committee for the Prevention of Elder Abuse and National Adult Protective Services Association 2005), 30 percent of elder abuse reports came from clinicians. This represents nearly twice the number that came from family members, three and a half times that

from friends and neighbors, and five times the number that came from the victims themselves.

Victims may not report elder abuse, even when it is severe and long-term, out of fear of retaliation, their wish to protect the perpetrator, the lack of ability to report, fear of possible institutionalization, or a sense that nothing can be done. In addition, victims may redefine behaviors as other than abusive based on cultural background. For instance, in focus group discussions with older adults and baby-boom caregivers representing four ethnic populations, Puerto Ricans were much less likely to emphasize psychological abuse as the worst thing that family can do to elderly members than were Japanese Americans (Anetzberger, Korbin, and Tomita 1996). Family, friends, and neighbors may fail to report elder abuse out of a desire to remain uninvolved, a belief in the sanctity of the family to handle its own concerns, suspicion of authorities, or a lack or awareness that help is available.

Although elder abuse can be detected in clinical settings, it is more commonly uncovered through observation or interview in the older adult's own home. It is here that the signs of abuse occurrence tend to bombard the senses—seeing burnt flesh, smelling urine-soaked mattresses, hearing words that belittle or condemn the victim. It is here, too, that elder abuse risk factors are most likely to be revealed in the separate and group interviews with the victim and perpetrator. Masking signs and risk factors is difficult where life circumstances are most abundantly clear, as they are at home. Therefore, it should not be surprising that clinicians most likely to detect and report elder abuse are those who see older adults as clients or patients at home. These include visiting nurses, social work case managers, and home care aides.

Screening or risk assessment instruments come in various formats, such as the checklist employed by the Indicators of Abuse Screen or the narrative guidelines developed for diagnostic and treatment purposes by the American Medical Association. Similarly, the content and methods of these instruments vary. Most include questions on demographics, common signs and risk factors for elder abuse, and degree of endangerment. Beyond this, instruments can be simple or complex in their level of inquiry. The HALF assessment, for example, examines simply *h*ealth, *a*ttitudes toward aging, *l*iving arrangements, and *f*inances. In contrast, the Screening Tools and Referral Protocol (STRP) combines three screening tools (one each for examples, signs, and risk factors of elder abuse) and a referral protocol with twenty-four extended tools that further assess such identified risk factors as functional ability and depression. The greater the complexity and comprehensiveness of the instrument, the more costly its application and the less likely it is to be used. Conversely, instruments that lack comprehensiveness may have insufficient detail for abuse detection. This is a particular issue for elder abuse, estimated to affect only one in twenty older adults.

Few elder abuse screening and risk assessment instruments have universal acceptance, and few have been tested for reliability and validity. Instrument accuracy and efficiency are important, given the demands on clinicians' time and the potential negative consequences attached to mistakes in case identification. To address these concerns, some clinical settings use two levels of detection, with different instruments employed at each level. A prescreen seeks to identify situations of elevated risk within large vulnerable populations. A screen attempts to narrow detection to situations of such high risk that investigation is warranted.

The use of screening and risk assessment instruments is enhanced within a multidisciplinary or interdisciplinary team. Some such teams are created by specific organizations for their own use. Other teams are formed by and for communities or elder abuse networks. However, all multidisciplinary teams provide a more holistic evaluation of elder abuse situations than can be accomplished by any single clinical discipline alone. Team assessments tend to be more complete because they combine the orientations and expertise of several disciplines, typically medicine, law, social work, and nursing at least.

Screening and risk assessment instruments help provide clinicians with the special skills needed for elder abuse detection, documentation, and case referral. These instruments can improve the capacity of clinicians to penetrate situations involving vulnerable older adults and find out what might be going on that indicates risk or danger. They also can sequence discovery so that it represents judicious use of scarce resources and improves the prospects for elder abuse identification.

GEORGIA J. ANETZBERGER

See also **Batterer Typology; Elder Abuse, Consequences of; Elder Abuse and Neglect: Training Issues for Professionals; Elder Abuse by Intimate Partners; Elder Abuse Perpetrated by Adult Children; Intimate Partner Violence, Forms of**

References and Further Reading

Anetzberger, Georgia J. "Caregiving: Primary Cause of Elder Abuse?" *Generations* 24, no. 2 (2000): 46–51.
———, ed. *The Clinical Management of Elder Abuse.* Binghamton, NY: Haworth Press, 2005.
Anetzberger, Georgia J., Jill E. Korbin, and Susan K. Tomita. "Defining Elder Mistreatment in Four Ethnic Groups across Two Generations." *Journal of Cross-Cultural Gerontology* 11 (1996): 187–212.
Baumhover, Lorin A., and S. Colleen Beall, eds. *Abuse, Neglect, and Exploitation of Older Persons: Strategies for Assessment and Intervention.* Baltimore, MD: Health Professions Press, 1996.
Bonnie, Richard J., and Robert B. Wallace, eds. *Elder Mistreatment: Abuse, Neglect, and Exploitation in an Aging America.* Washington, DC: National Academies Press, 2003.
Comijs, H. C., A. M. Pot, H. H. Smit, and C. Jonker. "Elder Abuse in the Community: Prevalence and Consequences." *Journal of the American Geriatrics Society* 46 (1998): 885–888.
Erlingsson, Christen L., Sharon L. Carson, and Britt-Inger Saveman. "Elder Abuse Risk Indications and Screening Questions: Results from a Literature Search and a Panel of Experts from Developed and Developing Countries." *Journal of Elder Abuse and Neglect* 15, no. 3-4 (2003): 185–203.
Fulmer, Terry, Lisa Guadagno, Carmel Bitondo Dyer, and Marie Therese Connolly. "Progress in Elder Abuse Screening and Assessment Instruments." *Journal of the American Geriatrics Society* 52, no. 2 (2004): 297–304.
Hansberry, Maria R., Elaine Chen, and Martin J. Gorbien. "Dementia and Elder Abuse." *Clinics in Geriatric Medicine* 21 (2005): 315–332.
National Center on Elder Abuse. *The National Elder Abuse Incidence Study.* Washington, DC: Author, 1998.
National Committee for the Prevention of Elder Abuse and National Adult Protective Services Association. *The 2004 Survey of State Adult Protective Services: Abuse of Adults 60 Years of Age and Older.* Washington, DC: National Center on Elder Abuse, 2005.
Rathbone-McCuan, Eloise, and Joan Hashimi. *Isolated Elders: Health and Social Intervention*, Rockville, MD: Aspen, 1982.
Teaster, Pamela B., Lisa Nerenberg, and Kim L. Stansbury. "A National Look at Elder Abuse Multidisciplinary Teams." *Journal of Elder Abuse and Neglect* 15, no. 3-4 (2003): 91–107.
Wolf, Rosalie S., Michael A. Godkin, and Karl A. Pillemer. "Maltreatment of the Elderly: A Comparative Analysis." *Pride Institute Journal of Long Term Home Health Care* 5, no. 4 (1986): 10–17.

ELDER ABUSE, CONSEQUENCES OF

Statutory and Organizational Responses to Elder Abuse

The Older Americans Act (OAA) became law on July 14, 1965. Among the OAA's primary objectives was advancing the physical, mental, and financial well-being of older persons living independently in the community and in group residential settings and institutions. Title VII of the OAA explicitly includes protection against abuse, neglect, and exploitation. Congress established the Administration on Aging (AoA), the only federal agency responsible for the administration of programs under the OAA, to accomplish the act's objectives. These programs include training medical professionals and law enforcement officers to identify and respond to elder abuse, providing technical assistance, creating state and local elder abuse prevention programs and coalitions, and conducting public awareness and educational promotions (AoA 1965). AoA funds the National Center on Elder Abuse (NCEA), which serves as a source of information and assistance on elder abuse (NCEA website 2006).

All fifty states have some form of elder abuse prevention laws. In general, states define elder abuse as abuse against a person aged sixty or older who is handicapped by the infirmities of aging or who has a physical or mental impairment which prevents the person from providing for his/her own care or protection and who is (1) being abused physically or (2) sexually, (3) exploited financially/materially, (4) neglected, including (5) self-neglect, or (6) has been abandoned (see Bonnie and Wallace 2002; Brandl and Cook-Daniels 2002). *Domestic elder abuse* (DEA) generally refers to any of these several forms of maltreatment of an older person by someone who has a special relationship with the elder. This may be a spouse, a sibling, a child, a friend, or a caregiver in the older person's own home or in the home of a caregiver (NCEA website 2006).

All fifty states have set up systems to report elder abuse. Generally, state Adult Protective Services (APS) receive and investigate reports of suspected elder abuse, including DEA. Mandatory reporting laws, including penalties for not reporting elder abuse, exist in forty-four states and the District of Columbia (Daly, Jogerst, Brinig, and Dawson 2003).

Depending on the state, certain types of professionals, including social workers and elderly service and health care providers, are required to report DEA to APS. As of this writing, there is no federal law on elder abuse in the United States.

The "Hidden" Nature of Domestic Elder Abuse

There are no official national DEA estimates for three reasons: (1) Definitions of elder abuse vary across states, (2) state statistics vary widely and there is no uniform reporting system, and (3) comprehensive national data are not collected (NCEA website 2006).

Despite these limitations, each year hundreds of thousands of older persons are abused, neglected, and exploited by family members (most likely spouses or children) or other caregivers (AoA website 2006). This finding is based largely on four sources: (1) state APS reports, (2) a review of the fifty-four elder abuse and domestic violence studies done between 1988 and 2002 (see Brandl and Cook-Daniels 2002), (3) the results from national studies such as the National Elder Abuse Incidence Study (NEAIS) (see NCEA 1998) or the National Crime Victimization Survey (Rennison and Rand 2003), and (4) a growing body of single-state studies using data from women living in domestic or institutional settings (see, for example, Burgess 2000; Mouton, Rodabough, Rovi, Hunt, Talamantes, Brzyski, and Burge 2004; Teaster and Roberto 2004; Teaster, Roberto, and Duke 2000; Zink, Fisher, Regan, and Pabst 2005). Even with these resources, many elder abuse advocates have long suspected that any studies estimating elder abuse, especially DEA, are likely underestimating the "true" amount of abuse elders experience (NCEA 1998).

Much of DEA is shrouded in secrecy for two primary reasons. First, today's generation of older women grew up in a time when values and beliefs about family were rapidly changing. Anetzberger (1997) and others (see Flanagan 2003; Zink, Jacobson, and Regan 2003) argue that the current generation of older women are more willing to endure abusive situations due to (1) a set of cultural and social values that often discounted their abuse or (2) having no socially or morally acceptable options for financial, legal, or emotional support. For example, among the themes Zink et al. (2003) uncovered in their interviews with thirty-six older women who experienced domestic violence was being told by police, clergy, and their own families to return to the marriage and "try to make it work." Second, older women rarely report their domestic violence to any authorities such as clergy, law enforcement, or doctors, or someone they know, such as a friend. Zink et al. (2005) found that of the women aged fifty-five and older who experienced physical and sexual abuse, 68.7 percent and 33.3 percent, respectively, had told anyone about their abuse. If they told anyone, it was most likely a friend. Older women, like their younger counterparts, are more reluctant to report for a variety of reasons, including fear, shame, and/or isolation, a belief that their experience is a taboo, and/or a financial and emotional dependence on their abuser (see Zink et al. 2005).

Physical and Mental Health Consequences of Domestic Elder Abuse

Even after years of elder abuse research, only recently have domestic violence and elder abuse researchers and advocates collaborated to examine domestic violence, including intimate partner violence (IPV), in the lives of the elderly (see Fisher, Zink, Rinto, Regan, Pabst, and Gothelf 2003). Both research efforts and advocacy attention have been increasingly drawn to the dynamic between aging women and their spouses/partners, as witnessed by an increasing number of published works documenting that IPV is among the most common categories of elder abuse (see Harris 1996; Penhale 2003).

There is a paucity of studies that explicitly examine DEA and its consequences on older victims' physical and mental health. Isolating the source of DEA can be a daunting measurement task, as DEA can be a continuation of lifelong domestic violence incidents perpetrated by a chronic batterer, may have begun at the onset of the aging process due to dementia or caregiver stress, may change from physical abuse to neglect, or may be a function of all of these factors. Wolf (1997) asserts that unlike domestic violence experienced by younger women, the consequences of elder abuse may be confounded with the aging process and diseases common among the elderly. Disentangling the causal nature of these relationships, she argues, is not only very difficult but costly.

Research has only recently examined the relationship between DEA and health consequences.

This published research has focused on older women, not older men. Two studies done in the United States focused on the effects on postmenopausal women, and both come to the same conclusion: Domestic violence takes a negative toll on the physical and mental health of older women. First, Mouton, Rovi, Furniss, and Lasser (1999), using data from the Women's Health Initiative, examined domestic violence and its effect on general health among a clinical-patient sample of 257 women aged fifty to seventy-nine. They reported that women who were threatened with physical abuse had significantly lower mental health scores on the Medical Outcomes Study Short Form 36 (Ware, Kosinski, and Keller 1994). Women who were physically abused also had lower physical health scores, but the results did not reach statistical significance. More recently, Zink et al. (2005), using a sample of older women from primary care practices in southwestern Ohio, found that women experiencing abuse (psychological/emotional, threatening, controlling, sexual, physical) reported a significantly higher number of chronic health conditions than nonabused women. Abused women also suffered significantly higher rates of depression and chronic pain than nonabused women.

Supportive of the results from these studies done in the United States are studies conducted in Australia (Schofield and Mishra 2004), Ireland, Italy, the United Kingdom (Ockleford et al. 2003), and the Netherlands (Comijs, Penninx, Knipscheer, and van Tilburg 1999). To illustrate, Comjis et al.'s (1999) study of psychological distress as a result of verbal, physical, and financial abuse and neglect examined both older men and older women in the Netherlands. Using a case-control design, participants were selected from a larger random sample of four five-year strata groups between the ages of sixty-five and eighty-four; nonabused elder controls were matched. The abused elders had significantly higher rates of psychological distress, lower emotional support, less mastery and feelings of self-efficacy, and a more passive and avoidant style of coping than their nonabused counterparts. Similar to Mouton et al. and Zink et al., this study was cross-sectional; consequently causal inference cannot be established.

Ultimately the most alarming consequence of elder abuse is mortality. In a prospective cohort study with a nine-year follow-up of a cohort of 2,812 community-dwelling adults aged sixty-five and older, Lachs, Williams, O'Brien, Pillemer, and Charlson (1998) reported that older people seen for elder mistreatment had significantly higher mortality than self-neglecting or nonabused subjects at the end of the study. Those who suffered self-neglect also had significantly higher mortality than those with no substantiated abuse reports.

A second study of morbidity and mortality, Shields, Hunsaker, and Hunsaker (2004), conducted a ten-year retrospective chart review of morbidity and mortality among elders age sixty and over in a large metropolitan area of Kentucky and Indiana. They reported that of the 1,099 autopsy cases, fifty-two victims age sixty and over were homicide victims and twenty-two persons age sixty and over were victims of neglect. They found that 50 percent of the gunshot victims died at the hand of a spouse or other family member; however, one case involved a wife who shot and killed her husband after being beaten and then doused in Drano by him. Of the twenty-two persons who suffered from neglect, 31.8 percent were living with a family member and 9.1 percent were alone with a family member at the time of death. Nearly 82 percent of the neglect cases were found, postmortem, to have physical injuries, including abrasions and contusions.

Programmatic and Service Consequences

DEA is often hidden from the advocacy efforts of the aging, domestic violence, and medical communities and the investigations of the APS and law enforcement (see Fisher et al. 2003). DEA resources, including domestic violence shelters and hotlines, are not tailored to the specific needs of older abused victims, little outreach is done to older domestic violence victims, and cross-training of domestic violence and aging experts is infrequent (Fisher Zink, Pabst, Regan, and Rinto 2004; Vinton 1992; Vinton, Altholz, and Lobell-Boesch 1997). Consequently, nationally, services and programs targeted specifically to DEA victims are woefully lacking.

There are very few elder domestic violence support groups across a limited number of states, with Wisconsin having the most support groups (eleven) for older abused women (Brandl, Hebert, Rozwadowski, and Spangler 2003). In Florida, as part of the Elder Domestic Violence Collaborative Project, interagency collaboration has led to the development of model policies for making their domestic violence centers more elder ready and a training manual for elder domestic violence case managers (Vinton 2003).

Research has shown that the health care needs of older DEA victims are largely not routinely addressed. Many health care providers, including primary care physicians, do not routinely screen for IPV among older patients (Kennedy 2004; Zink, Jacobson, Regan, and Pabst 2004).

Conclusion

Demographic projections signal that elder abuse, notably DEA, will remain a policy issue for some time. The elderly population is expected to increase from approximately thirty-six million today to about eighty-five million by the year 2050, in which over 56 percent will be older women (U.S. Census Bureau 2004). The projected increase in the number of older women will likely increase the number of DEA victims. DEA will continue to take negative tolls on the health and well-being of our elders and society if the current level and content of interventions and responses provided by the health care, law enforcement, domestic violence, and aging communities are not tailored to the needs of aging adults and their perpetrators.

SAUNDRA L. REGAN and BONNIE S. FISHER

See also **Elder Abuse, Assessing the Risks of; Elder Abuse and Neglect: Training Issues for Professionals; Elder Abuse by Intimate Partners; Elder Abuse Perpetrated by Adult Children; Neurological and Physiological Impact of Abuse**

References and Further Reading

Administration on Aging. *Older Americans Act. Public Law 89-73*, 1965. http://aoa.gov/about/legbudg/oaa/oaa_1965.pdf (accessed August 17, 2006).
——— website. http://www.aoa.gov (accessed August 17, 2006).
Anetzberger, G. "Elderly Adult Survivors of Family Violence: Implications for Clinical Practice." *Violence Against Women* 3, no. 5 (1997): 499–514.
Bonnie, R. J., and R. B. Wallace, eds. *Elder Mistreatment: Abuse, Neglect, and Exploitation in an Aging America.* Washington, DC: National Academies Press, 2002.
Brandl, B., and L. Cook-Daniels. "Domestic Abuse in Later Life," 2002. VAWnet Research Forum. http://www.vawnet.org.
Brandl, B., M. Hebert, J. Rozwadowski, and D. Spangler. "Feeling Safe, Feeling Strong: Support Groups for Older Abused Women." *Violence Against Women* 9, no. 12 (2003): 1490–1503.
Burgess, A., and A. Frederick. "Sexual Violence and Trauma: Policy Implications for Nursing." *Nursing and Health Policy Review* 1, no. 1 (2002): 17–36.
Comijs, H. C., B. Penninx, K. Knipscheer, and W. van Tilburg. "Psychological Distress in Victims of Elder Mistreatment: The Effects of Social Support and Coping." *Journals of Gerontology: Series B, Psychological Sciences and Social Sciences* 54, no. 4 (1999). P240–P245.
Daly, J. M., G. J. Jogerst, M. F. Brinig, and J. D. Dawson. "Mandatory Reporting: Relationship of APS Statute Language on State Reported Elder Abuse." *Journal of Elder Abuse and Neglect* 15, no. 2 (2003): 1–21.
Fisher, B. S., T. M. Zink, S. R. Pabst, S. L. Regan, and B. A. Rinto. "Service and Programming for Older Abused Women: The Ohio Experience." *Journal of Elder Abuse and Neglect* 15, no. 2 (2004): 67–83.

Fisher, B. S., T. M. Zink, B. A. Rinto, S. L. Regan, S. R. Pabst, and E. J. Gothelf. "Overlooked Issues during the Golden Years: Domestic Violence and Intimate Partner Violence against Older Women." *Violence Against Women* 9, no. 12 (2003): 1409–1416.

Flanagan, A. Y. *Elder Abuse: Cultural Contexts and Implications*. Sacramento, CA: CME Resource, 2003.

Harris, S. "For Better or for Worse: Spouse Abuse Grown Old." *Journal of Elder Abuse and Neglect* 8, no. 1 (1996): 1–30.

Kennedy, R. D. "Elder Abuse and Neglect: The Experience, Knowledge and Attitudes of Primary Care Physicians." *Family Medicine* 37, no. 7 (2005): 481–485.

Lachs, M. S., C. S. Williams, S. O'Brien, K. A. Pillemer, and M. E. Charlson. "The Mortality of Elder Mistreatment." *Journal of the American Medical Association* 280, no. 5 (1998): 428–432.

Mouton, C. P., R. J. Rodabough, S. Rovi, J. L. Hunt, M. A. Talamantes, R. G. Brzyski, and S. K. Burge. "Prevalence and 3-Year Incidence of Abuse among Postmenopausal Women." *American Journal of Public Health* 94, no. 4 (2004): 605–612.

Mouton, C. P., S. Rovi, K. Furniss, and N. Lasser. "The Associations between Health and Domestic Violence in Older Women: Results of a Pilot Study." *Journal of Women's Health and Gender Based Medicine* 8, no. 9 (1999): 1173–1178.

National Center on Elder Abuse. *The National Elder Abuse Incidence Study: Final Report*, 1998. http://www.elderabusecenter.org/default.cfm?p=nis.cfm.

———— website. http://www.elderabusecenter.org/default.cfm (accessed August 17, 2006).

Ockleford, E., Y. Barnes-Holmes, R. Moricelli, A. Morjaria, F. Scocchera, F. Furniss, C. Sdogati, and D. Barnes-Holmes. "Mistreatment Of Older Women in Three European Countries: Estimated Prevalence and Service Responses." *Violence Against Women* 9, (2003): 1453–1464.

Penhale, B. "Older Women, Domestic Violence, and Elder Abuse: A Review of Commonalities, Differences and Shared Approaches." *Journal of Elder Abuse and Neglect* 15, no. 3/4 (2003): 163–183.

Pillemer, K. "Ten (Tentative) Truths about Elder Abuse." *Journal of Health and Human Resource Administration* 12, no. 4 (1990): 464–483.

Pillemer, K., and D. Finkelhor. "The Prevalence of Elder Abuse: A Random Sample Survey." *The Gerontologist* 28, no. 1 (1988): 51–57.

Rennison, C., and M. Rand. "Nonlethal Intimate Partner Violence against Women: A Comparison of Three Age Cohorts." *Violence Against Women* 9, no. 12 (2003): 1417–1428.

Schofield, M. J., and G. D. Mishra. "Three Year Health Outcomes among Older Women at Risk of Elder Abuse: Women's Health Australia." *Quality of Life Research* 13 (2004): 1043–1052.

Shields, L. B., D. M. Hunsaker, and J. C. Hunsaker. "Abuse and Neglect: A Ten Year Review of Mortality and Morbidity in our Elders in a Large Metropolitan Area." *Journal of Forensic Science* 49, no. 1 (2004): 122–127.

Teaster, P. B., and K. A. Roberto. "Sexual Abuse of Older Adults: APS Cases and Outcomes." *The Gerontologist* 44, no. 6 (2004): 788–796.

Teaster, P. B., K. A. Roberto, and J. O. Duke. "Sexual Abuse of Older Adults: Preliminary Findings of Cases in Virginia." *Journal of Elder Abuse and Neglect* 12, no. 3/4 (2000): 1–16.

U.S. Census Bureau. "U.S. Interim Projections by Age, Sex, Race and Hispanic Origin," 2004. http://www.census.gov/ipc/www/usinterimproj.

Vinton, L. "Battered Women's Shelters and Older Women: The Florida Experience." *Journal of Family Violence* 7, no. 1 (1992): 63–72.

————. "A Model Collaborative Project Toward Making Domestic Violence Centers Elder Ready." *Violence Against Women* 9, no. 12 (2003): 1504–1513.

Vinton, L., J. A. Altholz, and T. Lobell-Boesch. "A Five Year Follow-Up Study of Domestic Violence Programming for Older Battered Women." *Journal of Women and Aging* 9, no. 1/2 (1997): 3–15.

Ware, J., M. Kosinski, and S. Keller. *SF36 Physical and Mental Health Summary Scales: A User's Manual*. Boston: The Health Institute 1994.

Wolf, R. "Elder Abuse and Neglect: Causes and Consequences." *Journal of Geriatric Psychiatry*, 30, no. 1 (1997): 153–174.

Zink, T., B. S. Fisher, S. Regan, and S. Pabst. "The Prevalence and Incidence of Intimate Partner Violence in Older Women in Primary Care." *Journal of General Internal Medicine* 20 (2005): 884–888.

Zink, T., C. J. Jacobson, and S. Regan. "Cohort, Period and Aging Effects: A Qualitative Study of Women's Reasons for Remaining in Abusive Relationships." *Violence Against Women* 9, no. 12 (2003): 1429–1441.

Zink, T., C. J. Jacobson, S. Regan, and S. Pabst. "Hidden Victims: The Health Care Needs and Experiences of Older Women in Abusive Relationships." *Journal of Women's Health* 13, no. 8 (2004): 898–908.

ELDER ABUSE AND NEGLECT: TRAINING ISSUES FOR PROFESSIONALS

Elder abuse in community settings (referred to as *domestic elder abuse*) has been the last form of family violence to receive multidisciplinary professional interest. Depending on the source, it is thought that the numbers of abused elders in America annually range from 500,000 to 2 million. The current literature suggests that domestic elder abuse is a complex phenomenon, which may or may not involve a malicious perpetrator and may also present severe health issues, even death, to those older people who self-neglect their own needs.

Elder abuse presents as physical abuse (any action by another that produces pain or injury to the older person), sexual abuse (any intimate behavior that is undesired or lacks competent consent by the older person), and emotional abuse (inducement of fear, intimidation, or a lowering of self-esteem to punish or control the older person). It also includes the financial exploitation of an elder (using the elder's goods, income, and assets for purposes other than the safety, benefit, and enjoyment of that elderly person). Elder abuse may be in the form of intentional or unintentional neglect at the hands of another or by elders themselves (self-neglect).

The U.S. government, although philosophically supportive of protecting older people from abuse and neglect, provides little national funding for protective services, professional training, and research opportunities (as compared with its provisions for such services regarding other forms of family violence) that would enhance the professional and public understanding of this issue. Thus, the incentive and cost for elder abuse training is usually the responsibility of those organizations and professionals who identify it as a priority and are willing to incorporate the costs into their own budgets.

There are several professional groups in need of training: (1) elder protective service professionals, often referred to as Adult Protective Services (APS) workers, who act as the responsible agents to accept reports of elder abuse and provide immediate assessment and intervention, (2) professionals who interface with the elderly as their client population (e.g., health care professionals such as physicians, nurses, therapists, and nutritionists; social workers and counselors; first responders such as fire-department and police personnel and emergency medical teams; paraprofessionals such as nurses aides), and (3) community service providers (e.g., volunteers who visit the homebound; meals-on-wheels drivers servicing abused or neglected elders). The intensity and scope of training varies with the professional duties, ethics, and sanctioned responsibilities to citizen safety.

This article will identify training themes necessary for a wide variety of professionals who interface with the aged population; it does not address the needs of paraprofessionals or volunteers.

Professional Knowledge of Reporting Responsibility

Clearly there are certain professionals who by nature of their work carry a professional obligation to know the law and file abuse and neglect reports. Typically this includes health care providers, social workers, counselors, and first responders. Some states are considering or have already introduced legislation that would require banking or financial agents (investment firms) to also be identified reporters of financial exploitation. Consequently, professionals must know the requirements of the state law where they practice or the laws of other states in which their clients may reside.

Elder abuse laws exist in every state and in the District of Columbia. Yet, these laws are not consistent in naming expected reporters, whether reports are mandatory and carry a legal consequence if not made, where and to whom to file reports, whether only "vulnerable" elders are protected, and the authority of APS agency to intervene. All state laws, however, are in agreement that the professional does not need to *confirm* if abuse or neglect is occurring, but only needs to *suspect* that it may be occurring. The designated agency receiving the report, typically APS, has the responsibility of substantiating the allegation while preserving the confidentiality of the reporter should he or she request anonymity. Additionally, all laws "protect" the reporter from being sued by the alleged victim or family as long as the report was made without malice.

Professionals have an ethical obligation to know what their legal responsibility is to their clients; therefore, they cannot use the excuse of ignorance of their state law for not filing a report. Several organizations have websites that are easy to access and can advise professionals as to the appropriate course of action. Particularly helpful and accurate websites are those of the National Center on Elder Abuse (NCEA) and the American Bar Association Commission on Law and Aging (ABANET). However, every state's Attorney General's Office would be able to provide professionals with the requirements of the law. Training specific to state law may also be received from the APS agency of that state. Additionally, many police departments would have protocols to accept reports of suspected abuse and refer them to the appropriate agency.

Assessment Skills

Requiring or encouraging professionals to report elder abuse and neglect does not provide the needed assessment skills to know who should be reported. Thus professionals must understand who may be perpetrators of abusive and neglectful actions and what the key factors are in assessing for possible abuse when interfacing with elders and their family members.

Professionals need to assess the older person's family relationships. This is because most elder abuse and neglect occurs at the hands of relatives—those very people assumed to have an interest in loving and caring for the older person. Professionals may not realize that it is the relative's needs that may motivate his or her involvement with the elder person. Therefore, exploring the reasons behind the family involvement and the older person's perception of that relationship is important information. For example, many older people are abused because their relatives are in need of the resources of the older person; the abuse is a tool used for controlling the older person's resources. For example, a homeless relative may seek shelter from an older, frail aunt; or an alcoholic adult son might steal his father's money because he cannot maintain a job. In both cases the perpetrator may threaten to

hurt, or actually physically abuse, the older person to keep control of the elder's home or money. Therefore, when a health professional assesses that an older person does not live alone, assumptions should not be made that the arrangement is for the care of the elder. Follow-up questions are often needed, such as: "Was it your idea that your granddaughter and her children move in with you? How much work has this created for you? Are you still able to use the rooms in your home or have you been restricted to one room?" Such questions will help the professional ascertain if the relationship is mutual and helpful or if it is coercive and possibly abusive.

Relatives who accompany older people to doctor appointments or emergency rooms and insist on being present throughout the examination may certainly be acting out of concern. But professionals need to be aware that relatives perpetrating abuse or neglect may request to remain with the elder because they fear that the older person will ask for help or share information that may expose the abuse or neglect. Therefore, professionals should insist on some time alone with older persons in order to ask questions about their well-being. Sometimes an older person is able to articulate some concerns by answering simple questions the professional might ask, such as: "Are you ever afraid that your daughter would purposefully hurt you?" or "I noticed that your daughter was upset when I asked her to leave us alone during this exam. Do you know why that would upset her?" Second marriages or late first marriages should be assessed for financial exploitation or for issues of domestic violence, including rape. Professionals should take an interest in asking about the adjustment to a new partner and if anything is making him or her feel uncomfortable or unsafe. Oftentimes older people are embarrassed by what they consider to have been poor choices, and consequently do not volunteer information unless the professional makes the time to show concern and is unhurried in listening to their responses.

Consistent with understanding the social network of the older person is also assessing for isolation. Isolation is a key factor in abuse and neglect and may present in either of two forms: the isolation that happens as one becomes frailer and physically or mentally less competent (e.g., losing the privilege of driving a car) or the isolation imposed on one person by another. The former may indicate a self-neglect scenario or the possible vulnerability to victimization. The latter may indicate a currently abusive or neglectful situation with isolation as a means of the perpetrator to control the victim.

Physical assessment of abuse should include the appropriateness of clothing with regard to the weather, as clothing may be used to cover cuts, burns, or bite marks. Examining the scalp not only for cleanliness but also for bruising due to hair pulling is necessary. Asking older people if they are able to fill their prescriptions, have groceries delivered, food prepared, and heat or air conditioning available helps in assessing environmental responsiveness to their needs. Health care providers, mental health professionals, and institutions of health care (e.g., hospitals, adult day-care facilities) should have standard assessment tools to screen for possible abuse and neglect.

Interfacing with Victims of Abuse and Neglect

For many professionals, understanding their reporting duties and becoming competent in assessing for possible abuse and neglect will be sufficient. But for professionals employed by APS agencies, intensive training is needed so that workers can provide clients with protection while preserving their autonomy (self-determination). APS professionals use many community services, such as meals-on-wheels and homemakers, for abused and neglected clients. However, such services were designed for frail elders in need of health supports, and not as supports for abuse and neglect monitoring. Agencies providing services to victims of elder abuse may not know how to provide services in an atmosphere where the perpetrator still visits or resides with the victim. Therefore, part of the training for APS professionals is learning the limitations of home services and how to develop more substantial services to meet client needs.

Several core competencies are necessary in elder abuse intervention work: understanding self-determination, completing mental competency and level-of-risk assessments, understanding the normal aging process, and knowing about ethnic and cultural norms of the victim and the victim's family.

Professionals need to fully understand self-determination in the context of vulnerable people whose decisional abilities may be compromised because abuse and neglect produce fear and hopelessness in their victims. The ability to access competent professionals to conduct mental competency assessments while simultaneously assessing for sensory changes or mental health issues is necessary. For example, a good competency exam should be done over several interviews, in various settings, and at different times of the day in order to be accurate. Some elder abuse experts believe that evaluating the victim's level of risk is more appropriate than competency evaluations for determining the ability of abused victims to make competent choices regarding their abusive situations.

Additionally, ethnic background and cultural norms influence the decisional process. For example, if an elderly woman of Asian heritage always depended on her husband to make difficult and complex decisions, then, although competent, she may neither have the practical skills, motivation, or cultural supports to make her own independent decisions.

The inability of clients to be compliant with agency objectives is often used by home-care agencies as the justification to discontinue services to very vulnerable people. For example, if the meals-on-wheels provider cannot navigate the garbage at the kitchen door and the client refuses or is unable to clean it, the service could be discontinued. Or if an abusive alcoholic adult child resides within the elder's home and the elderly parent refuses to ask the adult child to leave the residence, the homemaker/health aide might discontinue services. Understanding violence, maladaptive behaviors, alcoholism and enabling relationships, and compulsive behaviors to hoard junk or even animals (e.g., multiple cats) are all necessary training issues for professionals servicing abused and neglected elders.

Lastly, training is necessary for professionals servicing older neglected and abused elders who still rely on or wish to maintain contact with abusive family members. Older people are often unwilling to press charges against their children or to deny them contact. Learning how to supervise visits of former and perhaps current perpetrators of elder abuse is necessary, as is assessing, treating, and meeting the needs of perpetrators to reduce or eliminate their reasons to abuse the victims. Additionally, knowledge about actions that constitute crimes and when to engage the legal system is necessary training.

Conclusion

Elder abuse requires an array of core competencies: understanding the laws in respective states, assessing for abuse and neglect, learning how to interview elders who have sensory impairments, and understanding how ethical principles of self-determination, client abandonment, and providing protection work together. Professional competency in understanding the older person's cultural, ethnic, and family system is critical for presenting solutions and negotiating the client's decisions with level of risk. Training may come from a variety of sources,

ELDER ABUSE AND NEGLECT: TRAINING ISSUES FOR PROFESSIONALS

including accessing the literature on elder abuse and neglect. But as demonstrated in this brief essay, elder abuse and neglect is complex and requires training that is multidisciplinary and inter-active, allowing professionals to present difficult cases and explore possible solutions. Professionals interfacing with older people must insist that their agencies of employment, professional associations, community organizations, government funding, and local universities and colleges provide and in-clude ongoing training in assessment and interven-tion skills for working with clients vulnerable to elder abuse and neglect.

L. RENÉ BERGERON

See also **Assessing Risk in Domestic Violence Cases; Caregiver Violence against People with Disabilities; Elder Abuse, Assessing the Risks of; Elder Abuse, Consequences of; Elder Abuse by Intimate Partners; Elder Abuse Perpetrated by Adult Children; Health-care Professionals' Roles in Identifying and Responding to Domestic Violence**

References and Further Reading

American Bar Association Commission on Law and Aging. http://www.abanet.org/aging.
Anetzberger, G. J. "Caregiving: Primary Cause of Elder Abuse?" *Generations* 24, no. 2 (2000): 46–52.
———. "Elder Abuse Identification and Referral: The Importance of Screening Tools and Referral Proto-cols." *Journal of Elder Abuse and Neglect* 13, no. 2 (2001): 3–21.
Bergeron, L. René. "Servicing the Needs of Elder Abuse Victims." *Policy and Practice* 58, no. 3, (2000): 40–45.
———. "Elder Abuse: Clinical Assessment and Obligation to Report." In *Health Consequences of Abuse in the Family: A Clinical Guide for Evidence-Based Practice,* edited by Kathleen A. Kendall-Tackett. Washington, DC: American Psychological Association, 2004, pp. 109–128.
———. "Abuse of Elderly Women in Family Relation-ships." In *Handbook of Women, Stress, and Trauma,* edited by Kathleen A. Kendall-Tackett. New York: Brunner-Routledge, 2005, pp. 141–157.
Bergeron, L. René, and B. Gray. "Ethical Dilemmas of Reporting Suspected Elder Abuse." *Social Work* 48, no. 1 (2003): 96–105.
Brandl, B., and J. Raymond. "Unrecognized Elder Abuse Victims." *Journal of Case Management* 6, no. 2 (1997): 62–68.
Clearinghouse on Abuse and Neglect of the Elderly (CANE) website. http://www.elderabusecenter.org/default.cfm?p=cane.cfm.
Dunlop, B., M. Rothman, K. Condon, K. Hebert, and I. Martinez. "Elder Abuse: Risk Factors and Use of Case Data to Improve Policy and Practice." *Journal of Elder Abuse and Neglect* 12, no. 3/4 (2000): 95–122.
Dyer, C. B., V. N. Pavlik, K. P. Murphy, and D. J. Hyman. "The High Prevalence of Depression and Dementia in Elder Abuse or Neglect." *Journal of American Geriatric Society* 48 (2000): 205–208.
Fisher, J. W., and C. B. Dyer. "The Hidden Health Menace of Elder Abuse: Physicians Can Help Patients Surmount Intimate Partner Violence." *Postgraduate Medicine On-line* 113, no. 4 (2003). http://www.postgradmed.com/issues/2003/04_03/apr03.htm.
Freed, P., and V. K. Drake. "Mandatory Reporting of Abuse: Practical, Moral, and Legal Issues for Psychiatric Home Healthcare Nurses." *Issues in Mental Health Nursing* 20, no. 4 (1999): 423–436.
Fulmer, T. "Elder Mistreatment: Progress in Community Detection and Intervention." *Family and Community Health* 14, no. 2 (1991): 26–34.
Gerlock, A. "Health Impact of Domestic Violence." *Issues in Mental Health Nursing* 20, no. 4 (1999): 373–385.
Harris, S. "For Better or Worse: Spouse Abuse Grown Old." *Journal of Elder Abuse and Neglect* 8, no. 1 (1996): 1–33.
Jordan, Lisa C. "Elder Abuse and Domestic Violence: Overlapping Issues and Legal Remedies." *American Journal of Family Law* 15, no. 2 (2001): 147–156.
Kosberg, J. I., and J. L. Garcia. "Common and Unique Themes on Elder Abuse from a World-wide Perspec-tive." *Journal of Elder Abuse and Neglect* 6, no. 3/4 (1995): 183–197.
Krug, E., J. Mercy, L. Dahlberg, and A. Zwi. "The World Report on Violence and Health." *The Lancet* 360 (2002): 1083–1088.
Loue, S. "Elder Abuse and Neglect in Medicine and Law." *Journal of Legal Medicine* 22 (2001): 159–209.
National Center on Elder Abuse (NCEA) website. http://www.elderabusecenter.org.
NEAIS (National Elder Abuse Incidence Study). *Final Re-port.* Prepared for the Administration for Children and Families, and the Administration on Aging in the U.S., Department of Health and Human Services. Washing-ton, DC: National Center on Elder Abuse, 1998.
Penhale, B. "Bruises on the Soul: Older Women, Domestic Violence, and Elder Abuse." *Journal of Elder Abuse and Neglect* 11, no. 1 (1999): 1–22.
Peterson, M., and B. E. C. Paris. "Elder Abuse and Neglect: How to Recognize Warning Signs and Intervene." *Ger-iatrics* 50, no. 4 (1995): 47–52.
Ramsey-Klawsnik, Holly. "Elder Abuse Offenders. Types of Offenders: Comparison of Offenders." *Generations* 24, no. 2 (2000): 17–23.
Reis, M., and D. Nahmiash. "Abuse of Seniors: Personality, Stress, and Other Indicators." *Journal of Mental Health and Aging* 3, no. 3 (1997): 337–356.
Schiamberg, L. B., and D. Gans. "Elder Abuse by Adult Children: An Applied Ecological Framework for Under-standing Contextual Risk Factors and the Intergenera-tional Character of Quality of Life." *International Journal of Aging and Human Development* 50, no. 4 (2000): 329–359.
Shock, L. P. "Responding to Evidence of Abuse in the Elderly." *Journal of American Academy of Physician Assistants* 13, no. 6 (2000): 73–79.
Sijuwade, P. O. "Cross-Cultural Perspectives on Elder Abuse as a Family Dilemma." *Social Behavior and Per-sonality* 23 (1995): 247–252.
Teaster, Patricia. *A Response to the Abuse of Vulnerable Adults: The 2000 Survey of State Adult Protection*

Services. National Committee for the Prevention of Elder Abuse, the National Association of Adult Protective Services Administrators, the National Center of Elder Abuse. Washington, DC: National Center of Elder Abuse, 2003.

Vinton, Linda. "Battered Women's Shelters and Older Women: The Florida Experience." *Journal of Family Violence* 7, no. 1 (1992): 63–72.

Wei, Gina S., and Jerome E. Herbers. "Reporting Elder Abuse: A Medical, Legal, and Ethical Overview." *Journal of the American Medical Women's Association* 59, no. 4 (2004): 248–254.

Welfel, E. R., P. R. Danzinger, and S. Santoro. "Mandated Reporting of Abuse/Maltreatment of Older Adults: A Primer for Counselors." *Journal of Counseling and Development* 71, no. 3 (2000): 284–293.

ELDER ABUSE BY INTIMATE PARTNERS

Introduction

Elder abuse is one of the more controversial subjects in domestic violence. Many people do not want to hear about it, deny its existence, and do not know what to do when confronted with it. Researchers and academics cannot agree among themselves about the definition or extent of elder abuse. The term "elder abuse" was first used during congressional hearings in the late 1970s, when Congress was examining the mistreatment of the elderly in the United States. This article will examine various aspects of elder abuse by intimate partners.

Definition

Some scholars use the term *elder abuse* to refer to the abuse of persons over the age of sixty-five, while others who use the term include those who are much younger. Some well-respected researchers use the term to signify abuse perpetrated by someone who shares a home or residence with the elder victim, while other well-known researchers use the term to include acts of abuse that occur in an institutional setting. It is clear that attempts to reach agreement on the definition of elder abuse have generated controversy and debate. What is significant about elder abuse, and what makes it different from other forms of domestic violence, is that the age, psychological condition, and perspective of the elder victim in many cases make this abuse harsher and more life threatening.

For purposes of this essay, elder abuse will be defined as conduct that results in physical, sexual, psychological, or material neglect, harm, or injury to an elder (Wallace 2005); an "elder" being defined as someone who is sixty-five years of age or older. Physical harm includes inflicting bruises, scratches, cuts, or burns, or other acts that result in a nonaccidental injury by a person who has care, custody, or control of an elder. Sexual harm includes either nonconsensual direct or indirect sexual contact with or sexual exploitation of an elder. Neglect is the negligent treatment of an elder by a caretaker that may cause harm or threatened harm by the caretaker. Self-neglect occurs when an elder acts in such a manner that threatens his or her own health or safety. Psychological or emotional abuse includes acts or omissions that are judged by community standards and professional expertise to be psychologically damaging to the elder. Material abuse includes the direct or indirect use or exploitation of an elder's financial or material resources. This definition includes elders who are abused at home or in an institutional setting.

An intimate partner is usually viewed as someone who is married to or cohabiting with another person. However, with elder abuse, many times the abuser may be a child or relative of the elder. The elder's spouse or cohabiting mate may have predeceased the elder, leaving him or her with no other caretaker than another family member. Therefore, "intimate partner," for purposes of this essay, will be defined as any family member, by blood or marriage, who assumes primary caretaking responsibilities for the elder.

Extent

The extent of elder abuse, like other forms of domestic violence, is subject to continuing debate, since it occurs behind closed doors or in private. The National Elder Abuse Incidence Study (NEAIS) was the first nationwide study of elder abuse. It estimated that approximately a half million elders were abused or neglected in 1996. This study also set forth the proposition that for every reported case, there were at least five cases that were not reported. More recent studies estimate that one in fourteen incidents come to attention of the authorities (Pillemer and Finkelhor 1988). There have been other studies regarding the extent of elder abuse that set the number of cases at over two million per year. The complexity of defining elder abuse and the different reporting requirements in various states compound the task of accurately estimating its prevalence. Regardless of the actual numbers, it is obvious that elder abuse is a serious problem that must be addressed by society.

Theories or Reasons for Abuse

Why would an intimate partner commit these types of acts? Researchers and scholars do not have the answer to that question, but they do have some general information that may help in understanding why an intimate partner would commit elder abuse.

Cycle of Violence Theory

The Cycle of Violence theory is also known as the Intergeneration Transmission of Violence theory. This theory holds that violent behavior is learned within the family and bequeathed from one generation to the next. For example, if a child is raised in a family where there is abuse, the child may grow up to likewise become an abuser. According to the Cycle of Violence theory, the childhood survivor of a violent family thus develops a tendency toward violence as an adult. This theory fails to explain how some children who were raised in abusive families can grow up to not be abusive.

Psychopathology Theory

This theory is based upon the belief that abusers of the elderly have some sort of mental disorder that causes them to be abusive. Some researchers have found psychopathology present in abusers charged with physical and verbal abuse of elders, while others have found it lacking.

Social Exchange Theory

The Social Exchange theory assumes that dependency in relationships contributes to elder abuse. One aspect of this theory holds that the victim's

increased dependence on the abuser results in acts of abuse. This theory holds that when there is a loss of mutual sharing of resources between the elder and the intimate caretaker, the quality of the relationship degenerates. This results in the intimate partner perceiving the relationship as unfair, with an increase in hostility toward the elder. This imbalance may cause some intimate partners to abuse their elder victims.

Neutralization Theory

This theory was originally developed to explain juvenile delinquency (Sykes and Matza 1978). It holds that to commit crimes, the delinquents must develop techniques of neutralization. These techniques include denial of responsibility, denial of injury, denial of the status of the victim, condemnation of the condemners, and appeal to higher loyalty. Tomita (1990) has applied this theory to elder abuse and believes it may be employed by the intimate abuser to justify his or her acts.

Family Stress Theory

This is one of the most popular theories about the cause of elder abuse. The Family Stress theory is based upon the premise that providing care for the elder induces stress for the intimate partner. This stress may include the economic hardship of providing for medical care for the elder, the increased cost of having the elder live with family members, and payment for special transportation or other needs for the elder. This stress may also include loss of sleep due to getting up during the night to take care of the elder's needs and intrusions into the family privacy and activities.

There is no one accepted theory or reason that explains why intimate partners abuse elders. Scholars are still researching the causes and dynamics of elder abuse. Unfortunately, at this time, there is no "cure" for elder abuse. Therefore, it is important to understand the different types of elder abuse committed by intimate partners.

Types of Abuse by Intimate Partners

Abuse by intimate partners is one of the most controversial topics within the area of elder abuse. The definitions already given provide a broad overview of this form of abuse. This section will discuss these acts in more detail.

Physical Abuse

In some cases, the elder may not remember how, why, or when the abuse occurred. The victim may not disclose the abuse to innocent caretakers or other members of the family. Therefore it is essential that professionals in the field carefully document any unusual or unexplained physical injuries.

Common injuries may include bruising. Any unusual bruises that form a pattern or shape of another object such as a belt, cord, or hand should be investigated. Bruising that occurs after visits with relatives should also be carefully examined. Bite marks should immediately be reported to the authorities. These should raise immediate questions on when, how, and why the intimate partner was last alone with the elder. Bite marks are very seldom accidental in nature.

Burns are also possible indicators of physical abuse. Types include cigarette burns, burns with distinctive shapes such as that of a stovetop grate, and immersion burns which occur when the elder is held under or in extremely hot water. Fractures are common in elder abuse because as a person ages, bones become more brittle. However, multiple injuries to the head, multiple fractures or spinal fractures (where the bone is turned and broken in a circular pattern) should be reported and questions asked of the caretaker regarding the injury. Lacerations, abrasions, or hair loss can also be a sign of elder abuse. It is also true that hair loss can occur with aging for both men and women, and elders can bump against a wall and receive a laceration or abrasion. However, any of these injuries should be examined with care and concern and the possibility of elder abuse evaluated.

Sexual Abuse

In some cases, the intimate partner may sexually abuse the elder. This abuse may involve forced sex or indirect sexual exploitations such as taking pictures of the elder and selling them on the Internet. Sexual assault of an elder raises additional concerns, as it causes additional consequences. Some elders are so fragile that the assailant may break bones during the sexual assault.

Psychological or Emotional Abuse

This type of abuse is much harder to identify than physical or sexual abuse. However, as with other forms of domestic violence involving psychological abuse, its effects can be quite severe and long-lasting. The elder victim of psychological abuse may be deprived of other family support or may fear continued rejection by the intimate caretaker relative and therefore come to believe that there is no further purpose in living. These elders may suffer depression or may become overly

anxious or fearful of younger adults, especially if the abusive caretaker is younger. Psychologically or emotionally abused elders may also develop sleep disorders or hysteria.

Neglect

This type of abuse may be defined as the negligent treatment of an elder by a caretaker that may cause harm or the threat of harm. Neglect may occur in a number of different ways. The intimate caretaker may simply not feed the elder sufficient food to stay healthy. The caretaker may not change the elder's clothing if there is a need to do so—for instance, if the elder is incontinent and has soiled himself. The caretaker may also fail to take the elder to the doctor for proper health care and other medical treatment.

Self-Neglect

This is a very emotional topic for many in the field of domestic violence. Self-neglect occurs when an elder acts in such a manner as to threaten her own health or safety. Self-neglect may involve the elder's decision to refuse food or medicine. Elders in this situation may be mentally incompetent to act for themselves. While this type of abuse does not involve an intimate partner, it is included here for the sake of comparison with other types of abuse. This category excludes elders who are competent and make certain decisions as matters of personal choice.

Material Abuse

This type of abuse involves the exploitation of the elder's finances or resources. Similar to other forms of domestic violence, the definition of material abuse of elders is subject to conflicting definitions. However, the legal system has responded to this form of abuse. Forty-eight states and the District of Columbia have statutes that specifically mention financial abuse of elders (Roby and Sullivan 2000), but there is little if any uniformity among the statutes. Some states require dishonest tactics by the perpetrators, while others limit this form of abuse to neglect or at least reckless abuse or conduct. This is made more difficult by the acknowledgment that even professionals may have trouble distinguishing between an unwise financial transaction and an exploitative transaction that was the result of undue influence, duress, or fraud.

Material abuse is similar to other forms of elder abuse in that it is devastating to the victim and frequently can be traced to intimate partners,

287

whether they are spouses, children, or other family members. However, unlike other forms of abuse, material abuse may occur with the "consent" of the elder and thus is very hard in many situations to detect. This abuse may be as direct and open as taking money from elders' wallets or banking accounts. The use of undue influence may involve subtle or not so subtle pressure on elders to sign over their property to the abusers. Or the abusers may suggest that since they are caring for them, the elders should show gratitude by leaving property or other assets to them. The abusers may threaten to stop caring for the elders unless these assets are signed over. Additional forms of material abuse can be:

- Taking, misusing, or using without the elder's knowledge money or property
- Forging an elder's signature on a legal document
- Abusing the joint signature authority of a bank account
- Misusing credit cards
- Cashing an elder's check without permission
- Persuading an impaired elder to change his or her will or insurance policy
- Overcharging for caretaker services
- Denying elders access to their money

The risk factors associated with elder abuse are hard to determine, but some authorities suggest that most victims of elder abuse are white females over the age of seventy (Coker and Little 1997). One reason why this group is more likely to be victims of elder abuse has to do with the facts that women live longer than men and white females live longer than females from other races. A second reason is that the perpetrator perceives these women as weak and vulnerable. A third factor that applies to any victim is a lack of knowledge regarding financial matters in general.

Characteristics of Elder Abusers

Who would abuse an elderly family member in their care? What kind of person would beat, sexually assault, or steal from his or her elderly family member? These questions are for the most part unanswerable because of the lack of research in this area. However, the few studies that have been conducted provide some information, albeit conflicting, about the profile of an abuser. One study indicated that most perpetrators were between the ages of thirty-six and fifty (Teaster 2003), while another had figures to show that 75 percent of abusers were over the age of fifty (Pillemer and Finkelhor 1988).

While females are usually the caretakers, they do not commit most of the incidents of abuse. Fifty-two percent of the perpetrators in one survey were males (Teaster 2003). While spouses may account for most of the physical abuse and neglect, children appear to carry out most of the material abuse. What is known is that the perpetrators may be of either sex, come from various economic positions, and be of different ages. As with so many factors of elder abuse, more study is needed in this area.

Consequences

There are different types of consequences depending on the form of abuse. Physical consequences resulting from physical and sexual abuse and neglect take many forms. Elders heal more slowly than younger persons. Additionally, what may be a simple injury for a younger person may become debilitating for an elderly person. Mental consequences may include a crisis reaction to the abuse. Post-traumatic stress disorder may result from traumatic types of elder abuse, including physical assault. Susman and Vittert (1980) list some typical reactions that elders may feel as a result of abuse. These include pain and suffering, loss of affection or enjoyment of life, increased fear of crime, acute financial loss, unplanned change in lifestyle, increased isolation and loneliness, and reluctance to get involved in the criminal justice system. Finally, there are financial consequences to society as a result of elder abuse. These include increased costs of medical and mental health care, increased legal costs, and second-generation financial burdens on adult children for the costs associated with taking care of the injured elder.

Intervention

The Administration on Aging is a federal agency of the U.S. Department of Health and Human Services that has a strong commitment to protecting seniors from elder abuse. The Administration on Aging supports a wide range of activities at the state and local levels to raise awareness about elder abuse. These activities include training law enforcement officials and medical professionals in how to recognize and respond to cases of elder abuse.

All fifty states have enacted laws that allow Adult Protective Services (APS) to intervene in cases of elder abuse. APS comprises those services provided to elders and people with disabilities who are in danger of being abused and are unable to protect themselves and have no one else to care for them. Each state is responsible for establishing its own APS. In most states, APS workers are the first professionals to respond to reports of abuse, neglect, or exploitation of elders. The section or division of APS that works with elders has a number of different intervention responses. These include receiving and investigating reports of elder abuse, assessing the elder's risk of injury and ability to understand what is occurring, developing a case plan, arranging services, and monitoring and evaluating those services.

Some states designate professionals in certain occupations as "mandated reporters." In other words, people who work in these occupations *must* report suspected cases of elder abuse if they are involved with the elderly population within the scope of their job. For example, in California, mandated reporters include any person who has assumed full or partial responsibility for the care of an elder, whether or not that person receives compensation. Mandated reporters also include any care custodian in a public or private facility that provides services to elders and any health practitioner, including doctors, nurses, social workers, and counselors.

Once a mandated reporter or anyone else contacts APS about possible elder abuse, the process begins. If it is an emergency, APS will forward a copy of the report to the local law enforcement agency and emergency medical staff. If it is a nonemergency case of suspected elder abuse, it will be assigned a response time based upon the potential risk to the elder, and the report will be assigned to a staff person to conduct an investigation. If the report does not meet the definition of elder abuse, the reporting party will be given information regarding community resources that might be of assistance to the elder.

The APS investigator makes contact with the elder victim and assesses the alleged victim's risk factors. The investigator also assesses the victim's capacity to make an informed consent. If the victim can make an informed consent, he or she has the right to refuse intervention. If the victim desires to go forward with the case, a case plan is developed and services may be provided by a number of agencies, including law enforcement responses (e.g., the filing of criminal charges), counseling, temporary emergency shelter, assistance from advocates for the elderly if the elder cannot act on his or her own behalf, and referrals to other agencies as necessary.

Another important party who interacts with the elder victim is the health care professional. This person in many cases is not only a mandated reporter, but is tasked with evaluating injuries to the elder victim and recommending alternative courses of action. Health care professionals should assess not only the health status of elderly victims and the nature of the abuse, but also their financial status and living arrangements and the presence of emotional support or stress.

Finally, another intervention or prevention concept involves the use of *triads*. Triads are formed when local law enforcement agrees to work with senior citizens groups and community groups to prevent the victimization of the elderly. The three groups establish programs to prevent elder abuse through education and to address the care of elders. The essence of the triad program is cooperation. Triads allow law enforcement to work with senior citizens groups and advocates to establish programs that enhance the safety and quality of life of seniors. The use of triads continues to grow. In 1992, there were only fifty-six triads in twenty states. Today almost all states have triads. In 2000, the National Association of Triads was formed in an attempt to provide more secure funding for this approach.

Guardians and Conservators

Elders may be unable to care for themselves and the only family members available are the abusers. In those situations, the state has the authority to intervene and care for those who cannot care for themselves. The state uses the legal concepts and authority of guardianships and conservatorships to intervene and proceed with care.

In most states, a conservator is a person or entity appointed by the court to manage the estate or property of one who is unable to manage his or her own affairs. Guardians are appointed to tend to such matters affecting their elderly charges as where they live, what medications they take, and any other aspects of their well-being. In some states, a person is appointed as the conservator of both the estate and the person and is tasked with the dual responsibility of caring for both.

To establish guardian- or conservatorship, most states require a court hearing, which may be initiated by a caretaker or by the local government agency assigned the task of caring for elders who are helpless and alone. The first step is the filing of pleadings, which are formal documents alleging that the elder cannot care for herself. In most jurisdictions, the elder has a right to an attorney. The elder's attorney may contest the pleadings and has the right to cross-examine any witnesses who are called to prove that the elder cannot care for herself. If the court accepts the evidence of the pleadings, it imposes guardianship or conservatorship and lists the powers that the office may exercise. There is normally a review of the status of the case every year or two, depending on the jurisdiction. At these review hearings, the elder has the same rights she exercised in the first hearing.

Conclusion

Elder abuse by intimate partners is one of many controversial domestic violence topics. Elder abuse includes physical, sexual, psychological/emotional, and material abuse. These acts may be committed by strangers who work in an institutional setting which cares for the elderly or they may be inflicted by an intimate partner. This article has addressed elder abuse by intimate partners. The extent of elder abuse is underreported—according to some authorities by as low 1 in 25 cases.

There are a number of theories on why perpetrators commit elder abuse, including the Cycle of Violence theory, the Psychopathology theory, the Social Exchange theory, the Neutralization theory, and the Family Stress theory. However, as of this date, no one theory has explained all the different types of elder abuse. Much more research is needed in this area.

Similar to other forms of domestic violence, there are serious consequences suffered by victims of elder abuse, which may be more serious than those of other forms of domestic violence because of the special needs of the elderly. There are a number of agencies that work with and attempt to prevent elder abuse. These include federal, state, and local agencies and task forces whose concern is the health and welfare of the elderly.

Elder abuse is a critical topic in the area of domestic violence. With the "graying" of America and the aging of the baby boomers, elder abuse will take on a whole new significance in the near future. It is urgent that society understands its dynamics and is prepared to respond to it.

HARVEY WALLACE

See also **Battered Husbands; Battered Woman Syndrome; Batterer Typology; Coercive Control; Elder Abuse, Assessing the Risks of; Elder Abuse, Consequences of; Elder Abuse Perpetrated by Adult Children; Stockholm Syndrome in Battered Women; Women with Disabilities, Domestic Violence against**

References and Further Reading

Coker, Johnny, and Bobby Little. "Investing in the Future: Protecting the Elderly from Financial Abuse." *FBI Law Enforcement Bulletin* (February 1997): 1–5.

National Elder Abuse Incidence Study: Final Report. Washington DC: National Center on Elder Abuse, 1998.

Pillemer, Karl, and David Finkelhor. "The Prevalence of Elder Abuse: A Random Sample Survey." *The Gerontologist* 28, no. 1 (1988): 51–57.

Susman, Marjorie, and Carol H. Vittert. *Building a Solution: A Practical Guide for Establishing Crime Victim Service Agencies.* St. Louis: National Council of Jewish Women, 1980.

Sykes, Gresham M., and David Matza. "Techniques of Neutralization: A Theory of Delinquency." *American Sociological Review* 22 (1978): 664–670.

Teaster, Pamela B. *A Response to the Abuse of Vulnerable Adults: The 2000 Survey of State Adult Protective Services.* Washington DC: National Center on Elder Abuse, 2003.

Tomita, S. K. "The Denial of Elder Mistreatment by Victims and Abusers: The Application of Neutralization Theory." *Violence and Victims* 5, no. 3 (1990): 171–184.

Wallace, Harvey. *Family Violence, Legal, Medical, and Social Perspectives*, 4th ed. Boston: Allyn & Bacon, 2005.

ELDER ABUSE PERPETRATED BY ADULT CHILDREN

Estimates indicate that one million elderly people are victims of domestic violence every year. Forty percent of cases occur when adult children victimize their parents. The victimization includes psychological, physical, and financial abuse. Adult children perpetrating elder abuse are more likely to inflict psychological maltreatment than physical or financial abuse. Combining the fact that the baby boomer generation is graying and families typically provide care for aged loved ones, scholars believe that abuse of the elderly is growing. Also, due to the intimate nature of the parent–child relationship, researchers believe that elder parent abuse is one of the most underreported forms of violence.

Profiling Abusers

Previous research gives insight into the characteristics of abusers of elderly parents. An adult child abusive toward a parent tends to be financially dependent on the elder. Of adult children abusive to mothers, 77 percent are somewhat or fully financially dependent, and 65 percent are somewhat or entirely dependent for housing. Unemployment rates are higher among abusive adult children, and drug or alcohol problems are common. Many have histories with the criminal justice system and hospitalization for mental problems. They are also more reluctant to provide care for the parent, experience conflict with spouses over caring for the parent, and have unrealistic expectations of the parent considering the parent's reliant state. Low rates of social support in caring for the adult parent also perpetuate abuse. Situations involving one child as exclusive care provider are more problematic than when siblings are available to assist. One study found that 64 percent of parent abusers were sons, while 36 percent were daughters. Mild forms of psychological neglect are more likely to come from a daughter, and severe forms of psychological abuse are more likely to come from a son. Daughters are more likely to use physical violence than sons are. Younger perpetrators are more likely to be sons; older perpetrators tend to be daughters. Almost 30 percent of the abusers claim that the elderly person in the relationship previously abused them. This history of previous childhood abuse may serve as a justification for the adult child to abuse the elder parent. In general, adult children are more likely to abuse if they'd had poor relationships with their parents before the need to provide care arose. Old conflicts come back to life. Contradictory ideas on politics, religion, relationships, child rearing, education, work, or lifestyle renew anger, thus triggering abusive episodes.

Variations of Elderly-Parent Abusers

With abuser characteristics in mind, research provides a typology of adult children abusive to their elderly parents. Typologies are basic classifications or ideal types that help researchers understand social relations. In the literature, three variations of adult children who abuse their elderly parents exist.

They include hostile children, authoritarian caregivers, and dependents.

- *Hostile* adult children have long-term relationship problems with their aged parents, reporting that even at early ages they did not get along with them. This type also claims that the elderly parent has pathological problems. Deflecting their own actions as a source of conflict, they believe that the parent has mental or substance abuse issues that trigger most of the problems in their relationship. Pressure from other family members fosters a sense of obligation to provide care. Adult children of this type also indicate a preference to provide care for a passive parent. In some cases, they even convey a desire for the parent to die. Research often describes adult children in this classification as irate, mistrustful, and tense. Anger felt toward the elderly parent they are caring for is evident in their discussions about providing care. Their body language also indicates apparent hostility toward the parent. In addition, research indicates that the hostile adult child acknowledges general feelings of anger toward all people. These abusers tend to be highly educated but feel a sense of underachievement. Not surprisingly, they blame the elderly parent for holding them back and limiting their potential. They are less likely to live in the same house as the parent but are the most abusive. Moreover, life crises trigger episodes of abuse.

- *Authoritarian* adult children have a domineering, rigid, punitive personality. Research describes them as critical, impatient, and blunt. They are not typically substance abusers, are less educated than the hostile type, and see providing care as less of a burden. Their expectations are high in regard to care, possibly explaining why they choose to care for the elderly parent themselves. They do not believe that anyone can provide care as well as they can. While having high expectations for the elderly parent, they do not have sympathy for the dependency status of the aged parent. They feel that the elderly parent could do more to fight off dependency but will not put forth the effort. Regardless, children in this category have a need to control multiple aspects of the elderly parent's life. When the parent comes to live with them, they begin abuse by lashing out when a household rule is broken. Usually married, they treat the elderly parent like an infant or young child.

The few pleasures they report in providing care involve grooming or shopping for the aged parent. They resent the parent for discussing personal matters with others living outside of the house. In fact, they sometimes institutionalize the parent if information control cannot occur.

- *Dependent* adult children are financially reliant on elderly parents. Unemployed or in a low-paying job, they have lived with their parent continuously, occasionally, or during some period of time into their adulthood. Research indicates that they lack maturity and have never gained the economic or social status of others their age. They care little about their appearance, fail to adequately clean their surroundings, and are passive. However, their passivity subsides when abusive episodes occur. They are uneasy in social situations. Compared with the hostile and authoritarian categories, research indicates that they participate in fewer formal activities with others and are less likely to be married. Although their primary relationship is with the elderly parent, they provide fewer variations of care for them than members of the other groups. Compared with hostile or authoritarian types, dependents are more hesitant to discuss the abuse they inflict on aged parents.

Methods of Abuse

"Double direction" violence occurs with some children caring for elderly parents. This involves scenarios in which both the child and the parent try to control each other. Methods used by adult children to gain advantage in these situations vary. Studies indicate that 40 percent of adult children scream or yell at the parent to gain authority. Lower numbers use physical restraints (6 percent), overmedication and force-feeding (6 percent), threats of physical force (4 percent), and actual hitting (3 percent). Some play into stereotypical harsh conditions of institutionalized care such as alleged in nursing homes. In fact, a small percentage actually use threats of sending the parent to a nursing home to intimidate them.

Theory and Research

Existing literature shows six traditional theoretical explanations for elder abuse by adult children. Four of these explanations focus on the adult child as perpetrator. They include abuse socialization, pathology, stress, and social isolation. A fifth focuses on the elderly parent as the victim and deals with vulnerability. The sixth—exchange theory—concerns the imbalance of power that can occur with the adult child and elderly parent.

Abuse socialization theory suggests that adult children attain motives to abuse parents. They acquire norms and attitudes that promote abuse and negative feelings toward elders. Researchers base this theory on the social learning perspective promoted in the fields of psychology and social psychology. Studies in this area focus on the observation of and later participation in abuse. These studies frequently indicate that children and young adults imitate aggressive, violent behaviors they witness. In turn, as adults, they are more likely to abuse. Their offspring witness the behavior and repeat it as well. This generates what many refer to as a cycle of abuse. Generations of families ritualize a lifestyle characterized by an extensive acceptance of violence. Scholars often discuss this cycle in terms of child and spouse abuse. However, in the field of elder abuse, there is a widespread belief that abused children are more likely to abuse their parents if they provide care for them in old age. An abundant amount of research supports this concept of intergenerational transfer. It also indicates that there is an amplification of abuse by adult children when a cultural backdrop of ageism exists. However, some studies do indicate that a majority of children abusive to adult parents did not grow up in abusive families. Their parents typically dealt with highly charged disagreements by arguing and yelling. Regarding extended family, research finds that they also typically had positive, nonviolent relations with aunts and uncles.

The pathology perspective indicates that adult children abuse because of a mental defect or impairment. Research supports that individuals labeled with developmental disability, mental retardation, mental illness, or personality disorder are at a greater risk to abuse elderly parents. Studies find a positive history of psychotic illness in many elder abuse situations. Abused elders are three times more likely to report that their abusers have mental problems, and literature confirms high rates of abuse among mentally impaired adult children caring for parents. Altered cognitive states due to drug or alcohol use are included in this theoretical tradition. When present, drugs and alcohol reduce the ability to control violent, aggressive actions. Critics of the pathology perspective argue the emphasis on the individual. They agree that mental problems and substance abuse increase rates of maltreatment of elderly parents but view these as parts of the explanation. An additional limitation of the pathology perspective is failure to account for external factors that trigger repeated abuse. However, research shows that 38 percent of children abusive toward adult parents have a history of psychotic hospitalization, 56 percent are alcoholics, and 6 percent are drug users.

The stress explanation of abuse involves tension overload. Demands of providing care outweigh the resources available to those providing it. One study shows that 85 percent of abusive caregivers claim to have experienced at least five psychosocial stress events during the previous year. The source of the tension could be internal or external. Internal stress involves the inherited burdens of providing care for an elderly parent. External stress for the adult child involves environmental events such as a frustrated spouse, financial strain, time issues, or employment problems. When these events occur for an adult child caring for a parent, they compound the internal stress and lead to mistreatment. Psychosocial stress events need not be negative. Positive changes can also lead to stress, heightening a caregiver's sense of anomie, and increasing the probability of abuse. Regardless, research shows that not all children caring for elderly parents react to stress the same way.

Various factors influence how stress affects a caregiver. Some include the level of desire to provide care, individual responses to providing care, burden perceptions, magnitude of change, and nature of care provided. With desire for caring, resentment toward the parent may result when situations force an adult child to provide care. Concerning individual responses to providing care, adult children have different perceptions. As previously mentioned, this is influenced by issues such as gender, financial position, or the previous state of relations between the adult child and parent. In terms of magnitude of change, stress levels are dependent on how much change takes place in order to care for the aged loved one. For example, the stress level for someone taking care of a parent who has always lived down the street may qualitatively be lower than for someone caring for an aged parent living many miles away. Regarding the nature of the care provided, the type of care determines stress levels. Relating to issues of functional status, an adult child supplying financial support will have a different level of stress than one feeding and bathing an elderly parent on a daily basis. Moreover, research indicates that intimate activities, such as bathing, create psychological strain for both the child and the parent due to their personal nature, especially if the burden of care falls solely on one person's shoulders.

Social isolation theory implies that without social support, adult children caring for elderly parents are more likely to abuse. Isolation forces the adult child to handle the strains of elder care alone. Without others helping them, it is harder to obtain assistance and diffuse the responsibility of care. The marital status of an adult child caring for an elderly parent is also an important factor to consider. When the caregiver is single, no spouse is available to share in the burden of care. Strain and subsequent abuse are more likely to occur. One study supports this notion, showing 54 percent of elderly parent abusers are single. A socially isolated person caring for an aged parent also lowers the potential of outsiders to identify the presence of abusive attitudes and intervene before abuse occurs. On the other hand, an elder with low social support is more susceptible to having an abusive caregiver for the same reason. If multiple people live in the home of an elder being cared for by an adult child or if the elder has frequent visitors from outside of the home, abusers will be more likely to incur negative sanctions from others. Abuse rates then drop.

Vulnerability theory simply indicates that victim characteristics leave elderly parents open to abuse. Specifically, as parents get older, they become increasingly dependent on adult children. This dependence may be due to failing bodies, deteriorating minds, and depleted finances. As research in the field of victimology explains, the weak, feeble-minded, and monetarily challenged have higher risks of victimization. In addition, studies indicate that as elderly parents become older, their willingness to escape from abusive relationships lowers. This is due, in part, to a fear of the previously mentioned social isolation.

Exchange theory suggests that a lack of balance in the relationship between the adult child and dependent elderly parent promotes abuse. Using social psychological theories, this idea implies that the basis of interaction between the adult child and the elderly parent is a system of benefits and costs. When people equally contribute to a relationship, equality exists. However, once one person provides more benefits than the other does, control is established. That person will then have the power to continue the relationship as he or she pleases because the other person will be dependent on the benefits they provide. In terms of the adult child and elderly parent relationship, as the parent grows older, his or her resources may dissolve. Physically, mentally, and financially, the elder parent is unable to provide as much as they receive. They then become dependent on the adult child. With power and control in their hands, adult children can treat elderly parents as they please, knowing that their parents have few, if any, alternatives. On the other hand, research does imply that power in the hands of the child also leads to frustration and anger for the elderly parent. Negatively reacting to a state of dependency and lacking resources, older loved ones then become more likely to abuse the caregiver.

Limits of Traditional Theories

All of the explanations for elder abuse by adult children have limitations. The socialization approach does not tell us why some people who grew up in abusive environments do not grow up to abuse. Studies find a large number of abusers suffer from some mental or emotional impairment. However, pathology theory has timing issues. Do mental health problems and substance abuse promote elder abuse, or do the pressures of elder care promote mental health problems and substance abuse? The stress explanation implies that tension leads to abuse, but research shows that all adult children experience stress. They simply handle it in differing ways. Social isolation is a plausible explanation. However, it makes sense only when connected to other concepts. It is possible that pathological problems push others away from caregivers, increasing the likelihood of isolation. Finally, vulnerability and exchange theory rely on long-term relationship dynamics involving dependency. They deal little with acute stress responses to providing care that trigger abusive episodes. Due to limitations cited with each theory, scholars are promoting an integrated approach in describing the dynamics of elder abuse.

Integrated Theories

Several integrated theories involving elder abuse by adult children exist. They combine the best of traditional models, emphasizing that abuse of an elder parent is a process rather than a single act. Considering cultural influences, research is increasingly placing importance on internal relationship factors as well as external events leading to abuse. Three integrated theories worthy of note are the human ecology model, the theory of developmental dysfunction, and stage theory.

The human ecology model implies that people will fall back on widespread cultural beliefs when they have no experience providing care to an elderly parent. These cultural beliefs inadvertently promote abuse. For example, cultural acceptance regarding use of force, lack of worth of the elderly, and social isolation guide the type of care given.

Moreover, the lack of knowledge in providing care can create role confusion and push the adult child into abusive episodes.

The theory of developmental dysfunction views adult children as incapable of sustaining personal relationships with elderly parents. In part due to pathological issues, they abuse in the family context when external events push them over the edge. For example, the loss of a job or inadequate finances can trigger maltreatment.

The stage model consists of three phases, each of which contributes to the escalation of abuse. The first phase involves the point at which the adult child and the elderly parent establish that providing care for the latter is no longer a possibility but reality. Both the child and the parent define the situation by assessing social networks and types of care needed. The second phase involves the child and parent unconsciously processing their new roles and expectations. The third phase concerns abuse. It is the expressive stage, in which the child and the parent express their adjustment to their expectations and roles in a positive or negative way. Using this model, researchers indicate that a majority of abuse results from unreasonable and negative perceptions of the elder toward the caregiver and a lack of multiple people providing care.

It is relevant to mention *gero-criminology* in this discussion of integrated theories of abuse. Gero-criminology links ideas from multiple disciplines such as criminology, gerontology, psychology, sociology, and victimology to explain violence directed toward elders. Integrating concepts from multiple disciplines has theoretical potential. However, gero-criminology currently lacks a specific focus applicable to elder abuse perpetrated by adult children.

Abuse Reduction

Theory and research provide a backdrop for the possibility of abuse reduction. Guidelines currently in existence focus on the perpetrator and the victim. Measures include pre-care planning, coordinating with elderly service providers, personal education, medical screening, contacting the local police, documenting conflict, building social networks, and providing temporary relief for caregivers.

With pre-care planning, literature suggests that adult children encourage their parents, when still healthy, to purchase long-term care insurance. Adult children may have a stronger sense of resentment toward the adult parent when care provision suddenly becomes their own financial responsibility. As mentioned above, the sudden burden of caring for a mentally or physically dependent loved one generates stress. Health insurance and Medicare funds are limited when caring for an elderly parent. Long-term care insurance guarantees a pool of monetary resources when elder care becomes necessary.

Anyone who has observed or has a reasonable cause to suspect that an adult child is abusing an elder should contact Adult Protective Services (APS) immediately. APS screens allegations of abuse, including neglect or exploitation, from various sources such as witnesses, victims, and mandatory reporters such as health care providers, social workers, law enforcement officers, and firefighters. Depending on the state of residence, APS may be located within criminal justice or social service agencies. APS investigates claims of elder abuse and, depending on the claim, will intervene and provide victim support. APS may also serve as an external buffer when conflict occurs. For example, if the adult child and elder parent experience a dispute over the cleanliness of the adult parent's home, APS can step in before the situation escalates. They can serve as a mediator by providing information or making recommendations regarding sanitation. This deflects the parent's anger at the adult child, decreases the strain on the caregiver relationship, and lessens the possibility of an abusive episode. Aside from social support, APS will also provide the adult child and elder parent with emotional support and legal services.

In terms of personal education, it is extremely important for the child and elderly parent to learn as much as possible about the process of providing care and issues of mental impairment. APS sometimes offers elder care training for adult children at risk to abuse parents. For the adult child confronted with parental dementia or Alzheimer's disease, details regarding local support groups and information provided by the Alzheimer's Association should be obtained. The adult child should arrange an evaluation by a geriatric specialist. Physicians diagnose Alzheimer's disease in half of all people over eighty-five. Understanding the degenerative process of Alzheimer's disease helps the caregiver to realize that the elderly parent may not be consciously lashing out. The outbursts could be symptoms related to the disease, not rational or retaliatory in nature. However, the literature does suggest that sometimes, due to a lack of power in the caregiver relationship, elderly parents play the dementia role for control purposes. If the caregiver suspects this, the adult child should push for medical screening, such as a CAT (computed axial tomography) scan, to properly diagnose the possibility of dementia as a factor in any personal conflict.

Research recommends contacting APS not as an option, but as a requirement for anyone even suspecting elder abuse. In abuse situations, it may also be necessary to contact local police. Some departments treat reports of elder abuse with high priority and have personnel specially trained in response and investigation of this type of violence. With elder abuse cases being hard to prove, some scholars encourage the documentation of conflict to ensure that prosecutors will have enough information to press charges. Compiling evidence is essential to the validity of a formal complaint. Documentation is necessary for parental victims of adult children and caregivers who are victims of violence from elderly parents. For some, collecting evidence involves the use of hidden cameras or tape recorders. Overt ways of collecting evidence include taking photographs or home video. Filing the complaint of abuse will usually bring APS into the situation if they are not already involved. Research shows that the police and APS do not always have a positive working relationship. It is often difficult for police and APS to prove a case of elderly abuse against an adult child. There are cultural beliefs that elder abuse is not a major social problem. Victims are also reluctant to press charges against family members. In some cases, reporting abuse seems to harm more than help. APS may recommend removal from the adult child's care, potentially placing the victim in a less suitable environment. Consequently, the victim may then view reporting the abuse as punishment rather than a solution. Victims involved in substantiated cases are more likely than those in unconfirmed cases to refuse elder care support services.

APS contact helps to build social support networks for the adult child. To lower the potential for abuse, support networks for the elderly parent are important as well. The adult child can facilitate networks for the aged parent in a variety of ways. It is possible to privately hire home health care workers on a daily basis to visit with and assist in the care of the elderly parent. These workers provide companionship, but also help the adult child with a variety of tasks. While this type of assistance may benefit both the parent and the adult child, it is often difficult to locate quality, dependable workers. For some families, the cost of privately paying for assistance is unaffordable. To relieve the full-time pressure of providing care, it is also possible to enroll an elderly parent in Adult Day Care (ADC). These facilities typically operate during daytime hours and involve community programs specialized in providing services to older persons. They place emphasis on healthy rehabilitation and social activities and are located in a variety of settings, including churches, senior centers, and even hospitals. Having gained in popularity, there are over one thousand of these licensed facilities in the United States. Due to limited availability, enrolling an elderly parent in ADC may require a long-term contract. If long-term support is not what the caregiver needs, *respite care* is a possibility. This form of assistance provides adult children the option of temporarily leaving dependent parents at a facility where trained staff members provide care, or having a trained relief aid come into the home. Adult children commonly use respite services to meet an emergency need or as periodic relief from providing continuous care. In either condition, children providing care for elderly parents receive a break from the physical and emotional exhaustion that can trigger abuse.

Conclusion

The elderly will soon be the largest segment of society. With more elderly people, research indicates that elder abuse will increase. Since families still provide a majority of care for aged loved ones, analysts believe that adult children will continue to abuse. Research allows for the profiling of adult children who abuse elderly parents. It also offers a typology for understanding their actions.

Moreover, traditional theories provide a general understanding of this type of abuse, while new, integrated theories focusing on internal and external factors provide complex models for study. Applying these theories to abuse-reduction strategies offers a great deal of promise for alleviating the problem of elder abuse perpetrated by adult children.

JASON S. ULSPERGER and DEBORAH WILSON

See also **Coercive Control; Cycle of Violence; Elder Abuse, Assessing the Risks of; Elder Abuse, Consequences of; Exchange Theory; Intergenerational Transfer of Intimate Partner Violence; Parricide**

References and Further Reading

Anetzberger, Georgia J. *The Etiology of Elder Abuse by Adult Offspring*. Springfield, IL: Charles C. Thomas Publishing, 1987.

Brandl, Bonnie, and Loree Cook-Daniels. *Domestic Abuse in Later Life: Who Are the Abusers?* Washington DC: National Center on Elder Abuse, 2003.

Marcell, Jacqueline. *Elder Rage, or Take My Father . . . Please: How to Survive Caring for Aging Parents*. Irvine, CA: Impressive Press, 2001.

Payne, Brian K. *Crime and Elder Abuse: An Integrated Perspective*. Springfield, IL: Charles C. Thomas Publishing, 2000.

Quinn, Mary Joy, and Susan K. Tomita. *Elder Abuse and Neglect: Causes, Diagnosis, and Intervention Strategies*. New York: Springer Publishing Company, 1986.

ELECTRONIC MONITORING OF ABUSERS

Background

Battered women who appeal to the justice system for help are at heightened risk for abuse. To better protect domestic violence victims during the post-complaint period, some jurisdictions use electronic monitoring (EM) technology to supervise alleged and convicted batterers and to notify victims when they may be in danger. This technology provides crime control capability through varying degrees of surveillance and tracking of offenders and through alerting devices for victims, law enforcement, and community corrections agencies.

The criminal justice system's use of EM (also referred to as "electronic tagging") has grown steadily since its adoption by the courts in the mid-1980s (Vollum and Hale 2002: 2). EM has traditionally been used as an alternative to incarceration ("house arrest"), as an intermediate sanction (e.g., as part of intensive probation), or as a condition of release from jail (i.e., as a form of pretrial supervision). EM has historically been deployed in the context of noninterpersonal offenses, including drunk driving and drug- and property-related crimes (Crowe, Sydney, Bancroft, and Lawrence

2002; Vollum and Hale 2002). However, courts have increasingly applied EM in response to interpersonal offenses, including cases involving charges of sexual abuse and domestic violence. When administered in an interpersonal offense context, where one party is controlled or supervised via monitoring and a second party is protected from, or alerted to potentially untoward movement by, a potential abuser, EM is best considered "bilateral" rather than "unilateral" (Erez, Ibarra, and Lurie 2004). Such bilateral programs combine EM associated with home incarceration, originally intended to safeguard the general public, with individuated protection for specific victims named in pending or adjudicated cases (Erez and Ibarra 2006). Here, *bilateral electronic monitoring* (BEM) is used, not only to enforce liberty restrictions in the absence of traditional detention or incarceration, but also to monitor defendants' observance of "exclusion zones" around a complaining party's home, building an "accountability" mechanism into a judge's orders.

BEM typically operates on one of two technological platforms: radio frequency (RF) and global positioning system (GPS). RF-based BEM programs for domestic violence generally work as follows: As with a traditional "home detention" system, the offender is equipped with a tamper-resistant, ankle-worn transmitter; a receiver in his residence confirms his presence at home during court-ordered curfew hours, logging entry into and exit from the dwelling. Curfew is defined in terms of "out hours," i.e., the time frame during which the controlled party can be away from home (ordinarily aligned with his work schedule). A second receiver is placed in the protected party's home; it detects the presence of the offender when he enters a defined radius around the protected party's house. Radius penetration of a victim's home region by the transmitter-wearing offender results in an alert to a monitoring facility, which in turn notifies local law enforcement via a high-priority distress category call. The receiver in the victim's home may be equipped to emit an alert when the offender is detected within range, or the victim may be notified by a pager or cell phone. Having been alerted, the victim is supposed to take protective action, such as moving to a predesignated secure space within the house while awaiting assistance from law enforcement. In the event that she is not at home when the offender breaches the home region, the monitoring facility notifies her of the incident, so that she can stay away from home until the matter is investigated and resolved. The victim may also carry a field-monitoring device synchronized to the offender's ankle bracelet, alerting her to his approach while she is away from her home receiver, such as occurs during their simultaneous presence at a shopping mall. The defendant is not tracked while away from home, as is the case with GPS-based systems.

GPS-based EM operates on similar monitoring and alerting principles, though it has some additional capabilities: the tracking of offenders in time and space, and the capacity to define multiple zones of exclusion and inclusion, with broader ranges of detection, up to a 2,000-foot radius (Crowe et al. 2002: 67). This results in the ability to monitor the offender in areas beyond his and the victim's residences and to issue earlier alerts in the event of a radius penetration. In addition, GPS victims are less likely to be burdened with bulky equipment—they are ordinarily equipped with either a cell phone or a pager alone. Indeed, GPS programs can operate without the active participation of victims, since "geo-zones" can be programmed as "restricted" without a protected party's advance knowledge, and a victim need not be notified of the offender's breach of an exclusion zone. Instead, and depending on the nature of the breach and type of GPS platform in use, the offender may receive a cellular call from a supervisor alerting him to the geo-zone violation and warning him that he must remove himself from the area immediately, law enforcement may be dispatched to the scene, or the zone breach can be investigated in a follow-up supervisory meeting.

It is important to note that neither EM technology is capable of providing physical protection to the victim. Both monitoring systems can at best provide a warning to the victim (and notification to the police) that the offender is nearby, assuming that he is wearing his assigned transmitter. Thus the equipment will not prevent someone who is determined to hurt a "protected" party and is unconcerned about the personal consequences. Regardless of the technological platform adopted, enrollment in BEM is premised on the offender's ability to maintain or establish a residence apart from the victim (assuming that the two had been cohabitating before the arrest). Further, there is usually a lethality assessment of some kind that is administered before BEM enrollment will be permitted.

Research Findings

Until recently, most research conducted on the use of BEM in domestic violence cases was conducted largely "in-house," by agencies pretesting or administering BEM programs, and was not made easily available to other agencies/practitioners or to the scholarly community. An exception is a study of two RF-based BEM programs, reported in Erez, Ibarra, and Lurie (forthcoming) and in an ongoing series of publications and conference presentations, including Erez, Ibarra, and Lurie (2004), Ibarra and Erez (2004), Ibarra and Erez (2005), Ibarra (2005), and Erez and Ibarra (2006). These articles and papers have addressed such issues as the effectiveness of BEM at deterring contact between the two parties, the role of human supervision in BEM programs, the idea that BEM can operate as an alternative to relocation to a battered woman's shelter, the ways in which the controlled parties view the experience of enrollment, and the ways in which BEM functions as a kind of diversion program.

Contact Deterrence

The courts that were examined in the Erez, Ibarra, and Lurie study (in two jurisdictions in two different Midwestern states, "River County" and "Lakefront") were far likelier to use BEM during the post-arrest/predisposition period than during the sentencing phase. Typically, the stipulation that the arrestee enroll in the BEM program was attached as a condition of his release from jail on bond, although there was some variability by judge and by jurisdiction in how this took place.

BEM is premised on the notion that offenders under "no contact" orders, who know that they cannot approach a certain area without detection, are less likely to attempt to contact a victim, in spite of a history of violating such orders absent EM. According to this view, although some offenders will not be deterred in such circumstances, a sizable portion of batterers is likely to conform to protective orders if they know that they are being monitored electronically. A rationale often cited by court officials for placing offenders on electronic supervision is that it will strengthen protective orders and "give them teeth"; that is, restricted parties will take them seriously. The BEM study provides support for this view (Erez et al. 2004). Women participating in the program described how differently the offender had acted in prior cases, before BEM, when he would routinely ignore protective orders (Erez and Ibarra 2006). Victims attributed this contact-free period to the effectiveness of the technology.

Monitoring-facility logs backed up the women's perceptions. Records kept by River County (which averaged 183 cases per year) indicated that eleven "radius penetrations" were committed by seven persons over a two-year period, most of which were classified by staff as "informational violations" (Erez et al. 2004). These were essentially "drive-by penetrations"; the defendant was curious about whether the woman had a male guest at her home, or was testing the sensitivity of the monitoring equipment. These violations were often observed to have been committed while the defendant was intoxicated. Only one of the eleven cases could be classified as overtly hostile. In this case, a "jealous husband" was upset that his wife had a boyfriend at her apartment, for which the husband was still paying rent. After cutting off his anklet without being detected, he showed up at the apartment, broke down the locked door, and threatened to do lethal harm to both the woman and himself. The victim alerted authorities to her erstwhile partner's presence through the use of her duress pendant, and police in turn responded rapidly. At Lakefront, over a nine-year period, there were no "intentional" violations of the victim's home radius. "Incidental" penetrations were not considered intentional violations unless they formed part of a pattern, and the staff discerned none.

Certain kinds of contacts are not registered by electronic monitoring technology. For example, encounters at court, telephone calls, contacts by proxy, chance meetings on the street, sent flowers and mail, etc. Although victims were known to make complaints about these contacts to program staff, it is not known whether victims who participate in BEM programs report them at a higher rate than nonparticipating victims. However, it seems likely that victims in BEM programs who do report such contacts will find a more receptive ear, considering that they have already established relationships with program staff, whose duties include offering them support services (Erez and Ibarra 2006).

Face-to-face contact violations were the most common type of non–home-based violations reported by River County victims. There were few serious face-to-face violations reported by victims or program staff. One incident, at Lakefront, involved a "deranged" defendant (charged with stalking) showing up at the workplace of an unrequited former high school crush. Most face-to-face violations were the result of chance meetings in public places, during which the defendant might make a provocative comment to the victim. A common way in which defendants communicated face to face, albeit at a distance, was in the courtroom or in the courthouse hallway. Such communications were usually nonverbal gestures, and in some cases were done in the presence of unaware judges and attorneys (Erez et al., forthcoming).

It should be noted that RF technology does not track victims enrolled in BEM programs. Therefore, if victims try to contact the controlled parties, by telephone or in person at their residence, the surveillance system will be unable to detect it. In fact, both defendants and convicted abusers in the BEM study spoke about having been contacted and sometimes harassed by the victims, typically by telephone, and some mentioned that the women drove by their homes repeatedly, as if to taunt them. Some women admitted driving by the defendants' homes, claiming that they wanted assurance that he was where he was supposed to be during curfew hours; others admitted to driving past defendants' homes to check whether their field-monitoring devices were operational. Some defendants claimed that the victims made conjugal visits to their homes, which the victims denied. However, a probation officer, during a surprise home visit, found a protected victim hiding in a defendant's shower, leading to the latter's arrest for violating the no-contact order. Finally, some victims stated that they initiated telephone calls to the defendant, but only for some practical reason, such as to make arrangements for a child to be picked up or dropped off. According to these women, an intermediary, such as a friend, family member, or program support staffer, usually placed the call on their behalf (Erez et al., forthcoming).

Bilateral Electronic Monitoring as an Alternative to the Battered Women's Shelter

BEM provides abused women with an alternative to relocating to a battered women's shelter in the face of domestic violence. However, the gateway to BEM is through the criminal justice system: As a court-ordered measure, it presumes that a complaint has been filed against a putative abuser. Women who go to shelters need not officially report abuse in order to gain entrance there. BEM may be a viable alternative for women who are reluctant to relocate to a shelter; it allows them to remain in their current living conditions, undisturbed. As a result, they (and, if present, their children) are encouraged to resume a semblance of a "normal life," without fear of sabotage, and beyond the controlling presence of an abuser, something that most people take for granted but which many domestic violence victims cannot (Erez and Ibarra 2006).

Participation in BEM results in the diminishment of victim invisibility. BEM's protected parties

need not go into seclusion or be secretive about their location. Indeed, because the victim must file a complaint as a prelude to program entrance, she makes herself visible to a broad array of persons whose services she can seek in the event of need. The victim, for example, is not restricted to calling a police dispatcher lacking familiarity with her case, or seeking solace and protection in a personal support network (although women enrolled in BEM report a flowering of their social life during their tenure). She can mobilize a variety of functionaries with personal knowledge of her identity and the intricacies of her abuse history, including the program personnel with whom she develops relations (for an extensive discussion of this and other points related to the idea that BEM offers an alternative to shelter, see Erez and Ibarra 2006).

The Temporary Nature of Bilateral Electronic Monitoring

The BEM study found that participating women grow attached to the services and enhanced sense of personal safety that are associated with being a BEM enrollee, making the transition out of the program anxiety ridden. The temporary nature of BEM, however, is not a limitation unique to this program; it is common for society's responses to "social problems" to be temporary in nature. Residence in a shelter is temporary, as is an abuser's lock-up on domestic violence charges. In spite of the limited time that a victim might be in the program, participants feel that the existence of the BEM option should be conveyed to abused women by authorities as well as shelter personnel (Erez and Ibarra 2006).

The Role of Human Supervision in Bilateral Electronic Monitoring Programs

Although the nature of EM technology is important in that its capacities and limitations will circumscribe its reach and application, of greater significance is the program in which the technology is anchored. The program sets eligibility rules, defines expectations for participants' conduct while they are enrolled in the program, and directs how program personnel interact with participants and enforce program expectations. BEM programs can also be influenced to varying degrees by the research literature on domestic violence and the notion that BEM might be a type of intervention in an abusive interpersonal relationship (Ibarra 2005).

For example, one of the sites in the BEM study (River County) drew its cases from parties who were both in current and former relationships, while the second site (Lakefront) almost exclusively referred only parties whose relationship had undergone an irrevocable breach. Lakefront personnel went to great lengths to be certain that the victim wanted nothing to do with the defendant before ordering the equipment's installation, while River County personnel saw much merit in ordering the equipment precisely when the victim was ambivalent about her relationship with the defendant. Because the River County program enrolled many participants whose lives were still enmeshed with one another, emotionally, materially, and socially, program personnel approached interactions with male participants with a concern to detect "risk factors" in their living environments that might incline them to seek contact with the victim, and sought frequent encounters with them (e.g., through office and home visits) in order to gauge the presence of "red flags" indicative of elevated danger to the victim. Furthermore, the River County program was far more onerous in the imposition of liberty restrictions on male participants (Ibarra 2005). For instance, River County required defendants to make weekly office visits during which urine screens were administered, and to submit to surprise home visits. Lakefront did not have such rules and policies in place, deeming them too intrusive or burdensome for nonconvicted persons. Similarly, River County more strictly limited "out hours" to work and travel time, and required advance notice of up to one week for deviations from agreed-upon schedules. Lakefront was more flexible in setting curfews and had a "hands off" attitude toward defendants' whereabouts while they were not working, provided they returned home before 11 p.m.

Life on the Box: The Controlled Party's Perspective

Differences in the intensity of supervision appear to be the most salient experiential dimension for the men who participate in BEM programs as controlled parties (Ibarra and Erez 2004). Men participating in the more intensively structured River County program, for example, expressed anger and resentment about the "pains" associated with BEM (cf. Payne and Gainey 1998). Citing their status as defendants, they reported feeling that they were being treated as if they had been found guilty without trial and were now living under a demoralizing and unjust regime. Their lives were more transparent; their everyday practices open to scrutiny, correction, and sanction. River County men reported having been "tricked"

into consenting to enroll, because the extent of supervision had not been explained to them beforehand. Lakefront men, the overwhelming majority of whom were also defendants at the time of their enrollments, did not voice these criticisms or concerns. Instead, for the latter, BEM was more of an inconvenience rather than an injustice, notwithstanding the fact that they were required to subsidize the cost of administering the program by way of a weekly fee and that they were required to participate in BEM in order to be released on bond (Ibarra and Erez 2004).

Bilateral Electronic Monitoring for Domestic Violence as Diversion

Diversion programs attempt to meet several goals: providing services and assistance to violators, minimizing "unnecessary" social control, reducing recidivism, and decreasing the cost of justice administration. The use of BEM for domestic violence cases addresses these aims but also manifests a criticism often made of diversion. In particular, there is support for the idea that BEM exhibits the kind of "net widening" that critics have observed with other forms of diversion (Ibarra and Erez 2005). *Net widening* refers to the idea that alternatives to penal strategies represent an extension of penal control by the criminal justice system over civil society (Austin and Krisberg 1981; McMahon 1990). Net-widening occurs: (1) when people are brought into the system who would have otherwise exited it if not for the existence of a diversion program, (2) through the creation of new agencies and services that effectively supplement rather than replace the original set of control mechanisms, and (3) by the creation of diversionary programs that are more intrusive than would have been entailed by the justice system's ordinary handling of such cases.

Net widening is pertinent because domestic violence cases usually have high nonprosecution and dismissal rates relative to other violent offenses (Fagan 1995). The net-widening thesis would suggest that BEM participants are likelier to become enmeshed in criminal justice processing than nonparticipants. For example, although all domestic violence arrestees are arraigned prior to release, only some will end up on BEM, and these will tend to have a different experience with the criminal justice system upon release, owing to the greater transparency of their lives during the post-arrest period and the interest that the prosecution will take in their cases (Ibarra and Erez 2005).

Administrative data analyzed by Ibarra and Erez (2005) support the net-widening thesis. Dismissal rates for BEM participants with pending cases (i.e., defendants) over a two-year period are significantly lower for BEM than for non-BEM participants. The average number of days that BEM participants spend in the program is higher (mean = 48, median = 29) compared with the number of days that non-BEM participants spend in jail (mean = 30, median = 20). BEM participants' cases are likelier to last longer and culminate in verdict-based dispositions. These trends are contrary to the underlying premise of diversion: to divert offenders away from deeper or more extensive engagement with the system. The lower dismissal rates for BEM participants apparently reflect the continued participation of the prosecuting witnesses in the cases, which in turn results in defendants seeking continuances, either to build stronger defenses or to wear down complainants' resolve to remain involved with prosecution efforts.

Conclusion

BEM addresses longstanding concerns about the safety of domestic violence victims during a volatile period in an abusive relationship. When used in pretrial circumstances, it appears to direct participants on a course that is likelier to result in a verdict-based disposition, rather than toward the dismissal of the case, which is likelier with non-BEM defendants. BEM programs have the potential to empower victims who participate in them but also to result in arrestees who feel demoralized by the restrictions and supervision. The crafting of BEM programs is likely to continue to change, with the development of new technological capabilities, evolving concerns about the legal liabilities of jurisdictions that implement it, and as new categories of offenders continue to be brought under its purview. For example, questions about whether it is more or differently effective to administer BEM for post–separation-phase parties than for pre–separation-phase parties, or vice versa, and whether varying technological platforms should be used for parties in varying relationship phases also need to be addressed by future research. Similarly, future research might investigate agencies that are implementing BEM in conjunction with batterer intervention programs, as an alternative

to incarceration, and with varying degrees of supervision and program restrictions.

PETER R. IBARRA

See also **Batterer Intervention Programs; Domestic Violence Courts; Judicial Perspectives on Domestic Violence; Lautenberg Law; Mandatory Arrest Policies**

References and Further Reading

Austin, J., and B. Krisberg. "Wider, Stronger, and Different Nets: The Dialectics of Criminal Justice Reform." *Journal of Research in Crime and Delinquency* 18 (1981): 165–196.

Crowe, A. H., L. Sydney, P. Bancroft, and B. Lawrence. *Offender Supervision with Electronic Technology*. Lexington, KY: American Probation and Parole Association, 2002.

Erez, E., and P. R. Ibarra. "Making Your Home a Shelter: Electronic Monitoring and Victim Re-Entry in Domestic Violence Cases." *British Journal of Criminology* (June 12, 2006). http://bjc.oxfordjournals.org/cgi/content/abstract/azl026v2 (accessed August 17).

Erez, E., P. R. Ibarra, and N. A. Lurie. "Applying Electronic Monitoring to Domestic Violence Cases: A Study of Two Bilateral Programs." *Federal Probation* (2004): 15–20.

———. *The Electronic Monitoring of Domestic Violence Cases: A Study of Two RF-based Programs*. Report submitted to the National Institute of Justice, Washington, DC, forthcoming.

Fagan, J. "The Criminalization of Domestic Violence: Promises and Limits," 1995. *NIJ Research Report* http://www.ncjrs.org/txtfiles/crimdom.txt (accessed June 2, 2006).

Ibarra, P. R. "Red Flags and Trigger Control: The Role of Human Supervision in an Electronic Monitoring Program." *Sociology of Crime, Law, and Deviance* 6 (2005): 31–48.

Ibarra, P. R., and E. Erez. "Life on the Box: Electronic Monitoring and the Refashioning of Everyday Life." Paper presented at the annual meetings of the American Society of Criminology, Nashville, TN, 2004.

———. "Victim-Centric Diversion? The Electronic Monitoring of Domestic Violence Cases." *Behavioral Sciences and the Law* 23, no. 2 (2005): 259–276.

McMahon, M. "'Net Widening': Vagaries in the Use of a Concept." *British Journal of Criminology* 30 (1990): 121–149.

Payne, B. K., and R. R. Gainey. "A Qualitative Assessment of the Pains Experienced on Electronic Monitoring." *International Journal of Offender Therapy and Comparative Criminology* 42 (1998): 149–163.

Vollum, S., and C. Hale. "Electronic Monitoring: A Research Review." *Corrections Compendium* 27 (2002): 1–26.

EXCHANGE THEORY

An exchange theory of family violence is derived from the assumptions and propositions of social exchange theory (Blau 1964; Homans 1961; Thibault and Kelley 1959) and control theory (Hirschi 1969). The assumptions, concepts, and propositions of exchange theory are designed to explain all forms of intimate and family violence, ranging from corporal punishment to homicide and including violence and abusive acts in all intimate relationships.

The exchange approach to human behavior has a long history in both sociology and anthropology (Nye 1979). The key assumptions of the exchange perspective are:

1. Social behavior is a series of exchanges.
2. In the course of these exchanges, individuals attempt to maximize their rewards and minimize their costs.
3. Under certain circumstances, a person will accept certain costs in exchange for other rewards.
4. When one receives rewards from others, one is obliged to reciprocate and supply benefits to them in return (from Homans 1961; Blau 1964; Nye 1979).

The key concepts used by exchange theorists are rewards, costs, and reciprocity. Rewards are defined as pleasures, satisfactions, and gratifications (Thibault and Kelley 1959). Rewards also include gains in status, relationships, interaction, experiences other than interaction, and feelings that provide gratification to people (Nye 1979: 2). Costs are defined as any loss in status, loss of a relationship or milieu, or feeling disliked by an individual or group (Nye 1979: 2). There are two types of costs: (1) punishments and (2) losing out on some reward because another alternative was chosen (missing a good movie because you chose to go to a concert). Reciprocity is the key to social exchange. In brief, people are expected to help those who help them and not injure them (Gouldner 1960).

Control Theory

The assumptions and propositions of control theory were developed and defined by Hirschi (1969) to explain deviant behavior. Hirschi begins with the assumption that most people are tempted from time to time to engage in deviant behavior—including violence. For Hirschi, the central question is not "Why do people engage in deviant acts?" but rather, "Why do people conform most of the time?"

From this assumption, Hirschi develops the following propositions (which were originally developed to explain delinquent behavior):

1. The more attached people are to family, friends, and neighbors, the more involved they are in socially approved activities (e.g., school and work); and the stronger their belief in legitimate opportunities, the more likely they are to conform (i.e., not use violence toward loved ones).
2. Those with few or weak attachments, low levels of commitment and involvement, and lack of opportunities, or who hold the belief that conformity will not be rewarded, are more likely to engage in deviance and violent acts.

In his later work, Hirschi (Gottfredson and Hirschi 1990) focused on "self-control"—the willingness to defer gratification and exercise perseverance, caution, patience, planning, and sensitivity to others. The assumptions guiding this work include the notion that low self-control is due to faulty socialization. The key proposition, added to those above, is that low parental control leads to low self-control and thus to acts of deviance.

Applying Exchange Theory to Family Violence

As with the general exchange theory, the key assumption of an exchange theory of family violence is that human interaction is guided by the pursuit of rewards and the avoidance of punishment and costs. Simply stated, individuals will use force and violence in their relationships with intimates and family members if they believe that the rewards of force and violence outweigh the costs of such behavior.

A second assumption is that a person who supplies reward services to another obliges the other to fulfill a reciprocal obligation; and thus, the second individual must furnish benefits to the first (Blau 1964). Blau (1964) explains that if reciprocal exchange occurs, the interaction continues. However, if reciprocity is not received, the interaction will be broken off. Of course, family relations, including partner relations, parent–child relations, and sibling relations, are more complex and have a unique social structure compared with the exchanges that typically exist outside of the family. First, given the nature of family relations, including legal and blood ties, it is difficult to "break off" the interaction, even when there is little or no reciprocity. While one can break off a social interaction with a friend or coworker, can quit or be fired from a job, or leave one's church or synagogue and join another, breaking off an interaction with a spouse may require a formal legal divorce. Breaking off relations between parents and children is even more socially constrained and difficult. Even when one becomes an "ex-spouse," it is difficult to become an ex-parent. Parents can disown children or even petition family or juvenile courts to have their parental rights terminated. These, however, are difficult, complex, and rare occurrences. Unless a parent abandons a child, unless the child runs away, or unless there is court-imposed or court-approved termination of the parental responsibilities, parents and children are tied to one another for life, even if there is low or minimal reciprocity.

A second unique aspect of the family and intimate relationships is the substantial difference in power—personal, social, and psychological. Most, if not all, societies are patriarchal and thus grant men more social, economic, and legal power than is granted to women. Men are often older, larger, and stronger than their women partners. For much of their interaction with their children, parents are physically larger and more powerful than their children, and have more economic, personal, and social resources. Parents have a legal and constitutional right to raise their children without unwarranted interference by the state. Although child welfare agencies have the authority to investigate cases of abuse and neglect and to take short-term custody of maltreated children with *ex parte* court orders, state involvement in child rearing is rigorously constrained. Federal and state law require that state departments of child welfare make reasonable efforts to keep maltreated children with their birth parents, and the process of actually terminating parental rights is typically long and complex. Thus the exchanges between parents and children, especially young children, are inequitable, with the parents holding the most social power and social resources.

The family playing field, within which costs and rewards are calculated and reciprocity measured, is not an even one. Intrafamilial relations are more complex than those studied by traditional exchange theorists. In some instances it is not feasible or possible to break off interaction, even if there is no reciprocity. When the "principle of distributive justice" is violated, there can be increased anger, resentment, conflict, and violence.

Many students of family violence tend to view violence as the last resort to solving problems in the family. F. Ivan Nye (1979), however, notes that this need not be the case. Spanking, for instance, is frequently the first choice of action by many parents.

The Key Proposition

A central and oversimplified proposition of an exchange theory approach to corporal punishment is that people hit family members because they can. People will use violence toward family members when the costs of being violent do not outweigh the rewards.

There are a variety of costs for being violent. First, there is the potential that the victim will hit back. Second, a violent assault could lead to the arrest and/or imprisonment of the person who has done the hitting. Using violence could also lead to a loss of status. Finally, too much violence might lead to the dissolution of the family or the end of the relationship. Thus there are potential significant costs involved in being violent.

Formal and informal social control are means of raising the costs of violent behavior. Police intervention, criminal charges, imprisonment, fines, and loss of income are all forms of formal social control that could raise the costs and lower the rewards of violent behavior. Informal social control includes loss of status, the stigma of being considered an abuser, and social ostracism.

From these basic assumptions, there are certain structural properties of families that make them violence prone, and there are specific family and individual traits that make certain families more at risk for violence than other families. The structural properties of the family as a social institution, especially in the developed world, are intimacy, privacy, and inequality.

Intimacy

It goes without saying that across time and societies, family interactions are the most intimate of social interactions. Not only do family members have more intimate knowledge of one another, but membership in a family obligates other family members to share intimacies. Belonging to a family carries with it the right to influence other family members and the obligation to be influenced. As a result, the stake that people have in family interactions and relationships is much more than that which people have in other social relationships.

Privacy

The modern family is a private social institution. Law, custom, and culture combine to create a zone of privacy around the family as a social institution and an interaction setting. Behaviors, such as physical force or violence, that might provoke an intervention by an observer or bystander are responded to with selective inattention or even subtle approval if they are perceived to be between family members. The household has various levels of privacy. The public rooms—living room and dining room—are where what Goffman (1959) called "front stage" behavior occurs. The "family room" or "den" is a more private setting, and the bedrooms and bathrooms are the most private locations in the modern home. The more lethal forms of violence occur in the more private sections of the home—the bedroom and kitchen—out of sight of bystanders and even other family members (Gelles 1974). The privacy of the family reduces the visibility of family interactions and the likelihood of external informal or formal social control.

Inequality

This article has already alluded to the structured inequality in the family. Unlike most other interaction settings, the family is made up of individuals of different sexes and, most importantly, different ages and generations. The position of husband and father has traditionally been invested with greater status and power, parents have greater social and legal power than do their children, and older family members have more power in some societies (however, in Western societies, the oldest family members suffer from a loss of economic and social power when they leave the workforce). Because of differences in size, strength, and social power, some family members (e.g., husbands, parents, children with elderly parents) exercise force and violence with little fear of retaliation or harm.

Derived Propositions

From the main proposition that people hit family members because they can, and drawing on the three unique structural features of the family, one can expand the main proposition into three others that can explain and predict the occurrence of family and intimate violence:

1. Individuals are more likely to use violence at home when they expect the costs of being violent to be less than the rewards.
2. The absence of effective social controls (e.g., public disapproval, loss of status or a job, police arrest/incarceration) over family and intimate relationships decreases the costs of one family member using violence toward another.
3. Certain social and family structures reduce social control in family relationships and therefore reduce the costs and increase the rewards of being violent.

In addition to these propositions, exchange theory can be used to develop a testable hypothesis about individual behavior in families:

1. The more an individual anticipates costs and punishments for violent behavior toward a family member, the less likely it is that the individual will use violence in the family.
2. The greater the perceived costs of using violence in the family, the less likely an individual will be to engage in violent behavior.
3. The more an individual has a stake in conformity, that is, the more an individual has to lose in terms of social or economic status, the less likely the individual will be to use violence in the family, assuming that there is a likelihood of informal or formal social control and that there are specific costs for being identified as someone who engages in acts of family violence.

Goode (1971) offers an additional perspective on the balance of costs and rewards and how the calculus of costs and rewards can increase or decrease the likelihood of family or intimate violence. Goode explains that all social systems rest, to one degree or another, on force and its use. With regard to the likelihood of intimate violence, Goode states that the greater the nonviolent resources available to an individual, the more force that individual has the ability to use, but the less he or she will actually deploy the violence. Violence is a more common behavior among those who do not have access to personal, economic, social, and other nonviolent resources.

Tests of Exchange Theory

The sociologist Kirk Williams (1992) tested some of the main propositions of exchange theory of family and intimate violence using data from two national surveys of family violence and their follow-up studies. The findings from the study indicated that men who believed themselves more isolated from the police (greater privacy/lower likelihood of formal social control), who were more powerful in their relationship with their partners (greater inequality), and who approved of men hitting their partners (lower perceived costs of violence) were less likely to perceive arrest as costly to them. Men who perceived the costs of arrest as low were more likely to assault their partners. Thus, there is empirical support for the main propositions of an exchange theory of family violence.

RICHARD J. GELLES

See also **Attachment Theory and Domestic Violence; Battered Woman Syndrome; Battered Women: Held in Captivity; Control Balance Theory and Domestic Violence; Feminist Theory; Popular Culture and Domestic Violence; Social Learning Theory and Family Violence**

References and Further Reading

Blau, P. M. *Exchange and Power in Social Life*. New York: Wiley, 1964.

Gelles, R. J. *The Violent Home*. Beverly Hills, CA: Sage Publications, 1974.

————. "An Exchange/Social Control Theory." In *The Dark Side of Families: Current Family Violence Research*, edited by D. Finkelhor, R. Gelles, M. Straus, and G. Hotaling. Beverly Hills, CA: Sage, 1983, pp. 151–165.

Goffman, E. *The Presentation of Self in Everyday Life*. New York: Doubleday, 1959.

Goode, W. "Force and Violence in the Family." *Journal of Marriage and the Family* 33 (1971): 624–636.

Gottfredson, M. R., and T. Hirschi. *A Control Theory of Crime*. Stanford, CA: Stanford University Press, 1990.

Gouldner, A. "The Norm of Reciprocity." *American Sociological Review* 25 (1960): 161–178.

Hirschi, T. *Causes of Delinquency*. Berkeley and Los Angeles: University of California Press, 1969.

Homans, G. *Social Behavior: Its Elementary Forms*. New York: Harcourt Brace Jovanovich, 1961.

Nye, F. I. "Choice, Exchange, and the Family." In *Contemporary Theories about the Family*, vol. 2, edited by W. R. Burr, R. Hill, F. I. Nye, and I. L. Reiss. New York: Free Press, 1979, pp. 1–41.

Thibault, J. W., and H. H. Kelley. *The Social Psychology of Groups*. Morristown, NJ: General Learning Press, 1959.

Willliams, K. "Social Sources of Marital Violence and Deterrence: Testing and Integrated Theory of Assaults between Partners." *Journal of Marriage and the Family* 54 (1992): 620–629.

EXPERT TESTIMONY IN DOMESTIC VIOLENCE CASES

Introduction

Many people have seen an "expert witness" in a courtroom or at the scene of a crime on a variety of television shows. These popular shows depict a highly educated and sophisticated expert with several degrees, including a Ph.D., who has all the answers. These shows portray both the reality and the fantasy of expert witnesses and their role in the judicial system. This article will discuss the history of the use of expert witnesses, admissibility of expert opinions, and types of expert testimony. The final section will discuss the use of expert witnesses in domestic violence situations.

History

The use of expert witnesses in the courtroom to assist law enforcement officials dates back to the Salem, Massachusetts, witch trials of 1692, when a Doctor Brown first testified in a heresy trial. He informed the court that in his medical opinion, the defendant had bewitched the victims. From this dubious beginning, the use of expert witnesses has grown in both criminal and civil cases to include any relevant topic that is beyond the ordinary knowledge of everyday jurors.

In both civil and criminal cases, the justice system has come to depend on expert witnesses. For example, in 1996 there were 110 crime laboratories in the United States. By 1976 there were 240 active crime lab facilities, and in 1992 that figure increased to over 345 labs. This explosive growth of forensic facilities has not occurred without complications. Some personnel in these laboratories have incorrectly identified various physical items, including hair samples, blood typing, and bullets. The overwhelming majority of these facilities, however, have performed painstaking analyses that have assisted law enforcement agencies in their pursuit of finding the truth.

Admission of Expert Testimony

Frye vs. United States (1923) was the first major case that dealt with scientific evidence presented by expert witnesses. The Court of Appeals determined that the admission of expert testimony regarding a systolic blood pressure deception test was unacceptable. The ruling was based on the rationale that the test had not gained enough general acceptance or standing among physiological and psychological authorities. Thus the first guideline for admissibility of expert testimony is: The source from which the witness's scientific deduction is made must be sufficiently established to have gained general acceptance in the particular field in which it belongs.

Rule 702 of the Federal Rules of Evidence further details the guidelines that should be used in determining the admissibility of expert testimony. It states that expert testimony must assist the jury in understanding the evidence or material facts of a case. After *Daubert vs. Merrell Dow Pharmaceuticals* (1993) was settled, the rule was amended to include the following standards: The testimony must (1) be based upon sufficient facts or data, (2) be the product of reliable principles and methods, and (3) be the result of the application of these principles and methods by the witness to the facts of the case.

Qualifications

Expert witnesses come with a variety of different qualifications and backgrounds. Contrary to popular belief, an expert witness does not have to have a Ph.D. The expert witness must have special education, training, knowledge, or experience in an area that is the subject of his or her testimony. Experts may simply have a high school education, but must have worked in an area for a significant number of years and received special training that is unique to their profession. At the other end of the spectrum, experts may have a number of degrees and have conducted research in a particular area but have never worked in that area. Many experts will fall within the happy medium of the spectrum, having both an advanced education in the form of a bachelor's or master's degree and several years of work experience in a specific field. In the area of domestic violence, there are a number of victim advocates who do not have advanced degrees but have qualified as expert witnesses.

Types of Expert Opinions

Expert witnesses may testify about a number of different facts. Some experts may testify about physical evidence such as DNA samples; other experts, such as psychologists, may testify about a defendant's state of mind. Still others may testify about what occurred at a crime scene. No matter what an expert witness testifies to, he or she must be qualified as an expert in the area of testimony. This is especially true when dealing with expert testimony in domestic violence situations.

Expert Witnesses in Domestic Violence Situations

Expert witness testimony in domestic violence situations is still controversial. The controversy lies in the fact that many laypersons have misconceptions surrounding the complexities associated with domestic violence. Attorneys will therefore use expert witnesses in the hope of dispelling these misconceptions.

The testimony of such expert witnesses can take a number of different forms. In situations where it seems unfathomable why a victim would choose to stay with her abuser, experts are brought in to testify about the dynamics of battering and explain why this might occur. In other instances, a victim may attack or kill her abuser even though she was not being abused at the time. An expert witness is then used to testify about the victim's state of mind. The expert will discuss the issue of imminent danger and explain why the victim used deadly force as a method of defense.

Conclusion

More and more courts are accepting expert witness testimony in the area of domestic violence. The use of expert witnesses in these situations plays an essential role in explaining to jurors the dynamics of battering and why victims may act the way they do.

FRANCES MA and HARVEY WALLACE

See also **Battered Woman Syndrome as a Legal Defense in Cases of Spousal Homicide; Domestic Violence Courts; Judicial Perspectives on Domestic Violence; Legal Issues for Battered Women; Mediation in Domestic Violence; Violence against Women Act**

References and Further Reading

Holtz, L. *Criminal Evidence for Law Enforcement Officers,* 5th ed. Charlottesville, VA: Gould Publications, 2005.
Schuller, R. "Juror's Decisions in Trials of Battered Women Who Kill: The Role of Prior Beliefs and Expert Testimony." *Journal of Applied Psychology* 24 (1994): 316.
Wallace, H. *Family Violence: Legal, Medical, and Social Perspectives*, 4th ed. Boston: Allyn & Bacon, 2005.

Cases and Statutes

Daubert vs. Merrell Dow Pharmaceuticals, 113 S.Ct. 2786 (1993)
Federal Rules of Evidence 702
Frye vs. United States, 293 Fed 1013 (D.C. Cir. 1923)

F

FACTORS INFLUENCING REPORTING BEHAVIOR BY MALE DOMESTIC VIOLENCE VICTIMS

Introduction

Each year thousands of innocent men are victims of violence in their own homes. Domestic violence is an established fact for these men, whether their partner is a man or a woman. These men suffer the same type of assaults as women victims, in roughly the same or greater proportion, and yet they are far less likely to report their victimization than women. What makes these men so reluctant to report their abusers?

For many men in abusive relationships, their reasons for staying, and for not reporting the violence, are tightly enmeshed. They are also very similar to the reasons given by women in abusive relationships. They are in love with their abusers. They hope the abusers will change. They believe that they have done something wrong which warrants this treatment. They fear losing their partners, children, homes, friends, etc.

Male victims of domestic violence are, however, different in significant ways from female victims. In addition to the issues they have in common with female victims, there are particular issues unique to male victims. The lack of attention paid to these issues is the biggest hindrance to helping male victims of domestic violence.

Fear Issues

Fear is one of the major deterrents to reporting domestic violence among both women and men. Both genders fear that the police will not help them. Both also fear that calling the police will make things worse. They fear that their abusers will become even angrier and will return from police custody to abuse them more severely.

Men have special fear issues not generally shared by women. These include the fear that they themselves will be arrested by police. The police may believe that the woman accused of abuse was violent only in self-defense. This fear is more likely to turn into a reality if the man has used physical force to defend himself. Any mark he may have left on a woman batterer as he acted in self-defense—for example, from holding her off or shoving her away—may be perceived as evidence that he was the batterer and she was defending herself. If this scenario should actually happen to the man, he is even less likely to report future violence.

For a man in a homosexual relationship, calling the police about his victimization brings with it the risk of maltreatment and disbelief from a homophobic officer. Gay victims may also fear social repercussions from the gay community for airing such a problem when it is already so difficult for them to gain acceptance in the larger community. Admitting that problems exist within gay relationships simply fuels the discrimination leveled against the gay community. Gay male victims may also fear that their victimization will be seen as resulting from their "choice" of lifestyle and therefore deserved.

Gay victims suffer under the further threat that they will be exposed if they report their domestic victimization. For those who are not open about their sexual orientation, fear of being discovered in a gay relationship often outweighs their fear of the damage their partners will inflict on them.

Men with disability issues also live with the fear that if they report the abuse, their abusive caretakers will abandon them. In these cases, fear is intertwined with dependency. For the gay community, AIDS is in many ways comparable to a disability in the straight community. The man with AIDS, like the man with any other terminal illness, knows he will become progressively more ill and will become more dependent on his partner for his medical care. The further his illness progresses, the fewer options he has for survival outside of the relationship.

Masculinity Issues

The battered man may also fear a loss of self-respect, coupled with the fear that others—including the batterer, friends, family, and outsiders—will view him as being less than a man. Human society, over thousands of years and across virtually all cultures, has been organized around a patriarchal system in which the man is dominant and the woman subservient. When the woman is the batterer and the man the victim, this system is turned upside down. Both the man and the woman in this situation may be uncertain of how to renegotiate their relationship.

Traditional socialization of boy children includes admonitions against crying, against hitting girls, and against overreliance on others to solve personal problems. Boys are taught that a real adult man is strong, supports his family, and displays masculine characteristics such as daring, courage, and willingness to face danger. Boys are taught toward whom, when, and why they should use physical force. A man is not supposed to fight a woman—he is to come to her defense.

How is a man to translate his upbringing, which tells him to protect women, into useful action when a woman victimizes him? Fighting back is not viewed as an acceptable option. Crying is not viewed as an acceptable response. Admitting defeat and seeking help are also not options. These responses would be exactly the opposite of what almost every society's version of masculinity dictates.

Many men derive their male identities in relation to their spouses and families. Being viewed as a good provider is a source of self-esteem that may otherwise be lacking in the abused man's life. A good provider typically has a stable family with no outward problems. Admitting to victim status can be seen as revealing shortcomings as a man and as a provider.

For many couples their marriage vows are sacred and cannot be broken. This belief, combined with pressure from friends and family to stay together, creates a powerful deterrent to any behavior that would threaten the marriage. Add to this the pressure for the man to be a good provider and the man may feel that to report his wife's violent behavior would let down the people most important to him. He would not be living up to his responsibilities or their expectations. He would also be failing in his role as husband and provider.

If the man is seen as neglecting his role to provide, protect, and dominate in his household, then he is easily seen as being less than a man. Male victims may deny, even to themselves, that they have a problematic relationship; they attempt to assert that they can handle the situation or that the situation is not what it really is—abuse. Asserting that he can take his wife's abuse is a way of asserting manhood. Calling the police demonstrates a lack of manhood.

Denial also spares the man the public ridicule he fears if he should tell anyone of his plight. He wonders how his friends will react. He fears that they will belittle him and dismiss his problems as something he has foolishly allowed to develop by not taking charge of his home life. His self-image may thus be further damaged by admitting his victimization. His relationships with other men outside of his domestic situation may be the only arena he has to support some self-concept of being a real man.

Denial is also present when a man chooses not to seek medical attention when necessary for his injuries. If the damage a woman inflicts on him is bad enough to require a doctor's attention, how can he assert that he is a real man and is in charge of his life?

Emotional Issues

An often overlooked feature in men's lives is their emotional attachment to their mates. Men are taught from childhood to cover up their emotions. The level of success men have achieved in this cover-up has led to the belief that they do not possess emotions or that the emotions they do have are not as strong as those of a woman. This belief is incorrect. Men do form emotional attachments, and their behavior is often based on their attempts to preserve them.

A man's emotional attachment to his mate has an effect on him that is similar to the effect a woman's attachment has on her. He does not want to do anything to damage that attachment. Reporting his victimization may result in an end to that attachment. His mate may leave him or may be placed in jail. He is thus willing to tolerate behaviors from his mate that he would not accept from a stranger. His tolerance level for the violence may in fact be directly proportional to his attachment level and the level of threat to that attachment that reporting the abuse may pose.

Closely related to emotional attachment is sexual attachment. Ready access to sex would end if reporting the abuse caused an end to the relationship. Sex is often as much a need as an attachment. Maintaining a method of meeting one's needs is a strong motivation to tolerate a level of unpleasantness in a relationship. Again, tolerance is proportional to attachment and need levels.

For an abused man, the accumulation of fear and anxiety over his self-image and his ability to cope with his situation creates a feeling of helplessness. The symptoms are similar to those of women suffering from what has come to be identified as *learned helplessness*. This occurs when a person is repeatedly victimized and comes to believe that there is no escape from the situation and no one to whom to turn for help. He or she becomes depressed, suffers from lowered self-esteem, and feels powerless to change both the current situation and its prognosis for the future. Many persons of both genders also take on feelings of responsibility for the violence, believing that they have somehow caused it and are deserving of it.

Dependency issues, whether from illness, disability, economics, or other sources, will contribute to the guilt victims feel. In the eyes of the victim, the abuser is seen as justified in using violence. The victim feels that he is a burden on the abuser and that if he were better able to take care of himself this would not happen. This "if only" trap keeps the dependent man within his abusive relationship and even causes him to defend his abuser's behavior if anyone attempts to intervene.

Hope can also become a trap for the abused man. His hope that the woman will change or that the abuse will eventually subside keeps him in the relationship. Reporting the violence represents a loss of hope for the future. He remembers a time when the relationship was not so volatile and uses this memory as evidence that his hope is not in vain.

Image Issues

The news media contributes greatly to people's views of the world. How the media chooses to portray certain classes of people creates for the general public images of who is socially respectable and who is not. The wording and visual images used in media are powerful persuaders. Female victims of domestic violence are portrayed as innocent women who suffer frequent and unprovoked attacks at the hands of men who are barely more than monsters. Male victims are portrayed as provoking the "punishment" they have received through their own stupidity. Their batterers are long-suffering wives who have been given saintly status for putting up with such men.

Mass media such as movies and television project this stereotype of abusive relationships. Survival stories of women who have overcome their abuse are popular fodder for made-for-TV movies on Sunday nights or on the Lifetime or Oxygen networks. Very few stories depicting women as batterers of men are depicted in this type of programming; the rare male victim is characterized as not as saintly or heroic as the women survivors.

This demonstrates for a male victim a choice of remaining silent or being publicly denounced as a dolt. If the man internalizes this image as reality, his self-conception can be greatly altered. He may even begin to believe that he is not very smart and that his wife is right to correct him. Even if he does not take on this image of himself, he may still remain silent in order to preserve his self-image as a man. He would see himself as different from the men who complain because he takes the abuse without complaining.

Federal legislation is also contributing to an image problem, where women are the only victims. The Violence Against Women Act implies by its very name that women, not men, are victims. At the very least it implies that male victims are unworthy of legislative attention.

When things in the home are so difficult, professional reputation seems to be the last vestige of the kind of life the man has worked for. Professional reputation is often linked in a man's mind with respect, self-esteem, and his ability to be a good provider for his family. He may suffer from legitimate concerns over the damage to his reputation that would come from making his victimization public. This problem may be particularly acute for a man employed in a caring profession such as counseling or ministerial work. Status on jobs seen as requiring a masculine image—police officer, athlete, mechanic, etc.—may also be vulnerable to damage from revealing one's victimization. The image of such a tradesman as a victim of domestic violence does not seem to compute.

Legal Issues

Traditionally laws concerning violence in the family in America have been gendered in such a way as to imply or specifically state that the man is the abuser and the woman is the victim. These laws have been used to interpret what happens in violent homes and what the criminal justice system, including the police, should do about domestic violence cases. A woman's fear is that her husband may be able to convince legal authorities to side with him. This is based on her fear of her husband. A man's fear is that the legal authorities are automatically going to side with the woman. This fear is based on legal tradition. The wife's emotional response (i.e., her tears) also typically outweighs anything the man can contribute to his case.

Family law related to divorce, division of assets, and child custody has also traditionally focused on women. Custody of children is normally granted to the woman, unless she is totally unfit to care for them. The father may have visitation rights or even partial custody. This does not always leave the father feeling that he has adequate access to or input with his children. He may feel that he has failed in his role as a father, and may question the appropriateness of leaving custody of his children to a woman he knows to be abusive. He may wonder what will happen to them if he leaves. If he takes them with him, he may face charges of kidnapping or interference with parental custody.

Division of assets in a divorce, even in a community-property state, typically means the wife gets the family home, or the home is sold and the proceeds split. Since traditionally men have had more stable and higher-paying jobs than women, courts have seen the male as being more readily able to start over with less. They have also seen him as able to continue to pay alimony and child support, thus forcing him to continue to have some kind of connection with his abuser. The reality is that the man will need to find a new home, which means that he will have to furnish and supply it. The economic costs are staggering and do not include the emotional costs involved in such a permanent end to the relationship. This is particularly true if the man is marginally employed or unemployed.

In addition to these civil issues, male victims have reason to be concerned about the response they may receive from the criminal legal system. Police are generally the first representatives of the system that victims face. The traditional response of police, even to female victims, has been to do nothing and hope that the parties work out their problems without killing each other.

Mandatory arrest policies have existed only since the 1980s and have generally been aimed at male abusers. Even in jurisdictions with mandatory arrest laws, the police do not always make an arrest in cases of domestic violence. In some cases, mandatory arrest policies have given way to *preferred* arrest policies. This means that the police have more legitimate discretion regarding whether to make an arrest. Police are just now being trained to determine which partner is the primary aggressor in a domestic incident and to arrest that person, regardless of gender. In many cases this means that both parties may go to jail as the police wait for the courts to sort out the complex situation they find. Use of criminal justice resources may not seem an acceptable option for a male victim for several reasons. Aside from the aforementioned fear that he will be arrested instead of or along with his abuser, he may not want his abuser arrested. Putting his children's mother in jail may seem to be the ultimate betrayal of his manly responsibilities toward his family.

Another problem arises for the male domestic violence victim who has a criminal record. A man with a criminal record is more likely to be seen by police as the abuser, even if his record is not for violent offenses. If the police do arrest the abuser, prosecutors often choose not to pursue the case based on the difficulty of gaining a conviction. Juries often have a hard time believing that a man with a criminal record can be the victim, especially of a woman. The difficulty is compounded when the male victim has previously been arrested for domestic violence himself.

For some men the problem is related to their immigration status. Even if they are in the United States legally, if they are not citizens, they can be deported for criminal behavior. Language barriers and cultural beliefs such as prohibitions against airing family problems can also keep an immigrant male from seeking aid. Men who have immigrated from countries where the police and other government agencies are repressive often take great lengths to avoid interaction with such authorities in the United States. Their fear of the police in their home country was so great that they cannot believe that American police are to be trusted. For this reason, living with the abuse may seem safer than seeking aid.

In response to legal issues such as equal protection, gender neutral laws concerning domestic violence are now becoming the norm across the United States. The change in legal language is significant. Men are not labeled as abusers and women are not labeled as victims. With the recognition that families are not all composed of a husband, a wife, and their natural children, the definitions of *family, domestic,* and other terms denoting who is protected have also been expanded to provide coverage to a greater number of persons. However, these changes have been accomplished almost in secrecy. Agencies simply change their publications to reflect the new wording without so much as a thought to what it means to the public they serve or how their services might need to be changed. This leaves many male victims unaware that the laws have changed to provide them with protection. Ironically, these laws are ahead of the social trend rather than behind it.

Where Would the Male Victim Go?

Society has made a decent effort to see that battered women are provided with alternatives such as shelters and the many services available through them. There are limitations, however. There are not enough shelters, not enough beds, some shelters do not allow a woman to bring male children, pets, etc. Fund raisers, legal referendums, federal grants, and other tactics are constantly being used to overcome this lack of services for women, but what services are available to men?

Shelters are for women. Toll-free hotlines are for women. Emergency housing is for women. Legal advocacy is for women. The majority of free counseling services, job training, and other social-welfare services are for women. Even the pamphlets distributed by government offices concerning domestic violence are for women victims. If men turn to these services, they are turned away. Service providers cannot, will not, or do not know how to help male victims.

Physicians are being trained to screen the women who come to them with injuries to identify possible victims of abuse. If a victim is identified, she can be provided with an advocate, information on how to get help, and assistance with filing a police report and leaving the violent relationship. Physicians are not being trained to look for the signs of domestic violence victimization in the injured men they treat. The need for such training of physicians to screen injured males is not seen as an urgent issue. This opportunity to encourage men to report their victimization is thus lost.

In fact, many feminist advocates for women deny that men *can* be victims. They believe prima facie that the woman accused of abuse must have been fighting back against the violence of the man. If he was not being violent at the time, then he must have been violent in the past. They are also aware that if they acknowledge that men can be victims, it would take away from the limited funding, resources, and support available for women victims.

This leaves male victims with nowhere to turn for help except the police. However, once the male victim realizes that there is no help for him from the services generally provided to abused women, why would he assume that the police would be any different? The lack of services may be making these men feel even more hopeless and even less likely to report their victimizations. Experience has taught them that no one cares. As in the learned helplessness theory, they feel alone and see no escape.

Conclusions

Fear, lack of support, and limited options for seeking help have hindered the willingness of male victims of domestic violence to report their abuse. This lack of reporting in turn perpetuates the myth that men are not victims, they are only abusers. Advocates for abused men find themselves in a Catch-22 situation. It is difficult to draw attention to and create services for a population of victims who appear not to exist in official measures. And yet it is this very lack of attention and services that keeps male victims from coming forward.

Feminist denials that women can be perpetrators of domestic violence create blockages to creating services that are needed by both male victims and female offenders. Even if a woman recognizes that she has a problem, she cannot find help, as the batterer intervention programs are aimed at males.

Denying the existence of both the victim and the offender creates a mystique that hides this problem from public attention. It also gives the man one less option to try to salvage his relationship. He cannot convince his female partner to seek help when there is none available.

Social apathy and feminist hostility has deterred not only the victimized men from coming forward, but also would-be advocates, researchers, and policymakers. The silencing of these sources continues to deprive battered men of the resources, information, and role models they need. Many opportunities to encourage these men to come forward are lost.

Due to the overwhelming neglect toward the plight of male victims, there are no rallies, no sponsored events, and no spokesmen. There are no men who are held up as role models who have survived abusive relationships. In short, abused men have no examples to follow. They have no heroes to help them overcome their fears and step forward. The media images of male victims show exactly the kind of man most victims do not want to be.

Just providing services will not be enough to make men step forward and report victimization. Even just applying the services already available to females will not be enough. There will still be issues relating to what happens to his children and pets when he leaves. There will also still be issues of overcoming his fears, maintaining his masculine self-image, and providing legal remedies that will be truly responsive to his needs. Most importantly, social support, acceptance, and encouragement will need to be present in order to win the trust of men who have been victimized in their homes and neglected in society.

LORIE RUBENSER

See also **Battered Husbands; Community Responses to Gay and Lesbian Domestic Violence; Gay and Bisexual Male Domestic Violence; Gender Socialization and Gay Male Domestic Violence; Intimate Partner Violence in Queer, Transgender, and Bisexual Communities; Male Victims of Domestic Violence and Reasons They Stay with Their Abusers**

References and Further Reading

Cook, Philip W. *Abused Men: The Hidden Side of Domestic Violence*. Westport, CT: Praeger, 1997.

Dobash, Russell P., and R. Emerson Dobash. "Women's Violence to Men in Intimate Relationships." *British Journal of Criminology* 44 (2004): 324–349.

Gosselin, Denis Kindsch. *Heavy Hands: An Introduction to the Crimes of Family Violence*, 3rd ed. Upper Saddle River, NJ: Pearson, Prentice Hall, 2005.

James, Thomas B. *Domestic Violence: The 12 Things You Aren't Supposed to Know*. Chula Vista, CA: Aventine Press, 2003.

Mills, Linda G. *Insult to Injury: Rethinking Our Responses to Intimate Abuse*. Princeton, NJ: Princeton University Press, 2003.

Steinmetz, Suzanne. "The Battered Husband Syndrome." *Victimology* 2, no. 3/4 (1978): 499–509.

Stith, Sandra M., and Murray A. Straus, eds. *Understanding Partner Violence: Prevalence, Causes, Consequences, and Solutions*. Minneapolis: National Council on Family Relations, 1995.

Walker, Lenore. *The Battered Woman Syndrome*, 2nd ed. New York: Springer Publishing, 2000.

Wallace, Harvey. *Family Violence: Legal, Medical, and Social Perspectives*, 3rd ed. Boston: Allyn and Bacon, 2002.

FATALITY REVIEWS IN CASES OF ADULT DOMESTIC VIOLENCE HOMICIDE AND SUICIDE

The reviewing of cases of domestic-violence related deaths commenced in a handful of U.S. states beginning in the early 1990s. As of 2005, roughly thirty-five states conduct what have become known as fatality reviews. The term *fatality review* refers to the identification and analysis of cases of adult homicide and suicide where one or more parties die due to domestic violence. Reviewers seek to prevent further deaths, injuries, and abuse from domestic violence by suggesting and perhaps introducing preventive strategies involving service providers and community members at large. Reviews differ greatly by community and jurisdiction. Many reviews report aggregate statistical data or summary demographic details. Others dig deeply into fatalities, exploring the multiple and often hidden compromises faced by victims of domestic violence. A number of review teams combine both quantitative and qualitative approaches, bringing both depth and breadth to their deliberations.

Case Selection

Fatality review teams typically do not review all deaths caused by, related to, or somehow traceable to domestic violence. Rather, they select cases for review based upon the impact of the case on the community, the legal difficulties associated with reviewing a particular case, the resources of the team, and the potential the case might have for identifying innovative preventive strategies. Teams recognize that various types of cases qualify for review.

Roughly 1,000 to 1,600 people per year die in the United States as a result of intimate partner homicide. Men kill female intimates in anywhere from two-thirds to three-quarters of intimate partner homicides. In one-quarter to one-third of these cases, females kill intimate male partners. The vast majority of male perpetrators kill females after a long, highly stylized, and escalating pattern of woman battering. Conversely, women typically kill male intimates under circumstances in which their male partners have battered them, often over long periods of time. Although fatality review teams have traditionally paid more attention to the deaths of women than the deaths of men, both sets of cases display similar background characteristics and invite comparable intervention strategies.

Fatality review teams and researchers often distinguish between "single" and "multiple" forms of intimate partner homicide. In the former, the offender kills only the intimate partner. In the latter, the perpetrator kills the intimate partner and then commits suicide (homicide suicide) or kills the intimate partner and a number of family members, and then commits suicide (familicide). Men commit nearly all homicide suicides and familicides. Homicide suicide cases are particularly amenable to fatality review because there is usually no pending criminal prosecution or civil litigation that the review process might complicate.

Deaths attributable to domestic violence involve much more than intimate partner homicides. Researchers use the term "family homicide" to refer to that class of cases where one family member kills another (non-intimate) family member. Examples here include siblings who kill other siblings, parents who kill children, and children who kill parents. Although these killings qualify as domestic violence deaths under state statutes, they sometimes occur against the backdrop of adult intimate partner domestic violence. Fatality review teams analyze family homicides far less frequently than intimate partner homicides in part because these cases do not have the same potential for inviting intervention strategies in domestic violence cases and in part because child death review teams scrutinize a subset of family homicides (i.e., the killing of children).

A few teams have reviewed "sexual competitor killings." In these cases, men kill men over a woman they sexually compete for. Most of these cases involve at least one of the male sexual competitors battering the female. Although these cases are relatively small in number compared with intimate partner killings, they serve as a reminder that domestic violence spills over into other relationships.

Research suggests that a significant number of women might commit suicide to exit violent intimate relationships. Given that 6,000 women commit suicide each year, it is possible that more women commit suicide due to domestic violence than are directly killed by intimate male partners. In recognition of this fact, a small number of fatality review teams have begun to examine women's suicides. Evan Stark and Anne Flitcraft believe "battered women are provoked to attempt suicide by the extent of control exercised over their lives" (1995: 55). These researchers investigated the medical records of 176 battered women who were treated at the emergency room at Yale–New Haven Hospital. All of these women had attempted to commit suicide at least once during the study year. Over one-third of them "visited the hospital with an abuse-related injury or complaint on the same day as their suicide attempt" (1995: 53). The close correspondence between the battering and the suicide attempt suggested to Stark and Flitcraft that the battering may have triggered the suicide attempt. However, later research on sixteen female suicides recorded by the Bexar County, Texas, fatality review team revealed "no data yet on any abuse victim committing suicide as an apparent means of escape" (Thornton, Spears, and Brackley 2002: 12).

Working from data on sixty-five suicides identified by the Bexar County fatality review team, Thornton, Spears, and Brackley found twenty-seven reports of male suicide that contained some description of an intimate partner. Of these twenty-seven suicide reports, twenty-one displayed evidence of a "disturbance in the relationship" (2002: 12). In eleven cases the parties were estranged, in six the suicide occurred in the context of an argument, and in five cases men had a documented history of committing intimate partner violence. This preliminary research points to the role of suicidal ideations, threats, attempts, and completed acts as a control strategy in relationships involving domestic violence. Male suicide is therefore another form of death amenable to domestic violence fatality review.

The Philadelphia fatality review team examines a broad sweep of women's deaths in order to identify the extent of fatalities traceable to domestic violence. This team analyzes intimate partner homicides but has made a highly significant contribution by highlighting the deaths of women who die as prostitutes, with HIV/AIDS, or from causes related to homelessness. Prostitutes, homeless women, and women infected with HIV/AIDS all suffer disproportionate amounts of domestic violence. Team members contend that domestic violence contributes to many of these deaths, albeit perhaps in an oblique or indirect way. The work of teams such as those in Philadelphia raise important questions about what cases teams might select for review in order to highlight the magnitude of the problems associated with domestic violence.

Philosophy

It might be tempting to blame and shame police officers, medical professionals, judges, probation officers, or battered women's advocates for their failure to intervene appropriately or effectively to prevent a homicide or suicide. However, most fatality review teams recognize that the perpetrator is responsible for the death and do not attribute blame to local service providers. Teams acquired this "no blame and shame" philosophy from mortality review work in the fields of nuclear fuels and aviation (see Websdale 2003). In these fields reviewers soon learned that blaming individuals did not lead to open disclosure and actually reduced the likelihood of individual practitioners sharing compromising information about what might have contributed to a tragic outcome. In addition, the blaming of service professionals essentially perpetuates a style of thinking that parallels the abusive behavior of many perpetrators of domestic violence, who blame victims for much that goes wrong. Having said that reviewers seek to avoid blaming and shaming system professionals and

others, they nevertheless demand accountability on the part of involved agencies and others.

Team Membership

Given that domestic violence homicides and suicides are both complex and multifaceted, many teams have been careful to develop a broad membership that reflects the diversity of service providers and others who come into contact with victims of domestic violence. Put simply, anyone involved with or affected by a domestic violence–related death might serve on a team. However, up to the present, most teams have exhibited a strong criminal justice orientation and include powerful players such as prosecutors, senior police officials, probation and parole officers and, less frequently, public defenders. Also included are victim advocates. In some states, such as Washington, victim advocates have driven the fatality review initiative. In others, such as Florida, law enforcement and criminal justice agencies have played a more important role.

In addition to criminal justice professionals and advocates, teams often include public health professionals, emergency room staff, animal control officers, school counselors, child protective services workers, batterer intervention program specialists, members of the faith community, and drug and alcohol treatment providers. Less commonly and more controversially, some teams have reached out to the community in an attempt to create a more permeable and accountable team structure to gain fresh insights into deaths. This outreach has taken two principal forms.

In Montana, for example, the death review team has interviewed family members and others close to both victims and perpetrators in an attempt to gather comprehensive data on cases. In one review the Montana team spent five hours interviewing the mother of a perpetrator of domestic homicide. Reaching out to family, friends, neighbors, and workplace associates as a means of learning more about cases is slowly but surely emerging as a key development among teams. This tendency or trajectory finds a parallel in the research literature on intimate partner homicide, where more recently researchers have used proxy-informants, those close to the victim, who might have known of specific compromises and problems not revealed by police files, court documents, medical examiner materials and the like (see, for example, Campbell 2003a, 2003b).

The second development concerns the increased discussion of the role that battered women themselves ought to play on teams. Some teams have battered women at the table in the form of victim advocates and others who once experienced domestic violence. However, although state statutes often allow for the presence of battered women on review teams, teams have been slow to include these women other than in the team's capacity as system professionals, but this is changing. A number of teams are considering involving battered women directly in review work. For example, members of the West Palm Beach team have taken their deliberations to a group of survivors of domestic violence in order to get their feedback. This productive exercise may be the harbinger of major changes in team activity, seeking to somehow access the voices of battered women in an attempt to understand the complex compromises victims faced prior to their deaths.

Some have argued that these developments might serve to democratize teams, make them more sensitive to grassroots social and economic matters that affect battered women, and render them less bureaucratic and officious and more accountable. To the extent that domestic violence is much more than a criminal justice problem, these moves toward including survivors and the community appear promising. On the other hand, the presence of family members, victims of domestic violence, and others raises difficult ethical questions for teams about what they might share with these individuals. In addition, the involvement of family members also raises concerns about retraumatizing those close to victims (see Hauser 2005; Websdale 2005a, 2005b).

The Process of Reviewing a Case

Having identified an agency or organization to house the fatality review initiative, team members usually spend a considerable amount of time talking about how they will review cases. The nature of review often dovetails with the goals, purposes, and philosophical orientation of the team. The review process differs by team and is shaped in part by resources, levels of participation by various members, and the nature of any statutory guidelines. Members often take turns chairing or co-chairing teams. These individuals usually have the connections to orchestrate meetings, arrange for the flow of relevant information to the table, and have some political clout in the local domestic violence arena. Rotating chairs and co-chairs also limits burnout.

Notwithstanding certain difficulties with various types of private or confidential information, teams usually draw from some or all of the following:

police homicide logs; newspaper reports of homicides; crime scene investigation reports; detectives' follow-up reports; transcripts of interviews conducted by investigators with witnesses and other involved parties; data from prior protective orders; affidavits for protective orders; notices of service of protective orders; presentence investigation reports (probation); parole data including notification of victims; civil court data regarding divorce proceedings, termination of parental rights, child custody disputes, and child visitation issues; criminal histories of perpetrators and victims; child protective services data; summaries of psychological evaluations appearing in public record documents such as police files; medical examiners reports; autopsy reports; workplace information, perhaps regarding harassment or abuse; public health data, including emergency room data; shelter/advocacy outreach data; school data pertaining to abuse reports; statements from neighbors, family members, friends, workplace colleagues, witnesses, and others; and drug and alcohol treatment data.

Agency representatives and others bring their respective information to the table. Sometimes this is copied and circulated beforehand, other times it is analyzed only during review meetings. Some teams use documentary evidence only as a touchstone for ascertaining what they need. Teams that adopt this strategy sometimes destroy that documentary evidence at the close of their deliberations. Team members often present information deriving from their respective agency files, summarizing and interpreting those data as they proceed. Discussions ensue based upon the array of evidence presented, and detailed syntheses of at times disparate sources of data emerge.

Many teams find it helpful to generate a timeline of the case, a linear chronology that maps the primary events before the homicide in varying degrees of detail. They might also identify specific red flags, or warning signals, in the case that may or may not have been picked up by risk assessment instruments. Most teams address the nature and extent of interagency involvement and coordination in the case. Far fewer teams scrutinize the involvement of family, community members, and others prior to the death. Most teams complete their work by addressing the question of what is to be done. This question takes the form of recommendations for the development of more solid preventive interventions. More recently teams have focused on how to implement these recommendations.

In addition to thinking about the information to be gleaned from reviews, team members often think carefully about the way cases are reviewed. Of paramount consideration here are developing a climate that honors victims and their families and working to provide a safe and supportive climate for reviewers and those who work with teams. This means considering the emotional toll on reviewers and others and developing protocols that address these difficulties. Teams often reflect upon the culture they create, the language they use to talk about cases, the photographs members may or may not be asked to view, and the inevitable differences in perspective that surface during such challenging work.

Confidentiality

Whether or not fatality review statutes shield team deliberations and findings, most teams are careful to protect sensitive and confidential information from the public eye. Most teams understand the difference between public, private, and confidential information and work within these parameters, taking care not to break the law or infringe upon people's rights to privacy and confidentiality. In order to bring agency professionals to the table, it proved imperative in many states to develop protective statutes that rendered deliberations immune from subpoena and various forms of legal discovery. Such statutory shields ensure teams access to much, although not all, sensitive and confidential information. These confidentiality guarantees allow team members to come to the table in an open and honest manner.

The criticism of providing confidentiality shields is that they increase the likelihood of a cover-up. Such cover-ups might occur in cases where there is gross negligence or malfeasance. However, while it may be the case that confidentiality guarantees shield teams from civil suits and other legal or disciplinary actions, it is nonetheless the case that civil suits can still take place and any negligence or malfeasance challenged through tort law.

The need for confidential information speaks to the desire of many teams to produce thorough, comprehensive, and detailed reviews that maximize the opportunity to highlight systems failures and the like. However, it is also the case that perfectly thorough, detailed, and comprehensive reviews result from the analysis of public record data alone (see Thompson 2005). These reviews usually involve the examination of homicide suicide cases or other closed criminal cases where there are no pending civil or criminal legal issues, including appeals.

Fatality Review and Other Preventive Interventions

Domestic violence fatality reviews emerged alongside and as a part of a number of multi-agency and interdisciplinary initiatives in the field of domestic violence. In a number of states (e.g., Florida) fatality review teams arose out of existing coordinated community responses to domestic violence. In some states they arose in a review climate established by the work of multi-agency child fatality reviews. Fatality reviews also dovetail nicely with safety and accountability audits. These audits involve working closely with agencies and examining their modes of operation in minute detail. In a sense, safety audits scrutinize institutional ways of life that constrain and limit effective responses to domestic violence. Audits work with everyday procedures in police departments, the courts, and other agencies to improve communications and sharpen system effectiveness. Fatality reviews examine the everyday procedures, paper trails, and human practices through the lens of the death rather than everyday practice. If audits scrutinize everyday ways of providing services, fatality reviews approach service delivery through the rare but potent event of a death.

Although it is too early to say whether fatality reviews actually reduce domestic violence deaths, injuries, and abuse, it is clear that teams across the country report major improvements in inter-agency communication, the emergence of novel practices, an increased awareness of the significance of domestic violence as a social problem, and the development of increased understanding and appreciation among service providers. Fatality reviews also contribute to increasingly sophisticated appreciations of risk in local, statewide, and national contexts. In this sense fatality reviews and safety audits contribute to safety planning for victims of domestic violence and the coordinated and thoughtful delivery of services.

NEIL WEBSDALE

See also **Assessing Risk in Domestic Violence Cases; Battered Women Who Kill: An Examination; Compassionate Homicide and Spousal Violence; Domestic Homicide in Urban Centers: New York City; Female Suicide and Domestic Violence; Intimate Partner Homicide**

References and Further Reading

Campbell, Jacquelyn C., et al. "Risk Factors for Femicide in Abusive Relationships: Results from a Multisite Case Control Study." *American Journal of Public Health* 93, no. 7 (2003a): 1089–1097.

———. "Assessing Risk Factors for Intimate Partner Homicide." *NIJ Journal*, Issue 250 (2003b): 14–19.

Hauser, Jacquelyn. "Commentary on Websdale." *Violence Against Women* 11, no. 9 (2005): 1201–1205.

Stark, Eva, and Anne Flitcraft. "Killing the Beast Within: Woman Battering and the Female Suicidality." *International Journal of Health Services* 25, no. 1 (1995): 43–64.

Thompson, Robi. "Confidentiality and Fatality Review," 2005. National Domestic Violence Fatality Review Initiative.

Thornton, Jo E., William Spears, and Margaret H. Brackley. "Suicides Associated with Intimate Partner Violence: Perpetrator Suicides Underrecognized." *Fatality Review Bulletin* (Winter 2002): 12–13.

Websdale, N. *Reviewing Domestic Violence Deaths*. National Institute of Justice Special Research Bulletin on Intimate Partner Homicide, 2003.

———. "Battered Women at Risk: A Rejoinder to Jacquelyn Hauser's and Jacquelyn Campbell's Commentaries on R and B." *Violence Against Women* 11, no. 9 (2005a): 1214–1221.

———. "R and B: A Conversation between a Researcher and a Battered Woman about Domestic Violence Fatality Review." *Violence Against Women* 11, no. 9 (2005b): 1186–1200.

FEMALE SUICIDE AND DOMESTIC VIOLENCE

Domestic violence is a factor in up to one-quarter of female suicide attempts. Female victims of domestic violence have eight times the risk for suicide compared with the general population. Fifty percent of battered women who attempt suicide undertake subsequent attempts. Married females experience lower suicide rates compared with single females; however, if domestic violence is present in the marriage, the risk of suicide increases. If a pregnant woman is a victim of domestic violence, the risk of suicide increases. One in twelve pregnant women experience battering such as hits to the abdomen, breasts, or genitals, while 20 percent of pregnant female victims of domestic violence attempt suicide. Many female victims of domestic violence indicate that their rate of victimization increased when they became pregnant. Along with domestic violence, the prior loss of a child by miscarriage or a desire for abortion also increase suicidal tendencies. Research shows that in addition to married and pregnant women, young girls experiencing domestic violence also have increased rates of suicide.

Risk Factors

Various risk factors relate to suicidality among female domestic violence victims. Most obviously, the physical and psychological abuse by a partner may trigger suicidal thoughts. However, other underlying factors are relevant, which concern individual and social issues. Regarding individual issues, research alludes to genetic factors involving family histories of suicide, and points to problems involving mental disorders, including aspects of anxiety, nervous breakdowns, depression, and posttraumatic stress disorder. Depression and posttraumatic stress may be results of ongoing abuse from a partner or lingering aftereffects of a trauma occurring years earlier. For example, some battered females with suicidal tendencies indicate that they still deal with the psychological effects of sexual, emotional, or physical maltreatment experienced as a child. Combined with factors of low esteem, these psychological effects can trigger suicidal thoughts when victims blame themselves for their abuse. Regarding social issues, research emphasizes the importance of social bonds. Following sociological models of suicides, research shows that females in domestic violence situations are more likely to attempt suicide when low levels of social support exist. This includes friends and family networks. With all factors, the likelihood of suicide increases when victims use drugs as a coping mechanism.

Shifting Shame

Another motivation for female suicide in domestic violence situations involves a shift of shame. Here, the embarrassment of abuse causes battered women to fail to seek help from others. The suicide represents a transfer of shame to the victimizer or others in the battered woman's social network who did not step forward to help her. Not only does the suicide bring humiliation to others, but it also serves as a tool of revenge and a final act of empowerment.

The Impact of Divorce Laws

Research in the field of household economics indicates that females considering suicide in domestic violence situations benefit from unilateral, no-fault divorce laws. Traditional divorce laws require specific legal reasons for marriage dissolution. They also require both spouses to consent to the divorce. In states with traditional divorce laws, females experiencing abuse by coercive spouses experience legal entrapment. Even if a wife wants out of the relationship, she legally cannot dissipate the marriage contract without her husband's approval. This leaves suicide as a viable option. The balance of power in marriage shifts when states institute unilateral divorce. Abused wives have the power to legally end marriages on their own rather than experience the misery of an abusive relationship that could result in the taking of their own lives. Confronted with a possible divorce, husbands have the choice to correct abusive behavior or let the marriage end.

Work in this area examines domestic violence and suicide rates before and after states enacted unilateral divorce. It shows a significant decline in reports of spousal violence carried out by husbands against wives with the enactment of unilateral divorce laws. On the other hand, it also shows an increase in spousal violence carried out by wives against husbands. In relation to suicide, it indicates a 6 percent reduction in female suicides. There is a lag between the passing of unilateral divorce laws and the reduction of violence and suicide. In some areas, research indicates, the reduction of domestic violence and suicide may take up to twenty years. It sometimes takes that long before battered women comprehend new social norms associated with no-fault divorce and recognize the previously absent bargaining power available.

The Impact of the Battered Woman's Defense

Suicide and divorce are not the only alternatives for female victims of domestic violence. They may opt to kill abusive partners. Twelve percent of homicides by women in the United States involve the killing of a partner in an abusive relationship. This sometimes involves the murder of an abusive partner followed by a suicide. However, with legal defenses involving battered woman syndrome becoming more acceptable, judges and juries are acknowledging the detrimental impact of domestic violence on females. In turn, some scholars indicate that female suicide following the homicide of an abusive spouse is dropping.

Recommendations

If a female victim of domestic violence is contemplating or has attempted suicide, several recommendations exist. It is necessary to break the cycle of violence lying beneath the urge to commit suicide. Victims should confront embedded feelings and come to terms with self-blame. They should also break destructive patterns involving the use or abuse of alcohol or drugs. These substances have the potential to increase suicidal urges in situations of domestic violence. Victims should seek to build social bonds with friends and family. The increase of communication, intimacy, and recreational activity with people outside of the abusive relationship is critical. On a wider scale, a need for community-based prevention programs may be necessary. These programs should involve public service announcements to increase general awareness of female suicide and its link to domestic violence, but also to educate females on alternatives to suicide in domestic violence situations. Community programs should also involve official assistance organizations. If victims do not have the backing of friends and family, formal support groups composed of other abusers are beneficial. In addition, organizations that provide legal and economic resources to females in abusive relationships prove helpful.

JASON S. ULSPERGER

See also **Battered Woman Syndrome; Battered Woman Syndrome as a Legal Defense in Cases of Spousal Homicide; Coercive Control; Community Responses to Domestic Violence; Control Balance Theory and Domestic Violence; Cycle of Violence; Intimate Partner Homicide; Judicial Perspectives on Domestic Violence; Legal Issues for Battered Women; Pregnancy-Related Violence; Substance Use/Abuse and Intimate Partner Violence; Victim-Blaming Theory**

References and Further Reading

Counts, Dorothy A. "Female Suicide and Wife Abuse: A Cross-Cultural Perspective." *Suicide and Life-Threatening Behavior* 17, no. 3 (1987): 194–204.

Durkheim, Emile. *Suicide*. Reprint. New York: Free Press, 1897/1997.

Grant, Christine A. "Women Who Kill: The Impact of Abuse." *Issues in Mental Health Nursing* 16, no. 4 (1995): 315–326.

Lester, David, and Aaron T. Beck. "Attempted Suicide and Pregnancy." *American Journal of Obstetrics and Gynecology* 158, no. 5 (1988): 1084–1085.

McFarlane, Judith. "Battering during Pregnancy." *Women and Health* 15, no. 3 (1989): 69–84.

Meadows, Lindi A., et al. "Protective Factors against Suicide Attempt Risk among African American Women Experiencing Intimate Partner Violence." *American Journal of Community Psychology* 36, no. 1–2 (2005): 109–121.

Stark, Evan, and Anne Flitcraft. "Killing the Beast Within: Women Battering and Female Suicidality." *International Journal of Health Services* 25, no. 1 (1995): 43–64.

Stevenson, Betsey, and Justin Wolfers. "Bargaining in the Shadow of the Law: Divorce Laws and Family Distress." *Quarterly Journal of Economics* 121, no. 1 (2006): 267–288.

Thompson, Martha P., Nadine J. Kaslow, and Jeffery B. Kingree. "Risk Factors for Suicide Attempts among African American Women Experiencing Intimate Partner Violence." *Violence and Victimization* 17, no. 3 (2002): 283–295.

FEMINIST THEORY

Introduction

Feminist theory is a body of literary, philosophical, and sociological analysis that explores the inequality that exists between men and women in societies around the world. Specifically, this theoretical body of knowledge examines gender-based aspects that affect politics, power relations, and sexuality. Feminist theory consists of numerous subcategories that explain gender disparity through differing causal factors. Regardless of the subcategory of feminist theory that is examined, all of them contend that men and women should be equal within the political, economic, sexual, and social spheres of society.

The feminist movement has had a long history in the United States and an even longer history in some countries, such as France. There have been numerous women who have advocated feminist perspectives for hundreds of years. For instance, one eighteenth-century feminist writer and journalist, Mary Wollstonecraft, was highly cognizant of the feminist movement occurring throughout areas of Europe (Baird 1992). While in the United States, Wollstonecraft wrote what is considered the first book advocating women's liberation (Baird 1992). Wollstonecraft's book, entitled *A Vindication of the Rights of Women,* was written in 1792 in response to Thomas Paine's fairly biased treatise *The Rights of Man.* Naturally, Wollstonecraft's work underscored the fact that women were neglected and overlooked in almost all aspects of society, including the literary and scholarly circles (Baird 1992). While not popular among most of the male population of the time, her book was nonetheless widely read in the United States and parts of Europe (Baird 1992). This also served as the impetus of future actions that would come on behalf of women worldwide.

Though the work of Wollstonecraft is considered the first text on women's liberation, the true origins of feminism as a distinct school of thought are typically thought to have emerged in 1848 with the passage of the "Declaration of Sentiments and Resolutions" that was enacted at the women's rights convention held in Seneca Falls, New York (French 2005). Indeed, this has been dubbed the "first wave" of feminism and was also associated with an antislavery agenda (French 2005). Essentially, this period of feminism advocated for equality of all people and eschewed practices of exploitation regardless of the rationale presented for such unfair systems. This initial wave of feminism grew out of the movement to abolish slavery (Jurik 1999). Even though this initial period of feminism addressed various issues affecting women, the first wave ultimately centered around the acquisition of political rights, with the right to vote being its primary goal. Thus, this period lasted until 1920, when the passage of the Nineteenth Amendment guaranteed woman suffrage (French 2005).

The "second wave" of feminism emerged during the late 1960s and was referred to as the Women's Liberation movement. According to Jurik (1999), second-wave feminism drew its initial membership from women working in the Civil Rights, student, and anti–Vietnam War movements. Jurik (1999) goes on to note that during the Civil Rights movement, rights that were specific to women were largely ignored or placed as secondary to those advocated for racial minorities. Because of this, many white American women (and some minority women as well) disbanded from many of these movements and formed "consciousness-raising groups" that consisted of an all-female membership (Jurik 1999, p. 32). This period emerged in 1967–1968, and it is from this point that the Women's Liberation movement officially began. During this period, advocates of the feminist movement held that true equality consists of more than a mere ability to vote, hold a job, or engage in other activities (French 2005). Rather, true equality was also held to mean equality in the legitimate access to such opportunities (French 2005).

The "third wave" of feminism started in the mid- to late 1980s and focused on issues of patriarchy (French 2005). The basic contention of this movement was that men inherently seek to dominate and exploit women (French 2005). While third-wave feminists all desired to overcome the systematic subjugation of women, the women's movement had grown to encompass a wide variety of different and often conflicting subgroups of membership. Although feminists disagreed on many issues, they did share in the work of many projects, including work to support freedom in decisions pertaining to sex and sexuality, access to abortion services (particularly the right for women to choose), and the development of battered women's shelters (Jurik 1999).

It is from this point that any overview of feminist theory must address the variety of subcategories of feminism that have since developed. This essay will provide an overview of many of the primary categories of feminist theoretical thought in an effort to compare and contrast the bases for their development. In addition, the last section of this essay will discuss the importance of feminist theory in addressing issues related to domestic violence and sexual assault. Feminist theory has had a very distinct and important impact on services for victims of such crimes as well as the specific interventions utilized with perpetrators of violence against women.

Liberal Feminism

Liberal feminism contends that equality between men and women is possible but that any such equality will require substantive changes through social and legal reform. According to Hedges (1996), this type of feminism "attempts to reform or use existing political structures to advance women's interests along a civil rights model" and "argues that women deserve the same privileges, protections, pay, and opportunities that men do" (p. 1). Essentially, this type of feminist thought contends that the social system can accommodate the appropriate social change without the need to resort to an entire social revolution. This form of feminism is a bit more conservative than many other subcategories, since it does hold that men and women can coexist on equal terms and contends that the needed changes can be orchestrated within the current social system. One of the key challenges associated with this theoretical outlook revolves around achieving a balance, where women are afforded equality with men while not forsaking their identity as women (Hedges 1996). Finding such a balance has been touted as difficult, forcing women to act as if they must play the role of a man in the workforce rather than being free to have freedom of feminine expression in conjunction with equal access to opportunity there (Hedges 1996).

Radical Feminism

Radical feminist theory focuses on the uneven distribution of power that men hold over women in society (D'Unger 2005). According to radical feminists, violence is the ultimate expression of male dominance over women, and therefore domestic abuse and sexual assault (as well as other, similar crimes) are manifestations of such dominance and exploitation (D'Unger 2005). Views that provide tacit (as opposed to overt) approval of such dynamics are demonstrated in various forms of research pertaining to differing views on pornography, sexual assault, and violence that are held by men and women (Bromberg 1997). According to D'Unger (2005), radical feminist researchers tend to focus on issues related to women's sexual oppression and victimization, sexual harassment, and pornography. Further, the support for domestic violence interventions has been spearheaded by radical feminist supporters contending that such crimes were long unacknowledged due to similar tacit social approval of such violence within society (D'Unger 2005). The radical feminist contends that such violence is normalized through the lack of public resistance to this category of crime and also contends that women themselves begin to see this type of treatment as typical and acceptable because no contrary opinion is noted, particularly in the lives of those girls who are socialized within an abusive home.

Marxist Feminism

Feminist advocates under this subcategory draw much of their thought from the works of Karl Marx and Friedrich Engels (Jurik 1999). The original tenets of Marxist feminists held that women's subordination was the result of a system in which men held and controlled most private property in society (Jurik 1999). Indeed, not only do men hold more private property, but this ownership tends to be transmitted intergenerationally from the male parent to the male offspring, further perpetuating private property ownership among male members of society. Central to the works of Karl Marx was the emphasis on the division of labor. Marxists contend that the wage earners, officially termed the proletariat, are exploited and controlled by the wealthy bourgeoisie. This type of system is considered a form of economic oppression in which the rich control the masses by rewarding the wage earners for the production of desired goods and services at levels that are just high enough for them to exist, but low enough to ensure that they must continue to work in order to subsist. It is in this way that the wealthy maintain control over the working class and ensure that the latter must continue to consent to such a system of exploitation.

For feminists, this theory of power and exploitation goes one step further in defining notions of power through the division of labor in society. Within a capitalist framework, it is the males who tend to go into the workforce, and these men tend to develop the job skills to earn a higher wage than women who choose to enter the workforce. It is through this process and the unequal access to higher-paying job markets that women are further exploited, even though they may be members of the proletariat alongside their male counterparts. Thus it is that female members of the proletariat are doubly exploited, both by the bourgeoisie and by their male partners in the proletariat.

However, Marxist feminists do not contend that this imbalance will last forever. Rather, the purest of Marxist feminists contend that capitalism itself will be short-lived, similar to the contentions of any member of the Marxist school of thought. For Marxist feminists, this means that "capitalist expansion would eventually force all women into full-time labor force participation. The incorporation of women into the workforce would lead to the demise of the nuclear family" (Jurik 1999, p. 33). From this point, it is contended that the removal of demands from the family system will eventually make men and women equal because their primary value will be derived from their wage-earning abilities (Jurik 1999). Marxist feminists contend that such a system will be necessary so that women and men can come together to realize their mutual plight of being exploited by the wealthy bourgeoisie. Just as with traditional Marxism, the ultimate goal of Marxist feminists is to overthrow the capitalist power structure. Thus, it is the capitalist system that is thought to be the ultimate culprit behind female inequality. The removal of a capitalist system, according to these feminists, will also remove the gender bias within such a society.

However, it became apparent to many Marxist feminists that there was more to male and female inequality than was attributed to capitalism alone. It was clear that other factors did come into play when structuring this system of power and control. From observations in various socialist countries (particularly during the 1960s and 1970s) in Central and South America, as well as in Eastern Europe, it was clear that the removal of capitalism did not result in equality for women (Jurik 1999). Further, as time went on, family structures did modify and divorces were more prevalent, but it became clear to Marxist feminists that there was not necessarily a disintegration of the family (Jurik 1999). Further, it was clear that even with such changes in society, there still existed serious limits for women in the workforce that did not necessarily exist for men. Thus, women were subordinate to men in socialist societies as well (Jurik 1999). Adding to this was the fact that further equality of women in the United States had not caused the complete demise of the family. While it was true that the traditional nuclear family had been fragmented, family systems were morphing into new but cohesive groupings that consisted of the blended families and other familial groupings that had adapted and modified themselves to a more egalitarian society. Granted, problems did exist with this process of transformation, but it was clear that the family had not simply disappeared in the process.

Socialist Feminism

Because of these observed discrepancies in Marxist feminism, a movement developed to bridge Marxism with feminism while incorporating a social movement to include socialist and Women's Liberation groups (Jurik 1999). This eventually became the *socialist feminist* school of thought, which emphasizes that both capitalistic economic inequality and the existence of patriarchy are the core underlying causal factors for women's subordinate role in society (Jurik 1999).

For socialist feminists, the basis of inequality lies in the actual acquisition of material goods. This branch of feminism contends that there is a connection between class structure and the oppression of women (Stewart 2003) and that men maintain power in society because they engage in the world of work, being employed in the tangible workforce that produces specific remuneration for their efforts. Their production of goods and services translates into material wealth that is directly owned and controlled by the male rather than the female (Stewart 2003). This is compared with the traditional role of the female, who is stereotypically limited to work within the domestic arena. Domestic work seldom receives a specific form of remuneration within most family households and is undervalued by society when it is completed as a choice of vocation (Stewart 2003). This, along with the fact that women have not been conditioned to engage in the production of goods and services throughout much of history, provides men with power over women. This power comes by way of material production.

Another important aspect of socialist feminism is the rejection of biology in determining gender. According to socialist feminists, social roles are not inherent, and this means that both male and female roles can be pliable if there is sufficient social incentive to make changes in socialization and conditioning (Stewart 2003). Because socialist feminists do not attribute differences to physiology and emphasize a social basis for such differences in ability and opportunity, they make a specific point to challenge the basis of capitalism and the inherent forms of patriarchy that exist in most societies (Stewart 2003). Stewart notes that similar to the "views of radical feminists, socialist feminists believe that although women are divided by class, race, ethnicity and religion, they all experience the same oppression simply for being a woman" (p. 2). Thus, according to socialist feminists, true equality can occur only through the complete elimination of all class and gender distinctions. This would then mean that women would need to be in all spheres of social involvement in numbers equal to their male counterparts (Stewart 2003). In fact, the mere distinction between male and female is contrary to socialist feminism, since any true sense of equality would essentially consist of a completely nongendered society. With this view in mind, there would then be a basic unigender, where male and female distinctions would not even exist.

It should also be noted that other class distinctions would also be eliminated if a true socialist feminist view of society were to be formed (Stewart 2003). This means that economic distinctions would be removed, just as with any form of socialist government or social structure. Thus, wealth would be equally distributed among all members of society. Inherent in this would then be the lack of distinctions based on race and other criteria, since all members would have equal ownership of material goods (Stewart 2003). This would, by default, create a society in which all members would have equal power on an individual basis. At the macro level, this society would need to ensure that distinctions among groups did not exist. In essence and in its purest form, there would be no racial or economic categories (Stewart 2003). This demonstrates the broad view of socialist feminism and underscores the fact that it stands in direct contrast to much of the capitalistic thought of many Western industrialized nations.

Psychoanalytic Feminism

Psychoanalytic feminism is based on the work of Sigmund Freud and the psychoanalytic theory associated with him. This branch of feminism contends that gender is based upon the psychosexual stages of individual development. Feminists who support this theory contend that gender inequality stems from a variety of childhood experiences that are taught to and internalized by the child. Essentially, boys are taught to believe themselves to be masculine and girls are taught that they should view themselves as feminine. From this process, the male is ascribed characteristics that encourage competition and the ability to explore his environment, while the female is taught to remain docile and within the vicinity of the home. This theoretical orientation illustrates the manner by which language shapes subjectivity and gender definitions within the family (Hedges 1996). This process leads to a social system in which men are afforded more privilege and competitive advantage than are women. Much of the basis for this view on feminism is drawn from Freud's work in which he analyzed traditional heterosexuality and gender roles as being an arbitrary social construct rather than a matter of nature, physiology, or genetics (Hedges 1996). One interesting limitation to this theory questions the viability of its framework, which is based on Oedipus (for sons) and Electra (for daughters) complexes in a society in which the two-parent family (a natural dynamic of Freud's Oedipus/Electra nexus) is much less common than it was in the society that Freud knew (Hedges 1996).

Cultural Feminism

The term "cultural feminism" may seem a bit counterintuitive to many who are not familiar with this type of feminism. This is because cultural feminism does not contend that culture or socialization is the root cause of differences between men and women, as the term would seem to imply. Rather, cultural feminists contend that there are inherent biological differences between male and female members of society and that these differences are inevitable (Deegan 1986; Lewis 2006; Stewart 2003). Going further, these differences should be accepted as part of nature and embraced. This theoretical perspective holds that women are indeed superior in virtue compared with men (Lewis 2006). Cultural feminists specifically point toward moral deficiencies among men that have been viewed as socially acceptable (the "boys will be boys" mentality) while noting the emphasis on moral purity that has been the hallmark of a woman's self-worth and social value in a number of societies. According to Stewart (2003), cultural feminists see women as inherently more kind and gentle, and they "believe that because of these differences, if women ruled the world there would be no more war and it would be a better place" (p. 1). Stewart adds that cultural feminists are often nonpolitical and tend to focus instead on change within individual belief systems. This means that these advocates often address micro levels of change rather than the macro levels common in Marxist and socialist feminism (Stewart 2003).

Minorities and Feminism

Feminist scholars have bemoaned the fact that in addressing women's issues, the feminist movement has traditionally failed to provide adequate analysis of the unique issues presented to women of diverse racial and cultural groups (Hanser 2002). Because of this, critics have likened feminism to a concept that is limited to the historical and social experiences of middle-class white women (ibid.). However, these experiences have often been quite different from those of African American women, Latinas, and Asian American women (Hanser 2002). Indeed, during the early years of the feminist movement, there were documented cases of racism and discrimination between white American and African American feminists (Baird 1992). Issues of race, racism, and institutional oppression will likely be relevant to African American women but not to most white women (Baird 1992; Hanser 2002). The socialization of Asian American and Latin American women is likely to emphasize even further subservience and other dynamics that are laced with traditional values from their respective cultures. Further, there may be issues of religion as well as racial and cultural differences that should be taken into consideration (Shaheen 1998). This is particularly true for women who are of the Muslim faith and/or community (Shaheen 1998). Because of the vast array of differences that can be encountered among women and since many mainstream white American women are not necessarily likely to be well versed in these cultural differences, an awareness has developed of the need to have feminist schools of thought that can address these differences in an effective and supportive manner.

Feminism around the Globe

In addition to diversity and multiculturalism within the United States, there has been a growing awareness of the rights of women around the world. Reports from Human Rights Watch and Amnesty International make it clear that women and girls are victimized in various forms and to various degrees due to their status in societies throughout the world. Examples include domestic abuse and excessive restrictions in Afghanistan; genital mutilation in Africa and the Middle East; the stoning to death of women for adultery in Pakistan; the trafficking of women and their forced participation in the sex industry in eastern Europe; and the killing of women in India who do not bring an expected dowry amount for the groom's family. These and other actions necessitate advocacy for women around the world. Even in countries where crimes against women are not noted to be rampant, there are still concerns regarding their access to power and economic independence.

While it is clear that there is much ground to make up for feminist theorists around the world, Baer (2006) argues that various cultural and political hurdles may exist. For instance, "mainstream feminists are criticized by minority and Third World feminists for unexamined and unrecognized biases of their own" (p. 2). This points toward the necessity for feminists to expand their theoretical critiques while presenting a series of co-occurring pitfalls and challenges. Nevertheless, just as with the need for multicultural feminist perspectives in the United States, a similar diversification of views will be necessary to accommodate the global community. This means that it is likely that feminism will continue to contain further subdivisions as feminist theory grows to reflect cultural and international diversity of feminists around the world.

Feminist Theory in Relation to Domestic Violence and Other Crimes against Women

As the women's movement continued to gain momentum during the 1960s and 1970s, an increased awareness of domestic violence issues emerged within the United States. As women continued to demand equality within the professional arena, equality became an issue within the personal realm as well (Hanser 2002). Eventually, these personal demands extended to expectations within the marital relationship (Hanser 2002). Thus, feminist theory has provided a guiding framework for understanding and addressing domestic violence, as well as "explanations of how it has come about that men and women's unequal status in society . . . and the differential socialization of male and female children [have] perpetuated violence and abuse in the home" (Frances 1995, p. 395). Feminist theory has been instrumental in raising the public consciousness about sex role conditioning and how such conditioning can lead to belief systems that justify sexism, male privilege, and gender socialization (Healey, Smith, and O'Sullivan 1998). It is through the transmission of these belief systems that acts of domestic violence can reflect the patriarchal organization of society, with the male partner exacting forced subservience from the female partner (ibid.).

These views on domestic violence are consistent with many schools of feminist thought (particularly radical feminism), which contend that it is the use of violence that keeps women subjugated in the home and in society as a whole. Crimes such as sexual assault, stalking, marital rape, and domestic violence have two key underlying similarities: The perpetrator is most often male and the victim is most often female. In addition, all of these crimes serve to exploit and/or control the sexual and social freedom of women to have a lifestyle of equality both inside and outside the home. Since these crimes target women and are most often committed by males, it is easy to see the connection to feminist theory. This theoretical perspective has been used in therapeutic interventions for women (providing a framework and rationale for empowering victims), as well as programs designed for perpetrators (providing psychoeducation on the rights of women and enforcing accountability in the recognition of those rights). Thus it is that from the women's movement for equality in the broader society have come social changes impacting the responses to domestic violence issues.

Conclusion

While feminist theory has had a fairly lengthy history, it did not receive widespread acceptance until the 1970s. Even though feminist thought and critiques have faced many challenges in mainstream society, feminists have achieved substantial accomplishments that have considerably changed the social landscape as well as the personal dynamics between men and women. Throughout the development of feminist theory and against the backdrop of the substantive social change that has been generated, feminists themselves have not always agreed on their rationale or mode of operation. Indeed, there are a variety of subcategories to which a feminist may subscribe. As such, activists, researchers, and laypersons alike belong to various subcategory memberships. Regardless of their specific affiliation, all contend that women must have equality with men if society is ever to be free of oppression and discrimination.

Further still, women should be free of sex-based crimes and aberrant behaviors that provide men with the ability to exploit women. Crimes such as rape and domestic abuse are viewed as forms of specific and generalized control and therefore exploit women individually and collectively. Any society that is committed to equality between the sexes must then be particularly responsive to crimes that are based on sex or gender. It is with this in mind that feminist theory has impacted society on both the micro and the macro level, resulting in far-reaching and long-lasting change destined to change the course of human social development throughout generations to come.

ROBERT D. HANSER

See also **Attachment Theory and Domestic Violence; Battered Woman Syndrome; Christianity and Domestic Violence; Coercive Control; Control Balance Theory and Domestic Violence; Jewish Community, Domestic Violence within the; Qur'anic Perspectives on Wife Abuse; Rule of Thumb; Social Learning Theory and Family Violence; Stockholm Syndrome in Battered Women; Violence against Women Act; Worldwide Sociolegal Precedents Supporting Domestic Violence from Ancient to Modern Times**

References and Further Reading

Baer, J. "Five Minutes of Global Feminism," 2006. http://www.tjsl.edu/downloads/Judith%20A.%20Baer.pdf.htm

Baird, V. "Simply: A History of Feminism." *New Internationalist* 227 (1992). http://www.newint.org/issue227/simply.htm.

Bromberg, S. "Feminist Issues in Prostitution," 1997. http://www.feministissues.com/index.html.

Deegan, M. J. *Jane Addams and the Men of the Chicago School, 1892–1918.* New Brunswick, NJ: Transaction Books, 1986.

D'Unger, A. V. "Feminist Theories of Criminal Behavior." In *Encyclopedia of Criminology,* edited by R. A. Wright and J. M. Mitchell. New York: Routledge, 2005.

Frances, R. "An Overview of Community-Based Intervention Programmes for Men Who Are Violent or Abusive in the Home." In *Gender and Crime,* edited by R. E. Dobash, R. P. Dobash, and L. Noaks. Cardiff, UK: University of Wales Press, 1995, pp. 390–409.

French, M. "Feminist Criminology, Female Crime, and Integrated Theory," 2005. http://faculty.ncwc.edu/toconnor/301/301lect14.htm.

Hanser, R. D. *Multicultural Aspects in Batterer Intervention Programs.* Published dissertation (UMI). Huntsville, TX: Sam Houston State University, 2002.

Healey, K., C. Smith, and C. O'Sullivan. *Batterer Intervention: Program Approaches and Criminal Justice Strategies.* Washington, DC: National Institute of Justice, 1998.

Hedges, W. "A Taxonomy of Feminist Intellectual Traditions," 1996. http://www.sou.edu/English/IDTC/Issues/Gender/Resources/femtax1.htm.

Jurik, N. C. "Socialist-Feminist Criminology and Social Justice." In *Social Justice/Criminal Justice: The Maturation of Critical Theory in Law, Crime, and Deviance,* edited by B. A. Arrigo. Belmont, CA: West/Wadsworth, 1999, pp. 31–50.

Lewis, J. J. "Women's History: Cultural Feminism," 2006. http://womenshistory.about.com/od/feminism/g/cultural fem.htm.

Shaheen, A. "American, Ambitious, and Muslim." *WIN: Women's International Net* 8b (1998). http://www.geocities.com/Wellesley/3321/win8b.htm.

Stewart, C. "Different Types of Feminist Theories." Colorado State University, 2003. http://www.colostate.edu/Depts/Speech/rccs/theory84.htm.

FILICIDE AND CHILDREN WITH DISABILITIES

Filicide is the act of intentionally killing one's own son or daughter. Although filicide can refer to the killing of adult offspring, most filicides are murders of children, and, in most cultures, filicide is the most common variety of murder of children under the age of fourteen. In the United States, for example, the U.S. Department of Justice Statistics reports that between 1976 and 2002, 61 percent of children who died as a result of homicide were killed by their fathers (31 percent) or mothers (30 percent). An additional 6 percent were killed by other relatives, and 23 percent were killed by other people, mostly substitute caregivers, often acting in the capacity of parents at the time of the homicide.

This article addresses filicide as it affects children with disabilities. It addresses both unambiguous acts of intentional homicide and also more ambiguous acts and omissions resulting in death, such as the withholding of medical treatment or necessities of life, of which others are culpable with the knowledge and consent of parents. No data are available to establish a precise estimate of the relative risk of filicide for children with disabilities compared with the risk for other children. However, the available evidence suggests that the risk of death by filicide is higher, probably three to six times as high, for a child with a disability as for a child without a disability.

This evidence comes from a variety of sources. A large number of studies have been conducted comparing the risk of child maltreatment for children with and without disabilities. These studies generally have concluded that children with disabilities are more than three times as likely to experience child abuse as other children. However, applying this same figure to child homicides would require an assumption that the probability of maltreatment resulting in death is similar for children with and without disabilities. De Haan's (1997) study of fatal and potentially fatal child maltreatment, however, suggests that children with disabilities may be much more likely to die as a result of maltreatment than other children who experience maltreatment. Although many children experienced abuse categorized as severe, forty of forty-two children (95 percent) who actually died as a result of maltreatment had previously diagnosed disabilities or related conditions. Since children with diagnosed disabilities or related condition comprise only 10 to 15 percent of the general population, this suggests that they may be overrepresented among filicides by a factor of about six times. In addition, thousands of other children with disabilities die each year as a result of withholding or withdrawing medical treatment or other necessities of life, and few, if any, of these cases are included among child abuse or child homicide data.

Lucardie's (2003) content analysis of news media accounts of 1,967 homicide victims with developmental disabilities found that family members were implicated in 48 percent of all cases. Lucardie points out that the nature of this sample makes a direct comparison with similar statistics from the general population imprecise, but as a rough comparison, this suggests that homicide victims with disabilities are about 60 percent more likely to be killed by members of their own family than other homicide victims. Approximately 88 percent of the implicated family members were parents, while the remaining 12 percent were siblings (8 percent) or extended family members (4 percent). This suggests that about 42 percent of all homicides of people with developmental disabilities of all ages are filicides. When the same analysis was restricted to children fourteen and younger, 70 percent of all homicides were filicides. Restricting the data further to homicide victims age five and younger, 75 percent were filicides, suggesting that filicides make up a larger proportion of homicides among children with disabilities than among other children by about 20 percent.

While the nature of the data upon which these estimates are based requires great caution in their interpretation and more research is required to establish better estimates, these data strongly suggest that filicide is at least three times and probably four to six times more common among children with disabilities than among other children. However, if the deliberate withdrawal or withholding of medical care and necessities of life were to be included in these figures, the relative risk would be much higher. Technically, parents who withhold medical treatment or necessities of life, thereby causing their children's death, have committed filicide whether or not the death occurs under medical supervision. However, most people view many of these cases as substantially different from typical child abuse and neglect deaths. For example, some people argue that when imminent death is inevitable with or without treatment, withholding medical treatment should not be viewed as "causing death." However, in many cases, imminent death is not inevitable, and the decision to end the child's life

is based solely on the belief that the nature and extent of the child's disability makes death preferable to continued life. A classic study by Wall and Partridge (1997) made this distinction very clearly through the analysis of infant deaths in the pediatric intensive care unit of one American hospital. They found that 27 percent of all of these deaths occurred despite every effort being made to avert them, while 73 percent were the result of withholding or withdrawing treatment. While most of the decisions to withhold or withdraw care were based, at least in part, on the belief that death was unavoidable, 17 percent of babies who died of all causes died solely because a decision was made that their lives were not worth living, even though they were expected to survive if treated. This study did not address the nature or severity of disabilities among the children whose deaths were the result of decisions of parents and physicians. However, other studies have found that children selected to die include both those who would be expected to have relatively mild disabilities if allowed to survive and those who would be expected to have very severe disabilities. In addition, this study does not address the parents' roles as the decision makers who determine whether the child lives or dies, but medical ethics dictate that parents act as primary decision makers. Whether or not these deaths are viewed as socially acceptable or not, they clearly fall within the definition for filicide when they occur with the parents' knowledge and consent.

Historical and Cultural Context

Throughout history and across cultures, the killing of children with disabilities has been a recurrent phenomenon. In Korbin's 1987 study of the cultural context of child abuse and neglect, she described a list of reasons that legitimized filicide (the killing of children by their parents) in various cultures. For example, some cultures allow the killing of children born out of wedlock, children born as a result of rape, products of adulterous relations, or twins. Birth defects and disabilities were the most widely accepted reasons for killing one's own child.

While some cultures have required parents to kill children viewed as defective, others simply allowed it. The ancient Greek cities of Sparta and Athens typified this contrast. Sparta required parents to dispose of "defective" babies by casting them from Mount Taygetus. Their Athenian contemporaries, known for being less militaristic and authoritarian, allowed parents to place unwanted babies in urns outside the temple, where they could be taken home by anyone who wanted them. However, since potential parents typically rejected any baby with a perceptible imperfection, the result was often death for children with obvious disabilities.

Medieval changeling legends portrayed children with disabilities as the inhuman offspring of leprechauns or other mythical beings who replaced the parents' real human children. Parents were encouraged to drown them or throw changelings in the fire. These pagan myths were later incorporated into Christian versions. In the new versions, it was often the devil who replaced human children with his own, or, in a variation on this theme, children with disabilities were believed to be the result of an illicit union between the child's mother and the devil. Thus, the mother who refused to eliminate her child was sometimes eliminated along with the child.

Martin Luther in his *Table Talks* described his personal experience with a changeling, recommending that the parents drown their child, and when this recommendation was turned down, praying for the child's death. Luther's pronouncement that there is no sin in killing such a child, since it lacks a soul, provided a convenient rationale for killing children with disabilities. While his intentions were unclear in making this pronouncement, it continued to be a rationale for viewing children with disabilities as what he called a subhuman *massa carnis* (lump of flesh), unworthy of human rights, including the right to live.

With the coming of the scientific age, in which science replaced religion as the dominant paradigm for understanding the universe, religious rationales for eliminating children with disabilities were replaced with ones that claimed a scientific basis. In the late 1800s and early 1900s, the eugenics movement claimed to present a scientific rationale for eliminating people with disabilities through a variety of methods, including euthanasia of children with significant disabilities. As late as 1941, C. B. Farrar, editor of the *American Journal of Psychiatry,* published an editorial calling for the killing of children with severe disabilities when they reached the age of five. Farrar suggested that parental attachment to these children was the primary obstacle preventing adoption of a public policy that mandated these killings and that medical professionals must act to eliminate parental attachment to children with disabilities, which he described as a form of mental illness. The Nazi government in Germany had adopted a similar policy about two years earlier. What began with the government-endorsed mercy killing of one child with a severe disability at the request of his father in 1939 led to the mass execution of about 275,000 people with disabilities in Germany before the end of World War II, including thousands of children. Although many parents knew and some approved of these deaths, most thought that their children were only institutionalized and were subsequently told that they had died of natural causes. The skills, equipment, and personnel developed in these euthanasia programs were later redeployed to kill other victims of the Holocaust. For example, mobile gas vans, gas chambers disguised as shower rooms, and massive crematoria were all developed and used against children and adults with disabilities before being used against political prisoners, Jews, homosexuals, and other minorities.

After the euthanasia of children with disabilities was condemned as a crime against humanity in the wake of World War II, the eugenics movement lost much of its support and momentum. However, the emerging discipline of bioethics provided new rationales for the elimination of these children. There have been several primary bioethical arguments in favor of killing children with disabilities.

First, the *quality of life* argument suggests that children with disabilities are doomed to suffer with no potential for enjoyment of life, and therefore parents act in the children's best interests by ending their lives. Second, the *personhood* argument says that children must meet some criteria (e.g., minimum intelligence or communication abilities) before they can be considered to be human or to be persons with a right to protection of their lives. The taking of the life of a "nonperson" is therefore not an immoral act, since the life taken has no moral standing. Third, the *replaceability* argument suggests that even if it is possible for a child with a disability to enjoy life, he or she cannot be expected to do so as much as a child without a disability. Since families have limits to their size, these bioethicists suggest that eliminating the child with a disability can make room for another child with greater potential for a good life. Finally, the *burden* argument says that even if the child with a disability can be provided with a good life, the actions necessary to achieve this outcome for the child places an unfair burden on parents, siblings, and society as a whole. Therefore, families should have the right to eliminate this burden if they so choose.

Of course, there are many counterarguments to all of these, but one set of counterarguments frequently raised focuses on the unique status accorded disability in the bioethical rationales. For example, all children place demands on their families, and parents of children with or without disabilities may view these demands as burdensome. Yet, society does not generally accept the burden of child care as a rationale for filicides of children without disabilities. Similarly, many children with and without disabilities experience circumstances that threaten their quality of life. Children born in poverty, children who witness domestic violence, children who are abused, and children with disabilities all have disadvantages to overcome. If society views filicide as a compassionate response to one of these circumstances, why is filicide not an appropriate response to all of them?

Motivational Factors

While prosecutors and detective novels typically present solitary motivations as the sole reasons for crimes, filicides and other crimes that occur within families are typically the product of complex and interacting motivational factors. These factors fall into two major categories. First, there are instrumental factors, which can be understood in terms of desired outcomes for the perpetrator. Second, there are disinhibiting factors, which can be understood in terms of reducing the normal impediments to the commission of an antisocial act. Instrumental factors may include such things as reduced caregiving demands, gaining greater control over one's own life, or financial gain. Disinhibiting factors include rationalizations that justify filicide, the effects of alcohol or other disinhibiting drugs, depression, or anger. Parents who kill their children may be more significantly different from parents who do not kill their children in regard to disinhibiting factors than instrumental motivations.

Research on the motivations of parents who kill their children (with or without disabilities) suggests that about 50 percent of all cases are altruistic filicides—i.e., they are committed by the parents in the belief that they are acting in their children's best interests. These cases include so-called mercy killings of children with disabilities, but also a wide variety of other cases. Parents may believe that they are protecting their child from abuse by an estranged spouse or even from their own dysfunctional behavior. They may believe that killing their children is the only way to "save" them from eventually engaging in immoral behavior, having impure thoughts, or leading lives of suffering. The suicidal parent often comes to believe that his or her child is better off dead than surviving the parent's suicide. Thus, altruistic filicides are characterized by the construction of a rationalization in which killing the child can be viewed as an act of morality and love, rather than selfishness and violence.

These "altruistic" motivations are often combined with other potential motivations and function psychologically as disinhibiting factors that allow the parent to overcome natural reluctance to harm the child. For example, the parent of a child with multiple disabilities may find the caregiving demands overwhelming but is inhibited from eliminating the child through homicide. If, however, the parent comes to believe that the child's quality of life is so poor that death would be a kindness, killing the child becomes justified or even heroic in the parent's mind.

It is important to recognize that research repeatedly demonstrates that people with disabilities as a group do not rate their quality of life as significantly different from that of people without disabilities. While it is unquestionably true that some people with disabilities and chronic illnesses think that their lives are not worth living and want to die, it is equally true that a similar proportion of people who do not have disabilities or chronic illnesses feel the same way about their lives. Therefore, a parent's belief that the quality of life of a child with a disability justifies ending the child's life is always a reflection of the value that the *parent* places on the child's life and not the value that the child places on his or her own life.

Attitudes and beliefs that are common in a society or culture may support or conflict with the construction of such parental rationalizations. In one high-profile case, a parent indicated that she killed her children to spare them from suffering through their parents' divorce and her own intended suicide. In another, a mother indicated that she killed her children to spare them the difficulties that they would suffer growing up with a mentally ill mother. In a third high-profile case, a father indicated that he killed his daughter to end her suffering associated with having severe and multiple disabilities. The media and general public overwhelmingly attacked the first two parents as lying about their motivation or being out of touch with reality, while the third was enthusiastically supported as having taken heroic action. Research demonstrates that parental divorce, having a mother with a major mental health problem, and having a disability all pose real challenges for children, but society condemns the first two rationales for filicide while responding to the third with considerable sympathy and support. In this way, the social condemnation of some filicides and the social endorsement of others selectively encourages parents of children with disabilities to carry out filicides. In some cases, the children killed in so-called mercy killings had very severe disabilities, but in others the disabilities were very mild but were exaggerated in the parent's mind.

Displaced anger is another common motivational factor for filicide. The filicidal parent who acts from displaced anger often explicitly or implicitly sends a message of "look what you made me do" to the actual source of his or her anger. The filicide of a child by one parent as a means of hurting the other parent is not uncommon, in cases involving children with or without disabilities, and is particularly likely to occur when the source of the parent's anger is unavailable or viewed as too powerful to attack directly. A father who was enraged at his wife fatally stabbed his daughter, who had severe and multiple disabilities, after his wife had left the house to escape his rage. A mother who was struggling to manage the behavior of a preschooler with a severe behavior disorder beat him to death while her husband was away for a weekend golf trip. In some cases, the violence directed toward the child may stem from displaced anger toward non-parents—in the case of children with disabilities, these may be professionals and caseworkers in health care, education, or social service or even society in general. In this case, the act may communicate "I killed my child because you did not provide the support that I needed to be a better parent." A father, angry when doctors refused to provide the treatment he felt was necessary for his child, threw the child from a sixth-floor hospital window. A mother who was angry and depressed after being told that a government agency would not provide more funding for her son's program, killed her son and herself with motor vehicle exhaust. Filicides that are motivated by displaced anger are particularly likely to be accompanied by suicide, for which displaced anger is often a motivational factor.

The elimination of an unwanted child is a common motivational factor in filicides, particularly in the killing of neonates with or without disabilities. However, this motivational factor is often present in filicides of children of all ages, and appears to be particularly relevant to older children with disabilities, while it becomes less common with age for children without disabilities.

Fatal child abuse and extreme forms of punishment also apply to children with and without disabilities. Because children with disabilities often are more dependent at later ages and may have more difficulties with developmental challenges such as toilet training, this motivation appears to be particularly relevant to this group. Children with intellectual or behavioral disabilities may be particularly vulnerable because they have difficulty

learning how to avoid the rage of an irrational parent.

Parents of children with disabilities have also committed filicide to prevent detection of other crimes, typically abuse or neglect. These children are particularly likely to be reported as missing or to die in ways that have the potential to conceal evidence (e.g., fire).

Financial gain is an uncommon motivation in filicides, but it has occasionally been a prominent motivation in the filicides of children with disabilities. This may be a particular concern when infants and children who sustain serious lifelong disabilities as a result of medical negligence or motor vehicle accidents receive large settlements to compensate for a lifetime of care. Eliminating the child frees the settlement money to be used for other purposes. After a divorce, the noncustodial parent, who may be expected to contribute a large amount to support a child with a disability, may be particularly likely to be motivated by financial circumstances.

Finally, many filicidal parents are motivated by their need to feel like they are in control of their own life circumstances. This motivational factor is very common in so-called mercy killings, but also is a significant factor in many other varieties of filicide. Parents of children with disabilities may be particularly challenged by feelings that their lives are out of control. They may face uncertainty about their children's health and future or feel that life is a chaotic series of crises. They may feel frustrated by their inability to meaningfully improve the quality of their children's lives, and threatened by the specter of impending death. Paradoxically, killing the child appears to bring these challenges under control for some parents. Like falling on one's own sword to thwart the enemy or quitting one's job in order to avoid being fired, killing the child creates the illusion that the parent is in control of the situation.

Cases and Outcomes

Most filicides of children with disabilities often receive minimal attention from the public or news media. A few cases emerge periodically and become prominent locally, nationally, or even internationally. Cases that receive greater attention appear to fit a few specific patterns. First, some cases receive attention because they involve extreme violence against a particularly vulnerable child. For example, in 1996, the common-law stepfather of Matthew Brent Richmond immersed him in scalding water to punish the twelve-year-old, who had developmental disabilities, for a toileting accident; the case received widespread press coverage and led directly to changes in Ohio law expanding the death penalty to murders of children.

Second, cases in which the defense suggests that the parent had diminished responsibility due to the extreme stress associated with raising a child with a disability may receive substantial widespread public attention if the prosecution argues against this defense. This was the major defense offered by the mother of Casey Janine Albury who strangled her autistic seventeen-year-old daughter in New Zealand in 1997. The mother had tried unsuccessfully to push her daughter off a bridge before strangling her. Widespread public opinion, however, portrayed the mother as victim because she had had to care for a difficult child. The mother was sentenced to only four years in prison but appealed the sentence as being too harsh; she eventually served only four months in jail.

Third, cases involving parents who have claimed that they killed their children to free them from suffering resulting from or associated with their disabilities have received considerable public attention. In many cases, the distinction between these mercy-killing defenses and the previous category of diminished responsibility is unclear, because both claims are made. In many cases, the parent initially claims that the motivation was rational compassion but later acknowledges that his or her judgment had been impaired by stress or depression. In a few cases, the parent presents a defense based solely on the argument that killing the child was right or necessary for the good of the child. In 1993, twelve-year-old Tracy Latimer was killed in Saskatchewan by her father, who argued that killing her was necessary to prevent her from further suffering. Repeated trials and appeals followed over the next six years. Eventually, her father was convicted of second-degree murder and given a life sentence without a chance of parole for ten years. More than 2,000 newspaper articles were published about this case during these trials and appeals. Although the original charge of first-degree murder was downgraded to second-degree murder, of which Robert Latimer was convicted and given the lightest sentence possible under the law, polls overwhelmingly indicated that the public believed that even the minimum penalty was too harsh.

Finally, cases that involve children initially reported as missing often receive considerable public attention. In 1984, the father of Louise Brown reported that the family car had been stolen with his infant daughter, who had Down syndrome, in the car. The media and the public responded with a flurry of activity in a desperate search to find the missing baby. Eventually, it became apparent that her father had killed Louise Brown and the father's brother had helped dispose of the body. The defense focused on diminished responsibility of a remorseful father, and the court was sympathetic. The judge pointed out that the father had acted under extreme stress in the extraordinary circumstances of adjusting to his daughter's disability and was no threat to society. The father was portrayed as victim, as a loving father whose emotions had gotten the better of him under difficult circumstances. He was sentenced to five years for manslaughter and perverting the course of justice. He was released after serving less than two years. The case returned to the headlines in the 1990s, when Louise Brown's father killed his brother by stabbing him sixty-three times. This time, Brown's defense portrayed him as a loving brother whose emotions had gotten the better of him under difficult circumstances when his brother attacked him for swearing in front of his children. The court, the media, and the public were less sympathetic with these arguments of diminished responsibility of a remorseful brother, and Paul Brown was sentenced to life in prison.

Conclusion

Filicide, the act of a parent killing his or her own offspring, is the most common form of child homicide. Children with disabilities appear to be at least several times more likely to die as a result of filicide, but no precise estimate of their relative risk is available. Many interacting motivational factors appear to play a role in filicides of children with disabilities. Most instrumental motivations are similar to the motivations that lead to filicides of children without disabilities but may be intensified by the disability. For example, many filicidal parents of children with or without disabilities kill their children to escape from the responsibilities of caregiving. This motivation may be more intense and more enduring, however, in the case of a parent of a child with a disability, because the child requires much more care at perhaps high levels for many more years than a child without a disability. Disinhibiting factors may be much stronger for parents of children with disabilities because society encourages beliefs that support rationalizations for killing such children.

DICK SOBSEY

See also **Child Neglect; Child Sexual Abuse; Medical Neglect Related to Religion and Culture; Women with Disabilities, Domestic Violence against**

References and Further Reading

Catlin, Anita J. "Normalization, Chronic Sorrow, and Murder: Highlighting the Care of Carol Carr." *Pediatric Nursing* 29, no. 4 (2003): 326–328.

De Haan, B. "Critical and Fatal Child Maltreatment in Oregon." *Dissertation Abstracts International* 58, no. 8 (1997): 3307. (AAT No. 9805286.)

Jackson, M., ed. *Infanticide: Historical Perspectives on Child Murder and Concealment, 1550–2000.* Aldershot, Hants, England: Ashgate Publishing, 2002.

Lucardie, R. E. "Homicide of People with Developmental Disabilities: Content Analysis of Print Media." *Dissertation Abstracts International* 64, no. 7 (2003): 2653. (AAT NQ82135.)

Palermo, M. T. "Preventing Filicide in Families with Autistic Children." *International Journal of Offender Therapy and Comparative Criminology* 47, no. 1 (2003): 47–57.

Richards, C. *The Loss of Innocents: Child Killers and Their Victims.* Wilmington, DE: Scholarly Resources, Inc., 2000.

Schwartz, L. L., and N. K. Isser. *Endangered Children: Neonaticide, Infanticide, and Filicide.* Boca Raton, FL: CRC Press, 2000.

Sobsey, D. *Violence and Abuse in the Lives of People with Disabilities.* Baltimore: Paul H. Brookes, 1994.

Sullivan, P. M., and J. F. Knutson. "Maltreatment and Disabilities: A Population-Based Study." *Child Abuse and Neglect* 24, no. 10 (2000): 1257–1273.

Wall, S. N., and J. C. Partridge. "Death in the Intensive Care Nursery: Physician Practice of Withdrawing and Withholding Life Support." *Pediatrics* 99, no. 1 (1997): 64–70.

G

GAY AND BISEXUAL MALE
DOMESTIC VIOLENCE

Introduction

Domestic violence is not restricted to heterosexual couples. Gay and bisexual males have also been the victims and perpetrators of domestic violence and abuse. This article will examine some of the issues concerning gay and bisexual male domestic violence, with particular attention devoted to: defining what constitutes domestic violence; a brief historical perspective; some unique concerns for gay and bisexual domestic violence; profiles of the victims and offenders; discussion of the cycle of abuse; attempting to understand why victims stay; and prevention and treatment strategies. Because most domestic violence research has focused on male–female encounters, studies concerning gay and bisexual male domestic violence have been neglected. The few studies that do exist reveal that the frequency of gay and bisexual male domestic violence does not significantly differ from that of heterosexual domestic violence. For instance, one study found that approximately one-quarter of gay and bisexual men were victims of same-sex domestic violence. It is clear that domestic violence has no sexual or gender boundaries.

It is important to note that it is difficult to obtain accurate domestic violence statistics, for a number of reasons. First, domestic violence, in general, is underreported. Many victims believe that what happens in the home should stay in the home. This is particularly true for gay and bisexual men. They may not wish to disclose their victimization to the police or others for fear of outing—the nonconsensual disclosing of their sexual orientation. Second, socialization implies that "men should be men" and that they should be able to handle physical aggression without outside interference. Third, gay and bisexual men may be reluctant to report their victimization to authorities, particularly the police, for fear of further victimization through police ridicule, discrimination, or violence. Fourth, the concept of domestic violence may be vague. Is yelling considered domestic violence? Is pushing a violent act? Should the victim wait until blood is drawn before contacting authorities?

Defining Domestic Violence

Domestic violence has numerous definitions, ranging from narrow to broad. For the purpose of this essay, gay and bisexual male domestic violence will be defined broadly to include the control of others through power, including verbal and nonverbal harassment, physical and psychological threat or injury to the victim or to others, isolation (preventing or minimizing social contacts), economic deprivation, outing, sexual assaults (including being pressured into sexual activity), destruction of property, animal or pet abuse, withholding medication, or any combination of these methods.

Brief Historical Perspective

As noted above, domestic violence among heterosexual, bisexual, and gay couples has been around for as long as relationships have existed, although the focus of the majority of the research on domestic violence has been devoted to heterosexual relationships. Heterosexual domestic violence was first recognized as a problem only in the mid- to late twentieth century; at the start of the twenty-first century, much work remains to raise similar levels of awareness for gay and bisexual male domestic violence.

Prior to the women's movement of the late 1960s and early 1970s, domestic violence was minimized—often by blaming the victim—through the "you deserved what you got" mentality. Nearly forty years later, programs and resources for victimized women are well established. Ironically, while these resources exist for women, comparable resources are often unavailable to male victims—be they gay, bisexual, or straight. Gay and bisexual men are more likely to be killed by their partners than by gay bashers. For instance, Patrick Letellier found that in San Francisco in 1991–1992, one-third of murdered gay men were killed by their partners and one-third were killed by "roommates"—a term used by police who either do not know the relationship between the parties or do not wish to know.

As a consequence of the lack of attention devoted to gay and bisexual domestic violence, victims often believe that they must fend for themselves. Some have resorted to alcohol and/or drug abuse as a means of escape; others have attempted or committed suicide. There has been at least one documented case of a victim who went so far as to create a new identity, complete with a new name, Social Security number, change in physical appearance, etc., in order to avoid his abuser.

It would be unfair to simply blame the women's movement for the nonattention concerning gay and bisexual domestic violence. The gay and bisexual community must take some responsibility as well,

for keeping the topic in the closet. Measures to raise awareness are necessary and will be addressed in greater detail in the final section of this essay.

Some Unique Concerns

As noted above, previous studies have found that the prevalence of heterosexual domestic violence is roughly the same as that of gay and bisexual male domestic violence. However, gay and bisexual male domestic violence is complicated by homophobia (regardless of whether one self-identifies as being straight, gay, or bisexual) and the "HIV/AIDS effect." It is recognized that HIV/AIDS is not limited to the gay and bisexual male population; however, gay and bisexual men are considered to be within a "high risk" population.

Homophobia is a fear of homosexuals. Batterers frequently use homophobia to control the victim. This may include threats to disclose the victim's sexual orientation to friends, family, employers, etc., unless the victim complies with his demands. Basically, this amounts to emotional blackmail. In addition, homophobia can cause many in society, including victims' family members and law enforcement, to not recognize gay and bisexual male domestic violence as a problem.

Gay and bisexual male victims sometimes fail to leave an abusive relationship due to the HIV/AIDS effect. Some victims of HIV or AIDS fear an imminent death and do not wish to die alone (at the time of this writing, a cure for AIDS has not been discovered; however, the use of medications and positive personal health choices have substantially prolonged the quality of life of many HIV/AIDS victims). Some HIV/AIDS victims believe that finding another relationship may be extremely difficult due to their health status and would rather remain in their current relationship, even though abusive.

Research suggests that although the occurrence is rare, HIV-positive abusers may deliberately infect their partners to prevent them from leaving. As a means of controlling the victim, some abusers have used the "guilt card." For example, an HIV-positive abuser may actually feign serious illness to prevent his victimized partner from leaving or to make him return. The victim may not wish to abandon his abusive partner in a time of need (be it real or imagined), in part because of how he would be judged by others. Some abusers have prevented their partners from seeking medical attention, or have withheld medication, as a means to control the relationship and to promote future abuse. Some abusers have even threatened to communicate the status of their ill partners to others, including employers, parents, and/or health care providers.

Why would someone subject himself to such abuse? What would prompt a person to commit such abuse? In the next two sections, the characteristics of the victim and offender are profiled. Profiling is a process whereby people are placed into categories based upon shared characteristics. It is important to note that while profiling may prove useful for classification purposes, it serves merely to aid in understanding and should not be seen as a panacea for identification.

Profiling the Victim

Victims of domestic violence often share common characteristics. This holds true regardless of sexual orientation. It is important to note that individuals do not have to possess each of these traits to be victims of abuse.

Victims of gay or bisexual domestic violence often possess anger toward their partners, withdraw from social activities and other people, have a lack of trust, demonstrate or internalize fear, blame themselves for the abusers' actions, experience frustration, show signs of depression, and/or have low self-esteem. Additionally, victims may overestimate their ability to handle the violence; attempt to avoid conflict; deny the abuse; trivialize the abuse; attempt to leave the relationship only to return; find leaving the abuser to be difficult; believe they are trapped in the relationship and that there are no alternatives to leaving; and/or believe that they must endure the violence.

Victims often develop coping strategies as means to compensate for the violence, including appeasing or avoiding their abusers or simply justifying the abuse (i.e., believing that they "deserved it"). Sometimes the victim may actually attempt to seek some outside assistance, only to be ridiculed by the abuser. Many victims stay in the relationship because they believe (or imagine) that eventually the violence will cease.

Profile of the Abuser/Batterer

Abusers come in all sizes and shapes; they are not limited by socioeconomic status, age, physical strength, or racial, ethnic, religious, or occupational backgrounds. However, batterers do share some common characteristics. For example, many batterers deny the violence they inflict upon others; blame the victim by making statements such as, "He deserved what he got"; have anger management issues or explosive personalities; are loners—due to their lack of outside friendships, they may attempt to bully their partners into submission so they will not leave; lack control over their lives and therefore attempt to control the lives of others; and, like their victims, possess low self-esteem and self-worth.

In addition to the above characteristics, gay or bisexual batterers may also possess a number of other traits. These include tendencies to: manipulate, control, and dominate others; restrict the freedom and movement of the victim; use cruel, demeaning, and aggressive behavior to coerce the victim to submit to the batterer's demands; and attempt to stifle the victim through threats and physical violence, preventing others from learning of the abuse. Batterers often have histories of failed relationships and academic, occupational, and/or financial problems. They are prone to jealousy, insecurity, deceitfulness, and/or unrealistic expectations of self and partner; they may also exhibit a pattern of emotional dependency toward their victims, including obsession.

Furthermore, the profile of the batterer will most likely include a lifelong history of violence (known as the "cycle of violence" or "intergenerational transmission of violence"). Batterers in both heterosexual and same-sex relationships often experienced or witnessed violence in childhood prior to becoming violent themselves. As a result of the "cycle of violence," batterers often have experienced one or more of the following: witnessing physical and/or psychological abuse of family members; being victims of abuse or neglect by parents or siblings; bullying in school as either victims or abusers; and histories of victimizing previous partners. The abuser may also have threatened, harmed, or killed a family pet or other animal as a means to either control others or to show a propensity toward future violence. There is a strong relationship between animal abuse and human violence.

The abuser will most likely target those that he deems "weaker." Rarely will batterers display violence toward persons of higher status or authority. Batterers are also reluctant to seek assistance for their problem(s). It is not until they are mandated by law or have witnessed their lives completely at rock bottom that they ask for outside, professional counseling. Even then, batterers may not seek the help they desperately require.

It is not uncommon for domestic abusers (again, regardless of sexual orientation) to be under the influence of alcohol and/or drugs during the violent encounter. However, there is debate regarding the intensity of the abuse during intoxication. For instance, some research has found that alcohol intoxication may actually reduce aggression, whereas other research has found an increase in violence, particularly when drugs and alcohol are combined. Regardless of the impact of alcohol and/or drugs on an incident of gay or bisexual male domestic violence, voluntary intoxication is never the cause of the violence; it is merely an unacceptable excuse.

The Cycle of Abuse

One of the many problems associated with domestic violence is that once it begins, it rarely stops. While it may be true that relationship violence does not continue twenty-four hours a day, research indicates that there is a cyclical pattern to the abuse. Lenore Walker noted that there are three phases to domestic violence abuse. These stages pertain to all types of domestic relationships, including those of gay or bisexual males.

The first is the tension-building stage. This is characterized by verbal abuse (or the silent treatment) and may include assaults resulting in minor injuries. The second is known as the acute-battering stage. Violence often goes beyond inflicting minor injuries and escalates to severe battering of the victim, which may include punching, slapping, kicking, and/or choking. Often these injuries result in visible bruises or broken bones. The abuser may even resort to weapons to control the victim. This stage may last anywhere from a few minutes to days. The final stage is often referred to as the calm period. During this stage the abuser is apologetic for his actions and promises that he will never do it again. Along with his plea for forgiveness, he will likely shower the victim with gifts to show how much "he really cares" and repents for his actions. This "honeymoon" phase can last from days to years. This stage may actually be the most dangerous, since the victim is lulled into a false sense of security and decides to stay in the abusive relationship.

These three stages work together in a cyclical pattern. As the frequency of the cycle increases, so does the frequency and severity of the violence. In other words, the more times the cycle is completed, the shorter time it takes to actually complete the cycle. Without intervention, the cycle will likely continue.

Why Do They Stay?

People often ask, "Why would someone stay in an abusive relationship? If I were them, I would get out." Unfortunately, it is not that easy. Gay and bisexual men stay in abusive relationships for a number of reasons:

- *Fear of escalated violence.* Victims often fear that if they leave the relationship and return, their batterers will likely increase the violence level. This would be consistent with the cycle of abuse described above.
- *Threats.* Abusers often threaten their victims that if they leave or tell others, the violence will continue or become more severe. Some victims express concern that their batterers will harm not only them, but also others (i.e., friends, pets, etc.).
- *Poor self-esteem.* Many victims believe that they deserve the abuse and that they are at fault.
- *Loyalty.* Some victims remain loyal to their partners and believe that it is incumbent upon them to remain in the relationship. This may include a commitment to honoring their vows (whether personal or through a formal ceremony).
- *Fear.* This includes not just the fear of the potential consequences of leaving the relationship, but the fear of being alone. This may also include the fear of not finding another relationship because the victim deems himself as unworthy (having poor self-esteem).
- *Hope to change the batterer.* A victim often believes that he should remain in an abusive relationship because the batterer is really the victim and is in need of special care and attention that only the victim can provide. He may also believe the abuser's pleas of forgiveness and promises to seek help.
- *Lack of understanding.* It is not surprising that some victims do not even realize they are victims of abuse. They may be unaware that gay or bisexual battering actually exists, thinking that the violent act was merely an isolated incident and will not likely occur again; or victims may perceive that only severe cases of battery (violence that requires medical attention) are considered domestic violence.
- *Denial.* Similar to lack of understanding, victims may make excuses for the violence or pretend that it never occurred.
- *Stalking.* Some batterers will stalk their victims out of jealousy or in attempts to convince the victims to return to the relationship (providing they ever left).
- *Love.* Regardless of the abuse they have received, many victims remain in love with their abusers. Some victims believe that they

would be unable to fall in love again if they left the relationship.

- *Dependence.* This includes both financial and emotional dependence. There is some debate concerning financial dependence as an explanation for remaining in a violent gay or bisexual relationship. Some believe that gay and bisexual male relationships are no different than heterosexual or lesbian relationships in that whoever manages the financial purse strings possesses the ultimate control in the relationship, which can later be used as leverage in a domestic violence encounter. Others believe that gay men, in particular, have greater financial independence. Because gay men are (with few exceptions) not permitted to marry, partners often maintain separate financial accounts. In addition, because gay or bisexual male couples are less likely than heterosexual couples to have children, they may have more financial freedom than heterosexual couples with children.
- *HIV/AIDS.* As discussed earlier, HIV/AIDS plays a special role in gay and bisexual relationships. Victims of domestic violence who are HIV positive or who have AIDS may fear that if they do not abide by their abusers' demands, the abusers may withhold necessary medication. Fear of dying alone is also a concern; some victims would rather remain in an abusive relationship than deal with their illness in isolation. Additionally, a victim of domestic violence who is the caretaker of a partner with HIV/AIDS may not wish to abandon his partner in time of need.
- *Physical attraction.* Not to be confused with love, some bisexual and gay males may remain in an abusive relationship because they continue to possess a physical attraction toward their partner, which appears to outweigh the abuse. Although undocumented, this may apply for those who have abusive "trophy" boyfriends. The victim would rather endure the physical violence as long as he has an attractive boyfriend to parade around in public. If this is valid, it may coincide with the victim's low self-esteem and self-worth.
- *Socialization.* Men have been socialized to "take it like a man." A macho attitude is not isolated to the abuser. Victims often feel they need to stay in a violent relationship because they perceive that it would reflect negatively upon them to leave or report the incident to authorities, believing that men should be able to take care of themselves. Victims may also

fear that the police, or others to whom abuse is reported, would ridicule them for being unable to defend themselves.

- *Guilt.* Some victims who do engage in physical confrontations with their abusers may believe that they are no better than the abusers themselves. They may not understand the concept of self-defense and see themselves as being equally at fault.
- *Lack of support.* Gay or bisexual male victims who wish to seek help often find that there is a lack of available resources, including shelters and professional contacts, or that they simply do not know where to look for help.

Prevention and Treatment Strategies

Prevention and treatment programs for female victims of domestic violence are abundant. It certainly is not the purpose of this essay to minimize their importance; quite the contrary. The more resources available for abuse victims, the better. However, resources and treatment programs for abused men, be they gay, bisexual, or heterosexual, are severely lacking.

Shelters for men need to be established, complete with trained counselors to better serve male victims of domestic violence. These shelters or safe houses should also include services for pets. As previously stated, there is a strong relationship between a person who harms animals and one who commits physical violence toward humans. Batterers may threaten to harm or kill pets to control their victims and make the victims adhere to the abusers' demands. These may be household pets or even farm animals.

Due to the lack of available resources, some male victims of domestic violence may attempt to receive assistance from HIV/AIDS service providers or other social service agencies that focus on gay, lesbian, bisexual, or transgender issues, only to be told that these agencies are ill-prepared and ill-equipped to handle problems of domestic violence. Referrals to other agencies are unlikely (this is especially true if there are no agencies serving male domestic violence victims in a jurisdiction). If separate facilities are unavailable, partnerships with gay community centers may provide useful alternatives.

Professionals need to be trained in gay and bisexual male domestic violence issues. This is particularly important for criminal justice personnel, who are often first responders to domestic violence cases, and for health care professionals, who are mandatory reporters for domestic violence incidents. Research suggests that victims in same-sex relationships are often reluctant to report domestic violence to police personnel for fear of retaliation from their abusers, ridicule from officers, police homophobia (real or perceived), or officers' lack of understanding of male victims in domestic violence encounters.

For instance, police officers who respond to a gay or bisexual male domestic violence call may believe that since two men are involved, it is simply mutual combat. This is consistent with the socialization process exemplified by stereotypical statements such as: "Men should be able to fend for themselves" or "It is an equal fight, since two men are involved." Sometimes officers are unwilling to make an arrest where one is warranted; in other incidents, they may arrest the victim or both parties. The latter two options may be particularly true where a law enforcement agency is bound by a mandatory arrest policy, requiring officers to make an arrest whenever physical injury is present. Police academy and in-service training should include an awareness of and proper response to gay and bisexual male domestic violence encounters.

Additionally, other members of the criminal justice community should be educated concerning the special needs of gay and bisexual male victims of domestic violence. Research suggests that victims of gay and bisexual male domestic violence lack confidence in the court system. Accordingly, prosecutors should be encouraged to prosecute abusers in domestic violence cases and judges should be consistent in their sentencing when dealing with domestic violence victims, regardless of gender or sexuality.

Many health care professionals are also socialized to believe that gay or bisexual male victims of domestic violence do not need special treatment. This may be due to homophobia or perhaps a lack of knowledge concerning gay or bisexual male domestic violence. Mental health care training should include proper interviewing techniques for victims appropriate to gender and sexual orientation, with an assessment of history of abuse and previous injuries. Mental health professionals should be able to aid and counsel gay and bisexual male victims who miss work due to injuries suffered as a result of abuse. They should recognize signs and symptoms of abuse and serve as advocates for the victim, including during victim–police interactions.

Other solutions may include support or self-help group counseling for victims of gay or bisexual male domestic violence. Couple counseling is not recommended. The problem with couple counseling is that the abuser is sitting in the room with the victim. The victim may not feel free to discuss problems openly for fear of future retaliation and assaults; the abuser will likely deny the abuse and make it appear that the victim is to blame.

In addition, mental health counselors should work to develop counseling programs for the abusive partners in gay and bisexual male relationships. Some effective programs have been developed for counseling abusers in heterosexual relationships; programs of this type need to be extended to include issues pertinent to gay and bisexual relationships.

Policymakers should be aware of gay and bisexual male domestic violence issues. After identifying and acknowledging the problem, lawmakers should develop measures to ensure the safety of the victims, including recognizing and amending language within the law that does not appear to be inclusive of all victims. It is important that domestic violence be conceptualized as a potential problem in all types of relationships, regardless of gender and sexual orientation.

Finally, community education is critical. This includes the gay, bisexual, and heterosexual community. Communication must be open, not hidden behind a cloud of secrecy and shame. Information about gay and bisexual male domestic violence should be made available through gay establishments (including bars, clubs, restaurants, and shops), gay pride events, and gay community organizations. Gay media sources, including gay newspapers and magazines, gay Internet sites, and gay television networks, should be contacted and encouraged to provide domestic violence public service announcements that include contacts and referral agencies. Of course, this awareness should apply to all media sources, although it is unlikely that the "straight" or "mainstream" media will concern itself with gay or bisexual male domestic violence until the gay community itself initially acknowledges and addresses the problem.

Conclusion

The purpose of this article was to explore the various issues concerning gay and bisexual male domestic violence. As noted, little attention has been devoted to this topic. Community awareness and prevention strategies are needed to minimize the dangers associated with domestic violence, regardless of sexual orientation of victims and abusers. Without proper resources and treatment programs, the cycles of violence and abuse among gay and bisexual male couples will likely continue.

TOD W. BURKE and STEPHEN S. OWEN

See also **Animal Abuse: The Link to Family Violence; Battered Husbands; Batterer Intervention Programs; Community Responses to Gay and Lesbian Domestic Violence; Cycle of Violence; Factors Influencing Reporting Behaviors by Male Domestic Violence Victims; Gay Domestic Violence, Police Attitudes and Behaviors toward; Gender Socialization and Gay Male Domestic Violence; Intergenerational Transfer of Intimate Partner Violence; Intimate Partner Violence in Queer, Transgender, and Bisexual Communities; Lesbian Battering; Male Victims of Domestic Violence and Reasons They Stay with Their Abusers; Same-Sex Domestic Violence: Comparing Venezuela and the United States; Sexual Orientation and Gender Identity: The Need for Education in Servicing Victims of Trauma; Substance Use/Abuse and Intimate Partner Violence**

References and Further Reading

Burke, Tod W. "Male to Male Gay Domestic Violence: The Dark Closet." In *Violence in Intimate Relationships: Examining Sociological and Psychological Issues,* edited by Nicky Jackson and Giselé Oates. Boston: Butterworth-Heinemann, 1998, pp. 161–179.

Burke, Tod W., Michael L. Jordan, and Stephen S. Owen. "A Cross-National Comparison of Gay and Lesbian Domestic Violence." *Journal of Contemporary Criminal Justice* 18, no. 3 (2002): 231–257.

Coleman, Diane, and Murray Straus. "Alcohol Abuse and Family Violence." In *Alcohol, Drug Abuse and Aggression,* edited by E. Gottheil, K. A. Druley, T. E. Skoloda, and H. M. Waxman. Springfield, IL: Charles C. Thomas, 1983, pp. 104–124.

Cruz, J. Michael. "'Why Doesn't He Just Leave?': Gay Male Domestic Violence and the Reasons Victims Stay." *Journal of Men's Studies* 11, no. 3 (2003): 309–323.

Elliott, Pam. "Shattering Illusions: Same-Sex Domestic Violence." In *Violence in Gay and Lesbian Domestic Partnerships,* edited by Claire Renzetti and Charles Miley. New York: Haworth Press, 1996, pp. 1–8.

Harms, Bradley. *Domestic Violence in the Gay Male Community*. Unpublished master's thesis. San Francisco: San Francisco State University Department of Psychology, 1995.

Island, David, and Patrick Letellier. *Men Who Beat the Men Who Love Them*. New York: Harrington Park Press, 1991.

Letellier, Patrick. "Same Sex Male Battering." *Visions,* March/April/May (1995): 8.

———. "Twin Epidemics: Domestic Violence and HIV Infection among Gay and Bisexual Men." In *Violence in Gay and Lesbian Domestic Partnerships,* edited by Claire Renzetti and Charles Miley. New York: Haworth Press, 1996, pp. 69–81.

Leventhal, Beth, and Sandra E. Lundy, eds. *Same-Sex Domestic Violence: Strategies for Change*. Thousand Oaks, CA: Sage Publications, 1999.

Lundy, Sandra. "Abuse That Dare Not Speak Its Name: Assisting Victims of Lesbian and Gay Domestic Violence in Massachusetts." *New England Law Review* 28 (1993): 273–311.

Merrill, Gregory. "Ruling the Exceptions: Same-Sex Domestic Violence and Domestic Violence Theory." *Journal of Lesbian/Gay Social Services* 4, no. 1 (1996): 9–21.

Merrill, Gregory S., and Valerie A. Wolfe. "Battered Gay Men: An Exploration of Abuse, Help Seeking, and Why They Stay." *Journal of Homosexuality* 39, no. 2 (2000): 1–30.

Owen, Stephen S., and Tod W. Burke. "An Exploration of Prevalence of Domestic Violence in Same-Sex Relationships." *Psychological Reports* 95, no. 1 (2004): 129–132.

Sonkin, Daniel, and Michael Durphy. *Learning to Live Without Violence*. San Francisco: Gay Community News Volcano Press, 1989.

Walker, Lenore. *The Battered Woman*. New York: Harper and Row, 1979.

GAY DOMESTIC VIOLENCE, POLICE ATTITUDES AND BEHAVIORS TOWARD

Introduction

In order to understand police attitudes and behaviors toward gay domestic violence, it is necessary to consider two issues from an historical perspective: first, the attitudes of police officers toward homosexuality; and second, the attitudes of the gay community toward the police. Against this backdrop, the implications for police response to gay domestic violence may be more readily understood. It is also important to note that the body of research pertaining to gay domestic violence in general, and to police attitudes and behaviors more specifically, is very limited. As the gay community becomes less marginalized, it is likely that future research will continue to explore these important but heretofore largely neglected topics.

Law Enforcement and the Gay Community

Historically, the relationship between law enforcement and the gay community has been antagonistic. In the past, law enforcement officers were known to hold what would today be considered homophobic attitudes. After all, consensual homosexual sexual activity was once illegal (the last of the state sodomy laws were overturned in the 2003 U.S. Supreme Court case *Lawrence v. Texas*), and police departments sponsored both crackdowns on public displays of gay sexuality and raids on gay establishments. Public perceptions of the immorality of homosexuality also colored law enforcement actions, as police were seen as being moral exemplars within society. Finally, policing, as a vocational field, has long been a bastion of masculinity and machismo, resulting in institutionalized homophobia.

Even gay law enforcement officers have found it difficult to permeate the boundaries of a patriarchal heterosexual occupational culture. While gay police officers are more easily integrated into their agencies today than twenty, or even ten, years ago, they still face obstacles and discrimination that a heterosexual police officer does not. In part, the inclusion of gay officers into the ranks of policing appears to parallel two similar social movements: First, the reluctance of the military to accept openly gay soldiers on grounds that it could harm morale, and second, the struggle for acceptance that female officers continue to face, as they challenge the male domination of law enforcement.

Homophobic attitudes and values within police agencies have resulted in a discordant relationship with the gay community. In addition to the routine style of arrests for gay sexuality and raids on gay establishments noted above (for instance, the practices in Philadelphia became legendary examples of enforcement directed against the gay community), one higher-profile example comes readily to mind. In 1969, the so-called Stonewall Riots inaugurated the modern generation of gay civil rights activism. The riots were sparked by a police raid of the Stonewall Inn, a gay establishment in New York City, and served to galvanize the modern gay rights movement.

As noted below, the contemporary relationship between the police and the gay community is much healthier today than in the past. However, some homophobia remains within some police officers personally and organizationally, and it is difficult for gay citizens to forget the legacy of law enforcement's anti-gay practices. The evolving nature of the relationship between the police and the gay community shapes not only the enforcement of same-sex domestic violence, but also enforcement against hate crimes and other crimes against gay persons.

Policing Gay Domestic Violence

In many ways, gay domestic violence is not that different from heterosexual domestic violence. The issues of power and control, the cycle of abuse, and the devastation to victims' lives are products of all domestic violence, regardless of sexuality. The primary differences between gay and heterosexual domestic violence, as far as enforcement goes, are in the areas of outing, reporting, and officer attitudes.

Outing refers to the disclosure, voluntary or otherwise, of a person's homosexual orientation. The decision for a heterosexual person to call the police in a domestic violence incident is difficult enough. Gay persons face the added difficulty of revealing their sexual orientation to the responding officer(s); the victim may be fearful of a negative police or public response, especially if he or she is not openly gay.

A fear of outing can prevent a victim from reporting an act of domestic violence to the police. While domestic violence often goes unreported, it may be more difficult for gay persons to report an incident because they lack confidence in the police department or the legal system as a whole, or because they perceive law enforcement as homophobic.

Accordingly, a crucial variable to consider is law enforcement officers' attitudes toward both homosexuality and same-sex domestic violence. It is important to note the difference between perceptions of officers' attitudes, the officers' actual attitudes, and the officers' behaviors when responding to an incident of gay domestic violence. Here, the existing research is in need of further development. The body of literature on officers' attitudes and behaviors toward gay domestic violence is very limited; while some data suggest that homophobia remains as part of the police culture, other evidence suggests that discriminatory attitudes have faded. For instance, one 2002 study of police officers in a California city found that the officers did not perceive differences between gay and heterosexual domestic violence. However, another 2002 study of police officers (this time in a southwestern city) found that many officers believed that gay citizens would be treated less fairly than heterosexuals.

Furthermore, it is very difficult to draw conclusions about officers' actual behaviors when responding to same-sex domestic violence calls, absent anecdotal evidence (some of which suggests that some officers are effective and polite, whereas other accounts are less positive). Of course, it is also important to acknowledge law enforcement's historical reluctance to respond to domestic violence calls in general. This is in part due to beliefs in the privacy of the home, and in part due to officer safety concerns. In addition, officers sometimes are reluctant to view males as victims and females as perpetrators in domestic assaults. Victims of same-sex domestic violence may harbor these stereotypes as well, also serving to decrease incident reporting.

Even if all law enforcement officers were progressive and pro–gay rights, there is still the matter of the victims' perceptions of the police. Accordingly, a strategy for improving police response to same-sex domestic violence must occur along two fronts: First, as necessary, individual officers and departments must come to appreciate the importance of enforcing laws against abuse regardless of victims' sexual orientation or gender identification; and second, appreciation must be conveyed to the members of the gay community, to build their confidence in a legal system that has traditionally victimized them.

Fortunately, there is room for improving law enforcement response to gay domestic violence. There appear to be four keys to successful development of police response to gay domestic violence. First, interest group activism can stimulate attention to problems. Just as the women's movement of the 1960s began to spark concern about domestic violence in general, gay interest groups may promote domestic violence as a concern to the community. This activism can be directed not only at police agencies, but also at prosecutorial elections and state legislatures. The focus on state legislatures is particularly important, as they have the power to define what constitutes domestic violence, thus shaping the laws that police ultimately enforce. In communities with progressive (i.e., non-homophobic) police agencies, it is also important for gay interest groups to promote awareness of these sound police practices, stressing the importance of reporting domestic violence to law enforcement. Doing so can help bridge the gap that may exist between perceptions of the police and actual police attitudes and behaviors.

Second, police agencies should—and many increasingly do—promote an awareness of diversity (including, but not limited to, sexual orientation) and how it shapes both police and citizen behaviors and attitudes. Both sensitivity training and the presence of more openly gay officers within the police culture may help to erase the background of homophobia within departments. Requiring a college degree for police recruits may also enhance sensitivity toward diversity, because increased education is associated with tolerance.

Third, as gay culture continues to become mainstream, the social stigma of homosexuality may decrease. This could translate to lower levels of homophobia within the criminal justice system, and perhaps with a decreased fear of outing among victims. Police agencies have begun to demonstrate their recognition of sexual diversity by, in larger jurisdictions, designating liaison officers to gay communities. These officers can foster positive relationships between the gay community and the police, while also providing a nonjudgmental police resource to gay citizens. Some departments have gone so far as to recruit openly gay officers by advertising at gay pride events, in gay publications, and at establishments frequented by a gay clientele, such as gay bars. These openly gay officers can be liaisons between the gay and straight communities, and also between gay and heterosexual police officers.

Lastly, the police response to gay domestic violence will ultimately rest with the integrity of police leadership. Just as the initial efforts against domestic violence were more likely to be successful when supported by police administrators, so too will departmental efforts stressing tolerance and acceptance of gay citizens.

Conclusion

While not much is known about the actual attitudes and behaviors of police officers toward gay domestic violence, several observations are particularly salient. One, the gay community has traditionally had a difficult relationship with law enforcement, which shapes enforcement of all laws pertaining to gay citizens—not just domestic violence. Second, evidence suggests that police agencies are overcoming the institutionalized homophobia that was common not long ago. Third, with the proper organizational programs and leadership, it is possible to forge a positive relationship between the police and the gay community, which is likely to improve police response to not only gay domestic violence, but also to other issues of concern to gay citizens.

STEPHEN S. OWEN

References and Further Reading

Bailey, Robert W. *Gay Politics, Urban Politics: Identity and Economics in the Urban Setting*. New York: Columbia University Press, 1999. (See especially Chapter 9, "Sexual Identity and Police Practices in Philadelphia.")

Belkin, Aaron, and Jason McNichol. "Pink and Blue: Outcomes Associated with the Integration of Open Gay and Lesbian Personnel in the San Diego Police Department." *Police Quarterly* 5, no. 1 (2002): 63–95.

Bernstein, Mary, and Constance Kostelac. "Lavender and Blue: Attitudes about Homosexuality and Behavior toward Lesbians and Gay Men among Police Officers." *Journal of Contemporary Criminal Justice* 18, no. 3 (2002): 302–328.

Burke, Tod W., Michael L. Jordan, and Stephen S. Owen. "A Cross-National Comparison of Gay and Lesbian Domestic Violence." *Journal of Contemporary Criminal Justice* 18, no. 3 (2002): 231–257.

Faiman-Silva, Sandra L. *The Courage to Connect: Sexuality, Citizenship, and Community in Provincetown*. Urbana: University of Illinois Press, 2004. (See especially Chapter 6, "The Politics of Citizenship: Police-Community Relations.")

Kuehnle, Kristen, and Anne Sullivan. "Gay and Lesbian Victimization: Reporting Factors in Domestic Violence and Bias Incidents." *Criminal Justice and Behavior* 30, no. 1 (2003): 85–96.

Lawrence v. Texas, 539 U.S. 558 (2003).

Leinen, Stephen. *Gay Cops*. New Brunswick, NJ: Rutgers University Press, 1993.

Younglove, Jane A., Marcee G. Kerr, and Corey J. Vitello. "Law Enforcement Officers' Perceptions of Same Sex Domestic Violence: Reason for Cautious Optimism." *Journal of Interpersonal Violence* 17, no. 7 (2002): 760–772.

GENDER SOCIALIZATION AND GAY MALE DOMESTIC VIOLENCE

In understanding gender socialization and gay male domestic violence, it is important to recognize that domestic violence is not strictly the purview of heterosexual couples. In making the connection between gay male domestic violence and gender socialization, there are a number of important issues of which to be aware. First, in contemporary American society, "men are expected to be men," and fitting this role includes exercising their ability to defend themselves against physical aggression. Second, due to this stereotype, men are hesitant to report any kind of victimization or violence against them to authorities. Third, most domestic violence research has focused on male/female domestic violence. Fourth, all domestic violence is generally underreported to the authorities, and most of these victims, including gay or bisexual males, feel that much of what happens should stay in the home or area of residence.

Domestic violence is a major social and health problem in the United States that affects the families in which it occurs as well as all of society and has future implications for both. Some two to four million women in the United States are physically battered annually by their partners, and 25 to 30 percent of all U.S. women are at risk of domestic violence during their lifetimes (American Medical Association [AMA] 1996; Kerker, Horwitz, Leventhal, Plichta, and Leaf 2000). Having pointed this out, the risk is also prevalent in the gay community, occurring at a greater rate than heterosexual violence because both partners in the homosexual relationship are men and each has the same probability of being an abuser. Gay men are not less violent than straight men (Island and Letellier 1991). However, gay men, due to their socialization, are less likely to report the abuse and more likely to stay with their abusive partner because of homophobia, heterosexism, and ignorance in the community regarding domestic violence in relation to homosexuality (Island and Letellier 1991; Nolan 2000).

The definitions of domestic violence may cover a broad or narrow range. However, the classic definition of male violence is a pattern of violent and coercive behaviors whereby one attempts to control the thoughts, beliefs, or behaviors of an intimate partner or to punish the partner for resisting one's control (Ashcraft 2000; Jacobson and Gottman 1998; Lobel 1986). Intimidation and fear are the tools used to gain this control over another individual (Robertson 1999; Walker 2000). The legal definition of domestic violence is "any assault, battery, sexual assault, sexual battery, or any criminal offense resulting in the physical injury or death of one family or household member by another who is or was residing in the same single dwelling unit" (Title XLlll, Chapter 741, Statute 741.28). Others, including Dutton (1995) have postulated that this is too narrow a focus, that domestic violence is a learned behavior including any action or words that hurt another person. This broader definition, according to Ashcraft (2000), includes the use of threats, force, and physical, sexual, emotional, economic, and verbal abuse.

In considering types of abuse in same-sex relationships, the abusers may threaten to expose their partners' sexual preference to family, friends, community, church, and employers (Chung 1995; Island and Letellier 1991; Renzetti 1992). This may strongly impact men who are bisexual and have a family outside their same-sex relationship. Physical abuse occurs when one threatens, hits, kicks, chokes, pushes, shoves, pulls the hair of, slaps, punches, throws something at, or uses some type of weapon against another individual (Walker 2000). Lenore Walker also includes in this category the refusal to help partners who are injured or sick, restraining partners or keeping them from leaving, abandoning them in a dangerous place, and locking them out of their homes. Emotional abuse happens when one ridicules, insults, blames, humiliates, criticizes, and purposely ignores one's partner (Walker 2000). This may also include racial slurs or putdowns of another's beliefs or culture. According to Ashcraft (2000) and others, verbal abuse accompanies emotional abuse as the abuser says hurtful things and verbally belittles the partner. Dutton (1995) points out that financial abuse may keep the victim totally dependent on the abuser. Usually the abuser completely controls the

couple's monetary resources by keeping everything in his own name and making the abused partner ask for money, tell what it will be used for, and account for each expenditure. Social isolation is another type of abuse and with same-sex partners, it is especially prevalent, as the values of society generally do not accept gay lifestyles (Chung 1995; Nolan 2000; Renzetti 1992). Sexual abuse may involve using gay male pornography and acting out brutal scenes of sadomasochism, raping the partner, accusing the partner of affairs, treating the partner as a sex object, cheating on the partner, forcing the partner into group sex against his will, and general sexual coercion of the partner (Walker 2000). This all leads into the cycle of violence outlined by Walker (Walker 2000). It is difficult for the gay male abuse victim to break away from this cycle.

The batterer's traits come from behaviors designed to control another (Robertson 1999; Walker 2000). There is no profile of a typical batterer; he can come from any economic, social, ethnic, religious, professional, or educational group (Selinger 1996).

Why do gay males stay in abusive relationships? According to Dutton (1995) and Jacobson and Gottman (1998), the abuser and his partner may be extremely dependent on each other. Also, many gay men fear a backlash from those in the heterosexual society who think that the gay community is "sick, violent, or uncontrollable" (Lobel 1986; Oatley 1994). Other reasons gay men stay trapped in the cycle of violence are similar to those of abused heterosexual women who likewise stay trapped in their relationships. Leaving the abusive relationship may lead to financial loss, retaliation, publicity and embarrassment, and physical violence, or even death (Jacobson and Gottman 1998; Lobel 1986). Many times these gay men do not know where to get help and do not have support groups or any type of domestic shelter to which they may retreat (Friess 1997).

In summary, this essay has explored the various problems dealing with gender socialization and gay male domestic violence. It is interesting to note that there are many similarities as well as differences between gay and heterosexual partners in violent relationships. Abused gay and bisexual men become trapped in the same cycle of violence as abused heterosexual women, but with far fewer options for escape and rehabilitation. Gay and bisexual men, as well as the larger society, need to come to terms with the denial of same-sex abuse and violence by recognizing the patterns of abuse that occur in same-sex relationships. Society also needs to recognize the needs of gay and bisexual men and allow for services to fulfill these needs (Griffin 1995).

JOSEPHINE A. KAHLER and SHIRLEY GARICK

See also **Batterer Typology; Gay and Bisexual Male Domestic Violence; Gay Domestic Violence, Police Attitudes and Behaviors toward; Intimate Partner Violence in Queer, Transgender, and Bisexual Communities; Lesbian Battering; Male Victims of Domestic Violence and Reasons They Stay with Their Abusers; Mutual Battering; Same-Sex Domestic Violence: Comparing Venezuela and the United States; Sexual Orientation and Gender Identity: The Need for Education in Servicing Victims of Trauma**

References and Further Reading

American Medical Association. *Resident Forum* 275, no. 22 (1996): 6.

Ashcraft, C. "Naming Knowledge: A Language for Reconstructing Domestic Violence and Systemic Gender Inequity." *Women and Language* 23 (2000): 1–3.

Chung, C. *Pathways to Wellness: A California Statewide Resource Handbook for Asian Women and Girls.* San Francisco: National Asian Women's Health Organization, 1995.

Domestic Violence Legal Definition, la. Stat. § 741.28 (1995).

Dutton, D. G. *The Batterer: A Psychological Profile.* New York: Basic Books, 1995.

Friess, S. "Behind Closed Doors: Domestic Violence." *The Advocate* 748 (1997): 48–52.

Griffin, G. "Understanding Heterosexism—the Subtle Continuum of Homophobia." *Women and Language* 21, no. 1 (1998): 33–40.

Island, D., and P. Letellier. *Men Who Beat the Men Who Love Them.* New York: Harrington Park Press, 1991.

Jacobson, N. S., and J. M. Gottman. "Anatomy of a Violent Relationship." *Psychology Today* 31 (1998): 60–69.

Kerker, B., S. Horwitz, J. Leventhal, S. Plichta, and P. Leaf. "Identification of Violence in the Home." *Pediatrics and Adolescent Medicine* 154 (2000): 457–462.

Lobel, K., ed. *Naming the Violence: Speaking Out about Lesbian Battering.* Seattle, WA: Seal Press, 1986.

Nolan, R. "Domestic Violence in Gay and Lesbian Couples," 2000. http://www.psychpage.com/learning/library/gay/gayvio.html (accessed December 2001).

Oatley, A. "Domestic Violence Doesn't Discriminate on the Basis of Sexual Orientation." *Suncoast News* (1994): 19–21.

Renzetti, C. M. *Violent Betrayal: Partner Abuse in Lesbian Relationships.* London: Sage, 1992.

Robertson, N. "Stopping Violence Programmes: Enhancing the Safety of Battered Women or Producing Better-Educated Batterers?" *New Zealand Journal of Psychology* 28, no. 2 (1999): 68–78.

Selinger, J., producer. *Domestic Violence: The Faces of Fear* (television documentary), 1996. Trenton: New Jersey Network Productions/PBS.

Walker, L. E. *Battered Woman Syndrome.* New York: Springer, 2000.

GREECE, DOMESTIC VIOLENCE IN

Introduction

In the mythological *Theogony of Hesiod,* state and violence were brothers—children of the terrible Styx, who assisted Zeus in his struggle to attain divine authority. In myth and in reality, the meanings of "state" and "violence" are interlinked: The state represents power and force, while violence also means coercion. The state has no meaning without violence, and violence without the state has no reason to exist. A basic component of the state as a sovereign authority is the family. Thus, it follows that family violence exists as a reflection and extension of state violence.

Violence exists as various forms of coercion, exercised by a stronger party (the one who possesses power) against a weaker party (the one who has less or no power). Such relationships of coercion within the family can exist between husband and wife and between parents and children.

The use of violence and coercion is an everyday, ordinary social phenomenon. People are so accustomed to the occurrence of violence in everyday life that the more subtle and barely perceptible forms of psychological violence often go unnoticed. The practice and acceptance of violence—whether intentional or unintentional—follows a person throughout his or her lifetime. In other words, violence is a social reality, established and legalized by the state itself and deeply rooted in people's attitudes.

The abuse of one's wife, as it has occurred in all cultures and historical periods, constitutes the expression of unequal power relations which create and permit oppression and all forms of violence inflicted by the strong against the weak. The process by which violence is taught is circular: It begins in the family, expanding through the culture of the larger society in which children grow and mature, and then in turn is either reinforced or discouraged in the family.

Greek women, like women all over the world, have begun to tell their stories of violence in their homes, as feminists and psychologists increasingly encourage them to speak out on this issue. Comparisons of the underlying social and cultural issues in abuse of women in Greece with women in other countries, including the United States, indicate that power and control issues are important factors in spousal abuse across cultures. Using a feminist social-psychological analysis helps psychologists better understand the social impact of violence against women inside and outside the home, as well as ways to help such victims become survivors. Broadening the understanding of the psychology of women can broaden the understanding of the social construction of human behavior and make the analysis of the relationship among violence, leadership, and the physical and mental health of women clearer. Further, promoting the study and deeper understanding of the psychology of women will reinforce efforts toward achieving equality between women and men. These issues shall be discussed in this article in the context of the political climate as well as in a social-psychological frame.

In Greece, domestic violence is invisible violence which takes place behind closed doors and is considered strictly a family affair. It is a well-hidden secret kept by abused women in Greece. Walsh (2004) defines domestic violence as intentional, threatening, coercive, and controlling behavior in intimate relationships. This includes not only physical abuse, but also direct or indirect threats, emotional and psychological violence, sexual abuse, social isolation, economic control, and behavior that causes a person to live in constant fear. It is an abuse of power, a socially constructed phenomenon. Domestic violence constitutes a flagrant violation of fundamental rights, including the rights to dignity, freedom, safety and equality in the family, and protection by the law. In much of the world, there has been over the last decades of the twentieth century a conceptual shift in societal views on violence against women, and it is now considered a violation of human rights.

While there are many reasons why many women experience violence in secret, one significant reason is the way "violence" is understood—personally by women, by their partners, and socially. What exactly constitutes violence is a hotly contested issue and will continue to be debated for some time. One issue of note is that most of the research on violence focuses primarily on physical violence. Although as of the start of the twenty-first century large-scale research into domestic violence has not gained momentum in Greece, as it has in the United States and in other European nations, there have been efforts by feminists and professionals over the previous decade to begin researching this issue. It is important to mention that in academic circles in Greece, this type of research is not considered scientific and essential. Funds for research are not allocated for feminist studies, and research on issues such as family violence and sexual abuse is limited and not encouraged.

As of this writing, existing research has presented compelling evidence suggesting that the prevalence of physical violence experienced by Greek women is of serious concern. Given that the majority of the research studies available report on physical violence, it can be conjectured that using a definition of violence that includes psychological abuse may result in uncovering higher rates of violence experienced by Greek women. Artinopoulou (2004) reported that 56 percent of the women interviewed experienced verbal or psychological violence. Psychological abuse, which is often the most damaging to the victim, is not granted much importance by the law enforcement agencies and the courts. Physically violent behavior receives more serious penalties.

Since 1984 much has been done in the area of violence against women; however, the range of theoretical approaches demonstrates the continued lack of consensus surrounding this issue. Additionally, there is still a great need for victim advocacy and other resources promoting women's safety. Current research has demonstrated that there exist a number of structural and social barriers preventing Greek women from disclosing violence and accessing available support and assistance resources.

In Greece the patriarchal structure of society entitles men to certain advantages over women; this structure allows for a priority to be given to male rights in ways that often overwrite and/or exclude women's human rights. Not all men choose to abuse their power and violate women, but those who do can be said to benefit from that choice. These men demand to have their needs granted in their intimate personal relationships; in doing so, they often meet with few, if any, immediate sanctions. Antonopoulou, in her survey "Domestic Violence in Greece" (1999), reported that approximately half of the survey's 676 respondents believed that women's demands for equal access to work and independence provoke domestic violence.

Most women who reported experiencing domestic violence suffered alone and in silence, clearly indicating that in Greek society, domestic violence is a hidden phenomenon and a taboo subject of discussion. The silent suffering of women experiencing violence in intimate relationships is not new. The fact that violence against women continues to be a major social issue demonstrates the degree to which society undervalues women and their place within it.

Lenore Walker's books and research, including *The Battered Woman, Terrifying Love,* and *The Battered Woman Syndrome,* have been translated into Greek. A series of lectures given by Walker at universities and sponsored by feminist groups allowed professionals and non-governmental organizations (NGOs) the opportunity to come in contact for the first time with new theoretical understandings and approaches to therapy for battered women. Her book *The Battered Woman* became required reading in many university psychology departments. Walker's theories of the cycle of violence, learned helplessness, and the battered woman syndrome gave a new insight into and enriched the understanding of violence against women. Furthermore, Greek scholars and feminists became aware that many Greek women who were abused had been the victims of earlier violence, usually incest and other child abuse and emotional maltreatment. As Walker (1984) notes, for some of these women the experience of their victimization is too difficult to face, and they therefore find ways to numb themselves and black out their awareness of it.

There is still a great need to advocate for women's safety in Greece. As subsequent research has demonstrated, there are a number of structural and social barriers preventing women from disclosing violence and accessing support and assistance. As de Bruyn (2001) mentions in her research, some women feel that their partner's behavior is "not too bad," indicating that a level of internalized tolerance for violence and/or a degree of dependence on intimate personal relationships acts as a barrier to women's safety. In Antonopoulou's (1999) survey, one in ten women endorsed the marital obedience clause, whereas one in three men believed that women should be obedient in the home. There are

a number of reasons why women stay with their abusive partners (i.e., nowhere to go, economic reasons, lack of family support, and cultural beliefs that hinder the decision of abused women to leave their homes). It is well known that violence often does not stop even after the couple has separated. It is of utmost importance for protecting women's personal safety to improve public policy by creating a coordinated support system, including resources for social services and interventions and assistance from law enforcement and the justice system, so that women can feel safe when they feel they must leave their homes and not continue to be harmed if they decide to stay.

The development of the women's movement in Greece promoted the study of battered women, separating it from child abuse advocacy. This was a way to put the focus on women who were unable to protect their children, as they themselves were being abused. As the feminist movement grew stronger, so did the battered women's movement, and by 2000 there was advocacy for an end to the violence against both women and children.

Previous psychiatric theories that labeled battered women as masochistic and their batterers as sadistic still have some credibility in Greece as a result of both psychiatric studies and nonempirically supported misperceptions. Such attitudes tend to place the blame on the victim, permit the batterer to avoid taking responsibility for stopping the violence, make it difficult for the battered woman to terminate the abusive relationship safely, and prevent any meaningful recovery.

Greece's participation in the Council of Europe and its Committee on Equality for Women and Men as well as the rise of women in the political and economic structure of Greece has made its people more aware of the need to better understand and stop abuse against women. Encouraged by feminists, government ministries and the Equality Council use the survey information from Antonopoulou's (1999) research to develop and implement policies with the goal of better protecting women and ending men's violent behavior in intimate relationships. In accomplishing this, it was important to link policies and programs together with the prevailing psychological theories and research on domestic violence in Greece.

Attitudes toward male violence against women in Greece continue to change, along with other social and political changes that impact the Greek population. Women who have participated in the United Nations Decade on Women have brought its antiviolence stance to Greece. The old stereotype of the Greek man as being justified in beating his wife just because he had assumed the leading role within the family is slowly giving way to a more modern view of gender relationships. As might be expected, these social changes are more clearly reflected among the college-educated, urban, career-oriented population, as opposed to the Greek rural population. However, attempts to organize rural women around finding better ways to protect themselves against male violence have been increasingly successful.

The women's movement, combined with the reality of more women entering the workforce and becoming financially independent, has caused many women to change their expectations about how much they should be obedient to or coerced by men. While some men have followed a parallel path in their expectations and behavior, especially among the new generation, others have not. The fact that men and women perceive their family roles differently clearly remains a point of conflict. Persons who have learned to resolve conflict by physical violence may continue to do so, thereby socializing their children to accept violent behavior as a given.

Interventions

A number of interventions have been used in what has become known as the battered women's movement. These include efforts toward social changes to overthrow the patriarchal order of society and bring about equality for all persons. Furthermore, institutional reforms such as those necessary within the health, legal, and social service systems have been set up by the Greek government. Prevention services and crisis intervention centers to protect women and their children have been introduced.

In 1999, the General Secretariat for Equality established the Interministerial Committee for the Elimination of Violence Against Women. This committee plays a decisive role in policy planning and implements actions against violence. The Greek legislation regulates and confronts violence against women by means of provisions which generally deal with crimes against the life and integrity of the individual, against her personal freedom, against her honor and personality, and against sexual freedom. Violence against women is a crime, and women's safety and integrity are a priority.

In legislative terms, the forms of violence taken into consideration are those regulated by the general provisions of the civil or penal code and are classified as:

- Physical injury (art. 308, 309), light and dangerous bodily injuries

- Crimes against sexual freedom and crimes of economic exploitation of sexual life (art. 336–353)
- Violation of sexual dignity (art. 337)
- Offenses relating to marriage and family (art. 354–360)
- Disruption of family peace and order (a misdemeanor)
- Crime of rape, which is regulated by law 1419/84, which introduced the ex officio prosecution of the crime of rape. Rape in marriage does not constitute a separate crime.

The revision of the legislative framework and the introduction of special provisions regulating and confronting violence against women is an immediate concern of the Interministerial Committee and the NGOs. The Greek Parliament is expected to implement new legislation in the fall of 2005 against the abusers.

Although it is possible to obtain a civil restraining order in domestic violence cases or to obtain juvenile court intervention in child abuse cases, treatment usually cannot be mandated by court order. Yet if arrests are not made and treatment is not ordered, the abuser's behavior is regulated by few external controls and abuse is likely to continue. Under the present situation, an abused woman can call a special number at the police station for emergencies, file a complaint against her abuser, and request to have the abusing incident recorded by the police. This is very useful, since it can be used as evidence when responding to future incidents. Furthermore the abused woman can request from the public defender's office a court order to arrest and prosecute her abuser. An evaluation by the medical examiner to verify the physical abuse is strongly recommended.

Some of the efforts to help victims of violence and to bring about public awareness that have been made by the Equality Office and NGOs include:

- Creating hotlines to provide legal and psychological support to victims of violence
- Distributing print material providing information about services available to victims of violence (i.e., police, social workers, etc.)
- Offering educational seminars organized for professionals serving in the Reception Centers for Abused Women. The aim of these centers is to provide information and legal and psychological support for female victims of violence
- Offering special seminars implemented for police personnel dealing with abused women

It is worth noting that the Police Academy curriculum in Greece also includes a mandatory course which discusses issues of domestic violence, rape, human trafficking, and related issues.

The most important intervention in efforts to stop abuse of women has been the creation of shelter houses. In the Athens area, there are two shelters, one in Salonika. One is run jointly by the General Secretariat of Equality and the municipality of Athens. It offers temporary shelter to abused women and their children as well as legal and psychological support. Another, run by the Greek Archdiocese (KESO), provides shelter, support, and financial assistance for women and children. It is expected that the services of the Archdiocese will expand to house women and children victims of sexual exploitation and human trafficking.

There have been many unsuccessful attempts by NGOs to create shelter houses. NGOs undertake actions in support of female victims of violence and promote public awareness of violence against women. They provide services free of charge to abused women, such as legal advice, psychological support, and defense at court. Hotlines set up by NGOs offer advice and psychological support, especially to women who have decided to stay at home with their abusers. There are no comprehensive treatment or therapy programs for batterers. In violence cases, courts sentence batterers to prison.

Furthermore, the Units for Social Exclusion Intervention, run by KETHI (Research Center on Equality Matters, a governmental unit) in cooperation with the General Secretariat for Equality, offer supportive services to women in five large cities throughout Greece. Reports from these centers for 2003 mention that over 1,062 women who were victims of violence visited those centers. One out of three women was from the Balkan countries, with Albanian women representing 22 percent.

Psychologists, psychiatrists, and other providers of social services are still unable to meet battered women's needs because of a basic lack of understanding about domestic violence as well as their ingrained attitudes about the roles of men and women. Most therapists—mainly psychiatrists, who have not been trained in gender issues—have difficulty finding women's reports credible. They are critical of women's behavior and encourage women's guilt. They blame the victim and hold women responsible for their own victimization. "You must have done something" is still the phrase used most often by these professionals.

Victimization can produce psychological effects which are diagnosed under different mental health categories. The results of a study by Antonopoulou and Skoufalos (2004) can be used to infer that traumatic experiences faced by Greek females most likely occur during their thirties, thus causing acute and dissociative symptoms. Taking this and similar studies into consideration, mental health professionals should try to create and implement abuse prevention programs. Since domestic violence occurs across all levels of economic, social, and educational groups, some women who have been battered also may have a mental illness that existed prior to the abuse.

Child Abuse and Neglect

In Greece the phenomenon of physical and mental abuse of children occurs with the same intensity and frequency as in other countries. The little research that has been carried out to date indicates that the basic causes of child abuse have been determined as psychological disorders of the parents, poverty, and a low cultural and educational level. Also, in Greece, scientific research on this subject is based on the traditional approach to the reasons for the abuse. Hospitals and police report an estimated 4,500 cases of child abuse yearly, and about 36 children per year die as a result of abuse.

In the six months prior to this writing (2005), the emergency service division of the Athens Mental Health Center responded to 200 calls concerning child abuse. In 40 percent of the cases the father had committed the abuse. In the case of sexually abused children, the father was named as the perpetrator in 98 percent of the cases, while only 2 percent involved the mother. In 2000, the Athens public prosecutor stated that sexual abuse of children had reached alarming proportions. Girls aged ten to fifteen who reported being raped by their fathers usually did so without support from their mothers.

The Legal Aspect

The criteria used to constitute the offense of child abuse in Greece are the following:

- A doctor's verification of the abuse is required, followed by investigation and an inquiry into the conditions under which the abuse took place and a confirmation that the abuse is the result of the interpersonal relations between parent and child.
- In Greece, offenses relating to both child abuse and neglect are treated in accordance with regulations concerning bodily harm and exposure to danger contained in the criminal code. In particular, article 312 of the

criminal code concerns not only abuse through direct action (beatings, etc.), but provides penalties for abuse which is caused by neglecting the nutrition and care of the child which a parent or a guardian is obliged to supply.

- Any citizen aware that the offense of child abuse has been committed has the right to press charges, either with the police or with a public prosecutor. However, no legal responsibility is imposed on someone who is aware of the offense but does not report it.

Prison sentences which the court may impose range from three months to five years, unless there is evidence of acts more severely punishable, such as sexual abuse, child murder, etc.

Article 312 of the criminal code conflicts with the natural and legal right of parents to take disciplinary measures against the child, which, according to pedagogic tradition, also includes the use of physical punishment. The legislation does not clarify which physical punishments can be imposed and which cannot, although the more up-to-date law 1329/83 defines a framework of pedagogic measures which are necessary and which do not negatively affect the child's personality.

However, other kinds of queries arise concerning the competence of a judge to evaluate and decide on the personality of the child, the personality of the parents, and all the general and special social terms and conditions which are involved in the application of pedagogic procedures by parents or guardians. A Children's Ombudsman was established by law 3094/2003 and has the right to examine special cases and complaints. Furthermore, this office undertakes the responsibility of bringing information and awareness of child abuse to Greek society and to special groups who take care of children. Many people who work with abused children have little understanding of family dynamics or cultural characteristics of the persons they serve. Furthermore, reports indicate that outright bias may affect the evaluation of immigrant and poor families.

The entry of thousands of immigrants into Greece between 1993 and 2000 from economically weaker countries of eastern Europe, such as Ukraine, Georgia, Romania, and Albania, has resulted in an increase in incidents of abuse and sexual exploitation of women and children, or human trafficking. In a study by Antonopoulou and Skoufalos (2005), symptoms of post-traumatic stress disorder (PTSD) in victims of human trafficking were reported, and abused women were found most at risk for developing PTSD. Mental health professionals might be likely to misdiagnose these clients. The validation of these results has implications for the development of intervention programs to help abused women and children heal from this type of trauma. The Greece-based NGO "The Child's Smile" is very well qualified to offer child protection, provide sufficient services, and offer housing and legal protection to children all over Greece through its hotlines and centers.

Nevertheless, there is no family court institution in Greece, even though what constitutes family law in Greece is considered by European standards to be very progressive. Abuse cases referred to the judicial system are handled by the penal court, which punishes the perpetrator, but makes no provision for the children and other family members. For example, if a suspended sentence is given to a mother who has severely physically abused her baby, she will continue to "take care" of him at home after the court hearing, with no intervention from the state, unless the mother seeks help from a welfare agency.

Conclusion

Commencing with this overall scrutiny of the phenomenon of family violence in Greece, one could propose, as has already been done, a series of up-to-date preventive measures, although by their nature they will have limited scope and only temporary effects. There are measures which, although immediate, are too focused on short-term results to deal effectively and thoroughly with violence in the family.

Such measures have been adopted and implemented by all contemporary democratic societies, although with mediocre and disappointing results, as ascertained by relevant studies. This does not mean that these measures must be abandoned, particularly since no specific strategic planning (no new model) has crystallized to address this problem in modern society.

On the contrary, these measures must be intensified and improved, based on observations and conclusions that have emerged from their application on an even broader social scale. In addition, more pressure should be applied by progressive foundations, organizations, and professionals for more intensive implementation, better coordination, and more frequent and effective financing of these measures and resources.

Violence in the family will continue to exist and manifest itself in various ways, since the processes and machinery of violence (its practice or promotion) exist on a national level in every country in the world. The acknowledgment of this fact by scientific researchers would be a big step forward. It should constitute the starting point for the review of certain commonly held ideas which relate to the origin and the manifestation of violent behavior. At the same time, endeavors must be made toward formulating a long-term strategy aimed at a comprehensive examination and study of violence in society as a whole, as well as violence as manifested within the family.

The modern person still has values and attitudes which do not correspond to the technological and scientific standards of this century: very old ethics for a new technological and scientific era. There is a deep and widening gap between the socio-ethical standards of the individual and modern scientific achievements. Social progress has significantly lagged behind. As an essential element which would lead to a qualitative improvement of contemporary social relations and advance the long-term objective of gradually eradicating violence, it is necessary to upgrade and reexamine the framework in which the relative studies have been conducted to date.

The objective of all scientific studies on the subject of violence is to locate incidents of violence in the family, compile relevant data, and then make proposals of a social nature to deal with the problem. Contemporary research must locate and concentrate not only on the negative incidents which must be dealt with, but also on the majority of social behavior which is positive and healthy, free from the usual syndrome of the dominator and the dominated. The location and analytical examination of healthy behaviors can guide studies along new paths, through observation to fruitful conclusions, which often conceal the method and ways for the rectification and updating of social behavior.

Even though established social structures and rules systematically and methodically tend to keep positive behavior and events "under wraps," contemporary society is not a boundless field of negative phenomena and behavior. Kindness and harmony also exist in society, and their discovery and study through scientific analysis and formulation could provide valuable sources of information for the promotion of new ideas and the acquisition of knowledge. With this dual nature that scientific research must acquire, it should concurrently utilize—to the required degree—the achievements of modern science and technology.

For example, the effectiveness of and public response to the promotion of positive, nonviolent images by the mass media should be researched. The mass media, which promotes violence and its various manifestations as a way of attaining certain social ambitions, could reverse their thematic approach in many cases by proposing and presenting nonviolent tactics. They could publicize relationships which develop not with an intervening catalyst of violent acts and reactions, but through dialogue and peaceful procedures. This different kind of approach by modern scientific research would also assist in the creation and development of appropriate educational programs and training procedures in all facets of society, so that the individual would become socially aware at an early age.

Perhaps this quest for nonviolent elements and corresponding social relationships will lead to the comprehension, or at least the realization, of that positive inner strength which, through heightened social awareness of the individual, will one day regulate interpersonal relationships as a substitute for contemporary society's outdated reliance on state coercion.

The aim of all modern scientists and researchers on the subject of violence should be their contribution and participation in the creation and presentation of a new charter for a contemporary direction in research and social studies. It would be both effective and invigorating to promote women's studies, which would provide an opportunity for the formulation of new ideas and proposals concerning the handling of social violence in the present and future.

CHRISTINA ANTONOPOULOU

See also **Africa: Domestic Violence and the Law; Cross-Cultural Examination of Domestic Violence in China and Pakistan; Cross-Cultural Examination of Domestic Violence in Latin America; South Africa, Domestic Violence in; Spain, Domestic Violence in**

References and Further Reading

Anagnostopoulos, Ilias G., and Konstantinos D. Magliveras. *Criminal Law in Greece.* Kluwer Law International. Athens: Sakkoulas, 2000.

Antonopoulou, Christina. "Domestic Violence in Greece." *American Psychologist* 54 (1999): 21–29.

Antonopoulou, Christina, and Niki Skoufalos. "Age as a Risk Factor of Trauma in the Greek Female Population." Paper presented at the 8th Conference of the International Association for the Treatment of Sexual Offenders (IATSO), Athens, October 6–8, 2004.

———. "Symptoms of Posttraumatic Stress Disorder in Victims of Trafficking." Paper presented at the 2nd International Congress on Brain and Behavior, Salonika, November 17–20, 2005.

APA Presidential Task Force on Violence and the Family. *Issues and Dilemmas in Family Violence,* August 1995.

Artinopoulou, Vaso. "Family Violence in Greece: Identifying the Needs for Prevention." Paper presented at the 8th Conference of IATSO, Athens, October 6–8, 2004.

"The Child's Smile." NGO website. http://www.hamogelo. gr (accessed August 15, 2005).

de Bruyn, M. *Violence, Pregnancy and Abortion: Issues of Women's Rights and Public Health: A Review of Worldwide Data and Recommendations for Action.* Chapel Hill, NC: Ipas Publications, 2001.

General Secretariat for Gender Equality (Greece). National Report of Greece, 4th and 5th. U.N. Commission for the Elimination to All Forms of Discrimination Against Women, 2000.

————. International Day on Violence Against Women. Pamphlet, November 2004.

Giotakos, Orestis. "Personality Characteristics of Rapists in Relation to Their History of Childhood." Paper presented at the 8th Conference of IATSO, Athens, October 6–8, 2004.

Walker, Lenore E. *The Battered Woman.* New York: Harper & Row, 1979.

————. *The Battered Woman Syndrome.* New York: Springer, 1984.

————. *Terrifying Love: Why Battered Women Kill and How Society Responds.* New York: Harper & Row, 1989.

————. "Battering in Adult Relations." In *Encyclopedia of Women and Gender,* vol. 1. San Diego: Academic Press, 2001.

Walsh, Deborah, and Wendy Weeks, for the Support and Safety Survey, Australia. *What a Smile Can Hide.* Royal Women's Hospital Report, 2004. http://www.rwh.org. au/emplibrary/socialsupport/WhatASmileCanHide.pdf (accessed August 18, 2006).

HEALTHCARE PROFESSIONALS' ROLES IN IDENTIFYING AND RESPONDING TO DOMESTIC VIOLENCE

Introduction

This article focuses on the health professional's role in identifying and responding to domestic violence. The physician, nurse, dentist, physical therapist, or other health professional may be the first person to whom abuse is disclosed. As a result, the acute and chronic effects of domestic violence are healthcare issues that nearly every health professional encounters in the course of routine practice. Providers are expected to know the basics of recognition and intervention related to screening and identification, early intervention, and crisis care for those affected by domestic violence. Therefore, all health professionals are expected to routinely screen, diagnose, assess, intervene, and ultimately help prevent domestic violence.

Health Effects of Abuse

Domestic violence causes substantial short- and long-term morbidity and mortality. Acute injuries, long-term sequelae of prior injuries, and chronic illnesses are common manifestations of abuse. Although survivors can sustain life-threatening physical injuries, they may also suffer less obvious effects that are just as debilitating. In addition to physical trauma, survivors present with other medical problems, including chronic pain syndromes, somatization disorders, post-traumatic stress disorder, anxiety, depression, suicidality, and alcoholism and other forms of substance abuse.

According to a 2000 U.S. Bureau of Justice Statistics report, current or former intimate partners murdered 33 percent of all female homicide victims. The true figure is probably higher, as the victim–offender relationship was not discernible in an additional 31 percent of homicides. In contrast, only 4 percent of male homicide victims were killed by an intimate. Recent research has also shown that the leading cause of pregnancy-associated death is homicide, a substantial component of which is intimate partner homicide.

Guiding Principles of Care

Healthcare providers should observe four guiding principles of care, originally promulgated by the Family Violence Prevention Fund when addressing domestic violence: (1) victim safety, (2) victim autonomy, (3) perpetrator accountability, and (4) advocacy for social change.

Victim Safety

Every aspect of clinical care, including inquiry, assessment, documentation, safety planning, communication, intervention, and follow-up, must be conducted with utmost concern for the safety of the survivor and her/his dependent children. The provider should consider whether what she/he is asking, doing, and/or recommending is going to help the patient become safer or at least not place her/him at risk for further harm.

Victim Autonomy

Abused individuals have had their freedom to make informed, independent choices about their (and their children's) lives restricted by the batterer's controlling and intimidating behavior. Facilitating the patient's ability to make her/his own choices is key to restoring a sense of purpose and well-being for survivors, and can facilitate a patient's readiness to take proactive steps to seek safety.

Perpetrator Accountability

It is important to reframe the violence as occurring because of the perpetrator's behavior and actions, not the survivor's. It thus follows that the problem of violence in the relationship, and the need to take definitive steps to end the violence, is the perpetrator's responsibility. This guiding principle assumes the importance of victim safety but rejects victim-blaming and other excuses offered by the offender as "explanations" for the violence.

Advocacy for Social Change

Health professionals acting alone cannot meet all the needs of survivors of abuse. As healthcare professionals and systems grapple with the complex issues involved in responding to domestic violence, the need to collaborate with others in healthcare, law enforcement, the faith community, and society at large becomes apparent. Health professionals can be important catalysts for change so that domestic violence can be more effectively identified and ultimately prevented.

Barriers to Inquiry and Disclosure in the Healthcare Setting

Survivors present frequently in the healthcare setting, coming in contact with clinicians who are in a position to identify abuse and respond effectively. The vast majority of patients (victims and nonvictims alike) expect healthcare providers to know about domestic violence, and welcome being asked about it during the healthcare encounter. However, despite the substantial prevalence of abuse seen in the healthcare setting, most providers still do not routinely inquire about domestic violence unless clear indicators of trauma are present. Recognizing and addressing the barriers faced by clinicians and patients can increase clinicians' ability to detect domestic violence and to respond effectively.

Clinician Barriers to Routine Inquiry

Routine confidential inquiry about domestic violence is often omitted from the healthcare encounter, despite well-publicized recommendations and, in some cases, mandates in the guidelines and standards of professional associations and recognized experts. Many providers feel they have insufficient time to fully evaluate, support, and plan for safety with patients who have disclosed abuse. Some believe it is not their job to "pry" into patients' "private" lives, or may be hesitant to "open Pandora's box" and initiate a foray into time-consuming issues that they feel reluctant or poorly equipped to address. Far too many providers have had little or no education or training about domestic violence and lack both the knowledge and the skills needed to incorporate routine inquiry or even basic awareness into their practice patterns. Nearly 50 percent of the physicians in Sugg's landmark 1992 study expressed feelings of powerlessness and inadequacy when trying to help abused patients. Many providers feel ill-equipped to respond to a disclosure of abuse, in part because they are unaware of community-based referral resources. Time constraints, discomfort with the topic, beliefs about the acceptability of certain behaviors, and possible personal exposure as a victim, witness, or even perpetrator are additional barriers to inquiry and response in the healthcare setting. Finally, some find it difficult to deal with patients who cannot acknowledge their own abuse and leave the abuser, use alcohol or other drugs, or have psychological sequelae. Such challenges interfere not only with inquiry, evaluation, assessment, and safety planning, but also with clinicians' ability to establish trust and convey empathy.

Patient Barriers to Disclosure

Even after sustaining injuries, survivors of domestic violence rarely disclose without being asked in a sensitive and patient manner. Patients cite fear of retaliation, distrust of the healthcare system, fear of being reported to the police, fear of losing children, and fear of deportation. Long-term abuse is associated with shame, guilt, and low self-esteem, all of which impede the patient's ability to seek help from healthcare providers. Financial dependence on the abuser often makes leaving impossible and therefore renders disclosure futile. Patients from ethnic minorities may accept violence as a cultural norm and may not discuss it with their provider. Language differences may impede frank discussions of abuse, especially if the abuser acts as interpreter. Finally, language and cultural differences between patient and provider are barriers to both disclosure and identification.

Current Screening Recommendations

The American Medical Association recommends routine screening for domestic violence by all healthcare providers. This recommendation has been endorsed by other professional organizations, including the American College of Emergency Physicians and the American College of Obstetricians and Gynecologists. The Joint Commission on the Accreditation of Healthcare Organizations requires that hospitals institute protocols for domestic violence screening and referral. Research has yet to systematically investigate the impact of screening on long-term health outcomes. Efforts to elucidate this impact have been hampered by concerns over the inability to identify and follow survivors without jeopardizing safety. Given the low risk associated with screening (compared with other screening tests), the prevalence of domestic violence in healthcare settings, and the short- and long-term effects of abuse on victims' health, these recommendations are generally felt to be appropriate even in the absence of outcomes research.

Inquiry and Identification in the Healthcare Setting

Beginning the Conversation

Although survivors access medical services more frequently than do nonabused individuals, most do not volunteer a history of abuse even to their primary care physicians. Survivors are more likely to disclose their history in the healthcare setting if the provider is perceived to be knowledgeable, nonjudgmental, respectful, and supportive. Patients voice clear preferences for providers to take the initiative to inquire, as a matter of standard practice, about domestic violence during the course of routine healthcare. The gender of the provider or clinician is not an important factor in the willingness of most patients to disclose abuse. Indirect interventions such as placing educational posters or brochures in the waiting room, examination rooms, and lavatories also communicate concern and interest to patients, increasing their comfort in revealing abuse.

Inquiry in the Healthcare Setting

All adolescent and adult patients should be screened for current and past abuse in the course of routine care. Patients should be interviewed in private, without the partner, children, or other relatives present. The most dramatic yet relatively uncommon presentation of domestic violence in the clinical setting is that of an acute injury sustained from a recent assault. More commonly, survivors present with chronic, nonspecific "red-flag" medical complaints (e.g., back pain, headaches, nonspecific abdominal pain) or common medical or behavioral conditions (e.g., vaginal discharge, sprains and strains, anxiety, depression, panic, social phobia, alcoholism).

It is easiest to begin a conversation about domestic violence if posters, literature, or other practice-wide messages are visible. If this is not yet the case, it is still quite easy to broach the subject to individual patients, the vast majority of whom welcome such an overture. Clinicians can frame questioning about domestic violence by referring to posters or literature displayed in the office, if available, or by simply stating: "As you may know, abuse by a partner—a spouse, date, or even an ex-partner—is unfortunately very common in our society, including in my own practice. Because of this, I am now asking every patient if she/he is safe at home and in her/his relationships."

Once an appropriate framing statement is made, accompanied by respectful yet actively engaged body language and eye contact appropriate to the patient's culture, any one (or more) of the following simple, direct questions can be posed:

- "At any time [or, "in the past year" or "currently"] have you been hit, slapped, punched, strangled, threatened, made to feel afraid, or hurt in any way by a current or former partner/husband/date?"
- "Every couple has conflicts. What happens when you and your partner disagree?"
- "Do conflicts ever make you fearful or turn into physical fights?"

- "I see patients who are being hurt or threatened by someone they love. Is this happening to you?"
- "Do you ever feel afraid of your partner?"
- "Do you feel safe in your home and around your spouse or intimate partner?"

Domestic violence is indeed prevalent throughout the world, but by no means directly affects a majority of patients. Statistically speaking, therefore, the answer to an initial screening question is likely to be no. Even so, most patients are grateful to have been asked, as routine inquiry about domestic violence indicates a level of caring and compassion that many seek and appreciate from their healthcare providers. There are cases, however, in which a patient may be in an abusive relationship, yet is not ready to disclose to anyone, including physicians. Such individuals may offer a half-answer to a screening question, such as, "My husband loves me," or simply turn away and say nothing. Should this be the case, the clinician can gently follow up with an additional question, such as: "When I speak with someone with a situation/sadness/problem such as yours, it is sometimes because someone has hurt or mistreated her/him. Has someone been hurting you?"

When injuries are in suspicious locations or if the explanation does not correlate with the injury, probing gently for further details can uncover ongoing domestic violence. Even a simple question such as, "Can you tell me who hurt you?" can be an effective and sensitive way to ask about abuse.

Physical Examination

Typical injuries are located on the upper arms, chest, abdomen, thighs, head, neck, and mouth. Black eyes, contusions, and evidence of attempted strangulation are commonly seen. Multiple injuries in varied stages of healing or those that cannot be explained adequately or consistently typify chronic, recurrent trauma due to domestic violence. Any injury suspected to be a result of sexual assault should be cause to suspect ongoing domestic violence. In addition to acute injuries, patients can have multiple medical complaints without significant physical findings.

Observation of Partner Behavior

In addition to clues from the history or physical examination, certain partner behaviors should also raise suspicion for domestic violence. The partner may come into the examination room, exhibit overly attentive or controlling behavior, answer questions directed to the patient, or insist on being present throughout the encounter. If getting a domestic violence history is crucial, the partner should be asked to leave, or can be distracted by asking him/her to fill out forms or answer questions "privately," thus leading him/her to believe that he/she is being treated as an "expert," while the patient is being asked about abuse privately by another member of the healthcare team. It is best to create and enforce an office policy that permits partners and other family to come into the examining room only after the examination is completed. Such an "office protocol" serves to prevent and avoid the awkward situation of having to ask a partner to leave the examining room.

Time Management in the Clinical Setting

Healthcare professionals, particularly physicians, may be reluctant to engage in inquiry and identification because of concerns about having insufficient time to screen and respond in a careful and patient manner, given the multiple responsibilities and time pressures of daily practice. Judicious time management, however, will allow both for universal screening and for targeted follow-up. The most common scenario is for inquiry to produce a negative report (i.e, no history of abuse), in which case the patient is almost always grateful for having been asked. Most patients who have experienced abuse are not in immediate danger, even if the abuse is ongoing. The clinician can perform a quick danger assessment, validate and support the patient using brief supportive statements, offer emergency hotline numbers and other referral resources, and arrange a separate time to interview the patient in depth about her/his abuse history. It is rare to see a patient who presents in acute danger in the office setting. This unusual situation is nonetheless as urgent as a cardiac, respiratory, or diabetic emergency, and should be treated accordingly. Screening for abuse, therefore, should not add substantially to the clinician's schedule, and may ultimately save time by allowing for abuse to be addressed in a separate, dedicated visit.

Intervention

When a survivor seeks help following disclosure, the following questions, which deal with immediate safety, should be asked in a private setting:

- "What happened?"
- "Has this happened before? How did it begin?"

- "How badly have you been hurt in the past?"
- "Have you ever needed to get emergency help or go to a hospital because of an assault?"
- "Has your abuser threatened to harm or kill you, him/herself, or anyone else?"
- "Have you ever been threatened with a weapon, or has a weapon ever been used on you?"
- "Have you ever tried to get an order of protection?"
- "Have the children ever seen or heard you being threatened or hurt?"
- "Have the children ever been threatened or hurt by your partner?"
- "Are your children safe and cared for right now?"
- "Do you know where the abuser is right now?"
- "Is it safe for you to return home today? Do you need emergency help right now? Do you feel you need to flee for your safety?"
- "Do you have a safe place to go?"
- "Do you know how you can get help if you are hurt or afraid?"
- "Have you been able to talk to anyone else about this?"

As important as it is to ask the right questions, it is critical to refrain from asking questions in a manner that might frighten or intimidate the patient, increase her/his sense of humiliation and shame about the abuse, or be interpreted as "blaming the victim." Here are some pitfalls to avoid:

- Most survivors do not identify themselves as "abuse victims" per se because of the perception of shame, helplessness, and worthlessness associated with such a value-laden term. Therefore, avoid using labels such as "victim" or "battered" when speaking with patients. Instead, use resilience-promoting terms like "survivor" whenever possible.
- Do not inquire about abuse in the presence of the partner, friends, roommates, or family members.
- Do not break confidentiality by disclosing information, discussing your concerns, or providing advice to anyone without the survivor's explicit consent.
- Never ask a patient what she/he did to provoke the abuse, or why she/he has not terminated the relationship.
- Listen attentively, but do not ask a survivor of any type of sexual violence to provide you with more details than she/he feels comfortable offering.

Specific Interventions

Following disclosure, the primary roles of the healthcare provider are to communicate concern, provide information, review options and resources, initiate safety planning, provide medical treatment, and arrange for follow-up. The clinician also must evaluate the need to file a mandated report to the appropriate agency for children, elderly, or disabled patients, and in those states in which clinicians are required by law to report domestic violence. Care and/or referral for acute and chronic medical and psychological issues, plus referral for comprehensive primary care should be undertaken as indicated. A discussion of safer sex practices and protection against sexually transmitted infections and pregnancy, especially for patients who have been raped, should occur. Most importantly, the patient should be referred to community experts who provide direct service to survivors. Each clinical practice or healthcare facility should maintain a resource and contact list of local agencies to which patients can be referred. These programs can forge natural partnerships with the healthcare community, working together toward a sustained, coordinated community response to domestic violence. Local resources include police departments; domestic violence service, advocacy, and intervention agencies; batterer intervention programs; social service agencies; services offered by religious communities; local government or county court offices; culturally specific agencies, programs, and community centers; schools and other educational institutions; political and community opinion leaders; and companies that address violence in the workplace.

Providing Information and Validation

The provider–patient relationship is strengthened when the patient is reassured that she/he is being treated honestly and respectfully in the clinical setting. Clinicians should listen attentively and respectfully, communicating messages that can validate the patient and begin the difficult process of healing and recovery, specifically:

- Disclosure should be acknowledged as an act that is both difficult and courageous.
- Domestic violence is against the law, and survivors have legal rights.
- The abuser—not the victim—is at fault for perpetrating the abuse that has occurred.
- The patient is believed—she/he does not have to provide proof or verification that abuse has occurred.

- She/he is not to blame; no one deserves to be hit, hurt, or abused in any way.
- She/he is not alone; many have endured similar situations and have benefited from help from the healthcare system and from community agencies.
- Her/his safety is of utmost importance.
- She/he will set the pace for action and healing.
- Interactions and disclosures that take place in the healthcare setting are confidential to the extent possible under the law.
- Limitations of clinician/patient confidentiality, particularly in respect to mandated reporter responsibilities, will be disclosed and discussed honestly.
- Follow-up both for the presenting complaint and for comprehensive primary care will be arranged.

Safety Planning

A safety plan is a detailed, individually developed protocol that a survivor can use to get and stay safe. Although healthcare professionals should know the elements and importance of safety planning, the specific details of each plan should be worked out by the survivor in conjunction with an experienced domestic violence advocate. To develop a safety plan, the survivor's degree of danger and the specific resources needed to flee suddenly and to maintain violence-free, independent living must be addressed. The plan should include:

- A safe place to go along with an alternative, if possible (friends, family, shelter, or safe house)
- Preparation of necessary items including cash, driver's license, other identification, car keys, medications, and a change of clothing for survivor and children
- Records to take and/or keep secure, such as birth certificates, visas, passports, Social Security numbers, prescriptions, bank account numbers, credit card records, other financial information, school records, and work history or résumé
- Contact information for friends, relatives, spiritual leaders, and healthcare providers
- A copy of the survivor's order of protection, if one has been issued
- Other items deemed necessary when the safety plan is being developed

Each safety plan is individualized according to the immediate and anticipated safety needs of each patient, the needs of dependent children, identified financial resources and needs, and expected living arrangements. Since abusers often search their victims' belongings, before giving any written materials to a patient, ask her/him if it is safe to take written materials from the office. Quite often, safety planning and other vital information need to be provided more than once.

Many survivors choose to stay in abusive relationships because they believe it is safer to stay than to leave. Each survivor faces difficult and potentially volatile and dangerous decisions when preparing to leave an abusive relationship. Informed decisions by patients must be respected, regardless of whether the clinician is in agreement with the survivor's choices. A patient who remains in an abusive relationship should not be labeled as difficult or noncompliant. Choosing not to leave usually reflects the limited resources available to a survivor, or her/his reasonable assessment of available options and safety needs. Deciding to stay may also reflect fear of being ostracized by one's own family or of having the children lose a parent, or may represent reluctance to risk losing a significant relationship with someone who once seemed to be a loving and caring partner. For reasons of safety, time management, and treatment, the provider should not attempt to speak with or counsel an abuser in an acute or volatile situation. Couples counseling or marriage counseling in such situations is unwise and potentially dangerous and is therefore contraindicated.

The survivor's role is to decide when it is safe to leave and when the logistical, spiritual, economic, and emotional resources to support this decision are in place. The clinician's role is to provide the patient with options, support, and information about resources in a manner that is compassionate, concerned, and nonjudgmental. Disclosure of domestic violence may herald an especially dangerous period for both survivor and children. Therefore, once disclosure is made, particular attention must be paid to the safety and well-being of children and others living in a home in which domestic violence is occurring.

RADAR: A Practical Framework for Identification and Response

RADAR—an acronym for Remember to ask, Ask directly, Document findings, Assess safety, and Review options/Refer to appropriate services—is a model five-step approach to identify and treat survivors of abuse. The RADAR model, developed by Elaine Alpert for use by the Massachusetts Medical

Society, has been used extensively in clinical settings since 1992 (Alpert 2004). Using RADAR, clinicians can detect domestic violence, treat its effects, and refer patients to appropriate services. The RADAR five-step approach is as follows:

1. *Remember to ask.* Inquiry cannot take place unless healthcare providers remember to ask. Incorporating inquiry into routine clinical practice is now the recognized and recommended standard of care.

2. *Ask directly.* Identifying abuse can be accomplished either through routine screening during the clinical encounter or by direct inquiry if domestic violence is suspected. In either case, principles of respectful patient interviewing should be employed. Clinicians should use engaged body language, sit at the same level as the patient, make eye contact and allow the patient adequate time to respond to questions, listening carefully to the patient's responses and noting the patient's affect. The use of engaged body language and other nonverbal cues will underscore the clinician's interest in the patient's well-being and will facilitate disclosure of traumatic or otherwise difficult experiences. Physicians and other healthcare providers can also facilitate a safe atmosphere by training office staff to be sensitive to trauma issues and by placing patient education materials and helpful telephone numbers in waiting rooms, examination rooms, and restrooms.

3. *Document findings.* Careful documentation of abuse-related injuries and illnesses is an essential component of the healthcare response. Documentation can be useful in court proceedings, for risk management, and to justify services provided. Documentation should be clear and accurate, using written descriptions, freehand sketches, preprinted body diagrams, and/or photographs (including patient consent for photodocumentation). Written accounts should be clear and nonjudgmental, using direct quotations when applicable. Photographs, which can be taken in digital format, should be signed or initialed and dated by the healthcare provider with a notation that the photo image is both accurate and unaltered. At least one photograph should include the patient's face; the injury being documented; a ruler, coin, or other size guide; and a written notation of the date, in a single image.

4. *Assess safety.* Following disclosure, healthcare professionals can play an invaluable role in assessing danger, initiating safety planning, and making referrals to community-based services. Important determinants in assessing risk are the survivor's level of fear, and her/his own appraisal of immediate and future safety needs. Additional indicators of escalating risk include increase in frequency/severity of abuse, threats of homicide or suicide by the partner, presence or availability of a firearm or other weapons, and new or increasingly violent behavior by the perpetrator outside the relationship. Disclosure may herald a particularly dangerous period for both survivor and children. Therefore, once disclosure is made, particular attention must be paid to the safety and well-being of children and others living in a home in which domestic violence is occurring.

5. *Review options/Refer as appropriate.* Caring for domestic violence survivors is a team effort. While inquiry, immediate follow-up, and safety assessment in the clinical setting remain within the purview of the healthcare provider, follow-up often requires involvement of community-based domestic violence "specialists." Such specialists include shelter and legal advocates, court-based victim-witness advocates, social workers and other mental health clinicians, and community providers. Community-based programs provide hotlines, safety planning, emergency shelter, support groups, and legal assistance resources. Arranging to see the patient in follow-up is critical, as it conveys critical support and caring for the patient's welfare. Follow-up also can be both educational and reinforcing for the clinician.

Office Staff Training and Security

Office personnel can facilitate screening, referral, and patient assessment and provide crucial support when time constraints hinder clinicians. Office staff also can provide ongoing patient contact and follow-up, keeping in mind the safety and confidentiality needs of each patient.

All office staff should receive training about domestic violence. Training the entire "team" allows for sharing responsibilities, mutual support, and a lessening of the workload and emotional responsibilities for each individual. Each office should develop screening and intervention protocols that adhere to guiding principles of care, taking into account the security, logistical, time, and emotional needs of office staff. The office team can thus work smoothly and seamlessly for screening, response, and follow-up.

A suspected batterer should never be spoken to about any abuse-related behavior that he/she has not disclosed independently. Discussion of any survivor-originating information with the batterer violates the confidential relationship between clinician/office and patient/survivor, puts staff at risk, and increases the chance that the batterer will retaliate by injuring or killing the victim. Within the constraints of mandated reporter responsibilities, strict confidentiality must be maintained with respect to medical records and conversations concerning survivors. Suspicious behavior by a batterer in the office or vicinity can be reported to security staff or police more effectively when office personnel have been appropriately trained.

Conclusion

The healthcare visit provides an ideal opportunity for inquiry about domestic violence. Routine inquiry fosters the ability of patients to develop confidence in making informed choices that promote safety. There is no simple and easy solution for the complex problem of domestic violence; however, early diagnosis and efficient and compassionate intervention can ameliorate the serious effects of physical, sexual, and psychological abuse for current, as well as future, generations.

ELAINE J. ALPERT

See also **Assessing Risk in Domestic Violence Cases; Battered Woman Syndrome; Child Neglect; Child Sexual Abuse; Date Rape; Incest; Marital Rape; Medicalization of Domestic Violence; Sexual Orientation and Gender Identity: The Need for Education in Servicing Victims of Trauma**

References and Further Reading

Abbott, J., et al. "Domestic Violence against Women: Incidence and Prevalence in an Emergency Department Population." *Journal of the American Medical Association* 273, no. 22 (1995): 1763–1767.

ACOG (American College of Obstetricians and Gynecologists) Technical Bulletin. "Domestic Violence." Number 209—August 1995. *International Journal of Gynecology and Obstetrics* 51, no. 2 (1995): 161–170.

Adverse Childhood Experiences (ACE) Study. http://www.cdc.gov/nccdphp/ace.

Alpert, E. J. "Violence in Intimate Relationships and the Practicing Internist: New Disease or New Agenda?" *Annals of Internal Medicine* 123 (1995): 774–781.

———. "Have We Overlooked the Most Common Cause of Maternal Mortality in the United States?" (letter). *Journal of Midwifery and Women's Health* 46, no. 1 (2001): 3.

———. ed. *Massachusetts Medical Society Committee on Violence. Partner Violence: How to Recognize and Treat Victims of Abuse—A Guide for Physicians and Other Health Care Professionals*, 4th ed. Waltham: Massachusetts Medical Society, 2004.

Alpert, E. J., and C. L. Albright. *Massachusetts Medical Society Seminar Series on Domestic Violence*. Waltham: Massachusetts Medical Society, 1997.

American College of Emergency Physicians. "Emergency Medicine and Domestic Violence." *Annals of Emergency Medicine* 25, no. 3 (1995): 442–443.

American Medical Association. *Diagnostic and Treatment Guidelines on Domestic Violence*. Chicago, IL: Author, 1992.

———. Opinion H 515–965: Family and Intimate Partner Violence. Current Opinions of the Council of Ethical and Judicial Affairs, 2001.

American Psychological Association. http://www.apa.org.

Centers for Disease Control and Prevention, National Center for Injury Prevention and Control, Division of Violence Prevention. http://www.cdc.gov/ncipc/dvp/dvp.htm.

Domestic Violence and Sexual Assault Data Resource Center. http://www.jrsa.org/dvsa-drc.

Drossman, D. A., et al. "Sexual and Physical Abuse in Women with Functional or Organic Gastrointestinal Disorders." *Annals of Internal Medicine* 113 (1990): 828–833.

Eisenstat, S. A., and L. Bancroft. "Domestic Violence." *New England Journal of Medicine* 341, no. 12 (1999): 886–892.

FaithTrust Institute. http://www.cpsdv.org.

Family Violence Prevention Fund. http://www.endabuse.org.

———. *Preventing Domestic Violence: Clinical Guidelines on Routine Screening*. San Francisco: Author, 1999.

Felitti, V. J. "The Relationship between Adverse Childhood Experiences and Adult Health: Turning Gold into Lead." *The Permanente Journal* 6 (2002): 44–47.

Felitti, V. J., et al. "Relationship of Childhood Abuse and Household Dysfunction to Many of the Leading Causes of Death in Adults: The Adverse Childhood Experiences (ACE) Study." *American Journal of Preventive Medicine* 14 (1998): 245–258.

Foege, W. H. "Adverse Childhood Experiences: A Public Health Perspective" (editorial). *American Journal of Preventive Medicine* 14 (1998): 354–355.

Frayne, S. M., et al. "Medical Profile of Women VA Outpatients Who Report Sexual Assault in the Military." *Journal of Women's Health and Gender-Based Medicine* 8, no. 6 (1999): 835–845.

Frye, V. "Examining Homicide's Contribution to Pregnancy-Associated Deaths." *Journal of the American Medical Association* 285 (2001): 1510–1511.

Garimella, R., et al. "Physician Beliefs about Victims of Spouse Abuse and about the Physician Role." *Journal of Women's Health and Gender-Based Medicine* 9, no. 4 (2000): 405–411.

Gerber, M. R., et al. "Adverse Health Behaviors and the Detection of Partner Violence by Clinicians." *Archives of Internal Medicine* 165 (2005): 1016–1021.

Isaac, N. E., and V. P. Enos. *Documenting Domestic Violence: How Health Care Providers Can Help Victims*. U.S. Department of Justice Research in Brief, National Institute of Justice Office of Justice Programs, 2001. NCJ 188564.

Koziol-McLain, J., and J. C. Campbell. "Universal Screening and Mandatory Reporting: An Update on Two Important Issues for Victims/Survivors of Intimate Partner Violence." *Journal of Emergency Nursing* 27 (2001): 602–606.

McCauley, J., et al. "The 'Battering Syndrome': Prevalence and Clinical Characteristics of Domestic Violence in Primary Care Internal Medicine Practices." *Annals of Internal Medicine* 123, no. 10 (1995): 737–746.

———. "Relation of Low-Severity Violence to Women's Health." *Journal of General Internal Medicine* 13 (1998): 687–691.

Minnesota Center Against Violence and Abuse. http://www.mincava.umn.edu.

National Center for Children Exposed to Violence. http://www.nccev.org.

National Center on Elder Abuse. http://www.elderabuse-center.org.

National Online Resource Center on Violence Against Women. http://www.vawnet.org.

Rennison, C. M., and S. Welchans. *Intimate Partner Violence: Special Report*. U.S. Department of Justice, Office of Justice Programs, Bureau of Justice Statistics, 2000. NCJ 178247.

Saltzman, L. E., et al. *Intimate Partner Violence Surveillance: Uniform Definitions and Recommended Data Elements*. Version 1.0. Atlanta: National Center for Injury Control and Prevention, Centers for Disease Control and Prevention, 1999.

———. "Violence against Women as a Public Health Issue: Comments from the CDC." *American Journal of Preventive Medicine* 19, no. 4 (2000): 325–329.

Stark, E., and A. Flitcraft. "Killing the Beast Within: Woman Battering and Female Suicidality." *International Journal of Health Services* 25, no. 1 (1995): 43–64.

Sugg, N. K., and T. Inui. "Primary Care Physicians' Response to Domestic Violence: Opening Pandora's Box." *Journal of the American Medical Association* 267 (1992): 3157–3160.

Tjaden, P., and N. Thoennes. *Extent, Nature and Consequences of Intimate Partner Violence: Findings from the National Violence Against Women Survey*. U.S. Department of Justice, Office of Justice Programs, National Institute of Justice, 2000. NCJ 181867.

———. *Extent, Nature and Consequences of Intimate Partner Violence: Findings from the National Violence Against Women Survey, Research Report*. U.S. Department of Justice, National Institute of Justice, 2000.

Waalen, J., M. M. Goodwin, A. M. Spitz, R. Petersen, and L. E. Saltzman. "Screening for Intimate Partner Violence by Health Care Providers: Barriers and Interventions." *American Journal of Preventive Medicine* 19, no. 4 (2000): 230–237.

Warshaw, C., and E. Alpert. "Integrating Routine Inquiry about Domestic Violence into Daily Practice." *Annals of Internal Medicine* 131, no. 8 (1999): 619–620.

Weiss, J. S., and S. H. Wagner. "What Explains the Negative Consequences of Adverse Childhood Experiences on Adult Health? Insights from Cognitive and Neuroscience Research" (editorial). *American Journal of Preventive Medicine* 14 (1998): 356–360.

Whitfield, C. L. "Adverse Childhood Experiences and Trauma." *American Journal of Preventive Medicine* 14 (1998): 361–363.

Whitfield, C. L., R. F. Anda, S. R. Dube, and V. J. Felitti. "Violent Childhood Experiences and the Risk of Intimate Partner Violence in Adults: Assessment in a Large Health Maintenance Organization." *Journal of Interpersonal Violence* 18 (2003): 166–185.

Widom, C. S., and M. G. Maxfield. *An Update on the "Cycle of Violence."* U.S. Department of Justice, Office of Justice Programs, National Institute of Justice Research in Brief, 2001.

Womens Health.gov. "Violence Against Women." http://www.4woman.gov/violence.

HOMELESSNESS, THE IMPACT OF FAMILY VIOLENCE ON

Domestic violence is one of the primary causes of homelessness for women. Women who are financially dependent upon their violent partners often face an untenable choice: remaining in dangerous situations or becoming homeless. This choice is undeniably more difficult for women with children, for they are making decisions with consideration for their children's safety and well-being as well as their own. This essay will present a discussion of the extent of the problem, causes, and pathways of homelessness, policies and their implications, theories, and programmatic responses. In addition, two contemporary topics of debate will be explored.

What Is the Extent of the Problem?

There are two primary vantage points from which to understand the extent of the problem of domestic violence and homelessness: the proportion of homeless parents who have a history of domestic violence and the proportion of homeless parents who report that domestic violence is the primary reason they are seeking shelter. Some recent research is summarized below to provide insight into these two perspectives.

In one study, 47 percent of homeless parents reported a history of domestic violence, and one in four stated that a primary reason they sought shelter was domestic violence (daCosta Nunez 2004). The U.S. Conference of Mayors' 2004 survey of homelessness and hunger in twenty-seven cities reported that twelve cities identified domestic violence as a primary cause of homelessness; moreover, this survey has documented increases in the numbers of homeless families turned away from emergency shelters across the country. Choi and Snyder (1999) reported that 16.2 percent of their sample said that domestic violence was the primary reason for their homelessness, ranking as the second most common reason. A Chicago study found that 22 percent of homeless women interviewed stated that domestic violence was the immediate cause of their homelessness, and more than one-half (56 percent) said they had histories of domestic violence (Levin, McKean, and Raphael 2004). However, Metreaux and Culhane (1999) found that only 8.9 percent of their sample reported domestic violence in their households prior to shelter stays.

While the literature provides varying estimates of both elements associating domestic violence and homelessness (history and immediate cause), it is clear that such a relationship exists. What is less clear is the extent of causality, for domestic violence does not always lead to homelessness, nor is homelessness always caused by domestic violence. Potential factors that limit researchers' ability to draw conclusions include research methodologies (interviews and/or surveys versus use of administrative records), confidentiality practices that prohibit the reporting of domestic violence, poor record-keeping by service agencies, and reluctance of homeless families to self-identify as victims of domestic violence.

Causes of Homelessness

The causes of homelessness have been identified as generally falling into one of two categories: structural and individual. Structural causes of homelessness generally refer to the inability of society to provide sufficient resources for everyone to remain stably housed. These include lack of affordable housing, lack of jobs, skills gaps (differences in the skills demanded by the job market and those offered by potential workers), and lack of transportation to jobs. Structural causes of homelessness can also include those ancillary situations in which jobs lack health insurance, which results in the inability of poor workers to maintain their health and therefore their ability to work. Alternatively, the individual causes of homelessness include mental illness, substance abuse, lack of job skills, and domestic violence. These occur when the individual has internal characteristics that prevent him or her from finding and maintaining gainful employment, thus resulting in an inability to be self-sufficient. Although this discussion started by describing two categories of causes for homelessness, in reality these causes often interact for individuals and families. For example, if job training programs are offered to people who lack job skills but the community infrastructure does not provide sufficient jobs to employ newly trained individuals, homelessness may still result. Similarly, individuals who complete treatment programs for substance abuse may find that there is insufficient affordable housing and remain homeless.

Domestic violence as a cause of homelessness similarly presents a complex set of interrelationships among structural and individual causes. For women who have depended upon their partners for economic support, who lack work histories and/or job skills, these barriers to self-sufficiency and stable housing will be exacerbated by such structural phenomena as the feminization of poverty. Relevant evidence of the feminization of poverty includes the fact that on average, women earn less than men, female single-parent families represent the majority of all families living in poverty, and approximately 50 percent more women than men are poor. The implication of the feminization of poverty for women striving for self-sufficiency is that despite their best efforts to overcome their personal limitations, structural factors will limit their success.

Other risk factors that have been associated with homelessness and domestic violence include childhood abuse experiences where there was nobody to turn to for sources of safety and support (Anderson and Imle 2001).

Pathways of Homelessness

Homeless families are the fastest-growing subpopulation of the homeless; most homeless families are made up of women with children. Homeless families often follow a path that is characterized by housing instability. They often start out by staying temporarily with family or friends. This is called "doubling up." As their presence becomes burdensome on those they are staying with, they often shift to other family members or friends. Doubling up can become problematic for host families because of overcrowding, financial burdens, or interpersonal conflicts. Such situations are exacerbated when the homeless family is fleeing domestic violence and potential danger to the members of the host family is a realistic concern.

The path of housing instability may continue once the family unit has exhausted personal support resources such as family members and friends. The initial choice is typically a domestic violence shelter (and, indeed, may be the *first* choice, depending on the availability of host families and/or the extent of immediate danger). Domestic violence shelters offer safe havens and the assurance that the family unit can remain intact. However, such shelters usually have time limits for staying in them and may or may not offer second-stage, transitional, or other subsequent housing options following the termination of such time limits. In those communities where the domestic violence shelter system ends following emergency shelter stays, the family must turn to the mainstream homeless service system.

There are several reasons why mainstream homeless services are undesirable for both families in general and families that are fleeing domestic violence in particular. First, some homeless shelters have policies that restrict their residents to adults only. This means that the parent and child or children are likely to be separated. The children may be placed in foster care or youth shelters, depending on their ages. These options are destructive to the family unit, may exacerbate the trauma associated with the experience of domestic violence and the subsequent homelessness for both parents and children, and may increase the danger to both. Second, where shelters do allow children to stay with their parents, often only congregate, dormitory-style sleeping arrangements are available. This is true even when separate quarters are available for women with their children. Such sleeping arrangements produce concerns about safety for the children; also, school-aged children may not get the sleep they need to succeed in their classes. Third, specific to families fleeing domestic violence, mainstream emergency shelters for homeless people do not offer the level of security available in safe havens for victims of domestic violence. Fourth, reporting domestic violence is related to increased risk of multiple stays in emergency shelters and decreased likelihood of successful exits from shelter systems. This is likely due to the increased social and economic strains associated with domestic violence (Metreaux and Culhane 1999). Fifth, women who stay in emergency shelters are more likely than women either in transitional housing programs or in the community to score higher on clinical tests of psychological distress, anxiety, dissociation, sexual concerns, and intrusive experiences (Gorde, Helfrich, and Finlayson 2004).

Finally, there is considerable concern among providers of services to domestic violence victims due to federal reporting mandates. Later in this essay, the debate about sharing information via the national Homeless Management Information System (HMIS) will be presented; suffice it to say here that protections for the identity of domestic violence victims are not in effect once families enter the mainstream system of care for the homeless.

Policies and Policy Implications

The McKinney-Vento Homeless Assistance Act (42 USC 119) provides the following general definition of a homeless person:

(1) an individual who lacks a fixed, regular, and adequate nighttime residence; and
(2) an individual who has a primary nighttime residence that is—
   (A) a supervised publicly or privately operated shelter designed to provide temporary living accommodations (including welfare hotels, congregate shelters, and transitional housing for the mentally ill);
   (B) an institution that provides a temporary residence for individuals intended to be institutionalized; or
   (C) a public or private place not designed for, or ordinarily used as, a regular sleeping accommodation for human beings. (§ 11302)

Federal law defines homeless children as "individuals who lack a fixed, regular, and adequate nighttime residence" (42 USC 119, §11432 et seq.). Included are children who share housing with other persons because of economic hardship or loss of housing; live in motels, hotels, trailer parks, or camping grounds because they do not have alternative living arrangements; reside in emergency or transitional shelters; have been abandoned in hospitals; or, are waiting for placement with a foster care family.

Relevant to the discussion of domestic violence and homelessness is the disparity between federal definitions for general homelessness and for homeless children. As can be seen from the definitions provided above, an adult fleeing a domestic violence situation with one or more children may or may not be considered homeless, but the child or children may be. Specifically, children who are sharing housing with other persons because of economic hardship or loss of housing; or living in motels, hotels, or trailer parks because they do not have alternative living arrangements are considered homeless by federal law; however, their adult parents are not. These disparities in federal law mean that various rights and benefits for adults and children fleeing domestic violence situations may differ. In general, adults who are considered homeless according to the federal definition may be eligible for a variety of homeless assistance programs, including those providing food, counseling, job training, and other supportive services. These may be essential for the adult to establish economic self-sufficiency and therefore freedom from dependence upon abusive partners. Children who are considered homeless are entitled to free and appropriate education, and local education agencies must ensure that barriers to educational success such as segregation and lack of transportation are removed. These assurances can provide safety mechanisms and even supportive counseling for children who have left abusive situations.

Theoretical Perspectives

There is no single theory that explicates the relationship between domestic violence and homelessness. Two theories that have been discussed as relevant to domestic violence are learned helplessness and gendered entitlement. *Learned helplessness* refers to the long-term pattern of weakened resistance to violence in a relationship; it assumes that the victim is unwilling or unable to actively plan and execute strategies for leaving the abusive relationship. *Gendered entitlement* is a feminist perspective that places domestic violence in a cultural environment where male power is valued and attempts on the part of female victims to end abusive relationships are not supported by those in their lives (including family, courts, police, etc.).

Theories of homelessness include disaffiliation, abeyance, and liminality. Disaffiliation theory explains homelessness in terms of detachment from social bonds and social institutions. Abeyance refers to a structural condition where the needs of the many cannot be met by society; available resources are demanded by a surplus of users. Liminality describes the social, cultural, and physical limbo that homeless people experience: They are outside of society's network and therefore always in transition.

If these theories have anything in common, it is isolation: Victims of domestic violence are isolated from friends, family, and social support structures; similarly, homeless people are isolated from mainstream society. When victims of domestic violence become homeless, increased isolation is the logical result. It therefore becomes the work of the social service system to assist these individuals and families in reestablishing fragile ties and rebuilding resilient responses.

Programmatic Responses

For homeless people who have experienced domestic violence, services must be comprehensive and coordinated. First and foremost, the safety of parents and children must be assured. If this means increasing the length of time such families can stay in safe havens, then resources must be sought to allow this practice to flourish. If this means creating more safe havens, then resources must be directed to meet this need. Given that mainstream emergency shelters are often the only option left to families fleeing violent homes, these shelters can set aside private sleeping quarters for such families and increase security protocols.

Prevention is more challenging for families experiencing domestic violence than for others who are at risk of homelessness. It may increase the danger for victims to acknowledge their situations and seek help before leaving their violent homes. The only viable alternatives may be public education and parenting and relationship educational programs.

Transitional housing programs are viable responses to the needs of this population. They typically provide supportive services and affordable housing for up to eighteen months, an arrangement that can be very effective in assisting homeless families that have experienced domestic violence in achieving emotional, physical, and financial stability.

The creation of affordable housing options can assist those survivors who are able to work toward self-sufficiency. Communities can seek ordinances that require the creation of integrated affordable housing as well as advocate for increased subsidized housing vouchers from state and federal governments.

Debates

There are two topics relevant to this discussion that are the subject of national debate: initiatives on chronic homelessness and HMIS reporting requirements. The federal administration under George W. Bush has identified chronic homelessness as its top priority based on evidence that the chronically homeless spend a disproportionate amount of time in the service system and use a disproportionate share of the resources available for the whole homeless population. There are potentially negative implications for those experiencing both domestic violence and homelessness, as they are qualitatively different from those living on the streets for extended periods. Concerns have been raised about the diversion of scarce funding resources from generic service program approaches to those that focus on the chronically homeless. The kinds of programs that have been previously described as potentially effective for those experiencing both domestic violence and homelessness, namely extended-stay safe havens, humane emergency shelters, transitional housing programs, and community education efforts, are under threat of losing funding due to the emphasis on chronic homelessness.

The second area of debate concerns the national database that is being funded and required by the U.S. Department of Housing and Urban Development (HUD). Domestic violence shelters qualify for funding under many of HUD's program initiatives. Yet, HUD is inexorably moving in the direction of requiring organizations to participate in the national HMIS in order to qualify for funding for their homeless service programs. At the local level, this means that all of the service agencies in a given community will record and share information about the homeless people they serve. Ultimately, such data will be shared at the state and national levels as well. On the one hand, sharing data about service recipients can increase efficiency and document needed services. On the other hand, domestic violence shelters are at their core concerned with the safety of their residents, and sharing personal information on public databases threatens their very missions. Considerable communications have taken place between HUD and domestic violence advocates, but concerns persist about the perception that HUD's revised position on this point falls short of protecting service recipients. In these ways, the debate frames the very designation of people fleeing domestic violence situations as homeless, for to refrain from such designations may mean loss of precious financial resources for service provision.

Closing and Summary

This essay has provided a number of perspectives on the impact of domestic violence on homelessness. The extent of the problem, causes, and pathways of homelessness, policies and their implications, theories, and programmatic responses have all been presented. In addition, two contemporary topics of debate were explored. The convergence of domestic violence and homelessness as one social problem will persist as long as there is either domestic violence or homelessness. To effectively address this compound social problem, it is necessary to simultaneously develop and implement evidence-based service interventions for each problem individually and understand more clearly the unique attributes and needs of individuals and families experiencing both life situations.

WENDY P. CROOK

See also **Education as a Risk Factor for Domestic Violence; Social Class and Domestic Violence; Social, Economic, and Psychological Costs of Violence; Substance Use/Abuse and Intimate Partner Violence; Victim-Blaming Theory**

References and Further Reading

Anderson, D. G., and M. A. Imle. "Families of Origin of Homeless and Never-Homeless Women." *Western Journal of Nursing Research* 23, no. 4 (2001): 394–413.
Baum, A. S., and D. W. Burnes. *A Nation in Denial: The Truth about Homelessness.* Boulder, CO: Westview, 1993.
Choi, N. G., and L. J. Snyder. *Homeless Families with Children: A Subjective Experience of Homelessness.* New York: Springer, 1999.
Crook, W. P. "New Sisters of the Road: Homeless Women and Their Children." *Journal of Family Social Work* 3 (1999): 49–64.
daCosta Nunez, R. C. *A Shelter Is Not a Home . . . Or Is It?* New York: White Tiger, 2004.
Gorde, M. W., C. A. Helfrich, and M. L. Finlayson. "Trauma Symptoms and Life Skill Needs of Domestic Violence Victims." *Journal of Interpersonal Violence* 19, no. 6 (2004): 691–708.
Hopper, K. "Reckoning with Homelessness." Ithaca, NY: Cornell University Press, 2003.
Levin, R., L. McKean, and J. Raphael. *Pathways to and from Homelessness: Women and Children in Chicago Shelters.* Center for Impact Research, 2004. http://www.impactresearch.org/documents/homelessnessreport.pdf.
McKinney-Vento Homeless Assistance Act, 42 USC 119.
McLanahan, S. S., and E. L. Kelly. "The Feminization of Poverty: Past and Future." *Network on the Family and the Economy* (n. d.). http://www.olin.wustl.edu/macarthur/working%20papers/wp-mclanahan3.htm.
Metreaux, S., and D. P. Culhane. "Family Dynamics, Housing, and Recurring Homelessness among Women in New York City Homeless Shelters." *Journal of Family Issues* 20, no. 3 (1999): 371–396.
U.S. Conference of Mayors. *Hunger and Homelessness Survey: A Status Report on Hunger and Homelessness in America's Cities.* Washington, DC: US Conference of Mayors, 2004.
Williams, J. C. "Domestic Violence and Poverty." *Frontiers* (1998). http://www.findarticles.com/p/articles/mi_qa3687/is_199801/ai_n8772075.

HUMAN RIGHTS, REFUGEE LAWS, AND ASYLUM PROTECTION FOR PEOPLE FLEEING DOMESTIC VIOLENCE

The Case of Rodi Alvarado

In Guatemala in 1984, at age sixteen, Rodi Alvarado married Francisco Osorio, twenty-one, a former soldier. He became violent almost immediately and abused her for ten years without respite. He dislocated her jawbone, kicked her violently, and raped her repeatedly. Once she attempted suicide. The Guatemalan police and courts refused to intervene because it was a "domestic" matter. Finally, in 1995, she fled to the United States; she was forced to leave her two children behind with relatives. As of this writing, she has not seen her children since.

In 1996, her request for asylum was granted, but the immigration service appealed. The decision was reversed on appeal and it was ordered that Ms. Alvarado be deported to Guatemala. In its divided decision, the court stated:

> We agree . . . that the severe injuries [she] sustained rise to the level of harm sufficient (and more than sufficient) to constitute persecution. . . . [and] that she has adequately established . . . she was unable to avail herself of the protection of the Government of Guatemala in connection with the abuse inflicted by her husband. . . . [W]e find that [she] has been the victim of tragic and severe spouse abuse. We further find that her husband's motivation, to the extent it can be ascertained, has varied; some abuse occurred because of his warped perception of and reaction to her behavior, while some likely arose out of psychological disorder, pure meanness, or no apparent reason at all. . . . We are not persuaded that the abuse occurred because of her membership in a particular social group or because of . . . political opinion. We therefore do not find [her] eligible for asylum. . . .

The decision in the case known as *Matter of R. A.* has been widely criticized by scholars, lawyers, and activists in the fields of domestic violence and refugee law, particularly for its failure to understand basic concepts of domestic violence and to incorporate international human rights law principles. In the years following, the decision has been reviewed by Attorneys General Janet Reno and John Ashcroft, resulting in the withdrawal of the decision, denying her claim and calling for the immigration agency to issue regulations detailing the appropriate considerations for assessing women's asylum claims before Alvarado's case can be reviewed again. As of this writing, her case remains unresolved and the regulations, first called for in 2001, have not yet been issued. Although the decision has been retracted, its impact has led to denials of cases of women seeking asylum from human trafficking, honor killing, sexual slavery, and rape, as well as domestic violence. At the same time, violence against women has become better understood and some women have been able to gain protection in the United States.

Domestic Violence as a Violation of Women's Human Rights

Domestic violence against women occurs all over the world and transcends all boundaries—race, class, age, religion, education, culture, and ethnicity. Its very prevalence has made it difficult to gain the kinds of international protections and recourse for women that have long been available for other kinds of human rights violations. Historically, human rights standards have been defined and interpreted based on a male perspective. Inherent in this male-oriented view is a prejudice that addresses the "public" realm differently from the "private." Under this view, the worlds of politics, business, science, and social development are seen as the province of men, the "public" realm, and thus subject to outside regulation and governance. The home, the family, and the community are viewed as constituting the "private" realm and are therefore immune to interference from government and far from the jurisdiction of international human rights protections. Although this private sector is considered women's world, it is also seen as a sanctuary for men—where they are to be free from restraint and public scrutiny. Under this construct, domestic violence is seen as a woman's personal, private "problem" to be worked out within the family. At worst, it is considered the aberrant behavior of a particular man—it is not seen as a social, cultural, or political matter.

At the turn of the twenty-first century, this view of violence against women has been shifting. International human rights law has grown to recognize these harms as human rights violations. Rape is now considered a crime of war and a violation of the right to bodily integrity. At least under some circumstances, harms against women typically committed in the home or private sphere are seen as warranting governments to take preventative action and to enforce punitive penalties once they have occurred. As the international framework shifted to include the private sphere in its ambit, it allowed for a host of conduct against women, including domestic violence, to be understood as human rights violations.

One of the first documents to reflect this broadened understanding is the 1993 Declaration on the Elimination of Violence against Women, which states that violence against women is a "manifestation of historically unequal power relations between men and women" and that this is "one of the crucial social mechanisms by which women are forced into a subordinate position compared with men." Another historical marker was the 1994 inauguration of a new United Nations office, the Special Rapporteur on Violence Against Women, its Causes and Consequences. In her seminal report, the first Special Rapporteur, Radhika Coomaraswamy, stated: "Violence against women in general, and domestic violence in particular, serve as essential components in societies which oppress women, since violence against women not only derives from but also sustains the dominant gender stereotype and is used to control women in the one space traditionally dominated by women, the home."

As understood in the human rights context, violence in the family includes battering, rape, and sexual assault, and the threat of any of these by husbands, fathers, or other males in the household, and encompasses physical, psychological, emotional, and mental abuse. The understanding of violence against women has vastly improved over the course of the 1990s and into the 2000s, and many international documents recognize violence against women in all its forms as human rights violations. Nevertheless, a tremendous gap between theory

and practice remains. States still fail to provide necessary protection, to implement and enforce appropriate laws, to exercise the political will, and to create social climates that deter and penalize violations of these fundamental human rights. In spite of these persisting difficulties and the many women whose suffering goes unabated, much groundwork has been laid that may lead to greater opportunities for women to gain protection from violence. For many women, the only way to obtain protection is to flee to another country.

As is true of many women trapped in abusive relationships, women who flee such relationships seeking protection often do so only as a last resort when all else has failed. Few of these women think of themselves as refugees deserving of international protection. They simply want to escape. The question is, are they refugees?

Who Is a Refugee?

Refugees are people who have been forced to abandon their homes, family, friends, livelihoods, and homelands. Some flee hurriedly in response to an immediate threat. Others reach the decision to leave their country after a long period of uncertainty, fear, and anxiety, when all other options have failed. All have had their lives disrupted by forces beyond their control and would be at grave risk if forced to return to the place they fled.

People fleeing en masse from some terrible natural or political disaster such as the 2004 tsunami in Indonesia or the atrocities that occurred in the mid-1990s in the former Yugoslavia and in Rwanda are common images of refugees. Another classic image is the political dissident protesting against a despotic regime, arrested and detained in secrecy, held in isolation, and tortured into confessing to acts he may never have committed. People fleeing these kinds of harms most certainly exist, and every year a small number of them manage to arrive on U.S. shores seeking protection. Many other people flee equally appalling and desperate situations from countries where there is no protection available for them, where the harms they fear are condoned, if not practiced, by government officials.

There are no exact figures available on refugee populations, but in December 2004 the estimated number of refugees worldwide—people fleeing their country of origin due to fear of great harm—was between 11.5 million to as many as 19 million. Women and children are believed to make up between 50 and 80 percent of the refugee population. Of the total number of refugees in 2004, less than 500,000 were found in the North (Europe,

Canada, and the United States), where they could request the protection of asylum law, and the number of women among them was very small. Few records of refugees and asylum seekers are disaggregated by age or by gender, so exact numbers are not available. Estimates from early 2004 indicate there were approximately 500 asylum cases raising gender-related harm pending in the United States.

"Refugee" is both a descriptive and a legal term, with a precise meaning. Descriptively, whenever people flee their home due to circumstances beyond their control, they are commonly referred to as refugees. The many people living in refugee camps or restricted areas, such as the Burmese in Thailand or the Afghans in Pakistan, are considered refugees even if they have never received any official recognition as such. As a matter of law, to be deemed a refugee, each individual must have the reasons for his or her flight assessed by an official adjudicator, and if at the end of this process he or she is determined to be a refugee, certain protections are afforded, most notably that the person cannot be forced to return to the country he or she fled.

The definition of a refugee is found in the International Convention Relating to the Status of Refugees, as amended by the 1967 Protocol Relating to the Status of Refugees (Refugee Convention). The Refugee Convention states, in relevant part, that a refugee is "any person who . . . owing to a well-founded fear of being persecuted for reasons of race, religion, nationality, membership of [sic] a particular social group, or political opinion, is outside the country of his nationality and is unable or, owing to such fear, unwilling to avail himself of the protection of that country." Many countries, including the United States, use the same or similar language in their own definition of a refugee.

In the United States, there are two different ways a person can receive protection based on the refugee definition. One is by being determined to be a refugee by an immigration official stationed abroad to make these assessments. Those designated as refugees through this process receive papers identifying them as such and allowing them to enter and live in the United States and have certain legal protections. Very few people come to the United States as refugees through this overseas process. According to U.S. government records, in 2004 the total number of people allowed to enter as refugees was 52,835, up from 28,300 in 2003.

The other way of achieving protection as a refugee in the United States is to arrive at any official port of entry, which includes airports as well as other designated areas, and then request asylum.

This entails a thorough application and adjudication process in which the individual must establish that he or she meets the definition of a refugee. Anyone who ultimately prevails in doing so is granted asylum and is accorded permission to remain in the United States, to work, and to travel. Although in general more people receive protection through this process than by being granted refugee status abroad, the overall numbers of asylum claims that have been granted have been low. Government statistics reflect a total of 27,321 people granted asylum in 2004, not including those whose cases were decided on appeal, for which there are no numbers available; in 2003 that number was 28,753.

There are several other remedies under U.S. law that would allow a person fearful for their safety, life, or freedom in their country of origin to remain in this country. These have some similarities with asylum protections but have a higher burden of proof and include refraining from sending a person back to the country of origin if it is established that his or her life or freedom would be in danger, and protection under the Convention Against Torture, as provided for under U.S. law.

Seeking Asylum in the United States

The 1980 Refugee Act is the U.S. law governing the protection of refugees and asylum seekers. This law is based on the international Convention Relating to the Status of Refugees, as modified by the 1967 Protocol to the Refugee Convention. In the relevant part, the law states that a refugee is

> any person who is outside any country of such person's nationality . . . and who is unable or unwilling to return to, and is unable or unwilling to avail himself or herself of the protection of, that country because of persecution or a well-founded fear of persecution on account of race, religion, nationality, membership in a particular social group, or political opinion.

To receive the protection of asylum in this country, four essential elements must be satisfied. There must be a reasonable possibility that the individual would face harm if forced to return to his or her country of origin, or, in light of the harm the applicant suffered in the past, it would be inhumane to force him or her to return there. The harm feared or suffered in the past must constitute persecution as that term is understood and defined under U.S. law. The harm has been or would be inflicted by a government or by an individual or group that the government either cannot or will not control. The harm or persecution must be inflicted upon the person for reasons related to the person's race, religion, nationality, political opinion or membership in a particular social group, or any combination of these.

The term "persecution" is not defined in the Refugee Convention or in the U.S. Refugee Act. Over time, the courts have given the term meaning as they have examined whether the harm raised in specific cases could be said to "rise to the level" of persecution or not. The term is still not conclusively defined, but violations of fundamental human rights, severe harm, torture, and in some cases, threats of any of these, have been recognized as constituting persecution. In the context of women's asylum claims, some of the advances in the human rights field have been brought to bear, and harms that have been found to constitute persecution now include rape, female genital cutting, honor killing, domestic violence, and forced compliance with repressive social norms such as deprivation of education or employment opportunities or forced marriage. Among the harms raised by women asylum seekers, perhaps the most controversial is the fear of domestic violence, with no protection available in the home country.

Asylum Protection for Women Fleeing Domestic Violence

Domestic violence has been recognized as a basis for granting asylum protection in a number of countries, including the United States. In 1995 the United States issued guidelines for the adjudication of claims of women asylum seekers, and these state that domestic violence can provide the basis for an asylum claim. Yet essentially it remains at the margins of human rights and refugee protections and is an especially thorny area of asylum law. Some surmise that one reason for this is precisely because domestic violence is so pervasive and cuts across all distinctions such as race, class, religion, age, sexual orientation, socioeconomic background, education levels, and country of origin. Certainly, domestic violence occurs in the United States. The National Domestic Violence Hotline website estimates that in a given twelve-month period, four million women in the United States experience serious assault by a partner and that as many as one out of three women around the world has been beaten, coerced into sex, or otherwise abused during her lifetime. Under asylum law, the number of people potentially affected by a certain group or type of harm does not determine whether any given individual is eligible to receive protection. Each claim must be evaluated on its own merits and granted or denied accordingly. Nevertheless, the prevalence of domestic violence may interfere with an adjudicator's ability to assess a given asylum claim.

Two additional reasons given for the precarious status of domestic violence as a basis for asylum claims also raise complex concerns in meeting the definition of a refugee under the law. One of these is the question of state responsibility and its role in allowing or enabling a "private actor" to perpetrate the harm. Both human rights law and refugee law recognize state responsibility for human rights violations by nonstate actors, and asylum law has applied this principle in situations where it has been shown that the state either cannot or will not control the actor in question. The Refugee Convention and U.S. law are also clear that the state does not have to be actively involved in committing the persecution; the absence of state protection can be enough to support state responsibility.

In asylum cases raising domestic violence, a key component of determining whether the state can be responsible for failing or refusing to act depends on a variety of factors. Some countries have laws that condone violence against women or that simply do not include it as punishable conduct. Other countries have "obedience" or "modesty" laws that require a woman's submission to her husband or other male authority figures and give that person an explicit or implicit right to discipline his wife, relative, or partner. In other countries, women are deemed the property of their fathers or husbands. In still others, there may be laws against certain kinds of violence against women but they are largely unenforced or women lack the resources for or are denied access to the systems that might enforce them. In some situations, women are discouraged from seeking justice and protection because the system holds them responsible, blaming them for "inciting" or "instigating" it or for refusing to be compliant and submissive to their husband's demands. In some societies, family, religious, and community members support the husband and urge the woman to work out their differences, or to simply not complain and to stay with or return to her abuser. All of these factors and more present deep obstacles for women who wish to receive protection, support, and assistance in their home country, and can ultimately lead to the decision to flee and seek refuge and safety elsewhere. These same factors, if they can be established to the satisfaction of an asylum adjudicator, can support the view that the state is responsible, either through its own actions, such as laws that condone domestic violence, or through a failure to act, such as police refusing to take a woman's complaint.

In establishing the role of the state when the persecutor is a private actor—a spouse, partner, or family member—the lack of state protection can itself provide an essential element in establishing persecution. Where the facts and circumstances in the home country demonstrate it, this view states that the state has failed to take action because domestic violence is accepted by the state and society, precisely because it happens to women. Under this view, women are the targets of persecution by men in part because they know, or have reason to believe, that their crimes will go unpunished.

A second principal difficulty in being granted asylum based on domestic violence is establishing that the violence has been or will be inflicted "on account of" one of the five grounds—race, religion, nationality, membership in a particular social or political group. A woman might be able to show that her spouse or partner abused her because of religious differences. For example, in one asylum claim, a young woman showed that her father beat her because she would not comply with his strict, fundamentalist religious views. Even though they shared the same religion, she was able to convince the court that both her and her father's religious views were consistent with their faith and that her father abused her because she would not adhere to his narrower interpretation of the religion. Domestic violence claims that can be put in the context of religious differences seem to have the greatest chance of success, perhaps because the courts do not have to examine the underlying social and cultural context and can simply determine that different interpretations of religious views allow for greater or lesser control of women's behavior.

A woman might also be able to show that she suffered abuse due to her political opinion. Some women have raised feminist views, such as the belief in independence, the belief in the right not to be forced to submit to another's will, and the belief in the right to be free from physical abuse, as the reason a spouse or partner abused them. This approach is more difficult. Domestic violence is seldom perpetrated solely as punishment for specific "bad acts" and is rarely done rationally or predictably, although certain indicators may often be present, such as consumption of alcohol. Generally, it is very difficult to establish with specificity the exact trigger of domestic violence. In the context of asylum, where the actions occurred far away and there are not likely to be witnesses or documents proving the abuse, the burden of proving the facts can be daunting. Nonetheless, at least one U.S.

court found that a woman's husband subjected her to domestic violence because of her political opinion in opposition to his patriarchal views, finding that she established that he beat her only when she expressed opinions or acted in ways that defied his beliefs.

A request for asylum that raises race or nationality as the reason for the spouse's abuse might prevail if she can show that that was the reason her partner abused her. This is not a common approach to domestic violence asylum claims.

The reason for persecution most frequently presented in domestic violence asylum claims is membership in a "particular social group." This ground was added to the Refugee Convention because, according to many historians, the Convention was aware that it would not be possible to categorize every individual or group who might ever be in need of international protection. This category is viewed by many as a "catch-all" for claims that might not easily fall under any other ground. Under U.S. law, *social groups* can be defined by a variety of characteristics. For example, certain clans or ethnic groups have been found to constitute a social group, as have members of a family. In order to be convincing for asylum law purposes, a social group must be defined broadly enough that it encompasses more than just the person seeking asylum, yet it must be narrow enough that it is distinguishable from the rest of the population. For example, a group comprising all women in Afghanistan who wear the chador may be seen as too broad, while a group comprising women who refuse to wear the chador in public may be seen as a particular social group.

One position that has been successful in some countries is that women themselves constitute a particular social group. Proponents of this view consider that a fundamental understanding of the discriminatory laws and societal norms that give rise to and condone the persecution of women in the first place lead to the conclusion that women form a "particular social group" for asylum purposes. The failure or refusal of the state to intercede or protect them supports this view: Women are viewed as separate or different from others in the society, less deserving, and as such, unlikely to receive protection under circumstances where other members of that society would.

Established law provides clear criteria for identifying a "particular social group": groups defined by an innate or unchangeable characteristic; individuals who associate voluntarily for reasons so fundamental to their sense of self and human dignity that they should not be forced to change; and groups whose members are associated by a former, unalterable status. U.S. and other courts have determined that the first definition would include sex, or in contemporary terminology, "gender," yet no U.S. court has ever granted asylum to a woman based on her gender alone.

Courts have granted domestic violence asylum claims using the social group category, and the definitions of the social groups have varied widely. One immigration judge found the group to be "Ivorian Muslim women who have suffered spousal abuse at the hands of their husbands and who are perceived as having disgraced their husbands by obtaining a divorce and failing to conform to the subservient role of women in Cote d'Ivoire"; other groups have been defined simply as family members. Although membership in a particular social group is the category most often used when presenting a request for asylum based on domestic violence, because this area of the law is unresolved, requests that can rely on one of the other grounds of persecution may have a greater chance of success.

Conclusion

Following the retraction of the decision in Rodi Alvarado's case, no official precedent exists as of 2006 under U.S. asylum law concerning domestic violence, and although her request remains unresolved as of this writing, claims based on domestic violence have been granted since her case was first presented. Other countries have also given asylum to women fleeing domestic violence, including Spain, the United Kingdom, Canada, Australia, and New Zealand. Yet, the claims of women asylum seekers continue to meet denials due to erroneous interpretations of the refugee definition and a fundamental lack of understanding of applicable human rights norms and relevant country conditions. Many compelling cases of egregious human rights violations have been denied, contrary to controlling law and established norms. The treatment of asylum claims raising gender-based persecution, particularly domestic violence, remains controversial and uncertain. The law has moved both forward and backward, and the final outcome is far from determined.

PAMELA GOLDBERG

See also **Africa: Domestic Violence and the Law; Cross-Cultural Examination of Domestic Violence in China and Pakistan; Cross-Cultural Examination of Domestic Violence in Latin America; Greece, Domestic Violence in; Legal Issues for Battered Women; Multicultural Programs for Domestic Batterers;**
Spain, Domestic Violence in; Trinidad and Tobago, Domestic Violence in

References and Further Reading

Amnesty International USA Women's Human Rights and the Stop Violence Against Women Campaign. http://www.amnestyusa.org/women.

Center for Gender and Refugee Studies of Hastings College of the Law. http://cgrs.uchastings.edu.

———. "Gender Asylum Campaigns: Rodi Alvarado's Story," n.d. http://cgrs.uchastings.edu/campaigns/update.php.

Copelon, Rhonda. "Recognizing the Egregious in the Everyday: Domestic Violence as Torture." *Columbia Human Rights Law Review* 25 (1994): 291–367.

Gillespie, Shanyn. "Terror in the Home: The Failure of U.S. Asylum Law to Protect Battered Women and a Proposal." *George Washington Law Review* (2003): 131–158.

Goldberg, Pamela. "Any Place But Home: Asylum in the United States for Women Fleeing Intimate Violence." *Cornell International Law Journal* 26, no. 3 Symposium (1993): 565–604.

———. "Where in the World is There Safety for Me?: Women Fleeing Gender-Based Persecution." In *Women's Rights Human Rights: International Feminist Perspectives,* edited by Julie Peters and Andrea Wolper. London and New York: Routledge, 1995, pp. 345–355.

Hueben, Elizabeth A. "Domestic Violence and Asylum Law: The United States Takes Several Remedial Steps in Recognizing Gender-Based Persecution." *University of Missouri Kansas City Law Review* (2001): 453–469.

Human Rights Watch. "Women's Rights: Domestic Violence." http://www.hrw.org/women/domesticviolence.html.

———. "Women's Rights: Refugee and Internally Displaced Women. Gender-Based Asylum Claims." http://hrw.org/women/refugees.html.

Musalo, Karen. "Matter of R-A-: An Analysis of the Decision and its Implications." *76 Interpreter Releases* (August 9, 1999): 1177–1182.

National Domestic Violence Hotline. "Abuse in America." http://www.ndvh.org/educate/abuse_in_america.html.

Thomas, Dorothy Q., and Michele E. Beasley. "Domestic Violence as a Human Rights Issue." *Albany Law Review* 58 (1995): 1119–1147.

Von Sternberg, Mark. "Battered Women and the Criteria for Refugee Status." *World Refugee Survey* (2000): 40–47.

Cases, Statutes, and International Treaties Cited

1951 Convention Relating to the Status of Refugees, United Nations, *Treaty Series, Vol.* 189, p. 137, and the 1967 Protocol Relating to the Status of Refugees, United Nations, *Treaty Series, Vol.* 606, p. 267.

Declaration on the Elimination of All Forms of Violence Against Women, Adopted by General Assembly Resolution 48/104, 20 December 1993.

Matter of Kasinga, 21 I&N Dec. 357 (BIA 1996).

Matter of R-A-, Int. Dec. 3403 (BIA 1999), withdrawn pursuant to 22 I&N Dec. 906 (A.G. 2001).

Matter of [Name withheld], [number withheld], slip op. at 13 (IJ Oct. 24, 2001) (New York) (Chew, IJ).

Matter of S-A-, 22 I&N Dec. 1328 (BIA 2000) (father beat, imposed isolation, and deprived daughter of education because of his orthodox Muslim views concerning the proper role of women in Moroccan society and because her liberal Muslim beliefs were inconsistent with his own).

The 1980 Refugee Act, as codified in the Immigration and Nationality Act, 8 U.S.C. §§101(a)(42) and §1158; 8 U.S.C. §101(a)(42) and §1157.

United Nations Special Rapporteur on Violence Against Women: Its Causes and Consequences, Preliminary Report. UN Doc E/CN.4/1995/42; Report of the Special Rapporteur on Violence Against Women, Its Causes and Consequences, E/CN.4/1996/53; Report of the Special Rapporteur on Violence Against Women, Its Causes and Consequences, E/CN.4/2003/75.

I

IDENTITY THEORY AND DOMESTIC VIOLENCE

A variety of theories have developed in the study of domestic violence; these theories can be categorized into three general perspectives: (1) individualist, (2) interactional, and (3) sociocultural (Miller et al. 1999). Individualist theories focus on characteristics of the perpetrator or victim of domestic violence, but they do not address how the offender and injured party interact to produce a violent relationship. Interactional theories locate the cause of domestic violence within the interaction. Issues that are examined include how attached actors are to one another, what is exchanged, who has power, and the meanings individuals attribute to themselves and others in the situation. Sociocultural theories address how culture and social norms foster or, alternatively, discourage the use of violence to resolve conflict. For example, the ideology of patriarchy, or the belief that men should be dominant in a society, encourages the use of force by husbands, fathers, brothers, and sons when they do not have power or control in a situation.

A focus on identity theory grows out of symbolic interaction, particularly structural symbolic interaction (Stryker 2002), thus it falls within the second theoretical perspective above. In structural symbolic interaction, society is patterned and organized, and this organization can be seen within any one individual and between individuals as they interact. Within any one person, the self is conceptualized as organized into multiple parts or identities, arranged in an overall hierarchy (Stryker 2002). In the early development of identity theory, each identity was seen as the internal component of a role that one occupied in the social structure; thus individuals had role identities. Role identities were the set of meanings attached to the self while in different roles. Later developments in identity theory opened the analysis of identities to group identities (self-meanings while a member of different groups) and person identities (self-meanings that identified the self as distinct and unique from others) (Burke 2004; Stets and Burke 2000). Identities develop in interaction with others. Persons come to see themselves as they believe others see them. They then act toward other persons, and themselves, based on these meanings.

Identity theory provides an important avenue for theoretical development in domestic violence research because all behavior, including aggression, is rooted in issues of self and identity. To understand aggression, we need to understand the meanings individuals attribute to themselves in a situation, that is, their self-definitions or identities. In all interactions, the goal of individuals is to confirm their identities. When their identities are not confirmed, persons may control others in the situation to make them respond differently in order to confirm their identities. If control does not work, aggression may be used as a last resort to obtain control and, in turn, confirmation of identity (Stets and Burke 2005). Thus, identity theory can help explain domestic violence by showing how a lack of identity confirmation at the individual level is tied to the control process and aggression at the interactive level. This will be discussed in greater detail later. First, identity theory will be reviewed.

Identity Theory

Identity theory has three slightly different versions which focus on different aspects of self and identity (Stets 2006). One of the earliest versions, developed by McCall and Simmons (1978), addresses how identities get accomplished in an interaction through negotiation with others. Individuals may have different interpretations or meanings of the same identity, and they must work out how to resolve seemingly contradictory meanings so that interaction can proceed smoothly. A second version of identity theory is in the work of Stryker and his associates (Stryker 2002; Stryker and Serpe 1982, 1994). They emphasize how the social structure influences the identity that one invokes in a situation. The assumption is that social actors are tied to diverse social networks in society, and these networks are premised on particular identities being maintained within and across situations. Thoits's work (1991, 2003) also has this emphasis. The most active program of research is in the third version of identity theory by Burke and colleagues (Burke 1991, 2004; Burke and Reitzes 1991; Cast, Stets and Burke 1999; Stets and Burke 2000, 2005). These researchers focus on the internal dynamics of the self that emerge when an identity is invoked in a situation, as well as the interactional consequences of those dynamics. In particular, a perceptual control system is offered as a theoretical way of understanding the operations of the self when an identity is activated.

To understand the different versions of identity theory as outlined above, consider how each can be used to explain behavior in a situation. McCall and Simmons would argue that behavior in an interaction is a function of individuals attempting to fit the meanings of their identity with the meanings of the identity of others in the situation. Indeed, every identity in an interaction is understood as it relates to a counter-identity. For example, the identity of 'father' depends on the identity of a child (the counter-identity of the father) to engage in play activity. The identity of 'therapist' needs the identity of a client in order for the therapist to make a diagnosis. The identity of 'teacher' requires the identity of a student so that the teacher may instruct. If conflict emerges when identities interact in a situation, negotiation strategies will be used so that each person's identity can be confirmed and interaction can proceed smoothly.

For Stryker and his associates, behavior in a situation corresponds to a particular identity being salient for the self in the situation. A salient identity is an identity that is high in one's overall hierarchy of identities. More salient identities are more likely to be invoked across situations. Thus, behavior that corresponds to a salient identity will be more likely to be observed over time. An important factor that influences the salience of an identity is how committed one is to the identity. Greater commitment results when a person has deep network ties to a large social network premised on an identity.

Finally, Burke and his colleagues argue that behavior in a situation is an outcome of the relationship between how people see themselves in a situation and the identity standard that is invoked in the situation. When there is correspondence between peoples' views of themselves in a situation and their identity standard view, *identity verification* exists: The meanings of behavior in the situation match the meanings in their identity standard. When there is a lack of identity verification, people behave differently in the situation to restore correspondence between the self-view and the identity standard view. This third perspective, which has come to be labeled *identity control theory,* or ICT (Burke 2004; Stets and Burke 2005, Stets and Tsushima 2001), has theoretically informed the domestic area the most.

Identity Control Theory

Early Developments in ICT

ICT began almost thirty years ago with the development of a way to measure people's identity meanings. Since people choose behaviors whose meanings correspond to those of their identity (Burke and Reitzes 1991), identifying the meanings of an identity for individuals allows for the prediction of the meanings of their behavior. Burke and Tully (1977) developed a method for the measurement of the meanings of people's gender identities. They gave respondents (boys and girls) a set of bipolar adjectives such as "weak strong," "not at all emotional very emotional," and "not at all competitive very competitive." Respondents rated themselves along these adjective pairs to help locate their identity meanings. Then, through a statistical procedure known as discriminant function analysis, the items were selected that best discriminated between the meanings of different groups in the sample, and in Burke and Tully's sample, this represented boys and girls. From this, a measure of gender identity was derived. For example, items that distinguished between girls and boys in Burke and Tully's sample included being soft (versus hard), weak (versus strong), and emotional (versus not emotional).

Since any identity contains multiple meanings, multiple bipolar dimensions can exist for any one identity. In further analyses of gender identity, researchers found that femininity includes the multiple dimensions of noncompetitiveness ("competitive not at all competitive"), passivity ("very active very passive"), and sensitivity of feelings ("feelings not easily hurt feelings easily hurt") (Burke, Stets, and Pirog-Good 1988; Stets and Burke 1996). Additionally, different people can have different meanings for the same identity. For example, while one woman may see herself in feminine terms as described above, another woman may see herself as less feminine and more masculine, as in being more competitive, active, and less sensitive in her feelings. What is important about the Burke-Tully procedure for measuring identities is that it uses the meanings of the individuals in a particular subpopulation to develop a particular identity measure, rather than using the researcher's own view as to the meanings of an identity or the views from another subpopulation.

Domestic Violence Research from Early Developments in ICT

The discovery of a measure of gender identity was important because it helped in the investigation of how gender identity relates to physical and sexual aggression (Burke et al. 1988). The long-standing argument in the domestic violence area has been that violence is consistent with the masculine ideal; men are more likely to behave aggressively as a way of demonstrating their masculinity (Toby 1966). However, no research has actually evidenced this (Rosenbaum 1986). Burke and his colleagues tested this argument in a study of college students (Burke et al. 1988).

A random sample of college students was gathered. Their gender identity was measured using the Burke-Tully method as described above. Respondents' physical and sexual experiences in their dating relationships were gathered. The results revealed that men and women with more feminine gender identities, that is, those who described themselves as noncompetitive, passive, and sensitive in their feelings, were more likely to inflict and sustain both physical and sexual aggression in their dating relationships. In explaining these findings, Burke and his associates (1988) argued that compared with those with more masculine gender identities, those with more feminine gender identities were: (1) more emotionally expressive and (2) more oriented to their dating relationships.

In terms of inflicting sexual aggression, the researchers argued that a greater orientation to the relationship may lead to wanting to be more involved with the other. To obtain greater involvement, more feminine individuals may initiate sexual activity, and if others do not desire this, their need to be more involved, coupled with their emotional excitability, may result in forcing the issue of sex. If their partners resist and individuals who are more feminine ignore this resistance, then their actions become sexual aggression. Similarly, emotional excitability can lead to physical aggression, particularly when individuals desire, but lack, control of a situation. The idea that one loses control and strikes out aggressively to get control is consistent with other theoretical and empirical work, which will be discussed below (Stets and Burke 2005).

Finally, Burke and colleagues (1988) point out that since research reveals that violence is reciprocal—that is, individuals "get what they give"—individuals who are more feminine who inflict sexual and physical aggression will eventually sustain such aggression as well. What is interesting about this study is that it reveals how identity theory can explain not only male aggression but also female aggression. For both genders, it is a more feminine gender identity that helps researchers understand the violence that takes either a sexual or a physical form and is inflicted or sustained by the actors.

Further Developments in ICT

Further developments in identity theory expand on the idea of understanding people's identity meanings and their corresponding behavior by conceptualizing the identity process as a perceptual control system, based on the work of Powers (1973). The theoretical development of identity theory, as it became formulated into ICT, argues that individuals are goal oriented; they are motivated to control perceptions of who they are in a situation so that these perceptions match their identity standard (Burke 1991, 2004). A correspondence between self-perceptions in a situation and identity-standard meanings results in identity verification and positive emotion. Noncorrespondence between self-in-situation meanings and identity-standard meanings results in identity nonverification and negative emotion. This identity control system is described below.

An identity is a set of meanings that are attached to the self. It serves as the reference or standard for a person in situations. When an identity is activated in a situation, a feedback loop is established. This feedback loop has four components:

1. The *identity standard,* or set of meanings defining who one is in a situation
2. *Perceptual input,* or how one sees oneself, which is based in part on directly observing oneself and in part on feedback from others as to how they see the self in the situation
3. The *comparator,* which compares the perceptual input with the identity standard and registers the degree of discrepancy between the two
4. *Output,* or behavior, which is the result of the comparator. Behavior is modified if the comparator signals noncorrespondence between the input and the identity standard.

What is important about the identity process as outlined above is that instead of seeing behavior as strictly guided by self-meanings (the identity standard) or the meanings of self in the situation (perceptual input), behavior is the result of the relationship between identity-standard and self-in-situation meanings. When the comparator registers no discrepancy between perceptions and the standard (a value of zero), this is identity verification, and no change in behavior is needed. As the discrepancy departs from zero and, correspondingly, identity nonverification increases—generally because one's direct observations or feedback from others about the self in the situation do not match identity standard meanings—behavior changes to counteract the discrepancy. The goal is to realign perceptual input with the identity standard.

To illustrate the above, it is helpful to consider how it applies to one's gender identity. A man's self-meanings of masculinity may include being dominant, controlling, and aggressive. If at home he perceives that he is not as dominant, controlling, or aggressive as he feels he should be, or alternatively,

his friends give him this feedback, then there is a discrepancy between his self-in-situation meanings and the identity standard. In response to this discrepancy, he may work harder to be more dominant, controlling, and aggressive and may use violence as the ultimate resource to realign perceptual input with identity-standard meanings.

An important assumption in ICT is that individuals seek situations in which their identities will be verified. They may choose to interact with others who they know will confirm their identities and avoid those who they know will not confirm their identities. They may even "act the part" by dressing a particular way or using a certain style of speech so that others recognize who they are and confirm their identities. When individuals act to verify not only their own identity, but also that of others in the situation, a "mutual verification context" exists (Burke and Stets 1999). Two or more individuals may act to mutually support each other's identities. Disturbances in these situations are countered in order to protect and preserve the identities of the actors, the relationship in which the identities are embedded, and, by extension, the social structure in which the identity ultimately belongs. For example, a married couple often develops a mutual verification context in which each partner not only verifies his or her own spousal identity, but also acts to support and maintain the spouse's identity. In turn, the relationship—and the institution of marriage more broadly—is maintained.

At the individual level, self-verification sustains the belief that one's world is controllable (Swann 1990). As Pinel and Swann (2000, p. 133) have remarked, "Self-verifying evaluations are what the purr of the automobile is to the driver or the roar of the jet engine is to the pilot: a signal that all's as it should be." When others see the self in a verifying manner, it also provides an emotional anchor that leaves one less vulnerable to the slings and arrows of life events. Individuals know who they are, others come to know and support that view, and this keeps individuals on an even keel. These feelings get reverberated at the interactive level. Mutual verification contexts often produce very stable relationships and result in positive emotions and feelings of trust and commitment among individuals (Burke and Stets 1999).

Domestic Violence Research from Recent Developments in ICT

Identity nonverification threatens the maintenance of one's own and others' identities in a situation.

It also threatens people's sense of control over their environment. In response to identity nonverification, individuals may withdraw physically or psychologically from the interaction, may selectively dismiss nonverifying information or selectively recall verifying information, or may work harder in the interaction to counteract disturbances and seek a match between self-perceptions and their identity standard. If, in working harder, they are still unable to obtain identity verification, their sense of control over the environment will diminish further. In turn, they may increase their control over others in the situation so that others will respond in a way that verifies their identity and they regain the perception of control over the environment. Stets and Burke (2005) revealed how control provides the very seeds of domestic violence. They argued that when increased control in the situation fails to achieve identity verification, that is, one cannot get another to verify the self, aggression may be used as a last resort to regain control over the environment and obtain identity verification.

Individuals control others to compensate for a loss of control over the environment (Stets 1993, 1995). Since a major theme in the domestic violence literature during the 1990s has been the relationship between control and aggression (Johnson and Ferraro 2000), Stets and Burke's research attempts to theoretically develop this relationship by showing how it is importantly influenced by the underlying process of identity verification.

Stets and Burke examined couples in the first two years of their marriage in two mid-sized communities in Washington State. They obtained an identity verification measure of each partner's spousal identity by calculating the amount of agreement between an individual's *self*-rating of how he or she should behave with respect to a series of spousal role activities (the spousal identity standard) and how the partner *expected* the person to behave with respect to these spousal role activities. Thus, each partner in the marriage had a self-rating and a rating of how the partner expected the person to behave in terms of the spousal identity. The greater the agreement between the self-rating and the rating of the other, the more there was identity verification for that individual. They also obtained measures of how much control each partner felt that they had over the environment, how much they controlled their partner in the marriage, and how much each was physically aggressive toward the other.

The results provided support for the finding that nonverification of a spousal identity reduced the self's perceived control over the environment.

In turn, the self increased acts of control over the partner. And, heightened control over the partner was associated with acts of aggression toward the partner. Unfortunately, Stets and Burke found that using aggression in an attempt to regain control was disruptive to later self-verification. Specifically, the use of aggression in one year significantly reduced verification of the spousal identity in the following year. Further, aggression ultimately led to a spiral of more aggression, since aggression in one year significantly influenced aggression in subsequent years. In this way, identity disruptions at the individual level threaten established relationships at the interactive level by influencing controlling and aggressive behavior, and such controlling and aggressive behavior jeopardizes stable social structural arrangements such as the institution of marriage.

Stets and Burke found that the link between identity verification, control, and aggression was more likely to predict minor aggression than severe aggression. Since minor aggression is less likely to cause serious injury compared with severe aggression, individuals may be more likely to use minor aggression as a strategy to regain control when it is lost. Severe aggression may be more likely to be interpreted as deviant, if not criminal, and its use may lead to the irretrievable breakdown of a relationship. Given the lesser costs associated with minor aggression, individuals may be more inclined to use it as a last resort.

In general, the findings of Stets and Burke reveal that if interaction is to continue smoothly, each person must act to verify not only his or her own identity, but the identity of the other in the situation. When identity verification is not forthcoming and a person engages in maladaptive behaviors such as controlling or behaving aggressively toward the partner in order to coerce identity verification, the person will find it even more disruptive and costly to the relationship both in the short and in the long run.

Future Research

ICT is a rapidly developing area of study (Stets and Burke 2005), which includes application to domestic violence research. More research is needed to investigate whether the identity process can help one understand not only dating aggression and marital aggression but also child abuse, sibling violence, parental abuse, and elder abuse. Perhaps it might even help in the understanding of violence between strangers. To the extent that another person does not confirm who one is, one will work harder to obtain that confirmation, although the person may work harder for confirmation from someone with whom he or she is close, whose opinion matters, and with whom he or she will likely interact in the future.

If a lack of identity verification fosters increasing control over another and, in turn, leads to aggression, intervention strategies may need to be developed that teach individuals alternative ways of responding to nonverification. Since part of the identity processes within ICT are psychological, having to do with the self, including self-perceptions and others' perceptions of the self, intervention may involve therapeutic efforts to understand the inner workings of the self. For example, one may be misinterpreting others' feedback. Others may be verifying one's identity but the self sees it as nonverifying, perhaps as a result of low self-esteem. Thus, these misinterpretations would need to be identified. Alternatively, others may be ignoring the self's display of behaviors that correspond to his or her identity standard such that the self may have to point out the consistency to his or her audience in a clear way. Finally, nonverification feedback from others may imply that the self needs to change its identity standards. This change would likely occur at a very slow rate, if the person were open to it.

Conclusion

In general, ICT is a coherent, cumulative, and ever-developing theory in social psychology that shows promise in explaining domestic violence. By focusing on the internal dynamics of the self as an identity control system, and the relation between those dynamics and the interactional dynamics in interpersonal settings, one can study how disrupted identities in situations produce aggression in interaction. The key is identifying the mechanisms that disrupt the identity process and finding ways to minimize the effects of these disruptions so that individuals do not resort to aggression.

JAN E. STETS and SHELLEY N. OSBORN

See also **Attachment Theory and Domestic Violence; Coercive Control; Exchange Theory; Feminist Theory; Social Learning Theory and Family Violence; Victim-Blaming Theory**

References and Further Reading

Burke, Peter J. "Identity Processes and Social Stress." *American Sociological Review* 56 (1991): 836–849.

———. "Identities and Social Structure: The 2003 Cooley-Mead Award Address." *Social Psychology Quarterly* 67 (2004): 5–15.

Burke, Peter J., and Donald C. Reitzes. "The Link between Identity and Role Performance." *Social Psychology Quarterly* 44 (1981): 83–92.

———. "An Identity Theory Approach to Commitment." *Social Psychology Quarterly* 54 (1991): 239–251.

Burke, Peter J., and Jan E. Stets. "Trust and Commitment through Self-Verification." *Social Psychology Quarterly* 62 (1999): 347–366.

Burke, Peter J., Jan E. Stets, and Maureen Pirog-Good. "Gender Identity, Self-Esteem, and Physical and Sexual Abuse in Dating Relationships." *Social Psychology Quarterly* 51 (1988): 272–285.

Burke, Peter J., and Judy Tully. "The Measurement of Role/Identity." *Social Forces* 55 (1977): 881–897.

Cast, Alicia D., Jan E. Stets, and Peter J. Burke. "Does the Self Conform to the Views of Others?" *Social Psychology Quarterly* 62 (1999): 68–82.

Johnson, Michael P., and Kathleen J. Ferraro. "Research on Domestic Violence in the 1990s: Making Distinctions." *Journal of Marriage and the Family* 62 (2000): 948–963.

McCall, George J., and J. L. Simmons. *Identities and Interactions.* New York: Free Press, 1978.

Miller, JoAnn Langley, Dean D. Knudsen, and Stacey Copenhaver. "Family Abuse and Violence." In *Handbook of Marriage and the Family,* edited by Marvin B. Sussman, Suzanne K. Steinmetz, and Gary W. Peterson. New York: Plenum Press, 1999, 705–741.

Pinel, Elizabeth C., and William B. Swann, Jr. "Finding the Self through Others: Self-Verification and Social Movement Participation." In *Self, Identity, and Social Movements,* edited by Sheldon Stryker, Timothy J. Owens, and Robert W. White. Minneapolis: University of Minnesota Press, 2000, 132–152.

Powers, William T. *Behavior: The Control of Perception.* Chicago: Aldine Publishing, 1973.

Rosenbaum, Alan. "Of Men, Macho, and Marital Violence." *Journal of Family Violence* 1 (1986): 121–129.

Stets, Jan E. "Control in Dating Relationships." *Journal of Marriage and the Family* 55 (1993): 673–685.

———. "Job Autonomy and Control over One's Spouse: A Compensatory Process." *Journal of Health and Social Behavior* 36 (1995): 244–258.

———. "Identity Theory." In *Contemporary Social Psychological Theories,* edited by Peter J. Burke. Stanford, CA: Stanford University Press, 2006, chapter 5.

Stets, Jan E., and Peter J. Burke. "Gender, Control, and Interaction." *Social Psychology Quarterly* 59 (1996): 193–220.

———. "Identity Theory and Social Identity Theory." *Social Psychology Quarterly* 63 (2000): 224–237.

———. "Identity Verification, Control, and Aggression in Marriage." *Social Psychology Quarterly* 68 (2005a): 160–178.

———. "New Directions in Identity Control Theory." *Advances in Group Processes* 22 (2005b): 43–64.

Stets, Jan E., and Teresa Tsushima. "Negative Emotion and Coping Responses within Identity Control Theory." *Social Psychology Quarterly* 64 (2001): 283–295.

Stryker, Sheldon. *Symbolic Interactionism: A Social Structural Version.* Caldwell, NJ: Blackburn Press, 2002.

Stryker, Sheldon, and Richard T. Serpe. "Commitment, Identity Salience, and Role Behavior: A Theory and

Research Example." In *Personality, Roles, and Social Behavior,* edited by William Ickes and Eric S. Knowles. New York: Springer-Verlag, 1982, 199–218.

———. "Identity Salience and Psychological Centrality: Equivalent, Overlapping, or Complementary Concepts?" *Social Psychology Quarterly* 57 (1994): 16–35.

Swann, William B., Jr. "To Be Adored or to Be Known? The Interplay of Self-Enhancement and Self-Verification." In *Handbook of Motivation and Cognition,* edited by E. Tory Higgins and Richard M. Sorrentino. New York: Guilford, 1990, 408–450.

Thoits, Peggy A. "On Merging Identity Theory and Stress Research." *Social Psychology Quarterly* 54 (1991): 101–112.

———. "Personal Agency in the Accumulation of Multiple Role-Identities." In *Advances in Identity Theory and Research,* edited by Peter J. Burke, Timothy J. Owens, Richard T. Serpe, and Peggy A. Thoits. New York: Kluwer Academic/Plenum, 2003, 179–194.

Toby, Jackson. "Violence and the Masculine Ideal: Some Qualitative Data." *Annual American Academic Political Social Science* 364 (1966): 623–631.

INCEST

According to the U.S. Department of Justice, a rape occurs every ninety seconds somewhere in the United States. Of those cases, fewer than half are reported to the police. Current statistics also suggest that one out of four females will be sexually abused within their first eighteen years of life. Approximately 75 percent of those cases will involve individuals who are sexually abused by someone in their own family.

Sexual relations between two family members (excluding husband/wife) is called *incest*. Since biblical times, incest has been documented to exist, and today it is suggested that it is one of the most underreported and least discussed crimes in America (Wyatt et al. 1999). For clarity of law, a person is guilty of incest if he/she knowingly marries, cohabitates with, or has sexual intercourse with an ancestor, a descendant, a sibling of the whole or half blood, an uncle, aunt, niece, or nephew of the whole blood (Goldstein 1999). Since incest is a topic of international taboo, it often remains concealed by the victim because of guilt, shame, or fear of further and more severe abuse by their attacker. Therefore, these victims rarely receive help in ending their abuse. In families experiencing domestic violence, it is not unusual to discover incidents of incest.

Categories of Incest

Many cases of incest (or familiar sexual abuse) involve children. Those categories of incest are *molestation, rape,* and *assault,* based upon the degree of harm to the child (Mayer 1983). In these categories, incest may include not only intercourse, but also the fondling and sexual petting of a child by an abuser. In a majority of these cases, the child does not suffer physical signs of abuse such as vaginal tears or a bleeding rectum; however, the abused child is still left with feelings of betrayal and emotional scars (McCabe 2003).

The first category of incest, child molestation, may occur without the physical act of intercourse. A child is fondled or touched in a manner or location that is uncomfortable to the child or petted by an adult who is thus sexually aroused by the thought of a sexual relationship with a child. Molestation occurs more often than assault or rape in cases of child incest. Unfortunately, molestation cases, because of their lack of physical evidence, are the most difficult category to identify or prosecute. In addition, without eyewitness testimony or a confession by the perpetrator, law enforcement is at a major disadvantage in the investigation of these cases (McCabe 2003). Therefore, it is not unusual for incest cases of molestation to continue without penalty or the punishment of the perpetrator.

The second category of child incest is rape. A rape is sexual intercourse against one's will or by force. An incestuous rape, just as a nonincestuous one, contains three elements: anger, power, and sexuality. Perpetrators of such actions often rape as a means of expressing anger and rage. The goal of these perpetrators is often not to harm their victims (as they would like the relationships to continue), but to maintain power and control over the victims and to achieve sexual gratification through rape.

When a rape occurs the child has no control over the situation. In addition, during the time period (perhaps years) in which the sexual abuse is occurring, it is not uncommon for children to also experience both physical and emotional abuse. Undoubtedly, the more violent the encounter, the more harm there is to the child both physically and emotionally. Some research suggests that individuals, mainly children, are damaged more by the physical and emotional abuses than by the sexual abuse; however, sexual abuse at the hands of a family member is very traumatic for a child victim. The rape of a child by someone the child should look toward for protection is most damaging. Not only has this person sexually abused the child, but the force through which the rape occurred deems this the most violent of actions.

The third category of child incest is assault. An assault may involve intercourse; however, the intercourse does not involve the physically forced intercourse of rape (Mayer 1983). It is within this category of incest that defense attorneys portray the child as the "willing" victim. Since the child did not resist the abuse, it must have been consensual; therefore, the child is not a victim. In these cases, the child probably does not have the physical injuries associated with a violent rape, but the emotional scars of victimization remain (McCabe 2003). Incestuous assaults of children may occur willingly due to drugs, alcohol, or the ignorance of the children, or because they feel that their parent would never cause them harm. Historically, parents have had control over their children, and when they tell the children to do something, the children do it. It is in these cases of incest that parents urge their children to participate in the sexual activity, and the activity continues until the children mature physically and are no longer perceived as "attractive" by their perpetrators, or the children themselves end the incestuous relationship. Regardless of their "willingness" to participate in a sexual relationship with a family member, the action is still identified as incest and is still illegal.

Relationships

The most commonly discussed incestuous relationship is that of father and child, typically a daughter. In fact, quite often the public will become so focused on the father–daughter relationship that it will fail to recognize sexual relationships between other relatives as incest (Crosson-Tower 2002). In the overwhelming majority of father–daughter incestuous relationships, the father is the perpetrator and the daughter is the victim; however, there have been cases in which the daughter was the aggressor.

Researchers suggest that in order for the father to justify or lower his inhibitions, he will often distort the role of the child in order to rationalize the sexual encounter (Crosson-Tower 1999). The child, in most cases the daughter, takes on a role other than a child in the family. In some cases, the mother is absent from the home and the daughter assumes the roles of the mother, e.g., housekeeper, cook, caretaker. In these cases, it is not unusual for the daughter to also assume the roles of wife and lover to the father of the household.

There are also those researchers who suggest that sexual relations between a father and a child are a way for the father to display his authority over the family. Fathers who engage in incest with their daughters are attempting to maintain a position of power within the household (McCabe 2003). In these cases, daughters are viewed as the property of the fathers; therefore, the fathers have the right to use their daughters as they desire and for as long as the daughters remain under their roofs.

Incest between a father and a daughter is just one form of parent/child incest. There also exist cases of father–son incest, with quite often the same dynamics of power and control, perpetrator and victim. However, with the stigma often associated with homosexuality, father–son incest is even less likely to be reported than father–daughter incest. Sons, who may themselves question their own sexuality, will rarely report victimization through father–son incest, as they themselves are often aroused during the encounter and therefore perceive (in their minds) that they were a willing participant. It is in these cases that the sons will remain silent. With less of a chance of being reported, son victims of incest also have less of a chance to receive assistance in addressing and ending the abuse. It is not quite clear how or why one father can comfort his child in his/her bed after a nightmare, while another father upon entering the child's bedroom becomes sexually excited; however, the distinctions do exist, and the cases of father–child incest are common in the United States and worldwide (McCabe 2003).

Another form of parent/child incest occurs between mother and child. Historically, women are not considered as perpetrators of sexual crimes, much less of a crime such as incest; however, mothers also engage in sex with their children. Unfortunately, a mother who has initiated sex with her child would go not only unreported, but unrecognized by many in society. Mothers are, for the most part, the major caretakers of their children. In the day-to-day activities of child rearing, it is assumed that mothers will have formed close and intimate relationships with their children. Mothers diaper, bathe, and dress their children; therefore, the touching of a nude child is perceived as loving and normal; certainly it is not perceived as a sexual encounter. It is usually within her role of caregiver that a mother often begins her sexual relationship with her child. In fact, a mother perpetrating incest may easily "mask" the activity under the role of mothering, and the incest may begin at a very early age and continue to be unrecognized for years. The mother is in the most advantageous position to be a perpetrator of incest.

Attempted explanations of mother–child incest mirror those provided for father–child incest, including a history of the parent herself having been a victim of incest as a child. In addition, it is suggested that mothers may initiate a sexual relationship with their male children in response to sexual rejection from an adult male (perhaps the child's father). The mother, still wishing to maintain a relationship with her selected adult male partner, may choose his offspring as a substitute. Although unexpected and quite often unrecognized, sexual abuse between mothers and their children does occur more often than is perceived by the public (Crosson-Tower 2002). The mother, the caretaker, can be the abuser.

Another form of incest is sibling incest. Although parents or guardians are presumed to be the perpetrators of incest, some researchers suggest that the brother–sister sexual relationship is the most common form of incest (Wiehe 1997). This form of incest involves sexual relations beyond age-appropriate exploration in that an older sibling, who often differs significantly in age or by virtue of his or her power and resources, is the perpetrator and the younger sibling is most often the victim. What society may label as simply "adolescent exploration" may be terrorizing and traumatic to the victim of sibling incest. It is suggested that sibling incest is one of the worst forms of abuse for a child to overcome. Specifically, since the older sibling often has more knowledge or experience, he/she usually maintains the power and control in the relationship. The younger sibling is defenseless. As the siblings are often forced to remain in the company of each other in the role of babysitters, the incestuous relationships are not only more likely to occur, but also more likely to continue until either the perpetrator or the victim moves out of the household or the victim ends the abuse by reporting it to a third party or confronting the abuser.

Explanations of sibling incest include not only that it is an attempt by one sibling to control or humiliate the other (Laviola 1992), but that because many of these juvenile abusers have been abused themselves, their perpetration of abuse is a way for them to imitate what they had to endure or experience (McCabe 2003). The *cycle of violence* model suggests that children who are abused will become abusers later in life; therefore, it stands to reason that a child who is a victim of incest may mature to be the perpetrator of incest with the younger children that remain in the home.

Indicators of Abuse

In most cases of incest, there are no physical indicators. If the child does not report the abuse immediately after it occurs, any sort of physical evidence is either washed away or healed (McCabe 2003). In addition, most perpetrators of incest do not leave evidence such as sperm, blood, or lacerations in the child's genital area because vaginal or anal penetration usually does not occur. However, there are some clear indicators of incest.

The first indicator of incest is physical evidence that is collected immediately after the incident. Sperm and saliva are just two forms of such physical evidence. Another particularly unfortunate indicator of incest is the presence of a sexually transmitted disease (STD). An STD, especially in young children, will often provide the evidence needed to confirm incest—especially in those cases where the parent (or perpetrator) has the same STD. In addition to physical evidence, a child's preoccupation with touching his/her genital areas may also indicate incest, as the area is perhaps sore or injured or the child has discovered that masturbation of the area provides a feeling of pleasure.

Another indicator of incest is the presence of cuts or bruises on the child that are suspicious, either in shape or location. In addition and in reaction to the incest, the child may attempt to injure him/herself through drugs, alcohol, self-mutilation, anorexia, bulimia, or suicide.

Finally, children with very poor hygiene may be victims of incest. In attempts to make themselves less attractive to their perpetrator, they will often refuse to bathe, hoping that their dirty appearance or smell will discourage future sexual assaults (McCabe 2003).

In cases where there is no physical evidence (the majority), one must consider *behavioral* evidence or indicators. Often a child who is a victim of incest will provide hints of that abuse through actions and behaviors instead of physical indicators. In particular, such a child may avoid others (especially adults), appear angry, anxious, or depressed or display a drastic personality change. The victim of incest has been betrayed by an adult to whom the child entrusted his/her safety and security. Hence the child is hesitant and perhaps even fearful of any other relationship that might occur with an adult (McCabe 2003).

The child victim of incest may also experience problems at school in terms of attention deficits, slow progress, and showing disrespect for authority figures. It is not unusual for the victim of incest to use sexual language or descriptions of sexual acts in conversations that are not considered age appropriate. For example, a first grader might discuss sexual intercourse and include the mechanics of position and ejaculation. As noted previously, it is not unusual for children who are victims of incest to imitate their abusers and sexually abuse other children.

Finally, some child victims of incest demonstrate fear in performing everyday activities or fear of world dangers, as well as a fear of homosexuality (more the case for male victims) and the fear of being perceived as "damaged goods" (more the case for female victims). These children often appear nervous or stressed out and express the desire to be alone or in a quiet, noninteracting environment. These victims of incest do not trust others and, in many cases, do not love themselves. The more frequent and severe the incest, the more obvious and apparent the behavioral indicators are to the observer (McCabe 2003).

Progression of Sexual Abuse

In attempting to understand the dynamics behind the incest, once must first consider the conditions that exist, including the state of the abuser's mind, before the seduction of a child. Finkelhor (1984) suggested that before a sexual assault of a child occurs, there is a progression of stages (or conditions), which must be completed. At each one of the stages, there is a progression of events that must occur; if this progression is interrupted or terminated, then the likelihood of abuse (at least for this encounter) is forfeited. With incest, these progressions also occur. The four preconditions to a sexual assault are:

- Precondition I: Motivation to sexually abuse
- Precondition II: Overcoming internal inhibitors
- Precondition III: Factors predisposing to overcome external inhibitors

- Precondition IV: Factors predisposing to overcome a child's resistance (Finkelhor 1984).

In the first precondition, the focus is on the perpetrator and the victim. The two middle preconditions focus on elements other than the perpetrator or the victim. The last precondition focuses solely on the victim or child.

In precondition I, the perpetrator or abuser attempts to relate to the child on an emotional level. In this stage, the child is seen as the source of sexual satisfaction for the abuser. In many cases, other sources of sexual satisfaction (such as adults) are not available to the perpetrator, and the child is a suitable alternative (Finkelhor 1984). Or the child may be precisely the target of the adult's desire. It is during this stage that many perpetrators perceive the everyday actions of the child to be seductive (Crosson-Tower 1999). A child who sits on the perpetrator's lap or smiles at the perpetrator, which is common in the family environment, is perceived as "flirting" with the soon-to-be abuser; thus, the abuser responds with attention to the child. In this stage, the adult is socially comfortable. Perhaps because of his inability to relate to adults on a social or emotional level, the adult enjoys the company of children more than that of adults. The child welcomes the attention from the adult, who may in other cases fail to acknowledge the child.

In precondition II, the perpetrator must overcome internal inhibitors—i.e., his consciousness that sex with children is wrong—before the sexual abuse will occur (Finkelhor 1984). It is during this stage that alcohol, drugs, and perhaps pornography will be introduced to the child within the family setting, to reduce her/his inhibitions. Pornography's role in the sexual abuse of children has long been discussed (McCabe 2000). Quite often a child will be shown adult or child pornography by his/her sexual predator as a means of introducing the child to the "normalness" of adult and child sexual relations. The child, who is inherently curious about his/her body and feelings of sexuality, may view the materials while masturbating or while allowing the perpetrator to sexually stimulate them. Through the use of alcohol, drugs, or the viewing of child pornography, the child is sexually aroused and the abuser's internal inhibitors are overcome. The perpetrator may now focus on overcoming the child's resistance.

It is under precondition III that the perpetrator must overcome the external inhibitors of a child (Finkelhor 1984). The goal is to have a willing or at least nonresisting child victim. Before abuse will occur, the child must consent to the sexual activity. In many cases, this means that the child's internal inhibitors or the perpetrator's external inhibitors must be eliminated. Those external inhibitors may be the amount of supervision of the child or the child's social support system. Oftentimes, abusers (including family members) will select their child victims not simply based upon their physical characteristics, but also based upon their availability (McCabe 2003). A child who is unsupervised during a great proportion of the day and/or evening is an available child. Such a child who chose to report the abuse would have few options in doing so, and no adults around to take the report seriously; therefore, not only are the children vulnerable from an approachability/availability perspective, they are also vulnerable to repeat victimization from a reactive perspective. A child with little adult supervision, other than that of the perpetrator, is an ideal child for a sexual assault.

Precondition IV is the final stage prior to the sexual abuse of the child. Here, the factors that eliminate the child's resistance are the focus of the perpetrator (Finkelhor 1984). Whether creating an environment of powerlessness or a trusting relationship between the perpetrator and the child, the abuser must develop an atmosphere to eliminate the child's resistance to sexual activities with the adult. As the abuser places himself in a pseudo-caretaker role for the child, he becomes indispensable in that child's eyes. In turn, the child wants to please the adult and, in most cases, will do all that is asked by the abuser. Once this stage has been satisfied, the child's sexual assault will likely occur.

Incestuous Families

Research suggests that families that are involved with incest often share similar characteristics or traits (Crosson-Tower 2002; Sgroi 1982). In considering the physical characteristics of a family, Finkelhor (1980) and Russell (1984) suggest that incest is more likely to occur in large families. Explanations of this phenomenon include the proximity of many family members within a limited space, the lack of child supervision, and a cultural norm of incest within the family.

The social characteristics of a family are also related to an increased risk for incestuous relationships. Specifically, parents of incest victims are often either absent or uninvolved in their children's lives (Crosson-Tower 1999). With parent(s) absent for most of the child's life, the child is not only unsupervised, but also likely to be on his or her

own at an early age. This vulnerability, as discussed earlier, increases the risk of incest. In today's society, half of all parents are unavailable to child victims of incest because of death, alcoholism, or psychosis.

Another social characteristic of incestuous families is limited communications among family members on all subjects, but especially the subject of sex. Parents may have extremely rigid attitudes toward sex that lead to little discussion or few questions from their children about sex or sexuality (deYoung 1982). A child who has such questions may go to others (instead of their major caretaker) for answers.

Finally, some parents acknowledge the reports of incest but blame the victim rather than the perpetrator (Laviola 1992). In the minds of some parents, the victims themselves play an active role in the incestuous relationship (especially if the relationship was between the child and the parent's adult partner); therefore, the child is thought to have seduced the adult and is to blame for the encounter, and the protestations of the child are not believed by the parents (Wiehe 1997). The incest is likely to continue until the child victim ends the relationship.

Siblings who are not the victims of incest will often not provide aid to the victim. In fact, many siblings of incest victims are resentful of the attention given to the abused child by the perpetrator and often are among those who blame the incest on the victim—due to jealousy—without ascribing any blame to the perpetrator (Crosson-Tower 1999). In other cases, the nonvictimized sibling will not report the activity for fear of "breaking up" the family. In the sibling's mind, an incestuous family is better than none at all. In general, incestuous families are dysfunctional and either discount or ignore the incest (Laviola 1992); thus, the abuse continues.

Finally, like domestic violence, incest is also a subject not openly discussed by those involved. In fact, it is not unusual that families involved in incest are also involved in domestic violence, with the same wall of silence used to cover both. Again, the victims are generally the only ones capable of ending the abuse.

The consequences of any form of abuse vary from victim to victim. Although the physical wounds may heal in a short time, the healing of mental and emotional scars involves a much longer process, and some victims are never able to recover and address the consequences of their abuse. Research shows that sexual abuse at the hands of a family member is, in many cases, more damaging in terms of long-term consequences than is sexual abuse at the hands of a stranger (Gully et al. 1999).

A family's responsibilities include protecting, loving, and offering support for its members in both joyous times and times of crisis. It is the parents' job to raise and protect their children. The parents should provide an environment of trust. When that bond of trust is broken by incest, the family structure begins to fall apart. The repercussions of incest are both short-term and long-lasting, damaging and distorting the child victim's perception of family and other personal relationships.

KIMBERLY A. MCCABE and JOANNE M. YEDNOCK

See also **Animal Abuse: The Link to Family Violence; Bullying and the Family; Child Abuse: A Global Perspective; Child Sexual Abuse; Ritual Abuse–Torture in Families; Sibling Abuse**

References and Further Reading

Crosson-Tower, C. *Understanding Child Abuse and Neglect,* 4th ed. Boston: Allyn and Bacon, 1999.
———. *When Children Are Abused: An Educator's Guide to Intervention.* Boston: Allyn and Bacon, 2002.
deYoung, M. *The Sexual Victimization of Children.* Jefferson, NC: McFarland, 1982.
Finkelhor, D. "Sex among Siblings: A Survey of the Prevalence, Variety and Effects." *Archives of Sexual Behavior* 9 (1980): 171–194.
Goldstein, R. *Child Abuse and Neglect: Cases and Materials.* St. Paul, MN: West, 1999.
Gully, K. J., H. Britton, K. Hansen, K. Goodwin, and J. L. Nope. "A New Measure for Distress During Child Sexual Abuse Examinations: The Genital Examination Distress Scale." *Child Abuse and Neglect* 23 (1999): 61–70.
Laviola, M. "Effects of Older Brother–Younger Sister Incest: A Study of the Dynamics in 17 Cases." *Child Abuse and Neglect* 16 (1992): 409–421.
Mayer, A. *Incest: A Treatment Manual for Therapy with Victims, Spouses, and Offenders.* Holmes Beach, FL: Learning Publications, 1983.
McCabe, K. A. "Child Pornography and the Internet." *Social Science Computer Review* 18 (2000): 73–76.
———. *Child Abuse and the Criminal Justice System.* New York: Peter Lang Publishing, 2003.
Russell, D. *Secret Trauma: Incest in the Lives of Girls and Women.* New York: Basic Books, 1986.
Sgroi, S. *Handbook of Clinical Intervention in Child Sexual Abuse.* Lexington, MA: Lexington Books, 1982.
Wiehe, V. R. *Sibling Abuse: Hidden Physical, Emotional, and Sexual Trauma,* 2nd ed. Thousand Oaks, CA: Sage, 1997.
Wyatt, G. E., T. B. Loeb, B. Solis, J. V. Carmona, and G. Romero. "The Prevalence and Circumstances of Child Sexual Abuse: Changes across a Decade." *Child Abuse and Neglect* 23 (1999): 45–60.

INMATE MOTHERS: TREATMENT AND POLICY IMPLICATIONS

Despite recent laws and policies that have been developed to reduce domestic violence, this serious problem continues to have a significant impact on society that will quite possibly be passed on to future generations. It is currently estimated that two to eight million domestic assaults occur each year (Wallace 1999). More striking is that one-half of all the women in the United States will become victims of battering sometime in their lives. Other indicators also suggest that women are victimized by their partners at a rate five times greater than that for men (Tjaden and Thoennes 2000). In addition, while there is no exact number of children who experience domestic violence directly or indirectly, a national study on family violence estimated

that ten million children are exposed to violence within their families (Onyskiw 2003). This may help explain (at least in part) why female inmates report more often than male inmates higher rates of violence.

National and smaller sampled studies have consistently found that female inmates have significantly higher rates of being victims of physical and sexual abuse as children, as adults, or as both, compared with their male counterparts (Beck 2000; Gable and Johnson 1995; Greenfeld and Snell 1999). In fact, female offenders are more likely to have experienced violence in their lives than the general population (Beck 2000). Women who are imprisoned for violent crimes are also more likely to report abuse as well. In examining histories of abused women, some studies have found that they come to the attention of the justice system earlier than nonabused women. For example, a study conducted in Oregon found that 50 percent of the abused women had been arrested by the age of fifteen compared with only 11 percent of the nonabused women who had been arrested. In addition, the Oregon study found that a large portion (60 percent) of these abused women had run away at least four times compared with only 15 percent of the nonabused women who reported running away (Oregon Department of Corrections 1993, as cited in Pollock 1998). In examining female offenders further, one characteristic is particularly noteworthy: 70 percent are mothers of minor children.

Similar to the general population of female offenders, inmate mothers also have higher rates of physical and sexual abuse as compared with inmate fathers and the general female population (Mumola 2000). Inmate mothers come from extremely troubled family backgrounds that are also reflected in their adult lives. For many, there is a substantial family history of violence, neglect, incarceration, and addiction, which, among other consequences, significantly influences the likelihood of the women continuing the cycle of violence. Indeed, one study found that 85 percent of the women had been physically abused during their childhoods and that more than a quarter of these women had been placed in foster care (Dalley 2002). More significantly, 46 percent of these same women reported becoming involved in abusive relationships later in their adult lives (Dalley 2002). For many inmate mothers, life prior to imprisonment is so uncertain and at times so dangerous that imprisonment is viewed as a safety valve (Ferraro and Moe 2003). This is especially the case for those women in battering situations who feel that there is no protection from their abusers.

The negative consequences of violence on children's physical and emotional well-being can be devastating (Brazelton 1992; Earls and Reiss 1994; Wallace 1999; Widom 1996). An important and recently recognized phenomenon is that regardless of whether children witness family violence or actually experience the abuse firsthand, they are more likely to grow up and react to their own children or spouses in the similar ways. Thus, childhood survivors of domestic violence situations develop predispositions toward violence in their own families and are at risk of becoming either victims or batterers as adults (Wallace 1999; Widom 1996).

The critical developmental disruptions and impairments that accompany child abuse and neglect set in motion a series of events that increase the likelihood of children failing to achieve important developmental milestones, which in turn may result in developing psychopathologies (Wolfe 1999). Although not all children who are abused will develop psychopathologies, they are clearly at a higher risk than nonabused children (Cicchetti, Ganiban, and Barnett 1990). Children who are physically and sexually abused often have "irreparably damaged self-esteems" and find it difficult to trust anyone again (Hart and Brassard 1987). These children often exhibit a wide range of behaviors and emotional problems, including sleep disturbances, compulsive behaviors, suicidal thoughts or gestures, phobias, and other emotional disorders. This was the situation of many of the inmate mothers when they were children (and has now become the situation for their own children). Their poor self-esteem and other problems are perpetuated into their adulthoods as they continue the pattern of becoming involved in abusive relationships with their partners (Gable and Johnston 1995; Pollock 1998). In fact, most studies have found that at least one-quarter to one-third of the women who reported being physically and sexually abused as children also reported that they were subsequently involved in abusive relationships as adults (Beck 2000; Greenfeld and Snell 1999; Mumola 2000). This suggests that a similar prevalent cycle of abuse and violence that exists among the general population also exists generationally among inmate mothers.

Based on the reality that a history of domestic violence begets domestic violence, researchers have begun to study the lives of the inmate mothers' children. Studies have consistently found that the children of inmate mothers also have similar traumatic experiences and disrupted lives, much the same as the women did when they were children. More recent research is also finding that the children's problems are not the direct result of imprisonment but rather existed prior to maternal incarceration (Dalley 2002; Siegel 2005). Many of these children's problems include witnessing or being subjected to violence and neglect. They also often have problems with learning, delinquency, physical health, and mental health (Bloom and Steinhart 1993; Dalley 2003; DeAngelis 2001; Gable and Johnston 1995). A further concern for these children is that when they are emotionally and physically cut off from their mothers, they may be more prone to repeating destructive family patterns (i.e., domestic violence, crime, and substance abuse) in their own adult relationships (Gable and Johnston 1995; Laird 1981).

In addition to confronting their daily problems, children whose mothers are imprisoned are more likely to have to adjust to new homes, new schools, and new parenting/caretaking styles than children whose fathers are imprisoned. Most often, female offenders are single mothers whose spouses or significant others are absent, which leaves these mothers with few choices in selecting caregivers for their children during their imprisonment (Mumola 2000). Most likely, the women's children are cared for by an extended family member, and many children are later placed in the foster care system. As experts have noted, however, placement in the foster care system does not guarantee stability (Gable and Johnston 1995). Children may continue to move from one foster home to another for a variety of reasons. Most studies suggest that these children are difficult to manage because of their often complicated problems and the lack of foster parents who are trained in dealing with these types of problems (Dalley 2003; Pollock 1998; Siegel 2005). Often these children do not receive the long-term treatment and support they need in order to live healthy, productive adult lives. On the other hand, fathers who are imprisoned have more options for child care. Typically their children live with their mothers, stepmothers, girlfriends, or extended family members and are less likely to be placed in foster care (Mumola 2000).

Clearly, these problems will not disappear upon the inmate mother's release from prison. If anything, the problems will continue to exist and more than likely will increase, thus making the mother–child reunification extremely difficult. Studies have found that for many women and their children, the reunification is a terrible experience. The harsh reality confronting female offenders and their children is that most of them will be reunited with few (if any) new skills to maintain a healthy relationship (Carp and Schade 1992; Morash, Bynum and Koons 1998). The majority of inmate mothers report that reunification is an extremely stressful time. Much of the stress during the initial weeks of release is related to finding employment, housing, and day care (Dalley 2000). Often these women have difficulty managing the daily and necessary routines (working, parenting, and maintaining their household). More importantly, though, they must also focus on maintaining their sobriety and not developing relationships with abusive men.

Studies have found that many of these women have a tendency to return to their former lifestyles, either by reuniting with former abusive partners or developing new abusive relationships (Gable and Johnston 1995; Pollock 1998). Compounding these problems is that they must parent often angry, depressed, and resentful children who are distrustful and fearful that their mothers will again abandon them because of drug use and further criminality.

Female offenders need to be taught self-sufficiency, responsibility, and the development of healthy interpersonal relationships in order to live crime-free, productive lives (Carp and Schade 1992). However, in the prison's artificial world, the inmate mothers are not provided with these necessary life skills and are told what to do, when to sleep, and when to eat. They have no abusive relationships to deal with, children to parent, or concerns regarding employment, housing, or maintaining their sobriety. Without a focus on the real world and its temptations, prison necessarily continues to be a false world destined to encourage recidivism (Dalley 2002).

Despite the fact that numerous studies have documented that inmate mothers have significantly different problems compared with inmate fathers, few prison programs focus on treatment addressing the cyclical nature of domestic violence, abuse, addiction, and imprisonment. But more importantly postrelease programs for these women who were previously in oppressive and controlling environments often reinforce those dynamics. As such, prisons (at least at the end of the prison term) should develop an alternative system that fosters independence and the development of essential life skills. Postrelease programs such as these are the weakest link in all the formal systems today (criminal justice, social services, and mental health).

Clearly, incarcerated and formerly incarcerated women and their children need a variety of services from very complicated and bureaucratic agencies, which often creates more havoc and frustration for these families. Moreover, the availability of services and programs for these mothers and their children varies depending on the political climate in the particular state and the attitude that the community has toward prisoners in general but particularly toward female offenders who have children (Gable and Johnston 1995). In a society that views women as the primary caregivers of children, women with a history of incarceration are usually scorned for placing themselves in a position of not being able to raise their children. Coupled with this is the level of understanding that the correctional system and social service agencies have regarding the particular needs of this population. The most compelling finding of all the studies is that the majority of inmate mothers are reunited with their children, though many of the mothers will not be able to succeed in living independent, nonviolent, crime- and drug-free lives or maintain stable relationships with their children. Thus, if the criminal justice system continues to use the current punishment practices instead of establishing interventions that are actually designed to prevent reincarcerations, the continuation of the cycle of violence, addiction, and imprisonment will unfortunately remain an inevitable reality (Carp and Schade 1992; Dalley, 2002; Morash, Bynum, and Koons 1998).

LANETTE P. DALLEY

See also **Battered Women, Clemency for; Battered Women Who Kill: An Examination; Children Witnessing Parental Violence; Cycle of Violence; Social, Economic, and Psychological Costs of Violence**

References and Further Reading

Beck, A. J. *Prisoners in 1999* (NCJ 183476). Washington DC: Bureau of Justice Statistics, U.S. Department of Justice, 2000.

Bloom, B., and D. Steinhart. *Why Punish the Children?* San Francisco: National Council on Crime and Delinquency, 1993.

Brazelton, T. B. *Touchpoints: Your Child's Emotional and Behavioral Development*. Reading, MA: Addison-Wesley, 1992.

Carp, S., and L. Schade. "Tailoring Facility Programming to Suit Female Offenders' Needs." *Corrections Today* 54, no. 6 (1992): 152–159.

Cicchetti, D., J. Ganiban, and D. Barnett. "Contributions from the Study of High Risk Populations to Understanding the Development of Emotion Regulation." In *The Development of Emotion Regulation*, edited by K. Dodge and J. Garber. New York: Cambridge University Press, 1990, pp. 1–54.

Dalley, L. "Imprisoned Mothers and Their Children: Their Often Conflicting Legal Rights." *Hamline Journal of Public Law and Policy* 22, no. 1 (2000): 1–43.

———. "Policy Implications Relating to Inmate Mothers and Their Children: Will the Past Be Prologue?" *The Prison Journal* 82, no. 2 (2002): 234–256.

———. "Children of Imprisoned Mothers: What Does the Future Hold?" In *With Justice for All: Minorities and Women in Criminal Justice*, edited by J. Joseph and D. Taylor. Upper Saddle River, NJ: Prentice Hall, 2003, pp. 121–136.

DeAngelis, T. "Punishment of Innocents: Children of Parents Behind Bars." *Monitor on Psychology* 32, no. 5 (2001): 56–59.

Dobash, R. E., and R. Dobash. *Violence Against Wives: A Case Against the Patriarchy*. New York: Free Press, 1979.

Earls, J. E., and A. J. Reiss. *Breaking the Cycle: Predicting and Preventing Crime*. Washington, DC: U.S. Department of Justice, 1994.

Enos, S. *Mothering from the Inside*. Albany: State University of New York Press, 2001.

Ferraro, K. J., and A. M. Moe. "Mothering, Crime, and Incarceration." *Journal of Contemporary Ethnography* 32, no. 1 (2003): 9–40.

Gable, K., and D. Johnston. *Children of Incarcerated Parents*. New York: Lexington Books, 1995.

Greenfeld, L. A., and T. L. Snell. *Women Offenders* (NCJ 175688). Washington DC: Bureau of Justice Statistics, U.S. Department of Justice, 1999.

Hart, S. N., and M. R. Brassard. "A Major Threat to Children's Mental Health. Psychological Maltreatment." *The American Psychologist* 42, no. 2 (1987): 160–165.

Laird, J. "An Ecological Approach to Child Welfare." In *Parents of Children in Placement*, edited by P. A. Sinanoglu and A. N. Maluccio. New York: Child Welfare League of America, 1981, pp. 97–132.

Morash, M., T. Bynum, and B. Koons. *Women Offenders: Programming Needs and Promising Approaches*. Washington, DC: National Institute of Justice, 1998.

Mumola, C. *Special Report: Incarcerated Parents and Their Children* (NCJ 182335). Washington DC: Bureau of Justice Statistics, U.S. Department of Justice, 2000.

Onyskiw, J. E. "Domestic Violence and Children's Adjustment: A Review of Research." In *The Effects of Intimate Partner Violence on Children*, edited by R. A. Geffner, R. S. Igelman, and J. Zellner. New York: Haworth Maltreatment and Trauma Press, 2003, pp. 11–45.

Oregon Department of Corrections. *Childhood Abuse and the Female Inmate*. Unpublished manuscript. Information Services Division, Research and Analysis Unit, 1993.

Pollock, J. *Counseling Female Offenders*. Thousand Oaks, CA: Brooks/Cole, 1998.

Siegel, J. A. *Disrupted Childhoods: The Lives of Female Prisoners' Children*. Unpublished manuscript, 2005.

Straus, M. A., and R. J. Gelles. *Physical Violence in American Families*. New Brunswick, NJ: Transaction Publishers, 1990.

Tjaden, P., and N. Thoennes. *Extent, Nature and Consequences of Intimate Partner Violence: Findings from the National Violence Against Women Survey* (NCJ 181867). Washington, DC: National Institute of Justice and Centers for Disease Control and Prevention, 2000.

Wallace, Harvey. *Family Violence*, 2nd ed. Boston: Allyn and Bacon, 1999.

Widom, C. S. *The Cycle of Violence Revisited: Six Years Later* (NCJ 153272). Washington, DC: U.S. Department of Justice, 1996.

Wolfe, D. A. *Child Abuse Implications for Child Development and Psychopathology*, 2nd ed. Thousand Oaks: Sage Publications, 1999.

INTERGENERATIONAL TRANSFER OF INTIMATE PARTNER VIOLENCE

Each year, millions experience violence in their intimate relationships; most cases are of infrequent and noninjurious incidents, but an alarming number also experience physically and psychologically traumatic violence at the hands of a partner (Straus and Gelles 1990; Tjaden and Thoennes 1998). Clinicians, advocates, and social scientists have long cautioned the public health significance of such violence, not only for its effects on the adults in the relationship, but also because of the disproportionate number of these couples who have young children in the home. In fact, partner violence is most prevalent in young men and women of childbearing age (U.S. Department of Justice 1995). Correspondingly, each year, millions of children in the United States and elsewhere are exposed to physical violence between their parents. In the United States alone, over fourteen million children are exposed to some act of interparent physical violence, over six million children are exposed to severe violence (McDonald et al. 2004), and one million are brought to domestic violence shelters with their mothers (Jouriles 2000). Community studies of children suggest that about 25 percent recall seeing or hearing at least one physical fight between their parents, and 14 percent recall two or more such fights (Ehrensaft, Cohen et al. 2003).

Children are also exposed to other forms of familial abuse, many of which tend to cluster together in the same families. Some 10 percent of children are reported to authorities for cases of abuse or neglect at the hands of a caretaker. The National Child Abuse and Neglect Data System (NCANDS; U.S. Department of Health and Human Services [USDHHS] 2004) records nearly 2.6 million referrals each year to child protection authorities for suspected child maltreatment by caretakers. These numbers are not inclusive of millions of children whose victimization goes unreported or is never disclosed (Finkelhor, Cross, and Cantor 2005).

The notion of intergenerational transmission, whereby partner violence is transmitted from the parent generation to the subsequent generation of offspring, has been one of the most widely cited theoretical explanations for the etiology of partner violence. Whereas the idea initially grew from narratives of men and women reflecting on their experiences in abusive relationships, a wealth of empirical research on this issue has emerged since the 1990s (Stith et al. 2000). In fact, a good deal of theoretical and empirical research now supports this "cycle of violence" theory (Moffitt and Caspi 2003; Widom 1989). The definition of the intergenerational transmission of partner violence has evolved with emerging research to take into account the myriad ways in which other forms of violence, such as child abuse and punitive parenting, can interact with childhood exposure to partner violence to increase the odds of the continuity of partner violence within families.

This article has the following goals: (1) to familiarize the reader with definitions of intergenerational transfer of partner violence, (2) to review theoretical perspectives and evidence about the intergenerational transfer of partner violence and views about how it occurs, and (3) to highlight implications for the design and implementation of interventions intended to prevent and reduce partner violence. This article aims to demonstrate ultimately that not only does exposure to partner violence increase the odds of the next generation's involvement in abusive relationships, but violence between parents is one of the most potent social-environmental mechanisms for the transmission of antisocial behavior in general.

Definition of Intergenerational Transmission of Violence

Historically, research on the effects of partner violence on child development has been hampered by problems of definition. Some have conceptualized the intergenerational transfer of domestic violence as going from parents to offspring. Others have examined the effects of other forms of familial abuse, such as child physical punishment, child abuse, and child neglect, on partner violence perpetration and victimization (Straus 1980, 1991; Wolfe et al. 1998).

Still others have focused on broad definitions of antisocial behaviors (Simons et al. 1995). These variations are examined in greater detail below.

Exposure to domestic violence is a heterogeneous experience. Some children witness actual events of violence between their parents, others overhear violence, and, perhaps of gravest concern, still others are physically injured during episodes of violence between their parents (Holden, Geffner, and Jouriles 1998). Although substantial progress has been made since the 1990s in this domain, the field is still constrained by issues related to definitions of violence exposure, substantiation of reports of children's exposure to violence, developmental sensitivity of the measures used to assess the experience of exposure, and numerous other methodological difficulties (Mohr et al. 2000).

There is also wide variability in how scholars define the type, frequency, and severity of violence between caretakers, as well as the level of exposure that the child has experienced. Further definitional issues concern:

- Whether it is the perpetration of violence that is transmitted across generations versus the experience of victimization by a partner (Avakame 1998).
- Variations in the time-frame for measuring partner abuse (current versus lifetime reports of partner violence) (Stith et al. 2000).
- Sample selection, such as representative community samples and samples of women drawn from battered women's shelters, arrests for partner violence, or child protective services databases (Ehrensaft, Moffitt, and Caspi 2004).
- Retrospective versus prospective reports of partner-violence exposure in childhood (Ehrensaft, Cohen et al. 2003; Fergusson and Horwood 1998; Jouriles, McDonald, Norwood et al. 2001).

These definitions have resulted in variable reports of prevalence and correlate children's partner-violence exposure (Fantuzzo and Mohr 1999). Correspondingly, the magnitude of the association of partner violence from one generation to the next varies considerably across these studies. The field is in need of further research in this area.

Evidence for the Intergenerational Transmission of Partner Violence

Several reviews suggest that there is sufficient evidence to support a cycle of violence theory, in which the violent behavior between parents increases the odds of partner violence in subsequent generations (Moffitt and Caspi 2003; Widom 1996). Recent meta-analytic studies suggest that strength of association of partner violence between parents and offspring is moderate (Stith et al. 2000). This meta-analysis found that the magnitude of the association varies across studies and depends on a number of key factors. Much of the variability lies in the age of onset, chronicity, and severity of the violence. Moreover, research suggests that children's perceptions, cognitive appraisals of blame, and coping styles influence the degree to which partner violence is learned by offspring (Grych and Fincham 1990). Others find that the co-occurrence of other forms of violence and antisocial behavior in the home and community interact with the occurrence of partner violence to increase the risk of transmission to offspring (Ehrensaft 2005; O'Leary, Tyree, and Malone 1994).

Mechanisms of Transfer

Theoretical Perspectives

Numerous theories have been put forward to explain the observation that partner violence tends to repeat from one generation to the next (Widom 1989). Originally, social learning theories (Bandura 1977; O'Leary 1988) postulated that exposure to violence between parents may teach children that violence is an acceptable or effective means of resolving conflict with partners. That is, parents model the use of aggression as a means of resolving conflict, and children observe that such behaviors are reinforced by the partner's compliance. In fact, Bandura's (1977) research on observational learning of aggression suggests that children are most likely to model observed aggression by others when the behavior of the perpetrator is rewarded, or when the behavior results in the removal of an unpleasant stimulus. This theory has been particularly influential to a line of research investigating the association of partner-violence exposure with attitudes condoning the use of partner violence, both among children and adults (Avery-Leaf et al. 1997; Slep et al. 2001; Wolfe et al. 1998). Others, from the feminist perspective, have highlighted the role of patriarchal social norms condoning the use of violence against women (Johnson 1995; Walker 1989).

However, social learning theory cannot singlehandedly explain the intergenerational transmission of partner violence, since the transfer of violence is not 100 percent. That is, many adults who report partner violence do not have a history of such violence between parents, and not all children who were exposed to violence between parents report subsequently perpetrating or being the victim of violence against a partner in adulthood. Additionally, patriarchal theory has been criticized for failing to account for the high number of nonviolent men and for elevated rates of partner violence in same-sex couples (Dutton 1995). In fact, there is no support for a gender-specific or role-specific pattern of transmission of partner violence, that is, females are no more likely to become victims versus perpetrators of partner violence if they observed their fathers aggressing against their mothers, and males are not more likely to perpetrate versus receive partner violence if they observed father-to-mother aggression (Dutton 1995; Ehrensaft, Cohen et al. 2003; Kalmuss 1984; Kwong et al. 2003).

Until quite recently, theories of partner violence were limited by the field's near-divorce from the field of antisocial behavior in general (Moffitt et al. 2000). There is now a growing consensus among many scholars that a developmental model is essential to an understanding of the process of intergenerational transmission, because it accounts for the capacity of early experience to set in motion a series of problems in adjustment across the lifespan, but also because it accounts for the fact that the transfer from one generation to the next is less than perfect. One theoretical view integrates the findings from family relations, developmental psychopathology, and basic developmental research on romantic relationships (Ehrensaft, Cohen et al. 2003). Beginning in early childhood, children's relationships with caregivers affect their ability to regulate their behavior and emotions, and their expectations of the behavior of others within close relationships. Those who are raised in relatively warm, caring environments, with caregivers who are consistently responsive to their physical and emotional needs, learn to expect and reciprocate care and affection in these relationships, and they later generalize these models of close relationships to other adults and to their peers (Bowlby 1969). Those who have experienced maltreating home environments are more likely to expect others to have hostile intentions, and have difficulty solving social problems (Dodge, Bates, and Petitt 1997), particularly if the maltreatment occurred when they were very young.

Empirical Evidence for Mechanisms of Transfer

Effects of Direct Exposure to Partner Violence on Child Mental Health. Numerous studies have documented the association of partner-violence exposure

with children's mental health problems (Ehrensaft, Cohen, and Chen in press; Fantuzzo et al. 1991; Jouriles, McDonald, Spiller et al. 2001; Kolbo, Blakely, and Endleman 1996; Wolfe et al. 1985). Though the earlier evidence was almost exclusively from cross-sectional research designs assessing partner-violence exposure and mental health problems simultaneously, more recent prospective longitudinal studies suggest that externalizing behavior problems are more likely to develop in youth who previously reported exposure to partner violence (Ehrensaft, Cohen et al. 2003; Fergusson and Horwood 1998). Others have found elevated rates of anxiety (Christopoulos et al. 1987) and depression (Sternberg et al. 1993) among children exposed to partner violence. Several scholars have raised the question of whether the exposure *itself* exerts deleterious effects on child mental health, as opposed to the numerous other social problems that tend to go hand in hand with partner violence. On the other hand, there is evidence from several prospective longitudinal studies of direct effects on child mental health, even after controlling for other social and behavioral factors (Ehrensaft, Cohen, and Johnson in press). Genetically informed research suggests that exposure to domestic violence damages children's intellectual and behavioral development, even net of genetic transmission in the family and other co-occurring risk processes (Jaffee et al. 2002; Koenen et al. 2003; Yates et al. 2003).

The mental health effects of partner violence on children are quite variable and appear to depend on several factors. For instance, young age of exposure is estimated to have significant implications for child adjustment. Notably, young children are at highest risk of exposure to violence between their caregivers, or between a caregiver and an intimate partner, for two reasons (Ehrensaft, Cohen et al. 2003; Fantuzzo et al. 1997). First, young children spend more time at home than older children or adolescents and are thus more likely to be at home during arguments. Second, intimate partner violence is at its peak prevalence among young men and women of childbearing age and tends to decrease steadily thereafter (O'Leary 1999). These data are of special concern in light of research suggesting that children who experience maltreatment and other forms of familial abuse (e.g., partner violence) before age 8 are at highest risk for experiencing enduring effects (Dodge et al. 1997). Two other factors—higher frequency of children's exposure to partner violence and their appraisals of interparental conflict—have been shown to influence the odds of child mental health problems (Grych et al. 2000).

Effects of Violence on Maternal Mental Health and Parenting. A number of studies of adults suggest that being the victim of partner violence is associated with depression, anxiety disorders, substance abuse disorders, and suicidal behavior (Danielson et al. 1998; Golding 1999; Koss et al. 2003). Previously, the preponderance of evidence came from studies of women presenting to battered women's shelters, who represent only a tiny fraction of all women who experience intimate partner violence, or from more representative national surveys that asked women to recall their experience of violence and mental health symptoms. More recently, evidence is accumulating to show that partner violence, particularly among women, distinctly leads to mental health disorders, even after accounting for preexisting disorders (Ehrensaft, Moffitt, and Caspi in press). Others have found, among a sample of abused and neglected children, that domestic violence exerts its influence on child behavioral and physical health via its indirect effects on maternal health and well-being and the quality of the mother's interactions with the child (English, Marshall, and Stewart 2003; Graham-Berman and Seng 2005). Mental health disorders are known to negatively impact parenting practices (Ehrensaft, Wasserman et al. 2003; Wasserman and Seracini 2000), and these parenting practices have in turn been hypothesized to be a primary mechanism for the intergenerational transfer of psychiatric risk (including antisocial psychopathology) from parent to child (Serbin and Karp 2003).

Links of Partner-Violence Exposure with Child Abuse and Neglect. Children who live in households where there is intimate partner abuse are more likely to be abused or neglected than those who do not (English et al. 1999; Saunders 1994; Straus and Gelles 1990). First, there is significant overlap (30–60 percent) in the occurrence of child physical abuse and domestic violence (Appel and Holden 1998), child sexual abuse and domestic violence (Kellogg and Menard 2003), child neglect and domestic violence (Copps-Hartley 2002), and all three types of abuse and domestic violence (Dong et al. 2004; McGuigan and Pratt 2001; Rumm et al. 2000). Exactly how these two types of family violence are linked is not known. However, there is evidence that the effects may be additive; that is, the odds of perpetrating partner violence in adulthood are highest when children both witness partner violence and experience child abuse (Kalmuss 1984).

At the turn of the twenty-first century, researchers have begun to integrate research on exposure to partner violence with research on child abuse, in recognition that these two types of risk factors may have similar effects on the emotional and behavioral development of children across the lifespan (Ehrensaft, Cohen et al. 2003; Ehrensaft et al. in press; Maughan and Cicchetti 2002; Schechter et al. 2004). This approach is particularly promising, especially where there is an integration of the study of both social and biological factors.

Behavioral-Genetic Transmission. Perhaps the newest approach here has evolved with the growth in behavioral genetics research on antisocial behavior. DiLalla and Gottesman (1991) pinpointed the absence of behavioral genetic research on partner violence in explanations of the intergenerational cycle of violence. Although Widom (1989) proposed that physiological processes might mediate the "cycle of violence," whereby violence by one generation increases the risk for violence by the subsequent generation, she did not iterate a genetic component to this hypothesis. Widom's hypothesis was not specific to the transfer of partner violence, but as general violence and partner violence share many common risk factors and age-based trajectories, it is conceivable that the observed intergenerational transmission of partner violence has genetic components (Ehrensaft et al. 2003; Hines and Saudino 2002). That is, the interaction of a genetic vulnerability with environmental risk may be most strongly predictive of the intergenerational transmission of partner violence. However, despite the fact that partner violence and antisocial behavior share many characteristics, research shows that they also differ in crucial ways. For instance, partner violence is the only form of violent behavior which females report perpetrating as often as males (Moffitt et al. 2001), and though partner violence and antisocial behavior share a trait called "negative emotionality," antisocial behavior is predicted by high levels of impulsivity, whereas partner violence is not (Moffitt et al. 2000). To date, there exists no published behavioral genetic studies of partner violence, and we would certainly argue that this area is an important avenue of further research, in view of emerging findings about gene-environment interactions in the transmission of antisocial behavior (Carey and Goldman 1997; Caspi et al. 2003; DiLalla and Gottesman 1991).

Prevention and Intervention

In the 1990s, the National Research Council reviewed existing prevention and intervention programs for family violence and identified fragmentation of the field of family violence research as one of the greatest impediments to designing empirically informed interventions (Chalk and King 1998). Since that review, substantial progress has been made in integrating the findings on the causes and consequences of adult partner violence, child exposure to interparental violence, child abuse and neglect, and the development of antisocial behavior. It remains true that existing interventions for most types of serious partner violence are of limited effectiveness (Dunford 2000; McCord 1992; Stuart 2005). Therefore, it is advisable to advocate a preventive approach to the intergenerational transmission of partner violence. Three approaches, based on the individual's developmental stage, are proposed.

1. *Identify and treat antisocial behavior early.* Antisocial behavior appears to be an important mediator of the link between childhood exposure to interparental violence or child maltreatment and subsequent involvement in partner violence (Capaldi and Clark 1998; Ehrensaft et al. 2003). Numerous studies have found that child abuse predicts antisocial behavior (Dodge et al. 1997; Jaffee et al. 2004; Widom 1989). Research has shown repeatedly that antisocial behavior is most responsive to treatment when targeted at an early age, though several programs show effects with adolescents as well (Wasserman and Seracini 2000; Blueprints for Violence Prevention). Early intervention would have the advantage of stemming the worsening trajectory of symptoms before the individuals extend such behavior to their intimate relationships, and this would be equally true for males and females (Ehrensaft 2005; Moffitt et al. 2001).

2. *Public health programs could tie partner violence prevention into existing preventive services.* For instance, one could offer incentives to young, economically disadvantaged couples who are expecting a baby and who have a history of violence to participate in empirically supported relationship conflict prevention (Halford et al. 2003; Heyman and Neidig 1997; Holtzworth-Munroe et al. 1995). This intervention could be tied to prenatal counseling.

3. *Tie partner violence services to existing programs for delinquent youth.* Adolescents who are already receiving interventions for serious delinquent behavior are among those at highest risk for partner violence, but they are almost never provided with interventions that would prevent their involvement in partner violence

before it begins (Chamberlain and Moore 2002; Ehrensaft et al. 2005). Prevention programs could offer interpersonal communication skills and target the development of other deficits that are the likely outcomes of children's exposure to family violence, including behavioral and affective regulation, stress reactivity, mistrust of others, and interpersonal avoidance (Dutton 2003; Ehrensaft et al. in press; Ehrensaft, Moffitt and Caspi 2004; Hamberger and Hastings 1991; Holtzworth-Munroe et al. 2003; Moffitt et al. 2000; Stuart 2005).

Summary

In summary, the study of the intergenerational transmission has evolved to recognize the complex interactions of multiple forms of family violence and antisocial behavior. Most of the risk factors for such transmission are similar for females and males. The field is now moving to investigate the ways in which these factors interact, including some burgeoning behavioral genetics research. Because serious partner violence is highly resistant to intervention once it becomes entrenched, preventive approaches tied to the risk processes identified here are worthy of further attention.

MIRIAM K. EHRENSAFT

See also **Bullying and the Family; Child Abuse and Juvenile Delinquency; Cycle of Violence; Sibling Abuse; Social Learning Theory and Family Violence**

References and Further Reading

Appel, A. E., and G. W. Holden. "The Co-occurrence of Child and Physical Spouse Abuse: A Review and Appraisal." *Journal of Family Psychology* 12 (1998): 578–599.

Avakame, E. F. "Intergenerational Transmission of Violence and Psychological Aggression Against Wives." *Canadian Journal of Behavioural Science* 30 (1998): 193–202.

Avery-Leaf, S., M. Cascardi, K. D. O'Leary, and A. Cano. "Efficacy of a Dating Violence Prevention Program on Attitudes Justifying Aggression." *Journal of Adolescent Health* 21 (1997): 11–17.

Bandura, A. J. *Social Learning Theory.* Englewood Cliffs, NJ: Prentice Hall, 1977.

Bowlby, J. *Attachment.* New York: Basic Books, 1969.

Capaldi, D. M., and S. Clark. "Prospective Family Predictors of Aggression toward Female Partners for At-Risk Young Men." *Developmental Psychology* 34 (1998): 1175–1188.

Carey, G., and D. Goldman. "Genetics of Antisocial Behavior." In *Handbook of Antisocial Behavior,* edited by D. M. Stoff and J. Breiling. New York: John Wiley & Sons, 1997, pp. 243–254.

Caspi, A., K. Sugden, T. E. Moffitt, A. Taylor, I. W. Craig, H. Harrington, J. McClay, J. Mill, J. Martin, A.

Braithwaite, and R. Poulton. "Influence of Life Stress on Depression: Moderation by a Polymorphism in the 5-HTT Gene." *Science* 301, no. 5631 (2003): 386–389.

Chalk, R., and P. A. King. *Violence in Families: Assessing Prevention and Treatment Programs.* Washington, DC: National Academy Press, 1998.

Chamberlain, P., and K. J. Moore. "Chaos and Trauma in the Lives of Adolescent Females with Antisocial Behavior and Delinquency." In *Trauma and Juvenile Delinquency: Theory, Research, and Interventions,* edited by R. Geffner (series ed.) and R. Greenwald (vol. ed.). Binghamton, NY: Haworth Press, 2002, 79–108.

Christopoulos, C., D. A. Cohn, D. S. Shaw, S. Joyce, J. Sullis-Hanson, S. P. Draft, and R. E. Emery. "Children of Abused Women: I. Adjustment at Time of Shelter Residence." *Journal of Marriage and the Family* 49 (1987): 611–619.

Copps-Hartley, C. "The Co-occurrence of Child Maltreatment and Domestic Violence: Examining Both Neglect and Child Physical Abuse." *Child Maltreatment* 7 (2002): 349–358.

Danielson, K. K., T. E. Moffitt, A. Caspi, and P. A. Silva. "Comorbidity between Abuse of an Adult and DSM-III-R Mental Disorders: Evidence from an Epidemiological Study." *American Journal of Psychiatry* 155 (1998): 131–133.

DiLalla, L. F., and I. I. Gottesman. "Biological and Genetic Contributions to Violence: Widom's Untold Tale." *Psychological Bulletin* 109 (1991): 125–129.

Dodge, K. A., J. E. Bates, and G. S. Pettit. "Mechanisms in the Cycle of Violence." *Science* 250 (1997): 1678–1683.

Dong, M., R. F. Anda, V. J. Felitti, S. R. Dube, D. F. Williamson, T. J. Thompson, C. M. Loo, and W. H. Giles. "The Interrelatedness of Multiple Forms of Childhood Abuse, Neglect, and Household Dysfunction." *Child Abuse and Neglect* 28, no. 7 (2004): 771–784.

Dunford, F. W. "The San Diego Navy Experiment: An Assessment of Interventions for Men Who Assault Their Wives." *Journal of Consulting and Clinical Psychology* 68 (2000): 468–476.

Dutton, D. G. "Intimate Abusiveness." *Clinical Psychology: Science and Practice* 2 (1995): 207–224.

———. *The Abusive Personality.* New York: Guilford, 2003.

Ehrensaft, M. K. "Interpersonal Relationships and Sex Differences in the Development of Conduct Problems." *Clinical Child and Family Psychological Review* 8, no. 1 (2005): 39–63.

Ehrensaft, M. K., P. Cohen, J. Brown, E. Smailes, H. Chen, and J. G. Johnson. "Intergenerational Transmission of Partner Violence: A 20-Year Prospective Study." *Journal of Consulting and Clinical Psychology* 71 (2003): 741–753.

Ehrensaft, M. K., P. Cohen, and J. G. Johnson. "Development of Personality Disorder Symptoms and the Risk for Partner Violence." *Journal of Abnormal Psychology.* In press.

Ehrensaft, M. K., T. E. Moffitt, and A. Caspi. "Clinically Abusive Relationships in an Unselected Birth Cohort: Men's and Women's Participation and Developmental Antecedents." *Journal of Abnormal Psychology* 113 (2004): 258–271.

———. "Domestic Violence Is Followed by Increased Risk of Psychiatric Disorder in Women but Not Men:

A Longitudinal Cohort Study." *American Journal of Psychiatry.* In press.

Ehrensaft, M. K., G. A. Wasserman, H. Verdeli, S. Greenwald, L. S. Miller, and M. Davies. "Maternal Antisocial Behavior, Parenting Practices and Behavior Problems in Boys at Risk for Antisocial Behavior." *Journal of Child and Family Studies* 12 (2003): 27–40.

English, D. J., D. B. Marshall, and M. Orme. "Characteristics of Repeated Referrals to Child Protective Services in Washington State Child Maltreatment." *Journal of the American Professional Society on the Abuse of Children* 4 (1999): 297–307.

English, D., D. B. Marshall, and A. J. Stewart. "Effects of Family Violence on Child Behavior and Health during Early Childhood." *Journal of Family Violence* 18 (2003): 43–57.

Fantuzzo, J., R. Boruch, A. Beriama, M. Atkins, and S. Marcus. "Domestic Violence and Children: Prevalence and Risk in Five Major U.S. Cities." *Journal of the American Academy of Child and Adolescent Psychiatry* 36 (1997): 116–122.

Fantuzzo, J. W., L. M. DePaola, L. Lambert, T. Martino, G. Anderson, and S. Sutton. "Effects of Interparental Violence on the Psychological Adjustment and Competencies of Young Children." *Journal of Consulting and Clinical Psychology* 59 (1991): 258–265.

Fantuzzo, J., and W. K. Mohr. "Prevalence and Effects of Child Exposure to Domestic Violence." *Future of Children* 9 (1999): 21–32.

Fergusson, D. M., and L. J. Horwood. "Exposure to Interparental Violence in Childhood and Psychosocial Adjustment in Young Adulthood." *Child Abuse and Neglect* 22 (1998): 339–357.

Finkelhor, D., T. P. Cross, and E. N. Cantor. "The Justice System for Juvenile Victims: A Comprehensive Model of Case Flow." *Trauma, Violence, and Abuse* 6 (2005): 83–102.

Golding, J. M. "Intimate Partner Violence as a Risk Factor for Mental Disorders: A Meta-Analysis." *Journal of Family Violence* 14 (1999): 99–132.

Graham-Berman, S. A., and J. Seng. "Violence Exposure and Traumatic Stress Symptoms as Additional Predictors of Health Problems in High-Risk Children." *Journal of Pediatrics* 146 (2005): 349–354.

Grych, J. G., and F. D. Fincham. "Marital Conflict and Children's Adjustment: A Cognitive Contextual Framework." *Psychological Bulletin* 108 (1990): 267–290.

Grych, J. G., E. N. Jouriles, P. R. Swank, R. McDonald, W. D. Norwood. "Patterns of Adjustment among Children of Battered Women." *Journal of Consulting and Clinical Psychology* 68 (2000): 84–94.

Halford, W. K., H. J. Markman, G. H. Kline, and S. M. Stanley. "Best Practice in Couple Relationship Education." *Journal of Marital and Family Therapy* 29 (2003): 385–406.

Hamberger, L. K., and J. E. Hastings. "Personality Correlates of Men Who Batter and Nonviolent Men: Some Continuities and Discontinuities." *Journal of Family Violence* 6 (1991): 131–147.

Heyman, R. E., and P. H. Neidig. "Physical Aggression Couples Treatment." In *Clinical Handbook of Marriage and Couples Intervention,* edited by K. Halford and H. J. Markman. New York: Wiley, 1997, pp. 589–617.

Hines, Denise A., and Kimberly J. Saudino. "Intergenerational Transmission of Intimate Partner Violence: A

Behavioral Genetic Perspective." *Trauma, Violence, and Abuse* 3 (2002): 210–225.

Holden, G. W., R. A. Geffner, and E. N. Jouriles. *Children Exposed to Marital Violence: Theory, Research, and Applied Issues.* Washington, DC: American Psychological Association Press, 1998.

Holtzworth-Munroe, A., H. J. Markman, K. D. O'Leary, D. Leber, and R. E. Heyman. "The Need for Marital Violence Prevention Efforts: A Behavioral-Cognitive Secondary Prevention Program for Engaged and Newly Married Couples." *Applied and Preventive Psychology* 4 (1995): 77–88.

Holtzworth-Munroe, A., J. C. Meehan, K. Herron, U. Rehman, and G. L. Stuart. "Do Subtypes of Maritally Violent Men Continue to Differ over Time?" *Journal of Consulting and Clinical Psychology* 71, no. 4 (2003): 728–740.

Jaffee, S. R., A. Caspi, T. E. Moffitt, and A. Taylor. "Physical Maltreatment Victim to Antisocial Child: Evidence of an Environmentally Mediated Process." *Journal of Abnormal Psychology* 113 (2004): 44–55.

Jaffee, S. R., T. E. Moffitt, A. Caspi, A. Taylor, and L. Arseneault. "Influence of Adult Domestic Violence on Children's Internalizing and Externalizing Problems: An Environmentally Informative Twin Study." *Journal of the American Academy of Child and Adolescent Psychiatry* 41 (2002): 1095–1103.

Johnson, M. P. "Patriarchal Terrorism and Common Couple Violence: Two Forms of Violence Against Women." *Journal of Marriage and the Family* 57 (1995): 283–294.

Jouriles, E. N. "Gaps in Our Knowledge about the Prevalence of Children's Exposure to Domestic Violence and Impact of Domestic Violence on Children." Paper presented to the National Academy of Sciences, Washington, D.C., April 2001.

Jouriles, E. N., R. McDonald, W. D. Norwood, and E. Ezell. "Issues and Controversies in Documenting the Prevalence of Children's Exposure to Domestic Violence." In *Domestic Violence in the Lives of Children: The Future of Research, Intervention, and Social Policy,* edited by S. A. Graham-Bermann and J. L. Edleson. Washington, DC: American Psychological Association, 2001, pp. 12–34.

Jouriles, E. N., R. McDonald, L. Spiller, W. D. Norwood, P. R. Swank, N. Stephens, H. Ware, and W. M. Buzy. "Reducing Conduct Problems among Children of Battered Women." *Journal of Consulting and Clinical Psychology* 69 (2001): 774–785.

Kalmuss, D. "The Intergenerational Transmission of Marital Aggression." *Journal of Marriage and the Family* 46 (1984): 11–19.

Kellogg, N. D., and S. W. Menard. "Violence among Family Members of Children and Adolescents Evaluated for Sexual Abuse." *Child Abuse and Neglect* 27 (2003): 1367–1376.

Koenen, K. C., T. E. Moffitt, A. Caspi, A. Taylor, and S. Purcell. "Domestic Violence Is Associated with Environmental Suppression of IQ in Young Children." *Development and Psychopathology* 15 (2003): 297–311.

Kolbo, J. R., E. H. Blakely, and D. Endleman. "Children Who Witness Domestic Violence: A Review of Empirical Literature." *Journal of Interpersonal Violence* 11 (1996): 281–293.

Koss, M. P., J. A. Bailey, N. P. Yuan, V. M. Herrera, and E. L. Lichter. "Depression and PTSD in Survivors of Male Violence: Research and Training Initiatives to Facilitate Recovery." *Psychology of Women Quarterly* 27 (2003): 130–142.

Kwong, M. J., K. Bartholomew, A. J. Z. Henderson, and S. J. Trinke. "The Intergenerational Transmission of Relationship Violence." *Journal of Family Psychology* 17 (2003): 288–301.

Maughan, A., and D. Cicchetti. "Impact of Child Maltreatment and Interadult Violence on Children's Emotional Regulation Abilities and Socioemotional Adjustment." *Child Development* 73 (2002): 1525–1542.

McCord, J. "Deterrence of Domestic Violence: A Critical View of Research." *Journal of Research in Crime and Delinquency* 29 (1992): 229–239.

McDonald, R., E. N. Jouriles, S. Ramisetty-Mikler, R. Caetano, and C. Green. "Prevalence of Children's Exposure to Intimate Partner Violence." *Journal of Family Psychology* (2004).

McGuigan, W. M., and C. C. Pratt. "The Predictive Impact of Domestic Violence on Three Types of Child Maltreatment." *Child Abuse and Neglect* 25, no. 7 (2001): 869–883.

Moffitt, T. E., and A. Caspi. "Preventing the Intergenerational Continuity of Antisocial Behavior: Implications of Partner Violence." In *Early Prevention of Adult Antisocial Behavior,* edited by D. P. Farrington and J. W. Coid. New York: Cambridge University Press, 2003, pp. 109–129.

Moffitt, T. E., A. Caspi, M. Rutter, and P. A. Silva. *Sex Differences in Antisocial Behavior: Conduct Disorder, Delinquency, and Violence in the Dunedin Longitudinal Study.* New York: Cambridge University Press, 2001.

Moffitt, T. E., R. F. Krueger, A. Caspi, and J. Fagan. "Partner Abuse and General Crime: How Are They the Same? How Are They Different?" *Criminology* 38 (2000): 199–232.

Mohr, W. K., L. M. J. Noone, J. W. Fantuzzo, and M. A. Perry (2000). "Children Exposed to Family Violence: A Review of Empirical Research from a Developmental-Ecological Perspective." *Trauma, Violence, and Abuse* 1 (2000): 264–283.

O'Leary, K. D. "Physical Aggression Between Spouses: A Social Learning Theory Perspective." In *Handbook of Family Violence,* edited by V. B. Van Hasselt, R. L. Morrison, A. S. Bellack, and M. Hersen. New York: Plenum Press, 1988.

———. "Developmental and Affective Issues in Assessing and Treating Partner Aggression." *Clinical Psychology: Science and Practice* 6 (1999): 400–414.

O'Leary, K. D., A. Tyree, and J. Malone. "Physical Aggression in Early Marriage: Prerelationship and Relationship Effects." *Journal of Consulting and Clinical Psychology* 6 (1994): 594–602.

Rumm, P. D., P. Cummings, M. R. Krauss, M. A. Bell, and F. P. Rivara. "Identified Spouse Abuse as a Risk Factor for Child Abuse." *Child Abuse and Neglect* 24 (2000): 1375–1381.

Saunders, D. G. "Child Custody Decision in Families Experiencing Woman Abuse." *Social Work* 39 (1994): 51–59.

Schechter, D. S., C. H. Zeanah, M. M. Myers, M. R. Liebowitz, R. D. Marshall, S. W. Coates, K. A. Trabka, P. Baca, and M. A. Hofer. "Psychobiological Dysregulation in Violence-Exposed Mothers: Salivary Cortisol of Mothers with Very Young Children Pre- and

Post-Separation Stress." *Bulletin of Menninger Clinic* 68 (2004): 319–336.

Serbin, L., and J. Karp. "Intergenerational Studies of Parenting and the Transfer of Risk from Parent to Child." *Current Directions on Psychological Science* 12 (2003): 138–142.

Simons, R. L., C. I. Wu, C. Johnson, and D. Conger. "A Test of Various Perspectives on the Intergenerational Transmission of Domestic Violence." *Criminology* 33 (1995): 141–172.

Slep, A. S., M. Cascardi, S. Avery-Leaf, and K. D. O'Leary. "Two New Measures of Attitudes about the Acceptability of Teen Dating Aggression." *Psychological Assessment* 13 (2001): 306–318.

Sternberg, K. J., M. E. Lamb, C. Greenbaum, D. Cicchetti, S. Dawud, R. M. Cortes, O. Krispin, and F. Lorey. "Effects of Domestic Violence on Children's Behavior Problems and Depression." *Developmental Psychology* 29 (1993): 44–52.

Stith, S. M., K. H. Rosen, K. A. Middleton, A. L. Busch, K. Lundeberg, and R. P. Carlton. "The Intergenerational Transmission of Spouse Abuse: A Meta-Analysis." *Journal of Marriage and the Family* 62 (2000): 640–654.

Straus, M. A. "Wife Beating: How Common and Why?" In *The Social Causes of Husband–Wife Violence,* edited by M. A. Straus and G. T. Hotaling. Minneapolis: University of Minnesota Press, 1980, pp. 23–38.

———. "Family Violence in American Families: Incidence Rates, Causes, and Trends." In *Abused and Battered: Social and Legal Responses of Family Violence,* edited by D. D. Knudsen and J. L. Miller. Hawthorne, NY: Aldine de Gruyter, 1991, pp. 17–34.

Straus, M. A., and R. J. Gelles. *Physical Violence in American Families: Risk Factors and Adaptations to Violence in 8,145 Families.* New Brunswick, NJ: Transaction, 1990.

Stuart, R. B. "Treatment for Partner Abuse: Time for a Paradigm Shift." *Professional Psychology: Research and Practice* 36 (2005): 254–263.

Tjaden, P., and N. Thoennes. *Prevalence, Incidence, and Consequences of Violence Against Women: Findings from the National Violence Against Women Survey.* Washington, DC: U.S. Department of Justice, 1998.

U.S. Department of Health and Human Services. *Child Maltreatment 2002: Reports from the States to the National Child Abuse and Neglect Data System.* Administration on Children, Youth and Families. Washington, DC: U.S. Government Printing Office, 2004.

U.S. Department of Justice. *National Crime Victimization Survey: Violence Against Women: Estimates from the Redesigned Survey* (Special report no. NCJ-154348). Washington, DC: Bureau of Justice Statistics, 1995.

Walker, L. E. *Terrifying Love: Why Battered Women Kill and How Society Responds.* New York: Harper & Row, 1989.

Wasserman, G. A., and A. M. Seracini. "Family Risk Factors and Family Treatments for Early-Onset Offending." In *Child Delinquents, Development, Intervention, and Service Needs,* edited by R. Loeber and D. P. Farrington. Thousand Oaks: Sage Publications, 2000, pp. 165–189.

Widom, C. S. "The Cycle of Violence." *Science* 244 (1989): 160–166.

Wolfe, D. A., P. Jaffe, S. K. Wilson, and L. Zak. "Children of Battered Women: The Relation of Child Behavior to Family Violence and Maternal Stress." *Journal of Consulting and Clinical Psychology* 53 (1985): 657–665.

Wolfe, D., C. Wekerle, D. Reitzel-Jaffe, L. Lefebvre. "Factors Associated with Abusive Relationships among Maltreated and Non-Maltreated Youth." *Development and Psychopathology* 10 (1998): 61–85.

Yates, T. M., M. F. Dodds, L. A. Sroufe, and B. Egeland. "Exposure to Partner Violence and Child Behavior Problems: A Prospective Study Controlling for Child Physical Abuse and Neglect, Child Cognitive Ability, Socioeconomic Status, and Life Stress." *Development and Psychopathology* 15 (2003): 199–218.

INTIMATE PARTNER HOMICIDE

Basic Intimate Partner Homicide Facts

Femicide, the homicide of women, is a leading cause of premature death in the United States for women. Femicide rates are highest among women aged 20–49, according to the Centers for Disease Control and Prevention (CDC) and the U.S. Department of Justice. National statistics indicate that women are killed by intimate or ex–intimate partners more often than by any other category of perpetrator, and the majority of intimate partner (IP) femicides are perpetrated by male intimate partners (husbands, boyfriends, ex-husbands, ex-boyfriends). A current or former intimate partner is the perpetrator in approximately one in three femicides nationally, but a relatively small proportion of male homicides (5 percent) are perpetrated by a female intimate or ex–intimate partner. As of this writing (2006) there are approximately four women killed by their male intimate partners for each male killed by a female intimate partner.

During 1981–1998, IP homicides decreased by almost 50 percent in the United States. Overall rates of IP homicide among males decreased 67.8 percent, and rates among females decreased 30.1 percent. The rates have since stabilized. The decreases in IP homicides are temporally associated with the implementation of national social programs and legal interventions to reduce IP violence, and analysis by Browne, Williams, and Dutton shows that in states where the laws and resources (such as shelters and crisis hotlines) were the most available, there were the greatest decreases in women killing male intimate partners. However, the relationship was not supported for men killing their female intimate partners. Other researchers have shown that increases in women's resources, decreases in marriage rates, enforcement of domestic violence policies such as pro-arrest mandates, and reductions in gun accessibility are all associated with the decreases in IP homicides.

The vast majority (67–80 percent) of IP homicides involve physical abuse of the female by the male partner or ex-partner before the murder, no matter which partner is killed. Approximately two-thirds of the cases of IP femicide have a documented history of abuse of the female partner by the male partner prior to the murder. In 75 percent of cases where males were murdered by their female partners, histories of abuse of the females by the males were documented. A recent national case control study found the following *perpetrator factors* associated with increased IP femicide risk: having failed to graduate from high school, being unemployed and not looking for work, having access to a gun, being highly controlling of the partner, forcing sex, stalking, using alcohol or drugs prior to an assault, threatening to kill the partner, and previously having used weapons against the partner. *Victim characteristics* associated with increased IP femicide risk included having less education, having a child by someone other than the perpetrator, and being separated from the perpetrator after having lived together. Factors that increase IP femicide risk at the time of the incident included use of a gun by the perpetrator, the occurrence of events triggering jealousy, and the perpetrator perceiving that the victim is leaving him for another partner.

Homicide-Suicide

It is estimated that 1,000 to 1,500 homicide-suicide deaths occur annually in the United States. Understanding of the epidemiology of homicide followed by suicide, however, is hampered by the lack of a national surveillance system. With no means of capturing homicide-suicide events in homicide databases (such as the Supplemental Homicide Report), researchers have relied on police and medical-examiner record reviews and follow-up interviews (a reasonable task only for small studies) or searched newspaper clippings for case identification. Despite these limitations, a growing body of literature confirms that homicide-suicide has certain patterns. Homicide is more likely to be followed by suicide when there is a close bond between the victim and perpetrator, and the majority (approximately 70 percent) involved male perpetrators killing a female intimate partner. Across studies of IP homicides, approximately 25 percent of femicides in the United States, Australia, and Canada are followed by suicide, compared with less than 5 percent of nonintimate killings.

The large national case control study of femicide described earlier contained one-third homicide-suicide cases. The suicidal perpetrators were more likely to be married and employed and to report less illicit drug use and abuse during pregnancy. These differences suggest that men who kill their partners and then kill themselves may have a larger "stake in conformity" than those who kill their female intimate partners and do not commit suicide. In other words, they may appear to be somewhat less dangerous than others who are seen in domestic violence criminal justice systems. Even so, the femicide-suicide perpetrators and femicide-only perpetrators had a similar background in terms of prior arrest for violent crimes (18 and 23 percent, respectively) and they engendered a similar amount of fear in their partners (thinking her partner capable of killing her, 53 and 49 percent, respectively).

There have been several explanations offered in the literature for femicide-suicide. One explanation is that the perpetrator becomes remorseful after killing his source of nurturance and commits suicide. This explanation, however, is challenged by the premeditated nature of the majority of femicide-suicides and the immediacy between the two acts. Typologies that have been advanced to explain homicide often fail to take into account the gendered nature of homicide-suicides and the history of intimate violence within relationships. Several authors include mercy killing—when failing health prevents caregiving—as a homicide-suicide trigger among older adults. However, Dawson and Gartner, examining homicide-suicides in Ontario, Canada, in 1998 reported that in twelve of fourteen cases attributed to mercy killing, there was no indication that the victim had been involved in the decision that ended her life. Mental illness, most notably depression, is another contributory factor cited in the literature. However, the proportion of perpetrators reported to have been depressed varies widely across studies, from 15 percent to 86 percent. The majority of these studies did not standardize data concerning perpetrator depression or suicidality, and psychological reports were rarely available.

A more recent explanation for femicide-suicide relates to male proprietariness—"a pathological possessiveness" that addresses issues of power and control in intimate relationships. Femicide-suicides often occur following estrangement and are planned acts by the perpetrator, supporting the explanation of male proprietariness. However, this explanation is also incomplete. Combining male proprietariness and perpetrator mental health issues with a history of IP violence may more comprehensively account for high stakes placed on the relationship with the partner. Interestingly, the constant across the literature is the perpetrator's belief that "If I can't have you, nobody will." Yet this statement, along with estrangement and controlling behavior, are also significant risk factors for femicide without suicide. Most authors acknowledge that the explanations for femicide-suicide, where no witnesses survive, is difficult to prove and most likely involves, as Easteal describes, "a mosaic" of causes.

Same-Sex Intimate Partner Homicide

According to the Centers for Disease Control and Prevention, the proportion of IP homicide committed by same-sex partners is greater for gay men than for lesbians. Nationally, among male victims of homicide, 6.2 percent were murdered by a same-sex partner; and among female victims, less than 1 percent (0.5 percent) were murdered by a same-sex partner.

Using the data from the larger multicity study on femicide described above, a case study of the five (1.6 percent) female-perpetrated IP femicides was conducted. Among the five cases, prior physical violence, controlling behaviors, jealousy, alcohol and drugs, and ending the relationship were consistently reported antecedents to the murder. These preliminary findings support that power and control are central to models of IP femicide, whether perpetrated by a man or a woman.

Maternal Mortality and Intimate Partner Homicide

Similar to the methodological challenges of studying homicide-suicides, the national homicide database does not indicate whether a woman was pregnant or had recently delivered when she was killed. Even so, detailed record reviews in some urban areas and a review of the national mortality surveillance system data by the CDC have demonstrated that homicide is the second leading cause of maternal mortality or pregnancy-associated death (death during pregnancy or in the year after pregnancy termination by delivery or other means) in the United States, causing 2 maternal deaths for every 100,000 live births. In at least three major urban areas in the United States (New York City, Chicago, Washington, D.C.) and the entire state of Maryland, homicide was the leading cause of maternal mortality, causing as many as 20 percent of maternal deaths. The increased proportion related to homicide is attributed to decreases in other causes of maternal mortality, such as medical complications of pregnancy and delivery.

Although current limitations in data do not allow the identification of the perpetrator in these maternal mortality homicides, one can assume that the majority were by an intimate partner, as in cases where women were not pregnant. One can also deduce that the majority of those cases that were IP homicides had been preceded by domestic violence against the woman.

In related findings, abuse during pregnancy was associated with a threefold increase in risk of IP-completed or -attempted femicide in the multicity femicide study. Violent victimization during pregnancy has also been associated with detrimental health outcomes such as depression, substance use, smoking, anemia, first and second trimester bleeding, poor weight gain, and maternal death. These findings lend support to the need for health care settings that include prenatal care to assess and intervene in domestic violence, as has been urged by medical and nursing organizations.

Ethnically Specific Issues

Numerous studies since the 1990s have substantiated that IP violence is a major public health problem for African American women, as well as all women of color or ethnic/racial minority status. IP violence against African American women has a significant impact on their health as well as their children. Among African American women between the ages of fifteen and forty-four years, femicide is the leading cause of premature death. Recent national data reveal that African American women are murdered by men at a rate three times higher (3.31 per 100,000) than white women (0.99 per 100,000). African American women are also disproportionately affected by pregnancy-associated homicide.

American Indian and Alaska Native women also had slightly higher rates of femicide than white women (1.09 per 100,000), while Asian and Pacific Islander women were the least likely (0.89 per 100,000) to be killed by a male. Among the five states that report ethnic/racial background (Arizona, California, Nebraska, Oregon, and Texas), Hispanic women have the second highest rate compared with white women. The reported rates per 100,000 for these five states are: white, 1.40; Hispanic, 1.54; African American, 3.88. In New York City, immigrant women were found to be more at risk for IP femicide than those born in the United States. Near-fatal (attempted) femicide of African American and other ethnic minority women also contributes to long-term disabling injuries and conditions. In the majority of these fatal and near femicides, the men who kill or abuse these women are intimate partners (husbands, boyfriends, ex-husbands, or ex-boyfriends).

Several multiyear studies of femicide trends have also reported ethnically specific data. Among African American women, the largest majority (84 percent) are killed between the ages of eighteen and sixty-four, with the mean age being thirty-two. African American women, similar to other women in the United States, are more likely to be murdered by men they know, such as a spouse (59 percent) or an intimate acquaintance, not a stranger. In cases where the male perpetrator is known, 94 percent of the homicides of African American women were intraracial.

Hispanic women have the second highest rate of femicide victimization. The trends among Hispanic women are very similar to those among African American women, except for their age. The mean age of Hispanic victims of femicide is twenty-eight, younger than both white and African American women, with the overwhelming majority being killed between the ages of eighteen and sixty-four (86 percent). Similar to African American women, they are most likely to be killed by a spouse (69 percent) or intimate acquaintance, the majority of whom are Hispanics, although the intraracial percentage is slightly less (84 percent) than for African American women.

Risk Factors

In general, studies have shown that poverty, low educational level, partner unemployment, and young age are associated with increased risk of IP homicide. Among the few intragroup studies examining these risk factors and IP homicide rates among African American women, low socioeconomic status, lack of employment of the partner,

and the establishment of limited social networks within a community are significant risk factors for IP violence. Similarly, Hispanic women often find that the context of their lives is frequently characterized by poverty, lower levels of education, discrimination, and an environment with higher use of alcohol and drugs, often by their male intimate partners. Often both African American and Hispanic women live in communities where there is a high level of violence and limited resources in general, and even fewer resources to protect women and children from IP violence and ultimately homicide. In the multicity IP femicide study, unemployment was a stronger risk factor than ethnicity or race, suggesting that it is the context of lack of resources that drives the increased risk associated with minority status rather than any culturally or racially specific characteristics.

Health Outcomes

Many studies have established that IP violence is associated with poor health outcomes for women, including poor pregnancy outcomes. Although there are fewer studies describing health outcomes for women of color, the majority of the existing articles describe abused ethnic/racial minority women as having more physical consequences, poorer mental health, and lower quality of health compared with nonabused women. Not only do these women report poorer health, but among middle-class African American women, those who have a history of physical and psychological abuse are less likely to use preventive health care practices such as breast self-exams, gynecological exams, and physical exams. In a study of African American privately insured female enrollees in health maintenance organizations, abused women had more health problems (central nervous system, gynecological, sexually transmitted infections, gastrointestinal), more problems per health visit, and more emergency department visits compared with nonabused women.

The evidence is mixed regarding whether African American or Hispanic women are more at risk for violent victimization during pregnancy. There have been four major national studies, all showing disproportionately more African American women being abused during pregnancy. Several studies have shown Hispanic women at lower risk during pregnancy, but at least one study that differentiated among Hispanic ethnic groups found that Puerto Rican women were more likely to be abused during pregnancy, while Mexican American, Central American, and Cuban American pregnant women were less likely to be victimized than African American and Anglo-American pregnant women.

Help-Seeking

African American women's responses to IP violence may be influenced by their chronic experiences of racism and the social contexts in which they live (i.e., poverty, limited or no access to community resources). Such life experiences often result in different opportunities for and restrictions on their resistance to violence. Often, previous racist or other negative experiences may prevent African American women from seeking help from institutional and/or community resources, which have traditionally safeguarded and protected white women from partner violence. However, while patterns of help-seeking may be different across ethnic/racial groups, most women do seek help after violent incidents. The help may be from formal sources (medical, counseling, law enforcement) or informal sources (talking to family and friends). For abused Hispanic/Latina women in the Chicago Women's Health Risk Study, only one-fifth (20 percent) sought any kind of help, even after experiencing a severe or life-threatening violent event from their intimate partner. The multi-city femicide study was of a diverse sample of 311 women (African Americans, 44.8 percent; whites, 27.7 percent; Hispanic/Latina, 21.9 percent). The largest group (42 percent of those sampled) had been to a health care provider in the year before their death, while 30 percent had sought help from law enforcement; however, very few women (4 percent) had sought help from a battered woman's shelter or crisis hotline. These study findings suggest that failing to assess for IP violence at every health encounter is a missed opportunity for the prevention of IP homicide.

Conclusions

Intimate violence continues to be a major public health issue for all women, and even though its occurrence has decreased, it ends with an IP homicide all too frequently. Many studies have identified characteristics of IP homicide that distinguish it from other forms of homicide. Despite findings that enhance the understanding of IP homicide, there is still a lack of systematic research studies on several issues, perhaps especially on ethnically specific issues related to IP homicide. There have been very few studies resulting in very few findings related to IP homicide as it affects Hispanic, Native American, and Asian American women.

Among studies that consider ethnic/racial minority groups, most comparisons are made with white (Anglo-American) women; more studies are needed to examine variations in associated factors within ethnic/racial minority groups, including comparisons across the socioeconomic spectrum. The research to date suggests that disproportionate risk related to ethnic/racial minority status may be more of a reflection of poverty, discrimination, and unemployment and its negative consequences, which result in a lack of access to resources that could prevent IP homicide. Additionally, an increased number of studies are needed that clearly define and identify ethnic/racial minority groups rather than grouping all black women (i.e., African American, African, Caribbean), all Hispanic women (i.e., Puerto Rican, Mexican, Cuban), or all Asian women (i.e., Korean, Chinese, Japanese) together as if they were homogeneous groups.

Demonstration projects are needed that test and evaluate evidence-based interventions aimed at reducing IP violence and ultimately its homicide. Such interventions must reflect what is known about gender issues and cultural influences as well as IP violence and incorporate mental health (depression, post-traumatic stress disorder), substance use/abuse, and parenting issues simultaneously.

Advocates, health care providers, law enforcement officers, lawyers, and community activists must also continue to support coordinated community responses to reduce risks for IP homicide. When women are identified as victims of abuse in a health care, legal, law enforcement, or community setting, there is a need to assess the risk factors for lethal violence in the abusive relationship. Specifically, it is important to assess perpetrators' access to guns and warn women of the risk this presents. This is especially important in the case of women who have been threatened with a gun or another weapon and in conditions of estrangement. Under federal law, individuals who have been convicted of domestic violence or who are subject to a restraining order are barred from owning firearms. Judges issuing orders of protection in cases of IP violence should consider the heightened risk of lethal violence associated with abusers' access to firearms.

Often, battered women like the idea of a professional notifying the police for them; with the exception of California, however, states do not mandate health care or other professionals to report to the criminal justice system unless there is evidence of a felony assault or an injury from an assault. In states other than California, a professional can offer to call the police, but the woman has the final say, as she can best assess any increased danger that might result from the police being notified. An excellent resource for referral, shelter, and information is the National Domestic Violence Hotline (1-800-799-SAFE).

If a woman confides that she is planning to leave the abuser, it is critical to warn her not to tell him she is leaving face to face. It is also clear that extremely controlling abusers are particularly dangerous under conditions of estrangement. Asking a question such as "Does your partner try to control *all* of your daily activities?" can quickly help a professional assess this extreme need for control. Professionals can also expeditiously assess whether the perpetrator is unemployed, whether children are present in the home, and whether the perpetrator has threatened to kill the victim. Under these conditions of extreme danger, it is incumbent on professionals to be extremely assertive with abused women about their risk of homicide and their need for shelter.

Evidence suggests that where there are shelters, legal advocates, health care professionals, and police trained to intervene collaboratively in cases of IP violence and where communities are consistently made aware of the issues related to IP violence and IP homicide, women and children are more likely to survive the violence in their lives.

JACQUELYN C. CAMPBELL, PHYLLIS W. SHARPS and NANCY GLASS

See also **Battered Woman Syndrome as a Legal Defense in Cases of Spousal Homicide; Battered Women Who Kill: An Examination; Compassionate Homicide and Spousal Violence; Domestic Homicide in Urban Centers: New York City**

References and Further Reading

Browne, A., K. R. Williams, and D. C. Dutton. "Homicide between Intimate Partners." In *Homicide: A Sourcebook of Social Research,* edited by Dwayne M. Smith and Margaret A. Zahn. Thousand Oaks, CA: Sage, 1998, pp. 149–164.

Campbell, Jacquelyn, Phyllis Sharps, and Nancy Glass. "Risk Assessment for Intimate Partner Violence." In *Clinical Assessment of Dangerousness: Empirical Contributions,* edited by G. F. Pinard and L. Pagani. New York: Cambridge University Press, 2000, pp. 136–157.

Campbell, Jacquelyn, Daniel Webster, Jane Koziol-McLain, et al. "Risk Factors for Femicide in Abusive Relationships: Results from a Multisite Case Control Study." *American Journal of Public Health* 93, no. 7 (2003): 1089–1097.

Chang, Jeani, Cynthia Berg, Linda Saltzman, and Joy Herndon. "Homicide: A Leading Cause of Injury Deaths among Pregnant and Postpartum Women in the United States, 1991–1999." *American Journal of Public Health* 95, no. 3 (2005).

Dawson M., and R. Gartner. "Male Proprietariness or Despair? Examining the Gendered Nature of Homicides Followed by Suicides." Paper presented at conference of the American Society of Criminology, Washington, D.C., 1998.

Dugan, L., D. S. Nagin, and R. Rosenfeld. "Do Domestic Violence Services Save Lives?" *NIJ Journal* 250 (2003): 20–25.

Easteal P. "Homicide-Suicides between Adult Sexual Intimates: An Australian Study." *Suicide and Life-Threatening Behavior* 24, no. 2 (1994): 140–151.

Glass, Nancy, Jane Koziol-McLain, Jacquelyn Campbell, and Carolyn Rebecca Block. "Female Perpetrated Femicide and Attempted Femicide: A Case Study." *Violence Against Women* 10, no. 6 (2004): 606–625.

Goodwin, Mary, Julie Gazmararian, Christopher Johnson, B. Gilbert, and Linda Saltzman. "Pregnancy Intendedness and Physical Abuse around the Time of Pregnancy: Findings from the Pregnancy Risk Assessment Monitoring System, 1966–1997." *Maternal and Child Health Journal* 4 (2000): 85–92.

Harvey, W. "Homicide among Black Adults: Life in the Subculture of Exasperation." In *Homicide among Black Americans,* edited by D. Hawkins. Lanham, MD: University Press of America, 1986, pp. 153–171.

Office of Justice Programs. *Bureau of Justice Statistics Factbook: Violence by Intimates—Analysis of Data on Crimes by Current or Former Spouses, Boyfriends, and Girlfriends.* Washington, DC: US Dept of Justice, 1998.

Paulozzi L. J., L. E. Saltzman, M. P. Thompson, et al. "Surveillance for Homicide among Intimate Partners—United States, 1981–1998." *Morbidity and Mortality Weekly Report* 50, no. SS03 (2001): 1–16.

Schollenberger, Janet, Jacquelyn Campbell, Phyllis Sharps, Patricia O'Campo, Andrea Gielen, Jacqueline Dienmann, and Joan Kub. "African American HMO Enrollees: Their Experiences with Partner Abuse and Its Effect on Their Health and Use of Medical Services." *Violence Against Women* 9, no. 5 (2003): 599–618.

Sharps, Phyllis, Jane Koziol-McLain, Jacquelyn Campbell, Judith McFarlane, Carolyn Sachs, and Xiao Xu. "Health Care Providers' Missed Opportunities for Preventing Femicide." *Preventive Medicine* 33 (2001): 373–380.

Violence Policy Center. *When Men Murder Women: An Analysis of 2002 Homicide Data.* Washington, DC: Author, 2004.

Websdale, Neil. *Understanding Domestic Homicide.* Boston: Northeastern University Press, 1999.

Wilson M., and M. Daly. "An Evolutionary Psychological Perspective on Male Sexual Proprietariness and Violence Against Wives." *Violence and Victims* 8 (1993): 271–294.

INTIMATE PARTNER VIOLENCE AND MENTAL RETARDATION

Introduction

Until the 1990s there was little professional or scholarly attention paid to the problem of intimate partner abuse among people with disabilities. Since that time, attention to the problem of the abuse of individuals with disabilities has increased rapidly. Although much has been written on the topic of the abuse of people with disabilities in general, there is relatively little research on abuse among people with mental retardation or other developmental disabilities. Moreover, more has been written about sexual abuse than physical abuse in people with mental retardation, although there is almost nothing written about emotional or psychological abuse of people with mental retardation in intimate relationships. The focus here will be on intimate partner abuse as it affects adults with mental retardation, although the broader literature on intimate partner abuse among people with physical disabilities is also relevant (e.g., Hassouneh-Phillips and Curry 2002) to the extent that individuals with developmental disabilities are more likely than others in the population to have a co-occurring physical disability in addition to their cognitive impairment.

One of the factors that differentiates people with disabilities, including mental retardation, from nondisabled individuals is the extensive contact they have with others who provide personal care services and who exert significant power over them. Despite this contact, this essay will address intimate partner abuse—physical, sexual, or emotional abuse—in adults who have mental retardation in the context of intimate or romantic relationships rather than professional relationships, recognizing that the line between professional and intimate relationships often is blurred in this population.

Attention to the problem of intimate partner violence among people with mental retardation has become more pressing as such people have been moved out of institutions and into the community, thereby allowing for more normalized social interactions. At least half a million persons with mild or moderate mental retardation are said to be living in U.S. communities (Groce 1988).

Thus, they are more likely than ever before to have intimate relationships with romantic partners, including dating relationships, cohabitation, and marriage.

Prevalence

There is very little published research on the incidence or prevalence of intimate partner violence among those with developmental disabilities or mental retardation. To date, virtually everything that has been written on the topic, some of which is based on anecdotal reports rather than scientific research, notes that rates of physical and/or sexual abuse are higher among people with developmental disabilities (e.g., Strickler 2001). Although no specific prevalence rates are available, some have concluded that the majority of people with developmental disabilities will be sexually assaulted in their lifetimes, although not all of this abuse will necessarily be inflicted by romantic partners. Furey (1994) studied 171 cases of sexual abuse reported over a five-year period and learned that the majority of victims were female (72 percent). A survey of disabled women, some of whom had cognitive disabilities, found that 67 percent reported physical abuse and 53 percent reported sexual abuse (Power, Curry, Maley, and Saxton, 2002). Carlson (1998) found that physical abuse severity ranged from mild to severe, and frequency ranged from onetime events to daily occurrences.

Very little is known about emotional or psychological abuse among people with mental retardation. Professionals from the developmental disabilities field in Carlson's (1998) qualitative study perceived emotional abuse to be even more prevalent among this population than physical violence. Types of emotional abuse reported by participants with mental retardation included forced isolation, restricted contact with others, destruction of personal property, extreme controlling behavior, verbal abuse such as name calling (e.g., "retard"), and intimidating behavior such as threats with weapons. Almost half had been threatened with death, and all but one had been blamed for things they did not do (Carlson 1998).

Perpetrators of abuse toward persons with mental retardation are generally individuals known to the victim, usually a man with whom they have a trusted personal or professional relationship (Furey 1994). Almost half the abusers in one study also had mental retardation (Furey 1994). Research available at the time of this writing does not permit conclusions about how much abuse of mentally retarded people is perpetrated in the context of a romantic relationship versus caretaking (Sobsey and Doe 1991). Although the location of occurrence for such abuse can be in community or work settings, research suggests that it is most likely to occur in personal residences such as family settings or group homes (Furey 1994; Sobsey 1994). Compared with abuse of women without mental retardation, abuse of persons with mental retardation tends to be more severe and of longer duration and involves repeated episodes and multiple perpetrators (Schaller and Fieberg 1998; Sobsey and Doe 1991). It is also important to note that there may be "disability-specific" forms of abuse unique to individuals with specific disabilities: for example, preventing someone from accessing a telephone or transportation, threatening to abandon them, or saying that no one will want them because of their retardation.

Risk Factors

A wide variety of factors may help to explain the greater vulnerability to intimate partner abuse among persons with mental retardation, including the nature of their mental retardation, childhood history, factors pertaining to how mentally retarded persons are socialized in society, and current living circumstances. Individuals with mental retardation have a variety of cognitive, language, and communication limitations that interfere with their development of good social skills and recognition of abuse (Protection and Advocacy, Inc. 2003). Professionals who worked with mentally retarded individuals in one study noted deficits in reading and understanding social cues (Carlson 1998). A history of childhood abuse is known to predispose women in general to subsequent victimization, and research has documented that childhood abuse occurs more frequently among children with disabilities, including mental retardation (Sobsey, Randall, and Parilla 1997).

Mental retardation is a stigmatizing condition, and these individuals have been segregated historically from "normal" society and subject to a host of discrediting cultural stereotypes that portray them as "dangerous, diseased, or worthless," leading to "internalized devaluation" (Sobsey and Doe 1991, p. 253). Such dehumanizing stereotypes reduce the inhibition against violence and allow perpetrators to abuse them without guilt, while at the same time raising questions about the credibility of abuse allegations. These societal views have permitted individuals with mental retardation to be socialized in dysfunctional ways that train them to be overly compliant and disempowered (Protection and Advocacy, Inc. 2003). Thus, people with mental retardation tend to have more limited self-advocacy skills (Protection and Advocacy, Inc. 2003). From childhood, they become accustomed to high levels of dependency on others for assistance with tasks of daily living (Groce 1988; Strickler 2001). This can lead to learned helplessness and the belief that they lack control over their lives, as well as overly compliant behaviors, all of which increase vulnerability for abuse (Sobsey 1994; Strickler 2001). Low self-esteem, resulting from social devaluation and traditional ways of treating individuals with mental retardation, is also said to be common among people with developmental disabilities (Carlson 1998; Groce 1988), further contributing to vulnerability for abuse.

Another myth is that people with developmental disabilities are asexual or lack the need or desire for intimate or sexual relationships (Strickler 2001). This in turn has resulted in a lack of education provided to them on these topics (Lumley and Miltenberger 1997; Tharinger, Horton, and Millea 1990), which became increasingly problematic once deinstitutionalization occurred on a large scale. For example, many individuals with mental retardation may be unaware that they have the right to refuse unwanted sexual overtures (Protection and Advocacy, Inc. 2003). Social isolation (Strickler 2001) and limited opportunities and skills for social interaction are associated with an elevated desire to please and be accepted by others, as well as misplaced trust. Women with mental retardation have been said to value romantic relationships so highly that they are willing to place themselves in high-risk situations: "Thus they will compromise themselves rather than risk the loss of a lover, even if that lover exploits and abuses them" (Stromsness 1993, p. 147).

Sequelae and Consequences of Intimate Partner Violence

Little is known about the consequences of intimate partner violence among individuals with mental retardation. One obvious consequence is injury. In her qualitative study, Carlson (1998) found the full range of injuries reported, including the need for hospitalization. Other reported consequences include reduced self-esteem (Carlson 1998; Schaller and Fieberg 1998); shame and guilt (Schaller and Fieberg 1998); impaired sense of safety and trust in others (Carlson 1998; Schaller and Fieberg 1998); social isolation (Schaller and Fieberg 1998); reduced levels of functioning, including "extreme regression" (Carlson 1998); and impaired ability to self-regulate anger (Schaller and Fieberg 1998), which may lead to violence or aggression against others. A sizable body of research has documented the wide-ranging consequences of intimate partner violence among women in general, including depression, anxiety, posttraumatic stress disorder, and various medical complaints and illnesses such as migraine headaches. There is every reason to assume that women with mental retardation suffer similar effects. In fact, professionals in the developmental disabilities field have speculated that women with such disabilities have even more exaggerated effects than women without them. One professional noted that mentally retarded individuals "get into the cycle [of victimization] earlier, stay longer, and have more trouble getting out" (Carlson 1998, p. 109).

Terminating the Abuse: Reporting and Disclosure Issues

Cognitive impairments and deficits in communication skills may interfere with the ability to recognize, label, and report or disclose abuse (Tharinger et al. 1990). "[D]isabled adults, particularly those whose conditions make them dependent on others for support, may be unwilling or unable to report abuse or neglect. Many fear, with justification, that they will not be believed or that retaliation will occur" (Groce 1988, p. 236; Tharinger et al. 1990). Even if an individual experiencing abuse wants the abuse to stop and wishes to report it, he or she may not be able to develop and implement a plan to do so (Protection and Advocacy, Inc. 2003). Related fears include retribution or loss of services, employment, housing, or important relationships due to disclosure (Strickler 2001; Stromsness 1993). Another barrier to disclosure is the fear that one's children may be removed (Groce 1988), a fear shared by abused women without mental retardation. As a result of these barriers to disclosure, when individuals with developmental disabilities are abused, the abuse may last longer and get worse, because it is more likely to go undisclosed and unreported (Protection and Advocacy, Inc. 2003).

When agencies learn of abuse, there are many barriers to reporting it to appropriate authorities, even when mandated by law, including fear of reprisals, bad publicity for the agency, accusations of professional incompetence, fear of licensing implications, and so forth (Protection and Advocacy, Inc. 2003). Abuse cases among individuals with mental retardation are more difficult to investigate and prosecute due to victims' cognitive deficits that create communication problems, as well as investigators' (e.g., police) lack of knowledge about and expertise in working with developmentally disabled people: "[T]he presence of an array of communication difficulties frequently leads to frustration when officers taking a report cannot understand the victim" (Protection and Advocacy, Inc. 2003, p. 4). Furthermore, "encounters with the criminal justice system can be baffling and intimidating to people with cognitive impairments" (Protection and Advocacy, Inc. 2003, p. 34), as they are to abused women who are not disabled in any way.

Implications for Prevention

Preventing physical, sexual, and emotional abuse among individuals with mental retardation will require a multifaceted effort. The movement toward greater inclusion into society of people with all types of disabilities has initiated many positive changes that will help to prevent intimate partner abuse among and against them by addressing several of the risk factors or sources of vulnerability discussed above. These changes include better integration of people with mental retardation into the community and systematic efforts to empower people with all types of developmental disabilities. In fact, it has been said that the cornerstone of abuse prevention is empowerment in that abuse tends to occur in a context of power differentials between abuser and victim (Sobsey 1994). Also sorely needed are social skills training and sexuality education (Strickler 2001), as well as assertiveness training and self-protection skills. Several studies are reported in the literature evaluating sexual abuse prevention programs (e.g., Lumley and Miltenberger 1997). In addition, one intervention program to prevent domestic violence and sexual abuse has been developed and evaluated, with promising initial results. The intervention employs the Effective Strategy-Based Curriculum for Abuse Prevention and Empowerment (ESCAPE) curriculum, a combination of twelve didactic sessions covering knowledge of abuse, empowerment, and decision making, as well as six support group sessions to review and reinforce the presented material (Khemka, Hickson, and Reynolds 2005).

Implications for Intervention

At this time, there is no research on empirically based interventions for intimate partner violence in victims with mental retardation, nor are there guidelines on best practices. Given the seemingly high prevalence of intimate partner violence, a strong case can be made for universal screening for abuse of women with mental retardation by professional staff with expertise in both domestic violence and developmental disabilities. Such screening should occur in all organizational settings where such individuals predominate, such as residential and group homes, shelter workshop programs, abuse and rape crisis centers (ARCs), and so forth. Abuse screening tools exist that have been adapted by clinicians for women with disabilities, such as the *Abuse Assessment Screen–Disability,* available from the Center for Research on Women and Disabilities (CROWD). It is important for professionals working with the mentally retarded population to be knowledgeable about whether reporting of adult abuse is mandated by law in their state, and if so, whether they are a mandated reporter. Those in doubt should contact the state's Adult Protective Services agency. Professionals required by law to report suspected maltreatment should become familiar with details of such reporting, which can be very complex (Protection and Advocacy, Inc. 2003).

Although some in the mental retardation field and many counselors outside the field question the extent to which individuals with developmental disabilities can benefit from counseling (e.g., Strickler 2001), there is ample evidence that therapeutic intervention can be successful with people with mental retardation (e.g., Tharinger et al. 1990). However, accommodations need to be made (e.g., repetition, greater structure and directiveness, a more educational stance). It is important that treatment goals be attainable, taking into account the client's limitations as well as strengths. Interventions can occur on an individual level or in group settings. Groups are a widely utilized intervention modality with domestic violence generally, for both victims and offenders, and are a good format for victims to share their stories and obtain support as well as to acquire safety skills (Tharinger et al. 1990). Use of videos to stimulate discussion and role playing are other widely used techniques (Sobsey 1994).

As of 2006, few if any communities have service programs specifically for mentally retarded victims of intimate partner abuse. Referral to an existing domestic violence program should be considered for such victims; however, few such programs have staff or expertise in working with women with developmental disabilities. Therefore, before making a referral to a domestic violence program, one should check to determine if the program can accommodate the needs of a client with mental retardation. Primary considerations in working therapeutically with a mentally retarded victim of intimate partner abuse are gaining his or her trust and maintaining confidentiality. Empowerment and self-determination should be the foremost guiding principles in such work (Sobsey 1994). The first step is to establish a victim's safety, which may be difficult if he or she resides in the same setting as the abuser. Much has been written about safety planning in work with abused women (see, for example, Davies, Lyon, and Monti-Catania 1998). An important intervention is to impart personal safety skills, defined as "patterns of behavior that are intended to reduce an individual's risk for abuse, exploitation, and violence" (Sobsey 1994, p. 195).

One common source of help for abused women is support and practical assistance from family and extended family members, but many women with mental retardation and developmental disabilities have limited or nonexistent relationships with family members. In these cases professional staff will need to provide such support (Groce 1988).

Interventions by the criminal justice system are a critical component of the comprehensive package of needed interventions for victims of intimate partner violence, including arrest and prosecution of abusers. For example, protective orders are commonly issued for victims that instruct the abuser to stay away and impose serious sanctions if the orders are violated. The ability of victims with mental retardation to take advantage of this form of assistance can be compromised by several factors. The complexity of the justice system can present a daunting challenge for any victim, which is only compounded by cognitive limitations. Such limitations can make people with mental retardation poor witnesses (Protection and Advocacy, Inc. 2003). Lack of familiarity with mental retardation on the part of criminal justice agents can also serve as a barrier to mentally retarded victims being able to avail themselves of the protections of the justice system.

Implications for Social Policy

To address the pervasive problem of intimate partner violence among people with mental retardation, a number of policy changes can be made with the goal of enhancing detection and amelioration of such abuse. First, reporting systems need to be improved. Some states already have mandatory reporting of abuse of all adults, or of vulnerable adults such as those who are elderly or dependent, and this requirement should be expanded to all states. For states that do have such reporting requirements, changes may need to be made in how the requirements are implemented and/or processed. California found that law enforcement and Adult Protective Services workers lacked sufficient information and training to work effectively with people with cognitive limitations; prosecutors and judges may similarly lack necessary expertise (Protection and Advocacy, Inc. 2003).

A related change pertains to increasing the expertise in identifying abuse and facilitating its reporting among those who regularly come in contact with people with mental retardation, such as those who staff group homes, shelter workshop settings, and developmental centers, as well as professionals who might be the recipients of such reports, such as law enforcement. The prevalence of abuse against individuals with mental retardation is sufficiently high to warrant designation of a specific staff person or persons who are trained in intimate partner abuse and sexual abuse in agencies that regularly provide services to the developmentally disabled population. This person should be alert to the presence of abuse and familiar with its investigation and reporting to outside authorities. Increased education might best be accomplished by developing collaborations with local domestic violence and rape crisis programs which are knowledgeable about interpersonal violence and accustomed to providing education on these topics (Hassouneh-Phillips and Curry 2002). Such collaborations would be an ideal way to begin to educate those who staff these programs regarding how to increase their accessibility to clients who present a range of disabilities, including cognitive impairment (Groce 1988).

Another important innovation would be increased education and training of professionals who regularly encounter intimate partner abuse regarding how to work effectively with clients who present with mental retardation. This would include, at a minimum, those who staff domestic violence programs, including shelters, as well as agents of the criminal justice system, including law enforcement, prosecutors, and judges. It is strongly advised that criminal justice professions develop collaborations with disability and victim advocacy organizations in their communities in order to promote greater professional understanding of these issues and to better meet the needs of abused victims with mental retardation. Wisconsin

has been in the forefront of efforts to develop statewide coalitions on behalf of abused women with developmental disabilities. In the wake of an outpouring of stories during the 1990s of women with mental retardation being abused, a unique partnership was forged between the Wisconsin Council on Developmental Disabilities and the Wisconsin Coalition Against Domestic Violence, with goals of "cross-training," public education, system change, and improved advocacy on behalf of abused women with developmental disabilities. California has also undertaken innovations such as multidisciplinary statewide conferences to promote better understanding of the issues facing crime victims with developmental disabilities and funding pilot programs to address the needs of such victims (Protection and Advocacy, Inc. 2003).

Resources

A variety of resources on the Internet are available regarding abuse of people with mental retardation, e.g., Oregon Health Science University's Center for Self-Determination and the Wisconsin Coalition for Advocacy. In addition, state coalitions against domestic violence and state disabilities advocacy organizations have increasingly posted information on this topic, e.g., Wisconsin Council on Developmental Disabilities (www.wcdd.org). Most states have Developmental Disabilities Councils, which may be another source of information.

An excellent website for information on intimate partner violence in general that also includes information on abuse of people with disabilities is maintained by the Minnesota Center Against Violence and Abuse (MINCAVA) (http://www.mincava.umn.edu). Finally, the Center for Research on Women with Disabilities at Baylor College of Medicine in Houston (http://www.bcm.edu/crowd) has an excellent website with a section on violence against women with disabilities that features an extensive discussion of research on prevalence and risk factors as well as intervention and recommendations, including specific guidelines for professionals.

BONNIE E. CARLSON

See also **Filicide and Children with Disabilities; Women with Disabilities, Domestic Violence against**

References and Further Reading

Carlson, Bonnie E. "Domestic Violence in Adults with Mental Retardation: Reports from Key Informants." *Mental Health Aspects of Developmental Disabilities* 1 (1998): 102–112.

Davies, Jill, Eleanor Lyon, and Diane Monti-Catania. *Safety Planning with Battered Women: Complex Lives/Difficult Choices.* Thousand Oaks, CA: Sage, 1998.

Furey, Eileen M. "Sexual Abuse of Adults with Mental Retardation: Who and Where." *Mental Retardation* 32 (1994): 173–180.

Groce, Nora E. "Special Groups at Risk of Abuse: The Disabled." In *Abuse and Victimization Across the Life Span,* edited by M. B. Straus. Baltimore: Johns Hopkins University Press, 1988, pp. 223–239.

Hassouneh-Phillips, Dena, and Mary Ann Curry. "Abuse of Women with Disabilities: State of the Science." *Rehabilitation Counseling Bulletin* 4 (2003): 96–104.

Khemka, Ishita, Linda Hickson, and Gillian Reynolds. "Evaluation of a Decision-Making Curriculum Designed to Empower Women with Mental Retardation to Resist Abuse." *American Journal on Mental Retardation* 110 (2005): 193–204.

Lumley, Vicki A., and Raymond G. Miltenberger. "Sexual Abuse Prevention for Persons with Mental Retardation." *American Journal on Mental Retardation* 101 (1997): 459–472.

Power, Laurie E., Mary Ann Curry, Mary Oschwald, and Susan Maley. "Barriers and Strategies in Addressing Abuse: A Survey of Disabled Women's Experiences." *Journal of Rehabilitation* 68 (2002): 4–13.

Protection and Advocacy, Inc. *Abuse and Neglect of Adults with Developmental Disabilities: A Public Health Priority for the State of California.* Los Angeles: Tarjan Center for Developmental Disabilities, University of California at Los Angeles, 2003.

Schaller, James, and Jennifer L. Fieberg. "Issues of Abuse for Women with Disabilities and Implications for Rehabilitation Counseling." *Journal of Applied Rehabilitation Counseling* 29 (1998): 9–17.

Sobsey, Dick. *Violence and Abuse in the Lives of People with Disabilities: The End of Silent Acceptance.* Baltimore: Paul H. Brookes, 1994.

Sobsey, Dick, and Tanis Doe. "Patterns of Sexual Abuse and Assault." *Sexuality and Disability* 9 (1991): 243–259.

Sobsey, Dick, Wade Randall, and Rauna Parilla. "Gender Differences in Abused Children with and without Disabilities." *Child Abuse and Neglect* 21 (1997): 707–720.

Strickler, Heidi L. "Interaction between Family Violence and Mental Retardation." *Mental Retardation* 39 (2001): 461–471.

Stromsness, M. M. "Sexually Abused Women with Mental Retardation: Hidden Victims, Absent Resources." *Women and Therapy* 14 (1993): 139–152.

Tharinger, D., C. B. Horton, and S. Millea. "Sexual Abuse and Exploitation of Children and Adults with Mental Retardation and Other Handicaps." *Child Abuse and Neglect* 14 (1990): 301–312.

INTIMATE PARTNER VIOLENCE, FORMS OF

Intimate partner violence is a phrase that refers to acts of violence such as unwanted physical or sexual force, withholding of or damage to material or property, and psychological abuse which are inflicted by one person against his or her intimate partner as part of an ongoing pattern of abuse or controlling tactics. Occurring within a domestic relationship that is legally or socially recognized, the complex dynamics of intimate partner violence defy any single classification. Intimate partner violence is a single category of adult domestic violence perpetrated by an individual against his or her intimate partner through numerous forms of abuse. Definitions differ between the legal and social perspectives and according to the population that has been victimized. Intimate partner violence is also referred to as domestic violence, spouse abuse, or battering; the terms are frequently used interchangeably. *Wife abuse* was the early feminist label for intimate violence but is rarely used today. Intimate partner violence does not include domestic victimizations of child abuse, child against parent abuse, sibling abuse, or violence committed by a family member other than an intimate partner or spouse. Workplace violence, sexual harassment, and commercial acts targeting women are also not included.

From a criminal justice perspective, intimate partner violence is an altercation of sufficient severity to justify law enforcement intervention. Although spouse abuse is the most frequently cited form of domestic violence that involves police action, most intimate partner violence is never reported to the police. Noncriminal emotional abuse and neglect will also come to the attention of law enforcement officers. Numerous forms of abuse are socially unacceptable and are present in a violent relationship but do not rise to the level of criminal violations. From a social perspective, intimate partner violence is a pattern of violent or coercive behaviors with which one intimate partner attempts to control the other. Multiple forms of violence frequently exist within dysfunctional homes through the efforts of a dominant figure to maintain power and control of family members. Response strategies differ significantly, depending on whether the intimate partner violence is identified as a criminal act versus a social wrongdoing.

Violence within the context of an intimate relationship refers to any and all violent and nonviolent victimization behaviors and crimes against the person, including rape, sexual assault, robbery, aggravated assault, and simple assault. It is a broad categorization that describes an attempted or actual physical attack or unwanted sexual contact, verbal threat of physical or sexual harm, attempted or actual destruction of property, attempted or forcible entry of a home/apartment, or the removal of property without permission.

Standard categories of domestic relationships include married and previously married persons; those who live together as husband and wife; and persons who have a child in common. Some states expand on traditional definitions of domestic relationships through the recognition of persons who live under the same roof, regardless of affiliation. Substantial dating relationships may also be included in the classification of domestic relationship. Same-sex relationships and roommates may also constitute domestic partnerships. Both legal definitions and social recognition of a domestic violence relationship vary from state to state. How the relationship is defined is a critical factor that determines the availability of social services and legal responses to that population.

A common concern in all violent intimate relationships is the indication of a strong relationship between the excessive use of alcohol and/or drugs and domestic violence. Aggression has also been linked with psychoactive drugs such as barbiturates, amphetamines, opiates, phencyclidine, cocaine, and alcohol-cocaine combinations. Power inequality is among the many problems affecting dysfunctional relationships. Class differentials, jealousy, and poor communication skills may all contribute to domestic violence regardless of sexual orientation.

The major sources of information on domestic abuse come from arrest statistics and victimization studies. The FBI's Uniform Crime Reporting (UCR) program, which began in 1929, collects information about crimes reported to the police and provides arrest statistics. The UCR program is being expanded to the National Incident-Based Reporting System (NIBRS). NIBRS, which collects more comprehensive data on each reported crime incident, is being phased in to replace the UCR program. The National Crime Victimization Survey and the National Family Violence Survey represent the most significant examples of victimization studies.

The definitions that follow are general classifications under which various forms of intimate violence exist. The categories provide a cohesive framework for classifying intimate partner violence. These descriptions also provide insight into the various types of abuse that professionals encounter.

Defining Categories

Animal Cruelty

There is a recent renewed interest in the link between intimate partner violence and the killing, mutilating, or threat to harm a family pet, which is typically referred to as animal cruelty. Considered a severe form of intimidation and punishment for real or imagined injustices, there is a concern over an increased likelihood that the abuser will physically harm or kill the intimate partner. Animal cruelty is an intentional method of emotionally controlling and coercing the intimate partner. As a form of manipulation, the mutilation of pets is used to ensure that the partner stays in the home to protect the animals. National surveys conducted by various universities and the Humane Society of the United States since 2000 have found that 74 percent of pet-owning women in women's shelters reported that a pet had been threatened, injured, or killed by their abuser. Common types of animal cruelty include bone breaking, burning, cutting off of ears or tails, drowning, torture, shooting, and stabbing the pets or livestock.

Battering

Initially *battering* was a term used to describe a particular form of domestic abuse, hitting. The contemporary use of the term is to describe a pattern of violence or coercive behaviors; it is further defined by including the term "wife" or "husband" to designate the partner that is being victimized (i.e., wife battering or husband battering). Humiliation, constant criticism, jealous accusations, and controlling involvement with family and friends are forms of abuse that constitute the pattern of battering. The actions of batterers reflect the tactics used by individuals and groups in positions of power to dominate and control. The control may be accomplished through economic forms such as withholding or denying access to money or other basic resources, or sabotaging employment, housing, or educational opportunities. Social isolation is quite common, including the denial of communication with friends and relatives or making communication so difficult that the victim chooses to avoid it. Prohibiting access to a telephone or transportation and denying needed health care are also examples. Verbal and emotional forms include intimidation, coercion, threats, and degradation. Physical and sexual abuse may occur. Individual acts do not constitute battering; it is the ongoing violence that characterizes battering, regardless of the form, marital status, age, or living arrangement of the intimate partners.

Death Ritual

The term *death ritual* refers to the escalating pattern of abuse by death threats, which may lead to homicide. It begins when the abuser talks about weapons, escalates to displaying weapons, and then brandishes weapons. This occurs while the abuser is making threats to the victim. The offender may actually take the partner to a secluded area and threaten to kill her there if the partner ever tries to leave the relationship. The more frequently these rituals are acted out, the more likely it is that the abuser will carry out such threats.

Destruction of Personal Property

Destroying or defacing the intimate's personal property is a form of emotional abuse and may rise to the level of criminal conduct, depending on the severity of the act and the monetary loss to the victim. Victims are most vulnerable to destruction of personal property at the time in which the couple is separating or divorcing. These acts constitute emotional abuse because they are designed to cause fear and financial hardship and provide an outlet for the anger of the separated person.

Elder Domestic Violence

Abuse of an elder within the context of intimate partner violence refers to the neglect or battering of or acts of violence (including financial abuse) against an elderly person perpetrated by a spouse, ex-spouse, or intimate partner. The difficulty in determining the prevalence of elder abuse is that the definitions of who is an elder vary among states according to age and reporting practices. Crimes against the elderly include financial exploitation, fraud, homicide, misuse of restraints, neglect, physical assault, and sexual assault. Age definitions range from fifty-five (Alabama) to sixty-five (California, Maryland, and Nebraska), with the majority of states using age sixty as a measure (Jogerst et al. 2003). The protections against elder abuse are sometimes based on infirmity rather than age, such as a "vulnerable adult" category. Further complicating the data on elder abuse is that protective legislation sometimes combines child abuse reporting with elder abuse reporting. As of 1993, all states had legislated in some way against elder abuse in the domestic setting.

Spouses and intimate partners make up the largest category of individuals responsible for perpetrating elder abuse; approximately 30 percent of the abuse that is perpetrated against elders is at the hands of an intimate or partner according to the National Center on Elder Abuse. An early study found that in cases of spousal abuse among the elderly, perpetrators were equally likely to be either male or female partners (Pillemer and Finkelhor 1988). The National Center on Elder Abuse has estimated that for every reported incident of elder abuse, neglect, or self-neglect, approximately five go unreported. Elder domestic violence victims experience increased suicide idealization and depression.

Also called maltreatment, the abuse against an elder may be either active or passive. This refers to the difference between intentional abuse and benign neglect, some of which might be unintentional. Active neglect is a deliberate attempt by a caregiver to inflict injury or emotional stress. Passive neglect may include the lack of proper hygiene. The lack of heat, running water, electricity, or air conditioning may provide evidence that neglect is occurring. The majority of elders who are not institutionalized are living in a family setting. The elderly are most vulnerable to domestic abuse when they are frail or suffer from mental or physical illnesses. Heavy alcohol and prescription medication use by elders complicate recognition of and response to intimate partner violence, increasing the risk of domestic elder abuse. It is estimated that over two million Americans aged sixty-five and older are injured, mistreated, or exploited through elder abuse each year.

The categories of elder spouse abuse include those who have been victimized throughout their lives and have grown old; cases in which the abuse begins late in life, which may be associated with age-related conditions of dependency, retirement, or sexual dysfunction; abusive relationships that are entered though marriages late in life, including those centered around financial abuse; and situations in which a formerly abused spouse turns the tables on an infirm batterer. A pronounced decline in the well-being of an elder sometimes signals disease, which may be treatable. Depression, poor nutrition, and medication interactions may be factors that contribute to the elder's vulnerability. During a domestic crime, an older person is more likely to be seriously hurt and possibly die from the abuse. Multidisciplinary teams are forming nationwide as the best approach to elder abuse prevention. The design of these multidisciplinary teams varies from state to state, but they share common prevention goals. Professionals share information among themselves as well as addressing the needs of the victim. The team approach offers a forum for balancing the different agency goals and aids in case resolution in the best interest of the elder. Adult Protective Services (APS) is the agency to contact when elder neglect or abuse is suspected. A local police department may also be contacted to intervene.

Emotional Abuse

This is the willful infliction of emotional anguish by threat, humiliation, intimidation, or other abusive conduct. Isolation, name-calling, being treated like a child, and abusive verbal attacks are examples of this form of abuse. Although acts of emotional violence do not rise to the level of criminal acts by themselves, they may provide evidence to support patterns of violence and strengthen the case of an abusive relationship. Emotional abuse is often linked with psychological abuse and is frequently present in all other forms of intimate violence.

Failure to Provide Care

A deliberate attempt to inflict injury or emotional stress may be by omission: for example, failure to provide needed food, medication, hearing aids, or eyeglasses for the spouse. A caretaker may be held legally responsible for a failure to act on a duty of care for an elderly or disabled partner when an intimate partnership or spousal relationship exists between them. Challenging the traditional response to elder abuse and abuse against persons with disabilities, the criminal justice system approach now includes aggressive prosecution through numerous statutes intended to protect vulnerable populations of adults. As of this writing, California is one state among six that has adopted criminal statutes that address the failure to provide care or to permit a dependent elder to suffer harm when a legal duty to provide care exists because of a special relationship.

Financial Exploitation

The illegal or improper use of an elder's funds, property, or assets by an intimate defines financial exploitation. Theft, fraud, and unfulfilled promises of care in exchange for assets are examples of financial exploitation. Substantial monetary or property gain to another person is considered exploitation when the elderly victim consented to enrich that person as a result of misrepresentation, undue influence, coercion, or threat of force.

Gay Male Domestic Violence

Domestic violence is the third leading health problem facing gay men, second to substance abuse and AIDS. Gay and bisexual men are likely to deny or minimize the violence that is perpetrated against them. Gay male victims are less likely to report intimate violence incidents than are lesbian victims. Rates of battering victimization in gay male relationships range from 12 to 36 percent. The estimation is less than reported lesbian domestic violence and comparable to family violence among heterosexual women. Gay and bisexual male intimate partner violence is typified by physical, material, and psychological violence. It includes all of the forms of personal violence previously mentioned, such as destruction of personal property, kicking, hitting, humiliation, punching, psychological abuse, and slapping. Threatening to tell others that the victim is gay is singular to both lesbian and gay partner violence. Alienation and isolation of gay men situates them for partnership violence with few resources available to break the cycle. While it may be similar to battering in general, this form is differentiated by the minimization and shame felt by the male victim.

Reports compiled by the New York City Gay and Lesbian Anti-Violence Project are a major source of information relative to intimate violence committed by gay, lesbian, and transgender intimate partners. It estimates that partnership violence in the gay community occurs in 25 to 33 percent of relationships, which is consistent with the prevalence of violence in heterosexual relationships.

Homicide

Categories of homicide—the wrongful killing of a human being—include murder, manslaughter, and negligent homicide, with varying degrees of culpability. When a husband murders his wife, it is referred to as uxoricide. Femicide is a more general term used to describe the killing of a woman by her intimate partner, relative, or friend.

A woman is nine times more likely to be killed by her spouse, an intimate acquaintance, or a family member than by a stranger, according to the report *When Men Kill Women* (Brock 2003). Brock's analysis of male to female homicide found that over 60 percent of women murdered in 2001 were the wives, common-law wives, ex-wives, or girlfriends of their killers. The report further states that 327 women (nearly one woman per day) were shot and killed by either their husbands or intimate acquaintances during the course of an argument.

The risk of intimate partner homicide is increased fourfold if the abuser is unemployed. A batterer's unemployment, access to guns, and threats of deadly violence are the strongest predictors of femicide. Major risk factors include a prior history of violence with increased frequency and severity over time, addiction to illegal drugs, engaging in death rituals, and homicidal and/or suicidal ideation. For gay and lesbian intimate partner homicide, a large disparity between the couple's ages appears to be an increased risk factor.

Homicide rates of heterosexual intimates have been declining over the past two decades. The most pronounced decline has been in the number of men killed by intimate partner women; also declining to a lesser degree is murder of female intimates. Rates of homicide among gay and lesbian couples are unknown.

Husband Battering

Husband battering is used to clarify the subject of the intimate partner abuse in which a male partner is battered by his abusive wife. The characteristics of this form are found above in the general definition of battering. Constant criticism, humiliation, and the use of controlling tactics are common indicators of this type of abuse. Biting, kicking, hitting with objects, pushing, and slapping are also common. Serious physical abuse may occur but is rare. Intimate violence against men has remained fairly constant and is estimated to be at 15 percent of all domestic offenses, or 103,220 victimizations in 2001 according to the National Crime Victimization Survey. Common tactics of intimate partner violence against men include biting, groin attacks, kicking, physical attacks while sleeping, sleep deprivation, and throwing things at them, including hot coffee or food. Weapons used include shoes, phones, knives, and, in rare situations, guns. Despite official statistics that estimate husband abuse ranging between 6 and 10 percent of all intimate

partner violence, male abuse by women is frequently trivialized. Males appear far less likely than females to report abuse by an intimate partner or to pursue prosecution if a report is made to the authorities, adding to the invisibility of this form of intimate partner violence. Denial of the abuse is a typical victim response.

Lesbian Battering

Lesbian battering is a pattern of violent or coercive behaviors perpetrated against an intimate partner in a lesbian relationship; the physical violence in the relationship concerns attempts at enhanced control over the thoughts, beliefs, or conduct of an intimate lesbian partner or to punish her for resistance to the control. Threats of "outing" the closeted female lesbian and exploitation of internalized homophobia complicate the violence within a lesbian partnership.

Same-sex partnerships are controversial, and lesbian battering in particular may not be socially or legally recognized in some states. Current criminal justice reporting practices do not specify the gender or relationship of the perpetrator to the victim; therefore, it is unknown whether or not the numbers include lesbian victims.

Partner abuse within lesbian relationships became recognized as a significant problem during the 1980s. Battering within same-sex relationships is often described as being at least as prevalent as it is for heterosexual couples and may be occurring at a rate as high as 50 percent within the population. Lesbians are characterized as resistant to addressing the problem of battering through underreporting and as being in states of denial.

The strides that have been made for female victims of domestic violence within heterosexual relationships have not translated into social service and policy responses for women victimized by other women through intimate violence, and response strategies are extremely limited. Lesbian partnership violence is different from heterosexual abuse mainly because it includes homophobia as a controlling tactic; unique also to lesbian relationships is the cumulative effect of living in a homophobic and heterosexist world. Lesbian partner violence explanations generally rely on the feminist model of power and control. This approach causes problems due to its oppression being rooted in male–female gender dynamics. Alternative explanations suggest multiple oppressions of power exist which affect lesbian domestic violence, including racism, sexism, and capitalism, besides heterosexism and homophobia.

Maltreatment

Typically associated with the unintentional injury or neglect of a person who has an infirmity or is impaired, maltreatment affects elderly intimates and adults with disabilities. This form of abuse may include over- or under-medication, misuse of restraints, and emotional or psychological abuse against the vulnerable adult.

Marital Rape

Marital or intimate partner rape is defined as unwanted intercourse or penetration (vaginal, anal, or oral) through force or threat of force or when the partner is unable to consent. Either gender may be victimized sexually, although women are the overwhelming majority of rape victims. Some states exempt married persons from criminal liability in cases of marital rape when the spouse is infirm due to age or medical conditions. A minor is presumed unable to give informed consent in a number of states; therefore, any sexual contact with a minor may legally be considered rape even if the minor and the adult are consensual intimates or dating partners, unless a legal exemption for age exists in that state. The age at which a minor may legally consent to sexual contact varies by state.

Physical effects of marital rape are bleeding, bruising, lacerations, or pain to the genitals, rectum, mouth, or breasts. When bruising or pain is documented along with injury to the face, neck, cheek, abdomen, thighs, or buttocks, the patterns of bruising might be suggestive of grab marks or the use of restraints. The victims may experience torn muscles, fatigue, and vomiting in addition to broken bones, black eyes, bloody noses, and knife or burn wounds. Behavioral indicators include intense fear, anxiety, or mistrust of the intimate partner, along with other indicators of sexual maltreatment. Depression without any other explanation or cause and self-destructive behavior or suicide attempts without a history of mental illness may also be suspicious for sexual abuse. Posttraumatic stress disorder (PTSD) is the most common disorder seen in victims of rape.

Marital rape became a crime in all fifty states in 1993. However, as of this writing, thirty-three states still provide husbands with exemptions from rape prosecutions; for instance, an exemption may be granted if the wife is mentally or physically impaired, unconscious, asleep, or legally unable to consent. Marital rape is most likely to occur in relationships characterized by other forms of intimate partner violence. The majority of women who are raped by their intimate partner are also battered by that partner, and many report being kicked.

Official statistics place the frequency of marital rape at about 25 percent of all reported rapes. Pregnancy is a factor that places a woman at greater risk for both physical and sexual abuse. Miscarriages, stillbirths, bladder infections, infertility, and the potential contraction of sexually transmitted diseases, including human immunodeficiency virus (HIV), are specific gynecological consequences of marital rape. Other risk factors include drug and alcohol abuse by the abuser. As many as one in ten wives may have been sexually assaulted by their spouses at least once.

Intimate partner rape is typically divided into three categories: violent rape, force-only rape, and sadistic rape. The violent rape occurs when the intimate partner uses physical violence and causes injuries apart from those due to the rape itself. It includes punching or injuring with a knife. The rape becomes part of the violent physical attack used to intimidate and humiliate the victim or make her beg for forgiveness. A force-only rape is accomplished with minimal force to ensure compliance and to prevent the spouse or intimate partner from escaping or self-defending. Holding down the victim by his or her arms or wrists and a size differential between the perpetrator and victim are indicators. The sadistic rape includes additional actions by the perpetrator that are meant to degrade and humiliate. Torture, forced use of objects to penetrate the victim, and urinating on the intimate partner are examples.

To date there is no national study of marital rape that has included cohabitating gay and lesbian couples. It is difficult to approximate its prevalence, although several small sample studies have attempted to research the phenomenon. Researchers have estimated the prevalence of lesbian and gay domestic violence to be similar to that in heterosexual relationships, occurring in between one-fourth and one-half of all relationships.

Misuse of Restraints

While typically associated with elder abuse in institutional settings, misuse of restraints may also be identified as a problem in an abusive home as a manner of controlling or punishing any adult. Restraints are to be used only for the safety of an infirm individual, and never without a physician's order. Misuse involves the chemical or physical control of an adult of any age or disability that is beyond a physician's order or outside accepted medical practice. Physical restraints include any rope or cloth that restricts the movement of the person. If the use of restraints is used as a punishment or for the purpose of inflicting pain, prosecution may be a feasible option. Signs suggestive of the misuse of restraints include physical injuries such as gag marks from taping around the mouth, or rope burns on the ankles, wrists, neck, or torso that result from being tied up or restrained for long periods of time.

Partner Battering

This refers to violence between any two intimate partners. Its gender-neutral designation includes violence occurring within all adult intimate relationships regardless of sexual preference, marital status, or age of the intimates. Additionally, the use of the term *battering* suggests an ongoing complete pattern of violence behavior which conforms to the concept of battering.

Physical Abuse

Physical abuse is characterized by the use of force or threat of force that may result in bodily injury, physical pain, or impairment. Physical abuse may be recognized through external or internal signs. External signs include but are not limited to bite marks, bleeding, bruises, burns, crying, marks, missing or pulled hair, ripped clothing, and wincing. Broken blood vessels around the eye may indicate strangulation. Internal signs of physical abuse include but are not limited to bone fractures, broken bones, dislocations, internal bleeding, and sprains. Physical abuse occurs through beatings, biting, hitting, kicking, pulling of hair, pulling the individual, punching, slapping, shoving, strangulation, striking, and throwing things. Physical abuse victimizes one person at the hands of the intimate partner. Acts of physical abuse are crimes against the person and more often than not rise to the level of criminal offense.

Psychological Abuse

Psychological abuse may include forms of emotional abuse as well as manipulative behaviors that cause the victim to become psychologically unstable over time. There are a range of behaviors that would constitute psychological abuse; these are relationship dependent and meant to take advantage of the vulnerability of the victim for the purpose of increasing reliance on the perpetrator. Examples include intentional attempts to confuse the person such as moving household items while insisting that they were always in that position, convincing the victim that family and friends are out to harm him

or her, punishing the victim for insignificant transgressions, or staging false suicides for the victim to discover. Exploiting the intimate partner's fears (i.e., exposing the victim to snakes or bugs) may constitute psychological abuse. Attacks on the personal property of the person, against pets of the victim, or sleep deprivation by repeated hang-up phone calls are meant to frighten and mentally incapacitate the victim. Indicators of this form of abuse are changes in personality, increased agitation or fearfulness, and extreme dependence, behaviors which were previously out of character for the individual. If the victim becomes confused or unable to distinguish between reality and fantasy, psychological torment may rise to the level of criminal neglect or abuse.

Sexual Abuse

This general category refers to nonconsensual sexual contact of any kind; examples include indecent touching or fondling, forced prostitution or pornography by an intimate partner, and marital rape.

Stalking

The crime of stalking is defined as conduct directed at a specific person that involves repeated visual or physical proximity; nonconsensual communication; verbal, written, or implied threats; or a combination of these things that would cause fear in a reasonable person. Common behaviors include following, harassing, and threatening the victims. Violence appears to occur in 30 to 50 percent of stalking cases, with severe violence noted in approximately 6 percent of the cases. The most consistent indicator of violence are threats and a previous intimate relationship between the victim and the offender. Stalking is a serious criminal justice problem: The National Violence Against Women Survey estimates that 5 percent of women are stalked by a current or former spouse, cohabitating partner, or date at some time in their lives. Almost one in three victims sought counseling as a result of the stalking, 18 percent sought help from friends or family members, and 17 percent obtained a gun.

Woman Battering

Women are the most frequent victims of intimate partner violence. It affects women in every social and economic stratum; similarly, it may be perpetrated by persons regardless of their economic, education, or professional status. To signify the long-term suffering of these women, they are often referred to as survivors. Woman battering has reached epidemic proportions in the United

States and is considered a major social problem. Women's quality of life is severely affected by all forms of intimate violence. Health concerns that are associated with violence against women include gastrointestinal disorders, chronic pain or fatigue, depression, loss of appetite and eating disorders, and gynecological and urological disorders. Physical injury, psychological trauma, and death are associated with violence against women. According to the National Center for Injury Prevention and Control, abused women experience more physical health problems and have a higher occurrence of depression, drug and alcohol abuse, and suicide attempts than women who are not abused. Domestic violence has also been acknowledged as a contributing factor for pregnancy and birth complications, sudden infant death syndrome, brain trauma, fractures, sexually transmitted diseases, HIV infection, depression, dissociation, psychosis, and other stress-related physical and mental disorders.

The battered women's movement beginning in the early 1970s placed partner abuse within the context of economic and social subjugation. Battered women's shelters began to open in the United States in 1974; these gave safe refuge to women who had been abused. The criminalization of domestic violence emerged from this movement, along with other social service and policy responses.

Humiliation, constant criticism, jealous accusations, and controlling involvement with family and friends are forms of abuse that constitute the pattern of woman battering. The intervention process relies on the ability of responding social systems to send clear and consistent messages to batterers, including arrest, prosecution, and counseling. The theme in counseling is nonviolence, and the difference between anger and abusive action is expressly taught.

DENISE KINDSCHI GOSSELIN

See also **Battered Husbands; Battered Wives: Held in Captivity; Batterer Typology; Gay and Bisexual Male Domestic Violence; Lesbian Battering; Mutual Battering**

References and Further Reading

Brock, K. *When Men Murder Women: An Analysis of 2001 Homicide Data*. Washington, DC: Violence Policy Center, 2003.

Burke, T., M. Jordan, and S. Owen. "A Cross-National Comparison of Gay and Lesbian Domestic Violence." *Journal of Contemporary Criminal Justice* 18, no. 3 (2002): 231–257.

Jogerst, G. J., J. M. Daly, M. F. Brinig, J. D. Dawson, G. A. Schmuch, and J. G. Ingram. "Domestic Elder Abuse and the Law." *American Journal of Public Health* 93, no. 12 (2003): 2131–2137.

Moore, K. *Lesbian, Gay, Bisexual and Transgender Domestic Violence: 2001 Supplement*. New York: National Coalition of Anti-Violence Programs, 2002.

National Center for Injury Prevention and Control. *Costs of Intimate Partner Violence against Women in the United States*. Atlanta: Centers for Disease Control and Prevention, 2003.

Pillemer, K., and D. Finkelhor. "The Prevalence of Elder Abuse: A Random Sample Survey." *The Gerontologist* 28, no. 1 (1988): 51.

Rennison, C. M., and S. Welchans. *Intimate Partner Violence* (NCJ 178247). Washington, DC: U.S. Department of Justice, 2000.

Williams, R. [The Gay Men's Domestic Violence Project Survey]. Unpublished raw data, 1998.

INTIMATE PARTNER VIOLENCE IN QUEER, TRANSGENDER, AND BISEXUAL COMMUNITIES

Intimate partner violence among queer, transgender, and bisexual people is underresearched and undertheorized. Insights from studies of same-sex domestic violence apply to these populations, but such studies may not address identities that transcend or trouble conventional sex and gender categories. Mainstream domestic violence discourses, criminal justice interventions, and social services have marginalized queer, trans, and bi populations along with, and sometimes to a greater degree than, lesbian and gay populations. Some service agencies and community groups have begun to "queer" the discourse on domestic violence by acknowledging a fuller range of gender and sexual identities that contribute to multiple and divergent contexts for, and experiences of, domestic violence.

"Same-sex" violence in lesbian and gay relationships is addressed in a number of edited volumes (Kaschak 2001; Leventhal and Lundy 1999; Lobel 1986; Renzetti and Miley 1996) and in many additional articles from a range of academic, clinical, and social service fields. Several foundational studies provide in-depth analysis of lesbian partner abuse (Renzetti 1992; Ristock 2002), lesbian sexual assault (Girshick 2002), and battering among gay men (Island and Letellier 1991). Further information on lesbian and gay domestic violence is offered within this volume.

In contrast, extremely limited research specifically addresses intimate partner violence involving non-heterosexual people who do not identify as "lesbian" or "gay," including transgender, bisexual, and queer-identified people. Diana Courvant (1997) has written a landmark article on domestic violence affecting trans and intersex people. Sulis (1999) provides a groundbreaking article on battered bisexual women, and Crane et al. (1999) discuss lesbian and bisexual women's caucus work in a domestic violence intervention agency. Bisexual men's experiences of violence are discussed together with gay men's experiences (Johnson 1999; Letellier 1996) and as part of lesbian-gay-bisexual-transgender (LGBT) experiences in general (Merrill 1999; Toro-Alfonso 1999), but specific information on domestic violence involving bisexual men per se is sparse.

The shortage of empirical research results in part from impediments to obtaining accurate data. These impediments include pressures on queer, trans, and bi people to remain closeted, decreased reporting of violent incidents among these populations, lack of documentation of this violence by criminal justice and social service agencies, and widespread lack of general understanding of these populations and their differences from straight, lesbian, and gay populations. In 1997, the National Coalition of Anti-Violence Programs (NCAVP) began producing annual reports on LGBT domestic violence in the United States and Toronto. Compiling data on violence against transgender and bisexual people is integral to NCAVP's ongoing research efforts. The number of service sites contributing data, and the capacity of these sites to collect accurate data, has increased over time (Moore and Baum 2004).

Aside from the limited but productive and growing literature that documents and analyzes LGBT intimate partner violence, the vast majority of research on domestic violence focuses on heterosexual relationships, with two results pertaining to queer, trans, and bi communities. First, scholarly theories and institutional discourses on domestic violence have marginalized lesbian, gay, bisexual, transgender, intersex, and queer (LGBTIQ) populations, contributing to a scarcity of resources suited to LGBTIQ people experiencing violence in their intimate relationships. This scarcity is even more pronounced for trans, bi, and queer-identified people than for those who identify as lesbian or gay.

Second, most theories about, empirical research on, and criminal justice and social service approaches to domestic violence are constrained by heteronormative assumptions about the identities and roles of individuals in intimate relationships, intimate partner violence, interventions, and service provision. These assumptions have the effect of forcing both queer and nonqueer individuals seeking institutional or community support to fit themselves and their experiences into a narrow set of frameworks in order to garner recognition and support from the system.

Queer Movements and Identities: Terms and Concepts

Understanding intimate partner violence among queer, trans, and/or bi people requires some familiarity with concepts related to their identities. Especially among younger generations of LGBTIQ people, a growing proportion of nonheterosexual people do not identify themselves exclusively as "lesbian" or "gay." Many align themselves with queer identities and movements instead of, or in addition to, lesbian or gay ones. The word "queer," now commonly used in a variety of social, scholarly, and political contexts, has at least three interconnected meanings. First, it has been reclaimed from its original negative labeling purpose and deployed repeatedly as a positive expression of group identification and pride by various LGBTIQ communities and movements.

Second, "queer" is used as an umbrella term for individuals, communities, identities, and practices commonly defined as outside normative social constructions of sexual orientation and gender. *Sexual orientations* under the "queer" umbrella include lesbian, gay, and bisexual as well as other forms of desire that defy normative gender and sexual boundaries. For example, polyamory, sadomasochism (S/M), and the communities that practice them are sometimes referred to as "queer." "Queer" as an umbrella term also encompasses non-normative *gender identities,* namely those of people whose lives and forms of self-expression do not fit within society's binary system for categorizing bodies and gender identities as either male or female. Transgender(ed), transsexual, transvestite, FTM (female-to-male), MTF (male-to-female), transman, transwoman, and genderqueer are examples of gender identities often included under the "queer" umbrella. Bornstein (1994), Feinberg (1996), and Halberstam (1998) offer analyses of MTF, FTM, and transgender identities and histories, and Nestle et al. (2002) provide an edited volume of genderqueer narratives.

It is important to respect each individual's chosen language for identifying her or his own gender and sexual identity. Many self-identified queer people prefer not to be called "queer" by straight outsiders to their communities, and not everyone considered "queer" by someone else considers themselves so. For example, many transsexual and intersex people do not identify as queer, and although queer theorists may consider transvestitism queer as a practice, many transvestites do not claim a queer identity.

Third, queer theoretical and political movements challenge systems that construct and uphold binary categories of sex (i.e., male/female), gender (i.e., man/woman), and sexual orientation (i.e., straight/gay). Participants in queer movements tend to see gender and sexuality as fluid social constructs, rather than as strict binary systems for categorizing individuals and relationships. Queer communities, activists, and theorists deploy queer ideology and identities to dismantle polarized categories of sex, gender, and sexual orientation, along with the implications of these categories, in a range of social and institutional contexts (Butler 1990/1999; Gamson 1995). Transgender and intersex movements have gained visibility and influence in queer theory and politics as well as in medical and other arenas (Bornstein 1994; Chase 2002; Fausto-Sterling 2000).

Complete understanding of intimate partner violence in queer, trans, and bi communities requires attention to aspects of identity other than gender and sexuality. Numerous empirical and analytical studies highlight the importance of race, ethnicity, class, citizenship status, HIV status, age, parenthood, and physical ability or disability in the roles and experiences of LGBT people in intimate partner violence, criminal justice interventions, and service provision (Bograd 2005; García 1999; Hanson

and Maroney 1999; Letellier 1996; Méndez 1996; Toro-Alfonso 1999; Waldron 1996). Queer theory investigates intersections of gender and sexuality with race, ethnicity, nationalism, class, and other dimensions of identity (Butler 2004; Ferguson 2004; Gopinath 2005; Halberstam 2005), and the implications of these intersections for violence affecting LGBTIQ communities. Insights from queer theory and politics illuminate dynamics of violence, particularly those related to identity, that are ordinarily obscured in domestic violence discourse. These insights are valuable for developing more effective service and intervention models.

Queering Understandings of Domestic Violence

Several analyses of violence against LGBT people subsume bisexual, transgender, and queer identities under the populations and relationship categories they discuss, and insights from these analyses do apply in many respects to queer, trans, and bi populations. For example, Onken (1998) and Allen and Leventhal (1999) discuss contextual factors contributing to violence against and within LGBT communities, including trans, bi, and queer-identified people. Hate violence, dominant gender norms, and isolation contribute to violence in queer relationships and to the lack of resources available when violence occurs. Violence against LGBT people is socially sanctioned (Onken 1998), and acceptance of this violence may be reinforced by a cultural climate that supports anti–gay rights ordinances and anti–gay marriage legislation. Trans and intersex people experience elevated levels of violence beginning in childhood that may in turn contribute to future violence in relationships. As a result, it may be harder for LGBT people to stand up to violence or to ask for help in the face of violence. Further, LGBT people may internalize blame for violence that happens against them or other members of their communities (Allen and Leventhal 1999).

Gender norms play a significant role in domestic violence in queer, trans, and bi communities, as they do in all communities. There is general consensus in mainstream domestic violence discourse about how masculine and feminine gender socialization manifest in heterosexual relationship violence (although gender dynamics do not play out according to formula in every heterosexual relationship). Violence committed by men is linked with masculine gender socialization that reinforces sexism, misogyny, homophobia, and physical and sexual violence. Feminine gender socialization may lead women to internalize blame and to resist leaving abusive relationships.

Queer, trans, and bi people, too, are affected by dominant gender norms, but in ways rarely discussed in mainstream domestic violence discourse. Men and masculine-gendered people are not easily believed when they report violence, whether their partners are masculine or feminine. This disbelief may be heightened for a masculine person whose abusive partner is either a woman, feminine in gender expression, or perceived as feminine or effeminate. Masculine gender norms dictate that men should be able to defend themselves, are not victims, and enjoy sex at any time, in any place. These expectations delegitimize masculine persons' claims of physical and sexual abuse. For example, abusive partners of butch women, transgender people, and FTM transmen may suggest that they are not butch enough or man enough to take forced sexual activity (Allen and Leventhal 1999).

On the other hand, masculine-gendered partners' abusiveness may be overlooked by the community as part of being masculine. A butch woman or FTM transgendered abuser may garner more sympathy from the surrounding queer community as the more "out," visible, or at-risk member of a couple. At the same time, enduring abuse may be viewed as part of being feminine. For example, MTF transgender victims of abuse may be falsely blamed for acting too effeminate or "victim-like." Thus adherence to gender norms, rather than the behavior and motivations of the abuser, can become the defining feature that legitimates claims of violence. In all segments of the LGBTIQ community, internalized gender and sexual stereotypes may be used to justify intimate partner violence or to deny that it is damaging to its victims.

Masculine gender norms may be the main cause for the underrepresentation of domestic violence among bisexual and gay men in the literature, and for the secrecy surrounding male bisexuality in general. Discussions about domestic violence in the bisexual community have emerged in part from a growing bisexual feminist movement (Sulis 1999). Domestic violence against both bisexual women and men has received little research attention, perhaps because bisexual people are often misunderstood and maligned by straight, lesbian, and gay men's communities. These misunderstandings may contribute to increased violence and lack of appropriate services for bisexual victims of domestic violence. Although bisexual people's experiences and needs regarding domestic violence are often assumed to be identical or interchangeable with those of straight, lesbian, and/or gay people, this is not necessarily the case.

Isolation, Power, and Control

The U.S. domestic violence movement has converged upon the importance of patterns of power and control in relationship violence and abuse. Although patterns of coercion and control are fundamentally similar across relationships, conditions related to sexual orientation and gender identity influence how the batterer achieves control, how battering affects the battered partner, and the resources available for support. Power and control can take particular forms when abusers or their partners are queer, trans, or bi. Just as abusers in straight, gay, and lesbian relationships may draw upon sexism and homophobia to threaten and intimidate their partners (Allen and Leventhal 1999; Pharr 1988), abusers of queer, trans, and bi people may use intimate knowledge of their partners' particular gender and sexual nonconformities against them. On the other hand, queer, trans, and bi abusers may enact power and control in ways that are specific to their own identities and those of their partners.

Isolation is a central tactic of power and control, with profound effects upon queer, trans, and bi survivors of domestic violence. Social homophobia, transphobia, and biphobia force LGBTIQ people to constantly negotiate the socially constructed phenomenon of "the closet," and to decide, repeatedly, whether and how to "come out" (Sedgwick 1990). If not out in any of a number of contexts (family, work, social circles, faith community), a queer person is by definition socially isolated. For example, by coming out to one's family, one may risk homophobic hostility, emotional rejection, or being disowned outright. Any of these scenarios makes it difficult to return to one's family for support in a crisis such as relationship violence. Isolation from family, coworkers, or other social networks can give abusers greater power and their negative comments more weight in the minds of their partners.

Social conditions that stereotype and isolate trans, bi, and queer-identified people lend themselves to abusive power and control. As an example with regard to transgender, an abuser of a gender-transitioning person may say that the police or shelter won't help "a freak like you" or that s/he is physically or emotionally oversensitive due to the hormones s/he is taking (Allen and Leventhal 1999). Like transphobia, biphobia too can be exploited by an abuser. Sulis (1999) outlines power and control tactics used to target bisexual people. Outing is an especially effective tactic against a bisexual victim because the abuser may threaten to out the victim both to straight family members or coworkers and to the lesbian or gay community. As with lesbian or gay parents, partners of bisexual parents may threaten to expose their sexuality to the children's other parent or other family members. In addition, a bi person's partner may exploit internalized shame about being attracted to, or having relationships with, both women and men, and the surrounding community may justify the abuser's violence against a bisexual person because "s/he slept with a woman/man." If bisexual people's partners identify or pass as straight, they may exploit their heterosexual privilege. Trans- and biphobia are used against lesbians and gay victims as well as transgender and bisexual people. For example, abusers might accuse their partners of not being "real wo/men" or "real lesbians" in an attempt to undermine their sense of self.

Victim and Perpetrator Roles

Domestic violence in queer, trans, and bi relationships poses a challenge to the ways victim and perpetrator roles are theorized and applied in dominant conceptions of domestic violence. Most mainstream accounts assume that each participant in a domestic violence scenario assumes one of two polarized and mutually exclusive roles: either "victim" or "perpetrator." The attribution of these roles to participants is usually gendered—women as "victims," men as "perpetrators." These roles are functional in many, perhaps most, cases of domestic abuse, but clearly not in relationships that include some other arrangement or construction of gender identities than "man" and "woman." Roles in relationships, including roles pertaining to violence, can shift over time, perhaps more frequently in queer relationships than in straight ones. For example, women can take on a multiplicity of roles in violent lesbian relationships, and these roles can extend beyond or even rupture the traditional victim–perpetrator categories (Marrujo and Kreger 1996). Among bisexual and gay men, too, "being the victim in one relationship does not preclude abusing in future relationships" (Johnson 1999, p. 217).

Service providers to queer, trans, and bi communities repeatedly confront situations in which law enforcement, the legal system, or service providers themselves misidentify the victim as the perpetrator or vice versa (Goddard and Hardy 1999). Gendered assumptions may lead advocates, police, or others to assume that the more masculine-appearing member of a couple is the abuser, which may not be the case. In some cases, the abuser may initiate or compound this confusion by calling in and identifying her/himself initially as the abused member of a couple. In response to situations where police or the courts have mistakenly mandated anger management or abuser treatment for the survivor, agencies have developed their own intake procedures to determine what the client's specific role is in an abusive dynamic and channel that person toward the appropriate services (Holt and Couchman 2004). Goddard and Hardy (1999) offer helpful techniques for advocates sorting through the potentially confusing terrain of violence in a lesbian relationship.

A queer analysis of intimate partner domestic violence would argue that rather than mapping queer, trans, and bi people and their relationships onto the existing binary gender framework for understanding domestic violence, it is necessary to consider how construction of the victim and perpetrator roles frames understandings of relationship violence. The weight that these roles carry, and the gender assumptions with which they are associated, may discourage queer, trans, and bi people (as well as others) from seeking help and services when violence is occurring.

Interventions and Services

Fears that discourage lesbian and gay people from accessing services are also present, and likely compounded, for transgender people (Johnson 1999). Failure of law enforcement to protect members of LGBT communities and violence committed against LGBT communities by law enforcement have been particularly acute for transgender people and LGBT people of color (Whitlock 2005). Moreover, queer victims of domestic violence are not legally protected in several states (Fray-Witzer 1999). Transgender youth, particularly those who have fled or been kicked out of their homes, may have been particularly targeted for harassment, violence, and verbal abuse by law enforcement as well as by others. Transgender, bi, and queer individuals may be less likely to report abuse or seek support against violence, whether they are "victims" or "perpetrators," because of their justifiable fears that criminal justice and service institutions will repudiate them or subject them to further violence.

Although a growing number of LGBT-led agencies now serve LGBT communities, these agencies tend to be located primarily in urban centers with large concentrations of LGBT people (Moore and Baum 2004). In many areas, mainstream shelters are the only resources available to anyone dealing with domestic violence. Many mainstream domestic violence programs do not serve gay or bisexual men, FTM or MTF transgender people. There is a long tradition of straight women-only groups in domestic violence service, and many women's shelters struggle with how to effectively meet the needs of transsexual and transgender clients. Many programs designed for women inappropriately define transgender, MTF, and FTM people seeking support as men, regardless of how these individuals identify themselves or live their lives (Allen and Leventhal 1999), and deny them service on this basis. One battered women's program admitted that providing motel vouchers to MTF trans-women was "the best solution we [could] come up with" (Crane et al. 1999, p. 130).

Bisexual women face numerous barriers in addition to the lack of data on violence, policing, and services pertaining specifically to them. Battered women's programs have traditionally focused on heterosexual women in their services, outreach materials, and staff and volunteer trainings; many either have not offered services to openly bisexual or lesbian women or have not done the work necessary to make their facilities safe for participation by these women. This work would entail developing nondiscrimination policies, implementing procedures for interrupting homo/biphobic comments and behavior by staff or clients, providing comprehensive training to staff and volunteers on LGBT battering, and hiring lesbian or bisexual survivors of violence (Allen and Leventhal 1999). Even when programs are open to out lesbians, they may not be prepared to serve bisexual women. Bisexual women in relationships with women are not protected by heterosexual privilege when seeking help for intimate partner violence (Sulis 1999); yet lesbian support groups and lesbian-specific services often exclude them in part because some segments of lesbian feminist communities view bisexual women as "traitors" who can fall back on heterosexual privilege or relationships and therefore do not belong in lesbian groups (Crane et al. 1999).

Although some mainstream service agencies may consider themselves open to LGBT populations, queer, trans, and bi people's experiences of being treated as "other" or even threatened can extend from the greater society into the shelter or service agency. Assumptions made and questions asked by domestic violence advocates, whether on the phone, in person, or on intake forms, can be problematic. Without asking preliminary (and sensitively phrased) questions, service providers cannot know how callers and their partners identify with regard to gender. Yet unless a domestic violence agency

has specifically undertaken to provide comprehensive anti-oppression training to its board, staff, and volunteers, intake forms, procedures, and language can (albeit unintentionally) inhibit the ability of queer people to feel welcomed and accepted by the agency. Some mainstream programs have made strides by expanding their service approaches in collaboration with local LGBT communities. Some agencies have established relationships and collaborative programming with local S/M communities to promote community education about healthy relationships and the differences between consensual S/M and abuse (Crane et al. 1999; Margulies 1999).

Regarding queer, trans, and bi batterers, most mainstream and LGBT domestic violence programs continue to use models based on separate services for clients defined as survivors and perpetrators (Cayouette 1999; Garcia 2003; Goddard and Hardy 1999; Grant 1999). Some experienced LGBT service providers argue that it is crucial to determine who is the victim and who is the perpetrator in a given relationship in order to safely assign clients to appropriate support groups or other services. While some agencies view this system as the only appropriate way to deliver services, others have established mixed support groups in which participants include both survivors and abusers, although never from the same couple (Quirk 2004).

Some of the organizations that first organized against violence in LGBT relationships, such as The Network/La Red in Boston and the Northwest Network in Seattle, were initially founded with a focus on battered lesbians. Over time these organizations and others have expanded their conceptions of identity to include transgender, bisexual, and queer identities beyond "lesbian" (Burk 2005; NCAVP 2004). There are a growing number of LGBT-specific anti-violence agencies throughout the United States, but many are just beginning to tailor their work to transgender populations. A 2004 national meeting of these organizations featured panel sessions on transgender services, and agency representatives present acknowledged that their programs had not served transgender clients effectively in the past, mostly because they lacked the expertise and because of transphobia within LGBT communities (NCAVP 2004). Agencies in some local areas have tried mixed-gender groups; facilitators of such groups may find that they need to monitor gender dynamics to ensure equitable discussions (Johnson 1999).

Queering understanding of intimate partner violence requires acknowledging the experiences of queer-identified people, transgender and transsexual people, bisexual people, lesbians and gay men. These populations include people of color, immigrant people (documented and undocumented), working-class people, young people, elders, people with disabilities, HIV-positive people, and members of drag, leather, poly, and other subcultural communities. At a minimum, anti-violence agencies seeking to serve these populations must implement queer-, trans-, and bi-inclusive intake procedures, forms, and language. Making service agencies truly accessible extends beyond language, however. If domestic violence interventions and services are to interrupt cycles of violence based on gender, sexual, and other forms of oppression, service agencies must confront rarely examined assumptions and privileges associated with gender and sexual normativity.

In addition to service agencies in the nonprofit sector, community-based dialogues and strategies for intervention are a promising avenue for addressing intimate partner violence in queer, transgender, and bisexual communities (see Russo 1999). Emi Koyama (2005) points out that, contrary to what might be assumed, natural alliances do not exist among transgender, transsexual, bisexual, and intersex communities that defy gender boundaries; such alliances must be built. Community building efforts among queer, trans, and bi populations may yield productive innovations that challenge gender, sexual, and other binaries (including client/provider and agency/community) that inhibit successful interventions in domestic violence.

ELIZABETH B. ERBAUGH

See also **Community Responses to Gay and Lesbian Domestic Violence; Gay and Bisexual Male Domestic Violence; Gay Domestic Violence, Police Attitudes and Behaviors toward; Lesbian Battering; Sexual Orientation and Gender Identity: The Need for Education in Servicing Victims of Trauma**

References and Further Reading

Allen, Charlene, and Beth Leventhal. "History, Culture, and Identity: What Makes GLBT Battering Different." In *Same-Sex Domestic Violence: Strategies for Change,* edited by B. Leventhal and S. E. Lundy. Thousand Oaks, CA: Sage, 1999.

Bograd, Michele. "Strengthening Domestic Violence Theories: Intersections of Race, Class, Sexual Orientation, and Gender." In *Domestic Violence at the Margins,* edited by N. J. Sokoloff and W. C. Pratt. New Brunswick, NJ: Rutgers University Press, 2005.

Bornstein, Kate. *Gender Outlaw: On Men, Women, and the Rest of Us.* New York: Routledge, 1994.

Burk, Connie. Interview with director of Northwest Network. Seattle, May 31, 2005.

Butler, Judith. *Gender Trouble: Feminism and the Subversion of Identity.* New York: Routledge, 1990/1999.

———. *Undoing Gender.* New York: Routledge, 2004.

Cayouette, Susan. "Running Batterers Groups for Lesbians." In Leventhal and Lundy, *Same-Sex Domestic Violence,* 1999.

Chase, Cheryl. "What Is the Agenda of the Intersex Patient Advocacy Movement?" Paper read at the First World Congress: Hormonal and Genetic Basis of Sexual Differentiation Disorders, May 17–18, Tempe, AZ, 2002.

Courvant, Diana. *Domestic Violence and the Sex- or Gender-Variant Survivor.* Portland, OR: The Survivor Project, 1997.

Crane, Beth, Jeannie LaFrance, Gillian Leichtling, Brooks Nelson, and Erika Silver. "Lesbians and Bisexual Women Working Cooperatively to End Domestic Violence." In Leventhal and Lundy, *Same-Sex Domestic Violence,* 1999.

Fausto-Sterling, Anne. *Sexing the Body: Gender Politics and the Construction of Sexuality.* New York: Basic Books, 2000.

Feinberg, Leslie. *Transgender Warriors: Making History from Joan of Arc to Dennis Rodman.* Boston: Beacon Press, 1996.

Ferguson, Roderick A. *Aberrations in Black: Toward a Queer of Color Critique.* Minneapolis: University of Minnesota Press, 2004.

Fray-Witzer, E. "Twice Abused: Same-Sex Domestic Violence and the Law." In Leventhal and Lundy, *Same-Sex Domestic Violence,* 1999.

Gamson, Joshua. "Must Identity Movements Self-Destruct? A Queer Dilemma." *Social Problems* 42, no. 3 (1995): 390–408.

García, Martha Lucía. "A 'New Kind' of Battered Woman: Challenges for the Movement." In Leventhal and Lundy, *Same-Sex Domestic Violence,* 1999.

Garcia, Norma. Interview with Community United Against Violence Staff. San Francisco, October 6, 2003.

Girshick, Lori B. *Woman-to-Woman Sexual Violence: Does She Call It Rape?* Boston: Northeastern University Press, 2002.

Goddard, Alma Banda, and Tara Hardy. "Assessing the Lesbian Victim." In Leventhal and Lundy, *Same-Sex Domestic Violence,* 1999.

Gopinath, Gayatri. *Impossible Desires: Queer Diasporas and South Asian Public Cultures.* Durham, NC: Duke University Press, 2005.

Grant, Jennifer. "An Argument for Separate Services." In Leventhal and Lundy, *Same-Sex Domestic Violence,* 1999.

Halberstam, Judith. *Female Masculinity.* Durham, NC: Duke University Press, 1998.

———. *In a Queer Time and Place: Transgender Bodies, Subcultural Lives.* New York: NYU Press, 2005.

Hanson, Bea, and Terry Maroney. "HIV and Same-Sex Domestic Violence." In Leventhal and Lundy, *Same-Sex Domestic Violence,* 1999.

Holt, Susan, and Delena Couchman. Interview with LA STOP Partner Abuse/Domestic Violence Program Staff. Los Angeles, October 14, 2004.

Island, David, and Patrick Letellier. *Men Who Beat the Men Who Love Them: Battered Gay Men and Domestic Violence.* New York: Haworth Press, 1991.

Johnson, Robb. "Groups for Gay and Bisexual Male Survivors of Domestic Violence." In Leventhal and Lundy, *Same-Sex Domestic Violence,* 1999.

Kaschak, Ellyn, ed. *Intimate Betrayal: Domestic Violence in Lesbian Relationships*. New York: Haworth Press, 2001.

Koyama, Emi. An Evening with Emi Koyama. Albuquerque, NM, July 26, 2005.

Letellier, Patrick. "Twin Epidemics: Domestic Violence and HIV Infection among Gay and Bisexual Men." In *Violence in Gay and Lesbian Domestic Partnerships,* edited by C. M. Renzetti and C. H. Miley. New York: Harrington Park Press, 1996.

Leventhal, Beth, and Sandra E. Lundy, eds. *Same-Sex Domestic Violence: Strategies for Change*. Thousand Oaks, CA: Sage Publications, 1999.

Lobel, Kerry. *Naming the Violence: Speaking Out About Lesbian Battering*. Seattle: Seal Press, 1986.

Margulies, Jennifer. "Coalition Building 'Til It Hurts: Creating Safety Around S/M and Battering." In Leventhal and Lundy, *Same-Sex Domestic Violence,* 1999.

Marrujo, Becky, and Mary Kreger. "Definition of Roles in Abusive Lesbian Relationships." In Renzetti and Miley, *Violence in Gay and Lesbian Domestic Partnerships,* 1996.

Méndez, Juan M. "Serving Gays and Lesbians of Color Who Are Survivors of Domestic Violence." In Renzetti and Miley, *Violence in Gay and Lesbian Domestic Partnerships,* 1996.

Merrill, Gregory S. "1 in 3 of 1 in 10: Sexual and Dating Violence Prevention Groups for Lesbian, Gay, Bisexual and Transgendered Youth." In Leventhal and Lundy, *Same-Sex Domestic Violence,* 1999.

Moore, Ken, and Rachel Baum. *Lesbian, Gay, Bisexual and Transgender Domestic Violence: 2003 Supplement*. New York: National Coalition of Anti-Violence Programs, 2004.

NCAVP [National Coalition of Anti-Violence Programs]. Roundtable, at Denver, CO, May 2004.

Nestle, Joan, Clare Howell, and Riki Wilchins, eds. *Genderqueer: Voices from Beyond the Sexual Binary*. Los Angeles: Alyson, 2002.

Onken, Steven J. "Conceptualizing Violence Against Gay, Lesbian, Bisexual, Intersexual, and Transgendered People." *Journal of Gay and Lesbian Social Services* 8, no. 3 (1998): 5–24.

Pharr, Suzanne. *Homophobia: A Weapon of Sexism*. Inverness, CA: Chardon Press, 1988.

Quirk, K. C. Interview with director of Esperanza Shelter for Battered Families. Albuquerque, NM, December 5, 2004.

Renzetti, Claire M. *Violent Betrayal: Partner Abuse in Lesbian Relationships*. Newbury Park, CA: Sage Publications, 1992.

Renzetti, Claire M., and Charles Harvey Miley. *Violence in Gay and Lesbian Domestic Partnerships*. New York: Harrington Park Press, 1996.

Ristock, Janice. *No More Secrets: Violence in Lesbian Relationships*. New York: Routledge, 2002.

Russo, Ann. "Lesbians Organizing Lesbians against Battering." In Leventhal and Lundy, *Same-Sex Domestic Violence,* 1999.

Sedgwick, Eve Kosofsky. *Epistemology of the Closet*. Berkeley and Los Angeles: University of California Press, 1990.

Sulis, Sarah. "Battered Bisexual Women." In Leventhal and Lundy, *Same-Sex Domestic Violence,* 1999.

Toro-Alfonso, José. "Domestic Violence among Same-Sex Partners in the Gay, Lesbian, Bisexual, and Transgender Communities in Puerto Rico: Approaching the Issue." In Leventhal and Lundy, *Same-Sex Domestic Violence,* 1999.

Waldron, Charlene M. "Lesbians of Color and the Domestic Violence Movement." In Renzetti and Miley, *Violence in Gay and Lesbian Domestic Partnerships,* 1996.

Whitlock, Kay. *Corrupting Justice: A Primer for LGBT Communities on Racism, Violence, Human Degradation and the Prison Industrial Complex*. Philadelphia: American Friends Service Committee, 2005.

J

JEWISH COMMUNITY, DOMESTIC VIOLENCE WITHIN THE

Domestic violence occurs at the same rate in the Jewish community in the United States and Israel (the two largest Jewish communities in the world) as it does in non-Jewish communities in the United States. Approximately 20–25 percent of married Jewish women and 3–5 percent of married Jewish men suffer from battering or abuse by an intimate partner. Domestic violence in the Jewish community, as in the general population, is distributed among all age, economic, and educational levels. The 20–25 percent rate of occurrence among married women also holds in the liberal Reform, Reconstructionist, and Conservative movements, as well as the traditional Orthodox community. One of the major obstacles to uncovering and addressing domestic violence in the Jewish community is the difficulty that many clergy (rabbis), lay leaders, and other Jews have had in acknowledging that the problem exists. Many still hold to the myth that Jewish men are not capable of abusive and aggressive behavior toward a wife or intimate partner and that such inappropriate behavior does not happen in Jewish homes. As a result, there has been a tendency to sweep cases of domestic violence under the rug. The historical and textual ambivalence toward striking a spouse in Jewish law is another problem in addressing domestic violence in the Jewish community.

Domestic Violence in Jewish Texts and History

Historically, Judaism, like other Western religions, has been patriarchal and has excluded women from important rituals and from leadership roles. Traditional (Orthodox) Jewish males say a blessing every morning to thank God for not making them a woman (women say a blessing to thank God for creating them as He wished). In the last two decades of the twentieth century, however, the Reform, Reconstructionist, and Conservative movements have moved to complete gender equality. Judaism nonetheless remains a religion that is deeply rooted in its core texts and legal traditions. Discussions about contemporary matters in the Jewish world are often steeped in the words and rulings of texts, sages, and scholars going back to the Old Testament. However, it is important to note that there is no definitive central rabbinical authority in Judaism that makes laws or rulings that apply to all Jews. Rather, rabbis have made rulings (*responsa*) that generally have applied to the communities they served at that time. Jewish law can be seen more as an ongoing conversation across time and geography than as a set canonical law. Therefore, there are often conflicting rulings by different rabbis and sages on various issues. The likelihood of encountering contradictory rulings is greater when the matter at hand is not mentioned in the Hebrew Bible (Five Books of Moses, books of the prophets, and later biblical-era writings), as is the case with violence against spouses. Rabbis, traditionally, have been unlikely to contradict the Five Books of Moses, which have been viewed as being the word of God.

It is argued in the Talmud, the collected wisdom of the sages during the first 600 years following the fall of the Second Jewish Commonwealth in A.D. 70, that a man should love his wife as much as he loves himself and honor her more. At the same time, the Talmud and later rabbinic sources sometimes say that it is acceptable to use force to discipline "bad wives": those who disobey their husbands and do not do their household chores or serve their husbands when requested to do so. Maimonides, the revered Jewish philosopher of the twelfth century, wrote that it was a wife's duty to serve her husband and that she could be forced to do so with a whip if she refused. However, Maimonides qualified this assertion (as does the Talmud) by stating that a man cannot force his wife to do work that is not "customary" or that is degrading. Thus, the wife is under the control of the husband, but he is not to abuse his dominant position over her.

The debate over the acceptability of striking one's wife continued over the course of Jewish history. Rabbi Perez Elijah of Corbeil in thirteenth-century France strongly condemned striking one's wife and considered spousal violence to be a communal matter. The Rabbi of Speir in the twelfth century went as far as ruling that batterers had to take an oath (which was taken very seriously at the time) to cease their beatings or they would be compelled to grant their wives a divorce and possibly face excommunication. At the same time, the *Gaon* (wise man) of Jury in Poland proposed that an assault on a wife should be treated less severely than an assault on a stranger. Rabbi Moses Isserles (Poland) noted in 1554 that under certain conditions, such as disobedience, beating was justified. But unjustified battering was to be condemned and punished. This separation of justified and unjustified corporal punishment was also made by a number of other sages of the Middle Ages. In the twentieth century, Rabbi Eliezer Waldburg ruled that an abusive husband should be forced to give his wife a divorce on grounds of the husband's cruelty. This discussion among Jewish legal authorities demonstrates the lack of a clear position in Jewish law on wife beating, with a small number of sages allowing beatings, many permitting only "justified" beatings, and a number of sages categorically rejecting the use of violence against one's wife. It is important to note that these rulings usually only applied in the locality of the rabbis who made them. In turn, these rabbis and sages were influenced by the norms and needs of their societies in making their rulings.

Judaism, Jewish History, and Myths about Domestic Violence in the Jewish Community

The tenets of the Jewish religion and Jewish history have combined to produce a number of myths that discount the presence of domestic violence in Jewish homes. The perfect Jewish husband is one of these myths. Jewish men are stereotyped as being passive and docile men, who are good providers for their wives and families. The first half of this characterization comes from the long history of oppression of the Jewish people. Because of the subjugation of the Jews during the Diaspora, from A.D. 70 until 1948, Jewish men gained a reputation for being meek and not willing to fight. Consequently, it is hard to accept that a Jewish man can engage in acts of violence and cruelty such as domestic violence. Also, as Jews in the United States have gained affluence, Jewish men have been said to be good providers for their wives and families. As a result, Jewish women who claim that they are abused have often met with disbelief from rabbis, friends, and even members of their own family. It was difficult to accept that a "nice Jewish man" who is so respected in the community would abuse his intimate partner or spouse. Because of this stereotype, it is common for a Jewish victim of domestic abuse to believe that she must be the only one in her situation and that she must have done something to anger her kind Jewish husband and to deserve the beatings.

Two other related myths that have helped to keep domestic violence in the Jewish world unreported are "the perfect Jewish household" and *Shalom Bayit* (peaceful household). Rabbinic commentaries on the book of Genesis claim that God pairs couples in heaven. Similarly, the blessings recited at a Jewish wedding also refer to a divine role in bringing the couple together. How could a match made in heaven include an abusive husband?

The Jewish home created by the marriage is also given high status, as a Jewish home is a sacred place, where many important rituals and observances take place. Peace and harmony (*Shalom Bayit*) are supposed to characterize the Jewish home, ruling out conflict and violence. Consequently, many have difficulties accepting the fact that domestic violence could occur in Jewish homes. It is the role of the Jewish woman to provide *Shalom Bayit,* to maintain the sacredness of the home, and to protect the home from danger. Arguments or fights in the home are seen as a failure of the woman to fulfill her role as an *Ashet Chayil* (woman of valor). The victim often blames herself for the abuse perpetrated by her husband, believing that she has failed to provide a proper Jewish home. Many Jewish victims of spousal abuse think that they have failed in their primary duty as a Jewish woman, let their husbands down, and brought shame to their families.

The tendency to keep domestic violence a secret and to refrain from reporting it to authorities, although present in all societies, is particularly relevant to the Jewish community due to its longtime status as a persecuted minority. Historically, Jews have been concerned that any inappropriate behavior would bring disgrace in the larger community. The tenuous position of the Jews in most of the places where they have lived during the past 2,000 years has caused a strong fear of giving the non-Jewish world further reason, such as domestic violence, for looking down on the Jews. Consequently, Jewish victims of abuse have often been told to keep quiet and not report incidents to the police and other civil authorities for fear of bringing further disdain from their non-Jewish neighbors. At the same time, Jews have felt that they need to be better than their persecutors and the gentiles who surround them. Consequently, domestic violence has often been viewed as a problem that is limited to the *goyyim* (non-Jews), as Jews are not capable of such misbehavior. Jewish victims of domestic violence in the United States have sometimes reported difficulty in getting the police to take them seriously because the myth that Jews do not commit domestic violence, in combination with the myth of the passive Jewish male, has spread to the non-Jewish population.

The need for rabbinic rulings throughout the ages is evidence that domestic abuse has been a continuous problem in the Jewish community. Jewish law and rabbinical authorities continue to be of crucial significance in shaping the response to domestic violence in some parts of the Jewish world. The Reform movement, the largest Jewish movement in the United States (as well as the much smaller Reconstructionist movement), does not recognize Jewish law as being binding. The Conservative movement, which recognizes the authority of Jewish law as interpreted by the sages of the generation, strongly condemns domestic violence. Although victims of domestic assault in all three of these movements often go to their rabbis for advice and counseling, few—if any—would view their rabbi's advice as binding or authoritative. The situation is quite different in parts of the Orthodox community in the Diaspora, where the rabbi, as interpreter of Jewish law, is still viewed as an authority. In Israel, rabbinical authorities have tremendous influence on responses to domestic violence, because so-called issues of "personal status," such as divorce, are largely under the control of rabbinical courts. As a result, many Orthodox women in the United States and all Israeli women are dependent on rabbinical authorities to grant them a divorce—a crucial method of escape from an abusive husband.

The *Get* and *Agunah* Problem

Jewish women cannot divorce their husbands unilaterally, and rabbinic courts cannot grant Jewish women release from their marriages (in Hebrew, a *get*). The husband, in Jewish law, has the exclusive power to grant *get*. The rabbinical court only supervises the divorce proceedings. This balance of power in favor of the husband often leaves Jewish women in the Orthodox community and in Israel at the mercy of their abusive husbands, who refuse to grant them a *get*. Women can go to the rabbinical courts in Israel or to their community rabbinical authority in the Diaspora and ask that their husbands be compelled to grant them a *get*. In the United States, rabbinical authorities, even if they were to order abusive husbands to grant divorces, have no legal authority and cannot compel recalcitrant husbands to release their battered wives from their religious marriages. Most rabbis in the Orthodox community, with some notable exceptions, have often told battered wives to go back to their abusive husbands for the sake of peace in the household, *Shalom Bayit,* and to stop doing the things that "cause" their husbands to beat them. Sometimes the husband is brought in for admonishment or the rabbi counsels the couple. Rarely does the rabbi advise the victim to leave her husband or instruct the abuser that he must grant his wife a divorce. Without a divorce, the woman cannot remarry and any children that she would have would be considered *mamzerim* (illegitimate). A woman who leaves her husband without a divorce is also likely to be considered a *shonde* (source of shame) and to be ostracized by her own community and possibly her own family. As a result, many battered Orthodox women see themselves as having no choice other than to remain with their abusive husbands.

The rabbinical courts in Israel wield tremendous power in matrimonial affairs because there is no civil divorce in that country. Although the courts can order men to grant their wives divorces and enforce penalties if they do not, very few men, including batterers, are ever sanctioned. In the Diaspora, too, the courts often instruct battered women to go home and try and reconcile with their abusive husbands, as the courts feel that it is their duty to keep families together. One study of domestic violence victims in Israel found that 55 percent of abused women who went to the rabbinical courts had been advised to return to their abusive husbands. All of the wives who did return to their husbands reported that they continued to be beaten and a number said that the beatings became worse. Many men use the rabbinical courts to maintain their abuse through continued delaying of proceedings, undergoing rabbinical supervised mediation, or simply promising to change, while continuing to beat their wives. The courts frequently refer the batterer and the victim to family therapy, which the men use to strengthen their dominance over their wives, rather than sending the abuser for treatment for his abusive behavior.

Domestic Violence in Israel

The previously discussed myths about Jews and domestic violence have had a strong influence on how the problem has been handled in Israel. This is best seen in the words of a police officer in Haifa, a city with a mixed Jewish and Arab population, who said, "This [domestic violence] only occurs with the Arabs, not the Jews." However, when the issue was first given serious consideration in the Knesset (the Israeli parliament) and referred to a subcommittee for study (after the Knesset member who raised the issue was shouted at, mocked, and jeered), it became clear that Israel had a serious domestic violence problem. The study found that there was somewhere between 30,000 to 60,000 cases of abuse in a country with a population, at the time, of six million. The subcommittee also reported that there were no mechanisms in place to help the victims of domestic assault, who were often given tranquilizers and small payments. As was the case in the United States and other countries at the time,

domestic assault was seen as a "family problem" and the police would rarely make an arrest when called to a domestic assault incident. Abusers were usually given warnings or a "man-to-man talk," while victims were discouraged from opening cases and were not told to have medical examinations. The maximum sentence for domestic abuse was three years, and the typical punishment was a fine or suspended sentence, both of which allowed the abuser to continue his battering.

Domestic violence began to be seriously addressed in Israel during the 1980s and early 1990s. As in the United States and other Western countries, women's organizations, with subsidies from the government, opened shelters for battered women in Jerusalem and six other major cities. Currently, there are twelve shelters in Israel, all of which are full. A term for "battered woman," *isha muka,* was coined in Hebrew, and the issue was given significant coverage in the media, along with a government-sponsored public education program against domestic violence. The Ministry of Welfare established a special department to deal with domestic abuse that works with the Ministry of Housing and the Ministry of Health. The law was changed so that the police must open a case each time an incident of domestic violence is reported. Despite these advances, sentences for batterers still remain lenient, and shelters or programs for victims remain underfunded. Victims seeking a divorce still face the religious personal status courts, which refuse to change Jewish law to make it easier for them to get divorces. Generally, all social problems in Israel must take a backseat to addressing the Israeli-Palestinian conflict and related terrorism, presenting additional hardships to abused women who seek help.

Domestic Violence in the American Jewish Community

The myths about domestic violence in the Jewish community have had a profoundly negative effect on acknowledging and dealing with domestic violence in the American Jewish community. Several victims reported being told by their rabbis that this was the first time they had heard of domestic violence in their midst. Yet, a study of Jewish victims of domestic violence found that before reporting the abuse to authorities, victims suffered for seven to fifteen years from domestic violence, as opposed to the three- to five-year period found in the larger population. Jewish victims often suffer in silence, because they blame themselves, do not want to be seen as betraying their families and their husbands, and do not want to bring shame to their families and communities. When battered American Jewish women did come forward, like their counterparts in Israel, they were usually told by their rabbis to go home and work the problem out with their abusive husbands for the sake of *Shalom Bayit*. In short, rabbis, teachers, workers in social agencies, and doctors were not properly prepared or trained to deal with domestic violence. Jewish social service agencies commonly referred victims of abuse to family therapists rather than domestic violence counseling.

Advocates for victims of domestic violence in the United States, like their Israeli counterparts, have faced many obstacles in gaining attention and resources for their causes. Most major Jewish organizations, until recently, have been unwilling to take up the battering issue. There have been several cases of flyers about domestic violence being torn down in synagogues and even at the headquarters of the United Jewish Appeal (UJA), the umbrella organization for Jewish community federations in North America. Most rabbis were also unwilling to openly confront domestic violence, as few responded to the call from women's groups to give sermons on the issue. A 2004 survey by Jewish Women International (JWI) reported that most rabbis did not feel that domestic violence should be dealt with from the pulpit. Until recently, the major rabbinical seminaries did not offer training for their students on recognizing and dealing with domestic abuse. As a result, rabbis and other communal leaders found out about cases of domestic abuse only when victims came to them for help. Those rabbis who wanted to help did not know what to do and often did not advise victims to contact the police. It is important to note that domestic abuse is now part of the curriculum of most rabbinical training programs and that many rabbis have taken it upon themselves to learn the signs of abuse and to be able to refer victims to the proper channels for assistance.

Responses to Domestic Violence in the American Jewish Community

The 1988 murder of Zitta Friedlander by her husband in a parking lot near her place of employment in Virginia helped bring the domestic violence issue out from under the rug in the Jewish community. Friedlander had been going through a long and agonizing divorce, during which her husband had frequently threatened to kill her. Friedlander's story and other cases of abuse that were being reported in the Jewish media caused JWI, which had largely focused on the needs of emotionally and physically abused children in Israel, to make domestic violence issues its central concern. JWI, which has approximately 75,000 members, is the only Jewish organization that has made combating domestic violence its primary concern. In 1998, JWI hired a full-time director for its domestic violence programs and has published two manuals on domestic violence, one for rabbis and one for other communal workers. However, its most difficult challenges were convincing the Jewish world that a domestic violence problem existed, pushing for comprehensive domestic violence programs at rabbinical schools and training programs for Jewish communal workers, and lobbying the major Jewish movements to develop comprehensive programs to address domestic violence. JWI has held two conferences on domestic violence, in 1993 and 1995, which both drew over 500 participants.

Major national Jewish organizations, such as the UJA and the various movements, have been slow in taking up the issue of domestic violence and providing funding for programs. Some efforts have included a domestic violence task force at the UJA, a training program for attendants at *mikvah* (Jewish ritual bathhouses that Orthodox women must visit after menstruation) to recognize signs of abuse, and a campaign begun by the Union for Reform Judaism to distribute domestic violence literature at its member synagogues. However, most of the programs to help Jewish victims of domestic violence in the United States have been local and organized at the grassroots level. SHALVA, in Chicago, was founded by eighteen Orthodox women in 1986, who were led by Hanna Weinberg, the wife of an Orthodox rabbi. Today, SHALVA serves 300 families, providing civil court advocacy; financial assistance, including interest-free loans for transitional needs; safe-house referral services; rabbinical and community advocacy; and bilingual assistance. SHALVA also runs a community education program on domestic violence and offers training for rabbis and communal service workers and social workers.

Similar programs such as CHANA (Baltimore), Shalom Task Force (New York), Shalom Bayit (Atlanta), and NISHAMA (Southern California), have been founded in the past twenty years in other Jewish communities across the country. In total, there are approximately sixty service agencies in the United States dedicated to helping Jewish victims of domestic violence. The Shalom Task Force in New York provides the only nationwide 800-number hotline for Jewish victims. Project

Eden works with both the victims of abuse and the abusers in Brooklyn's Hassidic community. The project is unique in that it is housed in the Brooklyn District Attorney's office. The batterers, all Orthodox men, are placed in a court-ordered therapy program called *Brairot* (choices), which runs for fifty-three weeks. In addition to providing counseling, financial assistance, and legal aid to help compel recalcitrant husbands to grant their wives divorces, the program's founder, Henna White, has engaged in an active campaign to counter the myth that domestic abuse is a *shonda* that should be kept secret.

DANIEL PRICE and EDNA EREZ

See also **Africa: Domestic Violence and the Law; African American Community, Domestic Violence in; Christianity and Domestic Violence; Cross-Cultural Perspectives on Domestic Violence; Cross-Cultural Perspectives on How to Deal with Batterers; Greece, Domestic Violence in; Minorities and Families in America, Introduction to; Multicultural Programs for Batterers; Native Americans, Domestic Violence among; Qur'anic Perspectives on Wife Abuse; Spain, Domestic Violence in; Worldwide Sociolegal Precedents Supporting Domestic Violence from Ancient to Modern Times**

References and Further Reading

Adleman, Madeline. "No Way Out: Divorce Related Domestic Violence in Israel." *Violence Against Women* 6, no. 11 (2000): 1223–1254.

Gardsbane, Diane, ed. *Healing and Wholeness: A Resource Guide on Domestic Abuse in the Jewish Community.* Washington, DC: Jewish Women International, 2002.

Graetz, Naomi. *Silence Is Deadly: Judaism Confronts Wife-beating.* Montvale, NJ: Jason Aronson, 1998.

Jacobs, Lynn, and Sherry Berliner Dimarsky. "Jewish Domestic Abuse: Realities and Responses." *Journal of Jewish Communal Service* 68, no. 2 (1991–1992): 94–113.

Lev, Rachel, ed. *Shine the Light: Sexual Abuse and Healing in the Jewish Community.* Boston: Northeastern University Press, 2002.

Newman, Lisa. "Closed Shutters No More," 2004. http://www.momentmag.com/features/feat2.html.

Orenstein, Debra. "How Jewish Law Views Wife Beating." *Lilith* 20 (1998): 9.

Scarf, Mimi. *Battered Jewish Wives.* Lewiston, NY: Edwin Mellon Press, 1988.

Siegel, Rochelle. "Domestic Abuse and Jewish Women: Opening the Shutters." *Jewish Women's Journal* 2, no. 3 (1994): 17–19.

Swirski, Barbara. "Jews Don't Batter Their Wives: Another Myth Bites the Dust." In *Calling the Equality Bluff: Women in Israel,* edited by Barbara Swirski and Marilyn P. Safir. New York: Pergamon Press, 1991, pp. 319–327.

Walker, Lenore. "Jewish Battered Women: Shalom Bayit or Shonde." In *Celebrating the Lives of Jewish Women: Patterns in a Feminist Sampler,* edited by Rachel Siegel and Ellen Cole. Binghamton NY: Haworth Press, 1997, pp. 261–277.

JUDICIAL PERSPECTIVES ON DOMESTIC VIOLENCE

Introduction

Despite the steady accumulation of research findings on the criminal justice system's processing of domestic violence cases, relatively little is known about the beliefs and perceptions of a critical group of actors in that system, trial court judges and magistrates. For many reasons, it is important to understand how judges think about the nature and causes of domestic violence, and their perspectives on the efficacy of current practices and proposed reforms. Judges have considerable discretion at multiple decision points in criminal cases, so their decisions may be shaped by their beliefs as well as by legal aspects of cases. The overwhelming majority of domestic incidents are processed in the lower courts, where they receive even less time, documentation, and visibility than do felonies (Spohn and Cederblom 1991). Further, judges not infrequently express their views to their courtroom audiences and may thereby shape the expectations for justice held by victims, offenders, and bystanders. Finally, domestic violence has been the subject of a broad array of reforms, new programs, and legal mandates, some of which have challenged judges' traditional roles,

428

and few of which have enjoyed widespread endorsement from the bench. The implementation and success of many of these programs may hinge on judicial acceptance and support.

This article summarizes what social scientists have learned about judges' attitudes and perceptions about domestic violence. Very briefly noted are the legal and historical contexts that form the backdrop of judges' training and common-law understandings of domestic violence. The methodological challenges that have limited research on this question are then discussed. Lastly, theoretical and empirical studies that start to fill in the questions about judges' attitudes about domestic violence are addressed, concluding with some observations on fruitful directions for future research and implications of current knowledge for policy and practice.

The Historical Context of Judicial Decision Making in Family Violence Cases

The legal history of domestic violence law and policy is well documented. While traditional common law did not endorse partner violence, neither did it expressly prohibit it. As heads of households, husbands and fathers were authorized to control their family members, and physical "discipline" was deemed unlawful only in extreme cases. Case law began to develop on this topic as women sought not criminal convictions, but civil divorce, in cases of physical abuse; the courts concerned themselves for several decades with defining exactly how much physical violence, inflicted under what sets of circumstances, constituted grounds for cruelty and therefore dissolution of marriage (Friedman 1985; Pleck 1987; Ryan 1986). The notion that wife assault might constitute criminal behavior made only halting inroads into American criminal law.

This case law on spouse abuse, only a few generations removed from contemporary legal training, has yet to evaporate from criminal case processing, despite several decades of explicit reforms (Zorza 1992). It is true that in almost all states, statutory changes have reclassified violent acts among family members as equal to, or even more serious than, assaults committed by strangers. However, enforcement of such laws has been uneven (see, for example, Avakame 2001), evidence for the efficacy of these reforms has been mixed, and the most recent innovations depart from a strictly criminal law treatment of domestic assault. For example, in some states, such as New York, criminal charges of assault are eligible to be heard either in criminal court or family court (or both). The institutionalization of "integrated domestic violence courts" (which bundle criminal charges, child support complaints, visitation disputes, and the like into a single jurisdiction presided over by a single judge) inadvertently sustains the premise that criminal cases of partner assault cannot, and should not, be separated from other problematic relationship issues. Against this unresolved legal backdrop, judges, along with other criminal justice practitioners, must settle on norms for processing complaints of domestic violence.

The Challenges of Studying Judges' Attitudes and Beliefs

Social scientists have studied the beliefs of the public, as well as of criminal justice and social services professionals, about domestic violence. They have reached some consensus about these beliefs. For example, research shows that in general, the public condemns physical violence between family members and believes that criminal justice agents have a role to play in crisis intervention, but places more hope in prevention and rehabilitation than in punishment and deterrence (Klein et al. 1997; Worden and Carlson 2005). Studies of practitioners suggest higher levels of factual knowledge about the etiology of domestic violence and the law, although not much more optimism about the effectiveness of interventions (Belknap 1995; Ferraro 1989; Johnson, Sigler, and Crowley 1994) and lingering skepticism about victims' motivations and roles in violent incidents (Davis 1983; Worden and McLean 2000). However, these studies have seldom included judges. As a result, what is known about variation in judges' perceptions and beliefs, as well as factors that might account for that variation, is quite limited.

Why do social scientists know so little about judges' beliefs about domestic violence? In general, social scientists know little about judges' attitudes about most topics, for several reasons. First, many studies of courthouse decision making are limited to a single jurisdiction, so few judges become research subjects. Relatively few social scientists have succeeded (or perhaps attempted) to interview judges directly about their work, relying instead on social characteristics (such as age, sex, gender, and professional experience) as proxies for attitudinal constructs, and case outcomes as proxies for judicial decisions (despite the fact that decisions such as convictions, pleas, and sentences are usually the product of courtroom workgroup dynamics).

Data collection strategies that more directly address judges' attitudes are costly and subject to limitations. Some court researchers have relied on mail surveys to study topics such as sentencing preferences (Frank, Cullen, and Cullen 1987), attitudes about plea bargaining (Worden 1995), and preferences for handling child sexual abuse cases (Saunders 1987). However, these studies sometimes suffer from limited generalizability and are not always well suited for capturing complex attitudinal constructs.

Other methodological approaches include courtroom observational studies (e.g., Goolkasian 1986; Meyer and Jesilow 1997; Ptacek 1999); historical (Merry 1995) and more contemporary (Crocker 2005; Schafran 1995) content analyses of written case opinions; and intensive case studies (Nicolson 1995). These studies offer some purchase on the public legal choices and justifications judges select to resolve cases. However, they are still several steps removed from measures of judicial beliefs and attitudes.

Interviews with judges, designed expressly to tap their thinking about domestic violence, may be the most promising approach. As of this writing, only a few such studies have been undertaken, however, and not all involved judges (for example, Fahnestock's [1991] study of rural domestic violence provides useful insight into the values of court clerks and administrators, but not judges). These include Hartman and Belknap's (2003) study of Midwestern judges; Ptacek's (1999) interviews with progressive Massachusetts jurists; and McLean's (2003) interviews with a sample of rural New York magistrates. Coupled with the findings of survey-based studies and those relying on other methodological strategies, the results of these studies suggest that (1) most judges hold fairly decisive views about the nature and causes of domestic violence, as well as about appropriate social and legal responses, but (2) there may be little agreement among judges on these questions. A review of the findings of these studies is below, followed by a consideration of the factors that might explain variation in judges' beliefs.

Judges' Beliefs

The Nature and Causes of Domestic Violence

Judges differ in their thinking about the nature of domestic violence. Like most other criminal justice professionals, they tend to define domestic violence in terms of physical assault (Johnson et al. 1994), although this does not necessarily mean that they are oblivious to the toll taken by emotional abuse. Crocker (2005) observed that in written trial court opinions, Canadian judges tended to strongly condemn partner violence, seldom minimizing its gravity even when they found justification for mitigating its punishment.

When asked about the causes of domestic violence, judges give the same array of answers offered by the public (Carlson and Worden 2005). Many judges link violence to alcohol and substance abuse (Fahnestock 1991; McLean 2003, but see Crocker 2005; Worden and McLean 2000), dysfunctional relationships (McLean 2003; Schornstein 1997), and unemployment and financial stress (McLean 2003). There is ample evidence in early and more recent research to suggest that some criminal justice practitioners are wary of victims' motives and tolerant of perpetrators' behavior. Interviews with judges have uncovered these views (Hartman and Belknap 2003; Worden and McLean 2000). However, when asked to evaluate circumstances that should, or should not, factor into court decisions, judges provide little systematic evidence that these cynical attitudes have a significant impact on case dispositions. For example, few Midwestern judges agreed that victims were unlikely to testify, and most dismissed victims' continued relationships with abusive partners, their own substance abuse, or other victim characteristics as irrelevant to their discretionary decisions (Hartman and Belknap 2003). Similarly, Crocker (2005) reports that a major theme in judicial decisions is documentation of victims' credibility in court; most judges seemed not only sympathetic but also respectful of victims' statements.

But the regard for victims expressed by many judges is countered by suspicion and cynicism among others. Some court officers are quick to point out that complainants are vengeful (Fahnestock 1991; McLean 2003) and manipulative (Worden and McLean 2000). Further, even judges who hold victims blameless are inclined to fault circumstances, rather than personal culpability, for men's violence, going to great lengths to document perpetrators' reputations, economic standing, and community ties to dismiss what appears to be anomalous behavior (Crocker 2005).

In sum, research supports the statement that judges' beliefs about the nature and causes of violence vary considerably; however, researchers do not yet know enough to say how these beliefs are distributed.

Social and Legal Responses to Domestic Violence

A great deal of policy reform has centered on criminalization of partner violence, as well as on exhortation of criminal justice professionals and communities to collaborate in holding offenders accountable and keeping victims safe. These directives, while not always embraced by law enforcement and prosecutors, are at least consistent with their core missions of apprehending and convicting offenders. However, judges' professional roles are more complex: They are obliged to maintain neutrality and impartiality, to refrain from advocacy, and to sustain high standards of proof for conviction (Killian 2001). Judges' attitudes about appropriate responses to domestic violence tend to reflect this role conflict; furthermore, they mirror the views of the public and many other groups of practitioners in their pessimism about the effectiveness of criminal sanctions (Hartman and Belknap 2003; Johnson et al. 1994).

Research suggests that even judges and court workers who are sympathetic to victims may identify more strongly with their formal courthouse role than with policy reformers (Fahnestock 1991). Many judges are troubled by the problems of evidence and proof required for criminal conviction, especially when victims are unwilling or unable to help make the case. Meanwhile, many judges believe that reforms, such as mandatory arrest laws and calls for more aggressive prosecution and sentencing, have increased caseloads, reduced police discretion, and even prioritized one particular type of crime over other community problems (Worden and McLean 2000).

All the same, when judges are asked what they think should be done to reduce violence, they tend to answer in a criminal justice paradigm (Johnson et al. 1994): Many recommend restrictions on plea bargaining, no-drop prosecution policies, and harsher punishment. One might infer that these views stem from a belief in deterrence, and there is some evidence to support this inference (Crocker 2005). However, not all judges offer such recommendations. A study of misdemeanor court judges found that some recommended more specialized domestic violence courts and more coordination between family and criminal court authorities (Worden and McLean 2000). Still others adopted a more therapeutic approach, favoring counseling (for one or both parties) (Hartman and Belknap 2003; Worden and McLean 2000). An important question, still unanswered by research, is what sorts of counseling they would favor, and under what conditions: mandated batterers' treatment, aimed at adjusting offenders' attitudes and behavior? counseling for women to empower them to exit or manage violent relationships? or the traditional practice, now statutorily banned in most states, of "sentencing" victims and perpetrators to mediation and couples therapy?

To summarize, researchers have limited empirical purchase on judges' attitudes about what society should, and should not, do in response to domestic violence. What research suggests is that their opinions vary greatly. They range from traditional attitudes that effectively minimize violence, either through distributing blame across both parties and/or classifying such incidents as properly the province of civil courts and social services, to attitudes more collinear with contemporary policy reforms that emphasize formal mechanisms to ensure offender accountability and victim safety.

Factors Associated with Judges' Beliefs

There is a rich theoretical literature on models of judicial decision making, much of which taps into theories about the relationships between core values, such as religious views and political ideology, and legal decisions, such as appellate opinions and felony sentencing. Therefore, although there exists little in the way of empirical findings about explanations for judges' views on domestic violence specifically, it is possible to propose some hypotheses that are consistent with previous researchers' models.

First, judges' beliefs about gender and relationships may shape their thinking about the criminal courts' role in criminalizing violence. Previous research suggests that among the public and some groups of practitioners, traditional gender role attitudes are linked to beliefs that minimize violence, attach blame to victims, and justify offenders' actions. Even among judges who are protective of victims, Crocker (2005) observed paternalistic and chauvinistic themes. Likewise, fundamental attitudes about the purposes of criminal sanctions, rehabilitation, and personal responsibility may affect beliefs about how to deal with many types of crime, including domestic violence (Frank et al. 1987; Worden and McLean 2000).

Second, judges' decision context may influence their notions of what is, and is not, legitimate and relevant information in domestic violence cases. Courthouse setting may matter: For example, judges sitting in urban, bureaucratized courtrooms will seldom know anything more about cases than the facts included in a police report and perhaps a bit of testimony, but judges in small towns and rural areas may have a wealth of background information about one or both parties' lifestyles, characters, and problems. Such judges may define this information as relevant if only because it is almost impossible to disregard (Fahnestock 1991; McLean 2003; Websdale 1998).

Third, some have hypothesized that common social experiences associated with age or generation, gender, race, ethnicity, and professional background may indelibly stamp judges' attitudes about crime and justice long before they reach the bench. The intuitive appeal of these sorts of hypotheses is countered, however, by the lack of empirical research; most studies find few differences across groups of judges (or other criminal justice professionals, for that matter) defined by these variables (e.g., Spohn 1990), perhaps because individuals whose socialization left them with attitudes very different from those of most jurists are unlikely to seek (or find) positions on the bench.

Fourth, reformers have suggested that deliberate resocialization efforts, in the form of judicial education, might account not only for variation in beliefs but also for changes in beliefs about domestic violence. While some evidence lends support to this hypothesis (e.g., Fahnestock 1991; Schafran 1986), there is competing evidence to suggest that judicial education has no discernible effect on knowledge or attitudes concerning domestic violence (Morrill et al. 2005). One cannot say with much confidence that attitudes are easily manipulated. It is unlikely that judges, who enjoy little public scrutiny and considerable job security in most communities, would undergo significant attitude or behavioral change about the causes and blameworthiness of domestic violence simply because they were told that they should (Burt et al. 1996). However, judges who acknowledge that they know little about the causes and consequences of violence might be receptive to additional information and education, which might result in changed ideas about effective and ineffective responses.

Finally, a strong body of research has documented the fact that although criminal courts all work with the same laws in any state, their processes and outcomes vary considerably, and this is particularly pronounced at the misdemeanor court level. Attempts to understand this variability typically model court behavior as the collective product of interorganizational dynamics and of community political forces. To the extent that judges internalize the views of colleagues in the courthouse or have been socialized into the values of their communities, these levels of analysis would be relevant to the present topic as well. However, as of this writing, there are virtually no published studies that impose and test these models in domestic violence court cases.

Conclusions

From this review of what is known about judges' perceptions and attitudes about domestic violence, one can conclude the following:

- First, court actors' attitudes about domestic violence are probably influenced in subtle ways by the case law and common law, which historically resolved the conflict between husbands' roles as heads of households and their culpability as batterers in favor of the former. While such laws are long gone from the books, the fact remains that judges express difficulty and sometimes frustration in separating familial and legal relationships from conventional perpetrator–victim ones.

- Second, however, judges' attitudes about the causes of violence do not fit a single mold. While many judges, like most other practitioners and the public, equate domestic violence with substance abuse, judges locate the causes of violence in economic problems, social class identities, and temporary lapses on the part of offenders. Some judges blame victims; however, the authors of this entry have found no evidence to support the stereotype that most judges hold victims responsible for their abuse. Further, there is little systematic evidence that judges see most victims as reluctant or uncooperative.

- Third, research indicates that most judges define domestic violence as a legal rather than a social matter, for the purposes of their own decision making. However, at the same time, many judges are not optimistic about the impact of legal actions (such as arrest and incarceration) on offenders' behavior. Overall, they are more optimistic about social services interventions, particularly counseling, but do not necessarily see that as part of the legal system's responsibility.

- Fourth, although one can confidently conclude that judges' beliefs vary considerably on these matters, very little research has examined the factors that account for this variation.

Does it matter how judges think about domestic violence? Given their influence over court decisions and their ability to shape the policies and decisions of criminal justice agents such as police and prosecutors, the answer is surely in the affirmative. Courts are famously resistant to reform, especially those that are generated by outsiders. Domestic violence has been the subject of tremendous policy reform over the past decades, but the success of these reforms (and even researchers' ability to evaluate their effectiveness) depends on their implementation at the courthouse level. Future research should address the gaps in knowledge about the nature and causes of variation in judges' beliefs.

ALISSA POLLITZ WORDEN and SARAH J. MCLEAN

See also **Battered Woman Syndrome as a Legal Defense in Cases of Spousal Homicide; Battered Women, Clemency for; Batterer Typology; Divorce, Custody, and Domestic Violence; Domestic Violence Courts; Lautenberg Law; Legal Issues for Battered Women; Mandatory Arrest Policies**

References and Further Reading

Avakame, E. F. "Differential Police Treatment of Male on Female Spousal Violence: Additional Evidence on the Leniency Thesis." *Violence Against Women* 7, no. 11 (2001): 22.

Belknap, J. "Law Enforcement Officers' Attitudes about the Appropriate Response to Woman Battering." *International Review of Victimology* 4 (1995): 47–62.

Burt, M., L. Newmark, M. Norris, D. Dyer, and A. Harrell. *The Violence Against Women Act of 1994: Evaluation of the STOP Block Grants to Combat Violence against Women.* Washington, DC: Urban Institute, 1996.

Buzawa, E. S., and T. Austin. "Determining Police Response to Domestic Violence Victims: The Role of Victim Preference." *American Behavioral Scientist* 36 (1993): 610–623.

Crocker, D. "Regulating Intimacy: Judicial Discourse in Cases of Wife Assault (1970 to 2000)." *Violence Against Women* 11, no. 2 (2005): 197–226.

Davis, P. W. "Restoring Semblance of Order: Police Strategies in the Domestic Disturbance." *Symbolic Interaction* 6 (1983): 261–278.

Fahnestock, Kathryn. *Not in My County: Rural Courts and Victims of Domestic Violence.* Montpelier, VT: Rural Justice Center, 1991.

Ferraro, K. J. "Policing Woman Battering." *Social Problems* 36 (1989): 61–74.

Frank, J., F. Cullen, and J. Cullen. "Sources of Judicial Attitudes towards Criminal Sanctioning." *American Journal of Criminal Justice* 11 (1987): 2.

Friedman, L. M. *A History of American Law*, 2nd ed. New York: Simon & Schuster, 1985.

Goolkasian, G. *Confronting Domestic Violence: A Guide for Criminal Justice Agencies.* Washington, DC: National Institute of Justice, 1986.

Hartman, J. L., and J. Belknap. "Beyond the Gatekeepers: Court Professionals' Self-Reported Attitudes about and Experiences with Misdemeanor Domestic Violence Cases." *Criminal Justice and Behavior* 30, no. 3 (2003): 349–373.

Johnson, I. M., R. T. Sigler, and J. E. Crowley. "Domestic Violence: A Comparative Study of Perceptions and Attitudes toward Domestic Abuse Cases among Social Service and Criminal Justice Professionals." *Journal of Criminal Justice* 22 (1994).

Killian, M. D. "Judges Must Steer Clear of Victim Advocacy Groups." *Florida Bar Journal* 75, no. 8 (2001).

Klein, R., J. Campbell, E. Soler, and M. Ghez. *Ending Domestic Violence: Changing Public Perceptions/Halting the Epidemic.* Newbury Park, CA: Sage, 1997.

McDonald, W. F. "Judicial Supervision of the Guilty Plea Process: A Study of Six Jurisdictions." *Judicature* 70, no. 4 (1987).

McLean, S. J. *Rural Magistrates: A Study of Decision Making in Partner Violence.* Dissertation submitted to the University at Albany, State University of New York, 2003.

Merry, S. E. "Narrating Domestic Violence: Producing the 'Truth' of Violence in 19th and 20th Century Hawaiian Courts." *Law and Social Inquiry* 19 (1995): 967–993.

Meyer, J., and P. Jesilow. *Doing Justice in the People's Court: Sentencing by Municipal Court Judges.* Albany: State University of New York Press, 1997.

Morrill, A. C., J. Dai, S. Dunn, J. Sung, and K. Smith. "Child Custody and Visitation Decisions When the Father Has Perpetrated Violence against the Mother." *Violence Against Women* 11 (2005): 1076–1107.

Nicolson, D. "Telling Tales: Gender Discrimination, Gender Construction and Battered Women Who Kill." *Feminist Legal Studies* 3 (1995): 185–206.

Pleck, E. *Domestic Tyranny: The Making of American Social Policy Against Family Violence from Colonial Times to the Present.* New York: Oxford University Press, 1987.

Ptacek, J. *Battered Women in the Courtroom: The Power of the Judicial Response.* Boston: Northeastern University Press, 1999.

Ryan, R. M. "The Sex Right: A Legal History of the Marital Rape Exemption." *Law and Social Inquiry* 21 (1996).

Saunders, E. "Judicial Attitudes toward Child Sexual Abuse: A Preliminary Examination." *Judicature* 70, no. 4 (1987).

Schafran, L. H. "Educating the Judiciary about Gender Bias." *Women's Rights Law Reporter*, 1986.

———. "There's No Accounting for Judges." *Albany Law Review* 58, no. 4 (1995).

Schornstein, S. *Domestic Violence and Healthcare: What Every Professional Needs to Know.* London: Sage Publications, 1997.

Spohn, C. "The Sentencing Decision of Black and White Judges: Expected and Unexpected Similarities." *Law and Society Review* 24 (1990): 1196–1216.

Websdale, N. *Rural Women Battering and the Justice System: An Ethnography.* Thousand Oaks, CA: Sage Publications, 1998.

Worden, A. P. "The Judge's Role in Plea Bargaining: An Analysis of Judges' Agreement with Prosecutors' Sentencing Recommendations." *Justice Quarterly* 12, no. 2 (1995): 257–278.

Worden, A. P., and B. E. Carlson. "Attitudes and Beliefs about Domestic Violence: Results of a Public Opinion Survey: Beliefs about Causes." *Journal of Interpersonal Violence* 20, no. 10 (2005).

Worden, A. P., and S. J. McLean. *Judicial Attitudes about Domestic Violence.* Presented at the annual meeting of the American Society of Criminology, November 2000.

Zorza, J. "The Criminal Law of Misdemeanor Domestic Violence, 1970–1990." *Journal of Criminal Law and Criminology* (1992): 83.

L

LAUTENBERG LAW

The Lautenberg Law, more commonly known as the Lautenberg Amendment to the Gun Control Act of 1968, establishes a regulatory scheme designed to prevent the use of firearms in domestic violence offenses. More specifically, the Lautenberg Law makes it illegal for any persons who have been convicted of certain misdemeanor crimes of domestic violence to ship, receive, or possess firearms or ammunition affecting interstate commerce. This means that the Lautenberg Law imposes a lifetime ban on firearm possession following a qualifying misdemeanor conviction. The Lautenberg Law is controversial for two major reasons. First, its prohibitions relating to domestic violence offenses apply to misdemeanor crimes; more typically, prohibitions of this kind have been applied only to felony offenses. Second, the Lautenberg Law is controversial because it does not include a government exception for law enforcement and military personnel. Therefore, under the Lautenberg Law, military personnel and law enforcement officials such as police are prohibited from carrying firearms if they are convicted of certain misdemeanor crimes of domestic violence. Under this law, police officers and members of the military must turn in their firearms when the law is applied to them.

Congress passed the Lautenberg Law in response to a changed social, political, and legal climate concerning intimate partner violence. Historically, law enforcement often failed to intervene in domestic violence situations, and courts frequently did not prosecute batterers. This approach changed beginning in the early 1980s as a consequence of the women's movement and increased public awareness of the problem of domestic violence. Law enforcement officials in domestic violence situations moved away from a nonarrest and nonintervention policy to a policy that emphasized less tolerance for batterers and more assistance to victims. For example, many states have passed laws requiring mandatory arrest of perpetrators when police are called to domestic violence situations. In state courts, both prosecutors and judges increasingly held perpetrators of domestic violence accountable for their violence while, at the same time, providing protection for the rights of victims. The Lautenberg Law reflects this change in philosophy of accountability and victims' rights. Congress intended the Lautenberg Law to protect victims of domestic violence from harm by removing guns from individuals who have demonstrated a propensity toward violence against intimate partners.

Critics of the Lautenberg Law argue that its provisions violate the United States Constitution. Courts have decided constitutional challenges on several grounds, but the primary challenges concern the Commerce Clause, the Equal Protection Clause, and the Ex Post Facto Clause. Law enforcement officials and military personnel have been especially vocal in arguing that the government exception contained in other gun control laws should apply to them under the Lautenberg Law. In addition, members of Congress have introduced bills that would rescind the law or provide exemptions for law enforcement and the military, and there have been several court challenges to the law on the specific issue of the lack of a government exception for the military and law enforcement. However, thus far, the law has withstood all these challenges.

This essay will examine the Lautenberg Law in terms of the broader context of the rationale for federal gun control legislation, including as it applies to perpetrators of domestic violence. The essay will then provide a detailed description of the key provisions of the Lautenberg Law. Finally, we will examine the major constitutional issues upon which critics have challenged the law and how courts have ruled on these issues.

The Federal Gun Control Act of 1968

The purpose of the Federal Gun Control Act of 1968 (GCA) was to withhold access to weapons from dangerous individuals. Congress passed the GCA in response to the assassinations of Dr. Martin Luther King, Jr. and Robert F. Kennedy, as well as the increase in violent crime in the 1960s. The GCA placed licensing restrictions on the sale and manufacture of guns and criminalized certain conduct relating to the possession of firearms. Some sections of the GCA created disqualification classes in terms of individuals prohibited from possessing firearms. Disqualified individuals under the law included anyone convicted of a crime punishable by imprisonment for a term exceeding a year, fugitives, drug addicts, mental incompetents, illegal aliens, those dishonorably discharged from the armed services, and those who have renounced their United States citizenship. Under the GCA, a licensed dealer may not sell or distribute weapons to anyone who falls within one of the disqualification categories, and the law also prohibits disqualified individuals from transporting or possessing a firearm. The GCA exempts from its prohibitions any firearm or ammunition imported for, sold or shipped to, or issued for the use of the United States or any of its departments or agencies. It also exempts any state or any department, agency, or political subdivision of a state. This so-called government exception permits military, police, or government officials to possess a gun for official use, even after a felony conviction.

Congress passed, and President Bill Clinton signed, the first domestic violence–specific amendment to the GCA in 1994. This amendment, known as the Violent Crime Control and Law Enforcement Act of 1994, added a new provision to the list of individuals prohibited from possessing firearms. More specifically, the amendment prohibits anyone subject to certain orders of protection, also known as restraining orders, from owning or possessing a gun or ammunition. This amendment also prohibits anyone from selling or transferring a gun to someone who they know or should reasonably believe to be under a restraining order. In order to fall within this provision, the order of protection must restrain harassment, stalking, or threatening of an intimate partner. In addition, the amendment requires that the court make its determination after a hearing that includes a finding that the person subject to the restraining order represents a credible threat to the physical safety of an intimate partner or child.

Key Provisions of the Lautenberg Law

A few years after the passage of the Violent Crime Control and Law Enforcement Act of 1994, policymakers at the federal level argued for stronger gun control legislation because of research that indicated the frequent presence of guns in domestic violence situations. Proposed by Senator Frank Lautenberg in 1996, the Domestic Violence Offender Gun Ban was overwhelmingly passed by Congress, as an amendment to the GCA. President Clinton signed the law a few months later as part of the Omnibus Appropriations Act of 1997. The law added another disqualification category to the GCA. It provided that any person who has been convicted in any court of a misdemeanor crime of domestic violence is prohibited from owning or possessing firearms and ammunition. However, only certain kinds of domestic violence crimes qualify as requiring the firearms and ammunition prohibitions under the Lautenberg Law. More specifically, the misdemeanor crimes of domestic violence that qualify under this law require that the offense be a misdemeanor under federal or state law and have as an element the use or attempted use of physical force or the threatened use of a deadly weapon. The specific offense does not need to contain an explicit reference to domestic violence. Rather, the Lautenberg Law specifies that it refers to all misdemeanors that involve the use or attempted use of physical force when one of certain enumerated relationships exists between the perpetrator and the victim of the crime. Specifically, the perpetrator must be either (1) a current or former spouse, parent, or guardian of the victim; (2) a person who shares a child in common with the victim; (3) a person who is cohabiting or has cohabited with the victim as a spouse, parent, or guardian; or (4) a person similarly situated to a spouse, parent, or guardian of the victim.

The law contains a number of additional provisions that are important. It imposes two due process requirements; that is, constitutional protections to those charged under the law. First, the law states that a person shall not be considered to have been convicted of the domestic violence offense unless the person was represented by counsel in the case, or knowingly and intelligently waived the right to counsel in the case. Second, whether the person is entitled to a jury trial for a misdemeanor offense depends on state law or, in federal cases, federal law. However, the Lautenberg Law specifies that a person shall not be considered to have been convicted of the domestic violence offense unless the person convicted received a trial by jury, if so entitled, or knowingly and intelligently waived that right.

It is important to remember that only a "conviction" triggers the weapons prohibition of the law. Often state court practices make it difficult to determine whether a conviction has occurred in a particular case. States may utilize such procedures as an "adjournment in contemplation of dismissal" (ACD). Such a procedure permits a court to dismiss the charges against a defendant if the person has not committed another offense within a stated period of time and has complied with other mandates imposed by the court. Under the Lautenberg Law, the question of whether a qualifying "conviction" exists is made by reference to the governing state law; if it is considered a conviction under state law, it will support prosecution under the Lautenberg Law.

As part of the Lautenberg Law, Congress also enacted a provision that prohibits the sale or transfer of a firearm or ammunition to a person if the transferor knows or has reasonable cause to believe that the person has been convicted of a misdemeanor crime of domestic violence. Therefore, a court should not authorize the return of a firearm to a person that the court knows or has reasonable cause to believe has been convicted of a qualifying misdemeanor crime of domestic violence.

Punishment for violations of the Lautenberg Law can be a felony conviction, a fine of $250,000, maximum imprisonment of ten years, or any combination of the above. Although the law imposes a lifetime ban on firearm possession following a qualifying misdemeanor conviction, the Lautenberg Law does provide that firearm possession rights may be restored under certain circumstances—specifically, the conviction being set aside or the person having obtained a pardon which restores civil rights. But if the specific pardon or restoration expressly provides that the person may not ship, transport, possess, or receive firearms, then the restriction against firearms possession continues.

Constitutional Challenges to the Lautenberg Law

The provisions of the Lautenberg Law have been challenged on several grounds, three of which have received considerable attention by courts. First, opponents of the law maintain that it violates the Commerce Clause of the United States Constitution. Article 1, Section 8 of the Constitution gives Congress the authority "to regulate Commerce with foreign Nations, and among the several States, and with the Indian tribes." Critics charge that the Lautenberg Law violates the Commerce Clause because the law classifies as federal offenses activities that do not have an effect on interstate commerce.

Second, critics also argue that the Lautenberg Law violates the Equal Protection Clause of the U.S. Constitution. Amendment IV of the Constitution provides, in part, that "no state shall . . . deny to any person within its jurisdiction the equal protection of the laws." Opponents of the law state that it violates the Equal Protection Clause because it treats domestic violence misdemeanors more harshly than other misdemeanor offenses, it punishes misdemeanor but not felony offenses, and it excludes law enforcement officers convicted of misdemeanor domestic violence offenses from the government exception contained in the Gun Control Act of 1968.

Third, opponents criticize the Lautenberg Law as a violation of the Ex Post Facto Clause of the U.S. Constitution. Article 1, Section 8 of the Constitution states that "no bill attainder or ex post facto Law shall be passed." Critics argue that the Lautenberg Law violates the Ex Post Facto Clause because it prohibits the possession of a firearm by a person convicted of a domestic violence misdemeanor even if the criminal act occurred prior to the enactment of the Lautenberg Law.

Reviewing courts have rejected these challenges; however, the challenges represent a substantial debate concerning the Lautenberg Law. Each of these constitutional challenges will now be examined in more detail.

The Commerce Clause

Critics use as a basis for their challenge to the Lautenberg Law the U.S. Supreme Court's decision in *United States v. Lopez*. In *Lopez,* the Court was deciding whether a federal statute that prohibited the possession of a firearm on school grounds exceeded congressional authority under the Commerce Clause. The Court described three kinds of activities that come within the authority of Congress under the Commerce Clause. First, Congress possesses the authority to regulate the use of the channels of interstate commerce. Second, Congress may regulate the instrumentalities of interstate commerce, or persons or things in interstate commerce. Third, Congress may also regulate activities which have a substantial relation to, and effect on, interstate commerce. The Court in *Lopez* determined that the statute prohibiting the possession of a firearm on school grounds did not fall within any of the three enumerated activities. The Court stated that the law was a criminal statute that had no connection with commerce or any sort of economic enterprise and did not play a role in any larger regulatory scheme. The Supreme Court also found it significant that there was no jurisdictional nexus in the statute; that is, the statute did not require the government to establish that the firearm was possessed "in or affecting commerce" or was received after having "been shipped or transported in interstate or foreign commerce."

However, in the case of the Lautenberg Law, every court that has reviewed challenges based on the Commerce Clause has determined that the Lautenberg Law readily meets the minimum constitutional requirements under the Commerce Clause. Specifically, reviewing courts have determined that the Lautenberg Law contains an appropriate jurisdictional element because it provides that it will be unlawful for individuals convicted of domestic violence misdemeanors to ship, transport, or possess a firearm in or affecting interstate commerce. Therefore, the jurisdictional language contained in the law insulates it from constitutional challenges under the Commerce Clause.

The Equal Protection Clause

Opponents of the Lautenberg Law argue that the law violates the Equal Protection Clause of the Constitution by punishing domestic violence misdemeanors more harshly than other misdemeanor offenses, by punishing misdemeanor but not felony offenses, and by excluding law enforcement officers and members of the military convicted of misdemeanor domestic violence offenses from the government exception contained in the GCA. In instances where a law does not affect what the U.S. Supreme Court considers as a suspect class or a fundamental right, the court utilizes a "rational basis" review as its legal standard; that is, the Court requires only that a law be rationally related to the asserted governmental interest. Courts reviewing the constitutionality of the Lautenberg Law under the Equal Protection Clause have uniformly applied a "rational basis" review and have held that the Lautenberg Law does not violate the Equal Protection Clause. In examining the argument of opponents that the Lautenberg Law irrationally categorizes misdemeanor domestic violence offenses more harshly than other misdemeanors, courts state that the right to equal protection under the law does not strip Congress of the authority to treat different classes of persons in different ways. As such, in light of the Lautenberg Law's goal of reducing the likelihood that domestic violence could escalate into murder, Congress had rationally concluded that misdemeanor domestic violence offenders should not possess firearms.

Courts have also examined the argument that the Lautenberg Law unjustifiably discriminates between misdemeanor domestic offenders and felons. This argument rests on the fact that while convicted felons may regain the right to possess a firearm if they receive a pardon, have their conviction expunged, or otherwise have their civil rights restored, many jurisdictions do not deprive persons convicted of misdemeanors of their civil rights. Therefore, the Lautenberg Law creates a situation in which certain felons may be able to possess firearms, but individuals convicted of domestic violence misdemeanors will not. While courts recognize that such situations may exist, they have rejected equal protection challenges to gun control laws that rest on anomalies resulting from different state laws and regulations.

The final equal protection argument concerns whether the Lautenberg Law discriminates against law enforcement personnel and military personnel who have committed misdemeanor domestic violence offenses. Courts have rejected this argument, stating that while the ultimate effect of the Lautenberg Law may be to bar certain individuals who have committed domestic violence misdemeanors from careers that require the ability to possess a firearm, equal protection concerns are not implicated by the "uneven effects" of a rational classification, absent evidence of discriminatory intent. Applying the rationale to the Lautenberg Law, courts have determined that there was no evidence of discriminatory intent toward law enforcement or the military by Congress.

One of the most interesting cases concerning the equal protection challenges to the Lautenberg Law is the case of *Fraternal Order of Police v. United States*. The Fraternal Order of Police challenged the Lautenberg Law on behalf of two of its police officer members, each of whom had been convicted of domestic violence misdemeanors and hence had been required to relinquish their department-issued firearms. One officer was assigned to a position of lesser responsibility, and the other was put on leave. Off-duty, the officers, otherwise well suited to work as security guards, were unable to secure such employment because they were prohibited from possessing firearms. The Fraternal Order of Police challenged the statute, claiming that it infringed on the officers' constitutional rights to possess firearms, impeding their ability to serve as law enforcement officers, diminishing their job-related responsibilities, and resulting in termination of their employment. In 1998, the appeals court of the District of Columbia focused on the equal protection part of the Fifth Amendment's guarantee of due process (FOP I). The Fraternal Order of Police argued that because the statute did not provide a government exception for police officers convicted of a domestic violence misdemeanor, the result created an anomaly because a person with a prior felony conviction for domestic violence was eligible to carry a gun in connection with federal or state employment, while a person convicted of a domestic violence misdemeanor was not. In FOP I, the court could find no rational basis for barring police officers who commit misdemeanors from the government exception while imposing a lesser restriction on police officers who commit domestic violence felonies. The FOP I court held that the Lautenberg Law was unconstitutional because it withheld the public interest exception from those convicted of domestic violence misdemeanors. One year later, the United States was granted a rehearing by the same court, resulting in a reversal of the decision (FOP II). In this second decision, the court stated that while treating domestic violence misdemeanors more harshly than felonies seems irrational in the conventional sense of the term, it was not unreasonable for Congress to believe that existing laws and practices adequately deal with the problem of issuance of official firearms to individuals convicted of felonies but not to individuals convicted of misdemeanors. The court went on to explain that nonlegal restrictions, such as formal and informal hiring practices, may prevent felons from being issued firearms pursuant to the public interest exception, mitigating the apparent disparity created by the Lautenberg Law. Therefore, the court stated that there is a reasonably conceivable state of facts under which it is rational to believe that the felon problem makes a weaker claim to federal involvement than the misdemeanor one. The court's reversal in the case prevented a split among the federal circuit courts regarding the validity of the Lautenberg Law in the equal protection context.

Ex Post Facto Clause

A law violates the Ex Post Facto Clause of the U.S. Constitution if it applies to events that occurred before its enactment or if it results in a disadvantage to an offender by altering the definition of criminal conduct or increasing the punishment for a crime. Opponents criticize the Lautenberg Law as being retroactive and thus a violation of the Ex Post Facto Clause because it prohibits the possession of a firearm by a person convicted of a domestic violence misdemeanor even if the criminal act occurred prior to the enactment of the law. Reviewing courts have uniformly rejected this challenge. In *Hiley v. Barrett*, the court clarified why the law does not violate the Ex Post Facto Clause. The court explained that the prohibited activity is the possession of a firearm and not the domestic violence misdemeanor. In other words, the possession of the firearm is the crime that is punished under the law, not the commission of a domestic violence misdemeanor. Therefore, the Lautenberg Law is not retroactive and does not violate the Ex Post Facto Clause.

Conclusion

Congress intended the Lautenberg Law to protect victims of intimate partner violence from potential fatality at the hands of individuals known to be prone to violence. The Lautenberg Law remains a controversial piece of legislation, primarily because it does not contain a government exception for members of the military and law enforcement personnel, found in other federal gun legislation. However, reviewing courts have rejected all challenges to the constitutionality of the law.

PATRICIA E. ERICKSON

See also **Batterer Typology; Community Responses to Domestic Violence; Domestic Violence by Law Enforcement Officers; Domestic Violence Courts; Intimate Partner Homicide; Legal Issues for Battered Women; Mandatory Arrest Policies; Military Families, Domestic Violence within; Protective and Restraining Orders; Violence against Women Act**

References and Further Reading

Berns, Nancy. *Framing the Victim: Domestic Violence, Media, and Social Problems.* Hawthorne, NY: Aldine de Gruyter, 2004.
Buzawa, Eva S. *Domestic Violence: The Criminal Justice Response.* Thousand Oaks, CA: Sage Publications, 2003.
Ludwig, Jens, and Philip J. Cook, eds. *Evaluating Gun Policy: Effects on Crime and Violence.* Washington, DC: Brookings Institution Press, 2003.

Roberts, Albert R. *Handbook of Domestic Violence Intervention Strategies: Policies, Programs, and Legal Remedies.* New York: Oxford University Press, 2002.

Statutes

Gun Control Act of 1968, Pub. L. No. 90-618, 5801, 82 Stat. 1213 (1968).
The Domestic Violence Gun Ban of 1996, Pub. L. No. 104-208, 658, 110 Stat. 3009-371, 3009-371 to 372 (1996).
The Violent Crime Control and Law Enforcement Act of 1994, Pub. L. No. 90-618, 82 Stat. 1213 (1994).

Cases

Fraternal Order of Police v. United States, 152 F. 3d 998 (D.C. Cir. 1998), *rev'd* 173 F.3d 898 (D.C. Cir. 1999).
National Association of Government Employees, Inc. and William Hiley v. Barrett, 968 F. Supp. 1564 (N.D. Ga. 1997) *aff'd, Hiley v. Barrett,* 155 F.3d 1276 (11th Cir. 1998).
United States v. Lopez, 514 U.S. 549 (1995).

LEGAL ISSUES FOR BATTERED WOMEN

Introduction

It is a rare battered woman who does not find herself in the middle of a legal problem at some point in her relationship with the man who batters her. While it is acknowledged that at times the man is the victim and the woman is the perpetrator in heterosexual relationships, and same-sex partners also abuse one another, this article is written with the focus on the woman as the victim and the man as the perpetrator. Although the law is gender neutral, there is less experience in most areas of the law in dealing with the male domestic violence victims in heterosexual relationships or abuse victims of same-sex partners, who are still in many ways not protected by the law, especially under family law. However, where there are experiences in using the legal system in gender-neutral ways, these will be described.

The most common area of the law for the battered woman to have some contact with is family law, especially if there is a custody battle or disagreement about access to children as the marriage begins to come apart. Since so many of the children exposed to domestic violence in their homes are negatively impacted by the abuse they are exposed

to or experience themselves, juvenile court, where child abuse and neglect or delinquency are adjudicated, may be another area that battered women must deal with. If the police get involved or if a battered woman files for a restraining order, she may be faced with being a witness in criminal court where her partner will be arraigned and prosecuted, especially if he violates the court's no contact order. If she should try to kill her partner in what she believes is self-defense, then she will be under the criminal justice system's jurisdiction; if someone dies, then probate court might get involved. Finally, if she decides to file in court for damages due to personal injury by her partner, then her case will be handled in civil court with a personal injury lawsuit that may go to a jury trial. In all of these cases, forensic psychologists, who can provide expert testimony about the psychological impact of domestic violence, may be involved.

Family Court

It is often thought that battered women do not leave abusive relationships; in fact, those who are married stay in the marriage only about the same length of time as the national average—about six years (Walker 1984/2000). Even so, many battered women leave after a very short time, while others may stay twenty years or longer. When they are ready to leave, it still may take three to five attempts before they can make the final break. Battered women, like most people, do not want to break up the family. Batterers do not want to let the woman and children go. If there are young children still in the home when the battered woman leaves and ends the relationship, the batterer often engages in a custody battle that keeps him in control of his former wife and children.

Child Custody and Visitation

Typically, the custody problems begin when the legal papers are filed for dissolution of the marriage (Bancroft and Silverman 2002; Jaffe and Geffner 1998; Jaffe, Lemon, and Poisson 2003). If the abusive partner has not had a lot of contact with the children, which occurs in very traditional marriages where the father is the wage earner and the mother takes care of the children, then the typical visitation patterns that the court orders may give him more contact and time alone with the children than he or the children are used to. If the children refuse to visit their father or are difficult for him to handle, the mother is usually held responsible and she becomes in danger of losing access to her children (Johnston 2003; Kelly and Johnston 2001; Kuehnle and Walker 2003). In family law, the legal standard for anything that has to do with children is called "the best interests of the child."

Presumptions

There are assumptions, called presumptions, most of which are as yet scientifically untested, that legislators in the United States have accepted and that judges must follow when making a custody decision. If the presumption is challenged, evidence presented must prove more likely than not that it is in the best interests of the child. In most state courts in the United States, there is an assumption that it is best for children to have access to both parents, so the presumption is that parents must share custody and responsibility for their children. Despite the psychological evidence that it is not healthy for children to be exposed to a father who batters their mother (Drozd, Kuehnle, and Walker 2004; Margolin 1998; Rossman, Hughes, and Rosenberg 2000) and that the father's abuse may cause the mother to be less competent as

a parent than if she were not abused (Drozd et al. 2004), the burden of proof is still on the victim to prove both that domestic violence has occurred and that it is detrimental to the children's best interests for their parents to share legal custody and responsibility.

In most states, domestic violence advocates have been successful in persuading legislators to mandate that judges consider domestic violence when making custody determinations, but this still does not change the burden of proof to make the batterer prove his fitness to parent the children. Psychological studies demonstrate that batterers abuse their power in order to gain control over both their partners and their children, and some studies show that as many as 60 percent of those who physically and sexually abuse women also abuse their children. When psychological abuse is included, it has been found that almost 100 percent of all children exposed to domestic violence are negatively impacted (Holden, Geffner, and Jouriles 1998; Rossman et al. 2000).

A second presumption in child custody laws is that the parent who is friendliest toward the other parent and gives the other parent additional access to the child, speaks well about the other parent to the child, and seems most cooperative with the court is acting in the child's best interests. Therefore, in a custody battle, it would follow that the friendliest parent should get custody. Obviously, it is difficult for a battered woman to act friendly toward the batterer. She is caught between needing to prove that he is a batterer and is detrimental to the children's best interests on one hand and having to act friendly to him on the other (Drozd et al. 2004).

A typical child custody argument proposed by the battered woman uses psychological evidence that she has developed *battered woman syndrome* (BWS) as proof that domestic violence occurred, and she should not be forced to share joint custody with the batterer because both she and the children are in danger of future abuse and violence. The batterer's counterargument to prove that he is a more fit parent than the mother is to accuse her of *parental alienation syndrome* (PAS) or *psychological Munchausen by proxy,* two fictitious disorders that sound reasonable and are often accepted into evidence by unsuspecting courts (Walker, Brantley, and Rigsby 2005). While BWS may provide sufficient psychological data to demonstrate that domestic violence has occurred, it may be insufficient for the court to assume that awarding sole custody to the mother is in the best interests of the child, especially when experts testify that contact with the father is critical to overcome the fictitious PAS

(Johnston 2003; Kelly and Johnston 2001). Children who do not want to be in the middle of the abuse or who have already become alienated or even estranged from an abusive father may unwittingly demonstrate the symptoms that are said to be caused by PAS, leading judges to become confused and often paralyzed into inaction (a move that is supported by horrendous court schedules) or impulsively change custody from the mother to the father upon recommendations of guardians *ad litem,* who are untrained in recognizing domestic violence issues. Frequently, these custody hearings become battles of the experts, with as many experts testifying as there are therapists for children, each parent, and forensic child custody evaluators. Unfortunately, these cases fill the family court dockets (Drozd et al. 2004; Walker et al. 2006).

Parental Alienation Syndrome. PAS is so commonly used in cases against battered women that it is important to describe how this occurs. A psychiatrist, Richard Gardner (1992), formulated PAS based on his limited clinical practice, without any formal scientific studies to support his theory. A *syndrome* is defined as having interrelated core signs and symptoms due to the causative agent (American Psychiatric Association 2000). Most mental health professionals note that children who have been exposed to domestic violence prefer to be with one parent over the other, unlike children from homes without domestic violence, who wish to spend time with both parents. Sometimes this phenomenon is used as part of the confirmation that domestic violence is occurring in a particular home. A sensitive child may not wish to be bullied by a father who controls with threats and force. This is alienation, but it is based on the father's behavior. However, it is impossible to make a diagnosis of a parent based on the child; rather, the diagnosis must be made precisely with the parent.

There are many competing reasons why a child might prefer one parent over another besides exposure to domestic violence or child abuse. For example, it may be that a ten-year-old athletic boy prefers to be with a father who coaches his soccer team and takes him to football games, or a six-year-old girl prefers to be with a mother who has been her primary caretaker while her father traveled for his job. This is typically called *affinity for one parent,* because of interests and historical preference. In other cases, the child may have felt abandoned by a parent who has problems with alcohol or other drugs or has not been emotionally supportive of the child. This can produce what is labeled as *estrangement,* which

may look like alienation but is totally different (Drozd et al. 2004). It is important to recognize that the courts frequently and wrongly apply PAS to mothers who are trying to protect their children from abusive or neglectful fathers based on the child's refusal to permit the father to act as a parent (Zirogiannis 2001).

Psychological Munchausen by Proxy. Psychological Munchausen by proxy is another commonly used fictitious disorder, modeled after the rare but known disorder called Munchausen syndrome and its progeny, Munchausen by proxy. A parent, usually the mother, who claims that the child is being physically or sexually abused by a batterer, may be accused of making the child psychologically ill by fabricating false allegations against the father, just to bring positive attention to her heroic efforts as a protective mother. In some cases, the mother and child may even be accused of entering into a *folie-a-deux* or collusion against an innocent father. Obviously, it is difficult to prove that the child's psychological distress is not caused by the father's behavior, especially when the child is very young. Sometimes exasperated courts actually place the child in the father's custody in an attempt to prove whether or not abuse is occurring. However, children are resilient, often develop *child abuse accommodation syndrome* (CAAS), and adapt to the abusive situation by covering up the parent's abuse for fear of further retribution (Drozd et al. 2004; Kuehnle and Walker 2003; Walker et al. 2005).

During the 1990s, courts around the nation took testimony from citizens concerning gender bias in the courts (Shafran 1990). The reports confirmed dissatisfaction with child custody procedures as well as the allocation and collection of child support. Who was granted custody and how much child support the other parent was ordered to pay often depended on how much time a parent got to spend with a child or whether or not the parenting time was adequate or was even in the child's best interests. Data suggested by those reports estimated that upward of 70 percent of those obtaining child custody evaluations had faced allegations of domestic violence (Shafran 1990). Despite the evidence of gender bias against mothers when cases involving abuse allegations went to the judge to decide custody, nothing much has changed since then to protect women and children.

Removal of Children from the State

A battered woman who flees from a batterer may take her children across state lines without being arrested for kidnapping if there are no court orders to remain in a particular jurisdiction. Sometimes this precipitates a rush to file for divorce by one party before this happens, especially if a restraining order where another court has made a finding of fact that domestic violence occurred has not been obtained. If the batterer is a known stalker, it may be important to remove the mother and children from constant contact with him, and removal to another state may be in the children's best interests. This is also true if the battered woman and children have been kept isolated by the batterer and she wants to return to live with her family and others.

Most children do well after such a move, especially if it gets them out of the middle of a violent relationship between two high-conflict parents. Access and visitation can be creatively arranged so that the children get parenting time with the non-abusive father. This may include plans such as having the children spend the school year with one parent and the summers with the other parent or monthly visits for younger children if the parents can afford travel costs. Technology can keep the noncustodial parent in the child's life through telephone calls, videos, digital pictures, letters, and e-mails when the child is old enough to use a computer. Commensurate with the child's age, he or she should be given the responsibility of maintaining contact with the other parent without interference from the custodial parent. Often, the noncustodial parent provides a laptop computer or cell phone for older children so that the other parent does not have to be present for the contact times (Kuehnle and Walker 2003; Walker et al. 2005).

Validity of Prenuptial Agreements

Another area of contentiousness in divorce hearings with couples where there are reports of domestic violence is the validity of a prenuptial agreement that sets forth the distribution of assets should the marriage end in divorce or even death. Psychologists may be called as expert witnesses to testify that the battered woman signed a prenuptial agreement under the threat of further abuse, which may make it null and void; psychologists may also testify that the woman was not competent to knowingly sign the document because of the psychological effects from domestic violence (Walker and Shapiro 2004). Interestingly, if the prenuptial agreement is signed at the same time as the wedding, the court may also invalidate the marriage vows as having been made under duress, causing the marriage to be considered null and void. This would in turn make

division of property occur as if there were no marriage and therefore no accumulation of marital assets. Obviously, this would cause the victim to win the battle over duress and coercion of one agreement but lose the war for a greater share of the property. Sometimes civil torts for personal injury are filed simultaneously, as property or other assets may be used to offset the harm the woman has suffered.

Child Protection Dependency and Delinquency Courts

There are two other legal areas for families with domestic violence to become involved in child protection dependency and delinquency courts. In large cities, these may be separate from the court that hears dissolution of marriage cases; but in smaller towns, these courts constitute one entity. In fact, there is a movement to merge the courts so that all family matters may be heard under one unified family court rather than having cases go from one judge to another when children are at issue. However, this essay will describe each separately.

Dependency Court and Child Protection Issues

The state has the right to act as the parent under the doctrine of *parens patriae* when parents fail to assume proper responsibility for their children. Unless this occurs, the state usually does not challenge parental authority. Child abuse and neglect will trigger the threshold in all states for such intervention, while exposure to domestic violence will do so only in some states. In some cases, criminal charges may also be brought against the parties, so that cases involving the same acts or failures to act could be handled in both juvenile court and criminal court. Therefore, there are usually numerous lawyers and experts involved in these cases and different standards of proof.

To protect parents from undue interference by the state, there are laws that each state's legislature has passed which usually follow the model laws in the Uniform Child Protection Act requiring the presumption that reunification of the family is in the child's best interest. Therefore, if the state intervenes, its agents must put forth a treatment plan that, if followed, would lead to reunification of the parent and the child. Mental health professionals who work for the state's Child Protection Team are responsible for putting these plans together for the court, which will then incorporate it into orders of the court. It is often frustrating for a protective parent who becomes ensnared in the child protection system to prove that she is not abusive or to prove that the batterer is abusing both she and the children. Given the possibility that at least three courts may be involved simultaneously with one family, there can be even more confusion when judges do not agree or when different facts are accepted as evidence in different courts. For example, a woman who obtains a restraining order against an abusive partner in criminal or civil court may use that order to ask the juvenile court or family court to order that the batterer may have no contact with the children. Although judges are supposed to respect each other's findings of fact, jurisdictional problems are often rampant in domestic violence cases, especially when there is more than one state involved. Unfortunately, children do not have legal rights in these cases until their parents' rights are terminated (which is possible in some states), and their wishes do not get known to the courts. There is a worldwide movement to give children legal standing in the courts so that they may be represented by their own attorneys, who represent their wishes, not just what is believed to be in their best interest (Walker and Shapiro 2004).

Delinquency Courts

The U.S. Department of Juvenile Justice is responsible for prosecuting youth who are arrested for delinquency. Children who commit criminal acts are understood to have different needs than adults who do so, including the priority of rehabilitation. Studies have found a direct connection between child abuse and subsequent delinquency (O'Keefe 1994; Thoennes and Tjaden 1990). In most cases, except for crimes of violence, rehabilitation is recommended over punishment. However, when violence is used, especially in murder and sexual offenses, youths may be waived into adult court, tried as adults, and punished by prison terms if found guilty. Studies of youths who have been arrested and placed in detention centers have found that as many as 85 percent have been exposed to domestic violence and child abuse. Despite the high risk of delinquency in child abuse victims, there are almost no treatment programs for children who have developed post-traumatic stress disorder (PTSD) from family violence.

Other Civil Courts and Personal Injury Tort Cases

A battered woman who suffers serious physical and/or psychological injuries may sue the batterer in civil court for the damage he has inflicted upon her. These are personal injury tort cases that are similar to lawsuits against any party for negligence or malpractice. The laws specify that the injuries do not have to be intentionally inflicted but rather that the person should know or should have known that such behavior could produce serious and often long-lasting injuries. Most states have removed the laws, called interspousal immunity, barring married parties from suing each other. In some states, such as New Jersey, married parties must file a civil tort together with the action for dissolution of the marriage. Although such cases are heard in family court, if the parties wish, a jury trial may be elected.

Obviously, these actions are taken only when there are large sums of money available to pay off any judgment. Most often they are used as leverage to resolve financial settlements during divorce actions, as described earlier. However, they can be a deterrent to stop wealthy batterers from further stalking and harassment. Such legal actions may help a battered woman pay her medical and psychotherapy bills and live a comfortable life, especially if her injuries interfere with her ability to work outside of the home (Walker and Shapiro 2004).

Criminal Courts

The greatest changes in the laws in the United States to protect battered women and their children are in the criminal courts. Each state has passed laws to make it easier for law enforcement to arrest and prosecute batterers with or without the cooperation of the battered person, and some states even have special domestic violence courts. But perhaps the most important change is that women who killed their abusive partners in what they believed was self-defense may call expert witness testimony to the stand on their behalf. Although these changes began in the United States, they are now in effect in many other countries around the world.

Restraining or Protective Orders

Although the restraining order or other type of protective order is just a piece of paper and will not stop an act of violence if the batterer is determined to commit it, it does carry with it penalties for violation and has other benefits, one of which is that law enforcement officers are more likely to take a domestic violence call seriously when the victim has gone to the trouble of obtaining a protective order. In addition, obtaining a protective order requires a judge to make a finding of fact that the person has a higher than usual risk of being harmed or a finding of fact that the person restrained from contact with the victim did commit domestic violence. This finding of fact may be useful later on should the parties decide to terminate their marriage or become involved in a custody dispute over children, as the family court must then treat the case differently from those for which there is less risk of violence. Perhaps most importantly, the victim may become empowered by learning that a judge does take her reports seriously and is willing to try to protect herself and her children.

The process of obtaining a restraining order has been made very easy, to encourage victims to try to get protection from the court. Costs have been reduced for protective orders, and advocates rather than lawyers usually assist the victim in the process. In some jurisdictions, the batterer does not have to be personally served the order and it can be done by notice published in the newspaper. The alleged batterer has the opportunity to defend against the complaint within a certain period of time, usually thirty days. This is a court hearing in front of a judge. If there is a violation of the restraining or protective order, the allegation is brought before that judge, who may find the batterer guilty of contempt of a court order, which is punishable by fines or jail time.

Assault

Prosecution of abuse cases against both men and women now fill the criminal court dockets. Police officers are more likely to make an arrest knowing that there will probably be consequences for an abuser. Battered women are encouraged to use the criminal justice system to help protect themselves and their children, which means reporting assaults as well as obtaining restraining orders. First-time offenders are offered a deferred prosecution plan where they may choose to go into offender-specific court-ordered counseling programs. In some jurisdictions, this is a deferred prosecution which may be dismissed after a certain specified period of time without a reoccurrence of violence. In other places, the offender is required to plead guilty, and after a specified period of time with no further arrests, the offense is expunged from the record. Victims, who often wish to help the batterer stop his violent behavior, are more likely to cooperate with the court system if they believe that there is a chance for him to change. Victim witness programs provide advocates to encourage battered women to follow through and testify at the trials should the batterer not choose the deferral plan.

An unexpected consequence of making arrests easier occurred with police officers arresting both parties when it was not clear who was the aggressor during the initiation phase of the new arrest laws. Frequently, mothers, who have the responsibility for their children on their minds, plead guilty or no contest or enter a deferral program, so that they can be released and go home, preventing involvement by the Child Protection Team and dependency court if they were to be held in jail. They agree to go into a treatment program, usually court approved, to learn how to manage their anger and change their violent behavior despite the fact that they may have used violence only to defend themselves or their children against the batterers' abuse.

Women Who Kill in Self-Defense

Despite all the changes in the criminal justice system, it is still impossible to totally protect a battered woman from a batterer who is determined to kill her. Women who are desperate may choose to arm themselves with guns, the most common way for them to kill the batterer, and approximately 1,200 battered women each year shoot and kill their batterers, fearing that the batterers will kill them (Browne and Williams 1993). Prior to the 1980s, these women would have been encouraged to plead guilty to first-degree murder and risked being sentenced to spend the rest of their lives in prison. Today, it is less likely that they will be charged, and if they are, they are likely to present evidence of domestic violence at their trials. Many are acquitted on the grounds of self-defense, or convicted on charges of lesser responsibility, such as second-degree murder (meaning that it was not premeditated, but they should have known that their actions might result in the other person's death) or even manslaughter (which encompasses various ways in which emotional distress can interfere with good judgment).

The history of getting judges and juries to understand that women can meet the self-defense statute recommendations differently from men was a long battle in the appellate courts rather than in the state legislatures. Women who tried to admit testimony of how being repeatedly abused caused them to believe they needed to use deadly force even before their batterers had struck again were not permitted to do so because of the rules of evidence (Walker 1989). Most self-defense laws require evidence of a reasonable perception of imminent danger as the standard of proof to overcome the prosecution's evidence that a homicide did take place. It is not who committed the homicide but rather, why did she do it?

> The typical male case of self-defense may involve two men engaging in a fist fight, pretty evenly matched. However, women are not typically trained to fight with parts of their bodies, even if they did have the physical strength to fight with a man. Women who develop PTSD from trauma perceive danger sooner than someone who has not been traumatized. They startle more easily and in general have more anxiety than do those who have not experienced domestic violence or other forms of trauma. Descriptions of the look in the man's eyes or some other recognizable sign that his anger is rising are reasonable perceptions of danger for a battered woman. The issue of imminency also posed problems in the courts, as some wanted to define it as meaning immediate threat of danger. However, a review of the legislative intent indicated that it was meant to signify that danger was *about* to happen, allowing for some time gap, as if someone might be teetering on a precipice of sorts. Thus, the appellate courts broadened the use of self-defense to include battered women who knew that their partners could stalk and find them no matter where they went if they were to just leave their homes and that there was no escape for most of these women. Even so, the most often asked question is still, "Why didn't she just leave?" Rather, the question should be, "Why didn't he let her go?"

It is often necessary to have a forensic psychologist testify as an expert witness to help explain how both love and violence can coexist in the same relationship and how that can produce psychological effects such as learned helplessness, PTSD, and BWS, which then can impact on the woman's state of mind. Although the role of the expert witness is often debated in psychology and law, it may be critical to the understanding of the judge and juror to have such explanations about the woman's behavior and be able to relate it to other battered women and to this particular woman. Sometimes, the battered woman has other mental disorders that impact on her ability to perceive events and make good decisions about her behavior. For example, a battered woman may become so frightened that she goes into an automatic state where all her responses are governed by the autonomic nervous system and there is no ability to think and process information. This is called a dissociative state and is often seen in long-term victims of early child abuse as well as domestic violence. Other battered women may become paralyzed by fear, and still others may start to act—for example, by firing a gun for protection but not being able to stop until there are no more bullets left. Still others might be so frightened that they purchase a gun just to scare the man and take shooting lessons to

make sure the batterer cannot grab it away from them and use it to kill them. In other cases, the batterer may hand the woman the gun he has been threatening or hurting her with and tell her to shoot him, which she may do without even thinking, after so many years of being coerced into doing exactly what he tells her to do. Each case must be analyzed carefully to see how the woman's behavior during the incident fits into her typical psychological responses.

Legal Use of Battered Woman Syndrome

The psychology of domestic violence relationships has been ruled admissible as meeting the scientific standards that are currently in effect. Although it is often more difficult to get expert testimony admitted in criminal cases than in family court cases, where the scientific reliability is rarely challenged (Zirogiannis 2001), in fact, testimony on BWS has rarely been challenged anywhere since the early 1990s (Myers 1993; Slobogin 1999). In states where there were repeated challenges, the legislatures passed laws specifying the use of BWS either as a part of self-defense or a separate defense entirely in criminal cases. The fact that most state legislatures passed domestic violence protection laws also gives victims consideration as a special class or group of people, which makes it easier to argue that they need special protection in other areas that might not yet be covered by the law.

Psychological Evaluation and Battered Woman Syndrome

Forensic psychologists typically conduct clinical evaluations of people to determine their current mental status and cognitive abilities, and how their emotional status impacts on their cognitive abilities. In trauma cases, it is also important to assess for prior trauma history and its impact on how someone thinks, feels, and behaves. Psychologists use standardized psychological tests in addition to clinical interview data, to permit comparison of one person's responses with norms developed from others in similar groups (Otto, Edens, and Barcus 2000; Walker and Shapiro 2004). In domestic violence cases, it is also possible to use standardized tests that assess for psychological damage from trauma (Briere 1997). Unlike clinical psychologists or treating therapists, forensic psychologists also review data surrounding the incident(s) and understand the legal questions, to assist the triers of fact in understanding this person's state of mind in criminal cases or fitness to parent children in family law, or possible damages and the nexus

Table 1

Battered Woman Syndrome Legal Definition
PTSD Criteria:
   Re-experiencing the event
   Avoidance and numbing of responsiveness
   Hyperarousal
AND
Three additional effects:
   Disrupted interpersonal relationships/power and control
   Difficulties with body image/somatic concerns
   Sexual and intimacy problems
AND
Dynamics of battering relationships

---

with domestic violence in personal injury cases (Walker and Shapiro 2004).

The typical expert testimony describes the dynamics of the particular relationship and relates it to what is known about domestic violence relationships, with special focus on the abuse of power and control by the batterer and its resulting impact on the battered woman (Walker 1989). If the woman has developed BWS and PTSD or other diagnoses, then testimony about her clinical issues and how they impact her state of mind may also be presented. There has been some controversy in the forensic psychology literature about the scientific underpinnings of BWS and its limitations (Follingstad 2003). BWS does not appear as a diagnostic category in the DSM-IV-TR (American Psychiatric Association 2000). Rather, it is subsumed under the PTSD diagnostic criteria plus several additional psychological criteria that make it distinct. More recent research using a similar methodology to that used in the 1970s when BWS was first defined has reaffirmed its empirical basis across various cultures within the United States as well as among women living in several other countries around the world (Walker et al. 2005). The Battered Woman Syndrome Questionnaire (BWSQ) has been scientifically developed to measure BWS and has been translated in Spanish, Russian, Creole, Italian, and Greek. In most of the legal descriptions of BWS, an additional part of the definition includes the description of the dynamics of the domestic violence relationship. The criteria are summarized in Table 1.

Conclusions

It is a rare battered woman who does not have some contact with the legal system around various issues. This article has attempted to outline some of the more common areas where the courts may become involved despite the strong value of privacy in the United States. Early battered women advocates recognized the need to open the doors of the family and let the courts intervene as one way to help protect women and children who lived with domestic violence. Unlike in other countries where the public health system is the gateway into services (Malley-Morrison 2004), in the United States the gateway is through the criminal justice system. This has its problems in that psychological abuse, which most battered women claim is the most devastating form of domestic violence, is not taken as seriously by the criminal justice system as is physical and sexual abuse. Typically, once an arrest is made, the offender is offered the choice of psychoeducational group intervention and the battered woman is assigned a victim witness advocate from the prosecutor's office. In some jurisdictions, the victim and children might even obtain a grant for psychotherapy, while in others referrals to local agencies that provide counseling at a scaled fee are offered. Battered woman shelters that are located in most major cities also provide advocacy and psychoeducational counseling services and referrals to local professionals who specialize in domestic violence protection. Domestic violence remains a specialized area for lawyers as well as mental health professionals, which means that most lawyers do not have the necessary training to understand the psychological issues presented in this essay. However, law schools, like psychology programs, are becoming more likely to offer courses in domestic violence, and those professionals who are interested in practicing in this area have many continuing education courses from which to choose.

LENORE E. A. WALKER

See also **Battered Woman Syndrome as a Legal Defense in Cases of Spousal Homicide; Battered Women, Clemency for; Batterer Typology; Divorce, Custody, and Domestic Violence; Domestic Violence Courts; Expert Witnesses in Domestic Violence Cases; Lautenberg Law; Mandatory Arrest Policies; Violence against Women Act**

References and Further Reading

American Psychiatric Association. *Diagnostic and Statistical Manual of Mental Disorders,* 4th ed., text revision [DSM-IV-TR]. Washington, DC: Author, 2000.
Bancroft, L., and J. G. Silverman. *The Batterer as Parent: Addressing the Impact of Domestic Violence on Family Dynamics.* Sage Series on Violence against Women. Thousand Oaks, CA: Sage, 2002.
Briere, J. *Psychological Assessment of Adult Posttraumatic States.* Washington, DC: American Psychological Assessment Resources, 1997.

Browne, A., and K. R. Williams. "Gender, Intimacy, and Lethal Violence: Trends from 1976–1987." *Gender and Society* 7 (1993): 78–98.

Drozd, L., K. Kuehnle, and L. E. A. Walker. "Safety First: Understanding the Impact of Domestic Violence in Child Custody Disputes." *Journal of Child Custody* 2 (2004).

Follingstad, D. R. "Battered Woman Syndrome in the Courts." In *Handbook of Psychology*, vol. 11, *Forensic Psychology*, edited by A. M. Goldstein. New York: John Wiley & Sons, 2003, pp. 485–507.

Gardner, R. A. *The Parental Alienation Syndrome: A Guide for Mental Health and Legal Professionals*. Cresskill, NJ: Creative Therapeutics, 1992.

Holden, G. W., R. Geffner, and E. N. Jouriles, eds. *Children Exposed to Marital Violence: Theory, Research, and Applied Issues*. Washington, DC: American Psychological Association, 1998.

Jaffe, P. G., and R. Geffner. "Child Custody Disputes and Domestic Violence: Critical Issues for Mental Health, Social Service, and Legal Professionals." In Holden, Geffner, and Jouriles, *Children Exposed to Marital Violence*, 1998, pp. 371–408.

Jaffe, P. G., N. Lemon, and S. E. Poisson. *Child Custody and Domestic Violence*. Thousand Oaks, CA: Sage, 2003.

Johnston, J. R. "Parental Alignments and Rejection: An Empirical Study of Alienation in Children of Divorce." *Journal of American Academy of Psychiatry and the Law* 31 (2003): 158–170.

Kelly, J. B., and J. R. Johnston. "The Alienated Child: A Reformulation of Parental Alienation Syndrome." *Family Court Review* 39 (2001): 249–266.

Kuehnle, K., and L. E. A. Walker. *Children Exposed to Domestic Violence* (Home Study Continuing Education Program). Sarasota, FL: Professional Resource Press, 2003.

Malley-Morrison, K., ed. *International Perspectives on Family Violence and Abuse: A Cognitive Ecological Approach*. Mahwah, NJ: Lawrence Erlbaum Associates, 2004.

Margolin G. "Effects of Domestic Violence on Children." In *Violence Against Children in the Family and Community*, edited by P. Trickett and C. Schellenbach. Washington, DC: American Psychological Association, 1998, pp. 57–101.

Myers, J. E. B. "Expert Testimony Describing Psychological Syndromes." *Pacific Law Journal* 24 (1993): 1453–1455.

O'Keefe, M. "Linking Marital Violence, Mother–Child/Father–Child Aggression, and Child Behavior Problems." *Journal of Family Violence* 9 (1994): 63–78.

Otto, R. K., J. F. Edens, and E. H. Barcus. "The Use of Psychological Testing in Child Custody Evaluations." *Family and Conciliation Courts Review* 38 (2000): 312–340.

Rossman, B. B. R., H. M. Hughes, and M. S. Rosenberg. *Children and Interparental Violence: The Impact of Exposure*. Philadelphia: Brunner/Mazel, 2000.

Slobogin, C. "The Admissibility of Behavioral Science Information in Criminal Trials: From Primitivism to Daubert to Voice." *Psychology, Public Policy, and Law* 5, no. 1 (1999): 100–119.

Thoennes, N., and P. Tjaden. "The Extent, Nature, and Validity of Sexual Abuse Allegations in Custody/Visitation Disputes." *Child Abuse and Neglect* 14 (1990): 151–163.

Walker, L. E. A. *The Battered Woman Syndrome*. New York: Springer, 1984/2000.

———. *Terrifying Love: Why Battered Women Kill and How Society Responds*. New York: Harper/Collins, 1989.

Walker, L. E. A., and D. L. Shapiro. *Introduction to Forensic Psychology: Clinical and Social Psychological Perspectives*. New York: Kluwer/Plenum, 2004.

Walker, L. E. A., H. Ardern, R. Duros, H. Barry, C. Passeri, and K. Richmond. "Battered Woman Syndrome after 30 Years: Cross-National Comparisons in the U.S., Greece, Russia, and Spain." Presentation at the annual meeting of the American Psychology Law Society, St. Petersburg, FL, 2006.

Zirogiannis, L. "Evidentiary Issues with Parental Alienation Syndrome." *Family Court Review* 39 (2001): 334–343.

LESBIAN BATTERING

In the 1970s, the women's movement raised public awareness relative to the extent and magnitude of domestic violence in American society. Victim rights advocates urged the criminal justice system to increase the certainty and celerity of the legal response to domestic violence. They demanded that the system protect victims by arresting, prosecuting, and punishing batterers. By 1988, most states had adopted an array of legislative and procedural reforms, including mandatory arrest policies and stricter enforcement of restraining orders.

These reforms were intended to increase victim reporting as well as to encourage the arrest and prosecution of batterers. At the same time, researchers began to focus considerable attention on domestic violence, and numerous theories were advanced to explain its prevalence. Despite the increased attention, very few studies were conducted examining same sex battering.

A number of factors may combine to explain why researchers neglected to study the problem of same sex battering. First, many state laws limit domestic violence to couples who are married. By definition, these statutes fail to recognize same sex battering and therefore deny gay and lesbian victims legal protection and services. This further isolates victims of same sex battering making it that much more difficult to study this type of intimate violence. Secondly, the first domestic violence theories were developed by feminist scholars who attributed wife battering to patriarchy and male dominance over women. It was argued that men are socialized to control women and treat them as subordinates. Feminists maintained that battering is always perpetrated by men against women. Same sex battering challenged the perception that domestic violence is a gender issue. As a result, same sex battering was ignored because it was not compatible with early domestic violence theories. Third, the gay and lesbian community contributed to the lack of information on same sex battering. The gay and lesbian community was reluctant to recognize the problem of partner abuse among same sex couples. In particular, lesbians wanted to perpetuate the idea that women are less violent than men. In addition, many gay and lesbian leaders were afraid that the problem of same sex battering would be used by society to further condemn homosexuality. Lesbian and gay victims of intimate violence were often pressured by the community to remain silent. Consequently, the gay and lesbian community was slow to acknowledge or support victims of same sex battering.

Types of Abuse

In the early 1990s, a number of precedent-setting studies were conducted to gauge the prevalence of same sex battering. However, researchers studying same sex battering faced a number of obstacles relative to sampling. Researchers often had to rely on nonrandom sampling, which limited the generalizability of their findings. Some of the methods that have been used to generate data on same sex battering include: (1) advertising in gay publications, (2) surveying individuals at gay-identified events or locations such as pride parades or gay bars, (3) recruiting participants through a gay social service organization, and (4) snowballing. Participants secured through these various sampling techniques are in all likelihood not representative of the gay community. They usually have stronger ties to the community and do not reflect that segment of the population who remain "closeted." As a

result, studies examining gay and lesbian partner abuse are unable to measure the actual prevalence of same sex battering. This body of research, however, is still significant because it shows that gays and lesbians do experience violence in their intimate relationships.

Most of the research on same sex battering has focused on the problem of intimate violence in lesbian relationships. It has been reported that a significant number of lesbians suffer the same types of abuse as their heterosexual counterparts. Several studies discovered that between 25 percent and 46 percent of lesbians have been in an abusive same sex relationship. This pattern is comparable to partner abuse among heterosexual couples. It has been estimated that between 25 percent and 33 percent of heterosexual relationships are abusive.

Initial research revealed that many lesbians experience physical abuse and aggression at the hands of their partners. The violence can consist of slapping, biting, strangulation, or assault with a weapon to murder. Physical signs of the abuse include bruises, welts, burns, bleeding, broken bones, and internal injuries. In general, it appears that the most common forms of physical abuse involve pushing, hitting, and/or throwing objects. However, a significant percentage of battered lesbians endure serious personal crimes, including assault with a weapon and rape.

Preliminary research also found support for escalating violence in same sex relationships. In her seminal study of lesbian partner abuse, Elizabeth Leeder discovered evidence of what she referred to as chronic battering. Chronic battering involves abuse that intensifies over time, eventually escalating into a potentially life-threatening situation. A large percentage of battered lesbians have suffered prior abuse. A significant number of battered lesbians have disclosed that the abuse became more frequent and violent over time. In addition, repeat incidents tended to be more violent in nature than first-time incidents and therefore were more likely to require that victims seek medical attention.

Like heterosexual abuse, same sex battering involves sexual coercion, economic control, and psychological abuse. It has been suggested that lesbians suffer the same types of sexual abuse as heterosexual women, including unwanted touching, rape, and forced sex with others. However, there has been no definitive study examining sexual abuse in lesbian relationships. As a result, there is a lack of empirical evidence concerning this form of intimate violence.

Prior research has shown that batterers usually control the couple's assets and income in abusive heterosexual relationships. Thus, the victim may not possess the monetary means to leave the abusive relationship because she is financially dependent on the batterer. Interestingly, there is a lack of evidence supporting economic dependency among lesbian victims of same sex battering. Preliminary results actually suggest that victims and batterers are very similar in terms of employment status. However, victims tend to earn more money and have a higher level of educational attainment and greater occupational prestige than their partners. These findings are not consistent with heterosexual abuse.

Psychological abuse appears to be widespread among same sex couples. Research has found that lesbian victims of intimate violence frequently experience verbal assaults, insults, threats, humiliation, and manipulation. Psychological abuse tends to occur more frequently than physical abuse. Many battered lesbians report that the psychological abuse is as damaging as the physical violence. The verbal threats often serve as a harbinger of other types of abuse. Victims learn that the verbal threats usually precede the physical violence. As a result, victims will attempt to delay the onset of the physical violence by placating the batterer. The victim may engage in activities that will please the batterer, such as cooking her favorite meal.

Another form of psychological abuse is when the batterer threatens to harm the victim's children or pet(s) and/or destroy her property. When the batterer actually follows through on such threats, she is sending a clear message that she is capable of destroying the victim as well. This is intended to instill fear and terror in the victim.

A unique form of psychological abuse that exists in same sex relationships but not in heterosexual relationships is the threat of "outing." Here the abuser threatens to reveal to family, friends, employers, and others that the victim is a lesbian. The victim may fear being ostracized by her family and friends. She could also be afraid of losing her job or custody of her children. The abuser threatens to disclose the victim's sexual orientation in an effort to further control and manipulate her.

Correlates of Abuse

The contributors to partner abuse in homosexual relationships are similar to those in heterosexual relationships. Substance abuse, an imbalance of power between partners, violence or abuse in one partner's past, overdependency on one partner,

and personality disorders have been suggested as some of the factors. These factors appear to be interrelated, increasing the risk that abuse will occur in a lesbian relationship.

Substance Abuse

The "demon rum" theory of violence and abuse is one of the most widely believed explanations for family violence. Most research on the correlation of substance abuse and intimate violence show, however, that a number of variables intervene in the relationship between alcohol and interpersonal violence. Alcohol's effects appear to be mediated by several factors, such as the amount of alcohol consumed, the preconsumption personality of the drinker, and the expectations by both the drinker and others as to how alcohol influences behavior.

Research on the use of alcohol and same sex partner abuse has indicated mixed results, with some studies reporting that alcohol or drug use was related to violence. Recent research suggests that batterers may decide to be abusive even before they decide to drink. And while there appears to be a strong positive relationship between substance abuse and the frequency and severity of partner abuse, this relationship disappears when the batterer's dependency on her partner is statistically removed.

Hence both substance abuse and partner abuse in lesbian relationships may be related to dependency of one partner on another. Drinking may offer lesbians a way to overcome their dependency, and abusing a partner may also be a way to feel powerful. Lesbians who have been victimized often rationalize their partner's behavior, and substance abuse is a logical and acceptable way to do so.

Intergenerational Transmission of Violence

In interviews with victims, Claire Renzetti found that nearly one-third of same sex battering incidents occurred when neither partner was under the influence of alcohol or drugs. These women frequently cited a history of abuse in their own or their partner's family of origin. This suggests some support for the intergenerational transmission hypothesis that individuals who as children witnessed or experienced violence in their families of origin are more likely to be abusive toward their own partners.

A history of abuse may increase the risk of being both an abuser and a victim of abuse by an intimate partner. This "double whammy" effect has been found in studies of heterosexual battering, and the research on lesbian battering also suggests it. Lesbians who have witnessed and experienced intimate violence as children were significantly more likely to be victimized or to abuse their own partners.

Overall, the research has not provided strong evidence for the intergenerational transmission theory. Instead researchers have hypothesized that in those cases in which abuse had been present in the family of origin, this history of abuse was used by respondents and their partners to excuse the current violence. Similar to the use of substance abuse as a rationalization, the belief that exposure to abuse in the family of origin leads to abuse may be a way to justify the batterer's current abuse.

The Role of Power

The feminist emphasis on domestic violence as coercive control, as a way to get a partner to do what another wants even if she/he doesn't want to do so, has been applied to abusive same sex relationships. However, research on lesbian battering finds that power in intimate relationships is a complex, multifaceted phenomenon. A difficulty in the research stems from the measurement of power as a contributor to intimate violence. It has been measured in several ways; namely, which partner makes the most decisions and what status differences exist between partners in money and education.

Research on heterosexual couples has found a strong association between balance of power in the relationship and the incidence of battering; however, the relationship has been less strong in studies of abusive homosexual couples. In same sex relationships, an association has been found between the division of labor and victimization in that the partner who handled domestic issues was more likely to be a victim. Differences in social class and in intellectual abilities between partners were also factors in the likelihood of battering. In addition, when there was a difference between a partner's achieved status and expected status, given her background, this partner was more likely to be abusive. These studies on same sex couples highlight that the balance of power is multifaceted in intimate relationships.

Dependency

Emotional interdependence is generally a necessity in an intimate relationship, with each partner relying on the other for emotional support. In heterosexual relationships, it is often assumed that women are more dependent on their male partners. Men, while they may have a need for dependency, are less likely to express their need overtly according to cultural norms. Batterers are often individuals who are highly dependent on their partners but feel ashamed because they perceive it as a weakness. Research in heterosexual relationships has demonstrated that the likelihood of violence increases when a highly dependent husband attempts to control his wife and meets with resistance. A similar trend has been found in lesbian relationships. Research has found that the greater the batterer's dependency and the greater the victim's resistance, the more likely the batterer is to inflict more types of abuse. The abuse is also more likely to occur with greater frequency.

There are exceptionally high levels of attachment between partners in lesbian relationships. This is partly related to socialization and identity issues in females and partly related to lesbian couples' lack of support in the outside community. Lesbian couples insulate themselves by nurturing their relationships, creating emotionally intense relationships in closed systems. This closeness can generate insecurity, and one partner may feel threatened when the other partner has separate friends or different views. In particular, the dependent partner is likely to feel weak and ashamed. Researchers have suggested that self-destructive behavior, such as alcohol abuse, may be a way that some lesbians cope with their fear/shame of dependency.

Personality Disorders

Substance abuse, overdependency, a feeling of powerlessness, and the need to be powerful can be considered symptoms of an underlying personality disorder. Some support for underlying personality disorders of batterers has been found in heterosexual relationships. Research on personality traits or disorders has been limited with respect to same sex couples.

It has been argued, though, that batterers often have personality disorders, the most prevalent of which are borderline and narcissistic. The basis for this position is that characteristic symptoms for both disorders are often found in batterers. These symptoms include an unclear sense of self, a need for power, and a sense of entitlement. And all have been found to be associated with partner abuse in same sex relationships, as discussed in this section.

Victim Reporting

Despite the prevalence of intimate violence, a significant number of victims do not report the abuse to the police. Researchers have attempted to identify the factors that affect the reporting practices of crime victims. Studies have shown that crimes committed by strangers are more likely to be reported than those committed by relatives or intimate partners. As a result, many victims of domestic violence fail to bring partner abuse to the attention of law enforcement.

Domestic violence has a long tradition of underreporting. Moreover, the legal system for much of its history treated domestic violence as a private matter. Hence, victims of domestic violence may have been reluctant to report the abuse because they expected police to be unresponsive. Prior research has found that victims of domestic violence who did report the abuse to the police were often dissatisfied with how they were treated. Specifically, several studies revealed that victims of domestic violence identified police as the least helpful and most indifferent of all criminal justice personnel. These findings suggest that victims of domestic violence may not report the abuse because they do not want to be mistreated by police.

There are other factors that impact the decision of victims to report domestic violence to the police. Victims may fear that their batterers will retaliate and perhaps attempt to kill them if they report the abuse to the authorities. In addition, many victims love and are financially dependent on their batterers. As a result, a large number of victims will not report the violence because they do not want to get the batterer in trouble with the law. Lastly, some victims continue to believe that domestic violence is a private matter, and therefore they will not seek assistance from the criminal justice system. Lesbian victims face these as well as additional obstacles that contribute to the underreporting of same sex battering.

Specifically, there is a long history of police harassment against gays and lesbians. As a result, lesbian victims of intimate violence may be more distrustful of the police than their heterosexual counterparts. It has been estimated that only one out of four battered lesbians reports battering incidents to the police. Moreover, many battered lesbians who have contacted law enforcement claim that police reacted negatively to them and did not take their allegations of abuse seriously.

Furthermore, lesbian victims of intimate violence may fear that police will treat the incident as mutual battering and not recognize their victimization. Mutual battering implies that both the victim and the perpetrator are equally responsible for the violence. Police may minimize the abuse because they consider the incident "two dykes acting butch." Similarly, police may be uncertain about how to respond to lesbian battering. They have been trained that domestic violence involves a female victim who has been assaulted by a physically stronger male aggressor. When the incident involves two women, the ability of police to determine who is at fault becomes far more difficult. As with heterosexual abuse, the police may mistakenly assume that the larger or more "butch" female is the batterer. Conversely, the police may be more inclined to assign blame to both the victim and the perpetrator by arresting both parties. Consequently, lesbian victims may forgo seeking help from the criminal justice system because they fear being arrested and held partially responsible for the violence.

As noted earlier, police have not received positive ratings from heterosexual victims of domestic violence. It appears that the law enforcement response to lesbian battering is even less satisfactory. Evidence suggests that police are not only indifferent to lesbian victims of same sex battering—they are at times outright hostile. Therefore, lesbian victims may be more hesitant than heterosexual victims to report domestic violence to the police.

Another hurdle that gays and lesbians face is the fact that many states' domestic violence laws do not cover same sex couples. In these states, gay and lesbian victims of domestic violence are denied assistance and protection from the legal system. Consequently, there would be no reason for victims of same sex abuse to report the incident to the police.

Similarly, lesbian victims of same sex battering confront the added threat of "outing," which serves as another barrier to reporting. Lesbians who are "closeted" are likely to remain silent. They are not likely to come forward to report intimate violence to the authorities. Although it has been estimated that between 25 and 46 percent of lesbians have been in abusive same sex relationships, they have remained relatively invisible.

Obstacles to Leaving Abusive Relationships

Lesbian victims of same sex battering face many obstacles relative to leaving abusive relationships. In particular, many states narrowly define domestic violence and therefore deny legal protection to battered lesbians. By definition, a number of states restrict domestic violence to incidents involving members of the opposite sex. Several other states limit domestic violence to situations involving spouses, former spouses, or family members related by blood. Moreover, states that refuse to provide protection to gay and lesbian victims of same sex battering also hinder their ability to prevent further violence by denying them the opportunity to obtain restraining orders.

Some states subtly fail to recognize same sex battering. These states offer legal protections and services to unmarried couples who engage in "socially approved" sexual relations. In turn, these same states have laws prohibiting and criminalizing homosexual activities such as sodomy.

Many states offer protection to victims of same sex battering but fail to provide gays and lesbians with the same rights as their heterosexual counterparts. For example, a number of states restrict access to domestic violence shelters to heterosexual women, thereby excluding battered lesbians. It is not surprising, then, that many battered lesbians do not seek help from domestic violence shelters. They simply assume that these shelters provide assistance exclusively to female victims of heterosexual domestic abuse.

Claire Renzetti analyzed data from a survey of domestic service providers to determine whether the perceptions of lesbians were accurate relative to services being for battered heterosexual women only. She found that 96 percent of the respondents maintained that services were available to battered lesbians. However, the majority of respondents also reported that the agency did not engage in outreach to the gay and lesbian community to inform battered lesbians about the availability of services. Many of these agencies neglected to generate literature specifically addressing lesbian battering or offer support groups for female victims of same sex domestic violence. Furthermore, the staff in the majority of these agencies did not receive training on lesbian battering and its unique dimensions. Renzetti's findings suggest that many social service agencies profess to provide services to battered lesbians. At the same time, however, these agencies do little to make lesbians aware that such services are available to them.

Additionally, gay and lesbian victims of intimate violence, like their heterosexual counterparts, want to obtain restraining orders against their batterers. They are often informed that a mutual restraining order will be issued by the court. Mutual restraining orders serve to perpetuate the myth that same sex domestic violence constitutes mutual battering. In these cases, victims of same sex battering end up being held equally responsible for the abuse. As a result, battered gays and lesbians feel betrayed by the legal system when a mutual restraining order is issued because their victimization has not been validated. Rather, it has been called into question. A mutual restraining order also places the victim at risk for further abuse because the perpetrator may feel bolstered by the system's response. In other words, the perpetrator may believe that she can continue to abuse the victim with impunity.

Another problem that gays and lesbians often encounter is the homophobic attitudes of criminal justice professionals, including police, prosecutors, and judges, as well as social service providers. Many battered lesbians have reported that police responded negatively to them. Claire Renzetti recounts the actual experience of a battered lesbian who reported an incident of abuse to police. The victim maintains that the police told her that she deserved the abuse because she was a lesbian.

Similarly, the courts have been hostile to gays and lesbians. As noted earlier, battered lesbians often remain in abusive relationships because of the threat of "outing" and its potentially devastating consequences, such as losing custody of their children. The courts have done little to ease the fears of lesbian parents. For example, in a Florida case the court awarded custody of a young girl to her father, a convicted murderer, rather than to her mother, a lesbian. The judge ruled that the girl should be raised in a nonlesbian household, asserting that it would provide a better environment regardless of the fact that the father was a convicted murderer.

Strategies for Change

One of the first reforms that advocates for gays and lesbians need to pursue is equal protection for victims of same sex battering. Domestic violence laws in many states need to be revised to recognize same sex battering and to extend legal rights to gay and lesbian victims. Once these statutory changes have occurred, then advocates need to monitor the criminal justice system to ensure that police consistently enforce the law on behalf of victims of same sex battering.

This will require that police be educated about the nuances of same sex battering. Educators and trainers should dispel some of the myths associated with domestic violence. First, police have to learn that domestic violence is not exclusively a gender issue. It does not always involve a female victim and a male batterer. Similarly, police have to receive adequate training relative to investigating same sex battering so they will not treat these cases as mutual battering. When both parties show signs of injury, police need to be trained to take the time to consider the possibility of self-defense. Likewise, police cannot automatically assume that the physically larger partner is the aggressor.

Within the legal community, activities that have proved to be successful in confronting heterosexual violence can be used to combat same sex battering. Training and educating judges, lawyers, and advocates is necessary. Many states now require general domestic violence training for police and courtroom personnel. Some states, such as Massachusetts, have incorporated education about homophobia into the training.

In the courtroom, creative advocacy can empower lesbian survivors to insist on equal treatment under the law. Many states have codes of courtroom procedures that allow these cases to be heard in as private a forum as possible and that encourage judges and courtroom personnel to be sensitive to privacy interests. All states have procedures for impounding files or closing courtrooms. Creative advocacy can minimize the public airing of a case by utilizing different strategies. Sidebar hearings, impoundment motions, and motions to close the courtroom are ways to guarantee privacy. These strategies also allow the judge an opportunity to assess a case without the glare of the courtroom public.

A victim's safety is paramount in the prevention of further victimization. Therefore, the courtroom should be fully utilized to increase safety. In some states, though, judges routinely issue mutual restraining orders in same sex cases, and batterers often use the order as a basis to take out a criminal complaint against the victim, prolonging abusive contact. Mutual restraining orders can and should be appealed. In Massachusetts, for example, a person seeking an abuse protection order can ask the court for different relief measures to keep her or him safe. This opens up an array of protections for the victim: asking for no contact orders or orders to stay away from the workplace, the home, or a child's school. For increased safety, advocates have suggested requiring that car keys and garage door openers be returned. In addition, it is recommended that the victim be provided a police escort while moving out of the house.

Victims of same sex battering have lacked access to formal services within the community. Historically, battered women's programs have largely been heterosexually focused in their services, outreach materials, and staff training. Programs that do exist for lesbian victims are located in large urban areas; as a consequence, many victims can remain isolated from family as well as much needed services. However, it is important that lesbian victims seek out shelter when placed in danger. The primary problem in creating shelters specifically for battered lesbians is funding; therefore, lesbians must feel comfortable in seeking support from battered women's shelters. Staff and volunteers must be trained to understand the needs of lesbian victims better. Staff must also be trained to identify homophobia in other staff members and residents.

With little support from family and friends, some victims seek support from a therapist, psychologist, or member of the clergy. A number of experts have suggested that several issues be addressed during counseling. These include assessing the extent and severity of the abuse; assessing whether there is a question of mutual battering; distinguishing between abuse and appropriate behavior; developing protection plans; offering minimal cost support networking groups; and reassuring the victim that she is not to blame. It is also important for therapists to be patient and nonjudgmental; and heterosexual therapists must be able to determine any prejudgment they have toward lesbians.

Organizations within the gay, lesbian, bisexual, transgender (GLBT) community have emerged to provide services. One example is the San Francisco Network for Battered Lesbians and Bisexual Women that was formed in 1992. Its mission is the elimination of battering within the lesbian and bisexual communities. The network's goals are to support survivors, educate communities, and empower victims. The network consists of volunteers and relies on contributions from individuals. It offers training and educational presentations to the community and provides information, referrals, advocacy, and phone counseling.

Though resources for lesbians on college campuses have generally been geared toward providing a traditional social arena for white middle-class lesbians, GLBT organizations on campus can also be a resource for lesbian and bisexual women who are or have been in battering relationships. These organizations can act as an effective educational forum by sponsoring events that raise awareness about same sex battering, as well as through distribution of informational literature.

Many college campuses have developed policies on battering, though lesbian battering needs to be specifically addressed. College campuses should have policies on battering and complaint procedures that are separate from formal legal procedures. Lesbian organizations have recommended establishing a board to handle battering cases, and the board would be trained in the issues of domestic abuse, same sex battering, and screening. One area lacking services for battered lesbians is often campus security. Like traditional law enforcement, campus security has consisted primarily of white males, and therefore battered lesbians may be reluctant to report their victimization. Lesbians of color are also reluctant to report their victimization because of their orientation and their race. When campus security strives to develop a positive relationship with both the same sex community and communities of color, these segments can feel that services are accessible to them.

It is evident that, like their heterosexual counterparts, a significant number of lesbians experience violence in their intimate relationships. Similarly, the abuse often ranges from physical assault to sexual coercion to psychological exploitation. Victims of same sex battering have encountered more obstacles than heterosexual women to securing protection and services. Unlike their heterosexual counterparts, lesbians face the added threat of "outing" and possible loss of their children, job, and family ties. Clearly, more needs to be done by the legal system to ensure that battered lesbians are sufficiently protected from further violence and receive adequate services and that batterers are held responsible for their actions. Society as a whole, however, will have to accept homosexuality before the criminal justice system will be in a position to assist victims of same sex battering.

ANNE SULLIVAN and KRISTEN KUEHNLE

See also **Cohabiting Violence; Dating Violence; Feminist Theory; Gay and Bisexual Male Domestic Violence; Gay Domestic Violence, Police Attitudes and Behaviors toward; Intimate Partner Violence, Forms of; Intimate Partner Violence in Queer, Transgender, and Bisexual Communities; Same-Sex Domestic Violence: Comparing Venezuela and the United States; Sexual Aggression Perpetrated by Females; Sexual Orientation and Gender Identity: The Need for Education in Servicing Victims of Trauma; Stalking; Violence against Women Act**

References and Further Reading

Leeder, Elizabeth. "Enmeshed in Pain: Counseling the Lesbian Battering Couple." *Women and Therapy* 7 (1988): 81–99.
Renzetti, Claire. *Violent Betrayal: Partner Abuse in Lesbian Relationships*. Newbury Park, CA: Sage, 1992.
———. "The Poverty of Services for Battered Lesbians." In *Violence in Gay and Lesbian Domestic Partnerships*, edited by Claire Renzetti and Harvey Miley. New York: Harrington Park Press, 1996.

M

MALE VICTIMS OF DOMESTIC VIOLENCE AND REASONS THEY STAY WITH THEIR ABUSERS

Men represent half of all domestic violence victims (Archer 2000; Straus and Gelles 1990) and incur between 21 percent and 40 percent of physical injuries resulting from domestic violence (Archer 2000; Straus 2004; Tjaden and Thoennes 1998); the combined impact of physical and psychological abuse is comparable across genders (Pimlott-Kubiak and Cortina 2003). Children who witness their mothers assault their father are at risk for emotional distress (Mahoney et al. 2003), and for perpetrating relationship violence in adolescence (Foshee, Bauman, and Linder 1999; Moretti et al. in press) and adulthood (Kaura and Allen 2004; Langhinrichsen-Rohling, Neidig, and Thorn 1995; Straus 1992). Clearly, the problem of abused males is a serious one. And yet, male victims often remain in abusive relationships and do not get the help they need. Some of the reasons for staying are similar to those given by female victims, while others are particular to men.

Financial Dependency

A common misconception is that men, who typically have greater earning power than women, enjoy greater financial independence and can therefore more easily escape a violent environment. However, the advantage that men have in income levels when married is often lost after a divorce, when the female partner is awarded alimony and child support (Cook 1997; Pearson 1997). According to Steinmetz (1977–1978):

> If the husband leaves the family he is still responsible for a certain amount of economic support of the family in addition to the cost of a separate residence for himself. Thus the loss in standard of living is certainly a consideration for any husband who is contemplating a separation. . . . Leaving the family home means leaving . . . the comfortable and familiar, that which is not likely to be reconstructed in a small apartment. (p. 506)

457

Emotional Dependency

Like female victims, many male victims come from abusive, dysfunctional family backgrounds and seek to meet their stunted emotional needs with their partners, who may have had similar experiences. These couples "form a partnership of mutual dependency, shoring up each other's weaknesses and isolating each other from a world they believe is cruel and stress-laden" (Shupe, Stacey, and Hazlewood 1987, pp. 60–61). Most physically abused men (e.g., 95 percent of callers to the Domestic Abusive Help-line for Men; Hines, Brown, and Dunning in press) also report being controlled, verbally abused, and isolated from friends and family (Graham-Kevan in press). As a result, they suffer significant loss of self-esteem and may even become convinced that the violence is their fault. They do not believe that they could do much better in another relationship. When their partners apologize for their behavior and shower them with affection, male victims will recommit, rationalizing the abuse and viewing their partners as "really a good people" whom they must "heal," rather than dangerous people from whom they should flee (Migliaccio 2002; Pearson 1997).

Fear of Retribution and Concern for the Children

Men who contemplate leaving an abusive relationship may fear being stalked, enduring malicious rumors spread by their partners among friends and at their place of employment, or having to face false accusations of domestic violence (Cook 1997; Hines et al. in press; Pearson 1997). Men worry about losing their children in a custody dispute and are further motivated to stay if the children have been abused by the mother—a valid concern, given that abusive wives are as likely to hit their children as are abusive husbands (Margolin and Gordis 2003; Straus and Smith 1990). Given the bias within law enforcement toward arresting males (e.g., Brown 2004; Hamel 2005; Shernock 2005), calling the police may often be futile. One victim who sought to press charges was told by the police, "There's nothing to press charges on. She's half your size. The judge won't even look at it" (Cook 1997, p. 79).

Male Socialization and the "Wimp" Factor

Their identities "coded by masculine scripts" (Pearson 1997, p. 128), men are socialized to be responsible and competent, and this includes a commitment to marriage (Hines and Malley-Morrison 2001). As one man put it:

When you get married it's your responsibility to provide to make sure there is food on the table, clothes. Regardless of the fact that women are going out working these days, men are still taught that it is their responsibility to provide. So, if you leave, you are abdicating your responsibility, and you are less than a man. (Cook 1997, p. 61)

The needs to suppress pain and to appear strong and in control also inhibit men's ability to leave an abusive relationship and to admit they have been victimized. As children, males who are physically attacked have the choice of hitting back and being perceived as aggressive, running away and appearing weak, or minimizing the pain and appearing strong in the eyes of peers (Fontes 2003). In adulthood, male domestic violence victims are thus prone to minimize the abuse, out of fear of being labeled "wimps" (Cook 1997; Flynn 1990; Fontes 1998; George 2003) and becoming objects of ridicule. Society deplores wife abuse, but husband abuse is treated as a humorous topic (Steinmetz and Lucca 1988). Pat Overberg, past director of the Antelope Valley Oasis Shelter, relates the story of an ironworker whom she helped: "This guy was big, and his wife was tall, but thin, probably no more than a hundred pounds. . . . She kept beating him up with a baseball bat. Every time he came out of the hospital, they [his coworkers] were laughing him off the girders" (Cook 1997, p. 54).

When men do muster the courage to leave their abusers and seek help, they find few resources available. "I called eleven numbers for battered women," one man recounted, "and got no help" (Hines et al. in press, p. 15). As of this writing, only one out of approximately 1,800 shelters in the United States accepts male residents and their children. Some shelters help men in other ways, but only if men happen to contact them, and there is little if any outreach (Cook 1997; Fontes 2003). Faced with these obstacles, it is not surprising that abused men so often choose to stay.

JOHN HAMEL

See also **Battered Husbands; Battered Woman Syndrome; Coercive Control; Cycle of Violence; Stages of Leaving Abusive Relationships; Stalking; Stockholm Syndrome in Battered Women; Victim-Blaming Theory**

References and Further Reading

Archer, J. "Sex Differences in Aggression between Heterosexual Partners: A Meta-Analytic Review." *Psychological Bulletin* 126, no. 5 (2000): 651–680.

Brown, G. "Gender as a Factor in the Response of the Law-Enforcement System to Violence against Partners." *Sexuality and Culture* 8, no. 3-4 (2004): 1–87.

Cook, P. *Abused Men: The Hidden Side of Domestic Violence*. Westport, CT: Praeger, 1997.

Fontes, D. "Violent Touch: Breaking through the Stereotype," 2003. http://www.Safe4all.org.

Foshee, V., K. Bauman, and F. Linder. "Family Violence and the Preparation of Adolescent Dating Violence: Examining Social Learning and Social Control Processes." *Journal of Marriage and the Family* 61, no. 2 (1999): 331–342.

George, M. "Invisible Touch." *Aggression and Violent Behavior* 8 (2003): 23–60.

Graham-Kevan, N. "Power and Control in Relationship Aggression." In *Family Interventions in Domestic Violence: A Handbook of Gender-Inclusive Theory and Treatment*, edited by J. Hamel and T. Nicholls. New York: Springer. In press.

Hamel, J. "Fixing Only Part of the Problem: Public Policy and Batterer Intervention." *Family Violence and Sexual Assault Bulletin*, 21, no. 2/3 (2005): 18–42.

Hines, D., J. Brown, and E. Dunning. "Characteristics of Callers to the Domestic Abuse Helpline for Men." *Journal of Family Violence*. In press.

Hines, D., and K. Malley-Morrison. "Psychological Effects of Partner Abuse against Men: A Neglected Research Area." *Psychology of Men and Masculinity* 2, no. 2 (2001): 75–85.

Kaura, S., and C. Allen. "Dissatisfaction with Relationship Power and Dating Violence Perpetration by Men and Women." *Journal of Interpersonal Violence* 19, no. 5 (2004): 576–588.

Langhinrichsen-Rohling, J., P. Neidig, and G. Thorn. "Violent Marriages: Gender Differences in Levels of Current Violence and Past Abuse." *Journal of Family Violence* 10, no. 2 (1995): 159–175.

Mahoney, A., W. Donnelly, P. Boxer, and T. Lewis. "Marital and Severe Parent-to-Adolescent Physical Aggression in Clinic-Referred Families: Mother and Adolescent Reports on Co-occurrence and Links to Child Behavior Problems." *Journal of Family Psychology* 17, no. 1 (2003): 3–19.

Margolin, G., and E. Gordis. "Co-occurrence between Marital Aggression and Parents' Child Abuse Potential: The Impact of Cumulative Stress." *Violence and Victims* 18, no. 3 (2003): 243–258.

Migliaccio, T. "Abused Husbands: A Narrative Analysis." *Journal of Family Issues* 23, no. 1 (2002): 26–52.

Moretti, M., C. Odgers, and I. Obsuth. "Exposure to Maternal Versus Paternal Partner Violence and Aggression in Adolescent Girls and Boys: The Moderating Role of PTSD." *Aggressive Behavior*. In press.

Pearson, P. *When She Was Bad: Women and the Myth of Innocence*. New York: Penguin, 1997.

Pimlott-Kubiak, S., and M. Cortina. "Gender, Victimization and Outcomes: Reconceptualizing Risk." *Journal of Consulting and Clinical Psychology* 71, no. 3 (2003): 528–539.

Shernock, S. "Police Categorization and Disposition of Non-Lethal Partner Violence Incidents Involving Women Offenders in a Statewide Rural Jurisdiction with a Presumptive Arrest Policy." *Family Violence and Sexual Assault Bulletin*, 21, no. 2/3 (2005): 11–17.

Shupe, A., W. Stacey, and L. Hazlewood. *Violent Men, Violent Couples: The Dynamics of Domestic Violence*. New York: John Wiley & Sons, 1987.

Steinmetz, S. "The Battered Husband Syndrome." *Victimology* 2 (1977–1978): 499–509.

Steinmetz, S., and J. Lucca. "Husband Battering." In *Handbook of Family Violence,* edited V. Van Hasselt. New York: Plenum Press, 1988, pp. 233–246.

Straus, M. "Children as Witnesses to Marital Violence: A Risk Factor for Lifelong Problems among a Nationally Representative Sample of American Men and Women." Report of the 23rd Ross Roundtable on Critical Approaches to Common Pediatric Problems, M5796. September 1992.

———. "Prevalence of Violence against Dating Partners by Male and Female University Students Worldwide." *Violence against Women* 10, no. 7 (2004): 790–811.

Straus, M., and R. Gelles. *Physical Violence in American Families*. New Brunswick, NJ: Transaction Publishers, 1990.

Straus, M., and C. Smith. "Family Patterns and Child Abuse." In *Physical Violence in American Families*, edited by M. Straus and R. Gelles. New Brunswick, NJ: Transaction Publishers, 1990, pp. 245–262.

Tjaden, P., and N. Thoennes. "Prevalence, Incidence and Consequences of Violence against Women: Findings from the National Violence against Women Survey." NCJ172837. *National Institute of Justice,* 1998.

MANDATORY ARREST POLICIES

Domestic violence has traditionally been viewed as a private family matter. As such, the law has generally been more concerned with the protection of family privacy and the sanctity of the home, as opposed to the exposure of violence within this revered setting. Moreover, according to traditional and common law, husbands once enjoyed the privilege of chastisement, which not only allowed but encouraged the use of physical punishment to correct errant wives. In times past, assuming a husband's behavior was within the bounds of moderate chastisement, it was privileged and therefore not subject to legal sanction.

Sir William Blackstone is credited with the often-cited "rule of thumb" which allowed husbands to discipline their wives with a stick no larger than the diameter of their thumb. Ostensibly, this guideline was developed to ensure that punishment was moderate. Gradually, however, the law abrogated the rule of thumb and the privilege of chastisement. By the end of the nineteenth century, American appellate courts began to denounce the common law approach and refuse to recognize a spousal exemption in cases of assault and battery. During this same time, states began to amend divorce statutes to include cruelty as a ground for divorce.

However, while the black letter law appeared to be more responsive through such progressive changes, the criminal justice system did little to intervene in cases involving domestic violence. Thus, the mere elimination of common law defenses and privileges did little to improve the lives of battered women and children. Rather, the age-old notion that a man's home was his castle continued to dominate the official response to this issue. However, in response to the tireless efforts of advocates, states gradually began to appreciate the need for proactive policies designed to effectively assist victims of domestic violence. While different states have experimented with a variety of alternatives, policymakers continue to struggle with issues related to adequate and sufficient intervention in cases involving domestic violence. For many years, the most common law enforcement response to cases involving domestic violence was mediation. Mediation policies require the law enforcement officer to attempt to resolve the dispute between the parties. Essentially, officers were to serve as peacekeepers who, upon their arrival on the scene, assessed the situation and attempted to mediate the "dispute." With mediation, however, officers are discouraged from making an arrest except in the most extreme cases. Rather, they are encouraged to utilize informal mediation techniques to calm the parties down and offer constructive suggestions and referrals to social services, including counseling. The primary goal of the law enforcement officer following a mediation policy is to avoid further escalation of violence and to attempt to resolve the conflict between the parties. While mediation was the most common response in domestic violence cases for many years, it was rarely sufficient to resolve the underlying issues which fuel domestic violence. Thus, the use of mediation has been widely criticized on a number of grounds. First, mediation offers little to alter the dynamics of the relationship between the batterer and victim and in many cases affirms the position of the batterer through the lack

of any meaningful intervention. Others suggest that mediation contributes to common rationalizations of battering rather than forcing batterers to take responsibility for their actions. Further, critics claim that mediation responds to domestic violence as a family dispute among equal participants rather than treating the incident as a crime.

Incentives for Change: The Evolution of Mandatory Arrest

In 1977, Oregon was the first state to enact a mandatory arrest provision in cases of domestic violence. At first Oregon required an arrest in cases where abuse occurred unless the victim objected. However, in 1979, Oregon omitted the clause that allowed victims to object to an arrest and acted on behalf of the victim. Jolin (1983) found that Oregon's mandatory arrest legislation had both direct and indirect deterrent effects on domestic violence offenders. Thus, the uses of arrest as well as the threat of arrest were viewed as two very powerful tools that helped reduce the occurrence of domestic violence.

However, most states continued to rely on informal responses to domestic violence, including counseling and/or mediation by officers. In many cases the results of this relaxed and informal approach to domestic violence were deadly for women and children. Unfortunately, the official response to domestic violence continued to reflect the view that it was a family problem and not a crime. Despite long-standing approaches to domestic violence, the early 1980s would bring sweeping changes to the manner in which law enforcement responded to domestic violence.

In 1984, the now-famous Minneapolis Experiment was conducted. This research project was a joint effort between the Police Foundation and the Minneapolis Police Department (Sherman and Berk 1984). The study was designed to determine the most effective response to domestic violence calls for service. Three alternatives were available to officers. These included the following: arrest with one night in jail; perpetrator required to leave the scene or be arrested; informal dispute resolution or on-the-scene counseling. Prior to their arrival on the scene, officers did not know which alternative they would utilize. Rather, upon arrival the officer utilized the option that was indicated on preprepared forms. The study included only those calls for service which involved misdemeanor battery. The final sample included 314 calls. Following their response, officers completed a report detailing their response. In addition, researchers monitored the cases to determine the nature and extent of future violent behavior by the perpetrators. Victims were interviewed after the initial offense and thereafter for a period of twenty-four weeks.

The results of the research were enlightening. Official police reports and victim interviews revealed that in those cases where the arrest option was utilized, a lower incidence of repeat violence by the perpetrators occurred. In addressing claims that the incarceration, as opposed to arrest, accounted for the deterrent effect, the authors concluded that the limited period of incarceration was unlikely to have resulted in deterrence. As a result of the Minneapolis Experiment, policymakers and advocates urged lawmakers to enact mandatory arrest statutes. However, while the Minneapolis Experiment led to the widespread use of mandatory arrest, the authors of the study indicated a clear preference for presumptive or pro-arrest, as opposed to mandatory arrest, statutes. While arrest had a significant impact on the deterrence of future violence, the authors suggested that law enforcement officers retain the discretion to determine whether an arrest should be made.

That same year, a report issued by the Attorney General of the United States endorsed arrest as the preferred response to calls for service in domestic violence cases. The Attorney General's Task Force on Family Violence was created in response to the increased awareness regarding the prevalence of domestic violence. Following a review, the Task Force recommended that the criminal justice system's response to domestic violence reflect coordination and cooperation among law enforcement, the judiciary, social services, and therapeutic service providers. However, most important for purposes of this discussion were the recommendations regarding the role of law enforcement in domestic violence cases. The Task Force specifically advised that law enforcement agencies have a written protocol for domestic violence calls for service; respond to calls for service without delay; make forms and applications for orders of protection available for victims; monitor and maintain a system of tracking all existing orders of protection; document and report all violations of pre-trial release conditions; and utilize arrest as the preferred response in domestic violence cases.

While the recommendations of the Minneapolis Experiment and the Attorney General's Task Force clearly suggested necessary changes in the official response to domestic violence, a federal jury in *Thurman v. City of Torrington*, 595 F. Supp. 1521 (1984), had the opportunity to review and pronounce judgment upon the response of a

police department to a case plagued by domestic violence. In the Thurman case, a federal court awarded Tracy Thurman $2.9 million in damages from the City of Torrington, Connecticut. The jury determined that the Torrington police department failed to adequately protect Mrs. Thurman from domestic violence despite her repeated pleas for assistance. Law enforcement had consistently relied on informal mediation to "resolve the dispute" between the parties. However, the violence continued to escalate and culminated in a brutal attack on Mrs. Thurman and the couple's son. As a result of the attack, Mrs. Thurman was permanently disabled and disfigured. The case condemned the response of law enforcement and specifically called attention to the fact that the matter would have been handled differently if Mrs. Thurman and her child had been attacked by a stranger. The jury deemed the failure to protect Mrs. Thurman as a violation of the Fourteenth Amendment due process and equal protection clauses. The Thurman case sent a clear message regarding the civil liability which may be incurred for inaction in cases involving domestic violence. Thus, limitation of potential liability was an important incentive for the states to adopt new policies in cases involving domestic violence.

Ten years later, President Bill Clinton signed into law a major federal crime bill which included the Violence Against Women Act (VAWA). This act specifically provided millions of grant dollars to those states which adopted pro-arrest or mandatory arrest legislation. In light of these significant events, mandatory arrest has become an increasingly popular alternative in the mission to deter domestic violence.

Mandatory Arrest

Mandatory arrest or nondiscretionary statutes require law enforcement officers to arrest suspected batterers if there is probable cause that domestic violence has occurred. Moreover, most mandatory arrest statutes are coupled with a warrantless arrest provision which allows law enforcement officers to make a warrantless misdemeanor arrest in cases where the officer has probable cause to believe that violence occurred but did not personally observe the battery. Probable cause is a constitutional requirement and is specifically set forth in the Fourth Amendment, which states that "no warrant shall issue except upon probable cause." Moreover, the United States Supreme Court has specifically held that "probable cause to arrest exists when the facts and circumstances known to the officer are sufficient to warrant a reasonably prudent person in believing that the suspect has committed or is committing a crime" (*Gerstein v. Pugh,* 420 U.S. 103 [1975]; *Beck v. Ohio,* 379 U.S. 89 [1964]). Thus, in order to satisfy the constitutional prerequisite, an officer must believe that a crime has been committed and that the individual (to be arrested) is responsible for that crime. Determining whether probable cause exists can be a challenge in certain cases. However, it is generally suggested that acceptable sources from which to assess and conclude that probable cause exists include the following: the collective knowledge doctrine, knowledge about the suspect, behavior of the participants, reliable hearsay, and the observations by the officers (Gosselin 2000).

Mandatory arrest policies are unique in that they remove discretion from the victim as well as the officer. Victims no longer must decide whether they will press charges. Rather, these statutes mandate that the officer make an arrest of one or both of the parties involved. Thus, the presence of probable cause triggers a mandatory arrest provision and eliminates the discretion of the officer. The lack of officer discretion is an important distinction between mandatory and pro-arrest policies. Pro-arrest policies provide officers with significantly more discretion and allow an arrest to be made when the officer deems it necessary. Police agencies that adopt this approach typically encourage arrests through policy but ultimately leave the decision to the officers who will be responding to the calls for service. Such an approach assumes that the officer responding to the call for service will be in the best position to determine whether arrest is the appropriate response.

Types of Mandatory Arrest

There are typically two types of mandatory arrest policies adopted by law enforcement agencies. The first type requires the arrest of the primary aggressor. In certain cases, this determination is easily made based upon the extent of injuries sustained by the victim. However, in other cases it is extremely difficult to determine which party is the primary aggressor. These cases tend to occur where both parties have or lack injuries. However, because of the heightened scrutiny in cases involving domestic violence, the pressure upon law enforcement to make an arrest is significant. Unfortunately, in rare instances the victim may actually be arrested.

Dual arrest policies are also present. Dual arrest requires that officers arrest both parties and let the judge determine which is the victim. Again, such policies significantly diminish the amount of officer discretion in these cases. In cases where both parties

have serious injuries and a primary aggressor cannot be determined, this may be a satisfactory response, but it is not an ideal approach in all cases. Again, the danger is that a victim will be arrested and treated as a criminal rather than offered assistance traditionally provided to victims. Moreover, victim advocates argue that even in cases where both parties have sustained significant injuries, certain injuries could be sustained when an individual attempts to defend herself from an attack. Advocates therefore argue that dual arrest policies send the wrong message to victims of domestic violence and may cause more harm than good. Victims of domestic violence who are subjected to dual arrest policies may be less trusting of law enforcement officers and may avoid seeking help in future situations.

In order to ameliorate the harshness of mandatory arrest, some jurisdictions utilize crisis intervention teams. These teams allow law enforcement to enforce the mandatory arrest policies and provide needed assistance to the victim at the same time. Crisis intervention teams typically consist of police officers and social workers who work together to eliminate future abuse. The police officers will arrest the offender and focus on building a strong case against him. The social workers focus on building a relationship with the victim and making her aware of services that are available to her. These services include referrals to shelters, counseling, legal aid, and advocacy. The use of crisis intervention teams is still relatively new and has received both positive and negative responses from victims, law enforcement, and policymakers. While many believed that the coordinated approach was helpful, studies do not indicate a deterrent impact. However, the use of crisis intervention teams did result in increased reporting and trust in law enforcement (Adler 1999).

Critics of mandatory arrest statutes also argue that mandatory arrests result in a denial of due process rights. This argument suggests that an abuser could be arrested without the victim's substantiation or accusation. The critics assert that the arresting officer's probable cause may be subjectively biased. However, proponents of mandatory arrest policies insist that probable cause is one of the highest standards officers must meet, and this is not a subjective law enforcement tool (Adler 1999).

The Role of the Victim in Mandatory Arrest

For a variety of reasons, not the least of which is fear of reprisal, many victims refuse to "press charges" against their abuser. Domestic violence is not usually an isolated incident but rather a continuous cycle of violence. Consideration of the dynamics of a relationship marked by violence is instructive when attempting to understand the inability or unwillingness of a battering victim to press charges. One of the leading authorities in the area of domestic violence, Lenore Walker, developed the cycle of violence theory to explain the dynamics of a battering relationship.

Consideration of the legal process within the context of the cycle of violence is helpful to understanding the actions of battering victims. Three phases constitute the cycle of violence. The phases vary in terms of their length and frequency. However, despite their variance, these phases are remarkably apparent in most battering relationships.

The first phase, called the *tension-building phase,* is characterized by a gradual increase in the frustration level of the abuser. Minor incidents of battering tend to occur during this phase. In the hopes of minimizing the frustration and anger of the abuser, the victim attempts to placate the individual during this period of time. However, the victim's efforts are usually in vain and the tension-building phase transforms into the *acute-battering phase.* This second phase is characterized by significant battering of the victim. In the aftermath, however, the abuser attempts to reconcile with the victim by offering apologies, gifts, and what the victim wants most of all: a promise to change. Finally, there is the *calm and loving respite phase* or, more commonly, the "honeymoon" phase. Despite the battering that has occurred, the victim finds herself with a calm and loving partner who promises to change and showers her with love, attention, and affection. However, while this serves to reassure the victim that the abuser loves her and will change, this phase is temporary, and gradually the cycle begins again.

The victim is caught in a cyclical wave of emotions and battering which culminates with a loving partner promising the world. In many cases, the couple has entered the calm and loving respite phase by the time the victim is required to file charges against the perpetrator. This presents the battering victim with two alternatives: to press charges against the perpetrator and face an unfamiliar legal system, the loss of a partner, and financial loss or detriment, or alternatively to accept that the abuser will change this time. Battering victims often choose the latter due to the economic reality of separation, concern for their children, and their emotional attachment to the batterer. Physical abuse is often coupled with psychological abuse and leaves the victim feeling powerless and unable to leave the batterer. The batterer has usually separated the victim from any possible support system by alienating her from family and friends. The lack of any support system further fuels the victim's sense of dependency on the abuser. In circumstances involving children, the batterer often uses their welfare as leverage and is successful in pleading for forgiveness for the sake of the children.

Mandatory arrest statutes and no-drop prosecution laws remove the discretion from the battering victim. The responsibility to arrest and prosecute the batterer therefore lies solely with law enforcement. Removal of discretion or responsibility from the victim is intended to diminish the burden upon her. These statutes reflect an understanding of the nature of domestic violence and the dynamics of violent relationships. Moreover, such statutes illustrate an appreciation of the traits which often characterize victims of domestic violence. These include low self-esteem, guilt, self-blame, and learned helplessness.

In 1996, the Vacaville, California, police department developed a program called the Family Investigative Response Services Team (FIRST) to better handle domestic violence calls for service. This team comprised investigators, social workers, family support workers, representatives from the district attorney's office, and probation officers and was developed to obtain convictions through victimless prosecutions. The goal of the investigators was to obtain enough evidence without victim testimony to prosecute cases of abuse successfully. The use of photographs, dispatch tapes, medical reports, and witness statements helped relieve the pressure on the victim having to testify in the courtroom. For those women who wanted to reconcile the relationship, the victimless prosecution procedures made this an easier transition (White et al. 2005).

Mandatory Arrest: The Debate Continues

Mandatory arrest policies were adopted to deter future domestic violence. However, the widespread enactment of mandatory arrest statutes did not quell the debate regarding the deterrent effect of arrest in domestic violence cases. The Minneapolis Experiment was followed by a series of studies which attempted to replicate the findings regarding the deterrent effect of arrest in domestic violence cases. These studies were conducted in California (Berk and Newton 1985), Miami–Dade County (Pate and Hamilton 1992), Milwaukee (Sherman et al. 1992), Colorado Springs (Berk et al. 1992), Charlotte (Hirschel and Hutchinson 1992), and Omaha (Dunford 1992). The studies in Miami, Milwaukee, and Colorado Springs supported findings regarding the deterrent effect of arrest. However, those conducted in Charlotte and Omaha did not indicate that arrest was a sufficient deterrent to future domestic violence. In fact, three of the replicated studies indicated an increase in domestic violence following an arrest. Some researchers have pinpointed the lack of consistency among the judicial system as a contributing factor to recidivism in domestic violence cases. Those who do not face prosecution or who have their cases dismissed by the courts will be more likely to recidivate than those who are consistently punished for their abuse. Therefore, studies confirm that mandatory arrest policies are most effective when utilized in conjunction with a significant and consistent judicial response.

Moreover, research indicates that the deterrent effect of arrest is dependent upon the type of batterer involved in the case. A report by Edward W. Gondolf and Ellen R. Fisher identifies four types of batterers. These include the sociopath, the antisocial batterer, the chronic batterer, and the sporadic batterer. Gondolf and Fisher (1988) found that police were more likely to arrest the antisocial batterer. Although these arrests were justified, it was determined that arrest would have a more significant deterrent effect on sporadic and chronic batterers. The antisocial batterer was least deterred by an arrest.

There has been some evidence to suggest that those individuals who choose to conform to the norms and goals established by society are more likely to be deterred from future battering if they are arrested. Those offenders who were employed and/or married were less likely to repeat their abuse after an arrest. This had the opposite impact on those offenders who did not have a stake in conformity, i.e., were unmarried or unemployed; they did not respond well to the arrest. In fact, they were more likely to recidivate once arrested. The results of this study were troubling because a law enforcement agency cannot implement a policy of arresting only those batterers who are employed and/or married. Along the same lines, law enforcement officials cannot choose to avoid making arrests completely, nor can they arrest every offender when evidence indicates that it would result in future abuse.

Thus, the debate regarding the appropriate response to domestic violence continues. Consequently, states continue to utilize additional alternatives to augment their response to cases involving domestic violence. For example, it is common for states with mandatory arrest provisions to include no-drop prosecution statutes. No-drop statutes will not allow a victim of domestic violence to unilaterally dismiss charges against the perpetrator. Rather, depending on the jurisdiction, the judge,

prosecutor, or law enforcement officer must approve dismissal of the case. Like mandatory arrest, no-drop statutes reflect an appreciation of the dynamics of domestic violence. Given the cyclical nature of violent relationships, victims are often immersed in the "honeymoon" phase during the pre-trial period. At this time, the victim is plagued by pleas for forgiveness, promises to change, and suggestions that the victim is tearing the family apart by pursuing the prosecution. Victims are often unable to withstand the pressure and attempt to dismiss the case. In states with no-drop statutes, victims are unable to do so. The underlying purpose of no-drop statutes is to insulate the victim from the pressure to drop the charges.

In addition to mandatory arrest and no-drop prosecution policies, many states require that perpetrators remain in jail for twenty-four to forty-eight hours before bond may be set. This period functions as a cooling-off period for the perpetrator and allows the victim time to make temporary arrangements for housing and other necessities. Moreover, many states mandate judges to issue a temporary restraining order or order of protection in all domestic violence cases. Thus, once charges are filed, a temporary restraining order is imposed. Violation of the restraining order is grounds for immediate arrest.

While research continues to support the use of arrest as a powerful tool in the deterrence of future acts of domestic violence, it is, by itself, insufficient. The judicial system must continue to demand accountability from batterers. Thus, the successful deterrence of domestic violence requires a coordinated effort among law enforcement, the judicial system, service providers, and the public.

LISA S. NORED and ELIZABETH CORZINE MCMULLAN

See also **Police Civil Liability in Domestic Violence Incidents; Police Decision-Making Factors in Domestic Violence Cases; Police Response to Domestic Violence Incidents; Protective and Restraining Orders**

References and Further Reading

Adler, Jennifer R. "Strengthening Victims' Rights in Domestic Violence Cases: An Argument for 30-Day Mandatory Restraining Orders in Massachusetts." *Boston Public Interest Law Journal* 8 (1999): 303.

Attorney General's Task Force on Family Violence. Final Report. Washington, DC: U.S. Government Printing Office, 1984.

Berk, R. A., A. Campbell, R. Klap, B. Western. "A Bayesian Analysis of the Colorado Springs Spouse Abuse Experiment." *Journal of Criminal Law and Criminology* 83 (1992): 170–200.

Berk, R. A., and P. Newton. "Does Arrest Really Deter Wife Battery? An Effort to Replicate the Findings of the Minneapolis Spouse Abuse Experiment." *American Sociological Review* 50 (1985): 253–262.

Dunford, F. W. "The Measurement of Recidivism in Cases of Spouse Assault." *Journal of Criminal Law and Criminology* 83 (1992): 120–136.

Gondolf, Edward W., and Ellen R. Fisher. "Intervention with Batterers." In *Battered Women as Survivors: An Alternative to Treating Learned Helplessness*. Lexington, MA: Lexington Books, 1988.

Gosselin, D. K. *Heavy Hands: An Introduction to the Crimes of Domestic Violence*. Upper Saddle River, NJ: Prentice Hall, 2000.

Hirschel, J. D., and I. W. Hutchinson III. "Female Spouse Abuse and the Police Response: The Charlotte, North Carolina Experiment." *Journal of Criminal Law and Criminology* 83 (1992): 73–119.

Jolin, Annette. "Domestic Violence Legislation: An Impact Assessment." *Journal of Police Science and Administration* 11 (1983): 451–456.

Pate, A. M., and E. E. Hamilton. "Formal and Informal Deterrents to Domestic Violence: The Dade County Spouse Assault Experiment." *American Sociological Review* 57 (1992): 691–697.

Sherman, L. W., and R. A. Berk. "The Specific Deterrent Effects of Arrest for Domestic Assault." *American Sociological Review* 49 (1984): 261–272.

Sherman, L. W., J. D. Schmidt, D. P. Rogan, D. A. Smith, P. R. Gartin, E. G. Cohn, D. J. Collins, and A. R. Bacich. "The Variable Effects of Arrest on Criminal Careers: The Milwaukee Domestic Violence Experiment." *Journal of Criminal Law and Criminology* 83 (1992): 137–169.

White, M. D., J. S. Goldkamp, and S. P. Campbell. "Beyond Mandatory Arrest: Developing a Comprehensive Response to Domestic Violence." *Police Practice and Research: An International Journal* 6, no. 3 (2005): 261–278.

Case Law

Beck v. Ohio, 379 U.S. 89 (1964).
Gerstein v. Pugh, 420 U.S. 103 (1975).
Thurman v. City of Torrington, 595 F. Supp. 1521 (1984).

MARITAL RAPE

Marital rape is a serious and prevalent form of intimate violence. The legal definition of marital rape varies from one state to the next; however, marital rape is generally defined as unwanted intercourse or penetration (oral, anal, or vaginal) obtained by force or threat of force or when the wife is unable to give consent (Bergen 1996, 1999; Pagelow 1992; Russell 1990). Research on marital rape generally includes couples who are legally married, separated, divorced, or involved in long-term cohabiting relationships (Mahoney and Williams 1998; Russell 1990).

Researchers estimate that between 10 and 14 percent of married women experience rape in their marital relationships at least once (Finkelhor and Yllo 1985; Russell 1990). Based on findings from the largest study on violence against women in the United States, it is estimated that 7.7 million women have been raped by their intimate partners (Mahoney, Williams, and West 2001; Tjaden and Thoennes 2000). Rape by one's intimate partner may be one of the most common types of sexual assault. A Canadian study revealed that 30 percent of the women in one sample who were sexually assaulted as adults were assaulted by their intimate partners (Randall and Haskell 1995). Women who are battered by their partners may be at particularly high risk for sexual violence (Campbell 1989; Mahoney et al. 2001). Recent research indicates that women who are separated or divorced from their partners are also frequently at high risk for sexual violence (DeKeseredy, Schwartz, and Fagan 2005). Thus, marital rape is a serious problem that needs to be examined.

Marital Rape and the Law

Historically the act of forcing one's wife to have sex was not defined as "rape" in the United States. Rape was most commonly defined as "the forcible penetration of the body of a woman, not the wife of the perpetrator" (Russell 1990, p. 17). This traditional definition exempted husbands from being prosecuted for forcing their wives to have sex against their will. As many researchers, including Finkelhor and Yllo (1985) and Eskow (1996), have argued, this provided husbands with a "license to rape" their wives. This exemption is grounded in

English common law and is most frequently attributed to statements made by Sir Matthew Hale, chief justice in seventeenth-century England, who wrote, "But the husband cannot be guilty of a rape committed by himself upon his lawful wife, for by their mutual matrimonial consent and contract the wife hath given up herself in this kind unto the husband which she cannot retract" (quoted in Russell 1990, p. 17). Hale's statement established the understanding that with marriage, women gave an irrevocable consent to sex (Bergen 1996; Russell 1990). This understanding remained largely unchallenged until the 1970s when women in the anti-rape movement argued for the elimination of the spousal exemption (Finkelhor and Yllo 1985).

While reform of states' rape legislations has been slow with regard to the marital exemption, progress has been made. In 1978 John Rideout became the first man to be prosecuted for raping his wife while they still lived together (Russell 1990). In 1984 in the case of *People v. Liberta,* New York became the first state to legally overturn its marital rape exemption when it was ruled that the exemption did not provide equal protection to married women under the law (Finkelhor and Yllo 1985). On July 5, 1993, marital rape became a crime under at least one section of the sexual offense code (X 1999). However, there is still considerable variation by state with regard to prosecuting men for raping their wives. As of 1998 (when the most recent comprehensive study of state rape laws was performed prior to this publication) thirty-three states still provided some exemption to husbands from rape prosecution. Most commonly, husbands may be exempt from rape charges if the crime is not quickly reported or if force was not used because the wife was incapable of giving consent (Bergen 1998; Eskow 1996). In the latter case, some states assume consent unless the wife is resisting. Thus, rape in marriage is still treated as a lesser crime than rape by another perpetrator throughout most of the United States.

The legal status of marital rape has contributed to the popular perception that this is a less serious form of sexual violence than others, such as rape by a stranger. In their study of marital rape, Finkelhor and Yllo (1985) report on a 1974 study conducted by Rossi in which people were asked to rank 140 offenses in terms of severity. "Forcible rape of a former spouse" was ranked 62nd on the list, below selling marijuana and blackmailing someone (Finkelhor and Yllo 1985, p. 154). More recent research indicates that marital rape is still frequently perceived as less serious than other

forms of rape, and in some studies, rape in a marital relationship is not even perceived as possible (Monson, Byrd, and Langhinrichsen-Rohling 2006; Whatley 2005). In their study of college students, Monson, Byrd, and Langhinrichsen-Rohling (1996) found that marital rape was perceived as less serious than rape perpetrated by a stranger and that only 50 percent of the male students thought that it was possible for a husband to rape his wife.

Women's Experiences of Marital Rape

Despite popular perceptions, research with women who have been raped by their intimate partners reveals the severity of this form of violence against women. Not only do many women experience rape in their marital relationships, but women who are raped by their intimate partners are likely to be raped multiple times over the course of their relationships. Tjaden and Thoennes (2000) found that women experienced an average of 4.5 assaults per partner. When the focus is on rape by marital partners, the frequency of assaults is higher. Finkelhor and Yllo (1995) and Bergen (1996) found that 50 percent and 55 percent, respectively, of the women in their sample were raped more than twenty times over the course of their relationships. Women who are raped by their husbands not only experience vaginal penetration, but also commonly experience forced oral and anal intercourse (Mahoney et al. 2001).

Women who have been raped by their husbands commonly experience a wide range of violence that includes verbal abuse, battering, assaults with weapons, and forced intercourse with other people. Research indicates that between 20 percent and 70 percent of battered women experience sexual violence with their partners (Bergen 1996; Campbell 1989; Pense and Paymar 1993). The vast majority of women in Bergen's (1996) and Finkelhor and Yllo's (1985) studies experienced both battering and sexual assault. In "battering rapes" women experience physical abuse as well as sexual abuse in a variety of ways. Some women are battered and raped simultaneously, while others experience physical violence and then are raped afterward when their partner wants to "make up" (Bergen 1996). Some women's experiences are characterized as "sadistic" or "obsessive" rape when the violence involves torture, perverse sexual acts, and, frequently, the use of pornography (Bergen 1996; Finkelhor and Yllo 1985). Approximately 25 percent of Bergen's (1996) sample reported at least one experience of sadistic sexual violence with their partners.

It should be noted that not all women who are raped by their partners experience physical abuse in addition to sexual abuse (Bergen 1996; Finkelhor and Yllo 1985). In what Finkelhor and Yllo (1985) have called "force-only rapes," women are forced to have sex against their will but their experiences are not characterized by excessive physical violence. Twenty-five percent of the women in Bergen's (1996) sample experienced force-only rape, as did 40 percent of women in Finkelhor and Yllo's (1985) study. In Russell's (1990) study, 4 percent of the women who had been married had been raped but not battered by their partners. It is important to recognize marital rape as a distinctive form of violence and consider the multiple effects of this type of violence against women.

Women who are raped by their partners commonly experience a wide range of physical and emotional effects from the violence. As indicated above, women who are raped by their husbands are often physically assaulted, and common injuries include lacerations, broken bones, torn muscles, and black eyes (Adams 1993; Bergen 1996). Research indicates that when compared with women assaulted by other perpetrators, women who are raped by their partners report more physical injuries (Bennice and Resick 2003). Women who are raped by their husbands also commonly experience gynecological consequences as a result of the sexual violence, including vaginal and anal tearing, miscarriages, stillbirths, urinary tract infections, and bladder infections (Campbell and Alford 1989; Campbell and Soeken 1999).

Research indicates that the emotional consequences of being raped by one's husband can also be quite severe. Women who are raped by their partners, much like women raped by other types of assailants, frequently suffer from depression, post-traumatic stress disorder, intense fear, sleeping problems, and shock (Bergen 1996; Riggs, Kilpatrick, and Resnick 1992; Stermac, Del Bove, and Addison 2001). Long-term effects can include sexual dysfunction, eating disorders, poor body image, and depression (Bergen 1996; Frieze 1983; Ullman and Siegel 1993). When compared with other survivors of rape, research indicates that being raped by one's spouse is not less traumatic than being raped by another perpetrator (Bennice and Resick 2003). Indeed, it may be even more traumatic given that marital rape survivors often experience multiple assaults and that the assaults are perpetrated by someone whom they know and trust (Bergen 1996; Kilpatrick et al. 1988). Several studies have also attempted to examine the impact of sexual violence compared with physical violence on survivors of marital rape. When compared with women who have been battered by their partners, women who experience sexual and physical abuse experience higher levels of depression, anxiety, fear, and sexual dysfunction, and poorer self-esteem (Bennice and Resick 2003; Campbell 1989). Thus, it is clear that being raped by one's partner has serious emotional and physical consequences for the many women who experience this form of violence.

Assisting Survivors of Marital Rape

Rape is a highly underreported crime, and research indicates that women who are raped by those whom they know are particularly unlikely to report the violence to the police or seek medical assistance (Bennice and Resick 2003; Koss and Cook 1998). This may be particularly true for women who are raped by their husbands. Survivors of marital rape may not report the violence for many complex reasons, including fear of retribution by their abusers, fear that they may not be believed by the police, self-blame, or shame. Importantly, some women who have been raped by their partners may not identify their experiences as rape given the historic perception of stranger rape as "real rape" and because of cultural expectations that sex is an obligation in marriage (Bennice and Resick 2003; Bergen 1996). In her research on victims of marital rape, Basile (2002) found that the majority (61 percent) had unwanted sex with their husbands out of a sense of obligation. Women who perceive forced sex as a "wifely duty" are unlikely to report their experiences as rape or seek assistance. However, when women do choose to seek assistance for their experiences of marital rape, they may encounter significant barriers from service providers.

Law enforcement officials are often the first to respond to women who have been raped, and there has been little research that has systematically assessed the response of law enforcement officials to the problem of marital rape. Research by Frieze (1983), Russell (1990), and Bergen (1996) with marital rape survivors found that the police were largely perceived as unresponsive in that they tried to discourage the women from reporting, failed to respond to calls, or were unfamiliar with the laws. Frieze (1983) argued that police officers were less responsive to survivors of marital rape than they were to battered women. However, research by Stermac et al. (2001) found that when compared with other victims of sexual assault, women who were raped by their partners were more likely to be accompanied by police to the hospital and to have forensic evidence collected. The collection of forensic evidence is particularly important for prosecuting cases of rape in marriage. Bergen's (1996) research revealed that a positive police response can be critical in validating women's experiences of sexual violence and helping women to seek the resources to begin the healing process.

Battered women's shelters and rape crisis centers are two types of organizations that are in excellent positions to provide assistance to women who have been raped by their husbands. However, research indicates that historically many of these organizations have not provided comprehensive services to marital rape survivors (Bergen 1996; Russell 1990; Thompson-Haas 1987). A national survey of battered women's shelters and rape crisis centers in 1995 by Bergen (1996) revealed that 42 percent of battered women's programs and 79 percent of rape crisis centers trained their staff and volunteers specifically about the problem of marital rape. In terms of service provision, only 2 percent of programs provided support groups specifically for survivors of marital rape. Additionally, fewer than half (42 percent) of programs routinely ask women about their experiences of rape in marriage. This is particularly important given that women who are raped by their partners are unlikely to voluntarily speak about their experiences because of the shame and self-blame that many feel (Bergen 1996; Russell 1990).

When probing incidences of marital rape, it is important to ask women in a sensitive way about a wide range of experiences with their partners; for example, "Does your partner force you to have sex against your will?" and "Does your partner pressure you to do things sexually that you are not comfortable with?" rather than merely, "Has your husband ever raped you?" The latter is insufficient given that many women may not self-identify their experiences as rape, because their husband was the perpetrator. There are many services that battered women's programs and rape crisis centers can provide to survivors of marital rape, including outreach, shelter, medical advocacy, legal advocacy, and counseling.

Health care providers are also important for assisting women who have been raped by their partners to deal with the trauma that many of these women suffer. Given the prevalence of marital rape, health care providers (gynecologists and obstetricians specifically) should routinely screen their patients for experiences of sexual and physical violence with their partners. Research indicates that battered women are at risk for sexually transmitted diseases, HIV/AIDS, and unplanned pregnancy; therefore, health care providers should assess for this

as well (Bennice and Resick 2003). Women who are pregnant are not immune to physical and sexual abuse from their partners, and there is some evidence that the violence sometimes escalates during pregnancy (Pagelow 1984). Pregnancy may provide that rare window of opportunity when health care providers may have regular contact with their patients and can provide violence assessments, thorough examinations, and referrals for assistance (McFarlane et al. 1998). This assistance is also important when women may be most vulnerable following surgery or the birth of a child. Campbell and Alford (1989) found that 46 percent of the battered women in their sample had been raped by their partners after being discharged from the hospital—most after childbirth.

There are a variety of others who come into contact with marital rape survivors, including mental health professionals, marriage counselors, social workers, and religious leaders. As previously indicated, the emotional trauma associated with marital rape can be quite severe and long-lasting. Validating women's experiences of marital rape and challenging victim-blaming attitudes are particularly helpful strategies for assisting women who have been raped by their partners (Bennice and Resick 2003; Bergen 1996). Many women who have been raped by their partners have difficulty disclosing their experiences of violence, and if their disclosure is met with disbelief, resistance, or recrimination, women may not choose to disclose again or seek help to end the violence (Bennice and Resick 2003; Mahoney 1999; Russell 1990).

Conclusion

It is clear that rape in marriage is a prevalent and serious problem in contemporary society. While there have been many challenges to the historical existence of a husband's "license to rape," rape in marriage is still treated as a lesser crime in the majority of states. For many, rape in marriage is not perceived as "real rape." However, research indicates that marital rape survivors often suffer serious consequences as a result of the violence that they have experienced at the hands of their husbands. There are a variety of service providers, including law enforcement officials, advocates for battered women and rape victims, health care professionals, mental health care providers, and religious leaders, who routinely come into contact with survivors of marital rape and are important sources of support for women who have been raped by their husbands.

RAQUEL KENNEDY BERGEN

See also **Date Rape; Rule of Thumb; Social, Economic, and Psychological Costs of Violence; Victim-Blaming Theory; Violence against Women Act**

References and Further Reading

Adams, Carole. "I Just Raped My Wife! What Are You Going to Do about It, Pastor?" In *Transforming a Rape Culture,* edited by Emile Buchwald, Pamela Fletcher, and Martha Roth. Minneapolis: Milkweed Press, 1993, pp. 57–96.

Basile, Kathleen C. "Prevalence of Wife Rape and Other Intimate Partner Sexual Coercion in a Nationally Representative Sample of Women." *Violence and Victims* 17, no. 5 (2002): 511–524.

Bennice, Jennifer A., and Patricia A. Resick. "Marital Rape: History, Research and Practice." *Trauma, Violence and Abuse* 4, no. 3 (2003): 228–246.

Bergen, Raquel Kennedy. *Wife Rape: Understanding the Response of Survivors and Service Providers.* Thousand Oaks, CA: Sage, 1996.

———. "Marital Rape," 1999. http://www.vawnet.org/DomesticViolence/Research/VAWnetDocs/AR_mrape.pdf (accessed August 27, 2006).

Campbell, Jacquelyn C. "Women's Responses to Sexual Abuse in Intimate Relationships." *Health Care for Women International* 10 (1989): 335–346.

Campbell, Jacquelyn C., and Peggy Alford. "The Dark Consequences of Marital Rape." *American Journal of Nursing* 89 (1989): 946–949.

Campbell, Jacquelyn C., and Karen Soeken. "Forced Sex and Intimate Partner Violence: Effects on Women's Risk and Women's Health." *Violence Against Women* 5 (1999): 1017–1035.

DeKeseredy, Walter, Martin Schwartz, and Danielle Fagan. "Separation/Divorce Sexual Assault in Rural Ohio: Women's Views of Male Peer Support." Unpublished manuscript, 2005.

Eskow, Lisa R. "The Ultimate Weapon? Demythologizing Spousal Rape and Reconceptualizing Its Prosecution." *Stanford Law Review* 48 (1996): 677–709.

Finkelhor, David, and Kersti Yllo. *License to Rape: Sexual Abuse of Wives.* New York: Holt, Rinehart, and Winston, 1985.

Frieze, Irene H. "Investigating the Causes and Consequences of Marital Rape." *Signs: Journal of Women in Culture and Society* 8 (1983): 532–553.

Koss, Mary P., and Sarah L. Cook. "Facing the Facts: Date and Acquaintance Rape Are Significant Problems for Women." In *Issues in Intimate Violence,* edited by Raquel Kennedy Bergen. Thousand Oaks, CA: Sage, 1998, pp. 147–156.

Mahoney, Patricia, and Linda M. Williams. "Sexual Assault in Marriage: Prevalence, Consequences and Treatment of Wife Rape." In *Partner Violence: A Comprehensive Review of 20 Years of Research,* edited by Jana L. Jasinski and Linda M. Williams. Thousand Oaks, CA: Sage, 1998.

Mahoney, Patricia, Linda M. Williams, and Carolyn M. West. "Violence against Women by Intimate Relationship Partners." In *Sourcebook on Violence against Women,* edited by Claire Renzetti, Jeffrey Edleson, and Raquel Kennedy Bergen. Thousand Oaks, CA: Sage, 2001, pp. 143–178.

McFarlane, Judith, Karen Soeken, Jacquelyn Campbell, Barbara Parker, S. Reel, and C. Silva. "Severity of Abuse to Pregnant Women and Associated Gun Access of the Perpetrator." *Public Health Nursing* 15, no. 3 (1998): 201–206.

Monson, Candice, Gary Byrd, and Jennifer Langhinrichsen-Rohling. "To Have and To Hold: Perceptions of Marital Rape." *Journal of Interpersonal Violence* 11, no. 3 (1996): 410–424.

National Clearinghouse on Marital and Date Rape. *1998 State Law Chart.* Berkeley, CA: Author, 1998.

Pagelow, Mildred D. *Family Violence.* New York: Praeger, 1984.

———. "Adult Victims of Domestic Violence." *Journal of Interpersonal Violence* 7 (1992): 87–120.

Pense, Ellen, and M. Paymar. *Education Groups for Men Who Batter: The Duluth Model.* New York: Springer, 1993.

Randall, Melanie, and Lori Haskell. "Sexual Violence in Women's Lives: Findings from the Women's Safety Project, a Community-Based Survey." *Violence Against Women* 1, no. 1 (1995): 6–31.

Riggs, David, Dean G. Kilpatrick, and Heidi Resnick. "Long-Term Psychological Distress Associated with Marital Rape and Aggravated Assault: A Comparison to Other Crime Victims." *Journal of Family Violence* 7, no. 4 (1992): 283–295.

Rossi, Peter, Emily Waite, Christine Bose, and Richard Berk. "The Seriousness of Crimes: Normative Structures and Individual Differences." *American Sociological Review* 39 (1974): 224–237.

Russell, Diana E. H. *Rape in Marriage.* New York: Macmillan Press, 1990.

Stermac, Lana, Giannetta Del Bove, and Mary Addison. "Violence, Injury and Presentation Patterns in Spousal Sexual Assaults." *Violence Against Women* 7, no. 11 (2001): 1218–1233.

Thompson-Haas, Lynn. "Marital Rape: Methods of Helping and Healing." Unpublished manuscript, 1987.

Tjaden, Patricia, and Nancy Thoennes. "Prevalence and Consequences of Male-to-Female and Female-to-Male Intimate Partner Violence as Measured by the National Violence against Women Survey." *Violence Against Women* 6, no. 2 (2000): 142–161.

Ullman, S. E., and J. M. Siegel. "Victim-Offender Relationship and Sexual Assault." *Violence and Victims* 8 (1993): 121–134.

Whatley, Mark A. "The Effect of Participant Sex, Victim Dress and Traditional Attitudes on Causal Judgments for Marital Rape Victims." *Journal of Family Violence* 20, no. 3 (2005): 191–200.

X, Laura. "Accomplishing the Impossible: An Advocate's Notes from the Successful Campaign to Make Marital Rape and Date Rape a Crime in all 50 U.S. States and Other Countries." *Violence Against Women* 5 (1999): 1064–1081.

MEASURING DOMESTIC VIOLENCE

Understanding the nature and scope of the problem of family violence has been a daunting task for researchers, government officials, and practitioners. Measuring the extent of a social problem as pervasive as family violence is complicated by a number of different factors. First, there is no uniform definition of what constitutes abuse and neglect or what relationships delineate family. State laws vary in their definitions, as do different research study designs. Second, intervention methods and reporting mechanisms have evolved to handle specific populations of abused persons, creating a very complex and fragmented picture of the overall magnitude of abuse within families. Systemic barriers have created fractionalization in the data, limiting researchers' ability to understand the interrelationships that may exist within families and across systems. Third, even with appropriate reporting mechanisms in place, family members remain reluctant to report incidents of abuse. Various forms of family mistreatment are especially difficult to quantify, complicating the recall and documentation of acts of abuse. Therefore, reported cases of abuse or neglect represent only a fraction of the actual occurrence of mistreatment.

Research regarding family violence involves different areas of inquiry, including understanding the behavior patterns of family members, the consequences of abuse, the environmental or situational factors associated with maltreatment, and efficacy of various intervention strategies. Estimating the actual prevalence and incidence of family mistreatment has been a particularly arduous task, given the private sanctity of the family. Official estimates of the extent of family maltreatment are garnered utilizing two main categories of measurement: data, which reflect actual reports of mistreatment, and surveys, which attempt to capture incidents of abuse, whether or not they have been reported to authorities.

Reported Incidents

Official reports, generally prepared by governmental agencies, document cases of abuse and neglect that have come to the attention of officials. The Uniform Crime Reporting (UCR) data compiled by the Federal Bureau of Investigation (FBI) since 1930 is the official comprehensive measurement of crime in the United States. The UCR comes in the form of an annual nationwide summary of crime incidents known to the police. Crimes are categorized as Part I or Part II offenses. Part I offenses include murder, forcible rape, robbery, aggravated assault, burglary, larceny-theft, motor vehicle theft, and arson. A crime index is created with these eight offenses, whereby crime rates are calculated that allow for geographical and historical comparison. Part II offenses include twenty-one other less serious crimes and are recorded when the police make an arrest. The UCR system presents limitations in its ability to provide meaningful detailed information regarding family violence incidents, since it provides only summary counts of crime types known to the police.

The National Incident-Based Reporting System (NIBRS), developed in 1989 by the FBI, is intended to provide more detailed information about crime incidents. The NIBRS collects data on eight index crimes as well as thirty-eight other offenses, with specific details noted on the offense, victim, offender, and property. As of February 2004, twenty-four states have been certified to report crime statistics to the FBI in this venue. Sample findings suggest that the NIBRS will prove to be a useful tool in measuring family violence as its scope is expanded nationwide (Federal Bureau of Investigation 2000).

Reports of family maltreatment are also compiled periodically to estimate the extent of specific types of family abuse. The National Elder Abuse Incidence Study (NEAIS), conducted in 1996 by the U.S. Department of Health and Human Services, estimates the extent of elder abuse by examining reports of elder mistreatment as documented by adult protective service agencies and other sentinel agencies that work with the elderly (National Center for Elder Abuse 1996). The National Incidence Study of Child Abuse and Neglect, conducted in 1979–1980, 1986, 1993, and 2005, provides national estimates of the incidence of child abuse and neglect as recorded by child protective agencies and other sentinel agencies (see Administration for Children and Families [ACF] website). In 1994, the Bureau of Justice Statistics conducted a Study of Injured Victims of Violence from data collected from thirty-one hospital emergency rooms in which injured victims of violence sought medical treatment (Rand 1997).

Also, annual reports from various state agencies and local programs provide a reliable measure of reported cases of family maltreatment. For example, Medicaid Fraud Control Units Annual Reports (see Office of Inspector General website), Long-Term Care Ombudsman Reports (see Administration on Aging website), and the National Child Abuse and Neglect Data System (NCANDS) (see ACF website) compile data from reported cases. In addition, states document data on the number of fatal acts of family violence, criminal prosecutions, family court proceedings, etc.

Surveys

Social surveys provide an opportunity to measure the occurrence of family violence, regardless of whether or not such acts were reported to the authorities. Self-reports, despite their research limitations, can more fully capture the experiences of victims and perpetrators and explore more unique dynamics of family relationships. Survey results confirm that incidents of family violence occur with much greater frequency than is evidenced by what has been officially reported.

The National Crime Victimization Survey, conducted by the Bureau of Justice Statistics in cooperation with the U.S. Census Bureau, interviews more than 50,000 households, each twice per year, to estimate the occurrence of crime in the United States. Considered a major source of data on crime since 1973, this survey has been redesigned to better account for family-related crimes. The National Family Violence Survey, conducted in 1975 and 1985 by Murray Straus and Richard J. Gelles, provided data on a nationally representative sample and examines different family relationships using the Conflict Tactics Scales (CTS). The CTS tool is intended to measure a continuum of abusive behaviors within relationships, such as reasoning, verbal and nonverbal aggression, and physical violence (Straus and Gelles 1990). The National Violence Against Women Survey, conducted

between November 1995 and May 1996, was sponsored by the National Institute of Justice and the Centers for Disease Control and Prevention. The telephone survey interviewed 8,000 women and 8,000 men in the United States regarding their experiences of being victimized by an intimate partner. It also examined victims' experiences with the police, medical services, and the courts (Tjaden and Thoennes 2000).

KAREL KURST-SWANGER

See also **Analyzing Incidents of Domestic Violence: The National Incident-Based Reporting System; Conflict Tactics Scales**

References and Further Reading

Administration for Children and Families website. Department of Health and Human Services. http://www.acf.hhs.gov.

Administration on Aging website. Department of Health and Human Services. http://www.aoa.gov.

Bureau of Justice Statistics. *National Crime Victimization Survey.* http://www.ojp.usdoj.gov/bjs/cvict.htm.

Federal Bureau of Investigation. Uniform Crime Reports and the National Incident-Based Reporting System. http://www.fbi.gov/ucr/ucr.htm#nibrs.

———. "The Structure of Family Violence: An Analysis of Selected Incidents," 2000. http://www.fbi.gov/ucr/nibrs/famvio21.pdf.

National Center on Elder Abuse. *National Elder Abuse Incidence Study,* 1998. http://www.aoa.gov/eldfam/Elder_Rights/Elder_Abuse/AbuseReport_Full.pdf (accessed August 27, 2006).

Office of Inspector General website. Department of Health and Human Services. www.oig.hhs.gov.

Rand, Michael. "Violence-Related Injuries Treated in Hospital Emergency Departments." *BJS Special Report.* NCJ 156921. August 1997.

Straus, Murray A., and Richard J. Gelles. "Societal Changes and Change in Family Violence from 1975 to 1985 as Revealed by Two National Surveys." *Journal of Marriage and the Family* 48 (1986): 465–479.

———, eds. *Physical Violence in American Families: Risk Factors and Adaptations to Violence in 8,145 Families.* New Brunswick, NJ: Transaction. 1990.

Straus, Murray, Richard Gelles, and Suzanne Steinmetz. *Behind Closed Doors: Violence in the American Family.* New York: Doubleday, 1980.

Tjaden, Patricia, and Nancy Thoennes. "Extent, Nature, and Consequences of Intimate Partner Violence," 2000. http://www.ojp.usdoj.gov/nij (NCJ 181867).

MEDIATION IN DOMESTIC VIOLENCE

Introduction and Definitions

Mediation is a negotiation conducted by a neutral third party to resolve differences and reach agreements between two or more people or organizations. Many types of mediation exist. Mediation goals may include such things as improved communication; increased cooperation; reduced anger and hostility; healing; transformation of people, families, organizations, and communities; and assessment of strengths and weaknesses of legal positions.

Over the last decades of the twentieth century, an ever-growing tide of businesses, organizations, governments, and individuals have been steadily turning away from the rigid, gridlocked, adversarial criminal and civil justice litigation systems in hopes of finding new efficient, low-cost, low-stress, lasting mechanisms for resolving conflict and reducing crime. Two of those mechanisms incorporate mediation. One is *alternative dispute resolution* (ADR), which includes methods like mediation, arbitration, and domestic relations decision making. The second is *restorative justice* (RJ), a philosophy advocating that the most effective way to reduce conflict (especially crime) is by actively engaging victims, offenders, and the community in some form of dialogue or mediation.

While the goal of mediation is to enhance the relationship between those in conflict, the goal of litigation is to settle a conflict. Even so, they are not mutually exclusive. The civil and criminal justice litigation systems use mediation as a replacement for, as well as in addition to, usual legal processes. In the civil justice system, mediation occurs primarily in domestic relations (divorce) courts. Not only are judges in these cases increasingly likely to order mediation in domestic relations cases, but rising numbers of divorcing couples are hiring their own mediators to help them reach divorce agreements that they take with them to court. Recently, courts have begun to use mediators in permanent protection order proceedings called Restraining Order Conditions Shuttle Conferences (ROCSC). Even when there is a permanent protection order in effect, most people must have some ongoing contact. Rather than face-to-face discussions, the two people are placed in separate rooms while the mediator

"shuttles" between them as they work out an agreement. The purpose of these shuttle conferences is not to mediate the violence, but to help the parties negotiate the conditions of the permanent protection order as it relates to children and necessary future contact of the parties. The paramount concern of the process and the resulting agreement is present and future safety. The agreement is then reviewed and accepted, rejected, or modified by the judge.

In the criminal justice system, restorative justice mediation, such as victim–offender reconciliation, community accountability boards, and sentencing circles, is becoming increasingly common. During these mediations, the victim and offender meet face-to-face with a mediator/facilitator (and often, with family and community members) to discuss the crime, the harm done to the victim, the offender's responsibility, the reparation of that harm, and reintegration of the offender into the community.

Support for Litigation Only

After centuries of struggle, women have gained access to the legal system, enabling them to divorce, stop sexual harassment, and have batterers and rapists held accountable for their crimes. Many argue that just as females gain more power in the courts, those in authority have tried to trivialize issues faced by females and eliminate their access to effective legal remedies by implementing alternatives or add-ons to the justice system that critics say benefit victims less and exact fewer consequences for offenders.

Most domestic violence victims' advocates argue that the courts are physically safer because of metal detectors and searches as well as the diversion of some of the abuser's aggression away from the victim and toward the judge, attorneys, and other court personnel. They say it is also legally safer. Although there are countless complaints that mediators, judges, and attorneys lack basic education about domestic violence and hold negative views of females and their role in society, attorneys must at least know the law and are sworn to uphold it. While many mediators have voluntarily obtained mediation training and experience, there are no standards or requirements at the national or, in most cases, state level. Litigation is also safer because it sets legal boundaries and procedures, which, along with legal outcomes, are open to the public. Mediations are conducted in private and their proceedings are confidential. Finally, if the legal rulings or processes are flawed, higher courts can overturn the decisions.

Additional safeguards and advantages of litigation include the fact that courts can impose legal remedies and sanctions such as orders of protection, incarceration, restitution, and fines along with decisions about child custody and property division. Furthermore, unlike many agreements reached in mediation, the batterer's failure to comply with court orders may result in further sanctions (e.g., incarceration) by the court.

Support for Mediation

Mediation, according to its proponents, provides a nonadversarial opportunity for two or more parties, with the help of a neutral third party, to talk with each other with the aim of ironing out their differences and improving their relationships. The hope is that in the future they will be better able to work things out themselves. Instead of speaking through an attorney while being processed through the litigation system, mediation provides people an opportunity to engage in a discussion that fits their needs. Furthermore, there is mounting evidence that those who engage in mediation are more satisfied with the results and are more likely to stick to their agreements than people who use the litigation process.

Unlike the justice system, when mediation is used in a restorative justice context, it requires that the offender take full responsibility for abusive and/or violent behavior in front of those harmed. There is also an attempt to heal broken relationships and to strengthen the community so that all parties can move into more productive relationships.

Central Issues

Safety

People must feel sufficiently safe before, during, and after mediation or litigation to divulge information that will help in making decisions. Although significant steps have been initiated to increase safety, there is much criticism of both litigation and mediation for putting people in danger by failing to take domestic violence seriously.

Urban courthouses have become virtual fortresses, chiefly because of domestic violence–related murders occurring in justice centers over the past several decades. However, not only do these safeguards not exist in many rural areas, but the first place that most attorneys, prosecutors, or mediators meet their clients is in private offices that do not enjoy such safeguards.

Many mediators and attorneys screen for domestic violence. Because most clients will not or cannot acknowledge the nature or extent of the violence or abuse they have experienced or meted out, the effectiveness of screening is limited. Those who advocate litigation say that this is another reason to rely on litigation rather than mediation. If the domestic violence remains hidden, more safeguards exist through the litigation process.

Most mediators back victim advocates who state that there should be no mediation in cases where there is "severe," ongoing domestic violence. Disagreement arises when some suggest that only "milder" cases be mediated. These "milder" cases may include such things as a nonrecurring incidence of pushing or shoving years ago or violent threats without actual physical violence. Victim advocates say that these may be danger signs of brewing violence or a perpetrator's tactic in the cycle of violence, while mediators maintain that mediation will help people leave the past behind and move to more positive ways of interacting.

Mediators who are knowledgeable about domestic violence employ safeguards—such as helping victims develop safety plans—and conduct "shuttle" mediations, enabling people to speak freely, suggest options, express concerns, and ask for help they may have been too frightened or intimidated to give voice to if the two parties had to sit in the same mediation room or courtroom together.

There is little real protection once the victim leaves a secure location. Advocates of mediation submit that litigation is inherently adversarial, and therefore parties "win" or "lose." When this happens, the "loser" is likely to seek revenge, placing the victim and the community in more danger. Mediation advocates maintain that when both participate in deciding about issues affecting their lives, the perpetrator is less likely to retaliate; therefore, by avoiding the win/lose scenario, the victim is safer.

Neutrality

A key ingredient to successful mediation is the mediator's neutrality or "balancing" of power between the people engaged. The abuser typically holds more psychological and financial power in the relationship; therefore, the mediator attempts to decrease the abuser's psychological power while enhancing the victim's. Remaining neutral while attempting to shift power from one person to another is difficult enough, but professionals in most fields have long agreed that no one is truly neutral about anything.

It is not just lack of neutrality that many victim advocates fear about restorative justice's community accountability boards, sentencing circles, and similar processes. Victim advocates allege that many community members who take part in these processes are inclined to excuse the behavior of the batterer, force the victim to take responsibility for the batterer's abuse, and therefore increase the likelihood of further violence. Critics also say that asking victims of domestic violence to meet with their attacker will likely cause further psychological harm, thus re-victimizing the victim.

Information

To take full advantage of either litigation or mediation, people must have information that is meaningful to them. This rarely happens. Most people who come into contact with the civil or criminal justice systems do not have attorneys, have obtained their knowledge of litigation from friends, family, TV, and the movies, and have no awareness of mediation. They obtain information about mediation at the courthouse, where the stress of the situation at hand, coupled with short timelines and lack of written material or help with understanding their options, leaves people with limited comprehension of the mediation process or possible outcomes.

Likewise, attorneys, courts, mediators, or the people involved in the conflict rarely have all the facts related to the case. In mediation, the parties are asked to voluntarily divulge information as they negotiate agreements. During litigation, court orders, along with penalties for noncompliance, are likely to produce more information from those wishing to hide something.

Time and Expense

Few people can afford an attorney or mediator. While some courts have access to volunteer lawyers and mediators, there are not enough to meet the need. Wealthy people hire their own high-powered attorneys and mediators and take as long as they need to reach agreements. Poor people, on the other hand, must use the volunteer or court-appointed mediators and attorneys when they can get them. The judge gives them a set time, possibly by the end of court that day, to reach an agreement. If they do

not reach an agreement, they must come back to finish the case. This means incurring additional costs such as lost wages for missing another day of work, child care, and transportation. Thus, the effectiveness of mediation for the poor may be diminished as it becomes another tool of assembly-line justice.

Both litigation and mediation may extend the nature and extent of conflict. The batterer, whose financial resources usually far exceed the victim's, may manipulate mediation or litigation in a way that shifts his abuse to a new and more devastating level. Even when the batterer does not engage in these tactics, the costs and strains of navigating litigation and mediation may be beyond the emotional and financial resources of both the victim and the batterer.

Conclusion

Arising from the abuser's need to gain power and control over the victim and everyone else in his environment, domestic violence is complex and often deadly. Information is mixed about whether mediation, at a minimum, will "do no harm" or, at its best, will help those involved in domestic violence. Due to the complexities of domestic violence, the inadequacy of screening tools, and flaws in both mediation and litigation systems, particularly regarding the difficult task of finding mediators, attorneys, and judges who are well qualified to handle such cases, neither litigation nor mediation is a panacea. Because mediation is an ever-growing philosophy promising great benefits, and because legal systems are feverishly searching for alternatives as their budgets are cut, there is a clear need for the development of safe and effective court and community interventions that are directly linked to victim-based research.

JANET MICKISH

See also **Batterer Intervention Programs; Mandatory Arrest Policies; Police Response to Domestic Violence Incidents**

References and Further Reading

Cameron, A. *Restorative Justice: A Literature Review*. British Columbia Institute Against Family Violence, Vancouver, B.C., Canada, April 2005. http://www.bcifv.org/pubs/Restorative_Justice_Lit_Review.pdf.
Coker, D. "Enhancing Autonomy for Battered Women: Lessons from Navajo Peacemaking." *UCLA Law Review* 47, no. 1 (1999): 1–111.
Coward, S. "Restorative Justice in Cases of Domestic and Sexual Violence: Healing Justice?" 2000. http://www.hotpeachpages.net/canada/air/rj_domestic_violence.html.
Edwards, A., and Susan Sharpe. "Restorative Justice in the Context of Domestic Violence: An Annotated

Bibliography," 2004. http://www.mrjc.ca/forms/CM%20Documents/RJ-DV%20Bibliography%20PDF.pdf.

Frederick, L., and K. C. Lizdas. "The Role of Restorative Justice in the Battered Women's Movement." Battered Women's Justice Project, 2003. http://www.bwjp.org/documents/finalrj.pdf.

Hart, B. J. "Gentle Jeopardy: The Further Endangerment of Battered Women and Children in Custody Mediation." Mediation Quarterly 7 (1990): 317–330.

Johnson, N. E., D. P. Saccuzzo, and W. J. Koen. "Child Custody Mediation in Cases of Domestic Violence." Violence Against Women 11, no. 8 (August 2005): 1022–1053.

Mayer, B. The Dynamics of Conflict Resolution. San Francisco: Jossey-Bass, 2000.

Mickish, J., and M. Knapp. "Task Force Report on Safety, Justice and Mediation: Mediating Family Law Issues in the Face of Increased Violence against Women." Presentation at Working Group on Mediation and Domestic Violence, Denver University School of Law, 1996.

Mickish, J., and K. Schoen. "Restraining Order Conditions Shuttle Conference—Training Materials." Colorado Bar Association, 2001.

Moffitt, M. L., and R. C. Bordone, eds. The Handbook of Dispute Resolution. San Francisco: Jossey-Bass, 2005.

National Institute of Justice. "Restorative Justice: On-Line Notebook." U.S. Department of Justice, Office of Justice Programs. http://www.ojp.usdoj.gov/nij/publications/rest-just.

Salem, P., and A. L. Milne. "Making Mediation Work in a Domestic Violence Case." Family Advocate 17, no. 3 (Winter 1995): 34–38.

Strang, H., and J. Braithwaite, eds. Restorative Justice and Family Violence. New York: Cambridge University Press, 2002.

Taylor, A. The Handbook of Family Dispute Resolution. San Francisco: Jossey-Bass, 2002.

Ver Steegh, N., and K. Browe Olson. "Domestic Violence, Divorce and Mediation: Options, Discussions and Interventions," c. 2004. http://www.aals.org/clinical2004/VerSteeghOlsonClinical04.pdf.

Wheeler, L. "Mandatory Family Mediation and Domestic Violence." Southern Illinois University Law Journal 26, no. 3 (Spring 2002): 559–573.

MEDICAL NEGLECT RELATED TO RELIGION AND CULTURE

Despite the great advances of medical science over the past 150 years, there are still groups that reject one or more medical treatments because of their religious beliefs or cultural traditions. The largest of these are the Jehovah's Witnesses, with nearly seventeen million active members worldwide; while the Jehovah's Witnesses used to object to a range of medical practices, today their only objection is to blood transfusions.

Several small churches, however, advocate reliance on prayer and ritual to the exclusion of medical care in most cases of illness. Denominations that have lost children since 1980 because their religious beliefs led believers to forgo medical care for children include Followers of Christ, Faith Assembly, Church of the Firstborn, Christian Science, Faith Tabernacle, End Time Ministries, Church of God of the Union Assembly, Church of God Restoration, Twelve Tribes, Christ Miracle Healing Center, and followers of Ariel Sherman, Jon Lybarger, and Roland Robidoux.

Some parents have religious beliefs against immunizations but will seek medical treatment when their children are sick. The Worldwide Church of God, Upper Room Christian Fellowship in Indiana, and the Maharishis in Iowa have had measles outbreaks because of their religious exemptions from immunizations, but those affected sought medical treatment. Many chiropractors oppose immunizations and have joined the Universal Life Church so as to be able to claim a religious exemption from immunizations.

The Amish have low vaccination rates and in many cases have relied on folk remedies and health quackery. They have had outbreaks of polio, measles, and pertussis, and cases of tetanus among their children because of failure to immunize. However, their practices seem based more on a fondness for nineteenth-century culture than on theological precept.

In addition to an avoidance of immunizations, some religious belief systems call for following strict diets that may be harmful, especially to growing children and those who are sick. Furthermore, immigrants from some ethnic minority cultures have brought their own remedies to the United States and use them on sick children in lieu of Western medical care.

Beliefs that Cause Medical Neglect of Children

The Jehovah's Witnesses' opposition to blood transfusions is based on Bible verses such as Genesis 9:3–6, Leviticus 17:10,11, and Acts 15:22–29 and 21:25, which require abstinence "from blood" and prohibit eating "meat that has its lifeblood still in it." Because of Bible verses directing that blood be poured out on the ground, the Witnesses oppose the storage of blood. Witness theology holds that the soul is in the blood and that Christ offered a perfect atonement for human sin by shedding His blood. To accept a blood transfusion, according to this theology, constitutes eating blood and tramples on the sacrifice of Christ.

The Watchtower Bible and Tract Society, which makes policy for the denomination, also prohibits autotransfusions, in which the patient's own blood is stored for later use. The Society interprets Bible verses as prohibiting the storage of blood. It prohibits transfusions of whole blood and of its four primary components: red cells, white cells, platelets, and plasma. As membership has grown into the millions, however, the Society has added many caveats to its prohibition against transfusions. An early one was an allowance for hemophiliacs to take clotting factors VIII and IX. The Society explained those as acceptable because they were only "minor" components of blood. Then Witnesses were allowed to accept the blood products albumin and immunoglobulin. The Society said those were acceptable because, like the clotting factors, they were fractions of blood plasma.

Additional exceptions followed. A heart-lung or kidney dialysis machine was allowed because the blood flows through the machine continuously and therefore is not removed from the body. Blood-gas analysis tests on premature infants were also allowed. The tests involve removing 1–3 milliliters of blood, withdrawing a test specimen, and returning the remainder to the infant's bloodstream.

The Society continued to prohibit fractions derived from red cells, white cells, and platelets until 2000, when it published an anonymous statement that fractions derived from all the primary blood components were acceptable. Thus, Jehovah's Witnesses are now able to accept interferons and interleukins from white cells, and fibrinogen (a wound healing agent) from platelets.

Witness theology still prohibits the most common kind of transfusion, packed red blood cells. Furthermore, deviant Witnesses who voluntarily accept them run the risk of being disfellowshipped and shunned by family and friends. The AIDS pandemic as well as the Witnesses' strong opposition to transfusions have led to greatly reduced use of blood transfusions and to development of blood substitutes in medical practice. Nevertheless, many doctors consider blood transfusions necessary for certain conditions of infants and children who need immediate improvement in oxygen delivery.

Critics claim that the policy changes are given out so cursorily that members may not even understand they have occurred. They typically come in a column of questions from readers in the Society's publication, with brief anonymous answers and no acknowledgment that the policy is being changed.

Some countries have refused to grant Jehovah's Witnesses status as a religion because its prohibition of transfusions violates human rights agreements. Witnesses have been arrested, lost their property, and been forced to serve in the military because their faith was not recognized by the government. To gain recognition in Bulgaria, the Jehovah's Witness leadership pledged to the government in 1998 that its Bulgarian members had freedom of choice to accept transfusions without any control or sanction from the church. Reform groups distributed news of the agreement and charged that the Witnesses had a different policy in Bulgaria than in other countries. The Watchtower Society denies there is a difference.

The Pentecostalism that began in America in the 1890s encouraged exclusive reliance on faith healing, but as Pentecostal denominations, such as the Assembly of God, grew larger and more structured, they dropped their objections to medical care. Most faith-healing groups that withhold medical care from children today are charismatic and believe that St. Paul's "gifts of the spirit," described in I Corinthians 12 and including faith healing, have been restored to them. Some, such as Faith Tabernacle, emerged within the Pentecostal revival of the 1890s, yet some Christian apologists charge that the theology of contemporary faith-healing groups is not Pentecostal, but Plotinian.

Many sects that discourage medical care express the positive confession theology of Kenneth Hagin. This movement is also known as "Name-It-and-Claim-It," "Word Faith," and the "Health and Wealth Gospel." It teaches that the crucifixion was a vicarious atonement for both sin and disease. Christians must make "positive confessions" of their salvation through Jesus Christ and then the devil's temptation or disease will leave them. The positive confession, also called "pleading the blood" by some sects, is a legalistic argument that the crucifixion has already saved them from disease and therefore the disease has no "right" to affect them. Disease symptoms are regarded as a temptation from the devil to sway believers away from their God-given rights. After the believer has made this positive confession, he or she is, according to former Faith Assembly members, expected to stand firm on it and know that his or her healing is guaranteed. He or she should ignore disease symptoms as simply demonic temptations. This theology also encourages material prosperity. It teaches that God has promised Christians a right to material possessions, which they can get by ritually claiming them.

Critics charge that the movement teaches that God can be controlled by saying the right formulas. They also criticize it for the many preventable deaths of children that have occurred in its ranks. Several of the charismatic faith-healing sects advocate home deliveries of babies without medical attention. They believe that husbands are lords of the household and should be in control of childbirth. A former medical nurse named Carol Balizet has written books promoting what she calls "Zion Births" of babies that occur with no medical attention. She writes approvingly of a husband who orders his wife back into bed, though she wants to go to a hospital. She praises husbands who put their hands on their wife's hips and belligerently order God to enlarge them so the baby can be delivered. Balizet and Reverend Hobart Freeman, among other faith healers, claim that doctors deprive husbands of their God-ordained priesthood by touching their wives and babies and seeing them unclothed.

Research published in the *American Journal of Obstetrics and Gynecology* indicates that the mortality rate of infants in Freeman's Faith Assembly church was 2.7 times higher than among other Indiana infants, while the maternal death rate among Faith Assembly women was 86 times higher than that of other expectant mothers in Indiana.

The best-known church promoting exclusive reliance on spiritual means of healing is the Church of Christ, Scientist, commonly called the Christian Science church, founded by Mary Baker Eddy. This church does not have a charismatic style of worship, nor is the crucifixion central to its promises. Christian Science believes that matter and spirit are opposites. The material world is an illusion and a lie about God's creation. Man is God's perfect spiritual reflection, coexistent with God, never born into matter and never dying, according to Christian Science.

Christian Science theology holds that disease is caused by sin or fear and that the only effective way to heal or prevent disease is to draw closer to God. Its spiritual treatments for disease include denying that disease can exist and that a person can be tempted to believe disease is real. The theology opposes medical treatment and diagnosis for children and adults alike. It opposes not only drugs, but also hygiene, immunizations, therapeutic diets, manipulations, vitamins, and health screenings because they are "material methods" to evaluate, treat, or prevent disease.

Eddy did make a few exceptions in the prohibition of medical treatment, such as dental care, prescriptions for eyeglasses, and use of morphine, which she used herself. After criminal charges were filed in childbirth deaths, Eddy advised going to doctors for deliveries of babies. She also recommended that Christian Scientists have broken bones set by surgeons. The church has a rule that one cannot have Christian Science treatment while he or she voluntarily accepts medical treatment unless the medical care is for an exception approved by Eddy. Critics charge that the threat of refusing to pray for the church member frightens members away from considering medical care. The church counters that medical science and Christian Science have antithetical methods and beliefs, and, therefore, combining the two could harm the patient.

Many children have died or been permanently harmed by religion-based medical neglect. A 1998 *Pediatrics* study reported on 172 deaths of U.S. children whose parents withheld medical care on religious grounds between 1975 and 1995. Children died of diseases that have been routinely treated by physicians for decades. The authors of the study found that 140 fatalities were the result of conditions for which survival rates with medical care exceed 90 percent. Eighteen more had expected survival rates exceeding 50 percent, and all but 3 of the remainder would have had some benefit from medical care. In the ten years since the study was published, the authors have learned of more than 100 additional child fatalities in faith-healing sects.

Twenty-eight of the deaths in the *Pediatrics* study were of Christian Science children. The Christian Science church, however, claims that the mortality rate for Christian Science children is less than half that for children in the general population and that its spiritual treatments should be a legal substitute for medical care of sick children. The church's data cannot be independently verified because the church does not disclose how many children are receiving only Christian Science treatment for illnesses, what illnesses they have had, or what the outcomes have been.

For many critics of religion-based medical practices, the issue is not only that children die, but how they die. Many have suffered for long periods of time without sedatives. Some survivors have had permanent injuries because of religion-based medical neglect in childhood. Some have lost vision, hearing, or lung capacity or been permanently crippled.

Beliefs against Immunizations

Religious opposition to vaccines is not new. In colonial times many American Puritans opposed the new inoculation against smallpox on grounds that people would be more sinful if they were not afraid of the disease. Until the 1970s the Watchtower Society claimed that blood contained all personality characteristics. It opposed vaccines because they admitted "animal matter" into the human bloodstream and could cause moral insanity, sexual perversions, and criminal tendencies. In 1952 the Society dropped its opposition to vaccines that did not have blood products in them.

The Christian Science church opposes immunizations because it believes that disease is caused by wrong thinking rather than by bacteria and viruses. It also believes that disease should be prevented by understanding one's spiritual immunity as God's perfect child.

Many of the charismatic faith-healing groups oppose immunizations because they believe that life and death are determined by the will of God. Many also believe that the crucifixion of Jesus has redeemed them from disease. Some denominations oppose injecting "foreign" substances into the body because they hold that the body is God's temple. Lurid charges circulate that vaccines are made from monkey kidneys and began the AIDS pandemic. Some charge that vaccines are made from aborted fetal tissue. Tissue from fetuses aborted in Europe for therapeutic reasons was used to develop fully characterized cell strains, which are reconstituted from frozen stock to make vaccines for rabies, rubella, hepatitis A, and varicella (chickenpox). No further fetal tissues are used. The Catholic Church has not opposed vaccines.

Some fundamentalists have raised opposition to the hepatitis B vaccine, which states began requiring in the 1990s. They believe that hepatitis B is transmitted only by sexual contact and needle exchange and that their children will not have sex out of wedlock or use illegal drugs because of their Christian values. Having their children vaccinated against hepatitis B, they argue, suggests that they will be promiscuous and encourages them to be so. Hepatitis B, however, has modes of transmission other than sexual contact and needle exchange. It may be transmitted through an open skin wound or mucosal surfaces, regular household contact with a chronically infected person, or occupational exposure, particularly among health care personnel. Infants of infected mothers are at risk. The disease has been endemic in mental institutions, and deinstitutionalization has led to the placement of carriers in schools and child care centers. About 30 percent of infected persons do not show symptoms, making control difficult. The disease has a 15 to 25 percent risk of death from chronic liver disease or liver cancer.

Followers of Maharishi Mahesh Yogi have low vaccination rates (Maharishi Medical Centers website 2006). They claim that they are creating a "disease-free society" by reestablishing "balance between the body and its own inner intelligence through Vedic knowledge." They use "the complete knowledge of Natural Law" in "the 40 aspects of Veda and the Vedic literature" that were recently discovered by a medical doctor "as the basis of the 40 aspects of human physiology," the website says.

There are 152 schools in the United States, some of which are public schools, affiliated with the Waldorf Movement founded by Rudolf Steiner on the principles of Anthroposophy. Steiner also established anthroposophic medicine based on "spiritual science." While its treatment centers and practitioners are mostly in Europe, there are also some in the United States. Steiner's followers have claimed that vaccinations weaken the immune system and that allowing children to contract diseases naturally will strengthen their immune systems. In 2002, half the students at Shining Mountain Waldorf School in Boulder, Colorado, lacked some or all of the vaccinations mandated by state law. The Waldorf Movement claims the schools do not teach a religion, but simply use a pedagogy based on Anthroposophy. Critics charge that Anthroposophy is an occult religion.

Physicians point out that vaccines give adequate immunity in most cases and spare the child the risks and the pain of contracting the disease. However, the American Chiropractic Association opposes mandatory immunizations. It calls for states to grant exemptions from childhood immunizations based on the parents' conscientious objections. In states that do not grant philosophical or conscientious exemptions from immunizations, but only religious and medical exemptions, some chiropractors join the Universal Life Church and claim a religious exemption for their children.

Chiropractic theory includes supernatural elements. D. D. Palmer, the founder of chiropractic, believed that the body has a life force separate from the brain, which he called "innate intelligence." Later, he described it as a personified part of universal intelligence (God). His theory holds that spinal manipulation removes interference with the normal functioning of the innate intelligence and thereby allows the body to heal itself of all or most diseases. Like Christian Science, classic chiropractic theory simply does not believe that viruses and bacteria cause disease.

Groups with religious or philosophical exemptions from immunizations have had many outbreaks of vaccine-preventable disease. In 1972 a Christian Science boarding school in Greenwich, Connecticut, had one of the largest U.S. polio outbreaks in the post-vaccine era. Eleven children were left paralyzed. The epidemic was not discovered by health authorities until twenty days after the first student had become ill with the disease. The last U.S. cases of polio from the wild polio virus occurred in 1979 among Amish communities in Missouri, Iowa, Pennsylvania, and Wisconsin. One child died; two were permanently paralyzed.

Two Christian Science children have died of diphtheria since 1982. A California chiropractor's child died of diphtheria in 1998. In 1997 a twelve-year-old Amish boy in Pennsylvania contracted tetanus. His medical bills were $600,000. The Amish community refused to apply for Medicaid because of their religious opposition to accepting government assistance and were able to pay only $60,000 of the bill.

In 1990 the Followers of Christ in Oregon City, Oregon, had 69 cases of rubella. In 1991 there were nine outbreaks of rubella in Amish communities in New York, Michigan, and Tennessee. More than a third of U.S. rubella cases in 1991 occurred among the Amish. In February and March, 1991, Philadelphia had 492 cases of measles and 6 deaths among children of the Faith Tabernacle Congregation and the First Century Gospel Church. Between 1985 and 1994 there have been five large-scale outbreaks of measles at the Principia schools for Christian Scientists in the St. Louis area and at a Christian Science camp in Colorado. Three young people died of complications from measles in the first of the five outbreaks. The 1994 outbreak spread to 247 children, including many outside of the Christian Science community. It is the nation's largest measles outbreak since 1992.

Such outbreaks have also occurred in other countries where immunizations and other modern medical treatments are readily available. In 1993, five years after the last case of polio was reported in Canada, health officials found 21 cases of wild polio virus type 3 (primarily in children) among an Old Netherlands Reform Church congregation in southern Alberta. In 2000 the Netherlands had 3,000 cases of measles and 3 child deaths due to the disease. The outbreak began at a Dutch Orthodox Reformed school where most children were not vaccinated for religious reasons.

Such outbreaks are costly to society. Iowa spent $142,000 to control a measles outbreak started in 2004 by Maharishi University students. A 2005 measles outbreak among families who belong to the Upper Room Christian Fellowship cost Indiana an estimated $500,000.

Diet and Nutrition

Rigid beliefs about nutrition have caused harm to children. Babies and young children have a greater need for fat and protein than adults. Vegan diets can be dangerous for children without careful monitoring. Some parents who have endangered their children by vegan diets are deviant Seventh-Day Adventists who believe that plants are the only foods the Bible approves of. Ellen White, the founder of the Seventh-Day Adventist Church, did encourage vegetarian diets, exercise, and "natural remedies," but the church does not require them, nor does it encourage avoidance of medical care. The Adventists, in fact, have licensed hospitals and medical schools.

Church of Scientology founder L. Ron Hubbard has written that babies should be fed barley water rather than breast milk. He claimed to have "called up" the formula for barley water "from a deep past" some 2,200 years ago. He claimed that it heals babies because "Roman troops marched on barley."

The Black Hebrew Israelites practice veganism and other customs prescribed in the Pentateuch. Some avoid medical care. Literature about the Black Hebrew Israelites does not explain why some avoid medical care or whether veganism is practiced as the way to maintain health. They believe that they are descended from a lost tribe of ancient Israel, who were expelled by the Romans, migrated to West Africa, and later reached the United States as slaves. They believe that God has a plan to purify them through suffering and then lead them back to Israel. They are not recognized as Jews by Israel's rabbinate. Other African American groups with strict dietary rules are the Rastafarians and MOVE.

The International Natural Hygiene Society (website 2006) believes in eating only raw plant foods to cleanse the body of toxins and to maintain health. It claims that all disease is caused by "wrong behavior"—specifically, breaking "divine laws" about care for the body. The cure for cancer is to "stop all toxins, return to a pristine mode of living, [and] give the body maximal rest (including mental rest)" (website 2006).

Rigid vegan diets have caused deaths of children as well as vitamin deficiency, rickets, anemia, anorexia, lethargy, edema, kwashiorkor, marasmus, angular cheilitis, goiter, ketonuria, methylmalonic aciduria, tremors, hypotonia, pancytopenia, neurodisability, silver toxicity, and other maladies. Particularly common is deficiency in vitamin B12, because its significant dietary sources are only foods of animal origin. Adults may do well without intake of vitamin B12 for years because of their endogenous stores of the vitamin, while infants restricted to a vegan diet may become sick within a few months.

There are several reasons that parents allow their children to deteriorate with dangerous diets. When the dietary beliefs are based on religion, parents may not evaluate the children's conditions rationally. Also, parents believe that "natural remedies," including nutrition, take longer than drugs and surgery to become fully effective. Those on the raw-foods diet are often told to interpret discomfort as part of a detoxification process.

Beliefs in Nonbiological and Spiritual Causes and Cures

Some ethnic groups, such as Hmongs who have recently immigrated to the United States, adhere to spiritual explanations for the cause of disease and want to rely on rituals to cure it. In *The Spirit Catches You and You Fall Down,* Anne Fadiman tells of a Hmong child in California who suffered a seizure at three months old. Her family attributed it to the slamming of the front door by an older sister. They felt that the fright had caused the baby's soul to flee her body and become lost to a malignant spirit.

Her impoverished parents took her to Minnesota for treatment by a Hmong shaman called a *txiv neeb,* who tied spirit-strings around her wrist and gave her herbal potions. They purchased a cow, had it slaughtered, and put its head on their front porch to welcome the return of their daughter's soul. They paid $1,000 for amulets for her to wear. They also brought their epileptic daughter to a medical clinic and a hospital more than a hundred times in four years. But they did not follow doctors' orders for medications, partly because

the directions were too complicated for non-English speakers and partly because they had more faith in their traditional ritual cures. The girl is now brain-dead.

With the exception of the Jehovah's Witnesses and perhaps the Black Hebrew Israelites, these groups have in common nonbiological explanations for the cause and cure of disease. Moral, spiritual, or supernatural factors cause disease according to faith healers, natural hygienists, Maharishis, traditional Hmongs, and others. The cure, then, lies in realigning the patient with divine laws through prayer, ritual, and willful denial of evidence that does not fit the believers' overarching theory.

The Jehovah's Witnesses, by contrast, are not faith healers. They do not claim that God will heal them of the need for transfusions. They believe that they are following commandments in the Bible, and their literature has more than once conceded that their obedience may cost them their earthly life. The Witnesses generally seek medical care, but also want a contract from the physician that no transfusion will be used. In return, they offer to sign a statement absolving the physician of responsibility for harm. The validity of such agreements is questionable.

Public Policy

Largely because of lobbying by the Christian Science church, there are hundreds of state laws giving religious exemptions from child health care requirements. They are of two kinds: religious exemptions dealing with medical care for sick or injured children and religious exemptions from preventive or diagnostic measures.

The first type came into state codes primarily because of federal government coercion. In 1974, solely because of Christian Science lobbying, the federal government began a policy of requiring states to enact a religious exemption to child neglect laws. The policy was enforced through the power of funding: If states wanted federal money for child abuse and neglect prevention and treatment programs, they had to pass a religious exemption.

In 1983 the federal government dropped the policy and began requiring states in the grant program to include failure to provide medical care in their definitions of child neglect. This was partly because of child advocates' opposition to religious exemptions and partly because the Reagan administration wanted to require medical care for handicapped infants—the Baby Doe cases.

The federal government does not ask states to remove their religious exemptions. When the federal

Child Abuse Prevention and Treatment Act (CAPTA) was reauthorized in 1996, it included the statement that nothing in CAPTA "shall be construed as establishing a Federal requirement that a parent or legal guardian provide a child any medical service or treatment against the religious beliefs of the parent or legal guardian" (Public Law 104-235). The same federal law which requires states in the grant program to have laws requiring medical care of children allows these states to have laws letting parents withhold medical care from children on religious grounds—no matter how sick the child is.

Many organizations oppose religious exemptions from child health care laws, including the American Academy of Pediatrics, American Medical Association, Prevent Child Abuse America, National District Attorneys Association, National Association of Medical Examiners, and Children's Healthcare Is a Legal Duty. They have achieved the repeal of or significant improvement in the exemption laws of several states. Nevertheless, thirty-nine states still have religious exemptions in their civil child abuse and neglect laws, and two more have civil code exemptions for "nonmedical remedial treatment," which the Christian Science church has interpreted to include their prayers.

Religious defenses to crimes against children exist in thirty states, with twenty having religious defenses to felonies and ten to misdemeanors. Two other states have defenses against criminal charges for "nonmedical remedial" methods, while Florida's religious exemption, though only in the civil code, was grounds for the Florida Supreme Court's overturning of a criminal conviction of Christian Science parents in *Hermanson v. State*, 604 So.2d 775 (Fla. 1992).

The actual reach of the religious exemption laws varies widely. Some clearly give parents the right to withhold even lifesaving medical care from a child. Others just as clearly give parents only a right to pray. Most are ambiguous, and some have been interpreted by state courts in divergent ways.

Delaware has a religious defense to first-degree murder at 11 Del. Code §1103(c); Arkansas has a religious defense to capital murder at Ark. Code 5-10-101(a)(9). The Revised Code of Washington states at 91.42.005 that "[i]t is the intent of the legislature that a person who, in good faith, is furnished Christian Science treatment by a duly accredited Christian Science practitioner in lieu of medical care is not considered deprived of medically necessary health care or abandoned." New Hampshire Revised Statute 639:3 allows all parents to endanger children on religious grounds: "a person who pursuant to the tenets of a recognized religion fails to conform to an otherwise existing duty of care or protection is not guilty of an offense under this section."

The religious defenses of some states, however, protect only a right to pray. Rhode Island General Law § 11-9-5(b) states that "a parent or guardian practicing his or her religious beliefs which differ from general community standards who does not provide specified medical treatment for a child shall not for that reason alone be considered an abusive or negligent parent or guardian; provided the provisions of this section shall not (1) exempt a parent or guardian from having committed the offense of cruelty or neglect if the child is harmed under the provisions of (a) above."

Most religious exemptions to civil abuse and neglect laws do not prevent courts from ordering medical care for children over the religious objections of parents. The Delaware Supreme Court, however, prohibited state child protection services from taking custody of a Christian Science toddler with cancer, in part because of the religious exemption law (see *Newmark v. Williams*, 588 A.2nd 1108 [Del. 1991]).

The civil religious exemptions have, however, sometimes discouraged reporting of sick children in religious objector families. When statutory definitions of neglect say that withholding medical care on religious grounds is not neglect, people may feel that cases should not be reported to state child protection services. For example, Mississippi Code § 43-21-105(l)(i) states, "A parent who withholds medical treatment from any child who is under treatment by spiritual means alone through prayer in accordance with the tenets and practices of a recognized church or religious denomination by a duly accredited practitioner thereof shall not, for that reason alone, be considered to be neglectful under any provision of this chapter." Conversely, Michigan and Florida laws state that children at risk of serious harm for lack of medical care must be reported to state child protection services even though their parents have a religious exemption from being adjudicated as negligent (Mich. Compiled Laws § 722.634[14] and Fla. Statutes 39.01[30][f], respectively).

Among preventive and diagnostic measures, religious exemptions exist from immunizations, metabolic testing, newborn hearing screening, blood lead-level tests, prophylactic eye drops, vitamin K, and bicycle helmets. Two states, Oregon and Pennsylvania, have exemptions from laws requiring that children wear helmets when riding bicycles if parents believe they should wear religious headgear instead. The Christian Science church has led the lobbying for the other types of exemptions. Nationwide, forty-eight states have religious exemptions to immunizations, and forty-six have religious exemptions from metabolic testing or allow all parents to refuse the test.

Constitutional Issues

Since 1982 criminal charges have been filed in more than sixty U.S. cases of child fatalities or severe injuries when parents have withheld medical care on religious grounds. There have been convictions in forty-nine cases; convictions in six cases were later overturned on appeal: *Lybarger v. People,* 807 P.2d 570 (Colo. 1991); *Martin v. Commonwealth,* Va. Court of Appeals unpublished memorandum opinion in record #0863-90-2 (1992); *Hermanson v. State,* 604 So.2d 775 (Fla. 1992); *Commonwealth v. Twitchell,* 617 N.E.2d 609 (Mass. 1993); *Hernandez v. Florida,* 645 So. 2d 1112 (Fla. 1994); and *Walker v. Keldgord,* U.S. Dist. Ct., Eastern Dist. Calif., #CIV S-93-0616-LKK/JFM (1996). Most of the overturns were based on the parents' constitutional right to due process and fair notice of a crime, which the courts held was violated by a statutory religious exemption. Also, trial judges have dismissed the charges in three deaths of children on due process grounds: *State v. Miskimens,* 490 N.E.2d 931 (Ohio 1984); *State v. Miller,* Mercer Cty. Common Pleas Ct., #86-CRM30; and 31 (Ohio 1986), *State v. McKown,* 475 N.W.2d 63 (Minn. 1991), *cert. denied,* 328 U.S. 833 (1992).

First Amendment guarantees of religious freedom do not give parents a constitutional right to withhold therapeutic, prophylactic, or diagnostic medical care from children. The U.S. Supreme Court has ruled that "the right to practice religion freely does not include liberty to expose the community or child to communicable disease, or the latter to ill health or death" (*Prince v. Massachusetts,* 321 U.S. 158 [1944]). In *Jacobson v. Massachusetts,* 197 U.S. 11 (1905), the U.S. Supreme Court upheld a state's right to require immunizations without exception for religious belief. The Nebraska Supreme Court upheld a state law requiring metabolic screening of infants without a religious exemption (*Douglas County v. Anaya,* 269 Neb. 552 [2005]).

What remains unsettled is whether legislatures have a discretionary right to grant religious exemptions from child health care laws or whether children have a Fourteenth Amendment right to equal protection under the law and therefore the exemptions themselves are unconstitutional. Four state courts have ruled a state religious exemption law unconstitutional partially on Fourteenth Amendment grounds (see *Brown v. Stone,* 378 So.2d 218 [Miss. 1979]; *People v. Lybarger,* No. 82-CR-205 [Colo. 1982]; *State v. Miskimens, supra;* and *State v. Miller, supra*). As of this writing, the federal courts have not ruled on this issue.

RITA SWAN

See also **Child Neglect; Christianity and Domestic Violence; Munchausen by Proxy Syndrome; Ritual Abuse–Torture in Families; Worldwide Sociolegal Precedents Supporting Domestic Violence from Ancient to Modern Times**

References and Further Reading

American Academy of Pediatrics. "Religious Exemptions from Child Abuse Statutes." *Pediatrics* 99 (1997): 279–281.
Asser, Seth, and Rita Swan. "Child Fatalities from Religion Motivated Medical Neglect." *Pediatrics* 101 (1998): 625–629.
Balizet, Carol. *Born in Zion.* Grapevine, TX: Perazim House, 1996.
Bergman, Jerry. *Jehovah's Witnesses: A Comprehensive and Selectively Annotated Bibliography.* Westport, CT: Greenwood Press, 1999.
Bottoms, Bette, et al. "In the Name of God: A Profile of Religion-Related Child Abuse." *Journal of Social Issues* 51 (1995): 85–111.
Brenneman, Richard. *Deadly Blessings: Faith Healing on Trial.* Buffalo: Prometheus Books, 1990.
Campbell, James B., Jason Busse, and Stephen Injeyan. "Chiropractors and Vaccination: A Historical Perspective." *Pediatrics* 105 (2000): 43–51.
Christian Science Publishing Society. *Christian Science: A Sourcebook of Contemporary Materials.* Boston: Author, 1990.
Damore, Leo. *The Crime of Dorothy Sheridan.* New York: Dell, 1992.
Fadiman, Anne. *The Spirit Catches You and You Fall Down.* New York: Farrar, Straus and Giroux, 1997.
Fraser, Caroline. *God's Perfect Child: Living and Dying in the Christian Science Church.* New York: Holt Owl Books, 2000.
Gifford, Bill. "A Matter of Faith." *Philadelphia Magazine,* September 1997: 96–101, 154–156.
International Natural Hygiene Society website. http://www.naturalhygienesociety.org (accessed August 27, 2006).
Kaunitz, Andrew, Craig Spence, et al. "Perinatal and Maternal Mortality in a Religious Group Avoiding Obstetrical Care." *American Journal of Obstetrics and Gynecology* 150 (1984): 826–831.
Kohn, Alfie. "Mind over Matter." *New England Monthly,* March 1988: 58–63, 96.
Kramer, Linda. *The Religion That Kills: Christian Science, Abuse, Neglect, and Mind Control.* Lafayette LA: Huntington House, 1999.
Larabee, Mark. "The Faith Healers." *The Oregonian,* November 29, 1998. Several related articles by Larabee appear in the Nov. 30 and Dec. 1, 1998, issues of *The Oregonian.*
Maharishi Medical Centers website. http://www.maharishi-medical.com (accessed August 27, 2006).

Parker, Larry. *We Let Our Son Die.* Irvine CA: Harvest House, 1980.

Shepard, Suzanne. "Suffer the Little Children." *Redbook,* October 1994: 68–72.

Simpson, William. "Comparative Longevity in a College Cohort of Christian Scientists." *Journal of the American Medical Association* 262 (1989): 1657–1658.

———. "Comparative Mortality of Two College Groups, 1945–83." *Mortality and Morbidity Weekly Report* 40 (1991): 579–582.

Skolnick, Andrew. "Christian Scientists Claim Healing Efficacy Equal If Not Superior to That of Medicine." *Journal of the American Medical Association* 264 (1990): 1379–1381.

Swan, Rita. "Faith Healing, Christian Science, and the Medical Care of Children." *New England Journal of Medicine* 309 (1983): 1639–1641.

———. "Children, Medicine, Religion, and the Law." *Advances in Pediatrics* 44 (1997): 491–543.

Welsome, Eileen. "Born to Believe." *Westword* 24 (Oct. 12–18, 2000): 20, 22–24, 26–27.

Young, Beth. "Defending Christian Science Medical Neglect: Christian Science Persuasive Rhetoric." *Rhetoric Review* 20 (2001): 268–292.

MEDICALIZATION OF DOMESTIC VIOLENCE

The Trend toward the Medicalization of Society

The medicalization of domestic violence is part of a more generalized trend toward the medicalization of society. A definition of the term "medicalization" may be in order at the outset: The term suggests that the field of medicine is used as a foundation for providing a conceptual framework in interpreting whatever phenomena are in question. The reason for this trend toward the medicalization of society has to do with the fact that medicine has come to be viewed as the pinnacle of science; that is, the epistemological assumptions that guide the construction of medical knowledge are often perceived by those inside and outside the academy as having more validity than those epistemological assumptions that inform the so-called social sciences.

The field of medicine has shrouded itself under the value-neutral veil of positivism despite the fact that there is a considerable body of evidence that may call into question the notion of objectivity with regard to the social construction of medical knowledge. Nevertheless, the general public seems more than willing to place the whole of medicine on a pedestal and willingly accepts a medicalized view of all manner of phenomena. Examples of the trend toward the medicalization of society abound. Witness the medicalization of pregnancy, sexual function, sport, and old age, just to cite a few examples.

Perhaps one of the most invasive areas within which the trend toward medicalization can be seen is that of deviance or crime. Increasingly, in Western societies, those behaviors judged to be problematic are being explained as resulting from some sort of medical problem or disorder. In short, the jurisdiction of the medical field has been expanded to cover things that are not medical in nature. Historically one can see the trend initiate perhaps with Lombroso's theory of atavism, the mythical disease that the nineteenth-century Italian physician professed afflicted criminals. Atavism was diagnosed on the basis of the presence of various stigmata, the signs of atavism. Such symptoms included a protruding chin, pinched nasal nerves, ears set too far from the head, and hair growing in unusual places, among other symptoms. Today, atavism is regarded as one of the many mythical diseases that litter the history of medicine. One may also easily cite the early criminologists who practiced phrenology as evidence of an early trend toward medicalizing crime and deviance. Phrenologists studied the shape of the skull in an attempt to determine predispositions toward criminality in the individual. Bumps or "abnormalities" in certain places on the skull may have meant that the individual had a higher probability to engage in certain crimes. Today, of course, phrenology is a so-called dead science, once again pointing to the very social construction of knowledge that belies much of empirical science.

As the medicalization of deviance and crime began to evolve, it wasn't long before the expanding field of the study of mental illness would be employed as a ready-made rational system for explaining criminal behavior. In short order, sociobiologists, psychologists, psychiatrists, and the like began to reify all manner of crime as illness or disease. Consider the case of kleptomania, the stealing disease, which, argued here, has been socially constructed. In the wake of industrialization women entered into public life en masse as never before to take up the new pastime of shopping. The newly emerging marketplace created a new opportunity with regard to crime, namely, shoplifting. The shoplifting perpetrated by working-class women could easily be rationalized in that these women were tantalized by all the temptations of conspicuous consumption and stole either out of need or to acquire that which they wanted but could not afford given their class position. Simply put, working-class women who stole were easily tagged as thieves. However, the problem was that not only were working-class women involved in shoplifting but so were their middle-class and upper-middle-class counterparts. Given the social conventions of the day, it was unacceptable to call upper-middle-class women thieves, and so a disease was created for them, namely, kleptomania. What could be made of these curious women who stole that which they could well afford to purchase? Many writers have suggested that such phenomena may have been explained as a form of rebellion against upper-middle-class domesticity, that is, wealthy women acting out.

More recently, despite the somewhat torrid history with respect to the medicalization of deviance and crime, in many cases—some, in fact, bordering on the absurd—society seems fully willing to refer to all serial killers as psychopaths, problem drinkers as alcoholics, and hyperactive children as sufferers from attention deficit disorder. Such behaviors range from the deviant to the criminal and are obviously problematic for the individuals and the societies in which they live, but the extent to which they derive from illness or disease is ambiguous at best. More to the point of this article are the questions of the extent to which domestic violence is being medicalized and the consequences of such a conceptualization.

How Is Domestic Violence Medicalized?

One of the main ways in which one can bear witness to the medicalization of domestic violence is through examining the language that is often employed in the institutions that are most likely to have some dominion over either the victim or the perpetrator of such violence. It is in this instance that one becomes engaged in the deconstruction of a medical discourse that characterizes health care institutions and increasingly more and more the institutions associated with the criminal justice systems.

Frequently, the first responders to instances of domestic violence are either hospitals or law enforcement. Victims of domestic violence are often encouraged to seek medical attention for the injuries they sustain at the hands of their perpetrators. But whether they enter into the health care system of their own volition or at the direction of law enforcement or perhaps, on rare occasions, are taken to the hospital by their aggressor, these individuals' experiences are all informed by the medical discourse that engulfs them. From the outset these victims, who are predominantly women, are transformed into "patients," who are administered to by doctors and nurses, and soon enough the language of diagnosis, treatment, and medicine eventually extends to frame even the "disease" from which they suffer.

Both Wilkerson (1998) and Davis (1988) have written about the medicalization of domestic violence, suggesting that the epistemological assumptions employed in medicine, in conjunction with the language of medicine, may obscure the nature of such violence and in the worst cases serve to amplify the suffering of those who have been victimized. Wilkerson (1998) reflects on Foucault's *The Birth of the Clinic* (1975) to highlight the somewhat precarious claims to moral authority that inform medical discourse. She writes that the work "clarifies the relationship between the epistemology of medicine and its moral authority, tracing the processes by which the medicalization of society began to remap the moral domain from the soul onto the body" (Wilkerson 1998: 126). Such moral authority might also be seen as gendered inasmuch as science in general, and medicine in particular, has historically maintained an androcentric bias (Harding 1986).

Unfortunately the structure of patriarchal gender stratification that may be seen as informing domestic violence is the same structure that largely predominates in health care institutions. Though well meaning, health care professionals may be sabotaged in their efforts to extend aid to victims by the medical frame employed in the diagnostic process. Gelles and Straus, in their compelling *Intimate Violence* (1988), suggest that nearly all interested parties concur that the "medical system" has the greatest responsibility with respect to identifying, treating, and preventing domestic violence. Interestingly enough, given the discussion of the androcentric bias in medicine, the authors suggest that the medical system does a better job in the area of child abuse relative to wife abuse. "Wife abuse has not assumed the same place on the medical system's treatment and policy agenda that is held by child abuse and neglect. For the most part, doctors and psychiatrists are seen as even less helpful to battered women than are the police" (Gelles and Straus 1988: 178). Though in their own family violence survey Gelles and Straus (1988) found that the majority of women were satisfied with the medical treatment administered to them by health care professionals, the authors did cite the work of Stark, Flitcraft, and Frazier (1983), who found otherwise.

These three authors suggest that the medical system may contribute to the problem more than to the solution. The authors suggest that the patriarchal gaze of the medical practitioner may cast doubt on the mental health of the victim. The researchers found that women who were victims of domestic violence were often regarded as psychotic or malingerers, and like their precursors who suffered from hysteria, they would be best treated with sedatives or "nerve pills" and sent home. Taking a cue from labeling theory, the authors suggest that given this type of societal reaction, such battered women may have legitimate reason to question their own mental health and make an internal attribution about the violence they suffered.

Davis (1988) echoes the sentiment that casts suspicion on this androcentric bias in medicine that may complicate the understanding of domestic violence. Her research highlights a paternalistic character in the practice of medicine wherein "general practitioners [are] making moral judgments about women's roles as wives and mothers, psychologizing women's problems, not taking their complaints seriously, [advocating] massive prescription of tranquilizers, [and] usurpation of women's control over their reproduction" (Davis 1988: 22).

Most recently Kurz (2005) has found evidence of some resistance toward the medicalization of battering in at least some quarters of the medical establishment. Kurz (2005) studied emergency department staff at four hospitals. The author notes that at least one of those hospitals was engaged in efforts to encourage staff to view domestic violence specifically within a medical framework. Kurz (2005) made the following observation with respect to a physician's assistant working in the hospital so inclined to medicalize domestic violence: "She believes the battering aspect of a case is a legitimate medical concern and compatible with her own role.

She refers to battering as a 'syndrome' with distinct medical symptoms, and urges others to 'diagnose' the condition" (Kurz 2005: 215).

Despite the general trend toward medicalizing behavior and the specific efforts of hospital staff in at least one instance to have emergency department staff see battering as a medical problem, Kurz (2005) found widespread resistance amongst the first responders. Riding against the tide of many feminist writers, Kurz suggests that this resistance toward the medicalization of battering is problematic in that it serves to render many victims, particularly those who are judged by staff as being morally undeserving, invisible. "The second and third factors affecting staff's lack of response—that they feel there is little they can do, and that they don't see this as a legitimate medical problem—mean that staff feel that responding to battered women detracts from their 'real' work" (Kurz 2005: 217). Surprisingly, there appears to be some residual medicalization going on in the case of these deemed undeserving victims, that is, the author suggests, as has been discussed previously, that women who are labeled with "stigmatizing traits" are often not treated for battering per se, but rather are seen as suffering from drug abuse, alcoholism, or depression.

Rethinking Medicalizing Domestic Violence

While it is imperative to understand the intersection of the biological system and the social system with respect to making sense of and dealing with issues related to domestic violence, there is a present danger in reifying crime as disease or illness. Like many so-called conditions that have been appropriated by medicine of late, domestic violence may produce injuries that require medical attention, and writers such as Kurz (2005), Davis (1988), and Wilkerson (1998) have discussed at length the extent to which the ensuing medicalization process contributes to or detracts from the state of the domestic violence victim. Some have argued that medicalizing the problem in turn individualizes the problem, thereby isolating an individual in dire need of social support. "Pathologization also serves to obscure the group identity of women who are battered, perpetuating the sense that their suffering is an isolated personal problem, due to bad luck or their own inadequacy—rather than a common manifestation of relationships between men and women in this society" (Wilkerson 1998: 129).

Whatever the good intentions of the medical establishment in treating victims of domestic violence with respect to a pathological perspective, it is clear that there is considerable debate regarding the efficacy of medicalizing battering. Likewise it is important to raise serious questions regarding the medicalization of the abusers as well. Pathologizing perpetrators of domestic violence serves to obscure a social structure characterized by a patriarchal system of gender stratification that has historically afforded some tolerance for many forms of violence, and certainly that done to women in domestic life. Contemporary Western culture is filled with contradictions regarding violence and sex, which often become entangled in the popular culture. Simply the hypersexualization of women may objectify them sufficiently so that they are in a more vulnerable position with respect to the probability of being victimized by violence.

The fact that domestic violence was traditionally shrouded in the normalcy of family makes an understanding of the phenomenon limited to cases that have been observed. Nonetheless, the power differentials that define gender relations in the family are important to examine in an attempt to understand the problematic behavior. Although the social construction of gender is not static, and significant changes in gender relations have been observed in the past seventy-five years, power differentials in familial relations remain a constant. Couples' relationships may be informed by power differentials with respect to physical strength, sex, and economic position. Some religious ideologies may even validate the naturalness of a hierarchy with respect to gender relations. However, such structural and cultural factors in explaining domestic violence are undermined when theorists, practitioners, and criminologists employ a medical discourse with references to "battered syndrome" and discuss the "epidemiology of domestic violence."

While the notion of treating domestic violence as a disease may be appealing to some in that invoking treatment suggests the possibility of a "cure," we are by no means in a better position to seek social changes, indeed structural and cultural changes, that may serve to reorganize gender relations in such a fashion as to reduce the probability that women will be subject to domestic violence in their lifetimes.

CHARLES WALTON

See also **Community Responses to Domestic Violence; Popular Culture and Domestic Violence; Violence against Women Act**

References and Further Reading

Davis, Kathy. "Paternalism under the Microscope." In *Gender and Discourse: The Power of Talk,* edited by Alexandra Todd and Sue Fisher. Norwood, NJ: Ablex, 1988.

Foucault, Michel. *The Birth of the Clinic,* translated by A. M. Sheridan Smith. New York: Vintage Books, 1975.

Gelles, Richard, and Murray Straus. *Intimate Violence.* New York: Simon & Shuster, 1988.

Harding, Sandra. *The Science Question in Feminism.* Ithaca, NY: Cornell University Press, 1986.

Kurz, Demie. "Emergency Department Responses to Battered Women: Resistance to Medicalization." In *Violence against Women,* edited by Claire M. Renzetti and Raquel Kennedy Bergen. New York: Rowan & Littlefield Publishers, 2005.

Stark, Evan, Ann Flitcraft, and William Frazier. "Medicine and Patriarchal Violence: The Social Construction of a Private Event." In *Women and Health: The Politics of Sex in Medicine,* edited by Elizabeth Fee. Farmingdale, NY: Baywood, 1983.

Wilkerson, Abby L. "Her Body Her Own Worst Enemy: The Medicalization of Violence against Women." In *Violence against Women: Philosophical Perspectives,* edited by Stanley G. French, Wanda Teays, and Laura M. Purdy. Ithaca, NY: Cornell University Press, 1998.

MILITARY FAMILIES, DOMESTIC VIOLENCE WITHIN

Overview: Past, Present, and Future

The Defense Task Force on Domestic Violence, in its 2001 report, made it clear that services to prevent the ongoing escalation of domestic violence in military families were insufficient. It made over two hundred suggestions to improve both the quality and the quantity of the military's response to domestic violence. It recommended that the Department of Defense require the investigation of every reported incident of domestic violence. When subsequent investigations were conducted, they revealed precisely what the kindling conditions are for domestic violence explosions. The report stated that these factors must be explored in depth if the epidemic is to take a downturn. The risk factors include previous conviction(s), prior head injury exacerbated by military service, and observable patterns of traumatic reenactment. Treating at-risk individuals before they reunite with their families provides critical protection.

Identifying and taking seriously the precursors that are likely to resurface in the presence of the unrelenting stressors of military life can significantly shield innocent partners and children from predictable post-battle rampages. Canada has identified this need by providing integrative space for its returning military. After seeing action overseas, Canadians are sent to specified facilities to debrief, unwind, and prepare for peace and parenting. This antidote is showing success in Canada in decreasing domestic violence in military families.

In 2002, five women at Ft. Bragg in North Carolina were murdered by their Special Forces husbands who had just returned from combat in Afghanistan, drawing national attention to the issue of the rising rates of domestic violence in military families. Each of the killers was already known to be at risk because of prior domestic violence or similar behavior. Additionally, documented case studies that point to traumatic repetition are recorded in books such as T. S. Nelson's *For Love of Country* and Ed Tick's *Sacred Mountain*. By documenting the continuing impact of domestic violence within military families and pointing to traumatic reactivation as the causative factor,

hope is engendered that families and children will be better served. Stories of how domestic violence plays out in the lives of military families are not intended to shock or to cause despair but to evoke an understanding of how war does not end when it is declared over, and how the battles do not end when the soldiers come home.

Increasingly sophisticated knowledge of how the brain functions under stress and the patterns of head injury reactivation allow for new insights which in turn lead to the development of highly specific methods of early intervention. The military has been encouraged by many sources, including Congress, to take advantage of this heightened education so that fighting terror overseas does not result in terror for families at home.

The ways in which military families are segregated from civilian society contributes to the paucity of education about the origins and causes of domestic violence in military families. Some efforts are being made to remedy this and to find avenues of significant support both on and off military installations. The test of the success of these endeavors will be seen in whether or not military families feel safer reporting incidents of domestic violence before they escalate and whether or not more evolved treatment is presented that ultimately produces a true reduction in rates of domestic violence in military families.

Post-Traumatic Stress Disorder, Domestic Violence, and Military Suicides

The devastating effects of combat on veterans of the Vietnam conflict led to the awareness and the diagnosis of post-traumatic stress disorder (PTSD); it has also become evident that those with this condition may tend in the direction of committing domestic abuse. Vietnam veterans not only found themselves battering their wives and families, but also killed themselves in record numbers after their abusive behavior. Indeed, observing the aftereffects of the Vietnam conflict has led researchers to make the conclusive link between domestic violence, suicide, and PTSD. The combination of a propensity toward battering and suicidal tendencies is still common in veterans of more recent military actions. All of the most recent and highly publicized major incidents of domestic violence within military families have consistently included a suicidal component. Three of the five men convicted of murdering their wives at Ft. Bragg, North Carolina, in 2002 later committed suicide.

Rates of Domestic Violence in Military Families

The rates of domestic violence within the military are consistently higher than rates of domestic violence in civilian families. The most recent rate of reported domestic violence is 25 per 1,000 military personnel, according to Department of Defense figures. The lowest reported rate has been 18.6 per 1,000 military personnel. The civilian population reports three incidents of domestic violence per 1,000 people. In 2000, over 12,000 cases of spousal abuse were reported to the military's Family Advocacy Program (FAP). Eight women died that year, killed by their military husbands.

Rates of domestic violence within military families are likely to be much higher in reality than reported. Reporting is usually a complex process, driven by bureaucracy and imbued with shame. Abused spouses are rarely able or willing to risk the family's financial future by reporting to military channels. Complaints notoriously end up on the desks of commanding officers. Programs to ensure confidentiality have yet to be established. Attorney Phyllis Lonneman, who represents women abused by army husbands, suggests that it does not matter how good or bad the military programs are if the spouses are afraid to use them.

A recent army survey conducted by independent researchers (Behavioral Sciences Associates, which interviewed 55,000 soldiers on 47 bases) reported that rates of marital aggression are considerably higher than anticipated. One aspect of this report indicates that abuse escalates at bases scheduled to be shut down. This fits perpetrator patterns as documented by the National Coalition Against Domestic Violence (NCADV). Perpetrators become activated by changing conditions that undermine their control and security. This is another indication of the role of traumatic reactivation.

Statistics, including those from the Behavioral Sciences report, clearly state that domestic violence within military families, like domestic violence in civilian families, is classless. Commissioned and noncommissioned officers, commanders as well as ordinary soldiers, are all perpetrators of domestic violence. In civilian life, this equality of suffering applies to rich and poor, educated and uneducated alike.

Pregnancy, Children, and Domestic Violence

According to the NCADV, spousal abuse generally increases during pregnancy. Childbirth educators who work on military installations reported at a conference held in March 2005 on the subject of birth trauma that birthing mothers living in military households feel fear about returning with their newborns to a violent household.

Seventy-five percent of children in military families are under eleven years of age. These are, by far, the most vulnerable victims of domestic violence within military families, along with babies in utero. Babies' brains are shaped by experience. Limbic pathways encoded with terror, or young primitive brains that become conditioned by fear and panic, grow into the criminal minds of sociopaths and psychopaths. The research of such neuroscientists as Lise Eliot (1999), Allan Schore (1994), and Daniel Siegel (1999), as well as the work of public health experts Robin Karr-Morse and Meredith Wiley (1997), confirm the nature of this conditioning.

Army colonel Will Hatcher launched a Pentagon investigation into rising rates of violence against children in the military. Child deaths at Fitzsimmons Army Medical Center in Colorado, at Bremerton Naval Base in Washington, and at Travis Air Force Base in California aroused grave concern about the magnitude of suffering of innocent children as a result of domestic violence within military families.

According to developmental psychologist Joy D. Osofsky, existing research indicates that even in the earliest phases of infant and toddler development, there are clear associations between exposure to violence and emotional and behavioral problems. Infants and toddlers who witness violence show excessive irritability, immature behavior, sleep disturbances, emotional distress, fears of being alone, and regression in toileting and language. Reports have noted the presence of PTSD in these young children, including panic-ridden flashbacks to the traumatic event, avoidance, numbing of responsiveness, and increased arousal.

Raising consciousness and diagnostic skills about how war reactivates previous trauma is a giant step in stopping domestic violence in military families and protecting children from abuse. The resources to do this and to end the cycle of intergenerational violence are now available. The challenge is to use them. The Lautenberg Law and a

2001 Department of Defense directive prohibit soldiers with prior records of domestic violence or restraining orders against them from carrying a gun. These critical mandates require thoroughgoing enforcement at all military installations to be effective.

Shame

Removing the stigma of shame from traumatic reactivation is an essential step in lowering incidents of domestic violence in military families. There is an extensive history of blaming and condemning soldiers for their reactions to the horrors they witness during military service. This leads inevitably to repression, and repression is a step in the direction of explosion. Military spouses choose their wives and children as outlets for their explosions when they are not given other options for release or helped to understand what they have been exposed to in war.

Shame is isolating and ultimately backfires. Families and individuals who are separated from communication and external resources because of shame are put in harm's way, particularly during wartime, when emotions run high. Broadening and intensifying counseling services to families on military bases and to military families in general is required to identify and end this isolation. Isolation and domestic violence are virtually synonymous. The lessons of the past are pertinent here.

Shell shock was the term used for the disorder that affected soldiers serving in World War I who became withdrawn and paralyzed with fear. The diagnosis included marked physical trembling, often to the point of convulsive seizures. This trembling is characteristic of nervous system overload and adrenal exhaustion, natural outgrowths of the horrors of war. Treating it as such allows for true regeneration. One recorded attempt to address the behavior of shell-shocked soldiers during World War I was to require them to withstand even more battle. There has been much progress made since this blaming and shaming model of counterproductive treatment, but exposing vulnerability in the face of war is still often viewed as weakness. Education to counteract this misunderstanding is a component of domestic violence prevention.

A conference held at the University of Colorado in the summer of 2004, "The Unseen Costs of War," explored psychological services for military families. Attention was directed to the need to counteract shaming attitudes. In addition, the conference presenters emphasized that the availability of a diverse spectrum of services, rather than focusing only on chaplain-based counseling, is necessary to reach more military personnel. Chaplains are currently the only military personnel granted confidentiality.

Treatment and Services

Military families need access to psychological services that emphasize resources for all family members, including those that treat adrenal exhaustion. Services that include an understanding of the neurological and physiological origins of domestic violence inherently reduce feelings of shame.

There is a history of bureaucratic delay in organizations as complex as the military. This obstacle can be offset by direct services to military families from civilian agencies contiguous with military bases. Restrictions imposed on families to use only military facilities can be removed so that easy access to civilian resources can bypass unnecessary and often fatal delays. Military families experience a sense of isolation from the communities around them because of the physical and bureaucratic design of military bases. Indeed, alongside early intervention, combating isolation is central to preventing domestic violence within military families.

This is well said by Beals (2003) in her handbook prepared by the Battered Women's Justice Center. Military life, she reports, with its powerful control over the lives of service members, presents unique challenges for victims in need of help. Unlike the civilian world, where clear institutional boundaries exist between one's employer, doctor, judge, social worker, and advocate, the military system is, for the most part, seamless. Imagine, in the civilian world, that calling a local shelter or confiding in one's doctor automatically causes the batterer's employer to find out about his acts of violence and abuse. The risk of retaliation is obvious, and frightening. Of even greater concern to many victims is the fear that as a result of their reporting the abuse, their batterers may lose their jobs or otherwise face adverse career consequences, leaving the victims and their children impoverished and without housing or health care. Institutional practices may be unfamiliar; they differ among the services, and even among installations. As with any institution, the protocols that guide the military response on a given installation may vary dramatically, depending on the resources and informal relationships that exist at a particular installation, and the extent to which collaborative relationships exist with the surrounding civilian community.

The frequent moves required of military families contribute to the theme of debilitating isolation.

Most military families move every three years, ripping the military family from the support network of relatives and friends that they count on when times get tough. In addition, relocation often brings with it unfamiliar cultures, values, physical environments, and food. This cuts military wives and children off from comforting, sustaining, and familiar conditions, making them more vulnerable and dependent. When spouses are separated from their military partners, distrust and suspicion is generated, and many military husbands convicted of spousal abuse point to this distrust as the kindling for their fiery explosions. Services that address the specific impact of regular relocation on military families would help prevent domestic violence.

Perhaps the most significant change that could occur for military families dealing with domestic violence is increased access to civilian services and civilian advocates. Increasingly, civilian communities located near military installations either have or are developing *memoranda of understanding* (MOUs) with the installations for responding to domestic violence incidents involving military personnel. These agreements generally cover law enforcement response, prosecution, protective orders, shelter, and information sharing. Others have not yet taken these steps. Civilian advocates for military families dealing with domestic violence can play an extremely important role in conveying resources otherwise unavailable to military families.

Compared with civilian society, the military population is younger and drawn from lower socioeconomic ranks. Alcohol abuse is high, pay tends to be poor, and the military attracts people who have authoritarian tendencies. All of these factors play a part in the pattern of isolation and unreported abuse. Addiction counseling could help significantly if it could be added consistently to the services available to all military families now that drug and alcohol abuse have been documented as being problematic in the military, particularly for those in combat.

The military's response to domestic violence is centered in the FAP, whose primary role is to prevent, identify, assess, and treat domestic violence. However, the FAP operates under the installation commander, who oversees FAP services, including reporting and law enforcement. The service member's specific commander has responsibility for offender accountability. Some installations have reporting agreements with civilian law enforcement agencies.

As rates of domestic violence within military families have risen steadily since 2000, organizations of survivors have formed. While focused on serving military families, these organizations are outside the structure of the military establishment. Organizations such as STAMP (Survivors Take Action Against Abuse by Military Personnel) collect data, provide crisis counseling, and conduct investigations.

When the military process is too weighed down with bureaucracy or when it institutes policies that survivors feel are counterproductive, such as the Feres Doctrine, which bars survivors from taking legal measures to secure financial assistance when domestic violence has occurred within a military family, these organizations are useful in finding other resources. They offer a sounding board, group process, and overall support when domestic violence occurs within military families.

Combat Training and Domestic Violence

Studies conducted by the National Battered Women's Law Project in New York found a correlation between combat jobs and domestic violence. According to the study, troops trained to fight are more likely to batter women and children than their colleagues in noncombat jobs. This is corroborated by Murray Straus, a family violence expert. According to Dr. Straus, there is a spillover from what one does in one sphere of life into what one does in other roles. If one works in an occupation whose business is killing, it legitimizes violence.

In order for brutality, battering, and violence against women and children to occur, the victims have to be dehumanized. This is precisely what combat training is all about—the dehumanization of some portion of any given population. The humiliation of softness that is part of military training arouses traumatic rage. Women and children, as embodiments of the very softness disparaged in combat training, represent easy targets for this rage. Without an integrative transition period that differentiates the past from the present, soldiers are likely to continue, neurologically, in combat mode, even when they are not in battle.

Brain Structure and Domestic Violence

The long-held belief that the brain is a rigid structure has been dismantled by the discoveries of neuroscientist Paul MacLean, whose foundation research has been followed by writers such as Candace Pert, Antonio Damasio (expert in the field of head injury and recapitulation, which is so often a factor in domestic violence within military families), and Allan Schore (who writes extensively on the early origins of traumatic reactivation).

The brain, as is now known, has a triune structure that functions like three interconnected computers, each with its own intelligence. Two of these levels are below consciousness. These deeper, earlier brains are concerned almost utterly with survival, and it is vital to attend to them in order to end the cycle of violence. These are the brains that are trained to be aggressive in combat and which cannot easily differentiate the past from the present. They need assistance, support, and guidance to do so.

The responses of the primitive brain structures are not about time and appropriate behavior but are centered utterly on threat and survival. The link between primitive conditioning and adrenal firing is automatic and will proceed unless deliberate intervention to stop this activation is provided. Responses of both batterer and victim are lodged in the relationship between survival-based action and adrenal activation.

The midbrain's emotional memory is likewise not organized chronologically. Memory is conditioned by specific emotionally laden experiences that when rekindled do not differentiate past from present. Only the higher brain (sometimes divided into two components consisting of the cortex and the neocortex) has the capacity for perspective, understanding and the neutral state of reflection and witnessing. Accessing these higher brains and stimulating their integrative structural allies like the hypothalamus could substantially lower rates of domestic violence within military families, and perhaps even eliminate it completely.

There is no question that military service is extraordinarily activating and emotionally charged. This is particularly true of wartime service. Understanding the clear relationship between this activation, adrenal firing, and domestic violence in military families is fundamental to ending the cycle of violence.

The Cycle of Violence

Neil Jacobson and John Gottmann (1998) report that 80 percent of male batterers experience themselves as victims. They are, indeed, the victims of their own neurology that defines aggression as survival. Similarly, a person who is battered is neurologically driven to remain in the battered position.

Both the helpless person and the aggressor escape from these conditions by changes in consciousness that must precede action. These changes have to do with the growth of new neuronal options that allow perception to change. Thus, ending the cycle of violence means changing neurological firing. This is the newest and most profound

option available. Psychologist Steven Wineman sees battering as the acting out of powerless rage that is a response to feelings of oppression. Finding the source of the oppression is the ultimate solution to the cycle of violence. One step in ending the cycle of violence is seeing perpetrators not as others but understanding that an enormous amount of abuse is enacted by people who themselves have suffered profound violations and have themselves been crushed by oppression and power. New theories of trauma and new perspectives on brain function present perhaps the greatest hope for stopping domestic violence everywhere, including within military families. It is possible, even likely, that a perpetrator is subjectively powerless or victimized while simultaneously acting with enormous aggression. In fact, this combination is particularly lethal.

Culturally Endorsed Violence Encourages Domestic Violence

Saint Leo University in Saint Leo, Florida, sponsored twenty years of research showing the impact of violence in the media and in video games on children and adolescents, especially boys. The study showed that less than ten minutes of exposure to violence in the media creates long-lasting aggressive traits and actions. The key factor in video games in particular is that violence goes unpunished. Teachers of 600 eighth and ninth graders aged thirteen through fifteen said that children who spent time playing violent video games were more hostile than other children. Witnessing violence becomes the foundation for traumatic reactivation. An investigation into the maltreatment histories of U.S. Navy trainees who demonstrated abusive behaviors revealed that 94 percent had witnessed violence in some form prior to enlistment.

Research examining onscreen violence toward women finds that emotional desensitization can occur after viewing as few as two films with violent themes. Studies show that men who view a number of films in which women are portrayed in sexually degrading or violent situations become increasingly less disturbed by violence against women and less sympathetic toward female victims of violence.

Several studies support a link between early exposure to violence and aggressive behavior in school-age children. These studies also show that those who have been exposed to violence are more likely to commit crimes and to experience alcohol and substance abuse. A longitudinal study of eight-year-old boys found that those who viewed the most violent programs growing up were the most likely to engage in aggressive and delinquent behavior by the time they were eighteen and were the most likely to engage in serious criminal behavior (such as domestic violence and sexual assault) by the time they reached age thirty.

Domestic Violence in the Military and Gender

Most active-duty military personnel are men (85 percent). Fifty-one percent of active military personnel are married and most of them are married to civilian spouses who are dependent on them financially. Military wives earn less and are less likely to be employed than their civilian counterparts. In 66 percent of reported domestic violence incidents within the military, the victim was a female. There is, however, a small percentage of male victims (less than 30 percent).

According to the U.S. Department of Health and Human Services, the number-one health problem for women is violence. According to the Family Violence Prevention Fund, women in the military are particularly vulnerable to abuse due to geographical isolation from family and friends and the potential for social isolation within the military culture.

In the sample of active-duty military women from the greater Washington, D.C., metropolitan area, 30 percent reported adult lifetime intimate partner violence, defined as physical and/or sexual assault from a current or former intimate partner. African American women were significantly less likely to be abused during military service than were white women, but ethnic group membership was not a risk factor for lifetime abuse.

Summary

While rates of domestic violence in military families are not decreasing, there is cause for hope in the new understanding of the neurology of traumatic repetition, the willingness of the Department of Defense and other governmental agencies to take an unequivocal stand on domestic violence, and the intervention of civilian agencies and civilian advocates. Diane Stuart, director of the Office on Violence Against Women in the U.S. Department of Justice, said it simply when she stated that our ability to end domestic violence depends, above all, on building a coordinated community response to the needs of every survivor.

STEPHANIE MINES

See also **Domestic Violence by Law Enforcement Officers; Minorities and Families in America, Introduction to; Multicultural Programs for Domestic Batterers**

References and Further Reading

Beals, Judith. "The Military Response to Victims of Domestic Violence," 2003. Battered Women's Justice Center. http://www.bwjp.org/military/BWJPMIL-081803.pdf.
Damasio, Antonio. *Descartes' Error*. New York: Avon, 1994.
Eliot, Lise. *What's Going On in There?* New York: Bantam, 1999.
Hansen, Christine. *Report on the Study of Spousal Abuse in the Armed Forces*. Washington, DC: Caliber Associates, 1996.
Herman, Judith. *Trauma and Recovery*. New York: Basic Books, 1992.
Jacobson, Neil, and John Gottmann. *When Men Batter Women*. New York: Simon and Schuster, 1998.
Karr-Morse, Robin, and Meredith S. Wiley. *Ghosts from the Nursery: Tracing the Roots of Violence*. New York: Atlantic Monthly Press, 1997.
Mines, Stephanie. *We Are All in Shock*. Franklin Lakes, NJ: New Pages, 2003.
Nelson, T. S. *For Love of Country*. Binghamton, NY: Haworth, 2002.
Schore, Allan. *Affect Regulation and the Origins of the Self*. Hillsdale, NJ: Erlbaum, 1994.
Siegel, Daniel. *The Developing Mind*. New York: Guilford, 1999.
Tick, Ed. *Sacred Mountain*. Santa Fe, NM: Moon Bear, 1989.
Walker, Lenore. *The Battered Woman*. New York: Harper and Row, 1979.

MINORITIES AND FAMILIES IN AMERICA, INTRODUCTION TO

Introduction

This essay provides an overview of underserved populations. It will begin by explaining the dynamics of power and control in domestic violence and how it ties into common barriers that both underserved victims and victims in general face. However, the effects of the use of power and control intensify the suffering for underserved minority victims because of their special circumstances or negative perceptions held against them. The end-result barriers may include little awareness about domestic violence, minimizing and stereotyping the violence and the victims, economic hardships, hesitancy to report, and victim services issues. This essay will discuss the primary types of minority groups beyond the typical categories of race and ethnicity and will include issues concerning domestic violence of people with disabilities, military personnel and their families, and people in rural areas. It is very important to note that both males and females can be victims of domestic violence. However, due to the common understanding that the majority of victims are females, this article references women as victims. It is not its intention to negate the male population as victims.

Definitions of Special/Minority Populations

There is no universally accepted definition of what constitutes a minority group in America. For example, in the field of sociology, a minority group is a subgroup that is outnumbered by persons who do not belong to the same group. The term *minority* has also been used in a new way, referring to groups that are perceived to be worthy of preferential treatment. Some people claim that both minority and majority groups tend to be composed of individuals of the same racial or ethnic identity who are living under a particular government. However, the definition of minority victims of domestic violence goes beyond typical race- or ethnicity-based classifications and includes those groups that face problems and barriers in receiving services as a result of their culture, specific needs, and differences. The different types of minority groups besides those of race and ethnicity include, but are not limited to, different age groups, such as the elderly population; people with disabilities; military personnel and their families; and people in rural areas.

Dynamics of Power and Control

The dynamics of domestic violence involve a process that prevents the victim from leaving the relationship. For instance, repetitive physical assaults and/or constant verbal assaults, such as humiliating or blaming the victim, reduce her feelings of self-worth that could otherwise encourage her to leave. The "power and control wheel" developed by the Domestic Abuse Intervention Project lists categories of physical, sexual, and emotional violence that can trap victims in their abusive relationships. These are common techniques used by the abuser to perpetrate the victim's inability to leave the relationship due to fear, anxiety, and forced dependency. As a result, many victims believe that they have no choice but to stay. In addition to the dynamics of power and control, other compounded issues are usually faced by members of minority populations as barriers to leaving when they are abused.

Barriers

Awareness. Many women, for various reasons, do not understand that what is happening to them constitutes domestic violence. The primary reason is that women have accepted the violence as a normal part of their relationships. In addition, depending on their culture, men and women alike may possess the idea that women are men's property and believe that it is the male's right to do with the female as he wishes; this can lead to committing acts of domestic violence under the guise of discipline. Values regarding family unity, group orientation, and gender roles in which females are strictly limited to domestic chores and reproductive expectations are a few examples of beliefs commonly shared among various groups. Many victims believe that they have done something to deserve the violent treatment. Those beliefs could prevent victims and witnesses from disclosing the violence or intervening in some other way. New immigrants with limited knowledge of U.S. laws and systems especially tend to have little idea about domestic violence as criminal acts. In short, it is possible that both the abuser and the victim believe that the violence should be tolerated. Women are granted little or no power by social, cultural, and religious norms which socialize them to accept the power imbalance between males and females. Regardless of their cultural origins, the different belief systems of minority groups, in contrast to the laws and customs of the United States, pose difficulties for minority victims of abuse. Moreover, such differences also pose difficulties for law enforcement and other professionals who wish to support full recovery of these victims.

Isolation. Victims could be suffering from emotional and/or physical isolation. Oftentimes women in domestic violence situations are physically isolated in their homes. This is a form of emotional isolation also, due to the victim's lack of contact with family and friends. Additionally, not being allowed to see another person without the abuser's permission is a common characteristic of domestic violence. For example, living in an isolated area, with the nearest neighbors miles away, limits the ability to ask for help in a timely manner. Rural areas tend to have little public transportation services. Therefore, a simple act by the abuser such as disconnecting the phone line greatly limits opportunities for the victim to ask for help. In addition, there are several different types of isolation an individual can suffer, such as not being able to drive, not being allowed to learn a language spoken in the community, not being able to obtain an education, and having no financial control.

Economic Barriers. Economic hardship is one of the devastating preconditions and/or direct results of domestic violence. A victim may have little or no income to support herself (and her children) in the first place. In such cases, victims suffer from poverty, lack of resources, and a sense of immobility. Moreover, an abuser can prevent his victim from working, by either harassing her on the job, forcing her to take time off due to injuries, or not allowing her to obtain a job at all. Regardless of previous financial stability, many abusers seek total financial control. This compounds the financial problems of victims who live in economically challenged rural areas that suffer from high poverty rates and have

limited resources. The direct result is the victim's inability to support herself when she leaves the relationship. In fact, many victims choose not to leave because they cannot face the difficulty of regaining financial control. Other challenges related to economic issues can be any combination of the following: maintaining a current job while healing; being able to afford the costs of medical and mental health care, legal fees, relocation, and transportation; and finding and paying for child care. Most victims are forced to consider these multiple financial issues when thinking about leaving their abusers. Combined with other problems such as isolation, economic hardships truly discourage victims from standing up against their violent relationships.

Barriers to Reporting. Reporting is a difficult step for many victims. A victim's interpretation of the first response from law enforcement also discourages future reporting. If the response is negative toward the victim or supportive of the abuser, the victim may believe that the police cannot or will not help them.

Fear of being accused of lying or other illegal behavior could also cause victims to avoid contact with law enforcement. In the United States, many people are undocumented residents—as such, fear of police is an enormous factor for not reporting domestic violence. Illicit drug use by victims also may prevent reporting. Cultural dynamics may prevent a victim from leaving her abuser or even seeking help. For instance, victims who seek help from relatives or friends may be told to accept the abuse for family honor and reputation, or that violence is what she deserves. Certain cultures rely on elders to make decisions for their families. Such decisions made by others may not ease the victim's suffering or lead her to seek outside help because they may be based on strong family values or a lack of awareness about domestic violence in the culture.

Domestic violence committed by military personnel requires special attention for its setting. The military has its own criminal justice system, including law enforcement, corrections, and legal system. A unique aspect of the military culture is that it is an extremely closed system very similar to that of civilian law enforcement, though perhaps even more private and/or secretive. Generally domestic violence cases are investigated by the immediate commanding officer, who uses his own discretion as to the severity of the violence. Similarly, domestic violence by law enforcement creates unique issues for victims to face. Those issues include, but are not limited to, the abuser's access to personal information that can lead him to the whereabouts of the victim when she leaves and the abuser's access to weapons. When a victim decides to report her abuse at the hands of a partner in the military or law enforcement, it is possible that the case will be handled by someone who knows her abuser as a coworker and who might handle the report unofficially. This can lead to no record of the abuse by an officer, making it harder to build a complete history of violence, which is necessary to obtain a criminal protection order.

Reporting and disclosing the violence is usually the first step to recovering from the abuse. Therefore, barriers to reporting are considered serious problems which need to be solved, so that more victims feel comfortable asking for help and services when they are ready to take the initial step of recovery.

Lack of Services

Not every community offers services to domestic violence victims. Those that do may lack in service areas, such as multilingual staff, sufficient shelter capacity, twenty-four-hour hotlines, the ability to provide referrals to other local resources and service providers, transportation to the service location, and services for the disabled. A lack of knowledge of diversity, specific cultures, and religions on the part of service providers can have a direct impact on a victim seeking help. For instance, due to cultural or religious differences, a victim can feel isolated in a shelter and feel that being at home with the abuser is less stressful, which may be a compelling reason for her to return to him. In addition, many women who relocate to the United States with their husbands are ill informed about the availability of help from authorities and social services.

The current research indicates that the level of victimization of disabled people is as much as five times higher than that of the general public. Although people with disabilities have the same rights as any other victims, they are the largest group of victims that are neglected by the criminal justice system. This is because they are not afforded the same type of access, legitimacy, or respect as other victims. For example, not all criminal justice agencies have victim rights pamphlets or literature in Braille for blind people.

Minimizing and Stereotypes

Besides racial and ethnic identification, there seems to be unlimited ways to categorize people into small groups by any number of perceived common characteristics. As a consequence people tend to stereotype each other and divide others into groups. One common stereotype about domestic violence victims is that they are racial or ethnic minorities living in low-socioeconomic neighborhoods, whereas domestic violence crosses all economic, ethnic, and racial borders. Another common stereotype of victims is that the violence is their fault. These beliefs lead many people to minimize the severity of victimization. Stereotypes also perpetuate the harmful view that battered women are passive and helpless. Moreover, there are perceptions among law enforcement personnel that domestic violence is of a minor nature and of no concern to law enforcement. Likewise, court systems can also be discriminatory in nature. For example, victims can be highly emotional while going through the court process, which can lead to a negative view of the victim's credibility. Therefore, it is possible for victims to experience a sense of rejection, either perceived or actual, from the court personnel.

Conclusion

Domestic violence among minority groups is an important issue to be studied in order to understand the commonalities of domestic violence dynamics in general as well as the unique aspects and needs of each group of victims and perpetrators. The federal government, for example, continues to support studies and victim services related to domestic violence through the Violence Against Women Act (VAWA), enacted in 1994 and reauthorized in 2000. With VAWA 2000, the federal government committed itself to better serving victims of domestic violence, especially those with disabilities, elderly victims, and immigrant victims. Meanwhile, the study of underserved victims continues to evolve and become increasingly important.

TERI BERNADES and HARVEY WALLACE

See also **African American Community, Domestic Violence in; Asian Americans and Domestic Violence: Cultural Dimensions; Battered Woman Syndrome; Christianity and Domestic Violence; Coercive Control; Jewish Community, Domestic Violence within the; Military Families, Domestic Violence within; Multicultural Programs for Domestic Batterers; Native Americans, Domestic Violence among; Qur'anic Perspectives on Wife Abuse; Rural Communities, Domestic Violence in; Violence against Women Act; Women with Disabilities, Domestic Violence against**

References and Further Reading

Johnson, Rhonda M. "Rural Health Response to Domestic Violence: Policy and Practice Issues," 2000. http://rural-health.hrsa.gov/pub/domviol.htm.

Orloff, Leslye E., and Rachel Little. *Somewhere to Turn: Making Domestic Violence Services Accessible to Battered Immigrant Women: A "How To" Manual for Battered Women's Advocates and Service Providers.* Ayuda, Inc./U.S. Department of Health and Human Services, 1999. Available through www.vawnet.org.

Seymour, Ann, Jane S. Murray, Melissa Hook, Christine Edmunds, Mario Gaboury, and Grace Coleman. *2000 National Victim Assistance Academy.* U.S. Department of Justice, Office for Victims of Crime, Office of Justice Programs, 2000.

Siskin, Allison. *Violence Against Women Act: History, Federal Funding, and Reauthorizing Legislation* (Congressional Research Service report RL30871), 2001.

Ulbrich, Patricia M., and Jami Stockdale. "Making Family Planning Clinics an Empowerment Zone for Rural Battered Women." *Women and Health* 35, no. 2/3 (2002): 83–100.

Wallace, Harvey. *Family Violence, Legal, Medical, and Social Perspectives,* 4th ed. Boston: Allyn & Bacon, 2005.

Wilson, K. J. *When Violence Begins at Home.* Alameda, CA: Hunter Hose Publishers, 1997.

MOTHERS WHO KILL

Introduction

In recent decades, domestic violence has been accepted as a painful reality—one that law enforcement officials, social workers, health care providers, and many other professionals have sought to understand and eliminate. The topic of maternal filicide, or mothers who kill their children, might be seen as a subset of the problem of domestic violence, and yet, it remains mysterious to most experts in domestic violence. This essay aims to dispel some of the confusion surrounding this topic. It begins by describing research which identified five patterns associated with maternal filicide in the United States. It then discusses the implications of these findings and articulates strategies for preventing the deaths of children at their mothers' hands.

Research and Methodology

It is impossible to determine the *exact* frequency of contemporary filicide; however, evidence suggests that every three days in the United States, a mother kills her child. In 2001, Cheryl Meyer and Michelle Oberman published a joint study of U.S. mothers who killed, drawn from over 1,000 reports of maternal filicide in the United States from 1990 to December 31, 1999. The research involved a comprehensive search for media and court accounts of contemporary cases. Two hundred nineteen of the most thoroughly reported cases were selected, from which a typology of mothers who kill their children was created. After publishing that typology, these scholars designed a survey instrument, and Dr. Meyer interviewed forty women who had been convicted of killing their children and were incarcerated for their actions. The responses of the interview subjects inform the discussion below.

Typology: Patterns in Contemporary U.S. Filicide Cases

Filicide Due to Neglect

The most common type of filicide involves mothers whose children die accidentally, as a result of what the law might term "child neglect." This category of cases is marked by several striking patterns. The mothers typically have more than one child, and the deaths of the child or children are most readily viewed as accidental. Rather than intentional killers, these women typically emerge as well meaning, having attempted to raise their children under challenging circumstances. The vast majority of these mothers receive little or no support from the fathers of their children. They have limited financial means. Their living conditions are unstable, they have limited support from others, and they lack child care. All of these factors hinder the mother's ability to find work to support herself and her children, as well as to find ways to provide herself with the sort of respite care that all mothers, and particularly single mothers, need.

In the original study, there were a total of seventy-six cases of neglect. The majority of these women became mothers as adolescents. In addition, the overwhelming majority (85 percent) of mothers in this category were single parents. Moreover, among the cases reviewed, 41 percent of the families included three or more children. Not surprisingly, 90 percent of the cases in this category involved mothers living in poverty. Finally, in at least 41 percent of the cases, the mothers' lives were complicated by mental health problems such as depression or chemical dependency.

Filicide Related to an Ignored Pregnancy

The second most common form of maternal filicide involves the crime known as "neonaticide." Neonaticide is the killing of a newborn within twenty-four hours of birth, by a woman who typically had received no prenatal care and delivered her baby unattended, outside of a hospital setting. The women who commit this crime are disproportionately young, single, and emotionally isolated. They tend to become pregnant by accident, and they have mixed feelings about having a child. They suspect that their families will not accept their pregnancies and that the birth will rupture their fragile support systems. As young women, they worry about issues such as work, housing, and health care, fearing that they will be unable to support themselves and a child. At the same time, they tend to see the children as a potential source of love and affection in their otherwise lonely existences.

The fears triggered by their pregnancies led these women to ignore or conceal them. Some of the women studied managed to keep their secret because they gained little weight, or continued to bleed throughout their pregnancies. Others simply remained in a state of denial. It is important to note that these women were, in many cases, still girls, living at home with their parents. Although their families of origin often seemed loving, these girls felt unable to confide in any of the adults in their lives. Moreover, the adults did not notice any physical or emotional changes in these girls. In some cases, the adults also ignored or missed the broad hints that the girls dropped in their efforts to get an adult to help them. In such circumstances, it is not surprising that an adolescent might fantasize about the sort of affection and attention that a baby would bring to her life.

Purposeful Filicide

The set of cases involving mothers who *deliberately* take the lives of their children are the most varied and difficult to comprehend. Mental health problems are woven through the overwhelming majority of the cases in this category, and yet there is a remarkably broad spectrum of diagnoses relevant to these cases. At one end of the spectrum are cases in which the mother had little or no history of mental illness, and yet her violent actions clearly evidenced her extreme mental distress. For example, consider the case of Susan Smith, a South Carolina mother who killed her two small children in 1989 by leaving them in her car and rolling the car into a lake. Although she had long struggled with depression and suicide attempts, and even as a married adult continued a sexually abusive relationship with her stepfather, she was not under medical supervision at the time of her crime.

In other cases, the mothers had long histories of mental illness, often with scores of doctors and state agencies on notice about the risk that she posed to herself and to her children. For instance, Andrea Yates, a Texas mother who drowned her five children in a bathtub in 2001, had been treated for many years for depression and psychosis and was suffering from postpartum psychosis-related delusions when she killed her children.

Despite the diversity amongst these cases, there are striking and clear patterns. These commonalities include the killing of multiple children, the experience of a recent failed relationship, intense desperation and suicidal thoughts, and, finally, issues of cultural and religious ideology. Perhaps the most important of these fact patterns is that most of these cases involve suicide attempts by the mother. When the mother's suicide attempt fails, the criminal justice system often dismisses it as insignificant. Nonetheless, those seeking to understand and prevent these crimes must notice these attempts, in that it is the mother's determination that she can no longer go on living that typically leads her to take the lives of her children. Indeed, in many of these cases, the mothers tried to arrange alternative care for their children shortly before they killed them. It was only after their families and friends refused them that they decided to "take their children with them." Often, this decision reflects the mothers' deeply held religious convictions regarding guilt, forgiveness, and an afterlife. Another distinctive feature of these women's stories is their devotion toward their children. The overwhelming majority of these mothers had no history of abuse or neglect toward their children, and people who knew them described them as deeply devoted mothers.

Although postpartum mental illness receives a considerable amount of attention, a relatively small percentage of mothers studied by Meyer and Oberman within this category suffered from postpartum disorders (8 percent). Overall, when all 219 cases are included, the postpartum cases accounted for less than 3 percent of the sample. This is not to say that mental illness is not a key factor, as a significant number of women in this category sought treatment for mental health conditions. Unfortunately, those who did seek help did not necessarily disclose their thoughts of harming themselves or their children. In part, this may have been due to the shame they felt about being "bad mothers," but in addition, they may have feared losing custody of their children were they to reveal their darkest thoughts. Thus, their health care providers failed to recognize the immediate threat that these women posed to their children and to themselves.

Abuse-Related Filicide

Despite the considerable research on the subject of child abuse, little has been written about mothers who take it to fatal extremes. These cases involve chronic levels of abuse, typically taking place over the course of many months or even years. One of the most troubling aspects of this particular form of filicide as it emerged in the research discussed in this essay is that in the vast majority of cases, state child protection agencies *were aware* of the trouble in these families long before the children were killed. In the original sample of fifteen cases, child protective services had previously intervened in at least twelve, and possibly even fourteen. In two-thirds of these cases, the mother had previously lost custody and killed the child after reunification.

Some of the underlying commonalities in these cases included early child-bearing (many were adolescents when they had their first child) and substance abuse. Not only were many of the mothers abusing substances, but at least a third of the children-victims had been born addicted to substances. At least two of the women were pregnant at the time of the killings. In interviews with the women who had killed their children through abuse, it emerged that most of these women had themselves been abused as children. As others have suggested, there is considerable evidence that being abused as a child, or observing abuse as a child, is related to abusing as a parent.

Assisted/Coerced Filicide

The final category of cases in this typology refers to situations in which mothers kill their children while acting in conjunction with a partner—generally a romantic partner—who contributes in some manner to the death. In most situations, the mothers are passive participants, failing to protect the children from abuse at the hands of their male partners. The most noteworthy characteristic of women in this category of cases is that they typically are involved in violent relationships with their domestic partners, and the abuse carries over to the children. In most cases, state child protection agencies have been involved with the family. All of the children in this category of the original sample had been physically abused over a long period of time. For the most part, the deaths of these children resulted from discipline-related abuse that escalated into fatal beatings. These incidents typically occurred at particularly stressful times of day for the parents, such as bedtime.

Intervention and Prevention

This article has provided an overview of the five different categories of contemporary U.S. cases of maternal filicide. Each category is unique and presents distinct challenges for preventing future cases. There are at least two common problems that underlie all of the categories, however, and that might point to an additional path to prevention.

The first common problem is *maternal isolation*. Increasingly, motherhood is undertaken alone. The demise of the extended family, and indeed, of the nuclear family, means that mothers today experience a profound degree of isolation from support systems. In the past, and in other cultures around the world today, a new mother receives substantial support from her own mother, from her sisters, her aunts, and indeed, her entire community. With others who will shop, clean, cook, and care for her and her family, the mother of a newborn is free to devote her attention to her baby. In contemporary U.S. society, even a relatively wealthy mother is likely to spend long hours alone with her child, apart from her spouse, living at some distance from her extended family, and unconnected to her neighbors.

Although isolation is not ideal for any mother, for some women it is particularly problematic. Thus, the second problem common to cases of maternal filicide is that the mothers typically enter parenthood with preexisting vulnerabilities. These vulnerabilities might derive from factors such as one's relative youth or dire poverty, or the nature of one's mental health status, substance abuse, or intimate relationships. Obviously, most women manage to cope with these difficulties without killing their children. But not all harm to children takes the form of killing, which is simply the far end of the spectrum. The mere fact of becoming a mother does not automatically endow one with the coping skills needed to respond patiently and gently to the demands of a young child. Thus, the isolation of mothers with diminished coping skills creates an environment in which harm to a child becomes predictable, if not inevitable.

Nothing in this essay is meant to minimize the severity of the crime of filicide or to suggest that these mothers are not responsible. It is a crime to kill a child, and those who do so should be held accountable for their actions. What is particularly challenging about these cases emerges as researchers attempt to determine the extent to which these mothers are blameworthy. In this endeavor, one cannot help but notice the challenging circumstances that surrounded these mothers at the time that they took their children's lives. From this inquiry, one learns that filicide is not incomprehensible; it arises out of the toxic combination of isolation and despair. It is only with this understanding that researchers can chart the course toward change, so that one day, the death of a child at her mother's hands will indeed be truly incomprehensible.

MICHELLE OBERMAN

See also **Assessing Risk in Domestic Violence Cases; Child Neglect; Child Sexual Abuse; Corporal Punishment, Religious Attitudes toward; Divorce, Custody, and Domestic Violence; Filicide and Children with Disabilities; Medical Neglect Related to Religion and Culture; Munchausen by Proxy Syndrome; Postpartum Depression, Psychosis, and Infanticide**

References and Further Reading

Meyer, C. L., M. Oberman (with K. White, M. Rone, P. Batra, and T. Proano). *Mothers Who Kill Their Children: Understanding the Acts of Moms from Susan Smith to the "Prom Mom."* New York: NYU Press, 2001.

Milner, J. S., K. R. Robertson, and D. L. Rogers. "Childhood History of Abuse and Adult Child Abuse Potential." *Journal of Family Violence* 5 (1990): 15–34.

Cable News Network. "Nearly 5 Babies Killed Weekly, FBI Data Show," June 27, 1997. *CNN Interactive*. http://www.cnn.com/US/9706/27/killed.babies/index.html.

Oberman, M. "'Lady Madonna, Children at Your Feet': Tragedies at the Intersection of Motherhood, Mental Illness and the Law." *William & Mary Journal of Women and the Law* 10 (2003): 33–67.

———. "Mothers Who Kill: Cross-Cultural Patterns in and Perspectives on Contemporary Infanticide." *International Journal of Law and Psychiatry* 26 (2003): 493–514.

———. "Understanding Infanticide in Context: Mothers Who Kill, 1870–1930 and Today." *Northwestern Journal of Criminal Law and Criminology* 92 (2002): 707–738.

———. "Mothers Who Kill: Coming to Terms with Modern American Infanticide." *American Criminal Law Review* 34 (1996): 1–110.

Resnick, P. J. "Murder of the Newborn: A Psychiatric Review of Neonaticide." *American Journal of Psychiatry* 126 (1970): 1414–1420.

MULTICULTURAL PROGRAMS FOR DOMESTIC BATTERERS

Men from minority groups are mandated to treatment in numbers that are disproportionate to their representation in the general population (Healey, Smith, and O'Sullivan 1998). This is often attributed to a correlation with low socioeconomic status, lingering discrimination in the criminal justice system, and greater exposure to violence in the community (Healey et al. 1998; Williams and Becker 1994). Likewise, it is thought that resistance to treatment may be higher among minority men; for example, some African American men have likened their requirement to attend treatment to a mechanism of institutional racism. This potential racism is an issue that group facilitators and therapists have had to recognize while being careful to not allow it to become an excuse for battering (Healey et al. 1998). Such considerations can compound the complexity of therapeutic objectives and can serve to test even the most skilled and seasoned group facilitators.

Attrition Rates and Minority Clients

Research indicates that minority men, particularly African American and Latino men, have lower program completion rates than other cultural or racial groups (Chang 1996; Healey et al. 1998; Williams 1992). As a result, some researchers and practitioners have proposed that the effectiveness of interventions will be enhanced among minority men if programs are not merely culturally sensitive, but culturally competent as well (Healey et al. 1998; Williams 1992). While this can further complicate treatment programs, it seems that such considerations are crucial, given the overrepresentation of minority clients, the already high levels of attrition for batterer clients in general, and the even higher attrition rates cited for minority clients in particular.

Further, minorities have been discouraged from using mainstream social service agencies by racially and culturally insensitive attitudes and practices of service providers (Healey et al. 1998). Williams and Becker (1994) contend that batterer interventions must become "culturally competent" to improve retention and minority participation. According to Healey and colleagues (1998), a culturally competent intervention program purports to draw on the strengths of the culture (i.e., spiritual belief systems, family connections, communal social systems, etc.) and to address weaknesses within that same framework (such as alcoholism, harsh child discipline practices, rigid gender roles, etc.). While such programs have been developed, their existence is fairly uncommon in the published literature. What is more, evaluation studies of their effectiveness are rare, if at all existent. Lastly, any empirical comparisons as to the effectiveness of these few culturally competent programs with other traditional programs either do not exist or have not been disseminated in the mainstream literature. Because of this, it is imperative that such research be conducted to determine if minority clients can indeed be better served by programs that tailor their efforts to these specific clients. Currently, this research is scant, at best.

Williams and Becker (1994) conducted a survey of batterer intervention programs which indicated that for the most part, little or no special effort was being made to understand or accommodate the needs of minority populations. Rather, most of these programs instead implemented a "color-blind" approach where all clients were treated universally and identically. Williams and Becker (1994) contended that such an approach lacked the effectiveness of a culturally competent program, which fosters an environment that helps minority groups succeed in treatment. In specific, programs aiming to be culturally competent are advised to:

- Network with the minority community
- Locate outside consultants with expertise in working with minorities
- Obtain information concerning service delivery and programming for minority clients
- Have at least one bilingual counselor (Williams and Becker 1994, p. 287)

The need to examine cultural competence is quite apparent when one considers that clients most likely to successfully complete a batterer intervention program will tend to be white, middle-class, and educated (Saunders and Parker 1989; Tolman and Bennett 1990; Williams and Becker 1994). On the other hand, minority males who are referred to battering interventions tend to participate less, have lower completion rates, and are reported to be less successful than whites (Chang 1996; Healey et al. 1998; Saunders and Parker 1989; Tolman and Bennett 1990). As a result, some researchers seriously questioned the validity of such programs for minority battering clients (Williams and Becker 1994). According to Williams and Becker (1994), studies that examined characteristics of those clients who completed batterer programs may provide a picture that is cursory and cosmetic at best, not demonstrating the true underlying variables inherent to the minority client and batterer intervention programs.

For minority clients in particular, knowledge of social factors as a product of culture could be invaluable in overcoming abusive behaviors. For example, Williams and Becker (1994) pointed out that environments rampant with violence and poverty in which many African American men are raised can contribute to a coupling between violence and manhood. Minority males bring into treatment their cultural experiences as well as their violent tendencies with their partners. Both of these issues require attention throughout the treatment process (Williams and Becker 1994).

Interestingly, Sue and Sue (1990) have pointed toward the concept of internal-external dimensions in a person's locus of control. Research on generalized expectancies of locus of control have suggested that ethnic group members and those of lower socioeconomic status score significantly higher on the external end of the locus-of-control continuum (Sue and Sue 1990). Higher external end scores correlated with apathy, depression, and feelings of powerlessness regarding environmental factors. Whites, on the other hand, tended to score higher on the internal locus-of-control continuum. Higher scores on the internal end correlated with superior coping strategies, greater attempts at environment mastery, and lower predispositions to anxiety (Sue and Sue 1990).

The problem with an unqualified application of the internal-external dimension was that it failed to take into consideration the different cultural and social experiences of the individual (Sue and Sue 1990). Further, Sue and Sue (1990) pointed out that while the social-learning framework from which the internal-external dimension was derived may be valid, it was possible that different cultural groups and the lower socioeconomic classes have learned that control operates differently in their lives when compared with how it operates in society at large. It becomes obvious that Western and white approaches to counseling mimic many factors that are espoused by an internal locus-of-control ideology. Indeed, battering programs emphasize the ability of batterers to take responsibility for their actions. Most counselors are of the clinical opinion that people must take major responsibility for their own actions and can improve their lot in life through their own efforts (Sue and Sue 1990). However, when dealing with immigrant and/or minority clients, this worldview may clash with the ability of the therapist to build effective rapport (Sue and Sue 1990).

Further, clients who have high internal scores tend to be white and middle class, with such approaches seeming entirely appropriate (Sue and Sue 1990). With respect to batterer clients, this was not surprising due to the fact that white middle-class clients had the best prognosis toward completing treatment (Healey et al. 1998). Thus the internal-external locus of control seemed to produce attributional characteristics for behavior responsibility that correlated with attrition rates among whites and minorities.

According to Dobash et al. (2000), one primary mechanism for positive change among batterers centers around client views on external constraints and internal controls. The premise in this research was that movement from external forms of supervision maintained by others toward internal controls maintained by the batterer himself indicated the likelihood for successful intervention (Dobash et al. 2000). It was found that men acting relative to external constraints displayed more physically abusive behavior than men who were self-governed through internal controls. Further, clients relying on external constraints acquired fewer, if any, techniques to desist from battering than did those men who operated from an internal constraint paradigm (Dobash et al. 2000). Clients using internal controls seemed to have successfully acquired new techniques and orientations as a form of personal change (Dobash et al. 2000).

This research demonstrates the value of obtaining client self-responsibility in displays of violence. While this is indeed encouraging, the issue is nonetheless unanswered when considering minority clients who have externally driven worldviews. Studies such as those by Dobash et al. (2000) reflect positive movement for clients who are white and tend to hold middle-class values and beliefs. For the minority client, providing such a shift in worldview thinking may be difficult and inappropriate; a direct product of the structure of the program itself. In determining whether program curriculum could be a determining factor in achieving internal constraints among minority batterers, it becomes important to examine whether the treatment program is culture specific to the population it serves.

Cultural Competence: Latino American Populations

Providing therapeutic services for Latino Americans can be not only elusive, but also so varied, because of the multiplicity of ethnicities, as to seem impossibly fragmented and splintered. The complexity of this population is highlighted by Arredondo and Perez (2003), who note that to discuss Latino culture without consideration of within-group differences based on one's family heritage (i.e., Cuban or Puerto Rican) and other dimensions of Latino identity is to promote cultural stereotyping (also see Arredondo and Santiago-Rivera 2000). Further, to report research findings about Latinos without citing generational and socioeconomic differences may obscure the critical factors of acculturation and ethnic identity (Arredondo and Perez 2003). This is important because consensus on appropriate interventions for Latinos is extremely difficult to achieve. Any form of culturally appropriate intervention is going to require at least some degree of subjectivity and will not be as open to quantification (similar to the contentions made by Pedersen [2003]). This becomes even clearer when one notes the difficulty that has been associated with operationalizing multicultural competencies when counseling Latino clients (Arredondo et al. 1996).

Cultural Competence: African American Populations

It should be noted that focusing on one segment of the African American population hides the great diversity that exists among this population. Clients may vary greatly from one another based on factors such as socioeconomic status, educational level, cultural identity, family structure, and reactions to racism. Issues that may have to be dealt with are feelings about differences in ethnicity between the counselor and the client and issues of institutional racism. The need to discuss institutional racism is particularly relevant if the client is court mandated; this same issue is even more important if the counselor's racial/ethnic identity is of the majority population. This is also important when one considers the fact that African Americans are vastly overrepresented in America's current jail and prison systems.

Many African American clients will note the importance of the church or of spirituality in their lives. This should not be overlooked as a therapeutic tool in reaching this community and is discussed later as a specific cultural recommendation for improving current programs. It is important to note that African American values have been shaped by social class variables, experiences with racism, and a struggle for group identity. Because of this, the use of family, and more particularly the use of extended family, in African American culture has been widely noted as an important consideration in treatment.

Cultural Competence: Asian American Populations

When discussing Asian Americans, it should be mentioned that there is no general consensus on the number of disparate cultural associations that are grouped under the category "Asian" or "Pacific Islander American" (Sandhu, Leung, and Tang 2003). Indeed, as many as thirty-five distinct cultures have been identified as part of the Asian and Pacific Islander category (Sandhu et al. 2003). This points to the true difficulty in creating any blanket definition of cultural competence for this population. Unless this group is simply lumped together as a general category (obviously running the risk of oversimplification and even stereotyping), both the counselor and the researcher can end up with so many distinctions as to make their task seem scattered and overspecialized.

Nevertheless, it is true that each Asian group has its own distinctive cultural background, historical experiences, and reasons for immigration to the United States (Sandhu et al. 2003). Thus, any degree of general competence with this population may be best achieved by identifying variables and techniques that are found to be commonly effective with the Asian American population. For instance, the use of "matching" has been deemed effective by some researchers (Chin 1998). Researchers have found that counselors of the same race as the client population tend to be more effective than counselors of a different race (Gim, Atkinson, and Kim 1991; Sandhu et al. 2003). In general, counselors of Asian American ethnicity and counselors who have been culturally sensitized through training are given higher ratings for effectiveness by Asian American participants in therapy (Gim et al. 1991). Thus, while it may be difficult, if not impossible, to develop specialized competence with each specific ethnic group, it may be possible to find certain techniques that run as a commonality throughout the broader Asian American population.

Designing Feminist-Based Programs That Are Culturally Competent

Feminist scholars have bemoaned the fact that in addressing women's issues, the feminist movement has failed to provide adequate analysis of the unique issues faced by women of minority status. Feminism has been likened to a theory based on the historical and social experiences of white, middle-class women. Experiences have often been quite different for African American, Latino, and Asian American women. In regard to domestic violence issues, the distinction has been even more profound, particularly for those minority families that come from nations of origin other than the United States. For these women, a variety of issues surround their abusive relationships that many white women do not face. These differences also affect the means by which abuse is perceived, greatly modifying victim options available in coping with such problems. Further, some minority women may view certain credos of feminism to be contrary to their own cultural and personal viewpoints and belief systems.

With respect to batterer intervention programs, this becomes even more important as these belief systems are no doubt native to the battering males as well. Thus, within these abusive family systems cultural definitions and responses for coping may be quite different for both the minority victim and the minority perpetrator of battering. Just as feminist thought and theory has been criticized for overlooking the unique factors for minority women, by implication this theory may likely do the same for minority males as well. The need for feminism to tailor itself to these concerns has been addressed in the literature. However, many programs dealing with domestic batterers have failed to take such considerations into account. This can be particularly problematic for both the offender and the victim.

However, as mentioned earlier, many minority cultures operate on what is referred to as an external locus of control, where responsibility for one's behavior is seen more as the product of fate or chance rather than self-directed motivations (Rotter 1966). But if abusive beliefs include notions of centrality, superiority, and deservedness of the self, this runs counter to notions of minority self-beliefs that revolve around external loci of control. On the surface, this seems to be a bit of a paradox, with minority men feeling powerless on the one hand, yet superior and self-deserving on the other. However, research has shown that in Indian, Chinese, Japanese, and South Asian immigrant communities, strong patriarchal values are tied to domestic violence (Bonilla-Santiago 1996). In many Latino cultures, machismo and male entitlement, among other correlates, are prevalent connections to spouse abuse (Bonilla-Santiago 1996; Erez 2000; McWhirter 1999). In African American culture, issues of violence and black male masculinity have likewise been connected with domestic violence (Williams 1998).

Essentially, it is this paradox regarding behavioral responsibility in the home versus in the broader society that must be addressed among minority batterer clients. It is within this paradox that the justification, denial, and deflection of responsibility occur, and it is precisely this narrow paradox that warrants challenge. However, batterer intervention programs that focus on the values, belief systems, and experiences of Western, middle-class, white culture will be of little use among many minority clients (Healey et al. 1998).

The vast majority of batterer intervention programs (nearly 80 percent) are based on some form of feminist educational style of curriculum (Gondolf and Hanneken 1987). It is not surprising that these programs based on confrontation are more successful for Western, white, middle-class clients. Notions of individual responsibility, control over environment, and ability to achieve are all congruent with likely experiences for many of these white clients. While being challenged on their belief systems regarding sexism, male entitlement, and dominance are not warmly welcomed messages, white clients are nonetheless more apt to internalize self-responsibility due to socialization differences.

The assumption of responsibility within interpersonal relationships is no doubt interrelated with personal constructs of gender. One study by Anderson and Umberson (2001) specifically examined the construction of gender within batterers' accounts of domestic violence. These researchers found that batterers used diverse strategies to present themselves as nonviolent, capable, and rational men. What is directly important among these findings is that these men called on cultural discourses, such as innate masculine aggression (which, as men, they cannot help but have), feminine weakness, and men's rights, to explain their actions and support their notion of being typically nonviolent, capable, and rational (Anderson and Umberson 2001). Likewise, these men exhibited the stereotypical external locus of control for their own behaviors by blaming their partners for the violence in the relationship and depicted themselves as victims of a biased criminal justice system (Anderson and Umberson 2001). From this research, it was concluded that violence against female partners was a means by which batterers reproduced binary frameworks of gender (Anderson and Umberson 2001).

This is interesting because it demonstrates how cultural belief systems of batterers generate the violence in their relationships. These belief systems may in fact not only serve to justify their abuse actions, but also serve as a buffer against external criticism and challenges that they may receive from therapists and other community members. An interesting study supports this notion by using a symbolic interactionist perspective to examine perception of battering among male perpetrators (Goodrum, Umberson, and Anderson 2001). This study demonstrated that batterers minimized the negative views of them that were held by others. Further, they dissociated themselves from their partners' physical and emotional injuries (Goodrum, Umberson, and Anderson 2001). The researchers pointed toward the need for research that examines how batterers construct their violent versus nonviolent self-images in other contexts, such as with friends or colleagues (Goodrum, Umberson, and Anderson 2001).

The two studies by Anderson and Umberson (2001) and Goodrum, Umberson, and Anderson (2001) demonstrated how batterers use cultural and personal justifications to construct definitions of both gender and self-image, while simultaneously buffering against external challenges that may be presented. These justifications may indeed be the central issue in why such violence tends to occur. But for the minority client, this may completely overlook other crucial cultural variables. Issues such as family identity and honor, extended family support, and religious and spiritual contexts may all be extremely important in keeping minority batterers in therapy. Thus feminist theories of intervention, based on batterer responsibility for self-behavior, will likely have to modify their treatment approaches in creating egalitarian relationships among many minority clients. An infusion of minority awareness, sensitivity, and knowledge is paramount to effective change.

Psychotherapy and/or group treatment is none-theless a process of belief change (Russell 1995). Effecting this change requires that beliefs be brought clearly into awareness and confronted, with alternate beliefs developed (Russell 1995). Batterer treatment, to be effective, must go beyond a topical approach where simple behaviors are addressed (Russell 1995). Rather, underlying belief systems that condone battering must be confronted and modified. With this in mind, it is necessary for therapists to be multiculturally sensitive to their clients' worldviews. By the same token, therapists cannot allow minority status to become a tool to evade responsibility for batterer clients. Providing such a balance between sensitivity to culturally influenced, externally attributed worldviews and feministic orientations regarding power, equality, and gender can be very difficult and test the skills of even the most seasoned therapists. But because feminist-educational curriculums dovetail so well with goals of criminal justice systems (Healey et al. 1998) and because the need for multicultural competence among batterer programs seems to be so pressing (Williams and Becker 1994), each of the two components are essential to effective treatment programs for minority batterers.

Conclusion

According to Healey and colleagues (1998), tailoring interventions to the needs and values of specific racial, ethnic, or subcultural groups is consistent with the feminist and social learning theoretical frameworks inherent in a wide number of batterer intervention programs. The feminist model, used widely by a large number of intervention programs, takes into account only one social factor related to battering, that of sexism. However, other social factors may also promote violence among both minority and nonminority clients (Healey et al. 1998). Due to this, it is the contention of this article that those programs which infuse cultural competence and culturally specific techniques into a feminist theoretical framework will tend to deliver optimal results in completion rates for minority clients.

ROBERT D. HANSER

See also **Africa: Domestic Violence and the Law; African American Community, Domestic Violence in; Asian Americans and Domestic Violence: Cultural Dimensions; Batterer Intervention Programs; Batterer Typology; Cross-Cultural Examination of Domestic Violence in China and Pakistan; Cross-Cultural Examination of Domestic Violence in Latin America; Cross-Cultural Perspectives on Domestic Violence; Cross-Cultural Perspectives on How to Deal with Batterers; Greece, Domestic Violence in; Jewish Community, Domestic Violence within the; Mediation in Domestic Violence; Minorities and Families in America, Introduction to; Spain, Domestic Violence in; Trinidad and Tobago, Domestic Violence in**

References and Further Reading

American Psychiatric Association. *Diagnostic and Statistical Manual of Mental Disorders,* 4th ed., text revision. Washington, DC: Author, 2000.

Anderson, K., and D. Umberson. "Gendering Violence: Masculinity and Power in Men's Accounts of Domestic Violence." *Gender and Society* 15, no. 3 (2001): 358–380.

Arredondo, P., and G. M. Arciniega. "Strategies and Techniques for Counselor Training Based on the Multicultural Counseling Competencies." *Journal of Multicultural Counseling and Development* 29, no. 4 (2001): 263–274.

Arredondo, P., and P. Perez. "Counseling Paradigms and Latina/o Americans: Contemporary Considerations." In *Culture and Counseling: New Approaches,* edited by F. D. Harper and J. McFadden. Boston: Allyn & Bacon, 2003, pp. 115–132.

Arredondo, P., and A. Santiago-Rivera. "Latino Dimensions of Personal Identity (Adapted from Personal Dimensions Identity Model)." Unpublished document, 2000.

Arredondo, P., R. Toporek, S. P. Brown, J. Jones, D. C. Locke, J. Sanchez, and H. Stadler. "Operationalization of the Multicultural Counseling Competencies." *Journal of Multicultural Counseling and Development* 24 (1996): 42–78.

Bonilla-Santiago, G. "Latina Battered Women: Barriers to Service Delivery and Cultural Considerations." In *Helping Battered Women: New Perspectives and Remedies,* edited by A. R. Roberts. New York: Oxford University Press, 1996, pp. 229–234.

Chang, H. "An Analysis of Attrition in Batterers' Counseling." PhD dissertation, University of Wisconsin–Madison. *Dissertation Abstracts International* 57, no. 11A (1996): 4929.

Chang, H., and D. G. Saunders. "Predictors of Attribution in Two Types of Group Programs for Men Who Batter." *Journal of Family Violence* 17, no. 3 (2002): 273–292.

Chin, J. L. "Mental Health Services and Treatment." In *Handbook of Asian American Psychology,* edited by L. C. Lee and N. W. S. Zane. Thousand Oaks, CA: Sage, 1998, pp. 485–504.

Corcoran, J. "Solution-Focused Family Therapy with Ethnic Minority Clients." *Crisis Intervention and Time-Limited Treatment* 6, no. 1 (2000): 5–12.

Dobash, R. E., R. P. Dobash, K. Cavanagh, and R. Lewis. *Changing Violent Men.* Thousand Oaks, CA: Sage Publications, 2000.

Edleson, J. L., and M. Syers. "The Effects of Group Treatment for Men Who Batter: An 18-Month Follow-Up Study." *Research on Social Work Practice* 1 (1991): 227–243.

Erez, E. "Immigration, Culture Conflict and Domestic Violence/Woman Battering." *Crime Prevention and Community Safety: An International Journal* 2, no. 1 (2000): 27–36.

Gim, R. H., D. R. Atkinson, and S. J. Kim. "Asian-American Acculturation, Counselor Ethnicity and Cultural Sensitivity, and Ratings of Counselors." *Journal of Counseling Psychology* 38 (1991): 57–62.

Gondolf, E. W., and J. Hanneken. "The Gender Warrior: Reformed Batterers on Abuse, Treatment, and Change." *Journal of Family Violence* 2, no. 2 (1987): 177–191.

Goodrum, S., D. Umberson, and K. L. Anderson. "The Batterer's View of the Self and Others in Domestic Violence." *Sociological Inquiry* 71, no. 2 (2001): 221–240.

Hanser, R. D. "Multicultural Aspects in Batterer Intervention Programs." PhD dissertation, Sam Houston State University, Huntsville, TX, 2002.

Healey, K., C. Smith, and C. O'Sullivan. *Batterer Intervention: Program Approaches and Criminal Justice Strategies.* Washington, DC: National Institute of Justice, 1998.

McGoldrick, M., J. Giordano, and J. K. Pearce. *Ethnicity and Family Therapy,* 2nd ed. New York: Guilford Press, 1996.

McWhirter, P. T. "La violencia privada: Domestic Violence in Chile." *American Psychologist* 54, no. 1 (1999): 21–29.

Pedersen, P. B. "Culturally Biased Assumptions in Counseling Psychology." *Counseling Psychologist* 31, no. 4 (2003a): 396–403.

———. "Increasing the Cultural Awareness, Knowledge, and Skills of Culture-Centered Counselors." In *Culture and Counseling,* edited by R. D. Harper and J. McFadden. Boston: Allyn and Bacon, 2003b, pp. 31–46.

Ridley, C. R., D. M. Baker, and C. L. Hill. "Critical Issues Concerning Cultural Competence." *Counseling Psychologist* 29, no. 6 (2001): 822–832.

Rotter, J. B. "Generalized Expectancies for Internal and External Control of Reinforcement." *Psychological Monographs: General and Applied* 80, no. 1 (1966).

Russell, M. N. *Confronting Abusive Beliefs: Group Treatment for Abusive Men.* Thousand Oaks, CA: Sage Publications, 1995.

Sandhu, D., A. Leung, and M. Tang. "Counseling Approaches with Asian Americans and Pacific Islander Americans." In Harper and McFadden, *Culture and Counseling,* edited by R. D. Harper and J. McFadden. Boston: Allyn and Bacon, 2003, pp. 31–46.

Saunders, D. G., and J. C. Parker. "Legal Sanctions and Treatment Follow Through among Men Who Batter: A Multivariate Analysis." *Social Work Research and Abstracts* 25, no. 3 (1989): 21–29.

Sue, D. W., and D. Sue. *Counseling the Culturally Different: Theory and Practice.* New York: John Wiley & Sons, 1999.

Tolman, R., and L. Bennett. "A Review of Quantitative Research on Men Who Batter." *Journal of Interpersonal Violence* 5, no. 1 (1990): 87–118.

Williams, O. "Ethnically Sensitive Practice to Enhance Treatment Participation of African-American Men Who Batter." *Families in Society: The Journal of Contemporary Human Services* (1992): 588–595.

———. "Healing and Confronting the African American Male Who Batters." In *Family Violence and Men of Color: Healing the Wounded Male Spirit,* edited by R. Carrillo and J. Tello. New York: Springer Publishing, 1998, pp. 74–94.

Williams, O., and R. L. Becker. "Domestic Partner Abuse Treatment Programs and Cultural Competence: The Results of a National Survey." *Violence and Victims* 9, no. 3 (1994): 287–296.

MUNCHAUSEN BY PROXY SYNDROME

Munchausen by proxy syndrome (MBP) is a form of child abuse in which a caretaker, usually the mother, exaggerates, fabricates, simulates, or induces symptoms of illness in a minor child. The caretaker presents the child for medical care while denying knowledge of symptom origin. The caretaker wants the child to be regarded as ill in order to meet his or her own self-serving psychological needs. When first identified in the literature, the falsified symptoms of illness were physical (Meadow 1977). The falsification of physical symptoms, and thus medical illness, remains the most commonly identified and physically dangerous form of MBP abuse. The feigning of psychological/psychiatric signs or symptoms has come to be commonly included in MBP definitions as well. In addition, there has been professional realization that caretakers may use other falsified signs or symptoms such as learning disabilities, developmental delays, and the falsification of child abuse allegations to meet their own self-serving psychological needs as well.

The perpetrator is often quite ingenious in the methods used to attempt to deceive medical personnel and other professionals. Most cases present with some mixture of exaggeration, false reporting, and symptom induction. Methods for feigning symptoms are incredibly diverse. These have included ostensibly rather benign actions such as lying, falsifying medical charts, and presenting one's own blood or other specimens as the child's. However, many cases have involved such serious and potentially lethal actions as suffocating the child, introducing foreign substances (oral, fecal, and vaginal secretions) into an intravenous line, poisoning, overdosing with laxatives, and giving medications not prescribed for the child. The medical symptoms which are thus falsified or induced are quite varied but commonly include apnea, anorexia or feeding problems, diarrhea, seizures, cyanosis, asthma, allergy, fevers, pain, bleeding, infections, and vomiting. Victims typically present with more than one symptom, which may involve multiple organ systems. This results in an often dizzying array of medical subspecialists who are evaluating and treating the child. As a result, the child-victim may experience numerous medical procedures, which are sometimes painful and invasive. Child-victims may begin life entirely healthy, while other children start life with prematurity or compromising illnesses. The perpetrator may fabricate illness where none exists; the child might really have an illness, about which the perpetrator exaggerates; or the perpetrator may be abusing the child by over- or undertreating an existing condition. Symptom induction commonly occurs even while the child is in the hospital, and has been documented to occur even after the perpetrator has been told that she is under suspicion for abusing her child.

In Dr. Roy Meadow's original article (1977), a mother simply added her own urine or menstrual discharge to her six-year-old daughter's specimens and presented her repeatedly for medical care due to foul smelling, bloody urine. This created such concern for the child that the following occurred:

> 12 hospital admissions, seven major X-ray procedures . . . , six examinations under anaesthetic, five cystoscopies, unpleasant treatment with toxic drugs and eight antibiotics, catheterizations, vaginal pessaries, and bactericidal, fungicidal, and oestrogen creams; the laboratories had cultured her urine more than 150 times and had done many other tests; sixteen consultants had been involved in her care. (p. 344)

While the child's mother never admitted any wrongdoing, specimens collected under strict supervision showed no abnormalities, while the ones collected by the mother or left in her presence were grossly abnormal. Furthermore, analysis of the mother's urine sample suggested that the unsupervised specimens contained some of the mother's urine. While the mother was under psychiatric care, the child had no further urinary problems.

The other case reported by Meadow involved a toddler boy who was having sudden attacks of vomiting and drowsiness associated with hypernatremia only at home. Extensive investigations showed no

problems with his endocrine and renal systems. Between attacks he was otherwise healthy and developing normally. Furthermore, during a prolonged hospital stay, the mother was excluded from visiting the boy and he had no illness until the weekend she was allowed to visit. It was believed that his illness was caused by extreme sodium administration, probably by the mother. During the time arrangements were being made to address these suspicions, the child was again admitted to the hospital and died. Meadow (1994) subsequently reported that the mother twenty years later admitted to killing her son.

Nomenclature and Definition

"Munchausen syndrome by proxy" was the name applied by Meadow in 1977 to those two cases of abuse in which the mother falsified illness in her child. (Baron von Munchausen was a popular eighteenth-century Prussian storybook figure with a gift for lies and tall tales.) Since Meadow's original work, there has been debate about the proper name to apply to this form of abuse. Munchausen by proxy syndrome, Munchausen by proxy, Polle's syndrome, factitious illness by proxy, and factitious disorder by proxy have all been used as alternative names. Although the American Psychiatric Association has yet to recognize MBP as a formal psychiatric diagnosis in the *Diagnostic and Statistical Manual of Mental Disorders*, fourth edition (DSM-IV), factitious disorder by proxy has been listed and described in the appendix for proposed categories requiring further study. The DSM-IV lists the following criteria in its definition of factitious disorder by proxy:

- Physical or psychological signs or symptoms in a person under another individual's care are intentionally produced or feigned.
- The motivation for the perpetrator's behavior is to assume the sick role by proxy.
- External incentives for the behavior (such as economic gain) are absent.
- The behavior is not better accounted for by another mental disorder. (American Psychiatric Association, 1994)

Other terms which are sometimes used in the literature interchangeably with Munchausen by proxy are *doctor shopping, help seeking, extreme illness exaggeration, enforced invalidism,* and *doctor addiction.*

These varied terms have also been used in circumstances that are quite different than the original cases identified by Dr. Meadow, which can lead to confusion. The reason for using these terms to apply to other seemingly diverse circumstances is the perceived similarity in the motivations of the perpetrators. The internal dynamics that lead a perpetrator to falsify physical illness in her child often, though not always, involve using the child as an object to build and maintain a relationship with health care professionals, possibly in order to obtain their attention and approval. Thus, a parent may falsify sexual and physical abuse, psychiatric symptoms, behavioral difficulties, developmental delays, and learning disabilities in efforts to maintain relationships with authority figures such as police investigators, child protection workers, lawyers, mental health professionals, and school personnel. The perpetrator again uses whatever means are available to fabricate, exaggerate, simulate, or induce signs of these problems and then presents the child for abuse examinations, special educational services, psychotropic medication, and other services that the child does not truly need. Adding additional confusion is the application of these labels to situations as diverse as adults using other adults or their pets as the proxy.

In an effort to provide some unity of not only the terminology but the behavior being described, the American Professional Society on the Abuse of Children (APSAC) Task Force on Munchausen by Proxy developed a comprehensive set of definitions for the constellation of behaviors currently being defined as MBP that professionals could use to more accurately communicate (Ayoub et al. 2002). The APSAC framework identifies the broader behavior of *abuse by condition falsification,* in which the victim could be a child or adult. A subgroup, *pediatric condition falsification,* is defined as a form of child maltreatment in which an adult falsifies physical and/or psychological signs and/or symptoms in a child-victim, causing the victim to be regarded as ill or impaired by others. When the perpetrating adult is believed to have intentionally falsified history or signs or symptoms in a child to meet the adult's own self-serving psychological needs, then the perpetrator is diagnosed with factitious disorder by proxy. Within this framework it is indicated that there are other situations that are abuse by pediatric condition falsification that do not involve the internal dynamics of factitious disorder by proxy in the perpetrator. These situations may have consequences for the victim which are equally as serious as factitious disorder by proxy, but the interventions required to protect the child and the treatment of the perpetrator and family are different. These other situations include

falsified sexual abuse allegations to obtain custody or harm the child's other parent, parental desire to keep a child home from school by using illness, and blatant falsification of symptoms as a cry for help from an overwhelmed parent. Other situations which may need to be differentiated from pediatric condition falsification or factitious disorder by proxy include classic child abuse or neglect, difficult or psychologically impaired parents caring for truly chronically ill children, and children being in the care of overanxious parents.

Perpetrators and Victims

Although most cases of MBP in the published literature are in the United States and the United Kingdom, cases have been reported from many other countries, and MBP is clearly not confined only to countries with complex systems of medical care. Statistics related to MBP rely upon single case studies and two larger-scale studies using meta-analysis (Rosenberg 1987; Sheridan 2003).

Biological mothers are the most common perpetrators of this form of abuse, and this article refers mostly to the perpetrators as mothers. However, there have been documented cases in which the perpetrator was a nonbiological mother, the father, a relative, a babysitter, or a nurse. Mother-perpetrators are a diverse group, but certain features seem to reoccur in many, but not all, of the identified cases. These features may be used to assist in raising suspicion about MBP, but only along with medical evidence that raises suspicion as well; and they should never be used in isolation or as the determining factor in identifying a case of MBP, as that must come only from the medical evidence. Each of these features may have alternate explanations or might not be present in a particular case at all.

The mother-perpetrator often has a background in the medical field, through either education, training, or employment. Alternatively, she may have wished for a career in the medical field that never materialized or be exceedingly well versed in the technical details of her child's medical condition. She may lie about other aspects of her life, even about things that are relatively easily confirmed or disputed, such as educational attainments, prior relationships, past heroic acts, or job history. Reviewing the mother's educational and employment records as well as interviewing family members and friends will usually be sufficient to detect such fabrications. The perpetrator may have a history of falsifying illness in herself. The mother's past medical records should be reviewed beginning from childhood when possible.

Although psychological evaluation of the mother-perpetrator is useful to gather background information, understand the mother's motivations, and gather information pertinent to treatment and reunification, it is important to note that psychological testing and interviews will often indicate no psychopathology at all (Parnell 1998). There has been no evidence to suggest that MBP perpetrators are psychotic, delusional, or in any way not in touch with reality. They are quite aware of their deliberate and intentional fabrications and abusive behavior. They may have coexisting psychiatric disorders such as depression, anxiety, eating disorders, or somatoform disorders (i.e., physical symptoms not fully explained by a medical condition), but these are not the precipitating reasons for the MBP behavior.

The mother-perpetrator's specific motivations for abusing her child in this manner may vary. There is no single motivation that is essential to this diagnosis, but rather the diagnosis depends upon the general motivation of the mother needing a sick child to serve her own psychological needs. In fact, there are many self-serving psychological needs that have motivated this type of abusive behavior in confirmed MBP cases. Some mothers are escaping stressful or abusive home environments. Some are trying to obtain the attention of absent spouses or family members. Some crave the attention and approval they receive from family and health care professionals for their extraordinary care of the sick child. Others seem to be motivated by the need to control and manipulate doctors and other health care professionals, who they perceive as being in positions of authority. There may be different motivations at different times or simultaneously. In addition, although external incentives (i.e., money) are exclusionary criteria in many diagnostic models, they may co-occur with the primary motivation.

Child-victims are most often infants and toddlers who are unable to disclose what is happening to them. Yet there are some reports of older children in the literature, and in fact these older victims are sometimes coached to participate in the deception or even falsify illness themselves (Libow 2000; Sanders 1995). Male and female children are abused in relatively equal numbers when the perpetrator is the mother. When the much less common scenario occurs and the father is the perpetrator, then male children are more often victimized. Victimization is a repeated pattern of behavior, and those cases that have been eventually detected have gone on for months or years. More than one child in the family may be victimized, and often the method of victimization is the same among siblings. Symptoms are often produced while the child-victim is in the hospital. More than half of the time, the perpetrator actually does something physically to the victim to cause the symptoms, rather than just fabricating, exaggerating, or having the victim simulate illness.

The impact on the victim of MBP is not well understood, since this form of abuse is really still in the early stages of identification and case management. What is known is that the child-victim may suffer unnecessary physical pain either from the parent's actions or from the intrusive medical procedures ordered by the physician as a result of the deception. Over time the child may experience reduced opportunity to participate in age-appropriate social and educational activities due to repeated or protracted hospitalizations. This may result in long-term developmental disruption. Case reports and one larger-scale study (Bools, Neale, and Meadow 1993) have found conduct and emotional problems for the children, as well as problems related to school and limitations on their lifestyle by questionable or now real disabilities. In adults who had been child-victims of this type of abuse, problems include posttraumatic symptoms, feelings of inadequacy, relationship problems, and poor self-esteem (Libow 1995). In addition, there may be long-term physical damage which results, once again, from the mother's direct actions or from the unnecessary medical procedures performed to deal with the conditions she has created. MBP abuse can be fatal (Rosenberg 1987; Sheridan 2003).

It is important for survivors, practitioners, and others with healthy concerns in these children's lives to recognize that this form of child abuse violates the most basic sense of trust and security in the parent–child relationship—typically during the important early years of attachment.

Diagnosis

A significant obstacle to the diagnosis of MBP has been the failure of medical professionals to consider the possibility. Although physicians are trained to consider the reliability of a historian, they are not trained to consider the possibility that everything they hear from a parent may be a complete and elaborate fabrication. With the attention that has now been given to this form of child abuse, identification of cases is on the rise. However, suspicion will often hover around a case before an abuse report is made or other actions are taken to truly investigate the possibility of abuse. The diagnosis of MBP has been fraught with controversy

(Allison and Roberts 1998; McGill 2002). Under-pinning this controversy are three main issues. First, the perpetrators are primarily mothers and usually biological mothers. In our society it seems impossible that a mother could perpetrate such heinous abuse on her own child. Furthermore, most, although not all, of the mother-perpetrators present in a very positive manner to medical professionals, exhibiting behavior that is viewed as attentive, caring, and nurturing. In light of this, accusing such a mother of this bizarre form of medical child abuse is typically met with resistance and disbelief by other medical professionals and the perpetrator's family. In fact, these accusations are sometimes turned around to accuse the abuse reporter and/or the physician of formulating these accusations for their own gain (i.e., to cover up medical mistakes, to avoid acknowledging uncertainty regarding the child's problems). Not unexpectedly for any deceptive and ultimately criminal behavior, the perpetrator does not readily admit her MBP abuse of the child.

The second issue is the drama which often surrounds these cases. Even in the face of irrefutable evidence, the mother-perpetrator often maintains her denial and due to her otherwise stellar parenting and persuasive demeanor, family, friends, attorneys, and mental health professionals are drawn in to her deception and become zealous advocates. Some of these mothers seem to enjoy the excitement of the spotlight and seek attention from the media, politicians, and other high-profile public figures. These cases have also caught the attention of the popular media, being depicted in made-for-TV movies and TV series, novels, true crime books, and various news shows and documentaries. In addition, a few very sensational cases involving multiple child deaths have been labeled MBP cases and received extensive media coverage.

The third issue driving this controversy has been the process of identifying and confirming MBP cases. In early efforts to raise awareness of the possibility of MBP in seemingly caring families, features of the mother-perpetrator and the family system were identified as factors to consider in identification. However, even though it was cautioned that the indicators most salient for identification of cases were those involving the medical condition of the child (Parnell 1998), there was an overreliance on the behavior/personality features of the perpetrator and the family system. While these latter features are vitally important in the long-term management of the case, the initial diagnosis or identification must rely upon the current medical condition of the child, the child's past

medical record, and medical evidence of induction, simulation, fabrication, or exaggeration. If the medical evidence is not thoroughly and meticulously compiled, the likelihood of inaccurate identification of a case increases.

MBP concerns must be taken seriously due to the significant short- and long-term impact on the child-victim, including the possibility of death. At the same time, professionals must always consider and rule out other possible explanations for the concerns raised in a given case. In order to accurately include or exclude this diagnosis, suspected cases require an immediate and well-organized multidisciplinary investigation with a systematic approach to diagnostic clarification that relies primarily on the medical evidence.

The multidisciplinary team will consist of members of the child's medical team, a physician consultant, child protection team coordinator or child protective services worker, law enforcement officer, psychologist or psychiatrist, prosecutor, and, if hospitalized, nurses and the hospital social worker. The first goal of the team should be child safety, but each professional will have his or her own agenda. Legal, medical, mental health, and family issues are all represented. The medical information immediately available will be reviewed and a determination made regarding whether the case warrants further investigation and also whether the child requires immediate intervention to ensure safety. If the case requires further investigation and/or immediate intervention, the team will develop a plan for both of those issues. For instance, having the child hospitalized for monitoring or requesting court involvement to remove a child from the parent's custody could be pursued. Medical documents not readily available or prior medical professionals who need to be contacted will be identified. The team will decide the immediate steps required to intervene on the child's behalf.

As with other forms of abuse, determining whether MBP occurred will usually be based upon circumstantial rather than direct evidence. It is rare that the abusive act of the perpetrator is directly observed, although it does occur, as will be discussed below. However, more commonly, the diagnosis will be made based upon a thorough review of the child's medical history and current condition by a qualified medical expert. In essence, the goal is to review every piece of paper about the child-victim that can be obtained (i.e., inpatient and outpatient medical records, day care records, school records). The expert has a responsibility to review the information personally and not depend on someone else. The consequences of inaccurately diagnosing

MBP or of inaccurately dismissing the diagnosis are too grave. The review of medical records will offer an opportunity to determinate the accuracy of the medical history provided by the mother, confirm whether the mother has fabricated diagnoses or lab findings, and expose lack of continuity of medical care of the child. In addition, review of the records will highlight any inconsistencies between medical findings and reported symptoms, expose diagnoses that do not match medical findings, and confirm that all measures have been taken to exclude possible medical explanations for the child's condition. An attempt should be made to obtain and review the mother-perpetrator's medical records as well as the medical records for the mother's other children, as evidence of illness falsification may be obtained.

When necessary the history provided by the mother should be verified by personal contact with prior health care providers. The expert must be careful to trace every supposed diagnosis of the child back to the original health care provider. Often medical records simply repeat information stated by the parent and/or the history as reported in prior records. Information regarding the mother's interaction patterns with the child-victim and others is often noted by nurses and social workers in the records as well. The records may also provide evidence of the temporal relationship between the child-victim's symptoms and the presence of the mother. The expert should talk to anyone who has ever seen the child's reported symptoms from their beginning. Review of the medical records may reveal additional procedures which are needed to either rule out other medical causes for the child's condition or detect methods of symptom induction. This may include toxicology screens, monitor recordings of heart rate and respiratory patterns, hematology screens, microbiology studies, or other tests of blood, urine, and vomit samples. It is imperative that such actions be taken in a timely manner and that samples be treated in accordance with the handling of specimens as forensic evidence.

Thorough review of the medical records and history should be sufficient to confirm or dispute a diagnosis of MBP in most cases. However, there are times when more information may be needed because the medical expert is unsure of the diagnosis or there is insufficient evidence to ensure protection of the child-victim. Directed monitoring of the child's environment may be necessary while additional evidence is gathered. This can be accomplished safely only in the hospital. Directed monitoring means controlling aspects of the child's environment, not simply watching the family to see what happens. For instance, the child could be monitored closely at all times with special focus on documenting times when any visitors, including the mother, are present. At those times, there should always be medical personnel present in the room. In addition, no access to the child's records should be allowed, no food or drink should be brought in to the child except by nurses, and the parent should not participate in any medical care given to the child.

Another possibility is to separate the mother from the child by restricting her access to the child entirely. This could occur in a hospital setting after the multidisciplinary team has recommended such action and a court order has been obtained. However, such separation could also occur without hospital admission if a court order were obtained for an emergency shelter care placement. The shelter/foster home should be a medical shelter/foster home. The foster parent will need to document very carefully all aspects of the child's condition and functioning, especially specific to alleged medical conditions (e.g., food intake, allergies, symptoms, medications). Separation of mother and child sometimes provides very clear evidence as the child's condition improves markedly. However, this may not occur in cases where there is also a bona fide medical condition, the symptoms occur only infrequently, the perpetrator's abuse has now caused a true medical condition, or an older child is colluding in the falsification of illness.

In some cases, the best approach to diagnostic certainty is for the child to be monitored by video surveillance while in the hospital. The video surveillance is not disclosed to the parent and often not disclosed to all of the medical staff. Video surveillance is a controversial issue in which the child's right to safety is weighed against the parent's privacy. Video surveillance should never be undertaken without a multidisciplinary team of professionals first determining whether this is the appropriate action and then developing a detailed plan. Moreover, a court order for the surveillance should be obtained. However, when a child's safety can be protected as a result of the surveillance, the child's right to be free from future abuse and possible death must be paramount. Furthermore, visual evidence of the abusive behavior by the mother may be the only way to convince others, including a judge, that abuse is occurring and to protect the child during the often-lengthy child protective services process. Video surveillance has documented specific perpetrator acts such as choking or smothering a child, injecting substances into an intravenous line, and falsifying specimens. Clearly, this is a potentially dangerous approach to confirming abuse suspicions and should be done only in accordance with carefully defined protocols (Parnell 1998).

Case Management and Treatment

If suspicions of MBP were not quickly dismissed and the previously described investigation occurred, it is likely that the court will already be involved via the child protective services division. If the MBP diagnosis is then confirmed, the child will need to be removed from the care of the family and placed in an entirely neutral environment, usually a medical foster home, so that the child's condition may be carefully monitored and scrupulously recorded. Initial placement with extended-family members is not recommended. Although often cooperative with child protective services, extended-family members usually support the mother-perpetrator in her denial and will need additional information before being in a position to properly protect the child-victim. Contact between the mother and the child should not be permitted until the mother is fully engaged in psychotherapy.

Psychological evaluation is often useful during this time to gather more information about the mother-perpetrator and her relationship with the child-victim. The evaluation may establish the issues that led to the MBP abuse or, in the alternative, those issues that led to an erroneous suspicion of MBP. The psychologist can gather all of the pertinent psychosocial information, including medical, psychological, family, childrearing, and educational background. This will be accomplished through interviewing the mother and other family members, reviewing pertinent records of the mother, and conducting psychological testing. The evaluation will also identify any other individual or family issues that need to be addressed when considering reunification of the perpetrator and child. The psychologist will develop a plan for treatment of the perpetrator, including her prognosis and the estimated length of treatment. The evaluator may also address placement of the child and potential for reunification with the mother.

Psychological evaluation of the child may be beneficial to establish his/her emotional, social, and general developmental condition. Especially if the child-victim is preschool age or older, the evaluation should be done quickly to ascertain what the child's understanding is about what is happening, to determine the child's capacity to participate in play therapy, and to identify treatment issues. Of most importance, however, is to interview the child, even if full evaluation is not conducted. Older children can and sometimes do disclose the specific abusive behavior of the parent that led to the MBP allegations.

A swift resolution of the abuse investigation is very important as in all cases of suspected abuse. If the child has been abused, that needs to be clearly identified through proper investigation, a case plan should be developed, and a determination made regarding the possibility of reunification. If the child has not been abused, then reunification should occur quickly but with a plan to address any other problems which may have led to the suspicion in the first place. Unfortunately, it is not uncommon for an abuse report to be made and the child to be removed, but a thorough medical, psychological, and child protection investigation is not conducted and the case plan is merely a routine document of parenting classes and evaluation with an inexperienced psychologist. Professionals are often uncertain how to proceed, and the case lingers for a lengthy period of time. In such cases, sometimes the court has returned the child to the parents' care due to this passage of time and the inadequacy of the child protection response. Needless to say, this is not beneficial for the child or family.

Treatment of child abuse perpetrators represents many challenges, not the least of which is attempting treatment of an individual who denies wrongdoing. MBP perpetrator treatment is most effective with individuals who are able to admit to the specific acts of abuse toward their children and willingly participate in treatment and have few additional psychological problems. Treatment of perpetrators has been successful with intensive individual therapy (Parnell and Day 1998), a family systems approach (Sanders 1996), and an intensive inpatient program working with the individual and the family (Berg and Jones 1999). However, this success has been limited to a relatively small number of cases. Yet, reunification of the child-victim and mother-perpetrator should not be attempted without successful treatment of the mother. Some indicators of successful perpetrator treatment are continued acknowledgment of the abuse of the child, recognition of the emotional and physical impact of the abuse on the child, ability to put the child's needs first, resolution of internal or family issues which may have influenced the decision to engage in abuse of the child, and demonstration of alternative coping skills. In addition, in order to ensure child safety, long-term case management of the family must occur, which includes careful coordination of ongoing medical care of the child, monitoring by a child protective services worker, communication with the child's school, and family therapy.

Summary

MBP is a form of child abuse that may have both short-term and long-term physical and psychological consequences for the victim. While the mother-perpetrator's actions may be driven by complex psychological processes, the focus of these cases must remain the definition of the problem as one of a dangerous type of child maltreatment.

TERESA F. PARNELL

See also **Child Abuse and Juvenile Delinquency; Child Neglect; Child Sexual Abuse; Coercive Control; Medical Neglect Related to Religion and Culture; Mothers Who Kill; Postpartum Depression, Psychosis, and Infanticide; Stockholm Syndrome in Battered Women; Victim-Blaming Theory**

References and Further Reading

Allison, David B., and Mark S. Roberts. *Disordered Mother or Disordered Diagnosis? Munchausen by Proxy Syndrome.* Hillsdale, NJ: Analytic Press, 1998.

American Psychiatric Association. *Diagnostic and Statistical Manual of Mental Disorders,* 4th ed. Washington, DC: Author, 1994.

Artingstall, Kathryn. *Practical Aspects of Munchausen by Proxy and Munchausen Syndrome Investigation.* Boca Raton, FL: CRC Press, 1999.

Ayoub, Catherine C., Randell Alexander, David Beck, Brenda Bursch, Kenneth W. Feldman, Judith Libow, Mary J. Sanders, Herbert A. Schreier, and Beatrice Yorker. "Position Paper: Definitional Issues in Munchausen by Proxy." *Child Maltreatment* 11, no. 1 (2002): 105–111.

Ayoub, Catherine C., Herbert A. Schreier, and Carol Keller. "Munchausen by Proxy: Presentations in Special Education." *Child Maltreatment* 7, no. 2 (2002): 149–159.

Berg, B., and D. P. Jones. "Outcome of Psychiatric Intervention in Factitious Illness by Proxy (Munchausen's Syndrome by Proxy)." *Archives of Disease in Childhood* 81, no. 6 (1999): 465–472.

Bools, Christopher, Brenda A. Neale, and Roy Meadow. "Follow Up of Victims of Fabricated Illness (Munchausen Syndrome by Proxy)." *Archives of Disease in Childhood* 69 (1993): 625–630.

Eminson, Mary, and R. J. Postlethwaite. *Munchausen Syndrome by Proxy Abuse: A Practical Approach.* Boston: Butterworth-Heinemann, 2000.

Gregory, Julie, and Marc D. Feldman. *Sickened: The Memoir of a Munchausen by Proxy Childhood.* New York: Bantam Dell, 2003.

Lasher, Louisa J., and Mary S. Sheridan. *Munchausen by Proxy: Identification, Intervention, and Case Management.* Binghamton, NY: Haworth Maltreatment and Trauma Press, 2004.

Levin, Alex V., and Mary S. Sheridan. *Munchausen Syndrome by Proxy: Issues in Diagnosis and Treatment.* San Francisco: Jossey-Bass, 1995.

Libow, Judith A. "Munchausen by Proxy Victims in Adulthood: A First Look." *Child Abuse and Neglect* 19 (1995): 1131–1142.

———. "Child and Adolescent Illness Falsification." *Pediatrics* 105, no. 2 (2000): 336–342.

Mart, Eric G. *Munchausen's Syndrome by Proxy Reconsidered.* Manchester, NH: Bally Vaughan Publishing, 2002.

McGill, Craig. *Do No Harm? Munchausen Syndrome by Proxy.* London: Vision Paperbacks, 2002.

Meadow, Roy. "Munchausen Syndrome by Proxy: The Hinterland of Child Abuse." *Lancet* 2, no. 8033 (1977): 343–345.

———. "Who's to Blame—Mothers, Munchausen or Medicine?" *Journal of the Royal College of Physicians of London* 28, no. 4 (1994): 332–337.

Muttukrishna, Shanthi. *Munchausen's Syndrome by Proxy: Current Issues in Assessment.* London: Imperial College Press, 2001.

Parnell, Teresa F., and Deborah O. Day. *Munchausen by Proxy Syndrome: Misunderstood Child Abuse.* Thousand Oaks, CA: Sage Publications, 1998.

Rosenberg, Donna. "Web of Deceit: A Literature Review of Munchausen Syndrome by Proxy." *Child Abuse and Neglect* 11, no. 4 (1987): 547–563.

———. "Munchausen Syndrome by Proxy." In *Child Abuse: Medical Diagnosis and Management,* edited by Robert M. Reece. Philadelphia: Lea & Febiger, 1994, pp. 266–278.

Sanders, Mary J. "Symptom Coaching: Factitious Disorder by Proxy with Older Children." *Clinical Psychology Review* 15, no. 5 (1995): 423–442.

———. "Narrative Family Treatment of Munchausen by Proxy: A Successful Case." *Families, Systems and Health* 14, no. 13 (1996): 315–329.

Schreier, Herbert A., and Judith A. Libow. *Hurting for Love: Munchausen by Proxy Syndrome.* New York: Guilford Press, 1993.

Sheridan, Mary S. "The Deceit Continues: An Updated Literature Review of Munchausen by Proxy Syndrome." *Child Abuse and Neglect* 27, no. 4 (2003): 431–451.

MUTUAL BATTERING

Common beliefs about the form of domestic violence termed *mutual battering* assume that it involves physical, verbal, and/or psychological fighting between married intimate partners. The term can, however, be extended to include types of abuse between other family members such as siblings, cousins, and same-sex partners. In fact, many discussions about mutual battering seem to focus on same-sex partners (Asherah 2003; Haugen 2005; Renzetti 1993). Furthermore, it is also said to occur during adolescent dating (Ely, Dulmus, and Wodarski 2002). For purposes of this essay, however, the focus will be on abuse between adult intimates. The scenario plays as if the fault for the abuse lies equally with each individual who takes part in the conflict. Each person is perceived to be both perpetrator and victim. Each party seeks to control the behavior of the other by exerting some form of power over the other using whatever is at his/her disposal: wit, muscles, emotions, verbal criticisms, or psychological threats. Whatever works best for the abuser is what he/she will use to exert power and control over an intimate partner.

According to Ellen Pense and Michael Paymar (1993), mutual battering, like abuse by one partner against the other, is also "coupled with the threat or use of violence to control what the other partner thinks, does, or feels" (p. 2). In the case of mutual battering, there is often the assumption that both partners in the relationship exhibit abusive and controlling behaviors. When such conflict occurs, the perpetrator's intent is almost always to control the behavior of the other partner in the relationship. The above scenario of abuse is considered to be an age-old phenomenon. There are many instances where partners (homosexual or heterosexual) hit each other, and the conflict between the couple turns into an all-out brawl, tit-for-tat. One partner is considered to be just as much to blame as the other. Herein lies the dilemma in describing the form of domestic violence called mutual battering.

The Debate

The crux of the debate surrounding this form of domestic violence can be summed up with the following questions: Is mutual battering a myth? Should it more accurately be described as a form of self-defense? According to many advocates for abuse survivors, what accounts for mutually abusive behavior is the individual's response to abuse. It is considered a reaction, a defense mechanism used in order to thwart a partner's attempt to gain power and control in the relationship (Asherah 2003; Haugen 2005; Sarantakos 2004). It is also argued to be a person's way of controlling the resources (i.e., material or symbolic) within the course of the relationship (Renzetti 1993). The assertion here is that someone must "rule the roost."

In a relationship where abuse occurs, victims' advocates argue that victims of abuse often fight back to protect themselves against being controlled and to maintain an equal status with their partners within the relationships. Each individual is trying to assert him/herself to some degree, but the physically and emotionally stronger person may be the perpetrator of the abuse, while the other partner is (re)acting, either physically or emotionally, in defense of his/her life.

The other side of the debate holds that mutual battering is common in a culture characterized by violence. People tend to handle disputes through the use of violence; hence violence within the context of an intimate environment such as the home is no exception. Rapp-Paglicci, Roberts, and Wodarski (2002) assert that intimates deal with conflict in an aggressive way, especially when there is difficulty dealing with the stress of making a living in the larger society. One must therefore take into account the role that culture plays in shaping how partners cope with conflict. People tend to mimic what goes on in the larger society, and in a culture that seems to glorify violence, it should not be surprising that people living in that society cope with life stressors (e.g., work, school, finances) in aggressive ways.

Those who argue that women are just as likely to be abusive as men in their intimate relationships point out the prevalence of female aggression in many parts of the world (Sarantakos 2004). It is further asserted that women's violence toward their partners is not always an act of self-defense or a case of fighting back, though much of the research on domestic abuse focuses on women as victims, not perpetrators. Traditional research seems to dismiss abuse initiated by women against their partners. Again, the nature of the culture in which they live influences the perceptions of the role of women not only in the larger society, but in the household as well (Mills 2003). Some experts question claims of self-defense whenever women are the aggressors in abusive relationships (Haugen 2005; Lawrence 2003; Migliaccio 2001). They hold that women's violent behavior in their intimate relationships should not be viewed as an anomaly or as simply a case of fighting back. Rather, women's violence toward their partners should be viewed as an extension of the violence in the larger society. Both women and men are products of the larger culture, and as such, will mimic within the household the same kinds of responses to conflict exhibited in the larger society.

In research on domestic violence, mutual battering seems to be synonymous with female aggression in intimate relationships. There do not seem to be any studies devoted to cases of mutual combat where both partners engaged equally in abusive behaviors. Is there competition between partners within these relationships for power and control? Does this competition sometimes result in violence within the household? Does the outcome of these fights result in a "draw" between partners, and if so, does the mutual battering recur? Future research on the social problem of domestic violence is needed in order to address more seriously the issue of mutual battering. The gap in the existing literature shows the need to definitively prove the existence of mutual battering as a legitimate form of domestic violence and to more concretely debunk the myth that it does not exist.

CAROLYN E. GROSS

See also **Battered Husbands; Battered Woman Syndrome; Batterer Typology; Coercive Control; Cohabiting Violence; Dating Violence; Gay and Bisexual Male** Domestic Violence; Lesbian Battering; Marital Rape; Sexual Aggression Perpetrated by Females

References and Further Reading

Ammerman, Robert T., and Michel Hersen. *Assessment of Family Violence: A Clinical and Legal Sourcebook.* New York: John Wiley & Sons, 1992.

Asherah, Karen Lee. "The Myth of Mutual Abuse," 2003. http://www.nwnetwork.org/articles/4.html.

Burgess, Ann W., and Albert R. Roberts. "Violence within Families through the Life Span." In *Handbook of Violence,* edited by Lisa A. Rapp-Paglicci, Albert R. Roberts, and John S. Wodarski. New York: John Wiley & Sons, 2002, pp. 3–33.

Ely, Gretchen, Catherine N. Dulmus, and John S. Wodarski. "Adolescent Dating Violence." In Rapp-Paglicci, Roberts, and Wodarski, *Handbook of Violence,* 2002, pp. 34–53.

Hansen, Marsali, and Michele Harway, eds. *Battering and Family Therapy.* Newbury Park, CA: Sage Publications, 1993.

Haugen, David M., ed. *Domestic Violence: Opposing Viewpoints.* Detroit: Greenhaven Press, 2005.

Kurst-Swanger, Karen, and Jacqueline L. Petcosky. *Violence in the Home: Multidisciplinary Perspectives.* New York: Oxford University Press, 2003.

Lawrence, Susan. "Domestic Violence and Men." *Nursing Standard* 17, no. 40 (June 2003): 41–43.

McCuen, Gary E. *Crimes of Gender: Violence against Women.* Hudson, WI: GEM Publications, 1994.

Migliaccio, Todd A. "Marginalizing the Battered Male." *Journal of Men's Studies* 9, no. 2 (Winter 2001): 205.

Mills, Linda G. *Insult to Injury: Rethinking Our Responses to Intimate Abuse.* Princeton, NJ: Princeton University Press, 2003.

Pense, Ellen, and Michael Paymar. "Education Groups for Men Who Batter: The Duluth Model," 1993. http://menweb.org/throop/battery/commentary/duluth.html.

Rapp-Paglicci, Lisa A., Albert R. Roberts, and John S. Wodarski, eds. *Handbook of Violence.* New York: John Wiley & Sons, 2002.

Renzetti, Claire. "Violence in Lesbian Relationships." In Hansen and Harway, *Battering and Family Therapy,* 1993, pp. 188–199.

Sarantakos, Sotirios. "Deconstructing Self-Defense in Wife-to-Husband Violence." *Journal of Men's Studies* 12, no. 3 (Spring 2004): 277–292.

N

NATIVE AMERICANS, DOMESTIC VIOLENCE AMONG

The United States is a culturally diverse society, and the problem of domestic violence needs to be examined across all of its different cultures. When discussing domestic violence in relation to Native Americans, it is important to remember that only generalities can be used, as there is great diversity within this broad ethnic label. There are more than 500 federally recognized American Indian/Alaska Native tribal nations. Each of these tribal nations possesses distinct cultures and traditions. According to Census 2000, there are 2.5 million American Indians and Alaska Natives in the United States.

While some aspects of domestic violence may supersede culture, cultural considerations need to be made when developing community response mechanisms and designing treatment or other interventions and services. Acknowledging that domestic violence exists in Native American cultures may be viewed as criticizing the culture itself. Native Americans may fear that dominant society will use any information about domestic violence within their communities to reinforce negative stereotypes. Native American people still face many problems in addition to domestic violence, including racism,

prejudice, and discrimination. Yet, recognizing differences in history and experiences of racism and oppression, as well as differences in cultural and religious beliefs, is important in designing responses to address domestic violence.

Native Americans are victims of crime at more than double the national rate. For some crimes the rates are even higher; for instance, reported rape rates in 2004 were 2 per 1,000 for all races but 35 per 1,000 for Native Americans. According to the Department of Justice, Native American females are victimized by a partner at rates much greater than other ethnic groups. Their rate of 23 victims per 1,000 is more than double the rate of the next highest group, African American females. Native American victims of intimate and family violence are also more likely than victims of other races to be injured and need hospital care.

It is also important to note that at least 70 percent of the violence experienced by Native Americans is committed by persons of a different race, which is quite different than the typical intraracial violence experienced by other victims. Among Native American victims of violence, 75 percent of the intimate victimizations and 25 percent of the family victimizations involved an offender of a different race. This means that Native Americans are victimized outside of their own race more than other ethnic groups.

Traditional Beliefs

While it is impossible to make generalized statements about all aspects of Native American culture, most tribes share the same belief that every living thing has its own special place in the universe. Women were valued and honored in traditional native cultures. Almost all native creation stories have women being made first. Many of the spiritual teachings speak to the gifts of creation and wisdom brought by sacred women. Even the earth itself is thought of as female, and native people were taught to honor their connection to it. The teachings relate an important balance and interconnectedness between males and females who respect each other.

Historically, many Native American communities were matrilineal, both following the woman's bloodline and living in the woman's community. Either the husband or the wife could initiate a divorce if he or she wished. Traditionally, a high value was placed on the role of women, their linkage to the earth, and the giving of life; therefore, to abuse a woman would be like abusing Mother Earth and showing irreverence toward life, thus breaking a sacred bond. Domestic violence against women violates the Native American traditional belief that everything is sacred and bonded together, especially with regard to women, who are the bearers of life. As it is believed that everything has its own special place in the universe and should be respected, not abused, abuse of a family member is not "traditional," because it breaks the sacred bonds of respect.

To many Native Americans, family is part of a broad kinship and tribal network; its strength is based on interdependence and group affiliation, so a high value is placed on cooperation and harmony. Along with this interdependence, individuals are each expected to be responsible for their own behavior. Many Native Americans view themselves in terms of their role within the bigger group rather than as individuals. There may also be an emphasis on the importance of extended family and cultural spirituality.

In many tribes when violence has been committed against a woman, the community feels the need to respond to restore the harmony that is essential for survival of the tribe. A man who was violent within his family showed that he did not possess the self-discipline, respect, or spiritual understanding to lead his people; therefore, he would not be given any leadership opportunities within the tribe. The abuser could also be ostracized, be retaliated against by the male relatives of the victim, or even banished.

Traditionally, parenting methods and marital relationships were nonviolent and attempted to nurture the spirit of each individual and instill respect. With colonization by Europeans came the introduction of alcohol and corporal punishment teachings from Christianity. In the past two centuries, many youths also experienced violence in boarding schools. As reservations were established, the traditional male role of "protector" within many tribes was taken away by the American government. Native people were also exposed to the negative beliefs and behaviors toward women evident in the now-dominant culture. While Native American women often traditionally held key tribal positions and were honored for their role as life-givers and nurturers, this role was usurped by the European notion that women were little more than property. Unlike some native cultures that were matrilineal or others in which women were free to choose or reject their partners and in which men lived with their wives' people, the European practice was to have women take the last name of their husbands and wear a ring to show that they were no longer sexually available, since they belonged to the specific man who could treat his property however he chose.

Native people were taught, often through violent means and the passing of laws by the American government, to despise and fear their own cultural and spiritual ways. Language and traditions were often given up as the Native people experienced oppression bordering on genocide. This external oppression gradually created an internal oppression keeping native people divided and critical of each other, which in turn fostered further violence among native tribes, resulting in feelings of isolation, fear, and despair.

In the absence of traditional tribal ways of dealing with marital conflict, domestic violence has become a large problem for Native American women today. Native American victims living on reservations face many challenges when dealing with domestic violence, similar to those faced by other rural victims—such as limited access to telephones, transportation, and victim services. Additionally, Native Americans may face the complex issue of navigating tribal and state jurisdictions, where the jurisdiction depends on where the crime was committed, who committed the crime, and exactly what crime was committed. These jurisdictional issues may limit who will respond to calls for help from an abuse victim, and since many tribes do not have jails, there may be less incentive to arrest or enforce the laws. It is important to note that a protection order issued by one state or tribe is valid and enforceable in any other state or tribal jurisdiction.

Approaches to Dealing with Domestic Violence among Native Americans

There are two dominant approaches to dealing with domestic violence. One approach is often referred to as the "legal model," which is supported by dominant society and many feminists. The other approach is referred to as the "mediation model," which is supported by the informal justice movement and many Native American communities. The dominant legal model has focused on arrest and prosecution policies, treatment programs for batterers, and restraining orders for the protection of victims. The mediation model emphasizes the importance of the involvement of the community and urges reconciliation and addressing the problem.

Many minority groups have a deep-seated distrust of the dominant culture and thus may believe that the police, social services, courts, and others will not actually act in a protective fashion, and so they will not seek help from these resources. The stress of racism, discrimination in employment opportunities, and other economic inequalities may create additional barriers to leaving or changing a violent situation. Even simply the lack of bilingual capacity may force Native Americans to not utilize available services. Additionally, many services ignore or negatively label cultural beliefs which may be helpful in addressing interpersonal violence. Native American victims as well as batterers may also view therapy or treatment programs as another attempt by the dominant culture to be oppressive and controlling. This view may contribute to underutilization of treatment and premature dropout of those who do use such services.

In contemporary Native American communities, breaking a law or committing an act which is classified as breaking a norm or as being antisocial can cause tribal society to react with a sanction against the offender. Some alternative approaches to the intervention of the dominant society's criminal justice system include tribal justice systems and restorative justice, which turns to community support rather than the formal legal process to provide group conferencing and sentencing circles. Because

many of today's adult Native Americans were placed in foster care or sent to boarding schools when they were young, many have developed a deep-seated fear or resentment of state and federal government agencies; because of this, they may respond better to these alternative sanctions decided on by their tribal leaders. What is deemed an appropriate sanction for a particular act varies from tribe to tribe. Depending on the tribe involved and the traditional practices of that tribe, forms of redress for the victim of domestic violence often include some type of offering for the victim, for the benefit of the tribe, and/or to appease the spiritual beings associated with the tribe.

It is recognized that domestic violence affects more than the immediate couple. It also affects the couple's children, as well as the larger family, which traditionally includes many relatives and a greater number of people than the "nuclear family" of the dominant culture. Therefore, in tribal communities, there is typically a large supportive group of people able to help both the victim and the offender. When reentering the community, the offender has to ask forgiveness from the victims and their community. While the tribe has a say in what will happen to the offender, in many tribes the victim also has a say, but in some tribes the victim has no say in the matter.

Treatment for victims on the reservation is difficult because many reservations do not have sufficient funds to support treatment centers and programs. Therefore, victims usually have to go to an outside source for help. To date there has been little systematic research conducted and few clinical interventions developed specific to Native American domestic violence victims. To assist Native American victims of domestic violence, researchers need to examine why Native American women are more heavily victimized than many other ethnic groups. It will also be important to understand why domestic violence is committed predominantly by intimate partners of other races.

There are new programs which are designed to encourage an appreciation for indigenous cultures and foster pride in one's connection with one's culture and perhaps guide movement toward a more traditional lifestyle. Services and resources within such programs usually are culturally sensitive to Native American customs and traditions. Developing such programs can be difficult because in order to show respect for and protect the traditional Native American culture, many tribes do not print or share information about many of their traditional ways. Yet, ending violence against Native American women is integral to reclaiming traditional ways.

There is also an effort to develop community-based responses and examine tribal legal codes so crimes can be appropriately addressed. There has also been a push to develop methods to generate and record demographically specific statistics for the Native American population.

There is little research specifically on domestic violence in Native American communities. While most Native Americans do not condone domestic violence, they do view it differently. Because of the extended kinship networks and the general view that there is relative equality and interdependence between men and women, violence in the family is not seen as a gender or feminist issue where the man alone is to blame. Since both men and women bear responsibility for domestic violence, shelters and court systems that seem to blame and punish the man while not helping to resolve the underlying problem and ignoring the woman's behavior are avoided.

Improving links to local service providers, if there are any within the community, and accessing tribal or other resources are also important steps in offering culturally relevant victim services. Even in areas with high concentrations of Native Americans, there are few domestic violence shelters and few substance-abuse facilities despite the large number of Native American domestic violence survivors who are chemically dependent. Survivors would benefit from better availability of coordinated multidisciplinary approaches providing a broad range of services which would target abuse and addiction needs as well as acknowledge and support the woman's role as the traditional center of her family. Due to the complexity of domestic violence, a number of community resources may need to be involved, including tribal, health, social services, law enforcement, legal assistance, mental health services, and addiction treatment centers.

To address the issue of domestic violence among Native Americans, several improvements could be made. Beyond offering bilingual services for victims and batterers, workers in the system should reach out to those who could use their services, make them aware of the availability of services, and explain how the services work and what the procedures are to obtain them. Social service providers and other professionals who work with domestic violence victims should take the first step toward bridging any barriers, racial or otherwise. Partnerships with Native American communities should be made so close that relations can be maintained and needed adjustments to prevention, victim, batterer, and other programs will be recognized as early as possible. Efforts should also be made to address poverty and racism, which contribute to higher rates of domestic violence.

Conclusion

An examination of the history of a minority group may explain the presence of violence but it does not excuse it. Rather than simply incarcerating Native Americans who commit domestic violence and sending the abused to shelters, communities may benefit from integrating discussions of this problem and providing services for victims and batterers into community settings. Batterer programs may be viewed as better options than incarceration of the batterer as long as the victim's safety is ensured. Culturally sensitive service providers need to build trust with Native American communities, understand how social and cultural discrimination against the minority group has impacted that group over time, and how strengths within the Native American culture can be used to facilitate change and encourage a reduction in domestic violence.

WENDELIN HUME and SHERINA HUME

See also **African American Community, Domestic Violence in; Batterer Intervention Programs; Christianity and Domestic Violence; Cross-Cultural Perspectives on How to Deal with Batterers; Jewish Community, Domestic Violence within the; Minorities and Families in America, Introduction to; Multicultural Programs for Domestic Batterers; Rural Communities, Domestic Violence in**

References and Further Reading

Artichoker, Karen, and Marlin Mousseau. "Violence Against Native Women Is Not Traditional," Kyle, SD: Cangleska, 1993.

Malley-Morrison, Kathleen, and Denise A. Hines. *Family Violence in a Cultural Perspective: Defining, Understanding, and Combating Abuse.* Thousand Oaks, CA: Sage Publications, 2004.

Sacred Circle website (Rapid City, SD). http://www.sacred-circle.com (accessed August 28, 2006).

NEUROLOGICAL AND PHYSIOLOGICAL IMPACT OF ABUSE

The Evolution of Neurobiological Research

Typically, research connecting neurophysiology, victimization, and violence has sought to explain the criminal behaviors of offenders rather than the impact of abuse on victims. However, the new specialty of "developmental traumalogy" has evolved within the field of psychiatry in an effort to explain how trauma, abuse, and neglect impact the neurophysiology of victims of abuse. "During the past 20 years, the development of brain imaging techniques and new biochemical approaches have led to increased understanding of the biological effects of psychological trauma" (Solomon and Heide 2005). Technological advances such as functional magnetic resonance imaging (FMRI) and electroencephalogram (EEG) have permitted explorations into atypical concentrations of neurotransmitters, irregularities in brain wave patterns, inadequate integration of the right and left hemispheres, and size discrepancies within regions of the brain. This has allowed researchers to compare the brain activity and chemical responses of those who have experienced a history of abuse or neglect with others who have not experienced such stressful situations. Research inspired by these technological advances has placed a new twist on the age-old debate between whether "nature" or "nurture" more strongly influences the development of an individual's personality, well-being, and character. Researchers now seem to agree that the "process of early brain development is constantly modified by environmental influences" (Glaser 2000) and that "'nature' and 'nurture' interact continuously during the lifespan" (McEwen 2003).

The Functioning of the Brain

In order to understand the neurological, biological, and physiological impact of abuse on individuals, one must first establish a basic understanding of the functions of the body's main control center: the brain. The human brain controls both unconscious functions such as breathing and digestion, as well as more complex, higher-level cognitive activities that include functions such as thought, memory, and reason. In controlling the nervous system, the brain is composed of various critical structures. The cerebral cortex, which consists of four lobes, is responsible for the higher-level conscious functions, including memory, awareness, and language. It receives and processes information from sensory organs such as eyes and ears. The limbic system, also known as the emotional center, consists of a group of brain structures including the amygdala (involved in the response to aggression, fear, and pleasure) and hippocampus (involved in the formation of long-term memory). It is within the limbic system that emotions such as fear, pleasure, and aggression, along with memory formation, are processed. When the amygdala and hippocampus encode information and control behavioral responses, these regions of the brain are also changed structurally and chemically by those experiences (McEwen 2003). The hippocampus is the region of the brain involved in storing short-term memories and retrieving long-term memories. This region is exceptionally sensitive to elevated levels of cortisol which flow through the bloodstream for hours or days after stress. "The body's physiologic responses to stress are based on involuntary actions of the brain. Physical and mental abuse during the first few years of life tends to fix the brain in an acute stress response mode that makes the child respond in a hypervigilant, fearful manner" (Committee on Early Childhood 2000). As a person experiences a stressful situation, hormones such as adrenaline and cortisol inundate the brain to provide clarity and quick response. Unfortunately, continuous exposure and heightened levels of stress hormones alter the hippocampus, often leading to such ailments as posttraumatic stress disorder. Since childhood stress leads to initially high and damaging cortisol levels, prolonged stress leads to depleted cortisol levels in humans (Mukerjee 1995). Mukerjee describes this process with an analogy of a broken thermostat. As stress instigates a flooding of the brain with cortisol, the body's internal thermostat resets the threshold at which cortisol is produced, thereby resulting in low levels of future cortisol circulating the system.

Early Life Experiences

Stress, trauma, and abuse in the early years of life can alter the structure and function of the brain by changing the brain's chemistry. It appears that as the brain develops, excessive stress can stimulate chemical reactions that essentially "rewire" the brain. Since childhood represents the period when most of the brain development takes place, both positive and negative experiences influence how the brain will be "wired." Although the brain continues to develop and change throughout one's life-span, an infant is born with roughly all the brain cells he or she will acquire. "Early social, emotional and environmental influences exert significant organizing effects . . . on the brain . . . [that] shape and mold all aspects of intellectual, perceptual, social and emotional development" (Joseph 1998). Excessive stress "alters the production of both the stress-regulating hormone cortisol and neurotransmitters" (McEwen 2003), leading to chemical imbalances that may result in anxiety, depression, substance abuse, poor response to stress, aggression, and suicide. Brain scans reveal that those who have endured abuse and neglect are more likely to experience decreased brain activity and lack the ability to maintain a sense of emotional balance.

> During the first 3 to 4 years of life, the anatomic brain structures that govern personality traits, learning processes, and coping with stress and emotions are established, strengthened, and made permanent. . . . The nerve connections and neurotransmitter networks that are forming during these critical years are influenced by negative environmental conditions, including lack of stimulation, child abuse, or violence within the family. (Committee on Early Childhood 2000)

According to Schore (2001), "There is extensive evidence that trauma in early life impairs the development of the capacities of maintaining interpersonal relationships, coping with stressful stimuli, and regulating emotion." Schore claims that strong, stable, and healthy attachments between an infant and his or her caretaker are critical to the baby's neurological development and ultimately his or her mental health as an adult. Furthermore, Solomon and Heide (2005) claim that "[a]n infant's relationship with its primary caregiver has a direct effect on the hard wiring of neural circuits in the developing brain. Many of the neural circuits affected by early experience connect areas of the brain critical for emotional, physiological, psychological, and social development. Some of these circuits are necessary for adaptive coping in emotional and stressful situations" (Solomon and Heide 2005).

Prolonged and sustained stress causes the infant to experience negative emotions which trigger processes that alter the biochemistry of the infant's brain and alter the child's future coping capabilities. Schore claims that "the primary caregiver acts as an external psychobiological regulator of the 'experience-dependent' growth of the infant's nervous system." Greenough and Black (1992) explain "experience-expectant" development as growth that will not take place unless a specific experience occurs during its critical developmental period (Glaser 2000). These early social events are imprinted into the neurobiological structures that are maturing during the brain growth spurt of the first two years of life, and therefore have far-reaching effects (Schore 2001). Since the limbic system is thought to be "experience-expectant," normal infant development anticipates attachments between the infant and the caretaker (Joseph 1999). "The ability to form emotional attachments requires not just emotional stimulation, but the capacity to remember faces, people, objects, and even locations; functions associated with the amygdala and hippocampus. . . . However, as the amygdala and hippocampus may be injured by deprivation or abnormal rearing experiences, not just emotionality, but all aspects of short-term and long-term memory functioning may be disrupted as well" (Joseph 1999). Infants deprived of attachments to caretakers behave in ways similar to those whose limbic system has been damaged or destroyed.

Dr. Martin Teicher, a developmental neuropsychiatrist at Harvard University and director of the Biopsychiatry Research Program at McLean Hospital, has been at the forefront of research that compares the makeup and operation of the brains of individuals with and without a history of abuse and neglect. In his research, Teicher and his team expose how abuse provokes various neurobiological outcomes that alter the structure and function of specific regions of the brain, ultimately causing several identified abnormalities resulting from maltreatment.

These identified abnormalities include damage to the temporal lobe and cerebellar vermis, which represents the region of the brain involved in regulating language and the limbic system (the brain's emotional processing center). In studies comparing the MRI scans of those with no history of abuse and those who have endured abuse or neglect, the size of the left hippocampus or amygdala is smaller in size than that of persons with no history of abuse

(Teicher et al. 2004). When comparing abused or neglected children with a control group, Teicher and colleagues (2004) discovered a distinct difference in the size of the collection of nerve cells that connect the right side of the brain with the left side. In a comparison of the brain structure of twenty-two women reporting childhood sexual abuse with those of twenty-one women without a history of abuse, Murray B. Stein of the University of California at San Diego also uncovered an average 5 percent reduction in the size and volume of the left hippocampus (Mukerjee 1995). Furthermore, victims of abuse and neglect were less successful in integrating the functions of the left and right hemispheres when compared with those lacking a history of abuse. Harm to the left hemisphere resulted in abnormal brainwaves that mimic seizures. "Studies of the brains of human and animal subjects who have been victims of traumatic stress reveal differences in their brains when compared with control subjects who have not experienced trauma" (Teicher et al. 2004). These changes in brain structure and physiology are thought to affect memory, learning, ability to regulate affect, social development, and even moral development (Solomon and Heide 2005). Experiments at McLean Hospital have revealed that patients with a history of abuse are twice as likely to experience abnormal brain waves, or electrical activity, and five times more likely to experience suicidal thoughts than those who do not have a history of abuse. An abnormally developed left hemisphere of the brain is also linked to memory problems and depression (Teicher et al. 2004).

Solomon and Heide (2005) explain that non-traumatic memories are processed much like a roll of film. Personal experiences and events are temporarily stored in the limbic system and include a sense of time and self, such as in a photo of oneself at Disneyland with Mickey Mouse on a third birthday. The cognitive aspects of these memories are stored in the hippocampus, while the emotion attached to the memories is stored in the amygdala. "As the brain processes these memories over time, aspects of them are abstracted and transferred to the neocortex" (Solomon and Heide 2005). Upsetting experiences are processed at a much slower rate and linger in the limbic system for longer periods of time. "Because traumatic experiences are terrifying, the survivors avoid thinking and talking about what happened. This avoidance prevents processing. [As a result,] trauma alters physiology and gives rise to images, feelings, sensations, and beliefs that may persist throughout life" (Solomon and Heide 2005). The memories of traumatic events overwhelm the brain and become accumulated in the limbic system indefinitely. Those who suffer trauma through abuse or neglect experience impaired brain development, leaving them with an inability to cope with stress appropriately (Solomon and Heide 2005).

Physiological Ailments

Traumatic events not only affect an individual's brain functioning and memory capabilities, but they affect his or her physical health as well. "During the past few years, [researchers] have dramatically increased [their] understanding of the effects of traumatic stress on the brain, sympathetic nervous system, and endocrine system. Through a physiological domino effect, these changes affect many other body systems, including the cardiovascular system, respiratory system, and muscular system" (Solomon and Heide 2005). Although the negative consequences of abuse generate the greatest amount of damage during the early formative years, Solomon and Heide clearly articulate how maltreatment at any juncture of the lifespan impacts the vital organs of the body and produces negative health consequences even into adolescence and adulthood. In studies with adolescents, Juang and colleagues (2004) examined the existing correlations between adversity, depression, and headaches. Juang et al. found that "increased morbidity to depression and other psychiatric disorders is a long-term consequence of childhood adversity such as abuse and neglect" (Juang et al. 2004). Juang and colleagues's research also showed that chronic daily headache (CDH) in young people is "associated with family adversity, physical abuse, and parental divorce occurring during childhood." Researchers in countless studies have noted that abused women report experiencing inferior physical and mental health compared with women with no history of abuse (Garimella et al. 2000). In a study of 444 women responding to self-administered surveys in a small northeastern Italian town, Romito, Turan, and De Marchi (2005) examined the relationship between past and present abuse across "three indicators of current women's health—psychological distress, the use of psychoactive drugs, and a subjective evaluation of health" (Romito et al. 2005). The results showed that female "victims of partner violence were around six times more likely to be depressed and to feel in bad health, and four times more likely to use psychoactive pills than other women" (Romito et al. 2005), who had not endured any form of abuse.

Conclusion

It is difficult to study the impact of abuse on a person, since one may become a victim of abuse at various points throughout his or her life. Additionally, it is difficult to assess the time order of the symptoms and causes of abuse, since many trauma survivors do not seek assistance. It is possible that those born with a smaller hippocampus are more susceptible to acquiring disorders, including post-traumatic stress, rather than the abuse causing a decrease in the size of the hippocampus, which leads to physical or mental ailments. In addition, acts of neglect and physical, sexual, or emotional abuse during childhood also increase the risk of further victimization later in life (Romito et al. 2005), making it difficult to isolate the effects of each episode of abuse. A lack of interdisciplinary collaboration between various academic fields complicates the quest for knowledge further by yielding isolated bits of information that remain unknown to researchers in other academic fields.

As this research adds a new perspective to the question of nature and nurture's effect on human development, researchers are now beginning to examine whether there are evolutionary benefits to the physiological changes resulting from abuse. Childhood stress is not a new phenomenon, so new speculations have been raised as to "whether the increased stimulation for fight or flight may facilitate survival and reproductive success in hostile environments" (Cromie 2003).

Methodological impediments in research designs analyzing neurological processes have created numerous challenges in understanding the neurophysiological impact of abuse and neglect; however, understanding the impact of abuse and neglect on the mind and body provides the greatest information toward the development of adequate treatment and prevention. As researchers uncover the potential extent of physiological damage resulting from abuse and neglect, it becomes more evident that the best treatment for survivors is the creation of resources that aid in early intervention and prevention of abuse.

SILVINA ITUARTE

See also **Child Abuse and Juvenile Delinquency; Post-Incest Syndrome**

References and Further Reading

Committee on Early Childhood, Adoption and Dependent Care. "Developmental Issues for Young Children in Foster Care." *Pediatrics* 106, no. 5 (November 2000): 1145–1150.

Cromie, William. "Childhood Abuse Hurts the Brain." *Harvard University Gazette*, May 22, 2003.

Flinn, Mark V., and Barry G. England. "Childhood Stress and Family Environment." *Current Anthropology* 36, no. 5 (December 1995): 854–866.

Garimella, Ramani, et al. "Physicians' Beliefs about Victims of Spouse Abuse and about the Physician Role." *Journal of Women's Health and Gender-Based Medicine* 9, no. 4 (2000): 405–411.

Glaser, Danya. "Child Abuse and Neglect and the Brain—A Review." *Journal of Child Psychology and Psychiatry* 41, no. 1 (2000): 97–116.

Hawley, Theresa. "Safe Start: How Early Experiences Can Help Reduce Violence," 2000. *Practical Parenting Supporting Parents and Professionals*. www.practicalparent.org.uk/violence.htm.

Joseph, R. "Environmental Influences on Neural Plasticity, the Limbic System, Emotional Development and Attachment: A Review." *Child Psychiatry and Human Development* 29, no. 3 (Spring 1999): 189–208.

Juang, K.-D., et al. "Association between Adolescent Chronic Daily Headache and Childhood Adversity: A Community-Based Study." *Cephalgia* 24 (2004): 54–59.

McEwen, Bruce S. "Early Life Influences on Life-Long Patterns of Behavior and Health." *Mental Retardation and Developmental Disabilities Research and Review* 9 (2003): 149–154.

Mukerjee, Madhusree. "Hidden Scars: Sexual and Other Abuse May Alter a Brain Region." *Scientific American*, October 1995.

Raine, Adrian, et al. "Reduced Right Hemisphere Activation in Severely Abused Violent Offenders during a Working Memory Task: An FMRI Study." *Aggressive Behavior* 27 (2001): 111–129.

Romito, Patrizia, Janet M. Turan, and Margherita De Marchi. "The Impact of Current and Past Interpersonal Violence on Women's Mental Health." *Social Science and Medicine* 60 (2005): 1717–1727.

Schore, Allan N. "The Effects of Early Relational Trauma on Right Brain Development, Affect, Regulation, and Infant Mental Health." *Infant Mental Health Journal* 22, no. 1-2 (2001): 201–269.

Solomon, Eldra P., and Kathleen M. Heide. "The Biology of Trauma: Implications for Treatment." *Journal of Interpersonal Violence* 20, no. 1 (January 2005): 51–60.

Teicher, Martin H., et al. "Childhood Neglect Is Associated with Reduced Corpus Callosum Area." *Biological Psychiatry* 56, no. 2 (July 2004): 6–85.

P

PARENTAL ABDUCTION

Definition and Incidence

Parental abduction of a child occurs when a member of the child's family, or someone acting on behalf of a family member, takes action to deprive a parent of his/her lawful rights to have custody of or access to the child. Also referred to as "custodial interference" or "parental kidnapping," it includes attempts to remove, conceal, or refuse to return the child. Violations of court orders for custody and visitation, not uncommon between disputing separating and divorced parents, are not viewed as parental abduction unless they involve an indefinite or permanent effort to deny a parent's access to the child without good cause.

Parental abduction has become a serious concern in the United States and in many other Western nations. The second National Incidence Study of Missing, Abducted, Runaway and Thrownaway Children (NISMART II) estimated that in 1999 approximately 203,900 children were abducted by family members in the United States. By contrast, abductions by strangers during that year involved only 115 children but resulted in relatively extensive media coverage and public concern (see Sedlak et al. 2002).

Abductors are generally one of the child's parents but could also be grandparents, stepparents, or other relatives. Studies have shown that fathers are more likely to kidnap their children, although studies have also shown that mothers are almost as likely to do so. Boys and girls are equally likely to experience family abduction. Young preschool children are more likely to be abducted by a parent, perhaps because they are less able to verbally protest or resist, easier to transport and conceal, and are unable to tell others their history. Abduction of older children by a parent usually requires their participation and assent. The threat or use of force is relatively uncommon in abductions by a family member. Most parentally abducted children are recovered or returned relatively quickly, within the first few weeks or even within days. The large majority of the cases (more than three-fourths) are resolved within one to two months; only a small proportion of parentally abducted children may be gone for six months or more, and it is relatively rare that a child is never recovered (see Hammer, Finkelhor, and Sedlak 2002 for further demographic descriptors).

Historical Context

The emerging problem of parental abduction of children needs to be considered in the context of society's definition of who owns the child, the changing nature of the modern family, and gender roles. Historically, dating back to Roman times, and expressly incorporated within English common law, the doctrine of *patriae potestas* gave the father authority over his children. This legal doctrine was imported to the American colonies, where the presumption of paternal custody prevailed until the early part of the twentieth century. During this period, to some extent both women and children were viewed as men's property, and in this sense the male had the primary right to control and make decisions for his family. During the first half of the twentieth century, custody preferences changed to the "tender years doctrine," at which time society explicitly acknowledged mothers' primary role as birth parent and caretaker in the early years, bolstered by new psychological theories that stressed the vital importance of protecting the young child's emotional attachment to his or her primary caregiver.

During the 1960s and 1970s, the Women's Rights movement, an outgrowth of the Civil Rights movement, called for gender equality and helped set in motion both intended and unintended consequences for the family. Coincident upon the introduction of "no fault" divorce and equal division of property laws in the early 1970s, the "best interests of the child" legal principle was adopted by United States courts to decide who should have custody after parents separated, so that for the first time in history there was no gender preference for the custody of children. Subsequently, during the next two decades (1970–1989), divorce rates doubled and stabilized at the rate of about four of every ten marriages with children. In addition, the number of women bearing children out of wedlock increased substantially. As a result, by the latter half of the twentieth century, almost six in every ten children experienced living in a single parent home, for at least part of their growing-up years. An increasing number of mothers entered the workforce, and fathers assumed a greater role in their children's upbringing. At the beginning of the twenty-first century, at the same time that joint custody or shared parental caretaking became more widespread, divorced and never-married parents were increasingly geographically mobile. Consequently, when parents separate, the custody of their children tends to be "up for grabs"—that is, fit is more likely to be disputed. Whereas most custody-disputing parents appeal to the family courts to resolve their differences with one another, some individuals take the law into their own hands and kidnap their children (see Forst and Blomquist 1991 for further discussion).

Parental Abduction and Family Violence

What motivates some parents to abduct their children? Early explanations tended to focus on the nature of the conflict between spouses around the time of separation, noting that parental abductors may have a desire to blame, spite, or punish the other parent for leaving or may be trying to effect reconciliation. Others may be fearful of losing custody of their child and having a diminished role in the child's life. Subsequent studies have found that family violence plays a large role in parental abductions (Grief and Hegar 1993; Johnston, Girdner, and Sagatun-Edwards 1999). Whereas for some parents—usually fathers—kidnapping their children is a manifestation of their ongoing attempts to wield control and power over spouses who are trying to leave abusive relationships, for other parents—usually mothers—fleeing with and hiding their children is an attempt to protect the children from left-behind parents who are perceived to be molesting, abusive, or neglectful. In the aftermath of a failed marriage, however, which of these scenarios is true is often unclear and vigorously contested in counterallegations to authorities and in family courts.

Domestic violence and substance abuse—more often perpetrated by the male partner—are alleged to have occurred in two-thirds to three-quarters of families where children are subsequently abducted by a parent. In the majority of these cases there is some evidence to back up these claims. Allegations of child abuse occur in one-third to two-thirds of abducting families. Whereas allegations of child sexual abuse—primarily against fathers—are often unable to be substantiated, allegations of child neglect and endangerment—more often made against mothers—are substantiated in about one-fourth to one-half of the cases. Many of these concerned parents had sought the help of family courts and child protective services to protect their children; however, the response from these authorities was perceived to be too often inadequate and inconsistent. From the parents' viewpoint, counselors in the family and juvenile courts were often dismissive of their concerns, failed to thoroughly investigate their claims, and did not follow up or monitor the potentially unstable and neglectful environments to which their children were exposed. This either motivated them to "take the law into their own hands" and steal their children or resulted in the children becoming victims of abduction by the abusive parent (see Greif and Hegar 1993 and Johnston et al. 1999 for further details).

The study by Johnston et al. (1999) also found that abducting parents, compared with parents litigating custody, are more likely to have narcissistic and psychopathic personality traits wherein they feel entitled to flaunt the authority of the courts and law enforcement, exploit and control others with impunity, and do whatever they believe is best for the child, without consideration of the other parent's rights or feelings. Consistent with these attitudes, it has been found that these individuals are more likely to have prior arrests and convictions for other criminal offenses. This may also help explain why they do not expect the family courts to be sympathetic if they pursue their quest for custody through legal means. In a small number of cases, abducting parents are severely mentally ill, suffering from paranoid delusions and other thought disorders whereby they are convinced that the children's other parent, associates, and the legal system are conspiring against them. All of these parents who have severe personality and psychotic disorders are of relatively great risk to the children they abduct.

Other Factors Associated with Parental Abduction

Other indicators of risk for parental abduction need to be considered. Johnston et al. (1999) found that both abducting and left-behind parents, particularly women, are predominantly of low socioeconomic status, are more likely to be unemployed, have low incomes, have few occupational skills, and were poorly educated. They cannot afford neither the legal counsel that would help guide them through the courts nor consultation with mental health professionals to advise them on their family problems or help substantiate their claims for custody. Their difficulties are compounded if they are of cultural minority status, noncitizens, and not able to speak the language. Furthermore, a proportion of abducting parents are never-married women who do not consider that the biological fathers of their children have any rights to custody or visitation.

In all of these cases, distressed parents, who are dealing with a marital or relationship breakup and/or trying to rescue themselves or their children from abusive family situations, tend to turn to their own families and informal social networks for support

and help rather than rely upon formal agents like child protective services, police, and courts. Their informal networks often share more traditional views about gender roles that favor the custody of mothers and their extended families, or conversely, hold fundamentalist religious convictions about male authority and ownership of the child (in contradiction to prevailing custody laws that are gender neutral). In some cases, the abductor is given substantial assistance from cult-like groups or an underground dissident movement that provides not only practical assistance (food, money, and a place to hide) but also moral support to validate the abducting parent's actions. For this reason, many family abductors do not consider their actions to be wrong and are often surprised to find that they are illegal.

Parents who are citizens of another country (or have dual citizenship with the United States) may abduct their children following separation and divorce, particularly if they have strong, idealized ties to their extended families in their homeland, deprecate American culture, and categorically reject the other parent as important to the child. When these parents feel cast adrift from their mixed-culture marriage, they may turn to their ethnic or religious roots to find emotional support and reconstitute a shaken self-identity. Often, in reaction to feeling helpless and rejected or discarded by the ex-spouse, such a parent may return to his/her homeland with the child as a way of insisting that the homeland cultural identity be given preeminent status in the child's upbringing. Further, the family-of-origin may offer much needed financial support as well as a warm welcome home, in contrast to that provided by the left-behind parent.

Risk Factors and Preventive Measures

Indicators of risk for parental abduction exist in those separating/divorcing families with young children in which there have already been allegations of family violence—especially where a parent and her associates suspect or allege child abuse that has not been perceived, taken seriously, or properly investigated by authorities. There is also a heightened risk where one parent with a severe psychopathic or paranoid personality dismisses or denies the other parent's value to the child, uses the child as a weapon to punish a spouse who is trying to leave, or has paranoid delusions that he/she and the child are being persecuted by the left-behind parent. The risk may be increased where parents belong to cultural, ethnic, religious, or cult-like groups, or countries that hold strongly to different values about child-rearing, gender roles, and family compared with mainstream Western society; and where distressed parents, by virtue of their marginal social status and limited resources, feel alienated and disenfranchised from courts, mental health counselors, and social agencies that could ordinarily provide them some relief.

Imminent sign of an abduction is when a separating or divorced parent having the above characteristics makes credible threats to abduct, having already a history of hiding the child, withholding visitation, or snatching the child from the other parent. Furthermore, such a parent may be planning an abduction when he or she has no financial, occupational, or emotional ties to the geographic area, has resources to survive in hiding (like liquidated assets), or help from others to remain hidden from the left-behind parent or law enforcement.

To counter the threat of parental abduction, preventive measures may be sought from the family court, including: a detailed custody order designating which court has jurisdiction and specifying all parent–child access arrangements (times, dates, place of exchange, holiday periods); restricting travel outside the area with the child, requiring a bond to be posted if the child accompanies the potential abductor on vacations outside the area; placing a hold on the child's passport, birth certificate, and school and medical records, which may not be released without the written consent of both parents; or permitting visitation with the child only under the supervision of a third party. More restrictive measures are warranted when the risk of abduction is particularly high, when obstacles to locating and recovering the child are likely to be great, and when the child faces substantial harm from the abducting parent (see Johnston and Girdner 2001 for further preventive measures).

Effects on Victims

It is a commonly held myth that parental abduction is not consequential because a parent is unlikely to harm a child and that being kidnapped by a family member is not likely to be a stressful or traumatic event compared with stranger abduction. In fact the repercussions of parental abduction for children and their families vary greatly depending upon the circumstances of the case. It ranges from being fairly benign, where young children are located rapidly, cared for well, and voluntarily returned by the abducting parent, to having severe and long-lasting consequences, where children are physically, sexually, or emotionally abused or exposed to neglectful or violent environments by the abductor.

For the family left behind, searching for an abducted child is not only frustrating, but financially draining and emotionally exhausting. A study by Christopher Hatcher and associates in 1992 found that left-behind parents typically expend their resources, including borrowed funds, to hire attorneys and private investigators and to travel in search of their children. The researchers also found that the majority of parents and other family members of missing children experience substantial emotional distress as a result of the disappearance. Compared with the general population, their level of distress equals or exceeds the emotional distress of other groups of individuals exposed to trauma, such as military combatants and victims of violent crime.

Children appear to be most adversely affected when lengthy concealment is involved, when they are abducted by a psychologically disturbed or violent parent, and when they have been subjected directly to abuse by the abductor. For this reason, it should not be assumed that children are safe just because they are with a parent. Greif and Hegar (1993) found that almost 25 percent of the abducted children interviewed in their study had suffered physical abuse by the abducting parent, while 7 percent were sexually abused. Loss and trauma are also experienced when children are taken from a secure relationship with a primary parent by an abductor who tells negative stories such that they believe that they are no longer loved or wanted by the absent parent. Being in hiding or constantly on the run to elude authorities and having their identities changed is particularly disruptive to their healthy development.

Further trauma can occur to children as a result of some of the dramatic measures taken to locate and recover them—like being snatched back by a private investigator, apprehended by law enforcement, and placed in a children's shelter or foster care while their case is litigated in family or juvenile court. Their recovery and return home may not be a welcome rescue when it results in the sudden loss of the abducting parent on whom they feel entirely dependent and their precipitous transfer to the custody of the left-behind parent, whom they may not remember or may no longer trust. Those who have been indoctrinated with negative beliefs about the other parent can experience grief and rage such that they may strongly identify with one parent and reject the other.

The aftermath of the abduction, when children are recovered, does not necessarily signal relief for the child or the family. Often, a child is left upset and torn between the abducting parent and the custodial parent and the entire family is left to pick up the pieces of the life they once had with the child. Unlike in stranger abduction, the child can have feelings of love and longing for the abducting parent, which can be difficult for the custodial parent to hear, thereby putting a strain between the left-behind parent and the child. Indications of children's distress include anxiety and fright, nightmares, sleeping problems, clinging, and irritability. Regression disorders where a child reverts to behaviors inappropriate for his/her age (e.g., bed-wetting, thumb sucking) are not uncommon following the child's return home, along with behavior difficulties, declining grades, and health problems (Greif and Hegar 1993).

A review of studies by Nancy Faulkner (1999) concluded that the legacy of abductions is often an attachment disorder, where children are unable to develop a meaningful, healthy relationship with their left-behind parent after being reunited with him/her. Depression is also a common feature in these children. They may feel unable to trust anyone because they have lost stability in their lives and often feel angry, frightened, and abandoned. Moreover, even young children can be burdened by guilt, where they feel in some manner at fault for the abduction and secretly worry that they should have resisted being taken or found their way home. It is important also to recognize that these children are often lied to by their abducting parent and can be burdened with inculcated ideas of distrust, loneliness, and hostility regarding their family situations.

Long-term consequences have been explored by one researcher, Geoffrey Greif (2000), who followed up on his earlier study by interviewing the parents of teenagers and young adults who had been parentally abducted as children (Greif and Hegar 1993). Significant emotional and physical problems were observed by parents in more than two-fifths of the sample of youth—a minority, but hardly a small percentage. Greif (2000) also found that of those still having problems, many continued with therapy ten years after the parental abduction occurred. Parents reported that their teenage and young adult children were sometimes self-destructive and had a number of difficulties in their home, personal, and school lives. In 2003 Greif (2003) interviewed in depth a small group of adults who had been parentally abducted as children. He noted that the adults' relationship with both of their parents remained greatly ambivalent, as was their stance toward marriage and child-rearing. Feelings of loss and guilt, conflicts with siblings, and confusion about the use of their birth name upon recovery

also continued to haunt these individuals. It is not known to what extent the experiences of the relatively small number of individuals who participated in these studies are representative of the larger population of adults who were abducted as children. Further, more extensive research needs to be undertaken on short- and long-term outcomes for children and their parents.

In general, policymakers and researchers have argued that parental abduction constitutes more than the violation of parents' civil rights to have access to their children. Rather, because of the serious emotional problems that may result, parental abduction of children should be regarded as a form of child abuse in and of itself. In response, many laws and policies have been put in place to combat this type of abduction; however the justice system has a long way to go in implementing these laws in order to curtail and hopefully prevent the problem.

Justice System's Response to Parental Abduction

Before 1968, state laws governed all marriage, divorce, and custody matters, and any state could make or modify decisions about child custody based on the child's presence in the state. This led to "forum shopping," where some divorcing parents fled with the child to a state that appeared to favor their situation. Multiple, conflicting court orders could be issued from different states, with little or no willingness of law enforcement or courts in one state to enforce another state's orders. To address this problem, the Uniform Child Custody Jurisdiction Act (UCCJA) gave jurisdiction of the matter to the "home" state (defined as where the child had lived for the last six months prior to the court action, or where the child had significant connections to family, school, and community). All fifty states and the District of Columbia adopted versions of this act.

The Parental Kidnapping Prevention Act (PKPA), passed by Congress in 1980, acts as a "tie-breaker" when two or more states claim to be the "home" state. It also authorized the Federal Bureau of Investigation (FBI) to assist in locating and recovering children who are believed to have been taken across state lines. This means that in the United States, whenever there is a custody dispute between parents that involves different counties or states, the first order of business is to decide which court has the authority to hear the matter and make decisions for the family according to the "best interests of the child" principle. Once the court with continuing jurisdiction over the matter is determined, other courts in other counties or states are bound to enforce and not modify any orders that are made.

Essentially the same remedy at the international level, when children are transported across national borders, is provided by the Hague Convention on the Civil Aspects of International Child Abduction (signed by the United States in 1980 and ratified in 1988) and the federal statute that implements it (the International Child Abduction Remedies Act [ICARA]). That is, the Hague Convention is a reciprocal agreement between countries that identifies the "home country" which has jurisdiction in child custody matters and mandates the prompt return of parentally abducted or wrongfully retained children to their "habitual residence" in order for all decisions to be made about custody and visitation issues. Unfortunately, not all countries are signatories to the Hague treaty, especially those that are hostile to U.S. and European cultures, customs, and foreign policy (e.g., some countries in the Middle East). Furthermore, although a country may have adopted the Hague Convention, it may not have assigned the resources to a designated central authority to implement the treaty.

All of the laws cited herein treat parental abduction as a civil law violation rather than a criminal act. As early as the 1970s, frustrated left-behind parents urged lawmakers to treat parental abductions as serious crimes rather than private domestic disputes. During these early years, there was little or no awareness that family violence is a typical problem in abducting families, nor was it acknowledged that because of its detrimental effects on children, parental abduction may be a form of child abuse in and of itself. In fact, there was great reluctance to criminalize parental child stealing because it was argued that the new statutes would stigmatize and punish parents, resulting in more harm than good as essentially law-abiding parents were indicted and sent to jail or prison for seemingly no good reason. Eventually the advocates for criminalization were successful, and during the 1980s every state passed laws making parental child abduction a felony, carrying various penalties. In addition, the International Parental Kidnapping Act of 1993 made it a federal felony, punishable by up to three years in prison, to remove a child unlawfully from the United States. The Extradition Treaties Interpretation Act of 1998 is the basis for extraditing alleged abductors to the "home" country for criminal court proceedings.

During the last decade of the twentieth century, the movement to protect the victims of domestic violence spread across the country, gaining political momentum and resulting in the passing of federal legislation in 1994, specifically the Violence against Women Act (VAWA). This act provided for interstate enforcement of protective orders for domestic violence victims, along with many other provisions. Hence victims were on one hand being given explicit permission and protection to flee their abusers, including across state lines, but these rights and protections were potentially in conflict with criminal abduction/custodial interference statutes, whereby in some cases victims could be prosecuted for fleeing and hiding with their children.

The Uniform Child Custody Jurisdiction and Enforcement Act (UCCJEA) of 1997 helped resolve these anomalies, allowing victims these protections in emergency situations, provided their living arrangements were subsequently approved by the family courts. Also, this version of the act helped clear up other ambiguities in the previous statutes, like those that allowed parents to litigate excessively over which state was the "home" state and under what conditions another state could issue emergency orders. It also provided enforcement mechanisms for the act. Specifically, it authorized public officials (e.g., the district attorney) to assist in the recovery of the child and to provide the left-behind parent with legal assistance, in addition to their other responsibilities for prosecuting offenders. Subsequently, as of this writing, most states have adopted or are in the process of adopting the UCCJEA (see Hoff 2001 for a further discussion of these laws).

Congress has also enacted several laws relating to missing children that may apply to parentally abducted children, such as the Missing Children's Act of 1982 and the National Child Search Assistance Act of 1990. Among other provisions, these acts allow all missing children to be registered without any waiting period in a central national database at the National Center for Missing and Exploited Children (NCMEC) that can be accessed throughout the country by local law enforcement. With more sustained federal funding, the NCMEC has become the leading national organization offering assistance to local law enforcement and families affected by parental abductions, as well as providing a wide array of educational resources to the concerned public. All states now also have missing-children's clearinghouses, although it appears that they are not used as extensively as the NCMEC. Furthermore, the AMBER [America's Missing: Broadcast Emergency Response] alert system was developed in 1996 to assist law enforcement in coordinating and implementing emergency responses to children abductions in which the child is deemed to be in danger of serious injury, by broadcasting information to the public. All of these measures have been successful in the earlier recovery of parentally abducted children. However, it should be noted that not all parentally abducted children are missing. In almost one-half of the cases in the NISMART II study, the left-behind parent knew where the child was located and with whom the child was living but was having difficulty getting the child returned (Hammer et al. 2002). Furthermore, not all abducted children are perceived to be in serious danger, so an AMBER alert may not be issued for them.

At the local level, a number of private nonprofit organizations have sprung up throughout the United States to assist parents directly in locating and reuniting with their missing children; such organizations work in close cooperation with state and federal law enforcement and with the NCMEC. These include, among others, organizations like the Vanished Children's Alliance in California, Child Find of America Inc. in New York, and Operation Lookout in Washington State. Many of these grassroots organizations were formed in response to specific high-profile cases of child abduction and the extensive media response and public support the matter generated. They also identify much-needed gaps in services, lobby for legislation, advocate for victims, and provide education and prevention to the public, as well as offering technical assistance to law enforcement and other community agencies.

Despite all of these developments in law, community services, and legal protections, the criminal justice system pays relatively scant attention to the crime of parental abduction. Although NISMART II estimated that more than 200,000 children are abducted annually and more than one-half of these are reported to authorities, a national study by Kathi Grasso et al. (2001) showed that only about 30,500 police reports were officially registered, and only 3,500 charges were filed by prosecutors, half of which resulted in a criminal conviction. The justice system responded more harshly in those cases where there were clear violations of existing custody orders and where child endangerment was clearly indicated. This suggests that less than 1 percent of parent-abductors are convicted of the crime and punished. Instead, the large majority of cases are dealt with privately, without legal assistance, or settled in family courts as civil matters. Most, if not all, prosecutors believe that criminal prosecution is not in the child's or family's interest and that the most important priority is to recover the child safely and expeditiously.

There are many obstacles to the recovery of parentally abducted children and even more obstacles to the prevention of parental abduction in the first place. All of the laws and policies regarding this matter were made in efforts to assist families and the criminal justice system to combat parental abduction. However, attitudes that parental abduction is not a serious problem and is a private family matter persist and continue to affect the priorities given to this type of crime compared with other crimes. The relative invisibility of the extent of this problem in the justice system has led it to be seen as a specialist area of practice; consequently, most legal and mental health professionals and community agencies do not devote sufficient resources to training regarding relevant issues and implementation of relevant policies. It is important for the justice system and the general public, especially high-risk populations, to be better educated about parental abduction. Ongoing training and refresher courses are essential in order for police officers, attorneys, prosecutors, judges, and mental health professionals, as well as divorcing parents, to be better acquainted with the relevant laws. Court administrators need to put protocols and procedures in place for expeditiously handling these cases, and coordination between jurisdictions, states, and countries is essential. Finally, it is also important to develop and implement risk management assessment tools and strategies in order to forestall and prevent parental abduction of children (see articles by Girdner and Hoff 1994; Grasso et al. 2001; Johnston and Girdner 2001).

JANET R. JOHNSTON and SAMANTHA K. HAMILTON

See also **Battered Woman Syndrome; Child Neglect; Children Witnessing Parental Violence; Divorce, Child Custody, and Domestic Violence; Domestic Violence Courts; Shelter Movement; Stalking**

References and Further Reading

Faulkner, Nancy. "Parent Child Abduction Is Child Abuse." Paper presented to the United Nations Convention on Child Rights, June 1999. www.prevent-abuse-now.com/unreport.htm.

Forst, Martin L., and Martha-Elin Blomquist. *Missing Children: Rhetoric and Reality.* New York: Lexington Press, 1991.

Girdner, Linda, and Patricia Hoff. *Obstacles to the Recovery and Return of Parentally Abducted Children: Research Summary.* Washington DC: U.S. Department of Justice, Office of Justice Programs, Office of Juvenile Justice and Delinquency Prevention, 1994.

Grasso, Kathi L., Andrea J. Sedlak, Janet L. Chiancone, Frances Gragg, Dana Schultz, and Joseph F. Ryan. "The Criminal Justice System's Response to Parental Abduction." *Bulletin*. Washington DC: U.S. Department of Justice, Office of Justice Programs, Office of Juvenile Justice and Delinquency Prevention, December 2001.

———. "A Parental Report on the Long-term Consequences for Children of Abduction by the Other Parent." *Child Psychiatry and Human Development* 31 (2000): 59–78.

Greif, Geoffrey L. "Treatment Implications for Adults Who Were Parentally Abducted When Young." *Family Therapy* 30, no. 3 (2002): 151–165.

Greif, Geoffrey L., and Rebecca L. Hegar. *When Parents Kidnap: The Families Behind the Headlines*. New York: Free Press, 1993.

Hammer, Heather, David Finkelhor, and Andrea J. Sedlak. "NISMART: Children Abducted by Family Members: National Estimates and Characteristics." *Second National Incidence Study of Missing, Abducted, Runaway, and Thrownaway Children* (NISMART). U.S. Department of Justice, Office of Justice Programs, Office of Juvenile Justice and Delinquency Prevention, October 2002.

Hatcher, Christopher, C. Barton, and L. Brooks. "Families of Missing Children. Final Report." Washington DC: U.S. Department of Justice, Office of Justice Programs, Office of Juvenile Justice and Delinquency Prevention, 1992.

Hoff, Patricia M."The Uniform Child-Custody Jurisdiction and Enforcement Act." *Bulletin*. Washington DC: U.S. Department of Justice, Office of Justice Programs, Office of Juvenile Justice and Delinquency Prevention, December 2001.

Johnston, Janet R., and Linda Girdner. "Family Abductors: Descriptive Profiles and Preventive Interventions." *Bulletin*. Washington DC: U.S. Department of Justice, Office of Justice Programs, Office of Juvenile Justice and Delinquency Prevention, January 2001.

Johnston, Janet R., Linda K. Girdner, and Inger Sagatun-Edwards. "Developing Profiles of Risk for Parental Abduction of Children from a Comparison of Families Victimized by Abduction with Families Litigating Custody." *Behavioral Sciences and the Law* 17, no. 3 (1999): 305–322.

Sedlak, Andrea J., David Finkelhor, Heather Hammer, and Dana J. Schultz. "National Estimates of Missing Children: An Overview." *Second National Incidence Study of Missing, Abducted, Runaway, and Thrownaway Children* (NISMART). U.S. Department of Justice, Office of Justice Programs, Office of Juvenile Justice and Delinquency Prevention, October 2002.

Statutes Cited

Extradition Treaties Interpretation Act of 1998 Title II, Public Law 105-323. *Federal Register* 64, no. 15 (January 25, 1999): 3735–3736.

Hague Convention on the Civil Aspects of International Child Abduction, ratified in 1986, adopted by the United States in 1988.

International Child Abduction Remedies Act of 1988 (42 U.S.C. § 11601 et seq.).

International Parental Kidnapping Crime Act (18 U.S.C. § 1204).

Missing Children's Act of 1982 (28 U.S.C. § 534(a)).

National Child Search Assistance Act of 1990 (42 U.S.C. § 5780).

Parental Kidnapping Prevention Act of 1980 (28 U.S.C. § 1738A).

Uniform Child Custody Jurisdiction Act of 1968, 9(1A) U.L.A. 271 (1999).

Uniform Child Custody Jurisdiction and Enforcement Act (1997), 9(IA) U.L.A. 657 (1999).

Violence against Women Act of 1994; Violence against Women Act of 2000, 18 U.S.C. §§ 2265, 2266.

PARRICIDE

Parricide technically refers to the killing of a close relative. Since the 1980s, the term has become increasingly identified by the public as the killing of parents. Widespread interest in the phenomenon of youths killing their parents was generated by media coverage of several cases in the United States in the 1980s in which sons and daughters had acted alone or with others to kill parents who allegedly abused them. In one of these cases, sixteen-year-old Richard Jahnke and his seventeen-year-old sister gunned down their father in 1982 to end the man's physical abuse of Jahnke and his mother, his sexual abuse of the sister, and his verbal and psychological abuse of the entire family.

Interest in parricide cases has transcended the United States in recent years. A review of online media sources revealed that cases of sons and daughters involved in matricide (the killing of a mother) or patricide (the killing of a father) make headline news around the globe, particularly when the cases involve juveniles (children under eighteen, also referred to as minors) or are particularly heinous or atrocious. For example, news coverage was extensive in the case of Jeremy Bamber of Essex, England, who was charged and subsequently convicted of killing his adopted mother and father, his stepsister, and her two six-year-old twin sons by shooting them twenty-five times with a semiautomatic rifle, mostly at extremely close range. Bamber was twenty-two years old at the time of the multiple murders, which occurred in 1985.

The public's morbid fascination with parricide dates back thousands of years. The killing of fathers and mothers has been a recurrent theme in world literature, as is evident in the stories of Oedipus, Orestes, Alcmaeon, and King Arthur. The killing of parents has been viewed with horror across time and cultures. Such behavior is considered taboo, as reflected in two biblical commandments: Honor thy father and mother and Thou shalt not kill. When children kill their parents, the public wants to know why. Perhaps the reason behind the widespread curiosity since time immemorial is that all members of the public are children (either minors or adults), and many, if not most, are parents of (minor or adult) children. It is understandable to wonder whether "everyday people" are at risk of killing their parents or of being killed by their offspring.

The risk of an individual becoming a parricide victim or offender is actually very, very small. The act of homicide (killing of one person by another) is a low-base-rate event (an infrequent occurrence) in almost all countries that are not at war. Homicide data reflecting the relationship of the victim to the offender are not readily available across cultures. These data are collected in the United States and published by the Federal Bureau of Investigation (FBI) in its Uniform Crime Reports. The United States serves as a good reference point because the U.S. homicide rate is among the highest of the industrialized countries in the world. Yet, even in this country, where the relationship between the victim and offender is known, only about 2 percent of homicide victims are identified as having been killed by their biological sons or daughters. Perusal of arrest data from the mid-1970s through the end of the twentieth century reveals that annually, fewer than 365 parents in the United States—less than one per day—were killed by their biological children. In a country with a population ranging from approximately 220 to 280 million during this time frame, this number is not particularly large when one considers that there were between 15,000 and 25,000 homicide victims each year.

Interestingly, analysis of Supplementary Homicide Report data compiled by the FBI for the period 1976–1999 indicates that approximately 22 percent of children who kill their parents, often referred to as "parricide offenders," are under age eighteen. The question remains, Why do these kids do it? To what extent are their reasons different from those of adults who kill their parents?

In *Why Kids Kill Parents,* Heide (1992) identified three types of parricide offenders from the clinical and research literature: the severely abused child, the dangerously antisocial child, and the severely mentally ill child. In the years since its publication, this typology has proved useful in understanding the dynamics that propel offspring to kill their parents. Most children and adolescents who kill their parents tend to fall into the first two types: severely abused or dangerously antisocial. In contrast, when adult children are the killers, they cluster into the dangerously antisocial or severely mentally ill types. The reasons for these differences will be apparent following a discussion of the three types.

The Severely Abused Child

The severely abused child is thought to be the most frequently encountered type of adolescent parricide offender (APO). These youths are typically seen as "good kids" who kill under extraordinary circumstances. They are depicted as individuals caught up in intolerable situations. They murder their parents because they are in fear of their lives, often killing to protect themselves or others from death or serious physical injury, or because they feel desperate and see no other way to end the chronic abuse they and other family members suffer.

Close examination of these cases typically reveals that there has been long-standing patterns of abuse in the home. Physical abuse is commonly found in these homes, meaning that a parent intentionally inflicts physical injury or attempts to injure or cause pain to the child because of the parent's unresolved needs. The critical consideration is that the parent's behavior is not appropriate or proportional to anything the child has done. Although some abusive parents may claim that they are only "disciplining" their children, physical abuse is by definition excessive and disproportionate to any misbehavior by the child. In some physically abusive incidents, the parent's conduct is often not at all responsive to the child's behavior; that is, the parent strikes out against the child when the youth has done nothing wrong because the parent is unhappy, angry, or stressed. For example, parents have attacked their children as the youths sat watching television or preparing dinner. One girl who killed her father had earlier sustained a dislocated back after being severely kicked by him. A boy who killed his father had previously suffered bruises and welts on his arms, legs, and back from beatings by his dad. The boy's father also kicked his son, punched him in the head, nose, mouth, and stomach, and led the boy around by the hair. The man also threw things at his son—cutting him on occasion—and bent his son's thumb back so far that the boy was writhing on the floor in pain and thought the thumb would break. In these homes, the threat of serious injury or death is pervasive. Parents may threaten to kill their children, brandishing guns or knives and on occasion using them.

Verbal abuse is almost always present in these families. Parents say things to their children or make remarks in their presence about them that either are designed to damage their concepts of self or would reasonably be expected to undermine the children's senses of competency or self-esteem. Verbally abusive remarks include swearing at a child or insulting or belittling a child, by telling a daughter, for example, that she is "ugly" or "stupid" or saying to a son that he is "a sissy" or doesn't have the brains with which he was born.

Sexual abuse occurs in some homes in which sons and daughters kill parents. It is often harder to corroborate than physical and verbal abuse, because parents who sexually abuse their sons and daughters typically hide their activities from others. In addition, sexual abuse victims often feel partly responsible and ashamed, and are reluctant to tell others about the abuse, even when they are facing long prison sentences for killing the abusive parent. In some cases, the sexual abuse is characterized by gentleness on the part of the parent, who turns to the child to fill his or her needs for nurturance, love, or intimacy. In other cases, the sexual abuse is more appropriately characterized as brute force; the parent attacks the child to vent his rage and demonstrate his power, dynamics that are in fact similar to those seen in rape and sexual assault. Some parents expose their children to sexual issues that are age inappropriate and/or raise them in an environment that is sexually saturated or provocative. In the latter case, even though there may be no sexual contact with the child, the parent's activities are undeniably sexually explicit. These sexually abusive behaviors, although covert, are damaging to children because the children almost always know that these behaviors are "wrong" and feel confused about them. For example, one adolescent girl who killed her father was made to watch as her father's girlfriend performed oral sex on him; this man insisted on coming into the bathroom repeatedly

to converse with his adolescent daughter when she was showering.

In cases of severely abused children who kill their parents, psychological abuse is always present. Psychological abuse encompasses words and behaviors that undermine a child's sense of self, competence, and safety in the world. Verbal abuse is one type of psychological abuse. Physical and sexual abuse by a parent or guardian are also forms of psychological abuse because they destroy the child's sense of security and impede the development of competence in interpersonal relationships. Psychologically abusive messages take a variety of forms. Particularly undermining messages include repeatedly putting a child down by unfavorably comparing him with a sibling or another child, or characteristically expressing dissatisfaction with a child's accomplishments no matter how well she does. Psychologically abusive behaviors by parents are also myriad, and typically include repeated acts that are cruel or designed to humiliate the child into complying with parental expectations that a child may not be able to meet. One girl who killed her mother had endured many psychologically abusive acts by her. These included being prevented from seeing her godparents, who were very stable and good people and had practically raised the girl from the time she was a baby to about age twelve. One boy who had a bed-wetting problem killed his mother after she displayed his soiled bedsheets on a clothesline in the yard with a sign proclaiming the boy's problem for all the neighbors to see.

The Role of Neglect in Cases of Severely Abused Children

Not surprisingly, the focus in cases involving severely abused children is on the chronic nature of the abuse and its threat both to the child's psyche and to the child's very life. In nearly all of these cases, however, neglect accompanies the abuse in one or more forms, making it difficult to sort out the specific effects of each form of maltreatment. Physical and sexual abuse are often specifically defined incidents. In contrast, neglect is often chronic, and it is more difficult to identify. Four types of neglect are frequently seen in adolescent parricide offender cases.

Physical neglect has several components. Parents physically neglect their children by not providing adequate food or clothing, or by not providing a safe place to live. The failure to act to safeguard the child's physical and mental health also constitutes physical neglect. Failure to supervise the child properly is the most common form of neglect in the United States. Failure to set appropriate limits of behavior and to discipline one's child is also another common form of physical neglect.

An overlap in abuse and neglect occurs with youths who are physically, sexually, verbally, and psychologically abused, because these children are clearly not being protected by their parents; this constitutes a form of physical neglect. By the canons of good parenting, parents are supposed to provide a safe environment for their children. If one parent is being abusive, the nonabusive parent, if there is one, is responsible for protecting the child.

In addition to physical neglect, medical neglect is often encountered in cases of youth violence. The failure of parents to attend to their children's mental and physical health issues constitutes medical neglect. Adolescent parricide offenders are often seen by others as depressed and stressed for long periods of time preceding the killing.

Frequently in these cases, the youths are victims of emotional neglect. Neither the abusive nor the nonabusive parent, if there is one, is emotionally available to the child. In case after case, abusive parents are depicted as failing to provide loving messages and gestures and as not listening to their children. In abusive families, the nonabusive parent frequently escapes either physically or psychologically. The nonabusive parent is frequently physically absent from the abusive home and is therefore unable to protect the child or provide emotional support. A nonabusive parent who is in the home is often emotionally unavailable due to his or her own strategies for coping with the stress caused by the abusive parent. For example, nonabusive parents have reported turning to alcohol or "zoning out" on psychotropic drugs to cope with their spouses' destructive behavior. While this strategy may help the nonabusive parent cope with the situation, it often results in the emotional neglect of the child during a time of great need.

When the nonabusive parent leaves physically or emotionally, the child is at high risk of being a victim of emotional incest. In the absence of a spouse or age-appropriate mate, the abusive parent often expects the child to function like a surrogate partner, taking on the typical roles of a spouse and parent. The child may be expected to maintain the household (including cooking, cleaning, and raising younger siblings), as well as serving as a confidante to the parent. This type of neglect deprives the child of normal childhood experiences (such as participating in sports or extracurricular activities at school) and causes stress. Meeting expectations and assuming duties beyond their years is enormously stressful for children. When combined with other forms of abuse and neglect, the consequences can be devastating, with lifelong effects.

Child neglect typically begins at an early age and can seriously affect development. Children who experience early emotional neglect are at high risk for attachment disorders. The first two years, particularly the first six months, are critical periods for infants and young children. The foundation for trust of others is learned during this period when parents or guardians connect with children and meet their basic needs for food, physical comfort, and human contact. When the caretaker meets the child's needs, the child develops a healthy, secure attachment that becomes the basis for all future relationships.

The absence of a consistent, nurturing caregiver who forms a relationship with the child and takes care of the child's needs is developmentally traumatic. Children whose physical, emotional, and medical needs are not met learn very early in life that they cannot count on other human beings to respond to their needs and to comfort them. As a result, they disconnect from people and may not develop compassion and empathy for other human beings. They are often filled with distrust toward others and deep down harbor tremendous hatred and rage. Their pain and anger is a direct result of the parents' failure to nurture and care for them.

Children who have been neglected, like abused children, often have disorganized, insecure attachments to their caregivers. Without secure attachments, children cannot develop a healthy sense of themselves, and they often have difficulty connecting with other human beings throughout their lives. Because they do not form attachments to other people, they are more prone to acting out violently in relationships. Studies show that neglect is more devastating to a child than abuse by itself. Prolonged neglect can set the foundation for the development of the dangerously antisocial child.

The Dangerously Antisocial Child

Dangerously antisocial youths kill their parents for selfish, instrumental reasons. The term *dangerously antisocial child* here refers to individuals previously referred to by mental health professionals as "psychopathic" or "sociopathic" personalities. Today two more precise terms—conduct disorder (CD) and antisocial personality disorder (APD)—are used, depending on the age of the individual and the presence of specific criteria. Individuals who are diagnosed as having either of these disorders, unlike those who suffer from a psychotic disorder, are oriented in time and space and are free of delusions and hallucinations.

A youth under eighteen years of age may be classified clinically as having a conduct disorder when a long-standing pattern of violating the rights of others or disregarding major societal norms has been established. Diagnostic criteria include specific behavioral indicators of aggression to animals and people, theft or deceitfulness, destruction of property, and other serious rule violations. These indicators specifically target acts that constitute criminal behavior (e.g., battery, rape, vandalism, robbery, theft, arson) or behaviors that are deemed serious enough to warrant societal intervention (e.g., status offenses such as truancy, running away). CD is often the precursor to APD, a diagnosis reserved for adults (eighteen years of age and older) who engage in a similar response pattern.

The diagnosis of CD is to be distinguished from oppositional defiant disorder (ODD), often its forerunner. ODD is a pattern of long-standing defiant, negative, and hostile behavior (e.g., losing temper, arguing with adults, actively defying or refusing to comply with adults' requests) that is noncriminal. As diagrammed below, the three behavioral disorders can be placed along a continuum of defiance of authority and societal norms.

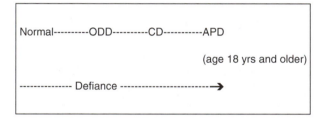

Abuse and neglect are often associated with behavioral disorders in children and adults. Children who are abused and neglected may adopt an antisocial way of responding to life as a means of psychic, if not physical, survival. Antisocial behavior can focus a youth's attention away from problems at home that are too difficult to handle. Criminal behavior can also provide an avenue for the youth to act out his or her pain. In the case of an adolescent parricide offender with a history of acting out, the question of whether the adolescent is truly sociopathic (that is, lacks a conscience) or has adopted a pattern of acting out as a coping strategy to maintain his or her fragile mental health is one best reserved for the mental health professional.

The family dynamics that set the stage for the development of ODD typically begin with parental neglect early in the child's life. ODD can often be traced to the failure of parents to set limits and to impose appropriate discipline for misbehavior, which is clearly a form of neglect. Children begin to learn societal rules and to accept authority and respect boundaries when they are between the ages of two and five years of age. Parents' acquiescence to their children's demands may not seem that significant when the child is three and wants a popsicle before dinner, or when the child is four and does not want to go to bed at the prescribed time. Unfortunately, the pattern becomes established and the stakes become higher and higher over time. The problem is often identified when youths are between ages twelve and fifteen and are obviously out of control, demanding to stay out until midnight and cursing their parents for "interfering" with their lives. Parents' attempts to set boundaries are ineffectual at this point. Adolescents who did not learn respect for authority in the home and lacked self-discipline as children can easily cross the threshold from defiant and oppositional behavior to criminal behavior, including violent acts. Parents are now seen by these children as obstacles, whose efforts to impede their goals are met with resentment, and on occasion with contempt.

Children whose parents do not set consistent limits are not the only ones at risk for development of ODD and CD. Children who have been severely neglected, as well as those who have been severely abused, are at risk for developing attachment disorders. As a result of their early childhood experiences, many abused and neglected youths fail to bond with others. These adolescents often lack attachments to teachers and conventional peers, as well as to parents. Consequently, they do not develop the values, empathy, and self-concept that foster self-control and could inhibit them from killing others.

Failure of parents to set boundaries was clearly present in the case of two brothers who viciously stabbed and bludgeoned to death their mother, father, and remaining sibling as the three slept peacefully in their beds. The boys were not mentally ill and there was no evidence of any type of abuse. The parents, however, were characterized as being "laid back" and as very tolerant about their sons' behaviors as the boys were growing up. Available evidence suggested that the parents were inconsistent about setting limits and imposing discipline. Both boys had extensive histories of antisocial behavior and alcohol abuse. In addition, previous mental health reports revealed that they had both been hospitalized for threatening to kill their mother. Both boys had physically assaulted their father and had told mental health professionals, as well as some friends, that they were going to kill their parents. The brothers had a history of involvement with an antisocial group known for endorsing a hate-filled ideology, engaging in violent tactics, and propagating anarchy. The parents were killed shortly after the boys learned that they were going to set some limits and were pursuing appropriate channels to hospitalize them.

The Severely Mentally Ill Child

Severely mentally ill children who murder their parents are psychotic or otherwise gravely mentally ill. They typically have a long-established psychiatric history. The killing of the parent is an underlying product of the mental illness. In one case, for example, an adolescent diagnosed with paranoid schizophrenia followed a detailed plan he had crafted to kill his mother to show his devotion to Satan.

Severe neglect and/or extreme abuse during early childhood can result in fragmentation of the child's mind, leading to dissociative identity disorder (DID) (formerly known as multiple personality disorder, or MPD) or to psychosis. Dissociation is a psychic response to overwhelming stress and hyperarousal. The child withdraws from the dangerous outside world and retreats into his or her internal world. With continued trauma, the internal world becomes increasingly complex and the child's personality may split into several parts, each specialized to cope with some aspect of the hostile environment.

Psychotic individuals have lost touch with reality. Typically their personalities are severely disorganized, their perceptions distorted, and their communications disjointed. They may experience hallucinations (hearing or seeing things that are not really happening) and bizarre delusions (beliefs that have no basis in reality and that would appear totally implausible to others in their environment; for example, a belief that one is the resurrected Jesus Christ returned to earth). Individuals with psychotic disorders do not understand that they are mentally ill and may behave bizarrely due to their belief systems or sensory experiences. They frequently need to be hospitalized until their mental disorder has been stabilized. Psychotropic medications are often helpful in reducing psychotic symptoms, including hallucinations and delusions.

Motivational Dynamics behind the Homicide

The key question in parricide cases is what propelled the child to kill his or her parent(s)? Cases are often not as simple and clear-cut as they initially appear. In-depth assessment of the offender and the circumstances behind the killing by a mental health professional experienced in domestic violence is essential. In addition, review of case materials and interviews with surviving family members and those who know the offender and the victim are important for corroborative purposes.

Abuse and neglect often exist in the histories of both juvenile and adult parricide offenders. The existence of abuse and/or neglect does not mean that the child was severely abused and killed out of terror or desperation. Abuse is unlikely to be the driving force in cases of adults who kill their mothers or fathers. Usually, adults have more resources and choices than do children and adolescents. A healthy adult who is living in a home with an abusive parent can move out of the dwelling or, if he or she stays, can seek help for the parent and set and maintain appropriate boundaries. For the healthy and prosocial adult, parricide is unlikely to be the answer. The research and clinical literature indicate that adults who kill parents often have documented histories of severe mental illness or of antisocial behavior. Depending on how they are viewed in the criminal justice system, they are likely to be sent to a psychiatric hospital or to be confined in prison for many years.

In contrast, when children and adolescents kill their parents, severe mental illness is almost always ruled out. Two competing theories are often argued by the defense and prosecution to win their cases. The defense is likely to maintain that the youth is a prosocial individual who was pushed beyond his limits and killed for reasons of physical or psychic survival. The prosecution is likely to stress that the youth is on his or her way to becoming a dangerously antisocial individual and warrants incapacitation (confinement in an institution to prevent further crime).

Regardless of how young parricide offenders are viewed, they typically do not fare well in the legal system. They are likely to be tried as adults, convicted, and sentenced to prison. The battered child syndrome, unlike the battered woman system, is not recognized in many states. Severely abused children typically are not criminally sophisticated. Thus, they exchange a life of abuse in their homes for a life of abuse behind prison walls.

Legal and Moral Dilemmas in the Twenty-First Century

Findings in the developmental neurophysiology of children subjected to severe and protracted abuse have important legal implications in how society deals with adolescent parricide offenders in the twenty-first century. Studies are increasingly linking extreme neglect and abuse with long-term changes in the nervous and endocrine systems. These changes affect cognitive, physiological, emotional, and social functions. A growing body of research literature indicates that individuals with extensive trauma histories often have difficulty thinking logically and behaving prosocially and are thereby at higher risk of behaving violently than those without such histories. Recent research findings also have indicated that neglect can have profound effects on children's development, including their ability to bond with others and feel empathy toward them, and to regulate and control strong emotions. These findings are best viewed in the context of recent research findings that have confirmed that the human brain is still developing through adolescence and is not fully developed until an individual is in his or her early twenties.

Advances in science are beginning to challenge fundamental notions of justice dating back thousands of years and may indeed pose a moral dilemma to the public: Should these youths be deemed as responsible for their behavior as other killers who have had different childhood histories, particularly if abuse and neglect have biologically compromised their ability to access higher cortical functions, regulate emotion, connect with other human beings, and respond adaptively to life's situations?

KATHLEEN M. HEIDE

See also **Attachment Theory and Domestic Violence; Battered Woman Syndrome; Child Abuse and Juvenile Delinquency; Child Neglect; Child Sexual Abuse; Children Witnessing Parental Violence; Coercive Control; Elder Abuse Perpetrated by Adult Children; Exchange Theory; Incest; Intergenerational Transfer of Intimate Partner Violence; Intimate Partner Homicide; Medical Neglect Related to Religion and Culture; Ritual Abuse–Torture in Families; Sibling Abuse; Social Learning Theory and Family Violence; Substance Use/Abuse and Intimate Partner Violence**

References and Further Reading

American Psychiatric Association. *Diagnostic and Statistical Manual of Mental Disorders,* 4th ed., text revision. Washington, DC: Author, 2000.
Beckman, Mary. "Crime, Culpability and the Adolescent Brain." *Science* 305 (July 30, 2004): 596–599. http://www.deathpenaltyinfo.org/article.php?scid=17&did=1112.
Boots, Denise Paquette, and Kathleen M. Heide. "A Cross-Cultural Comparison of Kids Who Kill Parents and What Happens to Them." Paper presented at the 56th annual meeting of the American Society of Criminology, Nashville, Tennessee, November 2004.
Bureau of Justice Statistics. *Homicide Trends in the United States, 1976–2004.* http://www.ojp.usdoj.gov/bjs/homicide/tables/urbantab.htm.
Ewing, Charles Patrick. *Fatal Families: The Dynamics of Intrafamily Homicides.* Thousand Oaks, CA: Sage Publications, 1997.
Federal Bureau of Investigation. Uniform Crime Reports. http://www.fbi.gov/ucr/ucr.htm.
Heide, Kathleen M. *Why Kids Kill Parents: Child Abuse and Adolescent Homicide.* Columbus: Ohio State University Press, 1992; Thousand Oaks, CA: Sage Publications, 1995.
———. "Parents Who Get Killed and the Children Who Kill Them." *Journal of Interpersonal Violence* 8, no. 4 (1993): 531–544.
———. "Weapons Used by Juveniles and Adults to Kill Parents." *Behavioral Sciences and the Law* 11 (1993): 397–405.
———. *Young Killers: The Challenge of Juvenile Homicide.* Thousand Oaks, CA: Sage Publications, 1999.
———. "Youth Homicide: A Review of the Literature and a Blueprint for Action." *International Journal of Offender Therapy and Comparative Criminology* 47, no. 1 (2003): 6–36.
———, Ph.D., Professor of Criminology, University of South Florida homepage. http://www.cas.usf.edu/criminology/heide.
Heide, Kathleen M., Denise Boots, Craig Alldredge, Brian Donerly, and Jennifer R. White. "Battered Child Syndrome: An Overview of Case Law and Legislation." *Criminal Law Bulletin* 41, no. 3 (2005): 219–239.
Heide, Kathleen M., and Thomas Petee. "Parents Who Get Killed and the Children Who Kill Them: An Examination of 24 Years of Data." In *Proceedings of the 2003 Homicide Research Working Group Annual Symposium,* edited by Carolyn R. Block and Richard L. Block. Chicago: Homicide Research Working Group, 2003, pp. 319–335.
Heide, Kathleen M., and Eldra P. Solomon. "Biology, Childhood Trauma, and Homicide: Rethinking Justice." Paper presented at the International Congress on Law and Mental Health, Paris, July 2005.
Magid, Ken, and Carole A. McKelvey. *High Risk: Children without a Conscience.* New York: Bantam, 1987.
National Association for Children of Alcoholics. http://www.nacoa.org/aboutnacoa.htm.
National Association of Counsel for Children. http://nacchildlaw.org/childrenlaw/childmaltreatment.html.
National Council on Child Abuse and Family Violence. http://www.nccafv.org.
National Council on Crime and Delinquency. http://www.nccd-crc.org.
Office of Juvenile Justice and Delinquency Prevention. http://ojjdp.ncjrs.org.
Straus, Murray, Ph.D., Professor of Sociology and Co-Director of Family Research Laboratory, University of New Hampshire homepage. http://pubpages.unh.edu/~mas2.

POLICE CIVIL LIABILITY IN DOMESTIC VIOLENCE INCIDENTS

Police serve as government's front-line service providers for victims of domestic violence (Friday, Metzgar, and Walters 1991). While some law enforcement officers effectively respond to domestic violence (Younglove, Kerr, and Vitello 2002), other police have been slow to appropriately enforce restraining orders, make mandatory arrests, be sensitive to victims' needs, and refer victims to social service agencies (Huisman, Martinez, and Wilson 2005). In an analysis of actual domestic violence calls for service, for example, victims perceived more domestic violence than the police reported (Harris et al. 2001), suggesting an increased need for police training and appropriate enforcement of existing domestic violence laws by police.

The tepid law enforcement response to family violence has led to the charge that police do not place a priority on domestic violence (Blackwell and Vaughn 2003). Some police continue to believe that domestic violence calls for service are for social workers to handle, not crime fighters (Sherman, Schmidt, and Rogan 1992). When empathetic police show sympathy toward victims at domestic violence scenes, many colleagues within the masculine police culture perceive this sensitivity to be a weakness (Adelman 2003). To the contrary, research shows that empathetic initial response by on-scene police at domestic violence incidents can lead to positive victim outcomes (Miller 2003). Moreover, when police refer victims to appropriate social service agencies, research indicates that law enforcement officers get a "broader understanding of [police] agency procedures and policies geared toward solving the social problem of family violence, as well as to understanding the general nature of family violence from a variety of perspectives" (Giacomazzi and Smithey 2001, pp. 118–119). Slow and inappropriate police response to domestic violence incidents, however, has resulted in police being held legally accountable through the courts via civil litigation.

Remedy for Violation of Federally Guaranteed Rights: Section 1983

The 1871 Civil Rights Act, also known as the 1871 Ku Klux Klan Act, has been codified into federal law as Title 42 of the United States Code, Section 1983 (del Carmen 1991). This federal law serves as a civil remedy for victims to recover monetary damages when their federally guaranteed rights are violated by defendants who are acting under color of law (Vaughn and Coomes 1995). Section 1983 was rarely used for the first one hundred years of its existence (Kappeler 2001). The statute did not have teeth until four legal developments occurred.

First, the U.S. Supreme Court ruled in a series of cases that officers acting outside the scope of their legitimate law enforcement authority could be considered to be officers acting under the "color of law"; therefore, under this interpretation of the "color of law" element, officers acting in violation of the law could now be sued under Section 1983 if they acted pursuant to the power given to them by the state and used their state-sanctioned authority to violate victims' federally guaranteed rights (Vaughn and Coomes 1995). Along these lines, in 1961 the U.S. Supreme Court ruled in *Monroe v. Pape* that officers could be sued under Section 1983 for an illegal search of a family's home, even though the search was outside the officers' legal authority.

The second development that led to more Section 1983 lawsuits involved the interpretation of who can be sued under the statute. According to the statute itself, only "persons" can be sued. Up until 1978, for purposes of Section 1983, municipal entities were not considered persons. The statute became much more appealing to plaintiffs' attorneys once the U.S. Supreme Court decided *Monell v. New York Department of Social Services* (1978), in which the Court held that municipalities are "persons" for purposes of Section 1983. The *Monell* case established that cities, counties, and police departments are subject to Section 1983 liability if a departmental policy, custom, or practice was the cause of the victim's constitutional violation. The *Monell* ruling made all municipal corporations, e.g., cities, counties, sheriff's offices, police departments, subject to suit under Section 1983, allowing plaintiffs to sue the "deep pockets" of governmental entities when their officers violate victims' federally guaranteed rights (del Carmen 1991).

A third development that increased police liability across a broad spectrum of issues was the Court's ruling in *City of Canton v. Harris* (1989), in which the Court held that municipal entities and police departments can be sued for failure to adequately train their officers. The *Canton* Court held that departments and municipal entities were subject to suit if their deliberate indifference in failing to adequately train their officers in "plainly obvious" areas was the moving force behind the victims' constitutional violation (*Board of the County Commissioners of Bryan County v. Brown* 1997).

A fourth important development in Section 1983 jurisprudence from the U.S. Supreme Court was *Pembauer v. City of Cincinnati* (1986), where the Court held that cities and, by extension, police departments can be held liable under Section 1983 for a single decision by an authorized departmental policymaker. The *Pembauer* decision led to increased lawsuits against police departments, cities, and counties whenever their officers became involved in a domestic violence dispute and a negative outcome resulted, especially when a chief of police or sheriff or other upper-level policymaking official gave direction, orders, supervised, or had knowledge of the domestic violence incident in question.

All Section 1983 litigation has increased because of plaintiffs' ability to sue:

- officers who act outside the appropriate confines of their behavior,
- police policymakers for a single decision that violates federally guaranteed rights,
- municipal corporations (e.g., cities, counties, sheriff's offices, police departments), and
- departments for failing to adequately train their officers in obvious areas.

Under this legal landscape, a logical prediction would be that lawsuits against the police for inappropriate response to domestic violence would increase, especially given the growing awareness of the scope and severity of the domestic violence problem. Indeed, research has confirmed that police liability for domestic violence is a concern among law enforcement administrators (Vaughn, Cooper, and del Carmen 2001).

Town of Castle Rock v. Gonzales: The United States Supreme Court Rules on Police Civil Liability in Domestic Violence Incidents

In *Town of Castle Rock v. Gonzales* (2005), the U.S. Supreme Court held that the police and the municipality for which they were employed were not liable for failing to properly enforce a domestic violence restraining order. Jessica Gonzales brought a Title 42 U.S.C. Section 1983 lawsuit against the City of Castle Rock, Colorado, and the Castle Rock police, alleging that the defendants violated her procedural and substantive due process rights as specified by the Fourteenth Amendment to the U.S. Constitution when they refused to enforce a restraining order against her estranged husband.

The facts of the case were undisputed. In May 1999, Ms. Gonzales, in connection with her divorce, obtained a restraining order against her estranged husband, Simon Gonzales. The restraining order limited Mr. Gonzales' contact with the couple's children to certain hours and indicated that the children could leave their house only with Ms. Gonzales' approval. In June 1999, two months after Ms. Gonzales obtained the restraining order, Mr. Gonzales abducted their three daughters (*Gonzales v. City of Castle Rock* 2002). When Ms. Gonzales discovered that her daughters were missing, she called the Castle Rock police to request assistance. Police officers were dispatched to Ms. Gonzales' home, where she told them that her estranged husband had abducted her daughters. She showed the officers the restraining order and requested the police to enforce it, so her children could be returned to her immediately.

Without specifying a reason, the on-scene officers told Ms. Gonzales that they could not enforce her restraining order. Rather, the officers instructed Ms. Gonzales to wait for her children to return home. After several phone calls to the Castle Rock Police Department requesting that the police attempt to find Mr. Gonzales and return her children, Ms. Gonzales drove to the police station, where a police officer took an incident report. A couple of hours after the incident report was filed, Mr. Gonzales drove to and opened fire in the Castle Rock Police Station. Mr. Gonzales died during a shootout with police. Later, the police discovered the bodies of the three Gonzales children in the cab of Mr. Gonzales' truck.

In bringing a Section 1983 lawsuit in the U.S. District Court for the District of Colorado, Ms. Gonzales claimed that the City of Castle Rock and its police violated her and her deceased children's

Fourteenth Amendment procedural due process rights under the U.S. Constitution by failing to enforce a restraining order that she had against her estranged husband. The district court dismissed Ms. Gonzales' lawsuit, holding that she failed to state a claim under the Fourteenth Amendment for violation of her procedural and substantive due process rights. On appeal, a three-judge panel of the United States Court of Appeals for the Tenth Circuit also rejected Ms. Gonzales' substantive due process rights claim under the "danger creation theory," which arose out of the 1989 U.S. Supreme Court case *DeShaney v. Winnebago County of Department of Social Services* (1989). The danger creation theory postulates that if a state's affirmative conduct places a person in jeopardy, then the state may be liable for the harm inflicted on that person by a third party. This is an exception to the general principle that the state is not liable for an injury that a third party inflicts on a member of the public (Black 1990).

DeShaney involved a social work agency that released a boy to his father even though agency personnel knew that the boy's father was abusive. Against the mother's pleas not to release the boy to the father, the boy was released, whereby the father beat the boy into serious brain injury. In denying the mother's suit under the Fourteenth Amendment's substantive due process clause, the U.S. Supreme Court held that the social work agency could not be held liable because of the public duty doctrine. Under the public duty doctrine, the government cannot be held liable for third-party victimization, and in *DeShaney* it was the father who injured the boy, not the government. The Court added, however, that substantive due process may be violated in very narrow circumstances: when someone is in custody, when a special relationship exists between the government and the victim, and when the government by its actions creates more danger or enhances the danger for the victim that sets in motion the third-party victimization. Under these three narrow exceptions, substantive due process liability may be pursued under Section 1983.

Using the U.S. Supreme Court's "danger creation" theory, the three-judge Tenth Circuit panel concluded that Ms. Gonzales' substantive due process claims failed because the Castle Rock police did not create or increase the danger to Ms. Gonzales or her children, or place them in jeopardy. With respect to Ms. Gonzales' substantive due process claims, the three-judge Tenth Circuit panel followed *DeShaney,* saying that the police were not constitutionally obligated to protect individuals against harm from nongovernment agents.

While *DeShaney* barred recovery for Ms. Gonzales under substantive due process, the three-judge Tenth Circuit panel turned to her procedural due process claim. The formation of a federal constitutional right under procedural due process originated with *Board of Regents v. Roth* (1972), where the Court recognized that citizens under certain circumstances have property interests entitling them to procedural due process protections. Under the *Roth* rubric, the three-judge Tenth Circuit panel ruled that Ms. Gonzales' procedural due process rights were violated.

According to the three-judge Tenth Circuit panel, the state statute mandated protection for Ms. Gonzales by the police pursuant to violation of the restraining order. The court interpreted the mandatory language of the statute to mean that when probable cause exists to show that a restraining order has been violated, police officers "shall arrest, or if an arrest would be impractical under the circumstances, seek a warrant for the arrest." The three-judge Tenth Circuit panel concluded that the protective order created a property interest specifically for Ms. Gonzales under the due process clause of the Fourteenth Amendment to the U.S. Constitution. The court was careful to point out that the property interest would not be a general obligation of the police to protect the public, but solely to protect Ms. Gonzales.

On rehearing *en banc,* the entire Tenth Circuit agreed with the three-judge panel, holding that Ms. Gonzales adequately stated a procedural due process violation against the City of Castle Rock, although the individual police officers were entitled to qualified immunity. The qualified immunity defense is never available to municipal entities or police departments, only to individual police officers (*Owens v. City of Independence* 1980). The *en banc* Tenth Circuit ruled that a reasonable officer in the same situation would not have known that the restraining order required mandatory arrest, or in other words, the law in the Tenth Circuit was not clearly established that arrest had to occur. In this instance, the court stressed that a reasonable police officer could not be expected to know that a property interest was created on the basis of the restraining order and a Colorado law that mandated arrest.

The *en banc* Tenth Circuit ruled that Ms. Gonzales was entitled to police enforcement of the restraining order against Mr. Gonzales from the state court judge. In reaching this decision, the Tenth Circuit was following a line of U.S. Supreme Court decisions on what has been termed the "negative implication jurisprudence" (*Greenholtz v. Nebraska*

Penal Inmates 1979; *Hewitt v. Helms* 1983), even though the U.S. Supreme Court questioned the legitimacy of this legal methodology, at least in prison cases, in *Sandin v. Conner* (1995).

Under the negative implication jurisprudence framework, mandatory language within state statutes, procedural rules, and/or policy manuals create due process property interests protected by the U.S. Constitution. The *en banc* Tenth Circuit said that the restraining order in the Gonzales case stated that police *shall* enforce the order, emphasizing that the language clearly intended its terms to be enforced by the police.

On appeal to the U.S. Supreme Court, Justice Antonin Scalia struck down the Tenth Circuit's ruling, declining to hold that a state-law restraining order created a property interest under the U.S. Constitution. In other words, the Colorado state law did not give Ms. Gonzales a right to police enforcement of the restraining order, which absolved the City of Castle Rock of civil liability under Section 1983.

According to the U.S. Supreme Court, although Colorado law entitled Ms. Gonzales to enforcement of her restraining order, she did not have a property interest in that enforcement. The Court explained that there were no due process rights violated, since an entitlement to enforcement of the restraining order did not create a constitutional property interest, but only an entitlement to procedure. Even if the statute did create entitlement to enforcement of the restraining order, Justice Scalia explained that such a right would not be a constitutional property interest.

As they did in *Sandin v. Conner* (1995), the Court rejected the legal methodology of the negative implication jurisprudence in *Town of Castle Rock,* explaining that entitlements are created by state law, not the U.S. Constitution, and a violation of an entitlement under state law does not necessarily violate a federally guaranteed right. An individual may have a benefit under state law, but he or she may not be protected by the U.S. Constitution whenever that benefit is violated. In contrast, to have an entitlement protected under the U.S. Constitution, the benefit must be described by a U.S. law, making such a benefit a federally guaranteed right and subject to suit under Section 1983. The Court was careful to stress that not every benefit is protected by the procedural due process clause, meaning that although Ms. Gonzales had the benefit of having her restraining order enforced, police had discretion as to which benefits were enforced.

Another justification the Court gave for finding no property interest was the Tenth Circuit's failure

to rely on "state expertise." Prior to finding a property interest in a state statute, the Court specified that the Tenth Circuit should have interpreted state law, instead of simply "quoting language from the restraining order, the statutory text, and a state-legislative-hearing transcript." Based on the restraining order language and Colorado state law, the Court concluded that police officers are not required to make arrests, but only to seek a warrant, which did not entitle Ms. Gonzales to a property interest; it entitled Ms. Gonzales only to the procedure that the police would seek an arrest warrant.

The Court concluded that police operate with discretion when interpreting mandatory arrest laws and restraining orders, which means that they are not truly mandatory. Interpreting Colorado state law, the Court said that the police maintained discretion, since the state law gave police officers two options: make an arrest or pursue an arrest warrant. The Court held that police use discretion to enforce restraining orders, especially when suspects are not present and their whereabouts are unknown. In fact, in the Gonzales case, the only proper response, according to the Court, was to pursue a warrant. Thus, the Court suggested that there is property interest in the Fourteenth Amendment due process clause when the suspect is present and his or her whereabouts are known. In other words, police officers have no discretion when they can identify immediately the suspect, because as soon as that happens, a procedural due process duty to arrest attaches (Black 1990).

Turning to the public duty doctrine, the Court held that police officers are not required to enforce restraining orders even under a state law mandate. The "public duty" doctrine specifies that police owe a general duty to protect general society, and no duty is owed to protect specific individuals. The public duty doctrine is a rule in tort law that a governmental entity (such as a state or municipality) cannot be held liable for an individual plaintiff's injury resulting from third-party victimization (Black 1990). Even if domestic violence restraining order statutes specifically mandate enforcement, under the public duty doctrine, an individual victim of nonpolice enforcement does not have a specific entitlement to enforcement of the restraining order. Similar to mandatory arrest laws that serve the general well-being of the public and not specific victims of domestic violence, the Court reiterated that the public duty doctrine also limits liability for nonenforcement of restraining orders.

The Court also emphasized that under *DeShaney,* the police cannot be held liable for third-party victimization. When victims are not directly harmed by the government, the victim's injuries are a result of a third party, not a state employee. When the government harms victims, there is a direct benefit to the state which triggers a property interest and due process protections because the Fourteenth Amendment protects the victim's life, liberty, and property from direct government actions; however, the Court ruled that indirect or incidental actions caused by third-party victimization remove due process protections from the victim.

The Court concluded that the "public duty" doctrine prevents police liability in Section 1983 cases under federal law when third parties injure domestic violence victims for both substantive and procedural due process violations. Thus, the Court ruled that there was no property interest in the police enforcing the restraining order under the procedural component of the Fourteenth Amendment's due process clause.

The Impact of the Violence against Women Act on Domestic Violence and Police Civil Liability

Congress enacted the Violence against Women Act (VAWA) in 1994 as a pioneering piece of legislation geared toward stopping both domestic and street violence against women. While VAWA was divided into seven lettered sections, the focus here, domestic violence, represents one of the multitude of problems that Congress was attempting to address when President Bill Clinton signed the legislation into law.

VAWA was enacted because previous institutional efforts to combat violence against women, including domestic violence, failed to receive adequate federal funding. By recognizing the extent of the problem, Congress funded VAWA grants specifically designed for "personnel, training, technical assistance, data collection, and other equipment." With increased federal funding, VAWA was designed, in part, to assist police agencies to reduce violence against women, especially domestic violence.

VAWA funded hotline training so that victims could receive emergency counseling and referrals for victim services over the telephone in a timely manner. VAWA funding also trained law enforcement personnel on the interstate travel patterns of domestic batterers, developing databases of domestic abusers who traveled across state lines and threatened and/or abused their victims. In an attempt to control post-separation domestic violence and stalking, VAWA funded police training on identification of criminal history records, protection orders, and wanted person records.

Because homelessness is highly correlated with domestic violence, VAWA addressed the need for temporary victim housing. In this effort, VAWA funded construction and maintenance of battered women's shelters. Also related to family life, since youth growing up in violent homes are at increased risk of engaging in violence themselves, VAWA provided youth grants to create programs to educate "young people about domestic violence and violence among intimate partners."

After Congress enacted VAWA, police training occurred on mediation, dispute resolution, verbal judo, and intervention without use of force in domestic violence incidents (Blackwell and Vaughn 2003). VAWA sparked passage of civil protection orders and mandatory arrest laws, requiring police officers to arrest batterers. VAWA also encouraged criminal prosecutions against batterers without the victim's consent (Catania 2005). Despite those laws, evidence suggests, and the *Town of Castle Rock* case demonstrates, that police officers need additional training on how to respond to domestic violence incidents.

An additional problem for domestic violence victims remains confidentiality and direct links to support systems that keep victims safe from their abusers. With VAWA, Congress addressed this need, stressing the importance of trust and respect as the foundations of the relationship between victims and their support team. VAWA monies helped to provide sensitivity training for police on the needs of domestic violence victims. Many departments have instituted victim-witness assistance programs and have hired specially trained victim advocates who respond to domestic violence calls for service. These domestic violence advocates are law enforcement employees, but they focus exclusively on the victims' needs (Herman 2005).

Of particular concern to police civil liability for inappropriate response to enforcement of an existing restraining order as discussed in this essay, VAWA also "encouraged states, Indian tribal governments, or local units of government to treat domestic violence as a serious violation of criminal law." As a result, VAWA grants were designed for implementation of mandatory arrest and protection order violation policies. Also part of the *Town of Castle Rock* case and addressed in VAWA was the heightened violence that often accompanies the separation of the abuser and the abused. A common misperception regarding women in abusive relationships is that if they would simply end the relationship, the abuse would end (Fugate et al. 2005); however, research shows that domestic violence may increase upon separation of the parties

(Fleury, Sullivan, and Bybee 2000), as was evidenced in the *Town of Castle Rock* case.

Discussion and Conclusion

Notwithstanding the outcome of *Town of Castle Rock v. Gonzales* (2005), where the U.S. Supreme Court ruled that there was no Section 1983 civil liability for inappropriate police response to domestic violence, liability remains a risk for law enforcement under various state tort laws (del Carmen 1991) and pursuant to Section 1983 under the Fourteenth Amendment's equal protection clause (*Thurman v. City of Torrington* 1984). Despite negative perceptions of police among some victims, a few studies report that domestic violence victims can favorably view police interactions at calls for service (Apsler, Cummis, and Carl 2003). Domestic violence victims trust police when they respond appropriately and enforce existing restraining orders, follow through on mandatory arrest of the primary aggressor, and steer victims to counseling and social service agencies (Apsler et al. 2003).

Research confirms what the *Town of Castle Rock* case demonstrates: Future domestic violence is likely when abusers make repeated violent threats, engage in actual violence, and have arrest histories for domestic violence. Hirschel and Hutchinson's (2003, p. 332) research also "supports the argument that officials should pay attention to the preferences of victims of domestic violence." Although not liable under Section 1983, the Castle Rock Police should have immediately, per Ms. Gonzales' request, attempted to enforce her restraining order. Kane's (2000) research also sheds light on the tragic outcome in the *Town of Castle Rock* case, reporting that in his sample, as the violent threats to victims escalated, a restraining order against the offender was less likely to be enforced by the police, thereby doing little to diminish the violence against the very individuals the restraining order was designed to protect.

While the field of domestic violence research enters its second decade, much more remains to be discovered (Rhatigan, Moore, and Street 2005). To the extent that community policing can improve police–citizen relations, it has a welcomed place in the overall law enforcement response to domestic violence (Giacomazzi and Smithey 2001). Research has shown that reducing violence against women is more nuanced than simply mandating arrest for all domestic violence perpetrators (Finn et al. 2004). Thus, more research, study, and analyses are needed regarding the most appropriate police response to lessen victim exposure to domestic violence

and lessen police exposure to legal action. Research also needs to identify the particular risk factors associated with victim injury when police respond to domestic violence incidents (Michalski 2004). In other words, more needs to be known about what police should and should not do in domestic violence incidents to reduce victim injury, increase offender deterrence, and provide faithful enforcement of statutory enactments and judicial precedents.

CLARISSA FREITAS DIAS, JESSICA L. EKHOMU and MICHAEL S. VAUGHN

See also **Domestic Violence by Law Enforcement Officers; Factors Influencing Reporting Behavior by Male Domestic Violence Victims; Gay Domestic Violence, Police Attitudes and Behaviors toward; Police Decision-Making Factors in Domestic Violence Cases; Police Response to Domestic Violence Incidents; Training Practices for Law Enforcement in Domestic Violence Cases**

References and Further Reading

Adelman, M. "The Military, Militarism, and the Militarization of Domestic Violence." *Violence Against Women* 9 (2003): 1118–1152.

Apsler, R., M. R. Cummis, and S. Carl. "Perceptions of the Police by Female Victims of Domestic Partner Violence." *Violence Against Women* 9 (2003): 1318–1335.

Black, H. C. *Black's Law Dictionary,* 6th ed. St. Paul, MN: West, 1990.

Blackwell, B. S., and M. S. Vaughn. "Police Civil Liability for Inappropriate Response to Domestic Assault Victims." *Journal of Criminal Justice* 31 (2003): 129–146.

Board of Regents v. Roth, 408 U.S. 564 (1972).

Board of the County Commissioners of Bryan County v. Brown, 520 U.S. 397 (1997).

Catania, S. "The Counselor." *Mother Jones* 30 (2005, July/August): 44–48.

City of Canton v. Harris, 489 U.S. 378 (1989).

del Carmen, R. V. *Civil Liabilities in American Policing: A Text for Law Enforcement Personnel.* Englewood Cliffs, NJ: Brady, 1991.

DeShaney v. Winnebago County Department of Social Services, 489 U.S. 189 (1989).

Finn, M. A., B. S. Blackwell, L. J. Stalans, S. Studdard, and L. Dugan. "Dual Arrest Decisions in Domestic Violence Cases: The Influence of Departmental Policies." *Crime and Delinquency* 50 (2004): 565–589.

Fleury, R. E., C. M. Sullivan, and D. I. Bybee. "When Ending the Relationship Does Not End the Violence." *Violence Against Women* 6 (2000): 1363–1383.

Friday, P. C., S. Metzgar, and D. Walters. "Policing Domestic Violence: Perceptions, Experience, and Reality." *Criminal Justice Review* 16 (1991): 198–213.

Fugate, M., L. Landis, K. Riordan, S. Naureckas, and B. Engel. "Barriers to Domestic Violence Help Seeking: Implications for Intervention." *Violence Against Women* 11 (2005): 290–310.

Giacomazzi, A. L., and M. Smithey. "Community Policing and Family Violence against Women: Lessons Learned from a Multiagency Collaborative." *Police Quarterly* 4 (2001): 99–122.

Gonzales v. City of Castle Rock, 307 F.3d 1258 (10th Cir. 2002), *aff'd,* 366 F.3d 1093 (10th Cir. 2004) (*en banc*), *rev'd, Town of Castle Rock v. Gonzales,* 545 U.S. ___ (2005).

Greenholtz v. Nebraska Penal Inmates, 442 U.S. 1 (1979).

Harris, S. D., K. R. Dean, G. W. Holden, and M. J. Carlson. "Assessing Police and Protective Order Reports of Violence: What Is the Relation?" *Journal of Interpersonal Violence* 16 (2001): 602–609.

Herman, J. L. "Justice from the Victim's Perspective." *Violence Against Women* 11 (2005): 571–602.

Hewitt v. Helms, 459 U.S. 460 (1983).

Hirschel, D., and I. W. Hutchinson. "The Voices of Domestic Violence Victims: Predictors of Victim Preference for Arrest and the Relationship between Preference for Arrest and Revictimization." *Crime and Delinquency* 49 (2003): 313–336.

Huisman, K., J. Martinez, and C. Wilson. "Training Police Officers on Domestic Violence and Racism." *Violence Against Women* 11 (2005): 792–821.

Kane, R. J. "Police Responses to Restraining Orders in Domestic Violence Incidents: Identifying the Custody-Threshold Thesis." *Criminal Justice and Behavior* 27 (2000): 561–580.

Kappeler, V. E. *Critical Issues in Police Civil Liability,* 3rd ed. Prospect Heights, IL: Waveland, 2001.

Michalski, J. H. "Making Sociological Sense out of Trends in Intimate Partner Violence: The Social Structure of Violence against Women." *Violence Against Women* 10 (2004): 652–675.

Miller, J. "An Arresting Experiment: Domestic Violence Victim Experiences and Perceptions." *Journal of Interpersonal Violence* 18 (2003): 695–716.

Monell v. New York Department of Social Services, 436 U.S. 658 (1978).

Monroe v. Pape, 365 U.S. 167 (1961).

Owens v. City of Independence, 445 U.S. 622 (1980).

Pembauer v. City of Cincinnati, 475 U.S. 469 (1986).

Rhatigan, D. L., T. M. Moore, and A. E. Street. "Reflections on Partner Violence: 20 Years of Research and Beyond." *Journal of Interpersonal Violence* 20 (2005): 82–88.

Sandin v. Conner, 515 U.S. 472 (1995).

Sherman, L. W., J. D. Schmidt, and D. P. Rogan. *Policing Domestic Violence: Experiments and Dilemmas.* New York: Free Press, 1992.

Thurman v. City of Torrington, 595 F.Supp. 1521 (D. Conn. 1984).

Vaughn, M. S., and L. F. Coomes. "Police Civil Liability under Section 1983: When Do Police Officers Act under Color of Law?" *Journal of Criminal Justice* 23 (1995): 395–415.

Vaughn, M. S., T. W. Cooper, and R. V. del Carmen. "Assessing Legal Liabilities in Law Enforcement: Police Chiefs' Views." *Crime and Delinquency* 47 (2001): 3–27.

Younglove, J. A., M. G. Kerr, and C. J. Vitello. "Law Enforcement Officers' Perceptions of Same Sex Domestic Violence: Reason for Cautious Optimism." *Journal of Interpersonal Violence* 17 (2002): 760–772.

POLICE DECISION-MAKING FACTORS IN DOMESTIC VIOLENCE CASES

Police officers are gatekeepers to the criminal court system for those who call on their assistance, including domestic violence victims; as such, police exercise much discretion regarding how to respond to domestic violence. This article examines what criteria police officers use to make arrest decisions in domestic violence cases and what community, departmental, and personal factors determine whether they follow laws indicating that officers are required to or may choose to arrest the perpetrator (i.e., mandatory and preferred arrest statues). Dual arrests, where both partners are arrested, have been identified as a problem because such arrests often punish the victims for using physical aggression in self-defense. Some states have implemented primary aggressor laws that encourage officers to arrest only the main perpetrator and not persons who may have used physical aggression to protect themselves. This entry examines how officers interpret conflicting stories to arrive at their decisions regarding whether and whom to arrest.

Three major sections of this article delineate how officers interpret, investigate, and respond to domestic violence situations. First, conceptual models describing how officers make decisions are reviewed. These models examine how officers interpret conflicting stories from intimate partners to decide who the primary aggressor is as well as how the police operate when mandatory or preferred arrest laws are implemented. Secondly, research on the criteria officers use to make arrest decisions is discussed. Lastly, this essay examines whether officers' gender, experience, or race influences how they interpret and respond to domestic violence situations.

How Officers Think about Domestic Violence Situations

Several environmental characteristics shape how officers think about domestic violence situations: officers' professional experience, departmental policies, and the extent to which the criminal justice system provides a coordinated response to domestic violence. Police officers have much discretion regarding how to handle domestic violence situations, even though all states have passed mandatory or preferred arrest statutes. Research shows that officers often do not arrest even if state law requires that they arrest when probable cause exists. *Probable cause* is a legal term meaning that evidence shows that it is more likely true than not true that a person committed a crime. Because there are no clear guidelines on when probable cause is met, mandatory arrest statutes cannot mandate arrest in all cases and do not eliminate police discretion.

Officers may use three overarching philosophies to integrate and interpret information: normative frame; efficiency, or pragmatic, frame; and legalistic frame. Decision frames are a set of rules about how to make arrest decisions and guide what questions are asked, what inferences are drawn, and what criteria receive the most consideration in arrest decisions. Decision frames derive from socialization and are connected to officers' values, attitudes, and worldviews. The normative frame emphasizes the question: What happened and who is to blame? Using the normative frame, officers examine what happened in the past and evaluate the moral appropriateness of each party's actions and their moral character. If both are equally blameworthy, officers will arrest both disputants. When the normative frame is used, battered women may be blamed for the violence when they deviate from social gender-biased norms. Research has found that officers' belief that violence was justified by infidelity reduced the likelihood of arresting the perpetrator (Saunders 1995). Several studies have found that officers place more blame on battered women who have been drinking; however, the effect of women's drinking on arrest decision varies widely across departments and is

determined by how officers interpret it. Moreover, research has found weak and inconsistent effects of officers' attitudes about women's role in society in their decisions to arrest, and situational characteristics have much stronger effect on arrest decisions (see Stalans and Finn 1995, 2000).

Using the normative frame, officers assess whether the husband or wife should have acted differently; whereas using the efficiency frame, officers focus on whether the disputants practically could have each acted differently and their potential for future violence. Officers using the efficiency frame are concerned with their own self-interest and how arrest will affect promotions, their time, and job security. Officers may be less likely to arrest if the case occurs close to the end of their shift and they are not allowed overtime pay to complete paperwork or processing of the defendant. Thus, they use arrest sparingly when they believe that arrests are not rewarded on their part. Officers do not attempt to unravel the past, but instead attempt to assess the likelihood of future danger or bad media publicity if an arrest is not made. Officers also judge the credibility of each disputant to determine whether claims can be substantiated and successfully prosecuted in court. Thus, the efficiency frame focuses on the self-interest of the officer and how likely it is that the arrest will lead to a successful conviction or decrease the danger.

The legalistic frame assumes that officers apply policies or statutes using only legal criteria and a strict interpretation of the statutes. There are several legal criteria that officers may consider in assessing the situation: the presence of physical injuries on one party, the use of a weapon, property damage, the couple arguing in front of the police, and third-party witnesses. The legalistic frame assumes a rational decision maker who does not use attitudes or stereotypes to interpret information. Much research refutes that the legalistic frame is an accurate portrayal of officers' decision making. Instead, research indicates that officers do not automatically arrest when mandatory arrest statutes are enacted and that they consider offender, victim, and personal characteristics that are not criteria specified in the statutes or policies. Research has found that officers were significantly more likely to arrest both parties, even though state laws discouraged such arrests, if their police department had a policy to arrest both parties when both claimed self-defense (see Finn et al. 2004 for a review of research on dual arrests). Officers are clearly selective about following policies and are more likely to follow policies that are consistent with their beliefs and attitudes. Moreover, officers do not consistently use legal criteria and expand their focus to include other situational and disputants' characteristics.

In summary, officers typically use either the efficiency or the normative frame to interpret information, guide the questioning of suspects, and make arrest decisions. Officers' use of the legalistic frame has received little support (for additional information, see Hoyle 1998; Stalans and Finn 1995).

Officers also use stereotypes about domestic violence, battered women, and categories of people based on social class, mental illness, race, gender, and other salient categories. Whereas the normative and efficiency frames guide the decision-making process, stereotypes and attitudes help officers to complete missing information, interpret conflicting stories, and make assumptions about likely outcomes or responses. Research has found that experienced officers considered their stereotypic beliefs about battered women's propensity to use self-defense in arriving at their arrest decisions. Officers also use their stereotypes about domestic violence when the wife is drunk, but stereotypes do not influence arrest decisions when the wife appears to be normal (Stalans and Finn 1995, 2000). Officers infer that men who abuse wives who are hallucinating or drunk are less dangerous and that these wives are more responsible for the violence, suggesting that stereotypes about mental illness guide their interpretations (Stalans and Finn 1995, 2002). These stereotypes thus affect officers' inferences about the situation and may lead them to provide unequal protection for mentally ill victims or victims who violate social or gender norms (Robinson 2000).

Criteria Officers Consider in Making Arrest Decisions

Numerous studies have examined what situational, offender, and victim characteristics officers consider in their arrest decisions. These studies have addressed several questions about how officers make arrest decisions in domestic violence cases. Are officers less likely to arrest when violence occurs in an intimate relationship than when it occurs against a stranger or acquaintance? What importance do officers place on the victim's preference for arrest? If the offender has fled, do officers investigate domestic violence cases differently than stranger or acquaintance violence cases? Do officers provide equal protection to all battered women or are they less likely to arrest the perpetrator when the victim violates gender or social norms or is a member of a minority group?

Are officers less likely to arrest perpetrators of intimate partner violence than those of violence against strangers or acquaintances? Research in the 1980s found that both intimate partner crimes and other violent crimes had similar arrest rates. But mixed findings from research in the 1990s, after mandatory and presumptive arrest statutes were passed, have still left the answer to this question unclear. Several studies also have found that arrest is less likely to occur in disputes involving intimate partner violence than in acquaintance or stranger violence, though many of these studies have not included cases where the offender is not present at the scene, have not controlled for situational differences, and have not examined differential arrest rates for only cases where the victim is the only witness, as in the typical domestic violence case (for a review, see Hall 2005). Contrary to these findings, when cases had only the victim as the witness, one study found that officers arrested 45 percent of the time in domestic violence cases and only 25 percent of the time in other violent cases. Moreover, domestic violence victims were significantly more likely to request arrest (42 percent) than were other violent-crime victims (33 percent), and officers placed more importance on victims' preference for arrest in making their arrest decisions about domestic violence cases compared with other violent cases. Officers also were more likely to arrest when the perpetrator was present at the scene in both domestic and other violent cases, and perpetrators were equally likely to be present at the scene in both domestic and other violent cases when officers arrived (see Eigenberg, Scarborough, and Kappeler 1996). Thus, officers under some circumstances may respond to domestic violence differently than to stranger violence, but future research is needed to determine these circumstances.

What criteria are most influential in officers' decisions to arrest, and do officers consider others than the legal criteria that should guide their decisions? Based on numerous studies, it is clear that officers consider several extralegal criteria in their decisions to arrest, such as suspect's alcohol use, presence of children, and marital status. These extralegal criteria have not been consistent predictors of arrest decisions, which indicates that other environmental circumstances may determine their influence. Legal criteria that have been found to consistently increase the likelihood of arrest include: disrespectful attitude toward the police, presence of witnesses, presence of a weapon, presence of the perpetrator, and a violation of an order of protection. Suspects flee the scene before the police arrive in about half of domestic violence cases, and officers are less likely to arrest perpetrators who have fled compared with those who are present at the scene, even though the absconded perpetrators could be easily located (Hall 2005).

Officers typically make an arrest in only 20 to 50 percent of the cases where there is clear evidence of a violation of an order of protection. This finding indicates that officers use their discretion and interpret the dangerousness and risk to the victim in determining whether to make such an arrest. Several studies have found that violation of an order of protection increases the likelihood of arrest, but its effect on arrest is no greater than other situational criteria. Moreover, other research found that violation of an order of protection did not increase the chance of arrest when weapons were present, and officers arrested in 76 percent of these cases. When weapons were not present, officers placed more importance on the violation of the order of protection and arrested in 44 percent of the cases compared with 12 percent of the low-risk cases that did not involve a violation of an order of protection (Kane 2000).

Other criteria have been inconsistent predictors of officers' arrest decisions: suspect's gender or race, victim's or suspect's use of alcohol, marital status, presence of children, presence of injuries, and victim's preference for arrest. Research based on police reports from actual cases has found mixed results for the suspect's gender. Moreover, based on two studies that manipulated the suspect's gender and mental state, officers were more likely to civilly commit and less likely to arrest female mentally ill perpetrators than male mentally ill perpetrators of domestic violence (Finn and Stalans 2002).

Research has found that arrest rates for cases involving visible injuries vary from 30 to 73 percent across police departments. In archival and vignette studies from the early 1980s through 2005, the presence or seriousness of visible injuries was not sufficient to invoke arrests, and its influence on arrest decisions depended upon other situational characteristics. For example, visible injuries increased the chance of arrest only when the perpetrator was present, and had no effect when the perpetrator had fled the scene before the police arrived. Officers also were more likely to use the presence of visible injuries in their arrest decisions when departments had clear policies to arrest when the victim had injuries or when the jurisdiction had a coordinated response to domestic violence (for a review, see Finn et al. 2004; Stalans and Finn 2000).

The importance of the victim's preference in arrest decisions clearly varies across departments, studies, and cases. Police officers often do not write in the police report the victim's preference even when it is a standard part of the police form, which suggests that it is not an important criterion. Thus, victims' preference for officers to arrest is not sufficient to prompt them to do so; for example, in one study, only 44 percent of the time did officers arrest when the victim requested it. Studies generally find that victims' preference for arrest has modest impact, accounting for 4 to 5 percent of variation in officers' decisions to arrest or not. Officers often are not persuaded by victims' preference because they think that most victims will drop charges, do not know what they want at that time, or are not providing an honest account of what happened. Officers' stereotypes about battered women and domestic violence also may affect how they interpret the victim's preference for arrest (see Stalans and Finn 2000).

Police officers do not provide all battered women with the same protection. As noted earlier, several studies have shown that police officers are less likely to arrest perpetrators who attack women who are drunk or having affairs. Officers who use a normative frame are more likely to arrest the husband if the battered wife is mentally ill because they believe that he is more blameworthy for hitting someone who cannot control her actions, whereas officers using an efficiency frame are less likely to arrest in this circumstance because they see the mentally ill wife as less credible and more dangerous (Stalans and Finn 1995). Thus, the guiding decision frame and stereotypes will determine which victims who violate social norms are more likely to receive protection.

Interview studies have found that police officers are less likely to make an arrest involving minority victims compared with white victims. Research based on domestic violence police reports found that after controlling for situational differences, the police were equally likely to arrest perpetrators on behalf of African American victims compared with other victims. However, police officers considered different criteria in arriving at their arrest decisions. Officers were less likely to arrest when the case involved an older African American battered woman compared with other older victims. Police were less likely to arrest the perpetrator if the African American victim had been drinking or taking drugs or had children present at the scene, whereas other victims' drug or alcohol use or the presence of children increased the likelihood that the perpetrator would be arrested (Robinson and Chandek 2000).

Officers' Personal Characteristics and Decision Making about Domestic Violence

Research has investigated how police officers' race, gender, academy training, and professional experience shape their interpretations and handling of domestic violence situations. Studies find that minority and white officers do not consistently differ in their interpretations or handling of domestic violence and that academy training also has little influence. However, men and women officers do have different stereotypes about and responses to domestic violence and consider different criteria. Rookie officers, with less than one year of actual law enforcement experience, and experienced officers also arrive at arrest decisions in different ways. These differences are further discussed in the following paragraphs.

Several studies have examined whether women officers are more empathic toward battered women and more likely to enforce the law. Women and men officers hold different stereotypes about domestic violence. Based on research, female officers responding to domestic violence calls, compared with their male counterparts, perceive that wives acted more often in self-defense and are more likely to be the only party injured, and that husbands acted more often intentionally and without justification. These gender differences in stereotypic views are related to the extent to which male officers support male-dominating relationships. Experienced male officers who are basically supportive of such relationships believe that a lower percentage of cases involve wives acting in self-defense, whereas female officers' attitudes toward male-dominating relationships are not related to their domestic violence stereotypes (Stalans and Finn 2000).

Despite these different attitudes, women and men officers have similar arrest rates in domestic violence situations, but they consider different criteria in making the decision to arrest. Women officers consider the battered woman's preference for wanting to settle the argument and are less likely to arrest if the victim is also willing to do so, whereas men officers do not consider this criterion. Thus, women officers tend to act in accordance with traditional feminist views and are more willing to arrest when the victim is unwilling to settle the argument. Both men and women officers consider the likelihood of severe injuries if the husband remained in the home and the presence of injuries on the victim in arriving at their arrest decisions. Moreover, men and women rookie officers typically recommend marriage counseling and only in one out of five cases refer the battered woman to

a shelter. These similarities reinforce research that shows that women and men officers hold similar views about their job and do not favor involvement in domestic disturbances. Thus, through professional socialization, women officers develop similar perceptions about their law enforcement role relative to men officers. However, once women officers achieve more experience in their profession and can defend their views, they may act on different stereotypic views of domestic violence. Research shows that experienced women officers are less likely to recommend marriage counseling and more likely to refer a battered woman to a shelter than are experienced men officers. Research also shows that women victims are more satisfied with women officers; thus, although women officers do not arrest perpetrators more often, they are more likely to provide support and information to victims and are less likely to hold gender-biased attitudes or stereotypes (see Stalans and Finn 2000 for a review).

Research has found that novice and experienced officers employ different frames for making decisions. Novice officers focus on normative considerations, such as the blameworthiness of each party, in making arrest decisions, whereas experienced officers focus on pragmatic considerations such as the ability to substantiate claims and the risk of future violence. The shift in focus from judicial norms to pragmatic issues occurs relatively swiftly, after one year of service. Inferences about dangerousness and wrongfulness predicted experienced officers' decisions to refer battered women to shelters much better than novice officers' referral decisions (for a review, see Stalans and Finn 2000; Stalans and Finn 1995).

Effective training to increase uniform enforcement of domestic violence statutes requires moving beyond officers' decisions to understanding what questions guide their investigations and how they interpret information and use stereotypes to make inferences. Effective training must begin to focus on the decision-making process rather than the final decision; research shows that officers still receive inadequate training in domestic violence, with most jurisdictions not requiring domestic violence training as part of their regular in-service training for experienced officers. Officers consider both legal and extralegal criteria in their arrest decisions, and their reliance on stereotypes may produce unequal protection; thus, future research focused on the decision-making process will be able to inform training curricula. Several departments have created specialized domestic violence units and have begun to offer more comprehensive services at the time of the initial response. Response units that consist of teams including service providers have improved the services and options available to victims. Moreover, police officers are increasingly relying on technology to obtain better information, and many jurisdictions now can obtain prior arrest histories on the suspect. Some jurisdictions are using phone bugs, silent hostage alarms, GPS tracking systems, and cellular phones to gather incriminating information against stalkers (see Hoyle and Sanders 2000; Roberts 2002; White et al. 2005).

LORETTA J. STALANS

See also **Domestic Violence by Law Enforcement Officers; Factors Influencing Reporting Behavior by Male Domestic Violence Victims; Gay Domestic Violence, Police Attitudes and Behaviors toward; Mandatory Arrest Policies; Police Civil Liability in Domestic Violence Incidents; Police Response to Domestic Violence Incidents; Training Practices for Law Enforcement in Domestic Violence Cases**

References and Further Reading

Eigenberg, H. M., K. E. Scarborough, and V. E. Kappeler. "Contributory Factors Affecting Arrest in Domestic and Non-Domestic Assaults." *American Journal of Police* 15, no. 4 (1996): 27–53.

Finn, M. A., B. S. Blackwell, L. J. Stalans, S. Studdard, and L. Dugan. "Dual Arrest Decisions in Domestic Violence Cases: The Influence of Department Policy." *Crime and Delinquency* 50 no. 4 (2004): 565–589.

Finn, M. A., and L. J. Stalans. "Police Handling of Mentally Ill Offenders in Domestic Violence Situations." *Criminal Justice and Behavior* 29, no. 3 (2002): 278–307.

Hall, D. L. "Domestic Violence Arrest Decision-Making: The Role of Suspect Availability in the Arrest Decision." *Criminal Justice and Behavior* 32, no. 4 (2005): 390–411.

Hoyle, C. *Negotiating Domestic Violence: Police, Criminal Justice, and Victims.* New York: Oxford University Press, 1998.

Hoyle, C., and A. Sanders. "Police Response to Domestic Violence: From Victim Choice to Victim Empowerment." *British Journal of Criminology* 40 (2000): 14–36.

Kane, R. J. "Police Response to Restraining Orders in Domestic Violence Incidents: Identifying the Custody-Threshold Thesis." *Criminal Justice and Behavior* 27, no. 5 (2000): 561–580.

Roberts, A. R. *Handbook of Domestic Violence Intervention Strategies: Policies, Programs, and Legal Remedies.* New York: Oxford University Press, 2002.

Robinson, A. L. "The Effect of a Domestic Violence Policy Change on Police Officers' Schemata." *Criminal Justice and Behavior* 27, no. 5 (2000): 600–624.

Robinson, A. L., and M. S. Chandek. "Differential Police Response to Black Battered Women." *Women and Criminal Justice* 12, no. 2/3 (2000): 29–61.

Saunders, D. G. "The Tendency to Arrest Victims of Domestic Violence: A Preliminary Analysis of Officer Characteristics." *Journal of Interpersonal Violence* 10, no. 2 (1995): 147–158.

Stalans, L. J., and M. A. Finn. "How Novice and Experienced Officers Interpret Wife Assaults: Normative and Efficiency Frames." *Law and Society Review* 29, no. 2 (1995): 287–321.

———. "Gender Differences in Officers' Perceptions and Decisions about Domestic Violence Cases." *Women and Criminal Justice* 11, no. 3 (2000): 1–24.

White, M. D., J. S. Goldkamp, and S. P. Campbell. "Beyond Mandatory Arrest: Developing a Comprehensive Response to Domestic Violence." *Police Practice and Research* 6, no. 3 (2005): 261–278.

POLICE RESPONSE TO DOMESTIC VIOLENCE INCIDENTS

Wife battering emerged along with child abuse as a social issue during the 1960s. The dominant view at the time held that marital violence was a private matter between the husband and his wife. Law enforcement intervention was rare, occurring in cases where the victim had been killed or severely maimed. The common forms of domestic violence that were prohibited by criminal law usually amounted to misdemeanors; unless police officers witnessed the violence, they had no power of arrest. Police officers were trained on how to respond to family violence crises by separating the parties for a cooling-down period. It was not uncommon for the officers to "counsel" the parties. In extreme cases the victim would be referred to the court to file a private complaint against her husband. These complaints were rarely taken seriously, however, and they resulted in fewer prosecutions than for any other crime.

Throughout the 1970s reformers sought changes that would ensure effective intervention. The debates centered on what type of intervention would be the most effective to protect victims and deter offenders; the no arrest policies of police came under strong criticism from victim advocates. Frustrations over the lack of effective remedies for women victimized through family violence gave rise to social science research exploration of potential approaches.

The Minneapolis Domestic Violence Experiment was the first empirical research to study the deterrent effects of arresting the family violence perpetrator (Sherman and Berk 1984). The preliminary report indicated that police *should* arrest abusers for crimes of intimate violence. Within ten days of the initial report, the New York Police Department became the first to require police officers to make an arrest in family violence situations, citing the experiment among the reasons for the new policy. Contributing to this policy change were the success of civil suits brought against police departments for their failure to provide equal protection to victims of domestic violence. A classic example is the successful 1982 suit brought by Tracy Thurman, who was permanently disabled when Torrington, Connecticut, police failed to protect her against her estranged husband.

The debate on the effects of arresting the perpetrator for domestic violence crimes still continues. Six replication studies following the Minneapolis Domestic Violence Experiment showed mixed results of the effects of mandatory arrest policies, including the expected deterrent effect in some cases and in others an opposite effect or no effect. Arrest was found to escalate future violence in some relationships involving unemployed and unmarried couples after an initial thirty-day respite. A flood of literature that questioned the efficacy of criminal justice intervention followed. A later recalculation of the replication research found mathematical errors—all of the studies do in fact indicate that arresting deters batterers better than other police responses (Maxwell, Garner, and Fagan 2003).

During the 1980s domestic violence was acknowledged as one of the most serious social problems in the United States. All states, the District of Columbia, and the Commonwealth of Puerto Rico have since enacted some form of legislation specific to domestic violence. The first domestic abuse statutes applied only to adult married spouses of abusers, and only to women as victims.

These legislative changes gave police officers the power to make arrests in cases where there existed probable cause to believe that domestic violence had occurred, regardless of whether the violence was witnessed by the officer. Mandatory and preferred arrest procedures in instances of domestic violence were adopted by police departments across the nation. Statutes have broadened the definitions and legislative protections; these definitions and provisions for protection and enforcement vary widely among jurisdictions. Contemporary police response to domestic violence incidents has been shaped by this history.

Definition of Domestic Violence

Domestic violence is an altercation of sufficient severity or harm to require police response where the parties are legally recognized as being in a domestic relationship and the allegation is that a crime has been committed or is being committed or that an order of protection has been violated. The most common types of domestic violence include child abuse, intimate partner abuse, and elder abuse. Other domestic-related persons may be involved in domestic crime, although intimate partner violence is the most frequently cited type of domestic violence that involves law enforcement intervention. Domestic violence is defined broadly in some states with terms such as "abuse," "harassment," "threats of harm," or "intimidation." In other states, the definition can include more specific behaviors such as burglary, criminal trespass, arson, sexual assault, denying an elder or person with disability access to needed care, and violation of a protective order.

The term *domestic* refers to the legally recognized relationship of the offender to the victim rather than a specific offense. For example, an ex-husband who burns down the house of his estranged wife may properly be charged with the crime of arson and identified as having committed a domestic crime. Examples of the crimes commonly committed against the person in domestic violence situations include assault, assault and battery, assault with a dangerous weapon, aggravated assault, rape, stalking, and murder. Domestic violence acts include but are not limited to beating, biting, kicking, punching, pulling hair, shoving, striking, slapping, throwing things, threatening, and sexual abuse.

Domestic Violence Relationships

For determination of full legal protections under domestic violence law, the victim-to-perpetrator relationship must be clearly identified. Typical relationships that have been recognized by legislation are:

- persons who are or were legally married (a spouse or former spouse),
- persons who reside or previously resided together without marriage (a cohabitant or former cohabitant),
- persons related through marriage (any person related by consanguinity or affinity within the second degree, related by blood or through marriage),
- persons who share a child in common, where the presumption is that the male is the biological father and the female is the biological mother (whether or not they were ever legally married),
- women who are pregnant and men who are presumed to be the fathers,
- persons who are having or have had a substantial dating or engagement relationship,
- biological children or stepchildren, and
- biological parents or stepparents.

Most states, the District of Columbia, and the U.S. Territories of Guam, the Northern Mariana Islands, and Puerto Rico include children as a class of protected persons in some way within their definitions of domestic violence. Five states include child abuse in their definitions of domestic violence, four states specifically include grandchildren as protected persons, and three states include foster children. Identifying the relationship entitles the victim to domestic violence civil and criminal orders of protection, family court options, and social systems responses.

Domestic violence crimes are not limited to any category of individuals; they transcend all social, racial, and gender boundaries. Intimate violence occurs within heterosexual and homosexual partnerships, though the most frequent victims are women who are abused by their male partners.

Arrest Policies in Domestic Violence

Aggressive law enforcement actions that include mandatory arrest policies have become the primary criminal justice response to family violence. Domestic violence arrest laws authorize warrantless arrests when particular conditions are met and encourage or mandate police officers to arrest for certain crimes. *Mandatory arrest* statutes require that police officers make warrantless arrests of abusers when called to the scenes of complaints of domestic violence and probable cause exists that

the abuse occurred. A hybrid statute mandates an arrest in some circumstances and grants discretion to police officers in some other situations. *Preferred arrest* statutes suggest that an officer make an arrest whenever probable cause to do so exists but does not require that the officer make an arrest.

The final determination of action lies in the hands of the responding police officers, even where a state mandates that an arrest be made. Individual officers must determine, based on their own knowledge and expertise, whether the situation they are investigating constitutes a domestic crime and whether probable cause exists. The form and substance of police training is critical to victim protection; the education of police officers relative to their responsibilities for the crimes committed within legally recognized domestic relationships should not be underestimated in its importance.

Incident Response

Police officers rely heavily on the dispatcher to obtain information about the likelihood of danger at the scene. Domestic violence incidents are no more dangerous than other forms of violence that police respond to. Prior to arriving at the scene the dispatcher obtains information about the people who are involved, their history of domestic violence, including the existence of protection orders involving either person, and whether there are any guns registered to the individuals in the home. On arrival, police officers secure the scene by limiting access and providing assistance to the people there. Entry into the home is legally permitted by consent or due to exigent circumstances. The individuals at the scene are separated and interviewed outside of the hearing of each other. First aid is rendered, and injuries, if present, are documented. Victim safety is the first concern of the responding police officers, yet determining who is in need of protection may not be as readily apparent.

An investigation at the scene is made through interviewing the victim, witnesses, and the suspect. Using the primary aggressor standard, the police officer makes a determination of who is the victim and who is the offender. An arrest decision is made based on the existence of probable cause that a crime has occurred and that a specific person committed that crime. Evidence is collected in the form of photographs and interview statements. Forms of domestic violence that do not meet the legal standard for criminal violation provide supporting evidence for domestic battering, a pattern of violent or coercive behaviors used for the purposes of control, intimidation, or punishment.

Police officers are often called to enforce domestic violence civil and criminal orders of protection. These may be called no-contact or restraining orders, since their intent is to restrain the perpetrator from further abusive behavior and to grant relief to the victim.

Entry into the Home

The "chief evil" against which the Fourth Amendment of the U.S. Constitution protects is the "physical entry of the home" (*Payton v. New York* 1980). The reasonableness of police entry into the home ordinarily requires that police obtain a warrant based on probable cause prior to entering, except in a few well-defined circumstances. The Fourth Amendment prohibition against entering a home without a warrant applies equally whether the police are there to conduct a search or seizure or for any other purpose.

Exceptions to the warrant requirement in cases of domestic violence generally fall into the categories of consent and exigent circumstances. Voluntary consent may be given to enter the home by the owner of the home or property or by someone with the apparent authority to consent. Exigent circumstances are situations in which immediate and serious consequences will most likely occur if the police officer postpones action to obtain a warrant. Circumstances are deemed exigent when: (1) hot pursuit is initiated against a fleeing felon, (2) destruction of evidence is imminent, (3) escape of a suspect is imminent, and (4) there is a risk of danger to the police or others (*Thacker v. City of Columbus* 2003). In some situations an emergency 911 call alone may be enough to support a warrantless search of a home. When a call for help originates from within the residence, the expectation of privacy is diminished. Courts recognize that police officers have a right and a duty to respond to emergencies, including domestic violence situations.

Primary Aggressor Determination

The challenge for the criminal justice community is in assigning blame. One party must be responsible and held accountable in the criminal justice paradigm. The practice of mutual arrest, where both parties in a dispute are arrested, is strongly discouraged by the courts in cases of domestic violence. Not only does it confuse the court as to how to proceed, it often results in neither party being prosecuted.

When police officers respond to intimate partner violence, they take action regarding a single allegation of harm, yet in determining the severity of that injury and the relative responsibility for that altercation, the police officer may consider previous harms. This is called the *primary aggressor determination.* A primary aggressor determination may be based on the prior history of violence between the partners or family members; the relative severity of injuries received by each person; whether an act of or threat of violence was taken in self-defense; the relative size and apparent strength of each person; the apparent fear or lack of fear between the partners or family members; and statements made by witnesses. For example, a woman who alleges that her partner placed her in a choke hold may tell the police officer that she thought he was going to kill her, so she bit his arm to release it from around her throat. The male partner may also allege harm by showing the police officer that she bit him on the arm. The police officer would determine if the bite mark is consistent with an act of self-defense based on the angle and location of the mark and whether the woman fought back in fear of her safety. A history of previous threats to kill her or prior beatings would provide further credibility for the claim of self-defense. When the harm against the woman is determined to be a criminal violation (strangulation, in this case) and her actions in biting the partner were consistent with her level of fear for her safety (due to prior assaults), then self-defense by that person is reasonable and her actions would not constitute a criminal violation.

In any relationship violence, including gay and lesbian partner violence, the victims may use self-defense during an attack. Traditionally police officers have looked at gender and physical size when determining who is at fault in a domestic dispute. A clearer picture of who is in need of protection is therefore made using the primary aggressor determination criteria.

It should be noted that the primary aggressor determination is not based on any one physical characteristic such as gender or size; it is a combination of factors. Common myths are that the victim can be determined by judging who is the passive partner, or the most agreeable to the police, or the one who is grateful for police intervention. These are misconceptions about the nature of family violence. Victims often appear defensive and may be either passive or aggressive; there is no proper way for a victim to act. Frustrations, anger, fear, and shame are just some of the emotions that victims may experience which cause them to react negatively against a person attempting to intervene. An objective interview will not be based on the sympathies of the police officer toward any party.

Probable Cause Determination

The manner in which the police officer responds in these diverse situations of domestic violence is based on a probable cause determination. The resolution regarding the primary aggressor is one part of the probable cause determination on whether to make an arrest.

Probable cause is a standard of proof that must be satisfied for any search or seizure to occur. An arrest is legally defined as a seizure and therefore falls under the same requirement for probable cause as a search. The requirement is stated in the Fourth Amendment of the U.S. Constitution and in state constitutions: "The right of the people to be secure in their person, house, papers and effects against unreasonable searches and seizures shall not be violated . . . and no warrant shall issue except for probable cause." In order to make an arrest, a police officer has the responsibility to determine whether probable cause exists, the likelihood that a crime has been committed, and which person(s) committed that crime. The standard is universal and must be met on both the state and federal levels before a person can be deprived of his or her liberty. Additionally, probable cause to arrest must exist at the moment of arrest. Facts and circumstances that come to the attention of the police officer after a person has been taken into custody may not be used retroactively to justify the arrest. The Fourth Amendment does not require that a police officer be absolutely certain that a crime occurred at the time of arrest, but it necessitates an inquiry into probability.

Sources for determining probable cause include the observations of the police officer, reliable hearsay, knowledge about the suspect, the suspect's behavior toward police, and the collective knowledge doctrine. The *collective knowledge doctrine* concerns the shared knowledge of the police as a unit rather than merely the knowledge of the officer who is acting. The doctrine therefore allows a police officer to act (make an arrest) if the officer reasonably relies on instructions from an officer who has probable cause.

In developing probable cause to effect an arrest in a case of domestic violence, the police officer relies heavily on interviewing skills. At the domestic dispute, the parties are separated; outside of the hearing of the other person, each is asked questions about what happened. These statements may become valuable evidence in the event the victim is unable to testify at trial; therefore they are well documented. The police officer views any complaints of injury and makes determinations of whether there are defense wounds or injuries caused by one person in self-defense from attack. This information is compared with statements from witnesses if they are available, including children, and with the physical condition of the place where the dispute took place.

When the victim is a child or an elder, the police officer makes the determination of who is the best agent to interview that victim. Again the officer documents injury and collects evidence. Through a probable cause determination, the police officer decides whether a specific law has been violated.

Federal Initiatives

Domestic violence has traditionally been within the jurisdiction of state law enforcement response. This changed in 1994 when Congress enacted the Violence against Women Act (VAWA). It encourages states to adopt mandatory arrest policies, supports state and local prosecutions of domestic violence, and provides federal penalties for criminalized conduct. Federal crimes of domestic violence now include interstate travel to commit domestic violence (18 U.S.C. §2261), interstate stalking (18 U.S.C. §2261A), and interstate violation of an order of protection (18 U.S.C. §2261). Federal law also prohibits an abuser subject to an order of protection from possessing firearms and ammunition (18 U.S.C. §9229(g)(8)). When a police officer determines that a valid order has been issued against an abuser, the officer should enforce the federal prohibition of gun possession.

VAWA directs police officers to enforce valid orders of protection properly issued by courts of other states, whether or not those orders are registered in the jurisdiction where the abuse occurs. This is known as full faith and credit. A responding officer must enforce the conditions of a valid criminal or civil order, including custody provisions and firearms prohibitions. Civilian orders of protection are given full force and effect on military installations under the Armed Forces Domestic Security Act (2002). Paving the way for the nationwide reciprocal enforcement of protection orders, the National Stalker and Domestic Violence Reduction Act (1997) authorizes civil restraining and abuse protection orders to be entered in all National Crime Information Center databases.

DENISE KINDSCHI GOSSELIN

See also **Domestic Violence by Law Enforcement Officers; Factors Influencing Reporting Behavior by Male Domestic Violence Victims; Gay Domestic Violence, Police Attitudes and Behaviors toward;**

Mandatory Arrest Policies; Police Civil Liability in Domestic Violence Incidents; Police Decision-Making Factors in Domestic Violence Cases; Training Practices for Law Enforcement in Domestic Violence Cases

References and Further Reading

Armed Forces Domestic Security Act (10 U.S.C. 1561a, 2002).

Maxwell, C. D., J. H. Garner, and J. A. Fagan. "The Preventive Effects of Arrest on Intimate Partner Violence: Research, Policy, and Theory." *Domestic Violence Report* 9, no. 1 (2003): 9–10.

National Stalker and Domestic Violence Reduction Act (28 U.S.C. § 534, 1997).

Payton v. New York, 445 U.S. 573 (1980).

Sherman, L. W., and R. A. Berk. "The Specific Deterrent Effects of Arrest for Domestic Assault." *American Sociological Review* 49 (1984): 261–272.

Thacker v. City of Columbus, 328 F.3d 244 (2003).

Thurman v. City of Torrington, 595 F. Supp 1521 (1984).

Violence against Women Act (VAWA 18 U.S.C., 2§ 40221, 1994).

POPULAR CULTURE AND DOMESTIC VIOLENCE

The Social Construction of Gender

The social construction of gender is central to the study of domestic violence. Ideas about gender permeate the culture in which domestic violence is staged. The identities of both victims and perpetrators are gendered. Given the hegemonic structure of gender relations, patriarchal constructions of masculinity and femininity position women and men relative to the site of such undesirable social interaction. At the risk of sounding flip, domestic violence is just that, an undesirable instance of social interaction. Therefore, just as gender organizes that social interaction one might define as normative, so does it inform that social interaction one might characterize as deviant, and in many cases criminal.

Nowhere are these constructions of gender that shape domestic violence more visible than in contemporary popular culture. Representations of domestic violence, especially the battering of women and sexual violence, abound in film, television, music, and print media. On some occasions the culture seems well aware of its own role in perpetuating domestic violence and portrays a sympathetic view of the victim; but on other occasions, and indeed, more often, the culture appears blissfully ignorant of the way in which it serves to construct gender myths and actively creates the real-life misogynist it so demonizes in many television movies. In an effort to expose some of the cultural contradictions with respect to domestic violence, particularly battering and sexual violence, this article will examine some aspects of the social construction of gender in contemporary popular culture.

To say that gender is socially constructed is to say that gender is distinct from the construct of sex, which is more generally construed as being rooted in biology or anatomy. However, many argue that sex may be less of a dichotomy and more of a continuum, and, as such, sex represents some socially defined criteria used to evaluate one's anatomy. Regardless, rather than referring to an anatomical or sexual category, *gender* refers to the social meanings that one attaches to either sex. For example, the hermaphrodite serves notice that sex may not be a dichotomous variable. Moreover, parents of the hermaphrodite will likely teach the child what it means to be a man or what it means to be a woman once a decision is made as to what the sex category of the child will be, which, of course, may be irrespective of the child's sex.

The popular culture is a ready-made reserve of ideas that foster such definitions of gender for the parents and society at large. Just as Berger and Luckmann (1966) suggested that there were processes that constituted the social construction of reality, so is gender subject to similar mechanisms. Given the social constructionist theory as it relates to gender, one might surmise that ideas about gender, or gender myths, are given rise out of social interaction and are eventually objectified through agents such as the popular media, schools, law, and family. The individual, in turn, incorporates such myths into the self, the site at which gender moves from the realm of objective reality toward subjective reality. Of course, individual experiences are judged against this baseline of cultural ideals. In this way, gender—the illusion of difference fabricated between men and women, in some cases where no difference exists—is made real.

One does not have to ponder too long to come to the conclusion that we live in a patriarchal society wherein maleness and masculinity are valued and femaleness and femininity are devalued to some extent. Contemporary society engenders a system based on male privilege, creating a social landscape wherein men, often unaware that they enjoy such perks, are able to navigate the social world with greater ease than their female counterparts. For example, when a husband and wife inquire about a house for sale, the attention is given to the husband, despite the fact that this particular wife earns more money than her husband. The estimate he gets to get the car fixed is always a bit cheaper than the estimate she gets. The car salesman would rather focus his attention on the husband than the wife. The husband's haircut is four times cheaper than the wife's, despite the fact that he generally gets more hair cut off. His clothing is cheaper, and his dry cleaning is cheaper. In short, it costs her more to be a woman in this world than it costs him to be a man.

Men enjoy more deference in banks and board meetings, civic organizations and courts. Moreover, beyond the simple fact that men may enjoy these economic or status perks, there is a fundamental difference in the experience of being a man or a woman that is grounded in the social construct of gender. The social world comprises gendered spaces, the locker room versus the hair salon. Even the home comprises such gendered spaces, the powder room versus the basement. Such socially defined spaces may well bear influence on the social interaction that takes place; and for the most part it has been "a man's world," as the saying goes, that is, despite pockets of feminine spaces, male spaces predominate in general. This fact rings true in the following anecdote. One night a man went to meet his wife as she got out of a graduate class she was taking at a mid-sized public university. She was unaware that her husband was meeting her; he had been in his office grading papers and thought he would catch her as she came upon her car in the parking lot. Parked beside her car he watched her as she left the building. As she came out of the building, he noticed that she reached into her purse, pulled out a cell phone, and appeared to have a conversation with someone. As she neared her car, she saw her husband and put her cell phone away. Her husband promptly asked her how she was and to whom she had been speaking. She quickly replied that she had not been talking to anyone—if she appeared to be involved in conversation as she walked to her car late at night, it was because she felt it made her less vulnerable to being attacked. The man, surprised, replied, "I don't know what that is like. That's not part of my experience." The woman perceived a threat not just this night but, indeed, every night, in a social space that her husband thought of in the most benign terms. In this way, the culture organizes the subjective experiences of men and women differently.

The Importance of Thinking Critically about Popular Culture

Boys and girls look to the popular culture for cues as to the scripts available to them to act out masculine and feminine identities. It is in the context of popular culture that boys learn how to see girls and girls learn how to see boys. Feminist observers of media have often written of the "male gaze," the voyeuristic way in which men learn to look at women. Gender becomes a frame within which to see the individual, and so one makes judgments as to the degree of masculinity or femininity a young boy may exude, just as one makes judgments as to the degree of masculinity or femininity a young girl may exude. Given the threat of being ostracized by one's peers, these young folks by and large amble on toward conformity to these socially defined scripts.

So, by the time a young girl reaches adolescence, she has already learned by careful observation of the popular culture that she is going to be valued for something other than what her male counterpart will be valued for, namely, her body. It is no surprise, then, that young girls become preoccupied with their bodies to a far greater extent than do young boys. Even at a young and innocent age, both young boys and young girls are cognizant of the sexualization of women that permeates the culture.

Given that media and the larger popular culture serve as agents of secondary socialization with regard to gender, it is imperative to take a critical view of said media and culture to better understand the ways in which gender is socially constructed. According to Denzin (1993), "Gender and sexuality arise out of the complex interactions that connect the texts, meanings, and experiences that circulate in everyday life, with the things the members of our culture tell one another about being men and women. Stories in the daily newspaper, in social science articles, comic books, daytime TV soap operas, nighttime family comedies, and melodramas, and in large box-office-drawing films like *When Harry Met Sally, Sex, Lies and Videotape, Blue Velvet, Driving Miss Daisy, Working Girl, Biloxi Blues,* and *Everybody's All-American* reproduce the gender stratification order" (p. 202). Denzin suggests that all cultural products serve as texts, be they popular, as in the case of daytime soap operas, or more obscure, as in the case of scholarly papers. Endorsing a poststructural view, Denzin is making the case that all of these texts are read by audiences, and meaning is generated as readers interact with these and other cultural texts. For Denzin and others taking this view, no one gender text is more authoritative or true than another. All of these texts provide different ways of knowing about gender relations: the feminist theorist writing about the sexual division of labor in the family, the beer commercial that features two scantily clad actresses engaged in a sexually charged "cat fight" over whether or not the beer "tastes great" or is rather "less filling," and the story of origins recounted in the book of Genesis all offer some account of the partial reality of a gendered world, while none of them holds any direct line to some objective truth about gender.

Moreover, it stands to reason that those accounts that are offered in the popular culture (such as the beer commercial noted above and other similar popular culture texts) are more accessible to the general public than the scholarly paper written by a feminist scholar (who herself is sometimes demonized in the popular culture as a "feminazi"). Further, those accounts that are made more accessible via the vehicle of popular media have a greater probability of informing the individual's conceptualization of gender, especially as society becomes more saturated with media and these secondary agents of socialization take on more salience as the influence of the nuclear family's primary socialization wanes.

One of the symptoms of a patriarchal society may be the variance with respect to the representation of women and men in popular culture. Despite the trend toward egalitarian marriages and the increasing presence and visibility of female filmmakers,

record producers, and television writers who have the ability to control their own images, the family and the representation of it still tend more toward the patriarchal. True, the United States may be exceptionally more liberated with respect to gender relations than, for example, Saudi Arabia, yet American culture, in large part, has been a bastion of androcentric stories and ways of knowing. Even the subtle gender hegemony institutionalized in the English language—"she," "woman," "female," all derivative of male pronouns—is reflected in the casting of male and female characters throughout the entire repertoire of popular culture devices.

When examining interpersonal violence, it is clear that victims are often subject to some form of dehumanization, which renders them an easy mark. The sexualization and continued objectification of women in popular culture may serve as an invitation to dehumanize real subjects in the realm of everyday life. If male consumers of culture are taught to see women as compilations of body parts, as in the case of pornography, then ultimately they may fail to see them as sentient human beings. If the culture continues to feature women as props for heterosexual male fantasies, then inevitably some men who are not moved to think critically about the cultural images they are fed may come to blur the distinction between such fiction and reality. In some cases such a reading of these cultural texts may end tragically, as in the following case:

> On July 17, 1981, David Herberg forced a 14-year-old girl into his car, tied her hands with his belt and pushed her to the floor. With his knife, he cut her clothes off, then inserted the knife into her vagina, cutting her. After driving a short distance, he forced the girl to remove his clothing, stick a safety pin in the nipple of her own breast, and ask him to hit her. He then orally and anally raped the girl. He made her burn her own flesh with a cigarette, defecated and urinated in her face, and compelled her to eat the excrement and to drink her own urine from a cup. He strangled her to the point of unconsciousness, cut her body several times, then returned her to the place where he had abducted her. In reviewing Herberg's criminal appeal, the Supreme Court of Minnesota noted that when Herberg committed these acts, he was "giving life to some stories he had read in various pornographic books." (Pacillo 1998: 139)

Though the preceding case would not be termed "domestic violence" proper, it does illustrate the extent to which women, no matter their station, may be vulnerable to individual men who are so influenced by misogynistic popular culture. Moreover, it lends support to the notion that deviance, and indeed criminal behavior, is not only learned in the context of direct interaction with others, but is fed by an ample supply of cultural references. In an age of media saturation, would-be abusers, rapists, and murderers have virtual handbooks to draw upon in the popular media.

The Representation of Domestic Violence in Popular Film

When examining the relationship between popular culture and domestic violence, there are at least two distinct angles to consider. One concern, as mentioned previously, is the extent to which the consumption of popular culture informs men's gender socialization in general, and the ways in which they see women in particular. To what extent has some level of domestic violence been normalized through the cultural content embedded in music, film, video games, comic books, commercials, and fiction? Does the hypersexualization of women so common in media make women more vulnerable to sexual assault in the home? Does the unquestioned indoctrination of conservative religious dogma result in women being viewed as men's property within their own homes?

The other concern has to do with the representation of domestic violence as a theme in a variety of cultural texts. When considering the representation of domestic violence in film, there are, of course, those productions that seemingly attempt to raise the profile of domestic violence, as it is problematic in the family as well as in the larger society. These films serve to expose a chronic societal problem that has often remained cloaked in the clandestine cover of family privacy. Perhaps no film made as much of an impact in this regard as *The Burning Bed* (1984), directed by Robert Greenwald and starring Farrah Fawcett. The film dramatizes the true story of a Michigan housewife, Francine Hughes, who was repeatedly battered by an abusive husband and, with nowhere else to turn, decided ultimately to kill her husband, dousing him with gasoline and burning down the house. The film highlights the failure of "the system" to protect women in these situations and raises questions as to what extent women are legally able to defend themselves with the use of force of their own volition. Hughes was prosecuted for her husband's death and subsequently acquitted.

Other films such as *Eye of God* (1997) show how domestic violence may be rationalized in the minds of perpetrators. In this film, a small-town Oklahoma diner waitress falls for a born-again convicted felon who, once out of prison, uses religious ideology to rationalize the subordination of his lover as well as the abuse that fells her.

The film *What's Love Got to Do with It?* (1993) offers a disturbing portrayal of the real-life breakdown of the marriage of soul music's most talented couple, Ike and Tina Turner. While the pair provided the counterculture generation with stellar grooves to dance to, with the likes of "Ooh Poo Pah Doo," from the ironically titled *Workin' Together* (1971), they were engaged in a tumultuous and often violent marriage. The violence wrought upon Tina Turner's character in the movie seems to be a by-product of Ike Turner's character's sense of a loss of control when faced with the prospect that his wife is emerging as a budding star well beyond his own fame. The violence appears to escalate the more disengaged Tina's character becomes from Ike's character.

The threat of violence is often used as a means of social control. One might infer that not only does Ike's character perceive that he is losing control of his wife's artistic talents and that her star is beginning to outshine his own, but he may well perceive, in addition, that he is losing control of her sexual being. In a capitalist economic structure wherein one is encouraged to commodify everything within one's grasp, it is no surprise that sex is subject to this process of commodification and that therefore there are those who may well come to view their partners' sexuality as their own property. Note the shift in the conceptualization of the socially constructed sentiment of jealousy, once a sign of flattery, a genuine show of one's love and admiration, now a fatal flaw in the relationship, a symptom that one claims ownership of another.

Many writers assert that violence is "often the outcome of an inability to control other people's sexual behavior, that is, other people's management of themselves as engendered individuals. This explains not only violence between men and women, but also mother-daughter, sister-in-laws [sic], and men themselves. In all such situations what is crucial is the way in which the behavior of others threatens the self-representations and social evaluations of oneself" (Moore 1994: 15). The irony, of course, in the case of Ike and Tina Turner is that it was Ike who was repeatedly unfaithful and not Tina. Fantasies of identity are often intertwined with those of power, which in turn inform the notion that violence is often the result of imagined rather than real threats (Moore 1994).

It is clear that the evolution of the representation of domestic violence in popular film has moved from the once-classic Hollywood position wherein it was dealt with so casually that it seemed not particularly problematic, or worse yet, that such violence was actually warranted, to a more self-aware and gender-sensitive

POPULAR CULTURE AND DOMESTIC VIOLENCE

position that such violence is depicted to raise consciousness about its ill effects for individuals and society at large. "A case in point is the representation of abuse in popular culture, specifically popular visual media. No longer relegated to daytime talk television and self-proclaimed women's channels like Lifetime and Oxygen, or social documentaries shown primarily on public broadcasting channels, or in art cinemas, the topic of abuse has been embraced by primetime television and the Hollywood movie industry. In 2002, for instance, domestic violence was featured on multiple episodes of the perennially popular television dramas *ER* and *NYPD Blue* and the much-lauded HBO series *Six Feet Under* and *The Sopranos*" (Shoos 2003: 60).

However, despite this new cinematic awareness of domestic violence as a theme in film, the social architecture of Hollywood is not often well suited for the treatment of such a complex issue. As Shoos (2003) goes on to state:

> The list [of shows and films] suggests that representations of domestic violence, like women directors and producers, seem to have finally broken through the celluloid ceiling. Yet, as I propose . . . despite their increased number and accessibility, there are nonetheless modes of invisibility at work in many of these representations. These modes include the tacit denial of the many complexities and contradictions of abuse, to which there are no easy Hollywood solutions; in the continued if continually disavowed construction of abused women and abusive men as the Other; and, most significantly, in the linking of this Otherness to particular categories of race and class. (Shoos 2003: 60)

Pornography

Without doubt, the most problematic genre of popular entertainment with respect to the representation of domestic violence is pornography. More so than any other genre, pornography serves to objectify and hypersexualize women to the extent that the subjects are so divested of any emotional or human content that they exist solely in the realm of some heterosexual male fantasy. The subject woman is reduced to a mere prop in the consummation of heterosexual male pleasure. A fair amount of so-called hard-core pornography does indeed commingle sex and violence such that they become part of the same hyperreal simulation.

Oddly enough there has been a debate within the often fractious world of feminist scholarship with respect to the effect that pornography may have on gender, as well as sexual relations. "Some liberal feminist scholars argue, for instance, that pornography advances women's rights by sexually liberating

women. On the other hand, anti-pornography feminist legal scholars argue, for instance, that pornography frequently acts as an instruction manual for perpetuating real-life sexual violence against women" (Pacillo 1998: 139–140).

While liberal feminists of the school that Pacillo refers to may reason that female porn stars, much like their fellow sex trade workers, are able to turn the tables on their oppressors and are empowering themselves at the expense of male sexual weakness, the truth of the matter is that such pornographic content makes horrifically problematic the gender socialization of adolescent boys and young adult men who have even greater access to such images in the Internet age. Even much of the so-called soft-core pornography features images that allude to the notion of rape as something erotic. The great harm in such visual content is not the sexual explicitness of the imagery, but rather the attitudes it encourages young boys and men to adopt with respect to women, relationships, sexual abuse, and assault.

Pornography has frequently been cited as at least an indirect factor in a number of high profile rapes, sexual assaults, and murders, the most infamous being the case of serial killer and rapist Ted Bundy. It is alarming to think of the number of young boys and even adult men that are first exposed to sexual content through pornography. As mentioned previously, there is great cause for alarm in the volume of young boys whose gender socialization process is informed by such disturbing content. Most problematic is that they may well come to see women through the distorted and misogynistic lenses of these hyperreal and hypersexual scenarios. Pornography, of course, offers the male viewer the illusion that he controls the sexual situation and outcomes, as these images are solely for his consumption and thus he may do with them whatever he pleases. These issues of control and power may figure into his real experiences once he moves beyond the virtual realm of sex. Will he have as much control as he exercised with the image in the magazine or the remote control? Will his lack of control of the sexual situation breed a sense of frustration and turn to violence? Surely this will not happen in every case, but, evidently, it happens often enough to cause concern.

Representation in Other Forms of Popular Culture

Other forms of popular culture such as popular music and video games are replete with allusions to domestic violence. Some of the same critiques of film in general, and pornography in particular, may be offered with respect to the treatment and representation of women in popular video games such as *Grand Theft Auto.* Even in the hugely successful Madden football video game, women appear only as grossly well-endowed cheerleaders who are there solely to shake and shimmy in the event of a touchdown—once again, serving as mere props for heterosexual male fantasy, only this time in the context of simulated professional sports.

The world of popular music is a bit more dynamic and diverse in its representation of women in general, as well as domestic violence as a theme. The synthesis of music and film in the production of music videos, which came to prominence with the creation of MTV in the early 1980s, fundamentally changed the way in which music was to be marketed and consumed. In the largely androcentric music industry, the representation of women in music videos as sexual objects to be used, dominated, and ultimately disposed of was originally a common feature of heavy metal videos and has become increasingly more and more a theme in rap videos. Once again, women most often appear in such music videos as sexual props that color the simulated world of the pop star.

As rap music moved from the margins of society to become one of the most dominant genres of music, the lyrical content changed as the demographic buying the music changed. Hip-hop, the cultural framework from which rap music emerges, grew out of a 1970s urban black sensibility. The music of early rappers like Chuck D, of Public Enemy fame, and KRS One was decidedly Afrocentric and socially conscious. However, as rap evolved and was commercialized and ultimately co-opted by the dominant culture, the content changed. Songs that promoted raising the consciousness of blacks, along with other Afrocentric themes, gave way to songs that celebrated the "thug life," raps that were fueled by misogyny and violence. In general, rap began to conform to the dominant culture's popular imagination of what urban black life must be like, and gangsta rap became the dominant subgenre in hip-hop. Black rappers like Ice Cube and Easy E, from the seminal Compton, California–based rap group N.W.A., along with sexually explicit rappers 2Live Crew and Too Short, set the standard for gangsta rappers to come, by degrading and dehumanizing women at every turn. One of the most successful rappers at the start of the twenty-first century is Eminem, a white hip-hop artist who makes claim to authenticity by virtue of his urban Detroit upbringing. Eminem has made a career out of incredibly popular songs that project fantasies of killing and raping the mother of his child as well as his own mother. In his song "Kim" (2000), the rapper warns the mother of his child, "Don't make me wake the baby / She don't need to see what I'm about to do."

However, it should also be noted that all of rap does not endorse such a view. Rappers affiliated with what some writers have called bohemian rap (e.g., The Roots, A Tribe Called Quest, Black Star) have put forth more supportive and sympathetic messages with respect to women. Perhaps the contradictions regarding domestic violence and hip-hop culture are best reflected in the well-known late gangsta rapper Tupac's anthem of support for "his sisters," "Keep Ya Head Up" (1993). The late rapper offers, "I know they like to beat ya down a lot / When you come around the block brothas clown a lot / But please don't cry, dry your eyes, never give up / Forgive but don't forget, girl keep ya head up."

Of course the theme of domestic violence is not specific to rap or heavy metal. Country music and bluegrass are filled with murder ballads like the standard "Knoxville Girl" and the Stanley Brothers' rendition of "Little Glass of Wine." On the Louvin Brothers' 1956 version of "Knoxville Girl," Ira Louvin laments, "I'm here to waste my life away / Down in this dirty old jail / Because I murdered that Knoxville girl / The girl I loved so well." Lou Reed, of the seminal late 1960s rock band The Velvet Underground, tells the listener, "You better hit her" in the group's classic "There She Goes Again." Singer-songwriter Tracy Chapman draws a sympathetic portrait of a victim and echoes the sentiment from *The Burning Bed* in her ballad "Behind The Wall" (1988): "Last night I heard the screaming / Loud voices behind the wall / Another sleepless night for me / It wouldn't do no good to call / The police always come late, if they come at all." Clearly, examples abound in multifarious genres. Finally, one is starkly reminded that in the mind of the batterer or rapist, it is as Belle and Sebastian sing in their 1999 tune "We Rule the School," wherein the singer advises the young female listener, "You know the world was made for men."

Conclusion

Clearly there are many contradictions that characterize American popular culture when it comes to domestic violence. The Lifetime TV movie that dramatizes the true story of the poor woman who eventually succumbs to the regular beatings by her husband is only a channel click away from the music video that features a whole harem of "hootchie mamas" who want nothing more than to be debased by "the mack on the mike." The ad in the newspaper for the Take Back the Night Rally at the local university is cut and pasted right next to the article recounting the case wherein the former community college president received two years in prison for murdering his wife with a two-by-four because she suffered from depression and was too troublesome to deal with. The radio spot announcing the wet T-shirt contest at the local strip club is cut and pasted right next to the public service announcement encouraging listeners to "end domestic violence now." In the end, these conduits of popular culture are just vehicles for all of these voices, some socially responsible, some hopelessly dangerous. Few films or songs are able to deal with the complexities and contradictions that shape the lived experience of domestic violence, and so the best popular culture can offer is some partial truth and some partial reality, always removed from any true and objective representation.

CHARLES WALTON

See also **Attachment Theory and Domestic Violence; Control Balance Theory and Domestic Violence; Exchange Theory; Identity Theory and Domestic Violence; Social Learning Theory and Family Violence;**

Worldwide Sociolegal Precedents Supporting Domestic Violence from Ancient to Modern Times

References and Further Reading

Berger, Peter, and Thomas Luckmann. *The Social Construction of Reality: A Treatise in the Sociology of Knowledge.* Garden City, NY: Anchor Books, 1966.

Denzin, Norm. "Sexuality and Gender: An Interactionist/Poststructural Reading." In *Theory on Gender/Feminism on Theory,* edited by Paula England. New York: Aldine de Gruyter, 1993, pp. 199–221.

Marshment, Margaret. "The Picture Is Political: Representation of Women in Contemporary Popular Culture." In *Introducing Women's Studies,* edited by Victoria Robinson and Diane Richardson. New York: NYU Press, 1997, pp. 125–151.

Moore, Henrietta. "The Problem of Explaining Violence in the Social Sciences." In *Sex and Violence: Issues in Representation and Experience,* edited by Penelope Harvey and Peter Gow. New York: Routledge, 1994, pp. 138–155.

Pacillo, Edith L. "Media Liability for Personal Injury Caused by Pornography." In *Violence Against Women: Philosophical Perspectives,* edited by Stanley G. French, Wanda Teays, and Laura M. Purdy. Ithaca, NY: Cornell University Press, 1998, pp. 139–151.

Shoos, Diane. "Representing Domestic Violence: Ambivalence and Difference in 'What's Love Got to Do with It,'" *NWSA Journal* 15, no. 2 (2003): 57–75.

POST-INCEST SYNDROME

Children are warned not to talk to strangers, but this focus is misguided. It puts the burden on (potential) child victims, and it is not "odd-looking" strangers who are most likely to molest children, but their teachers, coaches, priests, doctors, neighbors—and relatives. Children are not warned about their fathers, mothers, stepparents, siblings, foster parents, or mothers' boyfriends, but they should be.

This essay addresses the consequences of overt parental incest. Resources are provided regarding covert and sibling abuse.

Incestuous Abuse

Sexual abuse is not primarily about sex, but about power, conquest, and boundaries. Its traumatic impact increases in children, who are fragile and undeveloped. Because incest, which survivors have adapted to describe abuse based on emotional rather than blood bonds, combines all aspects of child abuse, it is arguably the most damaging trauma of all. Custodial or domestic incest increases that destructive power exponentially, due to children's absolute dependence and abusers' absolute authority.

For children, their family is their source of physical and emotional survival. From their parents comes their identity and sense of self-worth. To a child, caregivers and parents' partners often feel parental. They are older, bigger, in charge of everything—everyone older or bigger has more power than the child.

If a parent or other caregiver is sexually violating a child, it happens no matter what the child says, whether he or she cries or screams. Often, it hurts, though it may sometimes feel good—or special—confusing feelings the child does not understand or want to have. The abused child is cautioned never to tell, threatened, and warned that he or she will be blamed or not believed. In exchange for parental hugs and attention, is this the price the child must pay?

Not all survivors of incest will be affected in the same way; "nature" interplays with "nurture," and other relationships have an impact. The consequences of such a childhood do not fall into any neat categories. However, incest changes all survivors from whom they might have been. Blume (1997) calls this legacy "post-incest syndrome." It is not a scientifically established syndrome, per se. It is articulated in her "Incest Survivor's Aftereffects Checklist" and discussed further in her book *Secret Survivors*.

Incest Subverts Development

Love puts aside the parent's needs to attend to those of the child. Incest, however, is a supremely selfish act. Where love nourishes, incest takes. Incest creates emotional abandonment by sabotaging the caregiver role. To be violated by those who are supposed to love them best teaches children that they are not worth loving.

Unconditional love is given without strings. It teaches children that they are valued, with no expectations. Incest, however, teaches children that they must earn "love." Nonpossessive love allows children to be their own persons, to own their own lives. Incest victims, however, learn that they are extensions of abusers. Even their bodies do not belong to them. This destroys victims' ability to develop physical or emotional boundaries (where one person ends and someone else begins). Survivors frequently do not understand that all relationships have boundaries, where those boundaries should be, or how to establish them.

Validation supports children's feelings, rights, and values, affirming their existence. By allowing children to feel heard and acknowledged and to develop reality testing, validation helps them understand and accept themselves. Incest negates all of this, silencing survivors' voices.

Mastery is impact. It teaches children that what they do matters. Incest teaches children to be victims. Powerlessness leads to "learned helplessness"—paralysis, crippling passivity, and resignation.

Children molested in what should have been their safe havens must somehow build a life. What follows is a discussion of the aftereffects they face as adults—not "problems" to be "overcome," but survivors' inventive attempts to cope and to address needs they do not know how to meet in any other way.

The Secret

The only control most victims can exert over their intolerable reality is cognitive control. Incest becomes the secret that survivors keep even from themselves. They may be extremely private or verbally hypervigilant, monitoring every word, rigidly controlling every thought. They may feel an urge to tell but sense that no one would listen, or they may be terrified of anyone finding out. They may lie.

Some survivors employ classic defenses, such as suppression (pushing away thoughts) and denial; some minimize or rationalize their abuse. Incest material is also forgotten. This has been called "repressed memory"; it is really "traumatic dissociation."

Dissociation is commonly explained as people not remembering driving because they were distracted. In traumatic dissociation (also called "traumatic forgetting"), people block out emotionally significant events, separating traumatic material from consciousness. Survivors may dissociate locations, abusers, some or the entire trauma, or a period of childhood. Concomitantly, some create fantasy worlds or identities; for example, women see male identities as invulnerable.

Dissociative identity disorder (DID), formerly known as multiple personality disorder (MPD), is an extreme form of dissociation. The severely traumatized child's consciousness divides into parts, called "alters," with different names, ages, genders, or other characteristics. In times of stress, an alter will take control over consciousness. A five-year-old alter may hide in fear, a rageful part may come out and hit a wall. This generally results in "lost time" for the "host" (front person for the system), who, without treatment, usually cannot control and may not even be aware of "switching."

Alters are symbolic personifications of the aftereffects of post-incest syndrome, separated from each other by dissociation. Recovery includes communication, cooperation, and the eventual sharing of dissociated information, bringing it to consciousness.

There are different levels of traumatic dissociation, and different degrees of "dysfunction" in DID. Multiples, who lack a cohesive ego, may experience cognitive distortions, abilities that come and go unpredictably, and radical emotional or behavioral shifts. Internal communication, when "heard" as thought, is often confused with "hearing voices," a diagnostic criterion for psychosis. (Other misdiagnoses include bipolar disorder, also called manic depression.)

Alters can have different handwritings, brain wave patterns, eyeglass prescriptions, and blood pressure or blood sugar levels. Some have illnesses or allergies that others do not. Still, many multiples spend years struggling to find appropriate help. Some never do. DID is a remarkable and creative process that literally saves survivors' sanity, though they still pay a price.

Many features of posttraumatic stress disorder (PTSD), the common diagnosis for survivors of incest and other traumas, are dissociative. Flashbacks are intrusive recollections of trauma material, triggered by a person or event or sensory stimuli (e.g., scents, sounds, foods). They occur as nightmares/terrors, sensory flashes (brief images or feelings), and detailed, intense scenes, experienced as if they were currently happening. Flashbacks may feel and appear like, and are often misdiagnosed as, hallucinations. Dissociative survivors also experience strong, unexplained negative reactions to certain people, places, or things; "derealization" (a feeling of unreality); shock or shutdown in crisis; hypervigilance, or strong startle responses; and "hysterical" pain, numbness, and even paralysis.

Some parents participate in, or cooperate with, outside groups of abusers who intentionally create dissociative disorders in victims. Although this entire phenomenon has been called "ritual abuse" (RA), that term describes only the acts of groups associated with ritualized belief systems; other groups are also involved, for whom one label is "mind control" (MC). RA/MC employs sexual assaults along with pain stimuli (including cutting and electric shocks), confinement, sensory assaults, and mental manipulation. When joined with posthypnotic suggestion, this creates "programs" used to control victims' perceptions, beliefs, feelings, and behaviors for hedonistic, illicit, and political-influence purposes.

Parents are often programmed to abuse their children. The line between victims and perpetrators is very complicated. All are generally unaware of their involvement unless recovery brings dissociated material to consciousness. RA/MC creates absurd delusions, as well as the belief that others control their thoughts. RA/MC survivors often appear to meet the diagnostic criteria for psychosis; this "mental illness" is seen as organic and unrelated to family pathology. On the outside, daily life in such families appears "normal."

In the 1990s, a challenge to the validity of "repressed memories," DID, and RA/MC attained great acceptance. It was spearheaded by a group comprising people accused and convicted of child sexual abuse (all claiming to be innocent victims), their spouses, and a professional advisory board. They argued that sexual trauma was never forgotten; "overzealous" therapists were accused of "brainwashing" their clients, inducing a "false memory syndrome" (FMS).

Women who retracted their incest disclosures ("recanters") and accused parents presented wrenching (albeit "anecdotal," not validated scientifically) stories of "false accusations" that ruined their lives. Many legal and therapeutic professionals, and society at large, came to question the validity of incest disclosures. Accused abusers were acquitted, convictions (already rare) overturned. Therapists were charged with "memory implantation" in high visibility civil cases, though most did not go to court but were settled by therapists' insurance companies, for millions of dollars. Many therapists and facilities discontinued services to survivors.

Memory—both constant and recovered—is always vulnerable to numerous factors. Not all details of recalled abuse are literally true. Does science support the condemnation of dissociation, recovered trauma memories, and the therapists who work with them? Or, as some suggest, are FMS proponents a political advocacy group, based on unscientific concepts?

Research has found no difference in reliability between constant and recovered trauma memories. While peripheral details may not always be remembered accurately, the essence of the core event will be.

Some degree of traumatic amnesia following not only incest, but wars, natural disasters, and the Holocaust, has been found in roughly seventy studies. In thirty studies, about a third of subjects experienced total amnesia for childhood sexual abuse. No research to date has successfully demonstrated that trauma memories can be implanted.

The FMS position is that retractions are always true, and initial incest disclosures, always false. Yet retracting is a self-protective, comforting, predictable stage of recovery. At some point, many survivors claim they "made it all up." It should be noted that RA/MC perpetrators also intentionally reactivate victims' dissociative denial.

Are "recovered memories" valid? Not all abuse memories should be taken literally, but this does not invalidate the core reality of the claim. Programming, for instance, includes illusions of untrue or impossible events, which, when "remembered," support attacks on the veracity of RA/MC reports. Of course, studies depending on "self-reporting" are vulnerable to criticism. However, corroboration rates of 50 to over 70 percent for "recovered" incest memories have been established in twenty studies. Additional validation for survivors' memories is shown in their aftereffects, especially flashbacks, which replicate specifics of their disclosures. RA/MC survivors, for instance, may have aversions to such things as blood, pins, bugs, feces, raw meat, telephone ring tones, candles, chants or repeated words, boxes and coffins, holidays, or certain dates.

Every "false memory" claim should be evaluated on its own merits. As Ross Cheit (2005) demonstrates, public representations of these cases have not been accurate. Additional research on this topic has been done by Jennifer Freyd (2005) and Jim Hopper (2006a, 2006b), and in the scholarship of Brown, Scheflin, and Hammond (1998).

Inept or unscrupulous therapists can absolutely lead clients to develop untrue beliefs about their pasts; but are most therapists who accept the validity of DID, "recovered" memories, and RA/MC incompetent, or worse? Despite FMS advocates' criticism of "recovered memory therapy," experienced trauma therapists do not make memories the focus of incest treatment. They understand that memories are only one step in a complicated recovery process. They know that for either therapists or survivors to pursue memories aggressively would be reckless, because incest survivors remember when they are ready.

It might be helpful to discover what experience the scientists associated with the FMS movement have had with incest survivors. How many have they worked with clinically? How many have they interviewed? Experienced trauma therapists understand that remembering often begins with the least traumatizing event or abuser. Memories may change over time and details may shift; identities are clarified, faces appear from the shadows, and new, more painful abuse experiences come to awareness. This is not an FMS, but the normal process of trauma memories unfolding.

It may not be necessary to uncover all details or events of an abuse history. Still, it is important for trauma survivors to identify the fact of their trauma. Not recognizing the logical roots behind problematic behaviors or feelings often makes survivors feel crazy. Dissociated trauma memories—especially those related to programming—can strip survivors of their freedom.

PTSD, dissociation, and DID are reasonable reactions to extreme situations. They are not just psychological; they involve measurable neurological and other physiological changes. Many patients in psychiatric hospitals are incest survivors; they do not always belong there. What Denise Gelinas (1983) calls the "disguised presentation" of incest requires that therapists need to be aware of the prevalence of incest/RA/MC, their indicators and associated features, and the mechanism that hides them.

Guilt, Shame, and Self-Esteem

Secrets create, and are reinforced by, fear and shame. Sexual abuse nearly always involves shame. Incest becomes part of child victims' identity formation. Survivors often blame themselves for causing or allowing their victimization, especially when it happens more than once, as incest usually does. Guilt is preferable to powerlessness, and both are easier than acknowledging betrayal by someone loved and needed by the child. Survivors wear their abusers' shame, taking it on as their own.

Male survivors feel shamed by their sexual subjugation in a different way than women, who, ironically, "accept" the possibility of sexual abuse as a fact of life. Some survivors overcompensate by trying to be perfect. Of course, any such effort is bound to fail. Even the most outwardly perfect survivors can still feel soiled and spoiled inside. Some survivors feel marked. They may feel like damaged goods—as if there is something putrid and disgusting inside them. They may believe they are worthless. When belief becomes behavior, an indescribably destructive self-fulfilling prophecy begins.

Survivors are often unable to ask for anything. Many manifest "high appreciation"—totally disproportionate gratitude. Others have a sense of entitlement; they have been through this awful thing, and now someone, everyone, or the entire world owes them. Some develop a twisted sense of "specialness" for being "chosen."

Having learned that attention can be dangerous, survivors often try to be invisible or inaudible. They are silent when they laugh and soft-spoken, especially when needing to be heard. They sit in back corners of classrooms and walk with their heads down. Paradoxically, those who exploit or hurt the weak are drawn to these self-protective signals, often with horrendous consequences for already damaged survivors.

Conversely, for some survivors, all that is left is to be "perfectly bad." Some survivors adopt the most alienating lifestyles; some constantly provoke others with hostility and anger. Jails and prisons are full of survivors of incest as well as other kinds of childhood abuse.

Power, Control, and Boundaries

Power and control aftereffects are highly influenced by socialization. Women survivors, more likely to surrender to the belief that others are able—and entitled—to control them, often become passive. They cannot say no without experiencing abstract terror. They know that there is enormous danger in doing so, even if they cannot recall what it is and even if it no longer exists. On the other hand, just as women are not socialized to have power, it is more difficult for males to deal with being violated and powerless, because they are not supposed to be weak or submissive.

Survivors are often afraid of losing control—in general (which equals "going crazy"), of the secret, and of their feelings ("If I start to cry, I will never stop"). They may develop obsessive compulsive disorders, which are quite out of control in themselves, but provide survivors with the distorted illusion that they are in charge of *something*. Phobias (especially of containment or entrapment) provide a substitute focus for what survivors do not, or cannot, face.

To cope with having no courage, survivors often develop impenetrable emotional shells. Women may reveal all kinds of personal information, which others misperceive as vulnerability; others never reveal a thing. Some survivors are extremely protective of their boundaries, while others are seemingly indifferent to them. Some (mostly women) are exquisitely sensitive to other people's boundaries; others are invasive. Some are in a person's personal space when they talk to someone; others need be very far away. Some feel more secure socializing in another's home, because they can leave; others may require that people visit them on their turf, where they are in command. Some become socially phobic.

Some—mostly, but not always, males—become controlling, aggressive, or physically abusive. Being powerless as children may drive them to seek power at the expense of others in their adult lives. Incest may also create uncharacteristically aggressive women and passive men. However, the assumption that most of those who are abused become abusers is inaccurate.

Anger, Depression, and Suicide

Survivors have certainly earned the right to anger, an inevitable product of victimization. The feeling itself is not a problem, but what they do with it may be. Incest, like all child abuse, robs victims of the ability to properly manage anger. Some survivors harbor resentment, even rage, throughout their entire lives. Socialization leads women to suppress or deny their anger, which may result in depression; males are more likely to act it out.

Women abused by father-figures may idealize their abuser or men in general. Some survivors may pity their abuser and/or bear more anger at their mothers for not protecting them than at their actual abusers. Mother-blaming and idealization of men are both socially reinforced. Some idealize the nonoffending parent ("the good one"). Survivors may generalize their anger to all members of the abuser's gender or ethnic group, or misdirect it from its source to those closest to them, including therapists and other caregivers.

Anger can alert a person that something needs to be changed. Those who cannot interpret this valuable cue or take proper assertive action toward positive changes continue in damaging situations which in turn cause more anger, continued unhappiness, or depression.

Depression is a common, reasonable response to child abuse. Survivors already struggle with so much pain. The powerlessness and hopelessness of their childhoods have taught them despair, and they have many losses to grieve—the loss of their innocence, of their safety, even of their abuser. Their depression can be incapacitating. They may become emotionally paralyzed or cry for no apparent reason. Depression in incest survivors is often misdiagnosed as "biochemical," especially by psychiatrists who have not thought to ask about abuse experienced by their patients who have not mentioned or remembered it.

Some incest survivors maintain a lifelong "romance" with suicide. Like other aftereffects, this is a paradoxical survival tactic. As long as they always know that they can end their pain if it becomes unbearable, they can put one foot in front of the other and stay alive. Some become "passively suicidal." Some make real attempts at suicide which may in fact succeed.

Fear

Fear is a natural response to abuse at any age, even more so when the victim is a child. Repeated incest creates the sense of constant, imminent danger. The "fight or flight" reaction, an organically functional response to danger, remains always activated, thereby becoming counterproductive.

When the source is not identified, fear can turn to the more generalized state of anxiety. Survivors know the world is not safe, although, frighteningly, they may no longer remember why. They are often particularly fearful at dusk, which foreshadows the darkness that surrounded their abuse. Many cannot sleep alone or without a light. Many survivors develop panic disorders.

Because they know the world is unsafe, some never take any risks at all. Conversely, in acts of defiant overcompensation, some "dare the fates" by pursuing high-risk behaviors. For incest survivors, finding and creating safety in their lives and in the world are primary tasks in recovery.

Masking Pain

Incest survivors often misuse mood-altering substances or behaviors, such as alcohol, drugs, or sex. Some lose the ability to control this, becoming alcoholics or addicts. It should be noted that incest frequently occurs in families with an alcoholic parent, which predisposes survivors to alcoholism. Children from these families, where other abuses often occur, are called adult children of alcoholics, or ACOAs. They share many of the aftereffects associated with incest.

Many survivors (particularly, but not exclusively, females) develop eating disorders, which deflect or mask pain, provide a false sense of control, and offer a focus for displaced attempts at power. Anorexia provides an indirect way for survivors to rebel against abusive and controlling family members. Female survivors often feel sexually protected by the ways anorexia and bingeing change the body's size and features.

Many female survivors, and some male survivors, develop self-harming behavior. In recent years "cutting" has become an unfortunate trend, sometimes unrelated to abuse. It serves many purposes, including, paradoxically, comfort. Physical pain can feel more manageable than emotional pain. Hurting one's own body and seeing the resulting wounds externalize survivors' self-hatred. Wounds also provide visual representation of inner torment, or an external, physical excuse for denied incest pain. RA survivors are often programmed to self-injure—for instance, as punishment for remembering and telling. Some RA-related self-injuries specifically replicate locations or instruments used in torture. It is important for therapists to discuss not only the covered feeling, but also what body part the survivor hurts and in what way, in order to understand the function that self-injury serves and what abuse act it might represent. Survivors also engage in more "acceptable" mood-altering behaviors, like workaholism (commonly by males) or compulsive "busyness."

Most survivors must learn to experience, identify, tolerate, and express their feelings, and, especially, to self-soothe. Those who have made the choice of using substances or engaging in other behaviors to cover their feelings need to make a different choice. If they are no longer in control of how or when they use alcohol or drugs or engage in certain behaviors, or if they feel incapable of stopping, addictions have developed. Real emotional health is not possible until a foundation of abstinence and recovery has been achieved, although incest may need to be addressed along the way.

The Body

The body stores trauma's memories, feelings, and consequences. Survivors often feel betrayed by their bodies, which, to them, represent pain and powerlessness. For women, who also must cope with the risk of later sexual assault and negative, exploitive social messages about their bodies, incest sets a horrendous stage.

Survivors often have swallowing or gagging sensitivities. For many, even those not subjected to oral rape, water hitting the face stimulates suffocation feelings. Survivors also may ignore basic hygiene. This can serve a protective purpose, in their view, by keeping sexual interest at bay. Conversely, they may develop compulsive cleanliness. They may bathe in scalding water. Having become very self-conscious about bodily functions, survivors may have extreme needs for privacy or be unable to use public bathrooms. They may avoid mirrors. This connects with their problems of self-esteem or physical self-image and may also relate to DID (the face they "see" in the mirror may not be "theirs").

For some survivors, wearing heavy clothing feels safe, and baring any part of their body feels like exposure. Women survivors often "plain" themselves down. They may hide their faces behind unstyled hair or hide their bodies under baggy, formless clothes such as turtlenecks in summer. Many fail to remove clothing even where it would be appropriate—at the beach, for instance—or they may become flashy, exposing their bodies in very revealing clothes at inappropriate times.

Survivors can disown their bodies. They may miss or ignore their bodies' signals and needs. This can be dangerous, because a number of medical problems have been associated with an incest history, such as gastrointestinal disorders, thyroid dysfunctions, headaches, arthritis, fibromyalgia, and various gynecological problems, including unexplained pelvic pain, particularly during intercourse, and spontaneous vaginal infections. Incest histories also may underlie many cases of postpartum depression.

Survivors often "somaticize," displacing feelings into physical symptoms for which they repeatedly seek medical attention. Alternately, they may have strong aversions to doctors, especially dentists and obstetricians/gynecologists, and hospitals. This generally relates to invasive touch. For some it results from RA abuses involving medical personnel, procedures, or facilities.

Associated with neither affection nor comfort, touch can feel very unsafe for survivors. Literally, it can hurt. It can trigger flashbacks, especially when it is a surprise. Grabbing a survivor playfully from behind may earn the hugger an elbow in the ribs. It is advisable never to touch incest survivors without their permission.

Sex

Incest has been called premature sexuality. It is sexuality imposed on children who are neither emotionally nor physically prepared for it. Sex becomes an obligation, often shrouded in pain and fear. It can feel dirty and threatening. It can be difficult for the incest survivor to reconcile sex with love.

Women incest survivors often equate sex with rape; all sexual interest or pursuits feel like a violation. Many can say no only by "shutting down"—getting numb, or dissociating. Some avoid sex entirely, while some are compulsively oversexualized and consequently labeled "provocative," "seductive," or "promiscuous" according to social biases. They may be sexual with everyone they know and may inappropriately sexualize all of their meaningful relationships, except the ones they should. They often cry after orgasms.

Some incest survivors confuse sex and anger. Many overlap affection, sex, dominance, and aggression. Some use sex to achieve power. For men, this more often means dominating or violating others. Women, often sexually revictimized later in life, may attempt to "take power over" revictimization by "choosing" to work in the sex industry, dissociating themselves sexually so that it "doesn't matter," or tolerating unwanted sex for personal or professional gain.

Survivors of either gender may have strong aversions to, or need for, particular acts. Breath or touch on certain parts of their bodies or certain sex acts may trigger flashbacks. Some survivors can never be the aggressor, and some must always be. Involvement in sadomasochism (S/M) is associated

with an incest history, as are real, hurtful rape fantasies.

Although commonly believed to do so, incest does not cause homosexuality. Survivors may have an aversion to, or a need to act out with, the gender that abused them, but homosexuality is an emotional-sexual "orientation." Rape has nothing to do with who people love. Incest may lead some bisexual survivors to skew their future choices, but if there were no same-sex attraction to begin with, incest would not create it in its victims. However, incest does frequently make male victims of male abusers wonder if they might be gay, which, as a result of homophobia, can be very painful.

Survivors need to reappropriate their sexuality. After "reclaiming their virginity" by asserting abstinence while they separate sex from all of its negative associations, they can experience healthy sexual development on their own terms.

Relationships

Incest deeply affects survivors' social interactions, parenting (including childbirth), and, particularly, intimate attachments. Space allows only a brief discussion of aftereffects in committed relationships (explored further in *Secret Survivors*).

Survivors often re-create the dynamics of the abuse "relationship." However, it was not a relationship, as it was not reciprocal. Beginning in adolescence, female survivors often become involved with much older or more powerful people. This is also an exaggeration of a social norm. They may choose caretakers who exercise control over them. Such "teacher-student" power imbalances give survivors no room to grow.

Incest decimates trust. Having learned that they must "produce to be loved," survivors rarely expect to be taken care of without paying a huge price in return. What appears to be "safe" does not feel safe because it encourages them to let their guard down. Still, many survivors are desperate to satiate emotional hunger while simultaneously fearing intimacy, which is seen as having the power to destroy them. Barriers to intimacy arising from unhealthy relationships may meet conflicted survivors' self-protective needs. They become involved with partners who are unavailable, abusive, or unstable, or engage in "pursuer-withdrawer" arrangements, in which one partner retreats in fear of suffocation and the other engulfs his/her partner out of a desperate fear of abandonment.

Many survivors cannot reconcile the contradiction of incest. Their inability to hold in one consciousness two opposite views of a needed caregiver—both "loving" and "hurtful"—may lead them to "split" good and bad qualities as being mutually exclusive in people. They may elevate friends, lovers, or therapists into idealized, perfect caretakers who represent the fulfillment of their fantasies. Those who "fail" them, as will inevitably happen somewhere by someone, will then be dismissed as being entirely bad, whereas formerly they were seen as being entirely good. Often misdiagnosed as symptoms of borderline personality disorder (BPD) or other personality disorders (deep pathologies seen as very difficult to treat), such incest-based relational patterns are often logical reactions that can be explored and healed in therapy.

Intimate relationships with unhealed or still healing survivors can be extremely complicated for both partners. Survivors may be incredibly sacrificing or self-involved. Emotional and sexual intimacy often trigger memories of past abuse, leaving survivors traumatized and partners feeling (or being) neglected or even blamed. When survivors abandon sexual activity, partners often feel cheated or resentful.

Before survivors can have satisfying lives, let alone successful intimacies, they must develop healthy relationships with themselves, learning to recognize, balance, and meet their own needs. Their recovery comes first. This journey is totally out of their partners' control, as it should be.

As a consequence of all these factors, partners of survivors are "secondary victims" of incest. Partners may need additional support to examine their own needs, pain, behaviors, choices, and histories. Incest survivors often find each other.

Incest runs in families. Women survivors are often drawn to men who are perpetrators. Denial or dissociation may contribute to their not "seeing" what is happening when their own or other children are molested. That does not mean that they will necessarily fail to support their children if incest is disclosed. On the other hand, some survivors have a kind of sixth sense about perpetrators. Many are hypervigilant about abuse, and some become activists. They may not be able to change their pasts, but they have finally found their voices and are working to change the future for other survivors. This is an urgent task.

It has been said that there is no courage without fear. Incest survivors—especially those who were not believed or helped if they told—experience the world as a terrifying place. It takes enormous courage just to live their lives. No matter how weak, self-destructive, or helpless incest aftereffects make them appear, it is important to acknowledge that incest survivors are really strong. Their mere survival is a victory. It should be honored.

E. SUE BLUME

See also **Attachment Theory and Domestic Violence; Child Neglect; Child Sexual Abuse; Coercive Control; Feminist Theory; Identity Theory and Domestic Violence; Incest; Medicalization of Domestic Violence; Ritual Abuse–Torture in Families; Sibling Abuse; Stockholm Syndrome in Battered Women**

References and Further Reading

Adams, Kenneth. *Silently Seduced: When Parents Make Their Children Partners—Understanding Covert Incest.* New York: Bantam (reissue), 1991.

Blume, E. Sue. *Secret Survivors: Uncovering Incest and Its Aftereffects in Women.* New York: Ballantine (reissue), 1997.

Brown, Daniel P., Alan W. Scheflin, and D. Corydon Hammond. *Memory, Trauma Treatment and the Law.* New York: Norton, 1998.

Cheit, Ross. "The Recovered Memory Project," 2005. http://www.brown.edu/Departments/Taubman_Center/Recovmem.

Freyd, Jennifer. "J. J. Freyd's Trauma, Memory, and Betrayal Trauma Research," 2005. http://dynamic.uoregon.edu/~jjf/trauma.html.

Gelinas, Denise J. "The Persisting Negative Effects of Incest." *Psychiatry* 46 (1983): 312–332.

Herman, Judith Lewis. *Father–Daughter Incest.* Boston: Harvard University Press (reissue), 2000.

Hopper, Jim. Homepage, 2006a. http://www.jimhopper.com.

———. "Sexual Abuse of Males: Prevalence, Possible Lasting Effects, and Resources," 2006b. http://jimhopper.com/male-ab.

Leadership Council on Child Abuse and Interpersonal Violence. www.leadershipcouncil.org.

Noblitt, James Randall, and Pamela S. Perskin, eds. *Ritual Abuse in the 21st Century: Psychological, Forensic, Social and Political Considerations.* (In progress.)

Salter, Anna. *Predators: Pedophiles, Rapists, and Other Sex Offenders: Who They Are, How They Operate, and How We Can Protect Ourselves and Our Children.* New York: Basic Books, 2003.

Sarson, Jeanne, and Linda MacDonald. "Persons against Ritual Abuse-Torture." http://www.ritualabusetorture.org.

Simkin, Penny, and Phyllis Klaus. *When Survivors Give Birth: Understanding and Healing the Effects of Early Sexual Abuse on Childbearing Women.* Seattle: Classic Day Publishing, 2004.

Steinberg, Marlene, and Maxine Schnall. *The Stranger in the Mirror: Dissociation, the Hidden Epidemic.* New York: Harper Paperbacks, 2001.

Wiehe, Vernon. *Sibling Abuse: Hidden Physical, Emotional, and Sexual Trauma.* Thousand Oaks, CA: Sage Publications, 1997.

POSTPARTUM DEPRESSION, PSYCHOSIS, AND INFANTICIDE

Postpartum mood disorders are more common than is often realized: Up to 80 percent of new mothers experience mild depression within a year of giving birth. If the "baby blues" persist, depression can escalate to dangerous levels, influencing some women to experience psychosis and—in rare and tragic cases—to kill their offspring.

As many as 50 to 80 percent of all women experience some degree of emotional "letdown" following childbirth—the so-called "baby blues." The "baby blues" is common for numerous reasons. The baby's crying and the mother's interrupted sleep and soreness from breast-feeding are enough to make any woman feel irritable, if not overwhelmed and tearful. These feelings typically begin three to four days after the baby is born but normally dissipate on their own within a few weeks. In addition, rapid shifts in reproductive hormone levels, particularly progesterone, may contribute to a vulnerability to more severe depression among some new mothers. Fortunately, its more extreme sister disorder, postpartum psychosis, is rare, affecting only about 1 or 2 in 1,000 new mothers.

Postpartum Depression and Psychosis

Women are more likely to experience psychiatric illness after childbirth than at any other time in their lives. If the "baby blues" last for more than two weeks, however, the new mother may be suffering from a condition of intermediate severity, postpartum depression (PPD), a mood disorder on par with other forms of clinical depression. Ten to 22 percent of women experience PPD before the infant's first birthday. PPD is characterized by feelings of despondency, inadequacy as a mother, impaired concentration and memory function, as well as loss of interest or pleasure in activities that were formerly enjoyable. In addition, the mother experiences excessive anxiety about the infant's well-being. Mothers with postpartum depression are reluctant to share their upset emotions because they do not want others to think of them as bad mothers.

Some women also become paralyzed with fear and concern for the baby's safety. If such symptoms appear, it is important to seek professional consultation to help differentiate PPD from other conditions such as obsessive-compulsive disorder. Symptoms of anxiety are frequently an aspect of clinical depression, but true obsessive-compulsive symptoms signify a different disorder that needs proper diagnosis and treatment.

Though debilitating, the depressive emotional reactions that may accompany becoming a new mother are not as severe as those associated with postpartum psychosis. In psychosis, the hallmark symptom is a "break" with reality—a loss of the ability to accurately discern what is real from what is not. For instance, a woman with PPD may experience violent thoughts about her baby but recognizes that those thoughts are wrong and potentially dangerous. In that case, she will not act on them.

However, a woman suffering from a full-fledged postpartum psychosis will have lost, at least temporarily, the judgment needed to make this assessment. Very often, a woman with psychosis experiences a frightening sense of merger with her infant—she cannot differentiate where she ends from where her baby begins. Psychotic merger is so terrifying that she may try to avoid losing her sense of self by either committing suicide or killing the baby or both. Infanticide is the term used to refer to murder in which the killer is a parent of the victim.

In the month directly following childbirth, women are twenty-five more times likely to become psychotic than during other periods of their lives. Postpartum psychosis occurs following only 1–2 per 1,000 births. Furthermore, the risk of infanticide associated with untreated puerperal psychosis (occurring during childbirth or the period immediately following) has been estimated to be as high as 4 percent.

Women with puerperal depressive disorders experience a high relapse rate during subsequent pregnancies: 50 percent or more of women who had a previous episode of postpartum depression experienced a relapse following a subsequent pregnancy. However, for postpartum psychosis, the relapse rate is even higher—it is almost 80 percent.

Filicide and Neonaticide

There are two distinct types of infanticide. Filicide is the killing of a son or daughter older than twenty-four hours. Neonaticide is the killing of a newborn within twenty-four hours of birth. Neonaticide is a separate entity, differing from filicide in the diagnoses, motives, and disposition of the murderer. About 3 percent of all American homicides are filicides. The reported rate of murder for children less than one year of age has remained relatively stable over the past twenty years. The rate of killing children under one year is 4.3 per 100,000 live births.

Estimates of the occurrence of neonaticide in the United States range from 150 to 300 per year. The Uniform Crime Reports for the years between 1976 and 1985 show that on average about 384 filicides of children up to age eighteen were reported each year. Sixty-two percent of all homicides that occurred in children 0 to 5 years in the United States from 1976 through 1998 were committed by parents (U.S. Dept. of Justice 2000). The risk of filicide is greater among younger than older children.

Nevertheless, infanticide is a very rare phenomenon; only about 4 percent of women who become psychotic kill their babies. According to one study, 67 percent of women who kill their children are mentally ill, as opposed to only 6 percent of those who kill their spouses. Perhaps even fewer tragedies would occur, however, if proper education and treatment were more readily available to physicians and the public.

The ages of the filicide victims ranged from a few days old to as old as twenty years. The risk of filicide is greater among younger than older children and is greatest within the first year of a child's life. Among infants in the first week of life, mothers are almost always the ones who commit the filicide. The most dangerous period for the victims is the first six months of life. This is the time of maternal postpartum psychoses and depressions. The younger the child, the more likely is the suicidal mother to think of the child as a personal possession and feel inseparable from the baby.

Comparing mothers who commit neonaticide with those who commit filicide, only a few of the women who commit neonaticide were psychotic, but psychosis was evident in two-thirds of the maternal filicide group. In one study, serious depression was found in only 3 percent of the maternal neonaticide cases compared with 71 percent of the maternal filicide group. In contrast, suicide attempts accompanied more than one-third of the filicides, but none occurred among the neonaticide cases.

Although infanticide is now considered a crime by national governments all over the world, it has been and is still practiced on every continent and by people on every level of cultural complexity, from hunters and gatherers to highly evolved civilizations. Throughout history, the various motivations for infanticide have included population control, illegitimacy, inability of the mother to care for the child, greed for power or money, superstition, congenital defects, and ritual sacrifice. Researchers who study infanticide distinguish several different groups of parents who murder their offspring. Some kill as a result of psychotic delusions—the dread of parent–child merger or the belief that the child is trying to harm or kill them. Others murder their children out of profound depression and hopelessness. Often they carry strong religious ideas that killing their children will enable them both to enter an afterlife more peaceful than their current life.

Neonaticide

The great majority of neonaticides are committed simply because the child is not wanted due to the stigma of a pregnancy out of wedlock. Consistent with this observation, the most common reason for neonaticide among married women is extramarital paternity. Neonaticide is especially common among teenagers who are overwhelmed by dealing with their unexpected pregnancy.

In most neonaticides, the perpetrators are young women who live with their families but are psychologically isolated. Teenagers who commit neonaticide often lack relationships with open, caring, reliable adults who will recognize that they are pregnant and will initiate a conversation to help them make decisions about pregnancy and plan for its consequences. Many girls feel ashamed of having engaged in sexual relations and are fearful that their pregnancies will disappoint and even humiliate their families, causing the girls to experience shame and emotional paralysis.

Passivity is the most common single personality factor which clearly separates women who commit neonaticide from those who obtain abortions. In contrast to women who seek abortions (recognizing the reality of their pregnancy early and promptly and actively seeking to address the problem of an unwanted pregnancy), women who commit neonaticide often deny that they are pregnant altogether or magically assume that the child will be stillborn.

Neonaticide is not usually a premeditated act; frequently it is committed in the face of intense emotion such as shock, shame, guilt, and fear immediately following the delivery of a live infant. Generally no advance plans are made for either the care or the killing of the infant.

The methods of neonaticide listed in order of greatest frequency are suffocation, strangulation, head trauma, drowning, exposure, and stabbings. Suffocation is probably most frequent because of the need to stifle the baby's first cry in order to avoid detection. The crime is usually concealed. Following the murder, the body is usually disposed of and the mother denies that it has occurred.

Filicide

In contrast to neonaticide, the motives for filicide, in order of descending frequency, according to Resnick, are:

- "altruism" associated with the mother's suicide (38 percent)
- acute psychosis (21 percent)
- unwanted child (14 percent)
- fatal maltreatment (12 percent)
- to relieve suffering (11 percent)
- spousal revenge (4 percent)

The "altruistic" filicidal mothers see their children as extensions of themselves and do not want to leave them motherless in an uncaring world as seen through the eyes of their own depression. Varying degrees of pathological identification may exist between mother and child, ranging from the mother projecting her own suffering upon the child to psychotic merger.

The "altruistic" filicide raises particular medical legal issues. In most jurisdictions, the criteria for claiming "insanity" as a legal defense against the crime of murder are predicated upon the McNaughtan Rule: The defendant must prove that she did not appreciate the nature and quality, i.e., the wrongfulness and criminality, of her murderous act at the time that it was committed. Severe depression, even without psychotic features, may distort thinking to such an extent that a mother believes that her children will be better off in heaven with her than motherless in this world. In these cases, it is usually clear that the mother knows the nature and quality of her act and that killing her children is legally wrong. However, the filicidal mother often believes that she is also doing what is *morally* right by killing her child. When these mothers are brought to trial,

jury instructions in different jurisdictions vary widely on the meaning of "wrongfulness." The defense that the mother, although aware of the legal wrongfulness of her act, was conforming to a higher moral authority when she committed filicide has been acceptable in only a limited number of jurisdictions within the United States.

Acutely psychotic filicidal parents include those who killed under the influence of hallucinations, epilepsy, or delirium. However, this category does not include all psychotic child murderers and is the weakest because it includes cases in which no comprehensible motive could be ascertained. One striking example quoted by Resnick from the historical psychiatric literature is that of an "epileptic mother (who) placed her baby on the fire and the kettle in the cradle." Presumably she was suffering from a seizure disorder now known as psychomotor epilepsy, or "Jacksonian" seizures. A new mother in a similar neuropsychiatric state observed by the author of this essay held her newborn infant dangerously at fully extended arms' length and walked aimlessly around a room with one breast completely bare, oblivious to whether she was holding or dropping the child.

Unwanted child filicide requires no further explanation. Fatal maltreatment filicides are invariably the tragic outcome of child abuse such as "battered child syndrome." In these situations there was usually no clear homicidal intent and death is the unintended consequence of maltreatment that was intended to stop the child's "bad" behavior. Indeed, child abuse is the most common cause of filicide in the United States. A variation on this pattern includes child maltreatment with the participation of or coercion by a male partner.

"Spousal revenge" filicide is a final category, encompassing parents who murder their offspring in a deliberate attempt to make their spouses suffer. Infidelity, either proved or suspected, is a common precipitant for spousal-revenge filicide.

Paternal filicide is a related phenomena but one that is beyond the scope of this article. Suffice it to say that men are far more likely than women to commit familicide, i.e., killing the child's mother as well as the child, often followed by the father's suicide. In one study of ten paternal filicides from a psychiatric hospital, more than half of the men attempted suicide after the child murders.

There are also characteristic reactions to the deed of filicide. According to Resnick, after "altruistic" and "acutely psychotic" killings, there is often an immediate relief of tension. Resnick notes that "this explains the failure of some parents to complete their suicide. Furthermore, after the murder, these parents usually run to seek help and make no effort to conceal their crime." By contrast, parents who commit "unwanted child" and "fatal maltreatment" filicide often go to great lengths to dispose of or conceal incriminating evidence and to deny the crime.

In contrast to filicide, most neonaticidal murders belong to the unwanted-child classification. Furthermore, in the incidence of neonaticide, major mental illness in the mother is infrequent. These women tend to conceal the pregnancy, deliver the baby alone, and dispose of the baby secretly.

Conclusion

In summary, there is a spectrum of puerperal mental illnesses, ranging from "baby blues" (which is probably a normative response to rapid hormonal shifts immediately following delivery) to postpartum depression and psychosis, including the rare and tragic outcome of neonaticide by the mother. An effort has been made in this article to further delineate filicide from neonaticide, comparing and contrasting the two phenomena. It goes without saying that the best preventive measures to reduce the frequency of these tragic occurrences would be to increase the availability of educational and mental health services as well as emotional support during pregnancy and the puerperal period and to continue making such services more widely available to parents during at least the early years of childhood.

MARK I. LEVY

See also **Assessing Risk in Domestic Violence Cases; Child Neglect; Inmate Mothers: Treatment and Policy Implications; Mothers Who Kill; Parricide**

References and Further Reading

Campion, J. F., J. M. Cravens, and F. Covan. "A Study of Filicidal Men." *American Journal of Psychiatry* 145 (1988): 1141–1144.
d'Orban, P. T. "Women Who Kill Their Children." *British Journal of Psychiatry* 134 (1979): 560–571.
Gold, L. H. "Clinical and Forensic Aspects of Postpartum Disorders." *Journal of the American Academy of Psychiatry and the Law* 29 (2001): 344–347.
Green, C. M., and S. V. Manohar. "Neonaticide and Hysterical Denial of Pregnancy." *British Journal of Psychiatry* 156 (1990): 121–123.
Haapasalo, J., and S. Petäjä. "Mothers Who Killed or Attempted to Kill Their Child: Life Circumstances, Childhood Abuse, and Types of Killing." *Violence and Victims* 14 (1999): 219–239.
Jennings, K. D., S. Ross, S. Popper, and M. Elmore. "Thoughts of Harming Infants in Depressed and Nondepressed Mothers." *Journal of Affective Disorders* 54 (1999): 21–28.
Kunz, J., and S. J. Bahr. "A Profile of Parental Homicide against Children." *Journal of Family Violence* 11 (1996): 347–362.
Lewis, C. F., and P. J. Resnick. "Infanticide in the U.S." *Violence in America: An Encyclopedia.* New York: Charles Scribner & Sons, 1999, pp. 171–174.
Marleau, J. D., B. Poulin, T. Webanck, R. Roy, and L. Laporte. "Paternal Filicide: A Study of 10 Men." *Canadian Journal of Psychiatry* 44 (1999): 57–63.
Mendlowicz, M. V., M. H. Rappaport, K. Mecler, S. Golshan, and T. M. Moraes. "A Case Control Study on the Socio-Demographic Characteristics of 53 Neonaticidal Mothers." *International Journal of Law and Psychiatry* 21 (1998): 209–219.
Meyer, C. L., and M. Oberman. *Mothers Who Kill Their Children.* New York: NYU Press, 2001.
Resnick, P. J. "Child Murder by Parents: A Psychiatric Review of Filicide." *American Journal of Psychiatry* 126, no. 3 (1969): 73–83.
———. "Murder of the Newborn: A Psychiatric Review of Neonaticide." *American Journal of Psychiatry* 126, no. 10 (1970): 58–64.
Schwartz, L. L., and N. K. Isser. *Endangered Children: Neonaticide, Infanticide, and Filicide.* Boca Raton, FL: CRC Press, 2000.
Wilczynski, A. *Child Homicide.* New York: Oxford University Press, 1997.

PREGNANCY-RELATED VIOLENCE

Since the late 1960s and early 1970s, violence against women has been identified as a serious social problem in the United States. It is estimated that almost 2 million U.S. women a year will be physically assaulted and more than 300,000 will experience a completed or attempted rape (Tjaden and Thoennes 2000). More recently, the subject of violence against women has commanded even greater attention on the part of public health officials as an important reproductive health issue. In particular, there has been increasing concern about the relationship between intimate partner violence and pregnancy. This concern has come about as a result of a greater understanding of the changing dynamics of abusive relationships, particularly the awareness that the frequency, intensity, and impact of violence may change during the course of an intimate relationship and different stages of the life course, including pregnancy (Mahoney, Williams, and West 2001). In addition to a number of other risk factors, pregnancy and parenthood may be particularly risky life transitions, as they present both economic and psychological stressors to partners in an intimate relationship.

Prevalence Rates of Pregnancy-Related Violent Victimization

How much pregnancy-related violence occurs? Estimates of violence during pregnancy range from 7 percent (Campbell et al. 1992) to between 20 and 30 percent of pregnant women (Bullock and McFarlane 1989). In addition, researchers using national probability samples have found prevalence rates ranging from 15.0 percent (Gelles 1990) to 23.6 percent (Jasinski and Kaufman Kantor 2001). Using the most conservative estimates of pregnancy-related violence, approximately 150,000 to 300,000 pregnant women experience abuse every year.

Why is there such a wide range of reported prevalence rates? One of the first issues to consider when evaluating such diverse results is the type of sample being studied. For example, much of the research that examines the relationship between pregnancy and violence uses hospital- or clinic-based samples (e.g., samples of either postpartum women or women during prenatal care visits) (Martin et al. 2001, 2004; Rachana et al. 2002). These samples produce prevalence estimates of violence against women who are pregnant. In contrast, researchers using national probability samples are estimating the risk for victimization among either all women or all women of childbearing age regardless of pregnancy status. Although each type of research design has its purpose, the differences need to be noted, as they influence how prevalence rates are calculated. Moreover, regardless of which type of sample is being used, there is clear evidence that pregnancy-related violence has serious negative consequences for both the woman and her unborn child.

Are Pregnant Women at Greater Risk of Intimate Partner Violence?

An important question, particularly for public health officials, is that of risk. If being pregnant increases the risk for violent victimization, then certain interventions are warranted. This would seem at first to be a simple question to answer. However, once again researchers have reached different conclusions based on the type of sample they have included in their studies. Many researchers examining pregnancy-related violence, for example, use small samples of either postpartum women or women attending a prenatal clinic and do not include a comparison group of women who are not pregnant (Bullock and McFarlane 1989; Campbell et al. 1992; Stewart 1994). Unfortunately, this reliance on anecdotal reports from pregnant women or hospital samples of pregnant women does not make it possible to empirically test whether or not pregnancy, per se, increases the risk for violence. Furthermore, this body of research is focused primarily on examining the consequences of violent behavior for the infant (Parker et al. 1994; Webster, Chandler, and Battistutta 1996) as well as improving assessment techniques among physicians, rather than on establishing whether or not pregnancy is a risk factor for intimate partner violence (McFarlane et al. 1992; Norton et al. 1995). Although these are noteworthy endeavors and are likely to lead to improvements in health care outcomes for women and children, the question of whether pregnant women are at a greater risk of assault by their male partners compared with women who are not pregnant remains largely unanswered.

Research using national probability samples can address the question of risk because the sample studied includes both women who are pregnant and women who are not pregnant. Studies using these types of samples have consistently reported no difference in risk due to pregnancy. For example, Gelles' 1990 analysis of data from the 1985 National Family Violence Survey found that after controlling for age, pregnant women were not significantly more likely to be victims of assaults by their male partners compared with women who were not pregnant. Similarly, researchers analyzing the 1992 National Alcohol and Family Violence Survey found that for both Anglo and Hispanic families, there was no direct effect of pregnancy on violent victimization risk after controlling for age, socioeconomic status, and stressful life events occurring during the pregnancy year (Jasinski and Kaufman Kantor 2001). More recently Jasinski

(2001) found that pregnant women were no more likely to be victims of intimate partner violence than women who were not pregnant. However, persistent violence was more likely to occur among couples in which the male partner perceived that the pregnancy of the female occurred sooner than intended. Each of the studies discussed above did not find that pregnancy was a risk factor for intimate partner violence once other established risk factors were taken into consideration. Given contradictory evidence regarding pregnancy as a risk factor for intimate partner violence, what conclusions can be drawn?

Although studies using a probability sample seem to agree that pregnancy does not increase the risk for violent victimization, they were not designed to specifically look at this issue and consequently have not included all the necessary questions needed to create a complete picture of the violence/pregnancy relationship. Furthermore, it should be noted that these studies, although finding no increased risk for victimization, also have not found a decreased risk. Until there is more research on the dynamics of pregnancy-related violence, it would be unwise to state definitively that pregnancy is or is not a risk factor for violence.

What Are the Motives/Risk Factors for Pregnancy-Related Violence?

The life of a woman who is abused by her intimate partner is intertwined with her abuser's life, greatly reducing feelings of safety and security, as well as opportunities to leave the relationship. Each of these characteristics takes on new meaning if the victim is pregnant. What is known about the dynamics of pregnancy-related violence, however, is limited. It is unclear, for example, whether pregnancy precipitates abuse in previously nonviolent relationships or whether, for some, pregnancy offers any immunity to ongoing or intermittent assaults.

What can be concluded from this conflicting evidence? Regardless of the exact dynamics of pregnancy-related violence, most of the research finds that women who were abused while they were pregnant had a history of victimization (Glander et al. 1998; Horrigan, Schroeder, and Schaffer 2000; Smikle et al. 1996). This would suggest that women who have a history of victimization should be identified as an at-risk group with specific intervention efforts targeted to them. At the same time, it appears that although some women suffer abuse inordinately, the specific patterns and risk markers for abuse among these women have not been conclusively identified (Petersen et al. 1997). This gap in the research literature makes the development of comprehensive prevention and intervention programs extremely difficult and of primary concern to health care practitioners. Although the exact relationship between pregnancy status and intimate partner violence has yet to be identified, sufficient research does exist to be suggestive of the appropriate direction for prevention and intervention programs.

For example, research focusing on characteristics of the mother or the pregnancy as potential risks has produced several consistent patterns of risk that could be used to develop prevention programs aimed at reducing violence experienced during pregnancy. One factor that has emerged as a consistent risk factor for violence is low socioeconomic status (measured with educational levels, income, and/or employment) (Cokkinides and Coker 1998; Gazmararian et al. 1995; Goodwin et al. 2000; Martin et al. 2004). It also appears as if women who are abused do not have the same levels of social support as do women who are not abused (Glander et al. 1998; Sagrestano et al. 2004; Wiemann et al. 2000). Each of these two factors—low socioeconomic status and low levels of social support—may also be related to elevated levels of stress and in combination may increase the risk for violence. Other pregnancy-related factors that may increase the level of stress experienced by a couple and consequently increase the risk for intimate partner violence include first-time parenting (Jasinski 2001) and unplanned or unwanted pregnancies (Cokkinides et al. 1999; Jasinski 2001). Possible explanations for this pattern of behavior include jealousy of the unborn child and the perception that the pregnancy will interfere with the woman's role as caretaker for her partner (Campbell et al. 1995) and questions of paternity (Burch and Gallup 2004). It is also possible that a pregnancy not planned by the male partner might represent something that he cannot control and therefore increases the risk for violence.

Normative transitions associated with the entrance or exit into a social role, such as parenthood, may also increase the risk for victimization. As such a transition, pregnancy or the anticipation of parenthood for both new and experienced parents may increase the level of stress in the family and as a result increase the risk for violence (Curry and Harvey 1998). In addition, pregnancy or the birth of a child may intensify preexisting strains such as low socioeconomic status. Studies finding that young pregnant women are more likely to have been abused than older pregnant women also suggest that the combination of pregnancy and youth may be particularly stressful (Hedin et al. 1999; Muhajarine and D'Arcy 1999; Parker et al. 1994; Stewart and Cecutti 1993). Stress associated with financial hardships and chronic poverty and unemployment has the potential to tax family functioning, and the cumulative effect of multiple stressors can affect levels of marital conflict. Stress may also affect the ability to process information effectively and the selection of particular conflict resolution behaviors in given circumstances, potentially leading to frustration and perhaps violence.

What Are the Consequences of Pregnancy-Related Violence?

Violence during pregnancy greatly reduces the possibility that a healthy lifestyle leading to safe motherhood can be reached; instead, a number of negative consequences are likely to result for both the mother and her unborn child. These consequences include late entry into prenatal care, low-birth-weight babies, premature labor, fetal trauma, unhealthy maternal behaviors, and health issues for the mother.

Later Entry into Prenatal Care

In addition to this conceptualization of safe motherhood, one of the goals of the federal initiative called Healthy People 2010 is that 90 percent of pregnant women will begin prenatal care in the first trimester. Unfortunately, women involved in violent relationships often enter prenatal care later in their pregnancy than do women in nonviolent relationships (Dietz et al. 1997; Gazmararian et al. 1995; Goodwin et al. 2000; McFarlane et al. 1992; Parker 1993; Parker et al. 1993, 1994). Moreover, some women may delay their prenatal care as late as the third trimester (McFarlane et al. 1992). One study, for example, found that 38 percent of women in abusive relationships registered for prenatal care later than twenty weeks gestation compared with 23 percent of the women who were not abused (Norton et al. 1995). Late entry into prenatal care may be a risk factor for pregnancy complications, as it reduces or eliminates the possibility of early risk assessment of and education in healthy maternal behaviors.

Low-Birth-Weight Infants

Although researchers generally agree that violence and abuse are associated with delays in prenatal care, the same level of agreement is not present with regard to other outcomes of pregnancy-related violence, such as low-birth-weight infants. It has

been argued by some researchers, for example, that battered women are more likely than nonbattered women to give birth to preterm and low-birth-weight infants (Bullock and McFarlane 1989; Campbell et al. 1999; Curry and Harvey 1998; Parker et al. 1994). In one study, of the 100 patients who were victims of domestic violence, 16 percent had low-birth-weight babies, compared with 6 percent of the 389 patients who were not domestic violence victims (Fernandez and Krueger 1999). Other researchers have found that the percentage of victims with low-birth-weight babies was twice as high as that of nonvictims (Bullock and McFarlane 1989). In addition to the violence experienced by pregnant women, low birth weight may also be associated with late entry into prenatal care, along with other unhealthy behaviors by the mother (e.g., smoking, poor nutrition) (Bohn and Holz 1996).

In contrast, there are also a number of studies that have not found any relationship between violence and low-birth-weight infants. For example, Cokkinides et al. (1999) found that violence was not significantly associated with low birth weight. Their study used the South Carolina Pregnancy Risk Assessment Monitoring System (PRAMS) data from 6,143 women who delivered live infants between 1993 and 1995. Similarly, Shumway and associates' (1999) study indicated that birth weight and gestational age at delivery did not vary significantly with a history of, or the degree of, violence experienced during pregnancy. Some researchers, however, have suggested that the findings of no relationship between low birth weight and violence may be a function of confounding variables such as low socioeconomic status and poor nutrition (Bullock and McFarlane 1989). In other words, low-birth-weight infants are more likely to be born to mothers of low socioeconomic status with poor nutritional habits, and since many hospital-based studies use samples of women with these characteristics, it is difficult to untangle which factors are ultimately responsible for the negative outcome. Moreover, studies do not always control for gestation length when looking at consequences such as low birth weight. Differences in sample size and type as well as a lack of standard cutoff points for what constitutes low birth weight could also account for differences across studies.

Premature Labor

In addition to low birth weight, there is also contradictory evidence regarding the relationship between violence and premature labor. Several studies, for example, have concluded that women who are victims of intimate partner violence are more likely to give birth prematurely compared with women who are not abused. Berenson and associates (1994), for example, found that assaulted women were almost twice as likely to experience preterm labor compared with those who were not assaulted. Similarly, Shumway et al. (1999) found that women who were abused were 2.3 times more likely to experience preterm labor. In addition, an increased risk for preterm labor was associated with more serious violence. Fernandez and Krueger's (1999) study found that of the 100 patients who were victims of domestic violence, 22 percent had preterm deliveries compared with only 9 percent of the 389 patients who were not victims of domestic violence. Other researchers have found the risk of preterm labor to be as much as 5 times greater among victims of severe abuse compared to women who were not abused (Shumway et al. 1999). Although there are multiple studies finding a link between abuse and premature labor, there are also several studies that have not found a relationship between violence and premature labor (Cokkinides et al. 1999; Grimstad et al. 1997). As with much of the research on pregnancy-related violence, differences in empirical findings may be due to a variety of factors, including the failure to control for other variables related to preterm labor, as well as differences in research design and sample type.

Fetal Trauma

One of the most serious negative consequences of pregnancy-related violence is fetal trauma (e.g., miscarriage, spontaneous abortion, etc.). In contrast to some of the other negative consequences reviewed, research focusing on this type of negative outcome has been relatively consistent it its findings; abuse puts the unborn baby at great risk. For example, Jacoby et al.'s (1999) study of 100 women receiving prenatal care found that women who experienced any form of abuse were significantly more likely to miscarry (42.3 percent versus 16.2 percent, respectively). In addition, they found an association between current abuse and at least one spontaneous abortion (miscarriage) in the woman's obstetric history. Other researchers have also found an increased risk for miscarriages among abused women (Berrios and Grady 1991; Renker 1999). Violence has also been associated with fetal injury and death (Bohn 1990; Webster et al. 1996).

Unhealthy Maternal Behaviors

In addition to the direct effects of violence on the health and well-being of the unborn child, violence may also indirectly contribute to negative consequences by increasing the risk for unhealthy maternal behaviors (Plichta 2004). For example, several studies have found that abused women are more likely to smoke than women who are not abused (Cokkinides and Coker 1998; Cokkinides et al. 1999; Grimstad et al. 1997; Martin et al. 1996; McFarlane and Parker 1996; Wiemann et al. 2000). In addition, much of the same research has also found an association between violence victimization and alcohol and drug use. Martin et al.'s (1996) study of 2,092 prenatal patients in North Carolina found that during pregnancy, victims were more likely to smoke, drink, and use drugs than were women who were not victimized. Moreover, after controlling for demographic factors, victims were more likely to be in the more severe substance abuse categories during pregnancy than women who were not victims of violence. In one of the few studies with a racially and ethnically diverse sample, Berenson and associates (1991) found that drug use was related to battering for white and black women in their sample but not for Hispanic women. These unhealthy behaviors may be associated with negative consequences for the unborn child as well as for the mother.

Health Issues for Mother

After more than three decades of research focused on intimate partner violence, the negative psychological and social consequences of such victimization have been clearly identified. Victims of intimate partner violence report feelings of helplessness, depression, low self-esteem, suicidal thoughts, and anxiety, all indicators of psychological distress (Straus and Gelles 1990). Battered women are also more likely to visit emergency rooms and to have chronic health complaints (Stark and Flitcraft 1988). In addition, both experiencing and witnessing violence have been associated with a greater risk of violence (as both a victim and a perpetrator) in the next generation. All of these consequences are significant for women who are pregnant as well as for their unborn children. Besides the negative health consequences experienced by the unborn child, several studies have found that violence is associated with negative health consequences for the mother as well. Moreover, many of these health issues are also relevant for the health of the unborn child. Bohn and Holtz's (1996) review of the literature identifies health issues such as an unhealthy diet, severe postpartum depression, and breastfeeding difficulties that are associated with victimization. Other researchers have found that abused women suffer from more stress and receive less support from their partner, and others (Curry and Harvey 1998; Sagrestano et al. 2004). In addition, maternal health issues such as severe depression (Horrigan et al. 2000), lower self-esteem (Curry and Harvey 1998), kidney infections (Cokkinides et al. 1999), poor weight gain, anemia, and first- or second-trimester bleeding (Parker et al. 1994) have all been associated with violence victimization. Other researchers have focused on the interval between pregnancies, finding that victims of abuse tend to have very short intervals between pregnancies ("rapid repeat pregnancies"). Each of these consequences puts both the mother and the child at risk for long-term health-related consequences.

How Is the Medical Profession Working to End Pregnancy-Related Violence?

Although there are a number of areas with regard to pregnancy-related violence in which the research evidence is inconclusive, there is no dispute that intimate partner violence has only negative outcomes; and for women who are pregnant, these negative outcomes can have drastic consequences. Given this information, the most logical place for prevention and intervention efforts to begin is with health care providers. Pregnancy is often a woman's first entry into the health care system and perhaps her first contact with a helping profession; consequently professionals who deal with pregnant women and new mothers are in a unique position to screen for intimate partner violence along with other health-related factors and initiate intervention if needed (Sampselle et al. 1992). Despite the fact that violence during pregnancy may be more common than many of the items women are often asked about by their health care providers, most women report not being asked about violence (Friedman et al. 1992). Careful assessment, however, of both family risk markers (e.g., family-of-origin exposure, substance abuse), family stressors, and current conflict management strategies may provide a more complete picture of the patient and allow for the opportunity to prevent any occurrence of violence. For women who report that they have already been victimized, health care providers are in an excellent position to provide indi viduals with linkages to appropriate services. Screening for domestic violence is also essential among women presenting with trauma- and non-trauma-related symptoms in hospital emergency departments (Dienemann et al. 1999), as their injuries may be related to intimate partner violence.

Appearing to be most effective are screening questions that are direct (Naumann et al. 1999; Norton et al. 1995) and repeated. Naumann and associates (1999), for example, found that although women often find it difficult to start a conversation about abuse, they will answer direct questions. This concept of universal screening of women seeking any health care has been identified as an essential component of comprehensive health care for women (Koss, Koss, and Woodruff 1991). In addition to identifying victims and getting them assistance, the very process of assessment can be just as important, because it acknowledges that violence against pregnant women is a very serious issue (Parker et al. 1999). In other words, if women hear their health care providers asking about victimization, they may feel that the subject is okay to talk about. By making discussions of violence more commonplace in the health care setting, victims may be more comfortable in asking for help from their health care providers.

Summary and Conclusions

Increasingly, more attention is being devoted to violence against women as a reproductive health issue. However, empirical knowledge remains relatively scarce regarding the prevalence of pregnancy-related violence and the specific dynamics of violent relationships before, during, and after pregnancy. Differences in research designs and assessments have made it difficult to definitively conclude that pregnant women are at a greater risk for intimate partner violence compared with women who are not pregnant; however, the consequences for pregnant victims remain serious. What knowledge researchers do have suggests that the same dynamics present in violent relationships in which women are not pregnant are magnified when they are. In addition, there is the added impact of potentially harmful health consequences of physical and sexual violence for both the mother and her unborn child. Researchers are continuing to investigate the dynamics of pregnancy-related violence and, as suggested by some of the studies of practitioners, are taking a close look at how they interact with patients. Future work would benefit greatly from joint projects that unite researchers with practitioners with the ultimate goal of healthy women, healthy babies, and violence-free relationships.

JANA L. JASINSKI

See also **Assessing Risk in Domestic Violence Cases; Battered Woman Syndrome; Coercive Control; Marital Rape; Substance Use/Abuse and Intimate Partner Violence; Violence against Women Act**

References and Further Reading

Berenson, A. B., N. J. Stiglich, G. S. Wilkinson, and G. D. Anderson. "Drug Abuse and Other Risk Factors for Physical Abuse in Pregnancy among White Non-Hispanic, Black, and Hispanic Women." *American Journal of Obstetrics and Gynecology* 164, no. 6 (1991): 1491–1496.

Berenson, A. B., C. M. Wiemann, G. S. Wilkinson, W. A. Jones, and G. D. Anderson. "Perinatal Morbidity Associated with Violence Experienced by Pregnant Women." *American Journal of Obstetrics and Gynecology* 170, no. 6 (1994): 1760–1766.

Berrios, Daniel C., and Deborah Grady. "Domestic Violence: Risk Factors and Outcomes." *Western Journal of Medicine* 155 (1991): 133–135.

Bohn, Diane K. "Domestic Violence and Pregnancy: Implications for Practice." *Journal of Nurse-Midwifery* 35 (1990): 86–98.

Bohn, Diane K., and Karen A. Holz. "Health Effects of Childhood Sexual Abuse, Domestic Battering, and Rape." *Journal of Nurse-Midwifery* 41 (1996): 442–456.

Bullock, Linda, and Judith McFarlane. "The Birth-Weight/Battering Connection." *American Journal of Nursing* 89 (1989): 1153–1155.

Burch, Rebecca, and Gordon Gallup. "Pregnancy as a Stimulus for Domestic Violence." *Journal of Family Violence* 19, no. 4 (2004): 243–247.

Campbell, Jacquelyn, Sara Torres, and J. Ryan. "Physical and Nonphysical Partner Abuse and Other Risk Factors for Low Birth Weight among Full Term and Preterm Babies: A Multiethnic Case-Control Study." *American Journal of Epidemiology* 150 (1999): 714–726.

Campbell, Jacquelyn C., M. J. Harris, and R. K. Lee. "Violence Research: An Overview." *Scholarly Inquiry for Nursing Practice* 9, no. 2 (1995): 105–126.

Campbell, Jacquelyn C., M. L. Poland, J. B. Waller, and J. Ager. "Correlates of Battering during Pregnancy." *Research in Nursing and Health* 15 (1992): 219–226.

Cokkinides, Vilma E., Ann L. Coker, Maureen Sanderson, Cheryl Addy, and Lesa Bethea. "Physical Violence during Pregnancy: Maternal Complications and Birth Outcomes." *Obstetrics and Gynecology* 93, no. 5 (1999): 661–666.

Curry, M. A., and S. M. Harvey, eds. *Stress Related to Domestic Violence during Pregnancy and Infant Birth Weight*, vol. 9. Thousand Oaks, CA: Sage Publications, 1998.

Dienemann, J., D. Trautman, J. B. Shahan, K. Pinnella, P. Krishnan, D. Whyne, B. Bekemeir, and J. Campbell. "Developing a Domestic Violence Program in an Inner-City Academic Health Center Emergency Department: The First 3 Years." *Journal of Emergency Nursing* 25 (1999): 110–115.

Dietz, Patricia M., Julie A. Gazmararian, Mary Goodwin, F. Carol Bruce, Christopher H. Johnson, and Roger Rochat. "Delayed Entry into Prenatal Care: Effect of Physical Violence." *Obstetrics and Gynecology* 90, no. 2 (1997): 221–224.

Fernandez, F. M., and P. M. Krueger. "Domestic Violence: Effect on Pregnancy Outcome." *Journal of the American Osteopathic Association* 99, no. 5 (1999): 254–256.

Fisher, Philip A., Beverly I. Fagot, and Craig S. Leve. "Assessment of Family Stress across Low, Medium, and High-Risk Samples Using the Family Events Checklist." *Family Relations* 47, no. 3 (1998): 215–236.

Friedman, L. S., J. G. Samet, M. S. Roberts, M. Hudlin, and P. Hans. "Inquiry about Victimization Experiences: A Survey of Patient Preferences and Physician Practices." *Archives of Internal Medicine* 152 (1992): 1186–1190.

Gazmararian, Julie A., Melissa M. Adams, Linda E. Saltzman, Christopher H. Johnson, Carol Bruce, James S. Marks, and S. Christine Zahniser. "The Relationship between Pregnancy Intendedness and Physical Violence in Mothers of Newborns." *Obstetrics and Gynecology* 85, no. 6 (1995): 1031–1038.

Gelles, Richard. "Violence and Pregnancy: Are Pregnant Women at Greater Risk of Abuse?" In *Physical Violence in American Families: Risk Factors and Adaptations to Violence in 8,145 Families*, edited by Murray Straus and Richard Gelles. New Brunswick, NJ: Transaction Publishers, 1990, pp. 279–286.

Glander, Susan S., Mary Lou Moore, Robert Michielutte, and Linn H. Parsons. "The Prevalence of Domestic Violence among Women Seeking Abortion." *Obstetrics and Gynecology* 91, no. 6 (1998): 1002–1006.

Goodwin, Mary, Julie A. Gazmararian, Christopher H. Johnson, Brenda C. Gilbert, and Linda E. Saltzman. "Pregnancy Intendedness and Physical Abuse round the Time of Pregnancy: Findings from the Pregnancy Risk Assessment Monitoring System [PRAMS], 1996–1997." PRAMS Working Group. *Maternal and Child Health Journal* 4, no. 2 (2000): 85–92.

Grimstad, Hilde, Berit Schei, Bjorn Backe, and Geir Jacobsen. "Physical Abuse and Low Birthweight: A Case-Control Study." *British Journal of Obstetrics and Gynecology* 104 (1997): 1281–1287.

Healthy People 2010 website. http://www.healthypeople.gov/default.htm (accessed September 1, 2006).

Hedin, Lena Widding, Hilde Grimstad, Anders Moller, Berit Schei, and Per Olof Janson. "Prevalence of Physical and Sexual Abuse before and during Pregnancy among Swedish Couples." *Acta Obstetrica et Gynecologica Scandinavica* 78, no. 4 (1999): 310–315.

Horrigan, Terrance J., Andrea V. Schroeder, and Rose Mary Schaffer. "The Triad of Substance Abuse, Violence, and Depression Are Interrelated in Pregnancy." *Journal of Substance Abuse Treatment* 18 (2000): 55–58.

Jacoby, Mark, Daniel Gorenflo, Erin Black, Christine Wunderlich, and A. Evan Eyler. "Rapid Repeat Pregnancy and Experiences of Interpersonal Violence among Low-Income Adolescents." *American Journal of Preventive Medicine* 16, no. 4 (1999): 318–321.

Jasinski, Jana. "Pregnancy and Violence against Women: An Analysis of Longitudinal Data." *Journal of Interpersonal Violence* 16, no. 7 (2001): 713–734.

Jasinski, Jana, and Glenda Kaufman Kantor. "Pregnancy, Stress and Wife Assaults: Ethnic Differences in Prevalence, Severity and Onset in a National Sample." *Violence and Victims* 16, no. 3 (2001): 1–14.

Koss, M. P., P. G. Koss, and J. Woodruff. "Deleterious Effects of Criminal Victimization on Women's Health and Medical Utilization." *Archives of Internal Medicine* 151 (1991): 342–347.

Mahoney, Patricia, Linda Williams, and Carolyn West. "Violence against Women by Intimate Relationship Partners." In *Sourcebook on Violence against Women*, edited by Claire Renzetti, Jeffrey Edelson, and Raquel Kennedy Bergen. Thousand Oaks, CA: Sage Publications, 2001, pp. 143–178.

Martin, Sandra, April Harris-Britt, Yun Li, Kathryn Moracco, Lawrence Kupper, and Jacquelyn Campbell. "Changes in Intimate Partner Violence during Pregnancy." *Journal of Family Violence* 19, no. 4 (2004): 201–210.

Martin, Sandra L., Linda Mackie, Lawrence L. Kupper, Paul A. Buescher, and Katherine E. Moracco. "Physical Abuse of Women before, during, and after Pregnancy." *Journal of the American Medical Association* 285 (2001): 1581–1584.

Martin, Susan L., K. T. English, K. A. Clark, D. Cilenti, and L. L. Kupper. "Violence and Substance Abuse among North Carolina Pregnant Women." *American Journal of Public Health* 86 (1996): 991–998.

McFarlane, Judith, and Barbara Parker. "Physical Abuse, Smoking, and Substance Use during Pregnancy: Prevalence, Interrelationships, and Effects on Birth Weight." *Journal of Obstetrics, Gynecology, and Neonatal Nursing* 25 (1996): 313–320.

McFarlane, Judith, Barbara Parker, Karen Soeken, and L. Bullock. "Assessing for Abuse during Pregnancy." *Journal of the American Medical Association* 267 (1992): 3176–3178.

Muhajarine, N., and C. D'Arcy. "Physical Abuse during Pregnancy: Prevalence and Risk Factors." *Canadian Medical Association Journal* 160 (1999): 1007–1011.

Naumann, P., D. Langford, S. Torres, J. Campbell, and N. Glass. "Woman Battering in Primary Care Practice." *Family Practice* 16 (1999): 343–352.

Norton, Lynn B., Jeffrey F. Peipert, Sally Zierler, Bethany Lima, and Lucy Hume. "Battering in Pregnancy: An Assessment of Two Screening Methods." *Obstetrics and Gynecology* 85 (1995): 321–325.

Parker, Barbara, Judith McFarlane, and Karen Soeken. "Abuse during Pregnancy: Effects on Maternal Complications and Birth Weight in Adult and Teenage Women." *Obstetrics and Gynecology* 84 (1994): 323–328.

Parker, Barbara, Judith McFarlane, Karen Soeken, Concepcion Silva, and Sally Reel. "Testing an Intervention to Prevent Further Abuse to Pregnant Women." *Research in Nursing and Health* 22 (1999): 59–68.

Parker, Barbara, Judith McFarlane, Karen Soeken, S. Torres, and D. Campbell. "Physical and Emotional Abuse in Pregnancy: A Comparison of Adult and Teenage Women." *Nursing Research* 42 (1993): 173–178.

Parker, Robert Nash. "The Effects of Context on Alcohol and Violence." *Alcohol Health and Research World* 17 (1993): 117–122. Special issue: Alcohol, Aggression, and Injury.

Petersen, Ruth, Linda E. Saltzman, M. Goodwin, and A. Spitz. *Key Scientific Issues for Research on Violence Occurring around the Time of Pregnancy*. Atlanta: Centers for Disease Control, 1997.

Plichta, Stacy. "Intimate Partner Violence and Physical Health Consequences." *Journal of Interpersonal Violence* 19, no. 11 (2004): 1296–1323.

Rachana, Chibber, Khwaja Suraiya, Al-Sibai Hisham, Al-Mulhim Abdulaziz, and Abdul Hai. "Prevalence and Complications of Physical Violence during Pregnancy." *European Journal of Obstetrics and Gynecology and Reproductive Biology* 103 (2002): 26–29.

Renker, P. R. "Physical Abuse, Social Support, Self-Care, and Pregnancy Outcomes of Older Adolescents." *Journal of Obstetrics, Gynecology, and Neonatal Nursing* 28 (1999): 377–388.

Sagrestano, Lynda, Doris Carroll, Angela Rodriguez, and Bahij Nuwayhid. "Demographic, Psychological, and Relationship Factors in Domestic Violence during Pregnancy in a Sample of Low-Income Women of Color." *Psychology of Women Quarterly* 28 (2004): 309–322.

Sampselle, Carolyn M., Barbara A. Petersen, Terri L. Murtland, and Deborah Oakley. "Prevalence of Abuse among Pregnant Women Choosing Certified Nurse-Midwife or Physician Provider." *Journal of Nurse-Midwifery* 37 (1992): 269–273.

Shumway, Joseph, Patricia O'Campo, Andrea Gielen, Frank R. Witter, Adib N. Khouzami, and Karin Blakemore. "Preterm Labor, Placental Abruption, and Premature Rupture of Membranes in Relation to Maternal Violence or Verbal Abuse." *Journal of Maternal-Fetal Medicine* 8 (1999): 76–80.

Smikle, Collin B., Kimberlee A. Sorem, Andrew J. Stain, and Gary Hankins. "Physical and Sexual Abuse in a Middle-Class Obstetric Population." *Southern Medical Journal* 89 (1996): 983–988.

Stark, Evin, and A. Flitcraft. "Violence among Intimates: An Epidemiological Review." In *Handbook of Family Violence*, edited by Vincent B. Van Hasselt, R. L. Morrison, A. S. Bellack, and M. Hersen. New York: Plenum Press, 1988, pp. 293–317.

Stewart, D. E. "Incidence of Postpartum Abuse in Women with a History of Abuse during Pregnancy." *Canadian Medical Association Journal* 151 (1994): 1601–1604.

Stewart, D. E., and A. Cecutti. "Physical Abuse in Pregnancy." *Canadian Medical Association Journal* 149 (1993): 1257–1263.

Straus, Murray, and Richard Gelles. *Physical Violence in American Families: Risk Factors and Adaptations to Violence in 8,145 Families*. New Brunswick, NJ: Transaction Publishers, 1990.

Tjaden, P., and N. Thoennes. *Extent, Nature, and Consequences of Intimate Partner Violence*. National Institute of Justice, NCJ 181867. Washington, DC: Department of Justice, 2000.

Webster, Joan, Jenny Chandler, and Diana Battistutta. "Pregnancy Outcomes and Health Care Use: Effects of Abuse." *American Journal of Obstetrics and Gynecology* 174 (1996): 760–767.

Wiemann, Constance M., Carolyn A. Agurcia, Abbey B. Berenson, Robert J. Volk, and Vaughn Rickert. "Pregnant Adolescents: Experiences and Behaviors Associated with Physical Assault by an Intimate Partner." *Maternal and Child Health Journal* 4 (2000): 93–101.

PROSECUTION OF CHILD ABUSE AND NEGLECT

For the public, prosecution of child abuse is marked more by notoriety than knowledge. Ever since child abuse began to be prosecuted with some frequency in the 1980s, the news media have lavished enormous attention on several high profile cases like the McMartin Preschool trial (the longest trial in U.S. history), the Louise Woodward trial, and the Michael Jackson trial. But the average case receives little media coverage (Cheit 2003), despite the fact that tens of thousands of child sexual abuse cases alone come to the attention of law enforcement (Snyder 2000), and child physical abuse has begun to be prosecuted more frequently as well. The public and many professionals understand little in an area that can have enormous consequences for perpetrators, child victims, families, and communities. Despite professional disagreement over which cases should be prosecuted, there is broad consensus that prosecution of child abuse can be an essential societal response, and professionals involved with family violence need to have a working knowledge of it.

Prosecution of child abuse presents special challenges for everyone involved (National Center for Prosecution of Child Abuse 2004; Whitcomb 1992). Typically the key witnesses are the child victims themselves, and the emotional and cognitive demands of testifying can be enormous. Prosecution can hinge on already vulnerable child victims "retelling their stories" in adversarial proceedings. Usually the offender is someone the child knows and trusted: the father or mother, a sibling, relative, neighbor, caretaker, teacher, member of clergy, or other respected adult or adolescent. For sexual abuse—the most commonly prosecuted type of abuse—there is often limited evidence besides the child's testimony. Children's credibility in and out of court can be questioned; true allegations of child abuse can be met by disbelief if they are leveled against an apparently upstanding member of the community. Children testifying to abuse can be vilified by family members or others who side with the offender, and pressured to recant their allegations. Because of the Sixth Amendment right of defendants to confront their accusers, child victims who testify in court must often do so with their abusers facing them from the defense table. Child victims are sometimes ambivalent or even opposed to prosecuting their abuse, because of the difficulties involved, their relationship with the perpetrators, or both.

One major concern has been the stress that prosecution places on child victims and the potential for emotional harm (Quas et al. 2005; Whitcomb 2003). Testifying, it was thought, could negatively affect children's mental health, at worst leading to "secondary victimization" of child victims. Studies have found, not surprisingly, that children show stress and anxiety both before and during testimony. Testifying in court predicts poorer child mental health outcomes, particularly when children have to testify repeatedly, spend a long time on the witness stand, or undergo harsh cross-examination. However, most children recover within months after testifying, though some continue to have substantial behavioral problems. Despite the difficulties of testifying, *not* testifying can pose risks, too: Sas and colleagues' (1993) three-year follow-up study found that children were better adjusted and had a more positive appraisal of their court involvement when there was a guilty verdict—thus, testifying poses a risk but may lead to an outcome that helps improve children's later well-being. Quas and colleagues (2005) found a complex picture when they assessed alleged victims of child sexual abuse twelve years after their involvement in criminal court cases. They concluded that under certain conditions, testifying repeatedly in open court can contribute to a long-term trajectory of poor mental health functioning. On the other hand, they also found that children involved in trials who did *not* testify were more negative about their court experience. For the subgroup of less severe cases, nontestifiers reported higher levels of defensive avoidance. In total, the research suggests a need to balance the risks and benefits for children and society of both prosecuting and not prosecuting.

Another major challenge for prosecution, and an area of controversy, has been concern about the accuracy and credibility of children's testimony, both in forensic investigations and in court (see Ceci and Bruck 1999; Lyon 1999; National Center for the Prosecution of Child Abuse 2004; Saywitz, Goodman, and Lyon 2002). Children, especially very young ones, have developmental limitations to their memory, understanding, and ability to communicate that can be exacerbated by the stress of abuse and investigation. Getting accounts that are as accurate and believable as possible requires skilled interviewing. The skills apply mainly to forensic interviewing during investigation, but to some degree to questioning children at court hearings as well. Qualities of effective interviewing include:

- establishing rapport with children,
- obtaining as much information as possible through open-ended questions that allow children to "tell their story" in their own words,
- instructing children that it is all right to say "I don't know" if they lack the answer,
- phrasing questions in simple non-"legalese" that children can understand, and
- avoiding suggestive or leading questions.

Good interviewing should ease the stress on children, yield accurate information, and help forestall challenges by the defense. The stakes are high, since a mistake could lead to a failure to stop and punish actual abuse, or to sending an innocent person to jail. Despite the controversy, there is considerable evidence and agreement that most children of even surprisingly young ages can provide accurate accounts of their abuse or lack of abuse when questioned well. It is also widely recognized that children, especially the very young, can provide inaccurate accounts in some situations, particularly with poor interviews, and that false allegations are possible if interviewing is leading, suggestive, or overly repetitious.

A number of reforms have been developed since the 1980s in response to the obstacles and stresses of prosecuting child abuse (Whitcomb 2003). Many communities have developed multidisciplinary professional teams or joint investigation protocols to improve coordination and reduce the number of times children have to talk about their abuse. Recent research suggests that redundant interviewing has generally decreased as compared with the 1980s (Cross et al. 2005). Special child-friendly settings called Children's Advocacy Centers (CACs) have been developed to respond holistically to the needs of children in the criminal justice process. CACs aim to reduce stress on and increase support for children in investigations; facilitate delivery of needed mental health, medical, advocacy, and support services; enhance professional coordination; and improve investigations. Over 500 CACs have been developed nationwide since the first was founded in 1985 (Cross et al. 2005). The use of victim-witness advocates and family support programs in child abuse cases has expanded as well, whether connected to district attorneys offices, CACs, or other programs. In addition to their direct benefits for children and families, these aim to help foster nonoffending parents' support for children, a critical variable shown in numerous studies to buffer child victims against the stresses of the criminal justice system as well as the effects of abuse. A number of jurisdictions also have court preparation or "court school" programs for children. These programs educate children about court staff and functions and sometimes include an anxiety-reduction component as well. An evaluation of one such program found that it helped children gain knowledge of the legal system and reduce their fears of revictimization (Sas et al. 1993).

Motions for special courtroom procedures to help children have been used in many cases (National Center for the Prosecution of Child Abuse 2004; Whitcomb 2003). Courtroom seating can be rearranged to take the defendant out of direct view of the child or to place children in child-size chairs. A support person will sometimes be allowed to sit with a child witness. Children may be allowed to hold a teddy bear or blanket. Spectators can be removed from the courtroom. Children can swear to oaths adapted for their understanding, and attorneys can be directed to object by raising their hand rather than their voices. In *Maryland v. Craig,* 1990, the United States Supreme Court established that children may testify by prior videotape or closed circuit TV without having to confront the defendant, provided prosecutors can demonstrate that the child in question cannot reasonably testify otherwise.

Despite the challenges, the statistics on prosecution of child abuse are not dissimilar from those for other violent offenses (Cross et al. 2003). Child abuse cases are referred to prosecutors from both police and child protective services (CPS) investigations, though in many cases police and CPS work jointly or as part of a multidisciplinary team (see Finkelhor, Cross, and Cantor 2005). All child sexual abuse, defined as sexual activity between an adult and a youth under the age of consent, is a crime, while only serious child physical abuse and neglect are defined as crimes. Not surprisingly, a higher proportion of police cases than CPS cases are referred to prosecutors, though there are not enough data to estimate percentages. To decide whether to file criminal charges, prosecutors consider whether there is sufficient evidence that a crime has been committed and whether the probability of obtaining a just result justifies filing charges. The stress to the victim and family of prosecution and a possible trial is taken into account. Across thirteen studies reviewed by Cross and colleagues (2003), charges were filed in the majority of cases referred to prosecutors, but the rates varied from 28 to 94 percent. Much of this variation probably reflects differences in policy and practice across jurisdictions. The overall mean charging rate of 66 percent was somewhat lower than the mean rate for all violent offenses (79 percent), but not significantly different from the mean rate for all rape and other sexual assault cases (69 percent; this latter group does, however, *include* child sexual abuse cases). It is not clear to what degree charging rates reflect the base rate of true allegations; the characteristics of cases referred to prosecutors; the policy and skills of prosecutors; the influence of victim, family, and community wishes; or the inherent challenges of prosecuting child abuse cases, which the National Center for the Prosecution of Child Abuse (2004, p. 171) described as "some of the most difficult of all criminal cases to prove."

Once charges were filed, prosecution of child abuse did not appear to differ in outcomes from prosecution of other violent offenses. Most charged cases (72 percent or greater in most studies) were carried forward without dismissal, a somewhat higher percentage of cases than for other violent crimes (65 percent). For those cases carried forward, an average of 82 percent of defendants pleaded guilty, and 18 percent went to trial. Overall, 94 percent of those cases that were carried forward without dismissal ended in convictions (guilty plea or conviction at trial). The plea and conviction rates for charged cases were not significantly different than for other violent crimes. The number of trials in the research was not large enough to estimate separately the percentage of trials that ended in conviction. On average, 54 percent of convicted offenders were incarcerated. This was somewhat lower than for other violent crimes, perhaps because many defendants had familial or other close relationships with the victims. Thus the research suggests that, on the whole, child abuse prosecution is neither reckless, in that the rate at which charges are filed is not excessive, nor feckless, since child abuse prosecutions show outcomes that resemble those of other comparable felonies.

Prosecution will remain an important response as long as child abuse persists. Child-serving professionals and the public need to recognize its special difficulties and requirements, without being overly swayed by the horror stories told in the media. They also need to understand the criminal justice context in which it fits.

THEODORE P. CROSS

See also **Child Neglect; Child Sexual Abuse; Medical Neglect Related to Religion and Culture; Munchausen by Proxy Syndrome; Post-Incest Syndrome; Ritual Abuse–Torture in Families; Victim-Blaming Theory**

References and Further Reading

Ceci, Stephen, and Maggie Bruck. *Jeopardy in the Courtroom: A Scientific Analysis of Children's Testimony.* Washington, DC: American Psychological Association, 1999.

Cheit, Ross E. "What Hysteria? A Systematic Study of Newspaper Coverage of Accused Child Molesters." *Child Abuse and Neglect* 27, no. 6 (2003): 607–623.

Cross, Theodore P., Lisa M. Jones, Wendy A. Walsh, and Monique Simone. *The Multi-Site Evaluation of Children's Advocacy Centers.* Presentation at the 15th National Conference on Child Abuse and Neglect, Boston, 2005.

Cross, Theodore P., Wendy A. Walsh, Monique Simone, and Lisa M. Jones. "Prosecution of Child Abuse: A Meta-Analysis of Rates of Criminal Justice Decisions." *Trauma, Violence, and Abuse: A Review Journal* 4, no. 4 (2003): 323–340.

Lyon, Thomas. "The New Wave of Suggestibility Research: A Critique." *Cornell Law Review* 84 (1999): 1004–1087.

National Center for Prosecution of Child Abuse. *Investigation and Prosecution of Child Abuse,* 3rd ed. Thousand Oaks, CA: Sage, 2004.

Quas, Jodi A., Gail S. Goodman, Simona Ghetti, K. Alexander, Robin Edelstein, Allison D. Redlich, Ingrid M. Cordon, and David P. H. Jones. "Childhood Sexual Assault Victims: Long-Term Outcomes after Testifying in Criminal Court." *Monographs of the Society for Research in Child Development* 70, no. 2 (2005).

Sas, L., P. Hurley, A. Hatch, S. Malla, and T. Dick. *Three Years after the Verdict: A Longitudinal Study of the Social and Psychological Adjustment of Child Witnesses Referred to the Child Witness Project.* London, Ontario: London Family Court Clinic.

Saywitz, Karen J., Gail S. Goodman, and Thomas D. Lyon. "Interviewing Children In and Out of Court: Current Research and Practice Implications." In *The APSAC Handbook of Child Maltreatment,* 2nd ed., edited by John Myers, Lucy Berliner, Johen Briere, Terry Hendrix, and Theresa Reid. Thousand Oaks, CA: Sage, 2002, pp. 349–377.

Snyder, Howard. *Sexual Assault of Young Children as Reported to Law Enforcement: Victim, Incident, and Offender Characteristics.* Washington, DC: Bureau of Justice Statistics, 2000.

Whitcomb, Debra. *When the Victim Is a Child,* 2nd ed. Washington, DC: National Institute of Justice, 1992.

———. "Legal Intervention for Child Victims." *Journal of Traumatic Stress* 16, no. 2 (2003): 149–157.

PROTECTIVE AND RESTRAINING ORDERS

Introduction

Protective and restraining orders may be used in a variety of family violence situations. These protective and restraining orders are issued by a court to a specific person directing that person to stay away from or refrain from contacting the victim or victims. Protective and restraining orders can be used in other situations, but this article will focus on the types of protective orders that are issued in family violence situations. In order to discuss the concept of protective and restraining orders properly, it is important to define family violence. The definition of protective or restraining orders must also be set forth. This will include a discussion of the essential elements necessary to include in protective and restraining orders. The history of protective and restraining orders will be briefly examined. The full faith and credit provision in the Violence against Women Act will be discussed as well. Advantages and disadvantages of protective and restraining orders will be set forth. Finally, the effectiveness of protective and restraining orders will be evaluated.

Acts or Courses of Conduct Prohibited by Restraining Orders

The definition of family violence is controversial. Different authorities have defined it in a variety of ways. For the purpose of this essay, the term *family violence* is defined as any act or omission by persons who are cohabiting that results in serious injury to other members of the family. The term *family*, for the purpose of the definition, includes members of traditional households such as those who are married or are living together and related by blood, such as father and son. It also includes nontraditional households such as those of people who are living together but are not married or are not related by blood. In this context, family can also include those who were but are no longer living together.

Family violence subsumes several subtopics, such as spousal abuse, dating violence, gay and lesbian abuse, child abuse, and elder abuse. No single officially accepted definition for any of these types of violence exists among laypersons or professionals. For the purpose of this essay, spousal abuse is defined as any intentional act or series of acts by one spouse that cause injury to the other spouse. The term *spouse* includes individuals who are married, cohabitating, or involved in an intimate relationship. It also includes those who were once in these relationships and are no longer together. *Spouse* is a gender-neutral term that includes both males and females.

Dating violence is another form of family violence. The distinction between spousal abuse and dating violence is that spousal abuse occurs when individuals are married, cohabiting, or separated following marriage or cohabitation. Dating violence can occur between those who are involved in a romantic relationship or dating but not yet married or cohabiting.

In order to define gay and lesbian abuse, the terms *homosexual, gay,* and *lesbian* should be defined first. Homosexuality is defined as the manifestation of sexual desire toward a member of one's own sex. The term *gay* is defined as referring to a male homosexual or a socially integrated group oriented toward and concerned with the welfare of homosexuals. Lesbian is defined as a female homosexual. Gay and lesbian abuse includes the same or similar types of acts that are present in spousal abuse.

Child abuse includes physical child abuse, child sexual abuse, and child neglect. A number of scholars have defined these types of child abuse differently. For the purpose of this essay, physical child abuse is defined as any act that results in a non-accidental physical injury of a child by a person who has care, custody, or control of the child. Child sexual abuse is defined as sexual exploitation of or sexual activities with a child under circumstances that indicate that the child's health or welfare is harmed or threatened. This definition includes inappropriate sexual activities or behaviors that may occur between a child and an adult who is a stranger or a family member. Child neglect refers to any negligent treatment or maltreatment of a child by a parent or caretaker under circumstances indicating harm or threatened harm to the child's health or welfare. Child neglect is considered to be a continuum that ranges from momentary inattention to gross action or inaction.

The definition of elder abuse is another controversial issue among authorities. Some scholars may classify elders as those who are over the age of sixty, whereas others may include only those who are over the age of sixty-five. Elder abuse is composed of four different types of acts or omissions. These include physical, sexual, psychological, and financial abuse. Elder abuse can occur in both domestic and institutional environments such as nursing homes and long-term care institutions.

Stalking is defined as a knowing, purposeful course of conduct directed at a particular person that can cause a reasonable person to believe that she or he is in danger of physical injury or death or that such danger exists for a member of her/his immediate family. The object may be a celebrity, a complete stranger, or an individual who is related to the stalker by marriage or other intimate or casual relationship. Stalking may happen to a person who forms a relationship with the stalker or is found by the stalker on the Internet or other electronic or print media.

Cyberstalking involves sending e-mails or hacking into e-mails or other personal accounts while pursuing the victim on the Internet. Cyberstalking has become more prevalent as contemporary society relies more and more on the use of computers and the Internet. In many ways, cyberstalking and identity theft are the new crimes of the twenty-first century. Some cyberstalkers may obtain victims' personal data using the Internet and then attempt to destroy their credit or cause other damage. For instance, at a West Coast university, an ex-boyfriend accessed the university's registration website and disenrolled his former girlfriend from all of her classes without her knowledge or consent. This was a clear attempt on his part to injure or hurt his former girlfriend.

Stalking is composed of six elements that must be met before an act or a series of acts can be classified as such:

1. *Actions are conducted with knowledge of possible consequences.* This requires the perpetrator's knowledge that the acts undertaken by him or her will place the victim in fear of injury.

2. *Actions are conducted purposefully.* The acts must be conducted in a purposeful or conscious manner that a reasonable person would believe will cause the victim fear.

3. *Actions follow a course of conduct.* A perpetrator must engage in more than a single act in order to be classified as a stalker.

4. *Actions meet a reasonable-person standard.* A stalking crime is not judged by what the victim may personally feel. In other words, it is judged by what a *reasonable person* would think or feel if the reasonable person were in the particular situation that the victim is in.

5. *Actions cause victims' fear of injury or death.* The course of conduct by the perpetrator must comprise acts that would cause the victim to fear injury or death as a result of the perpetrator's actions.

6. *Actions are directed at the victim or his/her immediate family.* These include spouses, children, and parents. Many stalkers may also attack the victim's pet(s) as a way of intimidating or threatening the victim.

The four most common types of stalking behaviors are:

- erotomania,
- love obsession,
- simple obsession, and
- false victimization syndrome.

The erotomanic stalker has a delusional disorder. Oftentimes, the victim is a public figure or celebrity who does not even know that the stalker exists. The stalker believes that her/his love for the victim would be requited if not for external influences. These individuals do not accept any opposing evidence or suggestions and remain delusional for a long period of time.

The characteristics of love obsessional stalkers are similar to those of erotomanic stalkers. The main difference between them is that the former has a primary psychiatric diagnosis. The love obsessional stalker often engages in activities such as writing, telephone calling, or other activities to contact the victim so the victim will acknowledge the existence of the stalker.

Simple obsessional stalkers have been involved in a prior relationship with their victims. In this relationship they may have been spouses, cohabitants, boyfriends/girlfriends, employers, or neighbors. This type of stalking occurs after the relationship has ended or when the stalker perceives that the victim has mistreated him or her.

With simple obsessional stalkers, the purpose of the conduct is to solve a problem or seek revenge.

False victimization syndrome is the fourth classification of stalking. This is indicated when a victim believes that he or she is being stalked, but in fact there is no stalking. This is the rarest classification of stalking, and is an object rather than a subject perception. Although false victimization is not truly stalking, it is included for the purpose of comparison and understanding the stalking process.

What Is a Protective or Restraining Order?

Protective and restraining orders are court orders that restrict or prohibit the offender from having any contact with the victim or the victim's family. Under the terms of the Violence against Women Act (VAWA) of 1994, a restraining order is defined as "any injunction or other order issued for the purpose of preventing violent or threatening acts or harassment against, or contact or communication with, or physical proximity to, another person" (VAWOR 2003). Form, content, length, layout, and names of restraining orders may vary from state to state. Restraining orders are known by a variety of names, including protective or protection orders, stay away orders, orders of no contact, injunctions for protection, harassment orders, stalking protection orders, and orders not to abuse or harass (VAWOR 2005a).

Protective or restraining orders generally include various options such as a restriction regarding the offender's contact with the victim; prohibitions of abuse, intimidation, and harassment; child custody determination and visitation issues; mandating counseling for the offender; and firearm possession. The issuance of such an order requires sufficient evidence that supports and justifies it. Both civil and criminal courts have the authority to issue restraining orders (Office for Victims of Crime 2002). These orders are now available from federal courts and from all fifty states' courts and the District of Columbia's.

There are several essential elements of a valid restraining order. Any restraining order will be considered valid if all of the following criteria are met:

- The order gives names of the parties.
- The order contains the date the order was issued, which is prior to the date when enforcement is sought.
- If the order has an expiration date, the date of expiration in the order has not occurred.
- The order contains the name of the issuing court.

- The order is signed by or on behalf of a judicial officer.
- The order specifies terms and conditions against the abuser (VAWOR 2003).

The most common means used to enforce restraining orders are criminal sanctions. Depending on the state, violation of the order may be a felony, a misdemeanor, or contempt of court (Office for Victims of Crime 2002). In many states, however, repeat offenders are charged with a felony offense. Several states treat each violation of the order as a new offense. For example, the perpetrator may mail a threatening letter to the victim's home and may mail another letter to the victim's place of employment. The state that treats each violation as a separate offense would charge the perpetrator in this case with two distinct and separate crimes.

Sanctions for violating restraining orders differ among states. For instance, a violation of a restraining order in one state may subject the offender to criminal charges such as invasion of privacy. Entering a house or building in violation of a restraining order may be considered a crime of trespassing in another state.

In a few states, violation of restraining orders require the perpetrators to serve a minimum term of confinement. In other states, violations of restraining orders may affect other related criminal procedures or sanctions, including bail, pretrial release, probation revocation, imposition of supervision, and incarceration. Additionally, some states have created other types of sanctions, such as ordering the offender to attend counseling, requiring him to be subjected to electronic monitoring, or requiring him to pay court costs and attorney's fees incurred by the victim seeking a restraining order (Office for Victims of Crime 2002).

The act of stalking is a relatively new crime. Prior to the early 1990s, there were no laws at the state or federal levels that prohibited stalking. Law enforcement officers had to wait until the perpetrator committed a crime of assault or battery or a more serious offense before responding to the victim's pleas for help. In July 1987, an obsessed fan by the name of John Bardo committed the ultimate act of stalking when he confronted actress Rebecca Schaeffer, costar of the television sitcom *My Sister Sam*. He obtained her address, went to her apartment, and shot her at point-blank range with a .357 Magnum revolver, killing the twenty-two-year-old actress. This incident raised the nation's awareness of stalking. As a result, California enacted the first stalking law in the United States. Other states soon followed, and now every state in the union and the federal government all have stalking laws.

These newly enacted stalking laws were challenged in courts on a variety of grounds, including that they violated the constitutional rights of the stalker. Stalkers and their attorneys alleged that the issuance of the restraining order violated their First Amendment right of freedom of association and/or freedom of expression. The courts were uniform in upholding the validity of these stalking statues. Restraining orders have become one of the main law enforcement tools in family violence situations.

Full Faith and Credit

The federal full faith and credit provision of VAWA requires jurisdictions to enforce valid restraining orders, regardless of where the order was issued, to protect victims of family violence and stalking whenever the offender violates the order (VAWOR 2003). *Full faith and credit* is a legal term meaning that jurisdictions must honor and enforce court orders issued by other jurisdictions (VAWOR 2005b).

Under the full faith and credit provision, a valid restraining order must contain two essential elements. First, the court that issued the order has jurisdiction over the victim and the offender and also has jurisdiction over the case. Second, the offender has been given notice and has an opportunity to be heard (VAWOR 2005a). The full faith and credit provision also applies to *ex parte* orders. These are orders that have been issued by courts before the respondent or perpetrator has received notice or has had an opportunity to present evidence. Such orders are normally issued in emergency or high-risk situations in order to protect the victim before the regularly noticed temporary restraining order hearing. *Ex parte* orders are typically issued for a short period of time, such as three to fourteen days. They are valid in other jurisdictions only for the time that they would have been valid in the issuing jurisdiction. For instance, an *ex parte* restraining order that is issued for fourteen days before a hearing would be good in any other jurisdictions for fourteen days (VAWOR 2005a).

The full faith and credit provision has had a great influence on victims, abusers, and law enforcement officers. Victims who have a valid restraining order are entitled to full faith and credit throughout the United States. This is very important because many victims may travel to another state for various reasons, including visiting their families and friends or going to work. The full faith and credit provision is especially critical when dealing with cities that are located next to state or federal boundaries.

The full faith and credit provision requires an abuser to honor the terms and conditions of the restraining order no matter where he is physically located. Regardless of where the restraining order was issued and where it is violated, the abuser may be arrested and charged with a violation or violations of it (VAWOR 2003).

Law enforcement officers must enforce the terms and conditions of a restraining order as written. If an offender travels across a state line and violates the order, the offender can be arrested under the laws of the state where the act occurred. Therefore, responding law enforcement officers are not required to be familiar with the laws of the jurisdiction that issued the restraining order. Officers in the enforcing jurisdiction are required to comply with all laws and procedures of their jurisdictions if the order is violated (VAWOR 2003). For instance, if the enforcing jurisdiction has a mandatory arrest policy for violation of a restraining order, it will apply to a restraining order that was issued in another jurisdiction. Many jurisdictions have enacted laws to provide officers with statutory immunity from liability when they act reasonably to protect a victim in a domestic violence situation.

The full faith and credit provision establishes certain responsibilities for both the issuing and the enforcing jurisdiction. The issuing jurisdiction decides whether a restraining order should be issued, who is protected, terms and conditions of the order, and how long the order is valid. The enforcing jurisdiction determines how the order is enforced, whether the responding officers will arrest the offender, detention and notification procedures, and the issuance of criminal charges for any violation of the order (VAWOR 2003).

The full faith and credit provision does not require a victim to register or file a restraining order in the enforcing jurisdiction. Therefore, it is not uncommon that a restraining order is not registered in the enforcing jurisdiction where the violation of the order occurs. This situation frequently occurs because many victims may flee the issuing jurisdiction so that the offender cannot locate him or her (Carbon et al. 1998). If the restraining order appears valid on its face, responding officers in the enforcing jurisdiction are not required to conduct an independent verification of the restraining order's terms and conditions.

The National Crime Information Center (NCIC) has established the NCIC Protective Order File.

This is a nationwide registry for restraining orders. The purposes of the Protective Order File are to:

1. allow law enforcement officers, judges, and prosecutors to immediately access accurate information regarding restraining orders in domestic violence or stalking cases, regardless of where the order is issued;
2. inform law enforcement agencies across the nation of the existence, terms, and conditions of restraining orders; and
3. maintain information on the identification of offenders who are subjected to restraining orders and are prohibited from possessing a firearm (Carbon et al. 1998).

This nationwide registry will allow law enforcement officials in every jurisdiction to verify the status of restraining orders regardless of where the order was issued. However, as of this writing, some states and federally recognized Indian tribes are not participating in the program yet. Another problem with this process is that some participating jurisdictions have not forwarded all of their restraining orders to the Protective Order File. Therefore, if the Protective Order File is to become truly effective, all states must participate and send all valid orders to this file.

Advantages of Protective and Restraining Orders

Protective or restraining orders offer alternatives to arrest for victims of family violence. The use of a restraining order has several advantages. Most arrested offenders are released in a matter of hours or days. A restraining order can be valid for an extended period of time. In most cases, it is valid for up to three years.

When an offender is arrested, it may cause him to be fired or otherwise terminated from his job. This may increase the tension that already exists between the offender and the victim. A restraining order allows the offender to continue his employment. However, it prevents the offender from living with or contacting the victim.

A victim does not have to have an attorney to request a temporary restraining order or a regular restraining order. This is an advantage to many victims because attorneys' fees can be expensive, and the cost may be prohibitive or act as a deterrent to those victims who cannot afford it.

A restraining order carries the weight and gravity of a judicial edict. Thus, this may cause some offenders to think twice before violating an order of the court. Although some offenders may have

been involved with police and the judicial system a number of times, most offenders have not been issued a direct order from a judge stating that they shall not engage in certain conduct. This direct order from a judge may act as a deterrent.

Additionally, obtaining a restraining order can provide victims with peace of mind. Restraining orders may be issued in response to the victim's fear of personal injury, past actual injury, or threat of financial harm. A temporary restraining order may be issued by a judge on the same day that the victim requests it. This prompt issuance of a temporary restraining order provides much-needed relief to victims of family violence.

Disadvantages of Protective and Restraining Orders

Although there are certain valuable advantages of restraining orders, there are also disadvantages to this form of protection. It is important for victims to understand that they should not rely solely on the use of restraining orders, because the most obvious and dangerous disadvantage is that the offender may simply ignore their terms and conditions. This may result in injury or even death to victims. If offenders do not attach any meaning or value to the orders, they become merely pieces of paper that carry little, if any, force and effect. If offenders choose to ignore the orders, the only alternative available to the victims is to flee and contact the police, or perhaps prepare to confront the offenders with deadly counterforce.

Additional disadvantages to the use of restraining orders can be found in the very statutes that were enacted to protect victims of family violence. In some statutes, the victim is required to pay a filing fee before a restraining order is issued. Although most jurisdictions allow for this fee to be waived if the victim cannot afford to pay it, some consider the income of the abuser as a factor in determining the waiver of the fee. The payment of such fees may discourage the victim from requesting a restraining order.

In most states, personal service of the order is required for it to become effective. However, this can be a problem because many offenders are difficult to locate. The victim is not protected until the offender has been served with the order. Additionally, a lack of monitoring compliance exists with restraining orders. If the offender convinces or threatens the victim not to report the violation to the police, law enforcement officials will be unaware that the offender has violated the order. In some situations, the victim may go back to the offender because of the dynamics of family violence.

In many cases, offenders avoid violating the terms and conditions of restraining orders while continuing to harass or threaten their victims. Some offenders may actually measure the distance that is specified in the order. They may remain the proper distance from the victim, but their presence still acts as a form of harassment or threat.

Effectiveness of Protective and Restraining Orders

The effectiveness of restraining orders depends on various factors. In an attempt to understand the effectiveness of restraining orders from the victim's point of view, researchers studied three jurisdictions: the county court in Denver, Colorado; the District of Columbia Superior Court; and the family court in Wilmington, Delaware (Keilitz et al. 1998). All of these jurisdictions utilized different restraining-order processes and service models. The researchers conducted telephone interviews with 285 women who had received restraining orders, and conducted follow-up interviews with 177 of these women. Records from the civil case and criminal records of the respondent in the orders were also used in this study.

Before receiving a protecting order, the victims had experienced various forms of abuse. The study found that 37 percent of the victims had been threatened or injured with a weapon; more than 50 percent had been beaten or choked; and 99 percent had experienced intimidation, including threats, stalking, and harassment. The majority of the victims felt that restraining orders protected them against repeated incidents of physical and psychological abuse. They also reported that restraining orders were valuable in improving a sense of well-being. However, the study found that a restraining order alone was not as likely to be effective when the abusers had a history of violence.

In the initial interviews, 72 percent of the victims stated that the restraining orders were effective and reported no continuing problems from the abusers. More than 80 percent of the victims reported in the follow-up interviews that their lives had improved and that they felt safer. However, a relatively small percentage of the victims reported that problems increased after the issuance of the restraining order. These problems included calls at work or home, stalking, repeated physical abuse, and continuing psychological abuse (Keilitz et al. 1998).

As this study indicates, restraining orders may be effective in the great majority of cases. However, in some situations, the abuser simply ignores the terms and conditions of the restraining order and continues to engage in abusive behaviors. The Office for Victims of Crime (2002) states that restraining orders are effective only when the respondent is convinced that the order will be enforced.

Procedures

Many states have several different types of restraining orders. However, the majority of the states use the following four types:

- emergency protective orders,
- *ex parte* restraining orders,
- temporary restraining orders, and
- permanent restraining orders or protective orders.

An emergency protective order is issued by a local law enforcement agency and is effective upon service to the perpetrator. This procedure allows law enforcement officers to require the perpetrator to leave the home and not return for anywhere between twenty-four and forty-eight hours. During this time period, the victim must obtain an *ex parte* or a temporary restraining order. An *ex parte* order is issued by a judge without prior notice to the perpetrator. This order also is typically good for only a short period of time. Once the *ex parte* order has been issued, it must be served on the offender.

A temporary restraining order normally involves a notice and a hearing which both parties attend. Evidence is presented by the victim showing why such an order is necessary. The offender has an opportunity to present evidence or rebut the victim's evidence. At the conclusion of the hearing, the judge makes a decision of whether or not to issue the temporary restraining order, which is effective for a period longer than the emergency protective order or the *ex parte* order. Even so, it is normally valid for only several weeks or months. For the order to be permanent, another hearing must occur. A permanent protective or restraining order is issued after the hearing and may be valid for up to three years.

At the federal level, district courts can issue federal restraining orders. There are a number of federal crimes dealing with family violence. One crime concerns traveling from one state to another or to a foreign country or leaving or entering an Indian territory with the intent to kill, injure, harass, or intimidate a spouse or an intimate partner. There is also a federal law that makes it a crime to stalk the victim or a member of the victim's immediate family. This includes using the mail, telephones, faxes, or the Internet to engage in stalking.

Conclusion

Restraining and protective orders offer victims of family violence an alternative to arrest of the offender. This court order prohibits the offender from any contact with the victim or a member of the victim's family. While different states have different policies and procedures regarding the issuance of restraining orders, they generally fall into three broad classifications: (1) emergency protecting orders, issued in exigent situations by police or a judge without a hearing, (2) temporary restraining or protective orders, issued after a noticed hearing and valid for a short period of time, and (3) permanent restraining or protective orders, valid for up to a number of years.

Restraining orders offer several advantages to victims of family violence. However, there are also disadvantages to the issuance of such an order. Overall the research in the field tends to indicate that victims are safer and more satisfied when they receive a restraining or protective order.

SHIHO YAMAMOTO and HARVEY WALLACE

See also **Domestic Violence Courts; Judicial Perspectives on Domestic Violence; Legal Issues for Battered Women; Mandatory Arrest Policies; Police Civil Liability in Domestic Violence Incidents; Stalking**

References and Further Reading

Carbon, Susan B., Peter C. MacDonald, Michael Town, and Mary T. Wynne. "The Role of Judges in Enforcing Full Faith and Credit." *Minnesota Center Against Violence and Abuse,* 1998. http://www.mincava.umn.edu/documents/ffc/chapter6/chapter6.html (accessed September 2, 2006).
Keilitz, Susan L., Courtenay Davis, Hillery S. Efkeman, Carol Flango, and P. L. Hannaford. *Civil Protection Orders: Victims' Views on Effectiveness.* U.S. Department of Justice, Office of Justice Programs, National Institute of Justice, 1998.
Office for Victims of Crime [OVC]. "Enforcement of Protective Orders." *OVC Bulletin,* Legal Series no. 4. U.S. Department of Justice, Office of Justice Programs, 2002. http://www.ojp.usdoj.gov/ovc/publications/bulletins/legalseries/bulletin4/welcome.html (accessed September 2, 2006).
VAWOR [Violence Against Women Online Resources]. "Protecting Victims of Domestic Violence: A Law Enforcement Officer's Guide to Enforcing Orders of Protection Nationwide," c. 2003. http://www.vaw.umn.edu/documents/protect/protect.html.
———. "Increasing Your Safety: Full Faith and Credit for Protection Orders," c. 2005a. http://www.vaw.umn.edu/documents/survivorbrochure/survivorbrochure.html.
———. "An Advocate's Guide to Full Faith and Credit for Orders of Protection: Assisting Victims of Domestic Violence," c. 2005b. http://www.vaw.umn.edu/documents/ffc/pcadv/pcadv.html.
Wallace, Harvey. *Family Violence: Legal, Medical, and Social Perspectives,* 4th ed. Boston: Allyn & Bacon, 2005.

PSEUDO-FAMILY ABUSE

Pseudo-family abuse refers to the abuse that occurs in out-of-home care settings in which caregivers abuse the residents within their care. Such abuses are found in skilled nursing homes, residential treatment facilities, youth correctional programs, foster homes, and similar settings. Scholars also refer to this type of abuse as institutional, resident, or caregiver abuse.

The term *pseudo-family abuse* was first coined by Kurst-Swanger and Petcosky (2003) to place emphasis on the fact that caregivers function much like families in their role of caretaking. It is through this role of caretaking that abuses most often occur. The term *pseudo families* assumes two relevant factors related to family violence. "Families" reflects the fact that some individuals are cared for in places outside of the traditional family home, in which they are surrounded by staff, administrators, or foster families who provide for their daily needs. In that sense, residents and staff function together like a family. "Pseudo" reflects the fact that although they function like families, this type of family relationship is artificial at its core. There is no doubt that pseudo families are different from

587

traditional families in very important ways. Yet, in a quest to more fully understand interpersonal violence, it has been important to expand the definition of what constitutes a family. Scholars have long recognized that abusive relationships do not just occur within married couples and biological families, but in a wide range of familial relationships. Thus, today scholars consider abuse within all types of family structures, including stepfamilies, same-sex intimate partner relationships, adoptive families, extended families, and cohabiting and noncohabiting intimate relationships, and are also taking seriously the role of pets within a family.

Pseudo families, like other types of families, exist in many settings. For example, work environments, sports teams, church communities, fraternities, clubs, etc., are often viewed as tight-knit groups in which members might consider themselves a type of pseudo family. Since a great deal of time is spent with individuals in these social groups, close bonds and attachments are formed, and one might consider one's peers to be "like family" and embrace them as such. Abuse may occur in these relationships.

However, because of the intense nature of the caregiving relationship, this article will consider pseudo-family abuse in circumstances in which individuals are living in a twenty-four-hour congregate care setting or foster home where staff are paid a stipend or salary to provide some level of care. Although staff are biologically unrelated to the residents they care for, they are generally considered responsible for the emotional and physical well-being of the individuals in their care, unlike other types of pseudo families. In addition, the pseudo-family relationship assumes that the resident is living in the out-of-home care setting for a period of time.

Both children and adults are placed in out-of-home care settings for a variety of reasons. They may need specialized medical or psychological treatment, may be working toward developing independent living skills, may be in need of behavior modification, or may be unable to care for themselves due to their age or physical condition. Most are in need of some type of professional care or supervision. In some cases, individuals are placed in out-of-home care because their own homes are unsafe due to abuse and neglect. Most vulnerable to out-of-home placement are children, adults with disabilities, and the elderly. Examples of out-of-home care settings include facilities for children and adults with mental illness or developmental disability, long-term care or skilled-nursing facilities

for the elderly or adults with chronic illness or disease, residential treatment programs for youth, group homes, and foster families that provide care for children and/or vulnerable adults. For the sake of simplicity, this article will not cover adult correctional facilities, such as jails and prisons. Such facilities certainly represent a unique type of out-of-home care, and inmates are undoubtedly abused and neglected in those settings; however, adult correctional institutions serve a very different purpose and have different goals and responsibilities than other types of out-of-home care environments.

Although the term *family* means different things to different people, one might ask, why include pseudo-family abuse in a volume that focuses on domestic violence? Some scholars and practitioners may disagree, but there are a number of valid reasons for its inclusion. First and foremost, some of the factors involved in the abuse that occurs within traditional families and intimate partner relationships are markedly similar to the factors associated with the abuse that occurs in out-of-home care settings. In particular, the types of abuses endured by victims and the short-term and long-term consequences of such victimization are similar. In addition, the conditions that place individuals at risk for victimization and the characteristics of perpetrators are comparable. Therefore, researchers and scholars have much to gain by studying the intimate and complex nature of caregiving and the interpersonal and dynamic relationships that sometimes result in abuse. Second, the experiences of those children and adults who reside in these alternative living environments, even for relatively short periods of time, are crucial to their emotional and physical well-being. Abuses that occur while residing in an out-of-home care environment can have profound consequences for victims and occur with enough frequency to warrant public concern. In addition, some children and vulnerable adults are placed in such facilities by the courts and/or the human service system because biological families are unable or incapable of providing minimum standards of care and/or safety. Therefore, abuses that occur within institutional settings or foster homes only compound the difficulties originally experienced within families of origin. Finally, it is important to recognize the impact that institutional living has on its residents. There is often an emotional and/or physical price to be paid by residents once a move is made to institutional living. Since thousands of children and adults reside in out-of-home settings at any given time and the likelihood that the demand for out-of-home care settings will only increase in the future to accommodate a growing elderly population, it is imperative that attention be paid to the needs and safety of residents. Also, since taxpayer dollars finance these types of services, it is important to ensure that government funds are utilized in an appropriate manner.

The research on pseudo-family abuse is limited and there are currently no national prevalence data available that comprehensively consider all aspects of the problem. Researchers and scholars must rely on reported incidents of abuse, which is likely to paint only a very small picture of the actual abuse that occurs. Since several different human services systems operate to provide care for adults and children residing in various out-of-care settings, reporting mechanisms also differ across systems. Some states have established ombudsperson and protection and advocacy programs on behalf of the rights of residents and handle abuse complaints; however, these are fragmented and are meant to serve only discrete populations of people with specific disabilities or problems. Local law enforcement officials have historically followed up on reports of abuse; however, few police departments or prosecutors have had the resources to pursue investigations in a proactive fashion. As a result, sometimes it is unclear who is responsible for investigating and prosecuting crimes occurring in such settings. Since 1978, Medicaid Fraud Control Units (MFCUs) have had primary law enforcement jurisdiction over the investigation and prosecution of maltreatment occurring in facilities receiving Medicaid funding. These units are funded with both state and federal monies, and the vast majority of them are housed in state offices of attorneys general. With a dedicated commitment to the investigation and prosecution of such abuses, agents have been very successful in securing thousands of convictions for abuse and fraud and have recovered millions of dollars from out-of-home care providers who have committed fraud.

Forms of Abuse

The maltreatment of residents in caregiving institutions and/or foster homes takes many forms. As in traditional families, residents can be physically, emotionally, or sexually abused. Residents can suffer from neglectful care, which can have devastating consequences. Financial abuse, especially in the form of fraud, is of special concern in the case of pseudo families. Simply making the transition from independent living to an institutionalized setting can have negative consequences, even if no other abuses are present. Therefore, the impact of "institutionalization" will also be discussed.

Pseudo-family abuse encompasses acts of both commission and omission, meaning that both overt acts of abuse are considered as well as situations in which the caretakers fail to provide necessary care for the resident. Kurst-Swanger and Petcosky (2003) provide a working definition of pseudo-family abuse, which takes into consideration a standard definition of family violence (Pagelow 1984):

> Pseudo Family Abuse includes any act of commission or omission by individuals responsible for the daily care of others in an out-of-home setting, and any conditions resulting from such acts or inaction, which deprive individuals of equal rights, and liberties, and/or interfere with their optimal development and freedom of choice. (Kurst-Swanger and Petcosky 2003, p. 187)

This definition purposefully includes language to highlight the importance of equal rights, liberties, and freedom of choice. Congregate care, by its very nature, often is inherently void of such personal liberties, since institutions are often caring for a large number of people at once. Unlike one's own personal home, residents often have little choice or input into their daily activities, meals, physical living environments, roommates, etc. In fact, it is often the restriction of choice that makes living in an out-of-home placement so very difficult for residents, rendering them helpless and powerless. Although such caregiving institutions cannot reasonably replicate the type of freedom of choice and liberty one might be able to experience in his or her own home, institutions which exhibit total control over their residents may be at greater risk of maltreatment. Like traditional families, power differentials between staff and residents may increase the risk of abuse. However, some out-of-home settings may be providing care for a population in which the behavioral and emotional problems exhibited by the residents present many challenges for staff and administrators. In some instances, the staff is at greater risk of victimization, and therefore the abuse of staff will also be considered in this discussion of pseudo-family abuse.

Physical Abuse

The physical abuse of residents can involve a wide range of injurious acts. Physical abuse assumes the active engagement of maltreatment. The most common acts of physical abuse found within residential care facilities include but are not limited to hitting, kicking, pinching, slapping, punching, burning, scratching, and biting. Residents may endure hair pulling, being prodded with objects or having objects thrown at them, the inappropriate application of restraints, and/or excessive corporal punishment. In addition, residents may be given inappropriate doses of medications, such as sedatives or tranquilizers. Due to the physical vulnerability of many of the residents in care, even seemingly minor acts such as a push, shove, or shake can cause serious injury in some residents. Those at greatest risk of physical abuse are individuals whose age or physical limitations prevent them from protecting themselves or from reporting abusive acts. For example, young children, the frail elderly, and those who suffer from mental retardation or severe mental illness are among those likely to be at greatest risk.

Not all residents who are physically abused suffer physical injury, but many experience pain or hurt. However, at a minimum, even minor acts of abuse can impact the emotional well-being of victims and other residents who may witness such abuses. In some instances, residents might experience more critical physical injuries and in severe cases, residents might die as a result of the injuries they have received.

Individuals who are most closely associated with the direct care of the residents most often commit physical abuse. Staff who are responsible for the personal, daily care of residents are most likely to exhibit abuses, since their work places them in direct contact with residents. Activities such as serving meals, bathing, dressing, changing bedding, and transportation require staff and residents to engage in physical and often intimate contact, leaving opportunities for abuses to occur.

Emotional Abuse

As indicated above, emotional abuse, in the form of verbal attacks, is also a form of pseudo-family abuse. Emotional abuse occurs when a caretaker makes verbal comments or gestures toward a resident in which the resident is belittled, degraded, humiliated, taunted, or chastised. Residents may be subjected to verbal attacks such as yelling, screaming, name calling, or swearing. Further, residents may be intimidated by verbal threats or gestures. They may also experience emotional abuse if they are socially isolated from others or deprived of their possessions, activities, or food. Since staff tend to have almost if not total control over the environment in which residents live, staff can abuse that power by withholding things that have emotional value to the resident.

Regardless of the form emotional abuse takes, it leaves residents feeling helpless and fearful and compounds the negative impact of institutionalization. Like the emotional abuse that occurs in families, the emotional abuse in pseudo families tends to occur with greater frequency than physical abuse and often accompanies relationships in which other forms of abuse exist. Direct-care staff are more likely to engage in emotionally abusive behavior, since they have the most direct interaction with the residents. Staff members, as indicated earlier, are also at risk of being verbally assaulted by residents.

Sexual Abuse

The sexual abuse of residents is a phenomenon that is not well documented and is likely to be the least discussed form of abuse exhibited against children and vulnerable adults. Sexual abuse can involve a wide range of acts that may or may not involve direct physical contact with the resident. Acts in which residents are touched, rubbed, fondled, sodomized, or raped by the caregiver require physical contact with the resident. However, sexual gratification may also be achieved through watching residents undress or bath, exposing one's genitals, viewing the resident's genitals, or making residents engage in sexual activity with one another. In addition, any sexual act involving residents in which photographs are taken or which is filmed would be considered sexual abuse. In some instances, sexual contact between staff and residents may appear to be consensual; however, any type of sexual contact between staff and residents is inappropriate and therefore considered sexual abuse. Since the nature of the caregiver–client relationship is technically a professional one, any sexual contact between staff and resident is at a minimum unethical, but it is also likely to be considered illegal. Also, since many residents are unable to give consent legally because of their age, physical, or mental condition, the notion of consensual sexual relations between staff and residents is suspect.

Residents in out-of-home care settings are particularly vulnerable to sexual abuse because their age or physical or mental conditions often place them in a defenseless position and therefore put them at greater risk of being victimized. As is the case with physical and emotional abuse, direct-care staff are more likely to perpetrate sexual abuse. The personal and intimate nature of the caregiver relationship requires that residents rely on direct-care staff for personal hygiene support, placing them in direct physical contact with staff on an ongoing basis. Also, since many residents sleep in quarters which remain unlocked, residents are especially unprotected during the evening and overnight hours when staffing is limited and unsupervised.

Neglect

Neglect, a very serious form of maltreatment in traditional families, is equally, if not more, dangerous in pseudo families. Since residents are often socially isolated from others in the community, apparent signs of neglect may go undetected until it leads to serious injury, illness, or death. Caregivers have a legal responsibility to care for the residents in their care, and therefore any form of neglect, whether it is intentional, reckless, or careless, is subject to legal scrutiny and may be deemed criminal. Even relatively minor neglectful acts can have devastating consequences for residents, since residents tend to have preexisting emotional or physical conditions which require special medical treatment. Therefore, any neglectful act can have a potentially dangerous result. Administrators, facility owners, supervisors, and/or direct-care staff are all responsible for neglect.

Neglect can occur in a variety of forms, though the most common involves a failure on the part of the caregiver to do what is required for the resident based on a prescribed plan of care. This might include a failure to provide adequate and proper nutrition or hydration, climate control, dental care, supervision, transportation, medication delivery, or the proper assessment of a resident's physical or emotional condition. In addition, neglect may be evident when injuries or illnesses go unreported, soiled clothing or bed linens go unchanged, or residents are forced to live or eat in unsanitary conditions. Violations of state standards of safety and security because of carelessness may also constitute neglect.

At a minimum, neglect negatively impacts the quality of life for residents. However, neglect can also have catastrophic consequences, especially for residents who have preexisting health concerns. Neglect can result in bedsores, dehydration, malnutrition, illness, communicable disease, burns, broken bones, or countless other problems. In the case of children, neglect can have a profound impact on their cognitive, affective, and/or physical development and growth.

Financial Abuse

Financial abuse, also referred to as financial exploitation, is a unique problem that occurs on a variety of levels and can take different forms. It is likely to be the most common abuse committed against adult residents of out-of-home care and can have widespread impact. Not only are individual residents personally impacted by financial victimization when fraud occurs, but the health care industry faces devastating financial losses as well. In addition, since Medicare and Medicaid, two government health care programs, finance a considerable amount of out-of-home care expenses, taxpayers are victimized by fraudulent acts. Regardless of the form that financial exploitation takes, individuals who reside in facilities in which financial exploitation occurs are also at risk of suffering from a lack of quality care.

On a personal level, individual residents may have their personal effects stolen, bank accounts drained, or financial resources commingled with facility financial accounts. In these cases, residents experience personal financial loss, often leaving them penniless. In some cases, financial abuses are perpetrated by a resident's own family or professional advisors, such as a lawyer or accountant. In these cases, perpetrators obtain powers of attorney from residents and commit forgery or theft. Residents may also fall prey to a practice referred to as "patient dumping," in which they are systematically discriminated against for having Medicaid as their primary health insurer.

On a broader scope, billions of dollars are lost each year to health care fraud. Administrative personnel generally commit health care fraud in an effort to bilk health care insurance companies. Fraud can be committed in many different ways. According to the National Health Care Anti-Fraud Association (2005), the most common types of fraud include:

- billing for services that were never rendered,
- billing for more expensive services than were actually performed,
- executing medical procedures or services that are unnecessary, and
- submitting claims misrepresenting the medical necessity of certain procedures or services.

These and other fraudulent schemes mean significant financial losses for health insurers; however, they can also impact resident care. Fraud can drain a resident's finite health benefits; falsely record medical conditions and diagnoses, thereby altering a resident's medical history; and risk the health and safety of the resident through the performing of unnecessary surgeries, tests, or procedures.

Process of Institutionalization

Transitioning from a private home into an out-of-home care setting can be very difficult for residents and can have a detrimental impact on their cognitive, affective, or physical development. Although out-of-home care settings are critically needed to serve the physical, emotional, and behavioral challenges that residents face, the communal and institutional character of many out-of-home care settings may mitigate against the positive services that such settings can provide. Residents tend to have little decision-making power, even regarding personal decisions such as what time to eat, bathe, or sleep; their ability to leave the facility; what to watch on television; what personal items they are allowed to possess. Residents' lives become very structured, socially isolated, and controlled externally by staff.

Erving Goffman (1961) was one of the first to describe institutionalization as a process in which an individual has to shed elements of herself and her identity to assume the culture of the institution. Others refer to this process as the social breakdown syndrome, the syndrome of psychosocial degradation (Yawney and Slover 1973), or institutionalization syndrome. It can lead to apathy, depression, passivity, and even death. For example, some elderly people exhibit indirect self-destructive behavior in which they indirectly work toward death by refusing to take medication, eat, or drink. Residents, in effect, grow to disregard their health and well-being (Conwell, Pearson, and DeRenzo 1996). For young children, institutional living is associated with attachment and bonding problems (Bartholet 1999).

This form of maltreatment is very difficult to define and delineate, since no one person can be blamed. Even facilities which provide the highest quality of care can have residents who experience traumatic psychological and physical changes as a result of being institutionalized. Institutional factors associated with these negative consequences include lack of appropriate staff/resident ratios, high staff turnover rates, rigid rules, cold and uninviting physical spaces, lack of privacy, overcrowding, poor meals, and shared living spaces. Facilities tend to foster a culture of dependency, which can result in a loss of self-confidence, independence, and social interaction.

Maltreatment in Foster Homes

Foster homes are relied upon as a preferred alternative to institutional life for both children and adults. Foster homes can provide warm, nurturing environments in private home settings where residents can participate in normal family life. Foster families are paid a stipend to provide such care. Children are often placed in foster care when there is evidence that they have been abused or neglected by their parents. Approximately 500,000 children are in foster care in any given year. Vulnerable adults may be placed in foster care when they are in need of some level of care but can manage without the medical supervision of a skilled-nursing facility.

Like other pseudo families and traditional families, abuse also occurs in foster care, where residents may be physically, sexually, or emotionally abused or neglected. Abuse in foster care settings is especially troubling given the fact that foster homes should be considered safe havens, especially for those residents who have been removed from their own homes due to abuse or neglect. A growing concern over abuse and neglect in foster homes has led the federal Administration for Children and Families (ACF) to establish national standards for the incidence of foster care maltreatment of children (U.S. Department of Health and Human Services [USDHHS] 2000). Through ACF's Child and Family Services Review, states must demonstrate that of all the children who were in foster care in the state during a specific reporting period, only 0.57 percent or less were abused or neglected by a foster parent or facility staff member. In 2003, approximately 76 percent of the states were in compliance with this standard (USDHHS 2005).

Common Themes Identified in Pseudo-Family Abuse

It is difficult to determine why staff members would wish to harm or neglect their clients, since there appears to be little to be gained from doing so. If anything, staff who engage in such abuses are likely to run the risk of being reprimanded, fired, or arrested. The factors associated with the maltreatment of residents are varied and multidimensional, yet some common themes can be identified.

Institutional Factors

Scholars cite institutional problems as being central contributors to the occurrence of pseudo-family abuse and neglect. Residential facilities are notoriously understaffed and overcrowded. Staff-to-resident ratios tend to be very high, which causes great strain for both the direct-care staff and the residents. In addition, administrators find it difficult to attract highly qualified employees due to the low wages and the demanding schedules. The low pay and stressful working conditions often keep staff turnover rates high, which in turn results in inconsistent staffing levels and insufficient supervision of direct-care staff. Inadequate training and a lack of appropriate continuing education only compound any existing staffing problems.

Individual Factors

In addition to the institutional stresses noted above, one of the most prominent factors related to abuse is how individual employees navigate the demands of the job. The responsibility of caring for the personal needs of others is a demanding, stressful, and tiring job. Staff members are often asked to do the most unpleasant of tasks, such as changing soiled underclothing, bedding, and bedpans or cleaning up vomit or food that has been thrown across the room. Although some staff are trained in the nursing field and expect to perform such tasks, others are not emotionally prepared to handle the daily demands of the job. In addition, staff must negotiate the emotional, medical, behavioral, and cognitive challenges presented by the residents, often with little break or respite. Coping with the behaviors of emotionally disturbed or cognitively impaired individuals can be exhausting and especially difficult for staff unequipped with the types of communications skills necessary to be effective with a diverse population of residents. Individuals with disabilities or impairments are also at high risk of victimization within traditional families as well.

In addition, in some instances direct-care staff must endure frequent verbal and physical attacks from the residents or interrupt physical violence between residents. This is consistent with the dynamics of some violent families in that different family members may be involved in physical altercations with each other at different times. For example, a study done by Goodridge, Johnston, and Thomson (1996) found that nursing assistants in a long-term care facility in Canada were assaulted by residents on average about nine times per month and verbally attacked an additional eleven times per month. Conflicts were most likely to occur during personal hygiene care or when residents wanted to go outside. Parent and associates (1994), in a study conducted regarding the conditions of confinement for youth in detention or correctional facilities, reported that thousands of incidents occurred each year in which staff were injured by juveniles, compared with the hundreds of incidents in which youth were injured by staff. They also found that in any given year, approximately 24,000 incidents resulted in injury from acts committed by juveniles toward other youth, while an additional 17,000 youth engaged in suicidal acts. These studies highlight the challenges of providing out-of-home care for various populations.

While job stress may be a trigger for abuse, some staff engage in abusive behavior because there is simply ample opportunity to do so. Residents are easy targets for victimization because they often cannot fend off attackers and in some instances are incapable of even reporting abuse. A natural power differential exists between staff and residents, providing an environment in which abusive behaviors can flourish. Residents, in many instances, are at the complete mercy of the staff and must depend upon them to meet their basic needs. In addition, many facilities operate in isolation from the communities in which they reside, thereby placing residents at greater risk of victimization. These are also consistent themes in abusive families.

Financial exploitation is attractive because residents are often unaware of their own finances and are completely removed from the relationship between the administration and the health insurer. According to the National Health Care Anti-Fraud Association (2005), administrators have all the tools at their disposal with which to reap the great personal or corporate financial rewards of fraud. This includes the fact that there are generally a large number of insured patients to exploit and a wide range of medical conditions, procedures, services, and treatments on which false claims can be billed.

Aside from the factors noted here, research studies have yet to identify further the personal characteristics of perpetrators to determine whether or not abusive behavior is correlated with any other environmental, psychological, or biological factors, such as substance abuse, mental illness, personal stress or instability, or personal experiences with abuse and neglect. Since most caregivers provide care in a nurturing manner, yet are subjected to the same environmental factors as those who are abusive, it is likely that there are other social and personal factors associated with the abuse and neglect of residents.

Social Factors

Residents who live in out-of-home care environments represent some of the most vulnerable individuals in society. They are unable to care for themselves, and their families are in no position to provide adequate care. As such, they are often shunned and alienated by their own families, neighbors, or communities. Some are seen as social deviants. Institutional and foster care, therefore, provides an opportunity for them to be properly cared for, but out of the mainstream of society. Once removed from the community, they are often stripped of their personal identities and, in effect, dehumanized. Social isolation compounds the ambivalent and indifferent social attitude many have toward such a vulnerable population. Therefore, as a cohort, residents have little social power in society or within the out-of-home care placement. This places them at risk of victimization.

In summary, the pseudo family provides, for all practical purposes, many of the same functions as traditional families do, e.g., food, clothing, shelter, and social interaction. Maltreatment sometimes occurs within this surrogate family, not unlike in traditional families. In fact, factors such as power differentials, social isolation, stress, and lack of appropriate training and communication skills are found to exist in both types of families in which abuse and neglect is present. Yet, the abuse and neglect of individuals within pseudo-family environments has not, as of yet, been pursued with as much fervor as abuse within traditional family structures. Further research is necessary to determine the actual prevalence of abuse and neglect and the myriad of factors associated with its occurrence. In addition, an expansion of monitoring systems, protective and advocacy programs, and specialized law enforcement interventions are warranted.

KAREL KURST-SWANGER

See also **Animal Abuse: The Link to Family Violence; Bullying and the Family; Child Abuse and Juvenile Delinquency**

References and Further Reading

Bartholet, Elizabeth. *Nobody's Children: Abuse and Neglect, Foster Drift and the Adoption Alternative.* Boston: Beacon Press, 1999.

Benedict, Mary I., Susan Zuravin, Diane Brandt, and Helen Abbey. "Types and Frequency of Child Maltreatment by Family Foster Care Providers in an Urban Population." *Child Abuse and Neglect* 18, no. 17 (1994): 577–585.

Benedict, Mary I., Susan Zuravin, Mark Somerfield, and Diane Brandt. "The Reported Health and Functioning of Children Maltreated While in Family Foster Care." *Child Abuse and Neglect* 20, no. 7 (1996): 561–571.

Colton, Matthew. "Factors Associated with Abuse in Residential Child Care Institutions." *Children and Society* 16 (2002): 33–44.

Conwell, Yeates, Jane Pearson, and Evan G. DeRenzo. "Indirect Self-Destructive Behavior among Elderly Patients in Nursing Homes: A Research Agenda." *American Journal of Geriatric Psychiatry* 4, no. 2 (Spring 1996): 152–163.

Goffman, Erving. *Asylums: Essays on the Social Situation of Mental Patients and Other Inmates.* Garden City, NY: Anchor Books, 1961.

Goodridge, Donna M., Patricia Johnston, and Maureen Thomson. "Conflict and Aggression as Stressors in the Work Environment of Nursing Assistants: Implications for Institutional Elder Abuse." *Journal of Elder Abuse and Neglect* 8, no. 1 (1996): 49–67.

Hirst, Sandra P. "Resident Abuse: An Insider's Perspective." *Geriatric Nursing* 21, no. 1 (2000): 38–42.

Hobbs, Georgina F., Christopher J. Hobbs, and Jane Wynne. "Abuse of Children in Foster and Residential Care." *Child Abuse and Neglect* 23, no. 12 (1999): 1239–1252.

Hodge, Paul. "National Law Enforcement Programs to Prevent, Detect, Investigate, and Prosecute Elder Abuse and Neglect in Health Care Facilities." *Journal of Elder Abuse and Neglect* 9, no. 4 (1998): 23–41.

Kurst-Swanger, Karel, and Jacqueline L. Petcosky. *Violence in the Home: Multidisciplinary Perspectives.* New York: Oxford University Press, 2003.

National Health Care Anti-Fraud Association. "Health Care Fraud: A Serious and Costly Reality for all Americans," 2005. http://www.nhcaa.org/about_health_care_fraud (accessed September 2, 2006).

Pagelow, Mildred. *Family Violence.* New York: Praeger, 1984.

Parent, Dale, Valerie Leiter, Stephen Kennedy, Lisa Liven, Daniel Wentworth, and Sarah Wilcox. *Conditions of Confinement: Juvenile Detention and Corrections Facilities.* Washington, DC: U.S. Department of Justice, Office of Justice Programs, Office of Juvenile Justice and Delinquency Prevention, 1994.

Shaw, Mary M. Conlin. "Nursing Home Resident Abuse by Staff: Exploring the Dynamics." *Journal of Elder Abuse and Neglect* 9, no. 4 (1998): 1–21.

Stanley, Nicky, Jill Manthorpe, and Bridget Penale. *Institutional Abuse: Perspectives across the Life Course.* London: Routledge, 1999.

U.S. Department of Health and Human Services, Administration on Children, Youth and Families. *National Standards for the Child and Family Service Reviews.* Information memorandum ACYF-CB-IM-00-11, December 28, 2000.

———. *Updated National Standards for the Child and Family Service Reviews and Guidance on Program Improvement Plans.* Information memorandum ACYF-CB-IM-01-07, August 16, 2003.

———. *Child Maltreatment 2003.* Washington, DC: U.S. Government Printing Office, 2005.

Yawney, Beverly A., and Darrell L. Slover. "Relocation of the Elderly." *Social Work* 18 (1973): 86–95.

Q

QUR'ANIC PERSPECTIVES ON
WIFE ABUSE

There are two divergent schools of thought as to what constitutes the Qur'anic view of wife abuse. One modern school, following the Western feminist perspective, argues that the Qur'an legitimizes wife abuse by putting females under the hegemonic control of males. This is because the Qur'an is the ideological blueprint of Islamic patriarchy and formulates its social and legal relationships. The Qur'an allows men to marry up to four wives, maintain concubines, and control their wives and daughters within the family, depriving them of freedoms that women enjoy in modern democratic societies. In addition, women in Islamic countries are supposed to obey their husbands and cover their hair, faces, and bodies at home and in public. Worse yet, the Qur'an allows men to apply some form of corporal punishment to their rebellious wives. Finally, the Qur'an does not accord females equal rights in relation to education, inheritance, child custody, employment and remuneration, and legal witness and testimony. All these measures of the Qur'an have led to the rise of wife abuse in Islamic countries which continues at the present time. The remedy against wife abuse is to opt for modern egalitarian social and legal relationships in Islamic countries.

The second school is of the Islamic traditionalist genera and persuasion. The proponents of this school base their arguments on early and medieval Islamic sources, the majority of which have been written, constructed, and deconstructed by the Muslim men of the pen (ulema). These traditional Islamic sources approach the issue of wife abuse not within the construct of abuse per se, but in terms of the control of the female spouse as advised by the Qur'an. The intellectual thrust of this school is that Allah has put men in charge of women and allows husbands to control their wives through different means and methods that include even corporal punishments. The "inequalities" that the Qur'an advises are for the enhancement of marriage and the family institutions because women are the "weaker" sex, who need men's supervision at home and in public. Thus, the Qur'an does not condone wife abuse per se but allows husbands to control their wives for the good of the family.

There is a third emerging modern school of thought among Muslim intellectuals and academics that argues that wife abuse is a reality that is hard to deny in many Islamic countries. There are indeed verses of the Qur'an that, when read in isolation from the rest, sound as if female spousal subordination has been ordained by the text—for example, verse 34 of the chapter *al-Nisa* (The Women), which traditionally reads, "Men are in charge of women, because Allah hath made the one of them to excel the other, and because they spend of their property (for the support of women). So the good women are the obedient, guarding in secret that which Allah hath guarded." The verse continues, advising husbands how to deal with their "rebellious" (*nushuz*) wives, saying, "As for those from whom ye fear rebellion, admonish them and banish them to bed apart, and scourge them. Then if they obey you, seek not a way against them. Lo! Allah is ever High Exalted, Great." Verse 34 is one of the most controversial verses in the Qur'an because not only has it historically sealed the fate of women as dependent on men from birth to death, it has also provided a powerful means for those who see wife beating as the legitimate right of husbands to control their wives. This defense of wife beating is being practiced by and has been documented among some Muslim emigrant groups in Great Britain and a number of other western European countries.

The position of the third school is that the traditional reading of verse 34 is now defunct on several grounds: (1) It does not say that Allah has put *all* men in charge of *all* women, but only those men who spend their wealth to support their womenfolk (e.g., wives, daughters, widowed mothers); (2) it does not allow husbands to indiscriminately beat their spouses but makes corporal punishment the last resort for husbands who have exhausted other options for dealing with their rebellious wives; and (3) it is an integral part of the chapter *al-Nisa* that discusses spousal rights, duties, and responsibilities to one another. Approached from this perspective, the third school argues that verse 34, when read uncritically, seems to allow beating as a legitimate form of wife abuse in the Qur'an.

The feminist scholars have countered the third school on several grounds. First, they argue that verse 34 has centuries of tradition behind its application as the Qur'an's allowance for the use of corporal punishments against wives, rebellious or not. That is why wife beating and other abusive practices continue not only inside Islamic countries, but also among Muslim emigrant groups. Second, the defense of those who beat their wives is verse 34, whose traditional readings support the use of corporal punishment and do not accept the validity of the interpretive nuances that the third school has proposed. Third, a husband can claim that he has used the beating as the last resort as it is advised by the Qur'an. Thus the remedy against wife beating as advised by verse 34 is not in the interpretive nuances that the third school proposes, but in criminalizing such measures through modern and secular laws that Islamic countries must adopt in replacing the Islamic Shariah Law.

There are scholars who have proposed that short of replacing the Islamic legal tradition with modern secular laws, the remedy against wife abuse has a mechanism in the Qur'an itself. Accordingly, the Qur'an has two kinds of verses, as specified by verse 7 of the chapter *al-Imran*. It reads, "He it is Who hath revealed unto thee [Muhammad] the Scripture wherein are clear revelations—They are the substance of the Book—and others [which are allegorical]." Although the verse warns that all revelations are from Allah and believers are to take them as valid in their totality, there are those who try to explain the allegorical ones in a way so as to cause dissension among Muslims despite the fact that no one other than Allah knows the true meaning of the allegorical verses. The question is, which verses are the essence of the Qur'an and which ones are allegorical?

This question is not new but has been debated throughout Islam's long history without any definite resolution. However, traditionally speaking, Muslims believe that the Qur'an in its totality is a divine revelation whose injunctions the faithful must apply to their daily lives as earnestly as possible. Accordingly, one cannot arbitrarily pick and choose.

In modern times the debate has resurfaced because many Islamic countries are going through stages of modernity and development as they try to adapt to the global forces of a free market economy and its social and legal relationships based on secular laws. Thus scholars of the third school have proposed that those verses relating to social and legal aspects of marriage and the family carry in them allegorical aspects, as, for instance, verse 34 of *al-Nisa* discussed above. Other allegories relate to polygamy, divorce procedure and alimony, child custody, distribution of inheritance, and witness and testimonial rights of women, as well as those related to crime and punishment categories. Thus, allegorical aspects in such verses allow for time and social factors to enter into the interpretation process. For example, despite the fact that the Qur'an does carry injunctions concerning slavery, polygamy, and harsh punishment measures, to name but a few, many Islamic countries have abolished these practices altogether. This is because many Islamic countries have come to the realization that these measures no longer apply to the modern social and legal relationships that they want to construct for a functional engagement with the rest of the modern world. Thus, one could argue that verse 34 carries allegorical aspects that allow the verse to be subjected to reform. Islamic countries could prohibit wife beating as a practice that no longer has any utility behind its application.

The General Theological Thrust of the Qur'an toward Wife Abuse

The Qur'an does not condone any form of wife abuse because it is a form of transgression against the text's enunciated principle of righteousness and moral conduct. Accordingly, because it is Allah who is the source of all animate and inanimate power in all its manifestations; because it is Allah who entrusts power to, or deprives it from, whomever the Almighty chooses; and because it is Allah who entrusts all with varying degrees of power, it is incumbent on women and men of faith to utilize their shares of entrusted power for the highest amount of common good. Those who use their power to regularly abuse others (including their spouses) violate both the spirit and the letter of the Qur'anic advice that people of faith follow the route of righteousness and moral conduct ('amal saalih) in dealing with others. The verses of al-Nisa remind Muslims that Allah has entrusted married women to the "benevolent supervision" of their husbands, provided that the husbands are the principal breadwinners and spend their wealth for the maintenance of their wives. As to why this has been the case, the position of the Qur'an is not all that clear. Some verses give this impression that the power differential has been ordained by Allah, while some others seem to be saying that it is not the power differential that is the source of wife abuse, but the manner of its utilization. There are scholars who have argued that power-related verses seem to suggest that Allah uses the power differential as a deliberate measure for testing what the Qur'an calls the "impure human inclinations" (nafsi ammareh) that everyone possesses in varying degrees. Accordingly, access to power in conjunction with one's impure inclinations opens for some the road to abusive behavior, including spousal abuse.

The thrust of the Qur'an is that the faithful must recognize the fact that any course of action that one takes, be it good or evil, is consequential. The Qur'an is adamant that Allah watches over everyone as the ultimate judge (qaazi al-quzaat), who does not look kindly on those who regularly abuse their allotted shares of power. To the rhetorical question as to why there is the evil of abuse in this world, the response of the Qur'an is that Allah wants to check the level of people's transgressions against the Qur'anic injunctions. In due time, the Almighty takes action against the transgressors who raise Allah's wrath. This is so because Allah is the "mightiest of all the tyrants" (qaasim al-jabbaarin) and at the same time is also "the most compassionate and kindest of all" (al-rahmaan al-rahim) to those who use their power and wealth for the betterment of self and others in society. This divinely ordained principle of reward and punishment applies to the husband-wife duo, but more so to husbands because of power differentials between the spouses as discussed above. Simply put, the Qur'an reminds husbands that if they abuse their wives, they will have to face the wrath of the Almighty. Fear is a powerful anti-abuse factor in the Qur'an.

Wife Abuse Allows the Spouse to Seek Divorce According to the Qur'an

The Qur'an considers wife abuse as a form of abuse of the power that Allah has entrusted to those husbands who (1) are the principal breadwinners in the family and (2) put their wealth in the maintenance of the family and the household expenses. However, a husband who satisfies these conditions is not given a blank check to abuse his spouse or children. In fact the position of the Qur'an is that a husband who is a good provider should strive to be a good father, too. In case of conjugal, matrimonial, or parental conflicts, the Qur'an advises couples to try to resolve them through means that are least injurious to the sanctity of marriage and family life. If interventional methods of conflict resolution do not work, divorce is the last option that the Qur'an advises. During the stages of conflict resolution, couples are advised not to deviate from the road of righteous conduct toward one another, especially insofar as conjugal matters are concerned. The text warns believing men (al-muminin) and believing women (al-muminat) alike, especially if they are married to one another, that it is better for them to deal with one another based on the principles of righteousness (amali slaih), including, among others, fear of Allah (khoufallah). The Qur'an, nonetheless, allows for the dissolution of the marriage if the husband regularly abuses his wife or children or both, provided the aggrieved wife has sought divorce.

There are authentic Hadiths (revered sayings), attributed to the Prophet Muhammad and the succeeding caliphs, to the effect that such marriages were dissolved due to complaints of wives who had been subject to abuse at the hands of their spouses. Interestingly, the Qur'an does not prevent women from becoming the breadwinner and thus assuming the position of the head of the household. In practice, however, married women are considered their husbands' wards as a matter of both law and custom in the majority of Islamic countries. Even after divorce, the Qur'an allows for the couples to reunite through remarriage. The rationale of the Qur'an is both functional and realistic on the ground that marriage and the family are two of the most important social institutions in the context of which a loving and caring home environment is established. An abusive home environment, created by abusive practices, inflicts incalculable and long-lasting damage to the husband, the wife, and their offspring.

The Qur'an Does Not Consider Women (Wives) as an Afterthought

In *al-Nisa* (iv: 1) the Qur'an calls on the general populace to be vigilant of their responsibilities to Allah, who created the humankind from "a Unitarian living entity" (*al-nafsi wahid*) first, and then created women and men from a "clot" of blood, assigning to each their shares of rights, duties, and responsibilities. By attending to these responsibilities, believers perform their duties to Allah, society, and one another. In such an ideal environment, no rationale for spousal abuse applies.

Muslim scholars are in general agreement that the Qur'an does not portray women's creation as an afterthought that is perhaps wrongly attributed to the Bible, according to which God first created Adam and then, upon his complaints of loneliness, created Eve from Adam's left rib. There is a saying attributed to the Prophet Muhammad to the effect that women, in the same manner of a rib, are crooked. Among certain Muslim traditionalist circles, this saying implies that husbands must put their wives under a strict and harsh regime of treatment because women are inherently of a crooked nature. However, there are liberal-minded Muslim scholars who reject the authenticity of this saying on the grounds that the Prophet Muhammad would not have said something that so egregiously violates the egalitarian thrust of the Qur'an in relation to women's status in Islam. This rejection, of

course, does not mean that all Muslim husbands are egalitarian minded in their treatment of their wives as advised by the Qur'an. Wife abuse in Islamic societies is a concrete reality legitimated through various means, including attributions to the Prophet Muhammad and his deputies (caliphs). In fact, there is a lengthy work of Islamic literature, the *Hadith,* which covers about two million sayings and deeds attributed to the Prophet Muhammad. Although most of these are of a dubious nature, they play a very important legitimating role for those husbands who abuse their wives.

The Qur'an Does Not Portray Wives as Evil Tempters of Their Husbands

The general thrust of the Qur'an's view of marriage is that spouses are counselors to one another, helping one another toward the best course of action in household affairs. Allah has endowed both women and men with rationality to discern between good and evil. Those who choose evil rather than good will face the consequence of their choice. For example, in *al-Baqarah* (i, 30–38), the Qur'an portrays Havva (Eve) and Adam as the first female and male pair created by Allah as complementary to one another and placed in Paradise for eternal life. However, Iblis (Satan) beguiled them to transgress against the one and only injunction that Allah had warned the couple to observe in Paradise. In the Qur'an, this injunction is to not eat from a certain heavenly grain. Because both gave in to their temptations and were beguiled by Satan, Allah's wrath fell on both. Thus, Adam and Eve were expelled from Paradise to dwell on earth with all its dangers and miseries. However, once they repented, Allah forgave both and gave them dominion over earth and everything that roamed on it. The thrust of these verses is that Eve was not the primal evil "tempter" of Adam responsible for his fall, but one who was a victim to her own temptations, as Adam was. The Qur'an does not attribute "original sin" to women, married or not. By removing women from the list of "evil" forces tempting men to commit sin or crime, as envisioned by pre-Islamic civilizations, the Qur'an put a decisive end to the misogynist doctrine that women, especially wives, ought to be kept under a strict regime of control riddled with all kinds of social, legal, and psychological abuses.

However, as primordial Islam spread in different parts of the Middle East, North Africa, Asia, and southern Europe, coming face to face with older established civilizations, the misogynist view that women should be looked upon as the primal cause of men's malaise started creeping into Islamic circles to the effect that within a century after Islam's inauguration, married women were relegated to a secondary class status similar to their medieval Judeo-Christian counterparts. The general thrust of the Qur'an is that spousal abuse is not of an exclusively masculine nature, in that wives can also abuse their husbands through various means, such as, for example, deserting the conjugal bed to extort something from their husbands that they are not entitled to in the first place. Other abuses include lewdness (*fahshaa*), inchoate crimes, and maltreatment of the husband's children from previous marriages. However, the husbands' ability to abuse is of a more potent and varied nature because of the power-differential factor, as discussed above.

Qur'anic View on Spousal Rights, Duties, and Responsibilities

Muslims believe that the Qur'an is the most important repository of spousal rights, duties, and responsibilities within the institution of marriage and the family. The thrust of the Qur'an is that all believing men and women are given a set of legitimate rights (*huquq*) as well as duties and responsibilities (*masuliyat*) that they ought to perform. These are scattered among 114 chapters of the Qur'an. However, the specific chapter titled *al-Nisa* (The Women), as the name implies, is dedicated to women's status. *Al-Nisa* contains 177 verses, one of the longest of the Qur'anic chapters, the bulk of which was revealed to the Prophet Muhammad in Madina shortly after his emigration to that city in 622 C.E. It covers a wide range of issues in the context of which a Muslim woman's rights, duties, and responsibilities have been laid out. These pertain to property (*al-amwal*), education (*tahsil al-'ilm*), marriage (*al-nikah*), divorce (*al-talaq*), inheritance (*al-mirath, taraka*), and the family and its dynamics. Wife abuse takes place when a husband tramples upon any of these rights without any justification. What follows is a synopsis of this mechanism.

Prior to Islam, women owned property in both settled and tribal societies in the Arab Peninsula. For example, the primary Islamic sources mention women traders with financial capital in their possessions, such as Khadijah, a prominent woman in Makka who fell in love with her young employee and the future Prophet of Islam, Muhammad, and proposed marriage to him. However, there were financially abusive practices among pagan Arabs.

The Qur'an prohibited such practices and provided measures that it considered legitimate with regard to the utilization of property and financial capital. For example, the Qur'an (ii: 188) advises both sexes, "And eat not up your property among yourselves in vanity, nor seek by it to gain the hearing of the judges that ye may knowingly devour a portion of the property of others wrongfully." The term for "property" in its plural form is *al-amwal* (s. mal), which ranged from personal to fixed property (e.g., slaves, household items, arable land, orchards). This term is also repeated in various verses of *al-Nisa* as, for instance (iv: 29): "O ye who believe, squander not your wealth among yourselves in vanity, except it be a trade of mutual consent, and kill not one another. Lo! Allah is ever Merciful unto you." There is no doubt that the Qur'an recognized women's right to property ownership and allowed them to utilize their properties as they saw fit. At the same time, it warned and enjoined Muslim men and women against putting their properties to abusive practices, such as bribery, usury, loan sharking, prostitution, and gambling, which prevailed among Arab traders and commercial venturers.

Thus, financial capital gave women traders a cherished and powerful position in pre-Islamic Arab society, but it is doubtful if financial prowess adequately protected women and young girls from abusive practices that had their bases in pagan Arab tribal social and legal relationships. For example, female infants were subjected to infanticide by live burial in desert sands, and widowed women were not allowed to marry outside the king group unless no suitor came forward. Men of wealth were allowed to have an unlimited number of wives and concubines. In addition, male and female promiscuity prevailed to the effect that husbands encouraged their wives to copulate with men of distinction in the hope of getting in the line of noble lineage so as to link up with powerful kin groups. The Qur'an prohibited these types of abusive conjugal practices. Similar abusive practices in relation to inheritance, education, witness, debt financing, marriage, divorce, and child custody prevailed among pre-Islamic Arabs that the Qur'an prohibited, a synopsis of which is provided below.

Women in pre-Islamic times received inheritance, but the process was mostly of an arbitrary nature. The Qur'an regularized inheritance (*mirath, taraka*) by making it obligatory on both parents to apportion their wealth among their sons and daughters based on a written will (*wasaya*). The relevant verses are scattered throughout the text and are included, for instance, in (ii: 180, 240) and (iv: 7–9, 11–12, 19, 33, 176). The verse (ii: 180) advises believers to leave a written will so that those who possess property and feel the nearing of their death can ensure that the inheritance will be bequeathed to their family members (offspring, surviving parents, and known near relatives). The verse (ii: 240) regularizes the bequeathing of provisions (*nafaqa*) and inheritance by a husband among his wives as he feels his death approaching. The verses (iv: 7–9) regularize the share of the male and female members of a family from their parental inheritance, whereas the verse (iv: 11) regularizes the proportioning of the inheritance between male and female members of the family. It reads: "to the male the equivalent of the portion of two females, and if there be women more than two, then theirs is two-thirds of the inheritance, and if there be one (only) then the half."

The verse (iv: 12) regularizes bequeathing of inheritance by a husband's wives. It reads: "And unto you belongeth a half of that which your wives leave, if they have no child; but if they have a child, then unto you the fourth of that which they leave after any legacy they may have bequeathed, or debt (they may have contracted, hath been paid)." The fact that husbands could receive inheritance from their wives is, again, indicative of the fact that women did own property; property did change hands within the family passing onto the male and female offspring from both sides of the family. These verses give neither an exclusively matrilineal nor patrilineal, but a bilateral, character to the Islamic view of inheritance. However, there are verses in the Qur'an that have historically given rise to gender-based asymmetry in the distribution of inheritance that feminist scholars consider a concrete form of gender-based abuse in Islamic societies.

This has become a very sensitive issue in modern times and in a number of Islamic societies that strive for gender equity in their social and legal relationships. The battle cry is that these verses allow for unequal distribution of inheritance between the male and female family members of the deceased. There are progressive academic circles (women's liberation and feminist and liberal-minded scholars) that also see a definite form of wife abuse in this type of inequity, which they argue must be corrected through legal changes in the Islamic system of inheritance.

Scholars who defend the Qur'anic view of differences in the apportionment of inheritance propose that the inequity exists because daughters receive, upon marriage, a certain form of matrimonial wealth (*jahizah*) from their fathers next to a lump sum of money or jewelry that the prospective husband promises to his wife as dowry (*mahriyeh*). In addition, married women receive daily household provisions (*nafaqah*) from their husbands. Therefore, it is only fair that sons should receive a higher proportion of the inheritance. This argument, valid as it might have been in medieval agricultural societies, is now partially defunct in those modernizing Islamic societies in which the formation of wealth and acquisition of property follow nontraditional processes and dynamics. For example, in a good number of modernizing Islamic societies (e.g., Turkey, Lebanon, Jordan, Egypt, Tunisia, Morocco, Malaysia, Singapore, Pakistan, Iran, Kuwait, Iraq, Syria) women are highly educated and employed in different economic sectors earning wages and salaries that allow them to acquire property with all its empowering prospects.

In many Islamic countries women are legally allowed to petition family courts to divorce their husbands, or to get child custody in cases where their husbands were to be declared unfit for that responsibility. Employed women are also legally allowed to utilize their properties the way they see it fit within the dynamics of the free economy to which many Islamic countries in North Africa, the Middle East, and Southeast Asia adhere. Thus insisting on unequal distribution of inheritance can be considered as a form of wife and/or female abuse in those Islamic societies that have adapted modern free market economies and their dynamics.

There are generic Qur'anic terms and verses on the importance of writing and learning as well as on how to write and how to document transactions. These applied to traders and merchants (male and female) who conducted local and/or long-distance trade and thus had to deal with different aspects of trade such as debt financing. For example in (ii: 282), it is stated, "O ye who believe! When ye contract a debt for a fixed term, record it in writing. Let a scribe record it in writing between you in (terms) of equity. No scribe should refuse to write as Allah hath taught him, so let him write, and let him who incurreth the debt dictate, and let him observe his duty to Allah his Lord, and diminish naught thereof." The thrust of the verse is directed toward "O ye who believe," addressing the general populace. It is commonly observed that this verse was to regulate the abusive aspects of pagan Arab practice in debt financing whereby the lender imposed inordinate interest on the principal of the loan. What is immediately apparent from the tone and thrust of the continuing verse is that it was either directed toward males, who, as a general rule, were more powerful than females, or those males who were more powerful than other males. Concerning this point, the verse reads further, "But if he who oweth the debt is of low understanding (*safihann*), or weak (*zaifann*), or unable himself (*awla yastaiti'u*) to dictate, then let the guardian (*wali*) of his interests dictate in (terms of) equity." The verse also provides for a witnessing procedure for future references, advising that one should "call to witness, from among your men, two witnesses. And if two men be not (at hand) then a man and two women, of such as ye approve as witness, so that if one erreth (through forgetfulness), the other will remember. And the witnesses must not refuse when they are summoned."

Traditionally this verse has been interpreted as the Qur'an's allowance for equating the worth of two women's testimonies to one man's testimonial worth provided that the male party is not mentally deficient. The traditional defense of this measure has been based in the belief that women are more emotional, irrational, whimsical, or forgetful, along with a host of other such misogynist notions. However, the verse concerns itself with incurring debt and conducting trade and commercial activities that prevailed at the time. In such a society, equating two women's testimonies to one man's testimony was perhaps a cautionary practice. The verse reflects an historical perspective rather than a biological "truth," as traditionally the verse has been interpreted. Because it is an historical perspective, it easily lends itself to reinterpretation bound by time and social conditions. This being said, there is no doubt that this verse has been utilized to degrade female testimonial worth in Islamic court procedures, be they civil or criminal. This is a definite form of abuse that must be remedied through legal reform.

Conclusions

There are verses in the Qur'an which put women under men's control and supervision, thereby allowing for the abuse of power. There are also verses that admonish both sexes—but specifically males of means and power—who abuse those who are less fortunate and less powerful. However, there are also verses that advise husbands how to deal with their rebellious wives. These verses differ in their applications, ranging from attempts to reason with a wife who does not attend to her share of duties and responsibilities, to harsher ones that may even include beating in case of *nushuz* (some argue that it is a deviant form of sexual arousal accomplished through a mild form of beating).

Depending on one's approach to the Qur'an and interpretation of these verses, divergent schools of thought have emerged among students of the Qur'an as to whether wife abuse has a solid Qur'anic base or is a matter of time and social conditions.

Scholars inspired by Western feminist thought and methodology argue that wife abuse has a solid Qur'anic base because Islam, like its Judeo-Christian counterparts, is a patriarchal religion designed for the propagation of patriarchal interests and institutions and as such allows husbands to subjugate and control their wives through different means and methods including beating. Scholars of the traditional school argue that the Qur'an does not condone abuse per se, but puts females under the control and supervision of males because females are inherently the weaker sex and need men's supervision in all aspects of life. A third emerging school argues that the remedy for wife abuse is neither denial of the abuse that goes on in many Islamic countries nor a full-fledged de-Islamization process, considering the fact that wife abuse is a universal problem that takes place in other societies as well. Accordingly, the remedy for wife abuse has social, legal, and economic dimensions as well as a critical approach to the Qur'an and its views as to what constitutes married women's rights, duties, and responsibilities in the context of which spousal abuse occurs.

HAMID R. KUSHA

See also **Christianity and Domestic Violence; Cross-Cultural Examination of Domestic Violence in China and Pakistan; Jewish Community, Domestic Violence within the; Worldwide Sociolegal Precedents Supporting Domestic Violence from Ancient to Modern Times**

References and Further Reading

Ahmed, Lila. *Women and Gender in Islam*. New Haven, CT: Yale University Press, 1992.

Ali, A. Yusuf. *The Holy Qur'an: Text, Translation and Commentary*. Washington, DC: The Islamic Center, 1978.

Beck, Lois, and Nikki R. Keddie, eds. *Women in the Muslim World*. Cambridge, MA: Harvard University Press, 1978.

Encyclopedia of Islam. 9 vols. Leiden, Netherlands: E. J. Brill, 1913–1938.

Esposito, John L. *Islam: The Straight Path*. New York: NYU Press, 1988.

Goldziher, Ignaz. *Introduction to Islamic Theology and Law*. Princeton, NJ: Princeton University Press, 1981.

Kusha, Hamid R. *The Sacred Law of Islam: A Case Study of Women's Treatment in the Islamic Republic of Iran's Criminal Justice System*. Aldershot, UK: Ashgate Publishers, 2002.

Lemu, B. Aisha, and Fatima Heeren. *Women in Islam.* London: The Islamic Foundation, 1978.

Mernissi, Fatima. *Beyond the Veil: Male–Female Dynamics in a Modern Muslim Society.* Cambridge, MA: Schenkman Publishing, 1975.

———. *The Veil and the Male Elite: A Feminist Interpretation of Women's Rights in Islam.* New York: Addison-Wesley Publishing Company, 1991.

Mogahdam, Valentine M. *Modernizing Women: Gender and Social Change in the Middle East.* Boulder, CO: Lynne Rienner Publishers, 1992.

Muhsin, Amina W. *Qur'an and Women.* Kuala Lumpur: Penerbit Fajr Bakti, 1993.

Stowasser, Barbara F. *Women in the Qur'an: Traditions and Interpretations.* New York: Oxford University Press, 1994.

R

RITUAL ABUSE–TORTURE IN FAMILIES

Introduction

Before exploring the reality that there are pedophilic parents, families, and like-minded others who derive pleasure from inflicting ritual abuse-torture, it is useful to first present a continuum of parental pedophilic violence in order to challenge the myth that all parents are caring—a myth behind which pedophilic parents can hide.

Although "ephebophile" has been suggested as a term for perpetrators whose sexualized focus is the pubescent child (Paulson and Farragher 2002), for some parents there is no such age-specific demarcation—their sexualized violence is inflicted on their young children and extends into the children's adulthood. For this reason the term "pedophile" will be used throughout this article to refer to adults, specifically parents or guardians, who inflict sexualized violence on their children at any age from infancy to eighteen years.

Pedophilia is not about "having sex" with a child. It is about a parent's sexualized assault of his/her child. It is about a parent's abuse of the position of power and the responsibilities entrusted to him/her to care for a child within the parent–child relationship, by exploiting the dependency needs of the child. It is about abusing adult superior size and

knowledge. Depending on the age of the child, pedophilic parents can use grooming methods, such as tickling play, to break down the healthy physical touch boundaries of their children, gradually initiating sexualized touch and assaults. Threats, intimidation, coercion, mental-emotional manipulation, physical force, torture, or threatening to harm others or pets are tactics parents can use to hold their children silent captives. Neighborhoods, communities, and society at large embrace the role of parents to care for children; when the abuse of parental power is revealed, they too suffer, as their worldview is challenged, and they too experience a loss of trust and a sense of violation and vulnerability.

A Continuum of Parental Pedophilic Violence

An infant girl goes home and becomes the victim of sexualized assault at the age of seven days. Her pedophilic perpetrator is her father, a music teacher, who describes his acts of sexualized violence as having sex with his daughter. By the time he is arrested, his daughter has endured seven years of victimization (United States Senate 1985a). In another home, in another country, a father sexually assaults his twelve-year-old mentally challenged son in his bed because he thinks no one will believe his son if he tells (Colley 2004). Across the ocean, in another home, a nine-year-old girl is tied up and her mouth is duct-taped so she cannot scream as she is raped by her father; he forces her to tell hospital staff that her bleeding was due to a fall on her bicycle (O'Brien 2003). Another father rapes his daughter when she is nine years old and again when she is a young woman of twenty-three (Blais 2005).

But the continuum of pedophilic parental violence can go beyond sexualized physical assault—it can progress into the production by some pedophilic parents of pedophilic pornography using their own or their neighbors' children (Gillan 2003; United States Senate 1985b). For example, 90 percent of the child pornography recovered by the Sex Crimes Unit of the Toronto police involves interfamiliar violence against children and is made in "first-world" countries such as Canada, the United Kingdom, and the United States (Lamberti 2002). Terrorization and horrification expand when parents harm animals, such as pet dogs, to produce pedophilic pornography involving bestiality (United States Senate 1985c).

Pushing the reality of parental pedophilic violence even further along the continuum raises the question: Do some assaults involve acts so cruel, inhumane, and degrading that they ought to be considered torture? The authors of this article believe so. For example, one father sexually assaulted his eldest son but also physically beat, scalded, burned, and forced all his children to eat their own vomit and excrement (Canadian Press News Service 1998). In another case, a religious father used beer bottles, sticks, and a fishing knife, as well as his penis, to rape his daughter (Montgomery 2003) and forced her two brothers to rape her at age four (Cherry 2002). In the hospital with ovarian cancer at age twenty-two, she was sexually assaulted in her hospital bed by her father (Cherry 2003).

In these two examples, the degree of violence, degradation, and cruelty goes beyond the definition of abuse, passing into the reality of torture. The United Nations (1985) defines torture as "act[s] by which severe pain or suffering, whether physical or mental, [are] . . . intentionally inflicted . . . [as] an aggravated and deliberate form of cruel, inhuman or degrading treatment."

The continuum flows deeper: A father of an eight-year-old daughter rents her out to various members of a pedophilic group for one hundred dollars a session. For another one hundred dollars, her father agrees to allow one visiting pedophile to keep his daughter in his motel room for the night. The pedophile described this night as "the height of

my pedophilic experiences" (United States Senate 1985d). Another father, who drank and watched pornographic movies in his basement with his friends, forced his six-year-old daughter, whom he trained to mimic porn stars, to satisfy their pedophilic urges (Steed 1995). These fathers were involved in the pedophilic human trafficking of their daughters.

Women—mothers—are not invisible in the continuum of parental pedophilic violence. They cannot escape responsibility, nor can they hide behind the myth that all women are nurturers. A mother convicted of aggravated sexual assault of a child and for beating her daughters with belts and extension cords was aware her daughters were suffering sexualized assaults—one becoming pregnant—by her spouse. The mother was not only a pedophile, but a silent partner in her spouse's sexualized assaults on her daughters (Associated Press 2004). Another mother pleaded guilty to the sexualized exploitation of her thirteen-year-old daughter with a twenty-one-year-old man (Canadian Press News Service 2004). She is a human trafficker.

One woman describes her childhood filled with physical and sexualized torture inflicted by her mother, whose torturous delights came from sticking large sticks, broken glass, candles, wooden spoons, an old-fashioned potato masher, coat hangers, pencils, lit cigarettes, and thorny rose stems into her vagina. As she was tied to a coffee table, the woman writes, her mother poked a knitting needle into her rectum, used scissors to clip her vaginal folds, and smeared her with dog feces. This woman believes her torture stopped at about age twelve. Although she believes that her victimization started in infancy, her toddler memories are clear—by age three, she was forced to participate in sexualized acts by her mother (Elliott 1993).

Finally, the parental pedophilic continuum ends with ritual abuse–torture. It involves organized transgenerational family and like-minded group violence against children, including pedophilic victimization. The transgenerational lineage can originate with one or both parents. In other words, an adult can marry into a ritual abuse–torture family unknowingly, and their children can become the next generation of victims. One can also become a child victim of ritual abuse–torture while being "cared for" by paid child care professionals. Testimonial evidence also suggests that outsiders sometimes connect with ritual abuse–torture families and groups to access vulnerable children preconditioned to withstand hard-core pedophilic victimization.

Naming Ritual Abuse–Torture

The term *ritual abuse–torture* comprises three descriptive words—torture, abuse, and ritual—each emphasizing one specific aspect of ritual abuse-torture victimization. There is much research and literature explaining both abuse and torture, so the experiential realities of these words cannot be denied. Being tortured and being abused are not interchangeable as words or experiences. Although torture can encompass ordeals of abuse, abuse does not encompass torture. There are differences.

For instance, from an intuitive perspective, if a person were forced to choose between becoming a victim of abuse or a victim of torture, which option would the person select? A person would probably choose abuse over torture because, if for no other reason, intuitively they know that the degree of atrocity is different.

From a child-as-victim perspective, parental pedophilic abuse can involve sexualized touching and oral, vaginal, penile, or anal assault and include threats, force, or weapons. Pedophilic torture, however, progresses beyond abusive assaults. Physical, sexualized, and mind-spirit child torture can include electric shocking to the genitals, nipples, anus, or mouth. It can involve clothespins attached to a little girl's vaginal folds; it can involve objects forced into a child's vagina, penis, anus, or mouth—such as guns, knives, fish hooks, hot light bulbs, hot pokers, lit candles, and sticks or other objects identified in the ordeals described above. Torture means the infliction of burning, cutting, hanging, and ramming injuries; it can mean that a child is given a razor and forced to self-cut to draw his or her own blood. Torturous pain and drugging are intentionally inflicted to force the child into dissociative states—a form of mind-spirit torture. This describes some differences in the degree of atrocities of the actions of parental pedophilic abusers versus torturers.

This leaves one remaining word to be defined—ritual. Rituals organize, hence are to be understood for the organizational purposefulness they serve. They:

1. Organize people and practices within families and societies. The use of organizing ritualisms is seen in play, work, the arts, and religion, for example. Rituals provide a framework for planned group gatherings and have a purpose, a leader, and followers (Daft 1995).
2. Normalize and reinforce groupthink, beliefs, values, thoughts, perceptions, emotions, attitudes, motivations, and behaviors.
3. Involve actions that strengthen group bonding.
4. Design power and functionality within relationships such as: Does the parent believe his/her child to be a possession versus a person, and treat the child as such?

Thus, a Sunday morning ritual for one father is whipping up buttermilk pancakes for his family (Bokma 2005). Children in the Brownies or Cub Scouts use ritualism in their group pledges. Martial arts participants ritually bow to each other before beginning their sparring match. Initiating a newly promoted manager into the upper echelons of a major organization might include the ritual of affording the new manager entry to the executive dining room. Historically, opera lovers, emperors, and popes were entertained by castrati singers—Italian boys castrated so that they would retain their boyhood voices in adulthood, allowing them to sing beyond the normal limits of the male vocal range, a ritual that did not wane until the 1950s (Carroll 2001). The "sky burial" rituals of Mahayana monks of China involve leaving the cut-up body of a deceased monk as a gift for the vultures (O'Neill 1993).

Rituals used by ritual abuse–torture families and groups also serve to organize—establishing family and group cohesiveness and connectiveness and normalizing the torture of children. To maintain control over child victims, family leaders commonly use omnipotence themes associated with the characterization of a devil—Satan, Lucifer—a bishop, or a high priestess. Children are taught that they are special when selected to be the "chosen one" for a "consumption ceremony," a coded term used to disguise the planned pedophilic family and group rape and torture of the child. Manipulated to believe in the omnipotent power of the pedophile playing the role of Satan, the child is held in a state of horror, captivity, and enslavement. Therefore, rituals, as used in the term *ritual abuse–torture,* specifically function to organize the like-minded practices of family and group members' heinous actions of child torture.

The Modus Operandi for Ritual Abuse–Torture

Changing the Landscape: Ending Violence—Achieving Equality, a study conducted by the Canadian Panel on Violence against Women (1993), is a credible report funded by the national government that names "ritual abuse" as a definite phenomenon of violence, identified as occurring in every region of Canada (p. 45). Pat Freeman Marshall, co-chair of the panel, stated that it heard stories of violence that she could relate only to the torture endured within prisoner-of-war camps (Cox 1992). "Tortured" was the word frequently used by women who spoke to the panel of their childhood ritual abuse victimization. Victimized persons repeatedly reported that they were tortured, so the term "ritual abuse" does not fit for them. Nor does that term comprehend the brutality, degradation, and dehumanization that one bears witness to when listening to the universal and transnational childhood stories of women, youth, and men involving both abuse and torture. Thus, the term *ritual abuse–torture* (RAT) was coined.

A child, whether born into or taken into such families or groups, will endure the following violent ordeals in ways that reflect the idiosyncrasies of the perpetrators:

1. *Child abuse.* Going without food, being forced to sleep on the floor without bedding, and being called "good for nothing" may accompany pedophilic assaults that occur night or day. In these families or groups there is no safe place for children—they may be finger-raped in the car on the way to school or raped in bed or on a cold, hard barn floor.

2. *Terrorization.* Threatening, intimidating, and forcing the child to witness the harming of animals or other children delivers the message: "Don't tell. If you do, this will happen to you." If only one parent is involved in the ritual abuse–torture, he may threaten to kill the nonoffending parent.

3. *Human/animal brutality.* Using violence against a pet instills terror, promotes silence, and helps establish totalitarian control over the child. One woman, for example, described being forced to watch her father burn her pet rabbits alive. Such cruelty prevents the child from forming attachments to pets or to anything as they are made to feel that they are to blame for the harm animals suffer. Perpetrators know that nonattachment keeps the child feeling isolated, abandoned, and alone in his/her victimization. Another act of cruelty commonly forced onto animals and children is bestiality.

4. *Physical, sexualized, and mind–spirit tortures.* There are no limitations to creative brutality. Tools useful for torturing, many commonly found in ordinary households, include belts, wooden bats, and wire clothes hangers useful for whipping and beating. Rope is used for tying children down, hanging them by

their limbs, or looping around their necks. Knives, razor blades, and forks are cutting and scraping tools; hot spoons, hot stove elements, and lit cigarettes burn; toilet bowls, bath tubs, and sinks are used for holding the child's head and face under water; cattle prods are for electric shocking; and pepper blown into the child's eyes causes excruciating pain. Dog cages become child cages, a dog's dish and food become the child's dish and food, and a dog collar and leash control the child who is commanded to eat and be the dog she is told she is. Soiled cat litter, all forms of human bodily fluids—blood, urine, vomitus, semen, menstrual fluid, feces—are serviceable for smearing.

Physical and sexualized pain, dehumanization, and degradation inflict fatal wounds upon the child's relationship with herself, overwhelming her ability to cope, forcing her to have out-of-body experiences or to disconnect and dissociate. Feeling like an "it" and objectified further by enforced overdrugging, trained to self-harm, and schooled to be the "perfect victim," the child faces a reality so severely altered and distorted that she becomes a danger to herself—at risk for suicide. All these torturous actions are directed by the ritual abuse–torture parent, family, or group in an attempt to destroy the humanness of the child victim. Such intentionally destructive actions are acts of human evil (Staub 1993).

5. *Pedophilia.* Rampageous hard-core parental pedophilic violence can and does occur at any time. Weekends, holidays, and school breaks are ideal times for a child to "disappear"; absences are explained as visits to relatives or trips to summer camp. When the victim is the perpetrator's child, pedophilic victimization is convenient, happening right in the home, in commercial buildings owned by the perpetrator, in summer or winter cottages, campers, hotels, motels, on boats, farms, or simply outdoors.

6. *Necrophilia and necrophilic-like acts.* The child victim may be overdrugged, hooded, choked, beaten, near-drowned, or suffocated into unconsciousness. Such experiences are often expressed by the child as "the darkness came." This satisfies the ritual abuse-torturer's need to express domination over life and death. Raping the child's "dead-like" body gratifies the fiend's hunger for sado-necrophilism.

7. *Horrification*. Beyond a state of terror, horrification involves seeing, hearing, smelling, feeling, and experiencing heinous ordeals perpetrated without moral restraint. Horrification leaves the child speechless, voiceless, without verbal language, for there are no words that can describe horror. Shocked, shivering from the depth of inner coldness, the child's body tremors in response to being family- and gang-raped and forced into pornographic bestiality with large animals, such as horses, which are known to be used in bestiality (Associated Press 2005; *Chronicle-Herald* 2004; LifeSiteNews 2005).

8. *Organized violent family and group gatherings*. These gatherings are commonly coded as "rituals and ceremonies." Ritual abuse-torturers intentionally use rituals to orchestrate pedophilic torture, which is the defining characteristic and central purpose for family and group gatherings.

9. *Suicide and other self-harming acts*. Some children are forcibly taught, conditioned, or programmed to self-harm and self-cut as a way of "forgetting," replacing "remembering" with pain—then pain and forgetting with relief. Depending on the practices of the ritual abuse–torture family or group, the degree of self-harm conditioning and programming can include forcing the child to practice ways of committing suicide. This tactic provides protection for the perpetrators. If they fear a child is telling, they can attempt to force the child into committing suicide to prevent being exposed.

10. *Exploitation and trafficking*. Within ritual abuse–torture families and groups, a child can be exploited and trafficked locally, nationally, or transnationally, "off-street" or "on-street." Off-street exploitation—transportation and trafficking—happens when the child is taken to family and group gatherings to be victimized. Trafficking off-street also happens when outsiders—pedophiles who are not members of the ritual abuse-torture family or group—"rent" the child. When the child's body has developed, becoming unmarketable to pedophiles, the child might be forced by ritual abuse-torturers to work on-street. "In-house" or "on-site" trafficking happens when ritual abuse-torturers organize "a party" in their home, for example. Often forced into criminal activities such as drug trafficking, the child is also used in all forms of pornography.

How Does a Ritual Abuse–Torture Family Present to Outsiders?

Ritual abuse–torture pedophilic parents have a unique modus operandi because they have unlimited access to their children, who are not seen to be in a state of captivity and enslavement, although they are. The home is rarely considered a site of victimization and human trafficking. Disappearances designed to look like vacations go unquestioned, and the transportation of the children in the family vehicle or on airplanes to cities such as Toronto or Washington are above suspicion.

Besides having the normalcy of family or guardianship as the perfect cover, ritual abuse-torturers are master manipulators, organizing their functionality into three relational dimensions. The first dimension is that of the *community,* and the false social face that perpetrators present to it; they would be the proverbial "last person" that someone would suspect of violent organized pedophilic crimes. A family involved in ritual abuse–torture may appear normal, even ideal, to an outsider. It can include parents with professional careers, who may be sociable and well respected in the community, entertain in their homes, volunteer in community groups, and be active in their children's school and church activities. This all amounts to a grand performance for the outside world. The second dimension is *domestic.* The situation inside the family home can be violent or sociable depending on whether perpetrators or uninvolved neighbors/outsiders are present, respectively. The third dimension is *exploitative,* in that perpetrators may transform gatherings of the RAT family and group—the inner circle—into organized sex rings.

Corresponding to these three relational dimensions are the three realities that the victim of ritual abuse–torture must face. There is the community-face reality, as described above. A second reality—inside the family—is where incestuous violence can happen at any time, starting as early as when the child is an infant. Episodic domestic violence, threats with guns, and alcohol use may alternate with dinner parties. The parents may serve big meals and sit around the table talking and laughing with unsuspecting guests. However, when perpetrators are mixed with nonperpetrators at the table, the child knows that this is a dangerous situation for him or her. As a teenager, the victim may also be turned into a high school drug dealer by his or her own parents. The victim's third reality is very secretive—an insider-circle reality of victimization at violent family and group ritual and ceremonial gatherings. Often forcibly drugged, the victim is transported to these gatherings by his or her parents or other group members, some they know and some they do not. Like the child's parents, others involved in these gatherings may have professional careers and the respect of their communities. The child victim may be transported by plane to different group gatherings nationally and transnationally, discovering that there is an underground for this type of thing.

At these pedophilic necro-sadistic gatherings, the child victim survives much—nakedness, electric shocking, beatings, whippings, burns, being smeared with and forced to eat body fluids, being forced into bestiality, being leashed like a dog, made to walk on all fours, caged, encircled and repeatedly gang-raped by his or her parents and other women and men who may be dressed in costumes. The adults enjoy distorting the victim's reality with lights or darkness, incense, chanting, silence or noise, drugging, fear, terror, and torture pain.

Horrified into speechlessness, overwhelmed into dissociative states in order to survive, the child is taken home and taught to self-cut and self-hit in order to forget what happened and to return to the first relational dimension: the belief that he or she has the most normal, wonderful family. Children in these situations do as they are told.

Victimization and Traumatization Responses

Those who work with victims of ritual abuse–torture listen to women, men, and children tell of massive debilitating childhood victimization. They hear victims' expressions of shame, guilt, self-blame, self-hatred, worthlessness, objectification, dehumanization, of feeling non-human, robotized, disgusted at their bodies for becoming biologically and physiologically aroused in response to the sexualized violations inflicted on them. They also express anxiety, fear, and terror that they might harbor the evil of their perpetrators within themselves. Victimized and hurting, they struggle to sever a dangerous mixture of attachments—their child–parent bond mixed with the Stockholm syndrome paradox; the connective and cohesive bond of belonging "to the family"; and the conditioned-programmed torture bond that drives their urges to experience pain and degradation, to self-cut and commit suicide should they become "a traitor" by telling on the family.

Learning from persons who tell of their ritual abuse–torture ordeals will help social service providers identify ways to recognize the presenting behaviors of children who are being harmed; this will in turn help them promote early interventions.

Depending on their age, children harmed by pedophilic ritual abuse–torturers disclose their victimization, in complex ways. Behaviorally, victims can present as extremely compliant children constantly attempting to please, terrified of taking initiatives for fear they will do wrong and be victimized as a consequence. Or they may express their hurt through displays of anger and aggression, including acting out their victimization on animals, other children, or nonoffending adults. For example, one woman told the authors of this article that when she was a child, she went up to her nonoffending grandfather and started to unzip his pants. Having been forced to endure constant repetitive oral rape by her father, the outsider men he trafficked her to, and pedophiles in the ritual abuse–torture family and group, she had anticipated that her grandfather would expect the same. She expressed how confusing it was for her to see her grandfather's shocked response and hear him tell her that this behavior was inappropriate.

Little is known of the emotional victimization responses of infants or toddlers; however, nurses have seen fear and terror expressed in the eyes of infants subjected to painful intrusive medical interventions. This same "look of fear and terror" response would likely be triggered in infants or toddlers who had endured being repeatedly finger- and object-raped whenever their diapers were changed. Seeing this look of terror is likely pleasurable and satisfying to the parent, family, and group pedophilic perpetrators because victimized women have reported that their torturers often said to them that they like to see the terror in their eyes. Physical responses include pallor and anemia due to repeated blood loss from sexualized abuse and torture or a failure to thrive from neglect and the withholding of nourishment.

Although this essay is focused on children, some women suffer ongoing harassment and are stalked and assaulted. Additionally, victimized persons agonize over the likelihood that their pornographic images may remain in circulation, exploited by pedophiles and pornographers.

As the continuum of pedophilic violence that can be committed within guardian or parent–child relationships is acknowledged, the ability to identify children of all ages who are being ritually abused and tortured will continue to develop. Below are additional ways in which children's suffering may be revealed:

1. Memory attacks, or flashbacks, may occur. The authors of this article have coined the

term *memory attacks* because horrific memories do attack, obliterating the present and reinflicting all the feelings of torture pain, of being cut, burned, or gang-raped. The victimized person's body can even reexpress previous physical injuries: Welts, bruises, burning rashes, and vaginal or anal bleeding may appear suddenly, then suddenly or gradually disappear. These reexperiences can last a few minutes, hours, or days. Child-victims might reexperience their victimization as daymares or nightmares—glimpses into their horror.

2. Dissociative language may be evident when a child refers to him/herself as "you" versus "I" or objectifies parts of his/her body by referring to them as "the" body, "the" head, "the" hand, etc. (Sarson and MacDonald 2005).

3. "Accidents" such as falling out of a window, drowning, or running out in front of a car may indicate acts of suicidality because victimized adults have reported early-age suicide attempts, some occurring before age five.

4. Vague reasons for frequent school absenteeism can be covers for a child being too injured to be seen publicly.

5. Fearing people dressed in costumes or uniforms can relate to costumes worn by adults during the child's victimization.

6. A child might use the term "monster" when referring to the perpetrator's penis or vagina.

7. A child may present with or have a history of early-age sexually transmitted infections and pregnancies or abortions, or show abandon for high-risk behaviors such as dangerous driving and the abuse of drugs and alcohol.

8. A child's narrative about the treatment of pets can disclose a link between violence within the family and animal cruelty; there can be high pet losses in violent households (Ascione and Arkow 1999).

Best Practice Interventions

No single or series of responses shared above is proof that a child has been or is a victim of ritual abuse–torture. The child, in his or her totality and relationships with other persons and animals, needs to be considered before an impression statement can be made.

Best practices include:

1. *An evidence-based approach.* Investigating children's disclosure means listening to them tell their stories as free narratives, giving as much detail as possible. Asking children to draw pictures of their victimizing and traumatizing ordeals often adds clarity to the narrative. Having listened to and watched children draw such pictures, the authors were surprised at how effective and transformative this process can be. In our experience, when children talked about the first drawings in detail, later drawings were often void of these details, suggesting that the children had resolved some of the emotional hurt. Using audio and video documentation to record their first narrative might protect children from losing their information and prevents the need for repetitive disclosures. Collecting forensic evidence and conducting physical examinations using photo-documentation, if victimization is current, are necessary interventions, as children's bodies begin healing immediately after sexualized assaults (Heger et al. 2002). Knowledgeable listeners and investigators on ritual abuse–torture are vital.

2. *It's not sex—it's violence.* It is common to hear or read statements such as: "The father had anal or vaginal sex with the child" or "His mother gave him oral sex." Anal, vaginal, penile, or oral rape is not about "having sex." These are sexualized assaults against children—pedophilic crimes—and ought to be named as such. Reframing language is important because words carry meanings that hold harmful myths and distortions in place within society. To continue to use the words "sex with children" results in at least four negative reinforcing social and relational distortions:
   a. The disregard for the human rights and special needs of children to be protected from pedophilic crimes
   b. The minimization of the harm pedophilic crimes inflict upon children
   c. The sexualization of adult or parent–child relationships
   d. The normalization of pedophilic crimes against children.

3. *Disreality.* A word coined to describe the process of keeping horrific realities, such as ritual abuse–torture, at a distance, *disreality* can reinforce myths such as the belief that only strangers are pedophiles, ignoring the fact that some parents are also pedophiles. Developing a worldview that acknowledges the continuum of pedophilic violence that can exist within some parent–child, family,

and group relationships will accelerate civil society's ability to protect children.

4. *Educating children.* Pedophilic parents, families, and groups normalize the violence they inflict upon a child. Children need to be part of the solution, with educational opportunities that inform them:

a. about the differences between healthy and pedophilic adult or parent–child relationships, including the varied types of pedophilic violence that can occur;

b. that it is never a child's fault—a child is not to be blamed for the pedophilic crime an adult or parent commits;

c. not to hate their bodies for responding to pedophilic assaults. It is not their bodies' fault—pedophiles use this response to trick children into feeling ashamed and guilty so they will remain silent;

d. that it is healthy to be scared and hurt when they are being harmed, even if adults/parents try to manipulate them into believing that they are bad or weak if they cry or scream;

e. that pedophilic violence is not about teaching children about sex—it is a crime;

f. that adult or parent pedophiles will try to trick children into not telling. Some manipulative tricks are: telling children that they will destroy the family or that no one will believe them if they tell; making children feel that they are to blame; making children feel special so that the pedophilic assaults become a special secret.

Conclusion

Laws specific to ritual abuse–torture are required to hold perpetrators responsible. Dissolving myths and distortions and developing knowledgeable language will help promote understanding of ritual abuse–torture ordeals. Healing is enhanced when a victimized child's ordeals are truthfully named, thus validated, and when laws provide the child with the opportunity to seek justice for the actual crime he or she has survived. Embracing victimized children means acknowledging ritual abuse–torture as "an emerging human rights violation and a newly acknowledged form of torture that is inflicted by 'non-state actors' [parents, relatives, like-minded others] onto the girl or boy infant, toddler, child, youth" (Sarson and MacDonald 2004).

JEANNE SARSON and LINDA MACDONALD

See also **Animal Abuse: The Link to Family Violence; Child Neglect; Child Sexual Abuse; Corporal Punishment, Religious Attitudes toward; Incest; Medical Neglect Related to Religion and Culture**

References and Further Reading

Ascione, Frank R., and Phil Arkow. *Child Abuse, Domestic Violence, and Animal Abuse.* West Lafayette, IN: Purdue University Press, 1999.
Associated Press. "Mom Pleads Guilty to Assault of Daughters." August 29, 2004. http://www.chron.com/cs/CDA/ssistory.mpl/metropolitan/2767051.
———. "Hundreds of Animals Sexually Abused." *Edmonton Sun,* April 30, 2005.
Blais, Tony. "Deviant Dad Jailed 5½ Years." *Edmonton Sun,* May 27, 2005.
Bokma, Anne. "These Magic Moments." *Canadian Living,* June 2005, pp. 182–186.
Canadian Panel on Violence against Women. *Changing the Landscape: Ending Violence—Achieving Equality.* Ottawa: Minister of Supply and Services of Canada, 1993, pp. 45–47.
Canadian Press News Service. "Agency Failed Children." *Chronicle-Herald,* April 23, 1998.
———. "Mom Pleads Guilty in Teen Sex Case." *Ottawa Sun,* September 25, 2004.
Carroll, Rory. "Pope Urged to Apologise for Vatican Castrations." *The Guardian,* August 13, 2001.
Cherry, Paul. "Father Gave Sex Lessons with Daughter, Son Testifies at Incest Trial. Brothers Were Initiated at Young Age, Were Too Afraid to Disobey, Jury Told." *Montreal Gazette,* December 4, 2002.
———. "Molester Gets the Max Years of Incest: A Horrible Crime: Judge. Father Began Raping His Daughter at Age 4, Instructed His Two Sons to Do the Same." *Montreal Gazette,* March 11, 2003.
Chronicle-Herald. "Authorities Seize Child Porn, Bestiality DVDs." September 23, 2004.
Colley, Sherri Borden. "Man Jailed for Abusing Son." *Chronicle-Herald,* December 3, 2004.
Cox, Wendy. "Panel Hears Horror Stories of Violence against Women." *Chronicle-Herald/Mail-Star,* March 23, 1992.
Daft, Richard L. *Organization Theory and Design,* 5th ed. Minneapolis/St. Paul: West Publishing, 1995, pp. 333–338.
Elliott, Michele, ed. *Female Sexual Abuse of Children.* New York: Guilford Press, 1993, pp. 118–121.
Gillan, Audrey. "Race to Save New Victims of Child Porn." *The Guardian,* November 4, 2003. http://www.guardian.co.uk/child/story/0,7369,1077260,00.html.
Heger, Astrid, Lynne Ticson, Oralia Velasquez, and Raphael Bernier. "Children Referred for Possible Sexual Abuse: Medical Findings in 2384 Children." *Child Abuse and Neglect* 26, no. 6-7 (2002): 645–659.
Lamberti, Rob. "Teen Facing Kiddie Porn Charges. Toronto Police Make Use of New Law." *Toronto Sun,* December 1, 2002.
LifeSiteNews.com. "Bestiality on the Rise in Sexually Libertine Sweden." May 4, 2005. http://www.lifesite.net/ldn/2005/may/05050406.html.
Montgomery, Sue. "'Isabel Began to Die the Minute She Was Born.'" *Chronicle-Herald/Mail-Star,* January 21, 2003.
O'Brien, Jennifer. "Dad Gets 50 Months for Sex Assaults on Daughter." *London Free Press,* February 21, 2003.
Office of the United Nations High Commissioner for Human Rights. "Declaration on the Protection of All

Persons from Being Subjected to Torture and Other Cruel, Inhuman or Degrading Treatment or Punishment," 1985. http://www.unhchr.ch/html/menu3/b/h_comp38.htm (accessed September 4, 2006).

O'Neill, Thomas. "The Mekong: A Haunted River's Season of Peace." *National Geographic* 183, no. 2 (1993): 12.

Paulson, Michael, and Thomas Farragher. "Priest Abuse Cases Focus on Adolescents." *Boston Globe,* March 17, 2002.

Sarson, Jeanne, and Linda MacDonald. "Ritual Abuse/Torture: Identifying a Crime of Horror." *Royal Canadian Mounted Police Gazette* 67, no. 1 (2005): 32–33.

———. "Ritual Abuse-Torture: The Most Unspoken Face of Human Trafficking." Presentation at side-panel *The Many Faces of Torture* (Dana Raphael, facilitator) at the 48th Session of the Commission on the Status of Women, March 8, 2004, United Nations Headquarters, New York. http://www.ritualabusetorture.org/unspokenface.pdf (accessed September 4, 2006).

Staub, Ervin. *The Roots of Evil.* Cambridge and New York: Cambridge University Press, [1989] 1993, p. 25.

Steed, Judy. *Our Little Secret: Confronting Child Sexual Abuse in Canada.* Toronto: Random House, 1995, p. 64.

United States Senate. "Testimony of William Dworin, Los Angeles Police Department, and Lt. William G. Thorne, Bergen County Prosecutor's Office, Hackensack, NJ." In *Child Pornography and Pedophilia Hearings before the Permanent Subcommittee on Investigations of the Committee on Governmental Affairs, Ninety-eighth Congress, Second Session, Part 1, Nov. 29–30, 1984.* Washington, DC: U.S. Government Printing Office (hereafter *Child Pornography and Pedophilia Hearings 1984*), 1985a, p. 52.

———. "Testimony of William von Raab, Commissioner, U.S. Customs Service, Accompanied by Jack O'Malley, Customs Special Agent, Chicago." In *Child Pornography and Pedophilia Hearings 1984,* 1985b, p. 13.

———. "Testimony of Kenneth J. Herrmann, Jr., Professor, Dept. of Social Work, SUNY College at Brockport, Defense for Children International–USA, Accompanied by Michael J. Jupp and Toby Tyler, San Bernardino Co., CA Sheriff's Department." In *Child Pornography and Pedophilia Hearings 1984,* 1985c, p. 33.

———. "Testimony of Joseph Henry, Convicted Child Molester." In *Child Pornography and Pedophilia Hearings before the Permanent Subcommittee on Investigations of the Committee on Governmental Affairs, Ninety-ninth Congress, First Session, Part 2, February 21, 1985.* Washington, DC: U.S. Government Printing Office, 1985d, pp. 7–10.

RULE OF THUMB

Origins of the Rule of Thumb

Historically, the physical punishment of wives has been encouraged by most cultures. The legal and social mandates for appropriate punishment are attributed to the patriarchal basis of most civilizations. In patriarchal societies, males were the designated leaders of society and the home. Wives and children were relegated to inferior social and legal positions and in earlier times were regarded in many cultures as chattel or the personal property of the husband. The subjugation of wives to their husbands is evidenced throughout history and across civilizations. In order to maintain the patriarchal basis of socialization, husbands in most cultures were duty bound to mete out appropriate punishment for wives and children who committed transgressions. In many cultures, the failure of husbands to properly control their wives and children resulted in severe social and legal stigma or sanction.

According to O'Faolain and Martines (1973), in the first formal law of marriage, Romulus, the founder of Rome, required married women to "conform themselves entirely to the temper of their husbands and the husbands to rule their wives as necessary and inseparable possessions." A frequently cited example of the duty of husbands to discipline their wives is that of a Christian scholar, who, in the late fifteenth century, authored a treatise titled the *Rules of Marriage.* One rule required husbands with errant wives to "scold her sharply, bully and terrify her. And if this doesn't work, . . . take up a stick and beat her soundly, for it is better to punish the body and correct the soul than to damage the soul and spare the body" (Davidson 1977). Under the provisions of the Napoleonic Code, women were regarded as minors and thus possessed none of the legal or social privileges which males enjoyed (Pagelow 1984). The Napoleonic Code also authorized husbands to beat their wives for acts of disobedience.

British Common Law

Married women fared no better under British common law. In his *Commentaries on the Laws of England,* Sir William Blackstone (1865) offered a testament to the legal status of married woman. There, Blackstone stated that "[b]y marriage, the husband and wife are one person in law; that is, the very being or legal existence of the woman is suspended during the marriage, or at least is incorporated and consolidated into that of the husband; under whose wing, protection, and cover, she performs everything." As such, British common law provided no independent legal status for married women. Rather, at the time of the marriage, wives forfeited their independent legal existence. Thus, what did not exist could not be protected. Forfeiture under the convenient "single legal entity" theory justified other practices, such as the marital rape exemption.

The *single legal entity* theory provided the justification for the right of chastisement or the right of husbands to discipline their wives. Essentially, because the husband was to answer for the deeds and misdeeds of his wife, he also possessed the right to correct and chastise her with the use of corporal punishment. In *Commentaries,* Blackstone explains that a husband "could give his wife moderate correction." However, Blackstone emphasized that correction or chastisement must be moderate. In his attempt to define the proper and reasonable bounds of the privilege, Blackstone utilized the now-familiar *rule of thumb.* In his codification of the common law, Blackstone suggested that husbands could beat their wives with sticks which were no thicker than the husband's thumb.

However, while Blackstone is credited with the rule of thumb, his writings reveal serious doubts regarding its propriety, and he suggested that at least for members of the upper classes, wives "should have security of the peace against her husband." Blackstone noted, however, that the "lower rank of people, who were always fond of the old common law, still claim and exert their ancient privilege." Moreover, there appears to have been general agreement that husbands could not inflict permanent injury upon their wives. In extreme cases, wives could seek legal protection by petitioning a court for a writ of supplicavit. This writ bears a striking similarity to the modern-day order of protection or restraining order. If issued, the writ of supplicavit required a husband to post a bond or otherwise guarantee that he would not harm his wife in excess of that allowed by the right of chastisement.

The Rule of Thumb and American Law

The discovery and colonization of America by western Europeans brought about new opportunities to develop law. However, the most significant influences upon the development of American jurisprudence were Christianity and British common law—both of which strictly adhered to the view that husbands should serve as master of the household. As such, in many colonies the common law privilege of chastisement and rule of thumb were enacted into law and again institutionalized. Yet, despite the existence of the privilege, doubts soon began to emerge among legal scholars and jurists regarding the authority of a husband to discipline his wife. For example, Francis Wharton (1868) acknowledged the existence of the privilege at common law, yet stated that the "tendency of criminal courts in the present day is to regard the marital relation as no defence to battery" (§ 830).

Wharton also discussed, with some degree of trepidation, the now-infamous court opinion of *Bradley v. State,* 1 Miss. (1 Walker) 156 (1824). *Bradley* is often cited as the first published appellate court opinion in America in which the privilege of chastisement and the rule of thumb were officially endorsed by an American court. *Bradley* is the first in a trilogy of Mississippi Supreme Court opinions which address the right of chastisement in that state and is often cited for its tacit approval of the right of chastisement. The trilogy is particularly illustrative of the nineteenth-century debate regarding the ancient privilege of chastisement in American jurisprudence.

Moreover, there is a significant amount of misconception about the actual holding of the state high court in the *Bradley* decision, which should finally be clarified. Following a jury trial, Curtis Bradley was convicted of assault and battery against his wife. On appeal, Bradley challenged his conviction on the grounds that the trial judge erroneously denied a jury instruction which would have informed the jury that Bradley should be acquitted if the victim of the assault was his wife. The trial court refused to instruct the jury as requested and instead instructed the jury that a husband could legally commit an assault and battery upon the body of his wife. Thus, the sole issue before the state supreme court was whether a husband could, for purposes of the criminal law, commit an assault and battery upon his wife. Following review of Blackstone's *Commentaries* and guidelines for moderate chastisement, the supreme court affirmed the conviction. Apparently, the injuries in the Bradley case were sufficiently severe to overcome any argument that the same were inflicted for purposes of moderate chastisement.

However, while the court affirmed the conviction, it failed to abrogate the common law right of chastisement. Rather, it held that a husband could raise a defense based upon this right to demonstrate that injuries to his wife were the result of moderate chastisement. The court specifically acknowledged the judicial abhorrence of the common law rule, yet concluded that "every principle of public policy and expediency" required the rule to "prevent the deplorable spectacle of the exhibition of similar cases in our courts of justice." Thus, at the end of the day the Mississippi high court retained the privilege of chastisement to avoid the investigation of "family broils and dissentions before the tribunals of this country." The rule, as retained by the court, was as follows: "To screen from public reproach those who may be thus unhappily situated, let the husband be permitted to exercise the right of moderate chastisement, in cases of great emergency, and use salutary restraints in every case of misbehaviour, without being subjected to vexatious prosecutions, resulting in the mutual discredit and shame of all parties concerned."

Over a half a century later, the Mississippi Supreme Court was again faced with the privilege of chastisement in *Harris v. State,* 71 Miss. 462 (1893). Although the court reversed the conviction of the husband on the grounds of insufficient evidence, the *Harris* court, unlike the *Bradley* court, expressly abrogated the common law rule. In *Harris,* the court held that the "blind adherence shown in that case [*Bradley*] to revolting precedent has long been utterly repudiated in the administration of criminal law in state courts." The final installment in the chastisement trilogy occurred in *Gross v. State,* 135 Miss. 624 (1924). There, the Mississippi Supreme Court finally put to rest any doubts that remained following the *Harris* decision. In upholding the conviction of a husband for the assault and battery of his wife, the court concluded that there was no privilege in favor of the husband as against the wife in the common law offense of assault and battery.

While the Mississippi cases are illustrative, they are not isolated in their treatment of the right of chastisement in American jurisprudence. Rather, early court opinions throughout the southeastern and mid-Atlantic states endorsed the rule of thumb and the right of chastisement. A review of these early opinions reveals strong sentiment regarding the preservation of the sanctity and privacy of the home, coupled with patriarchal notions of discipline. Later opinions, however, repudiated the rule and eliminated any official endorsement of

the common law. In fact, by the late 1870s most appellate courts had officially eliminated any remnants of the common law privilege. Shortly thereafter, the elimination of the common law privilege was followed by the widespread amendment of divorce laws to include cruelty as a ground for divorce. As a result, wives now enjoyed greater legal protection in criminal and civil courts for violent acts by their husbands.

While the nineteenth century brought promising changes, the end of violence within the bonds of matrimony has yet to occur. Official efforts which produce meaningful results have been gradual and are attributable mainly to the tireless efforts of advocates who continue to demand that attention be paid to this enduring issue. Yet, despite the tremendous progress which has been made, statistics continue to demonstrate alarming rates of violence among intimate partners. According to the Bureau of Justice Statistics (BJS), in 2002 there were 494,570 rapes and physical and sexual assaults against women by intimate partners. Moreover, BJS found that violence among intimate partners was primarily a crime against women, with those between the ages of sixteen and twenty-four experiencing the highest per capita rates. Homicide rates consistently indicate that women are most likely to be murdered by an intimate partner. More unsettling, however, is the realization that official statistics do not reveal the full extent of violence within the home.

Thus, while laws have undergone significant modification to reflect a more enlightened view of the role and status of women in the context of marriage, the reaction of the legal system to violence within the marriage has been slow and in many situations continues to exhibit a tolerance for violence among intimate partners. In many cases, the system itself seems to cling to the philosophy that violence within the home is a "family matter" rather than an act which demands official intervention. As a result of his research for *The Violent Home,* Gelles (1974) concluded that "we are still convinced that in most cases a marriage license also functions as a hitting license." Such an assertion is confirmed by modern research which examines the perspective of abusers. Research continues to identify a sense of ownership and authority as justification for the infliction of physical pain and suffering upon intimate partners. According to Dobash and Dobash (1978/2005), "Male authority is still, regardless of the so-called liberation of women, revered and protected by social institutions and reinforced and perpetuated through the socialization of children." The socialized belief that males have a property interest in their partners and therefore may use physical injury as a means to maintain their domestic authority has yet to meet its unofficial end.

LISA NORED

See also **Christianity and Domestic Violence; Corporal Punishment, Religious Attitudes toward; Worldwide Sociolegal Precedents Supporting Domestic Violence from Ancient to Modern Times**

References and Further Reading

Blackstone, Sir William. *Commentaries on the Laws of England,* 1865.

Bureau of Justice Statistics. *Crime Characteristics/Summary Findings 1973–2004.* United States Department of Justice, Office of Justice Programs. http://www.ojp.usdoj.gov/bjs/cvict_c.htm#findings.

Davidson, Terry. "Wife Beating: A Recurring Phenomenon throughout History." In *Battered Women: A Psychosociological Study of Domestic Violence,* edited by Maria Roy. New York: Van Nostrand Reinhold, 1977.

Dobash, Rebecca Emerson, and Russell P. Dobash. "Wives: The Appropriate Victims of Marital Violence." In *Violence against Women: Classic Papers,* edited by Raquel Kennedy Bergen, Jeffrey L. Edleson, and Claire M. Renzetti. New York: Pearson, 1978/2005.

Gelles, Richard J. *The Violent Home: A Study of Physical Aggressions between Husbands and Wives.* Beverly Hills, CA: Sage, 1974.

O'Faolain, Julia, and Lauco Martines. *Not in God's Image.* Glasgow: Collins, 1974.

Pagelow, Mildred D. *Family Violence.* New York: Praeger, 1984.

Schelong, Katherine. "Domestic Violence and the State: Responses to and Rationales for Spousal Battering, Marital Rape and Stalking." *Marquette Law Review* 78 (1994): 79.

Schick, Lori. "Breaking the Rule of Thumb and Opening the Curtains—Can the Violence against Women Act Survive Constitutional Scrutiny?" *University of Toledo Law Review* 28 (1997): 887.

Siegel, Reva B. "'The Rule of Love': Wife Beating as Prerogative." *Yale Law Journal* 105 (1996): 2117.

Wharton, Francis. *A Treatise on the Criminal Law of the United States.* Philadelphia: Kay and Brother, 1868.

Cases

Bradley v. State, 1 Miss. (1 Walker) 156 (1824)

Gross v. State, 135 Miss. 624 (1924).

Harris v. State, 71 Miss. 462 (1893).

RURAL COMMUNITIES, DOMESTIC VIOLENCE IN

The rural setting for domestic violence can be a stark contrast to its large-city counterpart. For instance, in the 70,665 square miles of North Dakota live just over 600,000 people, among the lakes, forests, rivers, wooded bluffs, and prairies—fewer people spread across that much territory than reside in Chicago alone. Rural areas may differ from one another in geography, economics, demographics, and even culture. Rural life itself is not homogeneous across the United States, but there are certain characteristics and issues which are often found in rural areas.

For instance, there are typically few police officers to respond to calls, and there may be limited access to telephones or emergency services. The geography of rural areas may pose a significant hurdle to victims of domestic violence. The response time and speed with which support services may be provided in an emergency may vary greatly, and the typically lengthy response time may increase the lethality of certain forms of violence. In large cities about 27 percent of residents own a firearm, but in rural areas over 75 percent of citizens are gun owners. Additionally, a more accepting attitude toward ownership of weapons is common in rural communities. Hunting weapons are common, and domestic violence victims are often threatened with them. The increased availability of weapons in rural households increases both the likelihood and the lethality of domestic violence attacks on rural victims.

Rural women face many challenges when dealing with domestic violence, and few statistical studies of rural domestic violence exist. Often the significant problems of domestic violence victims are exacerbated by a variety of rural factors which may decrease access to resources and make it more difficult for victims to escape abusive relationships. Economic conditions in rural communities may pose obstacles to domestic violence victims, as many rural areas suffer from high and enduring levels of poverty. The eroding economic base in these communities makes it difficult to offer appropriate services and shelters to victims in the area and makes securing adequate employment quite difficult for victims trying to succeed on their own.

A strong allegiance to the land may discourage victims from leaving and losing a large part of their identity. Additionally, support for traditional gender roles may leave victims with a perception of few options and a risk of losing the support of family and friends if they attempt to question or leave the boundaries of expected role behavior. Rural living may make access to advanced education, job opportunities, and even adequate child care very difficult, thus increasing the victim's reliance on the batterer.

While rural culture cannot be precisely described, it often has several features which have implications for domestic violence victims in these areas. One common feature of rural culture is the influence of informal control. Social bonding is emphasized, structural conditions tend to foster conformity among the youth, and rural areas are often less tolerant of crime and deviance in general. The informal control is strengthened by the stability of the local population, with the same house or land staying within a family for generations. The resultant "density of acquaintanceship" can make it difficult for the victim of domestic violence to come forward and believe that her anonymity will be preserved.

With a greater reliance on informal social control in many rural areas, there can be less use of or need for governmental control, which can even lead to a mistrust of government. This mistrust of government can influence rural victims to be hesitant to seek help from welfare, housing, employment, or other government-sponsored programs. Even service providers without a link to government may be viewed with skepticism if they seem insensitive to local needs. This mistrust may even make victims hesitant to report abuse to law enforcement officials.

While some rural areas have experienced economic growth and development, there often tends to be an out-migration of the youth, leaving family relationships and support networks strained and thus further isolating many victims. Batterers characteristically seek to isolate their victims anyway, and the moving away of family members (who may have been mediators in the home) can cause an

isolation in rural areas that is extremely severe, as victims may literally be miles from the nearest friend or family member and have no public transportation available. There may be no telephones, and in some cases 911 services are lacking. To make matters worse, for those who can use a phone, there may be long distance charges for calling other communities that may be only a few miles away, making it difficult for victims to remain in contact with family and friends, and, in addition to the cost, longdistance charges are often monitored by the abusers. A victim may be alone with the abuser for several months over the winter if employment is seasonal. Alcohol use may increase during these periods of isolation and unemployment, fueling an already volatile situation.

A lack of anonymity and confidentiality in small towns and rural areas may make it more difficult to confide in the law enforcement officer or judge, who knows everyone socially and may even be related to the offender and therefore less likely to recognize the severity of the abuse. In addition to shortages of health care providers and underinsurance or lack of health insurance, rural health care providers may be acquainted with or even related to the abuser, thus creating a barrier to disclosing the abuse and further isolating the victim.

In relation to race, most rural areas tend to be quite homogeneous; most minority groups in rural areas tend to be underrepresented, and an importance is not placed on providing needed services to the victims who are members of minority groups. Native American victims living on reservations face many of the same issues as rural victims. Native Americans are the only minority group which is more routinely represented in rural areas than in central cities, though culturally relevant services for Native American victims are still typically absent.

Domestic violence is as frequent in rural areas as in cities. There are many difficulties faced by victims in rural areas in addition to the typical difficulties of victims no matter where they reside. There are also many unanswered questions which are deserving of future study, such as, How do the detection of and response to domestic violence differ in rural areas and what are the main problems of service delivery to battered women in rural areas? A better understanding of minority-group concerns and the complexities of domestic violence among Native Americans are also appropriate issues for further study and attention.

When discussing issues surrounding domestic violence and why victims may not leave an abusive situation, it is important to look at the particular realities of rural life:

No Transportation

Rural victims may not have access to a vehicle or even have a driver's license, so traveling to town to report a crime or to seek medical attention may not seem practical. Road conditions during winter may prohibit travel, especially on back roads where snow removal may be intermittent or completely lacking.

Nowhere to Go

Rural victims may not have access to a shelter, or the nearest one may be more than an hour away. Going to a shelter means uprooting children from school and extended family, and such a move takes advance planning. It cannot be a spontaneous response.

Security

Many rural victims have never lived anywhere else, and leaving the security of other family members to escape the actions of one is a frightening prospect.

Livelihood/Lifestyle

Many victims are business partners in farming or ranching operations. To leave the farm can be emotionally difficult and may mean giving up their only source of income and abandoning significant investments.

Generational Effects of Domestic Violence

Isolation can be pronounced in rural areas, and the family may be a closed unit. If victims grew up witnessing domestic violence, they may see domestic violence as normal.

Shortage of Resources

There is a lack of support services in rural areas to assist victims in leaving. If they are available, there may be a lack of public awareness as to how to access them. Consider that there may not even be 911 services. There are few, if any, programs for batterers in rural areas.

Rather than incarcerating batterers and sending the abused to shelters, rural communities may benefit from integrating discussions of and services for victims and batterers into their community settings. Batterer programs may be viewed as better options than incarceration of the batterer or having the victim leave the farm or ranch, so long as the victim's safety is ensured. Service providers sensitive to the needs of rural communities need to build trust with the communities and understand how financial and cultural issues have impacted that group over time and how strengths within the rural communities can be used to facilitate change and encourage a reduction in domestic violence.

WENDELIN HUME

See also **Community Response to Domestic Violence; Education as a Risk Factor for Domestic Violence; Native Americans, Domestic Violence among; Social Class and Domestic Violence; Social Learning Theory and Family Violence**

References and Further Reading

The Rural Womyn Zone website. http://www.ruralwomyn. net (accessed September 4, 2006).

Weisheit, Ralph A., David N. Falcone, and L. Edward Wells. *Crime and Policing in Rural and Small-Town America,* 2nd ed. Prospect Heights, IL: Waveland Press, 1999.

S

SAME-SEX DOMESTIC VIOLENCE: COMPARING VENEZUELA AND THE UNITED STATES

Most people are aware of domestic violence in one form or another, either through unfortunate personal experience, media accounts, anecdotal accounts through friends, and even public service advertisements on billboards. Some may believe that domestic violence is limited to heterosexual couples and/or that domestic violence is merely a family issue isolated in the United States. A comparison of same-sex domestic violence in the United States and Venezuela will reveal these statements to be false.

Studies concerning the prevalence of heterosexual domestic violence have been numerous and well documented. What has been lacking is the examination of same-sex domestic violence, both within the United States and abroad. What few studies exist regarding same-sex domestic violence in the United States have revealed alarming results. Same-sex domestic violence occurs at the same or higher frequency than heterosexual domestic violence. In fact, one study (Kelly and Warshafsky 1987) found that 47 percent of gays and lesbians were victims of

same-sex domestic violence compared with approximately 20 percent of women and 3 percent of men involved in heterosexual relationships (Rennison 2003).

It is important to note that statistics concerning same-sex domestic violence are problematic for a number of reasons. As with heterosexual domestic violence, not all violent acts are reported to authorities. The lack of reporting becomes magnified in the gay and lesbian community due to fear of "outing" (the nonconsensual disclosing of the sexual orientation of the victim). Additionally, gays and lesbians may be reluctant to report their victimization to the police for fear of police ridicule. Defining domestic violence also poses additional difficulties in accurate statistical reporting. For instance, if reported, how will authorities classify the incident? Will police officers report same-sex violent acts or simply reclassify them to a lesser crime to avoid paperwork or skirt mandatory arrest laws that may exist in some jurisdictions? Definitions of domestic violence may also differ

617

from jurisdiction to jurisdiction, state to state, and country to country.

There are numerous definitions of domestic violence, but for the purpose of this essay, same-sex domestic violence will include the control of others through power, including verbal and nonverbal harassment; physical and psychological threats or injury to the victim or to others; isolation (preventing or minimizing social contacts); economic deprivation; outing; sexual assaults (including being pressured into sexual activity); vandalism (destruction of property); animal abuse (pet abuse); withholding medication; or any combination of the above-named methods (Burke 1998). This definition may apply in the United States as well as internationally.

As previously stated, same-sex domestic violence studies have been limited, and as of this writing, with the exception of this evaluation, international comparisons have been nonexistent. Venezuela was chosen for comparison because one of the coauthors of the original study (Burke, Jordan, and Owen 2002) had extensive knowledge of Venezuela as a former resident and criminal justice researcher. The comparative results of the original study regarding same-sex domestic violence between couples in the United States (35 respondents) and in Venezuela (37 respondents) are noted later.

Same-sex couples in both the United States and Venezuela experienced domestic violence. While the two most frequent forms of domestic violence in both countries were verbal harassment and prohibition of social contact, victimization in other categories also proved disturbing. A large number of victims reported being physically attacked by their partners. The frequency of the attacks differed between counties. Venezuelan victims reported being hit once or twice during their relationships, whereas same-sex victims in the United States were often struck on three or more separate occasions. Same-sex victims in both countries were threatened with outing, reported property damage at the hands of their partners, and were pressured into sexual activities by them. Pressuring a partner to perform sexual acts appeared more problematic in the United States. A few Venezuelan victims reported that their medication had been withheld from them by their partners, thereby preventing them from receiving necessary treatment. These results indicate that being a victim of same-sex domestic violence is not isolated to the United States.

Attitudes toward the police and courts were also asked of those taking the same-sex domestic violence survey. Both United States and Venezuelan respondents were asked whether distrust of their

law enforcement personnel would prevent them from reporting an incident of same-sex domestic violence to the police. Venezuelans were much more likely *not* to report same-sex violence to the police. They also perceived that their local police departments were biased against gays and lesbians. United States respondents were more likely to have confidence in local law enforcement compared with Venezuelan respondents. However, this should not be confused with an outright trust of American law enforcement by gays and lesbians. In fact, respondents in both countries indicated that they would feel more comfortable seeking assistance from a friend or family member before asking the police for assistance.

Similar results were found when comparing Venezuelan and United States respondents' perceptions of the courts. While over half of all respondents indicated a distrust of the courts that would prevent them from reporting an incident of same-sex domestic violence, Venezuelans were much more likely to distrust the court system. What this means is that while gay and lesbian Venezuelans do not have a great deal of trust in their law enforcement and court system, United States law enforcement and courts could also do much more to support gays and lesbians, particularly those who have been victimized.

Questions were also asked about whether the respondents were aware of available resources for victims of same-sex domestic violence, as well as about fear of victimization and crime perception in the United States and Venezuela. Respondents in the United States reported greater awareness of resources for same-sex domestic violence victims, including information provided by seminars and workshops, newspapers, television, community groups, etc. Both Venezuelan and United States respondents indicated that they feared same-sex domestic violence; however, Venezuelan respondents were more likely to indicate that they believed that the victim was to blame. The vast majority of respondents from both countries believed that same-sex domestic violence is indeed a crime.

In conclusion, same-sex domestic violence is very real and is not isolated to one particular country. Information regarding same-sex domestic violence must be disseminated to the gay and lesbian population around the world. Resources also need to be made available to assist victims as well as abusers. The criminal justice system and its personnel must treat same-sex domestic violence as a real crime and take the necessary steps to aid the victim. Same-sex domestic violence is a serious cross-national issue that needs immediate attention and additional research.

TOD W. BURKE

See also **Gay and Bisexual Male Domestic Violence; Gay Domestic Violence, Police Attitudes and Behaviors toward; Gender Socialization and Gay Male Domestic Violence; Intimate Partner Violence, Forms of; Intimate Partner Violence in Queer, Transgender, and Bisexual Communities; Lesbian Battering; Male Victims of Domestic Violence and Reasons They Stay with Their Abusers**

References and Further Reading

Burke, T. "Male to Male Gay Domestic Violence: The Dark Closet." In *Violence in Intimate Relationships: Examining Sociological and Psychological Issues,* edited by N. Jackson and G. Oates. Boston: Butterworth-Heinemann, 1998, pp. 161–179.

Burke, T., M. Jordan, and S. Owen. "A Cross-National Comparison of Gay and Lesbian Domestic Violence." *Journal of Contemporary Criminal Justice* 18, no. 3 (2002): 231–257.

Burke, T., S. Owen, and M. Jordan. "Law Enforcement and Gay Domestic Violence in the United States and Venezuela." *ACJS Today* 24, no. 2 (May/June 2001): 1, 4–6.

Island, D., and P. Letellier. *Men Who Beat the Men Who Love Them.* New York: Harrington Park Press, 1991.

Jackson, N. "Lesbian Battering: The Other Closet." In *Violence in Intimate Relationships: Examining Sociological and Psychological Issues,* edited by N. Jackson and G. Oates. Boston: Butterworth-Heinemann, 1998, pp. 181–194.

Kelly, C., and L. Warshafsky. *Partner Abuse in Gay Male and Lesbian Couples.* Paper presented at the third national Conference for Family Violence Researchers. Durham, NH, July 1987.

Letellier, P. "Gay and Bisexual Male Domestic Violence Victimization: Challenges to Feminist Theory and Responses to Violence." *Violence and Victims* 9 (1994): 95–105.

Lie, G. Y., and S. Gentlewarrier. "Intimate Violence in Lesbian Relationships: Discussion of Survey Findings and Practical Implications." *Journal of Social Service Research* 15 (1991): 41–59.

Merrill, G., and V. A. Wolfe. "Battered Gay Men: An Exploration of Abuse, Help Seeking, and Why They Stay." *Journal of Homosexuality* 39, no. 2 (2000): 9–21.

Rennison, C. "Intimate Partner Violence, 1993–2001." NCJ 197838. *U.S. Department of Justice: Bureau of Justice Statistics Crime Data Brief,* February 2003.

Turell, S. "A Descriptive Analysis of Same Sex Relationship Violence for a DiverseSample." *Journal of Family Violence* 15 (2000): 281–293.

Waldner-Haugrud, L. K., L. L. Gratch, and B. Magruder. "Victimization and Perpetration Rates of Violence in Gay and Lesbian Relationships: Gender Issues Explored." *Violence and Victims* 12 (1997): 173–184.

SEXUAL AGGRESSION PERPETRATED BY FEMALES

While the phenomenon of sexual coercion in intimate relationships has been acknowledged for several decades, for the most part the research that has addressed it has focused almost exclusively upon males as perpetrators and females as victims. Sexual perpetration committed by women, especially against men, is often not taken seriously in contemporary American culture. Indeed, rape laws in the United States were based upon English laws that defined rape in terms of the sexual knowledge of a woman against her will and by force. Specifically, until fairly recently, for a behavior to be considered rape, it had to be perpetrated by a male against a female; it had to be extramarital; it had to involve the penetration of the vagina by the penis; and it had to involve force (Dixon 1991).

Thus, the concept of female-perpetrated rape or sexual aggression was foreign in the legal community. The recognition of female-perpetrated sexual aggression by the research community was almost entirely confined to the study of that which occurred in lesbian relationships. More than that, however, women's sexual coercion of men has often been treated as a topic of humor in contemporary culture. Few people are willing to acknowledge that men can be victims of sexual aggression perpetrated at the hands of women. Likewise, the topic has been neglected even among researchers who did not take the victimization experiences of men seriously or did not consider the phenomenon to be common enough to warrant empirical investigation.

619

This pattern began to change more recently with a handful of studies that have portrayed men as victims of unwanted sexual coercion by women. Nevertheless, many people remain skeptical that women are capable of physical aggression unless it is in the context of self-protection, let alone that they are capable of sexual coercion of male partners (Struckman-Johnson and Anderson 1998). However, a substantial number of research projects have emerged challenging the notion that women are not physically aggressive. Specifically, since the mid-1990s, a number of researchers have begun to demonstrate that women can and do coerce male partners sexually as well (Fiebert and Osborn 2001; Waldner-Haugrud and Magruder 1995).

Because it is important to recognize that women can assume the role of perpetrator in sexually coercive encounters and because this role has been ignored by many researchers, Stuckman-Johnson and Anderson (1998) argue that it is important that women and men be studied as both potential perpetrators as well as victims. To not explore the phenomenon of women as perpetrators and men as victims of sexual coercion ignores the potentially harmful effects of such experiences and implies that the experiences of the victim are not valid (Muehlenhard 1998). Consequently, the purpose of this article is to examine the phenomenon of female-perpetrated sexual coercion, especially against men, and to identify factors associated with such perpetration.

The Myth That a Women Cannot Be a Perpetrator

For some time, research on sexual coercion has perpetuated the myth that women are victims and men are perpetrators in sexually coercive encounters. This myth is perpetuated by a number of other myths and misconceptions. These include the idea that women have low sex drives, are less likely to be sexually deviant, are primarily responsible for controlling sexual activity, and do not have the size, strength, or ability to force a man to have sexual relations (cf. Finkelhor 1979). Furthermore, many believe that it would be impossible for a woman to force a man to have unwanted sexual contact with her because he would not be able to develop an erection. However, men can be sexually aroused by physical stimulation or even fear (Sarrel and Masters 1982). Moreover, unwanted sexual contact may include activities other than intercourse (Struckman-Johnson and Anderson 1998).

The Politics

While some may believe that women cannot be perpetrators and men cannot be victims, there may be other explanations for the reluctance of individuals and groups to acknowledge women as perpetrators. The politics surrounding the decision to study sexual aggression and perpetration by gender are indeed interesting. First, it is important to emphasize that ignoring the experiences of men as victims of sexual perpetration committed by women delegitimizes their experiences. Sexual perpetration against men, like that against women, is grounded in power differentials. While society at large may be patriarchal, not only do men who have been victimized in this manner have few places to which they can turn for assistance, but the neglect of the topic through systematic sampling bias by selecting only women to study symbolically sends the message that their experiences are insignificant. Second, there seems to be a double standard regarding what is acceptable behavior as well as how sexual aggression is conceptualized methodologically by researchers. For example, females may be allowed to be more assertive than males without being considered deviant if the encounter is motivated by intimacy and romance. At the same time, the same behaviors committed by males may be perceived as coercive or aggressive and motivated by power and control. It is plausible that the lack of concern about the sexually assertive behaviors of women is the result of society viewing women as less threatening than men (Struckman-Johnson and Anderson 1998), which in turn continues to symbolically subordinate women. Third, researchers may operationalize sexual assault by asking if one has ever been forced to have sexual relations when one did not want to by being given drugs or alcohol. In some cases, this may be defined through the instruments that are used. For instance, use of the Sexual Experiences Survey (Koss and Oros 1982) is common in the study of sexual coercion. Research relying upon this measure asks women to answer questions about their victimization experiences, while men are asked to answer questions about their perpetration experiences. Thus, the assumption is that women are victims and men are perpetrators, but not vice versa. Still other researchers may ask men about their victimization experiences but emphasize the incidence of female victimization. By extension, there is a tendency to consider only penile-vaginal intercourse as real sex and therefore only penile-vaginal sexual aggression as real sexual aggression

(Chalker 1994). Finally, when research on sexual aggression is limited solely to the experiences of men as perpetrators and women as victims, researchers are symbolically perpetuating traditional gender roles (Muehlenhard 1998).

Prevalence and Incidence

Existing literature reveals that women are more fearful of becoming victims of sexual aggression than are men and that those fears cause them to restrict their behaviors (Gordon and Riger 1989). The fears of women are based upon reality. Many empirical studies have demonstrated that women are far more likely to be victims of sexual assault and coercion as adolescents and adults. Similarly, individuals, both male and female, who were sexually victimized as children are more likely to be sexually victimized again as adolescents or adults and to report victimizing others (Brenner 1994).

One of the earliest studies of sexual coercion by women was conducted by Story (1986), who studied college women at a university in Iowa. While rates of sexual coercion perpetrated by women were lower than those typically found for coercion by men, she showed that 10 percent of the females in her college sample reported that they had forced some form of sexual intimacy. Nearly 4 percent reported that they had forced a partner to engage in sexual intercourse.

Similarly, Anderson (1998), in a study of nearly 500 college females, discovered that more than 40 percent had experienced some form of sexual victimization in the past, that between 26 percent and 43 percent had engaged in behaviors in order to obtain sex that would be defined as coercive if applied to male respondents, and that 26 percent to 36 percent of them had engaged in behaviors defined as abusive. According to Anderson, approximately 20 percent of the women in the sample reported using physical force, while more than 25 percent used the threat of physical force. Surprisingly, nearly 10 percent reported using a weapon to force their partner to engage in sex. Clearly, while the numbers of empirical research studies addressing the sexual aggression perpetration by women are not great, the results of these point to the need for increased attention.

In a study of 881 college students in 2001, Jasinski and Dietz found similar results using the Revised Conflict Tactics Scales to measure sexual coercion and assault. While males in the sample reported a statistically significant higher rate of perpetrating both minor and severe forms of sexual coercion against their partners than did females, 20 percent of females in the sample reported that they had committed at least one type of minor sexual coercion and 4 percent of females reported that they had committed at least one act of severe sexual coercion or assault in the year preceding the survey. Interestingly, those females who reported that they had engaged in sexually coercive behaviors were also likely to report perpetration of other types of physical and psychological aggression as well. In addition, they were more likely than their nonsexually coercive counterparts to report being victims of sexual coercion or assault as well as psychological or physical aggression. They also reported being less committed to the relationship within which the coercion had occurred. Finally, in a study of 248 women, Krahe, Moller, and Waizenhofer (2003) reported that nearly 10 percent of their sample reported using aggressive strategies to coerce a man to engage in sexual activities. They discovered that many of the women who reported that they used these strategies exploited men's incapacitated state or used verbal pressure, although a small group reported using physical force. Sexual aggression within this sample of women was associated with sexual victimization in childhood, higher levels of sexual activity, and peer pressure to engage in sexual activity.

Gender Differences in the Meanings and Consequences

While it is important to acknowledge the existence of sexual aggression perpetrated by women against men as a type of partner violence, it is nevertheless important to recognize that it is not the same as sexual coercion or aggression perpetrated against women by men. First, women have historically not had control over their own reproductive rights in the United States. Second, while laws may be made to treat the phenomenon in a gender-neutral way, there may be a disjunction between theory and reality. For instance, in applying the concept of force or threat of force for sex to both men and women equally, it remains true that for the average woman and man, it requires a much greater degree of exertion on the part of the woman to force a man to comply than it might for a man to force a woman to comply, unless a lethal weapon is being used. The same may not be said for some forms of threats. Moreover, women in America typically earn less money than men and have historically been more dependent upon men for their economic well-being. Thus, women may have been and continue to be more compelled to comply with the wishes of their male partners to engage in sexual relations.

Aside from those issues, it deserves noting that gender differences have emerged in empirical studies of the meanings associated with and reactions to sexual aggression experiences. However, the results of these studies are not conclusive. While many indicate that women report more negative reactions and emotions to the experience than men, Satterfield (1995) reported that some men reported being more distressed by the experience than did some women.

Potential Backlash and Cautions

It is acknowledged that researchers are compelled to share what the data reveal; but at the same time, this essay was written with some trepidation because there is some potential for the information to be used against those who have worked so diligently to end violence against women. Although it is important to reveal the truth about sexual aggression perpetrated by women, it remains clear that more women than men are sexually victimized (Brenner 1994; Koss 1993). When a woman is sexually assaulted, the perpetrator is almost always a man. When a man is sexually assaulted, the perpetrator is another man about one-third of the time (Michael et al. 1994). Consequently, men are by far much more likely to be the aggressors in cases of sexual assault. That women can be sexually aggressive should not be used to justify a reduction in efforts to prevent and treat violence against women or to support a viewpoint that sexual coercion should be viewed as a gender-neutral problem. Thus, it is with great caution that this essay is presented; it is in no way intended to be used as a justification for a decrease in attention given to the problem of violence against women, but rather to bring attention to the problem of violence against both men and women in contemporary society.

TRACY L. DIETZ

See also **Battered Husbands; Factors Influencing Reporting Behavior by Male Domestic Violence Victims; Marital Rape**

References and Further Reading

Anderson, Peter B. "Women's Motives for Sexual Initiation and Aggression." In *Sexually Aggressive Women,* edited by Cindy Struckman-Johnson and Peter B. Anderson. New York: Guilford Press, 1998, pp. 79–93.

Brenner, Lisa M. "Adult Patterns of Men and Women Who Were Sexually Abused as Children: Is There a Risk of Becoming a Victim or Perpetrator?" Unpublished doctoral dissertation, University of Kansas, Lawrence, 1994.

Chalker, Rebecca. "Updating the Model of Female Sexuality." SIECUS Report 22, no. 1 (1994): 1–6, 1994.

Dixon, Jo. "Feminist Reforms of Sexual Coercion Laws." In *Sexual Coercion: A Sourcebook on Its Nature, Causes, and Prevention,* edited by Elizabeth Grauerholz and Mary A. Koralewsski. Lexington, MA: Lexington Books, 1991, pp. 161–171.

Fiebert, Martin S., and Kelly Osburn. "Effect of Gender and Ethnicity on Self-Reports of Mild, Moderate, and Severe Sexual Coercion." *Sexuality and Culture* 5, no. 2 (2001): 3–11.

Finkelhor, David. *Sexually Victimized Children.* New York: The Free Press, 1979.

Gordon, Margaret T., and Stephanie Riger. *The Female Fear.* New York: The Free Press, 1989.

Jasinski, Jana L., and Tracy L. Dietz. "What's Good for the Goose Is Good for the Gender: Gender Differences in Sexual Aggression." Presentation at the annual meeting of the International Family Violence Conference, Portsmouth, NH, July 2003.

Koss, Mary P. "Detecting the Scope of Rape: A Review of Prevalence Research Methods." *Journal of Interpersonal Violence* 8, no. 2 (1993): 198–222.

Koss, Mary P., and Cheryl Oros. "Sexual Experiences Survey: A Research Instrument Investigating Sexual Aggression and Victimization." *Journal of Consulting and Clinical Psychology* 50, no. 3 (1982): 455–457.

Krahe, Barbara, Ingrid Moller, and Eva Waizenhofer. "Women's Sexual Aggression against Men: Prevalence and Predictors." *Sex Roles: A Journal of Research* 49, no. 5/6 (2003): 219–232.

Michael, Robert T., John H. Gagnon, Edward O. Laumann, and Gina Kolata. *Sex in America: A Definitive Survey.* Boston: Little, Brown, 1994.

Muehlenhard, Charlene L. "The Importance and Danger of Studying Sexually Aggressive Women." In Struckman-Johnson and Anderson, *Sexually Aggressive Women,* 1998, pp. 19–48.

Sarrel, Philip M., and William H. Masters. "Sexual Molestation of Men by Women." *Archives of Sexual Behavior* 11, no. 2 (1982): 117–131.

Satterfield, Arthur T. "The Meaning of Sexual Coercion: An Exploratory Study of Women's and Men's Experiences." Unpublished doctoral dissertation, University of Kansas, Lawrence, 1995.

Story, M. "Factors Affecting the Incidence of Partner Abuse among University Students," 1986, as referenced in Peter B. Anderson, "Women's Motives for Sexual Initiation and Aggression," in Struckman-Johnson and Anderson, *Sexually Aggressive Women,* pp. 79–93.

Struckman-Johnson, Cindy, and Peter B. Anderson. "'Men Do and Women Don't': Difficulties in Researching Sexually Aggressive Women." In Struckman-Johnson and Anderson, *Sexually Aggressive Women,* 1998, pp. 9–18.

Waldner-Haugrud, Lisa K., and Brian Magruder. "Male and Female Sexual Victimization in Dating Relationships: Gender Differences in Coercion Techniques and Outcomes." *Violence and Victims* 10, no. 3 (1995): 203–215.

SEXUAL ORIENTATION AND GENDER IDENTITY: THE NEED FOR EDUCATION IN SERVICING VICTIMS OF TRAUMA

Domestic violence first became a focal point of public and professional attention in the 1970s, but issues impacting lesbian, gay, bisexual, and transgender people (LGBT) have only slowly drawn the attention of domestic violence advocates. The growth of the lesbian and gay community in the 1980s, rooted in social activism and civil rights struggles, paved the way for a more concerted examination of issues of violence and trauma. In the 1990s, the lesbian and gay community expanded to include bisexual and transgender/transsexual people and their concerns. Understanding the diversity of sexual orientations and gender identities that can be expressed and the potential avenues for abuse, violence, exploitation, and trauma that exist requires a broad range of knowledge overlapping two areas of study: sex and gender identity on one hand, and the impact of traumatic and intimate violence on the other.

Like heterosexual people, LGBT people are impacted by violence and abuse in intimate relationships, including physical battering, emotional abuse, and sexual assault. LGBT people are, however, more vulnerable to other forms of violence, especially bias-related violence and sexual harassment directed at them specifically because their sexual orientation and/or gender identities differ from the proscribed heteronormative expression. LGBT people are potentially at greater risk of physical and sexual abuse as children, especially if their gender or sexual expression marks them as different from their peers. LGBT people are at a disadvantage within the justice system, where their relationships are often unrecognized, and it may be harder to obtain respectful treatment or legal redress and compensation when they are victimized. Additionally, it has been harder for LGBT people themselves to recognize violence within their own communities and families, since it can increase the stigma of having a socially marginalized identity.

Complicating an already complex issue, few service providers specializing in trauma treatment, domestic violence advocacy, or rape crisis counseling are educated about LGBT people and understand the diversity of sexual and gender identities potentially expressed within LGBT relationships and communities. Assisting victims in finding appropriate services and addressing the specific areas impacted by traumatic sexual violence require a commitment to education and a broader knowledge base than most providers have been able to access. The following section will serve as a primer for understanding human sexual identity, which is necessary for understanding the impact of trauma in the lives of sexual minorities.

Understanding Sexual Identity

The terms *sex* and *gender* are often used interchangeably, though they refer to very different components of human sexuality. *Sexual identity* is used descriptively here as a general term to include all aspects of human sexuality, although it is commonly used to refer to what is more precisely called sexual orientation. Sexual identity has four major component parts—biological sex, gender identity, gender (or sex) role, and sexual orientation—that together form an integrated biopsychosocial sense of self. Each component part is explained in further detail later.

The first component of human sexual identity is biological sex. Everyone is assigned a biological, or natal, sex generally based on a cursory examination of the visible genitalia at birth. Biological sex is actually a complex relationship of genetic, hormonal, morphological, chromosomal, gonadal, biochemical, and anatomical determinants that impact the physiology of the body and the sexual differentiation of the brain. Sex is simply defined as the bipolar categories of male and female; intersexuality is a combination, or mixture, of these two poles.

Those born with medically diagnosed intersex conditions are a small but stable part of humanity, approximately 1–2 percent of the population. Intersex conditions develop *in utero* and are caused by numerous genetic and hormonal variations in fetal development. Although chromosomal sex differences are established at conception (XY and XX), the primitive duct systems of male and female fetuses appear the same, and the biological differences between males and females do not manifest until about six weeks into gestation. At this time, the gonads produce various hormones that stimulate the development of both internal and external genitalia and differentiate male and female bodies. The female developmental process is considered a "default" system because without sufficient male hormones, the XY fetus will not masculinize and will therefore appear female at birth. An overproduction of male hormone will also masculinize a female fetus.

Due to the complexities of establishing correct gender assignment, many people with intersex conditions are not recognized and/or are wrongly assigned at birth. Physicians have, until recently, routinely surgically operated on people with visibly intersexed genitalia, causing potential psychological as well as physiological problems with sexual and gender identity development. People with intersex conditions often experienced shame for their sexual differences, and family members are rarely prepared to address the necessary support and education their children need for healthy sexual development.

Like all people, those with intersex conditions may be heterosexual, homosexual, or bisexual in their orientation, and may or may not struggle with issues related to their gender identity. Intersexuality has been publicly invisible and stigmatized, and people with intersex conditions have often been isolated. They are, however, at the same risk for domestic violence and trauma as other people, as well as at an increased risk of abuse from the medical establishment, whose interventions to help may be experienced as abusive. People with intersex conditions are also vulnerable to abuse from family, peers, and intimate partners, who may view their physiological differences as reason for emotional or physical battering.

The second component of sexual identity is gender identity. Gender identity is defined as the internal experience of gender, how a person experiences his or her own sense of self as a gendered being. Gender identity is a core identity, a fundamental sense of belonging to one sex or the other. "Being a man" or "being a woman" is an essential attribute of self; almost everyone has an understanding of themselves as a man or a woman, a boy or a girl. A person's self-concept of his or her gender is called gender identity, and may or may not correspond with the person's natal sex.

Gender identity is established early in life, between the ages of two and five, and is thought to be relatively impervious to change. The gender identity of most people is congruent with their assigned sex. This means that if they are "male," they experience themselves as "men," and if they are "female," they experience themselves as "women." For other people, however, gender identity—how they experience themselves in their bodies—is discordant with their natal sex and is in direct conflict with the biological facts of their bodies. Their gender identity is experienced as dysphoric, or dystonic, to their physicality.

Transgender is an umbrella term used to describe all gender-variant people. Transsexuals, some of whom are comfortable with the term *transgender* and others who are not, commonly "cross over" and are legally reassigned as a member of the "other" sex. Other transgender people live somewhere in the middle of this continuum and identify as bigendered, androgynes, or crossdressers. Some transgender people move back and forth from one gender expression to the other, experiencing their gender as a fluid and changing part of their identity. Cross-gender behavior is often present from a very young age. It is interesting to note that many intersex people also have stable male or female gender identities, even though their sex classification may be less easy to ascertain.

Like all people, transgender and transsexual people are at risk of domestic violence and sexual assault in intimate partnerships. They are also targeted for abuse through hate crimes and are especially vulnerable to sexual harassment, bullying, and sexual abuse from prostitution. Additionally, they are rarely protected within the criminal justice system and experience employment discrimination, complicated custody battles for children, and abuse at the hands of medical and clinical providers whom they depend on for sex reassignment treatments.

The third component of human sexual identity is gender role, which is defined as the socialized aspect of gender, or how masculinity and femininity are expressed. It is through the "performance" of gender roles (consciously or unconsciously) that people communicate their sense of gender identity. The acquisition of gender roles is a social process; through clothing choices, mannerisms, grooming, voice inflection, and social interests, people enact their gender expressions.

Gender is a social construct, meaning that the attributes of gender vary from one culture to another and are somewhat arbitrarily imposed (i.e., only men can wear long hair or only women can wear dresses). Due to the influence of feminism, gender role behavior in modern Western societies has become increasingly more flexible; however, deviations from socially defined gender expectations can still result in ostracism or severe societal punishment.

Men who deviate from proscribed sex roles by wearing clothing assigned to women are often called crossdressers; women who dress in masculine clothing styles are often referred to as butch. Many young people are especially flexible about gender role expression, enjoy stretching gender behavior past its approved edges, and often refer to themselves as gender benders.

The relationship between natal sex, gender identity, and gender role is multifaceted, and although these parts of sexual identity often "match up" (males are masculine men; females are feminine women), there is a great range in human sexual expression regarding gender role behavior. Since gender role is a public expression of underlying gender identity, appearances can be informative about a person's authentic identity; however, some people who appear to have conventional gender identities may be quite conflicted internally.

People who exhibit cross-gender expression in behavior, clothing, or mannerisms may be especially vulnerable to domestic violence and all forms of abuse. Partners of people who come out as transgender may be especially rageful and feel betrayed, increasing the possibility of physical and psychological violence. Young people coming out may be vulnerable to parental physical abuse, homelessness, prostitution, and medical misinformation regarding hormone and surgical treatments. Men who crossdress or are feminine in appearance, as well as women who present as butch or masculine, may experience difficulties in employment, which will impact their finances and their home lives. Males who defy traditional gender expectations may be targeted for particularly brutal physical violence, and both men and women who crossdress may be vulnerable to sexual violence.

The term *sexual orientation* describes both sexual preference and emotional attraction, which can be directed toward members of the same sex (homosexual), the opposite sex (heterosexual), both sexes (bisexual), or neither sex (asexual). Some people experience their sexual orientations as unchanging and essential parts of their natures, and others experience them as fluid. People with homosexual desires may not engage in homosexual sexual relationships, and people who do engage in homosexual relationships may not identify as gay.

Sexual orientation is itself a complex variable including physical preference, affectional preference, fantasy, and social relationships. Sexual orientation is particularly complex in a world where certain sexual expressions (i.e., homosexuality and bisexuality) have been despised and criminally punished. Due to the societal stigma surrounding homosexual behavior, lesbian, gay, and bisexual people have to "come out" of the assumption that they are heterosexual, not only to others but also to themselves.

Sexual orientation and gender identity represent two distinct components of sexual identity, although aspects of these identities often overlap. For example, cross-gender role exploration is very common among lesbian, gay, and bisexual people. Undoubtedly, some lesbian women express a more masculine identity than many heterosexual women, and some gay men express a more feminine identity than most heterosexual men. There is also a long history in the lesbian and gay community of "camp" or "drag," where men and women crossdress for entertainment purposes, or in the case of females, for employment in traditionally male professions. Additionally, the question of "same-sex" relationships becomes confusing when discussing intimate relationships with transgender and transsexual people (i.e., if a male-to-female transsexual is in a heterosexual marriage, is that a same- or opposite-sex relationship?). Sex reassignment can change the configuration of an intimate relationship (i.e., a heterosexual relationship is now a lesbian relationship; a lesbian relationship is now a heterosexual one), and understanding how people experience their relationships requires respectful and informed dialogue.

Although the gay and lesbian liberation movement has made same-sex relationships more visible, bisexual people sometimes feel that their sexual identity is not recognized within the lesbian and gay community, especially if the bisexual person is in a heterosexual relationship. Additionally, issues of sexual orientation and gender identity are often conflated, obscuring the diversity of sexual and gender expressions available. For example, men who crossdress or are more feminine in appearance (i.e., have a crossed gender *role*) are often assumed to be gay. Although they may be gay or bisexual, crossdressers are often heterosexual in orientation; concurrently gay men are often very masculine in their gender role and identity. Assumptions are often made that in lesbian couple relationships, one partner is more traditionally masculine and the other more traditionally feminine, mirroring a heterosexual ideal. Although some lesbian couples are butch and femme identified, it is not the only way to experience female same-sex relationships. In some lesbian couples, both are feminine, in other relationships both are masculine, and in most lesbian relationships, gender role is not an important component of their coupling. To complicate matters further, in some butch/femme relationships, the butch identifies as transgender, calling into question whether the relationship is functionally a "same-sex" relationship.

Lesbian, gay, and bisexual people are at risk for all forms of intimate partner violence, as well as bias-related crimes. Due to lack of laws protecting same-sex relationships, lesbian and gay couples are at risk for abuse from the legal system in child custody cases, as well as domestic violence. In order for violence to be considered "domestic" (versus assault and battery), the jurisdiction must recognize domestic partners of the same sex. Transgender and transsexual people are at even greater risk for abuse and bias-related violence than LGB people. For the most part, they have fewer civil rights—basic rights like the right to remain married, to retain custody of a child, or to remain employed, are often nonexistent. Additionally, people who appear gender ambiguous or are in the process of sex reassignment or transition are at enormous risk for physical, emotional, sexual, and economic violence. Undeniably, LGBT people are at great risk for multiple forms of violence, battery, and assault and generally have fewer options for assistance from social service and advocacy programs, police, or judicial systems.

Domestic Violence and Sexual Assault in LGBT Families

Same-sex domestic violence has been estimated to occur as frequently as it does in heterosexual families; approximately 25–30 percent of all couples experience battery. Gathering accurate statistics on LGBT domestic violence and sexual assault, however, is complicated, in part because researchers do not adequately identify LGBT people, and also because LGBT people do not volunteer information about their sexual or gender identities. It is generally assumed that LGBT people experience most forms of violence in equal or higher numbers than their heterosexual counterparts.

Due to the nature of homophobia and transphobia within the social service community, LGBT people rarely seek out services. From heterosexist intake forms to "women-only" shelters, services are rarely developed with an awareness of the unique needs of people with sexual and gender identities that differ from the heterosexual norm. The basic treatment model extant in the domestic violence field was developed within a gendered paradigm, i.e., that men are the perpetrators and women are the victims. Although this is often the case in heterosexual couples, this model does not give treatment providers a way to recognize abuse in same-sex couples, let alone to understand the complexity of gender identities expressed by both men and women.

There are few services available for gay men who are victims of spousal abuse, and sometimes service providers have difficulty discerning which of the partners in same-sex domestic violence is actually the perpetrator, especially since batterers often present themselves as victims. Support groups often leave lesbian, gay, and bisexual survivors of violence feeling isolated; perpetrators often have no options for assistance, especially outside of a few metropolitan centers. Transgender people have even fewer options for treatment and advocacy, and training within the social service field has been unavailable. Even programs developed within larger lesbian and gay social service agencies have rarely created specialized programs or provided education focusing exclusively on the needs of transgender and transsexual people.

There are many mythologies regarding domestic violence in same-sex relationships that serve to keep LGBT people isolated within abusive relationships. It is often assumed that lesbian relationships are always based on "equality," making it hard to recognize abuse. Violence in gay male relationships is often minimized and treated as if abusive behavior between men is just "boys being boys." Abused gay men may feel ashamed to be victims of violence, since it reinforces society's stereotype that gay men are not "real men." Domestic violence impacts all LGBT people, not just those who frequent bars, are into butch/femme relationships, are prostitutes, or are involved in consensual BDSM (bondage/discipline sadomasochist) relationships. Domestic violence can take place in all LGBT relationships, regardless of race, class, economic stability, lifestyle, or sexual and gender expressions.

Domestic violence in LGBT relationships, as in heterosexual ones, can take many forms, including physical battering, sexual assault, emotional or psychological abuse such as name-calling, yelling, and blaming; it can involve stalking or isolation from friends, economic abuse, destruction of property, and threats to children or pets. When violence is present in intimate relationships, it tends to escalate over time and can become lethal.

In heterosexual relationships, men are more often the perpetrators of domestic violence because of the power imbalance between men and women. In LGBT relationships, there are other power imbalances that can generate abusive patterns. These can include differences in financial or occupation status; class, race, or ethnic differences; disability or HIV status; and variables such as age and legal relationship to children. Additionally, LGBT relationships are always impacted by societal homophobia and transphobia—both internalized shame as well as institutionalized heterosexism. For example, LGBT people are often isolated within their coupled relationships from family, friends, and coworkers. This may make them more vulnerable to being "outed" by an abusive partner, where their status as LGBT becomes the focal point of the abuse. In many states, nonbiological parents have few legal rights to their children, and risking social service or legal involvement may jeopardize their parental status, as well as make them unable to protect their children. LGBT people of color have additional concerns regarding the racism of the helpers and abusive treatment from police and the criminal justice system. Attempts to leave relationships often escalate the violence, and even when violence ends in death, the crime is often not recognized as intimate partner violence.

All forms of domestic violence, abuse, and bias-related crime leave people traumatized. Victims of violence who seek advocacy and treatment should not have to be revictimized by the social service systems developed to assist them. Sadly, this is often the case for LGBT survivors of domestic violence, sexual assault, and bias-related abuse.

Treating LGBT Trauma Survivors

LBGT people experience multiple forms of trauma as members of sexual minorities for whom basic civil rights are not necessarily a given. Coming out as gay or gender variant can be very stressful for children and youth, and creating loving adult partnerships in a homophobic and transphobic culture can be a daunting task. The experience of LGBT people has often been one of betrayal, rejection, and marginalization. When LGBT people experience violence directed at them because of their sexual orientation or gender identity or when they are the victims of violence at the hands of family members and loved ones, the result is a compounding of trauma issues.

LGBT victims of trauma often feel isolated and afraid; they struggle with shame, financial fears, homelessness, and concerns for their children. Additionally, they lack safe houses, shelters, and professional advocates who can assist them through the transition. The silence regarding LGBT domestic violence and the absence of support and treatment programs make it especially challenging for people to leave abusive relationships. Few LGBT people are aware of issues of domestic violence and abuse or services that might be able to assist them. All victims of abuse can experience symptoms of posttraumatic stress disorder (PTSD) and can struggle years later with intrusive thoughts and flashbacks of the events that impact their ability to establish another, nonabusive relationship.

Lesbian, gay, bisexual, transgender, transsexual, intersex people, and all those addressing issues of being a sexual minority come from all races, ethnicities, class backgrounds, and walks of life and seek out services for themselves and family members at different stages of their life cycles. Few domestic violence workers, rape crisis staff, social work advocates, and clinicians have had training in sexual identity development, and there is a great need for quality and professional education and training of the issues impacting LGBT people.

Increased research regarding domestic violence, sexual assault, and bias-related violence in the lives of LGBT people who are victims, as well as those who are perpetrators, is also essential. LGBT people face a large array of social and environmental challenges, including a lack of employment protection, court bias in child custody decisions, lack of quality treatment by medical professionals when seeking routine medical care, and prejudiced treatment within the educational system from kindergarten through college. LGBT children and youth need educational policies that protect them within often hostile environments. Transgender, transsexual, and intersex people need medical and psychiatric social workers educated in gender issues who will advocate for them and their families during vulnerable times and recognize potentially abusive situations. LGBT people who are also dealing with mental illness and addictions present with complex challenges that are rarely addressed within clinical settings. Clinicians and law enforcement officials need increased training in LGBT domestic violence issues, and public policies must be developed that protect LGBT families impacted by all forms of violence.

Understanding the diversity of sexual and gender identity issues that LGBT people experience is necessary for the development of comprehensive service programs. Domestic violence workers, sexual assault advocates, and all psychologists, psychiatrists, social workers, and clinicians working with survivors of trauma need to be well versed in the diverse needs of LGBT people and their families to adequately offer educated assistance and quality services during times of vulnerability and crisis.

ARLENE ISTAR LEV

See also **Batterer Intervention Programs; Batterer Typology; Gay and Bisexual Male Domestic Violence; Gay Domestic Violence, Police Attitudes and Behaviors toward; Lesbian Battering; Training Practices for Law Enforcement in Domestic Violence Cases**

References and Further Reading

Bockting, Walter, and Eli Coleman, eds. *Gender Dysphoria: Interdisciplinary Approaches in Clinical Management.* Binghamton, NY: Haworth Press, 1992.

Boenke, Mary, ed. *Transforming Families: Real Stories about Transgendered Loved Ones.* Imperial Beach, CA: Walter Trook Publishing, 2003.

Brown, Mildred L., and Chloe Ann Rounsley. *True Selves: Understanding Transsexualism for Families, Friends, Coworkers and Helping Professionals.* San Francisco: Jossey-Bass, 1996.

Burke, Phyllis. *Gender Shock: Exploding the Myths of Male and Female.* New York: Anchor Books/Doubleday, 1996.

Califia, Pat. *Sex Changes: The Politics of Transgenderism.* San Francisco: Cleis Press, 1997.

Colpinto, John. *As Nature Made Him: The Boy Who Was Raised as a Girl.* New York: HarperCollins, 1999.

Cromwell, Jason. *Transmen and FTMs: Identities, Bodies, and Sexualities.* Champaign: University of Illinois Press, 1999.

Denny, Dallas, ed. *Current Concepts in Transgender Identity.* New York: Garland, 1998.

Devor, Holly. *FTM: Female-to-Male Transsexuals in Society.* Bloomington: Indiana University Press, 1997.

Ettner, Randi, and George Brown. *Gender Loving Care: A Guide to Counseling Gender-Variant Clients.* New York: W. W. Norton and Co., 1999.

Girshick, Lori. *Woman-to-Woman Sexual Assault.* Boston: Northeastern University Press, 2002.

Island, David, and Patrick Letellier. *Men Who Beat the Men Who Love Them: Battered Gay Men and Domestic Violence.* Binghamton, NY: Haworth Press, 1991.

Kaschak, Ellyn, ed. *Intimate Betrayal: Domestic Violence in Lesbian Relationships.* Binghamton, NY: Haworth Press, 2002.

Lev, Arlene I. *Transgender Emergence: Therapeutic Guidelines for Working with Gender-Variant People and Their Families.* Binghamton, NY: Haworth Press, 2004.

———. *The Complete Lesbian and Gay Parenting Guide.* New York: Berkley/Penguin Press, 2004.

Leventhal, Beth, and Sandy Lundy, eds. *Same-Sex Domestic Violence: Strategies for Change.* Thousand Oaks, CA: Sage, 1999.

Lombardi, Emilia L., Riki Anne Wilchins, D. Priesing, and D. Malouf. 2001. "Gender Violence: Transgender Experiences with Violence and Discrimination." *Journal of Homosexuality* 42 (2001): 89–101.

Mallon, Gerald, P. *Social Service with Transgendered Youth.* Binghamton, NY: Harrington Park Press, 1999.

McClennan, Joan C., and John Gunther, eds. *A Professional Guide to Understanding Gay and Lesbian Domestic Violence: Understanding Practice Interventions.* Lewiston, NY: Edwin Mellon Press, 1999.

Renzetti, Claire M. *Violent Betrayal: Partner Abuse in Lesbian Relationships.* Thousand Oaks, CA: Sage Publications, 1992.

Renzetti, Claire, M., and Charles H. Miley, eds. *Violence in Gay and Lesbian Domestic Partnerships.* Binghamton, NY: Haworth Press, 1996.

Ristock, Janice. *No More Secrets: Violence in Lesbian Relationships.* New York: Routledge Press, 2002.

Rottnek, Matthew, ed. *Sissies and Tomboys: Gender Nonconformity and Homosexual Childhoods.* New York: NYU Press, 1999.

Scarce, Michael. *Male on Male Rape: The Hidden Toll of Stigma and Shame.* New York: Insight Books/Plenum Press, 1997.

SHAKEN BABY SYNDROME

Definition

Shaken baby syndrome (SBS) is a form of child abuse resulting in an inflicted traumatic brain injury (TBI) thought to be secondary to a sudden deceleration which results in trauma to the brain of a young child. This sudden deceleration can occur when the child is violently shaken and the brain strikes the inner surface of the skull or when there is an impact where the head strikes or is struck by an object, such as a mattress, a fist, or a wall. The injuries which characterize the syndrome include some but not always all of the following: bleeding in and around the brain, bleeding in the retina of the eye, and fractures of the ribs and ends of the long bones. When there is an impact involved, additional injuries may include bruising to the body, often to the face and scalp, and skull fractures. In severely battered children, injury to abdominal organs, pancreas, liver, or intestines may occur, as well as midshaft fractures of the long bones and fractures of the spine.

Historical Perspective

As early as 1946, John Caffey, a pioneering pediatric radiologist in New York, noted the associated injuries of long bone fractures and hemorrhages on the surface of the brain (subdural hematomas) in infants. He was puzzled by the lack of history of trauma to these infants and described the causal mechanism as "obscure." In only one case out of the six he reported did he describe the infant as being "unwanted" by the parents, raising the question of "intentional ill treatment." As aware of child abuse as doctors and researchers are today, this seems an almost unbelievable conclusion; however, it is important to note that Henry Kempe, a pediatrician in Denver, Colorado, did not publish the landmark article on battered child syndrome until 1962. This was the first time that the concept of children receiving nonaccidental injuries at the hands of their parents was actually spelled out in the medical literature.

Further work by A. Norman Gulthkelch, a British neurosurgeon, identified whiplash shaking forces as a cause of subdural hematomas. Caffey later postulated that children who are violently shaken can develop the classic SBS triad of long bone fractures, subdural hematomas, and hemorrhages in the back of the eyes (retinal hemorrhages). More recently, the term *shaken impact syndrome* has been coined, as research has demonstrated that many victims of SBS also receive blows to the head that may be identifiable only at autopsy. Tina Duhaime, a pediatric neurosurgeon working with biomedical engineers at Children's Hospital of Philadelphia, developed mechanical models to study SBS. The conclusion of that work was that shaking alone cannot generate forces high enough to cause the injuries seen in SBS. This concept remains controversial, as many pediatricians experienced in the diagnosis and management of SBS have had parents confess to violent shaking of their crying infants until the infants went limp and were quiet. This event was followed in many cases by death or evidence of serious brain injury in the infant. James Peinkofer has written a detailed and fascinating history of the gradual recognition and acceptance of SBS by the medical community.

Epidemiology

By the middle 1980s Elaine Billmire and colleagues had established child abuse as the leading cause of serious trauma and death due to head trauma in infants. The majority of inflicted traumatic brain injury occurs in children younger than two years of age, with a mean age of four to eight months at the time of injury. Male children are more often victims than females. A recent population-based study in the United States has revealed an incidence of inflicted TBI of 17 cases per 100,000 person-years in children less than two years of age. The mortality rate for SBS ranges from 12 to 30 percent of those victimized. Fewer than 15 percent of the victims of SBS will have normal developmental outcomes. The remainder have moderate to severe problems which may include seizure disorder, cerebral palsy, loss of vision, cognitive impairment, emotional volatility, and living in a permanent vegetative state.

Victims

Several characteristics of infants are proposed as reasons they are the likely victims of SBS. Prolonged crying often triggers the abuse, and young infants cry a lot, up to three hours per day. They are small enough to be picked up and shaken and thrown by an adult. There are anatomical features that make them vulnerable: Their heads are large in proportion to their body size, they have relatively weak neck muscles, and the base of the skull is flatter than that of an adult, allowing the brain to move around more in the cranial cavity in response to shaking or direct blows as the head moves back and forth in a whiplash type movement.

Perpetrators

Suzanne Starling has looked at characteristics of perpetrators of SBS. Male caretakers, including biologic fathers, stepfathers, and mothers' boyfriends were perpetrators in 68 percent of the cases she studied. The preponderance of male caretakers as perpetrators of SBS has been confirmed in other studies.

Social Factors

Poverty, young maternal age, unmarried status at the time of the birth of the child, and low educational level of the mother have all been associated with increased risk of inflicting traumatic brain injury. Multiple births, premature births, and parents active in the military are other well-known risk factors for SBS.

Pathophysiology of Injuries

There are tiny blood vessels that course from the brain to the membranes overlying the brain and to a large vein coursing through the cranial cavity. With violent shaking or with a blow, the brain undergoes whiplash and rotational forces shearing through the blood vessels and at times through the brain tissue itself. There are membranes covering the brain. There is an outer dural membrane and an arachnoid membrane which is more tightly adherent to the brain. The resulting collection of blood pooling over the brain and under the dural membrane is called a subdural hematoma. Bleeding under the arachnoid membrane is called a subarachnoid hemorrhage. The brain itself may be bruised or sheared, resulting in damage to nerve cells. Subsequent brain swelling in response to injury can cause additional damage due to loss of normal blood circulation and lack of oxygen to brain tissues. The spinal cord may also experience bruising or hemorrhage secondary to whiplash forces.

Fractures of the skull result from blows to the head. Rib fractures are thought to be most likely secondary to compression as the adult hands circle the rib cage squeezing the child during the shaking maneuver. Fractures of the ends of the long bones, called metaphyseal fractures, occur from violent flailing or jerking of the limbs while the child is being shaken. The pathophysiology of retinal hemorrhages is not known, but actual separation of the layers of the retina during shaking has been proposed as the mechanism of this finding. Seventy-five percent or more of SBS victims will have hemorrhages within the layers of the retina or in the vitreous humor (the fluid within the globe of the eye). At times the retinal layers can be split and large collections of blood may layer out. This is called retinoschisis.

It is clear that the injuries of SBS are the result of violent acts and if witnessed by a layperson could not be seen as normal handling of a child and would be recognized as dangerous to the infant.

Signs and Symptoms of Shaken Baby Syndrome

Children with mild injury due to SBS may experience increased sleepiness, fussiness, and decreased interest in feeding. With more severe injury, the child may present with vomiting, seizures, apnea (cessation of breathing), and/or an altered level of consciousness. In many cases, infants are brought to emergency facilities when families call 911 because their infants have stopped breathing or have had seizures. Mild symptoms can be confused with a viral illness, and due to parents not providing accurate histories, as well as the young ages of the infants, the correct diagnosis may be missed. Carole Jenny has studied this phenomenon and has reported that missing the diagnosis often results in further injury, medical complications, and even death in these cases. Bruising of the face or head of an infant may be a clue to head injury and should call for further medical investigation.

Evaluation and Treatment

The development of computerized axial tomography (CAT scan) and magnetic resonance imaging (MRI scan) of the head have enabled physicians to more easily diagnose TBI in young children. Additional diagnostic techniques for SBS include a full skeletal survey, which is an x-ray of all the bones in the child's body, looking for fractures. Small, hairline fractures may not be easily seen, and other studies such as imaging with a small amount of radioactive material that localizes in bone (bone scan) or repeat skeletal survey in two weeks may be helpful. Once fractures are healing, they may be more visible on an x-ray. An eye exam by an eye specialist after dilation of the pupils to look for retinal hemorrhages is essential in a suspected SBS case. Additional laboratory testing is often necessary because of the life-threatening nature of the injuries and in order to eliminate other possible causes of the clinical findings in the child. If a spinal tap is performed to look for infection, bloody spinal fluid will be found if a subarachnoid hemorrhage is present. In cases of subdural hematoma, the baby may be anemic from loss of blood into the subdural space. Both bloody spinal fluid and anemia can be clues which help the physician establish a correct diagnosis of SBS.

A detailed discussion of treatment is beyond the scope of this article, but each injury to the brain, eyes, skin, and skeleton is managed individually. In cases where SBS is suspected, appropriate reporting to the local department of social services and law enforcement is mandated by law. Willingness of the doctor to testify in both juvenile and criminal courts is an important part of the management of SBS. It will be the decision of social services and the courts to determine whether the child has been abused and to ensure a safe environment after the child's discharge from the hospital. Law enforcement, district attorneys, and criminal courts are responsible for determining who the perpetrator is in an SBS case and what the punishment will be if there is a criminal prosecution and conviction.

Victims of SBS will need very careful follow-up for medical and developmental assessments. Appropriate services need to be provided to enable the child to reach full potential after injury.

Cost

The financial cost of SBS has been difficult to determine. Several research studies have shown that children with inflicted traumatic brain injury who survive have longer hospital stays and poorer outcomes than victims of accidental traumatic brain injury. In 1997, Jose Irazuzta and colleagues estimated charges for inflicted traumatic brain injury at an average of $35,641 per case seen in a pediatric intensive care unit. However, children left with severe disabilities may incur millions of dollars in medical costs over their lifetimes, and that cost is often borne by public programs instead of private insurance. These severe disabilities and accompanying financial costs, as well as loss of life, make attempts at prevention of SBS very desirable.

Prevention

SBS prevention programs have been established in many communities. The idea behind these efforts is that if caretakers have knowledge of how dangerous it is to shake a baby, they would not do it, even in anger. Other experts working in the field believe that adults who shake infants are so angry and out of control that educational efforts may not be successful in many cases. There are other prevention efforts directed toward educating parents about how to understand and manage crying in a young infant, since crying is often a trigger of the shaking. In general, providing support to young families, particularly through home visitation by nurses, has been successful in preventing all types of child abuse.

SARA H. SINAL

See also **Assessing Risk in Domestic Violence Cases; Child Neglect; Mothers Who Kill; Munchausen by Proxy Syndrome**

References and Further Reading

Alexander, R. C., C. J. Levitt, and W. L. Smith. "Abusive Head Trauma." In *Child Abuse Medical Diagnosis and Management,* edited by Robert M. Reece and Stephen Ludwig. Philadelphia: Lippincott, Williams, and Wilkins, 2001, pp. 47–80.

Billmire, M. E., and P. A. Myers. "Serious Head Injury in the Infant: Accident or Abuse?" *Pediatrics* 75, no. 2 (1985): 340–342.

Caffey, J. "Multiple Fractures in the Long Bones of Infants Suffering from Chronic Subdural Hematoma." *American Journal of Roentgenology* 56, no. 2 (1946): 163–173.

———. "The Whiplash–Shaken Infant Syndrome: Manual Shaking of the Extremities with Whiplash-Induced Intracranial and Intraocular Bleeding, Linked with Permanent Brain Damage and Mental Retardation." *Pediatrics* 54, no. 4 (1974): 396–403.

Canadian Paediatrics Society et al. "Joint Statement on Shaken Baby Syndrome." *Paediatrics and Child Health* 6, no. 9 (2001): 663–667.

Dias, M. S., K. Smith, K. deGuehery, et al. "Preventing Abusive Head Trauma among Infants and Young Children: A Hospital Based, Parent Education Program." *Pediatrics* 115, no. 4 (2005): e470–e477.

Duhaime, A. C., T. A. Gennarelli, L. B. Thibault, et al. "The Shaken Baby Syndrome: A Clinical, Pathological and Biomechanical Study." *Journal of Neurosurgery* 66, no. 25 (1987): 409–415.

Gulthkelch, A. N. "Infantile Subdural Hematoma and Its Relationship to Whiplash Injuries." *British Medical Journal* 22, no. 2 (1971): 430–431.

Irazuzta, J. E., J. E. McJunkin, K. Danadian, et al. "Outcome and Costs of Child Abuse." *Child Abuse and Neglect* 21, no. 8 (1997): 751–757.

Jenny, C., K. P. Hymel, A. Ritzen, et al. "Analysis of Abusive Head Trauma." *Journal of the American Medical Association* 281, no. 7 (1999): 621–659.

Keenan, H. T., D. K. Runyan, S. W. Marshall, et al. "A Population-Based Study of Inflicted Traumatic Brain Injury in Young Children." *Journal of the American Medical Association* 290, no. 5 (2003): 621–626.

———. "A Population-Based Comparison of Clinical and Outcomes Characteristics of Young Children with Serious Inflicted and Non-Inflicted Traumatic Brain Injury." *Pediatrics* 114, no. 3 (2004): 633–639.

Kempe, C. H., F. N. Silverman, B. F. Steele, et al. "The Battered Child Syndrome." *Journal of the American Medical Association* 181, no. 1 (1962): 17–24.

Olds, D. L., J. Eckenrode, C. R. Henderson, et al. "Long-Term Effects of Home Visitation on Maternal Life Course and Child Abuse and Neglect: Fifteen-Year Follow-Up of a Randomized Trial." *Journal of the American Medical Association* 278, no. 8 (1997): 637–643.

Peinkofer, J. R. *Silenced Angels.* Westport, CT: Auburn House, 2002.

Showers, J. "Don't Shake the Baby: Effectiveness of a Prevention Program." *Child Abuse and Neglect* 16, no. 1 (1992): 11–18.

Sinal, S. H., and M. R. Ball. "Head Trauma Due to Child Abuse: Serial Computerized Tomography in Diagnosis and Management." *Southern Medical Journal* 80, no. 12 (1987): 1505–1512.

Starling, S. P., J. R. Holden, and C. Jenny. "Abusive Head Trauma: The Relationship of Perpetrators to Their Victims." *Pediatrics* 95, no. 2 (1995): 259–262.

SHELTER MOVEMENT

Historical Development

A battered woman's shelter is a temporary residence where victims of domestic violence (usually female victims) and their children who have no other recourse can escape violent living situations as well as work toward gaining other resources such as financial means, health care, child care, and social resources that can aid them in working toward a stable and independent violent-free life. Domestic violence, specifically violence against women, was not recognized as a social problem until the mid-1970s. As a result, women seeking help had few options available to them. It was this lack of resources that started the shelter movement. The battered women's/shelter movement emerged from grassroots activists involved in the anti-rape movement, which focused on eliminating male violence against women. The movement was primarily feminist and focused on the notion that many of the problems women had been taught to define as private troubles were in fact widespread social problems. As the history of the battered women's movement reveals, the shelter movement in Great Britain and the United States took similar turns at roughly the same time.

The first refuge for battered women in the movement against domestic violence was Chiswick Women's Aid, which was established, quite by accident, in Britain in 1972. A consciousness-raising group had established a community center in which women could meet and discuss pertinent issues. A woman escaping domestic violence arrived and was immediately given shelter. As news of this available refuge spread, more women started to arrive requesting shelter. Within a year the facility, which was licensed to be used only for office space, had a daily residential population of twenty women and children. Due to the fact that no one was turned away, overcrowding soon became a problem. However, it was this very fact of overcrowding that revealed the dire need to establish a permanent shelter for battered women. It was not long after that the shelter was moved to a ten-room Victorian mansion. However, again, overcrowding became a problem and the idea of expansion quickly followed.

In the United States, Women's House, which was established in 1974 in St. Paul, Minnesota, is documented as one of the first, if not the first, shelters for battered women. As in Britain, a consciousness-raising group called Women's Advocates began it in 1972 with an eye toward social change. Through the implementation of telephone service in the county legal aid office, the group came to the realization that most calls for service were received from women experiencing domestic violence. In the attempt to help these victims and their children, volunteers opened their homes as temporary shelters. By 1973, Women's Advocates had rented a one-bedroom apartment to be used as a shelter. After being evicted, Women's House was established as a five-bedroom shelter in October 1974. Within a few months, Women's House was filled to capacity. Again, expansion was imminent.

By the late 1970s it was argued that the lack of shelters to house battered women was the primary obstacle to escaping male violence. By 1977, women's groups and organizations in England and Wales had established over 114 shelters, and in the United States over 130 shelters had been established. Funding usually came from rent, Social Security, and temporary government funding. Overcrowding was the norm and staffing comprised primarily volunteers. Shelters were usually found in the most dismal areas in houses needing extensive renovations. In England and Wales, the average stay was five and a half months, and in the United States the average stay was two weeks. A major difference between the shelters established in England and Wales and in the United States was that in the United States the shelters were available primarily to only the poorest women, while in England and Wales the shelters were open to all women needing shelter. By the late 1990s, over 1,200 shelters existed in the United States, housing over 300,000 women and children. In Great Britain, over 164 shelters had been established, housing over 20,000 women and children.

Philosophical Origins

Prior to the domestic violence/shelter movement, as well as the anti-rape movement, domestic violence was seen as a private trouble. It occurred within the privacy of a man's home. He was in charge of all affairs and persons residing in his home and he had the right to chastise his wife and children. In the 1970s, feminists adopted the concern of violence against women. Domestic violence came to be understood as the domination of men over women in all spheres of a patriarchal society. In opposition to a past liberal philosophy, feminists argued that male violence against women can be explained by the gendered social structure characterized by power, domination, and hierarchy. As such, male violence against women must be defined as a social problem. Using this framework, women's groups and shelters in Great Britain organized along self-help and nonhierarchical lines encouraging group support and empowerment. Within the United States, shelters took on a more structured and hierarchical form. The type of ideology adopted by the shelter staff determines how the shelter will be organized and how it will address the problem of violence against women in general and its residents in particular.

Shelters took on varying ideological foundations. In the United States one common ideological framework guiding the operation of shelters was the radical feminist focus on the politics of the mind and the body. According to this ideology, therapy can improve the female psychology and transform women to become independent, thus making them safer within their communities. Within Great Britain, radical feminist ideologies driving the operations of shelters focused on the social and material conditions of women. Another common ideological framework guiding other shelters' operations was the liberal feminist focus on equal rights. Within the United States, liberal feminist activists focused on the Bill of Rights, fighting for a change in the law and its enforcement which would require that domestic violence be given the same serious legal consideration that other acts of violence were given. Great Britain favored a more socialist-feminist approach to the liberal feminist focus in that shelters and activists focused more on the role of the state in ensuring economic independence through state-provided housing, social, health, and welfare benefits and services. Today, regardless of the feminist politics guiding the operation of shelters, most shelters emphasize individual help as well as structural change. However, not all shelters have a feminist focus.

Shelters operating under a feminist ideology, such as the Bradley-Angle House in Portland, Oregon, have come to be known as activists' shelters. However, other types of shelters, referred to as philanthropic shelters, organizational or bureaucratic shelters, and therapeutic shelters, have been established. Philanthropic shelters, such as the House of Ruth in Maryland, established in 1977, do not have a feminist focus. Instead, they focus on providing immediate material resources for the most needy and most deserving, with no focus on social change. Though not part of the original focus, philanthropic shelters today also place focus on counseling. Organizational or bureaucratic shelters give an emphasis to the coordination of community and governmental agencies in providing already existing services to battered women; one example is Community Effort for Abused Spouses (CEASE) in Alexandra, Virginia. These shelters have been criticized for placing too much focus on organizational efficiency and not enough on the residents of the shelter, and for not giving any attention to the widespread problem of domestic violence. Therapeutic shelters, such as Rainbow Retreat in Phoenix, Arizona, and Chiswick Women's Aid in Britain, take on the medical model and focus on the emotional and psychological shortcomings of battered women. Through therapy, the professional staff of the shelter tries to aid the women in overcoming their personal problems. Again, this ideology has been criticized both for ignoring the larger social problem of domestic violence and for blaming the victim.

Financial Backing

Since their beginning, domestic violence shelters have had to struggle to retain funding. For this reason, most shelter staff tend to be volunteers, with a small number of paid staff. Furthermore, many of the volunteers are themselves previous victims of domestic violence and previous shelter residents. Most early shelters operated through resident rent, which was usually obtained through state or federal benefits, such as Social Security or welfare. Because most government funding was temporary, most shelters also relied on private funding. More stable government funding within the United States was made possible through the Community Development Block Grants dispensed through the U.S. Department of Housing and Urban Development (HUD). In 1978 HUD made it clear that shelters qualified for such grants. However, in 1982, through the reorganization of HUD, the Community Development Block Grants were given local control, thus funding allocation received less federal oversight and became more difficult to obtain. By the late 1970s, fifteen state legislatures were providing funds for shelters. Many states have increased the cost of marriage licenses and established tax credit programs in order to fund shelter operations. Additionally, fines collected from civil and criminal court cases may be used, in part, to fund shelters. However, state and federal funding is given to the operations of less than half of all shelters in the United States. By 1981 only 30 percent of the shelters in England received some government funding.

Federal funding of U.S. shelters today can be obtained primarily through the Department of Health and Human Services (HHS) and the Department of Justice (DOJ). HHS programs that help to fund domestic violence shelters in various ways include Title IV-A: Temporary Assistance to Needy Families (TANF); Title IV-E: Foster Care and Adoption Assistance Programs; Title XIX: Medicaid Program (for shelters with medical or mental health staff); the Family Violence Prevention and Services Act (which stresses collaboration between child welfare agencies and domestic violence providers); and Title XX: Social Services Block Grant. Within the DOJ, the Office for Victims of Crime (OVC) provides grants to aid shelters through the Crime Victims Fund established by the Victims of Crime Act (VOCA). VOCA formula grants, in particular, provide significant funding to domestic violence shelters. Among tribal communities, the OVC provides a discretionary grant known as Victim Assistance in Indian Country (VAIC) to aid in funding domestic violence shelters. The Office on Violence against Women under the DOJ also provides grants to assist the operations of shelters; some of these grants are: the STOP Violence against Women Formula Grants program; the STOP Violence against Indian Women Discretionary Grants programs; Grants to Encourage Arrest Policies and Enforcement of Protection Orders; and Education and Technical Assistance Grants to End Violence against Women with Disabilities. Government grants tend to stress community collaboration and the organizational or bureaucratic model for shelters. As a result, there has been greater emphasis on individual counseling and less emphasis on social change.

Government funding is highly competitive and subject to renewal. Most shelter funding, however, is not obtained from local, state, and federal grant programs. Much of the funding is obtained from local community fundraisers, donations, private foundations, and corporations. Aside from monetary grants, shelters may receive public or private contributions of goods or services. This may include materials, transportation, office space, and professional services.

Services Offered

Shelters provide many services to their residents, the most important being shelter. As mentioned above, the average stay at a shelter in the United States is two weeks, while in Great Britain it is five and a half months. Short stays at shelters fall into the emergency shelter category. However, transitional living programs, which are extended stays, aid women and their children in moving from trauma to recovery. A major concern among shelter staff is residents' use of shelters for respite or transition. Most shelters offer a variety of services that tend to be designed to empower victims, thus enabling them to break away from their abusers and live violent-free and independent lives. Most victims who turn to shelters for transitional purposes are determined to change their lives and become independent of their abusers. These victims may experience the maximum use of the services offered at shelters. However, some victims turn to shelters for respite, that is, to take a break from the physical and mental exhaustion placed on them by their abusers. In these cases victims may not intend to use the services provided by the shelter. Some have argued that perhaps the intentions of the victims should be determined in order to improve the delivery of such limited resources; in other words, save the resources for those victims who intend to actually leave their abusers. On the other hand, it should be noted that in many cases it takes a few unsuccessful attempts before an abused woman is able to successfully leave an abusive relationship. With this in mind, shelter services may serve as building blocks that work to empower the victim over time.

Services offered by many shelters include legal assistance, health care, child care, and social support. Legal services include court advocacy and support, educating the victim on the criminal justice process, and assisting with visitation and filling out forms, such as victim compensation and protection orders. Health services include medical care as well as mental health care, including individual, family, and group counseling. Child care may include day care and recreation, education, medical services, and counseling services. Social support includes a gamut of services ranging from emotional and group support to assisting with employment and welfare needs. Many services may be provided within the shelter, especially if the shelter employs medical and mental health professionals. However, many shelters work in collaboration with community social service agencies who may donate their services.

Current Problems

Current problems are twofold: (1) problems faced by shelters and (2) problems faced by shelter residents or victims requiring shelter. The primary problems confronting domestic violence shelters today are funding and staffing shortages, two problems which are intertwined. State and federal budget cuts have adversely affected shelter funding. Government budget cuts have directly hit the purses of domestic violence shelters, requiring them to look elsewhere for funding and to cut resources in the interim. Threats such as HUD's reorganization or its data collection policy for shelters, as well as the recent threat of the elimination of the Violence against Women Act (VAWA) add undue financial strains on shelters.

While most shelters do not rely primarily on government funding, these cuts affect the daily operations of shelters, including employing or retaining qualified full-time staff. The lack of funds also requires that shelters turn away needy individuals. Other problems facing shelters include cultural insensitivity by and a lack of response from criminal justice professionals, inadequate bilingual interpreters within criminal justice and social services agencies, poor public transportation (in suburban and rural communities), and increased need for legal assistance for victims, counseling for children, better technology, and more shelter space.

While most shelter residents view their experiences in a positive light, many encounter numerous problems. For those victims who are able to obtain shelter, problems include inadequate space, as well as inadequate legal, medical, social, and counseling services, and stressful time constraints. Due to funding shortages, many women and their children are turned away from shelters. Furthermore, lesbians and women of color, holding perceptions that they will not be treated fairly, are less likely to turn to shelters for help. Lesbian domestic violence victims generally report less positive experiences than heterosexual women. Lesbian victims have the added worry that because their abusers are themselves women, safety within a women's shelter may be harder to secure. So great were their worries and their needs that in 1985, Seattle founded the first support group for battered lesbians. Women of color fear that since shelters are operated predominantly by all-white staffs, they will experience cultural insensitivity from within the shelter itself. Furthermore, language barriers hinder many women from contacting a domestic violence shelter. In 1981, the first shelter for Asian women—Everywomens Shelter—was established in Los Angeles. Additionally, many shelters that are located in areas with large Hispanic populations, such as Casa de las Madres in Los Angeles, tend to stress multiculturalism and offer all services in English and Spanish.

Finally, male victims of domestic violence and their children tend to be turned away from most domestic violence shelters, most housing only women, and their children. There has been a recent media claim, though based on refutable research, that men make up 35 to 50 percent of all domestic violence victims. Additionally, the fact that VAWA grants do not apply to domestic violence shelters exclusively for male victims has been criticized. On the other hand, advocates and scholars alike argue that the focus should not be on the number of hits but on who has the power and control and who is living in fear. They argue that the historically institutional power structure between the genders has resulted in women as the most common victims of abuse and the ones left to seek shelter. This does not dispute the fact, however, that domestic violence shelters need to be established for male victims. In fact, the Montgomeryshire Family Crisis Centre provided a house that established the first exclusively male domestic violence shelter in south-west England.

Conclusion

Shelters have been greatly ignored by research as well as by the system itself. The low priority given shelters by the criminal justice system and by researchers is a result of (1) the small numbers of residents housed within these facilities, (2) the brevity of time during which domestic violence victims reside within the shelter, and (3) the complex collaboration shelters have with so many different agencies. As a result, these facilities tend to be invisible. They receive little attention and minimal funding. However, the large number of such facilities in operation today warrants further study.

The conditions and resources of shelters are far from ideal. Shelters experience financial hardships which affect their daily operations, from maintaining a trained staff to providing necessary services to victims to the upkeep of the physical conditions of their facilities. As a result, the victims seeking refuge suffer the consequences. These problems have been identified both within the United States and internationally. Furthermore, the lack of criminal justice sensitivity and responsiveness hide from public view the extent of domestic violence as a social problem and the need for shelters.

VENESSA GARCIA

See also **Battered Woman Syndrome; Cross-Cultural Perspectives on How to Deal with Batterers; Domestic Violence Courts; Human Rights, Refugee Laws, and Asylum Protection for People Fleeing Domestic Violence; Legal Issues for Battered Women; Protective and Restraining Orders; Violence against Women Act**

References and Further Reading

Dobash, R. Emerson, and Russell Dobash. *Women, Violence and Social Change.* New York: Routledge, 1992.

House of Ruth website. http://www.hruth.org (accessed September 7, 2006).

Krishnan, Satya P., Judith C. Hilbert, Keith McNeil, and Isadore Newman. "From Respite to Transition: Women's Use of Domestic Violence Shelters in Rural New Mexico." *Journal of Family Violence* 19, no. 3 (2004): 165–173.

SafeNETWORK. "Herstory of Domestic Violence: A Timeline of the Battered Women's Movement," 1999. http://www.mincava.umn.edu/documents/herstory/herstory.html#schec.

Schechter, Susan. *Women and Male Violence: The Visions and Struggles of the Battered Women's Movement.* Boston: South End Press, 1982.

Trujillo, Olga R., and Gretchen Test. "Funding the Work: Community Efforts to End Domestic Violence and Child Abuse," 2005. http://www.aphsa.org/Policy/Doc/fundingstreams.pdf.

SIBLING ABUSE

Introduction

Sibling abuse is one of the more controversial topics in the area of domestic violence. Society places a great value upon sibling relationships, as exemplified by the use of such common terms as "brotherly/sisterly love" to indicate strong attachment, love, and caring. However, several studies indicate that incidences of sibling abuse occur in more than 60 percent of families (Straus, Gelles, and Steinmetz 1980). This would make it the most common form of domestic violence. It is also one of the areas needing more research.

Many people do not want to talk about sibling abuse. Contemporary society tends to minimize it. There are a variety of reasons for this, including the fact that parents tend not to view physical aggression by one sibling toward another as abuse. Many parents and family members find excuses for such abuse. They use statements such as: "Don't worry about it, it's just normal sibling rivalry," "They were just playing doctor," "He really didn't mean to hurt his sister/brother. He loves her/him," and "They will grow out of it" (Wallace 2005).

Prior to discussing sibling abuse, several key concepts need to be defined. *Domestic violence* is any act or omission by persons who are cohabiting that results in serious injury to other members of the family/household. Clearly, violence against a sibling falls within this definition. For purposes of this essay, *sibling abuse* is defined as any form of physical, mental, or sexual abuse inflicted by one child in a family unit on another. This definition covers various types of acts that will be discussed later. Additionally in this age of blended families and second marriages, this definition does not require the siblings to be related by blood. The definition also uses the term *child.* In this case, a child is a person under the age of eighteen. While there are reported instances of one sibling being abused by another when the victim is over eighteen, this is so seldom that it is not included in this discussion. It is also clear by the definition that sibling abuse does not include abuse by an adult member of the family against a child. However, there is a situation that involves siblings and adults that is so important that it will be briefly mentioned later in this article. That situation deals with what is known as serial abuse of siblings (Alexander 1990).

Theories about Sibling Abuse

Researchers cannot accept any one theory or theories regarding the cause or dynamics of sibling abuse; however, there are several theories that have received some support for their explanations of the cause of this type of abuse (Wallace 2005). These theories include the feminist theory, the conflict theory, and the social learning theory.

The feminist theory holds that violence and abuse are methods used by some men to control their female partners. It also argues that important social institutions tolerate the use of physical violence by men against women. These concepts create and encourage a social environment for spousal abuse and other forms of domestic violence, including sibling abuse. Relative power and its abuse are important concepts in domestic violence as well as sibling abuse.

The conflict theory holds that when different interests produce conflict, aggression and violence are techniques that individuals may use to resolve these situations, especially when other alternatives fail. Conflict among siblings may be based upon jealous rivalry, especially when they are competing for parental attention and affection.

The social learning theory provides another explanation of sibling abuse. This theory is based upon the assumption that behavior is learned through imitation and reinforcement. Aggression is adopted as a response to certain situations because there are rewards instead of punishments resulting from this form of activity. If parents use aggression or physical punishment, they are providing a model for their children to imitate in their relations with each other, since a parent may be a desired role model for the perpetrator of sibling abuse.

Types of Abuse

There are different forms of sibling abuse. Physical abuse may include any actions causing injury, including striking, kicking, punching, and use of instruments such as sticks or other items. Wiehe, one of the leading authorities in this area, includes prolonged tickling as a form of abuse practiced by siblings (1997). Emotional abuse includes name calling, ridicule, degradation, increasing an existing fear, destroying a prized possession, and torturing a pet. Sexual abuse of a sibling includes sexual exploitation or sexual activities with a child under circumstances that indicate that the child's health or welfare is harmed or threatened. Some authorities argue that some acts may be simple curiosity, while others are clearly sexual abuse.

Characteristics of Sibling Abuse

There has been limited study in the area of sibling abuse. What researchers do know comes from several clinical studies. Sibling abuse occurs at a higher rate among children in families where child abuse and spousal abuse are also present. Of those families with spousal abuse or child abuse, sibling abuse is higher in families with child abuse. Although boys are more likely to engage in sibling abuse, both sexes can be perpetrators of this form of domestic violence. Sibling abuse, like other forms of domestic violence, crosses all racial and socioeconomic lines. Finally, as the siblings grow older, the abuse decreases.

Serial Abuse of Siblings

What happens when one sibling is abused and removed from the home and another sibling is left in the home where the abuse occurred? Should all children in a home where sibling abuse occurs be removed? If so, how do the authorities justify such actions? Serial abuse of siblings occurs when a perpetrator first abuses one child and then abuses another sibling. This type of abuse may include physical, emotional, or sexual abuse or a combination of various types of abuse. The most publicized cases involve an older female sibling who is sexually abused and runs away without disclosing the abuse but returns to confront the abuser when her younger sister is reaching the age at which she was first abused. There have been several television documentaries dealing with this form of sibling abuse.

The perpetrator may abuse one sibling and immediately abuse the other sibling, or he or she may wait months or even years before abusing the second sibling. Several authorities have studied serial abuse and concluded that there are significant risks to the second sibling if left in the home of the abuser (Alexander 1990).

Consequences of Sibling Abuse

The consequences of sibling abuse include both immediate and long-term effects. Sibling abuse appears to result in negative relationships with peers in preschool and elementary school. It also may affect and influence the use of violence by the victim in adulthood. The perpetrator socializes the victim to the use of violence. Thus, the victim may accept violence as a method of dealing with others in certain situations as an adult. The victim may become dependent, may not be able to leave future abusive situations, or may become a perpetrator of abuse himself.

Interventions

Whenever a child is placed at risk by a parent or caretaker, the law gives the government the right to take actions to protect that child from further injury or harm (Tower 1996). In the case of domestic violence, children may be removed from their homes by local or state agencies. If a parent or caretaker fails to protect one child from abuse by a sibling, the abused child may be removed from the home or environment that endangers him or her. In the case of abuse of one sibling by a parent or caretaker, the law is clear that the other sibling(s) may also be removed to protect them. Courts have held that a number of jurisdictions support the proposition that based upon a parent's abusive behavior, courts have the power to remove siblings from the home because other siblings are in danger of abuse and should be removed for their own safety.

What becomes more controversial is the termination of parental rights based upon the abuse of a sibling by a parent or caretaker. Contemporary American society places great importance on the rights of parents to raise their children without interference. Many states authorize the removal of children in abusive situations but require that the courts establish a reunification plan to reunite the parents and the child. Many states have adopted a two-step process: First, the courts must find a specific statutory ground or basis for termination of the parent–child relationship, and second, the court must find that such action is in the best interests of the child.

There are a number of grounds or reasons for termination of the parent–child relationship. These include the parent's failure to improve or take the necessary steps for the sibling's safe return. This failure to improve may include failure to complete mandated counseling or a number of other court requirements. If there is a long-standing pattern of abandonment or extreme parental disinterest for the abused child and/or the abusive sibling, the courts may find this sufficient for the termination of parental rights. The parent may be suffering from long-term incapacity that renders him or her incapable of caring for the abused child, the abusive sibling, or another sibling or siblings. This type of mental illness may be sufficient grounds to terminate parental rights. Prior abuse with unsuccessful agency attempts to rehabilitate the parent may also be a reason. Finally, another reason may be that the original abuse of one of the siblings was so extreme that returning the victim or his or her sibling to the home presents an unacceptable risk.

Conclusion

Sibling abuse is one of the more controversial areas of domestic violence. It is also one of the more common forms of domestic violence. Despite this commonality, there is very little research being conducted into the dynamics of sibling abuse. Additionally, parents tend to minimize such conduct when they become aware of it. While no one theory can explain sibling abuse, various authorities have embraced the explanations offered by feminist theory, conflict theory, and social learning theory as the most popular frameworks in this area of domestic violence. Serial abuse of siblings involves the perpetrator abusing one sibling and then another. Sibling abuse, like all forms of domestic violence, has immediate and long-term consequences to its victims. There are a number of interventions in cases of sibling abuse, including removal of the sibling(s) from the home and even, in extreme cases, termination of the parent–child relationship.

HARVEY WALLACE

See also **Animal Abuse: The Link to Family Violence; Bullying and the Family; Intergenerational Transfer of Intimate Partner Violence; Parricide; Ritual Abuse–Torture in Families; Social Learning Theory and Family Violence**

References and Further Reading

Alexander, Randell. "Serial Abuse in Children Who Are Shaken." *American Journal of Disabled Children* 144 (January 1990): 58.

Straus, Murray, Richard Gelles, and Suzanne Steinmetz. *Behind Closed Doors: Violence in the American Family.* New York: Doubleday, 1980.

Tower, Cynthia. *Understanding Child Abuse and Neglect,* 3rd ed. Boston: Allyn & Bacon, 1996.

Wallace, Harvey. *Family Violence: Legal, Medical, and Social Perspectives,* 4th ed. Boston: Allyn & Bacon, 2005.

Wiehe, Vernon R. *Sibling Abuse: Hidden Physical, Emotional, and Sexual Trauma,* 2nd ed. Thousand Oaks, CA: Sage, 1997.

SOCIAL CLASS AND DOMESTIC VIOLENCE

The highly personal nature of domestic violence frequently prevents accurate assessment of the phenomenon. However, despite difficulties in ascertaining precise measurement of its occurrence, a plethora of research has been conducted examining correlates of reported domestic assaults. Among the identified correlates of this particular type of violence, which often mirrors the established correlates of crime in general, are gender, race, and social class. Gender remains perhaps the most salient factor influencing both victimization and perpetration, with women as likely victims and men as likely perpetrators. Race and social class remain a closely interwoven social reality and are often discussed concurrently. This essay documents recent research focusing on the relationship between social class and domestic violence with attention to the related link between race and domestic assault.

Generally, it is argued that domestic violence is not class specific, with victimization occurring in all corners of society. Although victimization can certainly occur anywhere, it is not randomly distributed throughout society. Instead, the extant literature base situates prevalence of domestic assault in lower-class families and communities. Isolated studies have reported higher incidence among middle- and upper-class families (see, for example, Davidson 1978), although the vast majority of empirical evidence overwhelmingly suggests a strong, significant relationship between domestic assault and lower socioeconomic status. Race is also closely linked to victimization for women, with minority groups significantly more likely to experience victimization in terms of physical assault, rape, and stalking. However, racial and ethnic differences tend to disappear after controlling for socioeconomic status (i.e., class).

As noted above, it is difficult to separate race and class realities in sociological research. Consequently, the bulk of research simultaneously reports findings pertaining to the intersection of the two. For example, results from a 1989 study examining the incidence of marital violence within the black community found that social class was among the most salient predictors of domestic assault (Lockhart and White 1989). Using a sample of 155 married or cohabiting black women living in a major southeastern metropolitan city in the United States, the authors found that lower-class women experienced both more general conflicts and more conflicts leading to violence in their relationships than did their middle- and upper-class counterparts. Greater incidence of violence wherein men were victims was related to interaction between class and the extent of discord present in the relationship. Interestingly, the proportion of women who engaged in physical violence, as well as its frequency, was equal to or exceeded that used by the men against them. Relationship discord was also found to be a significant predictor of domestic violence, even after controlling for social class.

Rennison and Planty (2003) analyzed the relationship between race of victim and intimate partner violence utilizing data from the National Crime Victimization Survey. Although univariate analyses typically indicate a significant relationship between race and domestic violence (as was the case in this study), further multivariate assessment revealed that racial differences disappeared after controlling for annual household income. Findings from this research again illustrate the importance of class in understanding the relationship between race and victimization.

Several studies have chosen to investigate the effects of socioeconomic characteristics along with other mitigating individual and environmental features, including substance abuse, mental illness, and community disorganization. Field and Caetano (2004), for instance, investigated ethnic differences in domestic violence as they related to socioeconomic status and alcohol use. Findings indicated that although ethnic minorities reported higher rates of domestic violence, differences were reduced after controlling for social class and alcohol use. Black couples, however, were found to be at greater risk of domestic violence as compared with whites and Hispanics even after controlling for risk factors. Not surprisingly, alcohol use tends to exacerbate conflictual situations, which may then lead to increased violence.

Environmental or structural variables have long been associated with higher incidence of virtually all types of crime and delinquency (Bursik 1988; Bursik and Grasmick 1993; Shaw and McKay 1942), and domestic violence is no exception. In a multilevel examination of partner violence, Van Wyk, Benson, and Fox (2003) attempted to identify the neighborhood-, partner-, and individual-level factors that were associated with domestic assault. Using data from the National Survey of Families and Households and the U.S. Census, their findings suggest that neighborhood effects interact with partner- and individual-level characteristics to explain male-to-female violence. Additionally, couples experiencing dissatisfaction with their finances and those with relatively short unions were more likely to experience violence regardless of neighborhood. Another macro-level study examining the relationship between social disorganization and domestic violence rates similarly found that neighborhoods with greater resource deprivation had significantly higher rates of violence between intimates (Miles-Doan 1998).

More recently, Benson, Wooldredge, and Thistlethwaite (2004) investigated racial differences related to participation in domestic violence. Several significant findings were generated, including the importance of community in predicting violence between intimates. Specifically, rates of domestic violence for both blacks and whites varied consistently by community type, and the correlation between race and violence was significantly reduced or disappeared altogether when ecological contexts were controlled. Additionally, individual-level risk factors appeared to operate similarly for both races.

Although most empirical evidence identifies class as an important predictor of domestic violence, these results are not without caveat. The true nature and extent of crime in contemporary society is unknown, and domestic violence is among the most underreported crimes. Hence, determinations about the scope of domestic violence remain questionable. Given the tendency to underreport this particular crime, researchers also remain unsure about the validity of the data they do have. Specifically, it is possible that the reporting of domestic violence itself varies by social class, presenting an inaccurate picture of the relationship between victimization and socioeconomic status. Only through continued research incorporating mixed-methodological approaches can the actual status of domestic violence be ascertained.

HOLLY E. VENTURA and J. MITCHELL MILLER

See also **Batterer Typology; Education as a Risk Factor in Domestic Violence; Victim-Blaming Theory**

References and Further Reading

Benson, M., J. Wooldredge, and A. Thistlethwaite. "The Correlation between Race and Domestic Violence Is Confounded with Community Context." *Social Problems* 51 (2004): 326–342.

Bursik, R. J. "Social Disorganization and Theories of Crime and Delinquency." *Criminology* 26 (1988): 519–551.

Bursik, R. J., and H. G. Grasmick. *Neighborhoods and Crime: The Dimensions of Effective Community Control.* New York: Lexington, 1983.

Davidson, T. *Conjugal Crime: Understanding and Changing the Wifebeating Pattern.* New York: Hawthorne Books, 1978.

Field, C., and R. Caetano. "Ethnic Differences in Intimate Partner Violence in the US General Population: The Role of Alcohol Use and Socioeconomic Status." *Trauma, Violence, and Abuse* 5, no. 4 (2004): 303–317.

Lockhart, L., and B. W. White. "Understanding Marital Violence in the Black Community." *Journal of Interpersonal Violence* 4, no. 4 (1989): 421–436.

Miles-Doan, R. "Violence between Spouses and Intimates: Does Neighborhood Context Matter?" *Social Forces* 77 (1998): 623–646.

Rennison, C., and M. Planty. "Nonlethal Intimate Partner Violence: Examining Race, Gender, and Income Patterns." *Violence and Victims* 18, no. 4 (2003): 433–443.

Shaw, C. R., and H. D. McKay. *Juvenile Delinquency and Urban Areas.* Chicago: University of Chicago Press, 1942.

Tjaden, P., and N. Thoennes. *Full Report of the Prevalence, Incidence, and Consequences of Violence against Women.* Washington, DC: National Institute of Justice, 2000.

Van Wyk, J., M. Benson, and G. Fox. "Detangling Individual-, Partner-, and Community-Level Correlates of Partner Violence." *Crime and Delinquency* 49, no. 3 (2003): 412–438.

SOCIAL, ECONOMIC, AND PSYCHOLOGICAL COSTS OF VIOLENCE

The topic of domestic violence and its associated social, economic, and psychological costs may elicit strong reactions from the public as well as from individuals involved with domestic violence scholarship and professional and social services. Domestic violence knows no boundaries in relation to class, race, gender, or age. It is generally accepted as the most frequent form of violence in the United States and is considered a major social problem. Domestic violence is the leading cause of injury and death to American women. It is estimated that over 4 million American women experience a serious assault by their partners during an average year. Nearly one in three adult women experiences at least one physical assault by a partner during adulthood. Half of the men who frequently assault their wives also frequently abuse their children. Each year an estimated 3.3 million children are exposed to domestic violence and many domestic homicide victims are children. The main purpose for discussing the "costs" of domestic violence is to more clearly show the importance of the phenomenon to everyone in society.

The costs of domestic violence can be most easily broken down into the two main categories of "direct" costs and "indirect" costs. For instance, one study showed that the health-related costs of rape, physical assault, stalking, and homicide committed by intimate partners exceeded $5.8 billion each year. Of that amount, nearly $4.1 billion was for direct medical and mental health care services, and nearly $1.8 billion was for the indirect costs of lost productivity or wages. Although the categories overlap to some degree, the direct costs of domestic violence are usually measured rather superficially in terms of dollars lost, injuries suffered, and lives taken. Direct costs could include direct expenses such as medical bills, legal fees, costs of incarceration, security measures, decreasing property values, sick leave taken, and employee turnover. The majority of direct costs are often borne by the government. The federal government typically bears the costs of income support, housing, and medical care. State governments typically cover the costs for court and legal services, child welfare, and family support programs. Businesses and employers may bear the direct costs of absenteeism, staff turnover, lost productivity, and employer liability.

Indirect costs are also prevalent and important but typically are even more difficult to measure. Indirect costs pertain to the actual human costs of domestic violence, which typically cannot be measured in dollars and cents. Mental and emotional trauma are very real consequences of domestic violence for many victims, but they tend not to be measured or reported in official government studies. The intangible costs of pain and suffering are also not usually measured. Indirect costs include but are not limited to pain and suffering, lost productivity, loss of freedom, fear, lost opportunity, reduced quality of life, replacement of lost or damaged property, vicarious trauma, and compassion fatigue. The majority of indirect costs are borne by female victims of domestic violence. Overall, the largest cost element of domestic violence is reduced quality of life and its related fear, pain, and suffering. Thus it is the direct victims who bear the greatest share of the costs of domestic violence.

Determining the cost of domestic violence is further complicated by the fact that most crime and economic statistics are often not broken down by crime type; and even when they are, domestic violence is generally overlooked. Research on domestic violence is further complicated by the fact that this term has a range of definitions. Domestic violence, by its barest definition, is violence within the domestic sphere of a home. In a broader sense, domestic violence could include any act of physical or sexual violence, threats or intimidation, emotional or social abuse, or willful neglect or economic deprivation where the victim-to-offender relationship is based on current or former marriage, family ties, or romantic relationship. Under this latter definition, domestic violence could take the form of child abuse, elder abuse, spousal abuse, or dating violence. Domestic violence harms more than its direct victim. It also harms the abuser and any children involved or witnessing the abuse, as well as the health and well-being of members of the community. In essence, domestic violence has a high price socially, economically, and psychologically.

Social Costs

Domestic violence financially impacts more than the immediate victim. As taxpayers, donors to private service providers, or consumers of government programs and services, everyone is impacted by the financial costs of domestic violence. Record highs in probation and parole caseloads and increasing jail and prison inmate populations have made a substantial impact on American society. Additionally, the necessity of investing resources in the criminal justice system to combat domestic violence and deal with its perpetrators means that there are fewer resources available for other socially valued uses such as education and social service programs, thus lowering in yet another way the quality of life for many.

From a broad perspective, even the time that a batterer invests in committing a crime or in serving a sentence represents a cost to society, since that batterer could perhaps have engaged in a legitimate and/or revenue-producing activity instead. Perhaps the greatest cost to society at large is primarily moral in nature, as the continuation of domestic violence forces many citizens to deal with a type of domestic terrorism within their own homes in communities across America. Even those who have not been directly victimized may suffer from a form of psychological victimization known as "fear of crime." This fear is most pronounced in women and may result in less social interaction and faith in society, which may in turn start to destroy the social order of the community and perhaps even the nation. This increased fear and suspicion of interacting with others, especially others who are "different," may reinforce existing racial and ethnic prejudices, thus lessening the rewards and knowledge offered by cultural diversity and perhaps even triggering further domestic violence and social isolation. Increased fear among citizens may not only create barriers and distrust among individuals but also weaken public belief in the legitimacy of the government, as individuals become dissatisfied with the criminal justice system's ability to "protect and serve."

Even by conservative estimates, each year over one million women suffer nonfatal victimization by an intimate. By other estimates, like those provided by the American Psychological Association, annually over four million American women experience a serious assault by a partner. According to findings from the Study of Injured Victims of Violence, approximately one and a half million people are treated each year for nonfatal injuries sustained in violence. A higher percentage of women than men are treated for injuries inflicted by an intimate.

On average 1.7 million violent victimizations happen each year to persons who are at work or on duty. Additionally, about 900 work-related homicides happen each year. Police officers tend to experience the highest rates of workplace violence. Whites have higher rates of workplace victimization than minorities, which contrasts with the overall violent crime trends. About 3 percent of workplace victimizations are committed by husbands or boyfriends.

Homes and businesses can be forced to carry the cost of cyber victimization. Computer viruses as well as vandalism and sabotage meant to harm or scare a domestic violence victim can easily create losses in the millions for many businesses, whereas online stalking or harassment and intense monitoring of what one has done on the computer are often concerns for individual victims of domestic violence.

Economic Costs

Evidence suggests that it is the public sector of society in general which bears much of the economic burden of domestic violence. For instance, many of the medical costs of treating domestic violence injuries are either directly paid by public financing or not paid at all. If the medical costs are not paid, they are absorbed by the government and society in the form of uncompensated care financing, which results in overall higher payment rates for all citizens. Financing that is used to cover these costs of violence results in less money being available for direct public expenditures such as education, Social Security, housing, and recreation; this in turn may have negative effects on investment and economic growth. Few if any studies examine the costs to faith-based communities as well as to government.

Many studies have shown that preventive measures to stop domestic violence cost less than the money that such measures save. For instance, the 1994 Violence against Women Act has resulted in an estimated net benefit of $16.4 billion, including $14.8 billion in averted victims' costs. Other studies have shown that providing shelters for victims of domestic violence results in a benefit-to-cost ratio of between 6.8 and 18.4. Similarly, the cost of a program to prevent child abuse through counseling equaled 5 percent of the cost of child abuse itself.

Some interventions with juvenile offenders have resulted in economic benefits that were more than thirty times greater than the corresponding costs.

While it might theoretically be possible to determine the amount of funding that communities and programs allocated to domestic violence across the United States, this research has not yet been done as of this writing. Some costs of domestic violence can be inferred by examining the overall economic costs of crime. Crime victims lose over $17 billion in direct costs each year. Direct costs include property loss or damage, cash losses, medical expenses, and income lost because of injury or activities related to the crime. Lost property is typically not recovered, and medical expenses typically exceed $250. Medical expenses may continue to accumulate for months or even years after victimization, and domestic violence victims are typically revictimized.

About one out of every six victims who were injured survives serious injuries from gunshot or knife wounds, broken bones, teeth knocked out, or injuries requiring hospital stays of two days or more. Injuries caused by crime account for more than 700,000 days of hospitalization each year. Although not yet studied, long-term health problems could result from serious as well as minor injuries. Many women who suffer serious injuries were assaulted by a significant other. Despite a lack of standardized research on the economic costs of domestic violence, it is important to examine the psychological costs of domestic violence as well.

Psychological Costs

It is difficult to assign "costs" to the more qualitative aspects of victimization, but crime has real emotional and behavioral consequences for domestic violence victims as well as their family, friends, and communities. Emotional reactions can range from slight to extreme in intensity and can include multiple emotions such as fear, sadness, guilt, alienation, and rage. These emotions can lead to a wide range of behavioral consequences, from difficulty sleeping and lost work productivity to avoiding public places, withdrawing from relationships, and even suicide.

Women who have been exposed to domestic violence have a greater risk of developing a range of health problems, including stress, anxiety, depression, eating disorders, sleeping disorders, loss of self-esteem, pain syndromes, phobias, and somatic and medical symptoms. In addition to poor health overall, victims are more likely to engage in drug or alcohol use and other activities that are harmful to their physical and psychological health. These costs are often magnified by the difficulties in accessing health services. It is important to note that the more severe the abuse, the greater its impact on the victim's health; furthermore, the impact over time of different types and multiple episodes of abuse appears to be cumulative. Typically, the mental health effects persist long after the violent episode(s).

The effect of domestic violence on children can be severe. It is estimated that between 3.3 and 10 million children witness domestic violence annually. Besides witnessing domestic violence, roughly half the children themselves may be the targets of physical, sexual, or verbal abuse by the perpetrator. Children's psychological problems precipitated by domestic violence may include bed-wetting, nightmares, withdrawal, loss of self-confidence, lack of self-esteem, tantrums, and emotional outbursts. In addition to these immediate costs, living with domestic violence may affect children's school performance and emotional development. The long-term costs may include diminished educational and employment opportunities, as well as increased likelihood of future criminal behavior.

Studies have shown that domestic violence has severe and persistent effects on the victim's physical and mental health and even carries with it the enormous cost of disability and premature death. When psychological symptoms are severe, a syndrome such as post-traumatic stress disorder (PTSD) or battered woman syndrome might be identified. In PTSD, victims may reexperience the traumatic event through intrusive thoughts, nightmares, or flashbacks. There may also be symptoms of emotional numbing, leading to diminished interest in activities and increased physiological arousal, causing difficulty in sleeping or concentrating. When one suffers from battered woman syndrome, one's thoughts about safety, expectations of future violence, and views of oneself may be negatively transformed. These syndromes illustrate that the psychological costs of victimization may last for years after the crime and that victimization may even alter one's perception of safety and the availability of alternatives.

Psychological harm comes not only at the hands of the batterer, but from the way the criminal justice system often neglects victims' needs or, worse yet, tends to blame them for their own victimization. The response of the criminal justice system may have a negative impact on the fresh emotional problems of victims; this is often referred to as being "revictimized." People such as family members and friends who are emotionally close to victims of domestic violence may also experience emotional problems and costs. Often these indirect victims experience difficulties and symptoms such as anger and fear, which are quite similar to the actual victim's reactions. The development of psychological problems in the indirect victim may inadvertently worsen the symptoms of the direct victim. For instance, if a child reacts with guilt and anger instead of love toward the mother when she tries to leave the batterer, this reaction may influence the woman to stay in the situation. In the case of the death of a domestic violence victim, close family and friends often feel anger and vengefulness in addition to the feelings of normal bereavement. Also, necessary extensive contact with the criminal justice system may interfere, sometimes severely, with the normal reorganizations and healing processes taking place.

Working with traumatized people can have long-term impacts like "burnout," where the worker becomes frustrated with her environment, or "compassion fatigue," where the worker grows weary from the nature of the work. There may be "vicarious trauma," where the worker's views of the world change and there is a shift in her belief system which may trigger behavioral and social changes. This outcome is sometimes referred to as secondary trauma disorder or secondary PTSD. Thus, there can be an emotional cost in working with victims of domestic violence.

Domestic violence deprives victims as well as family members, friends, the community, and even the broader society of their sense of emotional well-being. Although the causes of domestic violence are complex, various factors in social, economic, and cultural environments play a significant part. Addressing these factors, including the unequal distribution of power and resources between men and women and among various racial groups, can help to lessen the occurrence and consequences of domestic violence. Sharing information about domestic violence will be important to further prevention efforts and advocacy for policy reform and program development. When it comes to program development, studies suggest that domestic violence warrants attention at least equal to that of many other well-established diseases and risk factors for health

problems such as high blood pressure, high cholesterol, and obesity. Further research to understand domestic violence and to assess the effectiveness of various prevention strategies will be important.

At this point it is impossible to accurately gauge the cost of domestic violence, but it is expensive. How can one measure the costs of damaged lives and generations? Conservative estimates are that child abuse alone costs the United States $94 billion annually, or 1 percent of the gross domestic product. In terms of a dollar value, it is estimated that domestic violence costs range from $1.7 billion to over $300 billion annually, depending on which variables are considered. Given the importance and difficult nature of this topic, there is a clear need for systematic future research into the costs of domestic violence. Future research should follow rigorous guidelines, include both direct and indirect costs, and ideally be comparable across regions and countries.

WENDELIN HUME

See also **Battered Woman Syndrome; Battered Woman Syndrome as a Legal Defense in Cases of Spousal Homicide; Children Witnessing Parental Violence; Community Response to Domestic Violence; Cycle of Violence; Elder Abuse, Consequences of; Intimate Partner Homicide; Legal Issues for Battered Women; Workplace, Domestic Violence in**

References and Further Reading

Gosselin, Denise Kindschi. *Heavy Hands: An Introduction to the Crimes of Family Violence,* 2nd ed. Upper Saddle River, NJ: Prentice Hall, 2003.

Jackson, Nicky, and Gisele Oates. *Violence in Intimate Relationships: Examining Sociological and Psychological Issues.* Boston: Butterworth-Heinemann, 1998.

Karmen, Andrew. *Crime Victims: An Introduction to Victimology.* Belmont, CA: Wadsworth/Thomson Learning, 2004.

Straus, Murray A., and Richard J. Gelles. *Physical Violence in American Families.* New Brunswick, NJ: Transaction Publishers 1990.

Walker, Samuel, Cassia Spohn, and Miriam DeLone. *The Color of Justice: Race, Ethnicity, and Crime in America,* 3rd ed. Belmont, CA: Wadsworth/Thompson Learning, 2004.

SOCIAL LEARNING THEORY AND FAMILY VIOLENCE

Social learning theory is one of the most popular explanatory perspectives in the marital violence literature. Often conceptualized as the "cycle of violence" or "intergenerational transmission theory" when applied to the family, the theory states that people model behavior that they have been exposed to as children. Violence is learned through role models provided by the family (parents, siblings, relatives, and boyfriends/girlfriends), either directly or indirectly (i.e., witnessing violence), is reinforced in childhood, and continues in adulthood as a coping response to stress or as a method of conflict resolution (Bandura 1973).

During childhood and adolescence, observations of how parents and significant others behave in intimate relationships provide an initial learning of behavioral alternatives which are "appropriate" for these relationships. Children infer rules or principles through repeated exposure to a particular style of parenting. If the family of origin handled stresses and frustrations with anger and aggression, the child who has grown up in such an environment is at greater risk for exhibiting those same behaviors, witnessed or experienced, as an adult. Gelles (1972) states that "not only does the family expose individuals to violence and techniques of violence, the family teaches approval for the use of violence." Children learn that violence is acceptable within the home and is an effective method for solving problems or changing the behavior of others.

The primary hypothesis for the intergenerational cycle of violence is that violent and abusive adults learned this behavior as a result of being the victims of or witnesses of aggressive and abusive behavior as children. If children are abused by their parents, they may internalize beliefs and patterns of behaviors that lead them to abuse their own children; if children observe parents who hit each other, they may develop a greater propensity toward abusing their own spouses. Transmission of violent behavior occurs through processes of modeling, failure to learn appropriate ways to manage conflict, and reinforcement for violent behavior. Normal coping mechanisms may not be learned or may become impaired, leading to violence as the ultimate resource.

Research Supporting the Intergenerational "Cycle of Violence" Theory

There are numerous studies that support the cycle of violence theory, showing that the experience of violence in childhood is associated with general patterns of violent behavior (Widom 1989), as well as later violence in one's intimate relationships (Browne 1980; Burgess, Hartman, and McCormack 1987; Fagan, Stewart, and Hansen 1983; Gelles 1972; McCord 1988; Roy 1982; Steinmetz 1977; Straus, Gelles, and Steinmetz 1980; Walker 1984). Early support for the cycle of violence was buttressed by two reviews of the literature. A review of findings from six studies (Okun 1986) indicated that 23 to 40 percent of battered women witnessed violence between their parents, while in four studies 10 to 33 percent of battered women were also abused as children. Hotaling and Sugarman (1986) reviewed fifty-two case comparison studies of marital violence, finding that witnessing violence between parents was a consistent risk marker for spouse abuse among both males and females. Although not a consistent risk marker, the majority of studies also found an association between being a victim of childhood violence and spouse abuse.

Much of the early work on intergenerational transmission was derived from small cross-sectional studies of distinctive populations, such as clinical populations and children of battered women in shelters. Appropriate control group comparisons were often missing, making it difficult to establish cause and effect. Results from these studies have generally supported the association between witnessing or experiencing violence in childhood with later negative outcomes, such as partner violence. The linkage is somewhat less pronounced in non-referred, community samples (Margolin 1998; Stith et al. 2000). This may be a result of the less severe nature of most violence that occurs or a result of better controls. Women in shelters report an average of sixty-five to sixty-eight assaults per year, which is about eleven times greater than the average of six assaults per year reported by abused women in the National Family Violence Survey (Straus 1990a). Other limitations of the early studies included the use of retrospective data. Retrospective assessments rely on long recall periods, with the possibility of selective recall biases and memory reconstruction problems. Discrepant findings using retrospective versus prospective designs have been documented. For instance, a study that examined whether child-hood victimization increased the risk for drug abuse in young adulthood found increased risk with retro-spective self-reports, but no risk when prospective data was used (Widom, Weiler, and Cottler 1999). A better approach for studying the linkage between early exposure to violence and later partner violence is to utilize longitudinal studies.

Overcoming the issues of retrospection and lack of comparison groups, White and Widom (2003) used a prospective study to trace long-term out-comes for men and women with official records of child abuse and/or neglect prior to age twelve, and a control group of nonabused matched cases. Both groups (n = 939) were interviewed twenty years later to discover that the abused and neglected children were slightly more likely than controls to *ever* hit their partners (53 vs. 41 percent). This difference held for both males and females.

Another twenty-year prospective study using a randomly selected sample of youth and their mothers residing in two upstate New York counties in 1975 followed 543 children to test the indepen-dent effects of parenting, exposure to domestic violence between parents, maltreatment, adolescent disruptive behavior disorders, and emerging adult substance abuse disorders on the risk of violence to and from an adult partner (Ehrensaft et al. 2003). Consistent with social learning theory, ob-serving violence between parents, childhood power-assertive punishment by the mother, and adolescent conduct disorder (which appeared to mediate the effects of childhood physical abuse) were predictors of later perpetration of partner violence. Observing parental violence also predicted later victimization by a partner. Childhood physical abuse significantly predicted injury by a partner, as well as injury to a partner.

Support for the theory that direct or indirect (i.e., witnessing) childhood exposure to parental violence is related to engaging in later partner vio-lence is also supported by nationally representative samples, such as the 1975 and 1985 National Family Violence Surveys (Straus 1990b; Straus et al. 1980). Relying on retrospective data, Straus found that males and females who endured more (i.e., higher frequency) ordinary physical punishment as chil-dren had higher rates of both ordinary and severe marital violence as adults. They also reported higher rates of ordinary physical punishment and child abuse toward their own children. Men and women who had witnessed parents hit each other were three times more likely to abuse their own partners compared with those who had not. Respondents with the experience of being both abused as children and witnessing parental vio-lence—the "double whammy"—had a one in three chance of encountering marital violence in the study year, double the overall rate for annual marital violence. Subsequent analyses confirmed that dually exposed, compared with singly exposed, women had significantly increased risk for adult perpetration of child abuse and for partner abuse perpetration and victimization. Similarly, men ex-posed to both forms, rather than one form, of family-of-origin violence had double the risk of partner abuse victimization. Men's risk for perpe-tration of child abuse or partner abuse was elevated by exposure to any form of family-of-origin vio-lence but was not increased by exposure to multiple forms of family-of-origin violence.

As evidence mounted in support of the cycle of violence theory, a new criticism arose that studies failed to separate witnessing violence from experi-encing violence. These two types of exposure to violence may differentially affect the learning of marital violence. Kalmuss (1984) explored the rela-tionship between childhood family aggression (by those children who directly experienced violence and those who only witnessed it in their families) and severe marital aggression in the next genera-tion, using data from 2,143 adults in the 1975 National Family Violence Survey. In this retro-spective study, she found that severe marital ag-gression was more likely when respondents, males and females, observed hitting between their parents than when they were hit as teens by their parents, although both forms of first-generation violence resulted in increased levels of second-generation marital aggression. Exposure to both types of childhood aggression led to a dramatic increase in the probability of marital aggression.

Recent support for the intergenerational cycle of violence theory comes from meta-analysis, which is a systematic review of the relevant literature allow-ing for statistical aggregation of results that can be reported as an average effect size. A meta-analysis of thirty-nine studies that examined the relationship between witnessing or experiencing family violence in childhood and receiving or perpetrating violence in an adult heterosexual cohabiting or marital relationship demonstrated that growing up in an abusive family is positively related to becoming involved in a violent marital relationship (Stith et al. 2000). The relationship is weak to moderate, with r values ranging from .08 to .35, depending upon the relationship examined.

Intergenerational Transmission and Gender

Although boys and girls rely on both parents as a relevant source of information in constructing their own beliefs and behaviors, a major question has been the degree to which the process of intergenerational transmission operates differently for males and females. Are boys and girls vulnerable to the same degree (i.e., does childhood exposure to marital violence have the same effects on males and females)? Bandura's (1973) social learning theory states that the ability to influence through modeling depends upon the degree to which the child identifies with the model. This suggests another research question: Do gender differences exist in the modeling of behavior? e.g., are boys more likely to imitate their fathers and girls their mothers?

A community sample of adolescents, some with histories of childhood maltreatment, sheds some light on the first question. The maltreated adolescents, compared with nonmaltreated youths, showed differential patterns of adjustment problems and dating violence. Female adolescents with maltreatment histories reported considerable emotional distress (such as anger, depression, and anxiety), posttraumatic stress–related symptoms, and acts of violent and nonviolent delinquency compared with girls without such histories. Male adolescents with maltreatment histories reported fewer symptoms of emotional turmoil and delinquent behavior but were significantly more likely to be abusive toward their dating partners than boys without a maltreatment history (Wolfe et al. 2001).

Overall, the study of gender effects has produced mixed findings (Stith et al. 2000), with some studies showing that direct and/or indirect exposure to violence in childhood is more salient for females (Forsstrom and Rosenbaum 1985), some studies showing stronger effects among males (Rosenbaum and O'Leary 1981), some showing a same-gender modeling effect (Heyman and Slep 2002), and some showing no sex-specific differentiation (Cappell and Heiner 1990). A review of eight recent studies (Cummings, Pepler, and Moore 1999) examining the impact of interparental violence on children ranging in age from four to sixteen showed that girls exposed to interparental violence displayed higher internalizing scores than did exposed boys in the six studies that reported on internalizing outcomes. Of the five studies that reported externalizing scores, three studies reported higher scores for girls and two for boys. These studies suggest that the social context of the home may be more salient for girls than for boys. Data from the National Youth Survey also support the premise that prior experiences with violence may be more salient for females than for males. In this study, which examined both witnessing parental violence and experiencing child abuse, only witnessing violence had an effect on later violence and only for females. However, this effect was not direct and operated through other variables, such as marital satisfaction (Mihalic and Elliott 1997). A longitudinal study of parenting practices experienced in three distinct developmental periods while growing up also provides evidence of intergenerational transmission for females only (Belsky et al. 2005).

In contrast, Rosenbaum and O'Leary (1981) found that the effects of witnessing parental violence as children on later violent behavior were especially strong for males. Women who were victims of physical marital violence were no more likely than women in two control groups (composed of women who had suffered no physical abuse; one group claimed to have satisfactory marriages and the other group discordant marriages) to have witnessed spouse abuse between their parents. However, abusive husbands were much more likely to have come from families characterized by marital violence than husbands in the two control groups.

Others theorize that modeling of marital aggression is not sex specific, but is role specific. The 1975 National Family Violence Survey examined this perspective, finding that females who had observed fathers hitting mothers were just as likely to be the perpetrators of violence as the victims, and males were as likely to be the victims as well as perpetrators of marital violence. Kalmuss (1984) concluded that the intergenerational transmission of aggression involves both generalizable and specific models. Generalized models increase the likelihood of any form of family aggression in the next generation, and specific models increase the likelihood of particular types of family aggression (e.g., children who observe aggressive acts between their parents are more likely to model aggressive behavior in their own marriages) (see also Seltzer and Kalmuss 1988). A later analysis using the 1975 National Family Violence Survey also found evidence that the existence of spousal violence in the family of

SOCIAL LEARNING THEORY AND FAMILY VIOLENCE

origin increased the likelihood that the respondent, whether husband or wife, would be the target of aggression, but no evidence was found for sex-specific acquisition of the perpetrator role (Cappell and Heiner 1990). Findings from the 1975 National Family Violence Survey are in direct contrast to the 1985 National Family Violence Survey, which provided support for a same-gender modeling effect for perpetration of violence toward partners and children. Men's risk was increased by exposure to father-to-mother violence, and women's risk was increased by exposure to mother-to-father violence (Heyman and Slep 2002).

Sex-Role Theory

A subtype of social learning, sex-role theory suggests that early sex-role socialization teaches boys to be the dominant partner, major wage earner, and head of the household, while women are socialized to accept male dominant relationships and taught to meet the needs of others through their main roles as wives and mothers. These roles may leave males and females vulnerable to becoming offenders and victims of marital violence. Most empirical studies have failed to validate a sex-role interpretation of marital violence (Hotaling and Sugarman 1986; Mihalic and Elliott 1997). Walker (1984), contrary to her original supposition, found no evidence in a clinical sample that battered women had traditional sex-role attitudes. Instead, they perceived themselves as more liberal; however, they perceived their mates as traditional. Her research suggested that the discordance in perceived sex roles might lead to conflict within the marriage and hence to marital violence. This hypothesis was tested by Coleman and Straus (1986), who found that equalitarian couples had the lowest rates of conflict and violence, while male- or female-dominant couples had the highest rates. Consensus about the legitimacy of the power structure reduced the rate of conflict and violence in male- or female-dominated families, but when conflict did occur in these families, it was associated with a much higher risk of violence than that of equalitarian families encountering the same level of conflict. This suggests that disagreement over sex-role orientations may be a bigger factor in marital aggression than the actual orientation held.

Is Aggression Generalizable?

A key element of social learning theory concerns its generalizability. Is violence learned in one context generalizable to other contexts? Social learning theory

predicts a generalized pattern of learned aggression that may be modeled in both family and nonfamily relationships. Bandura (1971, 1973) proposes that aggressive models transmit general lessons, as well as specific ones, and that observers learn general aggressive strategies that go well beyond the specific modeled examples. The perspective of generalized modeling has much empirical support in both the family violence literature and the delinquency literature (McCloskey and Lichter 2003; Mihalic and Elliott 1997; Thornberry 1994). A review of twenty-three articles on the effects of observing parent aggression provided evidence that children observers are at risk for a variety of externalizing behaviors, including increased aggression at home and school and in the community (Fantuzzo and Lindquist 1989). The effects on child witnesses of domestic violence are not confined only to behavioral development, but also affect emotional development, although meta-analyses suggest that these links may be weak (Kitzman et al. 2003).

Data from the 1975 and 1985 National Family Violence Surveys and a 1972 university student survey demonstrated that children assaulted by parents were more violent toward brothers, sisters, parents, and persons outside the family. They were also more likely to be involved in property crimes and with the police (Hotaling, Straus, and Lincoln 1990). This study also found that adult offenders and victims of family assault had higher rates of violent and nonviolent crime outside the family. The relationship existed even with controls for socioeconomic class, gender, and severity of violence, although the relationship was, in general, stronger for males and blue-collar families. These authors suggest that it is not just the direct experience of being assaulted that leads to violence, but the experience of living in a multi-assaultive family (i.e., the highest rates of outside family violence were reported by those respondents who were from families where they witnessed violence between their parents and were directly assaulted by a parent). These findings suggest that there are common links in all types of violence.

A prospective sample of 299 children, ages six to twelve, were interviewed with their mothers in 1991 to examine gender differences in adolescent delinquency five years later against a backdrop of witnessing marital violence and being a victim of child abuse (Herrera and McCloskey 2001). This study indicated that 31 percent of children who experienced abuse and 33 percent who witnessed marital violence, compared with 18 percent of those children without abuse in their childhoods, were referred to juvenile court at least once. Additionally,

17 percent of abused children and 17 percent of those who witnessed violence were referred for a violent offense, compared with 5 percent without a family background of violence. Being a victim simultaneously of both forms of abuse failed to predict delinquency above and beyond that of either of the other two categories. There was an interaction between sex and child abuse, with girls at higher risk of arrest for violence if they had a prior history of physical child abuse.

Evidence that exposure to violence in childhood is related to antisocial behavior outside the home also comes from longitudinal delinquency surveys. The Rochester Youth Development Study, which tracks 1,000 seventh- and eighth-grade students in the Rochester public school system, found that a history of substantiated cases of physical or sexual abuse or neglect prior to age twelve increased the chances of youth violence by 24 percent. Adolescents growing up in homes with partner violence or a family climate of hostility also exhibited higher rates of self-reported violence. Exposure to multiple forms of family violence doubled the risk of self-reported youth violence. These analyses controlled for gender, race/ethnicity, family structure, and social class (Thornberry 1994). In the National Youth Survey, females who witnessed marital violence had higher rates of minor adolescent violence and felony assault (Mihalic and Elliott 1997).

Another study followed 1,575 cases from childhood through young adulthood, comparing 908 substantiated cases of childhood abuse or neglect with a group of 667 matched children not officially recorded as abused or neglected. Being abused as a child increased the likelihood of arrest as a juvenile by 59 percent, as an adult by 28 percent, and for a violent crime by 30 percent (Widom and Maxfield 2001).

A question that arises is whether there is a threshold in one's early experience of violence that must be surpassed before the aggressive lessons become salient. To answer this question, a national representative sample was used to compare the effects of minimal, moderate, and frequent spanking on children's physical aggression against siblings and parents. A linear relationship for preschoolers, preadolescents, and adolescents was found for all levels of spanking. This supports the idea that "violence begets violence" and that any punishment that uses violent means may be harmful. It is important to note that the degree to which the parent reasoned with the child moderated the effect in several models (Larzelere 1986).

The cycle of violence theory assumes that if physically aggressive parents end up with aggressive children, it is because the child has learned a patterned response to violence. An alternative explanation is that the child has a predisposition toward aggressive behavior and that the punitive parental behavior is a response to the child. Parents often cite child misbehaviors as leading to greater use of severe corporal punishment. Thus, corporal punishment may be a response to aggressive child behavior, rather than its cause. A test of the social learning model against the temperament model provided support for the social learning model, which suggests that temperament does not adequately explain the process by which corporal punishment is passed on intergenerationally (Muller, Hunter, and Stollak 1995).

While there appears to be support for a link between family violence and youth violence, others have argued that the claim that child maltreatment is the leading cause of delinquency relies upon methodologically flawed studies and that the few rigorous studies are inconclusive or offer only a weak connection, which often disappears when other variables are controlled in the analyses (Schwartz, Rendon, and Hsieh 1994).

Mediators of Childhood Exposure to Violence and Intimate Partner Violence

A large problem with the intergenerational violence studies is that too much emphasis is often given to the simple association found, even if weak, and people assume that everyone who had a violent childhood will be violent to their own spouses and children. In fact, researchers have identified both child and spouse abusers who came from nonviolent families and nonviolent individuals who came from violent families. Kaufman and Zigler (1987) reviewed the literature cited to support the intergenerational theory of violence and postulated that the best estimate of the rate of intergenerational transmission was about 30 percent, plus or minus 5 percent. Thus, while approximately one-third of those who have suffered physical or sexual abuse or neglect as children will subject their own children to some form of abuse, two-thirds will not.

Researchers know little about why the majority of abused children do not become violent. Most studies reflect only the linkages between observations of violence and direct experiences with violence during childhood and later behavioral outcomes in adulthood and have not incorporated the intervening variables which ultimately may be responsible for determining whether a person will perform a learned behavior. According to Bandura (1969), exposure to violence does not ensure observational learning. A comprehensive theory of observational learning includes four component processes that influence its nature and degree: attentional processes, retention processes, motor production processes, and incentive and motivational processes. Some people fail to learn the essential features of the model's behavior, memories may be lost or altered with the passage of time, physical capabilities may restrict performance of a learned observation, and a learned behavior may not be expressed if it holds no functional value for the person or if the behavior is not reinforced. Breakdowns in any of the above processes may result in a failure to translate observational learning to behavior.

Hotaling and Sugarman (1990) updated their earlier review of the literature on intergenerational transmission using multivariate statistics from a national probability sample and could find no link between current marital violence and earlier family-of-origin violence. They now conclude that the relationship that is typically found between current and past childhood violence disappears when other risk factors are controlled, such as socioeconomic status and marital conflict.

There are several potentially confounding social, family, and contextual factors that may be associated with both childhood exposure to violence and increased risks of later adjustment problems or intimate partner violence. Families who experience intimate violence often experience other mental health risks, such as unemployment, drug and alcohol abuse, divorce, incarceration, and other family stressors. Other variables that might mediate the relationship include frequency and duration of exposure, severity of childhood violence, age, gender, perceived legitimacy of violence in family relations, quality of attachment with caregivers, maternal stress, family disadvantage, marital discord, and other stressful life events (Kolbo, Blakely, and Engleman 1996). Other mediators include elevated depression (McCloskey and Lichter 2003) and childhood neglect (Andrews and Brown 1988).

The extent to which confounding factors such as parental criminality, alcoholism, drug use, and adverse life events might explain the relationship between interparental violence in childhood and psychosocial adjustment in young adulthood was examined in a 1977 New Zealand birth cohort of 1,265 children who were followed into adulthood (Fergusson and Horwood 1998). At age eighteen, retrospective reports of interparental violence were obtained. A substantial amount of the association appeared to reflect these social and familial contextual factors. Statistical control of family context was sufficient to explain all or most of several outcomes, including depression, suicide attempts, substance abuse (other than alcohol), nicotine dependence, and violent crime. Associations persisted for anxiety, conduct disorder, alcohol abuse/dependence, and property crime.

It has been suggested that child abuse affects later intimate aggression by enhancing the development of a problem syndrome in adolescence and young adulthood. Using a longitudinal community study, a direct effect between harsh physical punishment in childhood and perpetration of violence against an intimate partner later in life was found. Over half of the effect was indirect through problem behaviors in adolescence and young adulthood (Swinford et al. 2000). In contrast, Mihalic and Elliott (1997) found no direct or indirect effects between self-reported child abuse ("beaten as a child") and partner violence later in life.

Path models have demonstrated an indirect path between observing violence as a child and later severe marital violence via sex-role egalitarianism and approval of marital violence, both of which directly influenced the use of severe violence (Stith and Farley 1993). As egalitarianism decreased and approval of marital violence increased, the level of severe violence increased. In this same study, observation of parental violence was also related to decreased self-esteem, which increased the level of alcoholism and marital stress, both of which had an effect on the approval of marital violence. The variables in this study were not measured in temporal sequence; hence no conclusions regarding causality can be made. A national longitudinal study that provided temporal sequencing showed that the path between witnessing parent violence and later partner violence among females was mediated by the development of adolescent delinquency, which resulted in lower marital satisfaction. There was no direct or indirect path between witnessing violence and later partner violence for males (Mihalic and Elliott 1997). Other path models have demonstrated that antisocial personality disorder mediated the effects of abuse/neglect on interpartner violence for men and women, and hostility and alcohol problems also mediated the effects for abused and neglected women (White and Widom 2003).

A review of the mediating factors that diminish the likelihood of abuse being transmitted across generations suggests that the cycle of violence is less likely to repeat itself if as a child one had the love and support of at least one parent; a loving, supportive relationship as an adult; fewer stressful events in life; and acknowledgment of the childhood abuse and determination not to repeat it (Kaufman and Zigler 1987). Past or current life stresses or supports are influential in determining whether or not the cycle of violence is repeated. Respondents who were not physically abused as children but who abused their own children reported more neglect, more stresses, and less nurturance in the family of origin than those who did not abuse their own children. Abused respondents who did not abuse their children reported fewer stresses in their families of origin than those abused respondents who had abused their own children (Herrenkohl, Herrenkohl, and Toedter 1983).

Summary

This essay provides a complex picture of the role of social learning during childhood in explaining later intimate partner violence. While many of the earliest studies show associations between childhood exposure to violence (either as a witness or as a victim), most of these studies have methodological weaknesses, such as the use of clinic or shelter samples (which generally show a stronger relationship between early and later violence), small samples, lack of comparison groups, and use of retrospective data and analyses. The relationship, however, is also supported in the stronger studies employing national samples. However, more sophisticated analyses, using multivariate statistics, have commonly demonstrated that the relationship between parental violence in childhood and later intimate partner violence could be explained by other social, family, and contextual factors.

The preponderance of evidence suggests that while social learning is a viable explanation for intimate partner violence, its explanatory power is weak to moderate, and the mechanisms for intergenerational transmission of abusive parenting are complex and remain unspecified.

Prevention Implications

There are many reasons for preventing child abuse and child exposure to violence—one reason is some moderate potential to reduce intimate partner violence in later adulthood. Early intervention may restore normal developmental processes, such as empathy and self-control, that promote healthy nonviolent relationships. Since the family provides a context for early learning of violence, programs that intervene with the family should have far-reaching effects. Children are especially vulnerable to the effects of harsh, permissive, and inconsistent parenting. High levels of parental negative affect and hostility are disruptive to children's ability to regulate their emotional responses and manage

conflict appropriately. Patterson, Reid, and Dishion (1992) use social learning theory to describe an interactive pattern of behavior between parent and child, the "coercive process," whereby children learn to escape or avoid parental criticism by escalating their negative behaviors. This, in turn, leads to increasingly aversive parent interactions and escalating dysregulation on the part of the child. These negative parent responses directly model and reinforce the child's deviant behaviors. This suggests the need to teach parent skills that emphasize changing negative parenting practices, such as coercive discipline and punishment, and that teach parents how to handle conflict, maintain self-control, and problem-solve to effectively manage children. Clinical experience indicates that coercive discipline patterns among parents are difficult to change as children reach adolescence; thus families should be targeted before the children reach late childhood and before patterns of physical abuse become entrenched in the child and reproduced in later relationships.

There are several selected (secondary prevention) evidence-based parent training programs that target high-risk families. The Nurse-Family Partnership (Olds et al. 1998) is an effective method of reducing child abuse and neglect and later antisocial and criminal behavior on the part of children. It provides supports for first-time and other high-risk mothers during pregnancy and through the child's second birthday. Parents are provided educational content, supports, and skills designed to improve pregnancy outcomes, improve the child's health and development, and improve the mother's own personal development. The Incredible Years Parent, Teacher, and Child Training Series (Webster-Stratton et al. 2001) is designed to promote emotional and social competence in young children, ages two to eight, at risk for or presenting with conduct problems. The program for parents imparts skills such as how to play with children, ways to help children learn, effective praise and use of incentives, and effective limit-setting and strategies for handling misbehavior. In the advanced program, parents are also taught interpersonal skills such as effective communication, anger management, and problem-solving between adults. The Child Program intervenes with children who exhibit particular behaviors that place them at risk for later adolescent and adult violence. Although the program has not been tested to determine its effects on child abuse, the skills that parents gain and the reduction in conduct disorders among children may ultimately impact child abuse.

There is also evidence that a well-developed capacity for empathy inhibits or prevents aggression, suggesting that programs that work with children to develop social and emotional competencies may have long-term benefits. Promoting Alternative THinking Strategies (PATHS) is a universal (primary prevention) school program for children in kindergarten through grade 5 that teaches empathy and behavioral regulation to prevent initiation of aggressive behavior (Greenberg, Kusche, and Mihalic 2002).

Indicated (tertiary prevention) programs target populations already exhibiting the problem, such as domestic violence perpetrators and victims. Although numerous treatment options for batterers (e.g., cognitive-behavioral therapy, individual and group counseling, mandated arrest) have been evaluated, there is little empirical support that any of these treatment modalities stop the violence. Few studies have evaluated advocacy studies for victims, but at least two studies show promise for this approach (Goodman and Epstein 2005; Stover 2005). Until programs can be found that have demonstrated effects working with adult perpetrators and victims, early intervention models appear the most promising.

SHARON MIHALIC

See also **Attachment Theory and Domestic Violence; Children Witnessing Parental Violence; Identity Theory and Domestic Violence; Intergenerational Transfer of Intimate Partner Violence**

References and Further Reading

Andrews, B., and G. W. Brown. "Marital Violence in the Community: A Biographical Approach." *British Journal of Psychiatry* 153 (1988): 305–312.

Bandura, A. *Principles of Behavior Modification.* New York: Holt, Rinehart, and Winston, 1969.

———. *Psychological Modeling.* Chicago: Aldine-Atherton, 1971.

———. *Aggression: A Social Learning Analysis.* Englewood Cliffs, NJ: Prentice Hall, 1973.

Belsky, J., S. R. Jaffee, J. Sligo, P. A. Silva, and L. Woodward. "Intergenerational Transmission of Warm-Sensitive-Stimulating Parenting: A Prospective Study of Mothers and Fathers of 3-Year-Olds." *Child Development* 76 (2005): 384–396.

Browne, S. F. *Analysis of a Battered Women Population.* Denver, CO: Denver Anti-Crime Council, 1980.

Burgess, A. W., C. R. Hartman, and A. McCormack. "Abused to Abuser: Antecedents of Socially Deviant Behaviors." *American Journal of Psychiatry* 144, no. 11 (1987): 1431–1436.

Cappell, C., and R. B. Heiner. "The Intergenerational Transmission of Family Aggression." *Journal of Family Violence* 5, no. 2 (1990): 135–152.

Coleman, D. H., and M. A. Straus. "Marital Power, Conflict, and Violence in a Nationally Representative Sample of American Couples." *Violence and Victims* 1, no. 2 (1986): 141–156.

Cummings, J. G., D. J. Pepler, and T. E. Moore. "Behavior Problems in Children Exposed to Wife Abuse: Gender Differences." *Journal of Family Violence* 14, no. 2 (1999): 133–156.

Ehrensaft, M. K., P. Cohen, J. Brown, E. Smailes, H. Chen, and J. G. Johnson. "Intergenerational Transmission of Partner Violence: A 20-Year Prospective Study." *Journal of Consulting and Clinical Psychology* 71, no. 4 (2003): 741–753.

Elliott, D. S., and S. F. Mihalic, eds. *Blueprints for Violence Prevention Series.* Books 1–11. Boulder: University of Colorado, Center for the Study and Prevention of Violence, 2003. www.colorado.edu/cspv/blueprints.

Fagan, J. A., D. K. Stewart, and K. V. Hansen. "Violent Men or Violent Husbands? Background Factors and Situational Correlates." In *The Dark Side of Families,* edited by D. Finkelhor, R. J. Gelles, G. T. Hotaling, and M. A. Straus. Beverly Hills, CA: Sage, 1983.

Fantuzzo, J. W., and C. U. Lindquist. "The Effects of Observing Conjugal Violence on Children: A Review and Analysis of Research Methodology." *Journal of Family Violence* 4 (1989): 77–94.

Fergusson, D. M., and L. J. Horwood. "Exposure to Interparental Violence in Childhood and Psychosocial Adjustment in Young Adulthood." *Child Abuse and Neglect* 22, no. 5 (1998): 339–357.

Forsstrom, B., and A. Rosenbaum. "The Effects of Parental Marital Violence on Young Adults: An Exploratory Investigation." *Journal of Marriage and Family* 47, no. 2 (1985): 467–480.

Gelles, R. *The Violent Home: A Study of Physical Aggression between Husbands and Wives.* Newbury Park, CA: Sage, 1972.

Goodman, L., and D. Epstein. "Refocusing on Women: A New Direction for Policy and Research on Intimate Partner Violence." *Journal of Interpersonal Violence* 20, no. 4 (2005): 479–487.

Greenberg, M. T., C. Kusche, and S. F. Mihalic. *Blueprints for Violence Prevention: Promoting Alternative Thinking Strategies.* Boulder: University of Colorado, Center for the Study and Prevention of Violence, 2002.

Herrenkohl, E. C., R. C. Herrenkohl, and L. J. Toedter. "Perspectives on the Intergenerational Transmission of Abuse." In Finkelhor et al., *The Dark Side of Families,* 1983.

Herrera, V. M., and L. A. McCloskey. "Gender Differences in the Risk for Delinquency among Youth Exposed to Family Violence." *Child Abuse and Neglect* 25 (2001): 1037–1051.

Heyman, R. E., and A. M. Slep. "Do Child Abuse and Interparental Violence Lead to Adulthood Family Violence?" *Journal of Marriage and Family* 64 (2002): 864–870.

Hotaling, G. T., M. A. Straus, and A. J. Lincoln. "Intrafamily Violence and Crime and Violence Outside the Family." In *Physical Violence in American Families: Risk Factors and Adaptations to Violence in 8,145 Families,* edited by M. A. Straus and R. J. Gelles. New Brunswick, NJ: Transaction Publishers, 1990.

Hotaling, G. T., and D. B. Sugarman. "An Analysis of Risk Markers in Husband to Wife Violence: The Current State of Knowledge." *Violence and Victims* 1, no. 2 (1986): 101–124.

———. "A Risk Marker Analysis of Assaulted Wives." *Journal of Family Violence* 5 (1990): 1–13.

Kalmuss, D. "The Intergenerational Transmission of Marital Aggression." *Journal of Marriage and Family* (February 1984): 11–19.

Kaufman, J., and E. Zigler. "Do Abused Children Become Abusive Parents?" *American Journal of Orthopsychiatry* 57, no. 2 (1987): 186–192.

Kitzman, K. M., N. K. Gaylord, A. R. Holt, and E. D. Kenny. "Child Witnesses to Domestic Violence: A Meta-Analytic Review." *Journal of Consulting and Clinicial Psychology* 71, no. 2 (2003): 339–352.

Kolbo, J. R., E. H. Blakely, and D. Engleman. "Children Who Witness Domestic Violence: A Review of Empirical Literature." *Journal of Interpersonal Violence* 11, no. 2 (1996): 281–293.

Larzelere, R. E. "Moderate Spanking: Model or Deterrent of Children's Aggression in the Family?" *Journal of Family Violence* 1, no. 1 (1986): 27–36.

Margolin, G. "Effects of Domestic Violence on Children." In *Violence against Children in the Family and Community,* edited by P. K. Trickett and C. J. Schellenback. Washington DC: American Psychological Association, 1998.

McCloskey, L. A., and E. L. Lichter. "The Contribution of Marital Violence to Adolescent Aggression across Different Relationships." *Journal of Interpersonal Violence* 18, no. 4 (2003): 390–412.

McCord, J. "Parental Behavior in the Cycle of Aggression." *Psychiatry* 51, no. 1 (1988): 14–23.

Mihalic, S., and D. Elliott. "A Social Learning Theory Model of Marital Violence." *Journal of Family Violence* 12, no. 1 (1997): 21–47.

Muller, R. T., J. E. Hunter, and G. Stollak. "The Intergenerational Transmission of Corporal Punishment: A Comparison of Social Learning and Temperament Models." *Child Abuse and Neglect* 19, no. 11 (1995): 1323–1335.

Okun, L. *Woman Abuse: Facts Replacing Myths.* Albany: State University of New York Press, 1986.

Olds, D. L., P. L. Hill, S. F. Mihalic, and R. A. O'Brien. *Blueprints for Violence Prevention: Prenatal and Infancy Home Visitation by Nurses.* Boulder: University of Colorado, Center for the Study and Prevention of Violence, 1998.

Patterson, G. R., J. Reid, and T. Dishion. *Antisocial Boys: A Social Interactional Approach,* vol. 4. Eugene, OR: Castalia Publishing, 1992.

Rosenbaum, A., and K. D. O'Leary. "Children: The Unintended Victims of Marital Violence." *American Journal of Orthopsychiatry* 51, no. 4 (1981): 692–699.

Roy, M. *Battered Women: A Psychosociological Study of Domestic Violence.* New York: Van Nostrand Reinhold, 1982.

Schwartz, I. M., J. A. Rendon, and C. Hsieh. "Is Child Maltreatment a Leading Cause of Delinquency?" *Child Welfare* 73, no. 5 (1994): 639–655.

Seltzer, J. A., and D. Kalmuss. "Socialization and Stress Explanations for Spouse Abuse." *Social Forces* 67, no. 2 (1988): 473–491.

Steinmetz, S. K. *The Cycle of Violence: Assertive, Aggressive, and Abusive Family Interaction.* New York: Praeger Publishers, 1977.

Stith, S. M., and S. C. Farley. "A Predictive Model of Male Spousal Violence." *Journal of Family Violence* 8, no. 2 (1993): 183–201.

Stith, S. M., K. H. Rosen, K. A. Middleton, A. L. Busch, K. Lundeberg, and R. P. Carlton. "The Intergenerational Transmission of Spouse Abuse: A Meta-Analysis." *Journal of Marriage and Family* 62 (2000): 640–654.

Stover, C. S. "Domestic Violence Research: What Have We Learned and Where Do We Go from Here?" *Journal of Interpersonal Violence* 20, no. 4 (2005): 449–454.

Straus, M. "Injury and Frequency of Assault and the 'Representative Sample Fallacy' in Measuring Wife Beating and Child Abuse." In Straus and Gelles, *Physical Violence in American Families,* 1990a.

———. "Ordinary Violence, Child Abuse, and Wife Beating: What Do They Have in Common?" In Straus and Gelles, *Physical Violence in American Families,* 1990b.

Straus, M., R. J. Gelles, and S. K. Steinmetz. *Behind Closed Doors: Violence in the American Family.* Garden City, NY: Anchor Press/Doubleday, 1980.

Swinford, S. P., A. DeMaris, S. A. Cernkovich, and P. C. Giordana. "Harsh Physical Discipline in Childhood and Violence in Later Romantic Involvements: The Mediating Role of Problem Behaviors." *Journal of Marriage and Family* 62 (2000): 508–519.

Thornberry, T. P. *Violent Families and Youth Violence. Fact Sheet #21, December.* Washington DC: U.S. Department of Justice, Office of Justice Programs, Office of Juvenile Justice and Delinquency Prevention, 1994.

Walker, L. E. *The Battered Woman Syndrome.* New York: Springer, 1984.

Webster-Stratton, C., S. Mihalic, A. Fagan, D. Arnold, T. Taylor, and C. Tingley. *Blueprints for Violence Prevention: The Incredible Years: Parent, Teacher and Child Training.* Boulder: University of Colorado, Center for the Study and Prevention of Violence, 2001.

White, H. R., and C. S. Widom. "Intimate Partner Violence among Abused and Neglected Children in Young Adulthood: The Mediating Effects of Early Aggression, Antisocial Personality, Hostility and Alcohol Problems." *Aggressive Behavior* 29 (2003): 332–345.

Widom, C. S. "The Cycle of Violence." *Science* 244 (1989): 160–244.

Widom, C. S., and M. G. Maxfield. *An Update on the "Cycle of Violence." Research in Brief.* Washington DC: U.S. Department of Justice, Office of Justice Programs, National Institute of Justice, 2001.

Widom, C. S., B. L. Weiler, and L. B. Cottler. "Childhood Victimization and Drug Abuse: A Comparison of Prospective and Retrospective Findings." *Journal of Consulting and Clinical Psychology* 867, no. 6 (1999): 867–880.

Wolfe, D. A., K. Scott, C. Wekerle, and A. L. Pittman. "Child Maltreatment: Risk of Adjustment Problems and Dating Violence in Adolescence." *Journal of the American Academy of Child and Adolescent Psychiatry* 40, no. 3 (2001): 282–289.

SOUTH AFRICA, DOMESTIC VIOLENCE IN

South Africa, often called the "rainbow nation," is a country of great contrasts. Its landscape has deserts and forests; large urban cities and sprawling rural areas. Some live in great wealth and comfort; almost half of the country's population lives in poverty. South Africa's forty-four million people come from a range of rich and diverse cultural backgrounds, some adhering to age-old customs and traditions, and others to modern beliefs and values. South Africans represent some thirteen ethnic groupings and speak eleven different languages.

South Africa remains a fledgling democracy. Since the fall of apartheid in 1990 and the holding of the country's first democratic elections in 1994, the "new" South African state has had to grapple with many problems created by the apartheid government. Poverty, education, health, and social welfare have been critical challenges for a state struggling to establish its legitimacy and deal with the day-to-day business of governance. Crime has burgeoned, and crimes against women such as rape and domestic violence have become endemic. Fulfilling the promises set out in South Africa's progressive constitution has not been easy, as the majority of South Africans have traditionally not received equal status in society, let alone useful services from the state. Women have been a particularly forgotten group, as the struggle for women's rights took a back seat to the fight for racial equality.

Since 1994, the government has made significant commitments to protect women from domestic violence by both ratifying international instruments and developing policy and legislation to better protect women. It has ratified the 1994 United Nations Declaration on the Elimination of Violence against Women (CEDAW), which provides a framework for states to develop policy and legislation to deal with violence against women. Furthermore, the South African Constitution specifically entrenches the right of all South Africans to be "free from all forms of violence from public and private sources." Constitutional court judgments, such as *Carmichele v. the Minister of Safety and Security and Another,* 2001 (4) SA 938 CC, have underlined that this not only requires the state to respect the right of women to be free from violence, but requires the state to take reasonable steps to protect those rights. The court has itself noted that domestic violence in South Africa is "systemic, pervasive and overwhelmingly gender-specific, [and] ... both reflects and reinforces patriarchal domination ... in a particularly brutal form."

The Prevalence of Domestic Violence in South Africa

It is notoriously difficult to obtain reliable, comprehensive statistics on the incidence of domestic violence the world over. Many incidents go unreported as women fear retaliation or experience self-blame and shame at having been victimized by their intimate partner. A single domestic violence incident often includes a number of different kinds of abuses, making it difficult to keep accurate numbers. In South Africa, collecting domestic violence statistics is made more difficult by the fact that domestic violence is not a criminal offense. Police statistics record only criminal offenses which may have occurred as part of the domestic abuse, such as assault, rape, malicious damage to property, or theft. There is no differentiation within the crime statistics produced by the South African Police Service that indicates the percentage of each crime type (assault, for example) which occurred between domestic partners. Quantifying the incidence of domestic violence using police measures is therefore impossible.

While no official statistics exist on domestic violence in South Africa, research and service provision organizations hold that the levels of domestic violence have reached alarming proportions, with little or no indication that this trend is likely to recede. A commonly cited estimate is that one in every six women in South Africa is regularly abused by her intimate partner. Some studies have shown that as many as 80 percent of women interviewed have experienced some form of physical abuse perpetrated by someone within their domestic environment. Often, the injuries they sustain are serious and can even be fatal. Recent research on intimate femicide suggests that in South Africa a woman is killed every six hours by her partner.

Understanding Domestic Violence in South African Society

Domestic violence in South Africa cuts across all classes, races, religions, ethnicities, and regions. There is no universal definition which adequately represents all South Africans' experience of domestic abuse. Similarly, it is impossible to identify a single root cause for domestic violence: It stems rather from a complex interplay of factors at the individual, family, and community levels. However, despite the difficulties in defining, quantifying, and explaining domestic violence, it is clear that, left unchecked, it has severe implications for the physical and mental health of its victims and exacerbates other social problems, such as teenage pregnancy and sexual health.

South Africa is a complex social environment: It has high illiteracy levels, inadequate and inaccessible government and criminal justice structures, poverty, male-dominated societies, and a blend of traditional and Western social norms. Many South Africans operate at a survival level, with the need for housing, food, water, and health care being as important as living a violence-free existence. South African society is furthermore very violent. Decades of apartheid state-sponsored violence and community mobilization have meant that physical violence has become accepted as a legitimate means of resolving conflict and achieving social ascendance. There is a deep-rooted sense that there is no legal recourse for most of the issues facing men and women daily: losing jobs, homes, possessions. Bodily integrity and physical safety have come to be conditions that cannot be guaranteed. Even within this context, there is a sense that women suffer under a "double standard" of justice: that problems like domestic violence are not as serious as others but are rather recognized as part of the realities of living as a South African woman.

Given South Africa's violent political history, the very traditional, patriarchal nature of its society, and the fact that violence against women is commonplace, it should hardly be surprising that violence is frequently found in relationships. Violence against women is one of the consequences of men's strain under external factors such as poverty, conflict, and rapid political and economic change. In South Africa these challenges are profound: High levels of (male) unemployment and women's simultaneous entry into the workforce through economic restructuring combined with the lack of opportunities has meant a challenge to men's authority. As parts of society have gained political power and control, they have simultaneously perceived a *loss* of control on the family front. Men have experienced a failure to "match up" to the masculine myths and promises that are transmitted as part of South Africa's macho culture. Violence in the liberation struggle was seen as noble and necessary, but in the new South Africa it has become criminal and destructive. South African men lack personal power but live in a society that expects them to be powerful. A crisis of masculinity results, and because violence against women is condoned in custom (and until relatively recently in law), it has escalated as men have attempted to reassert their power and control over women.

While many divisions exist in South African society, South African men are ironically unified in their shared patriarchal identities. Whether black or white, change and insecurity has meant emasculation and powerlessness for men. Deteriorating social and economic circumstances have led to high unemployment, which has been experienced as personal rather than social failure. Violence has become the means for increasing self-esteem, and women, as the less powerful group, have become the victims of this symbolic reassertion of control. Domestic violence is used to punish women who step outside of their assigned gender role, in much the same way that the apartheid government justified white-on-black violence as socially justified and a necessary means of showing black South Africans their place. Women are policed and immobilized by the fear of violence, keeping them in subordinate roles through rigidly enforced cultural and ethnic beliefs upheld by families, tribes, religion, villages, and neighborhoods.

But, while conflict and rapid change in society may influence men's violence toward women, it does not cause it. Such a deterministic view is altogether too limited: All South African men do not beat their partners, even though domestic violence would appear to be the norm. Rather, poverty and crisis exacerbate violence that already exists in society at the intersection of social forces and individual choices.

Poverty and Domestic Violence

Poverty and economic dependency cannot be emphasized enough as factors which limit the choices that women have to escape abusive relationships. Poverty in South Africa is feminized in nature, with women and children disproportionately suffering under the poorest socioeconomic conditions. Living in poverty makes women particularly at risk of male violence, and economic need compels some women to accept strategies that make them vulnerable. The political and social dimensions of women's poverty affect their ability to challenge the violence against them. Women's economic dependency on men, and the cultural value attributed to women as "proper wives" or "good mothers" and "loyal" to the family may lead women to decide that the repercussions of contradicting the gender ideologies are worse than those of staying with an abusive partner.

The poverty in which many South African women find themselves has meant that sex has become an economic commodity. Women engage in extrarelationship sex for food or money—putting themselves not only at risk of contracting HIV and other sexually transmitted diseases, but also of violence from their partners. Practices such as "age-mixing"—where young girls are coerced, raped, and enticed into sexual intercourse and relationships by men who are older, stronger, and richer than themselves—have taken root and underpin abusive contexts. Trading sex for resources increases the risks of rape and physical violence from men who anticipate that their financial outlay earns them certain rights, often outside of sex. Women who have experienced some form of gender violence (particularly while children or adolescents) are also more likely to subsequently trade sex for money or drugs.

Women living in poverty tend to have limited access to formal institutions that might offer assistance in resisting violence, including health, education, social, legal, and police services. Women and their dependents may be deterred from going to such institutions because of the costs of such actions. These costs include both financial costs and the social cost of facing disapproval for having discussed the violence in public. Women (and particularly unemployed women) choose not to access the state system because of the possibility that the male partner will be arrested, leaving no one to provide for the family. This dependency often forces women to seek a more conciliatory process, such as those offered by churches, counselors, and informal justice mechanisms, as a way of ensuring that they are not left destitute.

Family, Culture, and Tradition

A discussion of domestic violence in South Africa is incomplete without reference to the family system:

The family in its various forms plays a very important role in many African cultures. For most women, the family is simultaneously their sanctuary and their site of abuse. It is inherently biased as power balances within a marriage are tipped in favor of men. Yet the family is also the place where young women and men begin to learn their social and gender roles and develop an understanding of acceptable and normal relationship behavior.

For most South Africans, the family is an extended network encompassing many generations and often living in close proximity. In traditional South African societies, households within an extended family are not autonomous units in which the marriage bond between a couple means that their union has privilege over other relationship ties. Rather, marriage is conceptualized as the union of two families for the purposes of procreation and survival. Taken against the intensely patriarchal nature of African society, this means that marriage gives men as a group control over women's procreative and productive capacities.

Notably, the family is distinguished for its right to sanction and control its members, particularly women. Women are viewed as "appropriate victims" of violence aimed at reinforcing gender roles, as men have the right (and obligation) to control a woman's behavior and can therefore justify beating her. Violence is therefore not viewed as a breakdown in social mores, but rather an affirmation of the way that society operates. In this sense, violence is not seen as dysfunctional to the system, but rather integral to the smooth functioning of the society.

Cultural norms which are entrenched in South African society further justify, sustain, and perpetuate men's coercion of women. Violence against women and girls—whether physical, emotional, or sexual—is a product of the social construction of masculinity which condones male dominance over women. It reflects preexisting social, cultural, and economic disparities between men and women and happens in many contexts, including the home, marriage, workplace, and public spaces. The relatively low status of women affects many areas of their lives in allowing for poor access to education, housing, health care, and social welfare services, which in turn serves to compound problems in accessing treatment and legal remedies for victims of domestic violence.

Culture and tradition are not synonymous with one another and are neither all good nor all bad. Indeed, South African culture, tradition, and practices change according to the area where people live, across different classes in society, and across time. However, throughout history, powerful men have had the responsibility of declaring and defining culture and tradition, and as a result notions of culture have developed which emphasize male rights at the expense of women. Culture plays a large role in maintaining the view, held by many South Africans, that women are subservient to men. Culture is used as an excuse to uphold the belief that it is an acceptable traditional practice for men to beat or abuse their wives.

The increase in domestic violence in South African communities has been linked by some to the demise of traditional values and women's challenges to the patriarchal order. The notions of "honor" and "shame" are deeply entrenched in South African culture. Honor is actively sought and prized by men, while shame is conferred on women for stepping outside of the boundaries that society prescribes. Shame is furthermore not only the burden of the individual woman, but of her entire family. The honor of mothers, daughters, and sisters are guarded by men as a group, yet at the same time this paternalism undermines the position of women.

Large sectors of South African society are tolerant of polygamous practices. Both men and women believe that a variety of sexual partners is acceptable and essential for men but not for women. Although male promiscuity has traditionally been accepted among many groups, a woman's sexuality is jealously controlled by her husband and/or family. This double standard produces violence when the woman attempts to ask about her partner's extramarital involvement(s). Women experiencing domestic abuse are further limited in their ability to demand mutually monogamous relationships, as the threat of being chased from their homes or being replaced by a second (and additional) wife are stark realities. A woman's access to housing, economic resources, and maintenance are often dependent on her male partner.

Certain customary practices have been shown to contribute to domestic abuse and the oppression of women. The payment of lobola (a bride price) by the husband's family to the family of the bride-to-be undermines women's status dramatically. Lobola has an intensely negative influence on the equality of power relations within the family and reinforces the idea of the man's proprietary ownership of his wife. Correspondingly, a latent understanding of having been "paid for" is entrenched among women, along with the belief that women must succumb to men's needs and wishes. Educational (and hence career) opportunities are curtailed through this practice, making women more

dependent on men for survival. Many young women are joined in marriage to old men who are able to afford to pay large lobola amounts of cattle and money. Practically, lobola restricts a woman's ability to leave an abusive relationship through the inability of her or her family to refund the lobola amount. Where this refund is not possible, a woman is sent back to her family to learn to be a "good wife" (as defined by the husband's family). No attention is paid to whether the wife wishes to return to her husband's home.

South Africans speculate that the acceptance of cultural norms and attitudes is waning among the younger generation. Some attribute the increase in domestic violence in South Africa to the demise of traditional values and women's challenge to the patriarchal order. However, there is still considerable personal agreement or acceptance expressed with patriarchal gender relations. In many cases women themselves still seem to uphold beliefs such as the subservience of women, punishment of the woman by the husband, male ownership of women, and male sexual entitlement. Women often implicitly believe in the authority of their male partners—ideas which are symbolized by the traditional marriage contract and reinforced by religion and the church.

Women are consequently forced to engage in various strategies to ensure their survival and security within a social, economic, and political context that is shaped and dominated by men. Oftentimes a woman will sacrifice the interests of women as a group in order to guarantee an individual reward. She bargains with patriarchy and makes her choices depending on where she feels most loyalty. If a woman sees that her best interests are served by protecting the family, she holds that institution above all others, even if it means perpetuating violence against other women. While the concept of the patriarchal bargain is useful for understanding why women inflict violence on other women in a social, political, and economic structure which furthers the interests of men, it should not be interpreted as absolving all women from responsibility for their violence. Taken against the backdrop of other social, cultural, and economic factors, it provides further evidence that a more nuanced approach is required to combating violence against women.

Legislative Reform

The Prevention of Family Violence Act (PFVA) (113 of 1993) was the new regime's first attempt at dealing with the problem of abuse within the home. The promulgation of the PFVA constituted a gain for victims of domestic violence in that it signaled recognition on the part of government that domestic violence was a serious problem. However, the PFVA was mired by many shortcomings, particularly its narrow application. The act covered only individuals who were married (by either civil or customary law) and those living in common law marriages. This excluded many people from accessing an interdict—for example, those in dating relationships, unmarried couples living together, and same-sex partners. The PFVA furthermore did not define what constituted domestic violence, resulting in widely disparate definitions used in courtrooms across the country.

The government responded to criticism of the PFVA by assembling a team of experts tasked with the development of a new act that would remedy many of the concerns raised by legal reform advocates. The task team, consisting of nongovernmental organizations, magistrates, lawyers, and academics, set about drafting legislation that both reflected women's experience of domestic violence and provided victims the maximum protection afforded by the law.

The Domestic Violence Act (DVA) (116 of November 1998) was implemented in courts and police stations across South Africa in December 1999. The DVA aimed to shift the commonly held notion that domestic violence was limited to physical abuse, and the act rested on the recognition that domestic violence was linked with other social and welfare issues, such as divorce, custody, and maintenance. The act explicitly recognizes that domestic violence takes a number of forms and occurs in all types of relationships.

Specifically, the DVA defines an exhaustive list of abuses, including:

- Physical abuse, including any act or threatened act of physical violence
- Sexual abuse, which is defined as any conduct that abuses, humiliates, degrades, or otherwise violates the sexual integrity of the complainant
- Emotional, verbal, and psychological abuse through patterns of degrading or humiliating conduct, including repeated insults, ridicule or name calling, threats to cause emotional pain, or the exhibition of obsessive possessiveness or jealousy
- Economic abuse, including the unreasonable deprivation of financial resources (such as household necessities and mortgage or rent payments), or the disposal of household goods and property

- Intimidation, which means uttering or conveying a threat which induces fear in the complainant. This includes threats which are conveyed through a third party
- Harassment, which is a pattern of conduct that causes the complainant to fear harm. Examples of harassment include repeatedly watching or loitering outside a complainant's home, business, or school, or repeatedly making telephone calls or sending packages, faxes, e-mails, or other correspondence
- Stalking by repeatedly following, pursuing, or accosting the complainant
- Damage to property
- Entry to the complainant's residence without consent where the parties do not share the same residence
- Any other controlling or abusive behavior where it may cause harm or imminent harm to the safety, health, and well-being of a complainant

The act's wide definition of a "domestic relationship" also broadens the range of complainants able to access legal protection from domestic abuse to include:

- People who are married by any law, custom, or religion
- People who live or lived together (whether of the same or opposite sex)
- Parents of children or people who have shared parental responsibility for a child
- Family members (whether related by affiliation, consanguinity, or adoption)
- People in an engagement, dating, or customary relationships, including actual or perceived romantic, intimate, or sexual relationships of any duration
- People who share or recently shared the same residence

Importantly, the DVA does not criminalize domestic violence. It allows the complainant to begin a civil legal process by applying for a protection order from the court. Upon application, the complainant may be granted an interim order, which sets out the prohibited behaviors. At the interim protection order stage, a return date is set, at which any challenges from the respondent are heard. Notice is served on the respondent of the existence of the interim order and of the date of the final hearing. At the final inquiry, the order may be confirmed, varied, or set aside. If the interim order is confirmed, a warrant of arrest is issued, which the complainant lodges with the local police station, to be used should the respondent breach any of the conditions of the order.

A complainant may also simultaneously begin criminal proceedings against the abuser for any crimes which may have occurred as part of the abuse. Examples of these may be rape and assault. Any criminal charges which are filed proceed independently of the application for a protection order under the DVA.

The DVA, however, does criminalize a breach of the protection order. Such a breach results in arrest and automatically in a criminal trial. Neither the complainant nor the prosecutor is permitted to withdraw a case where a breach of the protection order has been reported. If convicted of a breach of the order, the abuser may be sentenced to a maximum of five years in prison or a fine.

Implementing the Domestic Violence Act

Despite the existence of such progressive legislation, there remains, as in many other African jurisdictions, a discrepancy between the law as it is written and its application in practice. The years since the promulgation of the DVA have seen the criminal justice system struggle with the realities of implementing the new legislation.

Many of the problems in implementation have been practical in nature and are often symptomatic of the difficulties of "doing" justice within a resource-poor context. Police stations and courts are housed in basic buildings, often lacking the facilities necessary to deal sensitively with domestic violence issues. Police complain of a shortage of police vehicles and manpower, which impacts their ability to respond to complaints and serve protection orders on the respondents. Court rolls are long, meaning that women often have to wait in inhospitable conditions to see a magistrate or return on a following day to obtain a protection order. Many orders are granted on the basis of the papers alone, as the workload does not afford the magistrate the time to see the complainant at the interim order stage. A shortage of interpreters in courts and police stations makes communication difficult, particularly where the police officer or magistrate does not speak the local language.

The application process requires the participation of both the courts and the police, and there is seldom any coordinated interdepartmental workflow. The absence of imperatives for the health sector to act (often the first place that women go for help) where domestic violence is involved further weakens the act's meaningful implementations, and

a lack of complementary support services outside of the criminal justice system compounds the problem.

Implementation of the act fell largely to criminal justice personnel struggling to make the ideological shift to the more victim-centered approach underpinning the legislation. Scant, often ineffective training in enforcement of the DVA left police, court clerks, and magistrates grappling with the intricacies of interpreting and applying the act in real-life domestic violence cases where the distinctions between right and wrong are less often as clear-cut as set out in the law and more often reflect the grayness of human interactions.

For victims of domestic violence the difficulties of accessing legal remedies are even more complex. While the DVA undoubtedly provides the scope for women to access protection from their violent partners, the patriarchal and paternalistic criminal justice system is unfamiliar and daunting. Courts are often far from the victim's school or home, and transportation costly. Shelters and nongovernmental organizations providing services to victims of domestic violence are woefully unable to accommodate the numbers of women requiring care. Some South African women express dissatisfaction with the criminal justice process, as they often have to deal with unintended consequences of reporting the incident, such as additional abuse as a result of obtaining the protection order. Many complain that their intention in accessing the criminal justice system was resolution rather than the arrest and/or incarceration of their partner.

Even within the context of a single problem, such as domestic violence, many South African women access a range of different structures in the process of seeking resolution. Their help-seeking choices depend on the nature of the violence they have suffered, as well as the nature of their relationship with the perpetrator. Power relations within their communities and economic dependence on their husbands are powerful factors influencing their choice of justice mechanism. For many women the family often remains the first (and sometimes only) agency through which to resolve problems of domestic abuse, failing which they are taken to other dispute resolution structures, such as the church, street committees, headmen, traditional healers, and nongovernmental or community-based organizations. The formal court system is often the last resort, when all other options have been exhausted.

The debate continues as to whether the problems with the DVA constitute teething troubles or a system failure. Government and civil society continue to engage in reform initiatives aimed at improving the law and its application. Some of these initiates include piloting specialized domestic violence courts, intersectoral training, and conferences covering all related areas of family law (e.g., maintenance, domestic violence, child custody). Police, prosecutors, clerks of the court, and magistrates continue to receive focused training on both the content of the law and the social context within which it is applied.

Conclusion

The law is undoubtedly limited in dealing with a problem that is more often about human relationships, power dynamics, and gender inequalities, and only tangentially about legal resolution. In addition, the public is faced with a criminal justice system that is itself flawed, underresourced, and plagued with inequalities and biases. Eliminating violence against women is a profoundly political challenge—it necessitates challenging the unequal social, political, and economic power held by women and men and the ways in which this inequality is perpetuated through human institutions at all levels of society. The criminal justice system is attempting to do its part in ensuring that South African women enjoy protection from domestic violence through the DVA.

Legal reformers and campaigners for women's rights must support the development of a progressive and inclusive system that will protect women and marginalized populations, not only in theory, but also in financial and practical terms. They need to create a model for appropriate response to domestic violence that fundamentally shifts unequal social relations in real terms. However, the responsibility for altering these deeply entrenched notions does not end with either the criminal justice system or the government. Directives that come from outside may be effective at the level of individual change, but the re-patterning of relationship norms can come only from within. The call to engage with domestic violence faces each and every South African.

KELLEY MOULT

See also **Africa: Domestic Violence and the Law; Africa: The Criminal Justice System and the Problem of Domestic Violence in West Africa; Cross-Cultural Perspectives on How to Deal with Batterers; Dating Violence among African American Couples; Intimate Partner Homicide**

References and Further Reading
Carmichele v. the Minister of Safety and Security and Another, 2001 (4) SA 938 CC
Domestic Violence Act (116 of 1998)
Prevention of Family Violence Act (113 of 1993)

SPAIN, DOMESTIC VIOLENCE IN

Introduction

Many people hope to find protection and safety within the family from the slings and arrows of outrageous fortune. Unfortunately, as statistics on domestic violence reveal, this expectation is not often fulfilled. Domestic violence takes many forms that imply the use of force or coercion to generate or maintain the dominance of men over women. As stated by the Spanish Organic Act 1/2004 of December 28, 2004 (Integrated Protection Measures against Gender Violence): "It is violence directed against women for the mere fact of being women; considered, by their aggressors, as lacking the most basic rights of freedom, respect and power of decision."

Violence against women has been present since the beginning of the dominance of men over women and is so widespread that many people have become accustomed to seeing it as a normal and appropriate practice. Its recognition is very difficult, since it has been invisible for centuries. The attempts of women's organizations to fight domestic violence and media coverage have contributed to the fact that Spaniards have gained a great deal of awareness of domestic violence. After 1997, the media played a fundamental role in bringing the suffering of many women who were victims of domestic violence to the public eye. The murder of Ana Orantes by her ex-husband, after she had spoken on a television program about the abuse and a court decision that forced her to continue sharing a house with her former husband, triggered the attention of the media that is still present today. Since then, it is no longer an "invisible crime" but an offense that is clearly rejected by society. Moreover, domestic violence is a cause of social alarm as is reflected by the Centro Investigaciones Sociologicas (CIS) barometer (CIS 2004).

Gender violence is a clear symptom of the gender inequality that unfortunately persists in contemporary society. Most domestic violence situations are minor, but they are very frequent. In fact, if low-intensity cases were made visible, there would appear to be more abused women than nonabused, more abusive partners than nonabusive, and more families in which domestic violence occurs than those in which it does not. It is very common to hear every week in the Spanish news that yet another woman has been murdered by her partner or ex-partner (Villavicencio 2001).

In 1999 the Women's Institute conducted a macro telephone survey (N = 20,552 women over eighteen years old), with the main goal of quantifying violent acts against women in the home (Medina-Ariza and Barberet 2003). This study found that 12 percent of the sample group suffered some form of domestic abuse and that 4 percent admitted having suffered some type of violence in their immediate social contexts in the past year—in over 75 percent of these cases by their partners. Eleven percent of the participants, although they did not admit it, recognized that they had endured behaviors from their partners that were deemed by experts to indicate a certain level of violence. Their educational levels and employment status were similar to those of Spanish women in general. More recently, Bosch and Ferrer (2004) analyzed a sample of 142 battered women from different socioeconomic levels and regions of Spain attending specialized and nonspecialized centers. Their results corroborate that abuse victims come from all types of sociodemographic backgrounds and that they are not significantly different from non-abused women from the same environment.

According to official data facilitated by the Ministry of the Interior, police reports of domestic violence have been increasing dramatically during the last twenty years. In the 1980s and 1990s, the number of reported cases was under 20,000 per year, with a significant rising trend in the last five years (Instituto de la Mujer 2005). In 2004 more than 57,000 women filed legal complaints against their partners or former partners. Up until May 2005, 34,651 women had already filed complaints. Alberdi (2005) argues that this increase in the number of reported domestic violence incidents is a by-product of the new social definition of gender violence producing an attention effect that has made it more visible. However, every year, as a brutal symbol of the presence of gender violence, there are more than sixty women killed by their partners or ex-partners.

In Spain, gender discrimination and violence against women are still realities, although they are seen as politically and morally incorrect conduct. Patriarchal values prevail; otherwise it would not be feasible to find such rates of domestic violence, high levels of unemployment among women (twice that of men), high numbers of women in part-time and temporary jobs, and women receiving lower pay for the same work or bearing the brunt of the unequal distribution of domestic tasks.

Evolution of Cultural Risk Factors for Domestic Violence

The cultural issues of concern for researchers and professionals that deal with the effects of domestic violence are quite similar across countries. However, it is clear that there are specific factors in each particular country, such as political structure, religious beliefs, migration, civil conflicts, wars, etc., that contribute to women's vulnerability to domestic violence (Hasanbegovic 2001; Walker 1999).

The roots of the patriarchal family structure are quite old. In the Middle Ages, women within the family were considered more as objects of trade than as human beings. After marriage, the man acquired the condition of master of the house, supported by the principle of *fragilitas sexus,* the assumed physical, mental, and moral frailty of women that justified her submission to a man. The authority of the husband was so great that he could kill his wife under certain circumstances, such as adultery. This situation was upheld in Spanish legislation up until 1963 under the figure of law called *uxoricidio* (Lorente 2001).

Moreover, prominent Spanish Catholic religious authorities have reinforced the idea that a woman's destiny and role is determined by marriage, that her duties involve the rearing of offspring, and that man has the "noble obligation" to control his wife's behavior. Even today, Roman Catholic bishops suggest that sexual liberation since the 1960s has led to more men beating their wives (Directory of the Pastoral Family. . . 2003).

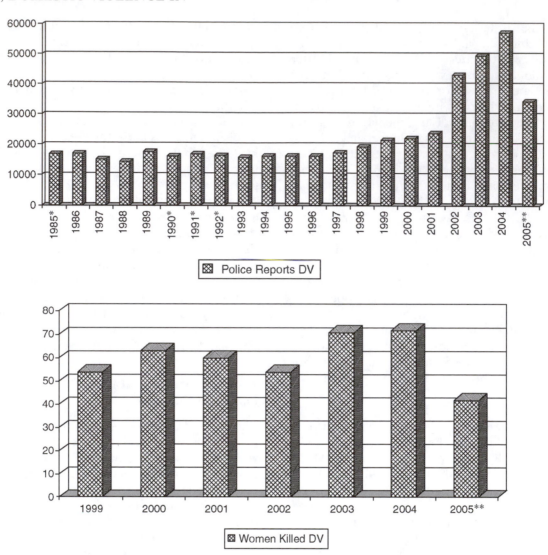

Data by Spanish Ministry of Interior.* = missing one month data; ** = until July 2005. http://www.mtas.es/mujer/mujeres/cifras/tablas/W805b.XLS.

Additionally, as is reflected in the term *machismo,* sadly an internationally known Spanish term, within the traditional Spaniard family the man is considered superior to the woman. In the recent past, the social expectation was that men as the head of the family had the last word on any type of decision, and his authority was not to be questioned. This type of family structure is full of inequalities and power differences which are closely linked to violence (Alberdi 2005). During Francisco Franco's dictatorial regime (1939–1975), this kind of family structure was strengthened. At that time, there was a substantial reduction of human rights and freedom in general; and in particular, women lost the right to vote, which they had attained in 1931 under the democratic regime of the Second Republic. Additionally, Spanish

women could not travel, have a bank account, or work without the explicit permission of their husbands or tutors. Franco's period, notably antifeminist, not only classified domestic violence as a crime of passion, but also delayed legal reforms and support services for female victims. Violence was justified as a means to achieve discipline and as an appropriate punishment. It was not until 1978—after Franco's death—that the Spanish Constitution recognized explicitly equal rights for men and women. Afterward, in the 1980s, Spain evolved rapidly, as is shown by the creation of the Instituto de la Mujer (IM) [Women's Institute] in 1983, within the Ministry of Labor and Social Affairs. Since its establishment, one of its main priorities has been the eradication of domestic violence (Valiente 1999).

European legislation sees gendered domestic violence no longer as an offense against honor, but as an offense against freedom. This process took shape in the Spanish Organic Act 3/1989 of June 21, 1989, which considered domestic violence an offense incompatible with democratic social order. Up until then, Spanish society had tacitly given domestic violence a legitimate place by considering the violence of men against women as a private family matter, a crime of passion, or a method of correction and punishment. Since the transition to democracy, the idea of equality for women has been expanding, and women have gained fundamental rights (i.e., changes in the civil code that allow separation and divorce).

Alberdi (2005) argues that Spain has had a revolution in the way it understands domestic violence, with a growing explicit refusal to tolerate violent behaviors and an increase in support given to the victim. This is reflected in the institutional response to the problem, as explained in the following section.

The Institutional Response to Domestic Violence

The recognition of domestic violence as a public issue means that the problem is no longer seen as a private matter—one that should and could be resolved privately—but instead requires state intervention. Domestic violence in Spain nowadays is considered mainly a public matter (primarily a human rights issue) of concern for the entire society, and especially for the state, which is supposed to protect its citizens. However, as in other countries, the recognition of domestic violence as a public issue, and subsequent state intervention, is a quite recent, although intense, phenomenon.

The creation of the national agency IM in 1983 is considered to be the starting point not only for state feminism but also for public policies regarding gender equality in Spain (Gil Ruiz 1996; Valiente 1995). In 1988, IM launched the First Plan for the Equality of Women (1988–1990), which, as of this writing, has been followed by the Second (1993–1996), the Third (1997–2000), and the Fourth (2003–2006). The seventeen regional Spanish governments (Comunidades Autónomas), plus a variety of local administrations, have also followed the national format and have been developing equality plans of their own. Equality organisms or "women-specific" agencies develop these plans, but they are also supposed to involve a cross-section of other governmental departments.

These plans have been the main instruments for articulating the public equality policies in Spain since the 1980s. They comprise a structured set of initiatives approved by the cabinets in different areas affecting women, including traditional measures for dealing with violence against women. The beginning of public equality policies in Spain came with the initial campaign against domestic violence in 1983 and the opening of the first shelter for battered women in 1984. In 1989, for the first time, Spanish legislation called for the punishment of physical violence between spouses or two people in an emotional relationship as a legal offense. This same legislation became stricter in 1995, following pressure by the "Anti-aggressions Committee" of the feminist movement (i.e., the women's demonstration in Madrid against violence in 1992).

However, it was not until December 1997, when Ana Orantes was killed, that the problem of domestic violence acquired the status of a public issue. The media impact of this case was so big that there were public reactions, even from the state, and IM launched the First National Action Plan against Women's Violence 1998–2000. Also in 1998, the Socialist Party finally took up the challenge of starting to prepare—along with feminist associations—the first draft of a comprehensive law against gender violence, a vindication that had been repeatedly claimed by the feminist movement since 1993. In the same year, the National Ombudsman presented a report on domestic violence, with fifty-one recommendations to public administrations for the improvement of assistance to women victims. In 2000 the Socialist Party, at that moment in the opposition, presented its legislative proposal backed by the feminist movement in parliament; it was rejected, due to the fact that the Conservative Party, with an absolute majority in the Congress at that time, opposed it. Another legislative proposal was presented and rejected again in 2002, having gained the support of all the political parties except the Conservatives. In 2001 the second specific National Plan against Violence was approved, and three regions—Madrid, Andalusia, and La Rioja—also launched their specific plans on violence. Another five—the Basque Country, Catalonia, Castilla-León, Aragón, and Galizia—did so in 2002. In 2001 the first regional law against violence was passed in Castilla–La Mancha (as of this writing, another three regional laws against gender violence have been approved in Navarra, Canarias, and Cantabria), and in 2003 a national "restriction order" for protecting victims was finally approved, after many years of campaigning by the feminist movement.

In March 2004 there were general elections, which were won by the Socialist Party. One of the main points in the Socialist electoral program was to promote the "comprehensive law" on gender violence, and it was one of the first electoral promises that President José Luis Rodríguez Zapatero's government kept: The Spanish Organic Act 1/2004 on Integrated Protection Measures against Gender Violence was approved on December 28. The pillars of this law are:

- the rights of women victims of gender violence,
- measures directed at changing the patriarchal structures of society—including measures on education, awareness-raising, mass media, and health care, and
- a mixture of penal and judicial measures.

This is a pioneering law because of its comprehensive character and because it draws on the concept of *gender* violence. In Europe, only Sweden has a similarly explicit legislation for combating *masculine* violence against *women,* although Austria, Germany, Luxembourg, Finland, and the United Kingdom have legislation against domestic violence.

With the approval of the law on Integrated Protection Measures against Gender Violence, there has been a clear shift toward what has been already called a *gender inequality policy frame* (Bustelo et al. 2005). A symbolic and important indicator of this change is that the term mainly used now is "gender violence" and no longer "domestic violence." Within this gender inequality policy frame, domestic violence is defined as a problem related to gender inequality. Thus, gender inequality is not only a cause of domestic violence but also an effect of it, that is, gender inequality is at the same time perpetuated by domestic violence. In this way, domestic violence is considered to be a universal problem of all social classes and groups regardless of class, education, or ethnicity.

However, from 1996 to 2004 the Conservative Party ran the Spanish national government, and before the above-mentioned law was passed, the official frame was a different one. It considered domestic violence most often but not necessarily as a problem between women and men, not relating it to the structural gender inequality issues behind it. In other words, there was a tendency to *degender* the issue. However, important signs of the alternative and competing gendered frame were found in the policy documents during those years. Moreover, the European comparative analysis of the MAGEEQ project (Mainstreaming Gender Equity in Europe) shows that this "degendering" effect is more easily found in other countries. The results of the MAGEEQ project reveal that the gender inequality policy frame in domestic violence was more present and frequent in Spanish and European Union documents than in the other case studies analyzed (Austria, Greece, the Netherlands, Hungary, and Slovenia) (see www.mageeq.net).

The *genderedness* of the Spanish policy approach to domestic violence might be analyzed by looking at three different questions:

1. What are supposed to be the origins or causes of domestic violence? that is, what is the explanation of the phenomenon and how is the problem represented? Depending on the answer, different solutions to the problem will be proposed.
2. Whose problem is it? that is, who is supposed to be the "target group"?
3. Who is supposed to do something about it? that is, who is responsible for action?

Regarding the first question, the new law, which names the problem as "gender violence" and not domestic violence, clearly states that "it is violence directed against women for the mere fact of being women." Thus, the problem is represented mainly as a gender issue. The second question is the most contradictory because, as will be seen later in this article, domestic violence is still seen mainly as a "women's issue." However, the gender focus allows the possibility for a more ample vision that includes the whole society, including men as a target group. Not exclusively a women's problem, domestic violence is fundamentally related to unequal power and gender relations, which necessarily includes men. Finally, the third question recognizes that domestic violence is a public, structural (i.e., rooted in socially gendered relations), and complex issue, which requires the participation and coordination of different state structures.

Resources

Besides the general institutional response, gender violence in Spain has been addressed through different resources, as discussed later.

Women's Organizations

The issue of violence against women became a priority for activists in the women's movement around the late 1970s. At that time women's organizations started offering programs to women with problems related specifically to conditions that were the result of their gender. These programs shed light on the great number of women suffering abuse by their partners or former partners. Therefore, feminist organizations were the first to offer shelter and services such as emergency phone lines for rape victims and psychological and legal support. These resources are still useful and irreplaceable for women's full recovery from gender discrimination.

In the late 1980s many women's organizations and nongovernmental organizations started to benefit from 0.5 percent of the total income tax revenue contribution, a subsidy offered by the Ministry of Labor and Social Affairs for developing social projects, such as intervention programs for gender violence. Specifically, there are women's groups that have intervention programs for domestic violence. Some of the main pioneering groups in Spain are discussed later.

Since 1973 the feminist Federación de Mujeres Separadas y Divorciadas has provided counseling and legal services to women who want to start separation or divorce proceedings. In 1991 it opened a Center for Integral Recovery for Victims of Gender Violence. Women from any Comunidad Autónoma can stay for about eighteen months. Since the mid-1980s, the feminist Asociación de Asistencia a Mujeres Violadas (Association of Assistance to Raped Women) has supported programs for rape victims in several parts of the country. The Comisión para la Investigación de los Malos Tratos a las Mujeres (Commission to Investigate Women's Maltreatment) has provided direct assistance to victims of violence since 1982. In 1990 the Women's Association for Health opened the Espacio de Salud Entre Nosotras (Safe Haven among Ourselves), a feminist mental health center that offers specialized intervention programs for women. They have groups for survivors of sexual abuse and for battered women. The organization called Themis: Asociación de Mujeres Juristas (Association of Women Jurists), which started in 1994, offers a legal support program for battered women.

In the 1980s, the women's movement denounced the lack of services to help victims of gender violence (Marugán and Vega 2003). State institutions were forced to accept the feminist protests and the need to create public services for victims of gender violence. The main focus was on rape victims and battered women. The Spanish central state and the Comunidades Autónomas have created different services all around the country. Due to the limited length of this article, only some of them will be mentioned.

State and Regional Government Services

Support services for women victims of violence in Spain were delayed in comparison with those offered in other countries. The main reason was that immediately after the end of Franco's regime, the women's movement and state representatives' efforts were focused on constructing a democracy and on achieving basic rights. This explains why social services in Spain are still currently less comprehensive than those in other countries.

According to the National Ombudsman (Defensor del Pueblo 1998), decentralization has produced different action plans for combating domestic violence in each community or region; consequently resources and support services for victims are not always sufficient or evenly distributed throughout the country.

Informational Services. The IM has from its beginning set up women's rights information centers. In addition, it offers a free women's rights information hotline, which has also been adapted for deaf women. The IM has organized several information campaigns related to the specific issue of violence against women. Marugán and Vega (2003) claimed that these campaigns focused mainly on women reporting aggressions to the police, thereby assigning the responsibility for stopping violence to survivors. Amnesty International (2005) expressed its concern about the short duration of these campaigns and the absence of an evaluation of the impact on Spanish society.

Financial Support. The right of domestic violence survivors to receive financial support has been established in international norms or agreements as part of the overall support to survivors that nations should guarantee. In Spain, women with a protection order and limited financial resources are entitled to receive Renta Activa de Inserción (RAI), a type of unemployment benefit. The Spanish Organic Act 1/2004 also provides for financial help amounting to six months' unemployment benefit for women who have been subjected to gender-based violence and granted a protection order by the courts. This act has gone further and entitles survivors to the legal status of the unemployed when they voluntarily terminate or suspend their employment. Additionally, women lacking economic means are entitled to receive special assistance for improving their employability when their age, general lack of skills, or social circumstances could be a handicap or when they or a family member have a certified disability.

State Accommodation Resources. In Spain, the first shelter for domestic violence victims was set up in 1984. In 2003, according to the Report on Action against Domestic Violence (Instituto de la Mujer 2004), there were 33 emergency centers for survivors, 106 battered women shelters, 127 safe houses (*pisos tutelados*), and 27 other shelter facilities. It is important to bear in mind that the Organic Act 1/2004 regarding these kinds of resources has taken action to remove obstacles faced by women over sixty-five years old who were not previously allowed to enter the shelter system because of their age. The act underlines that they shall be considered a priority group for access to subsidized housing and residences for the elderly. It also promotes special access to subsidized housing for victims of gender violence in general. The stance of the Spanish state is that one should "speak of integral protection services and not of shelter homes, so linked to charity and protection" (Murillo 2005).

Legal Resources. There are free legal aid services specializing in "domestic violence" set up by different bar associations throughout Spain following agreements with public services. In this regard, the Organic Act 1/2004 establishes that victims are also entitled to free legal assistance and ensures provision of legal representation and counsel to those without the economic means to litigate.

Police Programs. The National Police have stations or departments to treat women and girls who are victims of violence. Specialized police units called Servicios de Atención a la Mujer (Services to Attend Women) are tailored exclusively for cases of violence against women and are staffed by only policewomen. The Civil Guard Stations have similar services (Guardia Civil 2006).

GSM (Global Services for Mobile) Cell Phones. The Spanish government has promoted the phone help line service for battered women. Women with a protection order can apply for mobile phones with GPS (Global Positioning System) tracking in order to send distress messages to local police whenever they feel in danger. The program has been pioneered in several Spanish cities but is still frequently unavailable to women in rural areas because of problems of reception that remain unresolved.

Health Resources. Although in the last twenty years in Spain many health protocols have been developed, the Organic Act 1/2004 establishes new measures in the health sphere regarding early detection, assistance, and the application of specific protocols in order to speed up legal proceedings. A special commission has been created under the Interterritorial Council of the National Health Service to advise on, coordinate, and evaluate the health care measures established herein. It is relevant that this Organic Act emphasizes that National Health Plans shall include a section on the prevention and integrated treatment of cases of gender violence.

Regarding this issue, the Hospital Clínico San Carlos of Madrid, following the *World Report on Violence and Health* (World Health Organization 2002), has started a program that assists women survivors of gender violence. This program started as a research project (Valiente and Villavicencio 2002; Villavicencio 2001), and fortunately the positive outcomes and receptivity of the board of directors of the hospital have allowed the implementation and continuity of this type of program as one more of the regular services provided by this general state hospital.

Batterer Intervention Programs. In Spain, very few programs for male perpetrators of violence against women exist. In 1995, Echeburúa and Corral (1998) created the first batterer intervention program, with a subsidy from the Basque Women's Institute and the local government. The feminist movement has denounced the establishment of measures for men, as they would detract from the already scarce resources for programs for women survivors. On the other hand, another sector asks for a unified intervention protocol for batterers and the state obligation of periodically checking the effectiveness of any of these measures.

Concluding Remarks

Despite all positive improvements achieved in this field, there are a few challenges still to be addressed in Spain. A few of them are emphasized herein.

Although the new Spanish law uses clearly the term "gender violence," there is still some confusion around the term and the representation of the problem behind it. An example of this is how Spaniards are asked about domestic violence in the public opinion barometer of the CIS (2004). Efforts should be made to clarify those terms. Also, a more ample definition of gender violence is needed. The new Spanish law addresses a very important expression of gender violence—what can be called domestic violence or family violence—but not the only one. Sexual harassment, rape, language violence, and other violent expressions of discrimination against women must also be tackled comprehensively as issues having the same origins as domestic violence. All these should be identified, thereby making them visible, and typified as violent behaviors that must be considered as an outrage against human rights.

Besides all the efforts for framing the violence issue in terms of gender inequality and through a gender perspective, it can be concluded that generally speaking, domestic violence is still seen as a "woman's issue" (Bustelo et al. 2005). This means that domestic violence is still considered a women's problem, so that women are both the main problem holders and sometimes the exclusive target group of the policies that address the problem. Additionally, most of the time they are represented as being responsible for dealing with and overcoming the problem. A more comprehensive and *gendered* perspective is needed, not only involving the whole society but also appealing directly to men, because the root of the problem is unequal gender relations. Thus, their direct participation and involvement is also necessary for dealing adequately with it.

Following on from this idea, this new law focuses mainly on women who file a police complaint and obtain a protection order. These victims represent only the tip of the iceberg. Regardless of whether they have filed a complaint or not, survivors' empowerment and protection should be the main focus of support and assistance services.

There is a need to reach all women who are at risk through prevention programs and campaigns. On the other hand, the persistence of patriarchal attitudes and stereotypes regarding the roles and responsibilities of women and men in the family and in society are among the root causes of gender-based violence. Therefore, it is essential to take steps to ensure that professionals working in the justice system, social services, health system, and all the services that are directly or indirectly involved in proceedings concerning gender violence receive specific training to deal properly with these kinds of survivors. Such training should be compulsory for judges presiding over cases of gender-based violence.

Support services for women survivors of gender violence should be seen as resources to correct civil and human rights violations. These resources have been designed as social services for women without financial resources, and so are linked to charity. The low social and economic status of women can be both a cause and a consequence of gender violence (United Nations 1995). The access to specialist assistance and protection resources provided for survivors of gender-based violence should not be made exclusively through social services, as has been done heretofore. This conceptualization makes gender-based violence a problem of women treated with low budget funding.

Women who have been excluded from the shelter network should be referred to services that meet their need for protection and help as survivors of gender-based violence. There is a special need for mental health programs, among others, designed for women survivors of gender violence with serious psychological reactions.

It is essential to establish effective channels to ensure cooperation among the police, social services, health service, specialists, shelter and assistance facilities, and the judicial system in order to guarantee a well-coordinated intervention action plan. This is the only way to avoid survivors being subjected to secondary victimization that causes additional suffering and increases lethality risk.

It is vital that the regulations developed from the new law address the proper drafting, dissemination, and effective implementation of a comprehensive plan for early detection and prevention in the educational system. Awareness-raising measures through the media and public education programs are advisable to reinforce the notion that such violence is unacceptable and constitutes discrimination against women. People in general have to feel that they have a role in preventing violence against women and girls. It is important to reach a zero-tolerance level of violence against women in society in order to stop this pandemic.

Finally, Spanish society welcomes the significant number of initiatives aimed at achieving gender equality and eliminating discrimination against women by the Spanish state, but it has the challenge of periodically checking their effectiveness and ensuring that the new law is properly and effectively implemented. Otherwise all these initiatives will be only empty words.

PATRICIA VILLAVICENCIO, MARIA BUSTELO, and
CARMEN VALIENTE

See also **Africa: Domestic Violence and the Law; Cross-Cultural Examination of Domestic Violence in China and Pakistan; Cross-Cultural Examination of Domestic Violence in Latin America; Cross-Cultural Perspectives on Domestic Violence; Greece, Domestic Violence in; Trinidad and Tobago, Domestic Violence in; Worldwide Sociolegal Precedents Supporting Domestic Violence from Ancient to Modern Times**

References and Further Reading

Alberdi, I., and N. Matas. *La violencia doméstica. Informe sobre los malos tratos a mujeres en España.* Barcelona: Fundación "la Caixa," 2002.

Amnesty International. "España: Más allá del papel. Hacer realidad la protección y la justicia para las mujeres ante la violencia de género en el ámbito familiar," 2005. Madrid. http://www.es.amnesty.org/nomasviolencia/sabermas20espana.php.

Bosch E., and V. Ferrer. "Battered Women: Analysis of Demographic, Relationship and Domestic Violence Characteristics." *Colegio Oficial de Psicólogos. Psychology in Spain* 8, no. 1 (2004): 3–15.

Bustelo, M. "La evaluación de las políticas de género en España." Madrid: La Catarata, 2004.

Bustelo, M., T. Dombos, M. Filiopoulou, A. Hadjiyanni, F. Kamoutsi, A. Krizsan, R. Platero, K. Tertinegg, J. Van Beveren, and M. Verloo. "Comparative Frame Analysis: Domestic Violence and Sexual Violence against Women." Report by MAGEEQ (Mainstreaming Gender Equity in Europe), April 2005. www.mageeq.net.

Bustelo, M., E. Lombardo, E. Peterson, and R. Platero. "Spain Country Study. Domestic Violence." Report by MAGEEQ, October 2004. www.mageeq.net.

Bustelo, M., and E. Peterson. "The Evolution of Policy Discourses and Policy Instruments within the Spanish State Feminism: A Unified or Fragmented Landscape?" Paper presented at the workshop *State Feminism and Women's Movements: Assessing Change of the Last Decade in Europe,* coordinated by Joyce Outshoorn and Johanna Kantola. European Consortium for Political Research Workshops (ECPR), Granada, April 2005.

CIS [Centro Investigaciones Sociologicas]. "Barómetro de marzo" (survey no. 2,558), 2004.

Comisión para la Investigación de los Malos Tratos a las Mujeres (Commission to Investigate Women's Maltreatment) website. http://www.malostratos.org

Defensor del Pueblo. "Informe sobre la violencia doméstica contra las mujeres," 1998. http://www.defensordelpueblo.es/index.asp?destino=informes2.asp.

Directory of the Pastoral Family of the Catholic Church in Spain. Report by the Spanish Catholic Church, November 2003.

Durán, M. "Fair Trial for Women: Legal and Feminist Analysis of the Spanish Organic Act 1/2004 of 28th December." Presentation at the 5th Congress of the European Women Lawyers Association (EWLA), Strasbourg, March 17–19, 2005.

Echeburúa, E., and P. de Corral. *Manual de violencia familiar.* Madrid: Siglo Veintiuno de España, 1998.

Echeburúa, E., J. Fernández-Montalvo, and P. J. Amor. "Psychopathological Profile of Men Convicted of Gender Violence: A Study in the Prisons of Spain." *Journal of Interpersonal Violence* 18 (2003): 798–812.

Federación de Asociaciones de Mujeres Separadas y Divorciadas (Federation of Separated and Divorced Women) website. http:/www.separadasydivorciadas.org (accessed September 8, 2006).

Gil Ruiz, J. M. *Las políticas de igualdad en España: Avances y retrocesos.* Granada: Universidad de Granada, 1996.

Guardia Civil. "Violencia Doméstica," 2006. www.guardiacivil.org/mujer/domestic.jsp.

Hasanbegovic, C. "Violencia marital en Cuba. Principios revolucionarios vs. viejas creencias." School of Politics, Social Work and Sociology. Canterbury, UK: University of Kent, 2001.

Instituto de la Mujer. Data on "Violencia contra las Mujeres," 1999.

———. *Memoria de actuaciones contra la violencia doméstica.* Madrid: General Administration of the State and the Regional Governments, 2004.

———. "La Mujer en cifras," 2005. http://www.mtas.es/mujer/mujeres/cifras/tablas/W300-2.XLS.

Lorente, M. *Mi marido me pega lo normal. Agresión a la mujer: Realidades y mitos.* Barcelona: Ares y Mares Ed., 2001.

Marugán, B., and C. Vega. "Acción feminista y gubernamentalidad." In *Gouvernementalitat. Ein sozialwissenschaftliches konzept in anschluss an Foucault,* edited by Pieper and Gutiérrez. Frankfurt: Campus Verlag, 2003, pp. 161–175.

Medina-Ariza, J., and R. Barberet. "Intimate Partner Violence in Spain: Findings from a National Survey." *Violence against Women* 9, no. 3 (2003): 302–322.

Murillo, Soledad. Statement by Ms. Soledad Murillo, Secretary General for Equality Policies and Head of the Spanish Delegation before the 49th Session of the United Nations Commission on the Status of Women, 2005. http://www.un.org/webcast/csw2005/statements/050302spain-s%20e.pdf.

Spanish Organic Act 3/1989. "Actualization of the Penal Code." *Boletin Oficial del Estado,* no. 148 (June 29, 1989).

——— 1/2004. "Integrated Protection Measures against Gender Violence." *Boletin Oficial del Estado,* no. 323 (December 29, 2004). http://www.boe.es/boe/dias/2004-12-29/pdfs/A42166-42197.pdf. English version: http://www.redfeminista.org/nueva/uploads/Organic%20ACT%201-2004.pdf.

Themis: Asociación de las Mujeres Juristas website. http://www.mujeresjuristasthemis.org (accessed September 8, 2006).

United Nations. *Beijing Platform for Action* (A/CONF.177/20), October 17, 1995.

———. *Report by the CEDAW Committee* (A/59/38), 2004. http://www.un.org/womenwatch/daw/cedaw/31sess.htm.

Valiente, C. "The Power of Persuasion: The Instituto de la Mujer in Spain." In *Comparative State Feminism,* edited by D. M. Stetson and A. Mazur. Thousand Oaks, CA: Sage, 1995, pp. 221–236.

———. "But Where Are the Men? Central-State Public Policies to Combat Violence against Women in Post-Authoritarian Spain (1975–1999)." University Carlos III, Madrid, Spain. Strasbourg, October 7–8, 1999.

Valiente, C., and P. Villavicencio. *Predictores de ajuste psicosocial de mujeres víctimas de malostratos.* Proyecto de Investigación del Instituto de la Mujer, 2002. (Expediente no. 22/98)

Villavicencio Carrillo, P. "Barreras que impiden la ruptura de una situación de maltrato." In *La violencia contra las mujeres. Realidad social y políticas públicas,* edited by Raquel Osborne. Madrid: UNED Ediciones, 2001.

———. "Tratamiento cognitivo-conductual para mujeres víctimas de malos tratos (Cognitive-Behavioral Treatment for Women Victims of Abuse)." Postdoctoral research granted by the Dirección General de Investigación de la Consejería de Educación de la Comunidad de Madrid, 2003. (Expediente no. 02/0268/2000)

Villavicencio Carrillo, P., and J. Sebastián Herranz. *Violencia doméstica y su impacto en la salud física y mental de las mujeres*. Ministerio de Trabajo y Asuntos Sociales, Instituto de la Mujer, 1999.

Walker, L. E. A. "Domestic Violence around the World." *American Psychologist* 54, (1999): 21–29.

World Health Organization. *World Report on Violence and Health,* edited by Etienne G. Krug et al. Geneva: Author, 2002.

SPOUSAL ABUSE, THE PHYSICAL AND PSYCHOLOGICAL IMPACT OF

There are multiple names for spousal abuse placed within the realm of intimate partner violence. According to Martin (1988) the definition of battering which is part of spousal abuse is the affliction of injury or physical pain intended to cause harm from punching, slapping, biting, and hair pulling. More serious assaults may include choking, kicking, breaking bones, stabbing, shooting, or forcible restraints. Campbell and Humphreys (1993) also define battering as repeated physical and/or sexual assault of an intimate partner within the context of coercive control. Gelles and Straus (1988) point out that most women who hit men do so in self-defense, while most physical abuse is initiated by men. Women, due to their smaller size and lesser strength, are more prone to serious injury and death as a result of male-initiated violence (Browne and Herbert 1997). Sadock (1989) describes spousal abuse as the mistreatment or abuse of one spouse by another. She describes injuries ranging from shoving and pushing to choking and severe battering. These victims may suffer from broken limbs, fractured ribs, internal bleeding, and brain damage. Injuries may also be inflicted on the face, breast, and, if the woman is pregnant, the abdomen. According to Edwards (1996), a woman is battered every fifteen seconds, and battering in the United States is the leading cause of injury to women between the ages of fifteen and forty-four. An epidemic of spousal abuse is occurring in the United States due to the frequency of battering among spouses or significant others.

Victim Profile

Dickstein and Nadelson (1989) describe battered women as representing all age, racial, educational, religious, and social/economic groups. They may be married or single, business executives or housewives. Walker (1979) points out that women who are battered tend to have low self-esteem, commonly adhere to feminine sex role stereotypes, and frequently accept blame for batterers' actions. They commonly exhibit feelings of fear, anger, shame, and guilt and may be isolated from family and support systems. Many of these victims grew up in abusive homes, and may have left those homes and even married at a very young age in order to escape the abuse. Other symptoms of abuse may include withdrawal from socializing, self-blame, denial of abuse, and making excuses for the abuser. These abused individuals may also wonder, "What did I do to make him react so violently?" and their families may reinforce this self-questioning.

According to Campbell et al. (2003), most women will stay with their male abusers because of children, financial problems, fear of living alone, emotional dependence on the abusers, a belief that divorce is shameful, and/or a fear of reprisals from the abusers.

Most battered victims view their relationships as male dominated; and as the battering continues, a victim's ability to recognize the options available to her and to make decisions regarding her life (and possibly the lives of her children) develops into a phenomenon of learned helplessness. This phenomenon occurs when an individual fails to understand that regardless of his/her behavior, there is usually an undesirable and/or unpredictable outcome. According to Barnett (2001), women will mainly stay in fear for their lives or their children's lives as the batterer gains more power and control with the use of intimidation (i.e., making threats such as

"I'll kill you and the kids if you don't do as I say"). As they continue, these threats compound the victim's low self-esteem and she sees no way out of her situation. She may try to leave, only to return and be confronted by her abuser and the psychological power he holds over her, or murdered when attempting to leave or after having left. Other authors, such as Moss (1991), cite three more reasons for a woman staying in the marriage: a lack of a support network for leaving, religious beliefs, and a lack of financial independence to support herself and her children.

Clinical Findings

Health care providers see a panoply of behaviors from abused women. The clinical picture of these victims will include physical, emotional, and psychological injuries. Most victims are treated in the emergency room for physical injuries. Assessment for intimate partner abuse should be mandatory and take place in whatever setting the victim chooses to seek help. When no injuries are obvious, assessment for abuse is best handled with a history about the victim's intimate partner relationship. Several themes expressed by victims who have been in spousal abusive relationships have been identified by Hall (2003) and Smith (2003). These include relational authenticity deficits, immobility, emptiness, and disconnection. Answers to questions about these types of relationships should be assessed for feelings of being controlled or needing to control. A relationship is more likely to be violent when it is characterized by a partner's excessive jealousy, emotional immaturity, neediness, strong feelings of inadequacy, low self-esteem, and/or poor problem-solving and social skills (Hattendorf and Tollerud 1997).

The victim may be asked about how the couple solves their problems; if one partner needs to have the final say or uses forceful verbal aggression, this partner can also be considered abusive and possibly dangerous. Another approach would be to ask the individual whether the couple's arguments involve "pushing or shoving." As the interview continues, questions about violence within the relationship help to normalize the patient's experience and lessen the stigma of disclosure. If the patient hesitates, looks away, or displays similar nonverbal behavior, or reveals risk factors for abuse, he/she may be asked again later in the interview about physical violence (Poirier 2000). A number of clinics, hospitals, and doctors' offices ask women about safety issues as part of the overall health history or intake interview.

Due to the delicate and sensitive nature of the topic, and with many abused women being embarrassed about admitting to a problem, health care workers must be careful with their questioning approach. One technique used is the SAFE (Stress/Safety, Afraid/Abused, Friends/Family, and Emergency Plan) technique. The first two categories (Stress/Safety, Afraid/Abused) are designed to detect abuse. If abuse is present, questions in the other two categories are asked of the patient. Ashur (1993) notes that the usefulness of these questions allows the health care provider to paraphrase or edit them as needed for any given situation. If abuse is revealed from questioning, the health care provider's first response is critical. An abused woman should realize that she is not alone and should not be afraid to reveal the frequency of the abuse. Careful recording is essential in order to identify the extent and type of abuse, along with documentation using a body map to identify the location of contusions, bruises, or cuts for potential legal actions related to the violence. Other recordings of old and new injuries must be documented, and obtaining the patient's permission to take x-rays as well as photographs is essential. The health care provider must also obtain the abuser's name and how the abuser injured the patient, taking direct quotes from her. Inclusive with this is educating the patient about abuse and giving her referrals to social services, as well as reassuring her that confidentiality will be maintained (Berlinger 2004).

Janssen, Holt, and Sugg (2002) indicate that the health care provider has an ethical duty to diagnose and treat domestic violence victims, pointing out that some health care providers have been held liable in the past for failure to ask about abuse. Introducing the concept of domestic violence is an overlooked health issue and has been compared to "opening Pandora's box." Unlike other health risks for which providers order routine screening, exposure to spousal abuse is known to be often avoided due to exposure to embarrassing situations. The excuse often given is that the health care provider does not feel competent in dealing with abuse once it is identified (Sugg 1992). Battering during pregnancy often leads to miscarriage and stillbirth, as well as future psychological and physical problems for the woman (Mattson and Rodriquez 1999; Scobie and McGuire 1999). Because of this likelihood, assessment forms for abuse screening are often included in patient charts and initiated on the arrival of the patient to the postpartum unit from the delivery suite.

SPOUSAL ABUSE, THE PHYSICAL AND PSYCHOLOGICAL IMPACT OF

When to Suspect Spousal Abuse

The health care provider should suspect spousal abuse in any patient with the following characteristics:

- Presents with unexplained bruises, lacerations, burns, fractures, or multiple injuries in various stages of healing (particularly in areas normally covered by clothing).
- Delays seeking treatment for an injury.
- Appears embarrassed, evasive, anxious, or depressed.
- Has a partner who is reluctant to leave the victim alone and is domineering and uncooperative, or insists on answering all of the questions for the patient (though one should also keep in mind that some abusers are excessively solicitous of the victim).
- Says her partner has a psychiatric history or problems with alcohol or drugs.
- Has injuries that do not reflect the nature of her "accident."
- Expresses fear about returning home or fear for her children's safety.
- Talks about harming herself.

The health care provider interviewing a patient in a case of suspected abuse should trust his or her instincts even when these characteristics are not present. It is important for the safety and care of the patient that she is given assurance of confidentiality and that the abuser will not be made aware of any information shared with the provider. The heath care provider should keep in mind his or her own nonverbal behavior, including facial expressions that reflect sincerity. It is important to ask open-ended questions of the patient in an empathetic, nonjudgmental manner. One of the key attributes of the provider is being a good listener. The provider should offer written materials on the phases and progression of abuse, characteristics of victims and abusers, and the reasons victims stay. It is important for the victim to devise a safety plan and discuss with her provider the effects of abuse on the children in the home (Berlinger 2004).

Cycle of Violence

Battery may include violent sexual assault as well as physical violence. It may go on for days, after which the abuser may be extremely apologetic, promising to never do it again. This pattern is endemic of the cycle of violence. According to Walker (1979), the cycle of violence has three phases. The first phase is the *tension-building phase,* in which the woman senses an exacerbation of the man's frustration. He becomes angry with little provocation, but after lashing out at her may be quick to apologize. At this point the victim may become very compliant and nurturing, trying to anticipate his every whim in order to prevent his anger from escalating. Minor battering incidents may occur during this phase, and in a desperate attempt to avoid more serious confrontations, the woman accepts the abuse as being legitimately directed toward her. Her ability to reason is impaired when she assumes the guilt for the abuse. The battering incidents continue to escalate as the tension mounts and the woman waits for the inevitable explosion. This first phase might last from a few weeks to even years. As the phase intensifies, the victim becomes greatly impaired by not recognizing that the abuser's jealousy and possessiveness has increased along with threats of abuse and brutality to maintain control and captivity of her.

During the second phase of the cycle of violence, the *battering phase,* the most violent behavior occurs, lasting for the shortest duration. A triggering event occurs, and violence most often begins with the batterer justifying his behavior to himself, though in reality he has lost control. It might begin with the batterer wanting to "teach her a lesson" or the woman intentionally provoking the behavior of the abuser. The woman will often initiate the battering phase when the situation has become unbearable, knowing that once it is over, things will be better. During this phase the beatings are severe, and physical damage will occur. Drugs and alcohol may be involved with this phase of the cycle of violence. The victim survives by dissociating from her body despite the severity of the abuse. Help for the victim is usually sought only if the injury is severe or the woman fears for the lives of herself and her children.

The *apologetic phase,* the third and final phase of the cycle of violence, is actually the so-called honeymoon phase, during which the batterer becomes extremely loving and contrite. The abuser makes apologies and promises in order to win the forgiveness of the victim, changes his behavior, and exhibits every bit of charm he can muster. The batterer believes he can now control his behavior, and since he has taught his victim a "lesson," he believes she will not act up again. The victim's feelings are played on by the abuser and she desperately wants to believe that she can change his behavior. Magical thinking is used by the victim, who focuses on the loving phase of the relationship and hopes

671

against hope that the previous battering phase will not be repeated. This third phase may last briefly and may be almost undetectable—in most incidences the cycle all too soon begins again.

Women and men need to understand this cycle of violence and be willing to leave if abused, or have the abusive spouse seek help. Lore and Shultz (1993) conclude that there is evidence to suggest that social pressure may be used on abusers to help them control their behavior. Overall, the health care professional must be aware of the signs of abuse through careful observation of the individual and her spouse, since many victims overuse the health care system with multiple pre-hypochondriacal complaints. Many of the symptoms of emotional and physical abuse include atypical chest pain, asthma, recurrent headaches, somatic complaints with no identifiable cause, eating disorders and other gastrointestinal complaints, anxiety/panic attacks, depression, drug overdose, forgetfulness, hopelessness/suicide attempts, guilt, low self-esteem, sleep disturbances, and an inability to make decisions.

Although spousal abuse is considered a crime in the United States, there may be the need for the victim to obtain a restraining order from her county of residence that legally prohibits the abuser from contacting or approaching her; however, a restraining order provides only limited protection. Holt et al. (2002) found that permanent protection orders were less likely to be violated, while the likelihood of abuse increased with temporary restraining orders, even when relationships had ended. Mullen and colleagues (1999) report that stalking or other attempts at communication may follow the issuance of a restraining order. Many times the victimized spouse will move into a shelter, though most shelters have a waiting list and provide only a temporary respite.

Thus, for the overall safety of the abused victim, the importance of recognition, assessment, and implementation of action by health care providers cannot be overemphasized. Asking the correct questions, doing careful observation, and following the right reporting and recording procedures may mean the difference between life and death for these victims.

JOSEPHINE A. KAHLER and SHIRLEY GARICK

See also **Battered Woman Syndrome; Cycle of Violence; Depression and Domestic Violence; Female Suicide and Domestic Violence; Homelessness, The Impact of Family Violence on; Neurological and Physiological Impact of Abuse; Social Learning Theory and Family Violence**

References and Further Reading

Ashur, M. L. C. "Asking Questions about Domestic Violence: SAFE Questions." *Journal of the American Medical Association* 269, no. 18 (1993): 2367.

Barnett, O. W. "Why Battered Women Do Not Leave, Part 2." *Trauma, Violence, and Abuse* 2, no. 1 (2001): 3–35.

Berlinger, J. "Taking an Intimate Look at Domestic Violence." *Nursing* 34, no. 10 (2004): 42–55.

Browne, K., and M. Herbert. *Preventing Family Violence.* New York: John Wiley & Sons, 1997.

Campbell, J. C., et al. "Risk Factors for Femicide in Abusive Relationships: Results from a Multisite Case Control Study." *American Journal of Public Health* 93 (2003): 1089–1097.

Campbell, Jacquelyn C., and Janice Humphreys. *Nursing Care of Survivors of Family Violence.* St. Louis: Mosby, 1993.

Commission on Domestic Violence. "Statistics on Domestic Violence," 1999. http://www.abanet.org/domviol/stats.html (accessed September 8, 2006).

Dickstein, L. J., and C. C. Nadelson, eds. *Family Violence: Emerging Issues of a National Crisis.* Washington, DC: American Psychiatric Press, 1989.

Edwards, R. E. "The Courage of a Woman," 1996. http://www.biz.Arkansas.net/lordandedw/book.htm.

Gelles, R. J., and M. A. Straus. *The Definitive Study of the Causes and Consequences of Abuse in the American Family.* New York: Simon and Schuster, 1988.

Hall, J. M. "Positive Self-Transitions in Women Child Abuse Survivors." *Issues of Mental Health Nursing* 24 (2003): 647.

Hattendorf, J., and T. R. Tollerud. "Domestic Violence: Counseling Strategies That Minimize the Impact of Secondary Victimization." *Perspectives in Psychiatric Care* 33, no. 1 (1997): 14–23.

Holt, U. L., M. A. Kernie, T. Lamley, M. E. Wolf, and F. P. Rivara. "Civil Protection Orders and Risk of Subsequent Police-Reported Violence." *Journal of the American Medical Association* 288, no. 5 (2002): 589–594.

Janssen, P. A., V. L. Holt, and N. K. Sugg. "Introducing Domestic Violence Assessment in a Postpartum Clinical Setting." *Maternal and Child Health Journal* 6, no. 3 (2002): 195–201.

Lore, R. K., and L. A. Schultz. "Control of Human Aggression: A Comparative Perspective." *American Psychologist* 48, no. 1 (1993): 16–25.

Martin, M. "Battered Women." In *The Violent Family: Victimization of Women, Children and Elders,* edited by N. Hutchings. New York: Human Sciences Press, 1988.

Mattson, S., and E. Rodriguez. "Battering in Pregnant Latinos." *Issues in Mental Health Nursing* 20, no. 4 (1999): 405–422.

Moss, V. A. "Battered Women and the Myth of Masochism." *Journal of Psychosocial Nursing* 29, no. 7 (1991): 18–23.

Mullen, P. E., M. Pathe, R. Purcell, and G. W. Stuart. "Study of Stalkers." *American Journal of Psychiatry* 156, no. 8 (1999): 1244–1249.

Poirier, N. "Psychosocial Characteristics Discriminating between Battered Women and Other Women Psychiatric Inpatients." *Journal of the American Psychiatric Nurses Association* 6 (2000): 144.

Sadock, V. A. "Rape, Spouse Abuse and Incest." In *Comprehensive Textbook of Psychiatry,* vol. 1, 5th ed., edited

SPOUSAL PROSTITUTION

by H. J. Kaplan and B. J. Sadock. Baltimore: Williams and Wilkins, 1989.
Scobie, J., and M. McGuire. "Professional Issues: The Silent Enemy: Domestic Violence during Pregnancy." *British Journal of Midwifery* 7, no. 4 (1999): 259–262.
Smith, L. S. "Battered Women: The Nurse's Role." *Associate Degree Nurse* 2, no. 5 (1987).
Smith, M. E. "Recovering from Intimate Partner Violence: A Difficult Journey." *Issues in Mental Health Nursing* 24 (2003): 543.
Walker, L. E. *The Battered Woman*. New York: Harper & Row, 1979.

SPOUSAL PROSTITUTION

Prostitution is commonly referred to as the "world's oldest profession" and has been documented to exist even before biblical writings. Considering that historically prostitutes were forbidden the privilege of marriage (Rathus 1983), the phrase *spousal prostitution* appears to be an oxymoron; however, spousal prostitution is a very real phenomenon in contemporary American society, as husbands, in exchange for money, provide sex with their wives as a service to others.

For clarity of definitions, prostitution is defined as the granting of nonmarital sexual access, by mutual agreement, between the prostitute or her employer and her client, for remuneration (Siegel 1998). As the term "prostitution" is not specific to gender, the prostitute may be either male or female and either heterosexual or homosexual; however, most literature on the topic of prostitution addresses only the female prostitute. When the term "spousal" is added to the term "prostitution," this is often indicative of the existence of a division of power and labor between the two married individuals. This division of power reveals itself as one individual prostitutes (or grants sexual access to) the other. In most cases, the husband, in exchange for either money or drugs, prostitutes his wife.

Hollywood is not ignorant of the arrangement of spousal prostitution, and this theme has been presented in several contemporary movies. However, in movies such as *Indecent Proposal* with Robert Redford and Demi Moore and *Honeymoon in Vegas* with Nicholas Cage and Sarah Jessica Parker, spousal prostitution is depicted as an arrangement of mutual agreements; this is not always the case in real life, as some prostitutes are not given the opportunity to say no. In reference to discussions on the relationship between spousal prostitution and domestic violence, often the prostitution of the wife by the husband is accomplished through abuse or the threat of abuse—not unlike other outcomes of domestic violence. Therefore, for the purpose of this essay, spousal prostitution is defined as the sexual exploitation of one spouse by the other spouse for some profit.

Over three decades ago, Winick and Kinsie (1971) suggested that the majority of prostitutes had a history that included abuse by either a husband or a boyfriend. In fact, Hotaling and Finkelhor (1988) suggest that a family member often introduces prostitutes to sexual exploitation as children; that exploitation, as suggested in the cyclic process of domestic violence (the cycle of violence), continues into adulthood. It stands to reason that, as many males have been socialized to view sex as a commodity and women socialized to view themselves as sexual objects (James 1977), the idea that a woman is "sitting on a goldmine" simply because she is a woman provides the foundation for entertaining the thought of spousal prostitution. Husbands perceive sex with their wives as a product worthy of trade and therefore use that sexual activity as a product for sale on the open market.

Few women imagine their married lives to include sexual relations with men to whom they are not married or sex with other men at the request of their husbands; for the majority of wives this never occurs. However, some wives, because of financial needs or substance abuse, discover themselves engaged in prostitution, with their husbands occupying the position of pimp. Just as a pimp controls the actions and life of the street prostitute (Williams and Cluse-Tolar 2002), the husband controls the actions and life of the wife. Therefore, it is not unusual for a husband, in need of money to support a drug habit or as a livelihood to support his family, to prostitute his wife. In addition, for some women, the activity of prostitution was originally the desired outcome by the husband, and marriage is simply the avenue to it. These women may be mail-order brides. In fact, some of these women volunteer themselves to be brought to the United States to fulfill the role of a bride but sometimes discover themselves in the business of prostitution.

It is suggested that the mail-order bride industry is a cold and heartless business that has provided a focus for human rights campaigns for years. Every year, thousands of women leave their countries to begin new and "rewarding" marriages in the United States (Cullen 2002). Unfortunately, many of these women become trapped either in an environment of slavery or in prostitution (Cullen 2002). For some men, the allure of a tax-free business through prostitution is enough to entice a civil marriage ceremony, thus allowing the wife/"breadwinner" to begin working for them. These brides, who end up in loveless marriages, are often forced into prostitution by their husbands in order to provide him financial revenue. They are deprived of freedom, money, and rights and are used simply as sex objects offered to the highest bidders. Therefore, not only are these women deceived into entering the trade of prostitution, they are now victims of domestic abuse and spousal prostitution.

In an attempt to address the problem of spousal prostitution, many states have written laws on prostitution that specifically prohibit spousal prostitution. As historically the legal system in the United States has been perceived as reactive instead of proactive, the fact that both federal laws and state statutes prohibit spousal prostitution indicates that spousal prostitution has been identified to exist and has been identified as a problem.

Specifically, in Virginia one is guilty of facilitating prostitution if the prostituted person is the facilitator's spouse. In Oregon, a person is guilty of compelling prostitution (a class B felony) if that person induces or causes his spouse to engage in prostitution. In Arizona, causing a spouse to become a prostitute is considered a class 5 felony, and in Maryland one is guilty of prostitution if one places a spouse in a house of prostitution. Obviously, these states, which are not unique, have recognized the phenomenon of spousal prostitution as an activity they choose to address and to end.

In summary, just as with other crimes that occur among family members, the prostitution of one's spouse, or spousal prostitution, exists within the United States as well as in other countries. As more information becomes available on the full reach of domestic violence, one should expect to read of more cases of spousal prostitution.

KIMBERLY A. MCCABE

See also **Battered Woman Syndrome; Battered Women: Held in Captivity; Coercive Control; Date Rape; Intimate Partner Violence, Forms of; Marital Rape**

References and Further Reading

Cullen, S. "The Miserable Lives of Mail Order Brides." *Women in Action* 3 (2002): 6.

Hotaling, G., and D. Finkelhor. *The Sexual Exploitation of Missing Children.* Washington, DC: U.S. Department of Justice, 1988.

James, J. "Prostitutes and Prostitution." In *Deviants: Voluntary Action in a Hostile World,* edited by E. Sagarin and F. Montaninos. New York: Scott and Foresman, 1977, p. 384.

Melrose, M., and D. Barrett. *Anchors in Floating Lives.* Lyme Regis, Dorset, UK: Russell House, 2004.

Rathus, S. *Human Sexuality.* New York: Holt, Rinehart, and Winston, 1983.

Siegel, L. *Criminology: Theories, Patterns, and Typologies,* 6th ed. Belmont, CA: West/Wadsworth, 1998.

Williams, C., and T. Cluse-Tolar. "Pimp-Controlled Prostitution: Still an Integral Part of Street Life." *Violence against Women* 8 (2002): 1074–1092.

Winick, C., and P. Kinsie. *The Lively Commerce.* Chicago: Quadrangle Books, 1971.

STAGES OF LEAVING ABUSIVE RELATIONSHIPS

With the advent of the women's liberation movement in the early 1970s, gender inequality and the subordination of women became the focus of activists working toward equal rights and protection for women. Among the priorities of the movement was a focus on domestic violence, the legal ramifications for abusers and victims, and the need to provide safety for women who were assaulted and battered. Shelters were initially designed to offer a temporary safe haven for women (Cardarelli 1997). More shelters for battered women now are including their children, who also need therapeutic and rehabilitative care and attention.

Despite the movement's advocacy, activism, and efforts to empower women to take charge of their lives, women continue to be victimized and controlled in intimate partner relationships. Though domestic violence issues were mainly ignored under the guise of family privacy prior to the women's movement of the 1960s and 1970s, public attitudes have since been altered in support of the police protection of victims and the enforcement by police of restraining orders to keep women safe from assaults in their homes. Nevertheless, violence against women remains a serious problem, often of disastrous proportions. For some women, victimization may result in posttraumatic stress disorder (PTSD), disabling injuries, or death. Victims still carry the stigma of blame for appearing to provoke the batterer to act out his anger toward them (Burman 2003). Additionally, children carry the remnants of parental verbal and physical fights for many years to come, in the form of psychological and social impairments that could reverberate throughout subsequent generations.

Staying in a relationship under such horrific conditions has been misunderstood. This has unjustly added to mistaken beliefs that these women are weak and masochistic and probably deserve the punishment inflicted on them. Victim blaming serves to transfer the blame from the perpetrator to the victim. Yet, many plausible reasons for battered women remaining in such relationships have been demonstrated, such as:

- financial need,
- fear of intensifying the abuse by leaving,
- the belief that the batterer can change,
- emotional attachment to the batterer,
- learned helplessness in reaction to situations women believe are beyond their control, and
- doubt that they can raise their children alone (Roberts 1996).

Therefore, rather than asking a seemingly condemning question, "Why do and how can women stay in these horrific, abusive relationships?" given the aforementioned predicaments, more meaningful questions would be: "What finally propels women to leave, frequently placing themselves at great risk?" and "What initiates and compels their departures, often under duress and dire circumstances?" Reframing the queries exhibits an effort to understand victims' circumstances and the rationale for promoting change.

Women reach the breaking point and decide to leave for various reasons. Some examples of circumstances and events that may trigger such a breaking point in battered women include:

- when the children also become at risk.
- when their injuries are so extensive and their self-esteem so damaged that they believe that leaving is the only way left to heal and regain what they have lost.
- when they arrive at the realization that there must be more to life than the constant fear, savagery, and pain they are experiencing.
- when they realize that family and community help, support, and resources are available and accessible.
- when they gain hope and optimism that they can make it on their own, using their own survival and coping skills and becoming independent.

It has been reported that women leave battering partners and return many times before the final separation. They place themselves at great risk by doing so. Beatings invariably continue and tend to

675

escalate after separation (Shalansky, Ericksen, and Henderson 1999). Under such dangerous conditions, planning to end abusive relationships necessitates unyielding courage and exceptionally high motivation. No matter how much and how long women have persevered with the hardships and pain, they must acquire the emotional stamina and coping abilities to be ready to make drastic changes in their lives. To take that final step and attempt to get out permanently requires a steady mindset and steadfast determination to develop and follow through with a plan of action. This often awakens boundless strengths, perhaps never recognized before. Such dramatic behavioral change generally occurs after serious consideration of the benefits and costs of staying versus leaving that promotes the readiness to take action.

The Stages-of-Change Model

According to the *stages of change,* people move through a process of defined stages that demonstrates a measure of their readiness to make significant changes in their lives. Progressing through each stage gets them closer to a desirable goal. Readiness to change and the corresponding stages-of-change model are innovative concepts and ways of thinking that have been developed from extensive research on self-changers (Prochaska, Norcross, and DiClemente 1994). The findings have revolutionized the understanding of how people alter their ingrained behaviors, feelings, and thoughts that have kept them stuck and unable to cope constructively with severe problems and issues. In doing so, the popular notion of "having to hit bottom" in order to make major life changes is challenged. Although generally modified to suit each individual's circumstances and beliefs, "hitting bottom" usually connotes a very limited and extreme position to reach before being able to take action to alter an adverse behavior or situation. People can (and do) begin the process of change long before excessive pain and suffering might arise. They no longer have to consider losing everything meaningful in their lives before making dramatic changes to prevent it.

As an approach to assessment and treatment planning, the model matches the readiness to change with the appropriate stage clients are vested in during a specific time period. This information will identify the level of client motivation for working toward overcoming problems. To progress to a succeeding stage in the cycle, a series of tasks must be completed. Unless one becomes stuck at a certain level, working through the beginning stage (precontemplation) will lead to contemplation, preparation, action, maintenance, and termination of the difficulties experienced. Rather common is the relapse stage that interrupts the cycle, thereby promoting a return to previous stages or ending the effort to make positive changes. Hopefully, this will be temporary and progress on the path will resume.

The stages-of-change model can aptly apply to innumerable problems that people experience, such as substance abuse, eating disorders, and depression (Prochaska et al. 1994). With growing familiarity with its approach and related positive findings and results, researchers and practitioners have expanded its use to an array of presenting problems, including domestic violence. In this realm, the stages-of-change model has furthered the knowledge and understanding of the unsparing impact and excruciating traumas women endure in physically and emotionally abusive relationships. The change process examines in initial stages the subjective reactions to the violence exacted from inhumane behaviors, while establishing the need for continued vigilance and safety tasks in the planning and action stages to end the violence and prevent a reoccurrence.

An illustration of the incorporation of each stage in dealing with the crisis of battering between intimate partners will follow. The process has assisted in developing individualized methods and strategies to utilize in establishing positive life changes.

Precontemplation Stage

It is not unusual for people (family, friends, neighbors, coworkers, etc.) who observe and/or interact with an individual to notice that the person is experiencing problems. Yet the one who is experiencing the problem may personally lack awareness of it, deny its existence, minimize its influence, or consider the problem too hopeless to improve or change. Under these conditions, it is not surprising that there would be no incentive to attempt to make changes that will make life safer and less threatening, and no willingness to take risks to make it happen, at this point in time.

In an abusive relationship, several identifying features are characteristic of the precontemplation stage. The battered woman refrains from viewing her spouse or partner realistically, preferring to recall good times together and the "honeymoon stage," when, after a beating, she was showered with gifts and affection. Yearning to believe promises that the battering will never happen again places her in a compromising position. She deludes herself into thinking that if *she* changes to please him and stops provoking his anger, the assaults will stop. She becomes defensive and will always have excuses when her injuries, bruises, and burns are noticed, even in the emergency room: "I'm accident prone and always falling," "I'm so absent-minded and don't look where I'm going," or "Can you imagine, I just didn't realize the stove was hot."

Within this stage, traumatic bonding is likely to be prominent. Dutton (1992) described this dysfunctional attachment and loyalty as a dependency that begins as an emotional connection at the beginning of the relationship and continues despite the treachery and torment. Increasing isolation of the victim encourages an unhealthy union and pact with the batterer that makes leaving hazardous, although at this stage the woman is mostly unaware of or will not accept how dangerous staying has become. Psychic numbing accentuates the denial and tendency to minimize the trauma experienced, while the growing learned helplessness promotes the feeling of hopelessness and powerlessness in the relationship.

The stories are easy to see through, yet the façade is sustained to such an extent that the victim of the battering mistakenly believes them. In this stage, self-blame is internalized and rationalized: "If I had not gotten so angry because he was late, I know he would not have struck me"; "If I had told my mother that she could not have dinner with us again, I'm sure he would have been in a better mood." This precontemplator is so bound by the deceptions and false beliefs that she tells herself and others, without reasonable evidence to prove otherwise, that she remains stuck and unable to reach out for help. The tragedy, therefore, is that the status quo is sustained. Without recognizing and acknowledging that there is difficulty or conflict of any magnitude, there will be no efforts to promote a change.

Yet if the victim is not totally entrenched in this stage, a window of opportunity can open to new insights. With this enlightenment, there is a possibility that the seeds of change will be sown. Whether on her own or in treatment, the victim must begin to doubt that her abuser will change in order to begin pondering the risks of remaining in the relationship. The probability of increasing abuse, leading to numerous hospitalizations, even death, must be faced directly. The gravity of this impending possibility can no longer be ignored. Safety is the key component to consider, for herself and her children.

Contemplation Stage

During the contemplation stage, battered women are ready to acknowledge the severity of problems and deficits that earlier were minimized or denied. However, even as they begin facing the probability of disastrous consequences, they still are for the most part unable to make decisions to take action and make constructive change. Ambivalence is prominent in this stage. Not ready to make a change, battered women find their feelings frequently shifting back and forth; the resulting dilemmas create high anxiety. Lingering feelings toward husbands/partners, who once provided loving concern and security (whether real or imagined), become difficult to relinquish.

When pondering leaving versus staying, at first the choices may be bewildering. It appears that there may be much to gain and much to lose either way. In order to move forward with the most beneficial decision, it is helpful to contemplate the advantages and disadvantages of alternatives using a cost/benefit analysis of each choice. For example, advantages of leaving might include:

- safety/survival for self and children,
- feeling empowered and gaining self-confidence in taking charge and control of critical decisions,
- having a second chance at finding peace and happiness,
- being a positive role model in protecting the children, and
- breaking the cycle of violence.

Disadvantages might include:

- fears of continued harassment, stalking, and abuse,
- not being able to obtain a satisfactory job that will provide financial security, depending on educational and employment background,
- fears of starting over and independently making a new life, and
- possibly having to move to a distant area and stay hidden for an indefinite period of time.

It can take many months, even years, of weighing how life would change for better or worse. Considering the ongoing fears that battered women experience when faced with making such a life-altering decision, it is understandable that there would be apprehension about the future. Nevertheless, with an awareness of the sharp disparity between positive (and often exaggerated) memories of a caring relationship and the painful reality of what life has become, reasons to change are magnified and weighed carefully. As the intensity of violence escalates to life-threatening proportions, the benefits of staying lessen. Research findings have shown that as children are threatened and also become targets of the abuse, the desire to stay becomes even more narrow. In this way, the decisional balance is tipped, establishing necessary, even crucial, reasons to change. Once this is accomplished, the move toward the preparation stage takes effect.

Preparation Stage

Making an important decision after much reflection and deliberation of the critical nature of its consequences increases the motivation to carry it out and make it work. For a woman who realizes that sustaining the status quo is fraught with peril, there is a perceptible awareness that she has no other recourse, excepting more of the same punishing injuries and possible death. The journey to this point has not been smooth. The entire process preceding and during this stage has been an emotional and cognitive roller coaster, with shifting moments of clarity of purpose and ambivalent reconsiderations. Yet safety concerns eventually take precedence as reminders of the agony of the abuse take hold.

Being committed to taking action, she is ready to make a viable escape and safety plan for her children and herself, including an assessment of the degree of danger in each step taken. Consideration of supports and resources that can be tapped, while utilizing various sources to ensure safety and protection, are important to include in a safety plan. Phone numbers, identifying items (driver's license, Social Security card, children's birth certificates), and money saved are just a few items to gather. Having isolated herself due to years of making excuses and covering up evidence of the battering, a woman reaching out for help hopes she will receive positive responses to her appeals. People can be skeptical under the circumstances. Frequently, women have called upon trusted individuals (for example, relatives and clergy) who may have offered solace but urged them to stay in the relationship for the sake of the children. Although frustrating and disappointing, these reactions must not interrupt her persistence in following through with the primary objective of seeking safety measures.

Shelters are open to women, and in some locations, to their children also. They provide time-limited housing, therapeutic services such as crisis intervention and problem solving, and referrals to the community for vital resources such as legal and financial assistance, job training and employment opportunities, and police protection. The greater the strategic planning and corresponding resources and supports, the more opportunities there will be for finding safety and well-being. This necessitates careful and methodical preparation in planning to accomplish well-constructed goals.

Action Stage

Taking action involves challenging fears, facing intermittent uncertainties about having made the right decision, and experiencing doubts about moving forward with the plan. It means affirming the necessity and ability to take action, after a great deal of deliberation in earlier stages. Having built up the momentum and made preparations for many months or even years, not proceeding toward the goals of stopping the beatings and ending the relationship can be even more anxiety producing than doing so. Nonetheless, it often takes another horrendous incident (possibly after a lull in the battering and a promise that it will not happen again) to drive the will to immediately take action to leave and end the abuse. This is often described as the final incapacitating assault, the proverbial straw that breaks the camel's back, and strategies already developed are implemented. Women have remarked that they did not realize their own strengths, survival skills, and ability to cope under such duress and hardships before having to do so. Affirmations such as these express personal accomplishments and, under the circumstances, are well deserved.

Maintenance Stage

Having advanced through grueling and stress-producing stages, undertaking tasks that beforehand would have been considered unimaginable if not impossible, women are next challenged to maintain the gains they made in leaving behind a life filled with injuries, pain, and fears. They often need lifetime support, or at least support until assured that the perpetrator of the violence will not offend again. This is the time when relapse prevention should be addressed. Unknowingly, when distant distressful memories fade, a longing for the affection and attention once shown can emerge and create a desire to regain the positive parts of the relationship that were lost.

This is a danger zone, where fragile emotions reign and rational thought processes plunge almost spontaneously. Feeling lonely and not having reinvested socially in acceptable outlets, the temptation to reconnect with the abuser can be hasty and very risky. Without contemplating ominous conse-quences, a reenactment of the past and a cycle of violence can be repeated. Support groups, tele-phone hotlines that offer information, and treat-ment resources are crucial to counteracting these urges. The most important things for the woman to do are to get back on track, renew goals, and avoid being discouraged.

Termination Stage

One might wonder whether it is ever possible to terminate an abusive relationship, mourn the loss, and start life anew, safely and securely. Women do it, with varied emotions, numerous uncertainties about what lies ahead, and frequently a feeling of relief that the horror is ending. If achieved under their own actions, an empowering reaction and enhanced self-confidence can emerge. They made a difference in their lives and their children's lives.

Discussion

There could be many misfortunes and tragedies that might interrupt the stages of leaving an abu-sive relationship and create a relapse. Unable to earn an income adequate to satisfy even the basic necessities, having recurrent mood swings, and feel-ing lonely and overwhelmed with added responsi-bilities may instigate a return. Self-medicating with alcohol and other drugs can be a temporary escape but often exacerbates the problems experienced during the time of change. Women have been known to take drugs with their partners (many having been introduced to drug use by them), making it more difficult to sustain the detachment. Too often, the consequences can be serious and unrelenting. Developing and adhering to protective policies, providing the wherewithal to sustain life-saving changes, and helping women free themselves and their children with obtainable community sup-ports, resources, and available treatment should be a priority. Only then will women believe that they

have achieved peace of mind and freedom from strife.

SONDRA BURMAN

See also **Battered Woman Syndrome; Battered Women: Held in Captivity; Cycle of Violence; Educa-tion as a Risk Factor in Domestic Violence; Social Class and Domestic Violence; Victim-Blaming Theory**

References and Further Reading
Brown, Jody. "Working Toward Freedom from Violence: The Process of Change in Battered Women." *Violence against Women* 3 (1997): 5–26.
Burke, Jessica, Andrea Carlson Gielen, Karen McDonnell, Patricia O'Campo, and Suzanne Maman. "The Process of Ending Abuse in Intimate Relationships." *Violence against Women* 7 (2001): 1144–1163.
Burman, Sondra. "Battered Women: Stages of Change and Other Treatment Models That Instigate and Sustain Leaving." *Brief Treatment and Crisis Intervention* 3 (2003): 83–98.
Cardarelli, Albert P., ed. *Violence between Intimate Part-ners: Patterns, Causes, and Effects.* Boston: Allyn & Bacon, 1997.
Dutton, Mary Ann. *Empowering and Healing the Battered Woman: A Model for Assessment and Intervention.* New York: Springer, 1992.
Frasier, Pamela Y., Lisa Slatt, Vicki Kowlowitz, and Patricia T. Glowa. "Using the Stages of Change Model to Counsel Victims of Intimate Partner Violence." *Patient Education and Counseling* 43 (2001): 211–217.
Miller, William R., and Stephen Rollnick. *Motivational Interviewing.* New York: Guilford Press, 1991.
Prochaska, James O., and Carlo C. DiClemente. "In Search of How People Change." *American Psychologist* 47 (1992): 1102–1114.
Prochaska, James O., John C. Norcross, and Carlo C. DiClemente. *Changing for Good.* New York: William Morrow and Company, 1994.
Roberts, Albert R., ed. *Helping Battered Women: New Per-spectives and Remedies.* New York: Oxford University Press, 1996.
Shalansky, Catriona, Janet Ericksen, and Angela Henderson. "Abused Women and Child Custody: The Ongoing Expo-sure to Abusive Ex-Partners." *Journal of Advanced Nursing* 29 (1999): 416–426.
Walker, Lenore. *The Battered Woman.* New York: Harper & Row, 1979.

STALKING

Introduction

The word "stalking" denotes and has long been associated with hunting animals; only in recent years has the word's definition been expanded to include people as prey and the actions making up stalking as criminal. That is not to say that stalking, in its more recently defined form, is a new phenomenon. Cases of stalking can be found throughout history and literature. For example, in 1704, a case was prosecuted in England against a Dr. Lane, a physician who "persistently pursued Miss Dennis, a young heiress, against the wishes of her mother" (Mullen, Pathe, and Purcell 2000, p. 251). Another example, from the following century, occurred in 1897, when an erstwhile actor named Richard Archer stabbed William Terris, a well-known actor, after yet another rejection by the theater's casting decision makers (Gallagher 2001).

In literature, Heathcliff in Emily Brontë's (1847/ 1975) *Wuthering Heights* is a tormented soul as he suffers for the love he feels for Cathy that is not returned in terms of commitment and marriage. In William Shakespeare's (1594/1942) "The Rape of Lucrece," Sextus Tarquinius is "inflamed with Lucrece's beauty" and later "treacherously stealeth into her chamber, violently ravished her, and early in the morning speedeth away" (p. 1025).

Today, movie plots often focus on the scenarios of girl meets boy, girl resists boy, boy follows girl, and then, as a result, girl falls for boy or realizes she loved him all the time. Popular movies built around this theme include *The Graduate, Tootsie, Fever Pitch,* and old classics such as *Gone with the Wind.* Also in the movies, if the male pursues the female, the pursuit is entertaining and generally successful, but if the female pursues the male, she is generally portrayed as pitiable, at best, and demented, at worst. Think of *Play Misty for Me* or *Single White Female* (deBecker 2002). However, in reality, most stalking perpetrators are male, and most victims are female.

Meloy and Gothard (1995) define stalking as "the willful, malicious, and repeated following and harassing of another person that threatens his or her safety" (p. 258). This definition is in line with stalking statutes that usually require that a victim be in "reasonable fear" of death or serious bodily injury (18 U.S.C. §2261A). Another definition, offered by Pathe and Mullen (1997), is "a constellation of behaviors in which one individual inflicts on another repeated unwanted intrusions and communications" (p. 12). Behaviors associated with stalking include:

- Following victims
- Loitering near victims' homes and workplaces
- Giving gifts
- Sending letters
- Transmitting e-mails
- Making phone calls
- Vandalizing property (car or home, for example)
- Photographing the victims or their families
- Making threats
- Approaching or confronting the victims in public places or near the victims' homes or workplaces
- Physical and/or sexual assaults

Many of the stalking behaviors are not illegal and are even innocuous, but the pattern and the purpose of the actions distinguish them as stalking.

The Laws

All fifty states and the District of Columbia have statutes concerning the crime of stalking. In addition there are federal and tribal stalking statutes. The first state to pass anti-stalking legislation was California in 1990 (Snow 1998). There were several tragic cases in California that led to this legislation. The best-known of these cases is that of Rebecca Schaeffer, a young actress who was murdered at her door by a stalker in 1989. In the following year, four more women were killed by stalkers in Orange County in California. Several years before these murders, another actress, Theresa Saldana, had been stabbed and slashed several times by a stalker but survived because her screams were heard by a delivery man. Other states followed California, and by 1993 all the states had passed legislation making stalking a crime.

Many of these statutes (including that of California) were later revised in response to perceived holes in the laws and court challenges on the bases that the statutes were vague and/or overbroad. The challenge to laws on the basis of being vague refers to whether they are sufficiently clear and concise so that a person of ordinary intelligence could understand the behavior prohibited or required by the laws. A law can be seen as overbroad if it infringes on a constitutionally protected right, such as the freedom of speech (Snow 1998). The first state statute that was challenged was that of Massachusetts, and the court determined that the phrase in the law "repeatedly harasses" was vague. The court further decided that to fulfill this phrase, "the defendant must perform at least two series of acts (i.e., at least four separate acts)" (Mullen et al. 2000, p. 265). Other state statutes on stalking were also declared vague, such as those in Kansas, Oregon, and Texas. In order to help states rewrite these statutes to conform to constitutional requirements, the U.S. Department of Justice developed a model anti-stalking law in 1993 (Snow 1998). However, states do not have to adopt the model anti-stalking law, and therefore there are still problems with many state statutes and a "lack of uniformity" (p. 268).

Other criticisms of stalking statutes have focused on the perception that there were already laws on the books that covered stalking behaviors, and the new statutes were a response to the public concern about rare incidences of stalking leading to murder, and that some of the behaviors delineated in the statutes are legal in other contexts (Morewitz 2003).

However, proponents of these statutes counter that even though laws against stalking behaviors were on the books, they were not used to any great extent, and therefore statutes specifically on stalking were needed. Supporters of these statutes feel that enactment of these laws should result in more arrests, prosecutions, and greater satisfaction for victims and cause police to intervene before violence occurs. Also, arrests of stalkers may be a deterrent and provide them with treatment they need. Finally, laws against stalking give victims a forum and method to exert some control over their disrupted lives (Morewitz 2003).

Even though state and federal statutes on stalking vary, there are some commonalities. One commonality is that most statutes require that there be a pattern of behavior and often use the term "repeatedly." For example, the California statute reads, "Any person who willfully, maliciously, and repeatedly follows" (California Penal Code §646.9), and the Alaska statute requires a "course of conduct," which is further defined as "repeated acts of nonconsensual contact" (Alaska Penal Code §11.41.260

and §11.41.270). The New York statute also calls for a "course of conduct" (New York Penal Code §120.45), and in West Virginia the state law reads, "Any person who willfully and repeatedly follows" (West Virginia Penal Code §61-2-9).

A second commonality among state and federal statutes is that most require "a credible threat against the victim," in those or similar terms (Morewitz 2003, p. 61). The term "credible threat" has been somewhat controversial, as threats are generally assumed to be communicated via verbal or written means. However, a pattern of harassing behavior without a specific threat can constitute stalking. For example, behaviors such as sending someone dead flowers, calling incessantly, or sending unwanted romantically worded notes do not include specific verbal or written threats, but to the recipient, these behaviors may indicate a threat because of the pattern of the activities and/or past encounters with the sender. Therefore, some statutes do not include the term "credible threat" or include provision for the crime of stalking without this requirement. For example, the Alaska code does not use the term "credible threat" but states that a person commits the crime of stalking "if the person knowingly engages in a course of conduct that recklessly places another person in fear of death or physical injury or the death or physical injury of a family member" (Alaska Penal Code §11.41.270). The West Virginia statute on stalking and harassment allows for repeated harassment without credible threats, or credible threats, or a combination of the two to establish a crime (West Virginia Penal Code §61-2-9). The New York statute also does not use the term "credible threat" but does require that the "course of conduct" be "likely to cause reasonable fear of material harm to the physical health, safety, or property of such person" (New York Penal Code §120.45). However, the California statute reads that a person is guilty of the crime of stalking if he/she "makes a credible threat with the intent to place that person in reasonable fear for his or her safety, or the safety of his or her immediate family" (California Penal Code §646.9). The majority of state statutes on stalking do have the threat requirement (Wells 2001).

The third common feature of these statutes is that the intent of the perpetrator must be to place the victim in reasonable fear. As noted above, the California and Alaska statutes, respectively, require that the perpetrator intend to "place that person in reasonable fear for his or her safety" (California Penal Code §646.9) and "in fear of death or physical injury" (Alaska Penal Code

§11.41.270). The New York law states that the perpetrator also must "cause reasonable fear of material harm" (New York Penal Code §120.45). In West Virginia, the law states that the intent of the perpetrator must be to instill "reasonable apprehension that he or she or a member of his or her immediate family will suffer death, sexual assault, kidnapping, bodily injury or battery" (West Virginia Penal Code §61-2-9).

Another commonality among the state statutes is that the crime of stalking is generally a misdemeanor, and therefore punishments for this crime usually involve at the most a few months in jail and/or fines. However, many states allow felony charges and enhanced sentences if the crime of stalking is combined with other crimes, such as violating an order of protection, possessing or threatening with a weapon, or having a prior conviction for stalking. Also, interstate stalking is a felony, 18 U.S.C. §2261 (b). For example, in California, the crime of stalking by itself is a misdemeanor but may be combined with other offenses, such as breaking and entering or violating a restraining order, which will together warrant a sentence to a prison of more than one year rather than to a jail for a maximum of one year (California Penal Code §646.9). In Alaska, stalking in the second degree and harassment are misdemeanors, while stalking in the first degree is a class C felony, but to achieve the first-degree charge, the stalking has to be included with other charges, such as violating a court order or possession of a weapon "during the course of conduct constituting the offense" (Alaska Penal Code §11.41.260). New York laws also have degrees of stalking. Stalking in the third and fourth degrees are misdemeanors. To be charged with stalking in the second degree, which is a felony, the perpetrator has to have a record of prior convictions of stalking, has to be an adult stalking a person under the age of fourteen, or has to be someone who "displays, or possesses, or threatens the use of a firearm, pistol, revolver," etc. (New York Penal Code §120.55). The charge of first-degree stalking, also a felony, is reserved for one who "intentionally or recklessly causes physical injury to the victim" or who has a specific history of past stalking convictions (New York Penal Code §120.60). In West Virginia, the crime of stalking is a misdemeanor, but a subsequent conviction is a felony if it occurs within five years of the first conviction (West Virginia Penal Code §61-2-9).

States are also enacting laws that prohibit cyberstalking. For example, the Michigan statutes on stalking include a section on "posting [a] message through [an] electronic medium" (Michigan Penal Code §750.411s). In West Virginia, the stalking law prohibits "obscene, anonymous, harassing and threatening communications by computer" (West Virginia Penal Code §61-3C-14a).

Even though the statutes on stalking vary across the country, there are commonalities involving the elements of the offense, the type of offense, and the punishments available. As with the prosecution of any crime, all involved, from the victim to the police officer to the prosecutor and judge, must work together. Laws are just words if they are not enforced; police officers will be reluctant to build cases that will not be prosecuted, and prosecutors will not want to waste time on cases in which perpetrators will receive light sentences that will place them back in the vicinity of their victims. Victims will become discouraged if their cases are not taken seriously and do not result in harsh sanctions and recognition of stalking as a crime. The entire criminal justice system has to work together if these criminals are to be deterred.

Types of Stalkers

In an effort to understand stalkers, researchers have developed typologies based mainly on stalkers' behaviors and motives for stalking. These typologies are designed to assist criminal justice or mental health professionals as they attempt to build a case against, arrest, or treat stalkers. The typologies are also useful to researchers as they design studies to assess the purposes of stalking and thereby make recommendations for combating this crime and managing and treating offenders.

One of the well-known typologies includes three categories of stalkers: simple obsessional, love obsessional, and erotomanic (Zona, Sharma, and Lane 1993). These categories are based on the relationship between the stalker and the victim, whether real or imaginary.

Stalkers typed as *simple obsessional* are the most common. This stalker has had a prior relationship with the victim. The relationship in most cases was intimate. On the other hand, stalker and victim may at one time have simply dated for a brief duration or been neighbors, roommates, friends, or professional acquaintances, such as teacher and student or physician and patient. According to victims of stalking, the primary reason they were being stalked was so the stalkers could have some degree of control over their lives (Tjaden and Thoennes 1998). These efforts to control other people would be particularly apparent in prior intimate relationships where domestic violence occurred, as one of the main characteristics of batterers is the tendency to try to control victims.

Because of the behaviors of most types of stalkers, it is apparent that they are angry with and feel hostility toward their victims (Meloy 1996).

The second category is *love obsessional.* In these cases, stalkers and victims do not usually know each other. The victim may be a local or widely known celebrity or just someone upon whom the stalker has fixated. The stalker believes that if he/she is persistent, the victim will come to realize that he/she really cares for this person. Many of these stalkers suffer from mental illnesses.

The third category is *erotomanic.* In these cases, the stalker truly believes that the victim loves him/her, although they have not had a prior relationship, and indeed have never met. Erotomanic stalkers also have mental health problems, as they have developed delusions or delusional systems based on the fantasy relationship they hope to have or believe they have with their victims.

The most dangerous stalkers are those classified as simple obsessional, and the least dangerous are those in the erotomanic category.

A more detailed typology, offered by Mullen and colleagues (1999) focuses on the "stalker's predominant motivation and the context in which the stalking emerged" (Mullen et al. 2000, p. 75). This typology also takes into account the prior relationship, if any, between the stalker and the victim, and any psychiatric diagnoses. The categories in this typology include the rejected stalker, the resentful stalker, the predatory stalker, the intimacy seeker, and the incompetent suitor.

Rejected stalkers want reconciliation, revenge, or both from a former intimate partner, family member, friend, or professional contact who no longer desires to see them. These stalkers are usually male and generally are overly dependent on others but have "poor social skills and a resulting impoverished social network" (Mullen et al. 2000, p. 82). They tend to be jealous and possessive of others in their lives. Of the categories in this typology, the rejected stalkers are those who are most likely to threaten and assault their victims. If the victim was an intimate partner, assaults are likely to have occurred during the relationship as well. The likelihood of violence increases if the victim and stalker have contact, and the stalking behavior is difficult to stop because the stalker believes that he/she has a right to have contact with this person. These stalkers also are likely to have knowledge of the day-to-day routines of the victims and therefore can easily reach them by mail or phone or through confrontation at their places of work or their homes.

Resentful stalkers have a grudge against the victims for real or imagined slights. It is they who are the victims, "who, in the process of defending themselves, [are] striking back at their oppressors" (p. 90). One of the purposes of these stalkers is to frighten their victims. The resentful attitude of these stalkers is not reserved for a particular person but is often a general attitude toward life and others.

Predatory stalkers generally follow and watch their victims with the purpose of attacking them, usually sexually. The stalking process provides excitement for these stalkers, and they generally have some type of sexual deviance, such as exhibitionism, pedophilia, or voyeurism. These stalkers are usually men, and their victims may be adults or children. They generally lead a "lonely and socially inept existence with a paucity of meaningful adult relationships" (p. 115). Their behavior tends to be of short duration and ends after they have assaulted their victims or have been arrested.

Intimacy seekers believe that they have found their ideal match and are obsessed with their victims. They generally believe that the other person is in love with them, and they fantasize about how their lives will be once this idealistic relationship begins. These stalkers have few or no friends and have had few or no relationships in the past. They are persistent and will stalk for long periods of time. They use various means to pursue their victims, including finding out as much as they can about them, calling them, and sending them gifts and letters. Generally, they suffer from a mental disorder "that underlies the stalking" (p. 123) and are not affected by actions of the criminal justice system.

Incompetent suitors are "impaired in their social skills and most particularly in their courting skills" (p. 123). They approach their victims as though they were entitled to their attention and affection. Their efforts to entice their victims are often punctuated by crude and offensive remarks, and they do not understand the effects they have on others. Their pursuits are usually only for short periods of time, as they quickly move on to someone else. These stalkers do not understand their victims' concerns and are also unlikely to be deterred long by court appearances and sanctions.

The categorization proposed by Mullen et al. (2000) also includes a second axis, "related to the relationship to the victims" (p. 76), and a third axis, "related to psychiatric status" (p. 76). When these three axes are combined, a more adequate assessment can be made of (1) the relative danger the stalkers represent, (2) the behaviors of the stalkers, including the length of the stalking, and (3) how to manage the stalkers through the criminal justice system and/or treatment. For example, "the rejected grouping used the widest range of stalking behaviors, often repeatedly approaching, telephoning, letter writing, and leaving notes" (p. 76), while the predatory stalkers used the fewest types of behaviors, mainly focusing on surveillance. Intimacy seekers sent the most gifts and also rivaled the rejected group in terms of having the longest durations of stalking.

In terms of mental illnesses, those who could be diagnosed with a type of psychotic illness, such as schizophrenia or delusional disorders, were more likely to send gifts and letters than those with a mental disorder that did not involve psychosis. However, the nonpsychotics were more likely to "follow and maintain surveillance" (p. 77). Stalkers with psychotic or nonpsychotic mental disorders are as likely to issue threats, but those with non-psychotic diagnoses are more likely to carry out those threats than those with a type of psychosis.

A third typology has been designed to assist police officers as they determine how to build a case and arrest stalkers (Sheridan and Boon 2002). The types in this typology are based on characteristics of the stalkers, their behaviors, and the best management approaches. The first type, *ex-partners,* are the most common type of stalker. These stalkers are motivated by bitterness, anger, and hostility and are likely to have assaulted their victims prior to separation. Their behaviors will tend to be aggressive and may include threats, assaults, and destruction of property. They are not concerned about being reported to the police, as they feel they are not doing anything wrong but only trying to retain what they believe is theirs. Law enforcement officers should be aware of the danger these stalkers represent to their victims and those in the victims' families. They should help victims seek assistance as they would in domestic violence cases.

The second type are *infatuation harassers.* There are two subtypes of infatuation harassment—young love and midlife love, and therefore the stalkers' ages tend to be either teenage or midlife. These stalkers are acquainted with their victims and have determined that they are the objects of their affections. They have built a fantasy around their victims and so their approaches are generally not threatening but include gifts, chance encounters, and love notes. Generally with these cases, legal intervention is not necessary, and police officers may deter future behavior by explaining to the stalkers that they have frightened their victims and how arrests and criminal charges could negatively affect their lives.

The third type are *delusional fixation stalkers—dangerous.* These stalkers generally have a mental illness and a history of sexual deviance and arrests. The victims tend to be well-known celebrities or professionals who do not know their stalkers. The stalking behaviors tend to be diverse and numerous, such as telephone calls, letters, and attempts to confront the victims near their homes or in their workplaces. They may also make threats, particularly sexually oriented ones, and often act on these threats with attempted assaults. Law enforcement officers should be aware of the potential danger of these stalkers toward their victims and realize that arrest without psychiatric intervention will have little effect on future behavior.

The fourth type are *delusional fixation stalkers—less dangerous.* In this type of stalking, the perpetrators may or may not know their victims, but they believe that their victims love them. They have constructed fantasy lives based on that belief. They are generally not dangerous toward their victims but may look on other people in their victims' lives as the real reason why their victims do not acknowledge love for them. Therefore, people who represent this impediment to the fancied relationships may be in danger. Stalking behaviors usually do not include threats but focus on letters, gifts, phone calls, and perhaps planned confrontations. Law enforcement officers should be aware that arrest will deter the behavior only briefly and that these offenders are "not responsive to reason or rejection" (p. 76). Therefore, psychiatric intervention is needed to deter the stalking behavior significantly.

The last category in this typology comprises *sadistic stalkers.* These stalkers are very dangerous and seek to control their victims' lives as much as possible. Thus their behaviors can include breaking into the victims' homes and leaving something or disturbing possessions so that the victims will know they have been there; following the victims; damaging property; communicating in a threatening or sexual nature; physically assaulting their victims; or placing their victims in danger by such acts as "disabling brake cables, disarming safety equipment, cutting power off" (p. 77). These stalkers may or may not know their victims but usually choose victims who have stable, good lives that the stalkers set out to disrupt as much as possible. Law enforcement officers should realize that these stalkers are potentially violent, and should tell victims about the possibility of assaults and that this type of stalker is often very difficult to deter. These stalkers may even continue their harassing behaviors from jail if they are arrested and may attempt to find the victims as soon as they are released. If they cannot find their former victims, they are likely to move on to others.

These typologies indicate that stalkers are diverse. Some are only lonely and socially isolated, while others have serious mental illnesses. Their behaviors include a wide variety of actions, from sending gifts to confrontations and assaults. Intervention by the criminal justice system may be meaningful to some types of stalkers who have much to lose from being charged with this crime and may be sufficient to deter future stalking, while others may not even be deterred by incarceration. Counseling in addition to criminal justice sanctions for any of these types of stalkers would be beneficial and may increase the chances that they will find other uses for their time. This is particularly the case with those who have delusions that are either part of an underlying mental illness or the primary symptom of the illness. It is important for mental health professionals, law enforcement officers, and others in the criminal justice system to understand these types of stalkers so that they can be given appropriate sanctions and treatment focusing on deterrence.

Stalking Victims

Victims of stalking are likely to be at least acquainted with their stalkers. The most common stalker is someone who has had an intimate relationship with the victim (Mullen et al. 2000). Stalking victims, however, can be chosen because of their prominence in the community, country, or entertainment industry and have never even met their stalkers.

Stalking behaviors are generally not by themselves illegal, but the pattern and purposes of the behaviors are designed to gain the attention of the victim and exert some control over that person's life. The pattern and response of the victims will lead to a determination that the crime of stalking is being committed. The average stalker persists for almost two years (Tjaden and Thoennes 1998). Less intrusive behaviors are more common, such as gathering information about the victim and then using it to send letters, gifts, and e-mails and make phone calls.

As behaviors become more intrusive, they are also less common (Mullen et al. 2000). Some of these behaviors include following victims or conducting surveillance on their workplaces or homes, trying to influence family and friends by giving faulty information about the victims, confronting the victims, vandalizing property, issuing threats, and making assaults.

Cyberstalking is another form of stalking behavior that is becoming more common and has potentially serious consequences. The Internet provides a medium for stalkers to send unwanted messages and can also aid stalkers by giving them information about their victims, such as addresses, phone numbers, e-mail addresses, employers, birth dates, and other types of personal and professional information.

Stalkers can use e-mails to try to meet victims online, manipulate them into meetings, and proceed to use further e-mails for harassment and threats. Stalkers can also commit a variety of other actions via computer to harass, frighten, and cause negative consequences to victims. They can try to disable victims' computers by downloading viruses, spread false information about victims, post private photographs on the Web, and even pretend to be the victim online in chat rooms, for example, and ask for messages from deviant sexual partners (Spitzberg and Hoobler 2002).

In terms of violence, about 50 percent of stalking victims will be threatened by perpetrators, but in most cases those threats will not be carried out (Meloy and Gothard 1995; Zona et al. 1993). Meloy (2002), in a review of stalking and violence, states that he found that "[i]n most studies of violence [. . .], base rates do not usually exceed 30% per year, even in the most violent groups" (p. 106). However, Meloy also notes that in some newer studies, the rate of violence is higher and states that "this may be an artifact of data gathering, or it may be a true finding" (Meloy 2002). Another significant finding of this review is that the chances of violence increase substantially if the stalkers and victims have had prior intimate relationships (usually over 50 percent). In terms of homicide, Meloy reports that this is a rare occurrence among stalkers and at the most occurs "in one in four hundred individuals who are stalked by prior intimates" (p. 112).

The most common victims of stalking are those who have had intimate relationships with their stalkers; most of these victims are female, and most of the perpetrators are male (Mullen et al. 2000). Other victims include casual acquaintances and friends. According to Hall (1998), male victims probably fall most often into this category, and the most common perpetrators would be neighbors who feel resentment toward the victims and retaliate by acts such as damaging property, making unwarranted complaints to authorities, and closely watching the victims. Other victims of stalking may be at workplaces or in professional capacities, such as physicians, counselors, and lawyers. In these cases, the purpose of the stalking may be because the stalkers have romantic feelings toward the victims, but they can also be because the stalkers feel that they have not been treated fairly by the victims or others in the same environment. For example, in the workplace, if someone receives a promotion that the stalker believes was rightfully his/hers, this could cause resentment and make the chances of threats or physical assault more likely than if the basis of the stalking were infatuation, even though the chances of such cases resulting in violence are extremely low (Mullen et al. 2000). The least common types of stalking involve victims who are strangers. These strangers may be people the stalkers admire from afar who live in their communities or go to the same school. They may also be people whom the stalkers will probably never meet, who are prominent in the community, national affairs, or the entertainment business.

The effects of this crime on victims can range from mere annoyance to fear and terror to severe physical injuries and even death. Most victims report that they are emotionally affected (Pathe and Mullen 1997). Victims may also feel anger toward the stalkers and want to retaliate against them for interfering so dramatically in their lives. Victims will often go to great lengths to avoid and discourage stalkers, particularly if the stalking has continued for some time and/or involves someone who has abused them previously. They will often feel a lack of control over their lives as the stalkers' behaviors invade their personal and professional environments (Pathe and Mullen 2002). Stalkers do not behave in ways that are logical and generally do not respond to efforts to reason with them. Therefore, victims will feel frustrated as their prior methods of dealing with people, even those they want to avoid, do not succeed.

They will also be affected by the response of law enforcement officers if they report the stalking. If the response is positive and the police work with them, this will give victims a reason to feel that there is some hope that the stalkers can be stopped, and that they are truly victims of a crime.

Victims of stalking may change their lives significantly as they try to cope with being stalked. These changes may result in further isolation and loss of support when such contact is most needed. Besides feelings of frustration, anger, and loss of control, victims may also feel guilty and search for how their behavior may have encouraged the stalking. This may be particularly true if the victims had prior dating or intimate relationships with the stalkers, and they may ask themselves if they could have been more firm when they had told the stalkers that they did not want to see them again (deBecker 2002). Other emotions experienced by victims of stalking can include a high level of anxiety as they wonder how the stalkers will contact them the next time, if they will be waiting for them outside their homes or workplaces, and if they will be threatened or physically attacked. This anxiety may affect the victims physically as they lose sleep or weight or experience increases in headaches, nausea, and weakness (Pathe and Mullen 1997). The range of symptoms experienced by victims of stalking may constitute a diagnosis of post-traumatic stress disorder (PTSD), as they feel a lack of control over their lives, high levels of anxiety and stress, and profound weariness and make extraordinary and elaborate attempts to avoid the stalkers (Mullen et al. 2000).

Victims often have to change their lives in response to the actions of their stalkers. For example, if stalkers follow their victims to work or conduct surveillance outside the workplace, this can affect the quality of victims' work and work attendance. If the victims do not have employers who understand stalking and the underlying reasons for the changes in their behaviors, they could lose their jobs. On the other hand, victims may be so frightened that they leave jobs.

Victims may also feel threatened in their homes. If they have families, the stalkers can affect these secondary victims of their crimes (Pathe and Mullen 2002). Spouses and children may feel that their lives are being directed by the actions of stalkers; they may have some of the same anxieties as the victims and worry about the safety of the victims as well as of themselves. In severe cases, victims may move in an effort to get away from their stalkers. Other dramatic actions by victims may include changing their names and/or appearances. However, the stalkers usually find their victims again (Pathe and Mullen 1997).

All of these activities increase the isolation of victims and affect them further emotionally as their efforts to be rid of their stalkers do not succeed. As victims give up their places of employment and their homes, they lose friends at work and in their communities. They may fear for the safety of their families and send their children to stay elsewhere or decrease contact with family members. The high levels of stress may also affect relationships with their spouses or significant others. Victims may even consider or attempt suicide as they begin to believe that the stalking will never end and they see the destruction of their lives (Pathe and Mullen 1997).

Advice to victims of stalking is different depending on the circumstances. Victims who have had prior intimate relationships with their stalkers will, in all probability, take different actions than would celebrities who have never met their stalkers. Victims of former intimate partners should also be aware that they are more likely to be physically assaulted than any other type of victim.

Victims are urged to trust their instincts and respond to the first warning signs (Spence-Diehl 1999). Whether the stalker is a past intimate partner, date, friend, or stranger, there will, in all likelihood, be some initial indications that there is a potential for stalking. People who had intimate relationships in the past with their stalkers probably at the time experienced efforts by them to control their lives, such as surveillance, confrontation, and physical assaults. In dating relationships, potential stalkers may exhibit extreme possessiveness and jealousy and make efforts to keep track of the other persons' whereabouts and otherwise exert control over their lives. Once the dating relationship ends, other signs are further contacts by phone, e-mails, letters, the sending of gifts, or attempts at manipulation by asking for one last meeting.

If people are ending relationships with others they feel have the potential to stalk them, they should be firm about the decision they have made to end them. This is not a time for negotiation (deBecker 2002). If the spurned others then do exhibit stalking behaviors, depending on the circumstances, the victims may want to make a "no-contact statement" (Spence-Diehl 1999, p. 16) the next time they see them. If they know the stalkers, victims should tell them in no uncertain terms that they do not want to have any further contact with them (Spence-Diehl 1999). This should, of course, not be done in circumstances where victims feel threatened or where stalkers have asked to meet victims alone.

If the stalking continues, victims should report the behavior to the police and help them build a case. Victims should consider who else may have witnessed the stalking behaviors, the physical evidence they have, how they are going to gather evidence in the future, and the legal requirements for the crime of stalking. They should keep a record of every occurrence of stalking. Victims also should consider whether they need to file for an order of protection (Spence-Diehl 1999). About half of stalking victims report these crimes to the police (Tjaden and Thoennes 1998), and only about 25 percent of these cases result in arrest. Of these, about 20 percent are prosecuted, and about half of those prosecuted result in conviction.

Once victims report the stalking behaviors to the police, they should continue to file police reports based on the facts of what occurs and keep contact with the police about what is happening in the case. Victims should inquire whether there are victim advocates in the police department or prosecutor's office or other types of support groups. By so doing, victims will help the police build their cases, will feel more in control of the situation, and will understand that they are not alone as victims of stalking.

In terms of safety, victims should consider installing an alarm system in their homes, letting their neighbors know about the stalking, and making sure that they have an escape route in case their homes are invaded. Victims should also tell their families, friends, employers, and coworkers that they are being stalked. If the stalking includes excessive phone calls, victims should consider installing another line for their use while leaving the first line attached to an answering machine to keep a record of the stalkers' calls (Spence-Diehl 1999).

Victims may also be stalked while they are outside their homes, while they are in their cars, at work, or in social situations. In the car, victims should travel different routes to work and other places they frequently go, consider increasing the security measures on their cars, and make sure all doors are locked. They should be aware of cars around them and try to have escape routes if they are being followed.

In the workplace, victims should let their employers know about the stalking and work with security so that stalkers cannot gain access to the workplace. They should have someone escort them to their cars. Other actions victims can take in the workplace include having someone else's voice on their voice mail, varying work schedules, or transferring to other offices.

In public while at social events, victims should tell others about the stalking, and if stalkers are seen or attempt to approach them, victims should avoid them and seek assistance from the police. If victims find that they are alone with the stalkers, they should try to get to places where there are others and even enlist the aid of strangers (Spence-Diehl 1999).

If the stalking continues and becomes more intrusive, victims may want to consider further actions, such as having mail sent to a post office box, changing residences, trading cars, not using credit cards, and not giving information about themselves or their whereabouts to others unless necessary (Spence-Diehl 1999).

In terms of helping themselves emotionally, victims of stalking should reach out to others in their social environments, their families, and support organizations (Mullen et al. 2000). Victims need to feel as though they still have control over their lives, and they can do this by working with the police, speaking out about the stalking, filing for restraining orders, and taking actions which make them feel safer, such as installing alarm systems, getting a dog, or taking self-defense classes.

The murder of a stalking victim is a rare occurrence (Pathe 2002), and most victims of stalking will not be physically or sexually assaulted. However, estimates of the percentage of victims who are assaulted vary from a very small percentage (Zona et al. 1993) to around 30 percent (Meloy and Gothard 1995; Mullen et al. 1999). One thing that seems clear is that the likelihood of physical and/or sexual assaults by stalkers increases dramatically if there was a prior intimate relationship (Mullen et al. 1999) and increases even further when there had been violence in that relationship (Tjaden and Thoennes 1998).

About 50 percent of stalkers threaten their victims, but most of these threats are not acted upon. However, "the risk of violence likely increases when there is an articulated threat" (Meloy 1998, p. 5). Therefore, threats should be taken seriously.

Besides a prior intimate relationship and threats, there are some other risk factors related to assaults and homicides among stalking victims. Substance abuse is a risk factor in terms of threats, assaults, and property damage to stalking victims, as is a criminal history (Mullen et al. 1999).

In terms of mental illness, those with mental disorders involving psychosis or not involving psychosis are as likely to issue threats to stalking victims, but those with disorders not involving psychosis are more likely to assault victims, particularly when the diagnosis involves paraphilias or personality disorders (Mullen et al. 1999). However, stalkers diagnosed with a psychosis who are also categorized as predatory stalkers, although rare, can be particularly dangerous.

As with any crime, victims will feel that their lives have been interrupted and changed. The difference between most crimes and stalking is that the victimization can continue over a long period of time (as with domestic violence) and therefore wear down the outer and inner supports of the victims. Therefore, recognizing the crime and responding to it effectively is crucial to reduce the emotional damage to victims.

Conclusion

Stalking can be a dangerous crime that affects every aspect of victims' lives. Stalkers vary in terms of why they stalk, whom they stalk, and the danger they represent to their victims. They will use different methods to stalk, and most will not be deterred by attempts at intervention, even by the criminal justice system. Therefore, those in the criminal justice system, as well as mental health professionals, need to understand these criminals and the effect they can have on their victims.

GAIL FLINT

See also **Battered Woman Syndrome; Date Rape; Dating Violence; Intimate Partner Violence, Forms of; Marital Rape; Protective and Restraining Orders; Rule of Thumb; Social, Economic, and Psychological Costs of Violence; Victim-Blaming Theory; Violence against Women Act**

References and Further Reading

"The Antistalking Web Site." www.antistalking.com.

Boon, J., and L. Sheridan, eds. *Stalking and Psychosexual Obsession*. West Sussex, England: John Wiley & Sons Ltd., 2002.

Brontë, E. *Wuthering Heights*. Westport, CT: Easton Press, 1847/1975.

Davis, J. A., ed. *Stalking Crimes and Victim Protection*. Boca Raton, FL: CRC Press, 2001.

Davis, K. E., I. H. Frieze, and R. D. Mauro, eds. *Stalking: Perspectives on Victims and Perpetrators*. New York: Springer Publishers, 2002.

deBecker, G. "I Was Trying to Let Him Down Easy." In Boon and Sheridan, *Stalking and Psychosexual Obsession*, 2002, pp. 35–47.

Gallagher, R. *I'll Be Watching You*. London: Virgin Books Ltd., 2001.

Hall, D. M. "The Victims of Stalking." In *The Psychology of Stalking: Clinical and Forensic Perspectives*, edited by J. Reid Meloy. San Diego, CA: Academic Press, 1998, pp. 113–137.

Meloy, J. R. "Stalking (Obsessional Following): A Review of Some Preliminary Studies." *Aggression and Behavior* 1 (1996): 147–162.

———. "The Psychology of Stalking." In Meloy, *The Psychology of Stalking*, 1998, pp. 2–23.

———, ed. *The Psychology of Stalking: Clinical and Forensic Perspectives*. San Diego, CA: Academic Press, 1998.

———. *Violence Risk and Threat Assessment*. San Diego, CA: Specialized Training Services, 2000.

———. "Stalking and Violence." In Boon and Sheridan, *Stalking and Psychosexual Obsession*, 2002, pp. 105–124.

Meloy, J. R., and S. Gothard. "A Demographic and Clinical Comparison of Obsessional Followers and Offenders with Mental Disorders." *American Journal of Psychiatry* 152 (1995): 258–263.

Morewitz, S. J. *Stalking and Violence*. New York: Kluwer Academic/Plenum Publishers, 2003.

Mullen, P. E., M. Pathe, and R. Purcell. *Stalkers and Their Victims*. Cambridge, England: Cambridge University Press, 2000.

Mullen, P. E., M. Pathe, R. Purcell, and G. W. Stuart. "A Study of Stalkers." *American Journal of Psychiatry* 156 (1999): 1244–1249.

Pathe, M. *Surviving Stalking*. Cambridge, England: Cambridge University Press, 2002.

Pathe, M., and J. R. Mullen. "The Impact of Stalkers on Their Victims." *British Journal of Psychiatry* 170 (1997): 12–17.

———. "The Victim of Stalking." In Boon and Sheridan, *Stalking and Psychosexual Obsession*, 2002, pp. 1–22.

Schell, B. H. *Stalking, Harassment, and Murder in the Workplace*. Westport, CT: Quorum Books, 2002.

Shakespeare, W. *The Complete Works of William Shakespeare*. Cleveland: World Publishing Company, 1594/1942.

Snow, R. L. *Stopping a Stalker*. New York: Plenum Trade, 1998.

Spence-Diehl, E. *Stalking: A Handbook for Victims*. Holmes Beach, FL: Learning Publications, 1999.

Spitzberg, B. H., and G. Hoobler. "Cyberstalking and the Technologies of Interpersonal Terrorism." *New Media and Society* 14 (2002): 7–92.

Stalking Behavior website. www.stalkingbehavior.com.

Stalking Resource Center website. http://www.ncvc.org/src/main.

Stalking Victims Sanctuary website. http://www.stalkingvictims.com.

Tjaden, P., and N. Thoennes. *Stalking in America: Findings from the National Violence against Women Survey*. Washington DC: National Institute of Justice and Centers for Disease Control and Prevention, 1998.

Zona, M. A., K. K. Sharma, and J. Lane. "A Comparative Study of Erotomanic and Obsessional Subjects in a Forensic Sample." *Journal of Forensic Sciences* 38 (1993): 894–903.

Statutes

Alaska Penal Code §11.41.260 and §11.41.270.

California Penal Code §646.9.

Michigan Penal Code §750.411h, §750.411i, and §750.411s.

New York Penal Code §120.45, §120.50, §120.55, and §120.60.

United States Code 18 U.S.C. §2261A.

West Virginia Penal Code §61-2-9a and §61-3C-14a.

STOCKHOLM SYNDROME IN BATTERED WOMEN

Battered women's paradoxical responses to their abusers have perplexed professionals and laypersons alike. These responses include expressing love for the abusers, denying or minimizing the abuse, blaming themselves for the abuse, continuing to stay with the abusers, returning to the abusers after fleeing, and refusing to testify against the abusers after they have been arrested for abuse. Laypeople and professionals alike often label these behaviors "masochistic," suggesting that these women seek out partners who abuse them so as to obtain some perverse psychological gratification. However, intimate violence is characterized by coercion, in which external, or situational, forces are likely to exert more control over behavior than are internal, or dispositional, ones. Consistent with such a social psychological perspective, Graham and associates (Graham 1994; Graham and Rawlings 1991) contend that these puzzling responses by battered women can be understood through a survival mechanism of bonding with the abuser, also known as "Stockholm Syndrome." Graham's Stockholm Syndrome theory (1994), based on the literature of hostage and hostage-like groups, aids in understanding the behaviors of battered women which many find confusing and frustrating.

Stockholm Syndrome was coined by Lange (1974), who described a curious bond which developed between bank-employee hostages and their captors after a failed bank robbery in Stockholm, Sweden. After exploring this account, as well as extensively surveying nine "hostage" groups (hostages, concentration camp prisoners, prisoners of war, civilians held in Chinese Communist prisons, cult members, abused children, incest victims, battered women, and pimp-procured prostitutes), Graham and associates identified conditions under which this bonding develops; the psychodynamics of the bonding; evidence that a bond (which is bidirectional) has developed; and psychological consequences of this bonding.

Each of these aspects of the theory is discussed in this essay. Since it addresses the issue of Stockholm Syndrome in battered women in particular, female pronouns have been used throughout when referring to the abuse victim, even though women and men are equally likely to develop Stockholm Syndrome, given exposure to the right conditions. Similarly, the abuser is referred to as male, though dynamics are the same whether the couple is heterosexual or homosexual and regardless of the sex of the abuser or victim.

Conditions Necessary for the Development of Stockholm Syndrome

Four conditions identified by Graham and associates as necessary precursors for the development of Stockholm Syndrome in victims of domestic violence are as follows.

1. The victim perceives a person threatening her survival. The threats may be physical or psychological. It is not important whether others view her survival as threatened, but rather whether she does.
2. The victim perceives the abuser showing her some kindness, however small. For example, the kindness may be that for one day out of the month he does not abuse her.
3. The victim is isolated from outsiders. This isolation may be physical—she is not permitted to have contact with family or friends—and/or ideological—she is permitted exposure to only the abuser's perspective.
4. The victim does not perceive a way to escape the abuser. Batterers use violence to help ensure that their partners do not leave them.

Bachman and Saltzman (1995) found that compared with married women, divorced women were almost nine times more likely to be victimized, and separated women were almost twenty-five times more likely to be victimized. Furthermore, although the criminal justice system is charged to protect all citizens, it fails battered women in many respects, making escape from an abuser extremely difficult when the abuser elects to continue his abuse even after "separation." For example, historically, despite the greater seriousness of intimate violence than stranger violence, arrest has been less likely when victim and offender are married (Berk et al. 1984), and sentences for convicted spouse assailants are lighter than those for convicted stranger assailants (Goolkasian 1986). Police have been slow to treat the home as a crime scene when there is evidence that domestic violence has occurred. They frequently fail to collect the evidence needed to convict the abuser, putting the onus of conviction entirely upon the woman's word in a misogynistic court. Graham witnessed a Cincinnati, Ohio, judge ordering an abuser to marry his victim or else go to jail, totally ignoring the woman's feelings about marrying a man who had battered her.

Psychodynamics of the Stockholm Syndrome

The psychodynamics of the Stockholm Syndrome as hypothesized by Graham and associates (1991, 1994) are as follows. A victim—who does not see a way to escape—perceives her survival being threatened. This traumatized victim, if isolated from outsiders who could provide nurturance and protection, must look to the abuser to meet those needs. If the victim perceives kindness, however small, from the abuser, the victim develops hope that the abuser will let her live. To further this end, she strives to make the most of whatever kindness he feels toward her. In an effort to increase any positive feelings he might have toward her, she strives to see the world from the abuser's perspective, doing what she can to keep him happy, and thereby helping to ensure her survival. In the process, the victim becomes hypervigilant to the abuser's needs and unaware of her own needs. She eventually views the world from the abuser's perspective, losing touch with her own perspective, which is unimportant or even counterproductive to her survival. By misinterpreting her own feelings of high arousal—created by the trauma of having one's survival threatened—as love, not terror, she is able to create and maintain hope of surviving and of a future without abuse, feel more in control, fend off feelings of terror and hopelessness, and feel less like a victim. She thereby begins a process of bonding to the positive side of the abuser, denying the side of the abuser that produces the terror. With the denial of the violent side of the abuser, and thus the denial of danger, the victim finds it difficult to psychologically separate from the abuser. Other mechanisms that make it difficult for the victim to psychologically separate from the abuser include: fear of retaliation for any show of disloyalty to the abuser; losing the only positive relationship available to her, due to her isolation from others; and losing the only identity that remains—her self as seen through the abuser's eyes (which, in the case of the adult victim of chronic abuse, has replaced any previous sense of self).

Indicators of Stockholm Syndrome

Graham and associates (1991, 1994; Rawlings et al. 1994) identified a number of indicators that Stockholm Syndrome has developed in a victim:

1. The victim is bonded with the abuser. Actually, the bond is bidirectional, with the abuser also being bonded to the victim. The bond works as a safety strategy because the batterer is bonded to his victim as well. However, and contrary to other hostage situations, in domestic violence cases wherein the abuser has borderline personality disorder, the bond may actually encourage the violence. Also, since the batterer uses violence to maintain the relationship, the bondedness of the abuser may put the battered woman at risk should she decide to leave him.

2. The attachment to the abuser is an anxious one, not the secure attachment one expects with a loving partner.

3. The victim is intensely grateful for small kindnesses shown by the abuser. These kindnesses can be so small that observers may not recognize them as kindnesses at all. An example would be the abuser buying the victim a hamburger for her birthday, and the victim viewing this act as proof that he loves her. (This example comes from a clinical case supervised by Rawlings.)

4. The victim denies, minimizes, or rationalizes the abuser's violence. She denies her own anger at his abuse. These cognitive distortions are essential for the victim to bond to the abuser.

5. The victim flip-flops in her perceptions of both the abuser and abusive events, seemingly being unable to hold on to a perception or maintain a belief regarding her own experiences. These observations suggest that she finds it difficult to know what is real and what is not.

6. The victim is hypervigilant to the abuser's needs and seeks to keep the abuser happy. To do this, the victim tries to "get inside the abuser's head" in order to predict what would calm or upset him. Because the victim is so focused on the abuser's needs, she loses touch with her own needs.

7. The victim sees the world from the abuser's perspective. If the abuser sees persons or situations as threats, the victim also sees them as threats.

8. The victim sees outside authorities trying to win her release (e.g., police, therapists) as the "bad guys" and the abuser as the "good guy." She sees the abuser as protecting her. The victim finds it difficult to leave the abuser even after her release is won. Due to her isolation, the abuser is often her only source of support and nurturance; also, her sense of self becomes dependent on her relationship with the abuser.

9. The victim fears that the abuser will come back to get her even after the abuser is dead or in prison.

10. The victim shows traumatic stress symptoms. These include physical and psycho-physiological complaints, depression, low self-esteem, anxiety reactions, paranoid patterns, and feelings of helplessness. After physically and psychologically separating from the abuser, full-blown post-traumatic stress disorder (PTSD) is experienced with classical PTSD symptoms, including nightmares and flashbacks. This is due to the split-off feelings and perceptions associated with trauma reemerging into consciousness, thus beginning the process of integration and healing (cf. Allen 1997).

Graham (1994) identifies sixty-six different indicators of Stockholm Syndrome, of which those listed previously are only a small subset. Graham et al. (1995) developed a three-factor scale to measure Stockholm Syndrome, and this scale was derived from the sixty-six indicators.

Cognitive Distortions

Perhaps the most prominent psychological feature associated with Stockholm Syndrome is the breadth of cognitive distortions associated with it. When discussing the abuser and the abuse with a battered woman evincing the syndrome, one feels unable to pin down facts, as though facts are slippery slopes that are forever changing. Why is this? Being able to bond with an abuser involves developing cognitive distortions that strengthen and maintain the bond, and thus maintain hope. Graham (1994) proposed that bonding with an abuser is a cognitive distortion maintained only when other cognitive distortions such as denial of abuse are in place. Many of the indicators of Stockholm Syndrome listed previously are examples of cognitive distortions (e.g., 1, 3, 4, 5, 7, 8, 10). An expanded list of cognitive distortions observed in Stockholm victims can be found in Graham (1994).

Personality Distortions

Bonding with abusers who provide abuse alternating with nurturance—known as the cycle of abuse (Walker 1979)—may eventually lead victims to develop borderline-like personality characteristics and behaviors (Graham 1994). Survival behaviors developed in the context of chronic, interpersonal abuse may be generalized to others in ways that appear, in their current context, as maladaptive and self-defeating. The Stockholm Syndrome theory gives an alternative understanding of behaviors listed later which are associated with borderline personality characteristics in victims of chronic interpersonal trauma:

1. Victims develop only superficial general relationships and exhibit intense "push-pull" dynamics in intimate relationships. The "push" is due to the abuse that is being denied, while the "pull" is due to the need to create and maintain a bond with the abuser so as to help ensure survival.
2. Due to taking the abuser's perspective, the victim lacks a sense of self and feels "empty." This continues after freedom is won until such time as the victim is able to begin viewing the world through her own eyes, not those of the abuser. To do this she must achieve the difficult challenge of feeling safe from the abuser, an event which may never happen.
3. The victim shows abandonment depression. She has catastrophic responses to loss, for it is the abuser's love of her, she feels, that is the only thing causing him to keep her alive. Bonding with an abuser leads to the loss of an integrated self; thus, she looks to others, as she did with the abuser, to provide self-soothing and protection.
4. The victim shows impulsive, self-destructive behaviors (e.g., drug abuse, promiscuity). These behaviors may reflect the victim's taking the perspective of the abuser, which is that the victim deserves to be abused.
5. Due to chronic terror, the victim may experience disturbed states of consciousness (e.g., depersonalization, dissociation, and de-realization) under stress.
6. Perceptions and cognitions seem to slip away, as the victim appears unable to maintain a stable view of an event or person. These flip-flopping perceptions, which suggest that she has difficulty knowing reality, make maintaining boundaries difficult, as even perceptions change regarding where boundaries should be. This waffling is due to the need to distort terror in order to see it as love or caring, so no perception can be trusted or really known.
7. The victim expresses rage toward safe, intimate others, rather than toward the abuser. This is because abandonment by the abuser threatens survival, diminishes hopes of surviving, and increases terror.
8. The victim shows "splitting." Abuse causes the victim to deny the abuser's violent side and to bond with his positive or nurturing side. There is a need to see the abuser as all-good or all-bad. Gray thinking permits anxiety, fear, and doubt to creep in. This black-or-white or all-or-none thinking generalizes to relationships with intimate or threatening others and events. Due to the flip-flopping of perceptions, a person may be idealized as all-good at one moment and all-bad the next. Some people or groups will be viewed as all-good or all-bad.
9. The victim shows a clinging, childlike dependency due to the experience of interpersonal trauma in which she was helpless and dependent of the whims of the abuser, whom she sees as all-powerful.

Questions Frequently Asked about Stockholm Syndrome

In presentations conducted by Graham and Rawlings on Stockholm Syndrome in battered women to both professional and lay groups, several questions are commonly raised. A few of these common topics are discussed later.

Women who develop Stockholm Syndrome do not do so because they have weak or defective personalities, because they have been previously abused, or because they were socialized in a certain way. Victims who develop Stockholm Syndrome do so because they have a desire to survive, and it is believed that bonding with an abuser is a survival strategy. Stockholm Syndrome develops in hostages taken at random (e.g., airplane hijackings), and there is no reason to believe that these people have weak personalities or have been subjected to a particular type of socialization experience (cf. Graham 1994). It is the abusers, not the victims, who are likely to have had personality defects and/or abusive backgrounds prior to the occurrence of spousal abuse. Battered women may exhibit behaviors that resemble personality distortions due to chronic, interpersonal abuse, as discussed previously.

Victims do not stay with their abusers because they are bonded to them. Other theories of traumatic bonding, such as those proposed by Dutton and Painter (1981) and Symonds (1979), identify the bond as the primary factor preventing the woman from leaving. In contrast, Stockholm Syndrome theory maintains that victims bond with their abusers because they see no other way to safely escape. The reality is that victims are at the most risk if and when they leave their abusers (Bachman and Saltzman 1995).

One would least expect to see Stockholm Syndrome in a victim of interpersonal abuse when the victim perceives a way to escape the abuser, when the victim perceives no kindness by the abuser, and when survival is not of paramount importance to the victim.

Battered women can break out of the Stockholm Syndrome once it has developed, as discussed later.

Breaking Out of Stockholm Syndrome: The Unbonding Process

Except for the work of Allen (1991, 1997), there is little empirical evidence as of this writing describing the struggles that battered women experience while extricating themselves from their abusive partners. When a battered woman flees to a shelter and subsequently returns to her abuser, she is viewed as a failure. Some shelters deny refuge to women who show a repeated pattern of leaving and returning to their abusive partners. Allen (1991, 1997) provided a different perspective on this pattern, viewing it as a process of unbonding. She argued that each time a woman leaves and returns to her abusive partner, she is working through a psychological process which may eventually lead to termination of the relationship. Allen (1991) developed a Stages of Unbonding Scale (SUS) to measure a battered woman's progress along a pathway of disengagement from her abusive partner, consistent with the psychodynamics involved in the development of the Stockholm Syndrome bond. The scale is made up of thirty-seven items designated as psychological "tasks." Participants are asked to indicate the level of priority they assign to working on each task. Based on a study of battered women in abuse shelters who filled out the SUS and other instruments, Allen constructed an empirically based clinical model of the psychological stages of disengagement from the abusive partner. She found that progression through the stages was characterized by an increase in self-reliance and a decrease in attachment to the abusive partner. Subsequently, Allen (1997) conducted a replication of the 1991 study. The 1997 study, which involved women in thirty shelters across the country, showed a substantial replication of the 1991 study. For simplicity, the discussion here will focus on the stages as described in the 1997 study.

Stage 1: Immersion with Partner

In this stage, women's bonds with their abusive partners are extremely strong. The women are enmeshed in their partners' thoughts and feelings as they attempt to anticipate the partners' actions in their efforts to keep their abusers nonviolent. As a consequence, they experience a profound loss of their own sense of self. An example of a high-priority task for these women was, "How to get my partner to forgive me for leaving him."

Stage 2: Out of Denial: Questioning Attachment to Partner

Unbonding begins to take place at this stage. These women are able to see both the abusive and kind sides of their partners. An example of a high-priority task for these women was, "To understand how I can love someone who treats me so badly."

Stage 3: Imagining Oneself with One's Partner: Confidence vs. Self-Doubt

The women begin to imagine living without their partners. They are seeking to address both sense of self and financial independence issues. An example of a high-priority issue for these women was, "Proving to myself that I can take care of myself apart from my partner."

Stage 4: Reclaiming the Self

The women at this stage are focused primarily on reclaiming their own sense of self and personal power. An example of a high-priority task for these women was, "To discover the strength and power within me."

Identifying a battered woman's progress along the unbonding process involves carefully listening to her. For example, women exhibiting a high degree of Stockholm Syndrome will obsessively focus on their abusive partners' needs, wants, and beliefs but appear clueless about their own needs, wants, and beliefs apart from their partners'. They also show a great deal of flip-flopping. Several conditions which Allen identified as facilitating movement through the stages were assigning the responsibility for the abuse to the batterer himself, feeling anger toward the batterer, using therapy, and having a spiritual faith to rely on. When dealing with a battered woman who exhibits a high degree of Stockholm Syndrome, some caveats are useful in distinguishing between helpful and unhelpful interventions. Unhelpful interventions for women highly immersed in the Stockholm Syndrome include the following:

- Attempting to persuade the battered woman to leave her abusive partner. Her attachment to her abuser is a survival strategy which she is probably not ready to relinquish. She will most likely break off a relationship with anyone who presses her to leave, since that person will be perceived as a threat to her survival.

- Criticizing her partner. If the partner is criticized, the woman will feel a strong need to defend him, and again, this places the critic in an adversarial position.
- Putting the woman on medication. Battered women are often misdiagnosed with psychiatric disorders such as depression, bipolar disorder, and anxiety, for which they are given psychotropic drugs. These medications may blunt negative affect, making it more difficult for a battered woman to access her anger at her abuser and, thus, reducing the likelihood that she will break out of Stockholm Syndrome.
- Involving the battered woman and her partner in marital counseling. Counseling is successful only when people can be open and honest about their relationships. If a battered woman is honest, she risks further retaliation and abuse.

Helpful interventions for battered women in the immersion stage include the following.

- Reducing the battered woman's isolation through involvement in supportive networks, support groups, and therapy groups.
- Facilitating the battered woman's development of an overlearned escape plan. This helps break through her denial that abuse is occurring.
- Providing support and helping her develop several sources of support so that nurturance and succor come from sources other than the abuser, thereby helping break down her isolation.
- Affirming both the loving and abusive sides of the battered woman's abusive partner to help reduce splitting.
- Developing safety and trust in one's relationship with the woman. This may involve going through numerous testing experiences.
- Indirectly educating the woman about Stockholm Syndrome by using stories and metaphors. These indirect techniques tend to bypass cognitive defenses and help her consider different perspectives on her situation.
- Helping the woman with practical concerns she has, by, for example, providing information on the availability of resources, even though she may not be ready or able to utilize them at the time.

Additional interventions which promote unbonding and healing at each of the four stages are discussed in Rawlings et al. (1994) and Allen (1997).

Stockholm Syndrome in Children of Battered Women

Children sharing the woman's Stockholm Syndrome pose additional difficult challenges for battered women. Children who have witnessed the abuse committed by their father figure are likely to be in the same untenable situation as their mothers: isolated, threatened, perceiving no way to escape, and shown at least an occasional kindness, however small. In fact, they are likely to be even less able to escape and even more dependent on the abusive father than the battered woman who is their mother. They too, therefore, are likely to develop Stockholm Syndrome. When this happens, they are put in the position of having to bond with the abuser and may even have to abuse their mother themselves, in order to win favor with their father. Any healthy love they feel toward their mother is likely to pale in intensity and salience compared with the bond they must create and maintain with their father in order to survive. The battered woman who is also a mother is therefore likely to be abused by both the abusive partner and by her children.

Even if the woman manages to leave the abuser, the children are often required by law to continue to see their father, who may have visitation rights or shared custody. In such a situation, the woman may commence unbonding with her abuser at a time when it is still unsafe for her children—who must continue to see their father—to do so. Thus, abuse by the children and/or abuse by the partner that is accomplished through the children is likely to continue long after divorce or separation has occurred for the battered woman who is also a mother.

Conclusion: Why Is It Important to Be Aware of Stockholm Syndrome in Battered Women?

Stockholm Syndrome helps one understand behavior in battered women that, in the absence of an understanding of its context, appears irrational and self-destructive and encourages victim blaming. Stockholm Syndrome explains why bonding to an abuser occurs; it comes from efforts to survive chronic, inescapable trauma and abuse, and not from personality defects of victims of abuse. In the absence of this understanding, one tends to blame the victims for their own abuse.

In a classic study, Lerner and Simmons (1966) found that people have a strong tendency to blame innocent victims if these people are not able to stop the victim's future suffering. How many people are able to successfully stop domestic violence upon learning it is occurring among their friends, family members, or neighbors? Lerner and Simmons found that victim blaming is least likely when people know that they have done something that will stop a victim's future suffering. On the other hand, if people do something to try to stop a victim's suffering, but they do not know whether their actions are effective, the tendency toward victim blaming remains strong. This is also the situation of most judges, prosecutors, police, doctors, psychotherapists, and even friends and family members who attempt to help battered women. It is no wonder then that Belknap (1995) and Kurz and Stark (1988) have found it commonplace for those responsible for helping battered women to rationalize their seemingly negligible assistance to this group by blaming the victims.

Unfortunately, the effects of victim blaming are likely to be cyclical and cumulative. Outsiders' victim-blaming attitudes encourage more abuse—and by extension, encourage the development of Stockholm Syndrome—by further isolating the woman and thereby making her escape more difficult. For example, hearing an outsider make remarks such as, "If she doesn't help herself, why should I help her?" "Battered women are masochistic. They seek out abusive partners," or "If a woman stays with an abusive man, she must not want to leave him" tells a victim that she can neither confide in nor expect assistance from that person. The increased isolation and inability to escape make the woman still more dependent on her abusive partner's kindness. Thus, outsiders' victim-blaming attitudes promote the development of Stockholm Syndrome in battered women. This is particularly true when these beliefs are held, expressed, and acted on by police officers, judges, prosecutors, psychotherapists, psychiatrists, and friends to whom the woman might turn for help. There is no better example of the fundamental attribution error—a denial of the power of the social context within which bonding occurs—than that provided by frequently heard victim-blaming attitudes expressed toward battered women.

Consider the effects on battered women of the general public blaming her for staying with her abuser, when so many factors, including the public's own attitudes, serve to preclude her escaping her partner's abuse. The more women appear bonded to their abusers, the more victim blaming people do, as they misperceive that love, not inability to escape, is the reason women stay with their abusers. Thus, the cycle repeats itself, each time increasing the victim blaming, the conditions conducive to Stockholm Syndrome, and the abused woman's bonding to the abuser.

EDNA I. RAWLINGS and DEE L. R. GRAHAM

See also **Battered Wives; Battered Woman Syndrome; Coercive Control; Feminist Theory; Victim-Blaming Theory**

References and Further Reading

Allen, P. Gail. *Separation Issues in Battered Women*. Unpublished master's thesis. University of Cincinnati, 1991.
———. *A Test of Validity and Reliability of the Stages of Unbonding Scale*. Unpublished doctoral dissertation. University of Cincinnati, 1997.
Bachman, Ronet, and Linda E. Saltzman. *Violence against Women: Estimates from the Redesigned Survey* (NCJ 154348). U.S. Department of Justice, 1995.
Belknap, Joanne. "Law Enforcement Officers' Attitudes about the Appropriate Responses to Woman Battering." *International Review of Victimology* 4, no. 1 (1995): 47–62.
Berk, Richard A., Sarah F. Berk, Phyllis J. Newton, and Donileen R. Loseke. "Cops on Call: Summoning the Police to the Scene of Spousal Violence." *Law and Society Review* 18, no. 3 (1984): 479–498.
Dutton, Douglas G., and Susan L. Painter. "Traumatic Bonding: The Development of Emotional Attachments in Battered Women and Other Relationships of Intermittent Abuse." *Victimology: An International Journal* 6 (1981): 139–155.
Goolkasian, Gail A. "The Judicial System and Domestic Violence: An Expanding Role." *Response to the Victimization of Women and Children* 9, no. 4 (1986): 2–7.
Graham, Dee L. R., and Edna I. Rawlings. "Bonding with Abusive Dating Partners: Dynamics of the Stockholm Syndrome." In *Dating Violence: Young Women in Danger*, edited by Barrie Levy. Seattle: Seal Press, 1991, pp. 119–135.
———. "Observers' Blaming of Battered Wives: Who, What, When, and Why?" In *The Psychology of Sexual Victimization: A Handbook*, edited by Michele A. Paludi. Westport, CT: Greenwood Press, 1999, pp. 55–94.
Graham, Dee L. R., Edna I. Rawlings, K. Ihms, Diane Latimer, Janet Foliano, A. Thompson, Kelly Suttman, Mary Farrington, and Rachel Hacker. "A Scale for Identifying 'Stockholm Syndrome' Reactions in Young Dating Women: Factor Structure, Reliability, and Validity." *Violence and Victims* 10 (1995): 3–22.
Graham, Dee L. R., with Edna I. Rawlings and Roberta Rigsby. *Loving to Survive: Sexual Terror, Men's Violence, and Women's Psychology*. New York: NYU Press, 1994.
Kurz, Demie, and Evan Stark. "Not-so-benign Neglect: The Medical Response to Battering." In *Feminist Perspectives on Wife Abuse*, edited by Kersti Yllö and Michael Bograd. Newbury Park, CA: Sage Publications, 1988, pp. 249–266.
Lang, Daniel. "A Reporter at Large: The Bank Drama." *New Yorker*, November 25, 1974, pp. 56–120.
Lerner, Melvin J., and Carolyn H. Simmons. "Observer's Reaction to the 'Innocent Victim': Compassion or Rejection?" *Journal of Personality and Social Psychology* 4, no. 2 (1966): 203–210.
Rawlings, Edna I., P. Gail Allen, Dee L. R. Graham, and June Peters. "Chinks in the Prison Wall: Applying Graham's Stockholm Syndrome Theory to the Treatment of Battered Women." In *Innovations in Clinical Practice: A Source Book*, vol. 13, edited by L. Vandercreek, S. Knapp, and T. L. Jackson. Sarasota, FL: Professional Resource Press, 1994, pp. 401–417.

Symonds, Martin. "Victims of Violence: Psychological Effects and Aftereffects." *American Journal of Psychoanalysis* 35 (1975): 19–26.

Walker, Lenore E. *The Battered Woman*. New York: Harper & Row, 1979.

SUBSTANCE USE/ABUSE AND INTIMATE PARTNER VIOLENCE

Substance use/abuse and intimate partner violence (IPV) often coexist. Victims of adult IPV, childhood physical abuse, or sexual violence are more likely to use illicit drugs or alcohol. Perpetrators of IPV also are frequently under the influence of drugs or alcohol. This article describes the prevalence of substance use in IPV incidents and the extent to which illicit drugs and alcohol may contribute to the perpetration of IPV. Questions that illuminate the connection between substance use/abuse and becoming a victim of IPV also will be addressed. For example, does IPV victimization increase the use of illicit drugs or alcohol? Do substance-abusing women have a higher risk of IPV than those who do not abuse alcohol or illicit drugs? These questions must be answered to fully understand the connection between substance abuse/use and victimization from IPV or childhood physical/sexual abuse. Explanations for the association between substance use/abuse and the commission of IPV also are explored, including whether substance use/abuse causes the perpetration of IPV. The article concludes with a section on how substance abuse complicates treatment of intimate partner batterers and victims.

Prevalence of Alcohol Consumption in Intimate Partner Violence Incidents

IPV often occurs when the batterer, victim, or both have been drinking alcohol (see Testa 2004). Much research has established that alcohol use/abuse and IPV often coexist. In the United States, nationwide probability surveys reveal that between 30 and 40 percent of male perpetrators and 27 and 34 percent of women perpetrators of IPV were drinking alcohol when they physically attacked their partners (Caetano, Schafer, and Cunradi 2001). Men in domestic

violence treatment report a rate of alcohol abuse or dependence four times higher than that of nonviolent men (Murphy et al. 2005). In longitudinal survey studies, wives reported that their husbands inflicted more severe violence when the husbands were drinking alcohol than when they were not drinking alcohol (see Murphy et al. 2005). In a study of men in treatment for alcoholism, there was a ten times higher rate of the men committing IPV on days of heavy drinking than on sober days, and heavy drinking also increased the likelihood of severe IPV (Fals-Stewart 2003). Between 33 and 50 percent of IPV incidents reported to the police involve a perpetrator who has been drinking alcohol (see Roberts 2002). Alcohol use also is frequently present in IPV homicides. About 40 percent of men convicted of murdering their female partners had been drinking at the time of the murder (see Wilson et al. 2000). Research also has found that non–substance using partners are at an increased risk of intimate partner homicide if they live in a home with an alcohol or illicit drug user (see Bailey et al. 1997).

Is heavy drinking or alcohol abuse more strongly related to IPV than socially drinking alcohol? Studies have noted that alcohol use alone has a modest relationship to IPV, whereas heavy or binge drinking has a stronger relationship with IPV (see Acierno, Coffey, and Resnick 2003). Research also suggests that IPV involving alcohol abuse is associated with more severe injuries and more chronic IPV. In samples of married men entering alcohol treatment, 50 to 70 percent have committed IPV in the past year and 20 to 30 percent report committing severe violence. Moreover, men with alcohol abuse problems have two to four times higher rates of perpetrating IPV than nonalcoholic men. Women with alcohol abuse problems, compared with nonalcoholic women, are twice as likely to perpetrate violence against their husbands, and wife-perpetrated IPV is twice as likely to occur when the husband has an alcohol problem.

Prevalence of Illicit Drug Use in Intimate Partner Violence Incidents

Several studies indicate that a significant proportion of domestic violence cases involve illicit drug use or perpetrators with illicit drug abuse problems. Prior studies of incarcerated domestic batterers indicate that 24 percent reported using illicit drugs alone or more commonly in combination with alcohol at the time of the offense and that 22 percent reported a history of illicit drug addiction. Based on reports from abused women, one assailant in five (21.8 percent) used both alcohol and drugs, and close to one-third used illicit drugs, with the most prominent drugs of choice being marijuana, cocaine, and amphetamines (see Wilson et al. 2000).

Stimulants, such as cocaine, heroin, and crack, are more consistently associated with IPV than are other types of illicit drugs (see Boles and Miotto 2003). Crack and cocaine use increased both the likelihood of IPV victimization and the commission of IPV. The relationship between marijuana use/abuse and IPV has not received as much attention compared with other illicit drugs. In a fifteen-month longitudinal study, researchers compared the likelihood of IPV on days when male partners were using substances and on days when they were not using substances. The use of alcohol and cocaine significantly increased the daily likelihood of male-to-female IPV, whereas the use of marijuana and opiates did not increase male-to-female IPV (see Acierno et al. 2003).

Based on self-reports from domestic batterers who were court referred to enter batterer treatment, illicit drug use predicts the perpetration of IPV and psychological abuse against a partner after removing the influence of alcohol use/abuse (Todd and Stuart 2004). Moreover, illicit drug use compared with alcohol abuse is shown to be a stronger predictor of IPV in several studies (see Wilson et al. 2000). In a sample of male addicts, an early onset of drug/alcohol-related problems and a history of illicit drug use—particularly cocaine use—were related to being a perpetrator of domestic violence. Illicit drug abusers may inflict more severe injuries than alcohol-only abusers and are much more likely to commit repeated IPV compared with domestic batterers who use only alcohol (see Wilson et al. 2000).

Is the Relationship between Substance Use and Intimate Partner Violence Spurious?

Research supporting the relationship between substance use and IPV does not explain why substance use/abuse is related to the perpetration of IPV. One possibility is that substance use/abuse does not really increase the risk of committing IPV. The linkage between substance use and IPV may occur because IPV and substance use/abuse are associated with the same demographic or environmental factors; in short, the relationship is spurious. For example, people holding attitudes supportive of IPV may be more likely to use alcohol and/or illegal drugs and more likely to commit violence ("drunken bum" theory); thus, the attitudes rather than substance use directly influence the perpetration of IPV, and substance use does not have any causal relationship to committing IPV (see Johnson 2001). Several recent studies have disconfirmed the spurious explanation. These studies have found that alcohol abuse and illicit drug use are the strongest predictors of the commission of IPV after removing the influence of demographic, environment, and background factors (see Coker et al. 2000). Research has found that problem drinking is related to violence even after the influence norms supportive of aggression and social class are removed (see White and Chen 2002). For example, in a sample of 772 women surveyed at a health clinic, their male partners' alcohol use was significantly associated with the commission of IPV after the effects of age, employment, race, the battered woman's substance abuse, violence in the family of origin, and access to guns were removed (Coker et al. 2000).

Does Substance Use/Abuse Cause Perpetrators to Commit Intimate Partner Violence?

Researchers still debate whether substance use/abuse causes perpetrators to commit IPV. The biological disinhibition explanation asserts that alcohol lowers inhibitions against aggression directly through biochemical or physiological changes; and because of these physiological changes, alcohol users become violent toward their partners. This explanation does not explain the linkage of alcohol use/abuse with IPV because experiments have found that when people are not given alcohol but think they are drinking alcohol, aggression increases. Alcohol does not cause biochemical changes that increase aggression; instead, people's expectations about the effects of alcohol determine the relationship between alcohol and IPV. Thus, what people *expect* alcohol to do is a better explanation than is biological disinhibition. Moreover, research has found that individuals who report strong expectations of aggression following alcohol consumption were three times more likely to perpetrate IPV than those who did not hold such expectations (Field, Caetano, and Nelson 2004). Cross-cultural research also supports the finding that expectations determine the relationship between alcohol and IPV. Thus, individuals may drink alcohol to provide an excuse for their planned violence (see Roberts 2002).

Moreover, most binge drinkers do not commit IPV, and treated alcoholics do not refrain from IPV. Battered women have reported that batterers increased threats, isolation, and psychological abuse when the batterers were abstaining from substance use as part of their substance abuse treatment (see Roberts 2002). Furthermore, research has not found a link between alcohol and other forms of coercive control such as limiting access to education or resources, limiting access to friends and family, and surveillance or stalking. Thus, as noted previously, a better explanation than biological disinhibition is that alcohol's relationship to IPV depends upon people's expectations about its effects. When people expect to become more aggressive after consuming alcohol, they are more likely to be violent than are people who expect to become relaxed after consuming alcohol.

Additionally, abuse of or dependence on alcohol or illicit drugs may indirectly increase IPV through lowering marital satisfaction and increasing conflict. Research has found that alcohol and drug use is a frequent topic of discussion during conflicts involving IPV (Murphy et al. 2005). Experiments in which intimate partners are asked to discuss their most serious area of conflict have found that partners had increased negative verbal interactions when under the influence of alcohol compared with those who were given no alcohol or who were given a placebo that they thought was alcohol (see Fals-Stewart 2003). Illicit drug or alcohol use/abuse over time may facilitate conflict between couples and have an indirect effect on IPV. Supporting this explanation, substance-using men are significantly more likely to engage in psychological abuse such as insulting their partners and calling them derogatory names (Coker et al. 2000). Moreover, in one study, the strongest predictor of IPV was name-calling and put-downs in the relationship, and after controlling for psychological abuse, alcohol abuse was not related to IPV (Johnson 2001). Research has found that problem drinking has an indirect effect on IPV through increasing marital dissatisfaction, and the direct relationship between problem drinking and IPV is eliminated when marital dissatisfaction is included as a predictor for both male- and female-perpetrated IPV (White and Chen 2002).

Other research, however, suggests that additional cognitive, environmental, or interpersonal processes may account for the link between substance abuse and the commission of IPV. Some research shows that marital discord and psychological abuse do not completely explain the link between substance abuse and IPV. For example, after controlling for demographic factors, hostility, and marital satisfaction, heavy drinking still substantially increased the risk of perpetrating IPV as well as becoming a victim of IPV. Moreover, other research has found that both psychological abuse and illicit drug use were significant predictors of repeat IPV (see White and Chen 2002).

The Link between Substance Use/Abuse and Intimate Partner Violence: Does It Vary across Contexts and Groups?

The relationship between substance use/abuse and IPV may differ across social groups and environments. The *differential threshold theory* asserts that some people may have lower inhibitions against committing violence or more motivation to commit violence than other people (see Fals-Stewart et al. 2005). Support for differential inhibitions against committing violence has been found in comparisons between men with antisocial personality disorder and men who do not have antisocial personality disorder. Fals-Stewart and colleagues (2005) found that men who have antisocial personality disorder are inclined to commit nonsevere IPV, whether intoxicated or not. By contrast, men who do not have antisocial personality disorder are more likely to commit IPV when drinking alcohol than when they are sober. The theory suggests that alcohol lowers inhibitions against nonsevere violence for men who do not have antisocial personality disorder, whereas those with antisocial personality disorder have few inhibitions against committing nonsevere violence. Alcohol drinking lowers inhibitions against committing severe IPV among men with antisocial personality disorder, and these men are more likely to commit severe violence when drinking than when sober. For men who do not have antisocial personality disorder, drinking alcohol is not related to committing severe violence, suggesting that alcohol does not sufficiently lower the inhibitions against severe violence among the general population.

Individuals who are living in poverty or facing racial discrimination or low wages and lack of advancement due to dropping out of high school experience much stress associated with struggling to meet basic needs. Studies have found that women living in poverty are particularly vulnerable to and have much higher rates of IPV victimization and that batterers who are unemployed and/or are high school dropouts are more likely to commit injury-related IPV (see Johnson 2001). Individuals having a low social status may also turn to drugs and alcohol to cope with daily stress, which in turn produces more stress by using their limited money for self-medication rather than to support their family. Substance use also may have a stronger relationship with committing IPV among minorities because of the additional stress due to racial discrimination.

Thus, this argument suggests that a very stressful environment or a relationship that involves much conflict also may need to be present for substance use/abuse to serve as a partial impetus for IPV. Based on empirical studies, the relationship between alcohol abuse and IPV varies across ethnic background. After removing the influence of childhood victimization, approval of aggression, impulsivity, and length of the relationship, alcohol abuse by men or women and IPV were strongly related for African American couples but were not related for Hispanic couples. Among white couples, only women's alcohol abuse was significantly associated with IPV (Caetano et al. 2001). Other research also has found that heavy alcohol use strongly predicts IPV for minorities but not whites (see Johnson 2001). Additional research needs to examine whether the relationship between substance use/abuse and the commission of IPV varies across living situations.

The research has produced inconsistent findings on whether the relationship between alcohol abuse and IPV is similar for men and women perpetrators. Alcohol abuse or dependence has been associated with IPV for both men and women perpetrators (e.g., Wilson et al. 2000); however, two studies suggest that alcohol abuse is more strongly related to male-perpetrated incidents of IPV (see Thompson and Kingree 2004).

Relationship between Substance Use/Abuse and Intimate Partner Violence Victimization

Numerous studies have found that women using or abusing alcohol or illicit drugs are more likely to be victims of IPV (for a review, see Logan et al. 2002; Roberts 2002). Research estimates that adult victims of IPV have a five times higher rate of alcohol abuse and dependence compared with non-victims. Women in alcohol treatment are twice as likely to have experienced verbal abuse, sexual abuse, and severe physical abuse as children. Moreover, across studies, battered women have an average prevalence rate of 18.5 percent for alcohol abuse and 8.9 percent for illicit drug abuse, whereas in the general population of women, the lifetime prevalence rate for alcohol abuse is 6.3 percent and 3.5 percent for drug abuse. Batterers also may force their partners to take illicit drugs (Roberts 2002). Across research studies, victims of child sexual abuse compared with nonvictims were significantly more likely to abuse alcohol or illicit drugs as adults and were more likely to start using alcohol and illicit drugs at an earlier age.

The relationship between substance use and victimization from partners may reflect the use of alcohol or illicit drugs to cope with previous victimization experiences. Victimization thus may stimulate individuals to begin using or increase their use of alcohol or drugs to cope with the pain and stress resulting from victimization. Moreover, some battered women may use substances to eliminate the fear of being physically attacked again by their partners (Roberts 2002). Longitudinal research supports the view that IPV victims increased their use of alcohol and drugs after their partners physically attacked them (Logan et al. 2002). Furthermore, research suggests that battered women who develop post-traumatic stress disorder may have the highest risk of developing an alcohol abuse or dependence problem.

Additionally, substance-using women may be more vulnerable and have a higher risk of becoming victims. Marijuana use and harder illicit drug use independently increased the chance of women experiencing IPV victimization across the following twelve months, but heavy drinking did not increase IPV victimization (see Acierno et al. 2003).

Substance-using individuals also may have a higher risk of IPV victimization due to their neighborhoods and social environments. Substance use, especially of hard illicit drugs, is associated with environments that have higher crime rates and cultures that are more supportive of violence. Supporting the risky-environment supposition, women who use crack or cocaine have an increased risk of being physically or sexually assaulted. Research has found that two-thirds to three-quarters of crack users reported that their partners physically attacked them after they started using crack. Several studies have found that the verbal and physical degradation of women is common practice in the crack-using population. Thus, illicit drugs may increase the risk of victimization through increasing exposure to more dangerous subcultures, neighborhoods, or social networks. Women who frequent bars or fraternity houses are more likely to be sexually assaulted because they come in contact with a greater number of young men who drink alcohol. Research has shown that women who more often visit bars have a higher rate of sexual assaults.

In addition, substance use may increase the risk of victimization because it impairs cognitive judgment and decision making. Studies show that a substantial percentage of victims were using illicit drugs or alcohol at the time of being physically attacked by intimate partners or being sexually assaulted. At least half of the sexual assault victims were using illicit substances or alcohol when they were sexually assaulted. Substance-using battered women are less likely to call the police because they believe that the police will be more likely to blame them or to discount their victimization due to their substance use/abuse. Thus, substance-using battered women are more vulnerable to possible victimization.

Treatment Modalities and Responsiveness

Substance use/abuse complicates the treatment modalities offered to domestic batterers. Although substance abuse may not cause the occurrence of domestic violence, substance abuse that is left untreated may impair batterers' ability to understand and participate fully in batterer treatment programs. Moreover, substance-abusing batterers who do not undergo treatment for their substance abuse are more likely to drop out of batterer treatment programs (Daly and Pelowski 2000).

Substance-using victims often face many barriers to obtaining the services they need. Only about 10 percent of substance abuse counselors assess whether clients have been victims of IPV (Roberts 2002). Even when substance abuse treatment programs are aware of women's IPV victimization, it is generally addressed only after completion of substance abuse treatment. Roberts (2002) identified several problems with making sobriety the top priority. The "sobriety first" approach ignores that women who are trying to stop substance use may be at an increased risk of being revictimized. Batterers generally do not tolerate their partners' attempts to improve themselves and will try to regain control through any means. Moreover, batterers may attempt to sabotage the treatment process by preventing their partners from attending meetings, by keeping drugs or alcohol in the house, by forcing their partners to use substances, and by threatening violence if their partners do not

drop out of treatment. Furthermore, women who are revictimized are more likely to relapse.

Substance-abusing victims also receive less assistance from domestic violence programs than victims without substance abuse problems. Most shelters will not admit substance-using battered women because they are perceived as a danger to themselves or others, neglectful toward their children, and unable to follow shelter rules. Even when shelters admit substance-using women, they often fail to conduct thorough assessments of their substance abuse treatment needs. The lack of integration and connection between substance abuse and domestic violence treatment providers further undermines their ability to provide the needed resources and help to substance-using battered women. Coordination initiatives and cross-training have begun. Philosophical differences in treatment, however, will need to be addressed before a truly intertwined and coordinated model of combined treatment can be developed. A few treatment models have started to address philosophical differences and create a more coordinated integrative treatment model for substance-using victims (see Logan et al. 2002; Roberts 2002).

LORETTA J. STALANS

See also **Depression and Domestic Violence; Education as a Risk Factor for Domestic Violence; Social Class and Domestic Violence**

References and Further Reading

Acierno, Ron, Scott F. Coffey, and Heidi S. Resnick, eds. Special edition. "Interpersonal Violence and Substance Use." *Addictive Behaviors* 28, no. 9 (2003): 1649–1667.

Boles, S. M., and K. Miotto. "Substance Use and Violence: A Review of the Literature." *Aggression and Violent Behavior* 8, no. 2 (2003): 155–174.

Caetano, R., J. Schafer, and C. B. Cunradi. "Alcohol-related Intimate Partner Violence among White, Black, and Hispanic Couples in the United States." *Alcohol Research and Health* 25, no. 1 (2001): 58–65.

Coker, A. L., P. H. Smith, R. E. McKeown, and M. J. King. "Frequency and Correlates of Intimate Partner Violence by Type: Physical, Sexual, and Psychological Battering." *American Journal of Public Health* 90, no. 4 (2000): 553–559.

Fals-Stewart, W. "The Occurrence of Partner Physical Aggression on Days of Alcohol Consumption: A Longitudinal Diary Study." *Journal of Consulting and Clinical Psychology* 71, no. 1 (2003): 41–52.

Fals-Stewart, W., K. Leonard, and G. R. Birchler. "The Occurrence of Male-to-Female Intimate Partner Violence on Days of Men's Drinking: The Moderating Effects of Antisocial Personality Disorder." *Journal of Consulting and Clinical Psychology* 73, no. 2 (2005): 239–248.

Field, C. A., R. Caetano, and S. Nelson. "Alcohol and Violence Related Cognitive Risk Factors Associated with Perpetration of Intimate Partner Violence." *Journal of Family Violence* 19, no. 4 (2004): 249–253.

Johnson, H. "Contrasting Views of the Role of Alcohol in Cases of Wife Assault." *Journal of Interpersonal Violence* 16 (2001): 54–72.

Logan, T. K., R. Walker, J. Cole, and C. Leukefeld. "Victimization and Substance Abuse among Women: Contributing Factors, Interventions, and Implications." *Review of General Psychology* 6, no. 4 (2002): 325–397.

Murphy, C. M., J. Winters, T. J. O'Farrell, W. Fals-Stewart, and M. Murphy. "Alcohol Consumption and Intimate Partner Violence by Alcoholic Men: Comparing Violent and Non-violent Conflicts." *Psychology of Addictive Behaviors* 19, no. 1 (2005): 35–42.

Roberts, A. R. *Handbook of Domestic Violence Intervention Strategies: Policies, Programs, and Legal Remedies.* Oxford and New York: Oxford University Press, 2002.

Testa, M. "The Role of Substance Use in Male-to-Female Physical and Sexual Violence: A Brief Review and Recommendations for Future Research." *Journal of Interpersonal Violence* 19, no. 12 (2004): 1494–1505.

Thompson, M. P., and J. B. Kingree. "The Role of Alcohol Use in Intimate Partner Violence and Non-intimate Partner Violence." *Violence and Victims* 19, no. 1 (2004): 63–74.

White, H. R., and Ping-Hsin Chen. "Problem Drinking and Intimate Partner Violence." *Journal of Studies on Alcohol* 63, no. 2 (2002): 205–214.

Wilson, P., J. McFarlane, A. Malecha, K. Watson, D. Lemmey, P. Schultz, J. Gist, and N. Fredland. "Severity of Violence against Women by Intimate Partners and Associated Use of Alcohol and/or Illicit Drugs by the Perpetrator." *Journal of Interpersonal Violence* 15, no. 9 (2000): 996–1008.

T

TRAINING PRACTICES FOR LAW ENFORCEMENT IN DOMESTIC VIOLENCE CASES

Introduction

This article discusses law enforcement training practices for handling domestic violence cases. It covers three broad topics: definitions of relevant terms, current training practices, and future training practices. It will begin with definitions of terms such as *child abuse, domestic violence, elder abuse,* and *spousal abuse.* However, realizing that there are many controversies as to the different forms and effects from these types of aggressive behavior, scholars of victimology, a relatively new academic field, have not come far enough to separate the definitions concisely. The following definitions are broad in nature and remain flexible until scholars and researchers learn more about the scope and ramifications of various types of violence to determine whether and where they fall within the realm of domestic violence. Subsequently, this article discusses the law enforcement training topics as they relate to domestic violence. It concludes with a series of recommendations for future training practices.

Definitions

Domestic Violence

Applying a simple term to describe violence between intimate partners is not easy; some prefer the term *family violence,* while others use the term *domestic violence.* For the purposes of this essay the term *domestic violence* is preferred. Domestic violence is defined as any act of violence, abuse, or mistreatment, either intentionally or uncontrollably inflicted on a current or former legal spouse, a person with whom one is cohabiting or has cohabited romantically, a person whom one is dating or with whom one has had a dating relationship, a person to whom one is engaged or has been engaged, or a person with whom one has a child in common. This includes heterosexual and same-sex relationships. This definition of domestic violence is extended to cover children who are dependent upon the intimate partners, as criminal justice agencies have gained a greater understanding of the effects of domestic violence on children. Some statutes have been altered to include emotional abuse. This definition may also be narrowed in scope to fit the definitions in each state law. There is no requirement as to how long ago an intimate partner relationship must have existed between an abuser and a victim.

Acts of violence include bodily injury or threat thereof, sexual battery, physical restraint, stalking, death threats or homicide, property crime aimed at the victim, and violations of a protective court order. Acts of violence can be perpetrated by both male and female partners, and in some circumstances, by both.

Domestic violence is not the same as domestic disputes. Domestic disputes are differences of opinion between family members that do not include acts or threats of violence, or violations of court mandates. Along the same lines, some statutes and criminal justice authorities include subgroupings in their definitions of domestic violence: elder abuse, spousal abuse, and sibling abuse. Because elder abuse, spousal abuse, and sibling abuse are included in some statutes, as well as in the research, it is important to include them in this discussion.

Child Abuse

Most statutes define child abuse in terms of physical abuse, sexual abuse, and neglect. Physical child abuse is the physical injury of a child, resulting from, but not limited to, strikes, shoving, shaking, biting, burning, poking, twisting limbs, and bodily throwing. Child sexual abuse can occur as a single act or a series of abusive behaviors. It can occur in a single event or over the course of many years. Child neglect occurs when a caretaker by act or lack of actions places the child in a dangerous situation.

Spousal Abuse

There is no nationally accepted spousal abuse definition among professionals in the field or authorities in the criminal justice system; however, all authorities and scholars agree it exists. Spousal abuse can be defined in terms of a continuum. On one end of the spectrum, it can be defined as yelling, calling names, and throwing objects; on the opposite end, it can be said to include striking, hitting, or killing. Among the many different definitions of spousal abuse, shades of gray exist. For the purposes of this essay, spousal abuse is defined as individual intentional acts or a series of intentional acts, either physical, emotional, or sexual, the purpose of which is to harm the spouse.

The definition of spouse in this case is gender neutral, which means that the abuse may be inflicted upon either a male or a female partner. The definition also includes heterosexual and same-sex partners who are legally married, cohabiting, or intimately involved in a monogamous or serious relationship.

Elder Abuse

Elder abuse is conduct that results in the physical, psychological, or material neglect, harm, or injury to an elderly person. This definition includes abuse by family members as well as institutional abuse. The term *material* in this definition refers to the exploitation of the elderly person's financial resources. An elderly person is usually someone over the age of sixty-five.

Law Enforcement

A law enforcement officer or peace officer is defined as an individual who is employed by a branch of government and is sworn to uphold the laws of the United States, the state, county, and/or city by which he or she is employed. American law enforcement encompasses three independent levels: federal, state, and local. Although these entities have commonalities in powers of arrest, search and seizure, and upholding their allegiance to protect and serve, each entity has unique characteristics. The unique characteristics involve the enforcement of the law. Depending on their jurisdictional authority, each entity may enforce different criminal laws. For example, local police departments may be engaged in a domestic violence call, the state highway patrol officers enforce traffic laws on highways and streets, and the U.S. Customs Service may be involved with arresting individuals who violate federal laws concerning the importation of goods into the United States.

There are also differences between the two local entities: city police and county sheriffs. There exists a geographic jurisdictional difference between city and rural areas. Sheriffs' deputies do not have access to immediate back-up from fellow officers when needed due to the vast area they cover. Therefore, deputies have to rely on community contacts, verbal skills, and intelligence when doing their jobs. Another difference is that sheriffs' deputies work as bailiffs in courtrooms. The sheriff is also responsible for the operation of the jail.

Training

Biblical and early legal principles allowed men to use physical force as a form of discipline on their wives, which should be distinguished from spousal abuse. For example, English men under English common law could apply the "rule of thumb," which allowed a man to beat his wife with a stick no thicker than his thumb. Women were looked upon as property, over which the husband was the absolute ruler. A woman was expected to obey her husband. These historical principles and ideologies relegate domestic disputes to private and family issues. Through much of the twentieth century, law enforcement held similar beliefs regarding domestic disputes, viewing them as intractable interpersonal conflicts and therefore inappropriate for police attention. It was not until the 1960s, with the rise of the women's movement, civil rights movement, antiwar movement, and changing views on the commission of crimes, that American society began to change its values and social norms. In the decades since, the criminalization of domestic violence has gained recognition, and legal and societal efforts to combat domestic violence continue to evolve.

Police training manuals taught officers to avoid arrests whenever possible in domestic violence cases. The officers were instructed to defuse the immediate crisis and make the appropriate referrals for long-term intervention. However, law enforcement has in recent decades focused on improving its responses to protecting women and punishing offenders. Other reforms took place within laws, such as mandatory arrest laws, which required immediate law enforcement action. Previously, women could not obtain a restraining order unless they were willing to file for a divorce; when they did, their restraining orders were rarely enforced. It was not until the 1980s that legislative mandates improved access to and enforcement of restraining orders. Women can now obtain a restraining order without filing for a divorce and can obtain emergency protective orders from law enforcement.

In 1984 Lawrence Sherman conducted one of the most famous evaluations of domestic violence in the United States. He was the architect of the Minneapolis Domestic Violence Experiment. This study evaluated the effectiveness of arrests on prevention and deterrence of domestic violence. As a result of the study, Sherman made three recommendations. The first was to change existing laws to allow police to make warrantless arrests for misdemeanor spousal assault not committed in their presence. The second recommendation implied that mandatory arrest of perpetrators would deter future acts of domestic violence. The third recommendation was that there be additional studies on prevention and deterrence of domestic violence conducted in other cities. In fact, there were five additional studies.

These studies were inconclusive as to the effect of arrests and deterrence on future violence. In 2001, the National Institute of Justice and the Centers for Disease Control and Prevention reevaluated the results of the original Minneapolis experiment and its five replications. This reevaluation supported the proposition that arresting batterers did in fact reduce subsequent aggression against their female partners.

As a result, police agencies changed their procedures in response to domestic violence calls. Police agencies nationwide began to adopt pro-arrest policies for domestic violence cases. Today, in every state, legislation gives law enforcement officers the authority to make warrantless arrests for misdemeanor and felony assaults and for violations of protection orders.

Law enforcement has met with barriers in its attempt to improve responses to domestic violence cases and ensure victims' safety. Typically victims of domestic violence will contact either a domestic violence hotline or call 9-1-1. Even a call to a domestic violence hotline can result in an officer being called to the scene. Law enforcement professionals need training regarding how to respond to domestic violence calls for service because an officer's response can influence a victim's future behavior. The officer's response is crucial to fostering the victim's belief that he/she is safe and that the offender will be held accountable. Moreover, the victim's decision to report future incidents or to participate further in the court process is impacted by the officer's initial response. In addition, sexual assault by one's partner poses a unique challenge for law enforcement because previously sexual assault was generally thought to be perpetrated by strangers, not husbands. Other challenging situations faced by law enforcement include dating violence, same-sex domestic violence (as they may find it difficult to determine which partner is the aggressor), stalking, and responding to domestic violence in rural communities. The Violent Crime Control and Law Enforcement Act of 1994 sanctions the approval of funds to be distributed to law enforcement agencies promoting community policing philosophies; Title IV of this act is the Violence against Women Act (VAWA), which offers grants for law enforcement training, domestic violence shelters, and assistance to victims of sexual assault.

As a result of all these factors, law enforcement in every jurisdiction receives a broad spectrum of training on how to respond to domestic violence. Historically law enforcement focused on the legal aspects of arrests when enforcing domestic violence laws. Since police work is complex and can be difficult, states have enacted Police Officer Standards and Training (POST) for all law enforcement officers. Academies provide basic instruction on various topics pertinent to law enforcement. There are twenty-four common topics covered by nearly all POST academies, one of which is domestic violence. Domestic violence training includes the nature of laws classifying domestic violence crimes, the dynamics of domestic violence, the consequences of domestic violence, and effective training responses to domestic violence calls. The median number of hours of instruction required for covering domestic violence is twelve. Officers' basic academy training should be reinforced through periodic in-service training.

Nature of Laws and Classifying Domestic Violence Crimes

Call screening is a law enforcement agency's process of assigning priority to the services it provides. Oftentimes domestic violence is downgraded in seriousness, resulting in slower response time by the police, as compared with responses to other crimes and concerns. This occurs partially because of a lack of understanding of the dynamics of domestic violence. The decision-making process involved in prioritizing services in and of itself is difficult for law enforcement because officers may have to choose between responding to two equally violent acts occurring simultaneously. For example, police personnel may be required to consider the history of recurring domestic violence incidents in their decision-making process. Nevertheless, domestic violence usually involves escalating violence, which is one of the dynamics that law enforcement personnel may not realize. In fact, several violent incidents may occur and victims may leave and return to the abuser several times before calling for help or terminating the relationship. The danger of downgrading domestic violence calls gives the perpetrator more time to either continue the violence or flee the scene. In addition, downgrading the priority of domestic violence calls gives the abuser more power over the victim, which may lead the victim to believe that he or she is truly alone and helpless.

Other factors affecting the classification of domestic violence crimes are the statutory limits on arrest for certain types of crimes. In the United States, state constitutions or statutes of criminal law violations are divided into two major classifications: felonies and misdemeanors. A felony is regarded as the most serious type of criminal act an individual can be charged with and is punishable by imprisonment. A misdemeanor is regarded as a less serious criminal act that is punishable by confinement in a local jail not to exceed one year. Normally, police have the power to arrest a person who has committed a felony if officers have probable cause. Probable cause is a set of facts that would lead a reasonable person to believe that the offense has occurred. It is not necessary for the police officer to witness the felony before he/she has the power to arrest a suspect. Misdemeanor arrests, however, require the officer to witness the criminal act. If the officer did not witness the offense being committed, he/she could ask for the victim to make a citizen's arrest and then, in support of the citizen's request, would take the offender into custody.

The nature and classification of crimes can have direct impact on the ability of police officers to make arrests for domestic violence assaults. For example, many statutes define battery as the unlawful use of force against a person. Battery is the unlawful touching of another, whereas assault lacks the required physical touching classification. Absent serious injury, state laws have generally placed battery under the classification of a misdemeanor. Thus, until recently, officers did not have the authority to make an arrest unless they witnessed the assault or the victim made a citizen's arrest.

The Dynamics of Domestic Violence

One of the most frustrating aspects of criminal law statutes for police officers is understanding the dynamics of domestic violence calls. Previously, law enforcement officers were unable to make arrests unless they witnessed the perpetrator committing the assault. This fact has put a strain on officers in doing their jobs because oftentimes the victims are unwilling to make a citizen's arrest. Thus, the usual course of action in domestic violence cases resulted in the officer verbally reprimanding the perpetrator and leaving the crime scene frustrated. Nonetheless, the laws have changed and officers are now able to arrest the abuser; however, they still leave feeling frustrated due to a recurring cycle in which the abuser is arrested and released and commits further abuse, subsequently requiring officer assistance once again.

One of the most often asked questions is, why do the victims remain in or return to abusive relationships? The reasons are intricate and multifaceted; a number of theories attempt to explain the complexity of battering relationships. Some of the obvious reasons are fear or terror, learned helplessness, low self-esteem, lack of resources, and minimization of the abuse. Obvious reasons aside, there are more profound reasons why women remain in abusive relationships. One of the leading scholars of domestic violence, Lenore E. Walker, coined the term *cycle of violence* as a result of her research with battered women. Although this theory does not attempt to explain the cause of domestic violence, it does attempt to show the dynamic of domestic violence.

The cycle of violence has three distinct phases: the tension-building phase; the explosion, or acute battering, phase; and the calm, loving respite phase. Each phase can vary in intensity and length.

The Tension-Building Phase

This is the first step in the development of a battering relationship and marks the onset of the cycle of violence. Throughout this phase, pressure builds within the relationship; eventually the abuser engages in an act of battering, usually minor, of his/her spouse. It is at this point that the victim will become more nurturing and attempt to calm or stay out of the abuser's path to avoid being abused. Also during this phase, the victim attempts to understand the abuser's faulty logic by rationalizing the behavior and perhaps even accepting the abuser's argument that the victim is at fault and deserves the abuse. The victim will try to remove him/herself to avoid conflict, but the tension continues to increase until the batterer explodes into rage.

The Explosion or Acute Battering Phase

This is the most dangerous phase. The abuser begins to exploit his control over the victim physically. Thus, the abuser engages in assaultive behavior. It is this violent aggression that distinguishes this phase from the previous phase of the cycle of violence. It is only when the violent attacks are over that both parties may feel stunned and express disbelief and denial. For example, the victim may rationalize the violent act as the result of an external stressor.

The Calm, Loving Respite Phase

This is the phase when the victim is the safest. The abuser will offer contrite apologies and exhibit loving behavior. He/she will beg for forgiveness, proclaim to understand that he/she has gone too far, and will assure the victim that it will never happen again. The victim will believe the enticing promises and behavior and stay in the relationship in the hope that the abusive partner will truly change.

Walker posits that victims of domestic violence increasingly become powerless as a result of their fear and have no options for escaping their abusers. As a result, women stay in abusive relationships, managing the best they can. Walker's theory is generally accepted by academia, experts in the field, and the legal system. It sets the foundation of relationships within the realm of power and control, rather than personality types or defects, or the socioeconomic status of the abuser or victim.

The Consequences of Domestic Violence

The obvious consequences of domestic violence are physical injuries suffered by the victim. The four general classifications of physical injuries perpetrated on victims include: immediate injuries that heal leaving no trace, injuries leaving visible scars, unknown permanent injuries, and long-term calamitous injuries.

Immediate injuries may be similar to those incurred by most people during the ordinary course of their lives. They include bruises, cuts, contusions, and broken bones. These injuries heal quickly and may be perceived as minor in nature. However, they can be severe for those suffering from other ailments. A diabetic person who suffers from a stab wound inflicted by a partner as an act of domestic violence may take three times longer to heal than the average person. An elderly person who has been shoved by an intimate partner could suffer a broken hip, which could lead to death.

Injuries inflicted by abusers may leave visible scars, including scars on the face or neck, loss of teeth, and loss of mobility in limbs due to incomplete healing. Although these scars are not themselves serious injuries, they are not without additional enduring consequences. For example, in domestic violence cases, one avenue an abuser can take in reducing a victim's self-esteem is to disfigure the person. In doing so, the abuser can maintain control over the victim.

Long-term serious injuries may also include those that damage the victim's heath or physical capabilities. For example, some victims have suffered severe liver damage and damage to bodily organs and functions as a result of repeated beatings by their abusers. An abusive partner may also knowingly infect the victim with a sexually transmitted disease such as HIV/AIDS, gonorrhea, syphilis, and herpes simplex virus. These viruses can result in additional health problems or even loss of life. The resulting changes in the victim's life span and quality of life are also damaging to the victim.

Physical injuries are not the only type of injuries that can result from domestic violence. There are both short- and long-term mental consequences that impact the victim. The leading scholar in crisis understanding is Eric Lindemann, who studied the effects of crisis on the mental health of humans. Gerald Caplin extended Lindemann's theories to include human reactions to traumatic events. The term *crisis* has many different meanings for different individuals, who react to crisis situations differently. What may be only a minor annoyance to one may be a crisis situation to another. Nonetheless, the common approaches to crisis situations involve three stages: impact, recoil, and reorganization.

The impact phase occurs immediately following the violence. This is also known as the *shock phase,* during which individuals have difficulty eating or sleeping and may even experience disbelief that the violence actually occurred.

Through the recoil stage, victims internalize the abuse and learn to accept or adapt to the violence. The victim moves through various steps during the recoil phase, commonly experiencing emotions of fear, anger, self-pity, guilt, and sadness. After a period of time exhausts these emotions, the victim finally puts these feelings aside and begins to initiate the healing process. Later in the healing process, victims are able to recall their feelings with renewed emotional resources.

After a period of time, the recoil stage will give way to the reorganization stage. The victim's feelings of fear, rage, and revenge diminish in intensity, leaving a greater ability to cope with daily life activities. In essence, the victim begins to feel "normal," or back to the state experienced prior to the abusive relationship. The victim's perspective on life is changed from living in the past to living in the present.

Victims may never forget the experience, and, as indicated earlier, they will respond in a variety of ways. Some victims may experience acute stress disorder, posttraumatic stress disorder (PTSD), or long-term crisis reactions.

In 1994, the *Diagnostic and Statistical Manual of Mental Disorders,* fourth edition (DSM-IV), added the term *acute stress disorder* (ASD). This is stress felt in the immediate aftermath of a traumatic event. Characteristic of ASD is the development of anxiety, dissociative symptoms, and other such manifestations that occur within one month of the traumatic event.

PTSD was first named after Vietnam War veterans began experiencing flashbacks of their combat experiences. Symptoms of PTSD may develop following the experience of psychologically traumatic events outside the range of normal human experience. Traumatic events experienced by victims of domestic violence include, but are not limited to, violent personal assault, kidnapping, being taken hostage, and/or torture.

The National Organization for Victim Assistance (NOVA), one of the earliest leaders in the victims' rights movement, identified that victims may suffer from a condition called *long-term crisis reaction.* This is a condition that occurs when victims do not suffer from PTSD but may revisit the feelings of their abuse reaction after certain triggering events call forth their remembrance of the trauma they endured. Triggers may include holidays, birthdays, weddings, divorces, graduations, the anniversary of the major traumatic event, or the anniversary of the death of a loved one.

Victims of domestic violence may suffer from other forms of mental disorders as a result of their victimization, such as depression and substance abuse. Depression is marked by episodes of diminished interest or pleasure and decreased energy in nearly all activities. Depression also creates difficulty in thinking, making decisions, and concentrating. For some victims of domestic violence, depression may impair day-to-day functioning.

Substance abuse is the maladaptive pattern of substance use leading to distasteful consequences. Substance abuse can involve alcohol and/or drugs. The victim may begin to suffer physical ailments, legal problems, and interpersonal problems as a result of substance abuse.

Effective Training Response to Domestic Violence Calls

The primary area of interest in which officers are trained should be aimed at officer and victim safety. Learning and being able to apply specific field strategies and techniques will ensure their safety, as well as the perpetrator's arrest. It is also important for officers to understand that simply responding to domestic violence calls has an impact on the circumstances. Police may have a positive impact through proper documentation and consistent responses to domestic violence calls. Officers should be informed during training that their procedures have an impact in three areas: They increase the chances of successful prosecution, they decrease possible repeat calls, and they provide closure for officers themselves.

Consistent with the training focus on ensuring officer and victim safety as well as arresting the offender, training topics should include: the approach, identifying the aggressor, police report/

identifying evidence, victim protection, and victim resources. Proper training in these topics will ensure a decrease in domestic violence repeat calls.

Training law enforcement to execute a proper approach that will ensure officer and victim safety involves officers obtaining all prior information on the call's location before making contact. The information includes mental health issues affecting the parties, the level of violence, the number of people involved, and the culture of the parties. Another important factor is entry into the premises. It is sometimes necessary for officers to determine the proper tactical approach to the call before entering the premises. The officers are trained to visually observe the location's surroundings, stand to the side of the door, listen at the door before knocking, and identify him/herself as a police officer. Upon entering the premises, officers are trained to ask for, visually scan for, and take possession of any weapons as well as immediately attempt to locate/ identify the aggressor. Officers are trained to subsequently locate any other parties involved. To establish control of the situation, the responding officer separates all parties involved; maintains a watchful eye on all persons concerned; determines the aggressor, if not already identified; and removes the alleged assailant from the presence of the victim. It is important for the officer to prevent eye contact between all parties, as the aggressor could be controlling the victim's statements in this manner.

Training law enforcement officers in identifying the dominant aggressor can be tricky. A dominant aggressor is the party who is the most significant aggressor; he/she is not necessarily the first aggressor in a situation. Factors that help officers determine the dominant aggressor include threats or the fear of physical injury, whether the act was in self-defense, and the history between the parties. Additional determining factors are the ages, weights, and heights of both parties, as well as any criminal records, including convictions, probations, and paroles. Other considerations include the strength or special skills of the parties, who called for help, the demeanor of the individuals involved, the existence of corroborating evidence, the use drugs and alcohol, and the seriousness of injuries.

Law enforcement officers need to have a knowledge of common injuries that may result from domestic violence incidents. Often injuries are located on the face, neck, back, chest, arms, and legs. There may also be injuries on victims that will show that they were protecting themselves from their assailants. For example, victims who attempted to defend themselves while on the floor may have injuries on the bottoms of the feet from kicking away the assailants. It is important for officers to discern injuries inflicted on the aggressor by the victim in self-defense. Such injuries may include, but are not limited to, scratches on the aggressor's face, back, neck, inner arms, hands, or chest.

Other subsequent procedures undertaken by an officer responding to a domestic violence situation include determining if medical assistance is required for the victim, establishing probable cause for arrest of the perpetrator, and reassuring the victim that he or she is safe. After the officer has secured the scene, he/she can begin interviewing the victim and any witnesses.

Training law enforcement to be sensitive toward the needs and concerns of victims is very important for reducing domestic violence. Victims who feel that officers do not care about their condition may stop cooperating with them. However, a positive impression of the officer will ensure the victim's willingness to talk with him or her. Ideally, interview procedures should include the history of violence between the parties involved, documentation of the incident, excited utterances by the victim, and questions about the aggressor's violations of protection orders, warrants, probations, or conditions of release. Other important documentation includes a completed body chart of the victim's injuries and photographs of physical evidence. In the process of ascertaining this information it is essential for officers to make certain that all information is detailed because this information will aid the victim's pursuit for protection orders and other legal remedies. It is imperative for successful prosecution of domestic violence cases that the reports include the following items:

- A full description of the crime scene with photos including the names, ages, and locations of the parties upon officer arrival
- A full description of the incident
- Details of any medical treatment required by the parties involved
- The names of parties present during the incident, including children and adults
- The relationship of the parties involved
- A description of perceived victim's and aggressor's emotional states
- A body map showing victim's and suspect's injuries
- Current and past protection orders
- The suspect's probation or parole status
- Weapons seized at the location

In addition, necessary physical evidence to be collected includes: torn clothing, blood samples, hair and fibers, firearms and/or weapons, and complete crime scene sketches of the incident and damaged items.

A fundamental area to address in the course of training law enforcement officers on how to deal with victims involves debunking the myths and misconceptions surrounding marital and nonmarital sexual assault and rape. It is crucial for officers to be taught to identify evidence of nonconsensual sexual violence. Another important area of training covers corroborating the victim's statement with physical evidence. In addition, it is vital for officers to learn how to follow investigative procedures that do not compromise the victim's safety if the victim has relocated or is living in an undisclosed shelter.

With a proper understanding of available resources, law enforcement officers are able to help victims regain control over their lives. A crucial time for the victim is immediately following the abuser's arrest because the victim may fear that the abuser will return and inflict more harm in anger over the arrest. Therefore, providing domestic violence victims with information about available resources for them will help them feel safe and regain control over their lives. Officers need to be aware of the resources available to domestic violence victims in the communities they serve and must be able to provide this information to victims. Among the most important recommendations an officer can give is information about the local domestic violence shelter and free legal resources. Other resources an officer can offer are his/her own name and contact information, the report or event number of the incident, and contact information for the proper investigative unit. Finally, it is vital to train law enforcement about the different types of protective and restraining orders, such as emergency protection orders, temporary restraining orders, criminal court stay away orders, and workplace violence restraining orders. If authorized by departmental policy, officers can offer and provide the victims civil police standby while removing personal property from the residence.

Future Training

There are two reasons for the necessity of continuous domestic violence training for law enforcement professionals. The first is obvious: The more understanding an officer has, the better he/she is at applying the laws to protect the victims. The second reason deals with the integrity of the profession. That is, communities trust that law enforcement officers do not break the laws they enforce. Even though this should be the case, law enforcement executives have recognized that officers are not immune from perpetrating acts of domestic violence against their own intimate partners. One way to prevent officers from committing domestic violence or to recognize the signs that an officer might be perpetrating this type of crime is to develop a zero-tolerance policy approach to domestic violence.

At the time of this writing, there is no mandatory training policy for law enforcement agencies to provide continuous domestic violence training to its officers. Because of the serious nature of domestic violence, a collaborative effort among the International Association of Chiefs of Police, the Office of Community Oriented Policing Services, and the Office on Violence against Women has developed. The efforts by these agencies has developed a proactive zero-tolerance domestic violence policy that law enforcement agencies can implement. The policy expresses a zero-tolerance stance toward officers throughout their careers. It is anchored in community-oriented policing concepts which concentrate on the issues of domestic violence in a comprehensive manner. The comprehensive policy components are: Prevention and Training, Early Warning and Intervention, Incident Response Protocols, Victim Safety and Protection, and Post-incident Administrative and Criminal Decisions.

Law enforcement agencies can learn prevention and training techniques from domestic violence professionals in their communities through developing ongoing collaborations with them. Domestic violence professionals include members of domestic violence coalitions and councils, social workers and other social services providers, shelter staff, and hotline crisis personnel. These professionals will help police agencies and officers by providing additional training and on-scene victim advocacy, offering knowledge of resources and making referrals, and helping the department in the development of policies and practices as they relate to domestic violence responses. Moreover, it is each law enforcement agency's responsibility to know what training is taught at its basic academy and to supplement that training by filling in any absent information. Law enforcement agencies should educate new recruits on domestic violence call policies and procedures, especially those that run counter to basic academy training.

In addition, law enforcement agencies should offer ongoing training regarding new research, should advocate for program changes, and should keep abreast of new available resources for victims. Ongoing training can be implemented during in-service training, as part of roll call, and through the field training of officers. In-service training should reinforce basic academy knowledge, offer new knowledge, and update resources. Roll call training is the most effective way to keep departmental policies and procedures on domestic violence at the forefront, as well as to offer updated news of cases in the jurisdiction. Roll call is also a time when advocates can present educational information, tailoring their training to ensure that officers learn interpersonal communication skills, support skills, and empathy skills. Advocates should ensure that officers comprehend the complexity of domestic violence and their responsibility to perform effective law enforcement in support of victims during these calls.

Conclusion

Society has come a long way in understanding the dynamics of domestic violence; consequently, law enforcement has also increased its knowledge and professionalism regarding domestic violence. This in turn has resulted in law enforcement agencies paying increased attention to domestic violence issues in their initial training academies. Many jurisdictions include training on domestic violence within their police academy curriculums. However, there is much left to be done. Law enforcement agencies and institutions responsible for advanced training of law enforcement officers need to continue to focus their efforts on ensuring that all officers understand the dynamics of domestic violence. This in turn will lead to more protection for its victims.

TERI BERNADES and HARVEY WALLACE

See also **Assessing Risk in Domestic Violence Cases; Attachment Theory and Domestic Violence; Coercive Control; Cohabitating Violence; Cycle of Violence; Intimate Partner Homicide; Mandatory Arrest Policies; Marital Rape; Mutual Battering; Police Civil Liability in Domestic Violence Incidents; Police Decision-Making Factors in Domestic Violence Cases; Police Response to Domestic Violence Incidents; Protective and Restraining Orders; Stages of Leaving Abusive Relationships; Victim-Blaming Theory**

References and Further Reading

Garner, Joel H., and Jeffrey A. Fagan. *The Effects of Arrest on Intimate Partner Violence: New Evidence from the Spouse Assault Replication Program.* Washington, DC: National Institute of Justice, June 2001.

Hickman, Matthew J. *State and Local Law Enforcement Training Academies.* U.S. Department of Justice, Office of Justice Programs, Bureau of Justice Statistics, January 2005.

International Association of Chiefs of Police. *Domestic Violence by Police Officers: A Policy of the IACP Police Response to Violence against Women Project,* 2003.

Seymour, Ann, Jane S. Murray, Melissa Hook, Christine Edmunds, Mario Gaboury, and Grace Coleman. *2000 National Victim Assistance Academy.* U.S. Department of Justice, Office for Victims of Crime, Office of Justice Programs, 2000.

Sherman, Lawrence W. *Policing Domestic Violence.* New York: Free Press, 1992.

Walker, Lenore E. *The Battered Woman.* New York: Harper and Row, 1979.

Wallace, Harvey. *Family Violence, Legal, Medical, and Social Perspectives,* 4th ed. Boston: Allyn & Bacon, 2005.

TRINIDAD AND TOBAGO, DOMESTIC VIOLENCE IN

The twin-island nation of Trinidad and Tobago (hereafter Trinidad) is located in the southern Caribbean Sea, off the shores of Venezuela. Its first inhabitants were indigenous peoples; the first colonizers were Spanish. The British took control of Trinidad in 1797, imposing their language and government. The economy was dominated by plantation slavery until emancipation in 1834. Thereafter, indenture schemes brought East Indians to work in the fields. Trinidad won independence from Great Britain in 1962 and became a republic in 1976. The population as of 2005 includes 1.3 million people. Today the economy relies on oil, natural gas, the service industry, manufacturing, agriculture, and tourism. There is a relatively large middle class, but underemployment and unemployment are widespread.

Trinidad's people are highly diverse. As of 2000, 43 percent of the population claimed Afro-Trinidadian heritage, another 43 percent identified as Indo-Trinidadian, and 14 percent were "mixed." "Other" citizens claim European, South American, Chinese, Middle Eastern, and Amerindian backgrounds. Christianity, Hinduism, and Islam are the three largest religions in Trinidad, but many smaller religious groups flourish.

Diverse family and household forms also prevail. Social scientists have identified an Afro-Trinidadian pattern characterized by youthful serial "visiting" relationships and single parenting, followed by common law or legal marriage. Three-generation households are common. In contrast, the Indo-Trinidadian pattern is characterized by early formal unions, larger families, marital stability, and residence near or with the groom's natal family (Barrow 1996). In both patterns, the structure of gender relations is generally patriarchal. Evidence of the inequity of gender relations is widespread throughout the Caribbean, although scholars have still to account for the precise relationship between family forms, gender hierarchy, and domestic abuse.

There are few academic studies of the causes or prevalence of domestic violence in Trinidad. Using data from official records and nongovernmental organizations, Gopaul and Cain (1996) found that domestic violence was widespread and persisted across ethnic, educational, occupational, and conjugal status groups. Rawlins (2000) found almost identical rates of domestic violence in a sample of 100 Afro-Trinidadians and 100 Indo-Trinidadians. Approximately 16 percent of the total sample experienced violence as adults, of whom 77 percent were women. Domestic violence was slightly more prevalent in rural than urban locales. Studies by Clarke (1998) and Pargass and Clarke (2003) of violence against women in the region more generally conclude that domestic violence is prevalent and affects women across class, ethnic, and racial lines. Domestic violence research in the Caribbean is still in its infancy, and much of the evidence for its origins and frequency remains anecdotal.

In 1991 Trinidad became the first nation in the English-speaking Caribbean to pass comprehensive domestic violence legislation. The Domestic Violence Act of 1991 was a precedent-setting accomplishment; almost every other Caribbean nation has since followed Trinidad's lead. Creque (1995) found that 8,297 applications for protection were processed by the magistrates' courts in Trinidad from the inception of the act in 1991 through April 1994. Thus the law garnered widespread and immediate response from the public.

The Domestic Violence Act of 1999 replaced the first law. Like its predecessor, this statute draws upon a global discourse that condemns domestic violence but also acknowledges in its language and coverage the diversity of domestic forms that prevail in Trinidad (Lazarus-Black 2003). For example, protection is offered to people in intimate or formerly intimate relationships, to those with a child in common, and to persons in financially dependent relationships. The act also protects children, other dependents, and household members, but not persons in gay or lesbian relationships. The 1999 Act established the new category of financial abuse, gives magistrates authority to compensate victims, and provides for increased police intervention. In keeping with the local emphasis on reconciling families, cases can be resolved by an "undertaking," a promise by an alleged first-time offender not to engage in future abuse, or a respondent's signature to a peace bond. Trinidad's law is a civil, as opposed to a criminal, statute; a magistrate renders a decision based upon the preponderance of evidence rather than upon reasonable doubt. Breaches of protection orders, however, are treated as crimes and are punishable by fines and incarceration. Besides the 1999 statute, Trinidad has also signed several international conventions condemning violence against women. Thus as Pargass and Clarke (2003) report, there is formal intolerance for gender violence.

Research analyzing the passage and implementation of domestic violence law in Trinidad shows that women file the majority of applications for protection orders, most against intimate partners (Lazarus-Black 2001, forthcoming). This study found about 75 percent of applications for protection orders were dismissed or withdrawn from the courts, while less than a quarter, about 22 percent, received protective action. Interviews with litigants, lawyers, and judges suggest that applicants for protection orders exit the legal system for myriad reasons. Some women reconcile with parties; others cannot take the time or finance the costs to appear in court. Still others are intimidated into dropping charges or do so when they fear the case may result in loss of economic support. Cases exit the system, too, because of events and processes that occur within the legal system. The adjournment of a matter, the intimidation of a witness by a clerk, or the silencing of a victim by a magistrate can influence dramatically the history of any case.

In addition to legal remedies, a twenty-four-hour domestic violence hotline in Trinidad provides information and referrals. In 2005, nine shelters were operating, although these vary in size and the services they provide. Many churches, mosques, and temples offer counseling programs. Counseling is also available at National Family Services and probation offices and through nongovernmental organizations. The subject of domestic violence is widely covered in the media, and schools have launched educational programs. Efforts are under way to train those who come into contact with victims, including the police, lawyers, and magistrates (Trinidad and Tobago Coalition against Domestic Violence 2005).

MINDIE LAZARUS-BLACK

See also **Africa: Domestic Violence and the Law; Cross-Cultural Examination of Domestic Violence in China and Pakistan; Cross-Cultural Examination of Domestic Violence in Latin America; Greece, Domestic Violence in; Spain, Domestic Violence in; Worldwide Sociolegal Precedents Supporting Domestic Violence from Ancient to Modern Times**

References and Further Reading

Barrow, Christine. *Family in the Caribbean: Themes and Perspectives.* Kingston, Jamaica: Ian Randle, 1996.
Clarke, Roberta. *Violence against Women in the Caribbean: State and Non-State Responses.* New York: United Nations Development Fund for Women (UNIFEM), Inter-American Commission of Women (CIM), 1998.
Creque, Merri. *A Study of the Incidence of Domestic Violence in Trinidad and Tobago from 1991 to 1993.* Port of Spain: Shelter for Battered Women and Trinidad and Tobago Coalition against Domestic Violence, 1995.
Gopaul, Roanna, and Maureen Cain. "Violence between Spouses in Trinidad and Tobago: A Research Note." *Caribbean Quarterly* 42, nos. 2 and 3 (1996): 29–41.
Lazarus-Black, Mindie. "Law and the Pragmatics of Inclusion: Governing Domestic Violence in Trinidad and Tobago." *American Ethnologist* 28, no. 2 (2001): 388–416.
———. "The (Heterosexual) Regendering of a Modern State: Criminalizing and Implementing Domestic Violence Law in Trinidad." *Law and Social Inquiry* 28, no. 4 (2003): 979–1008.
———. *Everyday Harm: Domestic Violence, Court Rites, and Cultures of Reconciliation.* Champaign: University of Illinois Press, forthcoming.
Pargass, Gaietry, and Roberta Clarke. "Violence against Women: A Human Rights Issue Post Beijing Five Year Review." In *Gender Equality in the Caribbean: Reality or Illusion,* edited by Gemma Tang Nain and Barbara Bailey. Kingston, Jamaica: Ian Randle, 2003, pp. 39–72.
Rawlins, Joan M. "Domestic Violence in Trinidad: A Family and Public Health Problem." *Caribbean Journal of Criminology and Social Psychology* 5, nos. 1 and 2 (2000): 165–180.
Trinidad and Tobago Coalition against Domestic Violence. *Domestic and Gender-Based Violence Judicial Training and Resource Manual.* Port of Spain, Trinidad: Author, 2005.

Statutes Cited

The Domestic Violence Act of Trinidad and Tobago, Act No. 10 of 1991 (repealed).
The Domestic Violence Act of Trinidad and Tobago, Act No. 27 of 1999.

V

VICTIM-BLAMING THEORY

Definition and Evolution

Although the study of victimology represents a relatively new field of inquiry, early researchers were drawn to the concept of shared responsibility between victims and offenders in the commission of a criminal event (Karmen 2004). These researchers focused on victim attributes as well as the interaction between the victim and the offender, with the assumption that their interaction led to reciprocal forces causing the victimization. Since then, the controversy over victim precipitation of a crime has come under scrutiny, yet the daily practice of shifting some, if not all, of the blame for the crime onto the victim continues.

Victim-blaming theory describes the practice of holding victims partly responsible for their misfortune. It represents the faulting of individuals who have endured the suffering of crimes, hardships, or other misfortunes with either part or whole responsibility for the event. Often, victim-blaming theories rely on the premise that individuals should recognize the dangers that exist in society and therefore should take the necessary precautions to maintain a certain level of safety. Those who do not take such precautions are perceived as blameworthy for their demise even if they have not acted carelessly. These perceptions in effect shift the culpability away from the perpetrator of the crime onto the victim. When discussing issues of family violence, violence against women, or sexual assault, one often hears victim-blaming statements such as, "Why didn't she leave?" or "She was asking for it." Within the context of family violence, victim blaming often includes condemnation of the victim for staying in an abusive relationship.

Scholars theorize that the phenomenon of victim blaming is the result of a belief in a "just world." In 1965, social psychologist Melvin Lerner coined the term "just world hypothesis" to reflect the belief that "individuals have a need to believe that they live in a world where people generally get what they deserve and deserve what they get" (Lerner 1978). Lerner conducted a series of experiments to test his hypothesis by documenting the respondents' eagerness to believe that those who triumphed deserved their victories, while those who suffered were responsible for their demise. According to Lerner, people have a need to view the world as an orderly, predictable, and fair place. This belief encourages individuals to strive toward goals with an expectation that each action leads to predictable results. Lerner explains that when faced with evidence that the world is unjust, "just world" believers make sense of the situation with claims that the victim "must have asked for it." Although the belief in a "just world" may provide some comfort and encouragement to attain one's goals, it also has the potential to provide a false sense of security.

Does Victim Blaming Have an Impact?

Do the expectations of a just world and the act of blaming the victim have any real significance in the understanding of intimate partner abuse and sexual violence? According to Martin (2001), "In addition to being unjust, blaming victims shows a lack of compassion by disregarding victims' suffering and by imposing additional suffering in criticizing the innocent." In a quest to effectively aid victims and minimize the reoccurrence of abuse, one must examine the social attitudes that endorse victim blaming and examine the training of the professionals who work with victims.

In an exploration of the trends of how social attitudes influence social policies, Davis examines how the policies of the 1980s demonstrated a shift away from creating the services necessary for women to leave an abusive relationship (i.e., providing or assisting with housing, employment, education, etc.) for the sake of interventions designed to stop individual acts of violence so that families could stay together (Davis et al. 1992). Davis explains that during this time, women in abusive relationships were encouraged to "gain control over their lives" by changing the behaviors that led to the abuse. Rather than providing the services necessary to escape an abusive situation, victims of family violence were encouraged to modify their behavior in efforts to stop the abuse.

As a result of social policies, family traditions, religious institutions, and cultural customs which often encourage victims of intimate partner abuse to remain in the relationship, survivors of family abuse often turn to social service, medical, and justice personnel for nonjudgmental assistance. One would expect that those choosing careers in "helping professions" such as social work, medicine, and law enforcement would not engage in victim-blaming attitudes, yet research shows otherwise. As described by Danis (2003):

> [F]rom the late 1970s through the early 1990s, the social work profession earned a reputation as uncaring, uninformed, and unhelpful to battered women. Social workers were faulted for blaming the victim . . . , failing to recognize abuse as a problem . . . , and failing to make appropriate interventions and referrals.

Until recently, little inquiry explored the question of whether or not "social workers feel academically prepared to address domestic violence." In answering this question, Danis (2003) found that "the majority of the respondents felt they had 'none to a little' academic preparation" to provide adequate assistance in family violence circumstances. Social workers not only felt underprepared to work with victims of intimate partner abuse, but expressed some victim-blaming attitudes. Furthermore, within health care settings:

> available information suggests that one barrier to appropriate healthcare for abused women may be physician attitudes. . . . Close to one third (30%) [of physicians] hold non-supportive (victim-blaming) attitudes about victims of spouse abuse, and the majority (70%) do not believe that they have the necessary resources to assist victims of domestic violence. (Garimella et al. 2000)

Although some specific medical associations such as Kaiser Permanente in Richmond, California, have implemented family violence awareness trainings for their staff, "two victim-blaming attitudes stand out: approximately half of all physicians (55%) believe that their patients' personalities lead them to being abused, and one third (34%) believe that a victim must be getting something out of the relationship, or she would leave" (Garimella et al. 2000).

Within the criminal justice processes, victims not only endure their personal suffering, but also the speculation from juries who may perceive them as not having done enough to prevent the victimization. Studies of mock juries have found that "when presented with negative outcomes, people often engage in counterfactual thinking, imagining various ways that events might have been different" (Goldinger et al. 2003). Hence, when faced with a victim who has been injured by an abusive partner or sexually aggressive perpetrator, juries often imagine ways in which the victim's behavior could have led the events to occur differently without consideration of the real factors affecting the decision-making process at the original moment. Victims may be blamed as "having poor judgment" without receiving acknowledgment for the fact that viewing information in hindsight yields opportunities for better responses than those determined within real-time life constraints.

Using simulations to examine the impact of a victim's social role in the attribution of contributory fault in sexual assault cases, Pugh (1983) examined respondents' perceptions of the victim's moral character in an array of criminal cases. Through the manipulation of "the victims' social roles (i.e., nuns, married women, and social workers vs.

prostitutes, divorcees, and topless dancers), the victim's attire (provocative vs. nonprovocative), and the victim's previous sexual conduct (virgin vs. nonvirgin) [Pugh discovered that] contributory fault on the part of rape victims will reduce the likelihood of a guilty verdict" (Pugh 1983). The culpability for the crime is shifted from the perpetrator's actions to the victim's attributes or behavior. "Because of the preoccupation with the victim's actions, the responsibility of the accused is diminished" (Rude 1999). Even more disturbing is the fact that discrimination may heighten the plight of victims of color. George and Martinez (2002) found that "in judgments about the certitude of rape, the victim's culpability, the credibility of her refusal, and the perpetrator's culpability, participants judged women raped interracially as more blameworthy than those raped intraracially" (2002). Although these issues are pertinent to the administration of family violence cases within the criminal justice system, one must also recognize the impact of the practice of victim blaming on the creation of social policies and the implementation of services for victims of crimes.

Social attitudes influence not only policies and services available for victims, but also the victim's willingness to report the offense and seek assistance. Oftentimes, victims may remain silent about their suffering and not report their victimization for fear of experiencing the secondary victimization that follows when social systems respond with statements such as "Why did you stay?" or "Why didn't you resist?" Victims of intimate partner abuse respond to the social cues of whether their plight will be taken seriously by responding to the reactions of those in "helping professions" as well as the media portrayal of abuse cases.

In an exploration of 150 cases of women killed in Zambia from 1973 to 1996, Rude (1999) found that

> newspaper accounts of such killings create a secondary level of silence about domestic violence and homicide by blaming the victims and concealing the brutality of the attacks. . . . Cases are simply described as domestic disputes [and] women are judged to have "provoked" their perpetrators, whose violent reactions are all too often seen as inevitable, understandable, and therefore somewhat pardonable.

In one account used to describe the newspapers' headlines, language, and tone when publicly describing abuse, Rude (1999) writes:

> In 1986, Theresa Mwale was killed by her husband after she questioned him about a girl he accommodated in a hostel. The article, which appeared under the headline of "Nagging wife killer freed after custody", suggested

the wife's behavior was the real crime, not the husband's fatal beating of her with a hosepipe.

Although the accounts from Zambia appear quite extreme, the silencing effects resulting from victim blaming are similar to those elsewhere in the world. Much like the work of Pugh (1983), who found that "the presumption of contributory fault . . . mitigates the behavior of the defendant," Rude also discovered that the framework in which the abuse is described (i.e., blaming the victim) has an impact on the handling and support offered to the victims. The silencing effects of the abuse are intensified by the silencing effects of placing blame on victims.

Conclusions

Victim blaming has been studied multiple times within the context of sexual assaults, yet the practice of blaming victims remains prevalent. Intimate partner abuse inherently incorporates the use of psychological blaming of the victim, and the impact of victim blaming from social support systems cannot be underestimated. The significance of understanding victim blaming lies in the limitations such practices place on the services and support for victims. Blaming victims for their pain not only limits the services and support systems available to them, but also "shows a lack of compassion by disregarding victim's undeserved suffering and by imposing additional suffering in criticizing the innocent" (Martin 2001).

Victim-blaming theories have received considerable attention from social psychologists, yet little has been done to end the practice of shifting the culpability of unfortunate events from the offenders to the victims. Taking responsibility for one's safety may ensure a specific level of protection, yet it does not provide a guarantee that no bad events will take place. Until the populace gains an awareness of the harm caused by the simple act of blaming victims, victims will continue to suffer needlessly.

SILVINA ITUARTE

See also **Attachment Theory and Domestic Violence; Battered Woman Syndrome; Battered Women: Held in Captivity; Feminist Theory; Social Learning Theory and Family Violence; Violence against Women Act**

References and Further Reading

Danis, Fran S. "Domestic Violence and Social Work Education: What We Know, What We Need to Know?" *Journal of Social Work Education* 39, no. 2 (Spring/Summer 2003): 215–224.

Davis, Liane V., and Jan L. Hagen. "The Problem of Wife Abuse: The Interrelationship of Social Policy and Social Work Practice." *Social Work* 37, no. 1 (January 1992): 15–20.

Garimella, Ramani, et al. "Physicians, Beliefs about Victims of Spouse Abuse and about the Physician Role." *Journal of Women's Health and Gender-Based Medicine* 9, no. 4 (2000): 405–411.

George, William H., and Lorraine J. Martinez. "Victim Blaming in Rape: Effects of Victim and Perpetrator Race, Types of Rape, and Participant Racism." *Psychology of Women Quarterly* 26, no. 2 (Summer 2002): 110.

Goldinger, Stephen D., et al. "'Blaming the Victim' under Memory Load." *Psychological Science* 14, no. 1 (January 2003): 81–85.

Johnson, Lee M., Rehan Mullock, and Charles L. Mulford. "General Versus Specific Victim Blaming." *Journal of Social Psychology* 142, no. 2 (2002): 249–263.

Karmen, Andrew. *Crime Victims: An Introduction to Victimology.* Belmont, CA: Wadsworth/Thomson, 2004.

Lerner, Melvin J. *The Belief in a Just World: A Fundamental Delusion.* New York: Plenum Press, 1980.

Lerner, Melvin J., and D. T. Miller. "Just World Research and the Attribution Process: Looking Back and Ahead." *Psychological Bulletin* 85 (1978): 1030–1051.

Lipkusa, I. M., C. Dalbert, and I. C. Siegler. "The Importance of Distinguishing the Belief in a Just World for Self Versus for Others: Implications for Psychological Well-Being." *Personality and Social Psychology Bulletin* 22, no. 7 (1996): 666–677.

Martin, Mike W. "Responsibility for Health and Blaming Victims." *Journal of Medical Humanities* 22, no. 2 (2001): 95–106.

Pugh, M. D. "Contributory Fault and Rape Convictions: Loglinear Models for Blaming the Victim." *Social Psychology Quarterly* 46, no. 3 (September 1983): 233–242.

Rude, Darlene. "Reasonable Men and Provocative Women: An Analysis of Gendered Domestic Homicide in Zambia." *Journal of Southern Africana Studies* 25, no. 1 (March 1999): 7–27.

VIOLENCE AGAINST WOMEN ACT

The Violence against Women Act (VAWA) of 1994 was the first and most comprehensive federal legislation to address violence against women in the history of the United States. Although some federal legislation was passed prior to VAWA to address privacy issues for rape victims, fund battered women's shelters, and compensate crime victims, many people recognized that violence against women existed in many forms and had to be addressed on a national level. This recognition grew out of the women's movement of the 1970s, itself a product of the earlier civil rights movement. As women talked with each other and organized themselves, they realized that rape, battering, and other types of violence were common experiences for many women. During the period of intense grassroots activism leading up to VAWA, women fought for the prosecution and prevention of rape, created shelters for battered women, and advocated for legislation that would make hurting women because they were women a crime. Until passage of VAWA, many people and some judges believed that if a woman's boyfriend or husband hurt her, it was less of a crime than if a stranger hurt her. Many states still had laws that did not recognize violence or rape in marriage as a crime.

VAWA was first introduced in Congress in 1990. After four years of work by a few key senators and representatives from both parties and lobbying by over one thousand groups, VAWA became law as Title IV of the Violent Crime Control and Law Enforcement Act of 1994. The Senate Judiciary Committee investigation of Anita Hill's allegations of sexual harassment by then Supreme Court nominee Clarence Thomas in 1991 and the murder of Nicole Brown Simpson (the former battered wife of prominent football star O. J. Simpson) and Ronald Goldman in June 1994 also helped set the stage for bipartisan support of this landmark legislation.

VAWA has seven sections or titles. Title I, Safe Streets for Women, strengthened penalties for repeating sexual abuse, mandated restitution to victims, and further protected victims when they appeared in court by restricting questions about their sexual behavior. It increased funding for women's safety in public and on mass transit and for victim services and created grant funding to train police officers and court personnel. Title II, Safe Homes for Women, had ten components. The first was the creation of the National Domestic Violence Hotline, a toll free information and referral service for victims. This title created two new federal crimes. It became a felony, first, to cross state lines to commit violence and, second, to cross state lines in violation of a protection order. A protection order is a court order preventing the perpetrator from having contact with a prior victim. In order to prosecute the second crime, VAWA mandated "full faith and credit" for protection orders. This meant that a protection order from any state or Indian tribe was to be honored in all others. These two new federal crimes were very important because the federal government, for example, the FBI or attorney general, could now investigate and prosecute crimes of domestic violence. Title II also emphasized the seriousness of violence against women by providing grants to encourage arrest of abusers. In some cases this meant new mandatory arrest policies. Prior to VAWA, many police departments did not arrest perpetrators or would arrest both the perpetrator and the victim. Mandatory arrest was especially important when perpetrators violated protection orders, as this put the victim's life in even greater danger. Confidentiality of the addresses of both individual victims and of shelters was also mandated in this section.

Title II provided extensive funding for shelters, domestic violence education for young people from primary through higher education, broad-based community coordination of domestic violence intervention and prevention, and addressing the needs of people who had been underserved due to racial, ethnic, or geographical barriers. Resources for rural victims of domestic violence and child abuse also received funding. In order to identify further interventions to prevent violence against women, Title II required the development of a national research agenda by a panel of experts under the direction of the U.S. attorney general, who was then to report their findings within one year of the enactment of VAWA.

Controversy over Title III

Title III, Civil Rights for Women (also called the Civil Rights Remedies for Gender-Motivated Violence Act), was the most contentious section of VAWA. It was not only a source of argument during the four years before passage, when Supreme Court Chief Justice William Rehnquist suggested to the American Bar Association that it could flood the Court with a variety of domestic relations cases, but afterward. The intent of Title III was to protect the civil rights of women and men to be free from violence motivated by gender. Congress enacted this legislation based on its findings that

victims of gender-motivated violence were not equally protected in all fifty states, in part because of discrimination based on gender; that existing law provided a civil rights remedy for victims in the workplace, for example, sexual harassment law, but not on the streets or in the home; and that state laws did not protect victims from gendered violence because it was considered different—and less serious—than random violence, especially when the victim had a prior relationship with the perpetrator.

Two parts of the Constitution were used to justify this new civil right. First, Congress argued that women, in particular, were not equally protected from gender-motivated violence by the states. This is a reference to section 5 of the Fourteenth Amendment. Secondly, they recognized that violence against women had a very negative effect on interstate commerce. As noted in Title II, prior to VAWA, if victims were pursued across state lines they lacked legal protection. In addition, Congress argued that violence was frequently used by perpetrators to prevent women from participating in interstate commercial activities such as working and traveling and that the impact was even greater after violence. This portion of Title III is based on section 8 of Article 1 of the Constitution.

Title III stated that individuals who committed gender-motivated violence were liable to the injured party for civil damages in addition to criminal penalties. For a victim to sue the perpetrator, the person needed to prove only that she or he had been a victim of a felonious crime of violence and that it was motivated, at least in part, by the victim's gender. Congress was careful to exclude other types of domestic relations claims such as divorce, alimony, and child custody in response to concerns voiced by the federal courts. Yet, after less than a dozen district court rulings upholding the constitutionality of Title III, in 2000 the Supreme Court in *United States v. Morrison* upheld the Fourth Circuit Court of Appeals decision stating that 42 U.S.C. Section 13981 (the majority of Title III) of VAWA was unconstitutional. In this case, a student at Virginia Polytechnic and State University, Christy Brzonkala, attempted to sue two students, Antonio Morrison and James Crawford, who had raped her, and the university. The Court ruled that although violence against women had an aggregate effect on interstate commerce, so did other types of violence. It therefore determined that Congress was not permitted to regulate violent conduct or to exercise police power via Title III. Secondly, it rejected the argument that a federal civil rights remedy was necessary because the states were not providing victims equal protection. Citing civil rights cases from the past, they ruled that the Fourteenth Amendment could be used only to prohibit state action, not to provide assistance to one citizen against another. Furthermore, Title III was to apply to all the states, and not all were discriminating against victims. They affirmed that Christy Brzonkala should have a remedy due to the assault but that it should come from the Commonwealth of Virginia, not the federal government.

Titles IV–VII of the Violence against Women Act of 1994

Title IV, Equal Justice for Women in the Courts, provided funding for states and Indian tribes to develop, test, and implement model programs for training judges and court personnel about the laws regarding various types of gender-motivated violence. Federal circuit courts were also encouraged to determine whether gender bias existed in their areas and to make recommendations for reform. Title V, Violence against Women Act Improvements, provided funding for testing victims of sexual assault for sexually transmitted diseases; a baseline study of sexual assault on college campuses; a report on the medical and psychological aspects of the battered woman syndrome and its use in criminal cases; and studies regarding the confidentiality of the addresses of domestic violence victims and of how records of domestic violence complaints are maintained. Title VI, National Stalker and Domestic Violence Reduction, allowed the sharing of national criminal information about domestic violence and stalking offenders with civil and criminal courts and provided funding to states and local governments to use that information efficiently. Protections for Battered Immigrant Women and Children, Title VII, recognized the unique protections necessary for immigrants and spouses and children of immigrants experiencing domestic violence. It enabled victims to petition the attorney general, on behalf of themselves and their children, to avoid deportation due to leaving an abuser. The VAWA of 1994 was funded through 2000 at $1.6 billion.

Violence against Women Act Reauthorization in 2000

VAWA was reauthorized for five years in October 2000 as part of the Victims of Trafficking and Violence Protection Act of 2000. Much of VAWA 2000 extended grants and programs from the original legislation, and funding through 2005 was nearly double at $3.1 billion. Title I, Strengthening Law Enforcement to Reduce Violence against Women, emphasized enforcing protection orders via pro-arrest grants and by giving tribal courts full jurisdiction to do so. Grants under the STOP program (Services and Training for Officers and Prosecutors) were reauthorized to help police and the courts work more closely with victims services providers, as were grants to encourage arrest, to provide services for rural victims of domestic violence and child abuse, and to reduce stalking and violence against women on campus. Title I also created a definition of dating violence and included it as an area for some grant funds. Title II, Strengthening Services to Victims of Violence, provided funding for civil legal assistance to victims, for shelters and transitional housing, for the National Domestic Violence Hotline, for victim counselors in the U.S. attorney general's office, and for enhanced protections for elderly and disabled women. It also mandated studies to develop recommendations for Congress on preventing insurance discrimination against victims and appropriate workplace responses to victims and to identify how state unemployment compensation affects victims who lose their jobs due to the violence.

Title III, Limiting the Effects of Violence on Children, provided funding for a pilot program of supervised visitation for children of victims, reauthorized the victims of child abuse program, and mandated a study of the effects of parental kidnapping in domestic violence cases. Title IV, Strengthening Education and Training to Combat Violence against Women, established a new grant to provide education and training for providers to assist disabled victims, reauthorized the Sexual Assault Education and Prevention Grant program and the collaborative community grant program, and continued funding to train federal and state judges. Battered Immigrant Women, Title VI, responded to unforeseen problems with protecting immigrant victims and to changes in immigration law by including access to VAWA provisions by Cuban, Nicaraguan, Central American, and Haitian refugees.

The Future of the Violence against Women Act

As of this writing, VAWA 2005 has been introduced into both the House and the Senate. Since 1994, the act has provided tremendous benefits to victims, but legislation is always subject to funding limitations and shifts in federal priorities. The proposed legislation goes beyond responding to violence against women after it has occurred to preventing it via interventions with children and youth and by facilitating community responses to the problem. Eliminating violence against women ultimately requires a societal and cultural change. Huge strides have been made in recent decades and VAWA has been a powerful force to accomplish this goal.

NANCY MEYER-EMERICK

See also **Analyzing Incidents of Domestic Violence: A National Incident-Based Reporting System; Battered Woman Syndrome; Battered Women, Clemency for; Community Response to Domestic Violence; Date Rape; Dating Violence; Feminist Theory; Inmate Mothers: Treatment and Policy Implications; Intimate Partner Violence, Forms of; Lesbian Battering; Mandatory Arrest Policies; Police Response to Domestic Violence Incidents; Protective and Restraining Orders; Shelter Movement; Stalking; Training Practices for Law Enforcement in Domestic Violence Cases; Workplace, Domestic Violence in the**

References and Further Reading

Brownmiller, Susan. *Against Our Will: Men, Women, and Rape.* New York: Bantam, 1975.

Hanmer, Jalna, and Mary Maynard, eds. *Women, Violence and Social Control.* Atlantic Highlands, NJ: Humanities Press International, 1987.

Koss, Mary P., Lisa A. Goodman, Angela Browne, Louise F. Fitzgerald, Gwendolyn Puryear Keita, and Nancy Felipe Russo. *No Safe Haven: Male Violence against Women at Home, at Work, and in the Community.* Washington, DC: American Psychological Association, 1994.

Nourse, Victoria F. "Where Violence, Relationship, and Equality Meet: The Violence against Women Act's Civil Rights Remedy." *Wisconsin Women's Law Journal* XI, no. 1 (1996): 1–36.

Pence, Ellen, and Michael Paymar. *Education Groups for Men Who Batter: The Duluth Model.* New York: Springer, 1993.

Schechter, Susan. *Women and Male Violence: The Visions and Struggles of the Battered Women's Movement.* Boston: South End Press, 1982.

Straus, Murray A., Richard J. Gelles, and Suzanne K. Steinmetz. *Behind Closed Doors: Violence in the American Family.* Garden City, NY: Anchor/Doubleday, 1980.

Yllö, Kersti, and Michele Bograd, eds. *Feminist Perspectives on Wife Abuse.* Newbury Park, CA: Sage, 1988.

Cases and Statutes Cited

United States v. Morrison, 529 U.S. 598, 120 S. Ct. 1740 (2000).

Victims of Trafficking and Violence Protection Act of 2000, Pub. L. No. 106-386, 114 Stat. 1464 (2000).

Violence against Women Act of 1994, Pub. L. No. 103-322, Title IV, 108 Stat. 1902 (1994).

Violence against Women Act of 2000, Pub. L. No. 106-386, Div. B., 114 Stat. 1491 (2000).

Violent Crime Control and Law Enforcement Act of 1994, Pub. L. No. 103-322, 108 Stat. 1796 (1994).

WOMEN WITH DISABILITIES, DOMESTIC VIOLENCE AGAINST

Domestic violence was hidden from most of mainstream society and largely ignored by health professionals until the late 1970s (Stark, Flitcraft, and Frazier 1979). As research on domestic violence has developed and programs have been instituted to address the needs of victims, one particularly vulnerable group of women has remained overlooked: women with disabilities (Chenoweth and Cook 2001; Jennings 2002; McCarthy 1998). The research on the experiences of women with disabilities who are victims of domestic violence is so sparse that little attention has been paid to the impact of culture, beyond gender and ability status (e.g., ethnicity, age, sexual orientation) on those experiences (Hassouneh-Phillips and Curry 2002).

Who are women with disabilities? According to Banks (2003), "Women who have disabilities represent a very broad spectrum in terms of ability to manage their personal and social affairs" (p. xxi). Disabling disorders can be visible (e.g., arthritis, limited mobility, limited vision, deafness) or invisible (cardiac disease, chronic fatigue syndrome, fibromyalgia, pain, traumatic brain injury, learning disability). Having one disability not only does not preclude having others; instead, it increases the probability of having additional challenges. Domestic violence further increases disability.

All women who are victims of intimate partner violence, a large subset of domestic violence, are treated like victims of torture most often associated with war and kidnapping (Beck-Massey 1999). Women with disabilities, on average, endure domestic violence for longer periods than women without disabilities (Coker, Smith, and Fadden 2005; Curry, Hassouneh-Phillips, and Johnston-Silverberg 2001; Li, Ford, and Moore 2000) and are at high risk for being abused by multiple perpetrators (Hassouneh-Phillips and Curry 2002). Beck-Massey (1999) and Curry et al. (2001) found that in addition to vulnerability to the kinds of physical and psychological abuse experienced by most women, women with disabilities are also subjected to specific disability-related types of violence.

Although most examinations of domestic violence focus on a single perpetrator, usually an intimate partner, defined by Tjaden and Thoennes (2000) as "current and former dates, spouses, and cohabiting partners, with cohabiting meaning living together at least some of the time as a couple" (p. 5), the vulnerability experienced by women with disabilities involves a wider variety of perpetrators. Other family members can perpetrate domestic violence on women with disabilities, including parents (Nosek, Foley, et al. 2001), adult children (Bergeron 2005), and siblings (Crawford and Ostrove 2003). As many women with disabilities are dependent on other people for personal assistance, they are at high risk for abuse from the people who provide that assistance (Saxton et al. 2001). Most personal assistance is provided in private, thus increasing the vulnerability of women with disabilities. This is further complicated by the large number of family members, including spouses, who provide personal assistance for women with disabilities (Saxton et al. 2001).

Manifestations of Domestic Violence against Women with Disabilities

It is critical to describe domestic violence as it pertains to women with disabilities (Hassouneh-Phillips and Curry 2002). Nosek, Foley, and colleagues (2001) found it expeditious to draw on definitions from others, as they broke domestic violence into the components of emotional abuse, defined as "being threatened, terrorized, corrupted, or severely rejected, isolated, ignored, or verbally attacked" (p. 180); physical abuse, defined as "any form of violence against her body, such as being hit, kicked, restrained, or deprived of food or water" (pp. 180–181); and sexual abuse, defined as "being forced, threatened, or deceived into sexual activities ranging from looking or touching to intercourse or rape" (p. 181). They found that women with disabilities described five types of domestic violence: "(1) disability-related emotional abuse, (2) disability-related physical abuse, (3) disability-related sexual abuse, (4) abuse related to disability-related settings, and (5) abuse related to helping relationships" (p. 182). Saxton and colleagues (2001) also identified financial abuse as a form of disability-related domestic violence. Examples of the types of domestic abuse experienced by women with disabilities include:

Disability-related emotional abuse:

- Actual or threatened abandonment (Nosek, Foley, et al. 2001)
- Isolation (Crawford and Ostrove 2003)
- "[Y]elling and screaming, threats of abandonment, violations of privacy, threats to neglect children or pets, and being ignored" (Saxton et al. 2001, p. 404)

- Difficulty leaving an identified abusive relationship due to reliance on an abusive spouse for "financial and/or emotional needs" as well as "most basic needs of mobility and physical access" (Saxton et al. 2001, p. 403)
- Power imbalance due to socialization of women with disabilities to be passively compliant and pleasant (Saxton et al. 2001)
- Intolerance and rejection (Nosek, Foley, et al. 2001)
- Refusal to acknowledge disability (Corbett 2003; Nosek, Foley, et al. 2001)
- Unrealistic demands on women with disabilities to carry out prescribed family roles (Nabors and Pettee 2003)
- Family prioritization of men's disabilities over women's disabilities (Nabors and Pettee 2003)
- Threats of losing custody of or access to children (Beck-Massey 1999; Curry et al. 2001; Olkin 2003)
- Family disavowal of relationship (Crawford and Ostrove 2003; Nosek, Foley, et al. 2001)
- Talking about a deaf woman in her presence by manipulating lighting so that she cannot read lips (Crawford and Ostrove 2003)

Disability-related physical abuse:

- "By withholding or otherwise preventing the use of orthotic devices or medication, a woman can be rendered helpless" (Nosek, Foley, et al. 2001, p. 184; see also Beck-Massey 1999; Curry et al. 2001)
- "[W]ithholding, immobilizing, or impairing assistive devices or other equipment and withholding or forcing medication" (Saxton et al. 2001, p. 405)
- Dismantling of or prevention from using assistive devices (e.g., wheelchairs, hearing aids) (Beck-Massey 1999; Curry et al. 2001)
- Adult children allowing access of known abusive relatives to women with disabilities (Bergeron 2005)
- Family refusal to allow access to personal assistants (Bergeron 2005)
- "Batterers use the problems women experience (e.g., substance abuse) as abuse strategies (e.g., supplying alcohol or drugs, not allowing women to take medication for mental health issues)" (Zweig, Schlichter, and Burt 2002, p. 168)
- Family members' refusal to develop skills to communicate with a woman with a disability (Corbett 2003)

Disability-related sexual abuse:

- Spousal rape (Nosek, Foley, et al. 2001)
- Threat of physical violence to coerce sexual activity (McCarthy 1998)
- "The line between appropriate touching as an essential part of the job of providers and inappropriate touching, which could lead to unwanted or ambiguous sexual contact, was not always clearly definable. . . . Bathing and dressing are such intimate activities that it is not surprising that blurry boundaries can create confusion" (Saxton et al. 2001, p. 401)
- "[F]ondling or forcing sexual activity in return for accepting help" (Nosek, Foley, et al. 2001, p. 184)
- Confusion between "helping an individual with sexual activity and participating in sexual activity" (Mona 2003, p. 220)

Abuse related to disability-related settings:

- "Sexual abuse by members of staff in learning disability services is a phenomenon which has happened for many years" (McCarthy 1998, p. 548)
- Sexual abuse under the guise of provision of health care (Nosek, Foley, et al. 2001)
- Lack of protection from males in inpatient settings; abuse discounted or excused as "symptoms" of males' disabilities (McCarthy 1998)
- "[U]se of seclusion, restraint, and rapid tranquilization with people with developmental disabilities" (Sequeira and Halstead 2001, p. 462)
- "In institutions men routinely pay for, and women routinely accept payment for, sex. . . . Sex is seen as a commodity that can be exchanged and it is a one-way exchange, i.e., the men pay the women, not the other way around" (McCarthy 1998, p. 547)
- Therapists' discounting of impact of disability (Farley 2003; Williams and Upadhyay 2003)
- Therapists' misattribution of psychological presenting complaints to physical disability (Mukherjee, Reis, and Heller 2003)
- Exposure of nude body to others without permission (Mona, Cameron, and Crawford 2005)

Abuse related to helping relationships:

- "[R]ough handling, delayed responsiveness of the provider" (Mona et al. 2005, p. 238)
- Lack of understanding by police and other helping professionals of the nature of personal assistance relationships, due to societal assumptions that women with disabilities are incompetent (Mona et al. 2005; Saxton et al. 2001)
- Infantilization (Nosek, Foley, et al. 2001; Saxton et al. 2001)
- Attempting to transform a business relationship into a personal friendship (Saxton et al. 2001)

Disability-related financial abuse:

- "[T]heft of jewelry, money, and personal belongings; forgery; purchase of personal items when shopping with the participant's money; and withdrawal of extra money during ATM transactions performed for the woman. A unique form of financial abuse commonly reported was assistants showing up late or not working their full time, but still receiving full compensation" (Saxton et al. 2001, p. 405)
- Abuse of durable power of attorney (Bergeron 2005)
- Family refusal to consider financial limitations of women with disabilities (Corbett 2003)

Women with disabilities are often isolated in ways that prevent them from realizing that abusive treatment is not normal (Saxton et al. 2001). Perhaps the greatest threat is that women with disabilities are repeatedly told that they will not be believed if they report abuse (Chang et al. 2003; Nosek, Howland, and Hughes 2001), especially if the perpetrator takes advantage of the woman's disability to claim that she has misinterpreted or misremembered the abuse (Gilson, DePoy, and Cramer 2001). This is consistent with research indicating that health professionals, police, and legal personnel are slow to respond and engage in considerable victim blaming of women with disabilities (Curry et al. 2001). Even when the women are believed, domestic violence support systems (e.g., shelters) and transportation are seldom accessible to them. Similarly, programs designed to address and support women with disabilities tend to be unprepared to deal with abuse.

In discussing women with disabilities as victims of domestic violence, it is important to consider the violence itself as a source of disability (Plichta 2004). Curry et al. (2001) and Campbell and Kendall-Tackett (2005) indicated that domestic violence could also exacerbate disabling health conditions (see also Zlotnick, Johnson, and Kohn 2006). Three major disabling consequences of domestic violence are traumatic brain injury (Ackerman and Banks 2003; Coker et al. 2005), severe depression leading to suicide (Curry et al. 2001), and pain (Kendall-Tackett, Marshall, and Ness 2003). Plichta's (2004) review reveals that older women report chronic ill-health effects from intimate partner violence, even after the abuse has ended.

Women with disabilities experience increased vulnerability in part due to conflicting social stereotypes. Some "asexual" stereotypes portray women with disabilities as unattractive, undesirable, and desperate for relationships (Beck-Massey 1999; Crawford and Ostrove 2003; Dotson, Stinson, and Christian 2003; Li et al. 2000; Mona et al. 2005; Olkin 2003), whereas other "oversexed" stereotypes involve exaggerated attractiveness to the point of exploitation (Elman 1997; Fiduccia 1999). Farley (2003) explained that the most hidden intimate partner violence against women with disabilities occurs within prostitution, where injury is inflicted with impunity. The injured women are trapped in ongoing dangerous situations and do not receive health treatment for disabling physical and psychological injuries; this is consistent with research by Plichta (2004), who found that women in abusive relationships had unmet health care needs. Prostituted women, in particular, are unlikely to receive legal or medical assistance (Farley 2003; Zweig et al. 2002). Some pornography suggests that inflicting disabling injury on women with disabilities is acceptable and includes recommendations on how to injure women (Elman 1997); women in prostitution who encounter consumers of such pornography are at very high risk of being killed.

Increasing Safety for Women with Disabilities

It is critical to consider ways to facilitate safety for women with disabilities who are in abusive relationships. An overwhelming sense of vulnerability can interfere with women with disabilities who might consider independent living (Hendey and Pascall 1998) or leaving abusive relationships (Olkin 2003). Beck-Massey (1999) suggested being alert for signs of abuse (both individual and in the interactions of a couple), sensitive listening, and individually considered recommendations for increased safety. Chang and colleagues (2003) noted that safety planning is particularly complex for women with disabilities who are being abused by people on whom they are physically dependent; they recommended developing creative ways to let others know that help is needed and having extra medical supplies and assistive devices available.

Some environments appear to be relatively safe for women with disabilities. Albaugh and Nauta (2005) found that college women with disabilities reported receiving "less psychological aggression and coercion" (p. 303) than college women without disabilities or health concerns. Implementation of the Americans with Disabilities Act may increase opportunities for women with disabilities to experience the relatively safe college environment.

Participants in the Saxton et al. (2001) focus groups recommended the following as techniques to minimize the potential of abuse from people providing personal assistance: (a) rigorous screening in the recruitment, interviewing, and hiring phases; (b) checking references, including a criminal background check with the police; (c) drawing up a written contract; (d) authorizing payment; (e) scheduling and following through with regular supervision meetings for direct feedback on how the job is going; (f) making time for the provider to discuss concerns; and (g) never firing a provider in anger (Saxton et al. 2001, p. 410).

Coble (2001) provided recommendations for the hiring of personal assistants, including development of a hiring process and being specific about tasks to be handled and the preferred manner in which they should be accomplished (e.g., order of assistance with dressing, management of laundry). In order to facilitate cooperation of personal assistants, Coble emphasized the importance of clear communication, assertiveness, empathy, careful listening, and focusing on "only the immediate issue of concern" (p. 8). In addition, Coble (2001) noted that relationships between women with disabilities and personal assistants could be enhanced with psychotherapy using "a combination of education, conflict resolution and enhancing communication skills" (p. 8).

There is a strong need to increase the accessibility of shelters for women with disabilities (Beck-Massey 1999). The necessary accommodations vary considerably due to the wide variety of disabilities experienced by women. Zweig and colleagues (2002) noted that women with substance-related or mental disabilities face multiple barriers to receiving assistance in escaping from domestic violence. Shelters struggle with severe financial limitations that serve as barriers to developing accommodations necessary to serve women with disabilities who are attempting to leave abusive situations (Chang et al. 2003). Some shelters have started to coordinate services with other agencies (Chang et al. 2003), but the reality is that such coordination seldom meets the needs of the broad range of disabilities experienced by women.

Summary

There is a need for much more research to fully understand the extent and variety of domestic violence experienced by women with disabilities.

However, enough vulnerabilities have been documented so that programs can be instituted to start to meet the needs of and enhance safety for women with disabilities. Information about domestic violence ought to be made available in multiple formats accessible to women with disabilities. Services for women with disabilities must include awareness of, education about, and the ability to screen for domestic violence, just as domestic violence services must be prepared to serve women with disabilities. Education of health professionals and law enforcement personnel must include the specific challenges faced by women with disabilities; such education must directly address and confront stereotypes about women with disabilities. Future research should include attention to a broad range of issues, including ethnicity, age, sexual orientation, religion, socioeconomic status, and types of disability, to ensure that culturally accessible and relevant services are developed and maintained.

MARTHA E. BANKS

See also **Battered Woman Syndrome; Caregiver Violence against People with Disabilities; Victim-Blaming Theory**

References and Further Reading

Ackerman, R. J., and M. E. Banks. "Assessment, Treatment, and Rehabilitation for Interpersonal Violence Victims: Women Sustaining Head Injuries." In *Women with Visible and Invisible Disabilities: Multiple Intersections, Multiple Issues, Multiple Therapies*, edited by M. E. Banks and E. Kaschak. New York: Haworth, 2003, pp. 343–363.

Albaugh, L. M., and M. M. Nauta. "Career Decision Self-efficacy, Career Barriers, and College Women's Experiences of Intimate Partner Violence." *Journal of Career Assessment* 13 (2005): 288–306.

Banks, M. E. "Preface." In Banks and Kaschak, *Women with Visible and Invisible Disabilities,* 2003, pp. xxi–xxxix.

Beck-Massey, D. "Sanctioned War: Women, Violence, and Disabilities." *Sexuality and Disability* 17 (1999): 269–276.

Bergeron, L. R. "Abuse of Elderly Women in Family Relationships: Another Form of Violence against Women." In *Handbook of Women, Stress, and Trauma*, edited by K. A. Kendall-Tackett. New York: Brunner-Routledge, 2005, pp. 141–157.

Campbell, J. C., and K. A. Kendall-Tackett. "Intimate Partner Violence: Implications for Women's Physical and Mental Health." In K. A. Kendall-Tackett, *Handbook of Women, Stress, and Trauma,* 2005, pp. 123–140.

Chang, J. C., S. L. Martin, K. E. Moracco, L. Dulli, D. Scandlin, M. B, Loucks-Sorrel, T. Turner, L. Starsoneck, P. N. Dorian, and I. Bou-Saada. "Helping Women with Disabilities and Domestic Violence: Strategies, Limitations, and Challenges of Domestic Violence Programs and Services." *Journal of Women's Health* 12 (2003): 699–708.

Chenoweth, L., and S. Cook. "Guest Editors' Introduction." *Violence against Women* 7 (2001): 363–366.

Coble, A. C. "When the Challenge of Maintaining Personal Care Attendants Becomes the Focus of Treatment." *Rehabilitation Psychology News* 28, no. 2 (2001, Winter): 7–8.

Coker, A. L., P. H. Smith, and M. K. Fadden. "Intimate Partner Violence and Disabilities among Women Attending Family Practice Clinics." *Journal of Women's Health* 14 (2005): 829–838.

Corbett, C. A. "Special Issues in Psychotherapy with Minority Deaf Women." In Banks and Kaschak, *Women with Visible and Invisible Disabilities,* 2003, pp. 311–329.

Crawford, D., and J. M. Ostrove. "Representations of Disability and the Interpersonal Relationships of Women with Disabilities." In Banks and Kaschak, *Women with Visible and Invisible Disabilities,* 2003, pp. 179–194.

Curry, M. A., D. Hassouneh-Phillips, and A. Johnston-Silverberg. "Abuse of Women with Disabilities: An Ecological Model and Review." *Violence against Women* 7 (2001): 60–79.

Dotson, L. A., J. Stinson, and L. Christian. "'People Tell Me I Can't Have Sex': Women with Disabilities Share Their Personal Perspectives on Health Care, Sexuality, and Reproductive Rights." In Banks and Kaschak, *Women with Visible and Invisible Disabilities,* 2003, pp. 195–209.

Elman, R. A. "Disability Pornography: The Fetishization of Women's Vulnerabilities." *Violence against Women* 3 (1997): 257–270.

Farley, M. "Prostitution and the Invisibility of Harm." In Banks and Kaschak, *Women with Visible and Invisible Disabilities,* 2003, pp. 247–280.

Fiduccia, B. F. W. "Sexual Imagery of Physically Disabled Women: Erotic? Perverse? Sexist?" *Sexuality and Disability* 17 (1999): 277–282.

Gilson, S. F., E. DePoy, and E. P. Cramer. "Linking the Assessment of Self-reported Functional Capacity with Abuse Experiences of Women with Disabilities." *Violence against Women* 7 (2001): 418–431.

Hassouneh-Phillips, D., and M. A. Curry. "Abuse of Women with Disabilities: State of the Science." *Rehabilitation Counseling Bulletin* 45 (2002): 96–104.

Hendey, N., and G. Pascall. "Independent Living: Gender, Violence and the Threat of Violence." *Disability and Society* 13 (1998): 415–427.

Jennings, C. *Triple Disadvantage: Out of Sight, Out of Mind,* 2nd ed., 2002. http://www.dvirc.org.au/UpdateHub/Triple%20Disadvantage%20Report%202003.pdf (accessed May 12, 2006).

Kendall-Tackett, K., R. Marshall, and K. Ness. "Chronic Pain Syndromes and Violence against Women." In Banks and Kaschak, *Women with Visible and Invisible Disabilities,* 2003, pp. 45–56.

Li, L., J. A. Ford, and D. Moore. "An Exploratory Study of Violence, Substance Abuse, Disability, and Gender." *Social Behavior and Personality* 28 (2000): 61–71.

McCarthy, M. "Sexual Violence against Women with Learning Disabilities." *Feminism and Psychology* 8 (1998): 544–551.

Mona, L. R. "Sexual Options for People with Disabilities: Using Personal Assistance Services for Sexual Expression." In Banks and Kaschak, *Women with Visible and Invisible Disabilities,* 2003, pp. 211–221.

Mona, L. R., R. P. Cameron, and D. Crawford. "Stress and Trauma in the Lives of Women with Disabilities." In K. A. Kendall-Tackett, *Handbook of Women, Stress, and Trauma,* 2005, pp. 229–244.

Mukherjee, D., J. P. Reis, and W. Heller. "Women Living with Traumatic Brain Injury: Social Isolation, Emotional Functioning and Implications for Psychotherapy." In Banks and Kaschak, *Women with Visible and Invisible Disabilities*, 2003, pp. 3–26.

Nabors, N. A., and M. F. Pettee. "Womanist Therapy with African American Women with Disabilities." In Banks and Kaschak, *Women with Visible and Invisible Disabilities*, 2003, pp. 331–341.

Nosek, M. A., C. C. Foley, R. B. Hughes, and C. A. Howland. "Vulnerabilities for Abuse among Women with Disabilities." *Sexuality and Disability* 19 (2001): 177–189.

Nosek, M. A., C. A. Howland, and R. B. Hughes. "The Investigation of Abuse and Women with Disabilities: Going Beyond Assumptions." *Violence against Women* 7 (2001): 477–499.

Olkin, R. "Women with Physical Disabilities Who Want to Leave Their Partners: A Feminist and Disability-Affirmative Perspective." In Banks and Kaschak, *Women with Visible and Invisible Disabilities*, 2003, pp. 237–246.

Plichta, S. B. "Intimate Partner Violence and Physical Health Consequences: Policy and Practice Implications." *Journal of Interpersonal Violence* 19 (2004): 1296–1323.

Saxton, M., M. A. Curry, L. E. Powers, S. Maley, K. Eckels, and J. Gross. "'Bring My Scooter So I Can Leave You': A Study of Disabled Women Handling Abuse by Personal Assistance Providers." *Violence against Women* 7 (2001): 393–417.

Sequeira, H., and S. Halstead. "'Is It Meant to Hurt, Is It?': Management of Violence in Women with Developmental Disabilities." *Violence against Women* 7 (2001): 462–476.

Stark, E., A. Flitcraft, and W. Frazier. "Medicine and Patriarchal Violence: The Social Construction of a 'Private' Event." *International Journal of Health Service* 9 (1979): 461–493.

Tjaden, P., and N. Thoennes. *Extent, Nature, and Consequences of Intimate Partner Violence: Findings from the National Violence against Women Survey* (NCJ 181867). Washington, DC: U.S. Department of Justice, Bureau of Justice Statistics, 2000.

Williams, M., and W. S. Upadhyay. "To Be or Not to Be Disabled." In Banks and Kaschak, *Women with Visible and Invisible Disabilities*, 2003, pp. 145–154.

Zlotnick, C., D. M. Johnson, and R. Kohn. "Intimate Partner Violence and Long-term Psychosocial Functioning in a National Sample of American Women." *Journal of Interpersonal Violence* 21 (2006): 262–275.

Zweig, J. M., K. A. Schlichter, and M. R. Burt. "Assisting Women Victims of Violence Who Experience Multiple Barriers to Services." *Violence against Women* 8 (2002): 162–180.

WORKPLACE, DOMESTIC VIOLENCE IN

All too often the media does not cover incidents in which domestic violence spills over into the workplace; hence the public and policymakers are unaware of the numerous acts of domestic violence that are committed in workplaces. Furthermore, work colleagues, and even employers, are rarely aware of the many ways domestic violence impacts their workplaces. Bruises perpetrated by a partner are hidden under long sleeves and masked by a forced smile, low morale and self-esteem are recorded as poor job performance, and the use of company resources to deliver verbal and written threats or stalk are examples of the many faces of domestic violence in the workplace.

The Extent of Workplace Domestic Violence

While there is no precise estimate of how much domestic violence occurs at work, it clearly represents a daunting challenge to both safety and productivity, affecting a sizable proportion of the approximately 140 million employees in the United States. Several national-level data sources shed some light on the extent of workplace domestic violence.

First, data from the Bureau of Labor Statistics (BLS) Census of Fatal Occupational Injuries (CFOI) shows that homicide is the leading cause of death for women on the job (BLS 1994). During 1992–1994, 17 percent of the alleged perpetrators who killed women at work were current or former husbands or boyfriends (BLS 1996).

Second, according to a Federal Bureau of Investigation (FBI) report, each year approximately 3 percent of workplace homicides are known to be perpetrated by an intimate partner. Of the workplace homicides committed by an intimate, 62 percent were committed by a husband (n = 122), and 37 percent were committed by a boyfriend (n = 72). Far fewer homicides, nearly 2 percent (n = 3), were committed by a wife (Rugala and Issacs 2004, p. 42).

Third, National Crime Victimization Survey (NCVS) data show that an annual average of over 1.7 million workplace violent victimizations (i.e., rape, sexual assault, robbery, and simple and aggravated assault) occur each year. Intimate partners were the reported perpetrators of these violent acts in an average of 1.1 percent of workplace violence victimizations each year, yielding an estimate of approximately 19,000 workplace violence victimizations by intimates each year (Duhart 2001). Data from the 1987–1992 NCVS confirm that a larger percentage of female employees were victimized by an intimate than their male counterparts. Five percent of the women victimized at work were attacked by a current or former spouse or boyfriend compared with 1 percent of the men (Bachman 1994).

These estimates, however, drastically underestimate the extent of domestic violence in the workplace. While there are existing data systems that can be used to identify work-related deaths (e.g., BLS CFOI), work injuries resulting from being victimized (e.g., Employer's Reports of Injury and Illness or Occupational Safety and Health Administration logs), homicides (e.g., FBI Supplemental Homicide File), and violent victimizations (e.g., NCVS), none of these sources was specifically designed to identify the nexus between domestic violence and the workplace or while at work. This inability to measure workplace domestic violence is, in part, because of measurement limitations in the existing data that include: (1) samples that are not selected from the currently employed population, and/or (2) the lack of a detailed victim/offender relationship measure (see Fisher and Peek-Asa 2005). Thus, the answers to many important questions about the frequency, types, and consequences of domestic violence in the workplace are largely unknown.

The Effects of Domestic Violence on Employees

In a 2002 survey of 100 senior executives and managers from Fortune 1000 companies, 56 percent were aware of employees who had experienced domestic violence (as cited in Randel and Wells 2003). The few workplace-focused studies have documented that domestic violence negatively impacts the safety and well-being of the abused employee, the perpetrator employee, coworkers, and the organization.

The Effects of Domestic Violence on the Abused Employee While at Work

Research has shown that many domestic violence victims miss days of work or are tardy due to the physical and psychological abuse their bodies endure while not at work. To illustrate, a 1997 national study reported that 24 percent of women between the ages of eighteen and sixty-four years old who had experienced domestic violence indicated that the abuse caused them to arrive late at work or miss days of work (Family Violence Prevention Fund 2005a, 2005b).

According to the Centers for Disease Control and Prevention (2003), victims of intimate partner violence lose a total of nearly 8 million days of paid work—the equivalent of more than 32,000 full-time jobs—and nearly 5.6 million days of household productivity as a result of the violence. Farmer and Tiefenthaler (2004) estimated that there are between 3 million (using NVCS data) and 7 million (using National Violence against Women data) lost work days per year, with a lower-bound estimate of losses of $192 million shared by the victims and their employers.

A large proportion of abused women lose their jobs or earn lower wages as a consequence of their violent experiences and the resulting absenteeism or poor performance (see Farmer and Tiefenthaler 2004; Lloyd 1997; Lloyd and Taluc 1999). In her report to the Taylor Institute, Raphael (1996) estimated that between 24 and 30 percent of abused working women lose their jobs due to their domestic violence situations. These studies do not identify whether or not victims disclosed their situations to their employers.

Although domestic violence victims suffer negative consequences at their workplaces, studies have also shown that domestic violence does not affect involvement in the labor market. Using three national-level data sets to build game theoretic models, Farmer and Tiefenthaler (2004) showed that domestic violence in fact has a positive effect on labor market participation. In other words, abused women are more likely to work than women who are not abused. Lloyd's (1997, 1999) interviews with and survey of randomly selected women in a Chicago neighborhood echo Farmer and Tiefenthaler's results: Women who experienced intimate partner violence were employed at a rate that was not significantly different from women who were not abused. Although this may seem to contradict findings of the negative effects of domestic violence on work performance, there are reasons that domestic violence victims would seek employment. One explanation is that abused women work to maintain or regain economic independence. Another reason could be that abused women feel safer at work than at home, although the workplace domestic violence research suggests that this may not always be true for some women.

These studies do not identify whether domestic violence victims have similar earning potential to that of nonvictims. It is likely that although victims are employed in equal or greater proportions than nonvictims, domestic violence negatively impacts the victims' wages, lengths of employment, and benefits status.

The Impact of the Perpetrator-Employee on the Job

Of the many domestic violence victims assaulted, stalked, or harassed at their workplaces, how many of the perpetrators of these acts were also at work? Little research has examined the behavior of the perpetrator-employee who uses job-related resources to execute his/her abuse against a partner, or the negative effects of abusive behavior on work performance. Reckitt and Fortman (2004), working for the nonprofit Maine Department of Labor and Family Crisis Services, interviewed participants in domestic violence intervention programs in six cities in Maine. Their results showed that 85 percent of the offenders reported that they had used company resources to contact their partners while on the job, with over three-fourths (77 percent) using the company phone. Nearly a quarter (24 percent) used the company cell phone to check up on, pressure, threaten, or express remorse/anger to the victimized partners. A quarter of the abusers used the company car during working hours to drive to victims' residences.

Their results also revealed that the abuser's job performance was impaired: 41 percent of the abusers reported that their abusive behavior toward their partners had a negative effect on their job performance. When on the job, nearly half (48 percent) admitted that it caused them to have difficulty concentrating on their work because they were thinking about their relationship. Slightly less (19 percent) provided anecdotes of accidents or near-miss accidents that were brought on by their abusive behaviors toward a loved one. Their abusive behavior while not at work resulted in 15,221 hours of work time lost because they were in police custody. At Maine's average hourly wage, this equals approximately $200,000 in lost wages.

The Massachusetts-based Employers against Domestic Violence conducted focus groups with twenty-nine male domestic violence offenders that supports negative effects of domestic violence perpetration on the workplace (Rothman, no date). Furthermore, offenders reported that supervisors were often sympathetic to them, rarely penalized or docked vacation or personal days for leaving work early or missing days to attend court dates, and, for a few, their supervisors posted bail. Supervisors were likely to address substance abuse issues, but rarely did they address issues concerning domestic violence with the abusers.

The Consequences for Coworkers

Outside the media's coverage of coworkers being killed or injured by the heinous acts of a fellow employee's loved one or estranged partner, there is, as of this writing, little, if any, published research documenting the effects on coworkers of workplace domestic violence or working with a domestic violence victim.

Costs to Businesses

Studies have shown that business executives and managers are well aware of the effects of domestic violence on the operation of their firms. Two surveys of 100 senior executives and managers from Fortune 1000 companies, one in 1994 and the other in 2002, were sponsored by Liz Claiborne. Results from the surveys revealed an increase between 1994 and 2002 in the percentage of employers who were aware of employees who had experienced domestic violence. In 1994, 40 percent of the corporate leaders were aware of employees within their organizations who were affected by domestic violence. This rose sixteen percentage points in 2002 to 56 percent being aware of employees who were affected by domestic violence (as cited in Randel and Wells 2003). Whether this represents increasing workplace domestic violence or an increased awareness is unknown, but these findings are likely a combination of both.

Almost all of the corporate leaders surveyed (91 percent) believed that domestic violence affected both the private lives *and* the working lives of their employees. Notably, 60 percent reported that domestic violence took a toll on their employees' psychological well-being, physical safety (52 percent), productivity (48 percent), and attendance (42 percent). Support for these results comes from a series of focus groups with twenty-five health benefit managers from small and large businesses around the country (Partnership for Prevention 2005). The managers identified effects of domestic violence in the workplace that included absenteeism, inability to focus, poor self-esteem, low productivity, and low morale.

Half of the respondents to a Liz Claiborne survey recognized that domestic violence had a negative effect on their company's insurance and medical costs. Nearly a third (32 percent) reported that their company's bottom-line performance had been damaged. Over twice as many respondents (67 percent) believed that domestic violence was a serious problem that warranted their attention (as cited in Randel and Wells 2003).

The direct financial cost of domestic violence on businesses is staggering. On average, one victim can cost an employer $1,775 more in medical expenses than an employee who is not abused. An estimated $100 million in lost wages, paid sick leave, and absenteeism linked to domestic violence is also spent by businesses (as cited in Partnership for Prevention 2005). Legal liability has a price tag, too. Employers can face a range of liabilities for failing to address threats, including failure to secure the workplace from known threats and indirect liability for not intervening in known dangers (Speer 2003). While these liabilities have not been tried extensively in courts, findings increasingly favor victims. Employers can also be liable under torts for negligent hiring, retention, supervision, and termination should an employer fail to screen or remove dangerous employees or situations (Speer 2003). For example, "Courts have held companies liable for negligent hiring, negligent retention and for failure to warn because domestic violence that crosses over into the workplace may be predictable and preventable" (Braun Consulting News 2004). Businesses may incur additional legal liability under various laws governing their responses to workplace domestic violence, including Occupational Safety and Health Administration (OSHA) regulations, the Americans with Disabilities Act, and antidiscrimination laws (see Dougan 2004).

Legal Rights and Employment Protections for Domestic Violence Victims

As the scope and toll of domestic violence are better understood, legal protections for victims are increasing, and many of these include work protections. Many new policies that protect domestic violence victims against employment discrimination are being implemented, such as policies in Illinois and New York City that prohibit any employment discrimination against domestic violence victims (Weiser and Widiss 2004). Many states are also implementing policies that prohibit employers from penalizing employees for taking time off to seek protection orders or medical care or for other activities related to being a victim of domestic violence. While some of these policies are specific to victims of domestic violence, such victims are also

protected under policies that address any victims of crimes. California, Colorado, Hawaii, Illinois, and Maine, as of February 2004, provide rights for victims of domestic violence to take unpaid leave (Weiser and Widiss 2004), with much state as well as federal legislation pending. Victims who need extended time off can also be protected under the Family and Medical Leave Act or the Americans with Disabilities Act (Weiser and Widiss 2004).

Other policies require employers to protect workers from the potential effects of domestic violence. The OSHA General Duty clause states that employers have an obligation to maintain a safe workplace. Some states have identified violence as a general hazard, and some have identified domestic violence in the workplace as an aspect of the violence hazard. California, for example, requires all businesses to implement an Injury and Violence Prevention Program that requires employers to identify all potential workplace hazards, including violence (Howard and Barish 2003). Cal/OSHA has provided comprehensive guidelines for violence prevention in the workplace in its *Guidelines for Workplace Security,* and this document identifies family members or acquaintances of employees as posing a potential threat (Howard and Barish 2003).

How Domestic Violence Is Being Addressed in the Workplace

The Family Violence Prevention Fund (2005a) reported that "an increasing number of corporations, foundations and unions are addressing domestic violence by implementing workplace policies, training employees and managers, and supporting community efforts to end domestic violence." Information about "best practices" addressing workplace partner violence is available through the Corporate Alliance to End Partner Violence (CAEPV), a national nonprofit organization whose mission is to reduce "the costs and consequences of partner violence at work and [eliminate] it altogether" through a variety of means, including education, policies and programs, and legal issues and legislation. Since 1995 over sixty businesses and organizations, including State Farm Insurance, Target Stores, Southwest Airlines, the National Football League, and Women Empowered against Violence, have exchanged information, collaborated on projects, and used their influence to instigate change in their fight against intimate partner violence in the workplace (Corporate Alliance to End Partner Violence [CAEPV] 2005).

Examples of the workplace initiatives that CAEPV members have implemented to address intimate partner violence include:

- CIGNA and Archer Daniels Midland providing easy access to education and prevention material via newsletters, payroll stuffers, and request faxes.
- McKee Foods/Arkansas developing "Project Ruth"—a cross-functional team dealing with partner violence at work. In its efforts to create an atmosphere of encouragement and support for victims, Project Ruth provides needed help to McKee employees who experience domestic violence (CAEPV 2005).
- Liz Claiborne, Inc., partnering in 2004 with the Family Violence Prevention Fund to launch the Founding Fathers Workplace Campaign (Randell and Wells 2003). This initiative increased awareness among employees about how they can both prevent domestic violence and support employees who are victims, and provided "educational materials to employees on how fathers can act as role models, and how to talk to boys and young men about violence, bullying and relationship abuse" (Family Violence Prevention Fund 2005b).

Outside of these few case studies, there has been little systematic research to identify how many employers are addressing the issue of domestic violence in their workplaces, what these employers are doing, and how successful they have been. Fisher and Peek-Asa (2005) conducted a content analysis of publicly available documents and found that few programs provided comprehensive strategies for addressing the problem, and no programs had been adequately evaluated. Two resources were found to be particularly helpful for employers:

- a Sample Policy of Domestic Violence, developed by the National Center on Domestic and Sexual Violence (2004), which provides information for developing a comprehensive domestic violence workplace policy, and
- a resource guide for employers, unions, and advocates, developed by the Family Violence Prevention Fund (2004).

A range of topics are included in these guides, including guidelines for supervising victims of domestic violence, pointers on how to talk with an employee who is a perpetrator of abuse, designing personal and workplace safety plans, securing the work area, identifying and treating domestic violence, legal issues, and union responses to domestic violence.

In spite of these and numerous other guidelines (see Fisher and Peek-Asa 2005), employers have few resources for proven programs to address domestic violence in their workplaces. They have even fewer resources about how these programs can be implemented in various work settings. A growing interest in this topic, which will be fueled by growing awareness and recognition of its toll and consequences, will hopefully lead to more informative state-of-the-art models.

Conclusion

The work setting is ideal for efforts to prevent domestic violence and support its victims. Work settings are relatively controlled environments in which protection strategies can be tested and implemented. Employers should be motivated to test these programs because they will likely positively impact worker morale and productivity and could prevent potential events for which they could be held liable. As this field of work moves forward, one can hope that victims will increasingly find their employers to be positive partners in assisting him or her, and also that the workplace will be an intolerant atmosphere for abusers.

CORINNE PEEK-ASA and BONNIE S. FISHER

See also **Batterer Typology; Intimate Partner Homicide; Legal Issues for Battered Women; Stalking; Substance Use/Abuse and Intimate Partner Violence**

References and Further Reading

Bachman, Ronet. *Violence and Theft in the Workplace* (NCJ 148199). Washington, DC: U.S. Department of Justice, 1994.

Braun Consulting News. "Domestic Abuse and Workplace Violence—A Liability Issue for Employers," Spring 1998. http://www.braunconsulting.com/bcg/newsletters/spring2.html.

Bureau of Labor Statistics. *Violence in the Workplace Comes Under Closer Scrutiny*. Washington, DC: U.S. Department of Labor, Issues Paper Summary, No. 94-10, August 1994.

———. *Domestic Violence: A Workplace Issue*. Washington, DC: U.S. Department of Labor, No. 96-3, Accessibility Information, October 1996.

Centers for Disease Control and Prevention. *Costs of Intimate Partner Violence against Women in the United States,* April 28, 2003.

Corporate Alliance to End Partner Violence. "Best Practices," 2005. http://www.caepv.org/membercenter/best.asp.

Dougan, Stacey. "Employers May Face Liability When Domestic Violence Comes to Work." *Employee Benefit Plan Review,* February 2003. http://www.gtlaw.com/pub/articles/2003/dougans03a.asp.

Duhart, Detis. *Violence in the Workplace, 1993–1999 Bureau of Justice Statistics Special Report* (NCJ 190076). Washington, DC: U.S. Department of Justice, 2001.

Family Violence Prevention Fund. "The Workplace Responds to Domestic Violence: A Resource Guide for Employers, Unions, and Advocates," 2004. http://www.mag.maricopa.gov/detail.cms?item=1983.

———. "The Facts on the Workplace and Violence against Women," 2005a. http://endabuse.org/workplace/display.php?DocID=33002.

———. "Violence Does Not Equal Strength: High-Profile Men from Sports, Entertainment and Business Urge American Men to Lead the Effort to End Family Violence That Affects 1 in 3 Women," 2005b. http://endabuse.org/press/releases.php3?Search=Article&ID=128.

Farmer, Amy, and Jill Tiefenthaler. "The Employment Effects of Domestic Violence." *Research in Labor Economics* 23 (2004): 301–334.

Fisher, Bonnie, and Corinne Peek-Asa. "Domestic Violence and the Workplace: Do We Know Too Much of Nothing?" In *Workplace Violence,* edited by Vaughan Bowie, Bonnie S. Fisher, and Cary L. Cooper. Devon, UK: Willan Publishing, 2005, pp. 97–120.

Howard, John, and Robert C. Barish. "Government Approaches to Reducing Workplace Violence." In *Violence in the Workplace: Clinics in Occupational and Environmental Medicine,* edited by Carol Wilkinson and Corinne Peek-Asa. Philadelphia: W. B. Saunders Company, 2003, pp. 721–732.

Lloyd, Susan. "The Effects of Domestic Violence on Women's Employment." *Law and Policy* 19, no. 2 (1997): 139–167.

Lloyd, Susan, and Nina Taluc. "The Effects of Male Violence on Female Employment." *Violence against Women* 5, no. 4 (1999): 370–392.

National Center for the Analysis of Violent Crime. *Workplace Violence: Issues in Response,* edited by Eugene A. Rugala and Arnold R. Isaacs, 2004. http://www.fbi.gov/publications/violence.pdf.

National Center on Domestic and Sexual Violence. "Sample Policy on Domestic Violence," 2004. http://www.ncdsv.org/images/sample_policy.pdf.

Partnership for Prevention. "Domestic Violence and the Workplace," 2005. http://www.prevent.org/publications/Domestic_Violence_and_the_Workplace.pdf.

Randel, Jane, and Kimberly Wells. "Corporate Approaches to Reducing Intimate Partner Violence through Workplace Initiatives." In Wilkinson and Peek-Asa, *Violence in the Workplace,* 2003, pp. 821–842.

Raphael, Jody. "Prisoners of Abuse: Domestic Violence and Welfare Receipt, a Second Report of the Women, Welfare and Abuse Project," 1996. http://www.uic.edu/orgs/rin/violence.html#Welfare.

Rickett, L., and L. Fortman. *Impact of Domestic Offenders on Occupational Safety and Health: A Pilot Study.* Augusta: Maine Department of Labor, Family Crisis Services, 2004.

Rothman, Emily Faith. "How Employees Who Batter Affect the Workplace: An Employers against Domestic Violence Initiative." Executive Summary. http://www.caepv.org/membercenter/files/eadv.pdf.

Speer, Rebecca. "Workplace Violence: A Legal Perspective." In Wilkinson and Peek-Asa, *Violence in the Workplace,* 2003, pp. 733–749.

Weiser, Wendy R., and Deborah A. Widiss. "Employment Protection for Domestic Violence Victims." *Journal of Poverty Law and Policy,* May-June (2004): 3–11.

WORLDWIDE SOCIOLEGAL PRECEDENTS SUPPORTING DOMESTIC VIOLENCE FROM ANCIENT TO MODERN TIMES

Introduction

Domestic violence is neither a new nor a localized problem. The myriad forms of domestic violence can be found all over the world, and evidence of its occurrence can be found as far back as written history goes. Through the various historical periods and different societies the world over, there have been many sociolegal precedents that either blatantly supported domestic violence or failed to condemn it. This long history of apathy toward the subject has created a huge mass of social, legal, cultural, and traditional beliefs and attitudes that contemporary societies have yet to overcome despite their best efforts. This article will explore these beliefs and attitudes to demonstrate how their influence far outweighs current attempts to create attitudes and beliefs against domestic violence in any form. By knowing what must be overcome, societies may be more successful in their efforts against domestic violence.

One of the issues encountered in viewing domestic violence from different times is that throughout history many of the behaviors now thought of as domestic violence have been both legal and socially acceptable. This demonstrates an evolving standard of what is acceptable behavior in personal relationships.

An underlying theme in each society which allowed for domestic violence against women and children is patriarchy. When men are the ultimate authority and women and children are considered property, the difference in human rights is staggering. Historically, the only human rights women were granted related to their value as a man's property. Children had no rights at all.

This legal subjugation is often combined with social acceptance and even pressure to conform. The historical criminal justice practice of returning women and children to their male guardians' homes for punishment rather than subjecting them to formal processing reinforces this idea. Cultural practices of punishing men for the crimes of their women also reinforced women's legal subjugation. Legal codes from various societies, particularly those of the distant past, also indicated social support of and pressure toward committing domestic violence by specifying that a man had the right to punish and even execute his wife without official intervention. This implies that the man had no other alternative for resolving his domestic issues.

The level of violence overall in a particular society or time period also plays a role in influencing the acceptance of domestic violence. The more violent society is, as fostered by warfare, violent entertainment, crime, and even punishment of criminals, the more violence is accepted in the home. When the societal violence level is combined with patriarchy, women are easily seen as targets for domestic violence.

Ancient Civilizations

Ancient civilizations are often hailed as belonging to a golden age of humankind where art and culture were highly developed. The basic foundations of more modern societies can be traced back to ancient times, where the beginnings of math, science, religion, and law emerged. For all their positive achievements, ancient civilizations are also where the legal and social traditions of permitting domestic violence toward women and children began.

The Code of Hammurabi is the oldest written legal code known to exist. In it are provisions for disciplining a wife and children by the husband/father. These provisions are state-sanctioned rights to privately discipline without intervention by legal authorities. They included the right of the male head of household to execute his wife and her lover if she was caught cheating. She could also be drowned in the river for spending too much money and gadding about. The husband had the ability to sell her and her children into slavery or bind them into slavery for three years in order to pay his debts. The husband was also able to terminate the marriage as he chose, but the wife was required to prove her innocence and his cruelty in order to terminate the marriage.

Children were even less protected. Not only could they be sold or bound out, but they could be executed for disobedience. A son who struck his father was to have his hands cut off. An unmarried virgin daughter who was raped by a man who was not already married was forced to marry her rapist. The rapist's only penalty was to marry the girl and pay her father a fine.

These legal provisions compare favorably with Hebrew laws (Mosaic Codes). If anything, the Hebrew laws were even stricter. The death penalty was available for more crimes. Sons could be executed for striking their fathers, cursing, general disobedience, and rebellion. Women and children who were bound out for labor to pay the man's debts could be held for up to six years.

In Greece, the original laws regulating families did not include penalties, but left it to the male head of household to enforce the laws as he saw best. This left the range of punishments wide open. The woman had no recourse, as she was under male guardianship for her entire life.

During the Roman empire, beatings, divorce, and murder were private rights of the male head of household. Women were allowed to divorce their husbands only in cases of excessive violence. This right was also limited to those in the upper classes. Women in the lower classes could not divorce their abusive husbands no matter how excessive the abuse might be.

The Christian emperor Constantine the Great was the first emperor to execute his wife. In 289 C.E. she was boiled alive for being suspected of adultery—not for actually being caught in adulterous behavior. Constantine was later canonized as a saint in the Catholic Church.

The level of violence available for a man to keep order in his home in these ancient societies was certainly greater than that now afforded, but it was based in part on the level of violence available in the general societies of the times. The death penalty was the prescribed punishment for many crimes, even minor ones such as pickpocketing. Wars were fought man-to-man with swords, clubs, and whatever other weapons could be found. The level of personal contact in these wars was immense. The Roman empire also made sport of violence through its gladiators. Armed personal combat to the death with other men or with wild animals was considered entertainment, not violence or cruelty. By comparison, domestic violence was not only acceptable, but a normal form of familial interaction. It was not considered violence at all.

Europe

European societies of the Middle Ages also demonstrated a level of social and legal acceptance of domestic violence that is now intolerable. Women were denied education and the ability to participate in political affairs. Marriages were often arranged between fathers and future husbands without concern for the wishes of the daughters. Women of all ages were no more than chattel to men to do with as they wished. Their prime value was as housekeepers and breeders.

During the Middle Ages various communities in Europe would burn women alive for their transgressions. Offenses included threatening their husbands, committing adultery, scolding, nagging, and having miscarriages. The cause of a miscarriage did not matter, even if it resulted from abuse by the husband.

Children were treated even more harshly than women. In many societies children were bonded out for labor, sold into slavery, and even abandoned to the elements. Abandonment of unwanted infants was particularly popular as a remedy for having a child of the wrong sex. This, of course, meant female.

Religion also contributed to this viewpoint. The *Rules of Marriage,* written in the late 1400s by Friar Cherubino, set out the guidelines by which a man might use violence to keep his wife in line. Scolding, bullying, and terrifying were the first steps. If that failed, then beating with a stick was in order. This would save the poor woman's soul from her evil ways rather than provide revenge for the man.

Perhaps the most famous domestic violence rule, the "rule of thumb," emerged in connection with English common law. This rule indicates that a man may beat his wife with a stick, but only if the stick is smaller in circumference than his thumb. This placed a limit on the violence in the family where no limits had previously existed. The rule was thus seen as improving the treatment of women. Although the rule was popular in England and America, it was never officially codified into law. It remained a court-based interpretation of existing laws.

English common law also contained other provisions for the master of the house to use physical discipline against his wife and children. The laws did place some limits on this power; however, these limits were largely illusory, as very few men were punished for their violations. As Sir William Blackstone explained, the power to use physical discipline was necessary as long as the law would hold men responsible for the crimes of their women.

French laws limited violence by a husband to blows of any kind so long as they landed on the back and left no permanent marks. The social pressure to follow the laws, not just by adhering to the limits but by actually using violence, can be seen in the warning that accompanied these rules; men were not really men if they were not masters of their wives.

Napoleon Bonaparte was responsible for solidifying the legal codes of France and exporting many of these legal principles to other countries, including Switzerland, Italy, and Germany. Women were defined as legal minors no matter their age. Permanent disfigurement was permitted for minor offenses such as scolding. The Code of Chivalry went so far as to call for breaking the woman's nose so she would be permanently marked and embarrassed. The woman could achieve divorce only if it could be shown that the man was attempting to murder her through his violence.

Societies during these times were also very violent. Warfare continued to be a face-to-face encounter; this included the Crusades and many other violent campaigns, such as those wrought by Napoleon himself. Infant mortality reached epic proportions, and several plagues raced through Europe, decimating the population. Life was by no means certain and thus was held at a lower value than today's societies hold.

Crime was at high rates, and punishments were public. The death penalty was again the preferred punishment for everything from petty theft to murder. The methods of extracting a confession and executing persons were refined to a particularly gruesome level during this time. Drawing and quartering, burning alive, and use of the rack and other instruments of torture showed a barbarism of spirit. Even worse, these punishments were held in public venues where massive crowds would come and cheer on the violence. Domestic violence obviously paled in comparison.

The United States

When the English established viable colonies in America, many persons from all over Europe immigrated in order to make a better life for themselves. Many fled religious oppression, poverty, lack of opportunity, and other social ills found in their home countries. In the colonial era, America derived its laws and social order from England. After independence, the new country, while forming its new political structure of democracy, continued to use many of the legal traditions of England.

White landowning males were given all the power, and women were not so much as mentioned in the new system. Nowhere in the Constitution or the Bill of Rights are women discussed. Women were not allowed to own property, enter into contracts, or even vote.

Social control in the colonies and the early states was a mixture of legal and religious forces revolving around local statutes and the Puritan faith. The Puritan faith was very strict and required absolute obedience. Puritans believed that if they did not punish those who committed transgressions, God would forsake them. This led to harsh punishments, social approval of the male head of household using some physical violence in his home, and public punishments where more private means were unsuccessful.

The need to punish sinners made physical punishment of wives and children acceptable, though excessive violence in the home was also a sin. If the level of violence exceeded that which the neighbors were comfortable ignoring, the local minister or other respectable gentlemen of the community would meet with the offending man and counsel him about improving his behavior. This avoided criminal charges and kept the family together. It did not, however, eliminate future violence. The man simply took greater pains to avoid attracting the attention of his neighbors.

Divorce and out-of-home placement of children were rare in Puritan life. The sanctity of the family was of utmost importance. Marriage was a covenant between man, woman, God, community, and church. Breaking this covenant was not undertaken lightly, particularly by the woman, whose position was most subordinate.

As members of the subordinate class, women were expected to take seriously the biblical commands to obey and submit to men. This contributed to the perpetuation of domestic violence by demanding that a good Puritan woman blame herself and seek to adjust her behavior rather than seek to escape.

Legal approval of domestic violence toward wives was also demonstrated through early court cases such as *Bradley vs. State* (1824). Here the Mississippi Supreme Court affirmed a husband's right to use physical force against his wife in "cases of emergency" so long as he did not cause permanent injury. What exactly constituted a case of emergency was not defined. In *State vs. Oliver* (1874), the North Carolina Supreme Court also permitted violence by a husband so long as it was not from malice or cruelty. The court felt that it would be better for the husband and wife to work it out privately.

In more modern times, politicians at all points of the political spectrum make family values a part of their platform. Family values include strong marriages, marriage before sex, counseling and other social services to hold the family together, and media images of families sitting down to dinner together.

In fact, Child Protective Services and other social services agencies are often so exclusively focused on keeping the family together that any alternative which includes removal from the family or household is ignored. Family-first advocates argue against shelters for battered women, as they promote the breakup of the American family. This "keep the family together at all costs" strategy stands in direct contrast to the efforts of women's advocates who fight to get women out of violent relationships.

Counseling and other services are the preferred options for dealing with family problems, but they would seem to depend on the openness of the family. If family members do not share their problems, how can they receive the help and support they need? Standing in the way of this ideal is the high value that contemporary American society places on individual and family privacy. Many believe that, as the saying goes, what goes on behind closed doors should stay there.

Throughout history, the privacy of the home was based on several ideas. The first was a separation of men's and women's roles into public and private spheres. Then personal and familial worship and prayer guided in the home by the male head of household set the home apart from the public on religious grounds. The idea of the home as a sanctuary where men could retire after a day in the rigors of the working world also separated the privacy of the home from the public sphere.

Conclusions

The history of civilization indicates that changes in patriarchy and societal levels of violence have been important indicators of social and legal approval of domestic violence against women and children. In ancient times, society was filled with brutal violence in wars, sports, and criminal punishments.

Patriarchy was at an all-time high, and the power of life and death was literally in the hands of the master of the house. Modern times have seen sports and criminal punishments become less gory, while warfare has moved away from man-to-man confrontations. Patriarchy has lost much of its former status. Women are reaching for equality and achieving some level of success. Domestic violence is now illegal and socially unacceptable in most societies. Why then does the problem still exist?

Patriarchy still exists, even in its weakened form. There is still debate over the proper role for women in society. Pregnancy-related issues are but one of the snags. The call for a return of traditional family values is also problematic. Family time, dinners, church attendance, etc., are difficult to argue against. These ideals leave people feeling nostalgic for the seemingly better times of the past. What is forgotten about these better times is that these family ideals were achieved by fathers who worked and mothers who stayed home. They were achieved in a time when inequality between males and females was high.

For many modern families, a single income is not enough. Both parents have to work outside the home. Now one asks questions about the effect of the woman making more money or having a better job. One asks about the effect of day care and latchkey children. How do these realities fit within the ideals of traditional family values?

What about contemporary forms of entertainment? Video games, popular movies, and even some forms of music have become more and more violent. Nudity, foul language, and a level of blood and gore that is unprecedented have taken over from the days of public executions and gladiatorial fights in the coliseum. One has only to look at music videos and horror movies to see that society has not progressed so far; only the nature of entertainment has changed. Where does this leave the contemporary world? The remnants of several thousand years of patriarchy are still being challenged by women who struggle to work, raise families, and be equal to their male counterparts. The level of violence in entertainment as well as in reality is also being challenged. Rating systems on movies, television programs, and music and protests against the continued use of the death penalty and other forms of state-sanctioned violence attempt to limit exposure to the brutal side of life. History is a difficult thing to overcome. Until equality is achieved and humankind evolves past the need for violence, the struggle will continue.

LORIE RUBENSER

See also **Christianity and Domestic Violence; Corporal Punishment, Religious Attitudes toward; Qur'anic Perspectives on Wife Abuse; Rule of Thumb; Shelter Movement; Violence against Women Act**

References and Further Reading

Davies, W. W. *Codes of Hammurabi and Moses.* New York: Kessinger Publishing, reprinted from Jennings and Graham, 1905.

Davis, Elizabeth Gould. *The First Sex.* Baltimore, MD: Penguin Books, 1973.

Gosselin, Denise Kindschi. *Heavy Hands: An Introduction to the Crimes of Family Violence,* 3rd ed. Upper Saddle River, NJ: Pearson, Prentice Hall, 2005.

Mills, Linda G. *Insult to Injury: Rethinking Our Responses to Intimate Abuse.* Princeton, NJ: Princeton University Press, 2003.

Pleck, Elizabeth. *Domestic Tyranny: The Making of American Social Policy against Family Violence from Colonial Times to the Present.* New York: Oxford University Press, 1987.

Schneider, Elizabeth M. "Society's Belief in Family Privacy Contributes to Domestic Violence." In *Violence against Women,* edited by Karin L. Swisher and Carol Wekesser. San Diego, CA: Greenhaven Press, 1994, pp. 19–25.

Sewell, Bernadette Dunn. "Traditional Male/Female Roles Promote Domestic Violence." In Swisher and Wekesser, *Violence against Women,* 1994, pp. 19–25.

Stith, Sandra M., and Murray A. Straus, eds. *Understanding Partner Violence: Prevalence, Causes, Consequences, and Solutions.* Minneapolis: National Council on Family Relations, 1995.

Taves, Ann, ed. *Religion and Domestic Violence in Early New England: The Memoirs of Abigail Abbot Bailey.* Bloomington: Indiana University Press, 1989.

Walker, Lenore. *The Battered Woman Syndrome,* 2nd ed. New York: Springer Publishing Company, 2000.

Wallace, Harvey. *Family Violence: Legal, Medical, and Social Perspectives,* 3rd ed. Boston: Allyn and Bacon, 2002.

INDEX

INDEX

American Journal of Obstetrics and Gynecology, 477
American Journal of Psychiatry, 329
American Medical Association, 275, 481
  screening recommendations by, 357
American Professional Society on the Abuse of Children
  (APSAC), 507
American Psychiatric Association, 25
  MBP and, 506
American Psychological Association (APA), 75
American Puritans. *See* Puritans
Americans with Disabilities Act, 731
America's Missing: Broadcast Emergency Response
  (AMBER), 528–529
Amish, 162
  Medicaid and, 479
  polio and, 479
  rubella and, 479
  tetanus and, 479
  vaccinations and, 475
Ammonia, as health risk, 26
Amnesty International, 6, 167
  feminism and, 325
  torture and, 68–69
Amphetamines, 408, 697
Amygdala, 519–521
Anal sex, rape and, 7
Anal tears, with marital rape, 467
Analyzing incidents, 18–21
  of aggravated assault, 19
  of alcohol abuse, 20
  of drug abuse, 20
  limitations of, 20–21
  of rape, 20
  weapons and, 20
Anatomically detailed dolls, 138
Ancient civilizations, 734–735
Ancient to modern times, 733–737
  ancient civilizations, 734–735
  Catholic Church, 734
  Code of Hammurabi, 734
  Constantine the Great, 734
  Europe, 735
  Greece, 734
  Judaism, 734
  Middle Ages, 734
  Puritans, 736
  Rome, 734
  United States, 735–736
Androgynes, 624
Anemia
  with vegan diets, 480
  victimization and, 399
Anetzberger, Georgia, 272
Anger, 46, 168
  of battered women, 669
  in batterer, 241
  of caregivers, 115
  CBT and, 94
  displaced, 331
  of gay perpetrators, 337
  incest and, 384, 563
  incestuous rape and, 381
  parental abduction and, 527
  during recoil stage, 708
  stalking and, 686

of victims, 551, 643
  violence and, 128, 159
Anger management, 136
Angina, from bullying, 107
Angular cheilitis, with vegan diets, 480
Animal abuse, 22–29, 23, 408. *See also* Pet abuse
  in circuses, 23
  emotional, 23
  as excessive labor, 23
  family violence and, 26–28
  as racing, 23
  sexual, 23–24
  as testing, 23
  zoophilia and, 24–25
Animal-assisted therapy, 28
Animal collectors, 25
Animal Cops, 22
Animal cruelty. *See* Animal abuse
Animal hoarders, 25–26, 283
Animal Precinct, 22
Animal testing, 23
Ankle bracelets, 297
Anonymous threats, 169
Anorexia
  incest and, 383, 564
  with vegan diets, 480
Antelope Valley Oasis Shelter, 458
Anthroposophy, 478
Anti-aggressions Committee, 663
Anti-depressants, 239
Antisocial personality disorder (APD), 101
  in batterers, 464
  in bullies, 107
  child abuse and, 394
  child sexual abuse and, 151
  in law enforcement officers, 257
  parricide and, 533
Anti-Vietnam War movement, 322
Anxiety, 81, 157, 238, 355
  as abuse sign, 357
  of battered wives, 61
  of bullies, 105
  CBT and, 94
  with children of divorce, 247
  child sexual abuse and, 150
  cycle of violence and, 225
  of elder abuse perpetrators, 273
  emergency shelters and, 365
  family bullying and, 106
  incest and, 384
  IPV and, 393, 405
  leaving and, 493
  of male victims, 311
  pregnancy and, 574
  PTSD and, 65
  risk factors for, 643
  suicide and, 319
  of victim, 243
Anxiety continuum, 43
Anxious-ambivalent attachment pattern, 42
Anxious-avoidant attachment pattern, 42
AoA. *See* Administration on Aging
APA. *See* American Psychological Association
Apartheid, 654
APD. *See* Antisocial personality disorder

INDEX

INDEX

INDEX

Intimidation, 19, 169, 345, 549, 669–670
  in battering, 84, 410
  in brick-wall family type, 105
  as bullying, 103
  in child sexual abuse, 603
  in coercive control, 166
    DVA and, 658
    IPV and, 199
    marital rape and, 413
Intrusive memories, PTSD and, 65
Invasion of privacy, 583
Investigation, of child abuse, 133–134
IPV. *See* Intimate partner violence
Irazuzta, Jose, 631
Isha muka (battered woman), 426
Islam. *See also* Sharia
  corporal punishment in, 596
  divorce in, 597–598
  feminism and, 596
  rape and, 2
Isolation. *See also* Social isolation
  of battered husbands, 58
  bullying and, 104
  BWS and, 65
  in coercive control, 166, 167
  of disabled, 724
  in elder abuse, 272, 274, 293
  as emotional abuse, 411
  family bullying and, 106
  gay men and, 336
  of homosexuals, 626
  intervention as, 96
  of law enforcement officers, 257
  maternal, 498
  neglect and, 145
  as risk factor, 272
  in rural communities, 615
  sexual orientation and, 418
  as torture, 68
  of victims, 494
ISPCAN. *See* International Society for the Prevention of Child
    Abuse and Neglect
Israel, 423, 425, 426
  battered husbands in, 56
Isserles, Moses, 424
Ivory Coast, female genital mutilation in, 7

J

Jacksonian seizures, 569
Jackson, Michael, 578
Jacobson, Neil, 491
Jacobson v. Massachusetts, 482
Jahizah (matrimonial wealth), 600
Jahnke, Richard, 530
Japan, 217
Japanese Americans, 35
  elder abuse and, 275
Jealousy, 47, 169, 408
  battering and, 409
  in BWS, 68
  CBT and, 94
  in DB batterers, 101
  as flattery, 556
  of gay perpetrators, 337

incest and, 385
  in intimate partner homicide, 398, 399
  in psychological abuse, 68
  as risk factor, 40
  of unborn child, 572
  woman battering and, 415
Jean's Way (Humphry and Wickett), 187
Jehovah's Witnesses, 475, 476, 480
Jellyfish family type, 105
Jewish community, 423–428. *See also* Judaism
  counseling for, 428
  legal assistance for, 428
  Nazi killings of, 329
Jewish Women International (JWI), 427
Job loss, 729
  from bullying, 107
Job training, for homeless, 366
Johnson, Michael, 170
Joint Commission on the Accreditation of Healthcare
    Organizations, 357
Joint custody, 524
Joint legal custody, 250
Joint physical custody, 250
Jokes, crude, 68
Jones, Ann, 167
Jones, Brereton, 80
Journal of Interpersonal Violence, 195
Journal of the American Medical Association, 203
Judaism, 734
  corporal punishment and, 205
Judges. *See also* Judicial perspectives
  in coordinated community response, 264
  law enforcement officers and, 256
Judicial perspectives, 428–433
Judicial process, 203
Juvenile court, 440
Juvenile delinquency
  child abuse and, 124–131
  child sexual abuse and, 151
  discipline and, 126
  neglect and, 125
JWI. *See* Jewish Women International

K

Kaiser Permanente, 716
Kalahari Bushmen, 217
Karma, 33
Karo kari, in Pakistan, 210
Karr-Morse, Robin, 488
Katzenjammer Kids, 54
"Keep Ya Head Up" (Tupac), 558
Kempe, Henry, 629
Kennedy, Robert F., 436
Kentucky, clemency in, 80
Kentucky Correctional Institution, 80
Kenya, domestic violence bill in, 1
KESO. *See* Greek Archdiocese
Ketamine (ketamine hydrochloride), 230
Ketamine hydrochloride. *See* Ketamine
KETHI. *See* Research Center on Equality Matters
Ketonuria, with vegan diets, 480
Khmer, 30–31
Khoufallah (fear of Allah), 597
Kibbutzes, battered husbands in, 56

INDEX

INDEX

INDEX

INDEX

INDEX

INDEX